STRATEGIC MANAGEMENT

A METHODOLOGICAL APPROACH

FOURTH EDITION

Alan J. Rowe
School of Business Administration
University of Southern California

Richard O. Mason
Edwin L. Cox School of Business
Southern Methodist University

Karl E. Dickel
The Boston Consulting Group
Stockholm, Sweden

Richard B. Mann
University of Pittsburgh
Johnstown, Pennsylvania

Robert J. Mockler
Saint John's University
New York, New York

STRATEGIC MANAGEMENT

A METHODOLOGICAL APPROACH

FOURTH EDITION

ADDISON-WESLEY PUBLISHING COMPANY
Reading, Massachusetts • Menlo Park, California • New York • Don Mills,
Ontario • Wokingham, England • Amsterdam • Bonn • Sydney • Singapore
Tokyo • Madrid • San Juan • Milan • Paris

World Student Series

Cover Designer: Leslie Haimes
Composition/Art Styling: Gex
Permissions Editor: Mary Dyer
Senior Manufacturing Coordinator: Judy Sullivan

112498-5

We want to express our utmost appreciation to our families, friends, and colleagues, for their patience, support, and understanding of the many hours spent on completing this book.

ISBN 0-201-60082-X
2 3 4 5 6 7 8 9 10-DOC-98 97 96 95

arise. Herein lies the crux of strategic thinking. Managers must think beyond current conditions and arrive at courses of action that respond effectively to problems. A sound strategic analysis provides the factual basis on which to formulate strategic alternatives and helps managers evaluate the consequences of a given strategy.

The perspective we have taken is that in a capstone course in business such as this, the material covered should stand on its own. Although considerable reference is made to material addressed in courses leading up to the strategic management course, the body of knowledge that has evolved over the past 10 to 15 years provides a solid foundation for strategic management. Many of the methods used at this level are distinct from those applied in other courses. For example, early courses in strategy relied primarily on the integration of prior knowledge. In our approach to the field of strategy, however, we have also included research findings and specific methods applied by major consulting organizations such as the Boston Consulting Group.

CHANGES IN THE CURRENT EDITION

In preparing the fourth edition of this book, we have paid special attention to the helpful suggestions made by the reviewers and by the many users of the previous three editions. We have also updated material in every chapter and have added new material and new chapters.

The changes include expanded material on topics such as organizational restructuring, competitor analysis, cost de-averaging, and the use of information technology to gain a competitive advantage. There is more emphasis on the management aspects of strategy, on industry analysis as part of environmental analysis, on leadership, and on the change process. We have expanded the material on global strategy, strategic alliances, and the impact of Europe ECC. New topics include time-based competition versus cost-based competition, total quality management, value-based strategies, concurrent design and manufacture, and the application of expert systems as a strategic support tool. In addition, we have expanded coverage of generic competitive strategies, sustainable competitive advantage, and strategic computer applications. Our new thrust retains the unique attributes that distinguish this text from the others in the field. But we have streamlined the text material by emphasizing critical methodologies and have placed supporting methodologies in appendices at the end of several chapters.

We have restructured the sequence of the chapters in the book to focus more clearly on the *process* of formulating strategy. Each chapter focuses on a step in the process of determining which strategy leads to the desired goals specified by the organization. Thus each chapter starts with an indication of where in the process the material fits and how it contributes to formulating an effective strategy. Each of these chapters helps meet the overall objective of formulating a strategy that contributes to a sustainable market penetration and profitability. The methods employed are used to help analyze the requirements that ultimately lead to "total value management."

In addition to the strategic process model that can be associated with each chapter, at the beginning of each chapter we show the four dominant factors that impinge on the organization and create the need for change. Strategic techniques

PREFACE

A new standard of performance is being applied to strategic managers, who must cope with an increasingly turbulent environment. No longer is strategy simply the analysis of alternatives, or determining what marketing approaches will beat out competitors. Rather, strategic management needs to parallel the approach that has been taken when applying total quality management (TQM). Our emphasis in this revision extends the TQM approach to considering total "value" management. Performance measures such as return on investment, earnings growth, and market share must be augmented to include such other measures as flexibility, responsiveness, adaptability, and social responsibility. To achieve these objectives, organizations need to utilize shorter development cycles, prepare designs that take manufacturing considerations into account, ensure zero defects, introduce concurrent design and manufacturing, develop shorter delivery cycles, and become more customer-oriented. Thus "managing value" casts what corporate strategy must achieve in a new light.

Today's organizations will need to have leaner staffs, to empower their employees by sharing decisions, to obtain commitment and innovation from employees, and to evolve a culture that promotes the ability to be adaptive and responsive. They also need leaders who have the vision required to shape meaningful strategies and deploy them throughout the organization. Is this asking too much of management? Perhaps, but what is the alternative? A faltering, ineffective management that will not survive the onslaught of competition and of ever-present corporate raiders. Accordingly, we dedicate the fourth edition of *Strategic Management* to helping managers and aspiring managers succeed in the 1990s. The tools provided here will help them understand all aspects of the environment and the organization so that they can formulate achievable and effective strategic plans.

Because organizations are dynamic—they have different cultures and values, are in different phases of their life cycles, employ multiple management styles, and have changing portfolios of products—there are few pat answers to the questions that

Istuan, William Kelly, Matt Klempa, Thomas Lewis, John Jaeger, Dewey Johnson, Peter Lorange, Craig Lundberg, Mike McGrath, Ian Mitroff, Bill Paisley, Alan Patz, Bill Paulin, Ray Price, Heinrich Rutt, Marcus Schwaninger, Hans Seifert, V. J. Seshan, Mel Shader, Arthur Sharplin, Herold Sherman, Richard Snyder, Ivan Somers, George Stalk, Jr., George Steiner, Bill Strassen, and George Walker. We are especially grateful to the following reviewers whose insights have helped to make *Strategic Management* an even stronger instructional tool: Kim B. Boal, Texas Tech University; Gary Dessler, Florida International University; Roy H. Gordan, Hofstra University; Charles Gowen, University of Northern Illinois; Dewey Johnson, California State University, Fresno; Richard Kolasheski, University of Maryland; Leland Lahr, Lawrence Tech University; Eugene H. Melan, Marist College; Michael Merenda, University of New Hampshire; Rebecca Morris, University of Nebraska, Omaha; Daniel Slate, University of New Mexico; Wayne Smeltz, Rider College; James Thurman, George Washington University; and Arieh Ullman, State University of New York, Binghamton. The authors of the cases deserve special thanks for their contribution to making the book a valuable educational vehicle. We also wish to thank our students, who diligently studied the material and provided invaluable feedback, and our secretarial staff, Johna Miller and Janet Andrews, for their steadfast help.

Thanks, too, to the Addison-Wesley staff and freelancers, who have helped this book come to fruition: Mac Mendelsohn, Beth Toland, Kim Kramer, Kathy Diamond, Connie Day, and Nancy Benjamin.

Los Angeles, California	A. J. R.
Dallas, Texas	R. O. M.
Stockholm, Sweden	K. E. D.
Johnstown, Pennsylvania	R. B. M.
New York, New York	R. J. M.

CONTENTS

CASES

LIST OF WORKSHEETS

CHAPTER ONE

A Framework for Strategic Management

External
Environment

Strategic
Planning

Strategic Thinking
Strategy Formulation
Total Value
Strategic Success
Strategic Planning
Systems Framework

Resource
Allocation

Resource
Requirements

Strategic
Management

Organizational
Structure

Organizational
Culture

Strategic
Control

Internal
Environment

Chapter 1	**Chapter 2**	**Chapter 3**	**Chapter 4**	**Chapter 5**	**Chapter 6**
A Framework for Strategic Management	Strategic Analysis	Strategic Visioning, Goals, Ethics, and Social Responsibility	The Competitive Environment	Capability-based Strategy	Market Dynamics and Sustainable Competitive Advantage

How to approach strategic management	*Application of strategic analysis*	*Understanding vision, values, ethics*	*Coping with competitive forces, stakeholders*	*Assessing company capability, timeliness, quality*	*Determining trends, gap analysis, and market dynamics*

Chapter 7	**Chapter 8**	**Chapter 9**	**Chapter 10**	**Chapter 11**
Strategy in a Global Environment	Financial Planning and Competitive-Cost Analysis	Entrepreneurship, Mergers and Acquisitions, Restructuring, and the Service Sector	Leadership Factor in Strategy and Implementing Strategic Change	Information Technology and Future Directions in Strategy

Assessing global trade, foreign markets, monetary exchange	*Preparing a financial plan and competitive-cost analysis*	*Importance of small business, entrepreneurs, restructuring*	*Strategy implementation, leadership, culture*	*Information technology, trends, new management*

INTRODUCTION

Why are some companies successful while others struggle just to stay afloat? Is the answer better products, better marketing, more efficient production, better quality, timely delivery? Is it a productive organization with a supportive culture and effective leadership? Or is it some combination of the way the organization operates and the quality of its management? Questions such as these demand answers if a company is to be successful in today's increasingly competitive and turbulent environment. The answers are many, but they all focus on one basic requirement. *In order to succeed, a company must offer value to its customers.* That is, it must provide *total value*. Value represents the customer's perception of what is delivered, at what price, and with what features that serve their real needs. Pages 7 and 8 describe value and total value in greater detail. *Strategic management* is the process by which organizations determine what value is needed and how to add that value. It is a means for ensuring that organizations can cope effectively with the myriad of demands placed on them from within and without. This book aims to provide an understanding of the strategic management process and of methods that can be used to formulate appropriate strategies. These tools can help companies achieve and sustain a competitive advantage.

As an illustration of why companies require effective strategic management, consider the issue of *Business Week* dated June 24, 1991. In it, the following stories appeared.

1. Clorox, which was once part of Procter & Gamble, is now battling P&G over a detergent–bleach combination product. The result is that Clorox has taken the new detergent–bleach combination off the market. But in the process, P&G has lost some of *its* market share for core bleach products.
2. Motorola, the company known for cracking the Japanese market, had a difficult time selling chips to IBM. After many years, Motorola decided to allow other companies to produce its high-performance microprocessors while it concentrated on producing the reduced-instruction-set-chip (RISC). Motorola is working with IBM to design a low-cost version of the chip to power both IBM and Apple work stations.
3. On the other side of the Pacific, Nippon Electric in Japan is working with American Telephone and Telegraph, along with Sun Microsystems Inc. and MIPS Computer Systems Inc., to produce the RISC chips that will be the heart of future work stations and advanced personal computers.
4. Across the Atlantic, Ford of Europe is working at breakneck speed to be ready for the opening of borders in 1992. Ford will launch an image-building "blitz" across Europe and will speed up the introduction of new models. It will cost Ford $11 billion to improve its technology, introduce new models, and upgrade dealers.
5. Goodyear's miracle man Stanley Gault will attempt to pull Goodyear out of its slump. It is estimated that it will cost $11 billion to remake the ailing tire-maker—and this during a devastating slump in auto sales.
6. Faced with a $400 million loss, USAir has had to close many of its facilities, ground aircraft, and furlough 7,000 employees. It has also had to defer orders for 28 Boeing jets and cut back on its expansion plans for Cleveland and Baltimore. CEO Seth Schofield faces the challenge of discovering exactly where USAir fits.
7. The recent plunge in real estate values has propelled the banking industry toward disaster. Office vacancies are the highest they have been in years, property values have fallen, and bad loans have been increasing at an alarming rate. By taking an aggressive approach to identifying bad real estate loans and building adequate reserves, banks now appear to be on the mend and expect their loan portfolios to stabilize by the end of the year.
8. In an attempt to introduce more pro-family policies, du Pont has appointed Faith Wohl as "in house conscience." Her job is to help employees balance family concerns with their careers. She has done this by setting up day care centers and promoting generous leaves on the occasion of the birth or adoption of a child or the sickness of a relative.

STRATEGIC THINKING

Strategic management is essential for dealing with the continuous stream of changes that flood all organizations. Managers need to cope with pressures of rapid change in order to achieve organizational goals effectively. Thus "strategic thinking" is an on-going process in which significant events are dealt with in a comprehensive manner. For example, Michael Porter (1987) describes strategic thinking as being intimately linked with implementation. He states, "There are no substitutes for strategic thinking. Improving quality is meaningless without knowing what kind of quality is relevant in competitive terms. Nurturing corporate culture is useless unless the culture is aligned with the company's approach to competing. Entrepreneurship, unguided by a strategic perspective, is much more likely to fail than succeed. And, contrary to popular opinion, even Japanese companies use strategic thinking. The successful ones are strong believers in planning and avid students of their industries and competitors."

In their article "The Anatomy of Strategic Thinking," J. Roger Morrison and James G. Lee (1989) describe strategic thinking in the following cogent terms: "The successful strategic thinker is guided by a clear business concept based on a thorough understanding of the economics of [the] business and of the success factors in [the] industry."

It is superior strategic thinking, not sophisticated planning systems, that underlies most successful competitive strategies. Effective strategic thinking focuses on achieving competitive advantage by gaining and holding the initiative. Good strategic thinking also implies an understanding of how situations will change over time. Business strategy, like military strategy, is a matter of maneuvering for superior position and anticipating how competitors will respond and with what degree of success. Successful strategists aim always to keep one step ahead of the competition. They plan their moves well in advance and have contingency plans for the most likely outcomes.

The research of James Brian Quinn (1980) indicates that strategic decisions often are made without the benefit of formal strategic planning, even where there is wide acceptance of planning in the organization. This implies a reliance on strategic thinking as a substitute for formal planning. Larry Greiner (1987) also found little evidence to support the contention that major changes in the direction of an organization are based on normative assumptions that result from the strategic planning process. Greiner found that successful strategic change relies on the core values of an organization rather than acceptance based on formal planning.

No matter how they are arrived at, strategic decisions affect the very survival of an organization, and consequently, they require some form of strategic thinking. The president of A&E Plastipak, Bernard Denburg, stressed this when he said, "Strategic thinking is the continuous process of managing strategy consistent with strategic goals and cultural values of the organization." Strategic thinking, then, starts with the strategy formulation process and moves beyond merely doing an analysis of data. As Porter, Greiner, and others have pointed out, a strategy must also be managed. Strategy formulation involves knowing the competitive environment and knowing how to allocate resources, how to restructure organizations, and how to implement plans. It also involves managing the strategy formulation process. To do this, executives must be leaders with vision who are also aware of the behavioral factors that influence performance and the cultures that support the core values and mission of the organization.

Examples of environmental forces with which managers have had to cope include

- The stock crisis of 1987 and its impact on raising equity capital
- The recession of the early 1990s and its effect on consumer spending
- Continued Japanese dominance of traditional U.S. markets
- The rapid increase in breakthroughs in technology, especially in electronics and biogenetics
- The establishment of whole new industries in telemarketing and biotechnology
- Intensified global competition and changes resulting from the European Economic Community
- Changing values of employees, customers, and other stakeholders
- Iraq's invasion of Kuwait in 1991 and its potential effect on oil prices
- Formation of a commonwealth in what was formerly the Soviet Union and the resulting trade considerations
- Reunification of East and West Germany, leading to changes in the unified Germany's competitive position
- The projected return of Hong Kong to China in 1997 and the potential for changes in trade restrictions

All these events have affected how well various organizations can compete. Such volatility in the external environment makes strategic management and strategic thinking a necessity.

STRATEGY FORMULATION

This book presents a number of methods that can help managers analyze requirements and formulate a strategy that will achieve a competitive advantage. For example, many organizations have found that to be competitive, they must provide customers with QVST: quality, value, service, and timeliness. Obviously, there are variations on the theme. McDonald's, for example, uses QVSC—quality, value, service, and cleanliness—as its guiding principles. Nonetheless, the basic approach still applies. Customers increasingly expect products or service that perform as specified; they expect the best possible value at a reasonable cost; they demand the service needed to maintain products and assurance that the products will perform as specified. In our frenetic, competitive world, an appreciation of the importance of time often spells the difference between winning competitors and companies who "also ran." For example, Ford is planning to spend billions to upgrade its ability to introduce new models more quickly. In the service industry, timeliness is often the difference between getting a client or an order and losing out.

Strategic managers faced with many complex factors must utilize strategic thinking. In today's rapidly changing environment, it is no longer sufficient to prepare a strategic plan once a year or even once a quarter. Strategic managers need to monitor conditions continuously and must be willing to modify strategic decisions whenever the need arises. They have to understand the consequences of actions that are proposed and to weigh the merits of a new strategic thrust. Given the complexity of coping with many problems, managers need to use aids to decision making that can ensure that they have taken all the relevant facts into account and dealt with them appropriately. The methods presented in this book can assist managers in their quest to be adequately prepared and can ensure that they will not make a decision that is obviously wrong. Such tools help strategic managers use all the relevant intelligence available when making strategic decisions.

A number of cases are used throughout this text to show how to formulate strategies and how to define the requirements of carrying out a strategy. The first illustrative case describes how American Hospital Supply Corporation succeeded in becoming one of the largest distributors of medical supplies. But, because they did not focus on maintaining a "sustainable competitive advantage," they were acquired by Baxter Tavenol. Nonetheless, the steps AHSC took to achieve its initial competitive position illustrate how a focus on "total value" can contribute to achieving a competitive advantage.

The second illustrative case examines the problems that Polaroid had when the company introduced "Polavision" without doing an appropriate strategic analysis. Juxtaposing these two cases shows how taking the right strategic actions led to a strong competitive position for one company and how lacking a formal strategy and adopting a take-it-or-leave-it attitude with customers led to dismal performance in the other.

Using the concept of total value management, we will examine how organizations develop and utilize their value concepts to meet changing customer demands. Peters and Waterman (1982), in their monumental book *In Search of Excellence*, provided a useful framework for examining how the basic values and beliefs of an organization affect strategic performance. We will look at some of their findings later in this chapter.

A basic premise of business is the need to create value for all stakeholders—but especially for customers. With this in mind, we attempt in this book to show how strategy contributes to the success of a business and point out where and how value needs to be added during the strategic planning process. Figure 1.1 offers a succinct roadmap that covers the major topics and tools used in the text.

STRATEGIC ANALYSIS

Decision-making tools are primarily used to help managers formulate strategic alternatives and to reduce uncertainty. However, such methods are only part of what is needed. To adequately formulate strategy, decision makers need to consider links among the key elements of strategy. Figure 1.1 shows some of the important topics that are covered in each chapter of this book and relates these topics to the chapter sequence. There is no convenient way to cover the linkage between key elements and chapter sequence; therefore, material will be used wherever appropriate, whether its appearance is shown in the chapter title or not.

WHAT IS VALUE?

The term *value* as used here refers to the contribution that management can make to the organization, the products, and the stakeholders, including the customers. A busi-

FIGURE 1.1 | Strategy Process Model

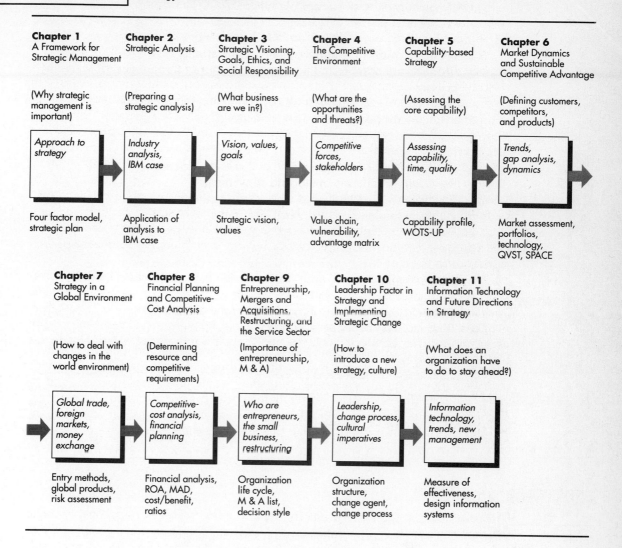

Chapter 1 A Framework for Strategic Management — (Why strategic management is important) — *Approach to strategy* — Four factor model, strategic plan

Chapter 2 Strategic Analysis — (Preparing a strategic analysis) — *Industry analysis, IBM case* — Application of analysis to IBM case

Chapter 3 Strategic Visioning, Goals, Ethics, and Social Responsibility — (What business are we in?) — *Vision, values, goals* — Strategic vision, values

Chapter 4 The Competitive Environment — (What are the opportunities and threats?) — *Competitive forces, stakeholders* — Value chain, vulnerability, advantage matrix

Chapter 5 Capability-based Strategy — (Assessing the core capability) — *Assessing capability, time, quality* — Capability profile, WOTS-UP

Chapter 6 Market Dynamics and Sustainable Competitive Advantage — (Defining customers, competitors, and products) — *Trends, gap analysis, dynamics* — Market assessment, portfolios, technology, QVST, SPACE

Chapter 7 Strategy in a Global Environment — (How to deal with changes in the world environment) — *Global trade, foreign markets, money exchange* — Entry methods, global products, risk assessment

Chapter 8 Financial Planning and Competitive-Cost Analysis — (Determining resource and competitive requirements) — *Competitive-cost analysis, financial planning* — Financial analysis, ROA, MAD, cost/benefit, ratios

Chapter 9 Entrepreneurship, Mergers and Acquisitions, Restructuring, and the Service Sector — (Importance of entrepreneurship, M & A) — *Who are entrepreneurs, the small business, restructuring* — Organization life cycle, M & A list, decision style

Chapter 10 Leadership Factor in Strategy and Implementing Strategic Change — (How to introduce a new strategy, culture) — *Leadership, change process, cultural imperatives* — Organization structure, change agent, change process

Chapter 11 Information Technology and Future Directions in Strategy — (What does an organization have to do to stay ahead?) — *Information technology, trends, new management* — Measure of effectiveness, design information systems

ness can succeed only when its products or services are perceived as having value. Thus, a key element in the determination of value is acceptance by the customer. Value is dependent on the vision of leaders, on the performance of the work force, on the imagination of the engineers, and on the support of all the functions in the organization and the suppliers outside the organization. The value of products or services can have the following qualities, which we have divided into four general categories.

I. Customer considerations
   a. Customers perceive value in the product.
   b. Price is attractive relative to that perceived value.

c. Products are reliable and consistent in their performance.
d. The product is aesthetically pleasing.
e. Products help customers be more efficient.

II. Capabilities
a. Products conform to standards or specifications.
b. Products are durable and perform satisfactorily throughout the warranty periods.
c. Products are safe and meet all environmental requirements.
d. Products are easy to use and to understand.
e. Products have unusual capabilities.

III. Service
a. Products can be readily serviced at a reasonable cost.
b. Service of products is timely and convenient.
c. Products are easily adjusted and easy to maintain.
d. Products can be upgraded when required.
e. Products are easily transported or moved when required.

IV. Competitive considerations
a. Products are highly differentiated and have desirable features.
b. Products are superior, or at least equivalent, to those of competitors.
c. Products are readily available.
d. Quality is built into the basic design of the product.
e. Products have superior warranties.

This list may seem long and exhaustive, but we could undoubtedly cite many more considerations. It is obvious that adding value to products or services involves more than incorporating uniqueness of design, price, location, and the like. Value is the end that is sought both by the organization and by customers. Achieving value is a total effort that requires careful coordination and planning. Strategic management can contribute to adding value and thereby ensure a competitive advantage.

TOTAL VALUE

"Strategy isn't beating the competition; it's serving customers' real needs" (Ohmae, 1988). When one recognizes that customers have changing expectations, it becomes obvious that the way to beat competitors is to deal directly with what the customer wants. Ohmae points out that the smartest strategy in war is to avoid the battle. There is no better proof of the validity of this statement than the price wars that ensue when strategy deteriorates into cost competition alone. The current battle in the PC computer field also illustrates that price wars simply erode the profits of all the suppliers of a product and rarely lead to a sustainable competitive advantage for anyone. Similarly, price clubs find that they cannot meet customers' need for service. In a provocative article entitled "Roaches Outlive Elephants," Drucker (1991) suggests that some of the largest corporations are in trouble and may not survive the current business environment. He places General Motors and IBM in this category.

Size alone is no longer enough to sustain current organizations; witness the linking of IBM with Apple and with Siemens in Europe. Flexibility and time to delivery may yield greater competitiveness than what used to be considered economies of scale, because economies alone no longer suffice.

According to Forker (1991), meeting customer needs is only a starting point. She insists that surpassing customer expectations should be the goal of every organization. Anticipate customer needs and then supply them in a "value added" mode to ensure that you keep a competitive edge. Bergsma (1989) maintains that there is a new standard of performance expected of top management: the management of value. He cites Deming, who considered quality of design, conformance, and performance as essential for meeting customer expectations. Managers increasingly will be called on to ensure that the organization focuses on the creation of value. But how does management make certain that the greatest value is achieved from the assets under their control? Thorbeck (1991) suggests that the best way to compete in the marketplace is to invigorate workers and focus on special skills. He points out that whereas unhealthy organizations lack coherence, healthy organizations are coherent and their personalities, capabilities, and attitudes help achieve desired goals. He describes a company where the factory was only an hour away from headquarters but no CEO had visited it in over four years. Building a cohesive team requires interaction and leadership. Involvement on the part of management is crucial to achieving an organizational culture that focuses on creating value and thereby competitiveness. This has been demonstrated by Levi Strauss, where CEO Robert Haas recognized that the company's major asset was the aspirations of its people (Howard, 1990). Haas employs company values to define what people are responsible for, and then he uses these responsibilities to shape performance and training. The result? A remarkably flexible and innovative company that has been one of the fastest growing in the apparel industry. At the same time, Levi Strauss has sustained its commitment to dealing with social issues.

Value marketing builds on the concept that quality, service, and pricing are the key to survival (Power et al., 1991). Value implies that the company is meeting customer needs and demands; however, that high quality does not mean higher prices. Value marketing ensures the customer that the product will perform as advertised and that customers will get even more than they expect. Guarantees reinforce consumer confidence and help build relationships based on the facts pertaining to the product. Finally, Power recommends that unrealistic prices be avoided, especially where a product does not justify the price. This, however, does not preclude specialty stores such as Tiffany Jewelers from charging higher prices, because the price incorporates prestige and special service. For example, one might wonder whether spending $175,000 for a Rolls-Royce reflects the pursuit of value or prestige.

The 1990s have been described as the era of the "quality imperative." This era was ushered in by highly competitive Japanese products and fostered by W. Edwards Deming and J. M. Juran, who are both pioneers in the field of statistical quality control (Port, 1991). A global revolution in marketing is clearly under way; every facet of the business is affected, and products and services will continue to improve. Port and Carey (1991) have cited a number of interesting statistics comparing the United States with Canada, Germany, and Japan on the attributes shown in the accompanying table. These data are based on 500 companies in the automotive, banking, computer, and health care industries. Although the United States is still a formidable competitor, it is obvious that in most categories, Japan leads the pack. In a comparison between U.S. companies and Japanese companies related to engineering and design, it was clear that the Japanese were much more responsive than were U.S. companies to the quality imperative. Japanese companies invest significantly more money in initial screening, evaluation, and planning. The result is that their average operating revenues are 42%, compared with the U.S. figure of 22%. Income from operations is 29% for the Japanese compared with 18% for the best American companies. These data depict the tangible benefits that can be derived from applying the quality/value approach.

	U.S.	Japan	Germany	Canada
Customer satisfaction reported	37%	41%	22%	43%
Competitiveness factors	29%	32%	6%	26%
Use of the time-based approach	21%	55%	7%	19%
Amount of process simplification utilized	12%	47%	6%	19%
Performance evaluation used	54%	59%	54%	51%

As the foregoing comparison shows, product design can contribute significantly to both quality and profitability. Hauser and Clausing (1988) have developed an approach that provides a conceptual map allowing for interfunctional planning and communications. The conceptual map groups the things customers want into bundles of attributes reflecting customer concerns. The preferences are weighted to reflect their relative importance and then related to competitive advantage. Engineering changes of the product are evaluated by team members. Thus the conceptual map shows how engineering decisions affect customer perceptions. Both of these are then related to process and production planning to yield the final desired quality. The authors of this approach call it "quality function deployment." Using it, Japanese auto makers completed 90% of their changes in an average of 17 months and had approximately half as many changes as the American automotive companies, who were much later in completing their design changes. Most of the design changes in American companies came between 1 and 3 months before final production, and many had a fair number of changes 3 months after completion.

Using an approach called "smart design" for the Mercury Sable, Ford was able to outsell General Motors (Nussbaum et al., 1988). Their approach to design blended form, function, quality, and style. In order to support this approach, companies such as IBM are using computer programs to analyze and simplify all the parts that go into their products. Another source of quality and value is the more intelligent use of time. A time-based competitive advantage can be achieved where flexible manufacturing with rapid response systems helps firms to expand the variety of products available in a shorter period than competitors (Stalk, 1988). To illustrate how the time-based approach works, consider that the United States produced 10 million automobile suspension components in 1987, compared to 3.5 million for the Japanese. But the United States required 242 employees to do so, the Japanese only 57. Not only were U.S. costs higher ($100 per part for the United States versus $49 for the Japanese), but the United States had only 11 varieties of finished parts whereas the Japanese had 38. It is obvious that when it is properly applied, the time-based approach significantly affects strategies. It will be an important factor to consider in the '90s.

Northern Telecom recognized that moving in the direction of a time-based strategy would mean rethinking almost every aspect of the business and would disrupt most of the company's current systems and practices. Here again, however, moving faster led to significant improvements. Over a five-year period, manufacturing intervals were reduced 75% to 80%, inventory was reduced approximately 30% over a 5-year period, and overhead was reduced approximately 30%. At the same time, customer satisfaction improved 25%. One of the major advantages of a time-based approach is knowing where costs occurred. Northern Telecom's new P&L statement showed that many costs were previously lumped into overhead. Now, with a flexible and knowledgeable workforce, company managers have adopted a "pay-for-skill" program. Northern Telecom considers improving delivery a never-ending process. When it reaches its 5-year milestone, it will reassess its strategy. If required, planners expect to modify their objectives. "There's no time to stand still in a time-based environment" (Merrills, 1989).

The well-known camping equipment company, Coleman of Wichita, Kansas, found that sales were grinding to a halt. By switching to a faster and more flexible approach, it made significant improvements in growth and is now considered a formidable competitor (Dumaine, 1991). Two years ago Coleman offered 20 models of ice coolers that could be had in three colors. With its new flexible approach, it now has 140 models in 12 colors—and was at the same time able to cut inventory costs by $10 million, reduce scrap by 60%, and increase productivity by 30%. Achieving flexibility required more than changes in equipment; it also required the cooperation of the union and workers. However, Coleman felt that if people were not deeply involved in understanding the business, they would not be able to perform well. The company's prior approach to design never allowed any mistakes, and meeting this standard required so many approvals that very little could be done. Now product development teams can make their own decisions without further approvals, a system that has resulted in significantly increased profits. As another example, Intel has found that the only way it can compete in the fast-changing chip market is to produce new designs in half the time it used to take and thus lock out competitors (Hof, 1992). However, even more rapid delivery may not be enough to stem Intel's losses. For example, Intel's 486 chip has a relative speed of 19, compared with IBM's RISC chip, which clocks in at 89—almost 5 times faster.

Most approaches to adding value have focused on improvements internal to the organization. Value marketing and total quality management illustrate the importance of dealing with the customer. Thus the customer is acknowledged as the key to achieving competitive advantage. (We have come full circle: for many years, the saying "The customer is king" stressed that the market's acceptance of products was the bottom line.) Flexible manufacturing, speedier delivery, and a greater emphasis on quality, service, pricing, and value have contributed to meeting customer expectations. An additional factor has now been added that can extend the ability of firms to increase value and better meet customer demand in order to beat the competition. Forging "strategic alliances" or "value-adding partnerships" helps to extend the firm's value-adding capability beyond the firm itself by combining the best of two or more organizations. There are many examples of strategic partnering. Ford and Mazda have built a strong team (Treece et al., 1992). Developing a new model car can easily cost over $2 billion. By using a strategic tie-in, the two companies can share these costs to the benefit of both, even where there appears to be obvious competition. Both organizations remain independent and continue their own research and development, but they work as partners on projects they feel will contribute to their mutual benefit. For example, Mazda wanted to develop a sporty utility vehicle and buy it from Ford. Ford was willing to provide a modified version of the Explorer, because this gave them the opportunity to manufacture pickups for Mazda.

One challenge facing computer chip makers may require strategic partnering to succeed. It is estimated that by the year 2000, electronic components will be etched on silicon chips that will require circuits to be less than 0.2 microns (millionths of an inch) in size (Pitta, 1992). Sematech, the consortium of U.S. chip makers, is using partnering to improve chip-making techniques. Nearly perfect cleanliness will be required to manufacture these new electronic devices. Motorola has already spent $650 million to build a Class I factory. Japanese chip makers have indicated that they would be willing to invest whatever is needed to produce the most advanced chips. Without strategic partnering, the United States might be left out in the cold.

A similar concern was noted by Johnston and Lawrence (1988). They consider partnering an alternative to vertical integration for small companies that do not have enough capital to acquire another company. The approach they advocate is for a group of independent companies to work together closely in providing goods and services along the entire value chain. For example, the McKesson Corporation, a $6.67 billion drug and health care distributor, relied on value-adding partnerships to compete with large drugstore chains. What McKesson did was to offer small, independent drugstore operators the advantages of the computer system it had developed (which no small drugstore could afford to develop on its own). By doing this, McKesson formed strong and lasting relationships with the firms in the value chain that were responsible for the final distribution of its products.

Partnering can build a viable infrastructure based on a stakeholder analysis to identify where the interdependencies exist. Value and ways to achieve it have become the key underlying elements in meeting customer needs.

STRATEGIC SUCCESS AND ORGANIZATIONAL VALUES

In 1982 Thomas Peters and Robert Waterman published *In Search of Excellence*, in which they summarized the results of years of study and consulting experience addressing the question "What lessons can we learn from the best-run companies in the United States?" Peters and Waterman came up with eight recurring attributes of excellence among the companies they studied. These attributes were based on operating values: beliefs strongly held and acted on by the executives involved.

Continuing our examination of "total value management," we will consider how organizations develop their value concepts. The factors researched by Peters and Waterman provide a useful framework for exploring the basic values and beliefs of an organization and their effect on strategic performance.

1. *A bias for action.* Excellent companies want to get things done. They "do it, try it, fix it," as the adage goes. They don't sit around waiting for good things to happen to them. Merrill Lynch acted on this value when it introduced "cash management" programs for its customers. Merrill Lynch put the service into effect before it knew what features customers would want and how best to operate the service internally. Then the company monitored performance and kept "fixing" it until the operation ran smoothly, beating others to the marketplace and achieving a competitive advantage.

   AHSC did much the same thing with its automated purchasing system. Early in the implementation of its strategy, the company made a commitment to developing a new computer telecommunications network that would provide full catalog and ordering services for its customers.

2. *Closeness to the customer.* Excellent companies are customer-oriented. They are deeply concerned with product quality and service, and they listen closely to their users' wants and needs. These companies realize that a customer buys not only a product but also utility. Utility is achieved when a product or service works as it's supposed to, when it lasts, when the customer knows how to use it, and when it's easy to use and achieves the desired results.

   IBM has been very successful at selling utility, largely because its founder, Thomas Watson, believed that one should offer "not machines for rent, but machine services." For Watson, services included timely advice and counsel on how to use the machines in the customer's place of business, as well as prompt repair and maintenance to ensure that the machines worked properly.

3. *Autonomy and entrepreneurship.* Excellent companies encourage innovation from within. In order to do this, these companies give their subunits or divisions considerable autonomy and foster an entrepreneurial spirit among their personnel. To ensure success, they often associate this value with another that "allows" individuals to make a reasonable number of mistakes.

   A chief feature of entrepreneurship within a large organization is almost always the emergence of a "champion": a person who believes strongly in an idea and who is willing to take risks for it. The successful champion finds a network of support people throughout the organization.

ILLUSTRATIVE CASE: AHSC

Our first illustrative case describes how American Hospital Supply Corporation achieved strategic success. Founded in the early 1920s, American Hospital Supply Corporation (AHSC) enjoyed modest success for the first 50 years of its existence. Just a few products, such as intravenous solutions, syringes, surgical gloves, and suction tubing, constituted its total product offering. In the late 1970s, executives took stock of what they believed to be a deteriorating situation. The company was not growing as fast as its president, Foster G. McGraw, and his associates thought it should. Inventories were accumulating rapidly. Profits were stagnant. They wondered what they could do to turn the company around. One thing they realized was that they had very little useful information about their customers' preferences and needs. They did not know why customers bought medical supplies from AHSC or from AHSC's competitors. Furthermore, they did not fully comprehend the forces that shaped the demand for their products and influenced their customers' purchasing decisions. As a first step to get a handle on its problem, AHSC undertook a comprehensive survey of the purchasing agents in hospitals, laboratories, and clinics throughout the United States. Hospital purchasing agents were considered the primary customers, because they were the ones who ordered AHSC's products.

When the results of the survey were in, the executives were rather surprised. The purchasing agents reported that they experienced great difficulty in placing orders for medical supplies. The agents were confused because there were so many different suppliers, and they were dissatisfied because sources of supply frequently were not dependable. There was also a morass of paperwork to deal with, and it was often a week or longer before they received the supplies ordered. Their hospitals' accounts payable were in disarray because of partial shipments, discounts, and complicated billings. Bookkeeping costs were mounting. It was nearly impossible to keep track of inventory. Consequently, each hospital generally carried 75–90 days of inventory for each item to ensure availability of supplies.

AHSC's executives viewed this chaotic situation as an opportunity because no single distributor met the hospitals' needs. AHSC decided to embark on a "full-line" product-distribution strategy. This meant adding a significant number of new products to the existing product line and developing a new distribution system. The company set the key objective of its strategy as follows: to place "at the purchaser's fingertips" the capacity to order all of the hospital's supplies directly from AHSC. It then set out to find the means to achieve this objective.

The essence of AHSC's strategy was to create a competitive advantage by developing the most reliable and responsive distribution system possible. AHSC placed a computer terminal in each hospital purchasing agent's office and linked it, via a nationwide network, to the central office. Purchasing agents immediately liked the system because it relieved them of a substantial burden.

AHSC's strategy proved successful. More and more purchasing agents ordered goods from AHSC, and they did so even if another vendor offered a particular item at a lower cost. By 1985, competitive bidding in the medical supplies market had virtually ceased. Customers became ever more dependent on AHSC, and business flourished.

Customer service was the key to AHSC's strategy. The driving force of that strategy was an efficient distribution system. Major strategic decisions about acquisitions, mergers, divestitures, and repositioning all revolved around this crucial resource. AHSC created a system to solve its strategic problem. It specified measures of performance for the system, including fast, easy ordering for the customer and 24-hour delivery. Finally, it committed the company's resources to achieving these strategic goals.

In order to diversify, managers at AHSC concentrated on a planned merger with Hospital Corporation of America. However, a rival firm, Baxter Travenol Laboratories, Inc. (now Baxter International), was making plans to acquire

AHSC, CONTINUED

AHSC. Baxter Travenol, itself a major manufacturer of hospital supplies, offered AHSC $50 per share. AHSC resisted Baxter's $50-a-share bid, and HCA attempted to stop Baxter by canceling a $100-million contract to buy intravenous solutions from Baxter and threatening to cancel nearly $1 billion in other purchase agreements. After several weeks, AHSC's resistance and HCA's threats failed, and Baxter Travenol acquired AHSC with a final bid of $51 per share (or $3.8 billion). The merger of AHSC, with $1.8 billion in sales, and Baxter Travenol, with $3.4 billion in sales (1984 figures), created the largest health care company in the United States.

Why was acquisition of AHSC a good strategy for Baxter Travenol? For one thing, the two companies were in the same business, which allowed Baxter to expand without diversifying. Another benefit of the merger was economies of scale. Baxter Travenol's acquisition of AHSC increased its sales volume, which enabled it to produce and distribute more products at less cost and thereby create more profit. Baxter's net income increased from $29 million in 1984 to $138 million in 1985, the year of the merger. By 1986 Baxter's sales totaled $5.6 billion, up from $3.5 billion in 1984. Net income jumped to $271 million in 1987, and based on first-quarter statistics, projected net income for 1988 was $364 million.

Finally, Baxter Travenol benefited from AHSC's strengths, particularly its computerized order and distribution system, called ASAP (Harvard Business School Case, 1985). Baxter expanded the ASAP system, which allows customers to order supplies directly through a central computer by means of a telephone-linked terminal. The system was tailored to individual customer needs, enabling hospitals, laboratories, and other customers to order products in predetermined groupings. It also provided price information, order confirmation, and a procedure for payment.

Shortly after it merged with AHSC, Baxter Travenol began to consolidate its operations to cut costs. After it swallowed American Hospital Supply, Baxter's size was tripled. Baxter's current posture is to trim down acquisitions, because they are not always the answer to achieving either profitable growth or a sustainable competitive advantage. Vernon R. Loucks, Jr. has restructured Baxter three times since 1986 by shedding plants, workers, and businesses. Loucks expected that these measures would be a means to respond to the constant pressure for cost control in health care (Siler, 1990). It was estimated that restructuring would save $275 million by 1993 on sales of $7.4 billion in 1989. In part, the problem stemmed from the struggle to absorb the 1985 hostile takeover of AHSC. Loucks expected to eliminate 6,000 jobs, but the number that it was possible to cut back proved far smaller. A vicious price war with Abbott Laboratories broke out shortly after the AHSC takeover devastated Baxter's profits. At the same time, hospitals began negotiating as a group and were able to obtain lower prices from suppliers. Following this was the loss to Abbott of a major contract with Voluntary Hospitals of America. As if all this were not bad enough, in Chicago a federal grand jury was hearing evidence to determine whether Baxter, the world's largest hospital supply corporation, was in violation of a federal anti-boycott law by pledging to Arab League officials not to do business with Israel (Siler et al., 1991). Baxter was eager to sever relations with Israel because of a lucrative joint venture with Nestlé in the $2 billion clinical nutrition market. And in addition to the anti-boycott case, Baxter was accused of paying physicians who make referrals. Medicare prohibits this kind of kickback.

Tracing the path of once-successful AHSC through to its takeover by Baxter illustrates that acquisitions call for continuous changes in strategy to contend with fierce competition and the unpredictable behavior of customers. Any unethical behavior that Baxter engaged in may also have contributed to its problems.

The 3M Corporation fosters internal autonomy and entrepreneurship through venture teams. A venture team at 3M consists of a small group of volunteers who represent various disciplines within the company—research and development, manufacturing, marketing, sales, and finance—and who, under appropriate leadership, make a full-time commitment to developing a new product. The members of the team are well motivated because each participates in the economic success of the product. Masking tape, 3M's first major product, is the result of just such an entrepreneurial approach, as is its famous Scotch tape. Most of 3M's current product line was generated by this system of venture teams.

4. *Productivity through people*. Excellent companies draw on the talent of their employees, seeing them as contributors of ideas, not just as a source of physical labor. In other words, they accord them respect. Many approaches encourage productivity through people: management by objectives (MBO), quality control circles, distributed decision making, and flat, interactive organizational structures are examples. Successful organizations tend to motivate employees by ensuring that

- Each person's job is reasonably demanding. (Sheer endurance does not count.)
- There is some variety and occasionally some novelty in each job.
- Each employee can learn and grow on the job.
- Each employee has an area of decision making that can be considered his or her own.
- Each employee gets social support and recognition.
- Employees can identify their jobs and the firm's products as part of their social life.
- Each job leads to some sort of desirable future goal for each employee.

During the 1970s and early 1980s, Hewlett-Packard (HP) built its personnel strategy around these ideas. From its inception, HP had never been a hire-and-fire company. During the 1970 recession, HP did not lay people off. Instead everyone was asked to work 10% fewer hours and take a 10% cut in pay. HP involved its employees in most corporate decisions and gave them considerable freedom and autonomy. This even included free use of electrical and mechanical laboratory equipment for personal projects. The value of respecting employees and encouraging them to stand out has been responsible for much innovation at Hewlett-Packard.

5. *Hands-on, value-driven executives*. One of the remarkable characteristics of a successful company is that its executives tend to "get their hands dirty" and participate periodically in some of the minute details of the business. These executives usually like hands-on, face-to-face engagements. They occasionally make sales calls on potential customers or operate a new piece of production machinery. These actions communicate their values to co-workers and customers and keep them in touch with the realities of doing business.

Peters and Waterman identified three characteristics of successful executives. (a) They have values they believe should guide the business: striving to be best, the importance of details, belief in people as individuals, the company as an extended family, the importance of profits, and the need for superior quality and service. (b) They know how to articulate and communicate these values to others. (They often choose slogans or almost ritualistic activities to do so.) (c) They use special indicators to monitor the company's progress. These indicators are in keeping with the company's values and do not alienate employees.

Author Tom Peters cited Willard J. Marriott, Sr., as a case in point. The founder of Marriott Hotels always believed strongly in quality, service, and cleanliness. He would read every customer complaint that his hotels received— a time-consuming task as his chain of hotels grew. But it kept him close to the business, and his dedication communicated to others the importance of the values he stood for.

All successful strategies are based on values like these. Furthermore, most successful companies develop measures of performance, or score cards, that tell them how well they are doing with respect to goals and values. (In Chapter 3 we will consider how values are determined, goals and objectives set, and measures of performance developed.) Values are derived from the deep-seated beliefs of a company's executives, and the companies that achieve excellence live by these values.

6. *Stick to knitting.* Excellent companies maintain a focus, even if they undertake a wide variety of activities and compete in many different markets. Unifying it all are an underlying theme and a definite sense of direction.

Too much diversification tends to diffuse a firm's focus. Richard Rumelt (1974, pp. 114–115) discovered this in his study of approximately 200 of the largest corporations in the United States. Rumelt found that companies that diversified into *related* businesses (especially when the related business involved a particular skill or resource that the company had perfected in its dominant business) outperformed companies that became conglomerates or acquired unrelated businesses. On the average, the related businesses had higher profits, higher rates of growth, and higher price-earnings ratios.

Rumelt's findings suggest guidelines for developing strategies. First, the successful company innovates and acquires other firms but does not venture far from its core skills and resources or from its executives' realm of experience. That is, the company "sticks to its knitting." Second, Rumelt's research revealed that product-division firms show average growth rates in earnings per share substantially larger than rates of firms without separate product divisions. This finding indicates the benefits of autonomy and entrepreneurship within an organization. It also shows why having product divisions yields so many benefits.

Ling-Tempco-Vought (LTV), the conglomerate brain child of flamboyant Jimmy Ling, is an example of a firm that diversified beyond its ability to focus. LTV lost track of its corporate strengths. It became involved in steel, meats, and high technology but found no common denominator with which to manage them. When LTV's Jones and Laughlin Steel holding suffered financial setbacks, the entire LTV structure nearly collapsed.

3M, on the other hand, identified its principal strength and strategic advantage—its coating and bonding technology—and forged a successful strategy based on this superior technological capability.

AHSC did much the same thing: it defined the medical-supplies field as its core capability and decided that excellence in distribution would be its driving force. Every acquisition and new venture fit into a carefully laid out product-line strategy. AHSC then focused on its three most distinctive competencies—telecommunications, computer-based order entry, and 24-hour delivery—in that order.

7. *Simple form, lean staff.* Excellent companies avoid excessive bureaucracy and red tape. A company experiences crises as it moves from the initiation or entrepreneurial phase of the cycle to the bureaucratic phase, then to the divisional, product group, and matrix phases.

One way to cope with each crisis is to incorporate more overhead. This means adding reports and forms, new managers and staff, and possibly luxuries if the company is profitable. This method of coping with crisis has led to the popularization of Parkinson's Law (work expands to fill the time available). The result is that the company becomes sluggish, and its profits tend to decline.

In the early 1980s, Schlumberger (pronounced "shlum-bare-zhay"), a little-known oil equipment and exploration information firm, was the world leader in making physical measurements of rocks, oil, and gas in newly drilled oil wells. It was one of the world's most profitable firms, and it practiced the "lean and mean" value. At the close of 1981, it had a total stock market value (price per share times number of shares in the market) of over $16 billion. This ranked it fourth, behind AT&T, IBM, and Exxon. Schlumberger employed approximately 75,000 people worldwide but ran its two major headquarters in New York and Paris with a total of 197 people, including its chairman and chief executive officer, Jean Riboud. Ken Auletta, in a *New Yorker* profile entitled "A Certain Poetry" (1983, p. 46), described Riboud's approach to form, staff, and surroundings as follows:

> Riboud's office has a single telephone with just two lines, and no private bathroom; there are white blinds on the windows, and a simple beige sisal carpet on the floor. His desk is a long, rectangular teak table with chrome legs; on it are a few memoranda but no "in" or "out" boxes and no books. His personal New York Staff consists of one secretary, Lucille Northrup, to whom he rarely dictates; memoranda and paperwork are frowned upon at Schlumberger, and when Riboud wants to send out a memorandum, he first writes it in long hand.

8. *Simultaneous loose–tight properties.* Finally, excellent companies find ways to be flexible, decentralized, and entrepreneurial while maintaining the ability to be inflexible, centralized, and controlled when necessary. These companies develop a corporate culture with a clear set of values, habits, and procedures—a "way of going." The individual who works with and promotes these core values is supported, rewarded, and given a great deal of freedom, whereas the individual who goes against these core values is disciplined, castigated, or chastised. If the violation is severe enough, the individual is fired.

McDonald's, under the leadership of the late Ray Kroc, mastered the balance between freedom and control. For instance, small groups within the company were given the freedom to experiment with ideas such as McDonald's breakfast menu, which, by 1985, accounted for about 40% of the company's total business. To this day, McDonald's operates with a very loose structure. Most major decisions are made in informal daily meetings of the home-office executives. The store managers and franchisees are given a great deal of autonomy.

Members of McDonald's top management team spend great amounts of time in the field inspecting operations and observing employees. In management's eyes, there are no greater offenses than serving stale or undercooked french fries, not being pleasant and courteous to the customer, leaving wrappings and paper cups strewn around the restaurant and parking lot, or serving food that doesn't meet McDonald's standards. These violations are dealt with rapidly and decisively. The perpetrators are warned, disciplined, and if need be, fired. Quality, service, cleanliness, and value (QSCV) are central to McDonald's strategy and firmly integrated into its culture.

These eight operating values have served as principles of management for some of America's most successful companies. The strategies of many successful companies are based on one or more of them. AHSC followed all eight to some extent.

In *A Passion for Excellence* (Peters and Austin, 1985), Tom Peters reemphasized the importance of several of the eight attributes contributing to success, particularly the hard-to-measure qualities embedded in attributes 2 through 5:

- Closeness to the customer (customer service)
- Autonomy and entrepreneurship (motivation and innovation)
- Productivity through people (quality)
- Hands-on, value-driven executives (leadership style)

Peters and Austin went on to say that the real success secret of well-run companies is their style of leadership, particularly a style that boosts productivity by empowering employees to be both motivated and innovative.

There are, of course, other values that might guide a successful company's strategy. A company could, for example, simply strive for technological superiority, following the adage that if you build a better mousetrap, the world will flock to your door. The essential point, however, is that *all strategies are based on values*. The first—and sometimes also the last—task of strategic managers is to determine what values will guide the organization.

MAINTAINING AND RENEWING SUCCESSFUL STRATEGIES

Success and excellence are temporary phenomena. Once achieved, they must be pursued continuously or they will erode. Strategic management involves constant monitoring of the methods and assumptions that underlie it.

In 1984, two years after Peters and Waterman published *In Search of Excellence,* *Business Week* ran an article called "Who's Excellent Now?" The article reported that some of the firms cited in the book as excellent companies had slipped from the top. At least 14 of the 43 excellent companies that Peters and Waterman identified were no longer considered among the nation's best. Hewlett-Packard no longer passed the test; neither did Atari, Delta Airlines, Disney, Kodak, or Texas Instruments. Why did these excellent companies falter? Was it because they abandoned attributes and values that made them successful? Were they victims of unexpected environmental forces? Or did they fail to recognize, in time, that they needed to formulate new strategies for changing conditions? The answers varied. Atari, for example, violated seven of the eight operating values identified by Peters and Waterman. Delta, at that time, was unprepared to deal with an external force—deregulation of the airline industry. As Robert Waterman wrote in response to the *Business Week* article, "Nobody said that excellence was forever" (Waterman, 1984).

STRATEGIC FAILURES

Perhaps the most striking example of the impermanence of excellence can be found in the U.S. automobile industry of the 1970s. From the 1930s until the early 1970s, the largest of the U.S. automobile manufacturers dominated the world market. Times changed, but the U.S. automobile industry did not.

In a talk entitled "The Failure of Success" (O'Toole, 1985, p. 55), Professor James O'Toole of the University of Southern California attributed the U.S. automobile companies' downfall to their failure to reexamine and challenge ten basic assumptions that had served them well for 40 years but were no longer appropriate. He recounted the obsolete assumptions of General Motors, Ford, Chrysler, and other U.S. companies, to which he gave the collective name "Monolithic Motors." Their obsolete assumptions follow.

1. *Monolithic Motors is in the business of making money, not cars.* This assumption focused managers' attention on finances and cash management and diverted it from their customers' changing wants and needs and from shifts in the marketplace.

2. *Success comes not from technological leadership, but from having the resources to quickly adopt innovations successfully introduced by others.* This failure to manage technology strategically permitted the Japanese manufacturers first to gain technological parity and then to surpass the American automobile manufacturers' technological advantage.

3. *Cars are primarily status symbols. Styling is therefore more important than quality to buyers who are, after all, "trading up" every other year.* Changes in economic conditions and in individual values changed this once-salient assumption. In the 1970s, many customers began to want utility, economy, and longevity more than status; several foreign-manufactured automobiles satisfied these desires better than U.S. models.

4. *The American car market is isolated from the rest of the world. Foreign competitors will never gain more than 15% of the domestic market.* Today the

United States is part of a global economy brought about by increased transportation, communication, and commerce. In a global society and economy, no one country can isolate itself effectively.

5. *Energy will always be cheap and abundant.* OPEC in the early 1970s ended the validity of this assumption.

6. *Workers do not have an important impact on productivity or product quality.* The prevalence of Henry Ford's great contribution, the mass-production assembly line, may have reached its limits. As the Lordstown plant's worker rebellion and other, similar events indicated, workers have a great deal of influence on production, quality, and quantity. Working together with the aims of the company in mind, they can enhance performance. Working apart and against the company, they can destroy performance. Interestingly enough, the more automated the plant (the more robotics it employs), the more important worker cooperation becomes.

7. *The consumer movement does not represent the concerns of a significant portion of the American public.* Ralph Nader's book *Unsafe at Any Speed* changed this assumption. Subsequent problems with product liability and financing reinforced the need for a change in thinking.

8. *The government is the enemy. It must be fought tooth and nail every inch of the way.* This assumption became a management cop-out for the U.S. automobile industry: an excuse for not addressing some real concerns about safety, pollution, and performance. By making the assumption universal, the automobile industry failed to address some legitimate issues and incurred substantial legal costs.

9. *Strict, centralized financial controls are the secret to good administration.* Like so many strategic assumptions, this is a half-truth that outlived its usefulness. When Alfred Sloan brought financial controls to General Motors in the 1920s, he brought order to chaos. But by the 1970s, the controls had become masters rather than servants. The result was that innovation, creativity, and long-range thinking were stifled.

10. *Managers should be developed from the inside.* Too much inbreeding in the U.S. automobile industry resulted in too little vision and much complacent thinking.

The failure of the U.S. automobile firms to monitor and challenge these ten assumptions—in short, their failure to think strategically and to change their strategies—permitted the Japanese and others to capture U.S. markets and prosper in them.

The automobile manufacturers have not been alone in basing strategies on incorrect assumptions. Robert F. Hartley summarized several such failures in a book entitled *Management Mistakes* (1983). Hartley's main conclusion after studying errors in strategic management was the same as O'Toole's. Success does not guarantee continued success; indeed, it can lead to failure.

In his book *Running American Business*, Robert Lamb (1987) looked at other reasons why some companies do not succeed. Lamb investigated failures in the executive suite and concluded that many chief executive officers are risk-averse and caught up in short-term thinking and that boards of directors are little more than rubber stamps. Lamb believes that executives give technology very low priority and are overly concerned about being members of the "phantom club" of chief executive officers (CEOs).

STRATEGIC RENEWAL

How can companies adapt their strategies to take advantage of changing conditions? Owens-Illinois, long a successful manufacturer specializing in glass containers, faced the classic dilemma of how to achieve growth in a declining industry. The solution was to refocus the company's business to include industries spurred on by population growth, particularly the growth of the elderly population. In 1984, under the leadership of chairman Robert Lanigan, Owens-Illinois began to refocus by manufacturing plastic containers and diversifying. The company phased out of glass-container manufacturing and invested $600 million to modernize production and increase output of its remaining product line. In addition, Owens-Illinois acquired a mortgage company—Alliance Mortgage—and began to invest in nursing homes. The change in strategy contributed to the profitability of Owens-Illinois.

The changes at Owens-Illinois exemplified corporate renewal through new strategies based on the recognition of new opportunities. Robert Waterman's book *The Renewal Factor* (1987) identified eight factors that companies should use in their corporate renewal efforts. Like the eight attributes he and Peters identified in *In Search of Excellence*, the eight renewal factors emphasize operating values and attitudes. Waterman's new directives follow.

1. *Informed opportunism.* Keep abreast of the latest information to maintain strategic advantage and flexibility.
2. *Direction and empowerment.* Identify what needs to be done and allow subordinates the freedom to find ways of doing it.
3. *Friendly facts and congenial controls.* Use financial controls as checks and balances but give managers the freedom to be creative.
4. *A different mirror.* Recognize that ideas can come from every source, including customers, competitors, and employees.
5. *Teamwork, trust, politics, and power.* Accept relentless fighting as a consequence of power politics while stressing teamwork and trust in getting the job done.
6. *Stability in motion.* Respond to changing forces with the recognition that some consistency must be maintained and norms retained; allow rules to be broken when necessary.
7. *Attitudes and attention.* Realize that attention is more effective than exhortation at getting things done and that symbolic behavior makes the words come true.
8. *Causes and commitment.* Maintain an awareness of the grand cause so that it permeates all action.

PREPARING AND COMMUNICATING A STRATEGIC PLAN

Strategic plans evolve from careful analysis of a firm's competitive advantage, threats posed by competitors, environmental forces, customer demands, and ways of measuring how well company goals are being met. The final plan should help executives make policy and operational decisions according to corporate guidelines, but it should not stifle creativity or prevent executives from dealing effectively with contingencies and changing conditions. The strategic plan also serves as the vehicle for communicating proposed strategy to individuals in the organization who are responsible for its implementation as well as soliciting input from those individuals.

A strategic plan can have the following components:

1. A definition of the desired future scope of the company, including a statement of identity. "What business is the company in or should it be in and what kind of company is it or should it be?" (Andrews, 1971, p. 28).
2. A description of the competitive advantage of the company, including its distinctive competence in relation to its competitors and the market niche it intends to occupy.
3. A statement of the purpose, mission, goals, and objectives of the company and the measures used to evaluate performance.
4. A statement of how to allocate resources needed to implement and execute the plan.

STRATEGIC PLANNING AT OMICON INDUSTRIES, INC.

Let us examine in detail the dynamics of strategic analysis at a major international corporation, Omicon Industries, Inc.

Omicon is a highly diversified company with $3 billion in sales and 24,000 employees. The company's core areas of expertise include processing paper and pulp, developing specialized chemical systems for paper and pulp factories, producing chemicals for forestry and agriculture, manufacturing heavy transport equipment, and engineering marine technologies. Omicon also develops, manufactures, and markets a wide variety of medical products and pharmaceuticals, serving doctors, nurses' committees, and hospitals. The 35 diversified business units are organized into the following four divisions:

- Engineering and distribution
- Pharmaceuticals
- Health care
- Consumer goods

Omicon's current return on investment of 11% is lagging behind that of its competitors.

To begin the analysis of the data, Omicon summarized the strategies of its business units by focusing on the economics and competitive nature of each business unit. Thus the process integrated information and creative insights from managers of each unit. It also involved these managers in the analysis, which usually leads to a more realistic action plan that the line managers understand and are committed to pursuing. The strategic planning helped higher-level managers to develop corporate strategy and more effectively allocate resources.

Omicon's strategic planning covered the following for each business unit:

1. Business definition: main thrust of the business, most important business activities.
2. Key success factors: manageable variables that can help Omicon gain competitive advantage in the industry.
3. Environmental assumptions: the market and competitive environment in which the strategy is to be pursued; major assumptions about the market; customers' purchasing criteria; technology; costs; and competitors' actions, which may represent opportunities or threats.
4. Omicon's competitive position: an assessment of Omicon's key success factors compared to key success factors of the major competitors.
5. Performance objectives: assessment of profits that can be made by improving competitive position and taking advantage of opportunities.
6. Action plan: major actions that need to be taken to maintain and improve competitive position and take advantage of opportunities.
7. The fit with corporate goals: an assessment of each business unit's compatibility with corporate goals and of the potential for improved fit.

Figure 1.2 shows how these seven components of strategy are related. Strategy, in this exhibit, is represented by the performance objectives. The arrows in Figure 1.2 show how the different components serve as a "reality test" for the entire strategic analysis. For example, component 3, environmental assumptions, is a key reality test for component 4, Omicon's competitive position, and component 5, performance objectives. An awareness of interactions among the seven components helps strategic planners to test the logic and assumptions of each one.

BUSINESS DEFINITION

The first objective in business definition was to distinguish each business unit at Omicon from the next. This was done by finding the point at which their key success factors started to differ significantly. Omicon defined its business units as having distinct products and/or services, target customer groups, and geographic regions in which they operated.

The business unit was further defined by specific customer needs and the manner in which they were satisfied. Figure 1.3 shows how key questions asked in defining each business led to key questions about other strategic components.

KEY SUCCESS FACTORS

The key success factors defined areas of possible competitive advantage. Why would a customer buy a product or be willing to pay more for it? How might a competitor succeed in persuading a customer to do both? In answering these questions, Omicon identified the most important key success factors and limited them to factors that could be acted on by competitors in the same business.

In Omicon's case, the most important key success factors were (1) increasing the product's value to the customer and (2) promoting cost-effectiveness. An

FIGURE 1.2 | **Seven Components of Strategy Formulation**

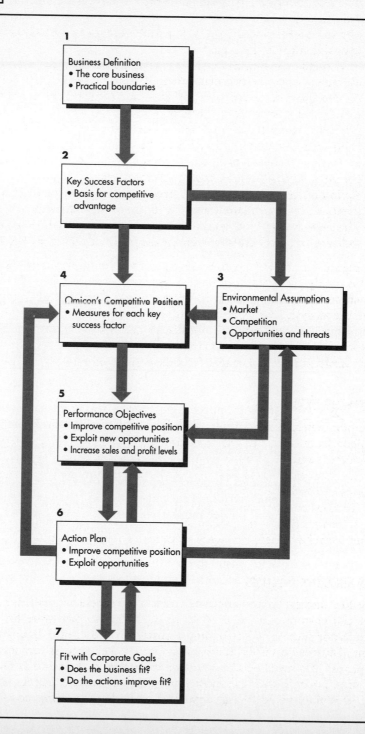

FIGURE 1.3	Key Questions Asked in the Analysis of Strategic Components One, Two, Three, and Six

Business Definition	Key Factors	Environmental Trends	Competitive Position	Opportunities
What are we selling?	Which competitors do we respect most?	Has the market been growing or declining? Will this trend continue?	Is the main competitor equal to us in all success factors or gaining?	Where are the weakest points in our competitive position?
How?	What do they do that we don't?	Are there any substitute products?	Is the main competitor losing money?	How quickly can we change things?
To whom?	What are the most important elements of cost?	Have there been any mergers or acquisitions?	Does the main competitor have a sustainable competitive advantage?	What do we have to do to succeed?
	Do customers want the cheapest product?	What is the position of imports?		
	What is a success factor and what is necessary to stay in business?	Does technology have much influence on costs?		
	Are the success factors the same for all businesses?			

assessment of customers' purchasing criteria was used to determine a product's value to the customer. Results were broken down into three categories of value:

- *Value of the product itself.* This value was a function of price, general performance, reliability, and up-to-date technology. These variables were applied to compare the value of Omicon's products to the value of competitors' products.
- *Value of customer service.* This value was a function of efficient communication of customers' service requests and promptness of service.
- *Value of start-up time.* This value was a function of how soon the customer could have a functioning product or equipment in place. It depended on manufacturing capacity, installation efficiency, and the effectiveness with which the customer was introduced to technological features or new system design.

Key success factors affecting cost-effectiveness included:

- Economies of scale in manufacturing or marketing
- Costs of raw materials and labor
- Productivity
- Manufacturing approaches
- Design, technology, engineering, or patents
- Location relative to the market

- Government subsidies or regulations
- Other considerations unique to the product

An alternative approach to the key success factors was developed by Kenichi Ohmae (1982). He evaluates a business strategy by using four categories:

1. Compete wisely.
   a. Old existing strategy—key factors for success
   b. New creative strategy—aggressive initiatives
2. Avoid head-on competition.
   a. Old existing strategy—relative superiority
   b. New creative strategy—strategic degrees of freedom

Ohmae then describes how to strengthen a company's competitive position.

1a. Focus resources in areas where the company can improve its competitive advantage.
1b. Challenge the accepted assumptions by using aggressive initiatives.
2a. Exploit relative superiority rather than competing across the board.
2b. Search for areas untouched by competitors and vigorously exploit these.

Ohmae summarizes his approach as "avoid doing the same thing, on the same battlegrounds, as competition."

ENVIRONMENTAL ASSUMPTIONS

The environmental assumptions made by Omicon integrated diverse information about the external business environment. These environmental assumptions were based on information about

- The market (size, growth, profitability, market shares of major competitors)
- Customers' purchasing behavior
- Technology
- Competitors
- Government regulations, politics, and so on

This information enabled Omicon to identify opportunities and threats.

COMPETITIVE POSITION

The determination of competitive position was based on the list of key success factors. Its purpose was to measure Omicon's market position for each factor relative to that of major competitors. Figure 1.4 shows Omicon's competitive advantages and disadvantages for three divisions. For example, a cost-effective advantage could be based on besting competitors with respect to economies of scale, productivity, product design, or efficiency of manufacturing.

Another important theme was innovation and new business opportunities. The strategy must not only maintain and improve competitive position but also continually upgrade Omicon's ability to innovate. Omicon could improve its competitive

FIGURE 1.4	Analysis of Competitive Position

Division	Competitive Position	Projected Profit Growth (1989)	
		Dollars (millions)	Percentage
Distribution division	Competitive disadvantage Control cost or provide full service? Have stock turnover or carry a full range?	$ 3.3	112%
Pharmaceutical division	Radical change in historic R&D focus Competitive position in raw materials Reduction of a key project Reduced investment plans	2.9	86
Health care division	Competitive disadvantage Need to focus geographically Cost reduction opportunities	0.8	118
Total		$ 7.0	105%

position by recognizing its sources of disadvantage and correcting them. For example, Omicon could increase its sales efforts to make the market aware of a product's advantage. Omicon could also improve its competitive position by recognizing entirely new sources of advantage, or *advantage innovation*. An advantage innovation might be a new manufacturing approach producing the same value at lower cost. Another form of innovation would be to identify an entirely new form of customer value. Such *value innovation* would represent new business opportunities. This difficult form of innovation involves predicting how the market, customer purchasing criteria, technology, and costs will evolve and how these developments might interact to provide new opportunities for increased value. Value innovation would also promote a spirit of entrepreneurship.

PERFORMANCE OBJECTIVES

Performance objectives emerged from assessments of competitive position and environmental assumptions. These objectives were designed to improve Omicon's competitive position, exploit new opportunities, and increase sales and profits as measured by

- Income level
- Change in income (percentage)
- Net income
- Return on sales (percentage)
- Operating cash flow
- Total assets
- Return on assets (percentage)
- Market share (percentage)

THE ACTION PLAN

The action plan was designed to achieve the performance goals. This plan included the specific actions required, capital investment proposals, and strategic expense (budget) proposals.

One important budget consideration for Omicon was to properly allocate funds in order to maintain its well-established competitive position. Capital investments and the strategic budget also had to be sufficient to achieve the strategies that would ensure continued strategic advantage.

FIT WITH CORPORATE GOALS

The next step in Omicon's strategic planning was to assist operating management in translating the corporate goals into a specific set of performance objectives for the individual businesses. This process was carried out in the context of the company's major purpose and goals, which are to build a balanced and growing portfolio of profitable and growth-oriented businesses based on

- Use of high-quality human resources
- Superior product design and engineering
- Delivery of value and service to the customer
- Focused international activities
- Lowest costs consistent with desired quality

By keeping corporate goals in mind, strategic planners could direct the company's resources into business units that had the highest chances of success. Planners were also able to allocate resources in directions consistent with corporate goals. Figure 1.5 shows where Omicon used corporate goals to guide the strategic-planning process.

One basic question that Omicon asked was "Can the business units create value through product engineering?" Although one of Omicon's corporate goals is to create value through design and engineering, Omicon had to consider costs. The company also had to ask, "Which business units have the best chance of success?" Omicon has a large number of business units. For each, the chance of success is obviously higher if it receives the time and attention of top management and budgetary resources. Businesses that were strong and closely related to corporate goals were likely to enjoy greater allocations of time and resources. Weak businesses less compatible with corporate goals and businesses without great sales potential were likely to be allocated less time and fewer resources. Figure 1.6 shows how Omicon based its final action plan on an assessment of its strengths and weaknesses.

A SYSTEMS FRAMEWORK FOR STRATEGIC MANAGEMENT

Unlike general management, which is primarily concerned with internal operations, strategic management is equally concerned with the external and the internal environment. A key objective of strategic management is to match the organization's

FIGURE 1.5	Role of Corporate Goals in Strategy Questions Asked at Omicon

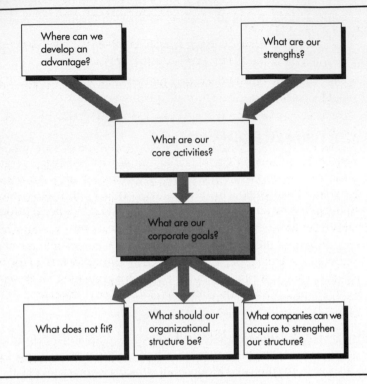

FIGURE 1.6	Action Plan Based on Omicon's Strengths and Weaknesses

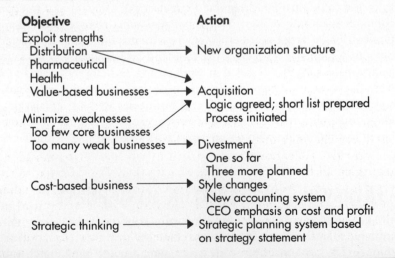

internal capability with the external opportunities and threats in order to formulate strategies that will achieve basic goals and maintain organizational values. Strategic management also enables the organization to adapt profitably to the vagaries of an unpredictable environment.

Any system of strategic management involves the five imperatives that C. West Churchman suggested in *The Systems Approach* (1968).

1. Identify the business's fundamental values and the goals and objectives that arise from them.
2. Assess the business's environment—forces outside the business itself that may be opportunities or threats.
3. Assess the business's resources and capabilities—those things within the control of the business, such as people, machinery, facilities, contracts, image, and goodwill—that can be allocated to achieve goals and objectives.
4. Identify or form the organization's components: (a) internal units that receive allocated resources and carry out the business's work and (b) an organizational structure that includes the units themselves and the relationships of authority, responsibility, and communication that they have with one another.
5. Develop the management and decision-making structure: the process used to allocate the business's resources to its components so as to realize goals and sustain values within the constraints of the environment.

THE STRATEGIC FOUR-FACTOR MODEL

The strategic four-factor model shown in Figure 1.7 illustrates a systems framework for strategic management. At the center of the model is embedded Churchman's first imperative: to identify the organization's values. Without knowledge of its values, an organization cannot develop its mission, goals, and objectives. Churchman's remaining four imperatives can be found within the four boxes in the circle. These imperatives are part of strategic planning, organizational structure, strategic control, and resource requirements. Outside the boxes are the forces and constraints that affect the four factors. The entire model shows how the organization's strategy must balance the demands imposed by external and internal forces, suit the overall functioning of the organization, and use resources in a manner that meets goals and satisfies values.

The arrows in Figure 1.7 show important interdependencies among the four factors of strategic management. Each of these factors links strategic management to the realities of the organization's internal or external environment, and each factor affects the other three directly or indirectly.

Strategic management, at the hub of the four-factor model, is the process of managing all four factors to achieve a strategy. The function of strategic management is to align the internal operation of the organization, including the allocation of human, physical, and financial resources, to achieve optimal interactions with the external environment. Strategic management is based on the organization's operational values—its fundamental beliefs about how the business should be conducted. The process of strategic management incorporates into strategies the types

FIGURE 1.7	Strategic Four-Factor Model

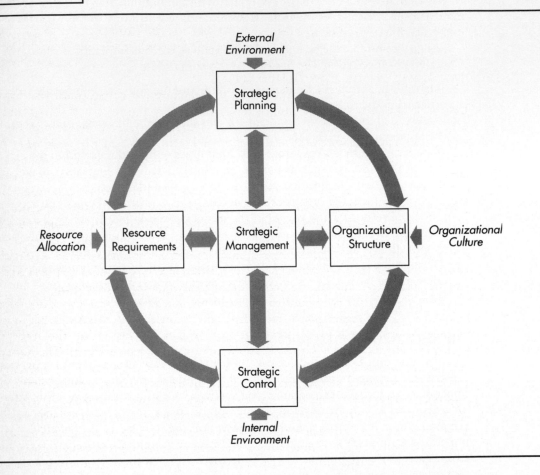

of values identified by Peters and Waterman (1982), Peters and Austin (1985), and Waterman (1987).

Strategic planning is the key link between strategic management and the organization's external environment. It is the one factor that requires a careful analysis of the external environment. Having identified external threats and opportunities, strategic planners analyze available resources and organizational strengths and weaknesses. The next step is to formulate alternative strategies that take advantage of external opportunities and internal strengths. Selected alternatives are then made into plans of action that have specific resource and organizational (structural and operational) requirements.

Resource requirements link strategic management to the organization's resources, including finances, facilities and equipment, land, access to information, goodwill, and personnel. Strategic planners have to determine resource requirements and their means of acquisition and allocation. In formulating strategic alternatives, planners must ask, "Can this strategy succeed, given the organization's available resources?" Various methods of analysis are used to assess resources and, if the strategy is feasible, to plan their allocation.

Organizational structure links strategic management to organizational realities. In formulating strategic alternatives, planners consider whether the organizational structure is suited to implementation of the strategy. Does the strategy fit the goals, objectives, labor pool, and operational procedures of the organization's units? Do the units have appropriate communication systems and procedures to monitor and control performance? Sometimes, as in the case of AHSC in the early 1980s, the organizational structure is changed to suit the strategy. Strategic planners must also determine whether the company's "unofficial" power structure, its culture, and the decision-making style of its managers will help or hinder implementation of a strategy. The style of leadership, operational values, and vision of top executives may be the most important factors determining whether an organization can succeed at implementation. Therefore, strategic planners must consider whether a strategy suits the leadership style of the organization's managers.

Strategic control is related to the implementation of a strategy. This factor links strategic management to the organization's internal environment because it involves evaluating how well the organization is implementing the strategy. Strategic control has two components, one internal and one external. The internal component involves monitoring resource allocation and organizational operations and suggesting changes needed to implement the strategy better. The external component involves measuring the strategy's success. Among the measures used are units sold, market share, gross sales, and profits. In a service-oriented business, the data might include customer evaluations of its service, such as the guest-comment cards read by Willard Marriott, Sr. Data related to specific performance goals may be as complex as the information analyzed by computerized management-by-objectives (MBO) systems. Strategic control is an ongoing process used to adapt implementation in response to (1) data about how well the strategy is doing and (2) changes in the internal or external environment.

In every chapter of this book, the strategic four-factor model and the strategy process model at the beginning of each chapter will be used to guide the reader through the phases involved in formulating an effective strategy for sustaining a competitive advantage.

ILLUSTRATIVE CASE: POLAROID

Our second illustrative case shows how a company in trouble can turn itself around with a careful strategic plan. In his article "Polaroid Struggles to Get Back in Focus," Peter W. Bernstein (1980) describes the stark evidence of trouble. In a warehouse near Cambridge, Massachusetts, where the company had its headquarters, piles of unsold Polavision sets were stored, testimony to the failure of Polaroid's highly touted instant-movie-camera system. Stockrooms from Santa Ana, California, to Paramus, New Jersey, overflowed with cartons of instant cameras and film. In Andover, Massachusetts, a vacant building that was once destined to house a film-assembly plant capable of producing millions of boxes of instant film stood empty, and then the building was sold. South of Boston, in Freetown, a building that was converted into a chemical factory went unused. After extensive layoffs, there were far fewer workers on the assembly lines of the camera production plants in Norwood than there had been in previous years.

A company in crisis, Polaroid paid heavily for past mistakes. Its miscalculation on Polavision was costly, and the company took a $68.5 million write-down, effectively reducing the inventory value of the sets to nothing. In addition, Polaroid misread the market for instant movie cameras; demand fell off just as the company was gearing up to produce more of them.

What went wrong at Polaroid? Why was top management unable to succeed at diversification? Was it a failure of leadership, or were the company's problems more deeply rooted? What could CEO William McCune have done? What information would he have needed to decide on a course of action? What sources of information could he have drawn on?

Polaroid's marketing of Polavision was at least as faulty as the technology. Consumers had been cool to home movies for a long time. Instead of coming to grips with Polavision's inherent marketing disadvantages, Polaroid chose to ignore them. Its strategy was simply to distribute this new product as broadly as it had the SX-70 five years earlier. But the public did not know what to make of the product, and Polaroid failed to devise a way for sales clerks to demonstrate its capabilities in a convincing and inviting way.

In the long run, how Polaroid solves its problems will depend on who is running the company. Edwin Land believed in developing the technology first, then selling consumers on its merits. "My motto," said Land, "is very personal and may not fit anyone else or any other company. It is: Don't do anything that someone else can do. Don't undertake a project unless it is manifestly important and nearly impossible. If it is manifestly important," Land continued, "then you don't have to worry about its significance. Since it's nearly impossible, you know that no one else is likely to be doing it, so if you do succeed, you will have created a whole new domain for yourself" (Chakrevarty, 1987). That was precisely what Edwin Land did with the Polaroid Corporation from his founding of the company in 1937 to his resignation as CEO in 1980. His motto proved successful until the late 1970s, when Land's blindness to the realities of the market led to severely declining sales.

In 1985 I. MacAllister Booth succeeded McCune as president and CEO, and McCune was made chairman of the board. Booth continued many of the policies that were in place in the early '80s. Booth paid off Polaroid's $130 million long-term debt and financed all growth out of cash flow. He assumed an accessible, open, managerial style, encouraging new ideas and inventions. He continued the change in marketing strategy by insisting that marketing was the key to increasing sales and therefore had to be more sophisticated. Accordingly, Booth used consumer research to develop the Spectra camera—the one that people really wanted.

In the style of Edwin Land, Polaroid has continued to invest in research and development, keeping a keen eye on marketability. In May of 1988, Polaroid revealed new technology that

POLAROID, CONTINUED

produces high-resolution black-and-white photographs from video images. The company also demonstrated a computer printer that produces color-photo images from television screens or computer screens. Although the payback for this type of long-range research is far in the future, Polaroid has worked toward financially firm ground today in order to invest in tomorrow. Polaroid has a strong brand identification, little long-term debt, and a stable film business. Management has combined Edwin Land's belief in undertaking nearly impossible projects of manifest importance with the profitability of well-researched markets. (In strategic terminology, Land subscribed to a highly differentiated strategy that provided a unique capability and a sustainable competitive advantage.)

The strategic planning of the '80s seems to be paying off for Polaroid. Shoring up its profitability for the '90s, Polaroid won the largest patent infringement case in history against Kodak. After a 15-year legal battle, Polaroid

forced Kodak to withdraw all its instant photography products (Weber, 1991). Yet in spite of its $925 million award from Kodak, shareholders are expressing dismay at the stock selling for $32 per share in 1992 compared with an offer of $45 per share in 1989 from Disney's Shamrock Holdings, Inc. (Alster, 1992). MacAllister Booth will have to look for other areas in which to expand beyond instant photography. The stockholders are not happy with the flat earnings that would make new-product development possible. To address these concerns, Booth is focusing on electronic scanners and cameras for Citicorp's photo credit cards. In the long run he hopes to move into the "imaging" business for medical equipment, slides, computer graphics, and digitized photos for computer storage. The Helios medical imaging system promises $100 million in sales in 1994. But even after 12 years of research on electronic image sensors, Polaroid still does not have a strategy for successfully introducing the product.

SUMMARY

A number of basic concepts were introduced in this first chapter. Strategic management is based on "thinking strategically," a continuous process that involves the interaction of every major strategic decision that is made. The AHSC case showed the vital link between strategic analysis and the key elements of strategy. A methodological approach to strategy formulation is considered important because it enables planners to avoid inconsistency, misallocation of resources, hazy focus, and the rigidity of blindly following policy. A methodological approach does not preclude creativity; rather, it ensures that appropriate data are employed in the formulation of a strategy that creates value.

A systems framework helps tie together the elements of strategy and identifies the four key forces impinging on the firm. The concept of "total value management" was described as the counterpart to "total quality management." The importance of an appropriate strategic focus, in terms of organizational values, was illustrated. We also saw how strategic failures often result from inappropriate strategy formulation or focus. An actual strategic plan followed at Omicon, a major international company, demonstrating the use of a methodological approach in preparing a strategic plan.

REFERENCES AND SUGGESTIONS FOR FURTHER READING

A troubled Polaroid is tearing down the house that Land built. 1985. *Business Week,* April 29, p. 51.

Alster, Norm. 1992. Double exposure. *Forbes,* September 14, pp. 408–410.

American Hospital Supply Corporation, *1987 Annual Report.*

American Hospital Supply. 1985. Let your customers work for you. *Executive Technology,* November, p. 47.

Auletta, Ken. 1983. A certain poetry. *The New Yorker,* June 6.

Barney, Jay B. 1986. Organization culture: Can it be a source of sustainable competitive advantage? *Academy of Management Review,* no. 11, pp. 656–665.

Bergsman, Ennius E. 1989. Managing value: The new corporate strategy. *The McKinsey Quarterly,* Winter, pp. 57–72.

Bernstein, Peter W. 1980. Polaroid struggles to get back into focus. *Fortune,* April 7.

Boston Consulting Group. 1991. Strategic platforms. *BCG Conference for Chief Executives,* Paris, January.

Chakrevarty, Subrata N. 1987. The vindication of Edwin Land. *Forbes,* May 4, p. 83.

Churchman, C. West. 1968. The systems approach. New York: Delacorte Press.

Clausing, Don and John R. Hauser. 1988. The house of quality. *Harvard Business Review,* May–June, pp. 63–73.

Drucker, Peter F. 1973. *Management: Tasks, responsibilities, practices.* New York: Harper & Row.

Dumaine, Brian. 1991. Earning more by moving faster. *Fortune,* October 7, pp. 89–90, 94.

Forker, Laura B. 1991. Quality: American, Japanese and Soviet perspectives. *Academy of Management Executive,* 5, no. 4, pp. 63–74.

Forrester, Jay W. 1961. *Industrial dynamics.* Cambridge, Mass.: M.I.T. Press.

G.E. keeps those ideas coming. 1991. *Fortune,* August 12.

Grant, Robert M. 1991. The resource-based theory of competitive advantage: Implications for strategy formulation. *California Management Review,* Spring.

Grover, Ronald and Keith H. Hammonds. 1988. Maybe I'll raid you—and maybe I won't. *Business Week,* September 5, p. 25.

Hamel, Gary, Yves Doz, and C. K. Prahalad. 1989. Collaborate with your competitors and win. *Harvard Business Review,* January–February, pp. 133–139.

Hammonds, Keith H. and Gail DeGeorge. 1991. Where did they go wrong? *Business Week,* October 25, p. 34.

Hamson, Ned. 1988. Visions of excellence and quality. *Forbes,* April 4, pp. 94–103.

Hartley, Robert F. 1983. *Management mistakes.* Columbus, Ohio: Grid Publishing.

Hauser, John R. and Don Clausing. 1988. The house of quality. *The Harvard Business Review,* May–June.

Heltzer, B. 1987. How Polaroid flashed back. *Fortune.* February 16, p. 72.

Hof, Robert D. 1992. Inside Intel: It's moving at double-time to head off competitors. *Business Week,* June 1, pp. 86–94.

Howard, Robert. 1990. Values make the company: An interview with Robert Haas. *Harvard Business Review,* September–October, pp. 133–144.

Hunsicker, F. Quincy. 1980. The malaise of strategic planning. *Management Review,* March.

Imai, Masaaki. 1989. *Kaizen, the key to Japan's competitive success.* New York: Random House.

Is Polaroid playing to a market that just isn't there? 1986. *Business Week,* April 7, p. 82.

Johnston, Russell and Paul R. Lawrence. 1988. Beyond vertical integration—The rise of the value-adding partnership. *Harvard Business Review,* July–August, pp. 94–101.

Jones, Dorothy E. 1985. Baxter Travenol calls it quits—and others may follow. *Business Week,* February 11, p. 42.

Katz, Robert L. 1970. *Management of the total enterprise.* Englewood Cliffs, N.J.: Prentice-Hall.

Lamb, Robert. 1987. *Running American business.* New York: Basic Books.

Merrills, Roy. 1989. How Northern Telecom competes on time. *Harvard Business Review,* July–August, pp. 108–114.

Nussbaum, Bruce, Otis Port, Rich Brandt, Teresa Carson, Karen Wolman, and Jonathan Kapstein. 1988. Smart design. Quality is new style. *Business Week,* April 11, pp. 102–117. In the same issue, see Paul Angiolillo, Ease and economy in the lab, p. 104; Katherine M. Hafner, Whimsy goes mainstream, p. 105; Katherine M. Hafner, Taking ideas from plant to plant, p. 106; and Joan Hamilton, Gray expectations: A new force in design, p. 108.

O'Toole, James. 1985. *Vanguard management.* Garden City, N.Y.: Doubleday.

Ohmae, Kenichi. 1988. Getting back to strategy. *Harvard Business Review,* November–December, pp. 149–156.

Ohmae, Kenichi. 1982. *The mind of the strategist.* New York: McGraw-Hill.

Pepsi keeps on going after number 1. 1991. *Fortune,* March 11.

Peters, Thomas J. and Nancy Austin. 1985. *A passion for excellence.* New York: Random House.

Peters, Thomas J. and Robert H. Waterman. 1982. *In search of excellence.* New York: Random House.

Pitta, Julie. 1992. Cleanliness is next to competitiveness. *Forbes*, February 17, p. 134.

Polaroid can't get its future in focus, 1983. *Business Week*, April 4.

Polaroid sharpens its focus on the marketplace, 1986. *Business Week*, February 13, p. 132.

Polaroid vs. Kodak: The decisive round, 1986. *Business Week*, January 13, p. 37.

Polaroid's Spectra may be losing its flash, 1987. *Business Week*, June 29, p. 31.

Popplewell, Barry and Alan Wildsmith. 1990. How to gain company-wide commitment to total quality. Gower Publishing Group.

Port, Otis. 1991. Dueling pioneers. *Business Week*, Quality Issue, p. 17.

Port, Otis and John Carey. 1991. The quality imperative. *Business Week*, Quality Issue, pp. 7–17. In the same issue, see Otis Port and John Carey, Quality: A field with roots that go back to the farm, p. 15.

Power, Christopher, Walecia Konrad, Alice Z. Cuneo, and James B. Treece. 1991. Value marketing. *Business Week*, November 11, pp. 132–140. In the same issue, see Christopher Power, Card wars: My value is bigger than your value, p. 138, and Christopher Power, Sears catches the value bug, p. 140.

Prahalad, C. K. and Gary Hamel. 1990. The core competence of the corporation. *Harvard Business Review*, May–June, pp. 79–91.

Quinn, James Brian. 1980. *Strategies for change. Logical incrementalism*. Homewood, Ill.: Irwin.

Rose, Frank. 1991. Now quality means service too. *Fortune*, April 22, pp. 97–110.

Rumelt, Richard P. 1974. *Strategy, structure and economic performance*. Cambridge, Mass.: Harvard Business School.

Rummler, Geary A. and Alan P. Brache. 1990. *Improving performance. How to manage the white space on the organization chart*. San Francisco: Oxford Press.

Schein, Lawrence. 1990. The road to total quality. *The Conference Board Bulletin*.

Siler, Julia Flynn. 1990. Will another round of surgery help Baxter? *Business Week*, April 30, p. 92.

Siler, Julia Flynn, David Greising, and Tim Smart. 1991. The case against Baxter International. *Business Week*, October 7, pp. 106–115.

Skousen, Mark. 1991. Roaches outlive elephants. *Forbes*, August 19, pp. 72–74.

Snow, Charles C. and Lawrence G. Hrebiniak. 1980. Strategy, distinctive competence, and organization performance. *Administrative Science Quarterly* 25, pp. 317–336.

Stalk, George, Jr. 1988. Time—The next source of competitive advantage. *Harvard Business Review*, July–August, pp. 41–51.

Stalk, George, Jr. and Thomas M. Hout. 1990. *Competing against time*. New York: The Free Press.

Stata, Ray. 1989. Organization learning—The key to management innovation. *Sloan Management Review* 36, Spring, p. 63.

Stevenson, Howard H. 1976. Defining corporate strengths and weaknesses. *Sloan Management Review*, Spring, pp. 51–68.

Sullivan, L. P. 1986. Quality function deployment. *Quality Progress*, June.

Teitelbaum, Richard S. 1992. Topps Co.: Timeliness is everything. *Fortune*, April 20, p. 120.

The Polaroid promise, 1987. *Forbes*, February 9, p. 8.

Thomas, Phillip R. 1990. *Competitiveness through total cycle time*. New York: McGraw-Hill.

Thomas, Rich. 1990. Spiraling out of control. *Newsweek*, September, pp. 17–18.

Thorbeck, John. 1991. The turnaround value of values. *Harvard Business Review*, January–February, pp. 52–62.

Treece, James B., Karen Lowry Miller, and Richard A. Melcher. 1992. Surprise! Ford and Mazda have built a strong team. Here's how. *Business Week*, February 10, pp. 102–107. In the same issue, see Karen Lowry Miller and James B. Treece, GM and Isuzu a waste of synergy, p. 107.

Waterman, Robert H. 1987. *The renewal factor*. New York: Bantam Books.

Waterman, Robert H. 1984. Who said excellence was forever? *Business Week*, November 26, p. 9.

Weber, Jonathan. 1991. Kodak settles Polaroid case for $925 million. *Los Angeles Times*, July 16, p. D3.

Who's excellent now? 1984. *Business Week*, November 5, pp. 76–78.

Wilke, John. 1988. Are sharks circling Polaroid? *Boston Globe*, June 7, p. 43.

Willoughby, Jack. 1985. Excellence isn't enough. *Forbes*, June 17, pp. 104–105.

CHAPTER TWO

Strategic Analysis

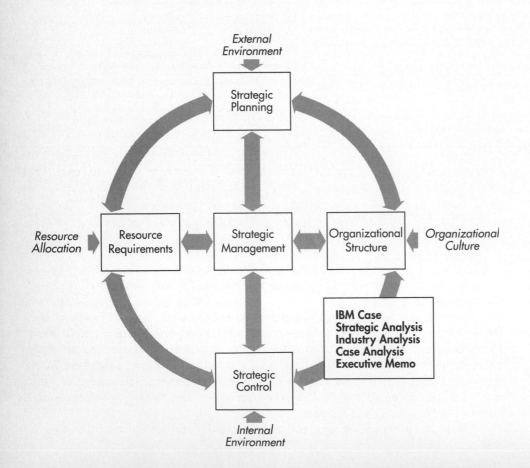

Chapter 1 A Framework for Strategic Management	**Chapter 2** Strategic Analysis	**Chapter 3** Strategic Visioning, Goals, Ethics, and Social Responsibility	**Chapter 4** The Competitive Environment	**Chapter 5** Capability-based Strategy	**Chapter 6** Market Dynamics and Sustainable Competitive Advantage
How to approach strategic management	*Application of strategic analysis*	*Understanding vision, values, ethics*	*Coping with competitive forces, stakeholders*	*Assessing company capability, timeliness, quality*	*Determining trends, gap analysis, and market dynamics*

Chapter 7 Strategy in a Global Environment	**Chapter 8** Financial Planning and Competitive-Cost Analysis	**Chapter 9** Entrepreneurship, Mergers and Acquisitions, Restructuring, and the Service Sector	**Chapter 10** Leadership Factor in Strategy and Implementing Strategic Change	**Chapter 11** Information Technology and Future Directions in Strategy
Assessing global trade, foreign markets, monetary exchange	*Preparing a financial plan and competitive-cost analysis*	*Importance of small business, entrepreneurs, restructuring*	*Strategy implementation, leadership, culture*	*Information technology, trends, new management*

INTRODUCTION

What business is a company in? Where should it be one, five, or ten years from now? How can it get there? We noted in Chapter 1 that part of the answer to these questions can be found in the values of the organization and of the executives who lead it. Today's business environment is characterized by rapidly advancing technology, keen competition within a world economy, increased government intervention, and vocal, informed stockholders. A major challenge facing executives is knowing how to introduce strategic change. To deal with this challenge an executive needs vision, creativity, flexibility, and entrepreneurship—in short, strategic thinking.

Although it is true that strategic management requires creativity, a framework for developing and executing strategy is also vital. Companies with multiple strategic thrusts, and especially companies that are multinational in scope, can no longer be managed by intuition. It is rare to find a major corporation anywhere in the world that does not have some form of systematic planning. The executive needs ways and means to deal with complex operations and to empower the organization to carry out a strategic plan.

What are the key elements of a strategic plan, and what must be done to ensure its success?

The strategic plan often starts with the gleam in the founder's eye—a vision of what might be achieved. Sometimes a formal document is prepared to encourage investment by venture capitalists. More typically, the chief executive officer's (CEO's) guiding principles clear the way through the maze of problems confronted during start-up. Once the company has a marketable product, process, or service, the difficulties that arise are typically operational. The strategy of a startup company is simple: survive and grow so as to achieve a position of stability. From that position, the company may be acquired, merge with other companies, or aggressively pursue its own growth. After a company has reached a stable point, formal strategic planning becomes essential.

For the larger or more mature organization, strategic planning is necessary for continued growth and profits. All organizations—like all products, industries, technologies, communities, and even nations—experience periods of growth and intervals of decline that may be followed by revitalization. Management itself goes through cycles as new members are brought in, mergers or acquisitions occur, or competitors take away market share. These inevitable changes demand strategic planning.

The problem with formal strategic-planning systems is that they tend to become ends in themselves as they are institutionalized within the firm. When too much effort is focused on meticulously developing "optimal" strategies rather than on challenging the assumptions on which these strategies are based, the mechanics of preparing the plan quickly overshadow the substance of a strategy. In a sense, the company is paralyzed by its own strategic-planning process. A rigid strategic plan can lead to misdirection, inefficiency, and waste by superimposing artificial guidelines and rules that prevent managers from making needed changes.

The illustrative case that follows is reprinted from a 1991 issue of *Fortune* magazine. It deals with John Akers's attempt to reinvent IBM and, by restructuring the organization, make it more competitive. A contrasting example was described in Chapter 1, where we saw the American Hospital Supply Corporation follow all the right strategies, but it became complacent and did not aggressively pursue a growth plan, and this error led to the company's acquisition by Baxter Travenol. These two cases illustrate that strategy is an ongoing process. When implemented properly it leads to success, whereas improper implementation spells poor performance or decline.

A number of updates for the IBM case are shown on pages 66 and 67. The latest change occurred in March of 1993. IBM's board announced that Louis Gerstner, Jr., an outsider, would be the next chairman and CEO. At an interview after the announcement, Gerstner commented, "The first thing I want to know is what is IBM's strategy and how does it relate to the competitive environment and customer needs." He went on to say, "Over the next few months, we will look at every single business with a no-holds-barred approach" (Scheier, 1993). Gerstner has a reputation for restructuring businesses and believes strongly in decentralization. As an outsider, he will take a fresh look at the problems confronting IBM. Based on his past experience, Gerstner believes in setting overall direction but allowing the division heads to formulate their own strategy. His principal view is that, like GE, IBM should be in those businesses where they are number one or two in terms of market share. John Akers was not able to turn IBM around—will Gerstner be able to do the job?

ILLUSTRATIVE CASE: CAN JOHN AKERS SAVE IBM?

To understand fully just what a disaster IBM has been, and just how blind its own management was to the depth of its problems, step back to a moment in late 1986. IBM was more than a year past a boom period and struggling. Revenue growth was miserable, earnings growth was nonexistent, and IBM's stock, then $125 a share, had lost nearly $24 billion in market value from a peak of $99 billion just seven months earlier. In an interview with *Fortune*, Chairman John F. Akers nonetheless exhibited gritty confidence: Four or five years from now, he asserted, people will look back and see that the company's performance has been superlative.

It is now 4½ years later. The stock was recently just below $100, which means another $18 billion in market capitalization has been shredded into megabits. IBM's total revenues have dragged, rising over the past five years at an average annual rate of only 6.6% against 13.4% for the data-processing industry as a whole. In unhappy concert, the company's worldwide market share has dropped from 30% to 21%. Each percentage point lost represents $3 billion in annual sales.

IBM's profits, though still the biggest of any company's in the world, have been roughed up as well. In 1990 the company made $6 billion on $69 billion in revenues and, mindful of four sour years just passed, bravely classed that as a "good" year. But the $6 billion was an embarrassing 10% less than IBM made in 1984 on only $46 billion of revenue. Then, IBM had a star return on shareholders' equity: 24.9%. For 1990 the figure was a mediocre 14.1%. Then, IBM perennially headed *Fortune*'s list of the most-admired U.S. corporations. In the most recent list, it was No. 32.

So far, 1991 has produced two shocks—IBM's last-minute disclosures in both the first and second quarters that it would earn much less than security analysts were estimating. The litany of continuing bad news has been only partly recession related: Price wars in the computer industry have grabbed the news and held it.

Unless IBM snaps back strongly in the last half, it will make less this year in regular profits (that is, not counting a special charge taken in the first quarter for retiree health benefits) than it did a decade ago, when it earned $3.3 billion. In short, this onetime symbol of corporate might—this national asset, by everybody's description—has had a serious industrial accident.

How did IBM get into this unprecedented trouble? Can John Akers pick up the pieces? Sitting in his Armonk, New York, office, his jacket off, Akers addressed those questions in a wide-ranging, more than an hour long interview with *Fortune*, his first with the press since the storm of 1991 broke. In his comments, Akers displayed a mixture of deep disappointment, resolve, and, in brief moments, a jarring insouciance. Asked just what went wrong—just why his forecast of superlativeness was so far off the mark—he replied with a stunner: "I don't think anything went wrong." Then why, one might reasonably ask, did he tell his managers in May that IBM was "in crisis," a characterization made in private and quickly leaked to the press? And, if IBM stock has lost $42 billion in value since 1986, just how far would it have fallen if something really had gone wrong?

Akers subsequently made clear that he meant only to emphasize that IBM is caught up in an industry moving so fast and changing so much that nobody in it can adjust quickly enough. But he conceded that no outside force was responsible for IBM's loss of market share. That could be laid, he said, first to the fact that IBM is so heavily in hardware—from which it gets 60% of its revenues—rather than software and services, the faster-growing parts of the industry. "And No. 2," he said forthrightly, "we didn't execute as well as we should have."

In fact the Big Blue machine crumpled in both products and marketing and left the company, in the words of a midlevel executive, "fighting for its life." The prognosis is uncertain, though clearly it includes good news and bad.¡ After a total remake, the product line is now

CAN JOHN AKERS SAVE IBM?, CONTINUED

much improved; Akers even calls it "sparkling." But marketing is still flawed, and that failing raises a momentous question as to how successfully IBM will perform even after the economy picks up again.

Unsure of the answer himself, Akers has a strategy for both now and then. Girding for the worst, though he expects better than that, he is pushing to cut IBM's expenses to where the company can tolerate revenue growth that barely crawls. Trying to remix the business, he is striving for growth in software, services, and what's called OEM—original equipment manufacturing, meaning production by IBM of its hardware for resale under another company's name. At the same time, in what amounts to a declaration of war on IBM's competitors, he says, "We're going to ship our spiffy product, and we're going to price it to maintain or gain market share."

In an industry already gone kamikaze on prices, that strategy may produce some not-so-spiffy profits. But Akers plainly has his back up about market share. He indicated as much repeatedly in the now-famous remarks he made to his managers in May. The leaked notes of his talk reveal Akers as angry, frustrated, and particularly aghast at the failure of his marketing strategies. Much of his optimism in 1986 sprang from his ongoing drive to increase the size of IBM's sales force and thereby get the company into closer touch with its customers. The U.S. marketing force grew 25%, from 20,000 people to 25,000. But for all this effort, U.S. revenues rose less than 7% over four years, from $25.4 billion to $27.1 billion. "Where's my return for the extra 5,000 people?" Akers demanded, in tones that caused the notetaker to escalate to capital letters, "Where's the beef? What the hell are you doing for *me*?"

That "me" resonates for special reasons. This is a man keenly aware that his time as boss is speeding by fast. No, that does not mean he is about to get fired or, as one particular rumor has it, that Ross Perot will be called in to replace him. IBM's directors appear to be solidly behind Akers. Says one of them, Thomas S. Murphy, chairman of Capital Cities/ABC: "John is doing all the right things. The situation is just incredibly difficult."

Because IBM executives are required to retire at 60, Akers, now 56, must step down by January 1995. He will then have been in office ten years. Unless matters improve drastically, the Akers era is going to be remembered, fairly or unfairly, as the period in which IBM dissipated its greatness. For this man with a lifetime of accomplishment behind him—as a Navy flier, as a standout IBM salesman, as a junior executive slated early for glory—that would be a bitter outcome. He told *Fortune* as much in 1986: "There have only been six chief executives of IBM. I hope that when my tour is over, people will look back and say, 'He deserved to be among them.'"

The scorecard at tour's end, as now, will be complex. In justice to Akers, appraisals of his tenure should take into account the complicity of his immediate predecessors as CEO, Frank T. Cary and John R. Opel, who handed him a fat, overconfident company. Any reckoning must also acknowledge, as Akers intimates, the chaos of today's computer industry. At its top are a few large, vertically integrated, globally spread companies, still very much headed by IBM. Its revenues are five times those of either Hewlett-Packard or Digital Equipment, the next-biggest U.S. companies, and more than twice those of the foreign leader, Fujitsu (*Fortune*, June 1). One size down is the latecomer crowd—such specialty companies as Apple, Compaq, and Sun Microsystems. All told, the computer and office products segment of the Fortune 500 includes 22 companies today, up from 15 ten years ago.

Layered further below is the industry's seething substructure, which by IBM's count includes a mammoth 50,000 competitors. Most of these are niche players. Many are startups, apt to be driving compulsively for revenues so they can cash in by selling out. In companies of all sizes, corporate alliances are so common that it's

CAN JOHN AKERS SAVE IBM?, CONTINUED

tough to keep straight who's competing, collaborating, or both. "We've all learned how to drink coffee together at ten and beat each other's brains out at two," Akers said in June, his envoys fresh from a strudelfest with archrival Apple at which they talked possible deals.

In between those kaffeeklatsches, the industry drums out technological advances with bewildering speed, constantly improving price–performance ratios. Price wars have turned the market increasingly into a spectacle of commodity economics. Allen J. Krowe, a former IBM executive who is now a senior vice president at Texaco, shakes his head in wonderment: "The industry has more Ph.D.s per square foot than any other. Yet its pricing calls to mind soybeans and sowbellies."

Amid this tumult, a revenue-hungry IBM is ever more flexible about how it conducts business. Credit Akers for that. Yet in a generally disaggregated world, IBM is still an asset-heavy, people-laden, bureaucracy-ridden aggregate. Another starkly important fact: Fortress IBM has patently lost its moat—its historical ability to get the business just because it is IBM, that nice, safe, fuzzy-blanket choice. Publications, including this one, have been saying for many years that the moat was drying up. Now the proof of the drought is there for all to see in IBM's deteriorated, and perhaps still deteriorating, financial results. IBM's executives themselves do not deny that the moat is gone.

But that does not mean they call the castle lost. President Jack D. Kuehler, 58, says everything is on the table to be reevaluated. "No company is going to survive in tomorrow's global marketplace by virtue of its history," he explains. Wouldn't past IBM managements have said the same? Sounding very much like a man recently deprived of a moat, he replies, "Ten years ago, I wouldn't have said it."

"Survive" is a serious word—but at least for the moment we are not talking survival with a capital S. Instead, IBM equates survival with a certain financial standard of living, a kind of compromise between the high style it once took for granted and the mediocrity it has lately been reduced to. Seven years ago, top management was confidently predicting that return on equity would continue to average above 20%. Today the goal is down to 18%. That rate, say IBM executives, will allow the company, after paying dividends, to meet all its capital needs and keep pace with an industry whose revenues it expects to grow annually at 7% to 10%. That range is an obvious comedown from the average of 13.4% recorded between 1985 and 1990. Growth came in lower as those years passed, to 5% in 1989 and 10% in 1990, and IBM has downsized its expectations accordingly.

It has also wrenched its annual growth in costs—what Akers calls "the expense machine"—down to under 10% and is clawing for 6%. From its top employment of 405,500 in 1985, the company has cut back 31,700 and has special offers on the table right now that could bring the total trimmed to 50,000. Among the departures this year are the 4,000 employees of the division making keyboards, typewriters, printers, and supplies, 90% of which was sold in March for $1.5 billion to the leveraged-buyout firm of Clayton & Dubilier. Inside IBM, many people opposed that move. But these products earned poorly, in large part because they got scant attention from IBM's computer-minded sales force. So Akers stepped up to the hard decision to sell.

When a division like that departs, the overhead that was allocated to it stays around. Severing thousands of employees also costs money. But Frank A. Metz Jr., senior vice president for finance, reckons that IBM has now built tremendous amounts of operating leverage into the business—that is, it has pared expenses to the point where a major portion of every incremental revenue dollar will come straight to the bottom line. That's fine if there happen to be any incremental dollars, which there certainly haven't been in the first half of 1991. "Shame on us," admits Metz. "We haven't demonstrated we can

CAN JOHN AKERS SAVE IBM?, CONTINUED

take advantage of the operating leverage that's there."

Nor has the company demonstrated that it spends investment dollars wisely. IBM's ability to do that matters enormously because its outlays are so huge. The puzzle for outsiders, who mainly see only the macro results, is to figure out whether the company is getting much for its vast efforts. Here the evidence is not reassuring. One miss, at least so far: IBM's purchase over the past five years of $6 billion of its own stock, at prices averaging $119 a share.

The much larger investment dollars at issue are those going into capital projects and research, development, and engineering. Last year outlays of this sort ran to a full $14.5 billion: capital expenditures of $6.1 billion, investment in software of $1.9 billion, and $6.5 billion for R&D and engineering. Over the past decade the total for these three kinds of expenditure was an immense $101 billion—about four times what the Reagan and Bush Administrations have spent on Star Wars.

Since IBM's return on equity has skidded, a presumptive case can be made that this wad, or major parts of it, has been ill spent. But the case is not provable. There is no way of determining, first, what the returns would have been had the money not been spent nor, second, how returns may benefit in the future because it was. One thing is certain, though: A delayed return—a bird in the bush—does not have the value of a revenue-generating bird in the hand.

The greatest perplexities about IBM's investments concern its huge spending on semiconductors. IBM is the largest manufacturer of chips in the world, though it produces only for itself, not for outside sale. The company searches unceasingly for technological breakthroughs. At its East Fishkill, New York, plant, it has recently sunk undisclosed but clearly colossal sums into an experimental manufacturing technology known as X-ray lithography, which may or may not prove out. In this process, a specially engineered cyclotron spins out the X-rays that engrave the

chips. There is only one other machine with similar capabilities in the U.S., owned by the government. In the semiconductor stronghold of Japan, Metz notes, there are 13 such cyclotrons. So IBM is extraordinarily proud of its machine.

But do these chip investments make economic sense? Jack Kuehler, who rose to the president's job through the technology side of the business, strongly defends the outlays as essential if IBM is to stay on the leading edge of chip technology and have recurring opportunities to be first in the market with "the best box." Buying chips from outsiders, he says, requires that these suppliers be clued in to IBM's product plans—an information handoff the company would prefer to avoid.

All this would sound more persuasive were it not that IBM buys chips by the carload from outside vendors for its low-end products all the time—as it is doing, for example, with its brand-new laptop computer, which uses an Intel microprocessor. On the other hand, IBM made a "best box" kind of announcement in June, when it said it was beginning production of new 16-megabit chips that it expects to have installed in its mainframe computers by next spring. That should give IBM a lead of perhaps six months—but no more than that—over several Japanese and South Korean companies that are also developing this next-generation technology.

An IBM announcement like that gladdens Akers's heart. True, he acknowledges the enormous cost of supporting IBM's semiconductor establishment. The tariff, in fact, has induced him to sign up both Siemens and Motorola as partners in bearing parts of the load. He also says that IBM's R&D budget is under a lot of pressure these days: "If you were to wander around our laboratories, you would find people waving their arms, saying, 'My God, what's going on around here?' I think that's healthy."

Even so, he argues that it is a huge plus for IBM to be the master of its own destiny in chip manufacture. He says he does not want to depend on the technology of his competitors,

CAN JOHN AKERS SAVE IBM?, CONTINUED

who are mainly Japanese. His thinking brings to mind the old Cold War days of massive deterrence. Just as skeptics sometimes questioned the merits of that military doctrine, so investors today sometimes scratch their heads about IBM's do-it-yourself approach. Lewis A. Sanders is president of Sanford C. Bernstein & Co., a money manager that is a huge, war-weary, and yet still optimistic holder of IBM stock. He once questioned the strategic advantages of IBM's approach as perhaps too nebulous, but now inclines to the company's view. In any case, those who choose to buy IBM stock should recognize that they are casting their lot with a company determined to carry the U.S. flag in chip technology.

Former IBM executive Allen Krowe seems to believe that some tough thinking about investments is a key to IBM's recovery. Asked what scenario might lift the company once again to a high return on equity, he focuses first on the thought that IBM needs to be "very prudent and very demanding" in the way R&D and engineering funds are spent to be sure each dollar provides a potential return. That indeed sounds like a reasonable top priority.

A related question about IBM's investments has to do with the company's delays and miscues in getting products to market. The new laptop, a major example, is the successor to two past failures. Also in the queue of much-delayed projects is OfficeVision, a software system that would help computer users network their machines. Then there are workstations—sophisticated, desktop computers for technical use. In this sector, such competitors as Sun and Digital Equipment leaped off to a lead while IBM just sort of hung around. Only last year did IBM finally come out with its own hot ticket, the RISC System/6000.

RISC, the prevailing technology for workstations today, stands for reduced instruction-set computing. Its history helps explain why IBM has struck out in revenue growth. The RISC semiconductor was an IBM baby, born in its Yorktown Heights, New York, lab in 1974. But internal arguments over how, and even whether, the chip should be used kept IBM fiddling while Sun and other companies decisively powered ahead. IBM finally put a RISC workstation on the market in 1985, but it was technologically a half-step behind the competition, says Kuehler, and did poorly. Andrew Heller, an IBM executive who had long led the development of workstations, later resigned with a blast at IBM's slow-moving culture: "Technology is like fish. The longer it stays on the shelf, the less desirable it becomes."

By the time IBM got its good product, the RS/6000, to market in 1990, the industry's annual sales of workstations were up to $7.5 billion and growing 40% a year. Playing a respectable game of catch-up, IBM snagged 7% of the 1990 total. But Sun got more than four times that much.

Says Kuehler of the workstation experience: "We just didn't really thoughtfully define the opportunity and make it happen in an efficient manner." Do insiders say IBM blew it? "Oh, yes. Oh, yes." But he notes that the RISC technology and the workstation market came along at a time when IBM wasn't listening much to its customers about the products they needed, something it is working to do in the Akers era. So Kuehler hopes that if IBM were to produce another RISC-like baby today, it would do a better job of bringing it up.

The RS/6000 is at least a solid component of what IBM has recently been describing as "the strongest lineup of products and services in our history." There is a certain pitifulness to the claim, given that this vaunted collection is producing so little in revenues and profits. But many outsiders agree with the company's contention—among them Naomi Seligman, co-director of the Research Board, whose 40 members are the management information chiefs at such huge computer buyers as American Airlines, State Farm, and Du Pont. Because of the potentates she represents, Seligman gets inside looks at what the major computer chefs have cooking. Four years

CAN JOHN AKERS SAVE IBM?, CONTINUED

ago, when *Fortune* interviewed her for an IBM article, she was not impressed with the company's product line. Today she thinks IBM has finally muscled a good array into place and also has important technologies in the wings.

Kuehler says that IBM's efforts to speed the development of products has it working simultaneously on three different generations of mainframes. IBM's more recent offerings include the first generation of those mainframes, called ES/9000, introduced last September, and a midrange or minicomputer, the AS/400. This machine got to the market later than it was needed, in 1988, but last year accounted for no less than $14 billion, or one-fifth, of IBM's revenues. About two-thirds of that business came from Europe, which has a big population of smallish businesses that have a particular need for minis.

The wobbler in IBM's wares is its personal computers, which sell in a soybean-and-sowbelly, price-driven market. They lack distinctive qualities that might allow them to command the premium prices IBM keeps trying to get. The company's interest in securing certain of Apple's technologies reflects its continuing search for an edge. Behind the scenes, also, Kuehler has focused IBM's formidable technological prowess on this underachiever by directing the heads of some key IBM labs around the country to make quarterly visits to Boca Raton, IBM's PC hub. Like smoke-eaters converging on the oil well fires in Kuwait, IBM specialists are flying in from the kingdoms of disk drives, AS/400s, mainframes, and basic research. Kuehler asks them all one question: "What is your contribution to the personal computer line?"

The extraordinary attention focused on the PC reflects, first, IBM's wish to hold its ground in every corner of the industry and, second, its awareness that a lot of the world sees a future in which little boxes, packed with cheap chips supplying evergrowing amounts of computing power, largely supplant the big, high-margin boxes that are IBM's pride. Long-held doubts about the viability of the mainframe business pushed James H. Gipson of Pacific Financial

Research, a well-regarded money manager, into writing a 1989 letter to his clients headed "Why We Don't Own IBM." Similar misgivings even seem to have invaded the households of key IBMers. Nicholas Donofrio, 45, recently told his daughter, Nicole, that he was moving from head of IBM's workstations division to head of mainframes. Said Nicole: "Dad, that seems like going from a quarter horse to a dinosaur."

Donofrio says he'd substitute Clydesdales for dinosaurs, but the statistics back up Nicole. According to estimates compiled by Gartner & Co., the industry's mainframe revenues grew at an annual rate of 8.9% from 1985 through 1990, against 21% for the desktop category that includes PCs and garden-variety workstations. What does the future hold for mainframes? An obvious downward pull is the ever-expanding ability of small computers to handle large, sophisticated jobs once considered big-box property, such as payrolls. Another is the fact that much of the computer industry's output goes to the service sector of the economy, where banks, insurance companies, and airlines, for example, are all feeling a pinch on the bottom line. Stephen S. Roach, senior economist at Morgan Stanley, estimates that about 85% of the installed base of computers belongs to service companies. Many of them, he thinks, have unused mainframe capacity.

The countervailing arguments include, not surprisingly, IBM's own view that the proliferation of desktop machines will create a continuing need for mainframes to serve up data and manage corporate networks. IBM wins some support from James Fischer of Andersen Consulting, which gets much of its $1.9 billion in revenues from advising corporations on their computer systems. Says Fischer: "As long as you have corporations controlled centrally, you're going to have a computing structure that is also centralized. And that is one of the forces that will not let the mainframe die."

Emphatic backing for these positions appeared recently in "The Future of the Mainframe Industry," a lengthy report by two

CAN JOHN AKERS SAVE IBM?, CONTINUED

Bernstein analysts, Philip Rueppel and Don Young (who has since gone to Shearson Lehman). Tracking the demand for mainframe computing power over the past five years, the analysts concluded that installed mainframe MIPS—millions of instructions per second, a measure of computing capacity—had grown vigorously, at an annual average rate of 39%. But that led to only a 5% rate of growth in mainframe units for two reasons: First, users added much of the power by upgrading the innards of existing computers rather than by buying new hardware. Second, responding to the growing reliability of their machines, users simply kept them on the job longer, slowing the retirements of MIPS from 15% of the installed base in 1985 to about 5% in 1990. Leaning on a survey they made of 50 big buyers of computers, the analysts predict that demand for mainframe MIPS will grow at perhaps a 33% annual rate over the next few years and that the decline in the retirement rate will stop. The result, they conclude, will be annual growth in IBM's mainframe revenues of around 9.5% through 1995, vs. 8.1% in the five years just past. Making a host of other assumptions—remember that this intelligence emanates from a firm that has long been bullish about IBM stock—the analysts estimated 1995 earnings for IBM at $11.6 billion, close to twice the figure for the "good" year of 1990.

They like that report at IBM. Unfortunately, the accuracy of neither its forecast about mainframes nor any other is provable until the results are in. One restrained conclusion about IBM's product line: It is better than it was a few years ago, still needs work, and is unquestionably getting it.

FOR WALL STREET, ONE SURPRISE AFTER ANOTHER

Speaking to a meeting of CEOs in May, John Akers began by recalling his days as an IBM salesman: "If we were behind on quota, we would come into the office on Saturday morn-ings to get some sales help from our managers. Well, on this Saturday morning I'm behind on quota, and I'm hoping one or more of you people in the room might be able to help me out." The audience roared, knowing full well what he meant: On March 19, a bare 12 days from the end of IBM's first quarter, the company had shocked the investment world by telling security analysts that earnings for the period were going to be about half Wall Street's estimates.

Three months later IBM did it again. On June 20, Big Blue said even the most bearish analysts were wrong: Second-quarter earnings would be off at least 80%. Corporate America takes it as gospel that large companies don't have earnings surprises of this kind. Ask other big-company CEOs about the IBM shockers and they just roll their eyes. So how to explain these bombs?

The story goes back to the third quarter of 1989, when IBM had another surprise shortfall—this one arising mainly from manufacturing problems with a new line of disk drives. Soon, a new director of investor relations, James Clippard, moved to the firing line as IBM stock fluctuated its way through 1990. Short sales of the stock were large. Then came the last quarter, traditionally strong for IBM, but this time a true rouser: $2.5 billion in earnings, or 40% of the year's total. Analysts got the good word on January 17 in a conference call. Reflecting IBM's pent-up frustration, Clippard let go a zinger: "This earnings release is dedicated to the shorts and pessimists on IBM."

Akers said in his May remarks to managers that he knew as early as November that first-quarter results would trail 1990's. IBM says now that it kept trying to "tamp down" analysts' estimates. Nobody paid much heed. Recession or no, war or no, the Street had seen the fourth quarter and had heard Clippard.

Along about the 15th working day of each month, IBM's management information system delivers to Armonk headquarters a quarterly forecast based on orders data from the company's marketing units. Business in January and

CAN JOHN AKERS SAVE IBM?, CONTINUED

February was poor, but the February forecast indicated that IBM could still have a decent, typically "back-loaded" quarter bolstered by strong sales in March. Nothing was certain, though: IBM customers can cancel an order at any time right up to the shipping date. Says analyst Don Young of Shearson Lehman: "IBM has a softer definition of 'order' than most computer companies do."

Sure enough, when it got to be "white-knuckle time"—what IBM salesmen call the waning days of a quarter—the business wasn't there. Orders had buckled all over the world. Akers has singled out business in Japan as "disastrous." The horrendous news was worsened by an adverse shift in currency rates—a rise in the dollar that made March sales in Germany and Japan less valuable when translated into dollars.

Once burned, twice shy, so after March 19 analysts handled the IBM hot potato nervously. The company said second-quarter business wasn't good, but didn't elaborate much. One veteran computer analyst, Barry Bosak of Smith Barney, visited Armonk in early June and gained so little knowledge he was embarrassed to put the trip on his expense account.

Probably IBM stayed mum because it knew white-knuckle time might again produce a shock. And so it did: When the June tidings arrived, there was no alternative to another conference call to analysts. The best news in it: In the third quarter IBM would begin shipping the high-end models of its new mainframe line on schedule.

A postscript: In between Earnings Surprises One and Two, a shareholder in Chicago sued IBM for failing to disclose the bad first-quarter prospects in a timely fashion. The lawsuit asks damages for all investors who bought IBM stock after November 30, 1990, and still held it on April 12, when the company officially released its earnings. IBM says the suit lacks merit.

By contrast, IBM's marketing skills don't seem any better than they did a few years ago and definitely trail those of the frontier days described by Thomas J. Watson Jr. in his 1990 book *Father, Son, and Co.*, written with *Fortune* editor Peter Petre. Said Tom Jr. of IBM's success in computers: "Technology turned out to be less important than sales and distribution methods. Starting with Univac [Remington Rand's first computer, in 1951], we consistently outsold people who had better technology because we knew how to put the story before the customer, how to install the machines successfully, and how to hang on to customers once we had them."

Oh, to have all that today! John Akers recognized the absence of those historical strengths around five years ago, when IBM's world began to disintegrate. His strategy then was to move those thousands of employees—the "redeploys," in IBM's lexicon—into the field, where they were going to help the company get closer to customers. Later on, as it became apparent in Armonk that the strategy wasn't delivering revenue growth, the U.S. marketing effort was reorganized several more times.

One customer who knows the consequences all too well is Thomas Pirelli, head of Enterprise Systems, a suburban Chicago company that sells specialized software to hospitals for computerized purchasing. Pirelli says the local IBM office was shaken up three different times in 1988 and early 1989. Three different sets of IBM managers called him, asking to drop by and explain how they were now doing things differently. "They wanted a day," says Pirelli. "By the third one, I was only giving an hour. And in those three sessions, they never asked about our needs. They don't listen. All they do is talk and show you the charts they've brought along."

In the confusion, Pirelli says, one IBM newcomer even had to ask how much business Pirelli did with the company. The answer then was about $2 million a year. "But since he plainly didn't know," says Pirelli, "I just made up a figure of $20 million. That got his attention—until he realized it wasn't true. I told him, 'We use an IBM computer for that kind of data. You ought

CAN JOHN AKERS SAVE IBM?, CONTINUED

to try it.' I'm not exaggerating about all of this. It was a parody!" Pirelli says that about 90% of the PCs in the hospitals he deals with used to be IBM's, but he estimates that these customers are buying only about one-third of their new ones from the company.

Can Pirelli's experience be explained by the fact he is a small-business man, a class of customer that IBM has never starred with? It appears not, since complaints from large customers also abound. The Research Board's Naomi Seligman says that most of the organization's members are "fed up with the mediocrity of IBM's marketing." These buyers, she says, complain that too many people were put on their accounts, that the "knowledge base" of the IBM sales force is poor, and that Big Blue is still not providing solutions their companies need to network their computers and get full value from their investments. "It's too bad," says Seligman. "The customers can't get what they want from small computer companies—they just aren't set up to provide solutions—and the customers are short of staff to do the job inside. IBM would have a real edge if it had the skills and particularly if it could find the right ways to motivate its employees."

In meetings, says Seligman, her organization's members discuss the kind of IBM salesman they would like—"and the model is always Al Johnson." Allen M. Johnson, 55, manager of the Bloomington, Illinois, office for 18 years, has only one customer, State Farm Insurance. In collaboration, State Farm and IBM have developed four generations of a sophisticated computer system for the insurer's 17,500 agents. The two companies are also working now with a California start-up, Go Corp., to test keyboardless hand-held computers on which the user—a State Farm claims adjuster, say—can write with a stylus.

Norman L. Vincent, head of data processing at State Farm, says he cannot say enough good things about Johnson: "From what I hear from other buyers, many IBM account execs just try to keep their noses clean for three years so they can get promoted. They say, 'If my customer wants something IBM doesn't want to give, I'm not going to the mat for it.' Well, Al is just the opposite. He'll go anywhere in IBM to get what State Farm needs. He'll run into some guy who says, 'My budget won't allow that,' and Al will ask, 'Okay, who controls your budget, and where do I find him?'"

In the late 1970s, Vincent recalls, Johnson's zeal got him into trouble. Johnson was then organizationally part of IBM's dataprocessing division, which sold the company's "big iron"—mainframes. But State Farm, trying to devise a computer system for its agents, needed small machines that were sold by another division. Johnson set about lining up the small stuff for State Farm. He says some "big-iron bigots" came after him, urging that he be fired.

Having survived, and having won nationwide repute for serving his customer well, Johnson rates a question: Has the IBM management ever asked him to teach other marketing people in the company how to do their job better? Answer: "No." That suggests a lack of judgment up the line. Indeed, the biggest indictment of Akers's management would seem to be that he has failed to fix IBM's marketing problems. He came from the world of sales. Surely he should have managed to whip it into shape.

He is still trying. Under way is yet one more revamping of U.S. marketing, which today is under the direction of George H. Conrades, 52, often mentioned as a prospect to succeed Akers. The new plan changes the way people are rewarded. Formerly, IBM's branch managers and sales reps were on a quota system that paid them best if they sold high-margin products, such as mainframes. That doesn't necessarily leave you pushing what's best for your customer.

So the new plan pays these folks according to what they produce in revenues—any kind of revenues. And top management is sounding tough about demanding results. In his much

CAN JOHN AKERS SAVE IBM?, CONTINUED

quoted May remarks, Akers said, "The fact that we're losing share makes me goddamn mad. I used to think my job as a rep was at risk if I lost a sale. Tell them theirs is at risk if they lose."

At management levels above the branches, a different incentive system now applies to 64 new geographical territories, organized into seven areas. The managers of all these units are paid primarily on profits and secondarily on the returns they achieve on assets under their control, mainly accounts receivable. That doesn't mean IBM has a receivables problem: Financial executive Metz says few companies have less of one. Instead, the standard is part of Armonk's drive to get management at all levels to focus on return on assets and cash flow. Says Metz: "This is a signal to middle management and the rest of the organization that these things are not just something Akers and Metz give speeches about, but are really, really something important."

This message might be coming through more clearly were there not considerable bitterness in IBM's ranks about the performance of management itself and, most particularly, about compensation at the top. Last year, counting his cash take and restricted stock grants (but not options, which would add another layer of pay), Akers earned $4.6 million, which is not all that extraordinary for the CEO of the biggest corporate earner in the world. But the $4.6 million was no less than a 138% raise over 1989. The four executives just below Akers also got increases over 100%. Unfortunately, the news of this largess hit the street just as the company was disclosing its bleak first-quarter earnings.

It did not look good—and never will. IBM's rationale for the raises was spelled out recently by Walton E. Burdick, senior vice president for personnel. The explanation harks back to 1989, when top management was docked slightly in pay because a $2.4 billion write-off knocked earnings down more than 30%, to $3.8 billion. Coming along next, the earnings of $6 billion in the "good" year of 1990 had a certain sheen to

them, and Burdick says that's why big pay raises were justified.

The trouble is that IBM's employees have been asked to buy this argument at a time when they are feeling stepped-up pressures to deliver sustained performance. Technically, IBM's hallowed principle of "full employment"—no layoffs—is still in place. Firings, though, are permitted. In IBMspeak these are called MIS, for "management initiated separations," and, by any name, Akers and crew want to see more of them. Says Burdick: "We are escalating standards of performance. We are raising the bar."

The words may seem discordant, given management's own lack of kick. But some employees—not to mention the shareholders—will deeply welcome the overdue tightening of standards and any resulting move toward streamlining. Despite Aker's vigorous efforts to decentralize and drive decision-making authority further down into the company, IBM's bureaucracy still lives and thrives. Almost everyone who deals with the company comes away with a numbing sense of how slowly it moves, how many people must weigh in on a decision, how the competing interests of one camp in the company must be balanced against those of other camps. Donald Coggiola, senior vice president of Policy Management Systems, a software developer and a business partner of IBM's, recently made a remark quoted in the *Wall Street Journal* that is likely to enter the lore about IBM. He described the company approval process as "giant pools of peanut butter we have to swim through."

The Japanese have a saying that it is hard for a large man to fully exercise his wits. The suspicion must persist that IBM is still oppressively rotund—a sumo wrestler, so to speak, trying to grapple with a whole gymnasium full of agile, clever, lesser weights. As the big fellow's designated manager for the next 3½ years, Akers faces a job that surely must be counted among the most difficult ever dealt an executive.

CAN JOHN AKERS SAVE IBM?, CONTINUED

Akers credits IBM with being able to adjust to shifting conditions, and history bears him out. IBM missed out early on minicomputers—and adjusted. It stumbled getting into PCs—and adjusted. His point, of course, is that this time too the company will make the requisite course corrections and ultimately prevail. The opposing argument is that those comebacks occurred in the days when the doubts about mainframes were small and the moat was wide. IBM could then make money with one hand and play catch-up with the other. Today, as IBM's results for 1991 show, it takes both hands—and both feet—just to stay in the game

Given the severity of that challenge and IBM's gymful of troubles, it is ironic that some knowledgeable outsiders still give the company high grades for depth of management, one of IBM's historical virtues. Says a critic of the company who is a fan in this respect: "IBM has ten people at the top who could run any other computer company." That may be true. But they certainly haven't yet proved they can run IBM.

Source: Carol J. Loomis, "Can John Akers Save IBM?" *Fortune,* ©1991 The Time Inc. Magazine Company. All rights reserved.

BACKGROUND FOR THE IBM STRATEGIC ANALYSIS

To illustrate how to analyze a company, we will first examine IBM's recent history and then analyze the foregoing illustrative case. The title, "Can John Akers Save IBM?" is provocative because IBM is such a well-known company. Following our discussion here, we will illustrate how to apply approaches that are covered in this book. As Figure 1.1 shows, strategic analysis begins with looking at the business itself and proceeds to examine the industry and the general economic and social environment in which the company operates. This external environment defines the context in which strategy needs to be formulated.

Starting with an examination of the business itself, we find that IBM dominated the computer field for many years, holding the largest market share in the sale of mainframe computers. Early competitors such as GE and RCA dropped by the wayside because they did not have the commitment or the competitive capability to withstand the IBM onslaught. In a bold attempt to ensure that the mainframe continues to be an important element of the computer industry, IBM is incorporating it as a key element of networking (Verity, 1989).

Can John Akers reinvent the IBM of the past? A look at some of the historic developments suggests that if properly managed, it can once again become a dominant force in the computer industry, which is itself being transformed into a telecommunications and computerized video industry. With the laser as a technological force behind many of the changes taking place, vast adjustments are needed to keep pace in the industry. Companies such as Dell Computer with only 1,900 employees can sell PCs cheaper than IBM, which has $69 billion in sales (Flannigan, 1991). To counter this threat, IBM will test selling its PCs by mail order

(Carroll, 1992b) and is planning to sell in Europe a PC clone made by an Asian firm (Carroll, 1992a). Over the years IBM has made significant contributions to developments in computers and software. As early as 1952, IBM introduced the 701 computer for scientific calculations. In 1958 it came out with the 7000 series, and in 1964 it introduced the system 360 computers. It continued to innovate in computer design in 1985, introducing the 3090 mainframe computer and the RISC computer (Lewis et al., 1988).

What happened at IBM to make one of America's most admired companies lose its luster? In 1988 IBM fell from America's most admired company to number 23 (Schultz, 1988). In 1992 IBM plunged to 118th on the list of most admired companies (Ballen, 1992). The criteria used by *Fortune* to assess a company's reputation included:

1. Quality of management
2. Financial soundness
3. Quality of products or services
4. Ability to attract, develop, and retain talented people
5. Use of corporate assets
6. Value as a long-term investment
7. Ability to innovate
8. Community and environmental responsibility

Fortune polled corporate directors, senior executives, and analysts, and 82% cited quality of management as the paramount factor (Ballen, 1992). What does this imply for IBM's future?

Analyzing the Industry

The next step in the strategic analysis is to examine the industry and the general economic and social system of which that industry is a part. An industry analysis includes an environmental scan to determine what forces external to the organization have a direct impact on its competitive position and what competitive actions need to be taken to achieve a sustainable competitive advantage. An industry analysis also helps determine what competitors are doing, what threats and opportunities exist, and whether the company should enter, remain in, or exit from an industry.

Determining in which industry a company fits can be a difficult task, because many companies are in several industries. It is often appropriate to begin an industry analysis by considering the "core" competency of the business that is its major source of income or by considering a specific strategic business unit (SBU). One can examine the standard industrial classification code; however, any conclusions based solely on the SIC code can be misleading if no additional information is used (such as what products are dominant in a given industry, what markets are served, and what percentage of the company's total sales are derived in a given industry classification). Nonetheless, the SIC code is a useful reference point because all companies are confronted with these same limitations. Where possible, industries are grouped by location, size, profitability, growth, or other factors that contribute to the direct or indirect competitive environment.

After an industry has been classified, it is useful to explore the strategic groups in that industry. This analysis includes those companies that compete in a given industry and how they affect the subject company's competitive ability. For example, although Apple might not be thought of as a competitor to IBM, Apple has taken away market share in the personal computer market and is a formidable force in that segment of the computer industry. Strategic groups can be found for most segments within an industry. Porter (1980), for example, looks at strategic groups as those companies that contribute to rivalry in an industry because of price, quality, product differentiation, overall size, market share, or willingness to take risks. The ease with which it is possible to enter or leave a group depends on the structure of the industry, which includes barriers to entry, maturity of the industry, cost structure, technology, product differentiation, and mobility of the company.

Having identified the group in which a company competes, one can draw a group map to show the member companies' relative size, importance, ability to compete, resources, and similar factors that contribute to rivalry among firms. An industry group map is shown in Figure 2.1.

Within a group, such as for mid-range computers, the relative percentage can be shown for each company in that group. The following are the relative percentages of the market for each of the dominant players (InfoCorp, 1993).

Company	Percentage
IBM	24
HP	17
DEC	13
NCR	8
Other	38

Using a similar approach for each of the groups, one can determine which companies are the major competitors within an industry and within a group. Developing an effective strategy depends on knowing who the competitors are and how strong they are. The industry group map can help planners determine how best to compete in a given arena.

Industry forces strongly influence what strategies are viable and whether the industry has growth potential or profit potential. Some of the major questions Porter (1980) believes are important to consider when examining an industry follow.

1. Is the industry fragmented, concentrated, mature, or declining? The personal computer industry is highly fragmented, whereas the automotive industry is highly concentrated. Steel has been both a mature and a declining industry.
2. How strong are competitors, what are their weaknesses, and how willing are they to compete vigorously? Philip Morris had considerable financial strength, but for many years it lacked technical know-how in industries such as wine making and eventually divested itself of its wine holdings.
3. How important is technology and how readily available is it? Does the industry have the infrastructure to sustain its differentiation against substitute

FIGURE 2.1   Industry Group Map

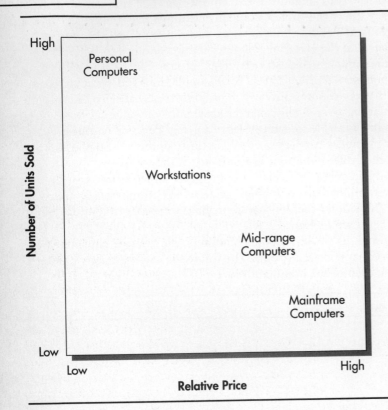

technologies? The electronics industry, which includes IBM, has suffered both from the need for new technology and from the proliferation of substitute products, especially computer clones.

4. What are the resources required to function effectively in the industry? Is it capital-intensive? Is there an adequate supply of skilled labor or technical and managerial personnel? Is the industry attractive to the financial community? Junk bonds have played havoc with banks, insurance companies, and stock brokerage houses because people relied on value that did not exist.

5. What are the long- and short-term trends in the industry? Are significant demographic changes taking place? Are suppliers and distributors reliable, and is their use cost-effective? What is the impact of global competition on the industry? The recession of 1991 and 1992 has had a direct impact on companies that make consumer products and has also affected those that depend indirectly on consumer spending. Global competition is increasingly becoming a fact of life that almost every industry must confront in order to survive.

6. What are the potential regulatory effects, especially in terms of pollution, labor, and restrictions on plant location or operation? Are significant laws

pending that would affect the industry? Is the industry subject to litigation, such as in health care or product liability?

7. What are customer expectations and needs? Do customers have significant power, are changes in buying practices under way, are customers subject to brand switching, and how price-elastic is the demand for the industry's products? Customers increasingly expect quality, service, timeliness, and performance, all of which contribute to what we call a product's value.

8. What are the channels for distribution of the products? Are needed services readily available? Is timing critical for delivery, and must inventory be kept on hand? What level of advertising and promotion is normal for the industry? Joint ventures, strategic alliances, and industry consortiums are becoming important ways to compete in today's turbulent environment.

9. Is the industry cyclic or seasonal in nature, or is demand predictable? Is there considerable uncertainty regarding the future of the industry (such as surrounds atomic energy, for example)? Is extensive R&D needed to maintain a technological edge? Motorola has shown that by spending large sums of money on R&D, it could reduce defects to the point where it was able to crack the Japanese market.

10. How is value added to products produced by the industry? Can cost be contained? Are mergers and acquisitions a problem? How vulnerable are companies in the industry to such takeovers as have occurred in the airline and cable industries?

IBM is still dominant in the mainframe segment of the computer industry, from which it derives 49.8% of its gross profits (Hammonds, 1991). Although the battle for mainframe customers has gotten really nasty, IBM still holds 69.7% of the U.S. market. Once the key computer company in Japan, IBM has dropped from number one to number two and most recently to number three, behind Fujitsu and NEC (Drefuss, 1988). IBM hopes that by making equipment for rival Mitsubishi it can recapture second place in Japan.

U.S. competitors such as DEC are striving to beat IBM in the mid-sized computer market. DEC is relying on an open system architecture to restore profits and market share (McWilliams, 1991). In order to compete in this market, IBM recently announced that it will offer a cheaper minicomputer, dropping the cost from $16,000 to $12,000 (*L.A. Times*, 1991). Using a "sizzling" RISC (reduced instruction-set computer) system, IBM hopes to position itself competitively in the workstation segment (Reinhardt & Smith, 1990).

IBM has had a major triumph with its AS/400, even though most companies had given up the mini-computer as dead (Verity, 1992a). IBM defied conventional wisdom and was able to build a $14 billion business. This success shows that IBM has the potential to remake itself. This theme is elaborated in the book *The Silverlake Project* (Bauer et al., 1992), which describes the transformation that took place in Rochester, Minnesota, over 1,000 miles from IBM headquarters in Armonk, New York. As the authors point out, IBM had become a product-driven company, as opposed to a customer-driven company. It had overlooked customer needs. But in the AS/400 venture, IBM vowed to change this. Against all odds—the project was completed in 2 years, involved 37 sites on 3 continents, used RISC technology, and entailed 10 million parts and 2,500 applications programs—the Silverlake Project succeeded. It did so by adhering to 10 basic principles:

1. Appoint a leader with the vision to release people's creative energies.
2. Pick the right people and give them a clearly defined mission.
3. Empower these people and trust them to use their own judgment.
4. Utilize work teams that criss-cross the organization.
5. Choose an appropriate market segment in which to position the product.
6. Gather data, and analyze it using a model of the markets and the business.
7. Allocate resources based on priorities, using tradeoffs.
8. Do things right the first time and break time constraints by using concurrent processes.
9. Recognize that the customer is your partner and tap into external expertise.
10. Meet and continuously exceed your customer's expectations.

Will all this be enough to offset competitors such as DEC and Sun who are targeting high-powered workstations that are beginning to look more like powerful minicomputers (Weber, 1991)? Other competitors include Apple, which has the dominant market share in the personal computer segment and AT&T, which recently purchased Teradata to tap into the database computer arena. These companies continue to nibble away at IBM's market share and profits (Moffat, 1991). Over the 10-year period from 1982 to 1991 the largest growth was in the personal computer segment, which rose from approximately $2 billion to $32 billion while the mainframe computers went from approximately $11 billion in 1982 to an estimated $20 billion in 1991 (Verity and Lewis, 1987).

The hardware portion of the computer industry is primarily an oligopoly of a few dominant companies. Segments such as the personal computer arena are highly fragmented because of the clones that have copied IBM's open architecture of the personal computer. Another important aspect of the computer industry is the software (computer programs) that makes the hardware useful. IBM has relied on companies such as Microsoft to supply programs that help it to be more competitive. IBM's own efforts in the software segment have been less than successful. In 1987 IBM promised to develop software that would link all its computers, but 30,000 programmers later, it still exhibits "software gridlock" in this one segment (Schwartz, 1991). Problems such as these and false starts on investments put an end to one of the most embarrassing chapters in IBM's history. IBM had hoped, for example, that its investment in Rolm would launch it into the rapidly growing telecommunications industry, but this effort failed because "people who understood the market best were not asked" (Hof and Keller, 1989).

ANALYZING INTERNAL PROBLEMS

By shifting our analysis from the competitive forces in the industry to the internal problems confronting IBM, we obtain additional information that we need for analyzing the case and formulating a recommended strategy to improve the situation. In its 1991 annual report, IBM noted significant improvements over 1989 operations because of "management's strategy to transform the company by increasing emphasis on quality and customer solutions, improving competitiveness of IBM's products and services, and achieving greater efficiencies from cost and expense management and strategic restructuring." The results included a 10.1% increase in revenue to $69 billion and net earnings of $6 billion, compared to $3.8 billion in 1989. However, *Business Week's* 1992 ranking of the top 1,000 companies showed that IBM lost $564 million in 1991.

Although there are many vocal critics, and IBM is far from being out of the woods, it is making progress toward improvement. By examining what led to the current situation, a strategic manager can determine what (if any) changes in strategy are needed to maintain and enhance a company's competitive position and profitability. IBM is under siege at every part of its vast empire as it tries to maintain its competitive position. It is a formidable competitor, but it no longer looks invincible. From a high of 46% of the personal computer segment, it now has only 23%, its mainframe share dropped from 80% in 1983 to 69% in 1991, and its stock price declined from a high of $168 in 1987 to $103 in mid-1991 (McCarroll, 1991). By the end of 1992, the stock had plummeted to $52. And this despite a major restructuring of its $69 billion revenue (Weber, 1991).

John Akers is taking some revolutionary steps to try to correct what he considers a crisis situation. "The fact that we're losing shares makes me goddamn mad. . . . The tension level is not high enough . . . the business is in crisis" (Byrne et al., 1991). Byrne reports that outsiders have criticized Akers for not accepting responsibility and for being reluctant to change the old way of doing things. Elsewhere, IBM has been accused of jettisoning paternalism in order to become more competitive (Evan I. Schwartz, 1991).

CORE COMPETENCIES

As we indicated at the outset, a case analysis should consider the environmental forces impinging on the organization, regulatory considerations (such as the 1980 antitrust suit brought against IBM), industry analysis, competitor analysis, customer analysis, and internal analysis.

At this point, we will examine the core competencies of IBM and what future options are open in its effort to formulate a sustainable competitive strategy. Prahalad and Hamel (1990) look at the roots of competitiveness by recognizing the need to rethink the corporation to determine where and how to develop organizational capability that can create products that customers need even though they may not be aware of them. For example, from 1980 to 1988 Cannon grew by 264% and Honda by 200%. Comparing this record with those of companies such as Xerox, Chrysler, and IBM makes it obvious that considerable potential exists for U.S. companies. In the short run, competitiveness depends on the company's ability to build an organization that can produce products at a lower cost, in a more timely manner, with value added in new products that were not previously anticipated. This was accomplished in the Silverlake Project that produced the AS/400. A core competency is not developed by spending more money on R&D; rather, it is an outgrowth of distinct advantages in the products produced. Furthermore, a core competency should be difficult for competitors to imitate. Skills have to be embedded in the organization and cannot be obtained from outside. Although it is appropriate for a firm to acquire portions of its products from other sources or to develop strategic alliances, the core competencies need to be protected. Prahalad and Hamel (1990) introduce a "competency map" that helps to identify the product areas in which a company can excel. This map shows where the competencies exist in the organization and what skills contribute to differentiated products. General Electric restricted its core competency to those product areas wherein it could be number one or two in the world. Using the competency map, a company can develop a "strategic architecture" that can be used to guide the deployment of assets in a way that builds the competitive structure of the company and helps to define in what products and in what areas it can compete most effectively.

It is not necessary to spend an excessive amount on R&D in order to exploit a core competency. The organization simply needs to identify its core competency and to allocate resources to develop a differential advantage. This competitiveness stems from the ability to produce at a lower cost, and more rapidly, than others. The source of competitive advantage is the ability to focus skills to produce competencies, which helps empower employees and enhances the company's ability to adapt rapidly to changing opportunities.

Taking this perspective, where do we find IBM's core competencies? The company seems to be focusing on the following areas (Verity et al., 1991):

1. Personal computers and workstations: $14 billion
2. Memory storage products: $10.8 billion
3. Software: $10.6 billion
4. Maintenance: $8 billion
5. Printers: $2 billion
6. Systems integration: $2 billion
7. Facilities management: $0.5 billion
8. Semiconductors: not sold outside in 1991

It has been suggested that the new IBM would resemble a holding company more than an integrated manufacturer. The restructuring has resulted in over 50,000 employees departing IBM for various reasons. The strategy of a cost-conscious IBM would sound the death knell for IBM's no-layoff practice. It would also pit the PC and workstation group against the mainframe group. The issue of redistribution of expenses, advertising, and corporate office costs is still unresolved (Loomis, 1991). IBM is fighting hard in Europe against the Japanese in a winner-take-all battle. To do this, IBM is cementing ties with former rivals (Levine and Schares, 1991). It has teamed up with Siemens to develop a high-capacity, 64-megabyte chip in 1995. (Today the 1-megabyte chip is fairly standard.) IBM is selling everything from chips to subsystems to European rivals and has become a major source of venture capital for small European companies, investing more than $100 million in 200 software and service firms. It has also linked up with Bull and with Italy's Olivetti. For an investment of $100 million, Bull will sell IBM a 5.7% stake in its equity; Bull, in turn, will base future computers on IBM's RS/6000 microprocessor (Levine, 1992).

While IBM looks to a brighter future, it reported a $2.8 billion loss for the first time in its 80-year history. IBM claims this was due to a sluggish economy and to the costs associated with reducing its workforce by tens of thousands (Moffat, 1992). This loss was incurred in spite of IBM's selling 11 of its $22.8 million System/9000 machines to Sears. Along with this news came the announcement that the RS/6000, which the company is hoping to sell to Bull in Europe, will have to be put on hold because of a faulty chip design (Hamilton, 1991).

With the PC now ten years old, IBM faces an uncertain future in this profitable segment of its business. There are some 60 million PCs in the United States today. To bolster its position in the '90s, IBM teamed up with Apple and will engineer a chip that will run both companies' programs. This design incorporates a major new method of writing software called OOP (object-oriented programming). The risks in developing such a product are high, but Apple is betting its whole company on it (Schlender, 1991). The estimate of PC sales worldwide is $93 billion, with U.S. sales estimated at $37.1 billion.

Multimedia computing is now here and will undoubtedly expand in the future. Laser disks are available that can hold encyclopedias, voice, video, text, drawings, dial-in videos, and data services of all kinds. Software will become increasingly easy to use and will extend into the realm of expert systems and "artificial intelligence" (Depke and Brandt, 1991). IBM envisions a growth in processing using its systems network architecture (SNA). IBM also will continue to support its large installed base of 3745 voice band processors (Horwitt, 1992). It has said it will provide support for the beleaguered semiconductor industry. This is a radical departure from IBM's policy of avoiding any interaction with competitors. In another move, it backed the purchase of Perkin-Elmer Co. to prevent Nikon Corp. from taking over the vital technology of sophisticated semiconductor manufacturing equipment (Lazzareschi, 1990). Thus, we see IBM changing in structure and behavior and even forging strategic alliances that previously were not done.

What should IBM do, given its situation in July of 1991, and what can we expect to follow? Six experts who were asked this question offered the following advice (Byrne et al., 1991).

1. Irving Shapiro, former director of IBM: It should continue to provide strong support for R&D so that it can remain competitive with the Japanese.
2. Kenneth Iverson, CEO of Nucor: Akers should create an environment where the focus is on costs and efficiency.
3. Rosabeth Moss Kantor, editor of the *Harvard Business Review*: Akers needs to communicate clearly to the organization what kind of company he expects it to be. He should also strongly indicate what is rewarded and what is valued. He should identify the "local heroes" who contribute to the long-term service thrust. Finally, he must examine the problems of bureaucracy, provide a statement of values, and articulate his vision for the company.
4. Thomas Peters, management consultant: It should not hesitate to break the company up into five pieces. Loosen up the atmosphere and reduce the top-heavy structure. It should try not to be heavy-handed and arrogant.
5. Amory Houghton, former IBM director: Shake the place up and loosen the horsepower and science that is already available.
6. Jeffrey Sonnenfeld, director of leadership studies at Emory University: Akers should avoid finger pointing and deal with the broad management issues. He

needs to take charge, explain his plan for correcting the situation, and accept responsibility for what has happened to date.

Each of these comments tends to focus on the main problem confronting IBM, the need to reinvigorate the management and the organization. IBM has abundant talent, outstanding technology and manufacturing capability, strong image and market position, and excellent potential. The critical issue is how to utilize these valuable resources to restore the luster to what was once the most admired company in the United States. All this can be accomplished, according to Schrage (1991), who suggests that IBM should adopt the approaches used by such enormously successful and innovative companies as Japan's Sumitomo and Mitsubishi. The question now confronting IBM is how to restructure so that the values and culture bind everyone together and encourage the release of highly innovative—though perhaps now dormant—forces.

ANALYZING THE IBM CASE

What went wrong at IBM? Why was top management unable to succeed? Was it a failure of leadership, or were the company's problems more deeply rooted? What could CEO John Akers have done? What information would he have needed to decide on a different course of action? What sources of information could he have used?

Asking these kinds of questions is generally a good way to begin a case analysis, the basic method used for many years to study strategic management and planning. Case analysis begins with pertinent facts about an organization and ends with possible solutions to problems that those facts reveal. This approach enables the strategic manager to become immersed in the complex, ill-structured, and sometimes chaotic circumstances in which organizations operate. Case analysis brings order to the statement of strategic problems and provides information that is useful in the development of strategic solutions.

Performing a case analysis gives students an opportunity to work as a team. While working on a strategic problem, members of the team hone their own communication and leadership skills and gain insight into group decision-making processes.

To be useful, the ideas developed must be stated clearly and buttressed by supporting arguments. A common failing in the preparation of written cases is the lack of a formal structure. All too often, excellent points are buried in excess verbiage.

Another important consideration is how best to prepare the case analysis. It is usually helpful to scan the case quickly in order to obtain a general impression of the key ideas and issues. This overview is followed by a more careful examination of the material and by the identification of relevant facts. The methodology covered in this book will be especially helpful in isolating and organizing the important facts from the mass of material presented.

SAMPLE CASE ANALYSIS FORMAT

A case analysis should follow a clear format to facilitate presenting ideas in a logical, consistent sequence. The sample format shown in Figure 2.2 readily fits a variety of strategic problems. The following example demonstrates how this framework can be applied.

Statement of the Problem

This statement identifies the main problem to be examined in the analysis. It is important to avoid such pitfalls as confusing symptoms with problems, making premature evaluations, taking information at face value, and applying old stereotypes to new problems. The problem has to be stated explicitly, and its short-term aspects distinguished from its long-term concerns. The statement should also include any assumptions to be made in the analysis. The following example illustrates a statement of the problem IBM was facing in 1991.

Example Statement of the Problem: IBM

IBM is confronted with a crisis of confidence and is facing continued loss of market share in both the mainframe and PC computer lines. The huge write-off of $5.4 billion has contributed to the lowering of IBM's credit rating by Moody's. Voluntary departures have resulted in the elimination of over 100,000 jobs worldwide since 1985, which has led to severe morale problems, with several key executives having defected. The economic decline in the United States and in Europe has contributed to the downturn in sales and to the losses incurred. Although management appears frustrated by the downturn, it is not clear that the changes that have come about were anticipated. Akers seems to be responding in a crisis mode rather than confronting the situation in a strategic manner with a carefully developed plan of action. He has tried to "reinvent" IBM but has not delegated enough authority to the new divisions for them to compete effectively.

Analysis of the Data

The first step is to identify important data to use in analyzing the case. Relevant data might include information about environmental issues, current economic conditions in the industry, market share, competitive strategy, customer reaction, available funding, profit, government regulations and their impact, product problems, productive capacity, work performance, and managerial style.

Managers can use a number of different methods to analyze these kinds of data and solve strategic problems, but they often rely on past experience or a cursory analysis of limited amounts of information. For example, managers who have had relevant experience with similar problems or are aware of research or other data may apply creative problem solving and estimate the risk of different outcomes. This informal approach does not, however, ensure that they will find appropriate solutions to complex problems. Rather than "winging it," managers

FIGURE 2.2	Sample Format for Case Analysis*

Topic	Methodology	Topic	Methodology
Statement of the Problem (What's going on?)		*Formulation and Evaluation of Alternatives (What can be done? Which alternatives are feasible, compatible, consistent?)*	
Company background	Situation audit		
Recent problems	Company capability profile	Status quo	Multiattribute analysis
Industry history	Strategic 4 factors	Concentration	Pareto law
Analysis of Data (What information do I need? Where can I find it?)		Horizontal integration	Heuristics
Industry analysis (What patterns and trends are important?)		Vertical integration	
		Diversification	
Growth	WOTS-UP analysis	Joint ventures	
Market structure	Environmental scan	Restructuring	
Competition	Growth-vector analysis	Divestiture	
Product analysis (Do our products have a competitive edge?)		Liquidation	
		Innovation	
Market share	Competitive portfolio	Others	
Pricing	PIMS analysis	*Recommendations (Are the recommendations specific?)*	
Promotion	Experience curve	Alternative(s)	
R&D	Product life cycle	Reasons for recommendations	
Distribution	SPACE analysis	Possible competitor reactions	
Key success factors	Critical success factors	Impact on the company	
Financial analysis (Financial performance? Projections?)		*Implementation (Can recommendations be implemented, and how?)*	
Profitability	Dupont formula	Resource allocations	
Liquidity	Strategic funds programming	Costs, returns	
Leverage		Feasibility	
Activity	Sustainable growth	Budgets, timetables	
Growth requirements	Baseline projections	Management commitment	
	Financial ratios		
Management and organization (What kind of organization is this?)			
Top-management strategy	Hierarchy of objectives		
	Key result objectives		
Values and mission	Decision styles		
Goals and objectives	Organization life cycle		
	Organization structure		

*Note: Terms used in this table will be explained in later chapters.

should augment their creative thinking with a systematic approach that does not overlook important factors that could affect the success of a strategic plan.

Formulation and Evaluation of Alternatives

Generally, several alternative strategies should be suggested. The following are some examples of such alternatives.

- Maintain the status quo.
- Broaden the product line.
- Expand into new areas through acquisition.
- Restructure the organization.
- Expand the firm's global alliances.

The next step is to evaluate the feasibility of each alternative. This involves examining the company's available resources or adding new information that supports one or another point of view. The preceding alternative strategies might be evaluated as follows:

- If IBM does nothing, its current problems will only increase.
- As a hedge against market maturation and competition, IBM should expand into other areas that would draw on either technology or marketing strategies similar to those now in use. Examples might include telecommunications and multimedia and wide area networks.
- IBM has the financial capability to make acquisitions, but the potential problems may outweigh the benefits.
- Restructuring the organization would be difficult but may be needed.
- Global alliances demand careful definition and analysis. For example, early expansion in Japan was initially successful but then encountered considerable local competition.

Recommendation of a Strategy

The choice of what strategy to recommend should be justified. For example, a "good" strategy that the company cannot implement is not acceptable. Some possible recommendations that IBM could choose are

- Expand into other lines of business where technology or marketing strategies similar to those used for current products could be employed.
- Restructure the organization into separate business units such as Johnson & Johnson has done.
- Prepare a management training program that emphasizes an entrepreneurial culture.
- Expand global alliances into Eastern Europe and Russia.

Implementation: Statement of the Plan of Action

The strategy that is chosen must be feasible and must also include a plan for carrying it out. The plan of action is often a series of steps needed to ensure that desired objectives are achieved. The following items illustrate what one might expect in a plan of action for the strategies shown above.

- Establish clearly defined criteria for accepting or rejecting new products
- Develop potential new products that IBM would find desirable and assess them using the criteria established.
- Examine the strategic fit of potential new products.
- Determine the resource requirements of new products.
- Examine the industry growth potential and the strength of competitors.

- Prepare a list of possible acquisition candidates.
- Exercise the necessary due diligence when considering an acquisition.
- Determine the strategic advantages of acquisitions and the resources needed for them.
- Examine alternative organization structures to determine which would best fit IBM's culture.
- Determine whether downsizing is needed, given IBM's recent losses.
- Establish a study team to explore how best to carry out any possible restructuring.
- Provide adequate communication and involvement to ensure acceptance of a reorganization.
- Examine IBM's policy of not outsourcing and its implications for restructuring.
- Expand the existing executive training to ensure that leadership, empowerment, teamwork, creativity, and an open culture are achieved.
- Provide for greater freedom of operation of individual units.
- Prepare a plan to find potential global partners.
- Explore the advantages and disadvantages of additional global strategic alliances.
- Determine whether forming alliances in Eastern Europe is desirable.
- Set a timetable to pursue the various options being explored.
- Assign responsibility for carrying out the various steps in the action plan.

PRESENTATION OF FINDINGS

Before a plan of action can be implemented, it must be communicated and accepted. Acceptance involves understanding and a sense of ownership to ensure that individuals are willing to commit themselves to undertaking a new strategy. In part, the material in Chapter 10 on organizational change deals with this issue. Empowerment and teamwork are two very powerful approaches that are being used increasingly to gain acceptance of a strategic plan.

When presenting a recommended strategy to top management or the board of directors, it is often advisable to summarize the material in an executive memo. This allows the executive to determine whether he or she is willing to pursue the matter further.

The executive memo serves two purposes:

1. It is a concise way of summarizing the findings and recommendations of the case analysis. Its one-page format forces the writer to address the issues clearly and succinctly.
2. It emphasizes that the case analysis is only a basis for arriving at viable strategic alternatives. The final choice involves a number of considerations, not the least of which is active involvement of the CEO.

A sample executive memo for IBM is shown in Figure 2.3. An effective executive memo presents

- Critical issues. What are the key problems, assumptions, and the like, and why? What are the expected results?
- Justification. Which methods of analysis were used, what data were considered, and how are they related to the proposed strategy?
- Action plan. What specific steps, resources, and timing are needed to carry out the recommended strategy?

Another purpose of the executive memo is to involve the CEO and other top managers in choosing and implementing strategies. Ideally, the CEO should enter the arena early in the process and set objectives, challenge assumptions, clarify options, and generally orchestrate the diverse elements that are needed to get a strategy formulated and implemented. In reality, top-management involvement in the strategic-planning process often amounts to little more than the allocation of corporate resources to implement proposals prepared by subordinates. This is unfortunate, because the effectiveness of implementation is often directly related to the level and visibility of the CEO's support.

FIGURE 2.3	Sample Executive Memo

To: John F. Akers
From: Alan Rowe, et al.
Re: The IBM business crises
Date: December 18, 1992

CRITICAL ISSUES

For the first time, IBM has reported $2.8 billion in losses, decreased market share both in PCs and mainframes, has had over 100,000 in staff reductions, has reported write-offs of $5.4 billion in 1992 which are expected to rise to $6.0 billion, and has been confronted by increasing competition, especially in the PC segment of the market. Morale is slipping with the defection of key personnel.

RECOMMENDED STRATEGY

Considering that the market is mature, fragmented, and price-sensitive, IBM needs to take forceful measures to counter the adverse forces that have caused serious problems. A number of alternatives were reviewed. Those that IBM should consider include

1. Expand telecommunications, multimedia, networks, and further development of the company's RISC chips.
2. Acquire companies that round out required technical competence in the foregoing areas. Expand the marketing of clones by subsidiaries, using mail order or telemarketing.
3. Restructure the organization into independent strategic business units to provide flexibility and the greater entrepreneurial spirit that fostered development of the original PC and the system AS 400 computer.

(continued)

| FIGURE 2.3 | Sample Executive Memo (continued) |

---

4. Obtain training support to smooth the organizational transition and to help foster a more open, less bureaucratic structure. Emphasize creativity, entrepreneurial spirit, and teamwork.
5. Expand strategic alliances both in the United States and abroad. Position the company to operate in a European common market and to exploit opportunities in such developing areas as Eastern Europe and Southeast Asia.
6. Provide superior service to users, and consider entering the "outsourcing" business. Timeliness, quality, value, and pricing need to be brought into line with competition.
7. Reduce the emphasis on the mainframe segment, and focus on the AS/6000 and related machines.

JUSTIFICATION

Using a number of analytical methods (including industry analysis, competitor analysis, technology analysis, financial analysis, and others), IBM can readily evaluate the merits of the proposed strategy. Worksheets covering stakeholders, core competency, product portfolio, and the like provide support to the other methods of analysis.

ACTION PLAN

The actual steps needed to carry out the strategy, including the timing and expected results, are crucial to ensuring a positive outcome. This phase is often associated with strategy implementation, which therefore also includes considerations related to organizational change. Some of the actions required for the foregoing strategic plan would include preparing a budget to allocate resources, preparing and communicating a new organization chart along with product and/or customer responsibility, determining the level of R&D needed to expand into new products, appointing a marketing team to re-examine all products and determine the potential areas for global expansion or alliances, preparing a training program reflecting the managers' assessment of which needs must be satisfied first, and developing an appropriate basis for evaluating and rewarding performance.

SUPPORTING MATERIAL

Append any worksheets, analysis, and supporting documents, and refer to them in the justification section.

UPDATE ON THE CASE

The following events have occurred subsequent to those described in the case presented at the beginning of the chapter.

1. A new SLC chip microprocessor for the IBM PC computers was introduced (Fitzgerald, 1992).
2. C. Michael Armstrong, chairman of IBM World Trade and the heir apparent to Akers, jumped ship to become chairman and CEO of Hughes Aircraft Co. (Margolis, 1992). He followed Ed Lucente, president of IBM World Trade, who left to join Northern Telecom.

3. To increase the sale of the PC, IBM has decided to sell clones in Europe that were made by an Asian firm (Carroll, 1992a) and to try selling PCs by mail order (Carroll, 1992b).

4. IBM has been courting Time Warner to develop a strategic alliance for transmitting video. The venture would rely heavily on technology development by IBM for "interactive" video using current cable TV systems.

5. Lucie Fjeldstad was appointed manager of IBM's multimedia business. Her formula for success is to
   - Bring in executives from outside the computer industry, which runs counter to IBM's culture.
   - Manage the multimedia business independent of IBM.
   - Offer incentives to ensure strong profit.
   - Exit from businesses that are not essential to IBM's future.

6. James Cannavino, who is in charge of IBM's personal computers and workstations, refuses to conform to Big Blue's bureaucracy. He has so far stopped the PC hemorrhage, and he is attempting to satisfy customer needs (Verity, 1992).

7. Considering strategic alliances or investments in other companies, IBM has
   - Talked electronic media with MCA, Disney, Lucas, and Speilberg.
   - Proposed using networking to deliver Time Warner movies into homes.
   - Considered equity positions in Sapiens, Northgate, Parallan, Group Bull, and Auspex.

8. IBM has announced that it may spin off its Personal Systems Division into a wholly owned subsidiary (Perratore, 1992).

9. With less than 12% of the PC market in Europe, IBM has disclosed that it would take 17,500 of its workers out of a contract with the I. G. Metall union (Templeman and Hollifield, 1992).

10. To oppose PC clones, IBM has decided to build its own clone called Value Point. This follows a drop in its PC market share from 21% in March 1992 to 16% in August (Arnst, 1992).

11. The electronics industry is facing "deconstructing" as a result of changes in the importance of the mainframe (Levine and Hof, 1992). Competitors will now become more responsive to customer needs by being smaller, leaner, and faster.

12. In its continued consolidation, IBM announced in December 1992 that 25,000 additional jobs would be cut. IBM has eliminated 100,000 jobs to date, using voluntary departures (Zonana and Weber, 1992).

13. Akers may have signaled his heir apparent by elevating five executives to the position of senior vice president. But analysts say that this may be misleading (Verity, 1992b).

14. In a surprise move, Akers rehires two of IBM's previous top executives, Paul Rizzo and Kaspar Cassani. Both men will act as advisors to John Akers (Associated Press, 1992).

15. Breaking with the past, IBM is expected to advertise the street prices of the new PS/ValuePoint line of personal computers. The message is that IBM intends to meet mail-order PC competitors head on (Perratore, 1992).

16. Nominated as the product of the year for 1992, IBM's "color notebook" shows that IBM can meet competition when it puts its technology to work (Seymour, 1993).

Giant firms such as GM and IBM need a new vision. They must either change or die, because worldwide, customers have a surplus of products to choose from and at declining prices (Flanigan, 1992).

It is clear from the actions being taken by IBM that it really does intend to "reinvent" itself. This will undoubtedly be accomplished by the breaking up of IBM reported in *Fortune* (Kilpatrick, 1992). The new company will have thirteen major "baby blues." These are divided into the following eight operating divisions and the following four marketing services:

Operating Divisions	Revenues in Billions	Product/Service
Enterprise Systems	$22.0	Mainframes
Adstar	$11.9	Storage devices
Personal Systems	$11.5	PCs, workstations
Application Systems	$11.4	Minicomputers
Programming Systems	$2.8	Software
Pennant Systems	$2.1	Printers
Application Solutions	$2.2	Software services
Technology Products	NA	Chips, circuits
Networking Systems	NA	Mainframe networks
Marketing Services		
Europe, Middle East	$26.1	IBM products
North America	$24.4	IBM products
Asia Pacific	$9.3	IBM products
Latin America	$5.0	IBM products

This breakup will give more autonomy to the separate businesses. However, IBM intends to retain a single sales force. In addition to the breakup, IBM is feverishly forming partnerships with other major computer companies. Time will tell whether this new strategy will pay off.

S UMMARY

This chapter discusses the important considerations that analysts must take into account before formulating a strategic plan. The chapter revolves around a case analysis addressing recent problems of the IBM Corporation. It also shows how to prepare an executive memo that summarizes a strategic analysis and the recommendations that follow.

REFERENCES AND SUGGESTIONS FOR FURTHER READING

Alster, Norm. 1991. IBM as holding company. Wonderful leverage. *Forbes,* December 23, pp. 117–120.

Arnst, Catherine. 1992. COMPAQ. *Business Week,* November 2, pp. 146–152.

Ballen, Kate. 1992. America's most admired corporations. *Fortune,* February 10, pp. 40–72.

Bauer, Roy A., Emilio Collar, and Victor Tang. 1992. *The Silverlake Project.* New York: Oxford University Press.

Byrne, John A., Deidre A. Depke, Stephanie Anderson Forest, Jonathan B. Levine, Robert Neff, and John W. Verity. 1991. IBM: What's wrong? What's next? *Business Week,* June 17, pp. 27–34. In the same issue, see Evan I. Schwartz, Hot dogs, roller coasters, and complaints, pp. 28–29; Keith H. Hammonds, Why big companies are so tough to change, pp. 30–31; and Judith Dobrzynski, What should Akers do next? Six gurus weigh in, p. 33.

Byrne, John A. 1992. IBM's heirs apparent? *Business Week,* December 14, p. 38.

Carroll, Paul. 1992a. IBM to see PC clone made by Asian firm. *Wall Street Journal,* March 11, p. B1.

Carroll, Paul. 1992b. IBM will test selling its PCs by mail order. *Wall Street Journal,* June 29, p. B1 and B5.

Coy, Peter. 1992. IBM needs a new network—but not too new. *Business Week,* April 20, pp. 95–96.

Depke, Deidre A. and Richard Brandt. 1991. PCs: What the future holds. *Business Week,* August 12, pp. 58–64.

Dreyfuss, Joel. 1988. IBM's vexing slide in Japan. *Fortune,* March 28, pp. 73–77.

Dvorak, John. 1992a. Inside track. *PC Magazine,* February 25, p. 95.

Dvorak, John. 1992b. Will IBM dump the mainframe? *PC Magazine,* June 15, p. 93.

Fitzgerald, Michael. 1992. IBM PC future rides on system advancements, SLC chip. *Computer World,* February 24, p. 1.

Flanigan, James. 1992. GM and IBM face that vision thing. *Los Angeles Times,* October 25, pp. D1 and D7.

Flanigan, James. 1991. What's behind IBM's contortion act? *Los Angeles Times,* December 11, pp. D1 and D12.

The Global 500. 1991. *Fortune,* July 29, pp. 245–246 and 265–266.

Hamilton, Rosemary. 1992. IBM tries casual approach to development. *Computer World,* February 24, p. 1.

Hamilton, Rosemary. 1991. IBM wins one, fumbles another. *Computer World,* September 23, pp. 1 and 10–11.

Hof, Robert D. and John J. Keller. 1989. Behind the scenes at the fall of Rolm. *Business Week,* July 10, pp. 82–84.

Horwitt, Elisabeth. 1992. IBM sees peer-to-peer future for processor. *Computer World,* February 10, p. 55.

InfoCorp. 1992. IBM, HP lead mid-range charge. *PC Week,* January 4, p. 21.

IBM 1990 Annual Report. 1991. Management discussion, pp. 38–42.

IBM offers cheaper minicomputer. 1991. *Los Angeles Times,* September 5, p. D3.

IBM rehires retired top executives. 1992. *Los Angeles Times,* December 22, p. D5.

IBM seeks alliance with Time Warner. 1992. *Los Angeles Times,* May 30, pp. D1 and D4.

Kirkpatrick, David. 1992. Breaking up IBM. *Fortune,* July 27, pp. 44–58.

Lazzareschi, Carla. 1991. IBM will build mainframes for rival Mitsubishi. *Los Angeles Times,* November, pp. D1 and D3.

Lazzareschi, Carla. 1990. Competitiveness. *Los Angeles Times,* April 1, pp. D1 and D8.

Levine, Jonathan B. 1992. Look who's helping defend fortress Europe. *Business Week,* February 17, p. 131.

Levine, Jonathan B. and Gail E. Schares. 1991. IBM Europe starts swinging back. *Business Week,* May 6, pp. 52–53.

Lewis, Geoff, Anne R. Field, John J. Keller, and John W. Verity. 1988. Big changes at Big Blue. *Business Week,* February 15, pp. 92–98. In the same issue, see John W. Verity and Geoff Lewis, The reorganization man's idea of fun, p. 95, and Peter W. Bernstein, How IBM cut 16,200 employees—without an ax, p. 98.

Loomis, Carol J. 1991. IBM's Akers turns revolutionary. *Fortune,* December 30, pp. 9–10.

Margolis, Nell. 1992. Armstrong jumps IBM ship. *Computer World,* February 24, p. 4.

McCarroll, Thomas. 1991. The humbling of a computer colossus. *Time,* May 20, pp. 42–44.

McWilliams, Gary. 1991. Open systems may be DEC's open sesame. *Business Week,* June 24, pp. 101–103. In this same issue, see Gary McWilliams, The big engine that hasn't, p. 102.

Moffat, Susan. 1992. IBM reports first loss—$2.8 billion. *The Times,* January 18, pp. A1 and A16.

Moffat, Susan. 1991. AT&T buying Teradata to tap into database computer arena. *Los Angeles Times,* December 3, pp. D1 and D5.

Moody's lowers stellar credit rating of IBM. 1992. *Los Angeles Times,* March 5, p. D2.

Perratore, Ed. 1992a. IBM may spin off personal systems division. *Byte,* October, p. 42.

Perratore, Ed. 1992b. New systems . . . new IBM? *Byte,* November, p. 50.

Porter, Michael E. 1980. *Competitive strategy.* New York: The Free Press.

Prahalad, C. K. and Gary Hamel. 1990. The core competence of the corporation. *Harvard Business Review,* May–June, pp. 79–91.

Redfern, Andy. 1992. European portable workstation project launched. *Byte,* October, p. 42.

Reinhardt, Andy and Ben Smith. 1990. Sizzling RISC systems from IBM. *Byte,* April, pp. 124–128.

Scheier, Robert L. 1993. Outsider will lead the new charge at IBM. *PC Week,* March 29, pp. 1 and 16.

Schine, Eric. 1991. Mike Armstrong's leap of faith. *Business Week,* March 9, pp. 66–67.

Schlender, Brenton R. 1991. Happy birthday PC. *Fortune,* August 26, pp. 40–48.

Schrage, Michael. 1991. IBM should use Japan's formula. *Los Angeles Times,* November 28, pp. D1 and D4.

Schultz, Ellen. 1988. America's most admired corporations. *Fortune,* January 18, pp. 32–52.

Schwartz, Evan. 1992. The Lucie show: Shaking up a stodgy IBM. *Business Week,* April 6, pp. 64–65.

Schwartz, Evan I. 1991. 30,000 programmers later, software gridlock. *Business Week,* July 15, pp. 134–135.

Schwartz, John. 1991. The blues at Big Blue. *Newsweek,* December 16, pp. 44–46.

Schwartz, John. 1990. Big Blue's new assault. *Newsweek,* September 17, p. 50.

Seymour, Jim. 1993. The product of the year: IBM's color notebook. *PC Week,* January 4, p. 97.

Templeman, John and Ann Hollifield. 1992. IBM drops a bomb on labor. *Business Week,* July 13, 1992, p. 45.

Van Dyk, Jere. 1992. Partners in opportunity. *Beyond Computing,* Premier Issue, pp. 33–37.

Verity, John W. 1992a. IBM's major triumph in minis. *Business Week,* March 16, p. 111.

Verity, John W. 1992b. Room at the top. *Business Week,* March 18, pp. 27–29.

Verity, John W. 1992c. Surprise! The new IBM really looks new. *Business Week,* May 18, pp. 124–126.

Verity, John W. 1989. A bold move in mainframes. *Business Week,* May 29, pp. 72–78. In the same issue, see Diedre A. Depke, The software that ties it all together, pp. 74–75; Gary Weiss, On the street, Big Blue is big blah, p. 76; and John W. Verity, Why IBM is cramping its biggest customers' style, p. 78.

Verity, John W. and Geoff Lewis. 1987. Computers: The new look. *Business Week,* November 30, pp. 112–123. In the same issue, see Geoff Lewis, PCs that can roar almost as loud as the giant, p. 118, and John W. Verity, Mainframes aren't ready for the mothballs yet, p. 121.

Verity, John W., Thane Peterson, Deidre A. Depke, and Evan I. Schwartz. 1991. The new IBM. Is it new enough? *Business Week,* December 16, pp. 112–118. In the same issue, see Deidre A. Depke, Any complacent IBMers left?, p. 115; Deidre A. Depke, Why even the Japanese are worried about IBM, p. 116; and John Carey and Peter Coy, The research is first class. If only development was too, p. 118.

Weber, Jonathan. 1991a. Traders wary of IBM pledges; stock off again. *Los Angeles Times,* December 10, pp. D1 and D6.

Weber, Jonathan. 1991b. Sun Microsystems aims at new market segment. *Los Angeles Times,* April 13, pp. D1 and D10.

Weber, Joseph. 1992. A big company that works. *Business Week,* May 4, pp. 124–132.

Zonana, Victor F. and Jonathan Weber. 1992. IBM will slash 25,000 jobs in restructuring. *Los Angeles Times,* December 16, p. A1.

APPENDIX A

Sample of Sources of Information for an Industry Analysis

1. *Business Week*
2. The Securities and Exchange Commission's 10K Reports
3. *Business Conditions Digest*
4. *U.S. Industrial Outlook*
5. *Conference Board, Business Outlook*
6. *U.S. Industrial Directory*
7. *Industry Week*, "Trends and Forecasts"
8. *Business Week*, "Survey of Corporate Performance"
9. *Forbes*, "Annual Report on American Industry"
10. *New York Times Index*

CHAPTER THREE

Strategic Visioning, Goals, Ethics, and Social Responsibility

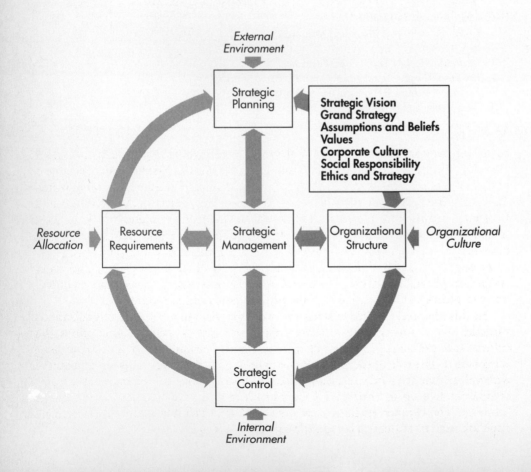

Chapter 1 A Framework for Strategic Management	**Chapter 2** Strategic Analysis	**Chapter 3** Strategic Visioning, Goals, Ethics, and Social Responsibility	**Chapter 4** The Competitive Environment	**Chapter 5** Capability-based Strategy	**Chapter 6** Market Dynamics and Sustainable Competitive Advantage
How to approach strategic management	*Application of strategic analysis*	*Understanding vision, values, ethics*	*Coping with competitive forces, stakeholders*	*Assessing company capability, timeliness, quality*	*Determining trends, gap analysis, and market dynamics*

Chapter 7 Strategy in a Global Environment	**Chapter 8** Financial Planning and Competitive-Cost Analysis	**Chapter 9** Entrepreneurship, Mergers and Acquisitions, Restructuring, and the Service Sector	**Chapter 10** Leadership Factor in Strategy and Implementing Strategic Change	**Chapter 11** Information Technology and Future Directions in Strategy
Assessing global trade, foreign markets, monetary exchange	*Preparing a financial plan and competitive-cost analysis*	*Importance of small business, entrepreneurs, restructuring*	*Strategy implementation, leadership, culture*	*Information technology, trends, new management*

INTRODUCTION

As the saying goes, "If you don't know where you're going, any road will take you there." A strategy, in a comparable sense, is just a means to achieve an objective or goal. Therefore, before a strategy can be proposed or implemented, the organization has to develop a clear idea of where it is going, and why. How is this accomplished? It usually begins with a *vision* of where the organization intends to be at some future date. The vision might call for continuation of a present strategy or for the development of a new strategy that would require radical organizational changes.

Choosing a goal and finding a strategy that leads there are fairly straightforward tasks. Complications enter in, however, because it is necessary to take into consideration the interests of stakeholders, of the organization, and of its employees.

In this chapter, we first discuss the strategic visioning process. Organizational variables that are difficult to measure objectively—values, beliefs, assumptions, and culture—are examined, and the role they play in the formulation of a strategic vision is explained. The role of specific strategies, goals, and objectives is discussed, together with values that are used to develop effective strategic visions. Values also affect how companies live up to their social responsibility and whether they pursue ethical behavior. The chapter explains how the social responsibility matrix and the ethics audit are used to evaluate a company's social posture.

THE CONCEPT OF STRATEGIC VISION

In his book *On Becoming a Leader* (1989), Warren Bennis describes the fundamental role that visioning plays in strategic leadership. To gain the support of stakeholders, executives need a challenging vision that translates what is essentially an act of the imagination into terms that describe possible future courses of action for the organization. Vision is the spark that is needed before the remaining steps are taken to achieve a successful strategy. To give the vision meaning, communication is vital. Executives must establish trust, to demonstrate their commitment to the vision, and act with confidence and positive self-regard in carrying it out.

Three principal factors materially influence how a strategic vision is created: the assumptions and beliefs of executives and leaders, their values, and the values reflected in the culture of the organization. Once a strategic vision is conceived, it is given substance and direction by three other managerial considerations: grand strategy, goals, and objectives. The relationships among these and other strategic-management concepts are shown in Figure 3.1.

ONE CHAIRMAN'S VISION: USAA

General Robert McDermott, the chairman of USAA (a major U.S. insurance company in San Antonio), had a vision for the company when he took it over in the late 1960s (Magnet, 1992). This company was originally organized to sell automobile insurance to military officers, but McDermott saw opportunities to expand the firm's product line and to offer the insurance to officers' dependents and relatives as well. At the same time, he focused on the need to provide high-quality, exemplary service to customers, especially in claims processing. As a result, USAA's phenomenal growth during the last two decades made the company one of the largest general insurance companies in the world.

Recently "Mac D," as he is usually called, sponsored a "Vision 2000" planning program to position USAA for its future. The company believes that its customer base could grow by at least 64% to 2.3 million clients by the year 2000. The median age of its primary customers is projected to increase to about 53, and that of their ex-dependents to about 37. The proportion of its customers who are permanently retired will probably increase by 12% to about 28% of its customer base. Meanwhile, USAA believes that its net worth will increase by about 20% or more. These represent significant changes in the business and require fresh thinking about the company and its mission. Vision 2000 was designed to provide this new insight and a new sense of direction.

The vision that emerged from the planning sessions includes several key concepts. First, the mission of the firm has been changed from providing insurance policies primarily in three categories: security (insurance products), asset management (banking and investment services), and quality of life (discount purchasing plans and loans.) To make the new vision viable it is necessary to focus on customers as individuals. This is a key element of USAA's vision that is "event-oriented services." Each active or potential customer of USAA is a member of what is called the life events program. Thirty-three pivotal events are considered, such as a

FIGURE 3.1 | **Strategic Vision**

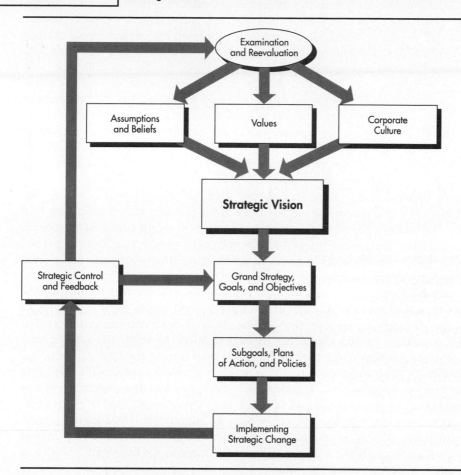

person receiving a military commission, a child reaching driving age, a household move, a vacation, a retirement, or the death of a loved one. Each event triggers a need for one or more of USAA's products and services. The company is positioning itself to respond to any life event in the simplest and most effective manner in order to convince members that they lose something of value if they go to a competitor. Carrying out this program has required an expansion and redirection of the company's information technology services. McDermott's approach is straightforward: "We should be able to satisfy a customer's needs with a single phone call. When a customer calls us for one reason, we should be able to make an assessment of what other services we might be able to provide (the life events concept aids in doing this) while the customer is still on the phone."

USAA's Vision 2000 is representative of what a good strategic vision should be. It is simple but not simplistic. It is specific, market- and customer-oriented, and focused on a problem or an opportunity rather than on how to carry out a program.

(The "how to do it" comes later.) Throughout USAA, General McDermott has also displayed the effective leadership that Bennis described. He initiated the effort to create a new vision, and now that Vision 2000 has been created, he is actively communicating it to all parties involved. He has made or supported the organizational changes and the investments in technology needed to achieve the vision. Using this approach, the company has remained on target in achieving its vision for the year 2000.

To be effective, a vision need not be so comprehensive as McDermott's. George David, the CEO of Otis Elevator, sums up his vision for the company in two basic ideas: "The only good elevator is an unnoticed one. Our objective is to go unnoticed" and "I want any salesperson in the company to be able to order an elevator with a single phone call." Ralph Lettieri, executive vice president of Benjamin Moore Paints, cast his vision as follows: "I wanted the customer to be able to walk into a home decoration center with a sample of color and walk out again with paint that exactly matched that sample." Another vision—one that resulted in major changes in the mutual fund industry—was stated simply by Ned Johnson, chairman of Fidelity Investments, who said "It might prove advantageous if we could give customers prices for our mutual funds on an hourly basis." Fidelity acted on the idea. Customers liked it, and Fidelity's competitors were forced to respond with comparable service.

One of the more famous and perhaps the most comprehensive visions in business history was that of David Sarnoff, who envisioned a new future for America and for the company that eventually became RCA. It demonstrates just how dramatically a strategic vision can affect an organization. In early 1914, as Sarnoff was sailing out of New York harbor, he listened to one of the first experimental radio programs of phonograph music that was being broadcast from the American Marconi station in New York's Wanamaker Building. He was enthralled by the experience and by the possibilities it suggested. Upon returning to New York, Sarnoff began to formulate his vision, which he summarized in a memorandum dated September 30, 1915, and addressed to Edward J. Nally, then vice president and general manager of the Marconi Wireless Telegraph Company of America (a predecessor of RCA). Called the "Radio Music Box" memo, it represents one of the rare cases in which a strategic vision was written and preserved for subsequent public review. Excerpts from Sarnoff's memo follow.

> I have in mind a plan of development which would make a radio a "household utility" in the same sense as the piano or phonograph. The idea is to bring music into the house by wireless.
>
> While this has been tried in the past by wires, it has been a failure because wires do not lend themselves to this scheme. With radio, however, it would seem to be entirely feasible. For example, a radiotelephone transmitter having a range of, say, 25 to 50 miles can be installed at a fixed point where instrumental or vocal music or both are produced. The problem of transmitting music has already been solved in principle, and therefore all the receivers attuned to the transmitting wavelength should be capable of receiving such music. The receivers can be designed in the form of a simple "Radio Music Box" and arranged for several different wavelengths which should be changeable with the throwing of a single switch or pressing of a single button.
>
> The "Radio Music Box" can be supplied with amplifying tubes and a loudspeaking telephone, all of which can be neatly mounted in one box. The box can be placed in the

parlor or living room, the switch set accordingly, and the transmitted music received. There should be no difficulty in receiving music perfectly when transmitted within a radius of 25 to 50 miles. Within such a radius, there reside hundreds of thousands of families; and as all can simultaneously receive from a single transmitter, there would be no question of obtaining sufficiently loud signals to make the performance enjoyable. The power of the transmitter can be made 5 kilowatts, if necessary, to cover even a short radius of 25 to 50 miles, thereby giving extra-loud signals in the home if desired. The development of a small loop antenna to go with each "Radio Music Box" would likewise solve the antenna problem (Sarnoff, 1968, pp. 31–34).

Later in the memo, Sarnoff predicted that sales of the Radio Music Box would reach "a gross business of about $75 million." RCA's actual sales of radios from 1922 to 1924 were $83.5 million. By the end of radio's "golden age" (1934–1941), over 830 AM stations were established, broadcasting about 270 hours of commercial network programming per week to radios in some 29,300,000 households (81.5% of the nation's households) and 8,750,000 cars (29.6% of the automobiles registered). In 1941, radio sets in households and automobiles represented an installed base worth about $1.5 billion. Annual industry income was in excess of $216 million, and annual radio advertising income was nearly $250 million (Sterling and Kittross, 1978).

The scientific knowledge that made radio possible was developed by people such as Michael Faraday, James Clerk Maxwell, and Henrich Hertz. Guglielmo Marconi, John Fleming, Lee de Forest, and Edwin Armstrong all produced innovations that helped convert the science into a workable technology. Both Marconi and de Forest started companies to commercialize their ideas. It was David Sarnoff, however, and his steadfast pursuit of the Radio Music Box vision, that made radio a large-scale, nationwide business that permeated nearly every aspect of American life. After a short period of experimentation during the 1920s, radio took off as a commercial enterprise. By the mid-1930s, Sarnoff's vision was realized. Radio is still a big business, even in today's era of television.

Other great entrepreneurs have realized their strategic visions in much the same way as Sarnoff. At a time when most office equipment was sold by "drummers," Thomas Watson, Sr. envisioned a company from which executives would purchase information solutions from professional businessmen who were backed by a strong service force. His vision became IBM. Ray Kroc believed that the concepts and assembly-line efficiencies pioneered by Henry Ford could be applied to popular foods, such as hamburgers, french fries, and milk shakes. His vision became McDonald's. Walt Disney dreamed that people would enjoy going to an amusement park dressed up as a fantasy world. His vision became Disneyland. Almost all successful companies begin with a strategic vision that is realized by means of effective strategies, plans, and policies.

A VISION OF REVAMPING: GE

Strategic visions often involve changing an established organization. Jack Welch, chairman and CEO of General Electric (GE), pioneered the revamping of that company. Long before most chief executives knew what corporate restructuring was, he was doing it. In 1981, after becoming GE's eighth—and, at 45, its youngest—chairman, he quickly eliminated thousands of jobs, removed entire echelons from the management hierarchy, and shifted assets from mature manufacturing businesses into fast-growing, high-technology, and service operations. In the five years between 1981 and 1986, GE sold 190 companies for a total of $5.5 billion and bought 70 companies for a total of $10 billion.

Welch's vision of a new, more competitive GE was based on two simple premises:

1. It is impossible to be outstanding in every field.
2. Laggard businesses tie up capital and management talent without earning a commensurate return. Individually they may be satisfactory, but overall they have a negative effect.

Based on these two premises, he divided the company into three groupings, which he sketched as shown in Figure 3.2. Within the three circles, Welch listed businesses with similar patterns of success:

- The traditional, core business, with 46% of profits
- High-technology businesses (31% of profits)
- Services (23% of profits)

FIGURE 3.2 | **The Shape of the New GE**

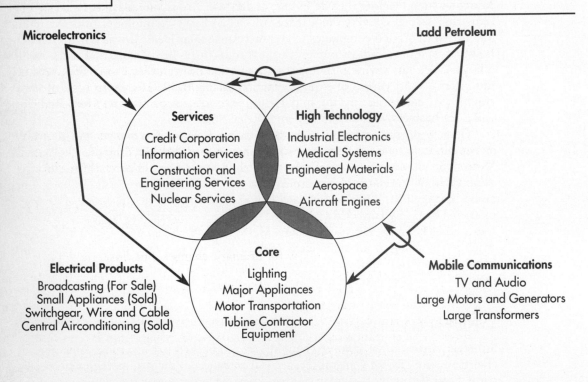

Source: Reprinted by permission of *Forbes* magazine, March 26, 1984. © Forbes, Inc., 1984.

Welch placed GE's remaining businesses outside the circles. Some were profitable; others were not. These "outside" businesses received word that they had to become the "top players" in their industries or they would be sold or closed. Two of the outsiders, Microelectronics and Ladd Petroleum, had links to all three core business groupings and thus were spared from this dictum.

Welch's simple drawing became a vision, or guiding principle, that was communicated readily throughout the organization. Welch's actions aroused considerable controversy. From 1981 to the start of 1988, he eliminated over 100,000 jobs (one in four) and increased revenues from $27 billion (in 1982) to $40.4 billion (in 1987). Operating profits increased from $3 billion in 1982 to $5 billion in 1987, and the price of GE's stock rose more than threefold.

Jack Welch's vision made GE more competitive. GE has become less bureaucratic and has pushed authority down to the operating divisions. Welch nurtured a new breed of manager who could thrive on turmoil and push for even stronger performance. At GE Medical Systems, the new management types are described as "win-aholics" (*Business Week*, 1987).

As the examples described illustrate, the vision of the CEO is extremely important. A successful strategic vision is an idea about a desirable future state that can gain broad consensus and support throughout the organization. A vision should be able to motivate employees and mobilize resources. This ability often makes the difference between a vision that leads to excellence and one that leads to mediocrity.

DEVELOPING A STRATEGIC VISION

Developing a strategic vision relies on being creative and intuitive. The methods described in this book can facilitate the thinking and analysis necessary for development of a new strategic vision, but they cannot make the final creative leap. That is the role of the strategist.

A *strategic vision* can be described as the concept for a new and desirable future reality that can be communicated throughout the organization. The organization's response should be to marshal its resources to achieve the vision. To accomplish these ends, a vision needs to be:

1. Simple, clear, and easily understood by most of the people. The key element of a strong vision is that it translates complex problems into understandable choices.
2. Distant enough in time to allow for dramatic changes, but close enough to gain commitment from the organization. The vision must be realistic, credible, and able to withstand hypothetical, cause-and-effect examination. The vision must also create a sense of urgency.
3. Able to focus the organization with respect to scope and time. The vision should focus the organization on the right things, particularly the things it does best.
4. Frequently articulated by top management to gain a solid consensus that the vision is desirable and achievable. The CEO must personify the vision and live by it. The vision must challenge the entire organization. Presentation of the vision is a very important step.

How can systematic analysis aid in the development of the vision? This question requires that existing and proposed businesses and products be assessed with respect to their potential. Assessment of potential involves two more questions:

1. Can this business/product be made more valuable to the customer? (Increasing a business's or product's value to the customer and the customer's recognition of it is known as *leveraging customer value*.)
2. Can this business/product maintain or increase its competitive cost advantage through *system innovation*?

These two questions form the basis for the *corporate development matrix* shown in Figure 3.3. To use this matrix, strategic planners categorize each business/product with respect to its potential for increasing in value to the customer (left axis) and its potential competitive cost advantage (bottom axis). Depending on its position in the matrix, a business/product is assigned high or low priority within the organization.

The "losers"—businesses/products with little potential for leveraged customer value or competitive cost advantage—should be sold or closed. Businesses/products listed in quadrants I ("watch and wait") and III ("unstable cash bonanza") need to be analyzed further. Those in quadrant I tend to be businesses/products that can,

FIGURE 3.3	Corporate Development Matrix

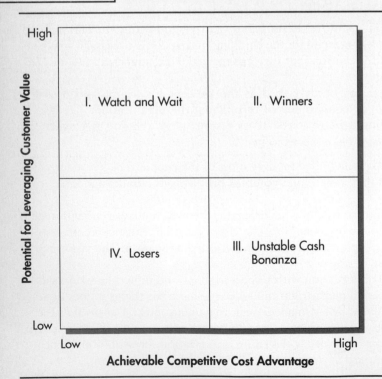

through specialization, carve out a profitable niche but that, because of the competitive situation, cannot establish a sustainable cost advantage. An example of a quadrant I business is GE's TV and audio business (see Figure 3.3). This business is driven by changes in consumer tastes and spending patterns and is under constant threat of price cutting by offshore suppliers. To retain a competitive advantage, GE must stay ahead of its competitors with respect to technology, customer service, new-product development, and so forth. But to stay ahead, top management must allocate time and resources in amounts disproportionate to TV and audio's contribution to the corporate portfolio. Thus GE's top management had to watch and wait for signals that helped them resolve TV and audio's status. Ultimately, GE sold its consumer electronics business to Thompson S.A. of France in exchange for Thompson's medical equipment business (*Fortune,* 1987).

The businesses listed in quadrant III typically manufacture products with high competitive cost advantage but little potential for further leveraging of customer value. While temporarily stable and very profitable, these products typically are vulnerable to severe margin and/or substitution pressures as the market matures. GE's turbine business is a classic example. Although GE holds a clear technological and market lead in this business, low-cost suppliers from the Far East are starting to erode this position. Only a significant technological breakthrough might increase the customer value of GE's turbine enough to offset this trend.

Only the "winner" businesses/products of quadrant II have the potential for continued value leveraging *and* competitive cost advantages that can be achieved through system innovation.

Jack Welch utilized the logic that underlies the corporate development matrix when he shaped his vision of the "new GE." And Table 3.1 shows how well GE was able to achieve that vision. With the exception of factory automation, it was either

TABLE 3.1	GE Business Ranking, 1989	
	United States	World
Aircraft engines	first	first
Broadcasting (NBC)	first	NA
Circuit breakers	first	first
Defense electronics	second	second
Electric motors	first	first
Engineering plastics	first	first
Factory automation	second	third
Industrial/power systems	first	first
Lighting	first	second
Locomotives	first	first
Major appliances	first	second
Medical diagnostic imaging	first	first

first or second in the businesses that remained after the restructuring (Carlson, 1991). Jack Welch transformed the GE bureaucracy into a formidable competitor built on a vision of core capability. He took a sleeping giant and built it into a $60 billion company with profits of $3 billion in 1992 (Smart, 1992). Fortunately, Welch knew how to "grow" a business. He took the $40-million-a-year plastics division and turned it into a $5-billion business. His entrepreneurial spirit also moved the medical technology unit and the financial division into highly profitable status. When asked about the upheaval he created and the layoffs, his response was that his only regret was that he might have been too cautious in making changes.

GRAND STRATEGY, GOALS, AND OBJECTIVES

Grand strategy is concerned with achieving the vision of the organization. A long-term, five-to-fifteen-year focus on the external environment is needed to develop a grand strategy effectively. A grand strategy is not formulated, put on the shelf, and dusted off every five years. Rather, the grand strategy is a firm's integrated approach to achieving a vision while responding to a constantly shifting external environment.

As indicated in the strategic four-factor model shown at the beginning of each chapter, formulation of a grand strategy (top of the model) involves a multidimensional approach that balances the external and internal considerations. A preliminary formulation of grand strategy takes into account the external and internal environment and must be analyzed for consistency and appropriateness in light of restraints imposed by the factors shown on the horizontal axis of the four-factor model (financial resources and organizational considerations).

The importance of considering financial resources and the organization's structure and culture can be seen from RCA's experience in the mainframe computer business. RCA in the 1960s chose to enter the business of manufacturing and distributing mainframe computers in direct competition with IBM, the industry giant, and several other major firms, such as Burroughs, Sperry Rand, and Control Data. RCA was strong in technical areas of electronics. For the most part RCA was reasonably successful in analyzing and evaluating the elements of the vertical axis of the strategic four-factor model. However, RCA did not do well in evaluating financial and organizational resources. IBM's financial staying power considerably outlasted RCA's. Most important, however, was IBM's ability to provide customer services that RCA could not develop quickly. This lack of responsiveness contributed to the ultimate failure of RCA's venture into computers.

Very much like the vision upon which it is based, a grand strategy reflects the values, interests, and personality of the CEO or founder. For example, the technical and cultural interests of Armand Hammer led Occidental Petroleum to pursue a strategy of developing business relations with the Soviet Union. The grand strategy of Mary Kay cosmetics reflects the personal style and marketing approach of its founder, Mary Kay. In a bureaucratic organization, however, a grand strategy is typically forged through bargaining, coalitions, and power plays among stockholders, top managers, and other stakeholders.

The grand strategy is a framework within which independent *substrategies* are developed. Substrategies generally are developed and implemented at the division or business-unit level and are likely to be concerned with resources (divestment of assets, sources of funds, capital allocation, asset management) or functions (production, marketing, distribution, research and development). At the division and unit levels of the organization, function and product/marketing substrategies tend to dominate. Most of the methodologies presented in this book are tools used to work through grand strategies to substrategies.

An *organizational goal* is a specific outcome that the organization seeks to attain or maintain. Organizational goals are chosen to implement the grand strategy or a substrategy or to align the organization more closely with its values and mission. One example of an organizational goal is to increase market share. Each goal is broken down into *objectives*—measurable accomplishments to be implemented within a specific period of time. An objective for the goal of increasing market share might be to increase it by 5% within six months to one year. The goals and objectives of substrategies are based on the same principle: the goals are aimed at implementing the substrategy, and the objectives are aimed at attaining the goal.

ASSUMPTIONS AND BELIEFS

Assumptions and beliefs about possible future outcomes are a key underpinning of vision and strategy. Data provide valuable input, but beliefs and value judgments inevitably color their interpretation. Managers have no choice but to make assumptions, because they cannot know the future. Assumptions carry risks and have consequences. For example, the stock market crash of October 1987 was predicted by some, but most investors blithely assumed that the bull market would last forever. This assumption had serious consequences. For some individuals and companies, the crash was merely a paper loss that would take effect only if the securities were sold. Some investors in this group assumed that the market would rebound. They figured that if they did not sell their securities, there would be no out-of-pocket losses. (In general, such investors were right.) The point is that any investment or managerial decision is based on assumptions.

Assumptions are made by strategic planners and by top managers who must determine the desirability of alternative strategies. Some managers are risk takers who envision a bright future with a strong growth market and limited competition. Others, who have the same set of facts, see a bleak future and favor conservative strategies. Who is right? Only the outcome, or consequences, will tell.

Unfortunately, strategic planners seldom identify specific consequences that could ensue from the strategic alternatives they are proposing. By ignoring possible consequences, these strategic planners invite disaster. The remedy is prevention. Strategic planners should carefully assess the assumptions, beliefs, and consequences—the ABCs of strategic management—of each strategic alternative they plan to propose. This assessment involves

1. Identifying every assumption associated with the strategy
2. Gauging the strength with which each assumption is felt
3. Specifying every possible consequence (good and bad) of each assumption

The ABCs are an important consideration in case analysis, particularly the first phase of case analysis, formulating a statement of the problem. Invalid assumptions and beliefs can be the cause of an organization's strategic problems.

What are beliefs, and how do they influence choices of strategy? In their book *In Search of Excellence,* Peters and Waterman (1982, p. 285) identified seven dominant beliefs held by executives in successful companies:

1. A belief in being the "best"
2. A belief in the importance of the details of execution; the nuts and bolts of doing the job well
3. A belief in the importance of treating people as individuals
4. A belief in superior quality and service
5. A belief that most members of the organization should be innovators, and its corollary, that the organization should be willing to support failure
6. A belief that informality enhances communication
7. Belief in and recognition of the importance of economic growth and profits

In each of the successful companies Peters and Waterman observed, the managers found a way to focus on these beliefs and get others at all levels in the organization, down to the lowest position, to share them.

Strategies are based in part on shared beliefs about the nature of the firm's environment. The validity and strength of these beliefs significantly affect the success of the organization. Beliefs also influence the way managers respond to situations. For example, managers who believe strongly in organizational stability are likely to reject strategies that would require organizational upheaval, no matter how much data is presented to support the potential for success. Many a merger has been rejected because of managers' belief in stability.

Beliefs that have led to success in the past tend to be reinforced and perpetuated by the organization. Success creates a powerful incentive to do more of what has worked, to do it more efficiently, to do it better, and to train the next generation of managers to do the same. Organizations reinforce successful behavior and build information systems, incentive plans, and organizational structures around beliefs that have worked in the past. For example, if an organization believes itself to be a specialist supplier, it adheres to a strategy of maximizing gross margin and price realization. If, on the other hand, the organization believes that it is selling a commodity, it stresses output, efficiency, and low costs.

Unfortunately, belief-driven mechanisms continue to push the organization in the same direction for some time, even after competitive conditions have significantly changed. The very same system that previously ensured success for the organization can become its worst enemy. U.S. car manufacturers, for example, took about 10 years to change their assumption-based beliefs about the realities of global competition. Early warning signals, such as a slow but persistent increase in the imports' market share, were certainly not ignored, but the domestic suppliers seemed unwilling or unable to take any action to stem the rising tide of imports. The U.S. manufacturers were too committed to their ingrained beliefs to recognize that these beliefs were based on eroding assumptions.

What this and countless other examples show is that change rarely results from proposing a strategy that is not consistent with (1) shared beliefs about what makes the business successful or (2) established organizational structures and methods of operating. Real change has to begin with changes in beliefs; new strategies and actions can then follow those changes.

Zakon (1985) devised a *beliefs audit,* which can be used to (1) test the validity of a set of beliefs against current realities and guard a strategy against possible threats, if appropriate, and (2) build a new set of beliefs appropriate for environmental changes that have occurred (or are foreseeable) so as to initiate new strategies.

Ideally, the beliefs audit should be continuous and ongoing so that it can detect early warning signals and emerging patterns. For practical purposes, however, a structured and managed group effort at critical junctures in the company's development is adequate. The beliefs audit involves careful articulation of the basic beliefs and belief-driven strategies and actions that characterize the firm. The beliefs can be elicited from the organization's employees, suppliers, and customers; inferred from the organization's actions; or determined from tests of the control system that show how beliefs motivate behavior. Most of the questioning can be informal, free-flow, and ad hoc, but it may be augmented by responses to questionnaires, particularly if large groups of stakeholders are involved.

The following set of questions should be asked during the beliefs audit:

1. What has made our business successful?
   a. Why do we make a profit?
   b. What do our customers particularly value (and pay for) in our products?
2. Will we still have today's advantages five years from now?
   a. What will happen if all competitors continue to operate as they do today?
   b. Will changes in the external environment change our business value to customers? If so, why and how?
   c. Which advantages will we be able to defend? Which will we be unable to defend?
3. How could we transform the means of gaining competitive advantage in this business?
   a. Could we change the entire system of delivering goods and/or services to customers (faster, better, more cheaply, more reliably)?
   b. Can new segments or subsegments be created?
   c. Can new advantages be gained through acquisitions or mergers?
4. How can we lead our organization in such a way as to exploit advantages in the future?
   a. Are our organizational structure and information systems still compatible with the market demands?
   b. Do our incentive systems still recognize the specific needs of each of our businesses?

    c. Are responsibility and authority properly balanced in the organization?

    d. Does our organization block rather than foster innovation?

    e. Can/should we improve communication within the organization?

Answers to these questions should be based on as much data and analysis as possible.

Early warning signals that beliefs may need to be changed can come from the following sources:

1. The marketplace
    a. Major accounts lost or gained
    b. Recent swings in overall volume
    c. Changes in price premiums paid for different products
    d. Changes in price–volume relationships
    e. Emerging substitute products
2. Distribution channels
    a. Change in distributors' margin or viability of the channel
    b. Change in the range of products sold by distributors
3. Competitors
    a. Counterintuitive behavior of a competitor
    b. New competitors emerging
    c. An established competitor suddenly gaining market share
4. The organization itself
    a. Unusual defection of key managers
    b. Systems not capable of answering relevant questions
    c. Misleading or erroneous information
    d. Management fumbles despite a seemingly adequate decision process
    e. Declining morale

Initial review and interpretation of the data should be confined to the top-management group, because the process can be a fairly painful and disruptive examination of the organization. Why alarm people in the organization when it may turn out that the company's beliefs and strategy are basically correct and need only minor adjustments? More often than not, the CEO's intuition about the validity of the organization's beliefs is what counts. If the organization is indeed no longer congruent with its environment, the beliefs audit can help top managers to develop a new vision for the organization.

VALUES

THE HIERARCHY OF VALUES

Corporate strategy, according to Christensen, Andrews, and Bower, is the "pattern of decision in a company that (1) shapes and reveals its objectives, purposes or goals, (2) produces the principal policies and plans for achieving these goals, and (3) defines the business the company intends to be in and the kind of economic and human organization it intends to be" (1978, p. 125).

Values are the general, abstract ideas that guide thinking; objectives are the well-defined, precisely stated, measurable targets to be achieved within a specified period of time. A business in high technology, for example, may be characterized by the value of discovering scientific truths before its competitors do. It may formulate a mission: to excel in research and development in electronics. This mission may lead to a goal: to become the number-one scientific firm in the industry. And this goal may lead to an objective: to obtain four new patents in electronics during the year 1993. In organizations, values fan out into mission, mission fans out into goals, and goals fan out into objectives. Corporate culture and beliefs determine how the values, mission, goals, and objectives are communicated to others and brought into being.

The grand strategy of an organization is generally based on satisfying this hierarchy. In this sense, vision and values set the stage for strategic management.

ORGANIZATIONAL VALUES

Values are abstract ideas that guide thinking and action. *Organizational values* are closely tied to the fundamental, underlying beliefs managers have about the business and about people. These values influence managers' choices of mission, goals, and objectives for the firm. In short, values dictate strategy.

Although they are often abstract, vague, and difficult to define, values are revealed by the actions people take, what people think, and how they allocate their time, energy, and skills. Willard Marriott, Sr., for example, valued the delivery of high-quality service at the Marriott Hotels. He is reported to have read every customer-complaint card, and he devoted large amounts of time, energy, and talent to ensuring that his high standards of quality were met. Quality was his first priority and, in his mind, the most critical factor for success. He devoted more time and energy to ensuring quality than he did to any other aspect of his business.

Milton Rokeach, a sociologist who has studied human values and their effect on public attitudes, defines values rather precisely:

> To say that a person has a value is to say that there is an enduring prescriptive or proscriptive belief that a specific mode of behavior or end-state of existence is preferred to an opposite mode of behavior or end-state. This belief transcends attitudes toward objects and toward situations; it is a standard that guides and determines action, attitudes toward objects and situations, ideology, presentations of self to others, and attempts to influence others. (Rokeach, 1973, p. 5)

The management theorist Chester Barnard considered the development and communication of appropriate operational values to be the highest calling of the executive. In The Functions of the Executive (1979), he summarized three key executive functions as "first, to provide the system of communications; second, to promote the securing of essential efforts; and third, to formulate and define purpose." Barnard's experience as an executive at the New Jersey Bell Telephone Company, and the extensive studies he made of other managers, led him to conclude that these three functions were essential to successful management. In Chapter 1, we saw how managers of America's most successful companies adhered to Barnard's prescription. They formulated clear operating values and communicated them effectively to all members of the organization, making sure to monitor activities and follow up persistently (Peters and Waterman, 1982). With effective leadership, then, values become infectious. They affect people's habits of thinking; their ways of relating to one another; the technology they employ; and the policies, rules, procedures, and job descriptions they work by.

PERSONAL VALUES

In 1928 the German philosopher Eduard Spranger identified six categories of people based on their dominant *personal values*. The six categories follow.

- *The theoretical person.* Truth is the dominant interest of the theoretical person. This person's interests are empirical, critical, or rational, leading to such occupations as intellectual, scientist, or philosopher. The chief aim of the theoretical person is to order and systemize knowledge.
- *The economic person.* Wealth (plenty) and efficiency (productivity) are the dominant interests of the economic person. This person wishes to create utility, is quite practical, and conforms well to the prevailing stereotype of the average American businessperson.
- *The aesthetic person.* Beauty and harmony are the dominant interests of the aesthetic person. Each individual situation is judged from the standpoint of its grace, symmetry, or fitness. For this person, the intrinsic value of each of life's events must be realized and enjoyed for its own sake.
- *The social person.* Love, cooperation, and humanism are the dominant interests of the social person. The social person prizes other people as, in Immanual Kant's words, "ends-in-themselves." In return, this person is kind, sympathetic, and unselfish and is likely to find theoretical and economic persons "cold and inhuman."
- *The political person.* Power is the dominant interest of the political person. The political person wishes to bring other people and resources together in order to achieve some personal goal. Leaders in any field generally possess this value in greater-than-average amounts. For some, this value is uppermost, driving them to seek personal power, influence, and recognition.
- *The religious person.* Unity is the dominant interest of the religious person. This person looks beyond human experience to comprehend the cosmos as a whole or delve deeply into the specific, infinitesimal aspects of experience to discover its limits. At either extreme, the religious person embraces the mystical and must rely on faith and belief.

Two researchers, William Guth and Renato Tagiuri, at the time professors at the Harvard Graduate School of Business, used Spranger's six-fold classification to demonstrate that "personal values are important determinants in the choice of strategy" (Guth and Tagiuri, 1965). Using a questionnaire developed by Allport, Vernon, and Lindzey, they found that U.S. executives attending Harvard's Advanced Management Program one year had the following average value profile:

economic, 19%; theoretical, 18%; political, 19%; religious, 16%; aesthetic, 15%; and social, 14%. The executive's average value profile differed from the average profiles of other professionals. Ministers, for example, prioritized their values as religious, social, aesthetic, political, theoretical, and economic—almost the reverse of the executives' priorities.

Guth and Tagiuri cited the case of National Duplicating Products Corporation, a small manufacturer of office equipment whose president's values were chiefly (1) social and (2) aesthetic. The company's strategy was consistent with these values: it produced very high-quality products with aesthetic appeal; emphasized product differentiation, not price competition; had an independent-agent form of sales organization; and promoted the security, welfare, and happiness of the employees.

The authors compared National Duplicating Products with Acoustic Research, Inc., a manufacturer of high-fidelity loudspeaker systems. The values of Acoustic's top executives tended to be (1) theoretical and (2) social. Consistent with these values, Acoustic's strategy stressed "truth and honesty" in relationships with suppliers, dealers, employees, other stakeholders, and the public. In order to carry out its strategy, Acoustic developed the concept of a "minimum acceptable level of profitability" and concentrated on developing high-quality products at the lowest possible price. This often meant that Acoustic's dealers received lower margins than their competitors were offering.

At both National Duplicating and Acoustic Research, the personal values categorized by Spranger guided corporate strategy. Spranger's six values are broad, abstract, timeless ideas that identify a person's strongest concerns. These values differ from the eight operating values of Peters and Waterman. Operating values identify preferred means rather than ends. Therefore, operating values (such as a bias for action, closeness to the customer, autonomy, and entrepreneurship) can be used to satisfy Spranger's more basic values. For example, an operating value such as "closeness to the customer" can satisfy aesthetic values through the production of attractive products and can satisfy social values through joint problem solving and cooperation.

Spranger's six values are applicable to every strategic situation. Some companies examine each strategic option to find out to what extent it incorporates each of Spranger's six values. Two of Spranger's values—the economic and theoretical values—are often regarded as rational. Economic analysis and the scientific method can be used systematically to achieve them. The other four values are sometimes called nonrational; they cannot be readily measured or applied systematically. For this reason, Churchman (1968) referred to them as "enemies" of the systems approach to strategic management. Though they may be "enemies" of systematic and logical thinking, the aesthetic, social, political, and religious values are always present in organizational life, and strategic managers should consider them.

SOCIETAL VALUES

Strategic managers must look beyond organizational and personal values to identify the values that are operative in society. *Societal values* are an important part of the organization's external environment—the environment in which it conducts its business.

The great social anthropologist Pitirim Sorokin argued in an extensive four-volume work (1937–1941) that society's values reflect its dominant socioeconomic pattern. In an agrarian society, the primary values are aimed at survival and security. People desire food, clothing, shelter, and protection from threats to their lives. As an agrarian society progresses and becomes able to produce a surplus of these basic needs, people are able to form cities and develop industries. These socioeconomic changes are accompanied by changes in values. The new values of industrial societies Sorokin called "sensate." Sensate values are the values of materialism. People want jobs, money, productivity, a higher standard of living, radios, television sets, automobiles, and vacation homes. In short, they want to participate in industry and the production process, increase their wealth, and enjoy material success.

As an industrial society achieves material success, it moves on to still another set of values. Sorokin labeled these new values "ideational." Alvin Toffler called them the third wave (1980). The post-industrial society is one where production shifts from tangible goods to services and information (a shift that took place in the United States somewhere around 1975). The new values come to center on the ability to express oneself in work and play. Maslow (1968) termed it "self-actualization." In highly developed, affluent societies, individuals strive for autonomy and control over their activities, enjoyment of the natural pleasures of life (a value that, if carried to its extreme, is referred to as hedonism), and becoming "at one with nature." Finally, despite a strong strain of individualism, ideational values include a desire for community and rewarding relationships with others.

A number of organizations have chosen to base strategies on current societal values. Volvo of Sweden, for example, incorporated ideational values into the redesign of its production procedures. Volvo did away with assembly line production and began having teams build cars from start to finish. This and other changes gave Volvo's workers more autonomy, freedom of expression, and sense of community. American firms such as Lincoln Electric, Donnelly Mirrors, Harwood Manufacturing, Harman International Industries, Hewlett-Packard, Dana Corporation, Delta Airlines, and Levi Strauss also have incorporated ideational values into their strategies.

IMPLICATIONS FOR STRATEGIC MANAGEMENT

Values, then, are fundamental to strategic management for a number of reasons. Values that are used to guide the business need to be appropriate for the time, place, and conditions in which the business operates. It is not a case of applying good or bad values (values are simply values), but rather of applying *appropriate* values. Some values, for example, are contrary to the laws of the society in which the company is to operate—a serious problem in international business. Other inappropriate values lead to the offering of products and services that customers are unwilling to pay for. In most situations, more than one set of values can be used to create a successful business. But whatever the values are, the success of the business depends on their appropriateness to the situation in which they are employed. In other words, the success of a strategy depends on the values that underlie it.

To be effective and operative, values must be embodied in the firm's *culture*— its atmosphere, norms, and attitudes about how business should be conducted. Perhaps the most important function of leaders is to ensure that organizational values become part of the firm's culture. Thomas Watson, Sr. understood this process very well. Among his values was to have customers perceive the company (IBM), and not individual salesmen, as providers of information systems and guarantors of high-quality service. One way he accomplished this was to impose a rigid dress code for the salesmen. Dressed in the IBM "uniform" (dark suit, white shirt, conservative tie, and well-polished shoes), the salesmen "disappeared" as individuals and became representatives of IBM.

One especially effective method of institutionalizing values within an organization's culture was developed at *The New Yorker* magazine. To appeal to its elite and sophisticated readers, the magazine set out to become known for superior writing, clear expression, and the absence of misprints and errors. At *The New Yorker,* extreme care is taken with the quality of every issue. Fact checkers retrace writers' steps, look up sources, and contact informants. The legal office examines every article for potential cases of libel. Editors and proofreaders comb every sentence for incorrect English usage and typographical errors. All of these procedures ensure that the magazine's values are part of its daily activities and culture.

The New Yorker reinforces its values by printing, as column fillers, humorous bloopers and examples of careless writing from other publications. Some are preceded by headings such as "How's That Again?" and "Letters We Never Finished Reading." Others are followed by sharp quips that highlight confusion created by the author's writing or the printer's errors. This practice serves a very useful purpose: it keeps the magazine's standards of excellence continuously in the minds of its employees, writers, and readers.

CORPORATE CULTURE

Corporate culture is the result of many factors. Among the most obvious are the type of business the organization is in, its products, its customers, its size and location, its competitive position, its financial and human resources, its formal structure, its methods of operating, and its facilities. Even more important, however, are the intangible factors: assumptions, beliefs, values, and the unwritten, often unspoken, and frequently unconscious norms and rules of the game that are *really* operating in the firm. Norms often reflect the values of the CEO or the founder of the firm.

Strategic managers ignore corporate culture at their peril because, to be implemented successfully, strategy must be consistent with the culture. New strategies almost always require changes in corporate culture. Strategic failures are often attributed to the inability of a firm to change its culture in ways that would make the new strategy work. There is often a gap between the existing culture and the appropriate culture for strategic success. Because culture consists largely of personal and social relationships and work tasks, such gaps are often defined as involving too much or too little of the following:

- Innovation in tasks and in task definition
- Support for task performance
- Attention to social and interpersonal relationships
- Personal freedom given to individuals

Studies show that the well-run businesses of the world have distinctive cultures that promote the creation, implementation, and maintenance of successful strategies (Schwartz and Davis, 1981). Because an organization's culture is crucial to the success of its strategy, part of strategic planning is to assess the culture and determine whether it would promote or defeat a proposed strategy. If it would defeat the strategy, can the culture be changed? Kilmann, Saxton, and Serpa (1985) suggested asking five basic questions about an organization's culture in order to assess its capacity for change.

1. What is the impact of culture on the organization's ability to carry out its activities and plans? The answer depends on the direction, pervasiveness, and strength of the culture. A *positive* culture supports the organization's mission and helps achieve its strategies. A *negative* culture, on the other hand, causes people to behave in ways that run counter to the expressed mission and strategies of the organization. A *pervasive* culture is widespread and shared by most of the organization's employees. *Strength* is the amount of pressure the culture exerts on employees, regardless of direction. A positive culture that is also pervasive and strong helps an organization carry out its activities and plans. "It points behavior in the right direction, is widely shared among the members of work groups, and puts strong pressure on group members to follow the established cultural guidelines" (p. 4). A negative culture that is strong and pervasive points people in the wrong direction and makes it hard to implement new strategies, policies, or plans.

2. How deep-seated is the culture? Kilmann, Saxton, and Serpa suggested three levels of depth: behavioral norms, hidden assumptions, and human nature. "Behavioral norms are just below the surface of experience . . . [and] describe the behaviors and attitudes that the members of a group or organization pressure one another to follow" (p. 5). "Wear only dark business suits to work" is such a norm. Hidden assumptions are the unstated beliefs people have about the organization's stakeholders—its suppliers, customers, competitors, allies, and regulators. (More will be said about stakeholders in the next chapter.) At the deepest level is human nature: employees' wants and needs, personal values, and the intellectual abilities they bring to the job. Cultures that penetrate all three are thus deep-seated and are the most difficult to change.

3. How many cultures does the organization have? Few organizations have just one culture, although some very successful corporations, such as IBM, General Electric, General Motors, and Texas Instruments, have an overarching, common culture. Different divisions of a company tend, however, to have different cultures, each with a direction, pervasiveness, strength, and depth of its own. The finance staff tends to have a much different culture than, say, the marketing group. Scientists in research and development view the world and the

company differently from managers and executives. Any successful change must deal with all the variations of corporate culture. Mergers and acquisitions often present very difficult problems of fusion—sometimes of diametrically opposed cultures.

4. How changeable is the culture? This answer depends on the answers to the three preceding questions. The direction, pervasiveness, strength, depth, and number of cultures present determine how readily an organization's culture or cluster of cultures can be changed. Another factor is the degree and type of cultural reinforcement offered by the organization's leaders. Executives can use rites, ceremonies, and reward systems to reinforce the current culture or to promote a new one. This leads to the last question.

5. Can culture alone be changed? The answer is generally no, because culture is made up of the assumptions, beliefs, and values of an organization's people and the tasks and activities they perform. What, then, must be changed to change corporate culture? Organizational structure, reward systems, work procedures, knowledge and skills, attitudes—all may have to be done if a new strategy is to succeed (see, for example, Kilmann, 1984, and Schein, 1985). In Chapter 10, we will describe methods for assessing an organization's culture and evaluating its ability to change.

CORPORATE SOCIAL RESPONSIBILITY

"America's top CEOs maintain that integrating the urban underclass into the national economy isn't just right—it's essential to everyone's prosperity" (Kirkland, 1992). This is the heart of the issue of corporate social responsibility. It is not a matter, as some would say, of being a do-gooder or ignoring the economic realities of the marketplace, and it is not solely an issue of what is right for business. It is nothing less than a matter of the survival of our economic system. Examples of socially responsible organizations illustrate that being a good "corporate citizen" is also good business. Baldor Electric CEO, Boreham, recognizes that restructuring that results in layoffs often means the loss of experienced and loyal workers who may be difficult to replace. Companies take this no-layoff approach in order to build a good company and sustain morale (Faltermayer, 1992). Joseph Vittoria, CEO of Avis, just says no to layoffs even when profits are down. Delta Airlines, in spite of a loss of $343 million, has not laid off a permanent employee in 35 years. Lincoln Electric believes in reducing the work week rather than losing experienced workers, and Nucor has been working four-day weeks for an extended period of time. While GM closes plants, Ford has refused to use dismissals and maintains that an experienced workforce helps ensure quality (Faltermayer, 1992).

The continuing downturn in business has, of course, led some companies to cut ethical corners in order to sustain profits. Yet James Burke, CEO of Johnson & Johnson, evaluated ten companies (J&J, Coca-Cola, Gerber Products, IBM, John

Deere, Kodak, 3M, Xerox, J.C. Penney, and Pitney Bowes) and showed that they grew an average of 11.3% from 1950 to 1990 while the Dow Jones industrial average increased only 6.2% for this same period. Each of the companies mentioned by Burke was considered an example of a responsible organization, and their growth records suggest a positive payoff (Labich, 1992). On the other hand, Steiner and Steiner (1991) reported on a study extending from 1972 to 1985 that showed that one could *not* conclude that socially responsible organizations have improved economic performance. They go on to specify what they consider a reasonable approach to social responsibility.

1. Each business must take into account the situation in which it finds itself in meeting stakeholder expectations.
2. Business is an economic entity and cannot jeopardize its profitability meeting social needs.
3. Business should recognize that in the long run, the general social good benefits everyone.
4. The social responsibility expected of a business is directly related to its social power to influence outcomes.
5. Social responsibility is related to the size of the company and to the industry it is in.
6. A business should tackle only those social problems in which it has competence.
7. Business must assume its share of the social burden and be willing to absorb reasonable social costs.

Though not prescriptive in an absolute sense, these seven guidelines provide a basis for reviewing each company's social responsibility posture. It is also possible to examine social responsibility by using Figure 3.4. This matrix helps explain both the basis for social choice (whether discretionary or legal) and how the company chooses to react to pressing social issues (proactive or reactive). Thus, for example, many companies respond on the basis of economics or beliefs because they only "react" to legal requirements such as mandated pollution control. Others are more "proactive" and choose to behave in an ethical or moral manner, as Johnson & Johnson did at the time of the Tylenol scare. More and more companies are expected to shift to this latter mode of social responsibility.

Historically, the term *responsibility* was used to describe moral actions. People were considered answerable for their actions and, accordingly, just recipients of the rewards, praise, blame, or punishment that flowed from their actions. Three central attributes of responsibility came from this idea:

1. *Obligation.* The notion that there are some actions a person can and must perform.
2. *Liability.* The notion that the neglect of a person's obligations is punishable. Legal liability makes a person bound to make good any loss or damage that occurs in a transaction.
3. *Incentive.* The notion that the fulfilling of a person's obligations should lead to rewards.

FIGURE 3.4	Social Responsibility of Business

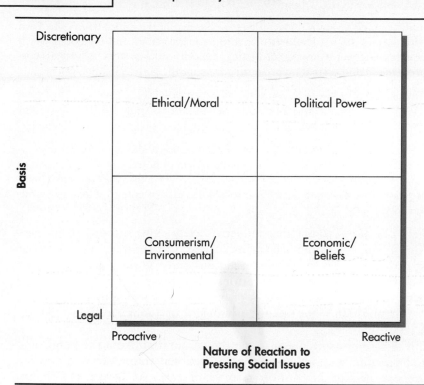

Underlying these attributes of responsibility is a fundamental psychological theory: motives cause human behavior. Motives can be conditioned by rewards and punishments, and they should be conditioned in such a way as to ensure that the resulting behavior is good, moral, or ethical.

This notion of responsibility was firmly held until the invention of the corporation as a legal entity. With the advent of the corporation, a single fictitious legal "person" was created who authorized a group of people to act as a single unit. This raised a new question: Do corporations have responsibilities just as people do?

In *The Wealth of Nations*, Adam Smith responded to this question and argued that corporations do have responsibilities. The profit motive and a well-functioning market, he argued, ensured that corporate behavior was socially good. The marketplace did this by regulating rewards and punishments via the profit mechanism and the free decisions of well-meaning customers. As a result, corporations that survived were socially responsible. The system guaranteed that only those firms that satisfied consumer needs would survive.

As late as 1919, this was the dominant legal view as well. In a classic case, *Dodge vs. Ford Motor Company* (S. Ct. Mich. 1919: 204 Mich. 459), the court opined:

> There should be no confusion (of which there is evidence) of the duties which Mr. Ford conceives that he and the stockholders owe to the general public and the duties which in law he and his co-directors owe to protesting, minority stockholders. A business corporation is organized and carried on primarily for the profit of the stockholders.

As corporations became more successful and more powerful, however, this view began to be challenged. Sylvia and Benjamin Selekman, in their book *Power and Morality in a Business Society* (New York, 1956), mounted their challenge as follows:

> The crisis which has led to the concern about social responsibility is much more complex. It stems from nothing less than the age-old problem of power—with its dangers as well as its beneficent aspects. Not until businessmen recognize that they are the administrators of power systems can they face realistically the task of how to discharge morally the power they wield.

Today there can be no doubt that modern society expects more of business than it once did. Ironically, as the Selekmans suggest, it is the very success of our economic system that has led to these expectations and has resulted in increased social demands being placed on corporations. And these demands extend far beyond the basic economic responsibilities of business. According to Davis (1973, p. 321), "Social responsibility has become a hallmark of a mature, global civilization," but the debate continues.

Along with these increasing pressures on the corporation from the public and from the state have come a steady erosion of institutional autonomy and, not surprisingly, a general decline in confidence in leadership. As Bennis (1977, pp. 36–37) puts it,

> What seems to have happened is this: the environmental encroachments and turbulence, the steady beat of litigation, the fragmentation of constituencies along with their new-found eloquence and power, multiple advocacy, win–lose adversarial conflicts between internal and external forces—all of this—had led to a situation where our leaders are paralyzed, or at least "keeping their heads below the grass," as Lyndon Johnson once put it. To grow and stay healthy an institution must strike a proper balance between openness to the environment and protection from too much permeability.

As corporations have come under increasing pressure on such issues as environmental protection, equal opportunity, and product safety, many have addressed these issues in their annual reports. Abbott and Monsen (1979), for example, found that the number of firms voluntarily reporting social responsibility disclosures increased from a little over 50% in 1971 to more than 85% in 1975. Society now demands that a modicum of corporate social responsibility take precedence over profit maximization. Moreover, it does not appear that this social involvement has been dysfunctional for the firm's stockholders. Socially responsible firms tend to perform as well as or better than those that are not.

This chapter is structured to help strategic managers assess the ethical and socially responsible dimensions of strategy. In the long run, an unethical or irresponsible strategy is as damaging to a firm as is an uneconomical strategy. This is because a corporation cannot survive without establishing the social legitimacy of its claim on social resources. In his book *Management: Tasks, Responsibilities, Practices* (1973), Peter Drucker describes succinctly the mutual relationship between strategy and legitimacy.

> The first job of management is, therefore, to identify and to anticipate impacts— coldly and realistically. The question is not, "Is what we do right?" It is "Do we do what society and the customer pay us for?" And if an activity is not integral to the institution's purpose and mission, it is to be considered as a social misfit and as undesirable.

Thus strategy becomes part of the social contract between an organization and its stakeholders. It is legitimate to the extent that it satisfies the functions and expectations for which these stakeholders allocate its resources. How can an organization's social legitimacy be determined? The methods described in the next three sections of this book were designed to help the strategic manager answer this question.

The first method, the *corporate social performance matrix* (CSPM), helps the manager evaluate the impact of a strategy on each of the firm's stakeholders with regard to pressing social issues influencing the firm. The result is a map of the critical issues and a scaling of the relative importance of each issue to the success of the strategy. (See Figure 3.5.) The CSPM also suggests which stakeholder demands may create liabilities and obligations for the firm.

The *ethical audit of strategy*, which we examine after an in-depth discussion of the relationship between ethics and strategy, penetrates deeper into the social legitimacy of a strategy. Drawing on basic ethical theory, it requires that a specific set of ethical issues be examined and discussed. The strategy is evaluated in terms of whether it violates or promotes a basic human right, produces good or harm to people, or is just or unjust in its assumptions about the distribution of organizational wealth.

Finally, a method that has been used successfully for role-playing in corporations and classrooms is presented. It is based on the writings of C. West Churchman, who has devoted his life to the pursuit of logic, systems analysis, and rational thinking as

---

FIGURE 3.5 | **Corporate Social Performance Matrix**

Pressing social issues	Stakeholders						
	A	B	C	D	E	F	...
1							
2							
3							
4							
5							
⋮							

a means by which the human intellect can solve social problems. His inquiry reveals the limitations of rational analysis as well. He calls these limitations "enemies" and identifies four key ones: politics, morality, aesthetics, and religion. The *enemies check* offers a creative way to go beyond the constraints of the CSPM and the ethical audit and to explore the full range of forces that may shape strategy.

CORPORATE SOCIAL PERFORMANCE MATRIX

BACKGROUND

There have been several attempts to operationalize the concept of corporate social responsibility, most notably Carroll's (1979) three-dimensional conceptual model of corporate performance and Halal's (1977) return-on-resources model of corporate performance. We will examine the former in detail.

Carroll defines *corporate social responsibility* as the entire range of obligations business has to society. These obligations must include economic, legal, ethical, and discretionary categories of business performance. It is often argued that businesses have traditionally emphasized their economic and legal responsibilities, whereas now there is also a growing response to ethical and discretionary aspects of social responsibility. However, these four categories are not mutually exclusive, and the boundaries between them are difficult, if not impossible, to define. Also, these terms are not value-free, and they will be interpreted differently by different people. Management, for example, may view a certain decision as discretionary, while another group of stakeholders may see it strictly as an economic response.

No corporate social posture will be value-free, and this is what makes corporate social responsiveness such a difficult undertaking. Halal (1977, p. 25) states that a firm can only attempt to unite "the diverse interests of various social groups to form a workable coalition engaged in creating value for distribution among members of the coalition." It is obvious that beyond a certain level of economic activity, the social issues at stake may become conflicting (an example is profitability versus pollution control) and that *tradeoffs* must be made by management. These tradeoffs involve both economic and ethical decisions that will not necessarily satisfy the needs of every stakeholder.

METHODOLOGY

The *corporate social performance matrix* (CSPM) is a tool that helps the strategic manager make these socioeconomic decisions. This method, which evaluates the total social performance of the organization on the basis of how well it is dealing with pressing social issues and satisfying stakeholder needs, is based on a simple model:

(organizational performance on an issue) × (importance weight of the issue)
= (evaluation on the issue).

| FIGURE 3.6 | A Checklist of Pressing Social Issues |

1. **Economics**
   a. Profitability
   b. Market penetration
   c. Customer loyalty, goodwill
   d. Financial stability

2. **Environment**
   a. Pollution control
   b. Repair of environment
   c. Recycling of waste material

3. **Discrimination**
   a. Minority employment
   b. Employment of women
   c. Equal opportunities
   d. Minority business partners

4. **Personnel**
   a. Occupational health and safety
   b. Salary level
   c. Training; education
   d. Counseling

5. **Products**
   a. Safety
   b. Quality
   c. Product improvement

6. **Community Involvement**
   a. Community activities
   b. Public health
   c. Education; arts

7. **Others**

Adding the resultant scores for all issues gives a measure of the corporate social performance for the organization as a whole.

This method should be extended, however, because the evaluation of performance on an issue is very much dependent on the point of view of the stakeholder involved. A thorough assessment requires the formulation of a stakeholder/issue matrix (see Figure 3.5). This matrix is used to evaluate the organization's performance with regard to each key stakeholder and for each pressing social issue.

To use this method, the strategic manager first identifies the pressing social issues facing the organization. Figure 3.6 can be used as a checklist for this task. Next the manager evaluates the organization's current performance for each stakeholder and each issue, using a scale of 0 to 9. A zero is assigned if there is no issue that is relevant for that stakeholder. A 9 is assigned if the performance needs significant improvement.

After completing these entries, the strategic manager has a more comprehensive picture of how the company meets the different social demands made by its stakeholders. Furthermore, weights can be assigned to reflect the importance of the different issues. Suggested weights are as follows: very important = 4; important = 3; moderately important = 2; marginally important = 1. When the values are summed across the rows and then multiplied by the "importance weights" of the different issues, this table provides an indication of what the company needs to address. The strategic manager can find out how the different stakeholders can benefit from the firm's performance. Finally, the combined total of *all* the evaluations on the different issues gives an overall indication of how well the company is addressing the social issues it faces. An application of this method is shown in Worksheet 3.1.

| WORKSHEET 3.1 | Corporate Social Performance Matrix |

Case ___Polaroid___

Date ___1990___

Name ___John Doe___

Stakeholders

	1	2	3	4	5	6	7	8
	Stockholders	Customers	Management	Employees	Government	Local communities	Suppliers	

Pressing social issues	Importance weights	Performance ratings								Row total	Performance evaluation
1. Economic	4	2	3	1	1	0	1	0		8	32
2. Environment	3	1	1	1	0	1	1	0		5	15
3. Discrimination	2	0	0	2	1	1	1	1		6	12
4. Personnel	2	2	0	2	3	1	2	0		10	20
5. Products	3	1	4	3	2	3	1	2		16	48
6. Community involvement	1	0	0	1	0	1	2	0		4	4
7. Other											
Stakeholder evaluation		6	8	12	7	5	3	3		Total	111

Discussion

Excellent performance in product safety and quality. Somewhat weak economic performance paired with low responsiveness to personnel and community needs (layoffs, shutdowns). Currently, the company rates rather low in terms of its responsiveness to social issues. Customers and management seem to benefit from the company's current performance, whereas shareholders, employees, and local communities presently gain little benefit from the company. Much of the company's below-average performance, however, is due to its current economic problems and should improve as these problems are solved. The company seems to be strongest in the treatment of environmental and product issues.

ETHICS AND STRATEGY

Two additional factors affecting the choice of a strategy are (1) the ethical norms of the society in which the firm does business and (2) the ethical principles of its leaders. Professor Mark Pastin, who is director of the Center for Private and Public Ethics at Arizona State University, believes that there is a strong link between ethics and strategy. Pastin argues that ethical thinking and strategic thinking are inseparable. Furthermore, ethical thinking teaches the executive some important lessons about strategic thinking because it opens up new pathways of analysis, often with surprising results. For one thing, ethical analysis alerts managers to social and political problems (and opportunities) that they might otherwise have ignored.

Ethics is also inseparable from the values that guide executives in the setting of organizational purposes, goals, and objectives. Ethics poses two key questions that need to be answered when formulating strategy:

1. Are the values that underlie the strategy defensible?
2. Are the effects of the strategy on the firm's stakeholders moral?

Answering these questions involves bringing to the surface the value assumptions that underlie the strategy and relating them to the various stakeholders. Next these assumptions must be examined from an ethical point of view. This evaluation requires ethical criteria drawn from the analyst's background on ethical thinking.

ETHICS IN PRACTICE

The strategic decisions managers make reveal the basic values and ethical principles to which they subscribe (Andrews, 1989). The size of most companies makes direct influence or control by management exceedingly difficult. Company policy can easily be ignored because of the communication problems posed by distance and by the many layers of management. As more companies decentralize and globalize, the possibility of corruption and misconduct expand. The CEO often helps to avoid these problems by making appropriate moral judgments, as in the case of the Tylenol recall. But leaders can also exert a bad influence: witness the S&L scandals and cheating on reports to the government by some aerospace companies. Ultimately, then, the executive is the one responsible for building a culture wherein trust, confidence, and honesty are rewarded. Quick action against offenders helps convince everyone that lapses in ethical conduct will not be tolerated.

Unfortunately, executives often exert pressure to compromise on ethical behavior (Richard, 1991). A survey done at Central Michigan University revealed that financial executives felt pressured to compromise on regulatory or legal requirements. In a number of cases, people were either "eased out" or terminated for refusing to act unethically. The majority of the respondents chose to do something about the situation (55%), compared with 18% who said they would do nothing and 27% who simply avoided the situation.

In a study of ethical codes of conduct at companies in the Fortune 500, Pelfrey and Peacock (1991) found some signs of improvement. For example, approximately half of the companies surveyed claimed they had a formal code of conduct. The survey revealed that 69% of the responding firms instruct their employees to contact legal counsel if they become aware of misconduct. Even so, in a number of incidents (such as the Watergate scandal and the explosion of one of the space shuttles), the "whistle blowers" suffered because of their willingness to speak up.

To help encourage ethical behavior, a number of companies are introducing training programs that foster an ethical culture by showing how it creates a competitive advantage (Harrington, 1991). Codes of ethics by themselves do not create a culture where ethical conduct is expected. To ensure that strategic decision makers will take ethical considerations into account, companies increasingly are turning to ethics training. However, to be successful, these programs must make it clear just how ethical behavior contributes to attaining a strategic advantage. Some executives complain that these programs have been a dismal failure, in part because participants sense that management is not sincere in its desire to support an ethical corporate culture. Ultimately, ethical behavior becomes meaningful when executives strongly support its incorporation into corporate culture and when there is clear evidence that ethics is an integral part of strategic decisions.

RIGHTS AND THE CATEGORICAL IMPERATIVE

In a school of thought that philosophers call "deontological ethics," there are said to exist rights and duties that should not be compromised under any circumstances. Thomas Jefferson referred to these as "inalienable rights" when he wrote the Declaration of Independence. It is the philosopher Immanual Kant, however, who is generally credited with the fullest development of the idea of rights. In *Foundations of the Metaphysics of Morals* (1787) he argues that society should strive to become a "kingdom of ends" in which all persons are treated as ends in themselves—never as only a means to achieve someone else's ends. The key to achieving this is in finding moral laws that are applied equally to everybody and from which no exceptions should be made (Kant thought "Thou shall not kill" was such a rule). This line of reasoning gives rise to rights—things a person has an inviolable and justifiable claim to—and to duties—obligations an individual cannot ignore.

An ethical strategy must adhere to the duties imposed on a firm by law or by custom. Furthermore, any strategy that would violate one or more stakeholder's rights is unethical. The following are some rights to be considered in strategic thinking (*Source:* Cavanagh, Moberg, and Velasquez, 1981, pp. 365–366).

1. *Right to life.* Acts taken under the strategy should not endanger the life of any stakeholder or subject a stakeholder unduly to injury.
2. *Right to property.* Acts taken under the strategy should not violate any stakeholder's claim to ownership of material possessions or "property."
3. *Right to free consent.* Stakeholders have a right to be treated by the firm only as they knowingly and freely consent to be treated.
4. *Right to privacy.* Stakeholders have the right to a private life and to choose what they share with others in intimate relationships.

5. *Right to freedom of conscience.* Stakeholders have the right to refrain from carrying out any order that violates the moral or religious norms to which they adhere.
6. *Right to free speech.* Stakeholders have the right to criticize conscientiously and truthfully the morality of actions taken by others so long as their criticism does not violate the others' rights.
7. *Right to due process.* Stakeholders have the right to a fair and impartial hearing whenever they believe that their rights have been violated.

Policies with respect to employees, consumers, and communities can be evaluated by means of the criteria suggested by these rights and others.

JUSTICE

The ideas of justice and rights are related, justice being the more general concept. John Stuart Mill, for example, listed the violation of rights as one sense of "injustice." In the general sense, justice is *fairness:* Is each stakeholder being treated fairly? In a more specific sense, justice has to do with *each stakeholder getting what he or she deserves.* Students who participate in a class expect to be treated fairly and to be given the grade they deserve. The stakeholders who participate in a corporate strategy expect the same treatment. When they receive it, justice is served.

John Rawls, in *A Theory of Justice* (1971), proposed two principles by which a just society would live. His carefully worded work may be summarized and paraphrased as follows:

a. Each stakeholder is to have an equal right to the same basic liberties every other stakeholder has a right to.
b. Social and economic inequalities among stakeholders are to be arranged so that they are:
   1) To the greatest benefit to the least advantaged stakeholder.
   2) Attached to offices and positions open to all under conditions of fair equality of opportunity.

Cavanagh, Moberg, and Velasquez (1981, pp. 363–374) have summarized the concerns for justice in terms of three canons, which they append to the list of rights that we have just examined:

8. *Distributive rules.* Acts taken under the strategy should distribute benefits and burdens equitably among stakeholders and on the basis of criteria relevant to tasks and goals. The strategy should not result in a worsening of the position of the least advantaged stakeholder.
9. *Fair administration.* The rules and policies of the strategy should be clearly stated and consistently and impartially enforced.
10. *Compensation norms.* Stakeholders should not be held responsible for matters over which they have no control, and stakeholders should be compensated by the parties responsible for injustices done to them.

UTILITARIANISM

Jeremy Bentham, in his *Introduction to Principles of Morals and Legislation* (1948), argued that "Nature has placed mankind under the governance of two sovereign masters, *pain* and *pleasure*." Thus he proposed that a pain/pleasure calculus (not unlike cost/benefit analysis) be developed and applied to all decisions. The option with the greatest balance of pleasure over pain was to be preferred. This has come to be summarized as "the greatest good for the greatest number."

Utilitarianism suggests that in assessing a strategy, the firm should choose strategies that satisfy Bentham's criterion in terms of either the ends they seek or the means they employ. More precisely,

11. *Ethical ends.* The strategic outcome should result in the greatest good for the greatest number for the longest period of time.
12. *Ethical means.* The actions taken in implementing the strategy should constitute an efficient means for stakeholders to realize the greatest good for the greatest number.

ETHICAL AUDIT OF STRATEGY

The twelve principles just described constitute a checklist for evaluating a strategy from an ethical point of view. Each principle forces the manager to think about some aspect of a strategy that may have been overlooked. Sometimes these principles yield conflicting advice. For example, a strategy may involve endangering someone's life yet potentially provide great benefits to a large number of stakeholders. Based on these considerations, the manager must decide whether the strategy is ultimately ethical or not. Worksheet 3.2 provides a framework for arriving at such decisions.

It should be pointed out that some well-respected observers believe that this kind of ethical audit is unnecessary. Nor is it necessary, in their view, to undertake a separate corporate social responsibility review. They argue that the free market effectively does this. One of the strongest proponents of this view, University of Chicago economist Milton Friedman, summarizes his position in *Capitalism and Freedom* (1962, p. 133):

> There is one and only one social responsibility of business—to use its resources and engage in activities designed to increase its profits so long as it stays within the rules of the game, which is to say, engages in open and free competition, without deception or fraud.

He goes on to conclude that

> Few trends could so thoroughly undermine the very foundations of our free society as the acceptance by corporate officials of a social responsibility other than to make as much money for their stockholders as possible. This can be a fundamentally subversive doctrine.

You should decide for yourself on this. But try Worksheet 3.2 before you make up your mind.

WORKSHEET 3.2	**Ethical Audit of Strategy**

Case _____

Date _____

Name _____

1. Impact on Right to Life

    Violates _____ Neutral _____ Promotes

2. Impact on Right to Property

    Violates _____ Neutral _____ Promotes

3. Impact on Right to Free Consent

    Violates _____ Neutral _____ Promotes

4. Impact on Right to Privacy

    Violates _____ Neutral _____ Promotes

5. Impact on Right to Freedom of Conscience

    Violates _____ Neutral _____ Promotes

6. Impact on Right to Free Speech

    Violates _____ Neutral _____ Promotes

7. Impact on Right to Due Process

    Violates _____ Neutral _____ Promotes

8. Impact on Distribution

    Just _____ Neutral _____ Unjust

9. Fairness of Administration

    Just _____ Neutral _____ Unjust

10. Norms of Compensation

    Just _____ Neutral _____ Unjust

11. Strategic Ends and Outcomes

    Great Good _____ Neutral _____ Great Harm

12. Strategic Means Employed

    Great Good _____ Neutral _____ Great Harm

THE ENEMIES CHECK

According to the philosopher G. W. F. Hegel, "Nothing great in the world has been accomplished without passion." It might also be said that many great intentions have been thwarted with passion. Criticisms of a business's products and policies, demands for new products and policies, and the changing attitudes of a business's managers, workers, customers, and clients all stem from people and their passions. *Any effective plan should mobilize the emotional force of the passion behind it and avoid those passions that might be directed against it.*

Unfortunately, most methods for formulating strategy are purely logical and rational. They depend on economic and technical analysis. Yet passions and the opportunities and threats they represent emerge from the nonrational—even the irrational—aspects of the environment. And they are generally neglected or ignored by rational analytical methods.

One example of the impact of passion on an organization comes from the Tennessee Valley Authority. The TVA was engaged in a major new dam building project when a group of impassioned environmentalists demanded that construction be stopped because the new dam endangered the only known habitat of a 3-inch fish called the snail-darter. As a consequence, a $120-million project was brought to a halt. Other examples include stockholders arguing that a firm should sell off its holdings in South Africa, citizens lashing themselves to trees so that lumbering companies cannot proceed with their work, protestors throwing themselves in front of trucks so that materials cannot be used to construct a nuclear power plant, strikes, sit-ins, and civil disobedience. These events are so well known that most executives and corporate planners use such terms as "show stoppers" and "wild cards" to describe them.

Is it possible to anticipate these rare, nonrational business forces? No surefire method is known. However, drawing on C. West Churchman's concept of the "enemies" of rationality, a simple, mind-expanding, brainstorming approach has been devised. In *The Systems Approach and Its Enemies* (1979), Churchman identifies four historical *enemies* of rational systems thinking: politics, morality, aesthetics, and religion. He argues that managers and planners should try to hear the "voices" of these enemies whenever they are developing a plan. It may be that one or more of these enemies will be responsible for the next show stopper. Each enemy, Churchman maintains, can have its own effect.

Politics affects a plan in that stakeholders, in the pursuit of their own interests—namely power, status, influence, and recognition—collect together to form a community around some aspect of that plan. That is, they form a *polis,* to use the Greek word.

Morality affects a plan in that stakeholders, as a part of their human spirit, possess a moral force. If some aspect of a plan impinges on that force, they respond with "that's wrong," "that's evil" or "that's right," "that's good."

Aesthetics affects a plan in that stakeholders respond to the beauty or ugliness of a plan, the "radiance" it gives off, its artistic form, or the tastefulness with which it is conducted. Considerations of form, symmetry, and harmony are part of the aesthetic dimension.

Religion affects a plan in that stakeholders react to it in terms of their orientation to unity in the universe and the creation of a satisfying and meaningful relationship with it. According to Churchman (1979, p. 173), the "religious approach to human affairs occurs *first* when we humans decide in terms of something we regard as superior, grander, more magnificent, than we feel ourselves to be" or "*second,* when we humans decide in terms of the small, minuscule, unique, which is not inferior to us, and is indeed superior because of its smallness." The Sierra Club's dedication to nature is an example of Churchman's first condition. E. F. Schumacher's passion for "small is beautiful" and "appropriate technology" is an example of the second condition. One company, Service Master, bases its mission on Christian values and sets as its goals "to honor God in all we do, to help people develop, to pursue excellence, to grow profitably," in that order.

The *enemies check* is a heuristic test to determine whether the nonrational forces of politics, morality, aesthetics, and religion are potentially working for or against the plan. It further aids in anticipating what form the wild card or show stopper might take. This method is based on the following thought-provoking questions:

1. Politics
   a. In what way might stakeholders be related to each other around a common issue such that they acquire power either to stop or to support the plan?
   b. Who are the agents likely to take action on this?
2. Morality
   a. What kinds of ethical issues, "wrongs" or "rights," does the plan raise?
   b. Who are the agents likely to take action on this?
3. Aesthetics
   a. What kinds of ugliness or beauty does the plan create?
   b. Who are the agents likely to take action on this?
4. Religion
   a. What basic beliefs about people and the universe are offended or supported by the plan?
   b. Who are the agents likely to take action on this?

The enemies check brings out threats to and support for a strategy that other methods usually fail to surface. Once an enemy of a strategy is identified, there are several actions one can take to deal with it:

- Confront, fight, or challenge it.
- Avoid it.
- Appease it.
- Surrender or concede to it.
- Convert it to a support.
- Love it.
- Incorporate it so completely that it becomes the plan.

Choosing one of these options for an identified enemy of the plan greatly enriches a strategy and improves its chances of success.

Summary

Effective strategic management, particularly strategic planning, requires a thorough understanding of the organization itself. The vision of the organization's founder, CEO, or strategic-management team cannot be realized if it is not consistent with the assumptions and beliefs, values, and culture that prevail in the organization. One of the tasks of strategic planners is to assess these organizational qualities and, where inconsistencies are found, decide whether to change the vision or the organization.

Another task is to evaluate prevailing assumptions, beliefs, and values to determine whether they are helping or hurting the organization. Appropriate assumptions, beliefs, and values have two main characteristics: (1) they reflect internal and external realities, and (2) they help the organization to achieve its vision. Inappropriate assumptions, beliefs, and values have opposite effects and must be changed *before* top managers attempt to introduce a new vision.

Sometimes a strategic planning team works with the CEO and top managers to develop a new vision for the organization. If this is the case, knowledge about the organization's internal environment helps planners to develop an appropriate vision. The emerging vision also should meet two criteria for profitability: (1) It should involve businesses/products with the potential for leveraged customer value, and (2) it should involve businesses/products with the potential for increased competitive advantage through system innovation. These criteria are essential because they involve changes in customer perception and organizational operations, both of which can be achieved through effective management and should not require extensive capital outlays.

The strategic planning team helps the organization to devise a grand strategy to achieve the vision and then develops specific goals, objectives, and plans of action. Where the CEO and top managers have difficulty thinking through the strategy, goals, or objectives, these can be analyzed via the critical-success-factor method shown in Chapter 5.

The strategic manager must be concerned with the social legitimacy as well as the economic vitality of the firm's strategy. As new social issues—such as product safety, occupational health and safety, employment, equal opportunity, and pollution—have surfaced, they have become a matter of strategy. Not only do most corporations want to develop socially responsible and ethical strategies; they *must* do so as a matter of survival. Modern corporate leaders must be able to explain the organization's position and to defend it.

The three methods presented in this chapter assist the strategic manager in this process of establishing social legitimacy and defending it. The *corporate social performance matrix* identifies salient stakeholders and issues. The *ethical audit* evaluates a strategy on fundamental ethical issues. And the *enemies check* determines the robustness of a strategy in the face of nonrational claims against it.

The results of these three reviews are used for two purposes:

1. To shape a responsible and ethical strategy.
2. To prepare the arguments necessary to explain the social legitimacy of the strategy to all stakeholders, including stockholders, employees, government agencies, community leaders, public interest groups, and individual challengers.

References and Suggestions for Further Reading

Abbott, Walter F. and Monsen, Joseph R. 1979. On the measurement of corporate social responsibility: Self-reported disclosures as a method of measuring corporate social involvement. *Academy of Management Journal* 22, no. 3.

Abegglen, James C. and George Stalk, Jr. 1985, *Kaisha, the Japanese corporation.* New York: Basic Books.

Andrews, Kenneth. 1989. Ethics in practice. *Harvard Business Review,* September–October, pp. 99–104.

Ansoff, H. Igor. 1972. The concept of strategic management. *Journal of Business Policy.* Summer.

Ansoff, H. Igor. 1965. *Corporate strategy.* New York: McGraw-Hill.

Barnard, Chester I. 1979. *The functions of the executive.* Cambridge, Mass.: Harvard University Press, p. 217.

Bauer, Raymond A. and Dan H. Fenn, Jr. 1972. *The corporate social audit.* New York: Russell Sage Foundation.

Bennis, Warren. 1989. *On becoming a leader.* Reading, Mass.: Addison-Wesley.

Bennis, Warren G. 1977. Where have all the leaders gone? *The McKinsey Quarterly,* Autumn.

Bentham, Jeremy. 1948. *Introduction to principles of morals and legislation.* New York: Hafner, Macmillan.

Carlson, W. Bernard. 1991. *Innovation as a social process.* New York: Cambridge University Press.

Carroll, Archie B. 1979. A three-dimensional conceptual model of corporate performance. *Academy of Management Review* 4, no. 4.

Cavanagh, Gerald F., Dennis J. Moberg, and Manuel Velasquez. 1981. The ethics of organizational politics. *Academy of Management Review* 3, no. 3, pp. 363–374.

Christensen, C. Roland, Kenneth R. Andrews, and Joseph L. Bower. 1978. *Business policy: Text and cases.* 4th ed. Homewood, Ill.: Irwin, pp. 247–259.

Churchman, C. West. 1979. *The systems approach and its enemies.* New York: Basic Books.

Churchman, C. West. 1968. *The systems approach.* New York: Delacorte Press.

Davis, Keith. 1973. The arguments for and against corporate social responsibility. *Academy of Management Journal* 16, no. 2.

Drucker, Peter F. 1973. *Management: Tasks, responsibilities, practices.* New York: Harper & Row.

Faltermayer, Edmund. 1992. Is this layoff necessary? *Fortune,* June 1, pp. 71–86.

Friedman, Milton. 1970. The social responsibility of business is to increase its profits. *New York Times Magazine,* September 13.

Friedman, Milton. 1962. *Capitalism and freedom.* Chicago: University of Chicago Press.

Garvin, D. A. 1983. Quality on the line. *Harvard Business Review* 6, no. 5. September–October, pp. 65–75.

General Electric—Going with the winners. 1984. *Forbes,* March 26, pp. 97–106.

Granger, Charles H. 1964. Hierarchy of objectives. *Harvard Business Review* 42, no. 3. May–June.

Guth, William D. and Renato Tagiuri. 1965. Personal values and corporate strategy. *Harvard Business Review* 43, no. 5, September–October.

Halal, William E. 1977. A return-on-resources model of corporate performance. *California Management Review* 19, no. 4.

Harrington, Susan. 1991. What corporate America is teaching about ethics. *Academy of Management Executive,* no. 1, pp. 21–30.

Hippel, Eric V. 1988. *The sources of innovation.* Oxford, England: Oxford University Press, p. 102.

Jack Welch: How good a manager? 1987. *Business Week,* December 14, p. 92.

Kilmann, Ralph H. 1984. *Beyond the quick fix: Managing the five tracks to organizational success.* San Francisco: Jossey-Bass.

Kilmann, Ralph H., Marry J. Saxton, and Roy Serpa. 1985. *Gaining control of the corporate culture.* San Francisco: Jossey-Bass.

Kirkland, Richard I., Jr. 1992. What we can do now. *Fortune,* June 1, pp. 41–48.

Labich, Kenneth. 1992. The new crisis in business ethics. *Fortune,* April 20, pp. 167–176.

Maslow, Abraham. 1969. *Toward a psychology of being.* 2nd ed. Princeton, N.J.: Van Nostrand.

Mott, P. E. 1972. *The characteristics of effective organizations.* New York: Harper & Row.

News/Trends: A Sweet Swap for GE and Thomson. 1987. *Fortune,* August 17, p. 8.

Pelfrey, Sandra, and Eileen Peacock. 1991. Ethical codes of conduct are improving. *Business Forum,* Spring, pp. 14–17.

Peters, Thomas J. and Robert H. Waterman, Jr. 1982. *In search of excellence: Lessons from America's best-run companies.* New York: Harper & Row.

Rawls, John. 1971. *A theory of justice.* Cambridge, Mass.: Harvard University.

Richard, Gary. 1991. Bosses pressure corporate financial executives to compromise ethics. *Program Manager,* July–August, pp. 34–41.

Rockart, John F. 1979. Chief executives define their own data needs. *Harvard Business Review* 57, no. 2. March–April.

Rokeach, Milton. 1973. *The nature of human values.* New York: The Free Press, p. 5.

Sarnoff, David. 1968. *Looking ahead.* New York: McGraw-Hill, pp. 31–34.

Schein, Edgar H. 1985. *Organizational culture and leadership: A dynamic view.* San Francisco: Jossey-Bass.

Schwartz, H. M. and S. M. Davis. 1981. Matching corporate culture and business strategy. *Organizational Dynamics,* Summer, pp. 30–48.

Selekman, Sylvia and Benjamin Selekman. 1956. *Power and morality in a business society.* New York: McGraw-Hill.

Smart, Tim. 1992. How Jack Welch brought GE to life. *Business Week*, October 26, pp. 13–15.

Sorokin, Pitirim. 1937–1941. *Social and cultural dynamics*. New York: American Book Company.

Spranger, Eduard. 1928. *Types of men*. Translated by P. Pigors. Halle, Germany: Niemeyer.

Steiner, George A. and John F. Steiner. 1991. *Business, government, and society*. New York: McGraw-Hill.

Sterling, Christopher H. and John M. Kittross. 1978. *Stay tuned: A concise history of American broadcasting*, appendix C. Belmont, Calif.: Wadsworth.

Toffler, Alvin. 1980. *The third wave*. New York: William Morrow.

Zakon, Alan J. 1985. The beliefs audit. *BCG Perspectives*, no. 282.

CHAPTER FOUR

The Competitive Environment

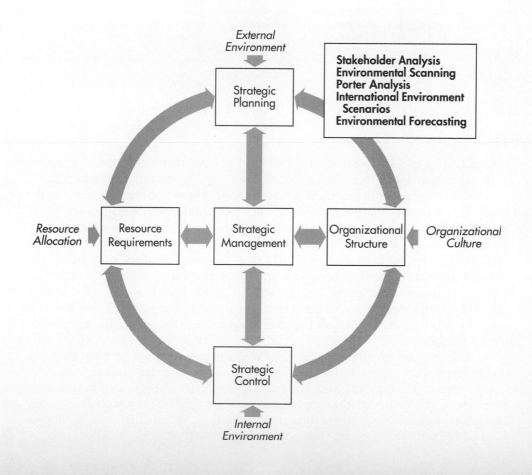

Chapter 1 A Framework for Strategic Management	**Chapter 2** Strategic Analysis	**Chapter 3** Strategic Visioning, Goals, Ethics, and Social Responsibility	**Chapter 4** The Competitive Environment	**Chapter 5** Capability-based Strategy	**Chapter 6** Market Dynamics and Sustainable Competitive Advantage
How to approach strategic management	*Application of strategic analysis*	*Understanding vision, values, ethics*	*Coping with competitive forces, stakeholders*	*Assessing company capability, timeliness, quality*	*Determining trends, gap analysis, and market dynamics*

Chapter 7 Strategy in a Global Environment	**Chapter 8** Financial Planning and Competitive-Cost Analysis	**Chapter 9** Entrepreneurship, Mergers and Acquisitions, Restructuring, and the Service Sector	**Chapter 10** Leadership Factor in Strategy and Implementing Strategic Change	**Chapter 11** Information Technology and Future Directions in Strategy
Assessing global trade, foreign markets, monetary exchange	*Preparing a financial plan and competitive-cost analysis*	*Importance of small business, entrepreneurs, restructuring*	*Strategy implementation, leadership, culture*	*Information technology, trends, new management*

INTRODUCTION

Organizations can be compared to ecological entities that have mutual relations with other entities in their environment. Like any ecosystem, an organization's environment holds opportunities and threats. Skillful strategic managers find in the firm's environment "market niches" that are particularly well suited to the products, services, and capabilities the organization has to offer. Failure to find a suitable niche leads the organization to encounter elements that can cause harm or even destruction. Successful strategic planning, therefore, requires a careful assessment of the external environment. Environmental assessment enables the organization to (1) find the best possible niche and (2) decide how it would respond to a range of environmental conditions that might occur in the future. Environmental assessment is a never-ending task for most firms because the environment is continuously changing.

Conducting an environmental assessment involves several different but interconnected layers see (Figure 4.1). In this chapter, we will discuss each of these layers.

As a start it is typically useful to conduct an environmental scan as a general overview. *Environmental scanning* is a method of identifying the economic, political, social, technological, competitive, and geographic factors that have an impact on the *firm* and then assessing their potential as opportunities or threats.

FIGURE 4.1	Levels of a Company's Economic Environment

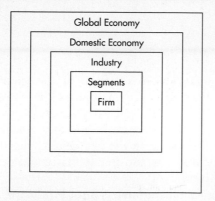

Strategic segmentation is essential in visualizing the competitive arena. The goal of strategic segmentation is to convert differences from competitors into a sustainable competitive advantage for the company. Understanding the different competitive environments and the forces driving an *industry* is essential in this process.

Stakeholder analysis covers the next level, that of the *domestic economy*. First, strategic managers identify the key stakeholders in the organization's business environment. Second, significant relationships among the stakeholders are charted to make a stakeholder map. The stakeholder map is a tool that strategic managers can use to identify the sources of environmental opportunities and threats and the ways they are transmitted to the organization. Third, managers identify and test assumptions about stakeholders, rank these assumptions, and determine which assumptions are most accurate and advantageous.

A discussion of the global economy follows. For most large companies today, global management is mandatory. It is also becoming increasingly important to medium-sized and smaller companies as countries around the world grow more closely linked culturally and economically. Entering foreign markets carries both significant opportunities and risks. Careful *assessment of the international environment* can be the basis for superior performance abroad.

Increasingly, companies are turning to environmental forecasting as a means of determining what strategies are needed to meet competitors' actions. Forecasting can be based on an analysis of such environmental data such as government or industry reports, industry trend analysis, competitor intelligence analysis, Delphi projections, or statistical analysis for predicting outcomes. Forecasting provides a basis for determining whether the courses of action under consideration will achieve the firm's goals and objectives.

An important forecasting approach that is fairly direct and has produced valuable results is scenario writing. This approach can utilize the expertise needed for a Delphi analysis or the knowledge of strategic planners who can project the likelihood of various outcomes. A number of approaches can be used to develop scenarios. These approaches, along with examples of how they are used, are discussed in this chapter.

ENVIRONMENTAL SCANNING

The external environment of an organization is defined by the set of forces with which that organization interacts. External forces include all kinds of stakeholders, economic trends, unforeseen events or crises, and various regulatory policies and laws. *Environmental scanning* is the first step in finding and analyzing external threats and opportunities. At this early stage in the strategic management process, managers need to identify all general events and trends that could be pertinent to the company's performance in the future.

Experience shows that environmental scanning is most productive when it consists of a brainstorming session by a group. Group sessions often result in a heightened awareness of reasons for strategic revisions or insights about future development. During the scanning session, managers try to identify environmental factors relevant to the following six key areas.

1. *Economics*: Factors related to the flow of money, goods and services, information, and energy
2. *Politics*: Factors related to the use or allocation of power among people, including dealings with local and foreign governments
3. *Social trends and demographics*: Factors that affect the way people live, including what they value
4. *Technology*: Factors related to the development of machines, tools, processes, materials, other equipment, and know-how
5. *Competition*: Factors that involve actions taken by current and potential competitors, market share, and concentration of competitors
6. *Geography*: Factors related to location, space, topography, climate, and natural resources

Scanning these six key areas reveals most of the environmental factors that need to be considered. Sometimes, however, managers find it useful to add another key area, such as the military, education, the law, medicine, or religion.

When all the relevant factors have been identified, managers can develop an environmental threat and opportunity profile (ETOP). The ETOP gives the first indication of potential external opportunities and threats. Depending on the impact and consequence of each factor, managers can determine whether that factor may pose a threat to the firm, is neutral, or represents an opportunity. To assess its impact and consequence, each factor is given a score. Scores for each factor's consequence and impact are multiplied to obtain a combined score that is used to assess the organization's overall position with respect to its environment. An application of the ETOP to IBM's situation in 1992 is shown in Worksheet 4.1. Although the scores are only estimates, their relative weight (rather than their absolute value) indicates the firm's position.

WORKSHEET 4.1	Environmental Scanning

Case ___IBM___

Date ___1992___

Name ___Mary Jones___

Factors	Potential Impact of Factor	Consequence	Environmental Threat
Economic	7	8	56
Political	2	1	2
Social	1	2	2
Technological	8	9	72
Competitive	9	7	63
Geographic	2	5	10

Impact from 10 (high threat) to 1 (low threat).
Consequence of factor ranked from 1 (unimportant) to 10 (very harmful).

Total ___205___

Comments:

Based on the analysis that was done in Chapter 2, IBM is in a fairly critical position
because of external threats. A total score in excess of 60 signals that a company is
"moderately vulnerable," and a score of 120 signals that a company is "vulnerable."
IBM's score of 205 shows that it is facing serious economic, technological, and
competitive threats.

Environmental threats do not have to be accepted as givens. It is often possible to develop a strategy that will change them in a favorable way. In other words, the organization can choose to be proactive rather than reactive. If the threat is restrictive legislation, for example, the organization can either accept the restriction as inevitable or lobby the legislature in an effort to prevent its being enacted. This ability to anticipate and minimize the effect of threats explains why environmental scanning is an important early step for managers who are developing new strategies.

Let us pause a moment to note a technique that is widely used in analyzing factors related to one of the key areas in environmental scanning: the competition. Assessing the competition can be achieved by what is termed "benchmarking" (Main, 1992). Copying the smart practices of competitors is an approach used by Ford, Xerox, AT&T, Motorola, and many others to stay abreast of changes in the field. Main found that of 580 companies he surveyed, 31% regularly use benchmarking to compare their products and services with those of competitors. For example, IBM has done over 500 benchmark studies in the past two years. How is it done? The following guidelines provide a basis for assessing the state of the art:

1. Focus on a specific problem and define it carefully. Then find out what other leading companies are doing.
2. Use persons who are responsible for a change in your own firm to obtain information. They have a vested interest in finding and implementing solutions.
3. Be willing to share information with others.
4. Avoid sensitive issues such as pricing. Don't look for new-product information.
5. Recognize that the information you receive is confidential.

The use of benchmarking as an assessment tool is growing, and the American Productivity and Quality Center has established a Benchmarking Clearing House in Houston.

STRATEGIC SEGMENTATION WITHIN AN INDUSTRY

Strategic managers must consider the full range of environments in which they might compete and the entire economic spectrum of a business activity, including suppliers, operations and production technology, distribution, marketing and sales, customer service, and so on. Only then can they identify strategic segments, or business activities, through which the company can

1. Establish an advantage relative to the competition
2. Defend this advantage over time
3. Enjoy secure and stable profitability

The key question in *strategic segmentation* is "In which parts of the industry can the company expect the highest long-term returns?" In other words, within which segments will it be possible for the company to

1. Develop a sustainable advantage relative to competitors in other, possibly adjacent, segments?
2. Deny competitors attractive returns on any investments required to enter the chosen segment?

The most important characteristic of a strategic segment is its defensibility. Proof that a segment exists is the barriers to competition that surround it. The higher these barriers, the higher the profit potential in that segment. Barriers can include

- Capital investment (such as the need for specialized equipment or a large-scale facility)
- Location (proximity to natural resources, for example, or transport-cost advantages for customers)
- Proprietary technological expertise and patents
- Established consumer franchise/trading relationships
- Tariffs and other trade barriers

Barriers can lead to a cost advantage, because of manufacturing, marketing, distribution, or a combination thereof.

As Figure 4.2 shows, strategic segmentation occurs at a more general level than market segmentation and involves decisions about production technology that entail long-term investment decisions. A *strategic segment* in the paper industry can be identified in terms of primary raw material (groundwood versus woodfree) and primary production process (uncoated versus coated). *Market segments* are identified by subdividing a strategic segment, such as artprint paper, on the basis of one or more product characteristics, such as quality, price, or weight.

Let's pursue a bit further the example of selecting a primary raw material for the production of paper. Woodfree papers, which are made from chemical pulps, require a completely different technology and production process from those made from groundwood. The decision to produce paper leads to considerable capital investments. Besides the paper machine, which can cost up to $500 million, coating equipment must be purchased. The choice of the strategic segment shown in Figure 4.2 can have a direct impact on which specific market segments will be served. Typically, a paper machine is built to produce a narrow range of paper weight. To switch to another range of weights requires that the firm rebuild existing equipment, incurring significantly higher capital costs. Coating can be done either by on-machine coaters, which are cheaper but produce lower-quality papers, or by off-machine coaters, which are more expensive but produce higher-quality papers. Therefore, the choice of machine (if that choice has already been made) determines which strategic segment the company should seek to compete in. These capital-investment decisions narrow down the number of market segments that are attractive for the company. For each market segment, further product differentiation can be pursued; for example, the company can choose to produce rolls or sheets and can choose to distribute the paper directly or through dealers.

Its choice of what product to offer also generally dictates in what region a paper company competes. Success in selling bulk papers, such as most groundwood grades,

---

FIGURE 4.2 | Strategic Segments and Market Segments in the Paper Industry

---

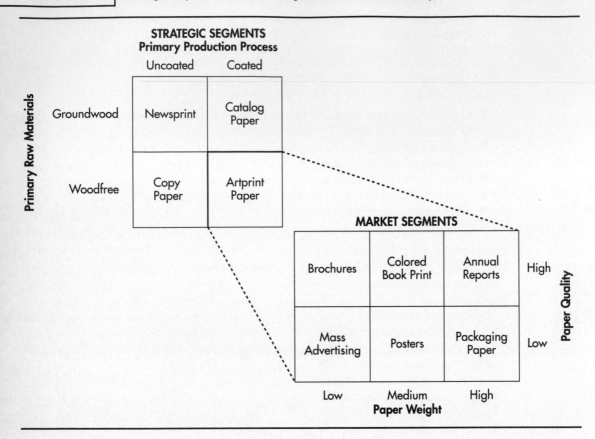

STRATEGIC SEGMENTS
Primary Production Process

MARKET SEGMENTS

is heavily dependent on making the right choice of location on a worldwide basis, as well as on a favorable exchange rate. North American producers of newsprint, for example, enjoy a very favorable cost situation, especially when the value of the dollar is low relative to that of other currencies. During this time they can make substantial inroads into Europe and other parts of the world. Consequently, all the major paper producers of these grades of papers are pursuing global strategies. Other specialty papers tend to be more domestic or regional in nature. For example, writing papers are typically regional products, because they depend more on regional standards and distribution strength than on lowest production cost.

Initial profitability does not ensure that a company has defined a strategic segment correctly. Above-average profits in an area may or may not validate the existence of a strategic segment. Profits do not guarantee that the segment is defensible or that profitability can be maintained. Many companies have found that short-term concentration on areas with above-average profitability can lead to long-term organizational decline. One such example is the motorcycle industry in the United Kingdom and the United States. In the late 1960s, these countries were the major producers of large motorcycles. The Japanese at that time produced small motorcycles. At this stage, manufacturers in both the United States and the United Kingdom apparently decided that "super bikes" (bikes with engine capacity greater than 500 cc) were a valid strategic segment exclusive of smaller bikes. Therefore, they abandoned the "small-bike segment" to the Japanese. This assumption about market segmentation was wrong. There were, in fact, no real barriers separating the design, production, marketing, and distribution of large and small motorcycles. The Japanese were allowed to dominate the small-bike market and, while doing so, were able to build a considerable competitive advantage in *all* motorcycle categories. A similar phenomenon occurred in the machine tool industry when U.S. companies abandoned their markets for smaller, numerically controlled lathes and machining centers to the Japanese. As a result, the U.S. machine tool industry has been almost obliterated.

COMPETITIVE ENVIRONMENTS

In the 1970s, the Boston Consulting Group (BCG) developed the *advantage matrix,* a useful first screen for identifying strategic segments. In this matrix (Figure 4.3), four generic competitive environments are defined on the basis of (1) the potential size of the advantage that can be gained by a competitor and (2) the number of different means by which a competitor can establish leadership in the industry. For commodities, which have little potential for product differentiation, the basic segment boundary is the cost advantage to be gained by serving more than one market segment, or class of customers. For differentiated products, the segment boundary lies in the combination of features built into the product and their cost/price ratio. In identifying segments with the advantage matrix, managers also include all conditions of the transaction process, such as service, vendor reliability, and delivery schedules.

The competitive environments identified in the advantage matrix are described in the sections that follow. Figure 4.4 shows the typical patterns of return on assets in these four competitive environments.

Volume Businesses

In volume businesses (see Table 4.1), basic or inherent costs are the largest part of the cost structure, and economies of scale or experience reduce costs. Examples of volume businesses include television sets, mid-sized cars, newspapers, and fast-food

FIGURE 4.3	The Boston Consulting Group's Advantage Matrix

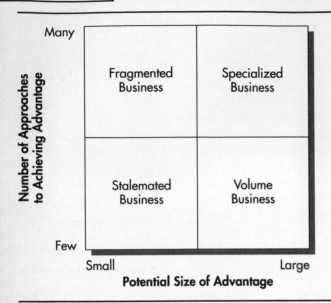

Source: Courtesy of The Boston Consulting Group, Inc. Reprinted with permission.

FIGURE 4.4	Patterns of Competitive Returns ROA=return on assets; S=segment; dots indicate different competitors

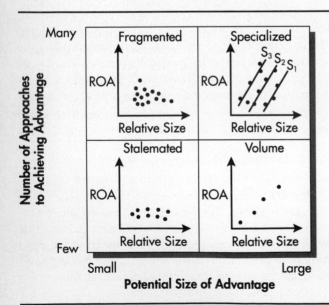

Source: Courtesy of The Boston Consulting Group, Inc. Reprinted with permission.

chains. A key strategy of a volume business is to be the cost and volume leader. Low costs and high sales volumes are two means of attaining competitive advantage. Followers survive only if the leader chooses to establish a price umbrella or if the business stalemates. Major threats to a volume leader are inadequate capacity for expansion relative to market growth (resulting in loss of market share), market maturation and differentiation, cost increases due to complexity, global competition, and technology stalemate.

TABLE 4.1	Competitive Environments Within the Machine Tool Industry

Competitive Environment	Examples of Products
Volume business	Small numerical control lathes, milling machines, machining centers
Stalemated business	Conventional lathes, drilling machines, sheet metal presses, mechanical forging presses
Specialized business	Multispindle lathes, single-spindle automatics, grinding machines, gear-cutting machines
Fragmented business	Vertical lathes, flexible manufacturing systems (FMSs), transfer lines

Stalemated Businesses

Stalemated businesses differ from volume businesses in that economies of scale do not have great cost benefits, often because technology and experience have stagnated throughout the industry and are widely shared among competitors. Examples of stalemated businesses include the steel, aluminum, shipbuilding, and paper industries. In these businesses, the cost advantages of high volume have shrunk, and establishment of a leadership position depends mostly on reducing factor costs, such as the costs of labor, energy, and capital. To reduce labor costs, many stalemated businesses move their manufacturing operations to newly industrialized countries, such as South Korea, Taiwan, or Brazil. Businesses that are sheltered by government subsidies can keep their domestic plants open, at least for a period of time.

Specialized Businesses

Specialized businesses are characterized by steep scale or experience effects in costs incurred by serving a specific market segment. They focus on a limited set of customers, or a "segment" of the market. Examples of specialized businesses include pharmaceuticals, cosmetics, book publishing, and luxury cars. By focusing on a selected part of the market, it may be possible to achieve significant price premiums, and a higher-than-normal price for a product. The main success factors for specialized businesses are market focus and segment leadership. Typically there are several highly profitable competitors, but each dominates a different market segment. Followers in each specific segment tend to be less profitable. Competitive battles are usually not head-on but rather tend to occur at strategic and market segment boundaries. It is also possible for a competitor to serve more than one market segment, which significantly lowers average costs. For a firm to do this, however, it must be possible to sell at different prices to each market segment, and the price in each segment must match value to the customer. One example is the entry of Japanese car manufacturers into the luxury car segment once dominated by Europeans.

Fragmented Businesses

The profitability of fragmented businesses is unrelated to size and strategic segmentation. Fragmented businesses are often regional businesses in which economies of scale are outweighed by the costs of complexity. Examples of such businesses include restaurants, engineering companies, handicrafts, and consulting firms. Competitive advantage can be sustained by innovation, operational efficiency, and market focus that is value-oriented. These factors are more important than relative competitive position in an industry that no one dominates.

Porter (1980) recommends a number of approaches for coping with fragmentation. First is to attempt an economic consolidation through franchising or mergers. He also advocates strategic segmentation that focuses on the customer, type of product, geographic location, or uniqueness of design. In addition, he recommends creating industry standards that make fragmented industries much more efficient because of their ability to reduce cost and to focus on value-added activities. Assumptions about the distribution of overhead and the allocation of new-product costs are covered in Chapter 8. Relying on a strategic discipline, a company can focus its efforts even within a highly fragmented industry.

COMPETITIVE FORCES

Strategic segmentation proceeds from identification of valid market segments and their competitive environments to a detailed analysis of the industry's competitive structure. Hence, moving outward in the levels of the economic environment shown in Figure 4.1, we find the next critical area that a strategic manager must assess: the industry in which the organization finds itself. One of the most comprehensive studies of the competitive environment in which a company operates was done by Porter (1980, 1985). His analysis will be covered in two parts. We will examine the impact of competition in an industry and some ways of dealing with industry evolution, fragmented industries, and strategic groups within an industry. Then we will present a means of assessing the attractiveness of a given industry. As is often the case, not all companies follow neat economic theory. Thus the guidelines described by Porter should be considered a useful overview, but they should be supplemented with other approaches. First we will examine the competitive forces in an industry using Porter's analysis. We will then use another approach called an "industry attractiveness analysis" to determine whether to enter or exit an industry.

PORTER'S ANALYSIS

According to Michael Porter, the key to competitive analysis is to identify the major competitive forces and assess their impact on the company's present and future market position (Figure 4.5). In particular, he singles out

1. Potential rate of growth in the industry
2. Threat of entry by new competitors
3. Intensity of rivalry among existing competitors
4. Pressure from substitute products
5. Dependence on complementary products and services
6. Bargaining power of buyers
7. Bargaining power of suppliers
8. Sophistication of technologies applied in the industry
9. Rate of innovation
10. Capability of management

These ten factors are discussed in the sections that follow. Analyzing them helps managers to formulate strategies that have a high likelihood of success, given the nature of the industry's competitive environment. Worksheet 4.2 evaluates each factor as it pertained to Polaroid's competitive situation in 1988.

| FIGURE 4.5 | **Competitive Forces** |

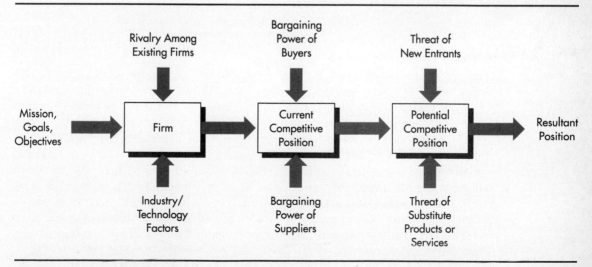

Source: Adapted from Porter, 1980.

WORKSHEET 4.2 | **Competitive Environment Analysis**

Case ___Polaroid___

Date ___1988___

Name ___John Doe___

1. Potential rate of growth of industry (in real terms)

   0–3% ____   9–12% ____   18–21% ____
   3–6% ____   12–15% ____   >21% ____
   6–9% ✓   15–18% ____

2. Ease of entry of new firms into industry

   No barriers– ___:___:___:___:___:___:✓:___:___ –Virtually impossible to enter
   (patent protection)

3. Intensity of competition among firms

   Extremely competitive– ___:___:___:___:___:✓:___:___:___ –Almost no competition
   (Kodak intense)

4. Degree of product substitutability

   Many substitutes available– ___:___:___:___:✓:___:___:___:___ –No substitutes available
   (alternative photographic sources)

5. Degree of dependency on complementary or supporting products and services

   Highly dependent– ___:___:✓:___:___:___:___:___:___ –Virtually independent
   (film processing, film suppliers)

6. Degree of bargaining power buyers and customers possess

   Buyers dictate terms– ___:___:___:___:___:___:___:✓:___ –Selling firms dictate terms
   (few large, concentrated buyers)

7. Degree of bargaining power suppliers and vendors possess

   Suppliers dictate terms– ___:___:___:___:✓:___:___:___ –Purchasing firms dictate terms
   (about average)

8. Degree of technological sophistication in industry

   High-level technology– ___:___:✓:___:___:___:___:___ –Very low-level technology
   (R&D essential)

9. Rate of innovation in industry

   Rapid innovation– ___:___:✓:___:___:___:___:___ –Almost no innovation
   (continual influx of new ideas)

10. General level of management capability

    Many very capable managers– ___:___:___:✓:___:___:___:___ –Very few capable managers
    (probably average or slightly better)

Source: R. O. Mason, Copyright © 1984.

Potential Rate of Growth

Strategic managers must first assess the industry's growth potential, because this potential determines the nature of the game to be played. Industries with low growth rates (under 6% per annum) present few opportunities for new firms but enable established firms to maintain profitability if they can protect their position. Modest growth rates (6–12% per annum) present opportunities for aggressive firms. High growth rates (over 12%) present substantial opportunities, but they attract large numbers of new competitors and require that most competitors make substantial capital investments to keep pace.

Threats of Entry

Under what conditions will a new competitor enter a firm's strategic segment? What can the firm do about it? In general, a new competitor will not enter a strategic or market segment if the barriers to entry are high and a strong competitive reaction can be expected from existing firms. As mentioned earlier, one of the most important barriers to entry is capital requirements. The more money and resources needed to start up a new business (that is, the higher the "ante"), the less likely it is that a new competitor will want to enter. In clothing manufacturing, for example, there are few barriers for new-apparel makers, some of whom use undocumented workers in "sweat shops" to achieve a cost advantage. The manufacture of fine textile designer clothes, on the other hand, requires considerably more capital investment and know-how.

Another barrier is the ability of established companies to practice economies of scale. As a firm's volume increases and it gains more experience, its costs tend to decrease. And, of course, it takes a certain volume of sales to cover fixed costs and to begin to return a profit on each sale. These factors give established firms a distinct cost advantage over new competitors.

Barriers to entry can also consist of exclusive access to patents, information, or raw materials; a preferred location; or superior facilities. Product differentiation, such as unique automobile styling, serves as a barrier for a company's market segments. Product differentiation also tends to give the established firm the advantages of brand identification and customer loyalty. This advantage is often gained by means of advertising, good quality, and service.

For some types of customers, the switching costs (the costs of changing from one product to another) serve as protective barriers. For example, programs written for one computer frequently will not operate (without modification) on another manufacturer's computer. Reprogramming becomes a switching cost and serves as a barrier to entry for new firms entering the computer field.

Intensity of Rivalry

Many factors account for the intensity of rivalry among existing competitors in an industry. The first factor is the number of existing competitors. In general, the more competitors, the greater the rivalry. The second factor is similarity among competitors. The more nearly equivalent the competitors' size, skills, and market power, the greater the rivalry tends to be. The third factor is barriers to exit. If it is difficult for firms to leave the industry, they tend to see no options but to "fight it out" within the industry, thereby increasing the intensity of rivalry. Fourth, as industry growth stalemates or declines, the pressure on each firm to maintain its market share gets higher. Added to all of these factors is that magical ingredient, personal commitment to being number one. Some people and the companies they manage are simply more determined to succeed than others. In some cases, intense competitiveness results from a determination to enter and defend a strategic or market segment. In others, it is generated by the aggressive personality of the firm's leader.

In analyzing the intensity of competition, then, strategic managers should determine whether competitors are

- Numerous
- Similarly positioned in the industry
- Unable to leave the industry
- In an industry that is stalemated or declining
- Extremely committed to a strategy or to an aggressive leader

In general, the more intense the competition in an industry, the more difficult it is for new firms to enter and for existing firms to survive.

Pressure from Substitute Products

Sometimes an industry is "hit from its blind side." This happened in clothing manufacturing as synthetic fibers substituted for cotton fibers, detergents replaced soaps, and coin-operated dry-cleaning machines substituted for dry-cleaning services.

Product substitution follows a typical pattern. While the established firms concentrate on each other, another firm, usually by means of technological innovation, creates a product that can be substituted for the existing product. The new product has a different form but performs the same function. Competition by substitution had disastrous consequences for the AddressoGraph Multilith Corporation. At one time, this company monopolized the mechanized-addressing market. Today, however, computer-printed labels have all but eliminated the need for AddressoGraph machines, which imprint addresses using embossed metal plates.

To prevent being surprised by a substitute product, strategic managers must continuously assess the external environment. Environmental scanning, technological assessment, and stakeholder analysis are all suitable methods.

In general, the greater the pressure from substitute products, the less attractive the industry.

Dependence on Complementary Products and Services

Some products, such as candy bars, are consumed independently of other products. Others have either a correlated demand or a derived demand. *Correlated demand* for a product is due to the fact that customers prefer to consume certain products together, such as meat and potatoes or recreation and food. *Derived demand* for a product is due to the fact that the purchase of one product creates demand for another product. The sale of an automobile, for example, leads to a demand for accessories, an audio system, gasoline and oil, repair services, replacement parts, and tires. The sale of a computer and printer creates a demand for computer paper.

These products exhibit a degree of mutual dependence. People buy automobiles because they know repair services are available, and they buy repair services because they purchased an automobile.

A review of the complementary, correlated, and derived characteristics of demand for an industry's products enables strategic managers to assess the organization's dependence on the success or cooperation of companies in other industries. A high degree of dependence is a danger signal. If the firms in the other industry are successful, healthy, dependable, and reliable, then a derived-demand situation can be quite profitable. In this situation, however, the firm's destiny is controlled in part by the actions of the other firms. This is seldom a comfortable circumstance. Firms in the complementary industries must be monitored constantly. One strategy that is often used in these circumstances is to merge with or acquire a firm that produces the needed products. If the other firm's products are complementary, the acquisition or merger is called *horizontal integration*. If the acquired firm's products create a derived demand, it is called *forward vertical integration*.

Bargaining Power of Buyers

Candy bars are sold to millions of individual buyers. The purchaser does not negotiate the price or the terms of sale. Commercial aircraft, on the other hand, are sold to just a few large airlines, which have the power to negotiate many aspects of the terms of sale. Defense weapons are often sold to only one purchaser—the U.S. government. Therefore, the government has a great deal to say about the terms of sale. In industries with many sellers and few buyers, the sellers are at a disadvantage. Price competition tends to ensue. In industries with few buyers and few sellers, the bargaining powers of sellers and buyers are often about equal. In this situation, a seller's ability to negotiate and to "cut good deals" often determines its success.

A review of the relative bargaining power of the buyers of an industry's products enables strategic managers to gauge the firm's market power. In general, the greater the bargaining power of buyers, the less advantage the sellers have.

Bargaining Power of Suppliers

The flip side of an assessment of the relative bargaining power of buyers is an assessment of the relative bargaining power of suppliers. The firm's buyers influence prices and marketing costs. Its suppliers influence production costs. Suppliers tend to be powerful if there are just a few of them, there are few alternative sources of supply, their product is important for the firm's business, and they are not dependent on the firm's purchases to have a successful business.

A review of the conditions of supply in the firm's resource markets—the markets in which it purchases labor, raw materials, facilities, and other important factors of production—enables strategic managers to determine how much bargaining power its suppliers possess. In general, the greater the bargaining power of the supplier, the less advantage the firm has. A process called *backward vertical integration* is often used to acquire suppliers with which the firm has weak bargaining power.

Technological Sophistication of the Industry

Some industries, such as retailing, currently employ a relatively low level of technology. Others, such as oil field information and services, depend heavily on scientific research and high-level technology. A high-tech firm must invest heavily in research and development, must often locate itself near a university or other research organization, and must strive to protect its position through secrecy, patents, and copyrights. The low-tech firm, on the other hand, always faces the possibility of intense competition because of its lower barrier to entry. Therefore, opportunities and threats are present whether technology is high or low.

Strategies for success are quite different depending on whether high or low technology is employed. In general, established firms in high-tech industries must emphasize research and development and offer specialized services to be successful. Established firms in low-tech industries must emphasize product identification, marketing, competitive pricing, value, and quality, as well as providing general services.

Rate of Innovation

Some industries, such as the table salt industry, are placid, stable, and subject to little change. Others, such as those in the computer field, are characterized by continuous, dramatic innovation. Innovation depends on two things: new ideas and the willingness and ability to carry them out.

Technological change is often the primary stimulus for innovation. The other main stimulus for innovation is new ways of thinking about service. Thirty years ago, Ray Kroc's new idea about fast food service created McDonald's; Walt Disney's vision of a family-oriented park created Disneyland; and Colonel Sanders's idea that homemade southern-fried chicken should be available nationwide created Kentucky Fried Chicken. None of these three innovators relied heavily on technological development. Rather, they depended on new ideas about products, services, and markets. These ideas revolutionized the industries involved.

A technological assessment and an environmental scan for new ideas about products, services, and markets, together with an estimate of the willingness and capability of the industry to adopt innovations, enables strategic managers to determine the rate of innovation in the industry.

In general, if the rate of innovations in an industry is high, the firm must have a flexible organization and be heavily committed to R&D and strategic planning to succeed. If, on the other hand, the rate of innovation is low, the firm must focus on marketing, sales, and cost reduction.

Management Capability

All of the preceding factors are tempered by one final consideration: What is the quality of management in the industry? Are there many competent and capable managers, or are there just a few? How many top managers does the industry have, and how highly qualified is each one? The long-term resiliency of an industry depends on the number of outstanding managers and on the chain of succession. During the last two decades the overall quality of management slipped in the American automobile industry, allowing the Japanese to gain an important advantage. Ultimately, quality management depends on entrepreneurship, sound decision making, and the "fit" of the manager's style with the demands of the situation.

A review of the breadth and depth of good management enables strategic managers to determine the general level of management capability in the industry. In general, when there are many capable managers in an industry, it is difficult for one firm to gain an advantage over another. If there are very few capable managers, a firm with a few exceptional managers can often gain an advantage. Strategic managers must also look out for firms that, out of ignorance or incompetent management, make stupid moves that can affect the viability of the industry. An industry that is especially vulnerable on this dimension may not be a good choice to enter.

INDUSTRY ATTRACTIVENESS ANALYSIS

Using the information obtained by applying Porter's industry analysis, one can now utilize Worksheet 4.3 to determine how attractive an industry might be. For example, is there potential growth, or is it limited? How easy is it to switch brands? What is the profitability? And so on. Examining the 15 factors shown, one can look at the forces applicable to each of these factors and assign a score from 0 to 10 to reflect the degree of attractiveness that industry has for a given company. Where the industry requirements fit the core capability of an organization, the attractiveness score is highest. On the other hand, if the company is unable to meet the industry requirements, the attractiveness score is low. Thus, for example, a company that is able to cope with all 15 of the factors shown might "ideally" have a score of 150. There are very few such companies. The majority of companies are likely to fall in the range of 75 through 120. (If each of the scores were 5, then the total would be 75, whereas if each of the scores were 8, the total would be 120.) Where a score is lower than 75, the strategic manager whose firm was already in that industry would have to consider significant repositioning in the industry in order to continue to operate on a profitable basis. One such approach, segmentation, was described earlier.

Other factors that need to be considered in analyzing an industry include resource requirements, government intervention, and industry structure. The availability of resources often becomes a critical aspect of carrying out strategy. For example, if funds are not available, a company could be headed for bankruptcy. Thus one must determine capital-investment requirements along with how much working capital is needed to sustain the company. This may depend on the capital-intensity in a given industry. For example, many companies "outsource" their computer operations to reduce the investment required in equipment, facilities, and personnel. The analysis of strategic funds programming, covered in Chapter 8, shows the capital requirements for various strategic options. If key

WORKSHEET 4.3	Industry Attractiveness Analysis

Case _____

Date _____

Name _____

Factor	Force	Score
1. Growth potential:	Increasing or decreasing size	_____ 0 10
2. Market diversity:	Number of markets served	_____ 0 10
3. Profitability:	Increasing, steady, decreasing	_____ 0 10
4. Vulnerability:	Competitors, inflation	_____ 0 10
5. Concentration:	Number of dominant players	_____ 0 10
6. Product sales:	Cyclic, continuous	_____ 0 10
7. Specialization:	Focus, differentiation, uniqueness	_____ 0 10
8. Brand identification:	Ease of switching, substitution, value, quality	_____ 0 10
9. Distribution:	Channels, support required	_____ 0 10
10. Price policy:	Learning effect, elasticity, industry norms	_____ 0 10
11. Cost position:	Competitive, low cost, high cost	_____ 0 10
12. Service:	Timing, reliability, guarantees	_____ 0 10
13. Technology:	Leadership, uniqueness	_____ 0 10
14. Integration:	Vertical, horizontal, ease of control	_____ 0 10
15. Ease of entry and exit:	Barriers	_____ 0 10

personnel are lacking, the company may be unable to function effectively. If critical materials cannot be had at a competitive price, or if physical facilities and equipment are not available, the company may be unable to maintain a competitive position.

Government intervention may significantly affect the ability of a company to compete within an industry. Often local governments (such as the state of California) impose stringent ecological requirements that force companies to either spend huge sums of money to correct the situation or move out of the state. For example, Kaiser Steel in Fontana, California, had to shut down its steel mill there because it was deemed uneconomic to implement the pollution-control equipment needed to reduce the emission of smoke and harmful particles as much as the law required. Increasingly, requirements for health and pension benefits are imposing costs that can make an industry noncompetitive. A critical function of an organization is to assess changes in government requirements, social legislation, bankruptcy laws, and the like in order to ensure that it is in compliance and is able to compete effectively given the industry demands.

It is possible to assess the industry structure by using Porter's approach to determining the intensity of competition. One can also examine strategic group maps to identify the major competitors in an industry and reveal how they impact the organization's ability to compete effectively. In a sense, such a map is comparable to a stakeholders' assumption graph (see Figure 4.8) applied to companies within an industry. Defining the strategic group, however, requires a careful analysis of the important factors that determine inclusion in a group and their effect on strategic competitiveness. For example, the variables used for these maps include markets served versus cost position, price/quality versus market segment, technology versus market served, and so on. The position of a company in the group map can be shown along with a circle describing the extent of penetration. (These group maps, in this form, are analogous to the product portfolios described in Chapter 6.)

In addition to considering the foregoing factors, one must ascertain how the industry deals with the "four P's" that are related to marketing practices.

Product What is the given product in the industry? Sometimes this is difficult to determine, especially in the field of electronics and high technology.

Prices How are prices established in the industry? Are they related to cost or the learning curve? Are products in the industry price-elastic or -inelastic?

Promotion An important consideration in gaining acceptance of products is the amount of funds spent on advertising and other promotional activities. Recent airline fare wars illustrate the importance of advertising in an attempt to gain new customers or increase utilization of air travel.

Place Geography, distribution channels, infrastructure, and location all influence performance in an industry. Whether the firm uses direct sales, telemarketing, representatives, or other channels of distribution often determines where a company is located.

One final consideration in the analysis of an industry is examination of the industry life cycle. The majority of companies in an industry go through life cycles, and the cumulative effect leads to changes in industry size, profitability, and performance. As companies accumulate knowledge and their products and processes undergo innovation, industries tend to reach a saturation point. Thus, for example, the aircraft industry has reached the point in its life cycle where the technology is fairly well known, physical facilities are in place, and capital is also made available to sustain the companies within the industry. As a consequence, the rate of growth in that industry is limited by variables such as alternative modes of transportation, access to airport, and cost of gasoline. As is evidenced by McDonnell Douglas's seeking to sell a part interest in its company to the Taiwanese government, sustaining oneself in the aircraft industry is becoming increasingly difficult. At the present time, there are two dominant players, Boeing and the European Airbus.

While some industries merely reach a point of saturation or low growth potential, others enter a declining stage. Decline is often due to technological obsolescence, but it can also be caused by government regulation or consumer needs. If there is a decline in demand (as has recently been true in consumer durables), there are just too many competitors and too much capacity. When confronted with the problems of a declining industry, many companies may choose to exit. For example, the automotive industry has gone through a major restructuring, including the shut-down of a number of facilities. On another front, Avery International actually paid an Italian company two million dollars to take over its business because the cost of exiting imposed such severe financial demands when considering the cost of laying off workers. It was cheaper to pay someone to take the business than to shut it down.

Another perspective on analyzing an industry is illustrated in Table 4.2 (Kichen, 1992). This table summarizes key points, which are explored in greater depth in the article itself, about major industry segments such as aerospace, chemicals, and construction. For example, the comment following Aerospace and Defense is "They have to prepare for even more draconian cuts." While somewhat superficial, this table does provide an overall picture of both the state of the economy and the condition of selected industry segments. (It also refers the reader to the place in the article where each segment is discussed.)

STAKEHOLDER ANALYSIS

A *stakeholder* is anyone whose actions can affect an organization or who is affected by the organization's actions. Because of these mutual interactions, each stakeholder has a stake in what the organization does, and vice versa. Stakeholders are also the organization's claimants; that is, they depend on the organization for the realization of some of their goals. The organization, in turn, depends on stakeholders for the full realization of its mission. Because of this mutual dependency, each stakeholder is, in effect, an advocate for any strategy that furthers its goals.

TABLE 4.2	Annual Report on American Industry

Aerospace and Defense
"Preparing for even more draconian cuts"
(Howard Banks, p. 96)

Business Services and Supplies
"Not much gain last year"
(Reed Abelson, p. 98)

Capital Goods
"Are in good shape to rebound"
(Brigid McMenamin, p. 102)

Chemicals
"Chemical exports increased"
(Randall Lane, p. 108)

Computers and Communications
"Little more than commodities"
(Julie Pitta, p. 112)

Construction
"Could be a construction industry turnaround in 1992"
(Claire Poole, p. 116)

Consumer Durables
"Too many competitors, too much capacity"
(Jerry Flint, p. 120)

Consumer Nondurables
"Americans weren't buying new houses, automobiles, or washing machines"
(Amy Feldman, p. 126)

Electric Utilities
"Capacity shortages, no-growth"
(Manjeet Kripalani, p. 130)

Energy
"1992 won't be so great"
(William Barrett, p. 134)

Entertainment and Information
"Forced into cost-cutting"
(Kathryn Harris, p. 140)

Financial Services
"Rescued by individual investors"
(Matthew Schrifrin, p. 144)

Food Distributors
"Slow sales and a trend toward buying less expensive"
(Toddi Gutner, p. 148)

Food, Drink, and Tobacco
"Profits keep rolling in for these companies"
(Edward Giltenan, p. 152)

Forest Products and Packaging
"Packaging materials, paper, and lumber just finished a dismal year"
(Linda Killian, p. 156)

Health
"Return on equity is still way above average"
(Mary Beth Grover, p. 158)

Insurance
"Industry is struggling to restore its credibility"
(Carolyn Geer, p. 162)

Metals
"Industry worked hard to prepare for the recession"
(Vicki Contavespi, p. 166)

Retailing
"Latest 12-month earnings were down almost 6%"
(Zina Sawaya, p. 168)

Transport
"Railroads enjoyed one of their better years in 1991"
(Roula Khalaf, p. 172)

Travel
"In the 1990s they have a new, and painful, situation"
(William Heuslein, p. 172)

Take, for example, a pharmaceutical company near Philadelphia that has just developed a new product. The question is whether this product, a drug, should be marketed as a prescription drug or one that can be sold over the counter. If it is sold as a prescription drug, the sales volume will be lower, so the price will be set higher. If it is sold over the counter, sales volume will be higher, and the price will be set lower. As the company's executives ponder this question, they realize that either answer will have substantial effects on strategies for the company's advertising, legal, marketing, sales, and distribution units. It soon becomes evident that to answer this important strategic question requires an understanding of the company's stakeholders and other aspects of the environment in which the company operates.

The success of the company's decision about the type and price of the new drug depends largely on actions taken by stakeholders in the pharmaceutical industry: competitors, government regulators, patients, physicians, pharmacists and other retailers, suppliers of the drug's raw materials, the parent firm of which this company is a subsidiary, and the company's managers, sales force, and stockholders. Success will also depend on inflation, world market conditions, and changing social and political trends in the external environment, especially those that affect major markets and suppliers.

MODELS OF STAKEHOLDER MANAGEMENT

The drug pricing problem is typical of many strategic-management problems. How can managers cope with the diverse priorities of many stakeholders? How can they structure strategic planning so as to consider the conflicting interests of many groups?

One of two models can be applied to this situation. The first is the *single-sovereign model* shown in Figure 4.6. In the single-sovereign model, the right and power to govern the organization are vested in a single ultimate authority—the chief executive officer (CEO). In the second model, the *steerer model,* the right and power to govern the organization are distributed among many individuals and groups, each of whom has a vital interest in the organization (Figure 4.7). The executive, as "steerer," attempts to achieve an equilibrium among the competing interests by forming coalitions and by creating synthetic and compromise solutions to organizational problems. The steerer's role is to guide the organization through the turbulent waters of diverse pressures and demands.

FIGURE 4.6	Single-Sovereign Model

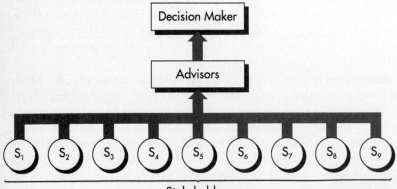

FIGURE 4.7 | Steerer Model

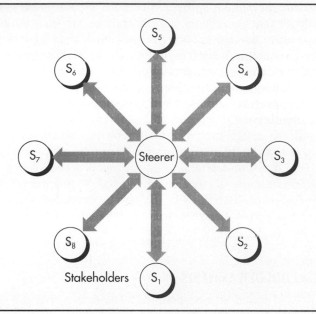

Stakeholders

Applying the steerer model helped the drug company solve its drug-pricing problem. The company decided to sell a higher-priced, prescription drug. Company executives carefully weighed the interests and possible actions of the company's stakeholders and charted a course that was consistent with the interests and actions of the most important parties involved.

Key stakeholders for the drug company turned out to be in the external environment: federal regulators of drug sales, physicians, and third-party payers. The interests of the main stakeholders within the company canceled each other out. The marketing unit that sold to physicians favored marketing a high-priced, prescription drug to physicians. The unit that sold to retail stores favored marketing a low-priced, high-volume drug. Not surprisingly, each group favored the strategy that would send the most business its way.

The Food and Drug Administration (FDA) had the final say in whether the new drug would have to be sold by prescription. While the FDA was deciding, market research focused on the physicians. If the physicians were sensitive to the issues of price and accessibility of the drug, then the low-priced, over-the-counter strategy would be better. If, on the other hand, they were not sensitive to these issues, then the high-priced, prescription strategy would be best. When the FDA indicated that the drug could be classified either way, and when market research revealed that physicians were not very sensitive to the issue of price—the physicians stressed professionalism—it became clear that the high-priced, prescription strategy would work better. Other forces in the environment, especially the willingness of insurance companies to pay for prescribed medications, lent support to this strategy.

Most executives do not make strategic decisions on the basis of the steerer model, despite evidence that this model is most appropriate for running an enterprise today. Increasingly, diverse groups are making claims as stakeholders in organizations. Federal, state, and local governments are stakeholders by virtue of regulation and taxation. Employees, through unions and employee groups, are gaining rights and powers as stakeholders. Consumer advocates, community action groups, public interest groups, creditors, suppliers, and competitors all demand a voice in organizational decision making. Yet many of today's executives still cling to the single-sovereign model of management. Executives choose strategies in the isolation of the executive suite, shut off from knowledge of stakeholder claims and deprived of a full understanding of the forces stakeholders might bring to bear. Such decisions almost always lead to mistakes and unrest. Frequently, they create new pressures and strife with which the executive must deal in the future. Stakeholder analysis is designed to help managers devise strategies that avoid these pitfalls.

METHODS FOR STAKEHOLDER ANALYSIS

A stakeholder analysis is based on two premises. The first is that the current state of an organization is the result of the supporting and the resisting forces brought to bear on the organization by stakeholders. Thus the present status of the organization is, at best, a temporary balance of opposing forces. Some of these forces provide resources and support to the organization; others serve as barriers or constraints. The forces are generated by stakeholders in the course of pursuing their own interests, goals, and objectives.

The second premise is that the outcome of an organization's strategy is the collective result of all the forces brought to bear on it by its stakeholders during implementation of that strategy. The organization is always in a state of quasi-equilibrium as it attempts to balance the various stakeholder forces. Every time an organization acts and its stakeholders respond, a new temporary balance is achieved. The status and performance of an organization at a given point in the future depends on the equilibrium it achieves throughout the implementation period.

These two premises lead to an important conclusion: *The validity of a strategic plan always depends on the assumptions that are made about the organization's stakeholders and about the actions they will take during the planning and implementation period.* Therefore, strategic managers should perform a stakeholder analysis in order to

1. Identify stakeholders.
2. Map significant relationships among the stakeholders.
3. Examine the stakeholder map for opportunities and threats.
4. Identify, or bring to the surface, assumptions about stakeholders and the forces they exert on the organization.
5. Assess the relative importance and certainty of these assumptions.

Following the stakeholder analysis, strategic managers undertake activities that provide more information about stakeholder assumptions, guard against or neutralize threatening stakeholder forces, and facilitate and build on the supporting and driving stakeholder forces. Let's see what each of the steps in a stakeholder analysis entails.

Identifying Stakeholders

A stakeholder analysis begins with identification of as many relevant stakeholders as possible. The following checklist is a useful beginning. It should, however, be expanded, refined, and "customized" for the organization under study.

- Owners and stockholders
- Creditors
- Customers and clients
- Employees
- Labor unions
- Labor communities
- Local government
- State government
- Federal government
- Scientific labs
- University researchers and faculty

- Suppliers
- Competitors
- Corporate management
- Sources of new technology
- Public interest groups
- Persons in the media
- Persons in education
- Persons in the arts
- Religious groups
- Military personnel

The major stakeholders of most business enterprises can be listed under one of the following categories:

- Customers
- Suppliers
- Competitors
- Owners

- Regulators
- Employees
- Important interest groups

Preparing a Stakeholder Map

Having generated a list of stakeholders, strategic managers next prepare a *stakeholder map* by positioning the key stakeholders in a system, or network, that indicates primary relationships. The principle is the same as that used by ecologists to depict food chains within a natural environment. At first the map may look like a tangle of spaghetti, but upon examination, patterns of interdependence usually emerge. These patterns are portrayed on the revised map. Figure 4.8 is a stakeholder map that might be drawn for a pharmaceutical company.

Examining Stakeholder Maps for Opportunities and Threats

Figure 4.9 shows some of the important external and internal stakeholder relationships Polaroid's executives had to manage in 1980 (see Chapter 1). External stakeholders appear outside the box, internal stakeholders within it. Polaroid's main

---

FIGURE 4.8   Stakeholder Map for a Pharmaceutical Company

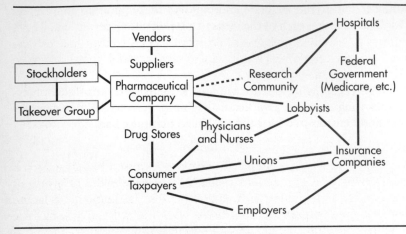

Source: Warsh, 1985.

FIGURE 4.9   Map of Polaroid Corporation's Stakeholders in 1980

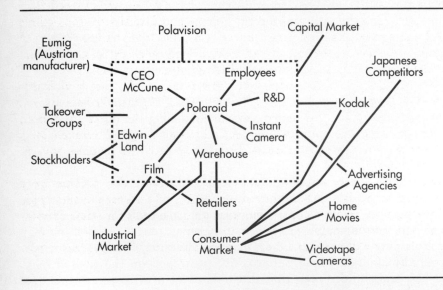

---

competitors are depicted at the upper right. Threatening substitute products, such as home movies and videotape cameras, are shown at the lower right. Polaroid's decision to segment its industrial and consumer markets is represented at the bottom. Other external forces being brought to bear include stockholders and takeover groups. The stockholders were putting pressure on the company to improve its profitability, while other investors viewed Polaroid's poor performance as a takeover opportunity. These pressures also concerned the primary supplier of Polavision, the Austrian manufacturing firm Eumig. Another important consideration was the effect that Polavision might have on Polaroid's film and instant camera businesses. Key internal stakeholders included Polaroid's founder, Edwin Land, and the (then) new CEO, William McCune. Polaroid's new strategy had to deal effectively with all of these relationships if it was to be successful and if it was to convince bankers to provide long-term loans.

Besides providing a "snapshot" of a company's current stakeholders, stakeholder maps can be used to identify trends based on past economic events and actions that were taken by various stakeholders. These maps are useful for tracking events as well as predicting the impact on future strategy.

Lessons from the Use of Stakeholder Maps   The central lesson to be learned from analysis of stakeholder maps is that actions taken by one stakeholder or group of stakeholders affect other stakeholders in the system. On the map, the affected stakeholders may be quite far removed from those who initiated the actions. The effects are propagated by means of economic, social, and political transactions among intervening stakeholders in the network. The technical term for significant changes in a stakeholder map is *structural change*.

Stakeholder maps for most organizations become more complex over time. As an organization grows, a variety of new stakeholders is added to the map. Some of the new stakeholders may be far removed geographically and culturally. The web of stakeholder relationships becomes more intricate, and the volume and diversity of transactions among stakeholders increase as time passes. Emery and Trist (1965) termed the web of relationships in a stakeholder map its "causal texture" and called the long-term trend toward increased complexity a movement toward a "turbulent environment."

The move toward increased complexity creates a need on the part of all stakeholders for (1) new responses that satisfy unmet needs, (2) faster responses, (3) more reliable responses, and (4) better ways of predicting the effects of chosen responses. These needs generate opportunities and threats for all the stakeholders involved in the system. Often, developing an effective response requires government action or cooperation.

Complexity also causes relationships among stakeholders to become more impersonal. Complexity, lack of personal relationships, and distance are among the reasons why stakeholder maps have become such valuable tools for strategic managers who are analyzing an organization's environment.

Strategic planners also use stakeholder maps to assess the effects of real or possible changes, such as

- New product technologies
- New process technologies
- Innovations in institutional relationships
- Changed demographics
- Deregulation by a government agency
- Regulation by a government agency
- Changes in the world economy
- Natural calamities

- Political crises
- Catastrophic accidents

Managers can assess each change by tracing its probable effects on the flow of materials, goods, services, money, information, and energy throughout the stakeholder map. In addition, planners consider where costs will accumulate, resources will be consumed, and revenues and benefits will be generated. Revenues and benefits are estimated for each stakeholder on the map to determine which part of the system is most likely to benefit from the change or to determine which part of the system is a beneficial niche.

Identifying (surfacing) and Testing Assumptions About Stakeholders   The success of any strategy depends on the validity of assumptions being made about the organization's internal and external stakeholders, particularly about how they are likely to respond as the strategy unfolds. Because the outcome of a strategy is the cumulative effect of actions taken by stakeholders during its implementation, strategic planners must identify and validate all of the assumptions being made about each stakeholder in the system. This process, called assumption surfacing and testing, involves

- *Assumption surfacing,* or identification of assumptions
- *Assumption rating,* or ranking of assumptions with respect to their importance and certainty
- *Assumption force-field analysis,* or determination of the net effects of assumptions that support a strategy and assumptions that do not support it

These three steps require information gained from all of the analytic methods described earlier, especially stakeholder identification and mapping.

Assumption Surfacing   Assumption surfacing is done to identify assumptions about how stakeholders will respond to a given strategy or to identify general assumptions about stakeholders. If the strategy has already been proposed, and the purpose of the analysis is to test the overall soundness of the strategy, then assumptions are surfaced by asking, "What are the most plausible assumptions the organization *must* make about each stakeholder for the strategy to be successful?" This is sometimes referred to as the "inverse optimal question." If no strategy has been proposed, and the purpose of the analysis is to uncover the most plausible set of assumptions upon which to base the new strategy, then assumptions are surfaced by asking, "What plausible assumptions can be made about each stakeholder?"

In either case, stakeholder assumptions can be classified into two categories:

1. Supporting or driving-force assumptions—those that indicate strategic opportunities and favorable conditions and are in keeping with organizational strengths.
2. Resisting or constraining-force assumptions—those that indicate threats, give rise to adverse and dangerous conditions, and take advantage of organizational weakness.

Worksheet 4.4 lists these two categories of assumptions for the Polaroid stakeholders of 1980.

WORKSHEET 4.4	Stakeholder Assumptions

Case   Polaroid
Date   1980
Name   John Doe

Stakeholders	Major Assumptions	Assumption Rating	
		Importance	Certainty
1. Major stockholder: Edwin Land	**Supporting**		
	a. Will continue to conduct research on new inventions	6	4
	b. Will not interfere with McCune's running of Polaroid	7	5
	Resisting		
	a. His "looser association" will deprive Polaroid of his leadership	5	8
	b. Corporate resources will be diverted to his research activities	6	9
2. CEO: William McCune	**Supporting**		
	a. Has the experience and background to manage	8	4
	b. His "broader-based" teamwork style will be effective at Polaroid	7	8
	Resisting		
	a. He will be diverted by oboe playing, silversmithing, auto tinkering, and vacationing	5	6
	b. He is associated with the rising problems with Polavision	7	9
3. Customers	**Supporting**		
	a. Price: prefer to pay $700 for Polavision, versus $1,800 for videotape set	7	7
	b. Will respond to personalized promotions such as "Santa Claus" delivery	6	2
	Resisting		
	a. Cool to home movies	7	1
	b. Performance: prefer reusable videotape	7	3
	c. Features: prefer sound, clear visible picture, more than 2½ minutes, etc.	9	4
4. Competitor: Eastman Kodak	**Supporting**		
	a. Polaroid will continue to hold off Kodak in the instant-camera market	8	1
	Resisting		
	a. Have stronger marketing and financial resources	9	9
	b. Will push easy-to-use, less expensive 35-mm cameras	6	3
5. Internal organization: R&D department	**Supporting**		
	a. R&D will produce the "new marvel"	8	0
	Resisting		
	a. R&D expense will continue to be a drain on corporate cash	4	8
6. Capital markets	**Supporting**		
	a. Polaroid can borrow at reasonable rates since there is unused debt capacity because it has no long-term debt	2	9
	Resisting		
	a. Polaroid has a declining cash position because of high inventor costs and lower-than-expected revenues	4	9

Assumption Rating   Assumptions about stakeholders vary with respect to the importance of these assumptions and the certainty with which they are held. Each assumption is rated on a scale of 0 through 9. For importance, the extreme values are as follows:

9 = very important assumption; one that has a most significant impact on the strategy and its outcome

0 = unimportant assumption; one that has very little impact on the strategy

For certainty, the extreme values are as follows:

9 = very certain assumption; one that is most likely to be true because either it is self-evident or there is substantial evidence to support its validity

0 = very uncertain assumption; one that has little or no supporting evidence, is questionable, and is likely to be invalid

These values are then graphed with the importance scale shown along the horizontal axis of the assumption-rating graph and the certainty scale shown on the vertical axis. An assumption-rating graph for the Polaroid case is shown in Figure 4.10.

FIGURE 4.10   **Assumption-Rating Graph for Polaroid's Stakeholders in 1980**

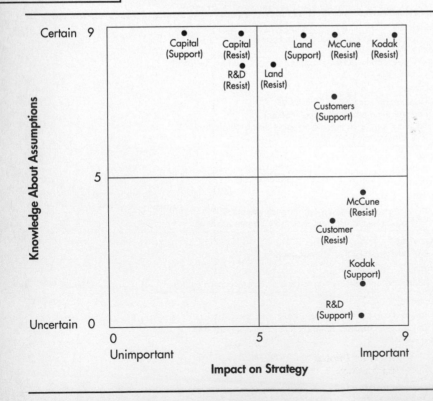

No manager is capable of dealing simultaneously with all the assumptions that underlie an organization's strategy. The assumption-rating graph helps by identifying the most critical assumptions. It also indicates how much is known about each assumption. Armed with this information, the manager can focus on those few assumptions that comprise supporting or limiting factors for the strategy. Certainty is a guide to the amount of knowledge the manager currently has about an assumption. Important but uncertain assumptions need to be investigated further. Importance is a guide to the amount of driving or resisting force an assumption exerts on the strategy. The importance rating is used in the assumption rating graph.

Referring to Figure 4.10, one can determine whether the stakeholders are supportive or will resist a proposed strategy. Stakeholders who are supportive and important will generally accept the proposed strategy, as shown in the upper right quadrant of Figure 4.11. Stakeholders in this quadrant who are expected to resist the strategy need to be convinced to change so that they are either neutral or accepting. The lower right quadrant covers both supporting and resisting stakeholders, because the level of their acceptance is uncertain. Their importance to the successful implementation of the strategy requires that management educate them to the benefits of accepting the strategy. The lower left quadrant covers those

---

FIGURE 4.11 | **Stakeholder Analysis Matrix**

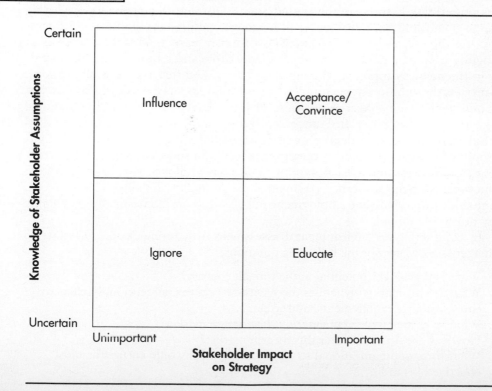

stakeholders whose acceptance is uncertain but who have a minimal impact on the outcome of the proposed strategy. This group can be ignored by management. Stakeholders in the upper left quadrant who are supportive can be ignored because their impact is unimportant. Stakeholders in this quadrant who are certain to resist the strategy need to be influenced by management in order to avoid possible interference with the strategy. Thus, we can see that the two right quadrants include the stakeholders who require the most attention. In some cases, the lower right quadrant is most important; in others, where there is strong opposition in the upper right quadrant, management must take remedial action to prevent interference with implementing the proposed strategy.

ASSESSING THE INTERNATIONAL ENVIRONMENT

Often strategic managers consider the external environment of the firm to be made up principally of those factors that are related to the national environment. However, as we will discuss more fully in Chapter 7, the global environment is becoming increasingly important. In some industries, it may be even more important than the national environment. Assessing the *international environment* is similar to assessing the domestic environment. An international assessment is more complex, however, because many more factors must be considered.

Doing business in a foreign country poses an entirely different set of problems than doing business in the United States. Distance, the difficulty of visiting foreign operations, and differences in language, culture, and political considerations are themselves barriers to entering a foreign market. Managers often have difficulty obtaining information about competitors and requirements for operating in the new environment. Personnel policies also differ; for example, in some countries the ethnic background of an individual may preclude his or her appointment to a managerial position. In Iran, Armenians are rarely appointed to key government posts. In France and Denmark, managers are often required to have an engineering degree or at least to have graduated from the right school or belong to the right professional society. In some countries, the government's permission must be obtained before an employee can be discharged. Sometimes, a huge severance payment must be made. To their chagrin, U.S. companies often find that employment policies that are domestically acceptable may not work abroad.

In conducting an environmental assessment of a foreign country, strategic managers seek to answer the following questions:

1. What is the market potential in the foreign country?
2. What are the market dynamics there with respect to competition, barriers to entry, resource requirements, and so on?
3. What risks are involved in entering this foreign market?
4. How can the firm best enter this foreign market?
5. What form of organizational structure and control would ensure the most effective operation?

REASONS FOR ENTERING FOREIGN MARKETS

A question that is frequently raised is why companies should be concerned with global strategies when there are ample opportunities at home. Vernon and Wells (1981) offered this answer: A firm should "go international" if there are profitable offensive or defensive functions it can perform in other countries. Among the possible objectives are (1) becoming a financial intermediary abroad, (2) becoming geographically diversified, (3) taking advantage of a technological lead, and (4) creating a market abroad. Let's look briefly at each of these objectives.

1. *Financial intermediary.* In this role, the multinational enterprise has access to foreign capital markets and can mitigate some of the problems of transferring funds from abroad where the dollar is devalued or there are differences in exchange rates.
2. *Geographic diversification.* The export of products to many nations increases the sales potential of the firm. By having a foreign subsidiary, the multinational firm may be able to overcome trade barriers, political considerations, transportation problems, or labor and material costs. Furthermore, a firm's presence in a foreign country can force its international competitors to protect that market, leaving the firm's home market more secure. Finally, geographic diversification enables the firm to make foreign investments that it can control.
3. *Technological lead.* In order to exploit a unique technological advantage that the firm may enjoy, it is often desirable to form a foreign subsidiary rather than to deal with the problems of exporting abroad. The larger market share obtained by successful penetration of foreign markets can also help cement the firm's lead at home.
4. *Foreign market.* Although it is possible to export or license products abroad, in many cases it is far better to create a foreign market that is under one's own control by expanding operations into one or more foreign countries.

As the world becomes smaller and distant countries more intertwined culturally and economically, people in business must reconsider assumptions about their markets. Domestic companies have significant opportunities to expand into foreign markets if they go about it in a manner compatible with the new cultures they enter. It is equally important to recognize that dangerous economic threats are mounting for firms that ignore foreign competition and fail to devise a strategy to deal with it.

Competing in international markets requires a different perspective than competing in domestic markets. How to enter a foreign market, how best to interact with customers, how to manage foreign joint ventures or subsidiaries effectively, and how to determine vulnerability and risk are examples of considerations pertinent to global competition.

International marketing operations cannot be undertaken by every business. For some, it may be a matter of survival to enter the global arena. For others, it may be a question of how to protect an existing domestic market from foreign competition. Few businesses, however, can afford to ignore the potential impact of foreign products or the growth potential that foreign markets offer.

The reason to go abroad is simple yet powerful: the world has become a single marketplace. National economics is being replaced by "globeconomics." Companies that ignore this fact find themselves in jeopardy. Today, over 70% of U.S.-made products face foreign competition.

Given these considerations, the question remains whether the entire business enterprise or just some part of it should become international. Rutenberg (1982) studied this problem and developed a checklist to help companies determine which aspects of the business should go international. His approach is based on three major considerations: (1) the current capabilities of the company's business units, (2) the nature of the external market, and (3) the potential costs and benefits of expansion. His list includes these questions:

1. What are the current capabilities of each business unit?
   a. Would it dilute management attention?
   b. Are products nontransferable?
   c. Are technology or marketing skills unique?
2. What are worldwide markets like?
   a. Do standards differ from those in the United States?
   b. Are most markets dominated by others?
   c. Is there market growth or potential?
   d. Are domestic markets threatened from abroad?
   e. Do tariffs or other restrictions exist abroad?
3. Can the business unit undertake expansion abroad?
   a. Is the unit already profitable and strong?
   b. Is technology unique, or is there a breakthrough?
   c. Does the unit have good domestic marketing skills?
   d. Does the unit have a strong market position in the United States?
   e. Is there real growth in demand for the products?
   f. Do the products have leadership positions in the United States?

Whereas Vernon and Wells's analysis helps the company establish objectives for international operations, Rutenberg's list is an aid to deciding which business units (that is, product lines and services) should be taken abroad.

RESEARCH ON FOREIGN MARKETS

Market potential is assessed by obtaining data about the foreign country and then determining the desirability of entering that country's market. Published sources of information regarding trade with foreign countries can be obtained from the consulates of those countries or from organizations that specialize in analyzing investment and trade in various countries around the world. Published sources are also listed in the Index to International Statistics, which can be found in large public and university libraries. Examples of such sources are

- *Business International:* One Dag Hammarskjold Plaza, New York, N.Y. 10017.
- *Eximbank Letter:* International Business Affairs Corp., Washington, D.C. 20571.
- *Foreign Exchange Review:* Manufacturers Hanover Trust Co., New York, N.Y. 10022.
- *Overseas Business Reports:* U.S. Department of Commerce, Washington, D.C.

Unfortunately, these sources of information seldom provide information on market potential or competitors' positions in the market. Obtaining the latter kind of information generally requires an in-country survey or information from foreign nationals or foreign organizations. The validity of the data may be subject to question because of the vested interests of such sources. Because of the uncertainty and sometimes the unreliability of information, organizations that are considering entering an international market may use either joint ventures or local agents to avoid the necessity of independent assessment and at the same time provide themselves with an opportunity to gain experience in a given country. In addition to gathering information, the company often has to work with legal counsel to be sure it does not violate specific laws, such as the Foreign Corrupt Practices Act.

Appendix A in Chapter 7 contains a list covering sources of information for international business. A description of the contents of each of the sources is included. Many institutions have direct access to these sources either through their library system or through computerized systems such as the National Trade Data Bank, which has over 30,000 entries covering a number of government agencies that deal with international trading.

ENVIRONMENTAL FORECASTING

The ability to forecast the future will become increasingly important in companies' efforts to plan appropriate strategies for a turbulent and complex world environment. The questions that strategic managers must consider are diverse: What will happen in the Middle East? Is a major world recession on the horizon? How will the break-up of what was formerly the Soviet Union affect the world economy? These and changing conditions of similar magnitude require a systematic response. Disappointed with using economics as the sole basis for forecasting (Linden, 1991), managers increasingly are looking for other ways to forecast the future meaningfully. Scenarios and the Delphi expert-opinion approach are two techniques that have been applied by the Center for Futures Research under the direction of Dr. Burt Manus. This organization formed the Club of 1000, which included a large panel of people actively engaged in understanding the future of the business environment. Using the data obtained from the Club of 1000, project director Selwyn Enzer covered areas with which business would be concerned. The topics covered included a forecast of when business might anticipate workable nuclear fusion, superbatteries, breakthrough pharmacy therapy, etc.

In their article "Manager's Guide to Forecasting," Georgoff and Murdick (1986) describe how managers at Compaq Computer Corporation chose the best combination of forecasting techniques to deal with difficult problems such as when IBM, Hewlett-Packard, and other companies would enter the portable computer market and how IBM's change in price would affect its potential profitability. They examined the problem of forecasting by taking into account the following considerations:

1. Time horizons—reasonable future period of time
2. Technical sophistication—expertise needed to forecast future events
3. Cost—the expense of updating forecasts
4. Data availability—currency, accuracy, and representativeness of data
5. Variability and consistency of data—relationships assumed among variables

Then they went on to examine four basic approaches that could be used for forecasting.

1. Judgment methods include the Delphi technique and scenario writing.
2. Data-oriented methods include market research, consumer surveys, and industrial and market surveys.
3. Time-series approaches include moving averages, exponential smoothing, and time-series extrapolation.
4. Casual models include correlation or regression models, leading-indicator forecasting, and econometric models.

The authors found that by combining forecasts, they were able to achieve results that were significantly more accurate than those yielded by any individual forecasting technique.

For many businesses, *quantitative forecasting* provides a basis on which current performance can be projected into future trends. Quantitative forecasting relies on the premise that the future can be predicted by identifying certain regularities in the past. This may be true in specific instances and for relatively short-term forecasting. For long-term forecasting, however, predictions based on past trends are not reliable. This is particularly true in times of instability, such as the months following the stock market crash of 1987. And it is becoming ever more true in the volatile global environment.

If managers cannot forecast critical events with certainty, then they need strategies to cope with uncertainty. Organizations today use sophisticated information and control systems to help them adapt to environmental changes. In addition, they make use of several *qualitative forecasting* techniques to overcome the shortcomings of quantitative approaches. Two key characteristics of qualitative techniques are that they (1) explicitly incorporate the subjective assessments of individuals or groups and (2) recognize that the decision makers have some influence on future developments.

One qualitative technique for predicting possible future events is the *Delphi method*. In this method, a panel of experts is queried repeatedly about possible developments in a particular area. In between rounds of inquiries, the experts review the responses of their fellow panelists. In most cases, the assessments converge very rapidly toward a set of assumptions that then becomes the basis for a prediction. The Delphi method is effective regardless of the forecast's planning horizon, but it is frequently very expensive.

Scenarios are often used in conjunction with the Delphi method. Scenarios are stories about the future that identify not only the likelihood of different new developments but also their impact and danger, as perceived by the individuals involved. This approach is discussed in detail in the next section.

In another qualitative forecasting technique, managers define future goals and objectives and then work backward to determine what assumptions are necessary to obtain the desired set of results. This method is not an attempt to forecast the performance of a particular strategy, but rather is an effort to predict the likelihood of its accomplishment, considering all the stakeholder and environmental assumptions necessary to make the strategy work.

SCENARIO WRITING

Scenarios have become increasingly powerful tools for developing strategic vision within organizations and for helping executives identify critical future paths. Peter Schwartz (1991), who has developed effective strategic-planning scenarios for a diverse set of organizations (including Royal Dutch/Shell, the White House, the EPA, Bell South, PG&E, Inland Steel, Volvo, Nissan, and London's International Stock Exchange) defines a scenario as: "a tool for ordering one's perceptions about alternative future environments in which one's decisions might be played out. Alternatively: a set of organized ways for us to dream effectively about our own future."

Two key characteristics of the scenario techniques are that they (1) explicitly incorporate the subjective assessments of individuals or groups and (2) recognize that the decision makers have some influence on future developments. A good scenario is based on facts and assumptions that have proved accurate in the past. Strategic planners then extrapolate the essence of these facts and assumptions to come up with alternative possible futures.

Some of the most useful information for strategic decision making comes from scenarios. Scenarios can be written or oral stories that describe the possibilities for a given set of conditions. They depict alternative futures and show how strategic decisions might lead to different outcomes. Scenarios help decision makers to "experience" the conditions imposed by these futures. They have the further advantage of providing a broad overview of the system and all its possibilities. Business scenarios can range from very simple depictions of future possibilities to highly sophisticated computer models.

One of the first companies to utilize scenarios in a significant way was Shell Oil. The article "Shell's 'Multiple Scenario Planning': A Realistic Alternative to the Crystal Ball" (1980) recounts how Shell's corporate planners described for their top management the bleak economic and political future for the 1980s. This forecast was based on an approach that forced managers continuously to question their assumptions about the future and to concentrate on qualitative arguments as a means of identifying significant and consistent patterns of economic and social development. In retrospect, one can see that this 1980 forecast was incredibly accurate. Shell does not try to forecast the future but rather examines reasonable potential happenings. Supplementing hard data with managers' opinions, Shell was one of the few companies that came through the 1973 energy crisis relatively unscathed: one of its scenarios predicted the possibility of a major disruption in energy supply.

Royal Dutch/Shell has continued to use scenarios as a planning technique that teaches managers how to think about unknown future possibilities. They separate what is predetermined from what is known or certain, and they separate what will happen from what cannot happen. The managers at Shell, based on the success of the 1973 scenarios, have come to accept this technique to cope with the necessity of constantly adapting and innovating in today's competitive environment (Wack, 1985). In a more recent article, Knowlton (1991) describes how Shell gets rich beating risk by utilizing scenarios. Over the years, Shell has developed a number of strategies to safeguard itself against unforeseen contingencies. With annual revenues of $107 billion in 1991, Shell is one of the world's largest industrial corporations. In addition to using scenarios, Shell also employs war gaming, which helps the company prepare for unexpected supply disruptions, accidents, or events such as the Gulf war. The two major scenarios on which they are working are called "Sustainable World" and "Global Mercantilism." These deal with major international economic disputes that can have environmental consequences. Regional conflicts in a destabilized world that has to deal with trade wars, recession, trading blocs, and similar uncertain events require the use of scenarios. Shell has clearly demonstrated the value of this approach by being one of the most profitable oil companies in spite of world turmoil.

Other industries have found that scenarios can be a useful tool in dealing with uncertain future environments. Southern California Edison introduced scenario planning. Mobasheri et al. (1989) described the need for scenario planning in order to have a meaningful resource plan. Based on a review of two decades of forecasting, the company was convinced that traditional techniques were inadequate. Top managers switched to writing scenarios wherein they could examine the implications of different conditions and the strategic responses required. The modern business environment is growing ever more chaotic, and understanding uncertainty and alternative actions has become a critical aspect of successful strategic planning.

Scenarios are used extensively by the Department of Defense to determine what military forces would be needed to deal with potential political and military conflicts. They are used in business to trace proposed strategies from their point of implementation through every outcome possible. A good scenario is based on facts and assumptions that have proved accurate in the past. Strategic planners then extrapolate the *essence* of these facts and assumptions to come up with versions of the future.

Scenarios help decision makers to "experience" the conditions imposed by these futures. They have the further advantage of providing a broad overview of the system and all its possibilities.

Most scenarios begin in the present. A series of assumptions is made about the present state of a system and about mechanisms likely to affect its future. The scenario spells out a future outcome for each alternative set of assumptions. All scenarios are intended to engage the imagination, stimulate discussion, and focus attention on critical strategic decisions. The following tasks are appropriate for almost all scenario writing.

SUMMARY

One of the most important determinants of an organization's success is its external environment. Some companies have quite effective internal operations and yet fail because of unfavorable conditions in the environment. Others are able to generate good or even outstanding profits, despite a number of internal problems, simply because they happen to be in the right place at the right time.

To be successful and to maintain a competitive advantage, an organization must constantly monitor events, trends, and stakeholder demands in its economic, political, competitive, geographic, social, and technological environments.

A comprehensive environmental analysis includes

1. A detailed examination of the stakeholders and the underlying assumptions being made about them
2. An overall scan of the environment
3. Assessment of the organization's vulnerability to environmental threats
4. Methods of predicting how the environment might change in the future

A stakeholder analysis is the key to understanding an organization's environment. By identifying the key parties and mapping important relationships among them, the strategic manager is in a position to see how changes that affect stakeholders will affect the firm. Environmental scanning complements and reinforces the stakeholder analysis by identifying trends and events that affect every element of the organization's business system.

Powerful strategies are based on exploiting differences between a firm and its competitors. Each competitor tends to inhabit a strategic segment of its industry, a segment whose boundaries define the limits of the competitor's advantage and profitability. The segment boundaries shift as competitors respond to one another's actions and the changing demands of the market. Segment boundaries are the main arenas of competition within the industry. The key task of strategic segmentation consists of identifying industry segments that the company should seek to enter and dominate. In the automobile industry, for example, a strategic segment might consist of luxury cars or sports cars. The goal of strategic segmentation is to convert differences among competitors into a sustainable competitive advantage for the company.

Around the segment boundaries are four main categories of competitive environments, which are defined according to the characteristics of businesses found there. To determine which strategic segment is most appropriate and to formulate strategies for sustaining competitive advantage within it, the manager needs to know whether competition at the boundaries is dominated by high-volume, stalemated, specialized, or fragmented businesses. A company can, for example, more easily develop a sustainable competitive advantage in a high-volume or specialized business environment than in a stalemated or fragmented one.

Another task of the strategic manager is to identify competitive forces that bear on the strategic segment. Among the twelve competitive forces are potential rate of industry growth, intensity of rivalry for domination of the strategic segment, and the bargaining power of customers. Analysis of the major competitive forces helps the strategic manager to determine whether a proposed strategic segment is a suitable one to enter.

Once a strategic segment has been targeted for entry, the task is to formulate strategies for segment domination. A company or business unit can seek to gain a competitive advantage by lowering cost, adding value or uniqueness to the product or service, specializing in a product or service for a very narrow market, intensifying its competitive tactics, or engaging in gamesmanship—manipulations resulting in temporary advantage. The goal of this analysis is to discover which strategy best suits the products and capabilities of the company.

All of these strategies can be applied to domestic or international strategic segments. International strategies, however, are necessarily more complex. The company must decide whether its products and organizational structure are suited to foreign markets and, if so, must devise strategies that match the company's strengths with the socioeconomic, political, and market characteristics of each foreign market it seeks to enter. Generally, foreign markets should be entered slowly, after much research and strategic planning.

Environmental forecasting is increasingly being used to determine how external forces affect strategic options. Methods include industry trend analysis, competitor intelligence, Delphi projections, and statistical forecasts.

One of the emerging forecasting approaches is scenario writing. The advantage of this approach is that there is more involvement by management, which leads to greater acceptance of the actions needed to carry out the strategy that is chosen. The variety of approaches for writing scenarios offer great flexibility and ensure that most managers will find one with which they feel comfortable.

REFERENCES AND SUGGESTIONS FOR FURTHER READING

Ackoff, Russell L. 1974. *Redesigning the future.* New York: Wiley.

Allan, Gerald. 1976. *A note on the Boston Consulting Group concept of competitive analysis and corporate strategy.* Boston: Intercollegiate Case Clearing House, Case #9-175-175.

Amano, Matt M. and Erik Larson. 1983. A longitudinal study of Japanese business expansion in southern California. Corvallis: School of Business, Oregon State University, pp. 1–12.

Bloom, Paul and Philip Kotler. 1975. Strategies for high-market-share companies. *Harvard Business Review* 53, no. 6, November–December.

Boston Consulting Group. 1979. *Specialization.* Boston: Boston Consulting Group.

Boston Consulting Group. 1974. *Segmentation and strategy.* Boston: Boston Consulting Group.

Buzzell, Robert D., Bradley T. Buzzell, and Gale and Ralph G. M. Sultan. 1975. Market share: A key to profitability. *Harvard Business Review* 58, no. 1.

Coyne, Kevin P. 1986. The anatomy of sustainable competitive advantage. *The McKinsey Quarterly,* Spring, pp. 50–65.

The dangerous folly called Theory Z. 1982. *Fortune,* May.

Davidson, W. H. 1982. *Global strategic management.* New York: Wiley.

Demaree, Allan T. 1992. What now for the U.S. and Japan? *Fortune,* February 10, pp. 80–95.

Doz, Y. Y. and C. K. Prahalad. 1981. Headquarters influence and strategic control of MNC's. *Sloan Management Review,* Fall.

Dreyfuss, Joel. 1988. How to deal with Japan. *Fortune,* June 6, pp. 107–118.

Emery, F. E. and E. L. Trist. 1965. The causal texture of organizational environments. *Human Relations* 18, pp. 21–32.

Fahey, Liam and William King. 1977. Environmental scanning for corporate planning. *Business Horizons* 20, no. 4.

Garvin, David A. 1987. Competing on the eight dimensions of quality. *Harvard Business Review,* November–December, pp. 101–109.

Georgoff, David M. and Robert G. Murdick. 1986. Manager's guide to forecasting. *Harvard Business Review,* January–February, pp. 110–120.

Ghemawat, Pankaj. 1986. Sustainable advantage. *Harvard Business Review,* September–October, pp. 53–58.

Gluck, Frederick W. 1982. Meeting the challenge of global competition. *The McKinsey Quarterly,* Autumn.

Green, Robert T. and Trina L. Larsen. 1987. Only retaliation will open up Japan. *Harvard Business Review,* November–December, pp. 22–28.

Haner, F. T. 1980. *Global business strategies for the 1980s.* New York: Praeger.

Hedley, Barry. 1977. Strategy and the "business portfolio." *Long-Range Planning,* February.

Hofer, Charles and Dan Schendel. 1978. *Strategy formulation: Analytical concepts.* St. Paul: West.

Hout, T., M. E. Porter, and E. Rudden. 1982. How global companies win out. *Harvard Business Review,* September–October.

Hurd, Douglas A. 1977. *Vulnerability analysis in business planning.* SRI International Research Report no. 593.

Japanese managers tell how their system works. 1977. *Fortune,* November.

Johnson, Chalmers A. 1982. *MITI and the Japanese miracle.* Stanford, Calif.: Stanford University Press.

Johnson, Richard Tanner and William G. Ouchi. September–October, 1974. Made in America (under Japanese management). *Harvard Business Review.*

Kahn, Herman and B. Bruce-Briggs. 1972. *Things to come.* New York: Macmillan.

Kichen, Steve. 1992. Annual report on American industry. *Forbes,* January 6, pp. 94–176.

Killing, P. J. 1982. How to make a global joint venture work. *Harvard Business Review,* May–June.

Kirkland, Richard I., Jr. 1988. Entering a new age of boundless competition. *Fortune,* March 14, pp. 40–48.

Knowlton, Christopher. 1991. Shell gets rich by beating risk. *Fortune,* August 26, pp. 79–82.

Kupfer, Andrew. 1988. How to be a global manager. *Fortune,* March 14, pp. 52–58.

Levitt, T. 1983. The globalization of markets. *Harvard Business Review,* May–June, pp. 92–102.

Linden, Dana Wechsler. 1991. Dreary days in the dismal science. *Forbes,* January 21, pp. 68–71.

Luke, Timothy and Stephen K. White. 1985. Critical theory, the information revolution, and an ecological path to modernity. *Critical theory and public life,* ed. John Foster. Cambridge, Mass.: M.I.T. Press.

McLuhan, Marshal. 1964. *Understanding media: The extensions of man.* New York: McGraw-Hill.

Main, Jeremy. 1992. How to steal the best ideas around. *Fortune,* October 19, pp. 102–106.

Main, Jeremy. 1984. The trouble with managing Japanese-style. *Fortune,* April 2, pp. 50–56.

Mason, Richard O. and Ian I. Mitroff. 1981. *Challenging strategic planning assumptions.* New York: Wiley.

Meeks, Fleming. 1991. Throwing away the crystal ball. *Forbes,* July 22, p. 60.

Micallef, J. V. 1981. Assessing political risk, *Columbia Journal of World Business,* Summer.

Mobasheri, Fred, Lowell H. Orren, and Fereidoon P. Sioshansi. 1989. Scenario planning at Southern California Edison. *Interfaces* 19, no. 5, September–October, pp. 31–44.

Morrow, Lance. 1992. Japan in the mind of America. *Time,* February 10, pp. 16–22.

Oh, T. K. and M. D. Oh. 1982. Measuring the extent and effects of Japanese-style management. Paper presented at the Academy of International Business, Washington, D.C., October.

Ohmae, Kenichi. 1990. *The borderless world: Power and strategy in the interlinked economy.* New York: Harper Press.

Ohmae, Kenichi. 1985. *Triad power: The coming shape of global competition.* New York: The Free Press.

Ohmae, Kenichi. 1982. *The mind of the strategist.* New York: McGraw-Hill.

Outlook 1992, state of the union. *U.S. News & World Report,* December 30, 1991/January 6, 1992, pp. 37–66.

Porat, Marc Uri. 1977. *The information economy: Definitions and measurement.* United States Office of Technology Special Publication 77-121(1). Washington, D.C.: Department of Commerce, Office of Telecommunications.

Peters, Thomas J. and Robert H. Waterman, Jr. 1982. *In search of excellence: Lessons from America's best-run companies.* New York: Harper & Row.

Porter, Michael E. 1990. *Competitive advantage of nations.* New York: The Free Press.

Porter, Michael E., ed. 1986. *Competition in global industries.* Boston: Harvard Business School Press.

Porter, Michael E. 1985. *Competitive advantage.* New York: The Free Press.

Porter, Michael E. 1980. *Competitive strategy.* New York: The Free Press.

Quelch, John A. and Edward J. Hoff. 1986. Customizing global marketing. *Harvard Business Review,* May–June, pp. 59–68.

Reich, Robert B. 1991. *The work of nations: Preparing ourselves for 21st century capitalism.* New York: Knopf.

Ronstadt, Robert and Robert J. Kramer. 1982. Getting the most out of innovation abroad. *Harvard Business Review,* March–April, pp. 94–99.

Rothschild, William E. 1979. Competitor analysis: The missing link in strategy. *Management Review,* July.

Rowe, Alan J. et al. 1989. *Strategic management.* Reading, Mass.: Addison-Wesley, p. 175.

Rugman, Alan M., Donald J. Lecraw, and Laurence D. Booth. 1985. *International business firm and environment.* New York: McGraw-Hill.

Rutenberg, D. P. 1982. *Multinational management.* Boston: Little, Brown.

Schein, Edgar H. 1987. *The art of managing human resources.* New York: Oxford University Press.

Schonberger, Richard J. 1982. Production workers bear major quality responsibility in Japanese industry. *Industrial Engineering,* December, pp. 34–40.

Schwartz, Peter. 1991. *The art of the long view.* New York: Doubleday.

Shell's multiple scenario planning: A realistic alternative to the crystal ball. 1980. *World-Business Weekly,* April 7.

South, Stephen E. 1981. Competitive advantage: The cornerstone of strategic thinking. *The Journal of Business Strategy,* Spring.

Special report—Japan's troubled future. 1987. *Fortune,* March 30.

Stalk, George Jr. and Thomas M. Hout. 1990. *Competing against time: How time-based competition is reshaping global markets.* New York: The Free Press.

Steiner, George A. and John B. Miner. 1977. *Management policy and strategy: Text, reading and cases.* New York: Macmillan. Chs. 7 and 8.

Stevenson, H. 1976. Defining corporate strengths and weaknesses. *Sloan Management Review* 17, no. 3.

Stewart, Thomas A. 1991. Brain power: How intellectual capital is becoming America's most valuable asset. *Fortune,* June 3, pp. 44–60.

A survey of Japan. 1987. *The Economist,* December 5.

Tanner Johnson, R. and W. G. Ouchi. 1974. Made in America (under Japanese management). *Harvard Business Review,* September–October, pp. 61–69.

Therrien, Lois. 1989. The rival Japan respects. *Business Week,* November 13, pp. 108–118.

Utterback, James. 1979. Environmental analysis and forecasting in *Strategic management: A new view of business policy and planning,* ed. Charles Hofer and Dan Schendel. Boston: Little, Brown.

Van Mesdag, Martin. 1987. Winging it in foreign markets. *Harvard Business Review,* January–February, pp. 71–74.

Vernon, Raymond and Louis T. Wells, Jr. 1981. *Manager in the international economy.* Englewood Cliffs, N.J.: Prentice-Hall.

Wack, Pierre. 1985. Scenarios: Uncharted waters ahead. *Harvard Business Review,* September–October, pp. 73–89.

Warsh, David. 1984. *The idea of economic complexity.* New York: Viking Press.

World Bank. 1987. *World development report.* New York: Oxford University Press.

Zuboff, Shoshana. 1988. *In the age of the smart machine: The future of work and power.* New York: Basic Books.

APPENDIX A

Example of a Foreign Environment: Japan

As competition between the United States and Japan intensifies, it tends to mask the important fact that the two nations really need each other. In many ways they have strong ties and admire one another (Morrow, 1992). The results of a survey conducted to determine what Americans admire about Japan and what the Japanese think about America are given in Tables 4A.1 and 4A.2. Both countries have obviously found things they admire about the other that are more important than the differences that tend to be exploited. The basic issue confronting Japan and the United States is how to live with the apparent differences and still benefit from the mutual interdependency that exists. The most significant bone of contention between the two countries is the large trade deficit that the United States has had with Japan. This condition leads to the obvious question of what will happen now with trade between the U.S. and Japan (Denaree, 1992). Nonetheless, companies such as Schick razors have 69.5% of the market share in Japan, compared to only 30.3% in the U.S. Coca-Cola has 33% of the Japanese market, compared with 41% for the U.S. market. Other companies such as Toys-R-Us and Apple Computer are making significant inroads into the Japanese market. Laying the groundwork is a complex task, but it is clear that Japan offers an opportunity for growth for those companies that can match the quality and price of Japanese products.

A number of U.S. companies are focusing on meeting the requirements of a very demanding Japanese consumer. One company that Japan respects is Motorola, which emphasizes strong R&D, built-in quality, and zealous service (Therrien, 1989). For example, defects have been cut from approximately 3,000 per million to less than 200. This achievement, of course, required significant investment in R&D, along with a passion for quality. With its sales approaching $1 billion in Japan, Motorola has achieved a significant return on its investment.

FIGURE 4A.1	What Japan and the United States Admire in Each Other

	U.S. Admires About Japan	Japan Admires About U.S.
Form of government	23%	63%
World leadership	31%	84%
Scientific/Technological accomplishments	82%	78%
Freedom of expression	27%	89%
Variety of lifestyles	25%	86%
Industriousness	88%	27%
Educational institutions	71%	48%
Leisure time for workers	15%	88%
Respect for family life	75%	87%

FIGURE 4A.2	Comparison of Japanese's and Americans' Views of Each Other

	Americans' View of Japanese	Japanese's View of Americans
Friendly	59%	64%
Competitive	94%	50%
Devoted to fair play	35%	43%
Lazy	4%	21%
Hardworking	94%	15%
Prejudiced	53%	41%
Violent	19%	23%
Crafty	69%	13%
Poorly educated	12%	21%

GLOBAL MANAGEMENT IN THE 1990s

In an article about global management for the 1990s, *Fortune* interviewed a number of senior executives, soliciting their views on a global economy poised for expansion. New technologies, productivity, integration of world markets, political and economic cooperation, and global alliances have set the stage for an era of unprecedented growth. Companies are exploring new management strategies to deal with future opportunities. The following comments suggest how various leaders whose firms are important in the Japanese economy are preparing for a global business environment.

Thomas F. Jordan—Du Pont, Japan

"This is the most competitive market in the world. Customers are demanding, quality standards are excruciatingly precise, and the culture is sometimes difficult to penetrate. But if you make it, the profits can be very attractive, and you'll have established a significant global reputation for yourself. Furthermore, you can use Japan as a base for expanding business in the Asia–Pacific region."

Rainer H. Jahn—Mercedes-Benz, Japan

"Japan is a tough market. Japanese consumers are among the most demanding in the world."

William J. Weisz—Motorola

"Cracking the Japanese market wasn't easy. After some initial resistance, Motorola was able to establish a string of joint ventures in the 1970s with such Japanese companies as Toshiba and NTT to manufacture and market radio communications equipment and semi-conductors."

Hiroshi Saito—Nippon Steel

"We have always been concerned with the environment. Over the past twenty years, we invested about $3 billion in antipollution facilities, and from 1973 to 1990 we spent about $1.5 billion on energy conservation. We have also trained environmental engineers and provided environmental technology to others overseas."

Joichi Aoi—Toshiba

"The nature of global competition is changing. The technological and financial resources required to develop many of tomorrow's markets are beyond the resources of most big international firms, and this is leading to new corporate alliances. That, in turn, is accelerating the trend toward globalization among Japanese companies."

Tsutomu Kanai—Hitachi

"Today's high technologies tend to be integrated in many fields. Manufacturers are expected to offer software together with hardware and to provide complete systems as well as industrial products and components."

Koji Matsuno—Hitachi Metals

"The global business structure has been changing as well as our own. In the past, Japan tended to export to get itself out of trouble, but that is not possible today. Overseas markets demand investment, not exports. Protectionism is a serious concern, particularly from the newly industrialized countries. The entire global atmosphere is different and there is no single cure available."

Yoshio Tateisi—Omron

"We need to focus more closely on our own specialty technologies, shift to new growth areas, develop new technologies and generally improve the efficiency of our operations from the plant to corporate headquarters."

Tadahiro Sekimoto—NEC

"Technology, especially in the area of electronic miniaturization and artificial intelligence, is progressing so fast that the barriers between man and machine are rapidly disappearing."

Toichi Takenaka—Takenaka

"The companies that will survive are those that already have established the administrative structures and technologies to keep productivity high and costs low. Some relief can be sought in overseas markets, but the job of cost control must be done at home."

Susumu Yamaji—Japan Airlines

"JAL's concern with global warming is just one example of the company's commitment to behaving like a responsible member of the global society—a good corporate citizen."

JAPAN'S SOCIOECONOMIC AND TECHNOLOGICAL ENVIRONMENT

The Japanese economy has been undergoing a radical transformation. In 1983, Japan exported 12–13% of its gross national product (Britain exported 20%). Japan held 165,000 patents, compared to 62,098 held by the United States and 28,683 held by West Germany. Capital spending was almost identical to that by comparable industries in the United States, even though Japan is a smaller country.

In 1987, though still one of the strongest industrial countries in the world, Japan began to re-examine its position. Fear and uncertainty tempered the exuberance that existed in the past. Profits were down by 25% in 1986 and by 26% in 1987. Japanese steelmakers faced a loss of $2.2 billion and planned severe layoffs. Unemployment, while low by world standards, was the highest yet at 2.8%, and Japan's cost advantage had slipped compared to that of the United States and West Germany. With its industrial slowdown, an aging population, and more restless youth, Japan is facing difficult decisions ahead. Most of the country's raw materials have to be imported; virtually all of Japan's supply of crude oil comes from abroad. Technological progress has put Japan on a par with (and in certain areas even ahead of) the industrialized West, but the country's labor reserves are nearing exhaustion. Low wages combined with a high rate of inflation have produced a standard of living that fades in comparison with the country's degree of economic success. And, by all accounts, Japan endures the most polluted environment in the world.

Despite these problems, the country is forging ahead on most fronts. Japan spends approximately three times as much as the United States does on industrial research and 20% more on services. Probably the most significant change in Japan's grand strategy is a planned shift to an information economy. Sugiichiro Watari, past president of Toshiba Corporation, explained that Japanese companies are moving toward a new corporate strategy based on "integration, intelligence, and information" (*Fortune,* 1987). The economic aspects of the information society depend to a large extent on Japan's computer industry and factory automation. Japanese mainframes had achieved parity with those in the United States by 1980. Japan now leads the U.S. in the race to develop a supercomputer and is working on a fifth-generation computer language, while the United States still uses the fourth-generation language. Japan is also going all out in its development of artificial intelligence and for a long time has led the U.S. in the field of robotics. Because domestic demand is now leading the Japanese economy and should remain strong through the year 2000, both trade and current-account surpluses should remain enormous for years to come (*Economist,* 1987).

How has Japan's socioeconomic environment contributed to its success in the global marketplace? The following characteristics are embedded in Japanese business culture.

1. The importance of harmony in the national culture
2. Unquestioning acceptance of standards of performance
3. Loyalty on the part of employer and employee that often leads to lifetime employment in one firm
4. Slow performance evaluations and promotions
5. Careful decision making that gives the appearance of consensus
6. Ability to adapt readily to new conditions because of support by the government
7. High level of savings: about 20% of the GNP
8. Willingness to carry out all decisions
9. Importance of ritual, as typified by the tea ceremony
10. Emphasis on religion and philosophy
11. Ownership of up to 25% of a company by banks that provide financing to those companies at attractive rates, typically 5–7% interest
12. High value placed on technological development

The Role of Government in Japanese Business   Explanations of Japan's great economic power have focused on Japanese management techniques or on the cultural aspects of Japanese society that cannot be copied. Yet neither of these two factors seem to have been as critical as the collaboration between the Japanese government and private industry (Johnson, 1982). This collaboration results in a "state-guided market system" dedicated to rapid growth. According to Johnson, the United States is a "regulatory" state, in which the government merely sets the rules for conduct and attempts to provide a favorable business climate. Japan, on the other hand, is a "developmental" state, in which the government takes a leading role in determining strategies for national economic growth and controlling investment and technology accordingly.

Although the Japanese government has the power to exert considerable pressure on companies, the pressure is not in the form of regulations. Antitrust regulation, for example, barely exists. This made it possible for Japanese automobile companies to develop a common design for antipollution equipment, a collaborative action that would be illegal in the United States. The U.S. economy is regulated by politicians who are replaced every few years, whereas economic policy in Japan is strongly influenced by career technocrats at the Ministry of International Trade and Industry (MITI). As a result, the Japanese economy is planned on a long-term basis, which promotes continuity and growth. As is the case in many European countries, companies are typically owned by banks, not by individual shareholders. Bank ownership is made possible by a staggering savings rate that is approximately 20% of the GNP, compared to less than

5% in the United States. A number of economists believe that the propensity to save is, in the final analysis, responsible for Japan's phenomenal growth (see, for example, Bronfenbrenner, 1970).

Homogeneity and Social Conformity   Beneath the surface, Japan is still a deeply traditional and conformist society. Individualism, in the Western sense, is no more an ideal in contemporary Japan than it ever was. In fact, the Japanese word for individualism, *kojinshugi,* connotes selfishness rather than independence. Even such marginal expressions of nonconformism as the *zoko* ("tribe") phenomenon—youths wearing outlandish gear and dancing in the streets—is in keeping with the Japanese tendency to seek security within a group. While social criticism is not as unthinkable as in the past, it is not readily accepted.

Sooner or later, Japan will have to shift its orientation from impressive economic growth to genuine social welfare, a process that simply cannot come from the top. The need to face up to the ever-increasing gap between economic prosperity and social progress will put Japan's economy to a test more difficult than conquering export markets or producing products of ever-increasing quality.

Competition   The aggressiveness that Japanese companies display abroad is an extension of their competitiveness at home. Although Japan is critically dependent on exports to pay for its imports of raw materials, surprisingly few products are developed solely for the export market. On the contrary, many of the country's most competitive products abroad had to weather a tough domestic market first. In fact, the demanding Japanese consumer may well be responsible for the high quality of Japanese products. The Japanese demand for quality sometimes borders on perfectionism, and many of the Japanese cars exported to the United States would be unfit for the Japanese domestic market.

Most Japanese companies use an ethnocentric strategy for penetrating a foreign market. The Japanese domestic market serves as a perfect testing ground for the production and sale of high-volume, low-cost items. Once economies of scale and benefits of the experience curve are established, they are used to undercut competition in foreign markets and attain dominance in the low-price end of the market. After the market has been penetrated, the company can work its way into more complex and more profitable market segments. This scenario unfolded in the electronics and automobile industries. Today, Japanese companies are exporting many high-priced, top-of-the-line models. They began, in the 1970s, by exporting less expensive bottom-of-the-line models.

The Japanese are willing to diversify to gain a competitive edge. Yamaha Companies, for example, produce many different products. They started with pianos, then moved into propellers, motorcycles, woodwinds, snowmobiles, and now jet skis. Finally, Japanese competitiveness is fueled by determination. Aggressiveness on the part of Japanese top managers has made Japan into one of the strongest industrial powers the world has seen.

ORGANIZATIONAL CHARACTERISTICS OF JAPANESE COMPANIES

One of the most common misconceptions about Japanese companies is that they use a high degree of participative decision making and reach decisions only after long and laborious deliberations that involve employees at several layers of the corporation hierarchy and end in consensus. As Kenichi Ohmae (1982), a consultant with many of Japan's best-known companies, has pointed out, nothing could be further from the truth. Decentralized decision making is a characteristic of Japan's giant trading companies, but this organizational pattern exists more out of necessity than by design.

Consensus is not the means but rather the end result of the decision-making process in most Japanese corporations. What Americans mistakenly call consensus management may merely be a means of ensuring that all levels of management are informed and prepared to execute the decision once it is made. What really happens is the process of *nemawashi,* through which an unofficial understanding is reached before any official decision is announced. In U.S. companies, the closest thing to this kind of decision making is the common practice of leaking information, be it correct or incorrect, in order to test responses or prepare employees to accept an upcoming major decision. In any case, unofficial information comes from the top, not the bottom. The Japanese can more openly engage in this type of office politics because of (1) the greater willingness of Japanese subordinates to conform with whatever comes from the top, and (2) the fact that many jobs are secure for life. Thus what may appear to be management by consensus is really management by compliance.

Most Japanese companies are run by a single man or a small group that makes all the crucial decisions. In fact, Japanese companies are much more autocratic than most people believe. As Schein (1981) noted, autocratic systems can outproduce democratic systems, at least in the short run. And high productivity, even when achieved by autocratic methods, can build high morale.

In companies such as Matsushita, Sony, Honda, Yoshida, Yamaha, and Casio, the CEO is personally responsible for all liabilities in the company and thus is likely to make final decisions personally. Subordinates learn how to "play to" the chief executive's style.

A study reported by Amano and Larson (1983) revealed how restrictive life in the Japanese firm can be. For example,

- To be hired by a major firm, a candidate must have graduated from a top-ranked university.
- All key candidates are male.
- Preference is given to men with no prior employment.
- Non-Japanese workers, such as Koreans and Chinese, are excluded. Ancestry is traced to country of birth.
- Moderate and harmonious employees are sought.
- Promotion depends on degree of conformity, loyalty, and harmony. Individual freedom and private life are given up because of politics, factions, and indoctrination.
- The elite retire at age 55, and those who are incompetent are fired or reassigned to undesirable posts.

DECISION-MAKING STYLE OF JAPANESE MANAGERS

How closely can the effectiveness of a particular management style be related to the cultural, sociopolitical, and economic framework within which it is practiced? Critics of Japanese-style management often argue that superimposing the Japanese style on U.S. business would be difficult because of the obvious differences in culture between the two countries. Yet management style is not simply a matter of principle—it is also a matter of degree. To assume that there is only one right management style for any U.S. company is tantamount to ignoring the considerable variety that exists among companies.

Several Japanese companies that have opened manufacturing plants in the United States have proved that their management techniques can be transplanted successfully. Tanner and Ouchi (1974), reported on 20 Japanese companies operating in the United States, many of which were outperforming American companies in the same industries. Schonberger (1982) demonstrated how manufacturing concepts such as just-in-time (JIT) provisioning of manufacturing inventories or quality circles can be successfully adapted without a complete changeover to Japanese-style management. Thus while the Japanese system may admittedly be unacceptable as a whole, parts of it may be useful in developing more effective management of a particular U.S. company.

A study conducted in the early 1980s explored the views of American and Japanese employees of several Japanese-owned companies in Southern California (Oh, 1982). A series of open-ended interviews with American personnel directors and top Japanese managers revealed the following specific business practices.

1. *Decision making by consensus.* In no company was consensus actually used. Group input was solicited, and the issues brought up by the top management were discussed.
2. *Concern for employees.* Japanese top executives avowed concern for their employees as people. American personnel managers believed this concern to be no greater than that of executives in American firms.
3. *Job rotation.* No firms in the sample practiced job rotation.
4. *Evaluation and promotion.* Americans felt that they would not reach a top position because of Japanese control of their firms.
5. *Groupism.* Most companies did not practice groupism. It was found incompatible with American employees' values of individualism, independence, privacy, and professionalism.
6. *Job security.* In general, the companies tried to avoid layoffs but did not rule them out. All the firms sampled were willing to dismiss unsatisfactory employees.

From another perspective, the style of Japanese managers can be seen in their manner of thinking. Rowe (1989) drew the following conclusions after studying a group of Japanese managers and American managers in high-technology firms. The American manager is highly analytic, uses logic and careful analysis, and is concerned with short-term results. The Japanese manager, by contrast, is much more concerned with the future and harmonious relations with people. Saving face is a basic value.

Japan is perhaps the premier example of a foreign market that American companies are trying to enter, but Europe 1992 can also offer new opportunities. Though there has been some success, entering the Japanese market is largely problematic because of Japan's protectionist policies. For more than a decade, during which time the U.S. trade deficit has soared to new heights, Japan has promised to open its markets. The reason that Japan will not open up, according to Green and Larsen, is that the products we seek to export are precisely the ones that Japan is trying to protect (Green and Larsen, 1987). The answer, then, is for the United States to adopt a new trade policy that is retaliatory rather than protectionist and that requires carefully targeting Japanese markets. Japan protects its automobile and electronics industries through its Ministry of International Trade and Industry. The Ministry uses every means possible to prevent local businesses from importing products. Customs procedures, restrictive standards, unrealistic certification requirements, and discriminatory procurement policies all act as barriers to imports.

Protectionist policies focus on one product rather than on one country. Therefore, the United States has considered placing a tariff on all foreign car imports without singling out Japan. The U.S. could also nurture key competing industries through subsidies, low-cost loans, tax relief, R&D grants, and exclusion of imports. While these strategies seem like a radical departure from free trade, allowing free trade in one direction alone has had devastating effects on U.S. industries and the trade deficit.

CHAPTER FIVE

Capability-based Strategy

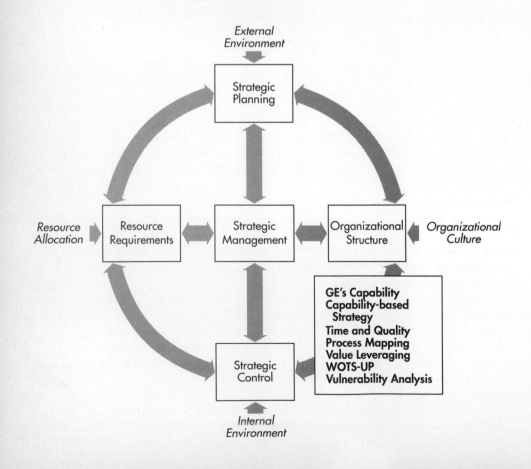

Chapter 1 A Framework for Strategic Management	Chapter 2 Strategic Analysis	Chapter 3 Strategic Visioning, Goals, Ethics, and Social Responsibility	Chapter 4 The Competitive Environment	Chapter 5 Capability-based Strategy	Chapter 6 Market Dynamics and Sustainable Competitive Advantage
How to approach strategic management	*Application of strategic analysis*	*Understanding vision, values, ethics*	*Coping with competitive forces, stakeholders*	*Assessing company capability, timeliness, quality*	*Determining trends, gap analysis, and market dynamics*

Chapter 7 Strategy in a Global Environment	Chapter 8 Financial Planning and Competitive-Cost Analysis	Chapter 9 Entrepreneurship, Mergers and Acquisitions, Restructuring, and the Service Sector	Chapter 10 Leadership Factor in Strategy and Implementing Strategic Change	Chapter 11 Information Technology and Future Directions in Strategy
Assessing global trade, foreign markets, monetary exchange	*Preparing a financial plan and competitive-cost analysis*	*Importance of small business, entrepreneurs, restructuring*	*Strategy implementation, leadership, culture*	*Information technology, trends, new management*

INTRODUCTION

Successful strategies for the 1990s will rely more on capabilities, which are often difficult for competitors to detect and imitate. Strategies are becoming more "intelligent." Advantage will dwell within the processes and behaviors of the organization: in the responsiveness of its operations, in its management of new customer needs, in its organizational simplicity and flexibility, in the innovativeness of its people, and in its use and management of information technology. In short, responsiveness is becoming a key success factor.

Arthur Shorin, CEO of Topps Company, recognizes the importance of timeliness because he is in the baseball card business, wherein "hot items" can come and go in a matter of weeks. For example, in six weeks Topps produced the cards describing the Gulf war weaponry. By staying agile, Topps has managed to outpace all its rivals (Teitelbaum, 1992).

Capability-based strategies are founded on the notion that internal resources and core competencies derived from distinctive capabilities provide the "strategy platform" that underlies a firm's long-term profitability. Evaluation of these capabilities begins with a company capability profile, which examines the company's strengths and weaknesses in four key areas: managerial, marketing, financial, and technical. Then a WOTS-UP analysis is carried out to determine whether the company has the strengths necessary to deal with specific forces in the external environment. This analysis enables managers to identify (1) external threats and opportunities and (2) distinct competencies that can ward off the threats and compensate for weaknesses. The picture revealed by the WOTS-UP analysis helps to suggest which type of strategy, or strategic thrust, the firm should use to gain competitive advantage. This can be described diagrammatically as shown in Figure 5.1.

A new threat to traditional organizations is the emergence of capability-based competitors relying on total quality and time-based responsiveness. These competitors often develop completely new and different delivery mechanisms and organizations. In order to ensure that the core competencies reach the customer with maximum impact, they institutionalize time and quality as critical variables in their operations. They achieve a faster and better operation by examining the whole process rather than improving many individual phases. As a consequence, they gain substantial and lasting benefits.

The new rules of strategy are dictating a shift to competing on capabilities. Stalk, Evans, and Shulman (1992) have identified four principles that serve as guidelines to achieving capability-based competition.

1. Corporate strategy does not depend on products or markets but on business processes.
2. Key strategic processes are needed to consistently provide superior value to the customer.
3. Investment is made in capability, not functions or SBUs.
4. The CEO must champion the capability-based strategy.

Following up on this latter point, they claim that "a CEO's success in building capabilities will be the chief test of management skill in the 1990s."

FIGURE 5.1   **Defining Core Competencies**

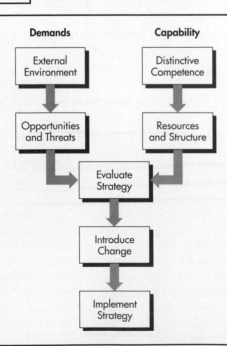

ILLUSTRATIVE CASE: GE'S NEW CAPABILITY-BASED STRATEGY

One firm that relies on capability-based strategy is General Electric, a company that has pioneered strategic planning and other management techniques and is in the process of revolutionizing U.S. management practices once again. This large, diversified company with a highly developed corporate management system is undergoing significant cultural change in order to become a more centrally managed firm. The key focus is on strengthening the firm's skills and resources in order to build a stronger foundation for its strategy.

The results of this effort are already showing. GE's new philosophy of running things more as a small business has boosted its productivity growth in the early 1990s to several times that of other large U.S. manufacturing firms. In 1990 the company's sales growth was $3.8 billion, more than the *total* sales of all but the largest U.S. companies, and with $4.4 billion in profits, it was second only to Exxon in earnings.

GE's new approach, which is bound to be emulated by many other companies in the 1990s, is based on speed, simplicity, and involvement of people at all levels in the organization. The three main management thrusts of this approach at GE are

1. *Work-out*, a way of getting employees involved in the decision-making process
2. *Best practices*, emulating the way other companies have sustained their competitive advantage
3. *Process mapping*, simplifying the way things are done, removing bottlenecks, and making the delivery system more effective

Work-out is essentially a forum where employees work on problems together in order to winnow unnecessary work out of their jobs. A group of 40 to 100 people from all ranks and functions within an organization gather for a three-day session. In many cases, some customers and suppliers are also invited to participate. The group members' main task is to develop as many practical solutions as possible to eliminate waste and to prune unnecessary tasks, meetings, paper-

work, and approvals from their daily work. The manager typically opens the proceedings and then leaves.

The group breaks into five or six work-out teams that for a day and a half list their problems, look for possible solutions, and prepare presentations. On the third day the manager returns, together with other senior executives, to listen to the groups' findings. The rules are such that the executives can make only one of three responses to the workout teams' proposals: agree immediately, say no, or charter a new team that will define a particular issue in more detail by a given date. This third day of the work-out session can be a grueling experience for managers. They often have to listen to complaints that have been built up over a long period of time.

The *best-practices* step is basically to ask, "What is the secret of success of companies who over many years were able to maintain faster productivity growth than their competitors?" For this purpose a group of GE executives, together with an outside consultant, screened a large number of candidates. Of the 20–30 companies examined, about half required more thorough joint fact-finding before conclusions could be reached.

The results of these in-depth comparisons were surprisingly similar. Almost all of the best-practice companies (such as AMP, Chaparral Steel, Ford, Hewlett-Packard, Motorola, Xerox, and some Japanese companies) emphasized the management process rather than the specific functions. Instead of considering individual departments or tasks, they focused on optimizing cooperation along the entire value-adding chain, including suppliers, and on being faster than their competitors in new-product introduction and delivery. Unlike most other companies, GE has installed measurement systems that include indicators of the effectiveness of its processes, not just the outcomes.

The best-practices effort provided an empirical basis for changing the way things were managed and measured at GE. Now the company regularly shares new ideas with other leading

GE'S NEW CAPABILITY-BASED STRATEGY, CONTINUED

companies, and it stresses the superiority of continuous improvement to one-time measurements.

Process mapping offers a set of tools to bring issues systematically to the surface and provide benchmarks. All the relevant functions along the value-adding chain are used to make a flow chart of each and every step that goes into creating or making a product. Process mapping can be a very difficult task for management, because what really happens often differs substantially from the way it was planned or written down in a company manual.

When a process is mapped, the participants often have developed, for the first time, the capability to manage the entire operation in a holistic way. The results of this approach, which will be described later in this chapter in the section on time-based management, are often quite different from the outcomes of traditional management practices. The results that GE has achieved by applying this approach have led to drastic improvements in several of its operations.

Top management at GE realizes that it will be a long time—perhaps a decade—before this new philosophy fully takes hold at the company. As this new management approach and its successes at GE become better known, the company may well not only change its own corporate culture by the year 2000 but may also start a revolution in management thinking throughout U.S. business.

FORMULATING A CAPABILITY-BASED STRATEGY

Traditionally, strategy has been defined as the process of aligning the internal capability of an organization with the external demands of its environment, as shown in Figure 5.1. The process has focused on the changes in the environment that led to opportunities and threats to which the firm had to adjust. The internal process of alignment to these changes was often taken for granted. Yet a number of studies have shown that differences in profitability *within* industries are more important than such differences *between* industries; that is, some companies consistently thrive in difficult environments while others do not succeed even though their industry is very healthy.

Recently, as the example of GE shows, the capability-based strategy has become prominent as a means of developing new sources of competitive advantage. Capability-based strategies, sometimes referred to as the resource-based view of the firm, are determined by (a) those internal resources and capabilities that provide the platform for a firm's strategy and (b) those resources and capabilities that are the primary source of profit for the firm. A key management function is to identify what resource gaps need to be filled in order to maintain a competitive edge where these capabilities are required.

Several levels can be established in defining the firm's overall strategy platform (see Figure 5.2).

At the bottom of the pyramid are the basic *resources* a firm has compiled over time. They can be categorized as technical factors (patents, brand identity, manufacturing skills), competitive factors (economies of scale, market share), managerial factors (organizational culture, speed of response to changing conditions), and financial factors (access to capital, cost-competitiveness). Taken together, these

FIGURE 5.2 | **Strategy Platform**

four factors establish the advantage base of the firm (Figure 5.3). We will examine the advantage base in detail in this chapter.

Core competencies, the second layer of the strategy platform, can be defined as the unique combination of the resources and experience of a particular firm. It takes time to build these core competencies, and they are difficult to imitate. Motorola, the maker of integrated circuits, mobile phones, automotive electronics, and other high-tech products, has succeeded in creating a flexible combination of its basic technologies together with generic management skills. This has allowed the company to be very competitive in a range of applications of its technologies and to stay ahead of its competition with innovative products. Other examples of firms that have succeeded in developing strong core competencies include Wal-Mart (fast-response systems in its distribution chain, combined with decentralized information flows), 3M (superior know-how in adhesive and coating technologies, combined with creative and fast new-product development), Honda (technical excellence in four-stroke engines, combined with flexible production), and Procter

FIGURE 5.3 | **Company Resource and Advantage Base**

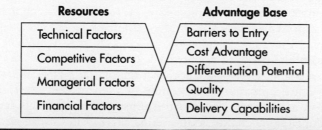

& Gamble (highly developed ability to understand market and customer trends, combined with strong management of international brands).

What seems to distinguish many of these successful firms is that they were able to combine strong technological skills or other know-how with unique and fast ways of (re)generating these skills and delivering them to the customer. Critical to sustaining these core competencies are their

1. *Durability*. Their lifespan is longer than individual product or technology life cycles, as are the lifespans of the resources used to generate them, including people.
2. *Intransparency*. It is difficult for competitors to imitate these competencies quickly.
3. *Immobility*. These capabilities and resources are difficult to transfer.

Successful firms have established effective mechanisms to safeguard and replenish these core competencies. At the same time, however, they are keenly aware that these core competencies will lose their strength if they are not constantly maintained and upgraded. Therefore, capability-based competitors realize that how they manage their processes is a critical component of their competitive edge. Excellence in delivering core competencies to the customer often requires organizational delivery mechanisms that are based on

1. *Speed of response*—the ability to preempt the competition with faster new-product introduction or a faster, more responsive service.
2. *Quality*—this increases customer satisfaction and allows the firm to win market share.
3. *Responsiveness to the customer*—the ability to better understand customer and competitive developments.
4. *Team organization*—the ability to be faster and more effective by breaking traditional functional departmentalization.
5. *Organizational learning*—the ability to learn through shared insights, models, knowledge, and experience and the ability to increase know-how and competencies within the firm.

PepsiCo is an interesting case in point. Besides its well-known cola brand, the company owns Frito-Lay, the highly profitable salty snack seller, as well as three restaurant chains: Pizza Hut, Taco Bell, and Kentucky Fried Chicken. PepsiCo has enjoyed some of the fastest growth in the food industry over the last ten years, and it is one of the most profitable companies in this industry. CEO Wayne Calloway jokingly identifies three main ingredients in PepsiCo's recipe for success: "Love change. Learn to dance. And leave J. Edgar Hoover behind." Learning to dance is Calloway's colloquialism for dealing with customers in radically new ways. PepsiCo's salespeople, for example, are making more daily sales contacts with customers than the representatives of any other company in the world. Leaving J. Edgar Hoover behind means managing those people in the "hands-off" way that the former FBI chief detested.

The most important element in PepsiCo's success is its passion for change. PepsiCo often revamps operations, marketing, or management even when things look fine, simply to keep a step ahead of the competition and retain its lead in its organizational delivery mechanism. Its main rule in making these changes is

"Simplify, simplify, simplify." Like other companies that compete on capabilities, PepsiCo concentrates on managing key delivery processes rather than on the measurement and refinement of goals. The emphasis is on delivering value to the customer, not on functional excellence.

The implications of a capability-based approach to strategy formulation are obvious. An analysis of the profit-generating potential of resources and capabilities shows that preservation and regeneration of these capabilities play a vital role in strategy development. The essence of strategy formulation, from this perspective, is to design a strategy that makes the most effective use of the firm's resources and core competencies and then to concentrate on developing the firm's mechanisms for effectively delivering these capabilities to its customers.

VALUE CHAIN ANALYSIS

Value chain analysis is derived from systems theory. Every entity on the stakeholder map (see page 138 in Chapter 4) is considered to be a system. Technically, each entity is a subsystem of the complex environment depicted by the stakeholder map. Each system receives inputs, performs transformation processes on them, and sends them as outputs to other systems on the map. These three activities are carried out via the *value chain*.

Input, transformation, and output involve the acquisition and consumption of resources—money, labor, materials, equipment, buildings, land, administration, and management.

How value chain activities are carried out determines costs and affects profits. A firm that seeks a cost leadership position reduces the amount of resources it consumes and the price it pays for them. Decisions governing each activity in the value chain determine the nature and quality of the output. A firm that seeks to gain an advantage through differentiation does so by performing its value chain activities, particularly transformation of the input, differently from or better than its competitors. Improving value chain functions is one of the best means of achieving competitive advantage.

Most organizations engage in hundreds—even thousands—of activities in the process of converting inputs to outputs. These activities can be classified generally as either primary or support activities that all businesses must undertake in some form. Figure 5.4 shows the primary and support activities of the value chain.

PRIMARY ACTIVITIES

According to Porter (1985), the primary activities are

1. *Inbound logistics*. Inbound logistics involve relationships with suppliers and include all the activities required to receive, store, and disseminate inputs. Materials handling, warehousing, inventory control, and vehicle scheduling are examples of these activities.
2. *Operations*. Operations are all the activities required to transform inputs into outputs (products and services). Machining, packaging, assembling, maintaining, and testing are examples of operations.

FIGURE 5.4	Activities Assessed by Means of Value Chain Analysis

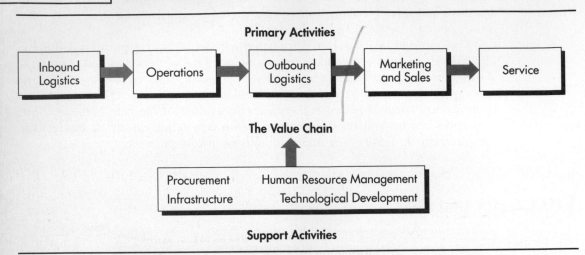

3. *Outbound logistics.* Outbound logistics include all the activities required to collect, store, and distribute the output. These activities focus primarily on the delivery of outputs to buyers. Warehousing, materials handling, delivery operations, shipping, order processing, and scheduling are examples of outbound logistics.
4. *Marketing and sales.* Marketing and sales activities inform buyers about products and services, induce buyers to purchase them, and facilitate their purchase. These activities focus primarily on the informational relationships established between the firm and its potential buyers. Pricing, selection of a distribution channel, channel management, advertising, promoting, selling, proposing, and quoting are examples of marketing and sales activities.
5. *Service.* Service includes all the activities required to keep the product or service working effectively for the buyer after it is sold and delivered. Training, consulting, installing, repairing, supplying parts, and fine tuning are examples of service.

Every firm performs all five primary activities to some degree and must ensure having a means for dealing with each. Which are emphasized, however, depends on the nature of the business. McDonald's and Disneyland, for example, have little need for proficiency in outbound logistics, but each must be very good at operations and at marketing and sales. Morton's Salt, on the other hand, must excel in outbound logistics in order to move its product into grocery stores efficiently. Computer and software firms increasingly must stress service in order to remain competitive.

Many of Polaroid's problems in the early 1980s derived from its operations (see the second illustrative case in Chapter 1). Polavision was an inferior product for which the company created too much production capacity and generated too large an inventory. Polaroid's marketing and sales activities were also deficient.

SUPPORT ACTIVITIES

Porter also identified four generic support activities. These are broad, systems management functions that support the primary activities and the firm as a whole. They are

1. *Procurement.* Procurement is the acquisition of inputs, or resources, for the firm. Although it is the designated function of the purchasing department, procurement is also carried out by every employee who purchases equipment, arranges for financing, gathers information, completes a real estate transaction, or acquires any but human resources for the firm.

2. *Human resource management.* Human resource management consists of all activities involved in recruiting, hiring, training, developing, compensating, and (if necessary) dismissing or laying off personnel. Human resource managers influence salary and wage levels and the overall cost of personnel. Through hiring and training programs, they promote levels of skill and motivation that affect the firm's overall performance.

3. *Technological development.* Technological development pertains to the equipment, hardware, software, procedures, and technical knowledge brought to bear in the firm's transformation of inputs into outputs. Its most important component is knowledge. Some forms of technological knowledge are scientific (chemical formulas). Other forms are more of an "art" (recipes used by restaurants). The use of computers and information systems also requires technological expertise. Technological development involves the identification, selection, adaptation, and (if necessary) creation of new technologies for use by the firm. Technology is embedded in the product itself and in the processes used to produce it. The function of technological development includes technology assessment to determine what new technologies a firm should consider adopting.

4. *Infrastructure.* Like cities, companies have infrastructures that serve their needs and tie their various parts together. In cities, the infrastructure includes roads, water lines, electrical lines, sewage systems, and government. In business organizations, the infrastructure consists of functions or departments, such as accounting, legal, finance, planning, public affairs, government relations, quality assurance, and general management. Though they are often referred to as "overhead," these functions are the glue that holds a firm together. If the infrastructure is working well, the firm can gain a substantial competitive advantage. If it is not working well, an otherwise effective firm can lose its competitive edge.

These four support activities permeate the entire organization. Therefore, strategic managers who are evaluating the support activities of a firm must look at how each activity is performed throughout the firm, *not* just by its designated unit. In fact, some of the most important support activities are not performed by the organizational unit that appears to be responsible for them. The hiring of senior executives, for example, is usually not done by the personnel department. The acquisition of major resources is usually not done by the purchasing department. Many important technological breakthroughs have come from "skunk works" where considerable freedom was accorded the managers, or other parts of the firm, not necessarily from the R&D unit. Every aspect of the firm needs to be examined to determine how support activities are conducted.

The success of many organizations depends on excellence in the execution of support activities. Consulting companies, such as the Boston Consulting Group and McKinsey and Co., sustain their competitive advantage by recruiting, training, and retaining high-quality personnel. The same is true of "big eight" accounting firms. The Corning Glass Works achieves competitive advantage through technological development. Its special processes for melting and molding glass into useful products have resulted in a long history of growth and profitability. Gallo Wineries has achieved a 15% cost advantage by growing and procuring grapes on a large scale. Federal Express has gained a competitive advantage in its industry by creating a comprehensive, computer-based infrastructure to keep track of each package from its point of origin to its final destination.

METHODOLOGY

The first step in performing a value chain analysis is to identify the key primary and support activities that the business conducts. A good way to start is to identify specific inbound-logistics activities. The manager uses the stakeholder map to determine the sources of incoming resources (inputs) and then asks, "What activities are necessary to obtain and handle these resources?" The next step is to identify activities needed to convert inputs to outputs. Then, using the stakeholder map, the manager identifies the destinations of the firm's outputs. The question here is, "What activities are necessary to move outputs from the firm to their final destinations?" The answer to this question defines outbound logistics. Marketing and sales activities and service activities are determined by focusing on each stakeholder who receives the firm's outputs. What activities are necessary to inform and persuade customers to buy the outputs, and what order-taking processes are necessary to complete sales? These constitute the marketing and sales activities. Finally, what activities are necessary to continue delivering value to the customer who has bought the product? What is required to maintain customer satisfaction? The answers define the service activities.

To identify the support activities—procurement, human resource management, technological development, and infrastructure—the manager reviews the primary activities and determines how each is helped by the support activities.

After the most important primary and support activities are identified, the manager assesses how each contributes to the company's competitive advantage. Does this activity give us a cost advantage? Does it help the firm differentiate its product from others in terms of quality or uniqueness? If the answers are yes, the manager asks, "Is this advantage sustainable over time?" Finally, the manager examines the sequence of activities in the firm's value chain for variations that decrease competitive advantage. The key question here is, "How does an error or deficiency in this activity affect an activity later?" The ability to correct or reduce key variations from competitive advantage determines whether the firm can implement a strategy successfully. Worksheet 5.1 is a value chain analysis that could have been done for Polaroid in 1988.

WORKSHEET 5.1 | Value Chain Analysis

Case __Polaroid/Polavision__
Date __1988__
Name __Dow Jones__

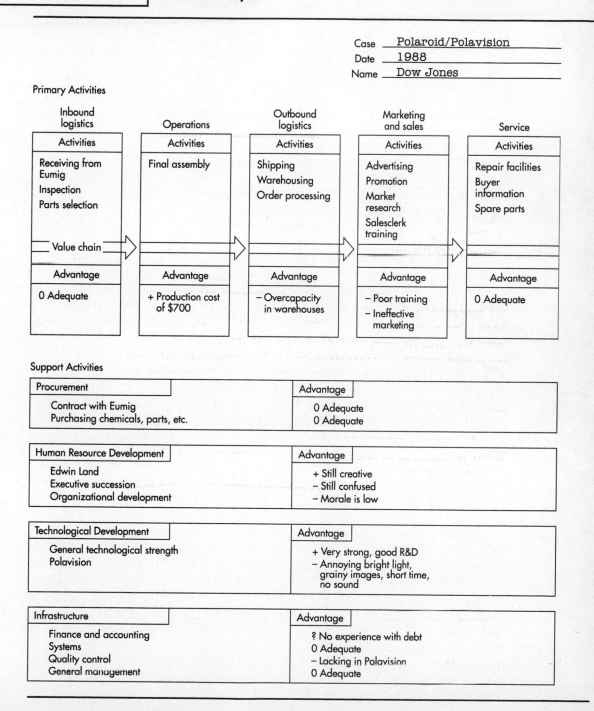

Primary Activities

Inbound logistics	Operations	Outbound logistics	Marketing and sales	Service
Activities	**Activities**	**Activities**	**Activities**	**Activities**
Receiving from Eumig Inspection Parts selection	Final assembly	Shipping Warehousing Order processing	Advertising Promotion Market research Salesclerk training	Repair facilities Buyer information Spare parts
Value chain				
Advantage	**Advantage**	**Advantage**	**Advantage**	**Advantage**
0 Adequate	+ Production cost of $700	– Overcapacity in warehouses	– Poor training – Ineffective marketing	0 Adequate

Support Activities

Procurement	Advantage
Contract with Eumig Purchasing chemicals, parts, etc.	0 Adequate 0 Adequate

Human Resource Development	Advantage
Edwin Land Executive succession Organizational development	+ Still creative – Still confused – Morale is low

Technological Development	Advantage
General technological strength Polavision	+ Very strong, good R&D – Annoying bright light, grainy images, short time, no sound

Infrastructure	Advantage
Finance and accounting Systems Quality control General management	? No experience with debt 0 Adequate – Lacking in Polavision 0 Adequate

TIME AND QUALITY

Capability-based companies execute the value-adding chain faster and more effectively than their competitors. In general terms, a process can be defined as effective when it delivers a desired outcome at a predictable, dependable quality, at low cost, and in a fast, timely fashion. Not surprisingly, many large international Japanese competitors use the triad of quality, cost, and delivery as their main criteria for designing their internal operations. Successful Western companies have similarly embraced two main concepts that are interrelated: total quality management (TQM) and time-based management (TBM).

Quality and time are the bases of customer satisfaction. They are closely linked. Quality without responsiveness does not maximize customer satisfaction. At the same time, "doing things right the first time"—that is, having reliable procedures—is a prerequisite for being fast. In turn, productivity increases and cost comes down as time is compressed.

The Malcolm Baldrige Award, created in memory of the late U.S. Secretary of Commerce, was designed to capture these elements of competitive capability and to reward those U.S. companies that have increased their international competitiveness. The Baldrige Award has come in for a lot of criticism, but it serves the useful purpose of stimulating business to change managerial approaches. It also offers a basic framework for determining how well managers are achieving the goals of satisfied customers and employee involvement (Garvin, 1991). The Baldrige Award was named after the Malcolm Baldrige National Quality Improvement Act in 1987. The award covers three types of businesses: manufacturing, service, and small business. The criteria whereon the Baldrige Award is based, which were formulated by the National Institute of Standards and Technology, are given in Figure 5.5. These criteria are designed to cover the overall business perspective of a company, its quality capabilities, and its general business capabilities. Winners of the award have included Xerox, Motorola, Westinghouse, and the Cadillac Division of General Motors.

Sims, in an article entitled "Does the Baldrige Award Really Work?" (1992), covers the industry reaction to the award. The consensus seems to be that the criteria used in the award help identify needs but do not reveal how to achieve world excellence. Ultimately, the award can be viewed as a guide to investing in organizational transformation that produces overall, significant results.

Beyond staying at the minimum required level, capability-based competitors painstakingly develop mechanisms to keep themselves at the leading edge in terms of their core competencies. They realize that process excellence is essential to delivering these core competencies to the customer. Therefore, a growing number of companies are focusing on the two complementary concepts of total quality management (TQM) and time-based management (TBM). With these approaches, they manage substantial physical and cultural change and often achieve substantial competitive advantage.

TQM

To better understand the meaning of quality and TQM, it is useful to take a historical perspective on the progression of "quality thinking." Obviously, applying

FIGURE 5.5	Criteria for the Baldrige Award

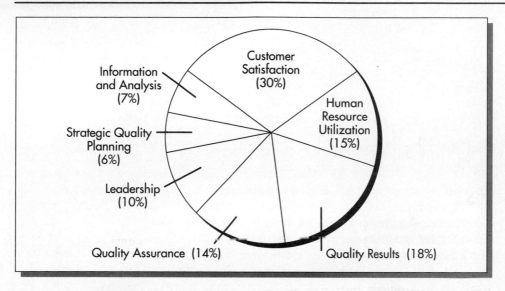

Criteria	Points
1. Leadership	100
2. Information and Analysis	70
3. Strategic Quality Planning	60
4. Human Resource Utilization	150
5. Quality Assurance of Products and Services	140
6. Quality Results	180
7. Customer Satisfaction	300
Total Points	1,000

quality as a strategic capability goes far beyond mere product quality. It permeates the entire system of creating, producing, selling, and servicing a product or service. A number of Americans have played a prominent role in the development of quality thinking, but much of the early efforts were made in Japan, and it took almost 40 years before U.S. companies started to wholeheartedly embrace these concepts. Here is a brief historical overview.

1948 In response to General MacArthur's request, Homer Sarasohn from M.I.T. and Charles Protzman from Western Electric designed a course to teach modern management techniques to the Japanese and help them become self-sufficient again, thereby reducing the need for U.S. economic aid. Over the coming years, they educated much of the elite of Japanese post-World War II industry. The result was that quality was measured using statistical process control (SPC).

1950   The Japanese Union of Scientists and Engineers (JUSE) invited W. Edwards Deming to come to Japan and introduce and teach his concepts. Deming introduced the concept of total quality control (TQC), which eliminated the need for final inspection by making quality the concern of *all* parts of the production process.

1954   Joseph M. Juran, a pioneer of statistical quality control (SQC) at Bell Telephone's Hawthorne Works, was invited by JUSE to evaluate its quality control processes. This resulted in quality control from an overall management perspective that evolved into quality improvement teams/quality circles (QCs).

1960   Philip B. Crosby, quality control vice president at ITT, began popularizing the concept of zero defects. He relied on four principles:

1. Quality is not an absolute measure but can be defined as conformance to requirements.
2. The approach to quality is prevention, not inspection.
3. The performance standard is zero defects.
4. The measurement of quality is the price of nonconformance (reworking, defects, warranty claims).

1966–1970s   Genichi Taguchi introduced his concept of design quality. Design quality is based on the notion of value to the customer. The outcome was the Taguchi method that was called quality function deployment (QFD).

Mid-1980s   Several U.S. companies (Ford, Xerox, Johnson & Johnson, Corning, Hoechst Celanese, Florida Power & Light, Westinghouse) began introducing continuous improvement programs. This is now known as total quality management (TQM).

1987   Congress established the Malcolm Baldrige award. The first winners were Globe Metallurgical, Westinghouse, and Motorola (1988) and Milliken, Xerox, and Florida Power & Light (1989).

What distinguishes TQM from earlier quality management approaches is that it provides a comprehensive framework for managing and improving all aspects of quality and that it involves all areas in a company in the process of achieving quality. This is well captured in the Total Quality Fitness Review diagram used at Westinghouse (Figure 5.6).

Total quality management (TQM) is used to improve activities in an integrated effort aimed at improving performance at every level of the organization. The company that uses TQM covers all the different phases of quality thinking, and it is constantly improving its customer responsiveness capabilities (Figure 5.7). Performance includes cross-functional goals of quality, cost, schedule, service, reliability, and customer relations. TQM integrates management efforts focused on continuous process improvement. These activities ultimately should increase customer satisfaction.

In TQM, an important element of timeliness is concurrent engineering, which integrates the design of a product with its manufacturing, operation, and support

FIGURE 5.6 | Total Quality Fitness Review at Westinghouse

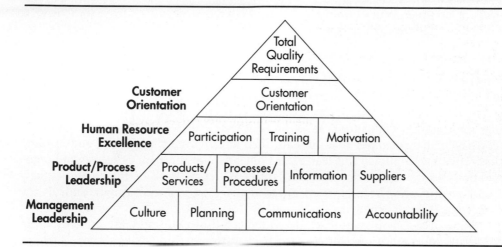

FIGURE 5.7 | Total Quality Management (TQM)

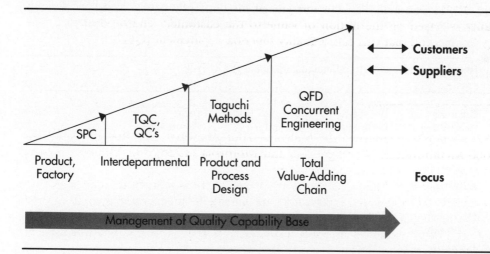

processes. Concurrent engineering helps the company achieve low-cost development, production, operations, and support with the shortest schedule possible that maintains the quality of the products and services. Unlike a sequential development process, this approach requires the simultaneous development of all the processes in the entire system. Concurrent engineering teams are needed to ensure that all functional groups are integrated. To be successful, the development process must change what people do and when they do it.

TBM

Time-based management is a complementary approach to TQM. It is a powerful tool for completely revamping a company's processes and systems to achieve a capability edge over the competition.

Time-based Competitors

These companies are ones that change the rules of competition. Rather than looking at time savings purely as a source for improving productivity, they look at their entire value delivery system and ask, "What if we could provide our product in half the time our competitors take, or even less?" Successful time-based competitors have cut throughput times in half, then have halved them again, and in some cases have accomplished this feat a third time. As a result, their processes and organizations today often look radically different from those of their competitors. Consequently, they have built up a lead that it becomes increasingly difficult for their competitors to challenge.

Some of the companies that have embraced this philosophy are listed in Table 5.1. The companies on this list are from different industries. Some, such as Citicorp, are well established; others are fairly new, fast-growing companies such as Wal-Mart. What all of these companies have in common is an innovative approach to creating fast, responsive delivery processes that give them significant time advantages over their competitors. What these companies also have in common is that each is the leader, or is fast becoming the leader, in its industry.

TABLE 5.1	Time-based Competitors (Estimated Performance)			
Company	Business Advantage	Response Differences	Growth vs. Industry	Profit vs. Industry
Wal-Mart	Discount stores	80%	36 vs. 12%	19 vs. 9% ROCE[a]
Atlas Door	Industrial doors	66%	15 vs. 5%	10 vs. 2% ROS[b]
Ralph Wilson Plastics	Decorative laminates	75%	9 vs. 3%	40 vs. 10% RONA[c]
Thomasville	Furniture	70%	12 vs. 3%	21 vs. 11% ROA[d]
Citicorp	Mortgages	85%	100 vs. 3%	NA

[a] Return on capital employed
[b] Return on sales
[c] Return on net assets
[d] Return on assets

Source: Adapted with the permission of The Free Press, a Division of Macmillan, Inc., from *Competing Against Time: How Time-based Competition Is Reshaping Global Markets* by George Stalk, Jr. and Thomas M. Hout. Copyright © 1990 by The Free Press.

Citicorp, for example, uses the vast customer database from its credit card business to evaluate the credit risk of individuals quickly. This way it can approve mortgages in a few days—in some cases within minutes—compared to the weeks or months other lenders often need. Citicorp used to have a small market share in mortgage lending; today it is number one.

Wal-Mart replenishes the stock in its stores twice a week, on average, and for many products, it replenishes daily. Competitors such as K Mart and Sears replenish their stock every two weeks. Compared to these competitors, Wal-Mart can maintain the same service levels with one-fourth the inventory investment, or offer its customers four times as much choice for the same inventory investment, or both. Wal-Mart is growing three times faster than the retail discount industry as a whole, and its return on investment has been consistently higher than average.

Ralph Wilson Plastics, a producer of decorative laminates, is another good example. The industry used to be almost completely dominated by Formica, the company whose name is often confused with the product. In the 1960s Ralph Wilson Plastics entered the business by offering ten-day delivery instead of the typical thirty-day delivery. Ralph Wilson Plastics' fast delivery appealed to the most time-sensitive market segments: the highly customized residential and the high-end commercial customers. Not fully aware of the value of fast delivery, Formica did not at first see this new competitor as a threat. Its market share was slipping, but the industry was still growing at a healthy rate. Ralph Wilson Plastics also used a unique process and machine set-up; Formica had difficulties in adopting this approach. As the growth in the industry slowed, Formica found itself much less able to sustain its price- and cost-competitiveness. Its sales and profitability fell while Ralph Wilson Plastics continued to grow, surpassing Formica as the industry leader in 1980.

How is it possible that companies with very similar backgrounds can differ vastly in delivery capability? The key differences of time-based competitors appear to be the following:

1. They view the entire system, including suppliers, distributors, and customers, rather than considering only individual functions.
2. They focus on reducing "non-value-adding" time rather than trying to make people or machines work harder or faster on value-adding activities.
3. They give the measurement of time and responsiveness the same priority as, if not higher priority than, the measurement of cost.

The idea of viewing operations as a system is not new; rather, it dates back to Jay Forrester's (1961) discussion of industrial dynamics in the 1960s. But only recently have large numbers of companies recognized the significance of this approach. A business can essentially be viewed as a series of interlinked operating cycles (Figure 5.8).

Time-based competitors put the customer first. Their view encompasses the entire time from customer order to delivery and payment. Customers are not interested in how their orders are put through the company, how many hierarchies are involved, when their orders are sequenced, and so on. They are concerned only about how fast, how new, or how unusual the product delivery is.

FIGURE 5.8	Business—A Series of Interlinked Operating Cycles

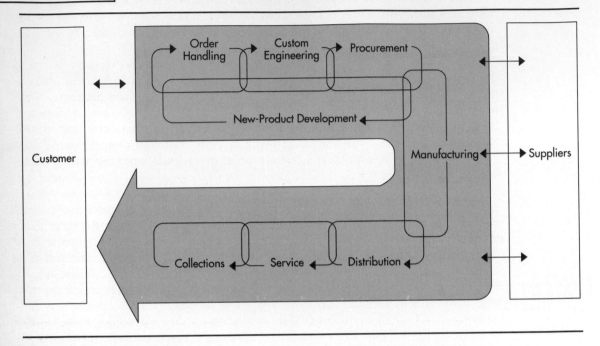

Process Re-engineering

Often bureaucracy grows as companies respond to changes by adding new functions or departments. As more departments are involved, additional time is consumed in hand-offs between departments and in checking and redoing work that was not completed correctly in other departments. Conversely, time is also wasted when individual functions are downsized at the expense of the overall operation. One car manufacturer, for example, reduced personnel in its order entry department to save several hundred thousand dollars. As a result, however, the quality of the code that was entered deteriorated. The entry of more errors into the system resulted in several million dollars of higher cost for rework on incorrectly ordered and manufactured parts.

The possibilities for eliminating wasted time in most traditional operating systems are great. Almost every traditional company adds value in only 5% or less of the elapsed time between order and delivery. The rest of the time, the product or service is waiting in queues to be processed or is being reworked. In most cases, the time spent in the white-collar part of the operations is significantly higher than in the blue-collar part. A car, for example, can be assembled in 20 hours. Yet, despite significant overcapacity in the industry, customers have to wait weeks or months for delivery.

Time-based competitors do not work harder, they work smarter. Instead of trying to reduce the value-adding time in the system with investments in ever more advanced machinery and information systems, they look at the tremendous amount of idle time and time spent "off the main sequence." Permanent coordination meetings, redefinition of tasks, frequent hand-offs and sign-offs, sequential procedures, waiting time in front of capacity bottlenecks, and rework can all be sources of significant waste and higher cost. Addressing these areas can often yield great improvements without major investments.

Lost Time

A useful tool for displaying the lost time in the system is called *white-space analysis* (Figure 5.9). By carefully following an order through the system, it is possible to measure the time during which this order was actually worked on (value-adding time) and the time it had to wait in in-baskets and out-baskets, queues, or inventories or when it had to be reworked (non-value-adding time). The company in Figure 5.9, a maker of electronics with fairly modern production facilities, spent 89% of the time in non-value-adding activities. Obviously, it was able to identify great potential for time savings without having to look at the value-adding activities at all.

Rework is a particularly deceptive part of the white space, because it can appear as a value-adding activity for an individual function, but for the system as a whole it is unnecessary or duplicate work. Rework is clearly an expression of lack of process quality, because things were not done right the first time. Therefore, a

---

FIGURE 5.9   **White-Space Analysis**

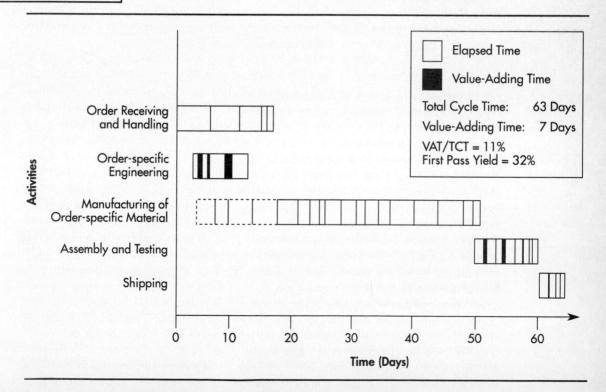

Source: Courtesy of The Boston Consulting Group, Inc. Reprinted with permission.

useful measure for process quality is *first pass yield*, the percentage of finished products that went through the system without requiring rework at any stage of the total process.

The first pass yield in most traditional, complex processes is extremely low. Suppose, for example, that an order has to pass through 20 stages with an average reject/rework rate of 5% at each stage. Statistically, the first pass yield is estimated at 36%. Thus 64% of the orders going through the system would require extra work in one form or another, which significantly adds to cost and time. To reach this same level of first pass yield in a process with 100 stages, the individual failure rate at every stage must not exceed 1%, on average. And in complex systems, such as car manufacturing, processes with several thousand stages are not uncommon.

A number of companies have begun to focus on this measure in their production processes, most notably in the electronics industry where extremely low failure rates are required. Some time-based competitors apply this measure of first pass yield throughout the entire company, which often reveals stunning levels of inefficiency, especially in the white-collar part of the operation.

The tracking of product teams is a key element in capability-based strategy. For example, Hewlett-Packard has over 50% of its sales from new products from the past three years, and over 50 products are in development (House and Price, 1991). Bill Hewlett said, "You can't manage what you can't measure." The measure his company uses is called a "return map," which captures both elapsed time and cumulative cost. By examining the relationship among development, manufacturing, and sales, H-P is able to track how well product teams are doing. This knowledge keeps management and the teams up to date.

Another important link in the delivery chain is the relationship with suppliers: time-based competitors establish partnerships with key suppliers and jointly reap the benefits. In this case, the white-space analysis can be extended to encompass the processes of the suppliers as well as the interfaces between buyer and supplier, including information exchange and the transport and storage of components.

Too many companies look only at the cost-savings and price-reduction potential; time-based competitors also take a careful look at the potential for realizing higher prices and then build the delivery performance needed. Fast, innovative product development often is the key to achieving such a position. Competitors with short cycle times can be first to incorporate changes in customer requirements into new products. The faster the pace of innovation, the more effectively the organization can use product variety to address specific market segments and increase overall market share. Through continuous learning from a rapid succession of product updates, the organization will out-compete slower competitors who wait for the great leap forward.

Product life cycles in many industries are getting shorter. Long development times can significantly cut into the time the company needs to earn a return on the initial R&D investment (Figure 5.10). The fast developer often spends less on the development of a product, introduces it earlier, reaches higher sales levels, achieves a faster payback, and attains higher overall profitability than its competitors. A case in point is the pharmaceutical industry, where some companies, such as Merck, consistently out-compete their rivals through fast product innovation.

FIGURE 5.10 | **Traditional vs. Time-based Product Developers**
(Dollar amounts in millions)

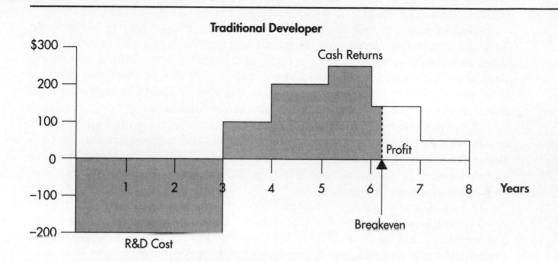

Traditional Developer

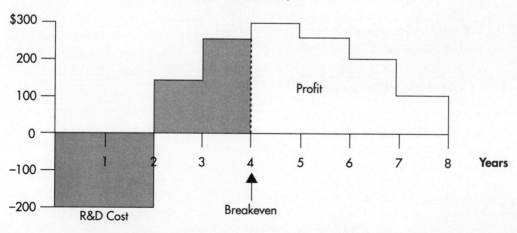

Time-based Developer

Process Mapping

The principal approach that time-based competitors use is mapping and measuring processes and then finding ways to simplify these processes. This can be done in repeated rounds of cycle-time reductions or, in other cases, through a completely different, innovative view of the business. Over a period of 15–20 years, Toyota went through repeated rounds of different approaches (Kanban, just-in-time, quality circles) to give it a commanding productivity lead over Western car manufacturers. An example of applying a new perspective is Federal Express, whose founder conceived a process for delivering mail that is markedly different from that of the U.S. Postal Service.

While conceptually simple, *process mapping* is often not easy in practice. To do it right, managers, employees, suppliers, and customers must work on the map together to make sure that what the company thinks happens really does happen. Typically, the actual maps of a process are substantially different from the designed behavior, which often does not sufficiently consider informal channels, feedback effects, exceptions, errors, rework, and other quality problems.

The main objective of mapping is to identify physical flows, stocks, and activities as well as information flows, decision points, and communication patterns. Those doing the mapping therefore begin by asking those involved what happens and the reasons behind what happens. In most cases, it is also helpful to track specific orders through the organization.

The display of this information can take on different forms, such as logistical flow maps, decision point maps, and maps of locational and functional information interfaces and hand-offs. Figure 5.11 shows examples of these different types of maps. After the process has been mapped and appropriate measures have been applied, those involved can start considering how to improve the processes. Several approaches to simplifying processes are available:

- Decentralize the organization so that it has fewer layers.
- Use process, not functional, organization form.
- Use parallel processing wherever possible.
- Use investments in areas that eliminate bottlenecks.

FIGURE 5.11 | **Three Examples of Process Maps**

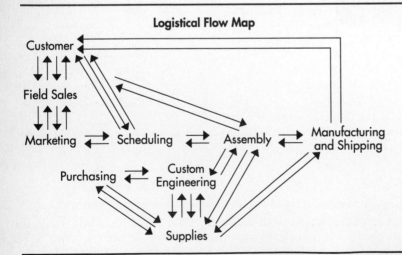

Logistical Flow Map

(continued)

FIGURE 5.11 | **Three Examples of Process Maps (continued)**

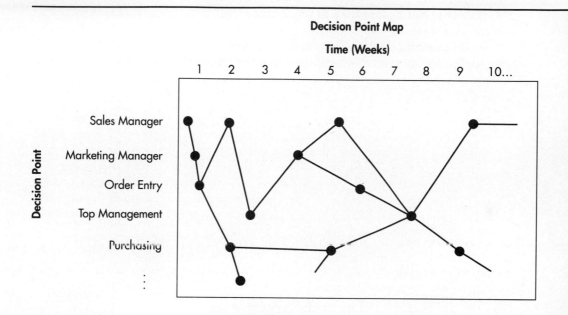

Decision Point Map

Time (Weeks)

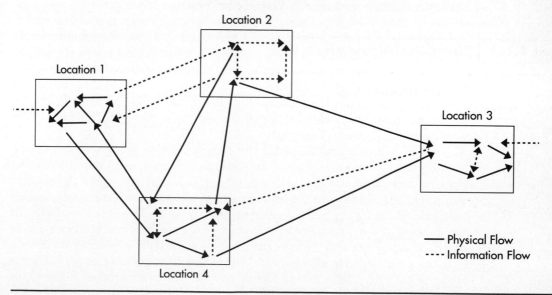

Locational Interface Map

— Physical Flow
---- Information Flow

- Produce smaller batch sizes.
- Synchronize procedures to balance work loads.
- Eliminate causes of rework at the source by not permitting incomplete work to be passed on.
- Apply flexible role definitions with a higher degree of integration.
- Implement standardization of the forms used and of work flows.

It is at this transition, from mapping and understanding the problems to making substantial physical and management changes, where good intentions often break down. Because of the sometimes radical changes needed to make the firm a more flexible, responsive organization, resistance builds up at several levels within the organization. Many companies are not able to go beyond the technocratic level of process redesign because of strong cultural barriers, such as resistance to change. Later in the book, we will discuss how to introduce the change process. Only those companies that are effective at bringing about change in the organizational culture and that exhibit strong leadership are able to achieve the flexibility needed for capability-based strategy.

VALUE LEVERAGING

Another approach that can be used to augment a capability-based strategy is to focus more directly on the customer. The leveraging of customer value, or *value leveraging,* begins with research designed to develop a thorough understanding of the customer's needs and problems. Various research tools are employed to gather information about customers: surveys, visit reports, analyses of competitive bids, panels, test marketing, and others. With the information it has gathered, the organization determines how it can serve customers better. Though this works well to satisfy customers' present needs, it seldom turns out to satisfy their future needs, perhaps because the information being analyzed is relevant only to the status quo. When it comes to innovations needed for the future, traditional suppliers to an industry often lag behind the market trends. Researchers at M.I.T. found, for example, that in the field of high technology it was the users (customers), not the manufacturers (suppliers), who developed the most new products (Hippel, 1988). These findings are shown in Table 5.2.

The key to value leveraging is for the organization to put itself "in the customer's shoes." This requires more than research and analysis of data; it requires imagination and vision. Coming up with innovations that will make the product more useful to the customer in the future is one means of value leveraging. Another is to increase the product's present value to the customer. This is accomplished by finding out how the customer thinks value can be increased or cost structure can be improved. The supplier may be concentrating on improving a product or service, whereas the customer may merely need help in using the product or service more efficiently. Thus rather than asking, "How can we make this product better?" the supplier should be asking, *"Can we increase the value of our product within the customer's system, and how?"* Answers to the second question often result in entirely different product/marketing approaches.

| TABLE 5.2 | Sources of Innovative Products First Tested in Practice |

New Product	User (%)	Manufacturer (%)
Measuring instruments		
First instrument of its kind	100	0
Major functional improvements	82	18
Minor functional improvements	70	30
Processing equipment		
First equipment of its kind	100	0
Major functional improvements	63	21
Minor functional improvements	20	29

Source: Eric V. Hippel, *The Sources of Innovation* (New York: Oxford University Press, 1988), p. 15.

Federal Express is a company based on value leveraging and competitive cost advantage through system innovation. The idea of overnight mail shipment certainly must have occurred to many mail distribution firms, but they concluded that overnight delivery was not feasible or cost-effective, given the delivery systems then in use. To accomplish overnight delivery via the U.S. Postal Service, for example, with its thousands of distribution and sorting points and its many different modes of transportation, would have required a monumental effort. It would also have required substantial investment in faster modes of transportation at a time when transportation was already the major cost.

Fred Smith, the founder of Federal Express, developed his vision from an entirely different set of assumptions. He realized that the major cost of overnight delivery would be sorting and handling, not transportation. To reduce the costs of handling, he decided to try a new system. Instead of establishing many small distribution points, which would be difficult to coordinate, he decided to have all incoming mail sorted at one central hub, in Memphis. His idea works. Every evening, at around midnight, some 65 Federal Express planes converge in Memphis to disgorge about 600,000 envelopes and packages. The mail is quickly sorted on 45 miles of conveyor belts and loaded back into the planes by 4 A.M. When the planes arrive at their destinations, the mail is loaded into small delivery vans and rushed to recipients before noon.

Another innovative approach to value leveraging is exemplified by the Swedish furniture company IKEA. IKEA's vision has revolutionized the furniture industry in Europe, and the company has set out to do the same in the United States. IKEA noticed that a significant segment of the market was made up of young buyers who wanted inexpensive, modern-design furniture. To attract these buyers, traditional manufacturers had cut costs by reducing the amount of material used to make the furniture. This measure reduced appearance and quality as well. IKEA looked at ways to cut costs without sacrificing quality. It examined the entire value-adding chain, from production to final installation in the customer's home, and realized that the greatest savings could be gained by reducing assembly and delivery costs. Therefore, IKEA designed pieces that customers could transport in their own vehicles and easily assemble at home.

The common theme in these two examples of value leveraging is that the companies involved looked for completely different ways to provide a service or a product rather than simply improving on existing approaches. Neither Federal Express nor IKEA is the low-price supplier in its market; that is, neither had to gain market share by offering lower prices. Rather, they leveraged customer value and were able to charge customers more.

Figure 5.12 shows how value leveraging and system innovation enabled Federal Express and IKEA to increase profits by raising prices and lowering costs.

SYSTEM INNOVATION

System innovation is vital in gaining a sustainable competitive cost advantage. Like IKEA, Toyota restructured its assembly and delivery system to create new value. Toyota's production system changed the rules of the game from cost-based

---

FIGURE 5.12 | **Effects of Value Leveraging and System Innovation on Costs, Price, and Profit Margin at Federal Express and IKEA**

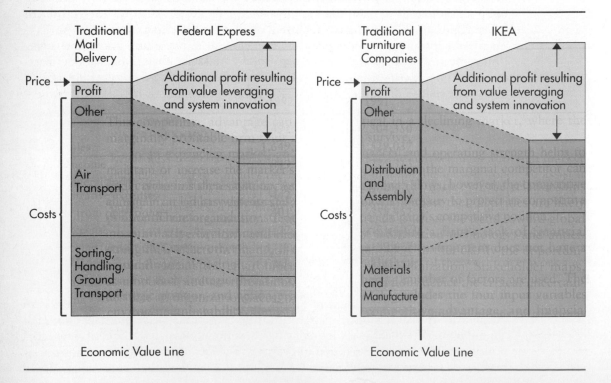

competition alone to cost-based competition plus time-based competition plus variety-based competition (Abegglen and Stalk, 1985). As shown in Table 5.3, this system allowed the Japanese manufacturers to produce cars at a faster rate and thus more cheaply than American manufacturers. Moreover, the Japanese learned to manufacture a more diverse line of products at virtually no cost penalty. The ability of the Japanese system—called the just-in-time (JIT) system—to respond rapidly to customers' demands for more variety is one of the major reasons that the system is now widely used.

Another system innovation that enabled the Japanese car manufacturers to gain a strong competitive advantage was their dedication to product quality. Initially, high quality was a requirement, because the distance between Japan and the United States meant that adequate service support could not be provided at acceptable costs. The Japanese were able to perfect a system that achieves higher quality and at the same time greater variety.

> Variety, at least in America, is often an enemy of quality. Reducing the number of design changes allows workers to devote more attention to each. . . . The Japanese, however, have achieved low failure rates even with relatively broad product lines and rapidly changing designs. . . . New designs account for nearly a third of all models offered each year, far more than in the U.S. (D. A. Garvin, 1983)

Poor product quality results in high after-sales costs. As a result of quality differences, U.S. manufacturers typically have significantly higher warranty costs than their Japanese counterparts. Garvin estimated the warranty costs of U.S. manufacturers to be about four times as high as those of the Japanese. Fortunately, though belatedly, many U.S. companies, such as Ford, have realized that "Quality is Job 1."

System innovation may depend somewhat on luck, but some organizations are consistently more successful at it than others. What are they doing right? These organizations have come to realize the hidden benefits of continuously demanding innovation from the system. One benefit of continuous innovation is that by the

TABLE 5.3	Impact of the Just-in-Time (JIT) Automobile Production System		
Factors Compared	U.S. Manufacturer	Japanese Manufacturer	Difference (%)
Cars	860	1,000	+16.3
Employment	2,150	1,000	−53.5
Employees per car	2.5	1.0	−60.0
Direct labor	1.25	.79	−36.8
Other labor, including salaried employees	1.25	.21	−83.2

Source: James C. Abegglen and George Stalk, Jr., 1985.

time the competition is able to understand and imitate it, the organization may already have moved on to something new. Another advantage is that people in the organization grow accustomed to change, which makes the firm more competitive.

The key to developing system innovation seems to be (1) sufficient vision to overcome functional specialization and look at the delivery system as a whole and (2) sufficient vision to consider quantum leaps, not just incremental improvements. To achieve significant results, strategic planners should consider the following three questions:

1. What kinds of changes in our delivery system would be valuable to our customers?
2. What would it mean to our customers if delivery cycle times could be cut in half, or if other performance criteria could be doubled?
3. What would a delivery system look like that could achieve these fundamental improvements?

If the organization is capable of making a quantum leap, the benefits of developing a new system of operation can be far-reaching. The more innovative the new vision, the greater its potential benefits to the organization.

Emerson Electric has consistently been profitable for the past 30 years (Knight, 1992). What accounts for this kind of performance, regardless of competition or business conditions? The answer is that Emerson focused on a strategy of being the best-cost producer (not the lowest-cost). Its success is attributable to the following six factors:

1. Commitment to total quality and satisfied customers.
2. Knowing the competition.
3. Competing on both process improvements and product design.
4. Involvement of employees and effective communications.
5. Continuous focus on cost reduction.
6. Supporting the strategy with the required capital expenditures.

Emerson implements these six factors by using careful planning and meaningful controls backed up with a value measurement chart that is used to assess value creation. Because operating managers are responsible for carrying out the planning, they have "ownership" of the decisions required to achieve performance.

ASSESSING COMPANY CAPABILITY

A key element in assessing its capability is knowing a company's strengths and weaknesses. Creating a capability profile can pinpoint strengths and weaknesses, and performing a WOTS-UP analysis can identify threats and opportunities as well.

THE CAPABILITY PROFILE

The *capability profile* is a means of assessing a company's managerial, competitive (or marketing), financial, and technical strengths and weaknesses. Worksheet 5.2 is a capability profile showing Polaroid's strengths and weaknesses in 1988. The

WORKSHEET 5.2 | Company Capability Profile

Case __Polaroid__
Date __1988__
Name __Mary Doe__

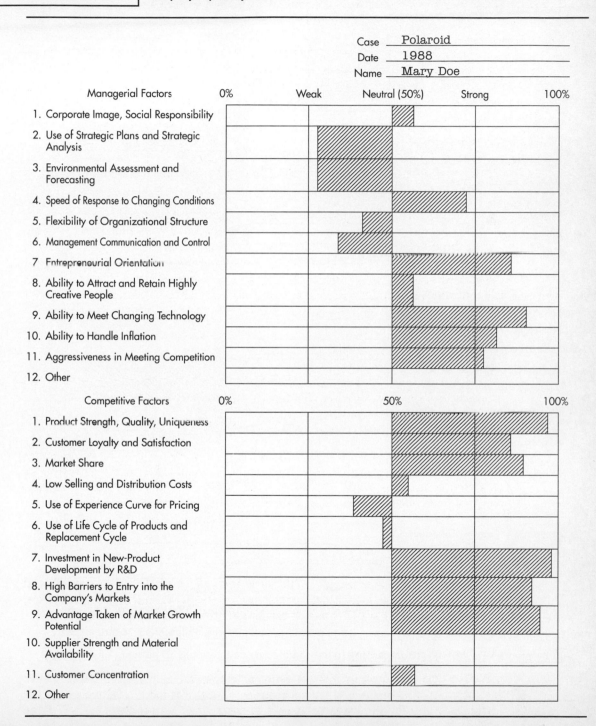

(continued)

| WORKSHEET 5.2 | Company Capability Profile (continued) |

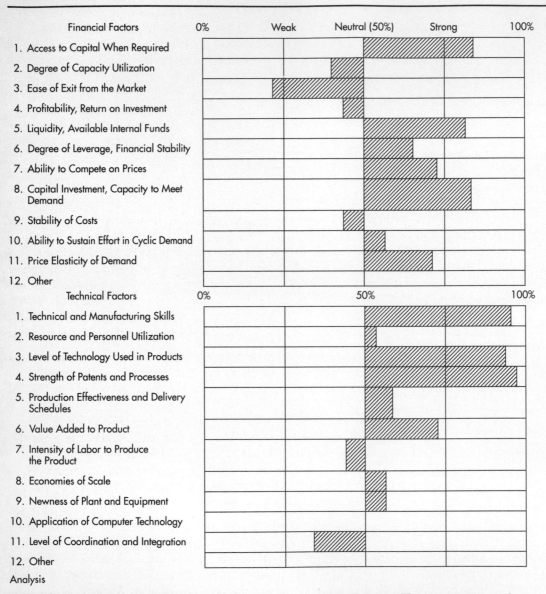

Financial Factors	0%	Weak	Neutral (50%)	Strong	100%
1. Access to Capital When Required					
2. Degree of Capacity Utilization					
3. Ease of Exit from the Market					
4. Profitability, Return on Investment					
5. Liquidity, Available Internal Funds					
6. Degree of Leverage, Financial Stability					
7. Ability to Compete on Prices					
8. Capital Investment, Capacity to Meet Demand					
9. Stability of Costs					
10. Ability to Sustain Effort in Cyclic Demand					
11. Price Elasticity of Demand					
12. Other					

Technical Factors	0%		50%		100%
1. Technical and Manufacturing Skills					
2. Resource and Personnel Utilization					
3. Level of Technology Used in Products					
4. Strength of Patents and Processes					
5. Production Effectiveness and Delivery Schedules					
6. Value Added to Product					
7. Intensity of Labor to Produce the Product					
8. Economies of Scale					
9. Newness of Plant and Equipment					
10. Application of Computer Technology					
11. Level of Coordination and Integration					
12. Other					

Analysis

Polaroid is quite strong in its competitive and technical capabilities. The company now has sufficient financial means to overcome its previous problems with Polavision. Management could be stronger in areas of forecasting, communication, and control. Expansion of market for the Spectra camera and video printouts should be undertaken.

graphic profile was created by drawing a bar opposite each factor that originated at the "neutral" center and extended into the "weak" or "strong" side of the graph.

The length of the bar drawn on the worksheet indicates the degree of strength or weakness for each factor. A blank line indicates that data are not available or are not applicable for the company being analyzed.

One can think of the bars as representing percentiles. "Neutral" signifies the 50th percentile. Therefore, strength can range from 50 to 100% and weakness from 0 to 50%.

A completed capability profile reveals "gaps" that need to be corrected and opportunities that should be pursued. It also helps managers to assess the relative position of the firm and decide whether aggressiveness or retrenchment is the proper strategic thrust.

WOTS-UP ANALYSIS

WOTS is an acronym for weaknesses, opportunities, threats, and strengths. (UP is simply added to make the term easy to remember.) As a companion methodology to environmental analyses and the capability profile, WOTS-UP analysis helps strategic managers to determine whether the organization is able to deal effectively with its environment. The more competent an organization is compared to its competitors, the more likely it is to gain market share and improve its profitability.

The issue of competency is central to three tasks of the strategic manager:

1. Identify the organization's distinctive competency. A distinctive competency is what the organization does particularly well. It includes the organization's unique resources and capabilities as well as its strengths and the ability to overcome weaknesses.
2. Find a niche in the organization's environment. A niche is a strategic and market segment to which the organization is well suited. Finding the correct niche enables the organization to take advantage of the opportunities that present themselves and avert threats from the environment and competitors.
3. Find the best match between the organization's distinctive competency and the available niches.

A WOTS-UP analysis helps find the best match between environmental trends (opportunities and threats) and internal capabilities. An *opportunity* is any favorable situation in the organization's environment. It is usually a trend or change of some kind or an overlooked need that increases demand for a product or service and permits the firm to enhance its position by supplying it. A *threat* is any unfavorable situation in the organization's environment that is potentially damaging to its strategy. The threat may be a barrier, a constraint, or anything external that might cause problems, damage, or injury. A *strength* is a resource or capacity the organization can use effectively to achieve its objectives. A *weakness* is a limitation, fault, or defect in the organization that will keep it from achieving its objectives. In general, an effective strategy is one that takes advantage of the organization's opportunities by employing its strengths and wards off threats by avoiding them or by correcting or compensating for weaknesses. The information in Figure 5.13 can be used to develop appropriate strategies.

A WOTS-UP analysis for Polaroid is shown in Worksheet 5.3. The first part of any WOTS-UP analysis is to collect a set of key facts about the organization and its environment. This database will include facts about the organization's markets, competition, financial resources, facilities, employees, inventories, marketing and distribution system, R&D, management, environmental setting (e.g., technological, political, social, and economic trends), history, and reputation.

The second part of a WOTS-UP analysis is to evaluate data to determine whether they constitute an opportunity, threat, strength, or weakness for the organization. Worksheet 5.3 shows how these evaluations are recorded.

WOTS-UP also can be used to analyze case studies in this text as follows:

1. Read the case rapidly for an overview.
2. Reread the case carefully, underlining key facts.
3. Evaluate each fact with respect to its potential as an opportunity, threat, strength, or weakness.

FIGURE 5.13   **WOTS-UP Matrix**

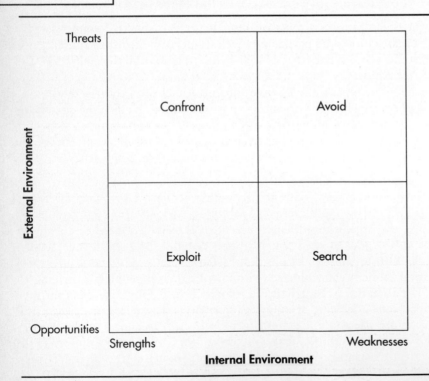

WORKSHEET 5.3 | **WOTS-UP Analysis**

Case   Polaroid

Date   1988

Name   John Doe

Opportunities

Maintain market leadership   ✓

New innovations; upgraded film   ✓

Vertical integration

Economy bouncing back   ✓

Improved financial position

New markets for the Spectra camera

Diversification into new products including

  video printouts

Threats

Technological problems continue

Market saturation

Strong competition from Kodak and

  35mm cameras   ✓

Internal resistance to change

Strengths

Market leadership in instant cameras   ✓

Strong R&D and marketing departments   ✓

Customers prefer Polaroid   ✓

High-quality products   ✓

High degree of self-sufficiency

Paid off $130M in debt

Weaknesses

Management changes   ✓

Too much capacity   ✓

Strategic management, forecasting   ✓

Price of film

Concentration on a few products

(Check if critical.)

When a WOTS-UP analysis is prepared, it is helpful to have each individual involved perform the analysis separately. Then the results can be compared and discussed in the group.

It is important to note that any given fact may give rise to more than one evaluation. For example, the increasing numbers of women who are employed outside the home may pose both an opportunity and a threat for a direct-sales cosmetics company such as Avon Products. It is an opportunity because it means that women have less time to shop and may therefore prefer a direct-sales cosmetics service. It is a threat because it implies that these women may be harder to reach at home. An effective strategy will take into account both possibilities.

It is also important to recognize that opportunities can contain hidden threats and hidden opportunities. Therefore, it is helpful to ask, "How might this threat also be an opportunity?" and "Does this opportunity contain threats as well?" It is also useful to ask, "How might this strength turn out to be a weakness?" and "How does this weakness really represent a strength?" The answers to these questions may give managers new insights into choosing appropriate strategies.

VULNERABILITY ANALYSIS

Another means of assessing threats to a company is the use of a vulnerability analysis. Executives tend to emphasize the strengths and opportunities on which their company's strategy is based and to downplay or even neglect threats and weaknesses. Vulnerability analysis can assist in strategy formulation by having the manager play the devil's advocate—one who criticizes the strategy or plan. Vulnerability analysis begins with the following simple question: What supportive elements, if suddenly taken away, might seriously damage or even destroy the business?

These elements are the *underpinnings* upon which the organization depends for its continued existence. Hurd (1977) identified the following twelve categories of underpinnings:

1. Customer needs and wants served by the product or service
2. Resources and assets: people, capital, facilities, raw materials, technological know-how
3. Cost position relative to competition, by major cost components
4. Consumer base: its size, demographics, trends
5. Technologies required
6. Special skills, systems, procedures, organization
7. Corporate identity: logo, image, products, corporate culture, role models
8. Institutional barriers to competition: regulations, codes, patent laws, licensing
9. Social values, lifestyles, common norms, ideals
10. Sanctions, supports, and incentives to do business, particularly in such fields as medicine, nuclear materials, restaurants, securities, import–export
11. Customer goodwill: product safety, product quality, company reputation
12. Complementary products or services in the stakeholder system

Vulnerability analysis involves seven key steps:

1. Identify underpinnings.
2. State how removal of an underpinning would threaten the business.
3. State the most conservative consequences of each threat.
4. Rank the impact of worst consequences of each threat.
5. Estimate the probability that each threat will materialize.
6. Rank the company's ability to deal with each threat, should it materialize.
7. Determine whether the company's vulnerability to each threat is extreme or negligible.

Worksheet 5.4 shows a complete vulnerability assessment that was done for the IBM Corporation in 1991, a time when IBM needed to assess the impact that failure of its strategy might have on the company.

The first step, the identification of underpinnings, is carried out by a group of top managers. It is helpful if participants have diverse backgrounds and interests.

After the basic underpinnings have been brought to the surface in a brainstorming session, each member of the group phrases them in terms of threats to the business.

The third step is to establish the most conservative assessment of the consequences, or *down-side risk,* should a potential threat materialize.

Fourth, by imagining a worst-case scenario, managers get a feel for the potential impact of each threat, should it materialize. They can now rank impact on a scale of 0 to 10, where zero denotes no impact on the organization at all, and 10 means catastrophic consequences.

The fifth step in vulnerability analysis is to estimate the probability that a particular threat will materialize. Very serious threats often have a remote probability of occurring, which forces managers to clarify their willingness to assume certain business risks. At the least, a probability assessment forces managers to decide whether they need more information before they can make a decision. Assessing probabilities is difficult, particularly in situations having a high degree of uncertainty. Strategic planners should be aware that top managers tend to be optimistic in their assessments.

The sixth step is to formulate possible reactions, or plans for dealing with threats that materialize. Even if the probability estimate elicits a wait-and-see attitude, this step will result in some degree of preparedness. The firm's ability to react or retaliate can be ranked on a scale of 0 to 10, where zero means defenselessness and 10 means that the company can easily absorb the blow.

The seventh and final step of vulnerability analysis is to place the company's overall vulnerability to each threat in the context of a *vulnerability assessment graph* (Figure 5.14), a four-quadrant matrix whose axes consist of rankings of the threat's impact and of the company's ability to react. In the case for IBM, the dot indicates placement of underpinning 4 (customer base), which had an impact rating of 7 and a reaction rating of 6 (see Worksheet 5.4).

Against threats that fall into quadrant D of the chart, a company is almost defenseless. Any entry in this quadrant demands immediate attention by top managers. If possible, they should remove such threats by abandoning a particular plan, strategy, or business unit. In cases where this is not possible, managers must

WORSHEET 5.4	Vulnerability Analysis

WORKSHEET 5.4	Vulnerability Analysis

Case   <u>IBM</u>

Date   <u>1991</u>

Name   <u>Doe</u>

Assumptions	Beliefs	Consequence	Impact 0–10	Probability 0–1	Capability 0–10	Vulnerability Assessment
1. Needs and wants served by product	Information processing	Compete with clones and others	9	.9	7	E
2. Resources and assets	Large and available	Current losses	9	.9	6	E
3. Cost position relative to competition	Recognized leader	Loss of position	6	.5	5	V
4. Customer base	World-wide	Difficult sales	7	.6	6	E
5. Technologies	Superior leader	Fallen behind	9	.6	9	E
6. Special skills	Sales and service	Cannot hold sales	8	.5	8	E
7. Corporate identity	Best managed company	Layoffs, restructure	5	.8	6	P
8. Institutional barriers to competition	Corporate accounts	Changing base	7	.6	8	E
9. Social values	Lifetime job, and care	Overhead expense	5	.3	8	P
10. Sanctions, supports, and incentives	Large sales of main frame	Declining market	8	.8	6	E
11. Customer goodwill	Proud of service	Changing expectations	5	.5	5	V
12. Complementary products or services	Software, mini-computers	Failed in software, AS 400	7	.8	6	E
13. Other						

FIGURE 5.14	Vulnerability Assessment Graph for IBM Corporation in 1991

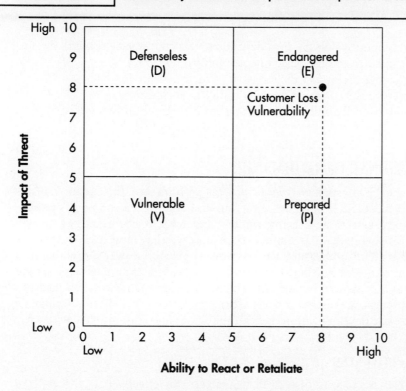

take immediate steps to upgrade the company's ability to react, thus moving the threat into quadrant E.

Threats in the second quadrant are still dangerous, but the company at least has sufficient capabilities to react or retaliate. For threats in this quadrant, managers should develop explicit contingency plans, particularly for those threats that are very likely to materialize.

Threats in quadrant P the company is prepared to deal with; therefore, very little monitoring of these possibilities is necessary.

The threats in quadrant V are light to moderate, and the company has very little to do if they materialize. Although explicit contingency plans do not need to be prepared, managers should at least try to monitor these threats for changes that indicate their escalation.

Figure 5.14 also shows how the vulnerability assessment graph can be used to evaluate a single threat, in this case the loss of underpinning 4, customer base (see Worksheet 5.4). Here, the loss of customer base falls into quadrant E, meaning that the company will be endangered by the loss of this underpinning. This graph can also be used to evaluate the overall vulnerability of the company. If IBM's impact and ability-to-react rankings were plotted for each underpinning listed in

Worksheet 5.4, eight of the underpinnings would fall in quadrant E, two in quadrant P, and two in quadrant V.

Vulnerability analyses, then, help managers to identify

- Underpinnings upon which the firm depends for its continued existence
- Forces that can destroy these basic underpinnings
- Factors that pose a threat and the strength of their potential impact
- The seriousness of the company's vulnerability to each threat
- The company's overall ability to compete effectively in its chosen industry

MEASURING ORGANIZATIONAL PERFORMANCE

Whereas TQM and TBM assess *internal* or process performance, this section considers *overall* effectiveness and how it can be measured. Looking at a company's performance measurement system and seeing what is and what is not measured can be quite revealing. For example, it is interesting to observe that most U.S. companies have very intricate financial measurement systems in place, but only a few measure their processes in terms of timeliness or responsiveness. On the other hand, some selectivity in what is measured is essential. This section focuses on ways to measure the overall effectiveness of the organization. These measurements help the company's managers monitor the development of its key capabilities and core competencies.

STRATEGIC EFFECTIVENESS

Strategic effectiveness consists of overall organizational effectiveness rather than just unit, product, or operational effectiveness. Therefore, assessment of strategic effectiveness involves evaluating the organization's ability to meet all its goals, subject to environmental uncertainty and internal politics and constraints. Strategic effectiveness also measures the organization's sustainable competitive advantage.

The following general statements emerge from definitions of strategic effectiveness.

- It is multidimensional.
- It involves the systems the organization uses to get things done.
- It includes organizational change and adaptation.
- It includes efficiency and individual performance.
- It requires strategic management.

Strategic effectiveness, then, is concerned with the manner in which strategies are chosen and implemented. To ensure strategic effectiveness, a strategic manager must be able to

- Establish priorities and develop goals and objectives.
- Utilize resources and eliminate nonproductive time.
- Solve problems and determine risk.
- Make decisions based on valid data and assumptions.
- Communicate, listen to feelings, and build trust.
- Resolve conflicts and differences in values.

- Involve individuals in the organization and obtain commitment.
- Achieve results and develop bases for accomplishment.
- Develop workable plans within policy guidelines.
- Maximize the organization's potential to achieve the strategic plan.

INDICATORS OF PERFORMANCE

Because strategy is a comprehensive perspective on what an organization must do in order to achieve its goals, measures of performance must be broader than simply profit or growth. Consistent with this view of the need for a broad basis for measuring performance are (1) efficiency, (2) effectiveness, (3) equity, and (4) responsiveness. These four key indicators are useful measures of performance, because they are often central to statements of goals and objectives. The indicators are measured as follows:

1. *Efficiency is the ratio of outputs produced to resource inputs consumed.* Inputs are frequently measured in dollars or in labor hours. Measures of efficiency include:
   - Return on investment = profit/investment
   - Sales productivity = sales/total labor cost
   - Sales profitability = profit/sales
2. *Effectiveness is the degree to which a goal has been achieved.* Effectiveness is not always directly related to the resources consumed. Measures of effectiveness include the degree to which the following have been achieved:
   - Market share
   - Sales growth
   - Stakeholder expectations
3. *Equity is the fairness, impartiality, or equality with which an organization's stakeholders are treated.* Measures of equity are shown in Table 5.4. Equity might be achieved as appropriate through
   - Equal monetary payments to stakeholders
   - Equal disbursement of goods and services to stakeholders
   - Equal allocation of resources to stakeholders

TABLE 5.4	Measures of Equity

Stakeholder	Measure
Stockholders	Dividends
	Earnings per share
Customers	Price
	Quality
	Reliability
	Geographic areas served
	Income classes served
Community	Contributions
	Taxes paid
	Scholarships
	Employment

Equity is directly related to social responsibility because of concern for stake-holders, who include customers, competitors, and so on. With increasing concern about an organization's social responsibility, equity becomes an increasingly important measure of performance.

4. *Responsiveness is the extent to which the organization satisfies demands placed on it.* Responsiveness does not depend on the source of the demands or even on the cost of satisfying them. Measures of responsiveness include
   ■ Average service time per customer
   ■ Number of complaints satisfied
   ■ Ability to react to organizational pressures
   ■ Capacity to satisfy quality and operational requirements

Many successful strategies are based on responsiveness. American Hospital Supply Corporation, for example, established a 24-hour delivery time (see Chapter 1). Marriott Hotels seek to satisfy quickly every customer who lodges a complaint.

Other indicators of performance are tied directly to a firm's objectives (Drucker, 1973). Drucker suggested eight key areas in which objectives must be set and measures of performance reported: marketing, innovation, human organiza-tion, financial resources, physical resources, productivity, social responsibilities, and profit. Many organizations use these eight areas as a basis for measuring key results and for analysis of their performance. An alternate approach used by Ohmae was discussed in Chapter 1.

An approach called the balanced scorecard (Kaplan and Norton, 1992) has been proposed as a basis for tracking performance in an effort to achieve continu-ous improvement in operations. The scorecard includes

1. *Financial*: measures cash flow, income growth, return on equity, etc.
2. *Internal business*: measures technical capability, time-cost, yield, design pro-ductivity, meeting schedules, etc.
3. *Customer*: Measures sales of products, on-time delivery, suppliers' perfor-mance, cooperative partnerships, etc.
4. *Innovation and learning*: measures technology leadership, learning time, time to introduce new products, etc.

Other measures reported for internal operations include

1. Survey in which customers, employees, and suppliers rated company performance
2. Break-even time for new-product development
3. Reduction in process time from receipt of an order to delivery of a product

A key element of responsiveness to customer needs is flexibility of the organ-ization. Comparing Japan and the United States makes it obvious why cus-tomers react more favorably to Japanese products. Table 5.5 shows these differences on two bases for flexibility: speed of innovation and meeting cus-tomer needs.

TABLE 5.5	Comparison of Flexibility Between the United States and Japan, Showing the Percent of Customers Whose Needs Have Been Met

1. Speed of Innovation	Japan	United States
Product features	82%	40%
High R&D content	80%	50%
Low price	78%	51%
Rapid change	81%	60%
Speed of product mix	78%	60%
Many new products	70%	52%
Advanced manufacturing	83%	66%

2. Meeting Customer Needs	Japan	United States
Handling orders	52%	77%
Supplier relations	72%	85%
Reliability of delivery	87%	98%
Distribution channels	36%	45%
Fast delivery	80%	88%
Durability	61%	68%
Flexible employees	75%	82%

Source: Thorton and Erdman, 1992.

CRITICAL SUCCESS FACTORS

John Rockart (1979) developed a three-step method for determining which factors contribute to meeting organizational goals. He had found that many executives tend to think in terms of what it takes to be successful rather than in terms of grand strategy, goals, and objectives. Therefore, Rockart developed a method that would help executives to derive a strategy, goals, and objectives from answers to the question "What does it take to be successful in this business?" Rockart termed the answers *critical success factors*. Once the critical success factors for the business are identified, executives can use them to develop strategies. The method can be applied by strategic planners within the company or by an outside management consultant or other advisor. The three steps in Rockart's method follow.

1. Generate success factors. In applying this approach in an organization, the strategic planner (advisor) meets with the organization's CEO and asks, *"What does it take to be successful in this business?"* The answers are recorded, as they are given, in a stream-of-consciousness fashion. A free flow of ideas is encouraged. The result is a preliminary list of critical success factors (CSFs).

2. Refine CSFs into goals and objectives. The advisor reviews the CSFs and evaluates and restates them in clearer and more precise language. Then the advisor asks, for each CSF, *"What should the organization's goals and objectives be with respect to this critical success factor?"* Once the list of CSFs is refined, the goals and objectives are stated for each one, the advisor meets again with the CEO. During this session, each CSF is discussed and restated. Unimportant factors are eliminated. If possible, the list is pared down to the seven to ten most critical factors.

3. Identify measures of performance. At this stage, the advisor reviews the organization's information system and other available sources of data to determine how to measure each CSF. The key question in this step is *"How will we know whether the organization has been successful with respect to this factor?"* The advisor constructs an indicator or measure that makes use of available data sources. In a third session with the CEO, the proposed measure of performance for each CSF is discussed and refined. If "hard" data are available, this process may be short and straightforward. If "soft" data must be used, however, the effort may be more time-consuming and will generally result in the identification of some indices, benchmarks, or milestones that can be used as indicators of how well the organization is doing in achieving its CSFs.

Rockart and his associates have applied the CSF method at several different organizations. Figure 5.15 is an example obtained from Microwave Associates.

Rockart's method can be used to identify and refine the CSFs named by top managers, not just by the CEO. Then the group discusses each CSF in turn and decides on its treatment. Sometimes subcommittees are appointed to consider a CSF and its performance measures in more depth. Finally, the top seven to ten CSFs are chosen.

FIGURE 5.15	Critical Success Factors and Their Measures of Performance

Critical Success Factors	Measures
Financial image	Price/earnings ratio
Technological reputation	Quality/reliability
Market share	Change in market (each product) Growth
Risk	Years of experience Customer relationships
Profit	Profit margin
Company morale	Turnover, absenteeism
Performance	Budgeted/actual

Source: John F. Rockart, 1979, p. 89.

SUMMARY

Once a company has established a general direction, it can determine whether it has the capabilities to proceed. To do this, managers need to evaluate the company with respect to key determinants of performance, such as efficiency, productivity, equity, responsiveness, quality, and service. Armed with an understanding of the firm's capabilities and of the threats and opportunities in the external environment, managers are in a position to determine which strategic thrusts and alternatives best suit its mission, goals, and objectives. This process enables them to find the best "strategic fit"—that is, the strategic thrusts and alternatives that best match the company's capabilities with the demands of the external environment.

A number of methods can be used to achieve a good match. They include the company capability profile and WOTS-UP analysis. Vulnerability analysis also helps identify key threats and determine how prepared a company is to meet them. Beyond staying at the minimum required level, however, capability-based competitors develop mechanisms to keep them at the leading edge in terms of their core competencies. They realize that process excellence is essential to delivering these core competencies to the customer. Therefore, a growing number of companies are focusing on two complementary concepts: total quality management (TQM) and time-based management (TBM). Value leveraging is another approach that companies can use to enhance their core capability to meet customer demand. With these approaches managers can determine whether they are capable of achieving a substantial competitive advantage. CSF and performance measurement are the final steps.

REFERENCES AND SUGGESTIONS FOR FURTHER READING

Barney, Jay B. 1986. Organizational culture: Can it be a source of sustained competitive advantage? *Academy of Management Review,* 11, pp. 656–665.

Boston Consulting Group. 1991. Strategic platforms. *BCG Conference for Chief Executives. Summary of Discussions.* Paris, January.

Drucker, Peter F. 1973. *Management: Tasks, responsibilities, practices.* New York: Harper & Row.

Dumaine, Brian. 1992. Is big still good? *Fortune,* April 20, pp. 50–60.

Forrester, Jay W. 1961. *Industrial dynamics.* Cambridge, Mass.: M.I.T. Press.

Garvin, David. 1991. How the Baldrige award really works. *Harvard Business Review,* November–December, pp. 80–93.

Garvin, David A. 1988. *Managing quality: The strategic and competitive edge.* New York: The Free Press.

Garvin, David A. 1987. Competing on the eight dimensions of quality. *Harvard Business Review,* November–December, pp. 101–109.

GE keeps those ideas coming. 1991. *Fortune,* August 12.

Grant, Robert M. 1991. The resource-based theory of competitive advantage: Implications for strategy formulation. *California Management Review,* Spring.

Hamel, Gary, Yves Doz, and C. K. Prahalad. 1989. Collaborate with your competitors—and win. *Harvard Business Review,* January–February, pp. 133–139.

Hauser, John R. and Don Clausing. 1988. The house of quality. *Harvard Business Review,* May–June.

Imai, Masaaki. 1989. *Kaizen, the key to Japan's competitive success.* New York: Random House.

Kaplan, Robert S. and David Norton. 1992. The balanced scorecard—measures that drive performance. *Harvard Business Review,* January–February, pp. 71–79.

Knight, Charles F. 1992. Emerson Electric: Consistent profits, consistently. *Harvard Business Review,* January–February, pp. 57–70.

Pepsi keeps on going after no. 1. 1991. *Fortune,* March 11.

Popplewell, Barry and Alan Wildsmith. 1990. *How to gain company-wide commitment to total quality.* Aldershot, Hampshire: Gower Publishing Group.

Prahalad, C. K. and Gary Hamel. 1990. The core competencies of the corporation. *Harvard Business Review,* May–June, pp. 79–91.

Rummler, Geary A. and Alan P. Brache. 1990. *Improving performance: How to manage the white space on the organization chart.* San Francisco: Oxford Press.

Schein, Lawrence. 1990. The road to total quality. *The Conference Board Research Bulletin.*

Sims, Arden C. et al. 1992. Does the Baldrige Award really work? *Harvard Business Review* 70, January–February, pp. 126–140.

Snow, Charles C. and Lawrence G. Hrebiniak. 1980. Strategy, distinctive competence, and organization performance. *Administrative Science Quarterly,* 25, pp. 317–336.

Stalk, George, Jr. and Thomas M. Hout. 1990. *Competing against time.* New York: The Free Press.

Stalk, George, Philip Evans, and Lawrence E. Shulman. 1992. Competing on capabilities: The new rules of corporate strategy. *Harvard Business Review* 70, no. 2, March–April, pp. 57–70.

Stata, Ray. 1989. Organizational learning—the key to management innovation. *Sloan Management Review,* 63, Spring.

Steeples, Marion Mills. 1992. *The corporate guide to the Malcolm Baldrige National Quality Award.* Homewood, Ill.: ASQC Quality Press.

Stevenson, Howard H. 1976. Defining corporate strengths and weaknesses. *Sloan Management Review,* Spring, pp. 51–68.

Sullivan, L. P. 1986. Quality function deployment. *Quality Progress,* June.

Teitelbaum, Richard S. 1992. Timeliness is everything. *Fortune,* April 20, p. 120.

Thomas, Phillip R. 1990. *Competitiveness through total cycle time.* New York: McGraw-Hill.

Thorton, Emily and Andrew Erdman. 1992. Flexibility as a key in manufacturing strategy. *Fortune,* September 21, pp. 63–74.

CHAPTER SIX

Market Dynamics and Sustainable Competitive Advantage

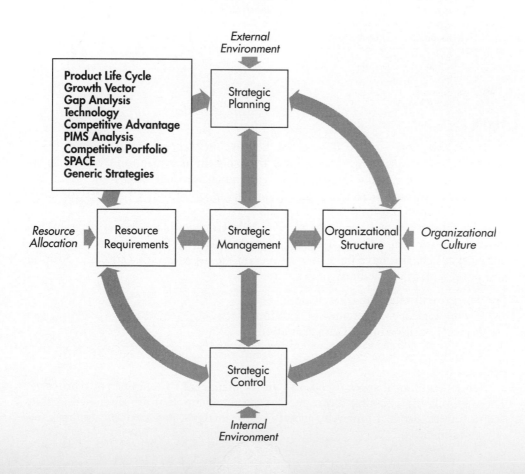

External Environment

Product Life Cycle
Growth Vector
Gap Analysis
Technology
Competitive Advantage
PIMS Analysis
Competitive Portfolio
SPACE
Generic Strategies

Strategic Planning

Resource Allocation

Resource Requirements

Strategic Management

Organizational Structure

Organizational Culture

Strategic Control

Internal Environment

Chapter 1 A Framework for Strategic Management	**Chapter 2** Strategic Analysis	**Chapter 3** Strategic Visioning, Goals, Ethics, and Social Responsibility	**Chapter 4** The Competitive Environment	**Chapter 5** Capability-based Strategy	**Chapter 6** Market Dynamics and Sustainable Competitive Advantage
How to approach strategic management	*Application of strategic analysis*	*Understanding vision, values, ethics*	*Coping with competitive forces, stakeholders*	*Assessing company capability, timeliness, quality*	*Determining trends, gap analysis, and market dynamics*

Chapter 7 Strategy in a Global Environment	**Chapter 8** Financial Planning and Competitive- Cost Analysis	**Chapter 9** Entrepreneurship, Mergers and Acquisitions, Restructuring, and the Service Sector	**Chapter 10** Leadership Factor in Strategy and Implementing Strategic Change	**Chapter 11** Information Technology and Future Directions in Strategy
Assessing global trade, foreign markets, monetary exchange	*Preparing a financial plan and competitive-cost analysis*	*Importance of small business, entrepreneurs, restructuring*	*Strategy implementation, leadership, culture*	*Information technology, trends, new management*

INTRODUCTION

Every organization's success depends on how well it competes in its primary "field of battle," the marketplace. Strategies that enable the organization to influence or control the market, such as creating or expanding into new areas and gaining a dominant position before the competition has an opportunity to enter the field, improve the organization's position overall.

This chapter focuses on methods that help strategic managers understand the market environment in which their company operates. Several aspects of product/market behavior have important effects on the organization's strategic position and development. Particularly relevant are

1. The growth rate of market demand
2. Technological changes and substitutions
3. Product positioning and differentiation

Equally important is sustaining a competitive advantage once the firm has achieved it.

Understanding market dynamics allows managers to assess trends properly. The methods for assessing future market developments that are discussed include decision trees, product life cycle, growth vector analysis, gap analysis, and technology assessment.

Growth vector analysis is a method of examining the firm's product and market position and alternative directions for growth. An existing product in a new market poses opportunities and challenges different from those of a new product in an existing market. A systematic analysis of the market options can often reveal unexplored growth opportunities.

Gap analysis and an understanding of the *product life cycle* help strategic managers to anticipate structural changes in the market early enough to adapt the company's strategy advantageously. Changes in sales, profitability, and investment recovery occur as products move through the phases of the product life cycle. The life cycle concept helps managers identify potential performance gaps, analyze them, and develop plans to reduce or close them.

In the long run, businesses may survive or fail depending on how effectively they harness technological change. New technologies can alter the life cycle of a product or service and the cost and performance characteristics with which the product or service is delivered. In extreme cases, such as the replacement of mechanical office equipment by computers, a new technology can change the entire functional characteristics of a market. Therefore, strategic managers have to monitor and take advantage of technological developments. Methods explained in this chapter include *technology assessment* and the analysis of *technology substitution*.

To complete an assessment of product/market strategy, strategic managers can perform a *competitive portfolio analysis* and a *profit impact of market strategy (PIMS) analysis*. The *product portfolio analysis* enables managers to position each of the company's products based on its growth potential and cash-generation capacity. This analysis also ensures that interproduct effects will be taken into account in developing each product's marketing strategy.

Strategic position and action evaluation (SPACE) goes further and helps define the appropriate strategic posture for a firm based on a range of different input factors. Accordingly, it can form a basis for specifying the *generic competitive strategy* for a business.

The appendices to this chapter are designed to provide methodological support for understanding market dynamics. Appendix A describes how to carry out the product/market mapping activity that is typically used in market research. It covers a number of topics, such as multidimensional scaling, cluster analysis, discriminant analysis, and conjoint analysis. These methods are designed to provide a sound basis for understanding product dynamics and customer perception. Appendix B describes in detail how to conduct a technology assessment. Because of the increasing importance of technology in sustaining a competitive advantage, the methods described provide an important basis for evaluating a company's relative technological position and the rate of substitution of new technologies. These inputs are increasingly becoming critical in formulating competitive strategies.

Chapter 6 is built around a new illustrative case—the AMP case. This case, which is about a company in the electronic connector industry, will be used in this chapter and others to demonstrate the applicability of various methods to strategic management. AMP started making connectors 50 years ago and has reached over $3 billion in sales as a diversified manufacturer of electronic connectors. As the case illustrates, in today's highly competitive market, where technology is critical, strategic management is vital to achieving a sustainable competitive advantage.

ILLUSTRATIVE CASE: AMP CONNECTS ITS ONCE AND FUTURE GOALS

AMP Inc. is entering the '90s with the goal of doing as well as it did in the '70s.

That's a respectable goal. The 49-year-old electronic connector maker intends to return to 15% growth in an industry that's projected to grow by only 7% to 9% per year over the next five years.

As the largest connector maker in the United States with $2.8 billion in 1989 sales, Harrisburg, Pa.-based AMP is four to five times bigger than its nearest competitor, Molex Inc. Industry observers say AMP has reached that status by doing a lot of things right for a long time: a strict focus on its market, a global presence, commitment to quality, a conservative financial approach, and a 9% investment in research, development and engineering (RD&E). "They are the industry's technology leader," says connector industry consultant Ronald Bishop, a principal at Bishop and Associates, Wheaton, Ill. "They also ensure their customers get improved quality and on-time delivery—they will continue to be the market leader for the next decade."

But the connector industry is changing. Consolidation, price pressure, and shorter supplier lists have prompted AMP to change its strategy. The company has closed 36 U.S. plants, restructured its workforce and expanded overseas, says Harold A. McInnes, AMP chairman and chief executive. The company has also been cautiously diversifying into connector-related markets and systems, expanding sales through distribution, and making small acquisitions to fill out its product line. But to reach 15% growth, says Bishop, "AMP will have to become more of a systems manufacturer and make more acquisitions—both of companies and technologies." In June, AMP did just that, acquiring fiber optic manufacturer Kaptron Inc. for an undisclosed sum.

AMP currently holds 18% to 20% of the $17 billion to $18 billion connector market, which still leaves AMP plenty of room to grow. "We believe we are in the strongest position in our history," says McInnes. "We're optimistic that given a reasonable environment, we can

return to our historic growth." AMP's 1989 sales increased only 5% over 1988's.

While different analysts estimate the current worldwide connector market anywhere between $14 billion and $25 billion depending on the connector-related products measured, AMP serves a market that includes connectors, terminals, splices, and packaging devices, according to AMP's head of investor relations, William Oakland.

AMP's greatest strength, industry watchers agree, is its consistent 9% investment in RD&E, which in 1989 amounted to $253 million—dollar- and percentage-wise the highest in the industry. Other strengths, according to connector industry consultant Kenneth Fleck of Fleck International Inc., Huntington Beach, Calif., include worldwide manufacturing with 70 locations in 26 countries, a direct sales force of more than 1,400 worldwide, superior application tooling and early customer involvement.

Fleck also mentions two managerial strengths: conservative financial practices and stable management. AMP's sales, general and administrative (SG&A) expenses are among the lowest in the industry: 18.1% of sales in 1989, and averaging for the past decade between 16.9% and 20.1%, compared with an industry range of 19.9% to 22.3%.

But there are some areas in which AMP hasn't been quite so strong. In the early 1980s, companies such as 3M Co., Thomas & Betts Corp., Augat Inc., Burndy Corp. and Robinson Nugent Inc. made inroads in the connector business at AMP's expense mainly by generating strong partnerships with electronics distributors, says Merrill Lynch Capital Markets' first vice president Jerry Labowitz. "AMP ignored the distributors until the early 1980s, and even then took a go-slow approach," he says. Even though AMP now runs a higher dollar volume through distributors, the current 10% volume compares with 30% for other connector makers.

Another weakness has been AMP's avoidance of the military market—part of a legacy

AMP CONNECTS ITS ONCE AND FUTURE GOALS, CONTINUED

from founder Uncas Whitaker who believed those markets were too entangled in red tape. But in 1988, in order to penetrate the military and commercial aerospace markets—the second-largest connector markets in the U.S. at around $1.3 bil-lion—AMP acquired Matrix Science Corp., a maker of circular connectors, widely used in military and aerospace applications. Prior to its purchase of Matrix, AMP concentrated mainly on flat rectangular connectors.

AMP at a Glance

Fiscal Year	1989	1988
Sales ($ millions)	$2,797	$2,670
Net income ($ millions)	$281	$319
Net income/sales	10.0%	12.0%
Cost of sales/sales	65.0%	62.7%
R&D/sales	9.0%	8.9%
Marketing, G&A/sales	18.1%	17.5%
Number of employees	24,400	24,100
Sales per employee	$114,616	$110,774
Net income per employee	$11,513	$13,242
Capital expenditures/sales	9.0%	8.3%
Current ratio	1.98	2.06
Debt/equity ratio	0.17	0.15
Foreign sales/total sales	54.2%	54.2%

All figures for fiscal year ended December 31.
Source: Company reports.

INDUSTRY DYNAMICS

AMP has been adapting to industry changes in other ways. Faced with overcapacity since 1984, industry pricing pressure has been enormous. OEMs have been paring their supplier lists. Customers increasingly are calling for more highly engineered, quickly developed products delivered early or on time. The industry is also restructuring and consolidating. "We feel the trend of the strong getting stronger through consolidation will continue," says McInnes.

Customers are also looking for systems capability, and AMP is increasing its systems business. The AMP Cooperative Electronic Subcontractor (ACES) program—third-party cable and panel subassemblers—is part of that focus. According to AMP president and COO James E. Marley, the ACES program is an effort to serve OEMs better. "They service the end-customer," he says, "and AMP gives them higher volumes and better pricing."

Both cable and backplane assembly are higher-tech operations than AMP provides in-house. But some industry observers question whether ACES makes sense, pointing out that some ACES are distributors for other brands and there may

AMP CONNECTS ITS ONCE AND FUTURE GOALS, CONTINUED

be no brand loyalty for AMP. Some fear AMP could erode its own profit margins and create price disparity among some groups of sellers.

As products using connectors—PCs, desktops and laptops—get smaller, the degree of interconnection in them decreases. As Shearson Lehman Hutton analyst Stephen J. Balog points out: "The rise of the PC is a negative [for the connector industry]. There is less connector content in PCs—maybe 2% to 3%."

McInnes does not see this as a disadvantage. "As the stuff gets smaller, it also requires more integration. There are fewer connectors per system but more systems sold. And these systems have to be connected into LANs."

AMP has excelled in spotting such opportunities and pursuing them. In Europe, AMP has targeted a new generation of customer premise communications equipment incorporating ISDN standards and has created cross-connect product systems. AMP has sold this product to Siemens AG, N.V. Philips GL, Alcatel, STC, and LM Ericsson. AMP has 15 European subsidiaries.

DIVERSIFICATION STRATEGY

Overseas sales account for 54% of AMP's total sales. According to Labowitz, AMP's geographic breakdown by sales shows 46% for the U.S., 30% for Europe, and 19% for the Far East.

AMP has managed to maintain its strong hold also in the computer and office equipment and automotive markets. In the United States, major AMP customers are IBM, Compaq Computer Corp., and Digital Equipment Corp. AMP has also begun in recent years to offset any market weaknesses through acquisition and strategic partnering. In January, it announced a 50–50 joint venture with $9 billion Dutch company Akzo N.V. to develop and produce additive-process printed wiring boards, 3-D molded circuits, and related products.

In 1989, AMP also acquired Garry Screw Machine Corp. and Decolletage S.A. St.-Maurice,

producers of metal parts used in coaxial connectors, and Lytel, a maker of electro-optic devices.

AMP's product diversification, though, has been cautious. AMP has begun to emphasize value-added assemblies: backplanes, which are combinations of PCBs and connectors; and cable assemblies, combinations of cables and connectors. Labowitz notes that on the more highly engineered cable assemblies and backplanes, margins can be substantially higher than on connectors themselves.

AMP positions itself in high-growth markets through its balanced product line. Of the 684 connector product lines in the U.S., according to Fleck, about 49 of them are high-growth, and AMP is well-positioned in 41 of them. Much of AMP's strategic advantage comes from its leasing of application-tooling machines, which allow customers to rapidly cut and strip wire and terminate connection devices at the ends. AMP has supplied 54,000 application-tooling machines to customers, and Labowitz estimates two-thirds of AMP's sales are of machine-applied products. "AMP's application tooling is the industry standard and it helps lower customers' costs," Bishop says.

AMP's Worldwide Sales

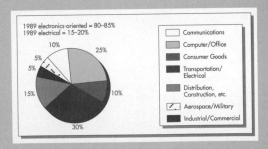

AMP has only recently begun to increase its sales through distribution; those sales now stand at nearly 10%, compared with less than 1% of total sales in 1979. But when AMP decided to sell through distribution, it did so with a vengeance. Says Steve Menefee, ex-vice president

AMP CONNECTS ITS ONCE AND FUTURE GOALS, CONTINUED

for sales and marketing with AMP distributor Hamilton/Avnet: "This company, in my opinion, acts and thinks like a semiconductor company. They're aggressive, cooperative, and a good listener. They've done many things to make their line look attractive to distribution."

From AMP's strategic standpoint, distribution broadened its customer base. "Ten years ago we looked at distribution," says McInnes. "We got involved in a casual way. Many components were moving through distribution and we knew some were coming out of direct sales and these were sales we were missing."

Chuck Poncher is president and CEO of Hawk Electronics Inc., Wheeling, Ill., a privately held specialty distributor that's carried AMP lines for eight years. "We've noticed changes in how AMP's been relating to distributors," says Poncher. "They've changed their price structure to benefit their distributors."

But could AMP's continued growth actually prove a hindrance? Bishop says AMP's size has made the company hard to do business with. "There were more procedures, red tape, and slow decision-making," he says. Bishop notes that AMP has been restructuring to push the decision-making down the line. "The people closer to the customer can serve him better," he says. "AMP's taking the slowness out of the machine."

Communication problems haven't gone unnoticed by AMP management. "In 1965 we first made the Fortune 500," says McInnes. "We've gotten bigger, and we've asked ourselves, 'How can we communicate around the world?'" As part of this effort AMP has created a "Planned Excellence" videotape for its employees, has formed international councils and has transferred employees between AMP's many regions.

FUTURE GROWTH

Observes analyst Labowitz: "The most important thing in the connector industry in the coming decade is that the U.S. will be the least exciting area for growth prospects. But connector makers have the most base in the U.S. If that's the case, AMP has to become inherently 'global'—in reality, they have to implement the things that have made them global so far. You have to communicate well—that's the challenge."

Marley says some of AMP's communication problems are being addressed, particularly overseas. "In order to participate in local markets you need a local team," he says. "In addition, a [global presence] enforces discipline: It suggests a product used in Japan can also be used in Europe. We've created a council to make sure we've addressed the nuances of every customer in every market."

Another challenge facing connector makers in a mature market is to know where the next opportunities will come from. Says McInnes: "We see growth in Europe with the economic community of 1992 along with potential of the Eastern Bloc. We should enjoy growth in the '90s in Asia and the Pacific." In the past five years, AMP has increased its overseas sales by 17.3%, says Bishop, compared with 2.6% sales growth in the U.S.

SMART BUILDINGS

Domestically, president Marley sees "smart" buildings and new technologies as areas of growth. There will be a need for rewiring of stores and buildings, and an area of major emphasis will be products and technologies that fit, he says. "Beyond that, there will be the impact of optical computers and superconductors."

But will these provide the environment necessary for 15% growth? Bishop foresees the emergence of new, smaller companies "niche-ing the heck out of AMP." He adds: "It's a conservative, well-managed company focused on engineering, but will have trouble maintaining its growth rate. As the industry matures, AMP is going to have competitors nipping at its heels. Where AMP will get beat up is where they can't turn a project around fast enough...."

Bishop also says the U.S. connector industry faces a very real Japanese threat, but AMP and

> ## AMP CONNECTS ITS ONCE AND FUTURE GOALS, CONTINUED
>
> Molex have excellent offshore manufacturing and are well-positioned to take advantage of the expanding marketplace. For instance, AMP's 10-year compound annual growth rate in the Far East was 15.6% and Molex's, 24.6%. The industry growth rate was 17.3%.
>
> "As [Far East] transplants come to the U.S. and start procuring products locally, AMP and Molex will benefit from that business," notes analyst Labowitz. "But if they are serviced through a Japanese company, AMP will have to compete.
>
> "AMP, along with Molex, are best positioned to be global companies—they have the ability and critical mass," Labowitz continues. "But to hold on to their business they have to effectively coordinate those things, and that's a real challenge to management."
>
> *Source:* Reprinted from *Electronic Business,* September 3, 1990, © 1990 Reed Publishing USA.

Now that we are familiar with AMP's record and have heard what several industry analysts have to say about the company, let's give CEO Harold McInnes the floor. The following are excerpts from two speeches he delivered: the first in 1990 at the International Connector Symposium, and the second in 1992 at the Fleck International Connection Congress.

DECADE OF THE 1990s—THE GAME GETS TOUGHER*

Here's the likely scenario:

Financial. It will be much more difficult to obtain funds, debt or equity, because of government budget deficits, rising demand for capital throughout the world—particularly Eastern Europe—and the tightening of credit by banks in the U.S., Great Britain, Japan, and other countries. Venture capital will be harder to obtain and more costly. Governments obviously need to encourage more savings and investment and less consumption, but this is politically difficult. In many companies, internally generated cash flow will be insufficient to fully finance new product development, modernization, and expansion—and they will have to look for financial help, usually equity investments, from other companies.

Technology. Will require ever higher levels of expertise and resources, and must move from the laboratory to salable product at an ever faster rate. Many companies won't have the resources to do this effectively without help. A critical aspect for the U.S. is the development of a national policy on government involvement and funding in non-military technology areas. If the U.S. is to maintain its technology lead, the laissez faire, i.e., "no policy" approach of the 1980s must evolve into a more pragmatic, long-term, results-oriented partnership among government, industry, finance, and academia that faces the realities of how technology is being managed nationally in Western Europe, Japan, and several other countries.

Manufacturing. Following the lead of the Japanese, it is now being elevated to equal status with R&D, marketing, and finance after decades of second-class status. The need is now recognized for multi-discipline teams who design from conception for manufacturability and quality—and who use a simultaneous engineering approach. Excellent progress is being made throughout the world on improving productivity and quality—and MRP, JIT, CIM, TQC and many other systems will continue to be developed and implemented. Outsourcing will continue to increase. Manufacturing will continue to migrate to lower-cost areas. While U.S. manufacturing employment will continue to decline, the U.S. will retain a sufficient higher-technology manufacturing base to support and enhance the leading role it has in advanced technology. To gain economies of scale and reduce investment, companies will increasingly "rationalize" their facilities through tighter controls on a regional or worldwide basis where each facility has an assigned role in an integrated whole—instead of a collection of companies primarily serving their local markets.

Marketing. Must be increasingly done on a regional and/or global basis to be effective. Global sourcing will increase. Quality requirements will rise steadily until leading companies reach six sigma levels in the late 1990s. Requirements will continue to rise for on-time delivery to more precise delivery times, better service, and higher-level technology support. Supplier lists will steadily shrink as customers reduce to the few best in each product or service category. Partnering between customers and preferred suppliers will slowly but surely move from lip service to implementation. Standards—national, regional, global—will become increasingly important in both the development and marketing of products. The niche player will have to be very creative—unique patentable products, alliances, superior service—to survive.

Pricing. After steady erosion since the mid-1980s, pricing will firm up in the next year or two in many products because of higher capacity utilization levels, more partnering between customers and key suppliers, and better understanding of value and of the need for healthy margins to fund improvement and expansion.

What are some of the conclusions we can draw from this scenario?

Human Resources. Increasingly, the most critical factor in success will be the extent to which a company, or any organization, empowers, trains, and motivates its people. Leadership, communications, teams, and gain sharing must supplant authoritarianism, secrecy, and bureaucracy. The key to continuous improvement is to have all people, from CEO to the machine operator, understand and work toward common goals in a results-oriented, customer-oriented culture. Education must, and will, become much better—particularly in the U.S. where science and math have been neglected and 20% of adults are functional illiterates. But this will take years. Thus, short term the answer is much more and better on-the-job training because over three-fourths of the employees of the year 2000 are already on the payroll today. In leading companies, training will be a continuous, integral part of each person's job. At AMP we launched our plan for excellence earlier this year to provide a more comprehensive, longer-term approach to continuous improvement of quality, productivity and service. A cornerstone is a quantum leap ahead in training, and our training expenditures have doubled in the last few years and will keep rising. This is happening throughout the industrial world.

A Global—or at Least a Regional—Approach. Will be increasingly needed in all functions. But, as AMP and most multi-nationals are finding out, fully implementing a truly global approach requires an extremely strong commitment from top management and great attention to detail for many years to bring about the required change in attitudes, culture, and practices. Pronouncements and coordination aren't enough. It takes very deliberate changes in systems, transfers of people, adjustments in inter-company accounting, creation of rewards and penalties—so decisions are made on what is best for the entire company rather than the individual division or subsidiary. The ultimate goal is a "seamless" organization with no internal barriers.

Multi-nationals. Will become more dominant because they can effectively raise funds, transfer resources, gain economies of scale, make large investments, and match up globally with customers. Successful multi-nationals will be the markets and channels through which many smaller, more localized companies will do business.

Strategic Alliances. Will be essential to success for even the biggest and strongest com-panies. The external support system—suppliers, subcontractors, acquisitions, minority interests, joint ventures, venture capital investments, research consortiums, consul-tants—will be as critical as internal capabilities. They provide valuable leverage as companies increasingly concentrate their main resources on their own unique in-house core capabilities. Doing this successfully is a very real challenge to most managements because their experience is primarily internally oriented. Done poorly, it can drain away resources and unduly divert management attention.

Broader Role for Key Suppliers. The most successful suppliers will be those who take full advantage of the customer's growing need for conservation of resources, cost reduction, cycle time reduction, quality and productivity improvement—thus increas-ing proclivity by outsourcing, partnering, subcontracting, and strategic alliances. Expanding into value-added products, assemblies, and services requires more resources, greater expertise, new approaches. Only a small fraction of all suppliers will end up being formally approved and able to do all this effectively.

Indirect vs. Direct Costs. A steadily rising proportion of total costs will be indi-rect—benefits, communications, commuter systems, legal costs, insurance, product liability, training and development, environmental protection, waste disposal, RD&E, marketing. The gap may narrow on direct wage costs as wage rates continue to rise more rapidly in the newly industrialized nations, but the disparity in indirect costs among different countries will widen and make it increasingly difficult for companies in the more advanced countries to compete in low-technology manufac-turing. Thus, managements throughout the world (but particularly in the advanced countries) will be under mounting pressure to limit or reduce benefits and shift more of this burden on workers and government, cut corners on environmental protec-tion, skimp on RD&E, and take other actions for short-term relief from margin pressures. The challenge will be to effectively control these indirect costs while meet-ing rising legal and societal requirements and managing for superior long-term—not short-term—results.

Let me conclude with a challenge to the connector industry. We at AMP believe the next frontier in the connector industry is reliability—i.e., *the effective performance of the connection system over the entire life of the equipment in which it is used.* As elec-tronic circuitry moves into further miniaturization and faster signal speeds, as elec-tronic equipment is placed into new environments, as servicing becomes more difficult and expensive, and as the consequences of failures becomes greater—reliability must become the top issue in the 1990s.

*Reprinted with permission of AMP Incorporated.

THE GLOBAL BUSINESS ENVIRONMENT IN THE DECADE AHEAD

Most companies have a good foundation to build on in the 1990s. Some of the principles and goals you'll see progress on will include:

- Further use of employee teams.
- Continuous training of each employee as an integral part of that person's development.
- Gain sharing and incentive pay linked as directly as possible to individual, team, and unit performance at the team, unit, and company level.
- Extensive non-monetary recognition of accomplishments.
- Much greater sharing of information within the company.
- Career counseling for all employees.
- Open posting of all job openings.
- More transfer of employees between U.S. and international operations.
- Formal executive/professional development and human resources planning programs to identify and provide for future needs.
- More commitment by the company to employment security, and
- Much benchmarking with companies who are leaders in what they do.

The days of command and control are over—replaced by leadership and empowerment. Management must communicate, set an example, share responsibility and authority, enable people to do more, and reward good performance. The payoff for doing this well will be enormous.

Excerpts from AMP's 1991 Form 10-K and financial statements and annual financial ratios follow.

EXCERPTS: 10-K REPORT FOR YEAR ENDED DECEMBER 31, 1991

PART I.

Item 1. Business

The foldout and inside front cover, pages 1–25, and Notes 14 and 15 on page 35 of the Annual Report to security holders for the year ended December 31, 1991 are hereby incorporated by reference.

The business in which the Company is engaged is highly competitive. The Company believes it is the leading producer of electrical/electronic connection devices, and associated application tools and machines. Over 95% of its business is in this single business segment. Within this segment there is great variety: over 100,000 types and sizes are included in over 200 product families. These product families generally involve the same or very similar basic technology, materials, production processes, and marketing approaches. Over 60% of sales are of products provided in strip form on reels and applied by customers with special machines provided by the Company. Another 10% of sales are of products provided in single piece form and applied by customers with special AMP tools. The balance of sales is of pre-assembled devices, which do not require application tools or machines. Nearly 80% of sales are of products in just two Standard Industrial Classification 4-digit codes—Electronic Connectors and Current Carrying Wiring Devices. In all cases, the Company's products are subject to direct and indirect competition. Generally speaking, most of the Company's products involve technical competence in development and manufacture and are subject to active competition with products manufactured and sold by many other companies. The Company competes primarily through offering high-quality, technical products and associated application tooling with emphasis on product performance and service and only secondarily competes on a price basis. The Company has several thousand patents issued or pending, with no one patent considered significant. The number of competitors is estimated at over 1,200.

The Company feels it has adequate sources of supply and does not expect the cost and availability of materials to have a significant overall effect on its total current operations.

The Company's backlog of unfilled orders increased from $514,000,000 at year-end 1990 to $525,000,000 at year-end 1991, and has risen slightly so far in 1992. A majority of these orders were for delivery within the next ninety days, and substantially all were scheduled for delivery within 12 months.

The Company is not aware of any material claims against its assets. However, it is potentially liable for all or a portion of environmental clean-up costs at several National Priorities List sites. At one site, which is the subject of a Corrective Action Order under the Resource Conservation and Recovery Act, the Company has incurred costs of nearly $1 million since 1984 and anticipates incurring additional costs of $75,000–100,000 per year indefinitely. At another site, for which the Company shares potential liability with several other parties, the Company spent $144,000 in 1991 and will spend another $144,000 in 1992; a cost determination as to subsequent years' costs has not been made, but based on cost estimates related to other NPL sites, the Company's cost at this site should not exceed $4 million, to be incurred over six to eight years beginning in 1993 or later. The remaining sites are involved in preliminary investigative activities and neither liability nor total cost assessments have been made. However, the Company's future environmental compliance costs are not expected to have a material impact on the Company's financial results, liquidity or capital expenditures. Over the five-year period 1987–1991 the Company has spent several million dollars annually for remedial and preventative actions in protection of the environment.

The primary seasonal effect generally experienced by the Company is in the third quarter when there usually is a temporary leveling off or modest drop in the rate of new orders and shipments because of the softening of customer demand in certain markets such as appliances, automotive, and home entertainment goods arising from model year changeovers, plant vacations and closedowns, and other traditional seasonal practices. This seasonal effect is most evident in the Company's European operations. Also there is usually some seasonal strengthening in domestic sales and orders in the first quarter, although this strengthening was mild in 1992 because of recessionary effects.

Presently, there are no foreign exchange or currency restrictions in the various countries which would significantly affect the remittance of funds to AMP.

Highlights and Financial Data: AMP
(Dollar amounts in millions, except per share data)

Years Ended	1991	1990	1989	1988	1987	1986	1985	1984	1983	1982	1981
Net sales	$3,095.0	$3,043.6	$2,796.6	$2,669.7	$2,317.8	$1,933.1	$1,636.1	$1,812.8	$1,515.5	$1,243.4	$1,234.3
Income before income taxes	423.6	462.0	455.3	529.2	430.5	294.0	192.5	362.7	292.6	213.5	241.0
Income taxes	163.9	174.9	174.4	210.1	180.8	129.7	84.5	161.4	129.5	94.6	106.2
Net income[1]	$ 259.7	$ 287.1	$ 280.9	$ 319.1	$ 249.7	$ 164.3	$ 108.0	$ 201.3	$ 163.1	$ 118.9	$ 134.8
Per share[1]	$ 2.45	$ 2.70	$ 2.63	$ 2.96	$ 2.31	$ 1.52	$ 1.00	$ 1.87	$ 1.52	$ 1.10	$ 1.25
Cash dividends per share[1,2]	$ 1.44	$ 1.36	$ 1.20	$ 1.00	85¢	74¢	72¢	64¢	53$\frac{1}{3}$¢	46$\frac{2}{3}$¢	40¢
Capital expenditures	$ 313.3	$ 338.4	$ 252.1	$ 220.3	$ 171.8	$ 151.7	$ 198.5	$ 255.7	$ 127.6	$ 121.9	$ 108.9
At December 31—											
Working capital	$ 738.0	$ 665.2	$ 711.7	$ 700.9	$ 625.3	$ 475.5	$ 356.1	$ 389.4	$ 446.5	$ 415.6	$ 410.7
Property, plant and equipment, net	1,180.2	1,121.5	953.8	894.6	865.4	793.6	750.2	620.4	461.9	413.5	362.9
Shareholders' equity	1,913.0	1,792.8	1,625.4	1,521.3	1,348.6	1,134.9	996.9	923.2	800.9	714.5	660.5
Backlog	$ 525.0	$ 514.0	$ 489.0	$ 475.0	$ 384.0	$ 326.0	$ 307.0	$ 340.0	$ 374.0	$ 254.0	$ 253.0
Number of employees	25,000	24,700	24,400	24,100	22,000	21,800	22,800	24,500	21,300	19,750	19,650
Shares of stock outstanding[1] (millions)	106.0	105.9	106.5	107.4	107.5	108.1	107.9	107.7	107.5	107.7	107.8

[1] Share data has been adjusted for the 3-for-1 stock split in 1984.
[2] On January 22, 1992 a regular quarterly dividend of 38¢ per share was declared—an indicated annual rate of $1.52 per share.

Consolidated Statements of Income (Unaudited): AMP
(Dollar amounts in thousands, except per share data)

	For the 3 Months Ended September 30	
	1992	1991
Net sales	$ 847,075	$ 736,318
Cost of sales	556,497	487,907
Gross income	290,578	248,411
Selling, general and administrative expenses	146,806	132,307
Income from operations	143,772	116,104
Interest expense	(6,826)	(9,761)
Other income (deductions), net	(8,019)	(4,605)
Income before income taxes	128,927	101,738
Income taxes	51,110	40,180
Net income	$ 77,817	$ 61,558
Per share—Net income	74¢	58¢
Cash dividends	38¢	36¢
Weighted average number of shares	105,188,969	105,850,212

	For the 9 Months Ended September 30	
	1992	1991
Net sales	$ 2,492,631	$ 2,304,350
Cost of sales	1,649,263	1,529,037
Gross income	843,368	775,313
Selling, general and administrative expenses	442,147	415,861
Income from operations	401,221	359,452
Interest expense	(22,982)	(31,407)
Other income (deductions), net	(15,595)	(9,627)
Income before income taxes	362,644	318,418
Income taxes	142,620	122,140
Net income	$ 220,024	$ 196,278
Per share—Net income	$ 2.08	$ 1.85
Cash dividends	$ 1.14	$ 1.08
Weighted average number of shares	105,634,132	105,900,503

Consolidated Balance Sheets (Condensed): AMP
(Dollar amounts in thousands)

	September 30, 1992*	December 31, 1991
Assets		
Current assets		
Cash and cash equivalents	$ 323,037	$ 370,829
Marketable securities	69,337	80,167
Receivables	630,876	589,212
Inventories—		
Finished goods and work in process	252,165	246,187
Purchased and manufactured parts	151,263	149,472
Raw materials	45,189	44,943
Total inventories	448,617	440,602
Other current assets	151,973	135,559
Total current assets	1,623,840	1,616,369
Property, plant and equipment	2,738,437	2,550,406
Less–accumulated depreciation	1,537,854	1,370,236
Property, plant and equipment, net	1,200,583	1,180,170
Investments and other assets	213,600	210,356
Total assets	**$ 3,038,023**	**$ 3,006,895**
Liabilities and Shareholders' Equity		
Current liabilities		
Short-term debt	$ 271,801	$ 336,660
Payables, trade and other	257,245	250,605
Accrued liabilities	305,521	301,142
Total current liabilities	834,567	888,407
Long-term debt	49,006	52,995
Other liabilities and deferred credits	184,814	152,450
Total liabilities	1,068,387	1,093,852
Shareholders' equity	1,969,636	1,913,043
Total liabilities and shareholders' equity	**$ 3,038,023**	**$ 3,006,895**

*Unaudited.

BUSINESS SEGMENTS

The Company's business is concentrated almost entirely in one product area—electrical and electronic connection, switching and programming devices—which are sold throughout many diverse markets. It is not possible, therefore, to divide AMP's business into meaningful industry segments.

However, the Company's operations are worldwide and can be grouped into several geographic segments. Operations outside the United States are conducted through wholly owned subsidiary companies that function within assigned, principally national, markets. The subsidiaries manufacture locally where required by market conditions and/or customer demands, and where permitted by economies of scale. Most are also self-financed. However, while they operate fairly autonomously, there are substantial intersegment and intrasegment sales.

Pertinent financial data by major geographic segments for 1990, 1989, and 1988 are:

(Dollars in thousands)	Sales to Unaffiliated Customers	Intersegment Sales	Total Sales	Pretax Income	Net Income	Total Assets
United States:						
1990	$1,237,237	$ 265,370	$1,502,607	$203,276	$133,249	$1,677,166
1989	1,281,864	234,705	1,616,569	186,953	124,511	1,574,894
1988	1,221,525	174,803	1,396,328	219,046	138,215	1,526,885
Europe:						
1990	$1,072,111	$ 19,828	$1,091,939	$165,535	$103,565	$ 755,881
1989	863,894	13,641	877,535	171,975	107,180	596,296
1988	809,785	14,971	824,756	193,403	113,938	505,477
Asia/Pacific:						
1990	$ 583,189	$ 20,067	$ 603,256	$ 74,671	$ 41,917	$ 567,772
1989	506,761	13,868	520,629	76,060	45,510	463,411
1988	514,138	10,876	525,014	95,492	47,597	457,560
Americas:						
1990	$ 151,052	$ 17,879	$ 168,931	$ 17,044	$ 7,692	$ 84,754
1989	144,117	15,227	159,344	23,866	11,263	81,398
1988	124,213	10,793	135,006	19,635	10,516	72,619
Eliminations:						
1990	$ —	$ (323,144)	$ (323,144)	$ 1,486	$ 689	$ (156,957)
1989	—	(277,441)	(277,441)	(3,567)	(7,557)	(186,240)
1988	—	(211,443)	(211,443)	1,647	8,857	(187,004)
Total:						
1990	$3,043,589	$ —	$3,043,589	$462,012	$287,112	$2,928,616
1989	2,796,636	—	2,796,636	455,287	280,907	2,529,759
1988	2,669,661	—	2,669,661	529,223	319,123	2,375,537

Transfers between geographic segments are generally priced at "large quantity customer prices less a discount" for items not requiring further manufacture and at "cost plus a percentage" for items subject to further processing.

Included in the assets of the United States segment are short-term investments at December 31: 1990—$405,946,000; 1989—$305,931,000 and 1988—$290,532,000; which generated interest income of approximately $18,371,000, $19,917,000, and $16,681,000, respectively.

Combined Balance Sheets: AMP Incorporated & Its Subsidiaries and Pamcor, Inc.
(Dollar amounts in thousands)

	December 31	
	1990	1989
Assets		
Current assets		
Cash and cash equivalents	$ 414,493	$ 309,164
Marketable securities	45,674	25,001
Receivables	557,484	520,028
Inventories	481,727	494,803
Deferred income taxes	69,565	56,144
Other current assets	49,468	32,098
Total current assets	1,618,411	1,437,238
Property, plant and equipment	2,803,328	1,927,541
Less—accumulated depreciation	1,181,784	973,786
Property, plant and equipment, net	1,121,544	953,755
Investments and other assets	181,661	138,766
Total assets	$2,928,616	$2,529,759
Liabilities and Shareholders' Equity		
Current liabilities		
Short-term debt	$ 378,636	$ 214,512
Payables, trade and other	244,655	224,924
Accrued payrolls and employee benefits	132,194	114,585
Accrued income taxes	151,384	129,765
Other accrued liabilities	46,341	41,711
Total current liabilities	953,210	725,497
Long-term debt	61,095	69,500
Deferred income taxes	79,840	71,609
Other liabilities	41,713	37,720
Total liabilities	1,135,858	904,326

(continued)

Combined Balance Sheets: AMP Incorporated & Its Subsidiaries and Pamcor, Inc. (continued)
(Dollar amounts in thousands)

	December 31	
	1990	1989
Shareholders' equity		
AMP Incorporated—		
Common stock, without par value—		
Authorized 350,000,000 shares,		
issued 112,320,000 shares	12,480	12,480
Pamcor, Inc.—		
Common stock, par value $1.00 per share—		
Authorized 64,000 shares, 20,000 shares	20	20
Other capital	77,746	77,156
Cumulative translation adjustments	114,108	67,911
Retained earnings	1,765,396	1,622,935
Treasury stock, at cost	(176,992)	(155,069)
Total shareholders' equity	1,792,758	1,625,433
Total liabilities and shareholders' equity	$2,928,616	$2,529,759

Combined Annual Income Statements: AMP Incorporated & Its Subsidiaries and Pamcor, Inc.
(Dollar amounts in thousands, except per share data)

	Years Ended December 31		
	1990	1989	1988
Net sales	$3,043,589	$2,796,636	$2,669,661
Cost of sales	2,012,394	1,816,821	1,672,718
Gross income	1,031,195	979,815	996,943
Selling, general and			
administrative expenses	543,437	505,191	467,045
Income from operations	487,758	474,674	529,898
Interest expense	(38,321)	(21,592)	(16,185)
Other income, net	12,575	2,255	15,510
Income before income taxes	462,012	455,287	529,223
Income taxes	174,900	174,380	210,100
Net income	$ 287,112	$ 280,907	$ 319,123
Net income per share	$ 2.70	$ 2.63	$ 2.96

Combined Statements of Cash Flows: AMP Incorporated & Its Subsidiaries and Pamcor, Inc.
(Dollar amounts in thousands)

	Years Ended December 31		
	1990	1989	1988
Cash and cash equivalents at January 1	$ 309,164	$ 247,788	$ 142,397
Operating activities			
Net income	287,112	290,907	319,123
Noncash adjustments—			
Depreciation and amortization	217,734	180,270	158,511
Deferred income taxes and investment tax credits	(5,765)	(15,720)	(22,120)
Increase to other liabilities	6,183	6,251	2,357
Other, net	17,881	7,879	20,116
Changes in operating assets and liabilities net of effects of acquisitions and disposition of businesses	55,780	(68,331)	49,728
Cash provided by operating activities	578,925	391,256	527,715
Investing activities			
Additions to property, plant and equipment	(338,389)	(252,122)	(220,257)
(Increase) decrease in marketable securities	(20,674)	58,843	(13,292)
(Acquisitions) disposition of businesses, less cash acquired, net	(3,466)	(13,971)	(25,725)
Other, net	(44,403)	(18,589)	(5,353)
Cash used for investing activities	(406,932)	(225,839)	(264,627)
Financing activities			
Changes in short-term debt	118,378	77,010	31,125
Proceeds from long-term debt	11,660	6,415	25,418
Repayments of long-term debt	(27,285)	(13,056)	(11,239)
Purchases of treasury stock	(26,037)	(44,881)	(92,596)
Dividends paid	(144,651)	(128,090)	(107,802)
Cash used for financing activities	(67,935)	(102,602)	(155,094)
Effect of exchange rate changes on cash	1,271	(1,439)	(2,603)
Cash and cash equivalents at December 31	$ 414,493	$ 309,164	$ 247,788
Changes in operating assets and liabilities			
Receivables	$ 6,465	$ (55,076)	$ (6,465)
Inventories	38,659	(15,048)	(55,923)

(continued)

Combined Statements of Cash Flows: AMP Incorporated & Its Subsidiaries and Pamcor, Inc. (continued)
(Dollar amounts in thousands)

	Years Ended December 31		
	1990	1989	1988
Other current assets	(14,184)	(346)	(2,249)
Payables, trade and other	(6,420)	9,654	50,642
Accrued payrolls and employee benefits	12,182	7,056	11,177
Other accrued liabilities	19,078	(14,571)	52,546
	$ 55,780	$ (68,331)	$ 49,728

Key Annual Financial Ratios: AMP

Fiscal Year Ended	December 31, 1990	December 31, 1989
Quick ratio	1.07	1.18
Current ratio	1.70	1.98
Net sales/cash	6.61	8.37
SG&A expense/sales	0.18	0.18
Receivables turnover	5.46	5.38
Receivables day sales	65.94	66.94
Inventory turnover	6.32	5.65
Inventory day sales	56.98	63.69
Net sales/Working capital	4.58	3.93
Net sales/Net plant and equipment	2.71	2.93
Net sales/Current assets	1.88	1.95
Net sales/Total assets	1.04	1.11
Net sales/Employees	123,222	114,616
Total liabilities/Total assets	0.39	0.36
Total liabilities/Invested capital	0.61	0.53
Total liabilities/Common equity	0.63	0.56
Times interest earned	13.06	22.09
Current debt/Equity	NA	NA
Long-term debt/Equity	0.03	0.04
Total debt/Equity	0.03	0.04
Total assets/Equity	1.63	1.56
Pretax income/Net sales	0.15	0.16
Pretax income/Total assets	0.16	0.18
Pretax income/Invested capital	0.25	0.27

(continued)

Key Annual Financial Ratios (continued)

Fiscal Year Ended	December 31, 1990	December 31, 1989
Pretax income/Common equity	0.26	0.28
Net income/Net sales	0.09	0.10
Net income/Total assets	0.10	0.11
Net income/Invested capital	0.15	0.17
Net income/Common equity	0.16	0.17

SUSTAINABLE COMPETITIVE ADVANTAGE

It is not necessarily difficult to achieve a competitive advantage by taking extraordinary steps. Sustaining it, however, is difficult. A *sustainable competitive advantage* has a reasonable lasting effect and helps the company to achieve its strategic goals. Three conditions of sustainable competitive advantage are

1. The customer consistently perceives a positive difference between the products or services offered by the company and those offered by its competitors. These differences include quality, uniqueness, value, or cost competitiveness.
2. The perceived difference results from the company's relatively greater capability.
3. The perceived difference persists for a reasonable period of time.

The positive difference is based on additional attributes, such as price, aesthetics, functionality, availability, visibility, and after-sales service. Positive differences in these areas help the company to establish a niche in the market.

Competitive advantage is durable only to the extent that it cannot be readily imitated. Four capability gaps have been identified that help to prevent imitation by competitors:

1. Business-system gaps such as good working conditions
2. Image gaps resulting from reputation, consumer awareness, and trust
3. Uniqueness gaps that limit competitors' actions, including patents, licenses, and regulations regarding consumer safety
4. Strategy gaps that reflect the organization's capacity for innovation, flexibility, and ability to adapt

To sustain its competitive advantage, the company must continue its expenditures for research and development, product improvement, performance enhancement, advertising, responsiveness to customer needs, delivery, and service. If a competitor can match these capabilities, the company may lose market share.

Ghemawat (1986) suggested that to sustain a competitive advantage, a company must focus on three areas: product innovation, new production processes, and marketing strategies besides pricing. In his view, sustainable competitive advantage depends on the company size in the targeted market, on superior access to resources or customers, and on restricted options of competitors.

An increasingly important factor in sustaining competitive advantage is maintenance of product quality. Garvin (1987) suggested eight absolute standards of product quality. They are, in order of customer preference,

1. *Performance.* The product must perform to specifications.
2. *Features.* Features in addition to basic performance can enhance the product's desirability.
3. *Reliability.* The product must perform consistently as specified.
4. *Conformance.* The product's design should meet established operating standards.
5. *Durability.* The product should function for a specified period of time, be repairable, and not become obsolete prematurely.
6. *Serviceability.* Product maintenance and repair should be provided with speed, courtesy, and competence. Maintenance and repair should not be difficult or complicated.
7. *Aesthetics.* The product should be a pleasing design, size, color, and so on.
8. *Perceived quality.* Reputation often is the basis of perceived quality.

Creating a sustainable competitive advantage requires a combination of different factors, the most important of which are shown in Figure 6.1. On the left side

---

FIGURE 6.1 | **Sources of Competitive Advantage**

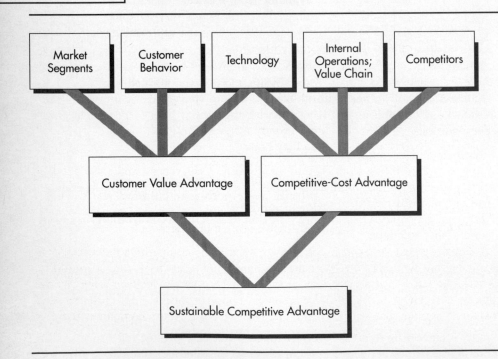

are customer-related areas in which a company can gain advantage, on the right side competitor-related areas. Technology affects both the potential for customer value advantage and that for competitive cost advantage.

Core competency can be created by finding new markets that are not currently there. Hamel and Prahalad (1991) describe how competitive battles were won in the 1980s by companies that used cost and quality advantages in known markets. In the 1990s, however, battles will be won by companies that use their imagination and create dramatically new markets for products that previously did not exist, such as speech-activated devices, multimedia computers, and genetically engineered medication.

Marketing strategy considers not only meeting competitive pressure but also identifying and serving real customer needs (Ohmae, 1988). In some instances, new products will generate a customer need, but in most cases, marketing means finding the need that matches readily available products. Ohmae describes the case of Yamaha, which had 40% of the global market for pianos but saw demand for them decreasing 10% per year. Recognizing that conventional pianos served a limited need, Yamaha added digital and optical technology to produce a modern "player piano." The results in sales have been explosive.

Consistent with our theme of total value, some of the ways of achieving a sustainable competitive advantage include

1. *Value.* The product is the best available for the price.
2. *Quality.* The product works well, looks good, and is very reliable.
3. *Service.* The customer can trust repairs that are timely and courteous.
4. *Price.* It is competitive but not the lowest.
5. *Distribution.* Able to meet demand at the lowest cost.
6. *Reputation.* Good image, name is known, location is convenient.
7. *Technology.* The product should be efficient and effective.
8. *Innovative.* Features are not available elsewhere.
9. *Functionality.* The product meets requirements as specified.
10. *Durability.* It doesn't break, can take abuse.
11. *Distinctive patent,* protection for unique features.
12. *Maintain relations* with suppliers, customers, networks.
13. *Flexible enough* to outpace competition—responsive to customer needs.
14. *Market focus.* Segmented, niche, or differentiated.
15. *Profitability.* Avoid price wars, discard obsolete products.

A company that recognizes the need to sustain its competitive advantage will choose ongoing strategies aimed at maintaining its market share and profitability. This requirement is not satisfied by preparation of a single strategic plan for the company as a whole or its SBUs but requires constant monitoring, updating, and focusing on actions that will sustain a competitive edge. Many companies that are now defunct did not recognize that the overriding "strategy" must be to stay ahead of the competition.

TREND ASSESSMENT

Strategic decisions deal with the future of the company. Therefore, understanding trends and exploiting them earlier than competitors can make for superior performance in an industry. Strategic managers must constantly assess market dynamics to determine which strategies are likely to be most advantageous for the company. Trend assessment is like playing a game of chess. Good players anticipate their opponents' moves and understand the second- and third-order effects of their actions. They also understand that future events are fraught with uncertainty and devise strategies to cope with that uncertainty.

DECISION-TREE ANALYSIS

The logical possibilities can be identified and the alternative outcomes can be assessed with the help of a diagram called a *decision tree* (Figure 6.2). The strategy

---

| FIGURE 6.2 | **Basic Decision Tree** |

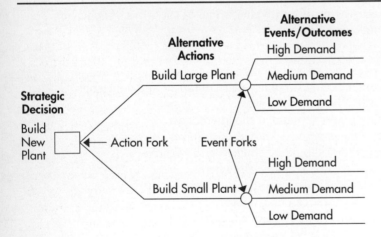

Result	Value
Disastrous	0–9
Critical	10–19
Negative	20–29
Marginal	30–39
Below average	40–49
Average	50–59
Better than average	60–69
Good	70–79
Very good	80–89
Outstanding	90–99

being considered is represented by a diagram whereon several branches show alternative courses of action. For example, if AMP needs to build a new plant to satisfy the demand for its products in a particular country over the next ten years, managers can use a decision tree to help them decide whether to build a large or a small plant. Any point at which they consider alternative actions is called an *action fork*.

Once the action branches have been drawn, managers have to consider how environmental conditions, or events, could affect the outcome of each action. Any point at which they consider events is termed an *event fork*. Event forks are represented by small circles. The events that the company wants to consider in Figure 6.2 are high, medium, and low demand for its product after the plant is built. These possibilities constitute the event/outcome branches. Other action forks, such as "expand/do not expand the small plant," or event forks, such as "competitive products enter/do not enter the market," can be added to this tree if they are germane to the problem.

Once the decision tree is complete, managers can use various criteria, such as profit margin or utility, to assess the outcomes of each action branch of the tree. Though monetary criteria are most frequently used, they exclude some relevant considerations. For example, trying to satisfy high demand with a small plant might be very profitable, but it could also result in considerable loss of sales and attract unwanted competition. Therefore, nonmonetary criteria should be used to measure the desirability of an outcome whenever appropriate.

If nonmonetary criteria are used, a scale of values can be applied to represent the desirability of outcomes (see the table in Figure 6.2). A value of 0 can, for example, be assigned to the worst possible outcome and a value of 100 to the best possible outcome. All the other possible outcomes are assigned some value in between. Experiencing high demand after a large plant has been built is the most desirable outcome. It would be assigned a value of 90 (Figure 6.3). Medium demand might be assigned a value of 50. Experiencing low demand with a large plant would be undesirable (negative) and hence would be assigned a value of 20. All other outcomes would be assigned values that lie between the two extremes.

After the decision tree has been structured and the value of each action/event branch has been defined, managers have to determine the probability that each event will occur. The AMP company, for example, might assume that there is a 40% chance of having high demand, a 35% chance of having medium demand, and only a 25% chance of having very low demand. The probabilities of all events on an action branch always add up to 100%.

Finally, managers have to decide which action to recommend. This involves computing the expected value of each action branch. *Expected value* is computed by multiplying the probability of occurrence (%) and the assigned value of each event/outcome and then totaling the results. Given the probability percentages and assigned values shown in Figure 6.3, the expected value of building a large plant would be computed as follows:

$$(.40 \times 90) + (.35 \times 50) + (.25 \times 20) = 58.5$$

As Figure 6.3 shows, the expected value of building the small plant is higher. Therefore, managers should recommend that the AMP company build the small plant.

FIGURE 6.3	Decision Tree with Probabilities and Assigned Values

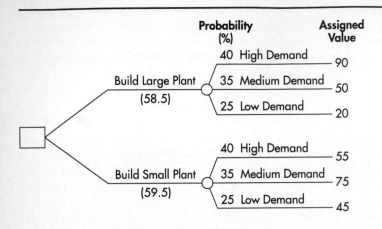

The riskiness of such a decision depends in part on the amount of information available about each possible event. If additional information can be obtained, even at additional cost, managers can come up with more accurate assigned values and probabilities of occurrence and thus arrive at a better decision. Suppose, for example, that the company had obtained additional information indicating that it should revise the probability estimates to 45% for high demand and 20% for low demand. Would the small plant still be the best alternative? It is always wise to verify a decision after gathering more information.

Because of the many variables impinging on a strategic decision and the degree of uncertainty associated with a long planning horizon, decision-tree analysis may be more valuable for defining a problem than for solving it. Decision trees are particularly useful for examining scenarios that contain many alternatives.

PRODUCT LIFE CYCLE

No strategic decision about marketing can be made without considering the phase of a product's or service's life cycle (Figure 6.4). What may be an appropriate strategy for one stage of a product's life cycle may be quite ill advised for another stage.

Most products have a life cycle of four stages: introduction, growth, maturity, and decline. The introduction stage is characterized by the creation of widespread awareness of the new product. Depending on the uniqueness of the product, the financial requirements of this phase can be extensive. In the second phase, growth, sales, and profits typically increase rapidly. As profits rise, competitors are attracted, and improved products or imitations enter the market. At this point, the product reaches maturity. Price competition intensifies, and growth in sales starts to

| FIGURE 6.4 | Characteristics of the Product Life Cycle |

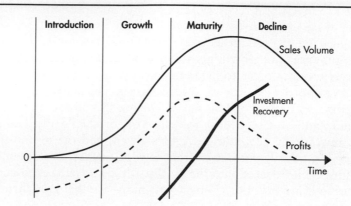

Characteristic	Introduction	Growth	Maturity	Decline
Concentration of competitors	High; few pioneers	Declining as more competition enters	Increasing after shakeout	High; few remaining harvesters
Product differentiation	Low, if any	Increasing; imitations and variations	High; increasing market segmentation	Decreasing as competitors leave market
Barriers to entry	High, if product can be protected	Decreasing; growing technology transfer	Increasing as capital intensity increases	High capital intensity, low returns
Barriers to exit	Low; little investment	Low, but increasing	High for large company	Decreasing; endgame
Price elasticity of demand	Inelastic, few customers	Increasingly elastic	Inelastic only in segments	Very elastic; bargaining power of buyers high
Ratio of fixed to variable cost	Generally low	Increasing	High	Decreasing
Economies of scale	Few, generally unimportant	Increasing capital intensity	High	High
Experience-curve effects	Large early gains	Very high; large production volume	Decreasing magnitude	Few
Vertical integration of competitors	Low	Increasing	High	High
Risk involved in business	Low	Increasing	Increasing	Declining exit barriers

decline, while profits reach their peak. In the decline phase, both sales and profits go down until the product is discontinued.

Investment in production capacity and market development takes place during the introduction and (in particular) growth phases. This investment often is not amortized until the product has entered the maturity phase. Companies can make the mistake of discontinuing products too early, before the products have fully contributed to investment recovery. The maximum contribution may well occur in the decline phase of the product life cycle.

Figure 6.5 lists several substrategies appropriate for each stage of the life cycle. In the initiation and growth phases of product life, operational controls should be relatively loose in order to facilitate expansion. At later phases, tighter control is needed to improve efficiency and reduce costs. The maturity phase represents a pivotal point in strategy formulation. During this phase, sales and market share decline rapidly. Consequently, to realize the product's potential to recover investment, operational procedures are formalized, and the responsibility for product strategy is gradually transferred from sales to finance. At the same time, new products must be introduced into the market if the company is to continue to increase its sales and income. The ability to maintain a stable growth rate depends on an "active" product policy.

Worksheet 6.1 shows sales and profit data for AMP indicating the products that are in the maturity phase of the product life cycle. As might be expected, profits have grown for the past few years and are now declining.

GROWTH VECTOR ANALYSIS

Growth vector analysis can be used to determine the position of each of the company's product lines and to identify all of the product/market options possible.

The two dimensions described are the company's product strategy and its market coverage. For companies with many different products, several product/market strategies will apply simultaneously. Different product and market strategies are shown in Figure 6.6. If, for example, a company focuses on a single product, it can build a strong distinctive competency that may enable it to dominate a particular market. AMP, for example, has concentrated on connectors and related tools and has become the leading supplier worldwide. Such a strategy can eventually, however, threaten profitability and growth as the market matures and becomes saturated. On the other hand, diversification into new and perhaps more profitable markets can be accompanied by unstable cash flows.

Worksheet 6.2 is an application of growth vector analysis to AMP. The company covers all product/market options. It has recently acquired several companies in related fields and is starting to expand its existing product range through value-adding services. The company seems well aware of the different market opportunities and takes well-planned and creative steps to exploit them.

GAP ANALYSIS

After strategic managers have isolated alternative growth strategies, they determine what the future sales potential of each alternative would be. This determination, which is based on a *gap analysis*, reveals (1) what the company can achieve, given its current performance, and (2) the sales it needs to have in 5 to 10 years, given its

FIGURE 6.5	Strategic Actions Appropriate for Different Phases of the Product Life Cycle

Product Strategy by Department	Life Cycle Phases			
	Introduction	Growth	Maturity	Decline
Marketing	Create widespread awareness; find acceptance	Concentrate on brand recognition; find niche; reduce price	Aggressively promote product, use defensive pricing	Phase out product
Production	Limit number of designs; develop standards	Add product variants; centralize production	Improve product and reduce costs	Prune product line
Finance	Plan for high net cash outflow and initial losses	Finance rapid expansion; still have net cash outflows but increasing profits	Redistribute increasing net cash inflows; declining profits	Liquidate unneeded equipment
Personnel	Staff and train new management	Add personnel in production, plan for overtime	Reduce workforce gradually; increase efficiency	Reallocate personnel
Research and development	Make engineering changes	Start developing successor product	Reduce costs; develop variants	Withdraw all R&D from product
Main focus of strategy	Engineering; market penetration	Sales; consumer loyalty	Production efficiency; successor product	Finance; maximum investment recovery

Source: Fox (1973, pp. 10–11).

FIGURE 6.6	Relative Advantage of Alternative Product/Market Strategies

Range of Product Strategies

Product Alternatives	Relative Advantages
Present Product	Builds distinctive competence; Economies of scale; Clarity and unity of purpose; Efficient utilization of resources
Related Products	Broader product appeal; Better use of sales force and distribution network; Motivation from doing something new; Flexibility to respond to changing market conditions
New Products	Reduced competitive pressure; Reduced risk of market saturation; Smaller fluctuations in overall sales

Range of Market Strategies

Market Alternatives	Relative Advantages
Present Market	Maximum market penetration; Possible market leadership; Expertise in specific market or market segment; Market visibility
Related Markets	Stable growth; Stable cash flow requirements; Increased plant utilization; Extension of company's expertise and technology
New Markets	Expansion of company's goodwill and reputation; Reduced competitive pressure; Diversification into more profitable marktets; Positive synergistic effects

WORKSHEET 6.1	Product Life Cycle

Case   AMP

Date   1992

Name   John Doe

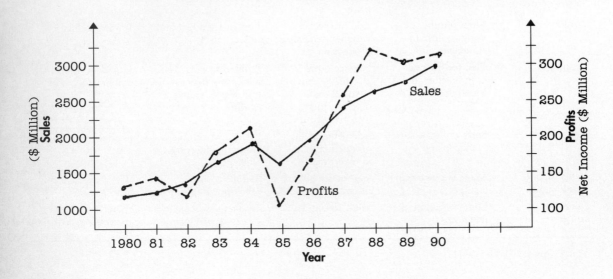

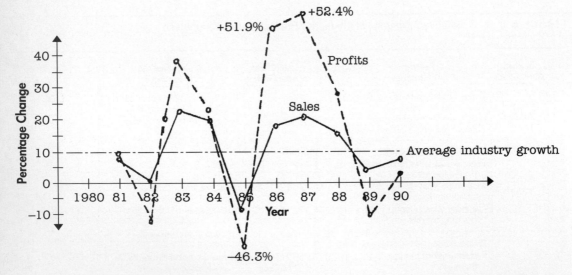

(continued)

WORKSHEET 6.1	Product Life Cycle (continued)

Case __AMP__

Date __1992__

Name __John Doe__

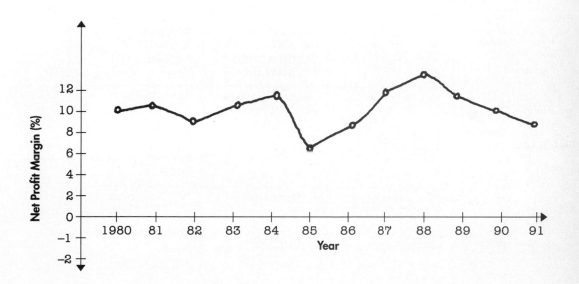

Analysis and Recommendations:

The chart of sales and profits indicates that AMP products have reached the maturity stage of the product life cycle. Profits are very cyclical, and growth in sales is declining. The second chart shows the strong decline in profit growth after 1987 and also indicates that the growth in sales has fallen close to the industry average. The net profit margin (third chart) has held very constant and solid. If these trends continue—that is, if AMP does not adjust its strategy—the growth in sales can be expected to fall further in the 1990s. The two major strategy recommendations for this phase of the product life cycle are to reduce the cost of the product and to look for potential successors of the current products. Increased efficiency will result in AMP having an increase in net cash inflows, which in turn can be used to introduce product variants. Control-oriented management with standardized procedures should help to ensure maximum efficiency.

WORKSHEET 6.2	Growth Vector Analysis

Case __AMP__

Date __1992__

Name __Mary Doe__

<table>
<tr><th rowspan="2" style="writing-mode: vertical-lr">Market Options</th><th></th><th>Market penetration</th><th>Product variants; imitations</th><th>Product line extension</th></tr>
<tr><td>Existing market</td><td>CONNECTORS, TERMINALS, SPLICES</td><td>PACKAGING DEVICES
VALUE-ADDED ASSEMBLIES</td><td>CIRCULAR CONNECTORS
BACKPLANES</td></tr>
<tr><td></td><td>Aggressive promotion</td><td>Market segmentation, product differentiation</td><td>Vertical diversification</td></tr>
<tr><td>Expanded market</td><td>COAXIAL CONNECTOR PARTS</td><td>ACES</td><td>ADDITIVE PROCESS
PRINTED WIRING BOARDS</td></tr>
<tr><td></td><td>Market development</td><td>Market extension</td><td>Conglomerate diversification</td></tr>
<tr><td>New market</td><td>CABLE ASSEMBLIES</td><td>ELECTRO-OPTIC DEVICES</td><td>FIBER OPTICS
ISDN
3-D MOLDED CIRCUITS</td></tr>
<tr><td></td><td>Present products</td><td>Improved products</td><td>New products</td></tr>
</table>

Product Alternatives

Identify and evaluate the company's current strategic position and its strategic alternatives:

AMP is pursuing product growth based on its core competency in electronics and connectors. It has achieved carefully planned growth by considering all nine options shown in the growth vector analysis. Generally, products move from left to right (market penetration to variants or extensions) as the product life changes. This is referred to as new uses for products. This shift is done for each of the three market options shown on the left axis of the matrix.

growth strategy (Figure 6.7). To forecast the sales increases likely to result from implementation of alternative growth strategies, managers estimate the following three measures of market structure (Weber, 1977):

1. Industry market potential (IMP)
2. Relevant industry sales (RIS)
3. Real market share (RMS)

To estimate IMP, managers assume that (1) everyone who can reasonably be expected to use this product will do so, (2) the product is used as often as possible, and (3) whenever this is the case, the product is used to its fullest extent. Given these three assumptions, IMP represents the maximum unit sales possible for a particular product. The difference between this maximum and current sales represents growth opportunities for the company.

Relevant industry sales (RIS) equal the firm's current sales plus competitive gaps, while real market share (RMS) equals current sales divided by RIS (Figure 6.7).

Weber described how these four components contribute to a gap between a company's sales potential and its actual performance:

1. *Product-line gap.* Closing this gap entails completing a product line, either in width or in depth, by introducing improved or new products. AMP attempted to close a product-line gap by producing cassette-player–radio systems for cars.
2. *Distribution gap.* This gap can be reduced by expanding distribution with respect to coverage, intensity, and exposure.

FIGURE 6.7 | **Gap Analysis**

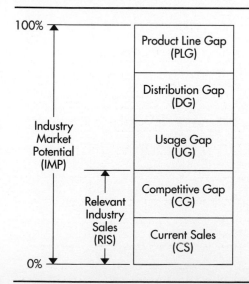

$$IMP = PLG + DG + UG + CG + CS$$

100%

Product Line Gap (PLG)

Distribution Gap (DG)

Industry Market Potential (IMP)

Usage Gap (UG)

Competitive Gap (CG)

Relevant Industry Sales (RIS)

Current Sales (CS)

Real market share

$$(RMS) = \frac{CS}{RIS}$$

0%

3. *Usage gap.* To close the usage gap, a firm must induce current nonusers to try the product and encourage current users to increase their usage.
4. *Competitive gap.* This gap can be closed by taking market share from direct competitors and those who sell substitute products.

Projected future sales or profit gaps can be closed by increasing the firm's total IMP, by increasing RIS while maintaining current RMS, or by improving RMS (Figure 6.8).

TECHNOLOGY ASSESSMENT

Technology often drives strategic planning. New products, new markets, new production processes, and new distribution systems usually originate from technological advances, which affect both productivity and profitability. Strategic managers have to monitor technological developments and manage their adoption by the company.

Different levels of technology have to be distinguished and managed appropriately (see Figure 6.9) and for this purpose the *technology pyramid* is useful. At the bottom of this pyramid are the *core technologies* of a company. These can be used in different product applications, and their development and protection are fundamental to the company's capability base. For example, optical technology is a core technology that is used in many of Canon's products from cameras to copy machines. Canon has unique and proprietary know-how in some of this technology, which enables it to offer products that often result in superior performance. A core technology for General Motors is its engine combustion technology, including electronics. This is why GM some years ago acquired Hughes and why it has recently taken a license on a new, revolutionary two-stroke engine in development. Production of computer chips is a core technology required for many applications.

FIGURE 6.8	Performance Gaps

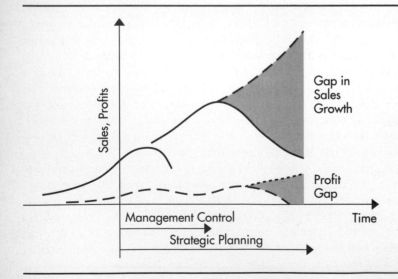

| FIGURE 6.9 | Technology Pyramid |

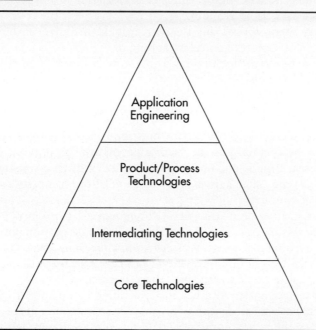

Not surprisingly, Japanese, North American, and European companies and consortiums are engaged in a fierce and expensive technology race.

The last example also shows that the maintenance and protection of core technologies today are often beyond the means of one company alone. Therefore, strategic managers must fully understand the significance and the financial requirements of different technologies, and they must often make tough choices about which technologies can and should be supported and which should not. Interestingly enough, Japanese companies often seem to be more focused on fewer core technologies than Western companies, and they spend more on these individual technologies. Instead, they rely more on partnerships and alliances where companies focus on developing different individual technologies but share the benefits in different final products. Western companies have a tendency to try to be competitive on many different technologies. As a result, they frequently either underspend on key development or are late with the newest generation.

Intermediating technologies are needed to arrive at complete final-product configurations. Canon, for example, needed technologies for making and cutting glass to maximize the impact of its core optical technology. In the case of combustion engines, there has been a growing trend toward four-valve technology, which makes for a cleaner burn and lower fuel consumption. To make this possible, new developments in metals and compounds, forging technology, and automotive electronics were needed. The strategic manager must be able to define

1. The "technology road map" that can deliver a core technology being developed. This entails understanding which intermediating technologies are needed and when they have to be available.
2. The necessary criteria for making the correct make-or-buy decision on these technologies. This requires an understanding of
   a. Whether to retain the technology know-how in-house or to rely on suppliers having the know-how.
   b. The potential for success of this technology.
   c. The cost associated with developing and marketing this technology.

The following technology check can be useful in doing the evaluation (see Figure 6.10). On one axis there is the success potential of technologies, which can be based on different inputs, such as market studies, growth estimates, or subjective evaluations. On the other axis is an evaluation of the company's own relative capability for this technology.

An interesting starting point is to take all ongoing R&D projects in a company and put them into this matrix. The circles shown in Figure 6.10 make up a portfolio that is not unlike those of many Western companies. The size of the circle indicates the relative numbers of dollars spent on projects A through K.

Concerning project A, for example, there is another company with a clear technology and time advantage. Rather than spending money on this R&D effort, management should ask whether it may be possible to outsource this technology or perhaps to acquire the other company, if necessary—similarly with projects G through K. They tie up valuable resources with questionable benefit. These resources could be redirected to give a much stronger push to projects B and C, which are vital to the company's future. Projects D, E, and F have a low success potential even though the company has a high technological capability in these areas. The recommendation is simply to maintain that capability and minimize the expenditure of resources for those projects.

Surprisingly enough, few companies do this technology check in a methodical and consistent fashion. Projects continue to be funded even though situations have changed. Yet, it is often this planned and deliberate technology portfolio choice that makes the difference between being first with new technologies or being a follower.

Product and process technologies are what is delivered to the customer. A car, for example, consists of many different technologies. It is the combination of technologies and the focus on specific features that determines the cost/price relationship and differentiates the product. The link between these features and the perceived customer value is discussed in Appendix A, on product/market mapping. One important point to keep in mind is that the timing of core technologies and new products should typically *not* be linked. Companies often make the mistake of linking the success of a new product to the development of a completely new technology. The result often is a costly delay. Connor Peripherals, the maker of computer hard-disk drives, applies a different strategy. Every year this company redesigns about one-third of its product, incorporating the latest technologies available at this stage. Thus it can offer a newly designed product every year, and every third year it has come up with a new generation of drives. This has allowed the company to outpace its competitors both in terms of technology and in terms of sales and profit growth.

FIGURE 6.10 | **Technology Check**

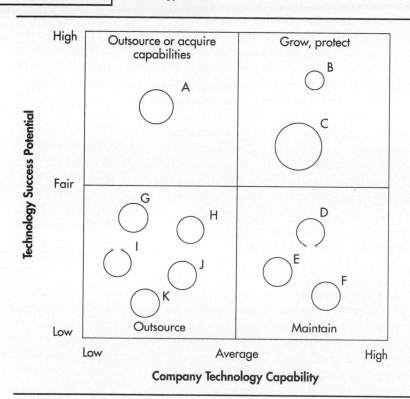

Finally, at the top of the technology pyramid is *application engineering*, which again should be clearly separated from product design. In today's world of "multiple choice," it is important to come up with customer-specific or segment-specific product variants, but it is also important to check the cost associated with this policy throughout the company, not just in the engineering department. Therefore, it is often wise to place application engineers closer to manufacturing and purchasing, rather than mixing them with R&D. Doing so limits costly product proliferation. It also involves suppliers as partners in the design process, thus speeding up design, reducing cost in the overall process, and enabling both to reap the benefits. Technological know-how and training within the company can be maintained through job rotation among the different technology and application areas.

When technology is used for competitive advantage, a low-cost strategy, used alone, is generally ineffective for achieving market dominance or rapid growth. This appears to contradict traditional arguments that favor economies of scale and first-mover advantages. Intel, for example, which moved into the 8-bit microprocessor field first, failed to maintain a dominant position despite economies of scale and first-mover status. Rather, it achieved market-share leadership by concentrating on customers' needs and on the actions required to sustain competitive advantage by providing superior customer service.

Does industry have to stay abreast of the very latest technology, or is familiarity with current technology sufficient to stay competitive? The answer depends on what competitors are doing, on what consumers demand, and on the ratio of the cost of switching technologies to the profit generated by the change. In many instances, new technologies become the driving force that creates demand. For example, 3-D printing could revolutionize product design and manufacturing (Allman, 1992). As another example, Sony engineers turn out an astounding average of four new products every day (Schlender, 1992). How does Sony do it? It hires generalists and turns them loose to work on advanced products. Its 9,000 engineers and scientists (out of 112,900 employees) work long hours to produce the advances that keep Sony out front. It spends $1.5 billion, about 5.7% of its revenues, on this effort. Closer to home, U.S. Surgical relies on its customers for new ideas that it can turn into products. Its salespeople visit operating rooms and doctors' offices to determine what is needed. In 1967 it was the first to bring out a "user-friendly" surgical stapler that revolutionized the closing of wounds. The result was a hundredfold increase in the company's stock value from 1987 through 1992.

To help maintain a competitive edge, the United States must have a viable technology policy. What is required in an era of global competitors is a policy that stimulates new ideas and products and that is flexible enough to meet urgent requirements. Sematech is one attempt at a collaborative approach in the electronics industry, but the United States may have to spend a significant amount to develop an infrastructure that emphasizes the ability to respond to competitors' advances and that can leapfrog their technology (Branscomb, 1992). Lewis Branscomb commented, "Whether it's tax cuts, collaboration, or hands off, U.S. technology policy needs a new twist." In today's global economy, he argues, what matters is not creating new technology but absorbing and applying innovations quickly. Instead of concentrating on the "supply" of new technologies, the U.S. government should stimulate "demand" for innovative ideas by encouraging collaborative research, investing in technological infrastructure, emphasizing the importance of precompetitive research, and helping companies improve their capacity to adapt innovations to specific business needs. Branscomb concludes that what we need is a "capability-enhancing technology policy." His proposal is to have the government support "generic technologies" that foster innovation across our industrial base. An example is congressional funding to upgrade a collection of over 2,000 computer networks that link university and research labs around the country and around the world.

PIMS ANALYSIS

In addition to a technology assessment, a company needs a means to assess the profit potential of its marketing strategy. The PIMS analysis provides a tool to make this type of assessment.

The *profit impact of market strategy* (PIMS) project was organized in early 1972 by the Marketing Science Institute at the Harvard Business School. A large database containing information on more than six hundred businesses was established and used to develop different PIMS profit models (Schoeffler, Buzzell, and Heany, 1974). These models were designed to answer the following questions:

- What factors influence profitability in a business, and how much influence does each one have?
- How does return on investment (ROI) change in response to changes in strategy and in market conditions?

The independent variables in the model were grouped under the following four major headings:

1. Competitive position of the business (relative market share, product quality, price, promotion, new-product development)
2. The business environment (growth in industry, rate of inflation, customers, replacement cycle)
3. Structure of the production process (capital intensity, degree of vertical integration, productivity)
4. Discretionary budget allocations (R&D budgets, marketing budgets).

The major findings of the study are summarized here.

- *Market share and relative market share.* Market share and relative market share (the company's market share divided by the combined shares of its three largest competitors) are strongly related to return on investment (ROI). Businesses with relatively large market shares tend to have above-average profits. The major determinants for the link between market share and profitability appear to be economies of scale, the effects of experience or learning, market power, and quality of management.
- *Product quality.* Leadership in a market appears to be based on unique competitive strategies and higher-quality products. This enables market leaders to sell at higher prices than businesses with smaller market shares.
- *Market growth.* Not surprisingly, market growth is positively correlated with ROI.
- *Vertical integration.* The degree of vertical integration of a business appears to have a positive effect on ROI later in the product life cycle. Early in the product life cycle, before experience and learning have reduced costs, the successful competitor concentrates on reducing manufacturing costs through gains in productivity. As the cost-reducing effects of experience take hold, ROI can be improved further by exploiting opportunities in the supply–production–distribution chain.
- *New-product activity, R&D sales ratio, and marketing sales ratio.* New-product activity and above-average ratios of R&D and marketing expenditures to sales play an increasing role in determining profitability in the later stages of the product life cycle. Businesses with weak market positions, however, may prefer

to seek new products without investing in R&D, simply by imitating successful products in the market. Furthermore, as market share increases, marketing expenditures may tend to become more effective; that is, marketing costs decline as a percentage of sales but without any noticeable decline in sales.

- *Investment intensity*. The higher the ratio of investment to sales (investment intensity), the lower the ROI tends to be. Businesses with high investments relative to sales are obviously not able to achieve sufficient profit margins. Investment in R&D tends to depress earnings sharply. High labor productivity appears to be vital to profitability when investment intensity is high.
- *Inventory levels*. High inventory levels damage profitability, particularly in businesses with few fixed assets.
- *Capacity utilization*. Adequate capacity utilization is very important for weaker businesses and for businesses with high capital intensity.

To perform a PIMS analysis, the strategic manager can use a checklist of variables, such as the one for AMP shown in Figure 6.11. After rating each variable in the checklist, the manager consults results of the PIMS study to determine which strategy will have the best chance of success.

COMPETITIVE PORTFOLIO ANALYSIS

Competitive portfolio analysis, which was developed by the Boston Consulting Group (BCG), is based on the close relationship between market share and cash generation. What distinguishes competitive portfolio analysis from PIMS is its focus on the specific role of each product in the overall strategy of the firm.

FIGURE 6.11 | **PIMS-based Evaluation of AMP's Professional Amplifiers**

Checklist		Ratings	
1. Market share	Low _____	Medium _____	High ✓
2. Relative market share	Low _____	Medium _____	High ✓
3. Product quality	Low _____	Medium _____	High ✓
4. Market growth	Low _____	Medium ✓	High _____
5. Vertical integration	Low ✓	Medium _____	High _____
6. New-product activity	Low _____	Medium ✓	High _____
7. R&D/sales ratio	Low _____	Medium _____	High ✓
8. Marketing/sales ratio	Low _____	Medium _____	High ✓
9. Productivity	Low _____	Medium _____	High ✓
10. Capacity utilization	Low _____	Medium ✓	High _____
11. Investment/sales ratio	Low _____	Medium ✓	High _____
12. Inventory level	Low _____	Medium ✓	High _____

Based on its cash flow characteristics and relative market share, each product can be positioned in a *product portfolio matrix* like the one in Figure 6.12. In the terminology used by the BCG, high-growth and high-market-share products are classified as "stars." These products usually have the highest profit margins, but they are also likely to require net cash outflows in order to maintain their market share. Eventually, stars become "cash cows" as growth slows and investment needs diminish in the maturity stage of the product life cycle.

"Question marks" are products with high growth potential but low market shares. They require large net cash outflows if market share is to be maintained or increased. If successful, these products become new stars, which will, in turn, become the cash cows of the future. If unsuccessful, they become "dogs," which are products with low market share and slow growth. Dogs generally remain in the product portfolio as long as they contribute some positive cash flow.

Each category represents a different stage in the product life cycle. Products start as question marks in the introductory phase, become stars as growth accelerates, develop into cash cows during the maturity phase, and finally become dogs as growth declines.

| FIGURE 6.12 | Product Portfolio Matrix |

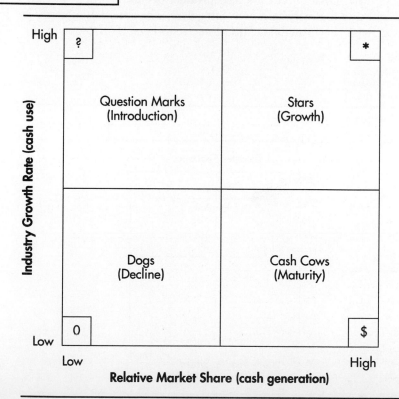

The product portfolio analysis can be used to allocate resources among products and to maximize long-run profits. The fundamental idea is to distribute cash generated by the cash cows to other products that will ensure future growth and profitability for the company. A financially balanced product portfolio contains products in each of the four categories. The different products also can be represented by different-sized circles that reflect their relative share of the company's sales. In this representation, a single, large cash cow might be balanced by several small stars and perhaps a few question marks and dogs.

Displaying each of a firm's products in a single matrix, such as the one in Figure 6.13, can help strategic managers to determine the products' competitive standing. To formulate an effective product/market strategy, it may also be necessary to develop product portfolio matrices for major competitors. Comparing the company's product portfolio with those of major competitors enables managers to avoid pitfalls. Attempting to increase a product's market share in a low-growth segment, for example, is very risky if the firm does not have a leadership position either in market share or in product strength.

Strategic managers can also use the product portfolio matrix to track the product life cycle through the four quadrants and adjust strategies as products move from one quadrant to another. As can be seen in Figure 6.13 successful product/market strategies bypass the decline/dog quadrant entirely. Products are eliminated from the portfolio or sold off when they evolve into this quadrant and cease to generate cash flow. Losses occur if a new product declines without passing through the growth/star and maturity/cash cow categories. The situation worsens if cash flow is directed from the growth/star quadrant to others. This sequence of

---

FIGURE 6.13   **Normal Sequence of Product Strategies**

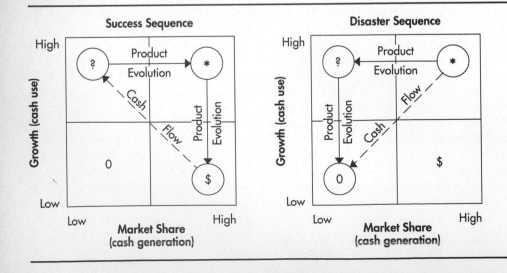

events, in which products do not evolve through the growth stage, keeps them from becoming cash cows. The result is seriously reduced profitability.

To develop a successful product/market strategy for each product, managers must first calculate its present market share relative to that of major competing products. The Boston Consulting Group has suggested that the market share of each product be compared to that of its single main competitor. Any product that has a relative market share greater than 1—that is, a product whose market share equals or exceeds that of its main competitor—is placed in the star/growth or maturity/cash cow category, depending on the market growth rate.

The BCG portfolio approach is used to evaluate products on the basis of their life-cycle phase and to ensure that products are optimally distributed among the four quadrants. If the product portfolio is unbalanced, the flow of products from question marks to stars to cash cows will cause cash flow difficulties. The portfolio analysis can also be used to evaluate business units within the organization. Like mature products, mature divisions can be spun off and new ones started to maintain a balance among the business units.

Strategic managers also use competitive portfolio analysis to establish product-development guidelines and targets, which are then finalized by top management. For example, management may set the cutoff point between low and high growth at 10% annually. Products exceeding this level receive funds for growth; other products are funded at a lower rate. The portfolio matrix for AMP is shown in Worksheet 6.3. The size of the circles is proportional to the sales volume for each product.

STRATEGIC POSITION AND ACTION EVALUATION (SPACE)

Strategic position and action evaluation (SPACE) is used to determine the appropriate strategic posture for a firm and each of its individual businesses. It is an extension of the two-dimensional portfolio methods, such as the BCG product portfolio.

Other methods include McKinsey's industry attractiveness/company strength matrix (Figure 6.14), General Electric's stoplight strategy, and the directional policy matrix (DPM) developed by the Shell Group (Figure 6.15). In each of these methods, one of the axes of the matrix measures the overall attractiveness of the industry in which the company operates, and the other axis represents the company's ability to compete in its market(s). The DPM, which uses market potential and company capability as its two dimensions, is perhaps more specific with respect to strategic implications.

The SPACE approach is an attempt to overcome some of the limitations inherent in the other methods. SPACE adds two key dimensions to the matrix (Figure 6.16). In a sense, the SPACE diagram can be viewed as a summary display of the findings of the PIMS study, because each dimension is viewed as a composite of several factors, which are evaluated separately. By including a large number of factors, the manager can examine a particular strategic alternative from several perspectives and will, therefore, be in a better position to select an appropriate strategy.

Financial strength and competitive advantage are the two major determinants of a company's strategic position, whereas industry strength and environmental stability characterize the strategic position of the entire industry. In the SPACE chart, these factors are rated on a scale of +6 to −6.

WORKSHEET 6.3	Product Portfolio Analysis

Case ___AMP___

Date ___1992___

Name ___John Doe___

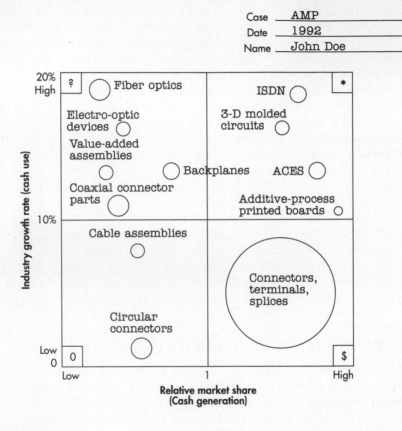

Comments and Recommendations:

AMP has started balancing its main business, connectors, which is becoming mature, by adding a range of new products and businesses. In some of these fields, such as ISDN connectors and 3-D molded circuits, AMP is an early technology leader. Fiber optics has high growth but is dominated by other companies already. AMP has to carefully define its niche, or area of specialization, if fiber optics is to avoid high cash outflows. Circular connectors, mainly for military applications, were added to round out the portfolio but have little growth potential. They should be managed for cash flow only.

FIGURE 6.14 | McKinsey's Industry Attractiveness/Company Strength Matrix

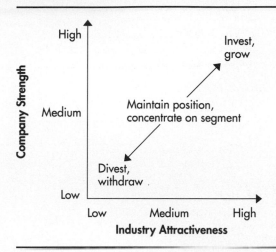

FIGURE 6.15 | Directional Policy Matrix (DPM)

	Unattractive	Average	Attractive
High	Diversification	Market segmentation	Market leadership; innovation
Normal	Phased withdrawal; merger	Maintenance of position; market penetration	Expansion; product differentiation
Low	Divestment	Imitation; phased withdrawal	Cash generation

Company Capability (vertical axis) — Market Potential (horizontal axis)

A company's financial strength is important when there are adverse economic conditions, such as rapid inflation or high interest rates. Equipped with a "cushion" to ease the pinch of difficult times, the financially strong company is in an excellent position to diversify into more attractive industries or to finance aggressive moves in its current industry at the expense of weaker competitors.

A company that enjoys advantages over its competitors in terms of market share, cost, or technology is usually able to maintain a higher profit margin as well.

FIGURE 6.16	SPACE Chart

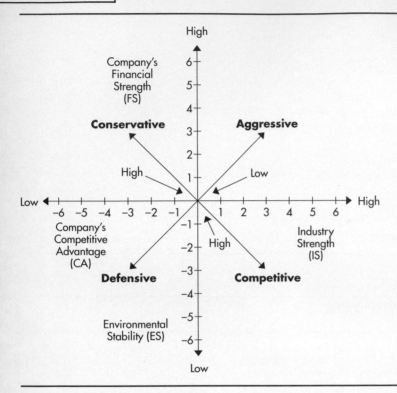

Source: K. E. Dickel, Copyright © 1984.

This competitive advantage can become critical in a declining market, where the marginally profitable firm finds it difficult to survive.

In an expanding market, an industry's financial and operating strength helps to maintain or increase the market's momentum, and even the marginal competitor can find a niche in such a situation. As the market's growth slows, however, the competitive climate in an industry deteriorates, and a firm finds it necessary to protect its competitive position. Therefore, industry strength can offset a company's competitive position.

Similarly, environmental stability can mitigate a firm's lack of financial strength. On the other hand, if a firm in a turbulent environment does not have a sound financial position, it finds survival very difficult.

For each strategic thrust in the SPACE chart, a number of factors are used. The strategic position and action evaluation (SPACE) includes the four input variables environmental stability, industry strength, competitive advantage, and financial strength to arrive at an aggressive, competitive, conservative, or defensive strategic posture for the firm. These postures in turn can be translated into generic competitive strategies, thus helping the manager define the appropriate strategic thrust for a business: overall cost leadership, differentiation, focus, or defensiveness.

1. Factors determining environmental stability (ES)
   Technological changes
   Rate of inflation
   Demand variability
   Price range of competing products
   Barriers to entry into market
   Competitive pressure/rivalry
   Price elasticity of demand
   Pressure from substitutes
2. Factors determining industry strength (IS)
   Growth potential
   Profit potential
   Financial stability
   Technological know-how
   Resource utilization
   Capital intensity
   Ease of entry into market
   Productivity; capacity utilization
   Manufacturers' bargaining power
3. Factors determining competitive advantage (CA)
   Market share
   Product quality
   Product life cycle
   Product replacement cycle
   Customer loyalty
   Competition's capacity utilization
   Technological know-how
   Vertical integration
   Speed of new-product introductions
4. Factors determining financial strength (FS)
   Return on investment
   Leverage
   Liquidity
   Capital required versus capital available
   Cash flow
   Ease of exit from market
   Risk involved in business
   Inventory turnover
   Use of economies of scale and experience

To apply this approach, a manager assigns appropriate numerical values to each of the factors. The averages determined for each group of factors are then plotted in the SPACE chart (Figure 6.16). By connecting the average values plotted on each axis, the manager obtains a four-sided polygon displaying the weight and direction of the particular assessment. It is important to recognize that the SPACE chart is a summary display and that each factor should also be analyzed individually. In particular, factors with very high or very low scores should receive special attention.

Another way of determining relative strategic position is to add the two scores on the axes opposite each other to obtain a directional vector that points to a specific location in the chart.

The basic strategic postures associated with the SPACE technique are illustrated and described in the following paragraphs and diagrams.

1. *Aggressive posture.* This posture is typical in an attractive industry with little environmental turbulence. The company enjoys a definite competitive advantage, which it can protect with financial strength. The critical factor is entry of new competition. Firms in this situation should take full advantage of opportunities, look for acquisition candidates in their own or related industries, increase market share, and concentrate resources on products that have a definite competitive edge.

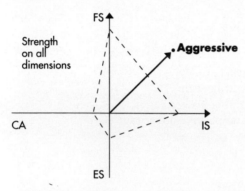

2. *Competitive posture.* This posture is typical in an attractive industry. The company enjoys a competitive advantage in a relatively unstable environment.

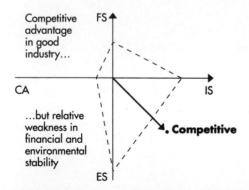

The critical factor is financial strength. Firms in this situation should acquire financial resources to increase marketing thrust, add to the sales force, extend or improve the product line, invest in productivity, reduce costs, protect competitive advantage in a declining market, and attempt to merge with a cash-rich company.

3. *Conservative posture.* This posture is typical in a stable market with low growth. Here the company focuses on financial stability. The critical factor is product competitiveness. Firms in this situation should prune the product line, reduce costs, focus on improving cash flow, protect competitive products,

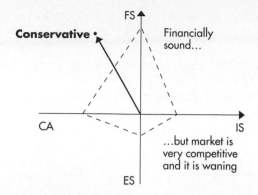

develop new products, and gain entry into more attractive markets.

4. *Defensive posture.* This posture is typical of an unattractive industry in which the company lacks a competitive product and financial strength. The critical factor is competitiveness. Firms in this situation should prepare to retreat from the market, discontinue marginally profitable products, reduce costs aggressively, cut capacity, and defer or minimize investments.

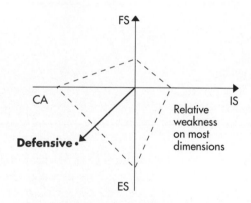

The four strategic thrusts identified by the SPACE method are very similar to the four strategic postures Miles and Snow (1978) discovered as a result of a historical analysis of hospitals and the textbook publishing, electronics, and food processing industries. In their study, they found the aggressive strategy to be the strategy of *prospectors*, who seek new product/market segments and employ broad planning approaches, decentralized controls, and extensive environmental scanning. Prospectors usually have some underutilized resources.

The defensive strategy is the strategy of *defenders*, who focus on a narrow product/market domain and guard it. Concentration, centralized control, and limited environmental scanning characterize this strategy. Defenders may, however, be rather cost-efficient; their products may be cash cows.

The conservative strategy is the strategy of *analyzers*. Endowed with financial strength but lacking a competitive advantage or industry potential, the company can pursue strategy that is based on careful analysis of the product/market opportunities and conservative development of them.

The competitive strategy is the strategy of *reactors*, who realize that the environment is unstable but the industry is strong. Unfortunately, they have neither the financial strength nor the competitive advantage to prosper in the face of environmental turbulence. This posture is generally an unstable strategic posture and frequently leads to failure.

Using Worksheets 6.4A, 6.4B, and 6.5 for AMP, we can determine which strategic alternative best fits under the conditions that the company faced in 1992. The diagram in Worksheet 6.5 shows that AMP should pursue an aggressive strategy because of its overall strong position.

SUPER SPACE

In order to enhance the use of SPACE, we have added two items: the relative importance of each factor (R) and the chance of sustaining the importance level of the factor (C). Multiplying these two items, we obtain a combined effect (E). The range of total value for E is approximately 0 to 50.

Total E Value	Expectancy
0–10	low
10–20	low/moderate
20–30	moderate
30–40	moderate/high
40–50	high
above	very high

The total E values indicate that the likelihood of maintaining a given factor is as shown above, whereas a basic SPACE analysis assumes they will continue at the current level in the future. Using Super SPACE yields the following results for AMP:

	Current	Sustainable
Company's financial strength	high	moderate
Competitive advantage	very high	moderate/high
Environmental stability	high	moderate
Industry strength	moderate	moderate/high

The advantage of Super SPACE is that it adds intelligence to the basic SPACE analysis. Thus strategic managers can assess their current position and determine whether additional effort must be invested in any of the factors in order to maintain the company's current competitive position in the future.

| WORSHEET 6.4A | Strategic Position and Action Evaluation (SPACE) |

		Relative importance of factor	Chance of sustaining	Combined effect

Factors determining competitive advantage:

			R	C	E
Market share	Small	0 1 2 3 4 5 ⑥ Large	3	.7	2.1
Product quality	Inferior	0 1 2 3 4 5 ⑥ Superior	8	.7	5.6
Product life cycle	Late	0 1 2 ③ 4 5 6 Early	5	.5	2.5
Product replacement cycle	Variable	0 1 2 3 ④ 5 6 Fixed	3	.3	.9
Customer loyalty	Low	0 1 2 3 4 ⑤ 6 High	7	.7	4.9
Competition's capacity utilization	Low	0 1 ② 3 4 5 6 High	5	.4	2.0
Technological know-how	Low	0 1 2 3 4 ⑤ 6 High	7	.8	5.6
Vertical integration	Low	0 1 2 ③ 4 5 6 High	3	.4	1.2
Other: Speed of new product introductions	Slow	0 1 2 3 ④ 5 6 Fast	8	.6	4.8

Average − 6 = __−1.8__   29.0

Critical factors:

AMP is benefiting substantially from its high market share and superior product quality.

Comments:

The company still enjoys strong competitive advantage because of quality and customer loyalty. This advantage can be expected to diminish, however, because of improving performance of competitive products and potential price aggressiveness of competitors with low capacity.

Factors determining financial strength:

			R	C	E
Return on investment	Low	0 1 2 3 4 ⑤ 6 High	5	.5	2.5
Leverage	Imbalanced	0 1 2 3 4 5 ⑥ Balanced	4	.6	2.4
Liquidity	Imbalanced	0 1 2 3 4 ⑤ 6 Solid	6	.4	2.4
Capital required versus capital available	High	0 1 2 3 4 ⑤ 6 Low	7	.3	2.1
Cash flow	Low	0 1 2 3 4 5 ⑥ High	9	.5	4.5
Ease of exit from market	Difficult	0 1 ② 3 4 5 6 Easy	5	.7	3.5
Risk involved in business	Much	0 1 2 3 4 ⑤ 6 Little	3	.6	1.8
Inventory turnover	Slow	0 1 2 3 ④ 5 6 Fast	4	.4	1.6
Economies of scale and experience	Low	0 1 2 3 4 ⑤ 6 High	7	.6	4.2

Average __4.8__   25.0

Critical factors:

Excellent financials, but some risk diversification may be warranted.

Comments:

Financial position very strong.

WORKSHEET 6.4B	Strategic Position and Action Evaluation (SPACE)

Factors determining environmental stability:

											R	C	E
Technological changes	Many	0	1	2	3	④	5	6	Few		6	.6	3.6
Rate of inflation	High	0	1	2	3	4	⑤	6	Low		4	.3	1.2
Demand variability	Large	0	1	2	3	④	5	6	Small		7	.4	2.8
Price range of competing products	Wide	0	1	2	③	4	5	6	Narrow		3	.4	1.2
Barriers to entry into market	Few	0	1	2	③	4	5	6	Many		8	.3	2.4
Competitive pressure/rivalry	High	0	①	2	3	4	5	6	Low		7	.6	4.2
Price elasticity of demand	Elastic	0	1	2	3	④	5	6	Inelastic		5	.3	1.5
Pressure from substitute products	High	0	1	2	3	4	⑤	6	Low		8	.8	6.4

Average − 6 = __−2.4__   22.3

Critical factors:

Fairly stable environment; strong competition.

Comments:

Necessary to observe competitors and potential new entrants carefully.

Factors determining industry strength:

											R	C	E
Growth potential	Low	0	1	2	3	④	5	6	High		5	.5	2.5
Profit potential	Low	0	1	2	3	4	⑤	6	High		8	.6	4.8
Financial stability	Low	0	1	2	3	④	5	6	High		4	.6	2.4
Technological know-how	Simple	0	1	2	3	4	⑤	6	Complex		7	.8	5.6
Resource utilization	Inefficient	0	1	2	3	④	5	6	Efficient		5	.5	2.5
Capital intensity	Low	0	1	2	③	4	5	6	High		7	.4	2.8
Ease of entry into market	Easy	0	1	2	3	④	5	6	Difficult		5	.5	2.5
Productivity, capacity utilization	Low	0	1	2	③	4	5	6	High		6	.4	2.4
Other: Manufacturers' bargaining power	Low	0	1	②	3	4	5	6	High		6	.5	3.0

Average __3.8__   29.5

Critical factors:

Good growth and profit potential; strong rivalry has led to lower capacity utilization.

Comments:

Very attractive industry, but bargaining power both relative to buyers and suppliers is

low due to intense competitive rivalry.

Source: K. E. Dickel and Alan J. Rowe, Copyright © 1984, 1994.

| WORKSHEET 6.5 | Strategic Position and Action Evaluation (SPACE) |

Case ___AMP___
Date ___1992___
Name ___John Doe___

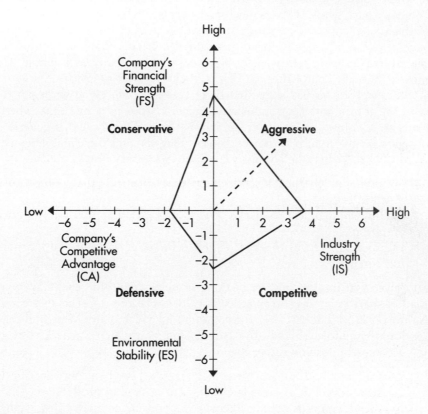

Analysis and Recommendations:

AMP is generally in a very strong competitive position, which makes it possible to take a fairly aggressive posture. Factors to watch out for are the potential future decline in competitors' capacity utilization, which could trigger a price war. AMP has also begun diversifying to reduce risk.

GENERIC COMPETITIVE STRATEGIES FOR STRATEGIC BUSINESS UNITS

Many companies plan their strategies on the basis of strategic business units (SBUs). The SBU is an organizational concept defined by the products offered to a market segment or strategic segment. It is used to determine the strategic action to be taken by the company in that segment and to evaluate the results. Some companies have only one SBU, in which case the SBU strategy is the same as that for the company as a whole. Others, such as General Electric, have many different SBUs. In this case the overall corporate strategy is related to the strategies of all the SBUs. Several authors have developed generalized concepts that can be used to describe the strategies being followed by SBUs or by a company as a whole. One of the most significant approaches to SBUs is Michael Porter's (1980).

Michael Porter has suggested three *generic competitive strategies* for dealing with the forces within an industry. A generic strategy is one that, when pursued, leads to a competitive advantage for the firm. The choice of generic strategies depends on the industry, the competitor analysis, and the capabilities of the firm. According to Porter, the company can base its strategy on

- Supplying its product or service more cost-effectively than competitors (overall cost leadership)
- Adding value to its product or service through differentiation (product differentiation)
- Narrowing its focus to a special product/market segment that it can monopolize (focus)

Successful implementation of these strategies typically results in the profit and market-share positions shown schematically in Figure 6.17. This figure also shows a fourth position that describes the condition in which many firms find themselves—stuck in the middle. This fourth position is not considered a generic strategy because it is a defensive position rather than one that leads to a competitive advantage.

1. *Overall cost leadership.* This strategy is based on the experience-curve concept: construction of large-scale facilities, tight control of production costs and overhead, vigorous pursuit of cost reductions associated with learning effects, and utilization of economies of scale for discretionary expenses such as R&D, promotion, and advertising. At a minimum, the prerequisites for successful execution of a cost-leadership strategy are access to sufficient financial resources, adequate process engineering skills, intense supervision of labor, and low-cost distribution capability.

2. *Product differentiation.* A product-differentiation strategy is intended to add value to a product or service and, accordingly, allows an increase in its price. To pursue such a strategy successfully, a company must be able to demonstrate the uniqueness of its product and justify the higher price. In general, this strategy requires strong marketing skills, superior product engineering and quality, and close coordination of the R&D, production, distribution, service, and marketing functions.

3. *Focus.* The first two generic strategies are aimed at an industry-wide market and, if successful, will result in above-average profits (Figure 6.17). To avoid getting caught in the middle, a company can isolate particular buyer groups,

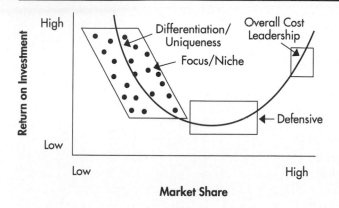

product lines, or geographic markets. By serving a narrower market segment, the firm can develop specific skills and reduce pressure from its industry-wide competitors. Firms that follow a focus strategy try, by definition, to monopolize a niche in the marketplace that may fall anywhere within the area on the left side of the Porter curve (see the area filled with dots in Figure 6.17). Their main competitive threat comes from other firms that are seeking the same focus.

The choice of generic strategy should be based on the firm's strengths and weaknesses vis-à-vis its competitors and on the number of strategic options available besides minimizing costs. Rarely is a firm as a whole suited for a combination of all three generic strategies. Figure 6.18 can be used as a guideline for selecting one of the three generic strategies based on the strengths and options of the strategic business unit (SBU). Each business unit can have its own generic strategy. For example, the light bulb division of GE would be considered cost-competitive, whereas the steam turbine division would more nearly fit the focus strategy.

Although not widely recognized as such, competition itself is a commonly used generic strategy. Aggressive competition is used to gain market share or high return on investment, and it always challenges the market position of established firms. Companies that engage in highly competitive marketing tactics may be new, in transition following restructuring, or in mature industries. They are constantly attempting to move into a cost-leadership position or a market niche. Competitive strategies typically involve fierce market-share battles, price wars, or other means of gaining customers from competitors. These actions are difficult to sustain and are not always successful, as the high failure rate of startup companies shows. In general, the competitive strategy is a defensive one that companies try to avoid because it seldom provides a sustainable competitive advantage. Furthermore, highly competitive moves invite retaliation and lead to price wars and other defensive measures. Restructuring has increasingly been used as a means of moving from a highly defensive position to a more competitive one.

FIGURE 6.18	Choice of Generic Strategy

Strong
High: Market Share
ROI

Weak
Low: Market Share
ROI

Market Position

Unique
(Differentiated)

Competitive
Advantage
(Skim Market)

Low Cost
(Dominance)

Aggressive
Competitor
(Expand Market Share)

Niche
(Focus)

Narrow
Market/
Product
(R&D)

Defensive
(Survival)

Stuck in the
Middle
(Restructure)

Focused
(Protected)

Growth
(Competitive)

Strategic Outlook

If market segmentation and product differentiation are not possible—that is, if no critical mass can be achieved by subdividing the marketplace or there are few ways to differentiate the product—a firm might try to become the cost leader if it is financially strong and if the market continues to grow until the experience curve can take effect. Competitors with weak positions in a mature industry do not have to withdraw from the marketplace if it is possible to harvest profits or use the SBU as a "cash cow," but these options generally are transitory.

If barriers to exit are low, one viable alternative is to liquidate the SBU. More often, the company faces a situation in which competitive advantage can be gained only at a competitor's expense. In this situation another generic competitive strategy—*gamesmanship*—can be implemented at the business level. The effective strategic planner makes use of a variety of financial maneuvers to strengthen the company's position, stalemate the competition, and facilitate eventual exit from the marketplace (Figure 6.20).

The best strategy for the weak SBU is to focus its resources on a particular buyer group (market segment) that is reasonably large and can be defended. The strong competitor can use its resources to build and exploit differences in the cost structure associated with producing, distributing, and marketing the product.

An alternative way of using the Porter curve is to add "Iso-quants." These are lines of equal return on investment that are not dependent on market share (Figure 6.19). A number of companies are neither stuck in the middle nor are they precisely on the curve. Figure 6.17 showed regions around the curve, but the iso-quants show that the company could fit almost anywhere on the chart. The value of such a chart is to show typical regions of return for alternative market shares. This is especially important in the low-market-share range, where PIMS analysis typically shows poor returns. In addition, other methods of return (such as ROA, ROE, and ROS) are rapidly gaining favor over ROI for measuring return.

The four generic strategies can be related to the earlier SPACE approach. SPACE can be used to "measure" the strategic position of each of the firm's SBUs and to help managers determine an appropriate competitive strategy for it (Figure 6.20 and Table 6.1).

The purpose of the SPACE approach is to identify which strategy fits the firm, taking into account industry strength, environmental stability, competitive advantage, and financial strength. SPACE displays the "bottom line" of a strategic review, and a thorough analysis is necessary to assess the particular strategic moves. However, at least two features make SPACE a valuable tool for strategic

| **FIGURE 6.19** | Use of Iso-quants with the Porter Curve |

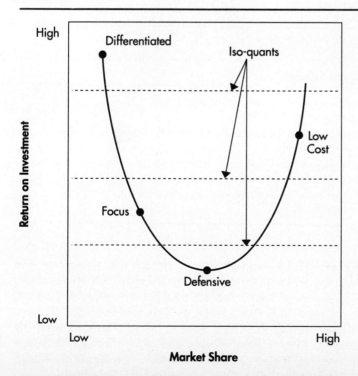

FIGURE 6.20 | **Strategic Options and Generic Strategies**
(FS = financial strength of the company; IS = industrial strength; ES = environmental stability; CA = competitive advantage of the company)

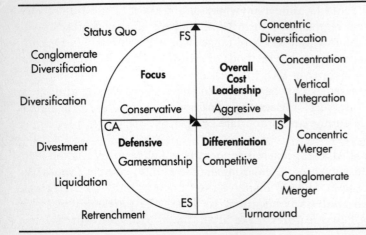

FIGURE 6.21 | **Application of Strategic Position and Action Evaluation (SPACE) to Strategy Choices for Business Units**

Strategic Posture as Determined by SPACE	Appropriate Generic Strategy
Aggressive posture	Cost leadership through concentration, concentric diversification, or vertical integration
Competitive posture	Differentiation, such as through strong R&D effort funded by merger with cash-rich company
Conservative posture	Focus and selective diversification through acquisition of companies in other market segments
Gamesmanship posture	Defensive, particularly survival tactics, such as retrenchment, divestment, or liquidation

---

management. First, SPACE provides a comprehensive approach that gives managers at all levels of the organization a means for considering the many different factors relevant to proposing a particular strategy. Second, and perhaps more important, SPACE provides a systematic approach that can be used to communicate different assumptions about important strategy variables. That is, when managers carefully assess each of the factors in the SPACE method, they can more effectively examine alternatives and achieve consensus. It also helps management to recognize the significance of each of the factors needed to maintain a competitive strategic posture.

SUMMARY

Two important responsibilities of strategic managers are (1) to understand how the organization's products or services are currently positioned in the market environment and (2) to determine how the organization can improve its position with existing or new products.

Knowledge about the status quo, with respect to the product and the market environment, enables strategic managers to identify the need for new product/market strategies. It is equally vital that the firm assess the trends that will affect the future of the company. In this chapter, we considered several tools available for this purpose. Decision-tree analysis helps managers identify alternative actions and their possible outcomes. Pinpointing existing products on the product life cycle also makes it easier to determine which strategies are appropriate. Growth vector analysis helps managers determine the most realistic and advantageous directions for growth, and gap analysis enables them to determine in advance where opportunities exist to pursue these new directions. Managers also have to consider whether new-product innovations or manufacturing technologies are needed to cut costs or boost sales. This requires continuous technology assessment.

PIMS analysis and competitive portfolio analysis help strategic managers to evaluate the financial consequences of product/market strategies. PIMS analysis enables managers to determine the impact on profitability of various strategies, based on models that have been developed from studies of hundreds of companies. Competitive portfolio analysis focuses on the cash flow that can be generated by a specific product/market strategy, such as having a balanced product portfolio or taking advantage of the experience curve.

In strategic position and action evaluation (SPACE), four input factors are used to arrive at different strategic postures for the firm: These postures identify generic competitive strategies and appropriate strategic thrusts for the business. Super SPACE adds importance of each factor and sustainability.

In this chapter, we also considered Michael Porter's three generic competitive strategies and how they are related to the SPACE approach.

REFERENCES AND SUGGESTIONS FOR FURTHER READING

Allan, Gerald and John Hammond. 1976. *The use of experience curves in competitive decision making.* Boston: Intercollegiate Case Clearing House, Case #9-175-174.

Allman, William. 1992. The ultimate widget: 3-D printing may revolutionize product design and manufacturing. *U.S. News and World Report*, July 20, pp. 55–56.

AMP Incorporated. 1991. *The Wall Street Transcript*, December 23, pp. 103, 763–765.

Barrett, Amy. 1990. Intimations of mortality. *Financial World*, September 18, pp. 30–33.

Birnbaum, Philip H. 1984. The choice of strategic alternatives under increasing regulation in high-technology companies. *Academy of Management Journal* 27, no. 3, pp. 489–510.

Birnbaum, Philip H. and Andrew R. Weiss. 1987. Competitive advantage and the basis for competition. Paper presented at the Seventh Annual International Conference of the Strategic Management Society, Boston, Mass.

Boston Consulting Group. 1974. Segmentation and strategy. BCG Perspective No. 156. Boston: Boston Consulting Group.

Specialization. BCG Perspective No. 240. Boston: Boston Consulting Group.

Branscomb, Lewis. 1992. Does America need a technology policy? *Harvard Business Review*, March–April, pp. 24–31.

Cardoza, R. N. and Y. Wind. 1985. Risk–return approach to product portfolio strategy. *Long-Range Planning* 18, no. 2, 77–85.

Cattin, P. and D. R. Wittink. 1982. Commercial use of conjoint analysis: A survey. *Journal of Marketing*, Summer, pp. 44–53.

Cohen, Warren. 1991. Spending on tomorrow today. *U.S. News and World Report*, July 22, pp. 45–46.

David, F. R. 1986. Evaluating alternative growth strategies—an analytical approach. *Long-Range Planning*, Spring.

Erdman, Andrew. 1992. AMP: Staying ahead of 800 competitors. *Fortune*, June 1, pp. 111–112.

Fox, Harold W. 1973. A framework for functional coordination. *Atlanta Economic Review* 23, no. 6.

Garvin, David. 1991. How the Baldrige award really works. *Harvard Business Review*, November–December, pp. 80–93.

Garvin, David A. 1987. Competing on the eight dimensions of quality. *Harvard Business Review*, November–December, pp. 101–110.

Ghemawat, Pankaj. 1985. Building strategy on the experience curve. *Harvard Business Review*, March, pp. 143–149.

Gould, J. M. 1983. Technology change and competition. *Journal of Business Strategy* 4, no. 2, pp. 66–71.

Green, Paul E. 1977. A new approach to market segmentation. *Business Horizons*, February, pp. 61–73.

Green, Paul E. and Frank Carmone. 1970. Multidimensional scaling and related techniques in market analysis. Cambridge, Mass.: Marketing Science Institute.

Green, Paul E. and V. Srinivasan. 1978. Conjoint analysis in consumer research: Issues and outlook. *Journal of Consumer Research*, September, pp. 103–123.

Hamel, Gary and C. K. Prahalad. 1991. Corporate imagination and expeditionary marketing. *Harvard Business Review*, July–August, pp. 81–92.

Hamermesh, Richard G. and Roderick E. White. 1984. Manage beyond portfolio analysis. *Harvard Business Review*, January, pp. 103–109.

Henderson, Bruce D. 1984. The application and misapplication of the experience curve. *Journal of Business Strategy* 4, no. 3, pp. 3–9.

Hofer, Charles. 1975. Toward a contingency theory of business strategy. *Academy of Management Journal* 18, no. 4.

Jorgensen, Barbara. 1990. AMP connects its once and future goals. *Electronic Business*, September 3, pp. 38–40.

Kehoe, William J. 1983. Strategic marketing planning: The PIMS model. *S.A.M. Advanced Management Journal*, Spring, pp. 45–50.

Kotler, Philip. 1972. *Marketing management.* Englewood Cliffs, N.J.: Prentice-Hall, Chapter 7.

Levitt, Theodore. 1965. Exploit the product life cycle. *Harvard Business Review* 43, no. 6.

McInnes, Harold. 1992. The AMP connection: Standard to strategy. National Center for Manufacturing Sciences, FOCUS, March.

Miles, Raymond E. and Charles C. Snow. 1978. *Organizational strategy: Structure and process.* New York: McGraw-Hill.

Ohmae, Kenichi. 1988. Getting back to strategy. *Harvard Business Review*, November–December, pp. 149–156.

Porter, Michael. 1985. *Competitive advantage.* New York: The Free Press.

Porter, Michael. 1980. *Competitive strategy.* New York: The Free Press.

Reese, Jennifer. 1992. Getting hot ideas from customers. *Fortune*, May 18, pp. 86–88.

Sarge, Dick. 1991. AMP is optimistic about global growth. *Sunday Patriot-News* (Harrisburg, Penna.), September 15, p. F-1, F-3.

Schiffman, Susan, et al. 1981. Introduction to multidimensional scaling. *Theory, Methods, and Applications.* Cambridge, Mass.: Academic Press.

Schlender, Brenton. 1992. How Sony keeps the magic going. *Fortune*, February 24, pp. 75–84.

Schoeffler, Sidney, Robert D. Buzzell, and Donald F. Heany. 1974. Impact of strategic planning on profit performance. *Harvard Business Review*, March–April.

Schuler, Joseph. 1991. 100,000 points of promise. *Pennsylvania Business and Technology,* Fourth Quarter.

Technology policy: Is America on the right track? 1992. *Harvard Business Review*, May–June, pp. 140–157.

The AMP connection: Standard to strategy. 1992. National Center for Manufacturing Sciences, *FOCUS*, March.

Urban, Glen L. and John R. Hauser. 1980. *Design and marketing of new products.* Englewood Cliffs, N.J.: Prentice-Hall.

Wasson, Chester. 1974. *Dynamic competitive strategy and product life cycles.* St. Charles, Ill.: Challenge Books.

Wasson, Chester. 1971. Product management. *Product life cycles and competitive marketing strategy.* St. Charles, Ill.: Challenge Books.

Weber, John A. 1977. Market structure profile and strategic growth opportunities. *California Management Review* 20, no. 1.

Willis, Clint. 1992. Cash in on U.S. companies that are hammering the Japanese. *Money*, April, pp. 69–72.

Wind, Y. and V. Mahajan. 1981. Designing product and business portfolios, *Harvard Business Review,* January–February, pp. 155–165.

Yelsey, A. A. 1984. Multiple image forecasting, *Planning Review*, pp. 27–29.

Zufryden, Fred S. 1988. Using conjoint analysis to predict trial and repeat-purchase patterns of new frequently purchased products. *Decision Sciences*, 19, pp. 55–71.

APPENDIX A

Product/Market Mapping

Product/market mapping and statistical analysis are typically used in market research. Strategic managers use the results of this mapping in making strategic decisions about how to differentiate products for sale to specific market segments.

Product/market mapping can help managers identify a product's key features or attributes in the eyes of its customers. With this input, managers can formulate successful product-differentiation and market-segmentation strategies.

The most commonly used product/market mapping techniques are

- Multidimensional scaling (MDS)
- Cluster analysis
- Factor analysis
- Adaptive perceptual mapping (APM)
- Discriminant analysis
- Conjoint analysis

We will look closely at the first and last of these. The choice of technique depends on the purpose of the analysis. Different techniques might be chosen, depending on

1. The focus of the analysis; whether information is available about physical/product features or psychological/demographic features
2. The depth of current knowledge about the market; whether information is needed to identify basic consumer choices or to fine-tune an existing market strategy

The data in Figures 6A.1 and 6A.2, developed by the Boston Consulting Group, constitute an index for the use of new digital telephone connectors in AMP's European market versus older analog standards. Between 1985 and 1990, the analog market grew from an index of 100 to 151, based on the continued addition of new telephone users. Digital connectors have slowly developed from 0.2% market share in 1985 to 7.4% in 1990.

Figure 6A.3 shows a forecast made using the S-curve computation. The substitution of digital devices for analog ones is projected to proceed rapidly and to lead to the quick demise of analog technology.

FIGURE 6A.1	Digital versus Analog Substitution Data for AMP

Index	Actual					
	1985	1986	1987	1988	1989	1990
Analog	100	112	123	132	143	151
Digital	0.2	0.5	1	2	5	12
Total	100.2	112.5	124	134	148	163
M (digital)	.2%	.4%	.8%	1.5%	3.4%	7.4%
	↓	↓	↓	↓	↓	↓
R	0.002	0.004	0.008	0.015	0.035	0.079

Index	Projected						
	1991	1992	1993	1994	1995	1996	1997
Analog	150.7	141.7	121.4	91.4	60.1	36.1	20.1
Digital	22.6	43.9	76.5	118.8	162.4	198.7	227.0
Total	173.3	185.6	197.9	210.2	222.5	234.8	247.1
M (digital)	13.0%	23.7%	38.7%	56.5%	73.0%	84.6%	91.9%
	↑	↑	↑	↑	↑	↑	↑
R	0.15	0.31	0.63	1.3	2.7	5.5	11.3

Note: M equals percentage of market share; R equals $M/(1 - M)$, which represents the rate of substitution, or the ratio of digital to analog technology.

FIGURE 6A.2	Digital versus Analog Substitution Graph

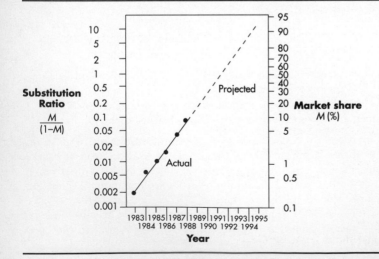

FIGURE 6A.3	AMP Digital Market Forecast Based on S-curve Computation

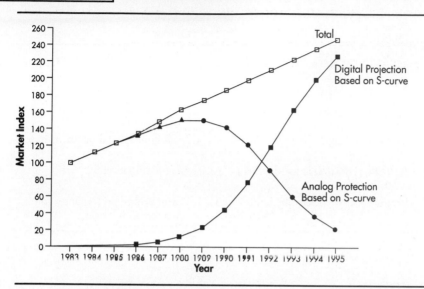

The matrix in Figure 6A.4 shows how each tool might be applied, given a focus and prior depth of knowledge about customer choices. Figure 6A.5 lists data input and output for each of the techniques. Because software for each of these techniques is available for personal computers, the user need only enter the data and interpret the results. The details of the technique are incorporated in the computer program. The articles and references at the end of the chapter provide sources of further information about how these tools can be applied. Strategic applications of two of them, multidimensional scaling and conjoint analysis, are described in the sections that follow.

FIGURE 6A.4	Use of Product/Market Mapping Techniques

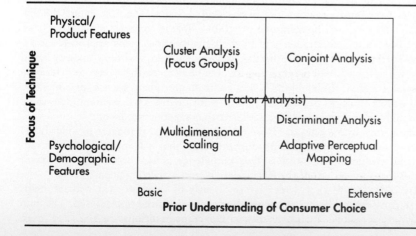

FIGURE 6A.5	Input and Output Data of Product/Market Mapping Techniques

Technique	Input	Output
Multidimensional scaling	Similarity rankings among products	Two-dimensional product map
Cluster analysis	Similarity ratings	Market groups or clusters with similar characteristics
Factor analysis	Attribute ratings	Factor loadings/collapsed dimensions
Adaptive perceptual mapping	Attribute ratings	Multidimensional product map
Discriminant analysis	Rating of consumers for different attributes	Group affiliation
Conjoint analysis	Product feature trade-offs	Feature share preference and market simulation

MULTIDIMENSIONAL SCALING

Multidimensional scaling helps strategic managers to evaluate similarities or dissimilarities between product attributes using indirect data provided by respondents. An indirect approach is used because, in many cases, the product attributes are not yet known or the respondents are unable or unwilling to represent their reasons for evaluation accurately. Computerized multidimensional scaling permits managers to identify product/market attributes based on simple input data, such as ratings on a scale of 0 to 10. On the scale, 0 means that the products are very similar with respect to an attribute, and 10 means that they are very dissimilar. The computer converts this information into a graphic representation in which the differences perceived by the respondents are seen as relative distances on the map. Figure 6A.6 shows such maps for automobiles and pain relievers. The task of the researchers is to add and describe dimensions, such as luxuriousness and sportiness for an automobile or gentleness and effectiveness for a pain reliever.

Figure 6A.7 illustrates the use of multidimensional scaling based on hard data, such as the airline distances between the major cities in the United States. The user enters the distances between pairs of cities, and the computer program is able to construct a map that positions all the cities relative to one another and in the right locations. This approach can be used to ascertain the relative position of products, services, or even a whole company based on differences ("distances") between pairs of objects. Researchers use these data to determine how "close" or similar each of these objects is to a competing product, service, or company. Multidimensional scaling is a proven strategic tool. It is invaluable for determining desirable product attributes and for positioning products relative to competing products.

Perceptual maps, such as the ones in Figure 6A.6 help strategic managers to identify (1) different customer or market segments, (2) product attributes that will appeal to specific segments, and (3) new-product opportunities. This knowledge guides product-development strategies and helps focus the efforts of the R&D, design, and marketing departments.

An MDS map of the car market, which is done yearly by the major car makers, helps them to identify weaknesses or "holes" in the product range that need to be closed. The map for 1970 (see Figure 6A.6) shows a void for cars with average luxuriousness and sportiness.

| FIGURE 6A.6 | MDS Maps of Consumer Perceptions of Automobiles and Pain Relievers |

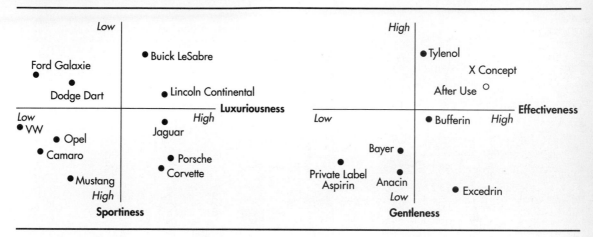

Source: Automobile map adapted from Greene and Carmone, 1970, p. 60; pain-reliever map adapted from Urban and Hauser, 1980, p. 221.

This gap was filled by Japanese manufacturers, who began to produce cars having the price and performance of a Volkswagen "bug" but more standard "luxury" features.

The map of the pain relievers (Figure 6A.6) was used to better position a new product in the market. After a careful market analysis, the pharmaceutical company planned to launch a new pain reliever (the **X** concept) that would approach Tylenol in gentleness but act faster and provide more pain relief. By collecting consumer ratings after the product was launched, the company discovered that its market position was not quite on target (after use **O**). The company then redesigned the product slightly to achieve the position targeted on the map.

CONJOINT ANALYSIS

Figure 6A.6 shows that perceptual mapping such as MDS typically focuses on psychological and demographic aspects of product positioning, not physical characteristics of the product. Once the desired position is identified, though, attention must be given to developing a product capable of achieving that position. Conjoint analysis is often used in this effort because it helps managers to

1. Quantify the relative value to the consumer of each individual feature of a product.
2. Identify feature-based segmentation patterns.
3. Assess the relative value of changing one or another product feature.
4. Predict consumer preference for new product features.
5. Predict relative market shares for existing or new products, and gauge the effect of feature and price changes on relative market shares.

FIGURE 6A.7 | Geographic Map Made from Hard Data; in This Case, Distances Between U.S. Cities

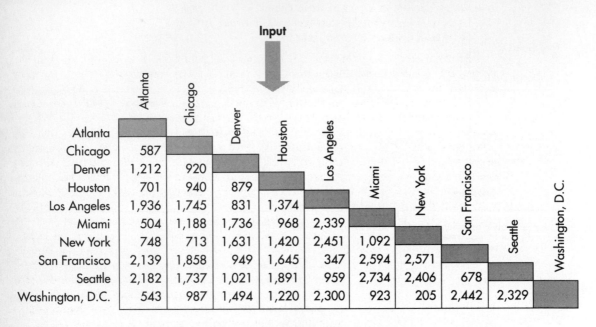

Input

	Atlanta	Chicago	Denver	Houston	Los Angeles	Miami	New York	San Francisco	Seattle	Washington, D.C.
Atlanta										
Chicago	587									
Denver	1,212	920								
Houston	701	940	879							
Los Angeles	1,936	1,745	831	1,374						
Miami	504	1,188	1,736	968	2,339					
New York	748	713	1,631	1,420	2,451	1,092				
San Francisco	2,139	1,858	949	1,645	347	2,594	2,571			
Seattle	2,182	1,737	1,021	1,891	959	2,734	2,406	678		
Washington, D.C.	543	987	1,494	1,220	2,300	923	205	2,442	2,329	

MDS Output

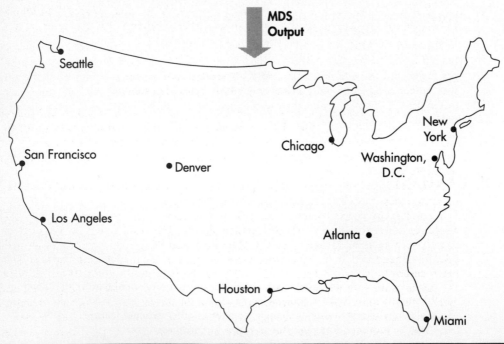

To conduct a conjoint analysis, managers must

1. Define the relevant attributes of the product.
2. Ask respondents (customers) to make a series of tradeoffs indicating their preference for one attribute from a pair of attributes.
3. Calculate respondents' preference scores for each attribute.
4. Simulate the effects of attribute changes.

Personal computer programs are available to perform tasks 2 through 4; the user defines the attributes (task 1) and then concentrates on analyzing the data. The following example illustrates an application of conjoint analysis.

A conjoint analysis that was performed to match products to market opportunities effectively explained the market dynamics seen in the personal computer industry. Late in 1983, a number of new personal computer (PC) models were prepared for market introduction in 1984, most notably the new Apple Macintosh and the IBM PC Junior. Conventional wisdom at the time was that the PC Junior would be a hit, because it was an IBM product, and that the Macintosh would be a flop like Lisa, an earlier Apple model with similar user-friendly features. At this point, a conjoint analysis of the PC market was conducted by the Boston Consulting Group (BCG). BCG surveyed more than 1,000 attendees at a Boston computer show. Only the responses of those who planned to buy a PC within a year were used.

The following product attributes were analyzed and a tradeoff prepared with respect to price, manufacturer's reputation, portability, data manipulation capability, database capacity, word processing capacity, and styling. For each attribute, variations were carefully chosen for their relevance to different products then available. Wherever possible, directly measurable attributes were used. For price, for example, three variations were set: $1,000, $2,000, and $3,000. Database-capacity (memory) variations were set as 256 K Bytes, 640 K Bytes, and 1 M Bytes. Other attributes, such as portability, required yes or no answers.

If asked which model would be ideal, people would, of course, say a 1 M Byte model for $1,000. In reality, this choice was not available. Therefore, for the conjoint analysis, respondents were asked to make tradeoff choices, such as:

Everything else being equal, which would you buy?

(a) A PC that has 1 M Byte of memory but costs $2,000.
(b) A PC that costs $1,000 but has only 640 K Bytes of memory.

The respondents ranked these tradeoffs, on a scale of 1 to 9, as shown in Figure 6A.8, where 1 means most desirable. This respondent to the price-versus-capacity question preferred answer (a) over answer (b); that is, he or she would prefer more computing power, even at a higher price. Only a further price increase would change this preference to a model with somewhat less power.

The combined responses were used to evaluate the relative importance of these attributes for segments as well as the total population (Figure 6A.9).

The next step was to enter the attributes of each of the products into the industry model in order to calculate the preference shares. The results showed how preference shares were likely to change when the Macintosh and PC Junior were introduced (Figure 6A.10). When the data on Macintosh were included in the model, with features based on press descriptions, it captured almost 50% of the first-choice votes. When data on the PC Junior were entered, on the other hand, they received no first-choice votes, and the market shares remained unchanged. At the time the model was tested, these results were counterintuitive. Yet in the spring of 1984, after the new computer models were launched, it became clear that the conjoint analysis had been quite accurate. The Apple

---

FIGURE 6A.8 | **Sample Response to Question in a Conjoint Analysis Survey**

Price

	$1,000	$2,000	$3,000
1 MBytes	1	2	5
640 KBytes	3	4	6
256 KBytes	7	8	9

Database Capacity

FIGURE 6A.9 | **Conjoint Analysis: Sequence of First Choices by Customers in Three Different Market Segments**

Business	Education	Home
1. Database capacity	Word processing	Price
2. Word processing	Portability	Data manipulation
3. Manufacturer's reputation	Price	Styling
4. Data manipulation	Data manipulation	Word processing
5. Portability	Database capacity	Portability
6. Price	Styling	Database capacity
7. Styling	Manufacturer's reputation	Manufacturer's reputation

---

FIGURE 6A.10 | **Preference Shares of PCs, Based on Conjoint Analysis**

	Share of Preferences (%)		
Product	Existing Models	Macintosh Introduced	PC Junior Introduced
IBM PC	46	30	30
Compaq	23	10	10
DEC Rainbow	19	9	9
Macintosh	—	47	47
PC Junior	—	—	0
Others	12	4	4
Total	100	100	100

Macintosh had an excellent start, whereas sales of the PC Junior quickly became an embarrassment for IBM.

IBM acted quickly to make changes in the PC Junior. Another conjoint analysis was used to predict the impact of alternative feature changes (Figure 6A.11). This analysis showed that dropping the price of the PC Junior, even by as much as 47%, would not solve IBM's problem. Increasing the memory of the PC Junior would significantly improve its market position but would seriously reduce preference for the more expensive IBM PC. If, on the other hand, the PC Junior were made portable, with no other changes, IBM would increase its total preference share from 25% (status quo) to 38% for both models.

As it turned out, IBM chose to increase the PC Junior's memory and not make it portable. Competitors started to take advantage of this situation and gained market share by adjusting their product policies and by offering portable models. IBM responded by introducing a portable version of the PC but never was able to duplicate its success in the desktop market. The PC Junior was finally abandoned in 1985.

This example shows the power of conjoint analysis as a method of simulating a product's reception in the market environment. Many companies have recognized this capability and regularly use conjoint analysis to test customer preferences for the attributes of a range of different products.

FIGURE 6A.11 | **Conjoint Simulation of Impact of PC Junior Feature Changes**

Product	Status Quo	Share of Preferences (%) IBM Options for PC Junior		
		Reduce Price from $1,900 to $1,000	Add Memory Without Price Decrease	Make Portable Without Price Decrease
IBM PC	25	23	7	23 ⎫ 38%
PC Junior	0	4	26	15 ⎭
Compaq	20	19	16	14
DEC Rainbow	7	7	4	7
Macintosh	46	45	45	39
Others	2	2	2	2
Total	100	100	100	100

Note: Compaq had reacted to competitors' new products by reducing its price from $3,400 to $2,750 in order to regain market share.

Source: Courtesy of The Boston Consulting Group, Inc. Reprinted with permission.

APPENDIX B

Steps in Technology Assessment

Technology has two basic components: (1) a tangible component, in the form of machines, tools, and material, and (2) an intangible component, in the form of technological knowledge and expertise. Knowledge, especially scientific knowledge, is by far the most important component. It dictates what skills and techniques employees need to learn; the layout and design of industrial plants; the operating principles of machines; the choice of computer software; and the procedures, patents, and copyrights originating from laboratories. Technology is a strategic resource, whether it is developed within the company or acquired from external sources.

A technology assessment involves two phases: (1) an information-gathering phase, termed *technology scanning*, and (2) an information-analysis phase, termed *technology evaluation*.

Technology Scanning

To perform a technology scan, strategic managers

1. Subdivide the business as a whole into strategic business units (SBUs).
2. Determine the following for each SBU:
   a. Technology currently used by the company.
   b. Technology currently used by competitors.
   c. New technologies on the horizon. (This should include any technological development that might accomplish the same *function* for the business.)
   d. Source of the new technology and its effects on all stakeholders in the system, as traced on a stakeholder map (see Chapter 4).

Technology Evaluation

To perform a technology evaluation, strategic managers ask two fundamental questions about each of the technologies identified in the scan.

1. *How important is this technology to the success of the business?* Does it add value? Is it changing? Will it open up new markets?

2. *How strong is our current and future position with respect to this technology?* This is indicated by expenditure, history, patents, publications, R&D, personnel skills, and ability to adopt or adapt the new technology. In general, a company is either a leader (strong position) or a follower (weak position) in the use of technology.

The answers to these two questions can be plotted in a matrix (Figure 6B.1). Answers in quadrant A, the high/high quadrant, indicate a strong position—one that should be pursued aggressively in order to retain a competitive advantage. Answers in quadrant B, the high/low quadrant, indicate that the technology is important to the firm but it is not being used to its full advantage. The firm can choose to

1. Commit resources in order to improve the technology position and turn it into a competitive advantage (more R&D, equipment purchasing, hiring, education, and the like).
2. Move out of this area. Reinvest in other areas.
3. Adopt an *adequacy stance.* Commit enough resources to maintain a satisfactory defensive or follower position. Monitor developments and wait to take advantage of the next technological breakthrough.

Answers in quadrant C, the low/high quadrant, indicate that the firm has a strong position in an unimportant or perhaps obsolete technology. This often happens when new technologies have become available and competitors have taken advantage of them. In this case, the firm should make the best of what it has and move toward new technologies or diversify into other areas where its technology can be more useful.

Answers in quadrant D, the low/low quadrant, indicate that the firm has a poor position in an unimportant technology. The firm's involvement in this area should be thoroughly reconsidered. The technology might be phased out or used in new ways. Technology is not the force driving strategy in this case. Rather, marketing aspects of the product strategy are most important.

As we noted in the chapter, it is generally ineffective to apply a low-cost strategy alone in using technology for competitive advantage in achieving market dominance or rapid growth. Furthermore, technology alone cannot sustain competitive advantage. Though it is vital for

| FIGURE 6B.1 | Technology Evaluation Matrix |

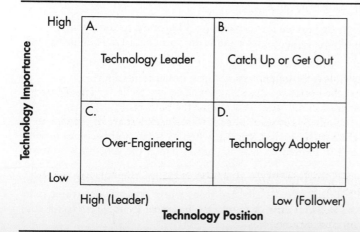

gaining advantage, especially during the introduction and growth stages of a product/industry life cycle, when a technology's relative importance to the industry is being determined, any technology must be backed up and supplemented by strategies that focus on marketing and customer service. One way to maintain competitive advantage from the maturity stage on is to focus on product changes that make the product easier and more advantageous for customers to use. This strategy might be useful for companies whose technological position falls in quadrant C or D of the technology evaluation matrix (Figure 6B.1).

TECHNOLOGY SUBSTITUTION

New technologies can radically change the demand for products that use an old technology. In addition, because many technological innovations do not come from the current technology leader, they tend to alter the competitive structure as well. The current technology leader is often put in a defensive position, from which it tries to ignore or thwart the growth of the new technological substitute. The leader slowly declines from quadrant A into quadrant C of the technology evaluation matrix, often without realizing it.

Why is it so difficult for the current leader to spot a new, superior technology? Mostly because the strategy is based on the old technology, which is still doing well and has achieved seemingly unassailable volume advantage. Take, for example, the slow adoption of reinforced fiberglass or plastics for the production of car bodies. Although these materials are potentially cheaper than steel, they are resisted because car manufacturers have made a significant investment in sheet metal presses and stamping machines. As these machines (which can cost up to $20 million and last up to 50 years) are taken out of the production process, the use of other materials for car bodies is slowly rising.

Technology substitution tends to succeed most easily if it enters or creates a new market segment. Because of high startup costs, plastic bathroom sinks were initially more expensive than the established ceramic ones. New extrusion technology, however, made it possible for designers to create more shapes and sizes. This enabled plastic sinks to penetrate the designer market and, eventually, to gain market share from ceramic sinks.

Plotted on a graph, technology substitution can be described as a gradual S-curve. Like an epidemic disease or other biological phenomenon, a new technology goes through an "incubation" period, during which it spreads relatively slowly, and then an "acute" stage, during which it spreads rapidly through an industry. The phenomenon of technological substitution proceeds by the following principles:

1. If a substitution has progressed even a few percent, it will proceed to completion.
2. The rate of substitution of new technology for old is proportional to the amount of the old remaining.

The process can be tracked by plotting the ratio of new to old technology:

$R = M / (1 - M)$

where R equals the rate of substitution and M equals the market share of the new technology. A characteristic of the S-curve is that R is 1.0 when M is 0.5 and becomes increasingly larger as M approaches 1.0. Plotted on semi-log graph paper, the substitution ratio R forms a straight line.

The substitution of front-wheel for rear-wheel-drive technology is plotted in Figure 6B.2. In 1960, less than 25% of the world's cars had front-wheel drive. Today, three times that number, or 75%, have front-wheel drive. Figure 6B.3 lists other examples of technology substitution, some of which occurred rather quickly.

Technology substitution data for the AMP case is shown in Figure 6A.1 (p. 274). First, the $M / (1 - M)$ ratios for the historical data are calculated and plotted on semi-log paper. As can be seen from Figure 6A.2, the resulting data points fall on a straight line that can be extended to project data points for future years. These points, which can be projected with simple linear regression or read directly from the graph, are then reconverted into market shares and a forecast for digital sales.

FIGURE 6B.2	**Technology Substitution: Market Share (*M*) of Front-Wheel-Drive Cars, 1960–1986**

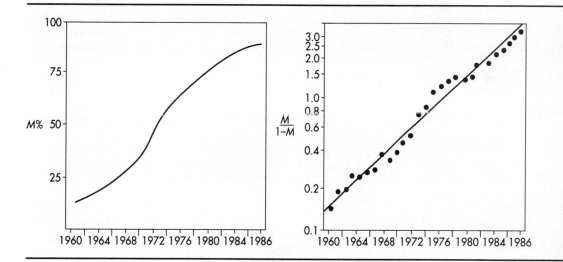

FIGURE 6B.3	**Examples of Technology Substitution**

| | New Technology | |
New/Old Technologies	Year of First Application	Years Until 75% Market Share Reached
Power/manual auto steering	1962	20
Polyethylene/glass bottles	1963	18
Organic/inorganic insecticides	1946	17
Air conditioning/natural auto cooling	1968	15
Basic-oxygen/open-hearth steels	1968	10
Diesel/steam locomotives	1949	9
Color/black-and-white television	1972	8
Detergents/soaps	1951	8
Turbofan/turbojet aircraft engines	1961	5

CHAPTER SEVEN

Strategy in a Global Environment

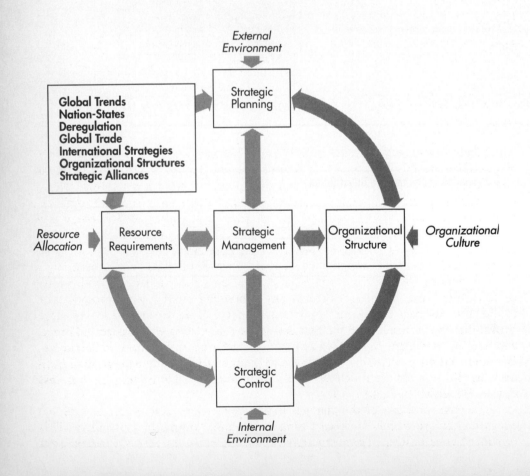

Chapter 1 A Framework for Strategic Management	**Chapter 2** Strategic Analysis	**Chapter 3** Strategic Visioning, Goals, Ethics, and Social Responsibility	**Chapter 4** The Competitive Environment	**Chapter 5** Capability-based Strategy	**Chapter 6** Market Dynamics and Sustainable Competitive Advantage
How to approach strategic management	*Application of strategic analysis*	*Understanding vision, values, ethics*	*Coping with competitive forces, stakeholders*	*Assessing company capability, timeliness, quality*	*Determining trends, gap analysis, and market dynamics*

Chapter 7 Strategy in a Global Environment	**Chapter 8** Financial Planning and Competitive- Cost Analysis	**Chapter 9** Entrepreneurship, Mergers and Acquisitions, Restructuring, and the Service Sector	**Chapter 10** Leadership Factor in Strategy and Implementing Strategic Change	**Chapter 11** Information Technology and Future Directions in Strategy
Assessing global trade, foreign markets, monetary exchange	*Preparing a financial plan and competitive-cost analysis*	*Importance of small business, entrepreneurs, restructuring*	*Strategy implementation, leadership, culture*	*Information technology, trends, new management*

INTRODUCTION

About midway between Hoteville and Bacavi Villages on the Third Mesa of the Hopi Indian Reservation, the Hopi Foundation has opened a not-for-profit solar electric enterprise. The enterprise will sell solar panels and systems to Hopis whose dwellings are sparsely scattered throughout the sun-baked, remote northern Arizona desert. Hitachi and other Japanese firms are the major source of technology and capital. Together with Arizona financial institutions, the Japanese are providing consumer financing for Hopi families. They are also supporting tests of solar hot-water heaters, which, when perfected, they intend to sell in Third World countries.

Just outside Denver, Colorado, a young real estate developer opened his one-person office. After striking a deal to buy a building from a local company, he found that his best financing opportunities came from German and Japanese banks, that the architect with the best design for remodeling was located in France, and that his first client would be a British firm with major operations in Singapore. (He later told his professors that because he planned to be a one-person small business, he did not devote much time to global studies while getting his business degree. He wishes he had.)

Indicative of some of the changes that organizations can expect in a global environment are trends such as China's renegade Guangdong province. This province has embraced an almost purely capitalistic economy that is growing faster than nearly any other in the world. It grew 27.2% in 1991 (Gibney, 1992). When visited by politicians from Beijing, local officials retorted, "What have you invested here? We pay for our railroads, our highways, and our power plants, and you have no right to tell us what to do."

When companies such as IBM, Toshiba, and Siemens decide to work together to develop computer components, the world really has changed (Weber, 1992). These three companies are expected to spend $1 billion in developing advanced semiconductors and advanced manufacturing processes. Schrage (1992) questions what's behind IBM's dutch-treat strategy. The answer seems to be that the next generation of advanced memory chips are needed to ensure global competitiveness and that the cost of development would be excessive for any one company alone. In another international venture, Fujitsu and Advanced Micro Devices have invested $700 million in sharing costs of development.

Asserting its clout in Europe, Germany is using its growing power to achieve what Helmut Kohl maintains that he wants, "a United States of Europe" (Templeman, 1992). As Germany flexes its economic muscle, the United States will have to accommodate to a changing market environment in Europe. Some individuals maintain that a strong Germany will actually enhance America's relations with Japan because Germany's markets are much more open to U.S. goods. Germany's new role in Europe made a major impact at the General Agreement on Tariffs and Trade (GATT). A new Western alliance may be forged, wherein Germany is firmly linked with the West.

These trends indicate that companies must change the way they conduct business if they are to remain competitive and profitable in the light of new consumer characteristics, such as

1. More particular and diversified lifestyles
2. An increased interest in fashion
3. Greater willingness to pay for intangible attributes in a product
4. Technology that saves time and is easy to use
5. A lack of interest in what country produced the product

In effect, we are becoming a truly borderless world where the successful corporation will be one that has a global outlook (Sera, 1992).

These few examples illustrate the global environment that affects enterprises of virtually all sizes and in virtually every industry. The task of strategic managers in today's business environment is to match and position their businesses in an increasingly complex, global environment. A business is like an ecological entity. It has mutual relations with other entities—called stakeholders—in its environment. A *stakeholder* is anyone whose actions can affect an organization or who is affected by the organization's actions. Successful strategic managers are able to identify the crucial stakeholders in their business's environment and to make realistic assumptions about them. These assumptions are used to develop business strategies. Increasingly, a firm's stakeholders are located at various and sometimes remote places all over the world.

Like any ecosystem, a business's environment holds opportunities and threats. Skillful strategic managers are able to find "market niches" in their firm's global environment that are particularly well suited to the products, services, and capabilities the organization offers. They are also able to develop organizational structures and arrangements that work effectively within the environment. Each of the four organizations described above was successful in doing this. Failure to find a suitable niche, however, can lead to damage or even destruction for an organization. For this reason, global environmental assessment is essential.

An organization's ability to cope with a changing environment is probably the most important determinant of its success or failure in a free-enterprise system. Changes in consumer tastes, political conditions, market structure, or technology cannot only affect individual companies but also make or break an entire industry.

Oil and automobiles provide a case in point. On October 16, 1973, delegates to the Organization of Petroleum Exporting Countries—five Arabs and an Iranian—met in Kuwait City and decided unilaterally to increase the price of oil to $5.11 per barrel. In September the price had been $2.90 per barrel; in December it reached $11.65. A panic set in as people everywhere in the world tried to reduce their dependence on petroleum. A few years later most American automakers were experiencing financial difficulties, and a few were on the brink of bankruptcy because they had failed to respond effectively to the price increases. They should have responded quickly by developing a line of more fuel-efficient cars. Foreign competitors looked upon the oil crisis as an opportunity. As a result, while Chrysler and American Motors were struggling for survival, Japanese manufacturers were thriving in the market by offering smaller, gas-efficient, low-maintenance automobiles. The lesson to be learned here is that failure to analyze the external environment for economic, political, competitive, geographic, social, and technological opportunities and threats can have a major disruptive impact on an organization.

A successful organization marshals its internal capabilities so as to interact profitably with its external environment. The many unknowns in the external environment introduce considerable uncertainty into strategic decision making. The concepts presented in this chapter are designed to help the strategic manager identify uncertainties in the external environment and plan how to deal with them. This chapter also presents an overall framework for global environmental analysis that includes a discussion of nine major trends that are affecting businesses of all types throughout the world. The basic concepts used to assess the global environment include the elements of competitive business strategies for global markets.

A FRAMEWORK FOR GLOBAL ENVIRONMENTAL ANALYSIS

Organizations do not exist in a vacuum. Rather, they are affected directly and indirectly by many stakeholders. Figure 7.1 is a graphical representation of an organization and its direct and indirect relationships with its stakeholders in a global environment. It is essential for an organization to understand who these stakeholders are, what their relationships are to the organization, and what assumptions the organization is making about them and their behavior. These assumptions should be tested for validity and appropriateness and should be reformulated as necessary. Classifying economic, political, social, technological, competitive, and geographic

---

FIGURE 7.1 | Global Environment: Generic Stakeholder Forces Map

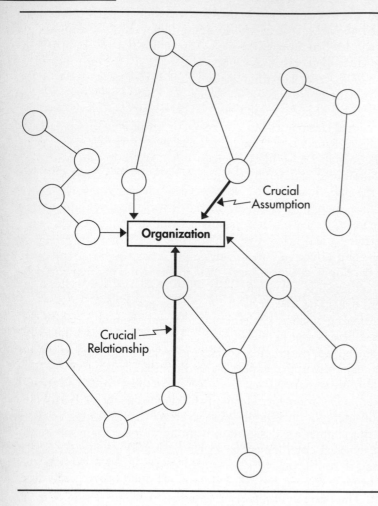

---

implications of these assumptions helps determine the nature of the relationships an organization has with its stakeholders and what impact their activities are likely to have on the organization. Tracing global trends (such as the trend toward global monetary superliquidity and increased use of information technology) and anticipating their effects on the organization's stakeholders further clarify the opportunities and threats the environment holds for the organization. Stakeholder maps, assumptions, and interpretations of those assumptions depict the critical uncertainties that an organization faces.

Some assumptions are pivotal and serve as the very underpinnings of the organization's policies, plans, and strategies. The organization is potentially vulnerable to changes and inaccuracies in these assumptions, so they must be examined carefully. The crucial stakeholders in an organization's environment also change over time, and today that change is rapid. Statistical forecasting and econometric modeling can be used to project some of these changes, as long as the fundamental relationships in the underlying stakeholder structure remain constant. Structural change in stakeholder environments, however, is common and frequent. Quantitative methods may not satisfactorily capture these major qualitative shifts. For this reason, qualitative environmental forecasting techniques are often used to describe and predict possible shifts in the web of relationships in the organization's stakeholder environment and to determine their probable effects on the organization.

A completed environmental assessment enables an organization (1) to find its best possible niche and (2) to decide how it might best respond to a range of future environmental conditions. Environmental assessment is a never-ending task for businesses, because their environments are constantly changing and they are continuously being affected by forces from abroad—and sometimes from the farthest reaches of the globe.

Major global trends

Today's business exists in a global political economy. National, regional, and local economies no longer are independent structures or isolated entities. Instead, a worldwide framework of interactions exists both within and between national, regional, and local economies. This interdependence is the result of a long-term trend in the evolution of civilization, including the development of improved methods of transportation, communication, and information handling and the exploits of merchant adventurers beginning with the Phoenician sailors and continuing through the Roman speculators. The Venetian traders, the Hanseatic League, the Portuguese explorers, the Spanish conquistadors, the Dutch merchants, the British imperialists—all served to create a strong dependent relationship among peoples of the world.

World War II furthered global integration, because it made people more aware of opportunities and threats to which they were exposed from other parts of the globe. Advanced technologies were developed in communication and computation and in massive destruction. The dropping of atomic bombs at Hiroshima and Nagasaki alerted the world to the possibility of global destruction and to the need to control the proliferation of such weapons and avoid a nuclear catastrophe. Having learned the lessons taught by the impotent League of Nations and the ill-conceived Treaty of Versailles that followed World War I, world leaders sought to create more effective global institutions. The United Nations, the International Monetary Fund, the Organization for Economic Cooperation and Development (OECD), Comecon (the Eastern bloc's version of the Common Market, which was disbanded in 1991), and the World Bank are among the institutions formed to help nations and organizations deal with the new global political and economic environment. Working together, all these factors accelerated the creation of a truly global economy until, in 1978, Senator Hubert Humphrey could claim that "There isn't a nation in the world which controls even the value of its money, the central symbol of independence. Inflation, recession, and stagflation are global in nature."

Fortune's report on the world's largest 500 industrial corporations provides a useful starting point for examining global trends (Woods, 1992). Table 7.1 shows what countries have the greatest numbers of large companies and what is the largest company in each. Of the ten countries shown, the largest companies in four of them are automotive and two are in petroleum.

TABLE 7.1   Countries with the Most Fortune 500 Companies

Country	Companies on the List	Largest Company
United States	157	General Motors
Japan	119	Toyota Motor
Britain	43	British Petroleum
Germany	33	Daimler-Benz
France	32	Elf Aquitaine
Sweden	14	Volvo
South Korea	13	Samsung Group
Switzerland	10	Nestlé
Australia	9	Broken Hill Propietary
Canada	9	Northern Telecom

Despite the number of its companies in the Fortune 500, the United States lags behind the rest of the world in fixed investments as a percentage of gross domestic product (Pennar, 1992). Table 7.2 shows these data for the major industrial nations.

TABLE 7.2   Percent of GDP Devoted to Fixed Investment

United States	15%
Britain	18%
France	20%
Germany	20%
Canada	22%
Japan	28%

Another perspective on global trends appears in Table 7.3 (Labate, 1992), where real domestic growth from 1987 projected through 1993 is shown for four major areas of the world. The forecast is for moderate growth for all four in 1993, as the world recovers from the 1991–1992 recession.

TABLE 7.3	Real Growth in GDP (in percent)						
Country	1987	1988	1989	1990	1991	1992	1993
Asia	12.0	9.5	6.0	7.0	8.5	7.0	6.8
Japan	4.0	6.5	4.8	5.5	4.5	2.5	3.4
Europe	2.7	4.0	3.5	3.0	0.8	1.5	3.0
United States	3.0	3.8	2.5	1.0	–1.0	2.5	3.0

ASSESSMENT OF THE GLOBAL ENVIRONMENT

Assessment of the global environment begins with a stakeholder analysis. First, strategic managers need to identify the key stakeholders in the organization's business environment worldwide. Second, significant relationships among the stakeholders are charted to make a stakeholder map. The stakeholder map is a tool that strategic managers can use to identify the sources of environmental opportunities and threats and the ways they are transmitted to the organization. Third, managers identify and test assumptions about stakeholders, rank these assumptions, and determine which assumptions are most accurate and advantageous.

Stakeholder analysis is supported by environmental scanning. *Environmental scanning* is a method of identifying the economic, political, social, technological, competitive, and geographic factors that affect the organization and then assessing their potential as opportunities or threats. A stakeholder map can then be used to show how these factors propagate through the environment and where they will have an important impact on the organization. Environmental scanning includes an assessment of the organization's vulnerability to environmental forces, such as price increases in oil by OPEC. Vulnerability analysis helps strategic managers determine whether the firm is in serious danger or is well prepared to cope with these forces. Because the global environment is becoming more uncertain, vulnerability analysis (described in Chapter 5) is becoming more important.

Another important aspect of environmental analysis is predicting global environmental trends and determining how they might affect strategic planning in the future. Qualitative environmental forecasting was described in Chapter 4 as a method for identifying possible future events and determining how they could affect the organization's performance. This method involves developing alternative scenarios and planning possible responses to them. Forecasting is important because the desirability of a strategic plan can easily change in light of events beyond the organization's control, such as actions of competitors or new government regulations.

Assessing the global environment should begin with examining basic forces at work and determining their effects on the organization or industry under consideration. Major global trends occur in the following areas:

1. Global money and capital markets
2. Information technology
3. A symbol-based economy
4. Diminished power of nation-states
5. Deregulation of markets
6. Global trade
7. Collapsing of the raw-materials economy
8. Demographic diversity
9. Transitional ecology

GLOBAL MONEY AND CAPITAL MARKETS

In today's global economy, money flows easily and quickly throughout the world. Generally it seeks the best interest rates or the best investment opportunities. One of the side effects of OPEC's 1973 increase in oil prices was that great amounts of cash (mostly dollars) began to pour into Middle East countries, from which it was deposited in European banks. Because, at the time, neither the U.S. trade position nor its gold stock was adequate to the task of providing a nesting place for these dollars, they were free to float around the world. This meant that there were a lot of dollars available to be invested or used without the control of U.S. banking authorities. These dollars came to be called "Eurodollars." By the late 1980s, Eurodollar deposits exceeded $1 trillion. In other words, for every $2 deposited in a bank or savings and loan inside the United States, there is another $1 deposited outside, beyond the reach of U.S. regulatory bodies.

This has become "stateless money." We can consider the world as having stateless money that has led to a stateless banking system without national boundaries. International business now relies on the stateless banking system. Another crucial event leading to stateless money occurred on August 15, 1971, when President Richard Nixon suspended the convertibility of dollars into gold and imposed a 10% surcharge on all imports to restore some balance to the United States's deteriorating international monetary flows. Before that, dollars had been convertible to gold at $35 per ounce. Now the value of the dollar was allowed to "float" according to market forces. By the end of 1973, all the major currencies in the world had stopped pegging their exchange rates to the dollar; true global floating had begun.

There are two major implications of stateless money. One is that money is free to flow to wherever in the world it is needed or demanded. The second is that floating exchange rates create volatility in the money markets. This means that a company that does business in other countries is directly vulnerable to changes in exchange rates (from which it may either profit or lose, depending on the nature of its investment). It also means that any company doing business in any country is vulnerable to changes in exchange rates in other countries that affect the relative prices of its goods or services compared to those of its actual or potential foreign competitors. And because the costs of international transportation and communication are decreasing, foreign firms have the capacity to invade other countries' markets rather effectively.

Stateless money has led to many profound changes in the U.S. and global economies. Foreign investment in other countries' economies has increased. In 1977, for example, foreign investment equaled about 2% of the total net worth of all non-financial corporations in the United States; by 1988, it exceeded 9%. It is expected to reach about 15% by 1995. In 1989 Americans were investing about 10% of their portfolios in foreign securities. Cross-border equity investments by the Japanese, British, and West Germans (before unification with East Germany) have been increasing at a rapid rate. Table 7.4 summarizes the extent of cross-border equity flows for 1989. This means that one nation's savings can easily be invested in another nation, depending on the rates of return. Consequently, our young real estate developer in Colorado may find his best source of capital in Germany or Japan, and these foreign banks may find attractive investments with him.

TABLE 7.4 | **Cross-border Equity Flows (Dollar amounts in billions)**

From \ To	United States	Britain	Other European Countries	Japan	Total Equity Imported
United States	X	83	50	84	217
Britain	97	X	110	76	283
Other European Countries	107	29	X	66	202
Japan	61	5	8	X	74
Total Capital Exported	265	117	168	226	$776 Billion

Source: The Economist, July 21, 1990.

The investments described above are equity investments and not the direct foreign investments made by companies abroad. Investments made, for example, by General Electric in its European plants and facilities are not included in Table 7.4. Direct foreign investment is also increasing. In 1987 all foreign countries, led by the British, invested some $35 billion in U.S. businesses and real estate. In the same year, however, U.S. companies invested over $50 billion in their subsidiaries and affiliates abroad, especially those in the European Common Market. At the end of 1987, total U.S. investment abroad was estimated to exceed $310 billion.

Equity investment and direct investment money is long-term money. Short-term money moves even faster globally. Every night, for example, about $1.5 trillion flows through New York's Clearing House Interbank Payment System (CHIPS), which processes all the domestic and foreign payments passing through New York banks. This amounts to about one-third of the United States's *annual* gross national product and, of course, it does not account for all short-term cross-border money flows. Trade payment accounts for only a very small portion of this volume, perhaps less than 1/300th. Advances in information technology have made this enormous change in the world's foreign exchange (FX) markets possible. In *The Borderless World* (1990), Kenichi Ohmae explains.

> At the root of these developments is the recent explosion of superliquidity in the Triad's [the U.S., Japan, and the EEC] financial markets. In Japan, for example, private savings and the corporate sector generate more than $1 billion in surplus capital every day that has to be invested somewhere. . . . The global, interlinked, tradable FX empire allows money literally to travel around the globe in seconds. Even if, for instance, the Bank of Japan decides to tighten up the money supply at home, desired funds are instantaneously available from abroad. During 1988 more funds were raised in Europe than at home for the entire Japanese private sector. (pp. 159–162)

Financial deregulation and technological breakthroughs in computers and telecommunications have created the world of fast-moving, stateless money. With it, many of our concepts about the economic environment of a firm have also changed. Exchange rates are no longer tied to the balances of trade among nations. Interest rates do not necessarily follow economic activities. The effects of national fiscal and monetary policies are no longer predictable. This means that every business—no matter where in the world it is located—is affected by events in the global financial markets. Increasingly, these events happen quickly and without warning. Successful strategic management requires that events taking place in global money and capital markets be monitored, examined, and evaluated for their impact on the business and its plans.

Two significant arenas are emerging as the dominant world markets. The first is a more unified Europe after 1992 and the second is the world's fastest growth area in the Pacific rim (Kraar, 1992). For example, Kraar describes the size and GDP of major Asian countries as follows:

China: GDP of $371.2 billion, 1,139 million people

Japan: GDP of $3,369.7 billion, 123.9 million people

South Korea: GDP of $283.5 billion, 43.3 million people

Taiwan: GDP of $175.7 billion, 20.4 million people

Indonesia: GDP of $107.8 billion, 179.3 million people

Thailand: GDP of $92.0 billion, 56.9 million people

Hong Kong: GDP of $82.7 billion, 5.8 million people

The fastest-growing country is China, which increased its GDP from $100 billion in 1983 to $371.2 billion in 1992. With its huge population, China can be a major outlet for U.S. goods and services, provided that Americans can compete with China's neighbors. The European market represents a key area for U.S. companies because of a longer history of trade and a number of restrictions placed on Japanese products. Tully (1992) claims that despite a recession in Europe, there is a growing drive to unify in order to serve a potential combined market of 340 million people who have funds to spend. The movement in this direction is obvious when one examines the objectives established to date:

Sector	Objectives	Results
Airlines	Open skies	Free international pricing by 1993
Telecommunications	Deregulation	Open competition by 1993
Automobiles	End quotes	National quotas until 2000
Borders	Remove customs	Barriers and free movement by 1993
Social policy	Heavy regulations	Lack of progress

Two important questions arise in any discussion of trade with Europe. First, will Germany lead the pack? Unification may be taking longer than anticipated, but Germany is Europe's largest economy and is on its way to becoming a global superpower (Rapoport, 1992). The GDP in eastern Germany is projected to grow 8% in 1992 and 10% in 1993, compared with growth of 1.5% in the western sector. Germany's trade surplus is expected to reach $33 billion in 1992 and $40 billion in 1993, which is second only to Japan's. (As evidence of Germany's clout, its unwillingness to reduce interest rates has wreaked havoc on all European countries.) It has been suggested that Germany offers a good model for American managers (Wever and Allen, 1992). The German market is based on social concerns and blurs the boundaries between what is good for business and what is needed by society. For example, the union used a government program as a strategy for modernizing industry. Even German banks reformed themselves without government intervention. Can U.S. companies follow Germany's model? The answer is: not "the work ethic." Rather, U.S. firms can compete on the basis of innovation and creativity.

The second question that arises is whether we can meet European standards. This has proved a real challenge for most American companies. The International Standards Organization in Geneva has issued the ISO-9000 guideposts, which can significantly affect the ability of U.S. companies to compete in Europe (Levine, 1992). Examples of the new requirements include design and service specifications, manufacturing process controls, supplier approval controls, after-sale service support, verification of inspection and testing, and record of training requirements.

In order to meet the hundreds and eventually thousands of EC rules, U.S. exporters—especially small ones—will have to make significant changes in the way they do business. Most exporters have not invested in European contacts, nor does the United States have a coordinated policy to deal with the coming standards (Oster, et al., 1992). The result is a major hurdle for U.S. exporters to overcome on many products that have never been regulated. One approach that has been suggested is for business and the government to coordinate their combined R&D expenditures, which can be critical to future competitiveness (Smith, 1992).

INFORMATION TECHNOLOGY

Technological advances in telecommunications and in computers have radically changed the flows of information throughout the world. As a result of the expansive use of fiber-optic cables, satellites, radio, television, and phone lines, it is possible for people and computers—be they large-scale "super" computers or "micro" or personal computers—to communicate with one another in seconds, wherever they are located in the world. Modern computer networks allow data, video, and voice communications to flow among entities and make it possible for organizations to share technological resources such as laser printers and mainframe computers. They also enable organizations to extend the size and scope of their operations by collapsing time and distance.

One of the results of these breakthroughs has been the advent of "interorganizational" systems and globally distributed systems. These are systems that permit direct communication and information exchange across organizational and national boundaries. Electronic data interchange (EDI) among organizations and their customers, suppliers, and other business partners is one result. Electronic mail (E-mail) and electronic funds transfer (EFT) are others. E-mail allows messages to flow quickly between one point and another. EFT makes possible the movement of funds between accounts wherever they are located. The CHIPs system and SWIFT (Society for Worldwide International Funds Transfers) are long-established worldwide electronic utilities that permit fully coupled, shared electronic business transactions to take place throughout the world. EFT has revolutionized the world's banking and financial services industries. Added to these technological tools are telephone systems—domestic and worldwide—and information product delivery services. Dow Jones News Retrieval Service, Reuters, and McGraw-Hill, for example, make news, commodity and financial quotes, and other information electronically available, worldwide, instantaneously. CNN and other television and radio networks also report on events soon after they occur.

The use of these technologies is characterized by both widespread cooperation and competition. Electronic alliances have led to standards such as the U.S. grocery industry's uniform communication standard (which is often bar-coded on products), the SWIFT EFT standard, EDIFACT and X.12 standards for moving business messages, and comparable standards in transportation, warehousing, automobiles, and aerospace. These standards have defined a playing field in which intense competition is taking place. Much of this was set in motion when Judge Harold Greene broke up AT&T into a long-distance carrier and seven regional telephone companies in the United States in 1984. Now, in most countries of the developed world, there is fierce competition for telecommunications business. AT&T has to contend with MCI, U.S. Sprint, and the seven Bell operating companies; British Telecom has Mercury; Nippon Telegraph and Telephone has three long-distance rivals; KDD, Japan's international carrier, has two competitors. Only in continental Western Europe, where telecommunications is centralized in state-owned postal telegraph and telephone companies (PTTs), and in Canada are telephone monopolies intact. Competition has been pushing the industry ahead rapidly, especially in the field of global information services. Most of these services have been deregulated throughout the developed world.

There are several important implications of the widespread use of information technology for strategic managers.

1. Technology can now be used for competitive advantage. Companies such as American Airlines with its SABRE system, Merrill Lynch, Citicorp, Baxter International, and Frito-Lay have developed systems that enable them to provide high-quality services, rapidly, to their customers and suppliers. This has helped them compete effectively in both local and global markets.

2. As we have noted, information technology is being used to move money and information to any place in the world. This has led to "superliquidity" and has permitted available funds to flow rapidly to those places in the world that offer the best financial opportunities. It has also increased the volatility of exchange rates among the world's currencies.

3. Information technology has enabled companies to coordinate and control their activities on a worldwide basis by greatly compressing time and distance. It can be used for collaborative work, electronic meetings, the exchange of knowledge and information products, bilateral communication, and many command and control functions. Texas Instruments, for example, operates manufacturing facilities in 18 countries and has sales and marketing operations in more than 30. In its Avezzano, Italy, facility an international team from the United States, Japan, Italy, Germany, and France worked together (in large part electronically) to build a new, advanced semiconductor facility. Some of its software products are designed in its European facilities, written in other countries, and incorporated in products produced in the United States. All of this and a myriad of other activities are managed electronically by means of a worldwide network operated out of Dallas, Texas. TI and many other companies whose products are information-intensive can move product knowledge and products themselves electronically around the world. This means that companies are able to disburse their value-adding chain and to perform functions wherever in the world it is most economically feasible. This flexibility redefines the comparative advantages of nations.

As the world continues to move toward a symbol-based economy, sometimes called the information society, and away from a material-based, or industrial, society, information technology will play an ever-increasing role in the strategies and management of firms. An environmental assessment should include an examination of global technological trends as they affect the firm and its industry. It should focus especially on the new opportunities and threats that information technology presents.

EMERGENCE OF A SYMBOL-BASED ECONOMY

The increased contribution of knowledge and information to the world's economies has created a symbol-based economy in which the creating and processing of symbols adds more economic value than the processing of raw materials. Drucker explains: ". . . in the world economy of today, the 'real' economy of goods and services and the 'symbol' economy of money, credit, and capital are no longer bound tightly to each other; they are, indeed, moving further and further apart" (Drucker, 1989, p. 12). Until recent times, few jobs required much in the way of knowledge. Today, however, knowledge and education have become the passport to good jobs and careers. Knowledge has become a developed economy's capital, and its knowledge workers and symbol processors are the group that sets the society's values and norms. Political economist Robert Reich (1991) calls the people who engage in this handling and processing of symbols "symbolic-analysts." *Knowledge workers* and *information workers* are other terms commonly used for these kinds of specialists, who include management consultants, architects, research scientists, design engineers, software engineers, civil engineers, biotechnology engineers, sound engineers, public relations executives, investment bankers, lawyers, real estate developers, and accountants.

Reich distinguishes these symbolic jobs from those that provide routine production (blue-collar) services and those that provide in-person services, such as attendants at fast-food outlets. Each of the three job categories plays a different role in the global economy. Routine production workers function in domestic economies and compete in world markets on the basis of their cost for manual labor. Personal service workers primarily serve the residents of their domestic economies and visiting tourists. Their services are not generally traded in global markets. As Rob Kling (1990) put it, "After all, one doesn't fly to Seoul just for a haircut or a cab ride, even if it is cheap! But a publisher may well have a book typeset in Southeast Asia, and thus displace clerical jobs in the United States" (p. 101).

Symbolic-analytic services, on the other hand, become distinctive competencies of firms and of the nations in which they reside. They are traded worldwide. Thus the people who offer these services "must compete with foreign providers even in the American market. But they do not enter world commerce as standardized things. Traded instead are the manipulations of symbols—data, words, oral and visual representations" (Robert Reich, 1991, p. 177).

Economic and social researchers have developed two different but related concepts to describe the global effects of the trend toward knowledge-based and information work. One is the *postindustrial society*. Proposed by Daniel Bell (1973), it highlights the importance of the service sector in modern economies and stresses the central role that credentialed experts such as scientists, engineers, and other knowledge producers play in them. Marc Porat (1977) offered the concept of the *information society*. He focused on the fact that in an increasing number of jobs, the processing of information has become a central and time-consuming activity.

Porat and others have found that information occupations have grown in size from 17% of the U.S. workforce in 1900 to over 50% in 1980. Since then the information sector has continued to provide a majority of jobs in the U.S. workforce and is growing rapidly in Japan, Western Europe, and other developed countries.

This trend has major implications for the management of organizations. In *In the Age of the Smart Machine* (1988), Shoshana Zuboff argues that organizations with highly "informated" jobs require specially skilled workers who can challenge traditional managerial styles and authority and whose skills become a novel resource upon which to base the organization's strategy. These special information skills often provide a comparative advantage in international markets. These forces are creating a new type of capitalism, *informational capitalism* (Luke and White, 1985). In an informational capitalistic society, "data-intensive techniques, cybernetic knowledge, and electronic technologies" are the crucial strategic resources. And, as Reich (1991) reminds us, they have also become the crucial resources in global trade. Reich summarizes: "In the emerging global economy, even the most impressive of positions in the most prestigious of organizations is vulnerable to worldwide competition if it entails easily replicated routines. The only true competitive advantage lies in [the symbolic-analysts'] skill in solving, identifying, and brokering new problems" (p. 184).

DIMINISHED POWER OF NATION–STATES

A trend toward fragmentation within nation–states is also prevalent. In what was formerly the Soviet Union, Eastern Europe, and the Middle East, factions are beginning to break away from the center and form local political economies, often around ethnic lines. Within the United States during the Reagan years, considerable power and responsibility, especially in the social realm, devolved to states and local governments. Consequently, Tennessee can compete directly with Ohio and Texas for a new Japanese auto plant without necessarily involving the federal government. Denver, Miami, Atlanta, Dallas, and Los Angeles can and do compete in the global market for foreign plants, conventions, conferences, international tourism, and special events such as the Olympics. According to *Time* (May 27, 1991), the competition is getting ugly.

> Virtually every state is going after a piece of the $400 billion worth of foreign investment in the U.S. . . . The number of state development offices abroad, which function almost like consulates, has doubled in the past five years, to 160. Illinois has more foreign offices than many small nations; it has outposts in Moscow, Shenyang, Brussels, Warsaw, Budapest, Toronto, Mexico City, Hong Kong and Osaka. No fewer than 38 states—plus San Bernardino, Calif. and Houston—maintain offices in Tokyo. (p. 42)

By engaging in these activities, local governmental units have assumed powers that previously were primarily the federal government's. In doing so they challenge the very core concepts that the country's founders invoked to bind the states (and cities) together.

This means that an assessment of a firm's environment must include an examination of stakeholders and forces in the broad global, transnational economy and political system. It should focus on the power and role of stateless corporations and on trading regions and blocs. The role of domestic regional, state, and local governmental units should also be carefully examined. Nation–states and their agencies and laws remain important, but long-term trends indicate that supranational and subnational entities are becoming even more so.

DEREGULATION OF MARKETS

A market is an idea, an artifact created by humans. No market is entirely open or free. Governments supervise and control many of the activities of private enterprises operating within their jurisdiction in the interest of economic efficiency, fairness, health, and safety. The rules and orders set by the executive authority to achieve these purposes are called regulations. Regulations usually take one of two forms. Either standards are established that must be adhered to, or limitations and controls are imposed on competition. Every nation sets different standards and controls competition in a different way and thus creates its own version of a market. There is a long-term trend, however, for these human-made markets to become similar and to become more open. This tendency fosters increased globalization.

In extreme cases of government regulation, industries are nationalized, such as coal was in the United Kingdom during the 1930s, or private natural monopolies are established, as were many U.S. utility companies. In the United States and other market-based economies, regulations are used to control activities in which normal market forces, operating alone, fail to achieve social objectives. In planned economies, such as the former Soviet Union, regulations are used to control almost all economic activities. In this case, market forces such as prices have little effect.

The origin of government regulations antedates the Industrial Revolution. Problems created by industrialization, however, brought on the need for more regulations. Child labor laws, foreign exchange controls, restrictive trade practices acts, employment protection acts, and licensing controls are among the regulations that governments have seen fit to impose as industry developed. Product standards, restrictions on entry, and trade barriers are among the other areas that have been regulated. Market externalities—consequences for public welfare or costs not fully accounted for in the market system—such as pollution, reclamation, visual impact, and noise have also required environmental and other controls.

In the years following World War II, a large body of regulations was put into effect in most Western, market-oriented nations. During the 1970s concern about the costs of these regulations began to rise, and substantial political pressure was brought to bear on governments to repeal, reform, or abolish some existing regulations. Under the Thatcher government in the United Kingdom, several large government-owned companies such as British Telecom were privatized. In the United States, the financial and airline industries (among others) were substantially deregulated. In Eastern Europe, efforts are being made to move toward a market economy. The People's Republic of China has established free trading zones in order to take advantage of market forces. The EC in 1992, the Pacific Rim "yen bloc," and the North American Free Trade Agreement all serve to lower trade barriers among the countries agreeing to the pact. These alliances are strong indications of a worldwide trend to liberalize markets both within and among nations. Such "deregulation" might better be referred to as "reregulation," because governments are still responsible for controlling for socially undesirable results.

As we have noted, global financial markets were among the first to become deregulated. During the last two decades, many restrictions on financial flows across national borders have been dropped. Several countries have deregulated their internal financial markets, and financial firms have developed innovations that separate the choice of currency and other aspects of contracts from the jurisdiction of the nation in which they originate. This has led to the increased integration of international financial markets. Originally, American securities firms benefited from this global integration, because the financial deregulation movement began in America, and many U.S. firms learned to deal with it first. A freer flow of funds across borders, permitted by deregulation, encourages a freer flow of other economic activities and serves as a stimulus to increased globalization.

GLOBAL TRADE

World trade has grown steadily since the end of World War II. In 1991 world trade reached almost two and three-quarters trillion dollars, of which about 73% was accounted for by OECD countries. *Since 1980 world trade has increased at a faster rate than has world output.* This means that the countries of the world have developed a greater propensity to trade goods and services among one another. As countries develop economically, they become more efficient at producing goods and services, frequently specializing in particular products for which they have a comparative advantage. At the same time, their populations tend to demand more complex, luxurious, and specialized goods and services. Together these factors provide a stimulus for imports and an opportunity for exports. Thus they encourage nation–states to trade with one another globally. This trend is facilitated by advances in transportation and communication technology. It also means that these trading nations become more dependent on each other and that their economies become more "exposed" to events that happen throughout the world. The companies that are directly involved in foreign trade and those that are indirectly dependent on it are also vulnerable to changes in world conditions.

In world statistics, trade is classified as either visible or invisible. *Visible trade* involves the exchange of physical goods and products. *Invisible trade* involves the exchange of services—such as financial, accounting, consulting, and advertising services—and includes financial transactions, profits, and interest payments. Invisible trade accounts for about 25% of the total world trade and is increasing at a faster rate than visible trade. (This confirms the fact that the world is being transformed from a material-based economy to a symbol- or information-based economy.) The United States is the world leader in invisible exports. When both visible and invisible exports are taken into account, the United States is found to have led all countries in world trade in 1988, with about 14.9% of the world total. (West Germany had 11.1%, Japan 10.4%, the United Kingdom 8.2%, and France 7.0%.) West Germany had a slight lead over the United States with respect to visible exports (11.9%) and Japan, France, and the United Kingdom followed in that order.

General Electric has nearly always been an international company. Formed in 1892 from Thomas Edison's old company, it soon began to work with Westinghouse, Siemens, and AEG in Europe to form a global oligopoly. After World War I, under the leadership of Gerard Swope, GE began to take an active role in Britain, Germany, France, Mexico, South Africa, Australia, and Japan. Following World War II, in 1953 GE was among the first companies to sell patents to the Japanese and help them build new factories. Since then the company has been an unchallenged leader in a large number of markets in the United States, including industrial machinery, medical electronics, and consumer electronics. As the global business environment began to change during the 1980s, however, CEO Jack Welsh and his management team crafted a new global strategy. They decided to get out of any business, anywhere (including the United States), in which GE could not attain a major position *worldwide*, even if the business was profitable. GE was restructured. It even sold off profitable U.S. businesses such as those marketing small appliances and semiconductors, because it was not a strong global competitor in those industries. About $10 billion of business was jettisoned. At the same time, the company acquired several new businesses abroad, especially in Europe, in which management believed GE could become a global leader. The total acquisition cost was about $19 billion; acquisitions were as diverse as the securities firm of Kidder, Peabody and the Tungsram lighting company of Hungary. Today the GE label goes on microwave ovens designed, fabricated, and assembled by Sansung in South Korea, and GE has become the largest private employer in Singapore and a major contributor to the Asian trading city's spectacular economic development.

As an editor at Kiplinger's (August, 1991, p. 22) put it, "Chief among GE's strategies is Welch's notion of a 'boundaryless' company that can do business in Cairo, Egypt, as easily as in Cairo, Ill." Welch's vision is to blend the company with its suppliers, customers, and other stakeholders into a global "seamless mass." The strategy seems to be working. GE's worldwide revenues topped $58 billion in 1990. The company has had 15 straight years of growth in earnings per share and expects earnings to continue to grow in 1991 and 1992. On May 31, 1991, GE had a total market value of over $67 billion, making it the fourth largest company in *Business Week*'s Global 1000 (behind Nippon Telegraph & Telephone, Royal Dutch/Shell, and Exxon).

COLLAPSING OF THE RAW-MATERIALS ECONOMY

There is a long-term trend in production to substitute knowledge and information for primary raw materials and for manual labor. This has changed the nature of industry in developed countries and placed additional stress on Third World countries. Most of the Third World labor force is engaged in agriculture, forest products, metals, minerals, and other primary materials. During the last 10 years, worldwide production of these primary materials has risen between 20% and 35%. Since about 1950, however, the prices of these products have been erratic and have generally trended downward. Demand has weakened. As the World Bank (1987) reported, the economic situation of those countries most heavily involved in exporting traditional primary raw materials deteriorated during the last 40 years, as prices declined relative to the prices of industrial goods.

Management theorist Peter Drucker (1986) sees major implications in this trend:

> The raw materials economy has thus come uncoupled from the industrial economy. This is a major structural change in the world economy, with tremendous implications for economic and social policy . . . in developed and developing countries alike. (p. 4)

He goes on.

> Why this decline in demand [for primary materials]? It is not that industrial production is fading in importance as the service sector grows—a common myth for which there is not the slightest evidence. What is happening is much more significant. Industrial production is steadily switching away from heavily material-intensive products and processes. One of the reasons for this is the now high-technology industries. In a semiconductor microchip the raw materials account for 1 to 3 percent of total production cost; in an automobile their share is 40 percent, and in pots and pans 60 percent. But also in older industries the same scaling down of raw materials needs goes on, with respect to old products as well as new ones. Fifty to 100 pounds of fiberglass cable transmit as many telephone messages as does one ton of copper wire. (p. 6)

The semiconductor industry is a good illustration of Drucker's point. It was born with the invention of the transistor at Bell telephone laboratories in 1947. Since that time its basic raw material, silicon (sand), has not changed. During the same period, however, the information that can be stored on a single wafer has expanded from about 1,000 bits to 64 million bits. The power of chip-based microprocessors has increased several thousand times. This has come as the result of research and development that has resulted in denser integrated circuits in which simple cells are replicated hundreds of thousands or millions of times. With each new infusion of knowledge, the relative role of raw materials has decreased. While the semiconductor industry has experienced exceptionally high technological velocity and innovation—as have the pharmaceutical, telecommunications, analytical instrument, and computer industries—the same trend is occurring less dramatically in many other industries. Since 1972 the number of beer and soft drink cans produced from a pound of aluminum has increased from less than 22 to almost 30. In the automotive industry, the cumulative value of quality improvements made in safety, fuel economy, emissions controls, and other intellectual inputs during the last 15 years has added about $3,500 to the retail value of cars. During World War II, bombs had to be deployed within about 3 miles of their target and were expected to land within a radius of about a mile of it. In the Gulf War of 1991, laser-guided bombs were released about 50 miles from their target and landed within 20 feet of it (*Fortune*, June 3, 1991). These are but a few indications of the fact that knowledge and information inputs into products are becoming ever more important. As a consequence, the economic forces affecting global raw-materials markets have become substantially uncoupled from those affecting global industrial markets.

DEMOGRAPHIC DIVERSITY AND THE WORLD DIVISION OF LABOR

Lewis Galoob Toys, headquartered in San Francisco, recorded sales of about $127 million on assets of approximately $75 million in 1990. Micro Machines®, mini-vehicles, dolls, games, and Game Genie™, are among the products it sells worldwide and the majority of its revenues come from North America and Europe. In addition to its own designers and engineers, the company engages independent designers and engineers from all over the world. It produces substantially all of its products under proprietary and character licenses obtained from toy inventors and designers also located around the globe. Some 40 "partner" factories in Hong Kong, Thailand, and the People's Republic of China manufacture Galoob's products. In order to reduce the risk of political or economic disruptions in its countries of manufacture, the firm has a $40 million insurance policy with Lloyds of London. For this global capability, Galoob relies on only about 100 employees of its own and about 199 in its wholly owned Hong Kong subsidiary.

A world market for labor is emerging as individuals and countries seek comparative advantage in the global division of labor. This means that most managers will be managing a more diverse workforce. As Jamieson and O'Mara (1991) have described it, in most countries today, and especially in the United States,

> the contemporary workforce doesn't look like, think like, act like, or have the same desires as the workforce of the past. Workforce 2000—and the workforce of today—is significantly different in its age distribution, increasing equality of men and women, cultural diversity, range of educational levels, inclusion of persons with disabilities, and mix of values and attitudes. These translate into portraits of diversity—a workforce of individuals who bring different resources and perspectives to the workplace and who have distinctive needs, preferences, expectations and lifestyles. (p. 14)

As a result, managers are confronted daily with new, complex challenges.

In the past, in most developed countries there was a dominant majority in the workforce (for example, white males in the United States). Often there was also a dominated minority, such as the black slaves in the antebellum South, who were imported to do hard, manual labor. William Johnson (1991) describes this as part of a long-term trend.

> The movement of people from one country to another is, of course, not new. In previous centuries, Irish stonemasons helped build U.S. canals, and Chinese laborers constructed North America's transcontinental railroads. In the 1970s and 1980s, it was common to find Indian engineers writing software in Silicon Valley, Turks cleaning hotel rooms in Berlin, and Algerians assembling cars in France.

> During the 1990s, the world's workforce will become even more mobile, and employers will increasingly reach across borders to find the skills they need. These movements of workers will be driven by the growing gap between the world's supplies of labor and the demands for it.

As a consequence, world economies are moving from an era in which large portions of the workforce are similar—and in which those who are different are expected to adapt or follow orders—to an era in which the workforce is composed of many different individuals. Johnson (1991) has identified several key trends in the global workforce:

1. The world workforce is growing rapidly. From 1985 to 2000, the workforce is expected to grow by some 600 million people, an increase of about 27%.

2. The vast majority of these new workers, about 95%, will come from developing countries such as Mexico and Pakistan.
3. Women will enter the workforce in great numbers, especially in the developing countries, where relatively few women have been absorbed to date.
4. The average age of the world's workforce will rise, especially in the developed countries.
5. People worldwide will be increasingly well educated. The developing countries will produce a growing share of the world's high school and college graduates.
6. Developed countries will send a higher percentage of their young to school.
7. Developing countries will supply a growing share of the world's educated people.

These trends will bring about pressures for workers, especially educated ones in developing countries, to emigrate to find better job opportunities. As Reich observed, the demand for these services will depend on levels and type of education and on class of job—routine production, in-person, or symbolic-analytic activities.

> Not all workers are equally likely to emigrate—or equally likely to be welcome elsewhere. . . . Typically, unskilled workers—janitors, dishwashers, or laborers—are recruited locally. At higher skill levels, companies often search across states or regions. Among college graduates, national labor markets are more common: New York banks interview MBA's from San Francisco; Midwestern manufacturers hire engineers from both coasts. At the highest skill levels, the labor market has been international for many years. Bell Laboratories physicists, for example, come from universities in England or India as well as from Princeton or M.I.T. At Schering-Plough's research labs, the first language of bio-chemists is as likely to be Hindi, Japanese, or German as it is English. (Johnson, 1987, p. 123)

This trend toward global demographic diversity in the workforce poses many opportunities and threats for strategic managers. First, firms will have to be prepared to compete in the global market place for the capabilities and skills they need. They may find these skills in a country other than the one(s) they operate in. Then they will be faced with deciding whether to import the labor from the other country or export the relevant business functions to it. If the required labor is physical—routine production, then the work should be transported to the other country. If the required labor is symbolic, however, it may be possible to "import" it electronically.

Second, managers will continually have to manage a workforce that is more diverse ethnically and in other major characteristics. They can no longer use management practices that are focused on the "average" worker. They must be able to treat people from different cultures and backgrounds equitably and effectively if they are to draw on the broad range of power that diversity provides and to compete effectively in global markets.

TRANSNATIONAL ECOLOGY

Nature does not adhere to the artificial boundaries that humans draw. Winds and waters flow according to the laws of the planet, not those made by governments. Humankind can, however, destroy the natural environment. If this lesson was not learned before, it was brought home forcefully during World War II with the dropping of atomic bombs on Japan. And the lesson has continued in the effects of modern technology. The nuclear catastrophe at Chernobyl, for example, reminded us that incompetent and sloppy control of local technologies can cause significant harm across national borders. The winds blew damaging doses of radioactive particles as far north as Scotland, Norway, and Sweden, and clouds still circulating the earth may affect other parts of the world. The effect of the use of chemicals on the ozone layer is another example. River pollution, acid rain, and smog easily cross borders. There is no longer any doubt that all human beings are united in their dependence on a natural environment that transcends national boundaries.

Nature is ordered in a different way from nation–states and other governmental units. The historian of cultures Thomas Berry (1988) refers to this ordering as dividing the earth into "bioregions," which he describes as follows:

> The planet presents itself to us, not as a uniform global reality, but as a complex of highly differentiated regions caught up in the comprehensive unit of the planet itself. There are arctic and tropical, coastal and inland regions, mountains and plains, river valleys and deserts. Each of these regions has its distinctive geological formation, climatic conditions, and living forms. . . . Each is coherent within itself and intimately related to the others. Together they express the wonder and splendor of this garden planet of the universe. (pp. 163–164)

Managing the world as a set of interrelated bio-regions requires a global set of institutions and a *transnational* point of view. Peter Drucker (1989) relates:

> The destruction of the ecology on which humankind's survival depends is thus a common task. To tackle it as a national (or local) task is futile—though obviously a good deal of national, and even local, implementation will be needed. It is futile too to try to tackle it adversarially, with one country accusing its neighbor of befouling the environment. . . . Inevitably the accused country will proclaim its innocence and deny that there is a problem. No effective action can be taken until we accept that serious environmental damage anywhere is everybody's problem and threatens all of us. (pp. 134–135)

As the leaders of cities, states, nations, and regions have sought to deal with the problems of pollution and mutual destruction and, more important, as concerned citizens in all nations of the world have sought better solutions, a global awareness has emerged. This too is serving to globalize our economic and political activities.

THE NEW GLOBAL ECONOMY RECAPITULATED

The nine major global trends that we have noted, taken together, paint a picture of a new global economy. The "global village" originally envisioned by McLuhan (1964) is becoming a reality, and its emergence has major consequences for strategic management and planning. The United States is no longer the preeminent political and economic power in the world. Together with the recovered economies of Japan, Germany, and the other EC countries, the United States now is part of an economic "triad" that collectively controls a large part of economic activity. For this reason, Ohmae (1985) has argued that corporations that hope to compete in the global arena must become "insiders" in the triad. Although it is possible for a few institutions, such as the ill-fated Bank of Credit and Commerce International (it conducted illegal transactions with other countries), to develop effective "outsider" strategies based on cornering business in Third World countries and the Middle East, insider strategies are likely to be the most effective overall. Even BCCI, operating out of Luxembourg, had its main offices in London, and surreptitiously tried to acquire several U.S. banks.

The U.S. multinational corporation also no longer dominates. Companies operating out of other countries, especially those from within the triad, are strong—sometimes dominant—global competitors. Equally important is the emergence of the stateless, global corporation that conducts activities and moves resources around the world without particular reference to national borders. These companies, and the nations in which they operate, now compete with each other on the basis of the overall value they add to their inputs during production.

The major contributor to value in production is knowledge, brain power, and intellectual capital. This fact has become the basis of competition among high-wage nations. Thus the knowledge workers whom Reich calls "symbolic-analysts" are pivotal to the long-term economic success of global corporations and of the developed nations of the world.

Newly industrialized countries (NICs) such as Korea, Taiwan, Hong Kong, Singapore, and Spain are seeking to move up toward a higher-value adding economy and will eventually become a threat to the economic competitiveness of developed nations. They also represent an opportunity for global corporations. The NICs, and Third World and developing nations as well, compete in producing low-cost, high-quality commodities and also such primary materials as agricultural produce, forest products, metals, and minerals. But as the world has become an information society and increased emphasis has been placed on high-value-adding, knowledge-intensive products and services, the industrial economy has been uncoupled from the raw-materials economy. Many manufactured goods and information products now react to forces different from those that influence materials markets.

A global division of labor is emerging as a result of nations capitalizing on their comparative economic advantages. Consequently, world trade continues to grow at about 4% per annum. World trade is growing faster than the rate of growth of world output. This means that the propensity to trade among nations of the world is increasing, as each seeks to exploit its national comparative advantage. Few nations or businesses can escape the effects of this trend.

There is also a global trend toward liberalization and deregulation of economies. Eastern Europe, Russia, and China are all shifting toward more market-oriented economies. The United Kingdom, especially under Margaret Thatcher, has made major strides in privatization of its industries and liberalization of its financial markets. In the United States, airlines, financial institutions, and other industries have been deregulated. Adding to this is a trend for nations to band together in regional trading blocs. The EC 1992, the informal Pacific Rim or "yen bloc," and the United States, Canada, and Mexico Free Trade Agreement are illustrations. The European Community will drop most trade barriers among its 12 nations, and perhaps other countries from the European Free Trade Association will join as well. This will create the largest single pool of freely flowing goods, services, capital, and people in the world. All these arrangements will promote greater competition among nations and among companies and will further fuel national and corporate attempts to draw on comparative economic advantages.

A greater political freedom has come at the same time during which markets have been liberalized, heralded most prominently by Gorbachev's policy of *glasnost*. This has encouraged the fragmentation of nations (most spectacularly that of the former Soviet Union) into smaller political (often ethnic) groupings and has spawned a new politics of secession.

As a consequence of all these forces, the 300-year-old political conception of the nation–state is losing sway. Global and regional economic and political forces are usurping and undermining, from above, many of most nation–states' former powers. At the same time, internal political fragmentation and pressures from state and local governments are tugging away from below. This means that although national sovereignty remains an important factor in strategic planning, it must be supplemented substantially with a deeper understanding of both global and local political and economic forces. Nation–states acting alone have also proved ineffective in dealing with ecological forces, the problems of pollution, and the threat of mutual destruction. The search for transnational institutions and solutions has further accelerated the trend toward globalization.

These trends have led to an absence of cohesive global economic leadership, as nations and stateless corporations jockey for preferential positions of comparative economic advantage. Political leaders no longer carry the global clout they once enjoyed. Multinational corporations may wield more power than they formerly did, but most are counterbalanced by strong competitors in many locations in which they operate. These global competitors serve to restrain the excessive use of political power. "Engine Charlie" Wilson's contention that what was good for General Motors was good for the United States, and vice versa, may have had an element of truth in 1953. It is not true today. It is probably not true of any corporation in any country today, and it is certainly not true of any global corporation with respect to the world. Yet in the overall balance of things, multinational corporations have gained power at the expense of nation–states.

The effects of increased competition are complicated by the emergence of new industries based on technological innovations and services and by the massive restructuring of old industries through leveraged buyouts, mergers, acquisitions, divestitures, and internal reorganizations. Global corporations such as General Electric and ASEA Brown Boveri are far different today from the organizations they were 10 years ago.

One of the consequences of these changes has been greater economic volatility. The rapid fluctuations in foreign exchange rates over the last decade or so have had substantial effects on businesses of all types and in all locations. Commodities have become pawns in bigger economic and political games. These games are serious because many nations have become dependent on foreign sources for basic supplies, as the growth in trade demonstrates. Nominal crude oil prices, for example, have varied from under $3 a barrel to nearly $40 since the mid-1970s when the OPEC countries began to control oil supply and prices. The United States, like many industrialized nations, depends on foreign sources for some 30 critical or "strategic" minerals such as stontium, beryllium, chromium, columbium, cobalt, graphite, natural rubber, tin, bauxite, and zinc. These minerals are essential inputs for such products as jet engines, TV screens, computer memories, home insulation, and automobile starter switches. Most of them come from Third World countries that are politically unstable. Trading patterns among nations and national balances of payments are also subject to wide fluctuations. The result of these forces is a higher level of global economic volatility that adds increased uncertainty to the strategic-planning environment.

Global competition and global trade are also affecting the global movement of labor. Knowledge workers (symbolic-analysts) move, compete, and contribute fluidly in the global markets as they are attracted to areas where they can add the most value. Manual labor and routine production work are being performed primarily by people who accept low wages and offer their employers the advantage of low overall cost. Thus, either these jobs are exported to low-cost locations or the workers themselves immigrate to places where jobs are available. These employment-related movements, coupled with the differential population increases among ethnic groups within countries and between countries (Third World countries in Africa, Asia, and Latin America tend to have higher population increases), mean that managers can expect greater demographic diversity within their workforces. This potential source of the benefits that diversity offers will at the same time complicate the planning of human resources management.

Two global developments mutually support and contribute to the globalization of the economy. One is the presence of global money and superliquidity. Short-term and intermediate funds and long-term investments now flow rapidly and easily across national borders in pursuit of the best opportunities. The other "globalizing" development is the considerable innovations in transportation and information technologies that allow information, people, and goods (as well as money) to go quickly anywhere in the world they are demanded. This has put a premium on speed. As George Stalk and Thomas Hout (1990) argue, the effective management of time has become the most powerful new source of corporate competitive advantage. And time-based competition is reshaping global markets. Among the corporations that have effective global, time-based strategies are Federal Express, Ford, Milliken, Honda, Toyota, Citicorp, and Mitsubishi. The activities of these companies and other global organizations have changed the economics of production, distribution, and marketing. Large scale and scope no longer necessarily lead to economies or lower costs. Micro-markets have become economically attractive in many areas. Products now grow obsolete or are redefined quickly. As a consequence, virtually all relationships between stakeholders are redefined. In short, global superliquidity and rapid information flow offer many new opportunities to organizations, but they can also pose considerable threat if they are not monitored and taken advantage of.

The new global environment of business is characterized by great uncertainty in its economic, political, social, technological, and competitive factors. The role of time and distance and geography are being redefined. This severely complicates the task of strategic management. It also invites—and can richly reward—entrepreneurship and innovative business practices.

COMPETITIVE BUSINESS STRATEGIES FOR GLOBAL MARKETS

To compete effectively in the global environment, the United States may have to change the rules by which it plays (Tumulty, 1992). Japan and Germany have such radially different approaches between business and government that the United States is finding it difficult to compete effectively in the markets in which those two countries compete. For example, the United States frowns on unwarranted collaboration among competing firms and has sent people to prison for it. In Japan and Germany, such collaboration is not only legal but also abetted by the government. For example, MITI, the Ministry of International Trade and Industry, helps formulate Japan's business policy on a global level. Recently, Mitsubishi and Daimler-Benz had their top strategic planners meet for two days of private talks in Singapore. Can the United States continue to compete when it ignores these kinds of pressures? In addition, the United States tends not to provide the support that small, growth-oriented corporations need. Without adequate financial support, such as SBA loans, these companies find it increasingly difficult to compete in a global marketplace where, for example, a number of smaller German companies have captured nearly 80% of their respective world market shares (Simon, 1992).

To be truly global, a company must have products that can be sold in the growing overseas markets. Differences in electrical requirements often make American products unsaleable in Europe and/or Asia. The potential economies of scale are needed in a growing global market. Companies will have to focus on outstanding, creative products rather than compromising by reducing cost. Manufacturing may provide the basis for sidestepping the economies of scale traditionally needed to compete effectively (McGrath and Hoole, 1992). For example, when Xerox in 1981 began to restructure its company in order to go global, it considered five basic changes:

1. Products would be designed only once in a way that fit the global marketplace.
2. Purchasing would consolidate sources of raw materials.
3. Economies in production would be achieved by larger capacity and geographic diversity.
4. Marketing and sales forecasts would become the basis for establishing production schedules.
5. Closer coordination would be sought between customer orders and distribution for the global market.

The key is matching manufacturing strategy to the business strategy to achieve well-integrated management practices and measurement systems. With this approach, manufacturing can coordinate its global resources to become a more responsive company.

GLOBAL BUSINESS DRIVERS

The emergence of the global economy and the fact that national and regional economies no longer exist as independent structures offer several new opportunities and threats for businesses. Among the responses that companies and their competitors are marshaling to cope with the changing environment are the following global business drivers.

1. Produce global or semiglobal products. Coca-Cola and Pepsi-Cola are globally standardized products sold almost everywhere. McDonald's hamburgers and french fries are becoming global products. Gucci bags are too. Some successful "semiglobal" products establish primary markets in selected countries and bolster these sales with lucrative secondary markets in other countries.

2. Supply the needs of global customers. For example, it is possible to design a car for select, perhaps top-of-the-line, customers around the globe. Ohmae (1990) cites the Rolls-Royce and the Mercedes-Benz as examples.

3. Serve global corporate customers. General Electric, General Motors, Royal Dutch/Shell, Toyota, British Petroleum, Daimler-Benz, Fiat, and Samsung are among the large corporations that have global operations. They answer a worldwide need for many products and services.

4. Buy from global suppliers. A domestic firm serving domestic customers may well find that its best source of raw materials and components or of financing lies outside its home nation. As more nations strive to trade on their comparative economic advantages, global sources of inputs will become more attractive.

5. Defend against global competitors. A global competitor can use cash flow, profits, and economies of scale secured in one country or business intelligence gained from operating in that country to improve its competitive position in another country. A company may have to go global to mitigate this advantage.

6. Disperse the firm's value-added chain globally. Companies such as Lewis Galoob Toys act like global strategic brokers and place their operations wherever in the world it is best to execute any business function in their value-adding chain. As more countries specialize for comparative economic advantage, and as the workforces of the world compete for jobs, this driver will become more attractive. It is important to note that quality considerations as well as cost considerations can influence the decision to disperse a firm's value-adding chain globally. Some spots in the world are "world-class" performers or "best of class" performers in executing certain aspects of the value-adding chain.

7. Disperse globally to minimize risk. Because of the increased uncertainty in the global environment, it may be necessary for a firm to spread its activities over several countries in order to reduce its exposure to political, economic, and social changes in any one country or location.

ASSUMPTIONS ABOUT DOING BUSINESS ABROAD

Some time ago, the government of Brazil decided to buy buses for interurban transportation. Rolls-Royce expressed interest in submitting a bid and asked the

Brazilians to send representatives to London to help work out the details. Rolls' communiqué, in typical British style, defined responsibilities: the Brazilians would have to manufacture their own spare parts and be responsible for all maintenance. Meanwhile, Mercedes-Benz sent a team of executives to Brazil. Before negotiations began, Mercedes executives announced that the company would build a spare-parts plant in São Paolo and train nationals for jobs in the plant and for maintenance positions in the field.

Mercedes got the deal, although its price was no lower than Rolls'. Why? Mercedes was chosen primarily because of its approach and style, which met the needs of the Brazilians better. Mercedes offered services that accommodated the community with which it sought to do business.

As the world becomes smaller and more intertwined culturally and economically, people in business must reconsider assumptions about how they do business. Domestic companies have significant opportunities to expand into foreign markets if they go about it in a manner compatible with the new cultures they enter. It is equally important to recognize that dangerous economic threats are mounting for firms that ignore foreign competition and fail to devise a strategy to deal with it.

In the following sections, we examine multinational competition and factors to consider in developing global strategies. Competing in international markets requires a different perspective than competing in domestic markets. How to enter a foreign market, how best to interact with customers, how to manage foreign joint ventures or subsidiaries effectively, and how to determine vulnerability and risk are examples of considerations pertinent to global competition.

International operations cannot be undertaken by every business. For some, it may be a matter of survival to enter the global arena. For others, it may be a question of how to protect an existing domestic market from foreign competition. Few businesses, however, can afford to ignore the potential impact of foreign products or the growth potential that foreign markets offer.

The reason is simple, yet powerful: the world has become a single marketplace. National economics is being replaced by "globeconomics." Companies that ignore this fact find themselves in jeopardy. Today, well over 70% of U.S.-made products face foreign competition.

TYPES OF INTERNATIONAL STRATEGIES

To compete effectively in a global environment requires an entirely different strategic thrust than that used in domestic markets. The multinational company usually does not have the luxury of allowing its units to compete as individual subsidiaries. Rather, successful multinational companies organize in ways that position their system of products, marketing, and fabrication so as to obtain the maximum leverage possible from economies of scale, lower prices, barriers to entry, standardization of components, and joint ventures or other actions deemed necessary to compete effectively. This view of global strategy is equivalent to creating a portfolio of markets that are highly interdependent and need to be balanced to achieve optimal performance.

The values outlined by Peters and Waterman in *In Search of Excellence* (1982) form a solid basis for determining what organizations are required to do in order to maintain a competitive strategic posture. The eight premises that these authors espoused (see Chapter 1) are equally applicable in domestic and international markets. Global strategies extend these premises into a more complex arena and require their augmentation. Exchange rates, stability of local governments, and culture are, for example, factors not normally taken into account in a domestic market.

To formulate global strategies, managers normally view the world as a group of interacting markets that have the potential of being mutually supportive. Four approaches to international strategy are shown in Figure 7.2. The axes represent two critical aspects of doing business in a foreign environment. One is the company's marketing orientation. The other is the company's approach to control of foreign operations. The four international strategies are defined below.

1. *Ethnocentric strategy.* The ethnocentric strategy is based on the presumption that one country's products or services are superior to those of another country. Consequently, the strategy is narrowly focused on that product. Under centralized control the product is sold in other countries wherever a market exists for it. Americans, for example, long felt that their automobiles were superior because they were made in the United States and attempted to sell them abroad with few changes in design or features. As has become painfully obvious, this is no longer a widely held view.

FIGURE 7.2	Four International Strategies

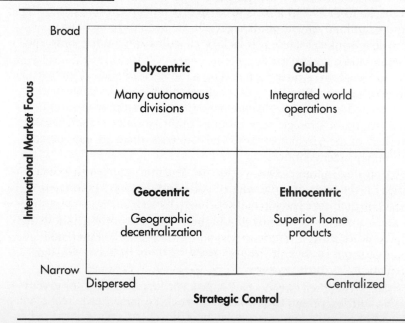

Although a multinational company pursuing an ethnocentric strategy would market its home products, it would have to be customized or modified to satisfy the tastes and desires of the host country. If the home product is clearly superior, the ethnocentric strategy should work well. But industrial nations around the world may develop products that better fit their own needs. In the aircraft industry, for example, where the United States dominated manufacturing for years, a consortium from England, Germany, and France produced the Airbus, which became a formidable competitor and contributed to the demise of two American airframe manufacturers.

2. *Geocentric strategy.* The second strategy is based on geographic decentralization with a narrow product line. This approach reduces risks by establishing markets, finances, and manufacturing in different countries. Therefore, if one country is having difficulty, the remaining divisions can continue to function normally.

   Geographic decentralization has both advantages and disadvantages. On the minus side, managing many different units in multiple locations poses a major management problem. On the plus side, each unit's performance can be evaluated easily by comparing it to the performance of other units. Funds, goods, and personnel can be shifted from one location to another, as needed. This strategy permits adaptation to local requirements and, if done correctly, is more effective than the polycentric strategy, which takes geographic decentralization to an extreme.

3. *Polycentric strategy.* The polycentric strategy is based on reducing risks by having a large number of autonomous units marketing a broad set of products. The many units are less vulnerable than one large subsidiary would be. Risk reduction is accomplished by a number of actions, such as the use of multiple currencies. The disadvantage of this strategy is that diversification and local autonomy limit the exchange of information among units regarding price, products, design, and movement of managers. If the need to reduce risks outweighs the disadvantages caused by lack of coordination among units, the polycentric strategy is a good choice.

4. *Global strategy.* The global strategy is based on an integrated view of foreign markets. Hout, Porter, and Rudden (1982) believe that the world is one market and should be treated as such. They recommend that the strategies of various subsidiaries, divisions, or strategic business units fit into a single comprehensive long-term strategy of the parent company. The countries, then, are considered a portfolio of interdependent entities.

   The global strategy assumes that worldwide distribution of the product can be justified on the basis of economies of scale and that R&D is related to the product rather than to a specific market. Lynn Townsend's attempt at Chrysler to build a world car—a base model that with appropriate modifiers in each country could be used everywhere—is an illustration of this strategy. Potential disadvantages include problems caused by trade barriers and fragmented distribution.

Whichever strategy is chosen—ethnocentric, geocentric, polycentric, or global—the social, political, and economic environment in each country needs to be analyzed carefully, and the firm's approach must be tailored to satisfy local needs.

When Mercedes-Benz offered its standard bus to the Brazilians, the company added other products and services to the package to meet the needs of Brazil.

Marketing theorist Theodore Levitt (1983) observes that because communications and transportation have become "proletarianized" and are available to all, the world is converging on commonality. Consequently, successful global companies will offer globally standardized products that are advanced (they are difficult to copy), functional (so they answer a real need), reliable (they meet quality standards), and low-cost (they are affordable and competitively priced). Only standardized products meet these requirements. Furthermore, this global market is enormous—potentially over 5 billion people. Only global companies with global products will be able to reach this large market. They will do it by "concentrating on what everybody wants rather than worrying about the details of what everyone *thinks* they might like" (p. 92). McDonald's hamburgers and fries, Revlon cosmetics, Levi's jeans, Sony TVs, Coca-Cola, and Pepsi qualify as global products.

If a pure global strategy is not possible, semistandard products can be designed and produced and customized after they cross national boundaries. Having products that are readily modifiable reduces lead time and cost. It still leverages a firm's development and manufacturing capabilities and permits global marketing and brand-name recognition.

Figure 7.3 shows four international strategies that reflect how multinational companies relate strategic thrust to segmentation of their markets. When a company serves a few market segments, it can choose either a global or a country segment as its main focus, depending on its products or services and on the competition. On the other hand, a company that serves many market segments must carefully choose whether to be the cost leader or to use trade barriers to exclude competitors from its local market segment. The strategic thrust that a company chooses depends both on the number of market segments that are being served and on whether its products or services can compete effectively in a global market.

An emerging requirement for ensuring effective marketing in a global environment is the development of strategic alliances (Ohmae, 1989). As we have noted, IBM, Toshiba, and Siemens—all major corporations in their respective countries—have recognized the global logic of strategic alliances. Managers will have to overcome their focus on competitor-oriented strategy and choose alliances that help reduce fixed costs and contribute to product enhancement. When examining ways of entering foreign markets, Bleeke and Ernst (1992) found that two-thirds of the 49 strategic alliances they analyzed had significant managerial or financial problems to overcome in the first two years. In the companies studied, 51% were successful and only 33% failed. These investigators advise that in order to improve their chances of success, managers should remember that

1. Alliances work as well as acquisitions and have the benefit of entering new markets with less capital investment.
2. Where a strong company forms an alliance with a weak company, the alliance rarely succeeds or, at best, turns in a mediocre performance.
3. Successful alliances require that the venture have autonomy and that the two organizations be flexible in their expectations.

FIGURE 7.3   Global Strategic Alternatives

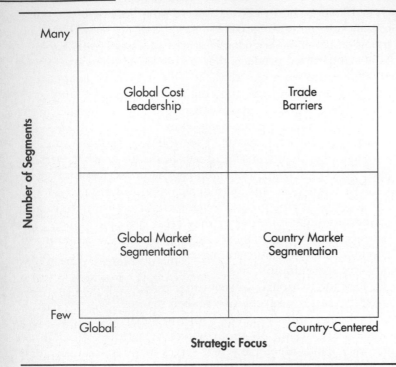

4. The alliance is most likely to succeed when financial ownership is shared equally between two companies.
5. In over 75% of alliances that were terminated, only one of the organizations needed the venture.

Thus, although strategic alliances are very attractive, business organizations must approach them more carefully than joint ventures or outright acquisitions.

Bartlett and Ghoshal (1989) have identified three sets of key thrusts and strategic capabilities that shape the way a firm conducts its international activities.

1. Build strong local presence through sensitivity and responsiveness to national differences. Companies that adopt this approach manage a portfolio of multiple national entities according to the needs of each location and compete on the basis of differentiation of their products and services. The authors call firms that take this approach "multinational." Phillips, ITT, and Unilever are cited as examples.
2. Build cost advantages through centralized global-scale operations. Such companies treat the world as an integrated whole and compete on the basis of cost leadership created by economies of scale. These "global" companies include the Japanese firms Matsushita, NEC, and Kao.

3. Exploit the parent company's knowledge and capabilities through worldwide diffusion and adaptation. Use of the firm's knowledge and skills is controlled but is modified by the local units to form products, processes, and marketing approaches that fit local requirements and to compete on the basis of their ability to leverage their intellectual capital instead of strict economies of scale. General Electric, Ericsson, and Procter & Gamble are examples of these "international" companies.

According to Bartlett and Ghoshal, however, these three thrusts and capabilities are inadequate for competing successfully in the emerging global economy. They argue that in the future, companies must embrace a fourth approach if they are to succeed. This "transnational" company is today an unrealized ideal because no firm yet exhibits all its characteristics. A transnational firm must be effective simultaneously in all of the three strategies summarized above. To achieve global competitive advantage, the transnational firm must manage both its cost and revenues together and must encourage innovations from all parts of the organization. It seeks global economies of scale where feasible, but it makes selective decisions about centralizing or decentralizing its assets primarily on an individual basis, depending on which approach will contribute most to the overall performance of the company. Its organizational form is an "integrated network" in which flows of components, products, resources, people, information, and funds between geographically dispersed units are managed dynamically. Local responsiveness is developed by building multinational flexibility. And, because differentiation is not necessary or desirable in all markets, a transnational varies its product and marketing approaches among different national operations. Above all, the transnational must be a learning organization that gathers knowledge and mines intellectual capital from all of the geographic areas in which it operates. The authors conclude, "In the future, a company's ability to develop a transnational organization capability will be the key factor that separates the winners from the mere survivors in the international competitive environment" (p. 212).

ENTRANCE STRATEGIES FOR SPECIFIC FOREIGN MARKETS

The choice of entrance strategy is as important as the decision to become a multinational company. If a company has had little or no experience in a foreign country, it should consider working with or through a foreign national. There are a number of ways in which an organization can work with a country's nationals. These include

1. *Employing local agents*. Local agents are presumed to know the territory and all the ramifications of doing business in a particular country or region. These individuals may have the connections needed to ensure the smooth entry of a product or subsidiary into the market. But because local agents are independent, they may be difficult to control, and there is no guarantee that they will pursue the product introduction forcefully.
2. *Employing local representatives*. Local representatives may be independent distributors or employees of the company. More than agents, these individuals

have a stake in both the sale of the product and the welfare of the company. Use of local representatives facilitates much better control and communication with the home office. Selecting representatives may, however, be more difficult than selecting local agents or distributors.

3. *Entering into licensing agreements.* The significant advantage of a licensing agreement is that it avoids the necessity of direct investment or involvement in the foreign country. If it is a high-technology product and the research for continued development is done in the United States, a foreign company is likely to want the license. On the negative side, there is no guarantee that the technology or product will be exploited appropriately. Other potential problems include patent infringements and poor execution of the technology locally, which can lower the product's reputation in the foreign market.

4. *Forming a joint venture.* The joint venture, unlike the first three approaches described, generally involves considerable investment and risk. The local requirements for a joint venture can also be prohibitive. For example, in many countries the foreign investor cannot own more than 49% of the joint venture, thus leaving control in the hands of the local company. On the positive side, the local company generally has an established position in the market and knows how to do business in the country. The joint venture is typically difficult to control and often results in a buyout by one of the partners.

5. *Acquiring local companies.* Acquisition ensures entry into the foreign market because the local company already has a market position. The physical facilities, workforce, distributors, and even managers are typically part of the arrangement. If the acquisition and the market potential are properly evaluated, this method of penetrating a foreign market is rapid and generally satisfactory. Risk is high, though, because key local personnel may quit, leaving an inexperienced U.S. company to run the acquisition. In addition, the tax and financial implications and obligations often far exceed those of other methods of market entry.

6. *Forming a foreign subsidiary.* This approach is analogous to the acquisition of a foreign company in that the multinational has complete control of the firm. Unlike acquisition, however, forming a subsidiary takes considerable time and effort. Obtaining the licenses, capital, and personnel necessary for formation of a subsidiary may be worth it if no appropriate company is available for sale. Sometimes the only possible way to enter a market is by investing in a subsidiary that will produce the product in the foreign country.

MARKETING STRATEGIES FOR SPECIFIC FOREIGN MARKETS

Global business not only involves working in a new and often radically different environment under different conditions, but it also poses difficult marketing questions. Most companies that decide to market internationally recognize their lack of expertise and tend to enter foreign markets gradually after careful strategic planning. This is wise because it helps international neophytes to avoid pitfalls. More often than not, a foreign country's way of doing business differs radically from that in the United States. Patents and copyrights, for example, are not equally protected in all countries; contractual or payment customs may differ from American practices; and local duties and restrictions can be formidable barriers to entry.

Having made the decision to market globally, a firm can choose from a number of entry strategies. It might, for example, consider one or more of Porter's four approaches (Porter, 1985).

1. Find a protected niche in which there is a minimum likelihood of interference from the local government.
2. Focus on supplying some particular need that the given country cannot supply locally. Large construction companies, such as Fluor, have pursued this strategy.
3. Choose a product that is unique in terms of cost, performance, or other attribute that can be marketed globally. McDonald's has succeeded with this strategy.
4. Choose an entire product line to market globally. This last approach requires that the company have a well-established product line and some experience in international marketing. The goal is to extend market penetration.

A fifth strategy for entering a foreign market is to customize the product or service to suit the unique demands of each country. Coca-Cola, for example, customizes its syrup and packaging for each country.

Quelch and Hoff (1986) identified four areas that a company should examine before customizing its strategy. Examination of these areas can help the company match its unique capabilities and products to the demands of each foreign market. The four areas are (1) the structure of the company's marketing function, (2) the types of products to be marketed, (3) the market mix in the country, and (4) other data about the country. Perhaps the most important factor is the way the company manages its marketing function. Problems can arise if marketing is controlled too tightly from corporate headquarters or is totally decentralized. To ensure a uniform marketing strategy, multinational companies such as Unilever employ marketing specialists who regularly visit the foreign locations to provide coaching and support. Kodak's approach is to control its worldwide operations from corporate headquarters. The most appropriate approach is to balance local autonomy with guidance and coordination from corporate headquarters. According to Quelch and Hoff, this balance can be achieved by

1. Encouraging field managers to generate ideas and participate in developing marketing strategies
2. Having country managers take on general management functions, such as control of their own budgets
3. Developing a product that permits economies of scale through use of both local and global resources

Porter (1985) stated that the following ten substrategies should be considered by companies seeking advantage in foreign markets.

1. Ascertain how to achieve comparative advantage, such as through the low cost of labor in a given country.
2. Determine how to achieve economies of scale and whether their achievement will involve a large capital investment.

3. Build on foreign experience rather than attempting to export products from a saturated domestic market.
4. Attempt to find economies of distribution so that these can be spread among the products sold.
5. Utilize large-scale purchasing to achieve economies of procurement.
6. Spread marketing costs by applying the same approach in many countries.
7. Differentiate the product whenever possible.
8. Incorporate unique technology into the product.
9. Maintain mobile production and service capability.
10. Avoid global impediments, such as high transportation costs, the need for specialized regional management skills, or restrictive regional government policies.

A number of emerging trends can have a direct impact on strategies for foreign marketing. International marketing practices are becoming less diverse, and distribution channels are reducing impediments to foreign competition. Intense competition among the Asian countries will affect some Western competitors. In particular, Asian countries will further protect their assets, making it more difficult for the United States to exploit cost advantages there. A freer flow of technology and the emergence of large new markets in China, what was formerly the Soviet Union, and developing nations such as Brazil will present new global opportunities and new sources of competition.

Global marketing often results from a desire to grow, especially if domestic markets are saturated. Growth must be managed, however, and entering foreign markets is no guarantee of growth or profitability. Blindly entering an overseas market can be disastrous. Like domestic strategy, global strategy requires research about markets, competitors, customers, and so forth. If research shows that a market exists and that the firm would have a competitive advantage, a well-planned and well-implemented global strategy can reap handsome rewards.

RISK ASSESSMENT

Regardless of a company's strategy for entering and marketing in a foreign market, managers need to consider the risks involved in doing business abroad. To assist in assessing such risks, Haner (1980) identified two major considerations: human and physical variables. The human variables relevant to risk assessment are

1. *Stability of temperament:* tendency toward violence, attitude toward corruption, emotional stability, and level of discipline prevalent in the culture
2. *Level of economic activity:* education and training of the workforce, work ethic, and attitude toward business typical in the country
3. *Social structure:* culture, traditions, elitism, distribution of wealth, languages, and religion of the people
4. *Political stability:* government-run or private enterprise, restrictions on foreign investments, and degree of regional autonomy

The physical variables that can influence the decision to locate in a given country are

1. *Availability of natural resources:* energy sufficiency, raw materials, agriculture, and water
2. *Severity of the climate:* seasons, storms, extreme heat or cold, and sunny days
3. *Geographic considerations:* desirability of location, historic or tourist concerns, and topology
4. *Infrastructure:* ease of access, communications, transportation, airports, roads, storage, support industries, financial support, and living accommodations

Haner also identified other factors that can directly affect the operation of a firm in a foreign market.

1. *Political stability:* attitudes regarding foreign investors, cost of social benefits, possibility of expropriation, preferential treatment of nationals
2. *Monetary considerations:* possibility of inflation and devaluation, balance of payment, currency convertibility, and exchange rate
3. *Infrastructure:* possibility of bureaucratic delays, support available in professional services and construction, communication, and transportation facilities
4. *Managerial considerations:* ability to enforce contracts, labor cost and productivity, sophistication of equipment, quality of local management, availability of skilled labor and of raw materials
5. *Economic and tax considerations:* rate of economic growth in the country, availability of short-term credit, availability of long-term capital and venture capital, tax benefits in that country

When addressing these five key factors, a strategic manager should be careful to identify and evaluate the overall goals and strategies of a country, its reigning ideology, and the policies it has adopted to achieve its goals—fiscal, monetary, income, foreign trade, and investment policies and policies with respect to various sectors such as health, education, welfare, housing, natural resources, telecommunications, transborder data flows, favored industries, and agriculture. Also important are the country's trading relationships with other countries, the global companies that operate in the country, and the country's relationships with international institutions such as the General Agreement on Tariffs and Trade, OPEC, the International Monetary Fund, the World Bank, and regional trading blocs.

An assessment of the riskiness of entering a given market in a country that might otherwise be considered appropriate is shown in Worksheet 7.1. The purpose of the country risk assessment is not to establish a precise mathematical model, but rather to quantify the key factors involved in determining the desirability of doing business in a given country. A simple weighting scheme is used to determine whether there is a high or low likelihood of encountering a risky situation in the country. To perform the risk analysis, the manager reviews the environmental data on the country under consideration and relates them to each of the five factors listed in the worksheet. For each factor, the manager assigns a numerical score from 1 to 100. A score of 50–70 indicates that the company's risks are moderate with respect to that factor. A score of 90–100 indicates a superior business environment. A score of 1–40 indicates unacceptable risks.

By averaging all the scores, the manager can approximate the riskiness of a given country.

WORKSHEET 7.1 | Country Risk Assessment

Case __Multinational__
Date __1992__
Name __John Doe__

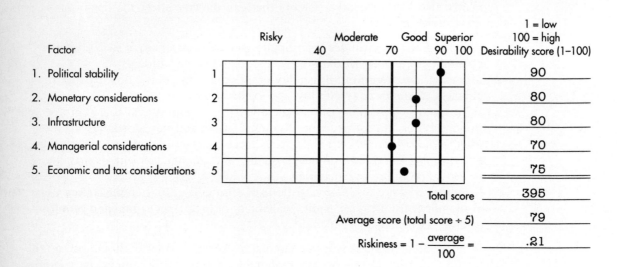

Factor		Risky 40	Moderate 70	Good Superior 90 100	1 = low 100 = high Desirability score (1–100)
1. Political stability	1			•	90
2. Monetary considerations	2			•	80
3. Infrastructure	3			•	80
4. Managerial considerations	4			•	70
5. Economic and tax considerations	5			•	75

Total score __395__

Average score (total score ÷ 5) __79__

$$\text{Riskiness} = 1 - \frac{\text{average}}{100} = \quad .21$$

Explanation:

The above analysis shows that there is a low risk for a multinational company wanting to enter the Singapore market. Thus the company would find this a potentially attractive environment from the perspective of riskiness.

The outcome of the analysis shown in Worksheet 7.1 would amount to endorsement entry by a multinational company. Singapore would be chosen because the risk of doing business there is low. This analysis does not indicate probability; rather, it is an assessment or subjective evaluation of the conditions that one is likely to find in a given country.

Another type of risk is inherent in the strategy used to enter a foreign market. A high risk of failure is associated with joint ventures, and such failures can be very costly (Killing, 1982).

The three main categories of risk factors can be rated and combined to form a *desirability index* for a given country. This involves rating the desirability of (1) the human and physical variables, (2) Haner's five risk factors (see Worksheet 7.1), and (3) the method used to enter the foreign market and averaging the scores of each. If Singapore's average desirability score were (.79), its human and physical variables averaged .30, and the entry variables averaged .51, then Singapore's combined desirability index would be .79 $\times$ .30 $\times$ .51, or .121. If another country had an index of .55 $\times$ .60 $\times$ .50, or .165, it would have a higher desirability index than Singapore.

It is difficult, of course, to anticipate catastrophic events, such as political upheavals or natural disasters, which can seriously disrupt foreign operations. Few companies, for example, anticipated the events in Iran prior to the Shah's leaving or the Persian Gulf operation that involved Iraq and Kuwait. Alternative future scenarios can define but not predict possible futures. As a minimum precaution, the multinational firm must constantly monitor the environment for signs that initial assumptions are no longer valid.

ORGANIZATIONAL ARRANGEMENTS FOR GLOBAL FIRMS

In his book *Scale and Scope: Dynamics of Industrial Capitalism* (1990), the noted business historian Alfred Chandler describes how successful, large industrial corporations developed at the end of the nineteenth century and grew during the first half of the twentieth century by exploiting economies of scale and scope. This required a "three-pronged" approach to innovation. Investments were made (1) in production facilities large enough to secure cost advantages, (2) in international and national marketing and distribution networks, and (3) in organizational structures capable of administrating large and far-flung enterprises. Chandler also discovered first-mover advantages. The first companies to make these three-pronged investments achieved the economies of scale and scope necessary to dominate their industries for decades.

The multidivisional, hierarchic structure (sometimes referred to as "M-form" by economists) proved to be the most effective organizational form for these purposes. DuPont and General Motors were the pioneers. American firms such as General Electric and Borden, British firms such as Lever, and German firms such as Bayer and Siemens also followed suit. Each became a competitive success in its industry. In each country, capitalism as a form of overall economic organization took on its own unique shape. In the United States it was competitive managerial capitalism; Germany fostered cooperative managerial capitalism; and in Great Britain personal capitalism flourished. In counterdistinction to America and Germany, firms in Great Britain were managed by "individuals or by a small number of associates, often members, of founders' families, assisted by only a few salaried managers, or they were federations of firms" (p. 235).

In *Scale and Scope* and elsewhere, Chandler maintains that a successful company's structure supports its strategy, and vice versa. These concepts will be developed in more detail in Chapter 10, where we discuss implementing strategic change. In this chapter we will explore some of the implications of the global environment for the choice of organizational structure and for a firm's ability to compete. We will also see why the M-form has become inadequate and why the network organization seems best suited for the new global environment.

ORGANIZATIONAL STRUCTURES

An organization may be conceived of as a collection of nodes. The nodes are individual units that do the work and add elements of value to the organization's final outputs. Materials, money, and information flow between the nodes. The term *structure* refers to the way the nodes are related to one another. In a multidivisional organization, for example, materials may flow horizontally—say, from sourcing to receiving to processing to distribution—but information and finances generally flow vertically. Information goes up to the central, controlling node, and instructions flow down to the operating nodes. A general organizing principle is that strategy and structure must be mutually supporting. This means that all the nodes must be carefully aligned with each other and well articulated with the global environment. As organizations become more complex, and as they add more diverse nodes dispersed throughout a wider geographic area, new ways of relating nodes to one another must be developed. When firms seek to implement truly global strategies, they typically find that the classical hierarchic M-form organization is wanting and must be modified. What modifications are appropriate depends on the strategies and capabilities of the organization as a whole and on how it adds value to its inputs.

Bartlett and Ghoshal (1989) have found that the particular organizational form that firms operating in several countries tend to employ depends on their individual strategies and capabilities. Specifically,

- Firms building on economies of scale and scope tend to seek cost advantages through centralized, global-scale operations. They employ an M-form organization in which overseas nodes are used to carry out the parent company's strategies. R&D and other knowledge-producing and learning activities are primarily conducted at the center. (Matsushita is an example.)
- Firms building on a strong local presence in various countries via sensitivity and responsiveness to national differences tend to be decentralized, each node being self-sufficient. Overseas nodes are used to sense and exploit local opportunities in each geographic location. For the most part, knowledge is developed and retained within each node. (Unilever is an example.)

■ Firms exploiting the parent company's knowledge and intellectual capital through worldwide diffusion and adaptation tend to rely on core competencies that are centralized, augmented by unique decentralized competencies. Overseas operations adapt and leverage these competencies. Knowledge is usually developed at the center and then transferred to overseas nodes where it may be adapted to local needs. (General Electric is an example.)

The nine emerging global trends described at the beginning of this chapter have caused managers and students of organizations to question the long-term effectiveness of these three organizational forms. Indeed, critical questions can be raised about whether the hierarchic, multidivisional form will continue to be the most effective in the global, postindustrial, information economy. As a rule, the M-form organization does not have the speed and agility necessary to compete in a time-based manner. Stalk and Hout (1990) and Keen (1991, 1986), for instance, argue convincingly that speed and agility are essential to competing effectively in today's global markets and explain why traditional organizational models may be inappropriate. The M-form, for example, emphasizes high-volume economies. It does not stress adding value by applying knowledge dynamically throughout the firm's value-adding chain. Thus it lacks the flexibility and swiftness to respond to a rapidly changing global environment.

Three related concepts have been put forth. As we have seen, Bartlett and Ghoshal (1989) developed the concept of a transnational firm. Miles and Snow (1986) also developed the idea of "network organizations," and Reich (1991) the notion of an enterprise web. All purport to overcome the deficiencies of the M-form. A successful transnational, network, or web organization is more flexible and better capable to learn from its diverse environments. These firms' assets and capabilities are clustered in nodes that have three general characteristics. They are dispersed, interdependent, and specialized. Differential contributions are made by all the overseas and domestic nodes, and these contributions are coordinated and integrated into worldwide operations. Generally speaking, learning is conducted and knowledge is developed jointly by the nodes and shared worldwide. This calls for a flatter organization consisting of many semi-autonomous nodes. There must be considerable horizontal communication among them. Bartlett and Ghoshal describe such a structure as an "integrated network configuration."

Reich (1991) provides imagery for such a network organization. Instead of a pyramid, his "new web of enterprise" resembles a spider's web. Strategic brokers (executives who manage ideas rather than things and who dynamically link problem identifiers with problem solvers) are at the center, but there are all sorts of connections that do not involve them directly, and new connections are being spun all the time. At each point of connection are a relatively small number of people—depending on the task, from a dozen to several hundred. Lewis Galoob Toys is an example of a global firm organized in this manner. The concept, however, is still evolving. As Miles and Snow (1986) explain, "New organizational forms are arising to cope with the new [global] environmental conditions. However, no new means of organizing or managing arrives full-blown; usually it results from a variety of experimental actions taken by innovative companies. . . . A few businesses, in the U.S. are on the verge of a breakthrough in organizational form" (p. 62).

The most thorough description of how this new type of organization works is provided by Miles and Snow. Their "dynamic network" organization has four major features.

1. *Vertical disaggregation.* Business functions such as product design and development, manufacturing, marketing, and distribution are performed by independent organizations within a network.
2. *Brokers.* Because each function is not necessarily part of a single organization, business groups are assembled by or located through brokers. (See the discussion of global brokering in the last section of this chapter.)
3. *Market mechanisms.* The major functions are held together in the main by market mechanisms (such as transfer prices) rather than by plans and controls. Contracts and payment by results are used more frequently than progress reports and personal, hierarchically based supervision.
4. *Full-disclosure information systems.* Broad-access computerized information systems are used as substitutes for lengthy trust-building processes. (Some degree of trust, however, is important to ensure the proper sharing of accurate and former proprietary information.) Each of the participants in the network agrees on a general structure of payment based on the value it adds. They all then hook themselves together in a continuously updated information system so that each others' contributions can be mutually and instantaneously verified. (p. 65)

The dynamic network organization requires a new managerial approach. To be effective it must be balanced.

> In order to understand all its ramifications, the dynamic network must be viewed simultaneously from the perspectives both of its individual components (nodes) and of the network as a whole. For the individual firm (or component, or node), the primary benefit of participation in the network is the opportunity to pursue its particular distinctive competence. A properly constructed network can display the technical specialization of the functional structure, and the balanced orientation characteristic of the matrix. (That is, it can achieve the best features of the other organizational forms.) Therefore, each matrix component can be seen as complementing rather than competing with the other components. (p. 70)

Matrix organizations and other forms are discussed more fully in Chapter 10.

Balance and dynamism are achieved through continual and active organizational learning, so the web that Reich describes is also learning-oriented. Actions are taken, and that experience is reflected on to gain knowledge. Knowledge and information are accumulated at each node and either communicated to other nodes or used as a resource in negotiating contracts and alliances. Nodes that do not learn or whose learning becomes obsolete are eliminated from the network. Learning creates distinctive competencies and skills at each node in the enterprise web. Each node, consequently, represents a unique combination of skills that can be drawn on when required. Exactly how these capabilities are drawn on is not so important as the fact that they are available when needed (or can be discarded if they become irrelevant). Direct ownership and control of each node in the web are not essential, perhaps not even preferred. Contractual and other agreements can serve just as well.

Miles and Snow conclude that in order for the organization to remain balanced, its major nodes must be "assembled and reassembled (frequently) to meet complex and changing competitive conditions." This requires forming strategic alliances with organizations well beyond the organization's boundaries and engaging in global brokering.

STRATEGIC ALLIANCES

Alliances are associations and agreements that define relationships between two independent entities. Frequently this is done by enforceable contract; occasionally it is accomplished by simple verbal agreement. Strategic alliances are coalitions that an organization forms with other organizations in order to achieve one or more of its strategic goals. An assumption of most large-scale, multidivisional corporations is that they must own and carefully control the assets and capabilities at every node in their network. Globalization is challenging this assumption. A corporation need not own every node in its value-adding network (or even most of them) as long as each node delivers its output on time and within cost objectives and meets quality standards. In fact, there are several reasons why, in the global environment, alliances are preferred to ownership. Alliances offer special capabilities that the firm can not acquire otherwise. They can be formed and disbanded quickly in order to respond to changing market conditions. They force a clear pinpointing of responsibility between nodes. And, by forming (or holding open the option to form) multiple alliances, a firm can use competitive pressure to hold down costs and manage risk.

The value of strategic alliances has been questioned by many companies because of the difficulties that can arise. This attitude is reinforced by the problems associated with carrying out agreements, maintaining trade secrets, and keeping the relationship viable for long periods of time. Sherman (1992) has shown that strategic alliances can work when there is considerable flexibility on the part of both partners and where there is an openness in sharing power between the two. In spite of any obstacles, many of the major companies in the United States have formed strategic alliances to improve their competitive position. For example, IBM formed an alliance with Siemens and Toshiba to develop DRAM chips. Other companies that have formed strategic alliances include AT&T, GE, Merck, and Time Warner. Although half of all alliances are failures, they do facilitate entering a new market, preventing a competitor from gaining position in a market, and exploiting new technology or the expertise of a partner. Often a strategic alliance is used as a prelude to an eventual acquisition or merger. Ultimately, successful strategic alliances depend on relationships that are built to persist rather than on those that simply take advantage of an opportunity for short-term gain.

Two terms are commonly used in the current management literature to describe the business decisions that surround forming strategic alliances: sourcing and outsourcing. *Sourcing* usually refers to the process of securing a source of supply for some basic component or product in the firm's product line. Apple Computer, for example, buys its laser printer engines from Canon, a very successful Japan-based global company with a reputation for quality. Laser printer technology is expensive and difficult to manage. Although the availability of quality laser printing is essential to Apple's strategy, it is not a primary basis for the company's competitive advantage. (Apple printers are sold in conjunction with Apple Macintosh microcomputers, and it is the unique software of the Macintosh that is at the core of Apple's strategy. The company owns and controls fiercely the "Mac look and feel.") By forming an alliance to obtain the engines for its printers, however, Apple has assured itself of a quality source of supply for an important complementary product. It also has been able to leverage its product and sales capacity without diluting its technical or financial resources on a secondary technology. Furthermore, laser printing technology changes rapidly, so the company has managed some of its risk of market obsolescence. If Canon does not continue to learn and innovate and keep current, Apple can turn to another supplier.

Outsourcing generally means contracting with an outside party to deliver some corporate service that is usually performed within the organization. Product design services and even janitorial services have been successfully outsourced. Recently the outsourcing of information systems services has become a much-discussed item on the management agenda. Eastman Kodak, the world's largest-selling scientific and photographic equipment manufacturer, formed "partnership alliances" with three companies to provide it with various information services worldwide. IBM will manage its data centers, which are located in various countries, via its global communications network; Digital Equipment will manage its voice and data telecommunications activities, which are also distributed worldwide. Businessland will procure, install, and support its personal computers and microcomputers.

Data entry, a tedious and time-consuming job, has been successfully outsourced by many organizations, including American Airlines. By offering lower labor costs and plenty of qualified workers, Ireland, South Korea, Jamaica, Haiti, Barbados, and even China have successfully bid on contracts to assume many firms' data entry functions. The global outsourcing of software programming is following suit. Countries such as India and the Philippines now have corps of trained programmers. A professional programmer in the United States costs about $100,000 per year on a full-cost basis, whereas an equivalent programmer in India or the Philippines works for about $35,000 a year. These factors have encouraged firms with considerable information systems activities to consider purchasing some of these functions abroad. A few small, information-intensive firms have also found global outsourcing profitable.

The decision to source or outsource by means of global alliances also entails a decision on the best organizational relationships to form. Reich identifies five basic forms of relationships between the organization and the nodes in its global network.

1. In *independent profit centers*, authority for product development and sales is pushed down to each node. In this case, each node is owned but is autonomous in decisions it makes.

2. In *spin-off partnerships*, independent businesses are spawned from the main organization, taking former employees and assets. The node then contributes to the organization on a contractual basis.
3. In *spin-in partnerships*, ideas and unique assets from external groups are acquired and become nodes in the organization itself.
4. In *licensing*, headquarters contracts with independent businesses to use its brand name, sell its special formulas, or otherwise market (that is, find applicable problems for) its technologies.
5. In *pure brokering*, headquarters contracts with independent businesses for identifying and solving problems as well as for production. This highly decentralized and flexible form is used by Lewis Galoob Toys.

All five of these arrangements can be used to construct a global organizational network.

GLOBAL BROKERING

One of the greatest challenges a business faces in establishing a global orientation is to *think globally* to begin with. Old habits of thought, reinforced by years of use and training, have rewarded us for thinking in a more traditional way, constricted by tacit local, national, and regional assumptions. The global environment renders many of these old modes of business thinking obsolete. Today it is possible—in fact, in many industries it may be necessary—to manage as a global broker. A global broker creates and manages a global network organization.

The global broker begins by breaking the business down into individual business functions according to the firm's value-adding chain. Typical functions include raw-materials sourcing, supplies, inbound logistics, production and operations of components and units, distribution, marketing, sales, customer service, finance, human resources, R&D, planning, product design, advertising, administration, government relations, legal services, technology development and evaluation, competitive intelligence, and the like. Then it is assumed that these subfunctions can be performed *anywhere*. The global broker then asks, "Where in the world *should* these tasks be performed?" The globe is scanned to determine where the candidate sites are. Each candidate location is next evaluated on the basis of such location factors as population, natural resources, existing products, trade conditions, markets, availability of labor and requisite skills, financing and capital, political stability, transportation infrastructure, communications, education, research capabilities, presence of allied or competitive businesses, and availability of the arts, entertainment, and hotels. The costs of land, taxes, utilities, and labor are also assessed. Now the subfunctions are matched to the candidate locations. A choice is made on the basis of feasibility, advantages, disadvantages, and the relative distinctive competencies of each location. Each location chosen becomes a node in the global network.

The firm must also decide whether to buy or build its own assets or to enter into an alliance and how much of each subfunction should be sourced or outsourced. The integrative organizational network must be formed, and patterns established for coordinating and controlling among nodes. This having been done, the proposed new business is ready to operate as a global, stateless organization. It could, for example, do its product design in the United States, the United Kingdom, and Italy, do its engineering in Japan, import raw materials from Brazil, produce parts in Taiwan and Malaysia, assemble and ship out of Singapore, finance in Germany and Japan, market primarily in Europe, and be headquartered in Toronto. The role of the headquarters node in this case is to perform the strategic brokering function. In the modern, global environment, more and more organizations will be developing their business strategies along these lines.

SUMMARY

All businesses today are affected by the global environment. A global economy is emerging in which local, national, and regional economies no longer exist as independent structures. Business today operates in a worldwide framework of interactions and interdependencies among all of these economies.

One of the most important determinants of an organization's success is its global environment. A business is like an ecological entity. It has mutual relationships with other entities, called stakeholders, in its environment, and it must be effective in managing these external relationships. Some companies have quite effective internal operations and yet fail because their managers overlook unfavorable conditions in the global environment, such as changes in foreign exchange rates. Others are able to generate acceptable—even outstanding—profits, despite a number of internal problems, simply because they positioned themselves in the right place at the right time.

To maintain its competitive edge, an organization must identify and understand its global stakeholders—all of the parties whose actions affect it and whom its plans affect. It also must monitor constantly changes in events, trends, and stakeholder demands in its economic, political, competitive, geographic, social, and technological environments. Nine basic trends toward globalization and their implications for the business must be observed and evaluated. These are (1) global money and capital markets and the trend toward superliquidity, (2) developments in information technology and their implications for worldwide services, (3) the emergence of a symbol-based economy in which symbolic activities such as handling money and information are core processes, and knowledge, know-how, and brain power are crucial resources,

(4) the diminished power of nation–states as institutions and the rise of stateless corporations and supranational institutions, (5) a movement toward the deregularization of markets, (6) the continuous expansion of global trade and an increasing propensity to trade on the part of almost all nations, (7) the uncoupling of the raw-materials economy from industrial, service, and information-intensive economies, (8) increased demographic diversity resulting from population shifts and the emerging world division of labor, with global mobility for workers to migrate to where work is or for work to be exported to where workers are, and (9) the growing awareness of a transnational ecology in which natural phenomena and human-made phenomena such as pollution move around the globe without regard to national or other artificial boundaries.

A comprehensive global environmental analysis is needed to interpret these trends and their effect on a business. Such an analysis would include (1) a detailed examination of the global stakeholders and the underlying assumptions being made about them, (2) an overall scan of the environment, (3) assessment of the organization's vulnerability to global environmental threats, and (4) the writing of scenarios and the use of quantitative and qualitative forecasting methods to predict how the global environment might change in the future.

Effective strategies are based on exploiting differences between a firm and its competitors and seeking competitive advantage based on those differences. Exploiting these differences, or just retaining competitive parity, may require doing business in foreign countries. Most international strategies must be positioned with respect to the developed world's powerful "triad": the United States, Japan, and the EC. International strategies are necessarily more complex than exclusively domestic ones. A business must decide whether its products, processes, and organizational structure are well suited to foreign markets and, if so, must devise strategies that match the company's strengths with the environmental characteristics of each foreign market it seeks to enter. There are several different ways in which a business can enter another country. These include employing local agents, employing local representatives, entering into licensing agreements, forming a joint venture, acquiring local companies, and forming a foreign subsidiary. Every candidate country and the method of entry should be assessed for risk with respect to that country's political stability, social structure, types of existing economic activity, and other factors.

Even in the face of considerable risk, there are forces at work that may still require the development of a global strategy. Among these "global business drivers" are (1) competing against global or semiglobal products, (2) supplying the needs of individual, mobile customers wherever they are located in the world, (3) serving corporations with global operations, (4) sourcing from efficient suppliers located around the globe, (5) defending against a global competitor, (6) dispersing each element of the firm's value-adding chain to that place in the world in which it is best performed, and (7) minimizing overall risk by diversifying globally. The business objectives that respond to these global drivers may help the firm meet these objectives: becoming a financial intermediary, securing geographic diversification, taking advantage of a technological lead, and creating a new or expanded market. This last objective grows important as domestic markets become mature and saturated. These global drivers may indicate a preemptive move. A proactive organization takes responsibility for creating its own environment whenever possible—and adapting to change when necessary—through a continuous process of long-range planning, objective setting, and forecasting of changes in the environment. The changing global environment has made proactive behaviors important for survival.

There are four pure forms of international strategies: (1) ethnocentric, which focuses on the supposed superiority of products made in the firm's own country, (2) geocentric, which focuses on specific regions, (3) polycentric, which treats every

location as a separate and unique entity, and (4) global, which focuses on standardized products and services marketed basically the same in all countries of the world.

Whatever strategy is adopted, the organization's structure must meet that strategy's requirements. Chandler has shown that during the first half of the twentieth century, a hierarchic, multidivisional form—the M-form—proved to be the most competitive for large industrial organizations. Although this may continue to be the most effective form for heavy industry, it is unlikely to be best for knowledge-intensive and other global organizations that require speed, agility, and flexibility. The choice of organizational strategy depends on the capabilities of the firm and the demands of the industry. Some firms should continue to stress economies of scale and scope. There are other alternatives, however. One option is to build on the strengths the firm developed by way of a strong local presence in various countries and to compete via sensitivity and responsiveness. Another is to exploit the parent company's special knowledge and intellectual capital by applying them appropriately in each geographic location. Finally, the solution may be to form a transnational, stateless corporation. A successful transnational firm employs an integrated network configuration, or web of enterprise. It is composed of nodes that are dispersed, interdependent, and specialized, and it communicates more horizontally than vertically. Hence it is more flexible and better able to learn from its diverse global environment than organizations that exhibit any other structure.

Transnational organizations need not own or directly manage all or even most of the nodes in their networks. Instead they can form strategic alliances with other organizations. These alliances may serve almost any function in the organization's value-adding chain and can take on any of several forms. Among these forms are independent profit centers, spin-off partnerships, spin-in partnerships, licensing, and pure brokering. Pure brokering involves contracting with a variety of independent businesses to perform general business processes such as research, product design, advertising, financial management, and information services, as well as to undertake production.

The transnational organization includes global brokering, in which an organization decomposes its value-adding chain into individual units and determines, on the basis of country characteristics, where in the world each function is best performed. Information technology and advanced transportation systems are then used to construct the network organization and to guide and coordinate its activities. Some nodes in the network are owned; others result from strategic alliances. As an archetype, the transnational organization is best suited to coping with the nine major global trends that are reshaping the business environment.

An appendix included in this chapter provides sources of information needed to support strategy development for a global environment.

REFERENCES AND SUGGESTIONS FOR FURTHER READING

Bartlett, Christopher A. and Sumantra Ghoshal. 1989. *Managing across borders: The transnational solution.* Boston: Harvard Business School Press.

Bell, Daniel. 1973. *The coming of postindustrial society: A venture in social forecasting.* New York: Basic Books.

Berry, Thomas. 1988. *The dream of the earth.* San Francisco: Sierra Club Books.

Bleeke, J. and D. Ernst. 1991. The way to win in cross-border alliances. *Harvard Business Review,* November–December, pp. 113–133.

Chandler, Alfred D., Jr. 1990. *Scale and scope: The dynamics of industrial capitalism.* Cambridge, Mass.: Harvard University Press.

Chandler, Alfred D., Jr. 1977. *The visible hand: The managerial revolution in American business.* Cambridge, Mass.: Harvard University Press.

Demaree, Allan T. 1992. What now for the U.S. and Japan? *Fortune,* February 10, pp. 79–95.

Drucker, Peter F. 1989. *The new realities: in government and politics/In economics and business/In society and world view.* New York: Harper & Row.

Drucker, Peter F. 1986. The changed world economy. *Foreign Affairs,* Spring.

Gibney, F. 1992. China's renegade province. *Newsweek,* February 17, pp. 35–38.

Haner, Frederick T. 1980. *Global business strategy for the 1980s.* New York: Praeger.

Holstein, William J. et al. 1990. The stateless corporation. *Business Week,* May 14.

Hout, Thomas et al. 1982. How global companies win out. *Harvard Business Review.* September.

Jamieson, David and Julie O'Mara. 1991. Managing Workforce 2000. San Francisco: Jossey-Bass.

Johnson, William B. 1991. Global Workforce 2000: The new world labor market. *Harvard Business Review,* March–April, pp. 115–127.

Johnson, William B. and A. E. Packer. 1987. *Workforce 2000: Work and workers for the 21st century.* Indianapolis: Hudson Institute.

Jordan, Thomas P. et al. 1992. Global management in the 1990s. *Fortune.* July 27.

Keen, Peter G. W. 1991. *Shaping the future: Business design through information technology.* Boston: Harvard Business School Press.

Keen, Peter G. W. 1986. *Competing in time: Using telecommunications for competitive advantage.* New York: Ballinger.

Kelly, K. 1992. Learning from Japan. *Business Week,* pp. 52–60.

Killing, J. Peter. 1982. How to make a global joint venture work. *Harvard Business Review,* May–June.

Kling, Rob. 1990. More information, better jobs? *The Information Society* 7, no. 2.

Kraar, Louis. 1992. Asia 2000. *Fortune,* October 5, pp. 111–142.

Kupfer, Andrew. 1992. Who's Winning the PC Price Wars? *Fortune,* September 21, pp. 80–82.

Labate, John. 1992. The world economy in charts. *Fortune.* July 27.

Levine, Jonathon. 1992. Want EC business? You have two choices. *Business Week,* October 19, pp. 58–59.

Levitt, Theodore. 1983. The globalization of markets. *Harvard Business Review,* May–June, pp. 92–102.

Luke, Timothy and Stephen K. White. 1985. Critical theory, the information revolution, and an ecological path to modernity. In *Critical Theory and Public Life,* ed. John Foster. Cambridge, Mass.: M.I.T. Press.

McGrath, Michael E. and Richard W. Hoole. 1992. Manufacturing's new economies of scale. *Harvard Business Review,* May–June, pp. 94–102.

McLuhan, Marshal. 1964. *Understanding media: The extensions of man.* New York: McGraw-Hill.

Ohmae, Kenichi. 1990. *The borderless world: Power and strategy in the interlinked economy.* New York: Harper Press.

Ohmae, Kenichi. 1989. The global logic of strategic alliances. *Harvard Business Review,* March–April, pp. 143–154.

Ohmae, Kenichi. 1985. *Triad power: The coming shape of global competition.* New York: The Free Press.

Oster, Patrick et al. 1992. 10,000 new EC rules. *Business Week,* September 7, pp. 48–50.

Pennar, Karen. 1992. One way the U.S. lags behind. *Business Week,* January 27, p. 99.

Peters, T. J. and R. H. Waterman, Jr. 1982. *In search of excellence.* New York: Harper & Row.

Porat, Marc Uri. 1977. *The information economy: Definitions and measurement,* United States Office of Technology Special Publication 77-12(1). Washington D.C.: Department of Commerce, Office of Telecommunications.

Porter, Michael E. 1990. *The competitive advantage of nations,* New York: The Free Press.

Porter, Michael E. ed. 1986. *Competition in global industries.* Boston: Harvard Business School Press.

Powell, B. 1992. Japan's Quality Quandary. *Newsweek,* June 15, p. 48.

Quelch, John A. and Edward J. Hoff. 1986. Customizing global marketing. *Harvard Business Review,* May–June.

Rapoport, Carla. 1992. What Germany will lead Europe? *Fortune,* September 21, pp. 149–158.

Reich, Robert B. 1991. *The work of nations: Preparing ourselves for 21st century capitalism.* New York: Knopf.

Riesenbeck, H. and A. Freeling. 1991. How global are global brands? *The McKinsey Quarterly,* no. 4, pp. 3–18.

Schonfeld, Erick. 1992. The global overview. *Fortune,* July 27, pp. 62–82.

Schrage, M. 1992. What's behind IBM's dutch-treat strategy? *Los Angeles Times,* July 16, p. D3.

Sera, K. 1992. Corporate globalization: A new trend. *Academy of Management Executive* 6, no. 1, pp. 89–96.

Sherman, Stratford. 1992. Are strategic alliances working? *Fortune,* September 21, pp. 77–78.

Simon, H. 1992. Lessons from Germany's midsize giants. *Harvard Business Review,* March–April, pp. 115–123.

Smith, Lee. 1992. What the U.S. can do about R&D. *Fortune,* October 19, pp. 74–76.

Stalk, George Jr. and Thomas M. Hout. 1990. *Competing against time: How time-based competition is reshaping global markets.* New York: The Free Press.

Stewart, Thomas A. 1991. Brain power: How intellectual capital is becoming America's most valuable asset. *Fortune,* June 3, pp. 44–60.

Templeman, J. 1992. Germany takes charge. *Business Weekly,* February, pp. 50–58.

Therrien, L. 1989. The rival Japan respects. *Business Week,* November 13, pp. 108–118.

Tully, Shawn. 1992. Europe 1992: More unity than you think. *Fortune,* August 24, pp. 135–142.

Tumulty, K. 1992. Global competition: Can U.S. still play by its rules? *Los Angeles Times,* June 8, p. A8.

Weber, J. 1992. Chipping away at national boundaries. *Los Angeles Times,* July 14, p. D5.

Wever, Kirsten and Christopher Allen. 1992. Is Germany a model for managers? *Harvard Business Review,* September–October, pp. 36–43.

Woods, Wilton. 1992. It was a bad year everywhere. *Fortune.* July 27.

World Bank. 1987. *World development report.* New York: Oxford University Press.

Zuboff, Shoshana. 1988. *In the age of the smart machine: The future of work and power.* New York: Basic Books.

APPENDIX A

Selected Sources of Information for International Business

Predicasts F&S Index Europe. Predicasts, Inc. (monthly, with quarterly and annual cumulations)

(Prior to the summer of 1978, *Predicasts F&S Index International* covered all countries other than the United States.) This is an excellent index for current information on companies and industries in the Common Market, Scandinavia, what was formerly the U.S.S.R., and other Eastern and Western European countries. It covers about 400 business, industrial, and financial periodicals and is arranged in three parts: (1) by SIC number or product, (2) by region and country, and (3) by company name.

Predicasts F&S Index International. Predicasts, Inc. (monthly, with quarterly and annual cumulations)

A companion to the above-mentioned index, this index covers articles on industries and companies in Canada, Latin America, Africa, the Middle East, Japan, Oceania, and other Asian countries that appear in more than 600 foreign and domestic periodicals. It has the same three-part arrangement as *Predicasts F&S Index Europe.*

INTERNATIONAL BUSINESS TRENDS

Business Asia
Business China
Business Eastern Europe
Business Europe

Business International
Business International Money Report
Business Latin America
China Hand (on reserve)

The reports issued for each series provide current news about companies, recent developments in laws and practices related to such topics as taxes, licensing, capital sources, politics and profitability, worldwide and regional trends, and news about specific countries. It also includes checklists and statistical tables. *Business International Money Report* provides weekly news about the international capital market, currency exchange rates, interest rates, credit controls, and related subjects.

TAX AND TRADE GUIDES

Common Market Reporter. Commerce Clearing House. (Looseleaf service, periodically updated)

This service provides information on law, regulations, decisions, and rulings relevant to conducting business in, and in competition with, the EEC.

Doing Business in Europe. Commerce Clearing House. (Looseleaf service, periodically updated)

This two-volume service provides an overall summary designed to help businesspeople and lawyers obtain a general understanding of relevant aspects of the European legal system.

Exporter's Encyclopedia. Dun & Bradstreet. (Annual)

This is a comprehensive world marketing reference guide in five sections. Section 2, "Export Markets," gives important market information for specific countries (import and exchange regulations, shipping services, communications data, postal information, currency, banks, embassies, and so forth). Other sections contain general export information.

FOREIGN AND INTERNATIONAL COMPANY INFORMATION

Business Week's "The Global 1000." (Issued annually in July)

Forbes's "Forbes International 500 Survey" (issued annually in a July issue) includes the 100 largest foreign investments and the 100 largest U.S. multinationals.

Fortune's "500 Largest Industrial Corporations Outside the U.S." (issued annually in July) includes the 100 largest commercial banking companies outside the U.S. and the world's 100 biggest industrial corporations.

Nomura Company and Industry Research on the Pacific Basin

Country Reports. Economist Intelligence Unit. (Quarterly, with annual summaries)

This report presents a wide variety of country-specific statistical and narrative information. Countries covered include China and North Korea, Philippines and Taiwan, Indonesia, Singapore, Japan and South Korea, Thailand and Burma, and Hong Kong and Macau.

International Financial Statistics. International Monetary Fund. (Monthly)

For each country this publication gives statistics on exchange rate, international liquidity, money and bank statistics, interest, prices, production, international transactions, government finance. Daily exchange rates, exchange transactions, international reserves, changes in money, and the like appear in comparative tables.

Marketing in Europe. Euromonitor Publications. (Monthly)

This is a research journal covering consumer goods markets, marketing, and distribution by country in Western Europe.

Markets of Asia Pacific. Facts on File. (Irregular)

Market analyses in this series are available on such countries as PRC, Malaysia, Singapore, Thailand, Philippines, and South Korea.

Statistical Yearbook. United Nations. (Annual)

This is a basic reference work for statistics in all UN countries. The sections cover population, manpower, agriculture, production, mining, manufacturing, construction, energy, foreign trade, transport, communications, consumption, balance of payments, wages and prices,

CHAPTER EIGHT

Financial Planning and Competitive-Cost Analysis

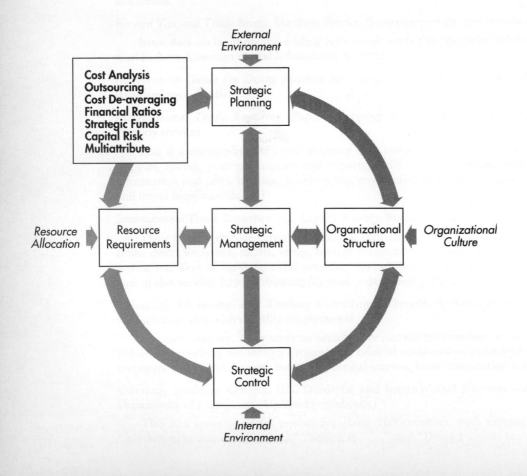

Chapter 1 A Framework for Strategic Management	**Chapter 2** Strategic Analysis	**Chapter 3** Strategic Visioning, Goals, Ethics, and Social Responsibility	**Chapter 4** The Competitive Environment	**Chapter 5** Capability-based Strategy	**Chapter 6** Market Dynamics and Sustainable Competitive Advantage
How to approach strategic management	*Application of strategic analysis*	*Understanding vision, values, ethics*	*Coping with competitive forces, stakeholders*	*Assessing company capability, timeliness, quality*	*Determining trends, gap analysis, and market dynamics*

Chapter 7 Strategy in a Global Environment	**Chapter 8** Financial Planning and Competitive- Cost Analysis	**Chapter 9** Entrepreneurship, Mergers and Acquisitions, Restructuring, and the Service Sector	**Chapter 10** Leadership Factor in Strategy and Implementing Strategic Change	**Chapter 11** Information Technology and Future Directions in Strategy
Assessing global trade, foreign markets, monetary exchange	*Preparing a financial plan and competitive-cost analysis*	*Importance of small business, entrepreneurs, restructuring*	*Strategy implementation, leadership, culture*	*Information technology, trends, new management*

INTRODUCTION

The financial viability of a firm determines its capacity to survive. Without a source of funds, internal or external, an organization cannot continue to exist. It is estimated that 90% of new ventures that file for bankruptcy do so because they lack working capital. Measures such as funds flow and financial indicators provide a basis for examining the performance of an organization and determine the value contribution of products, services, R&D, advertising, and other investments. Assessing the desirability of entering an industry, determining product value, and ascertaining whether the firm can meet competition also require appropriate financial analysis.

To compete effectively in today's global markets, companies must focus their efforts where they can achieve the best possible cost advantages relative to their rivals. To determine where the best cost advantages lie, strategic managers need to analyze the cost structure of their own company and the cost structures of their main competitors. The strategic manager can then develop strategies that reduce costs where possible.

Financial analysis has traditionally focused on an historic explanation of facts. Financial ratio analysis compares a company to its competition with respect to profitability, liquidity, leverage, and activity for the preceding period(s). The DuPont formula in Appendix D uses past data to show how the firm has managed its assets. And the flow-of-funds analysis highlights the past use of discretionary funds. Though all these techniques are widely used in industry, they were not designed for strategic planning. Nonetheless, they provide valuable data that can be used in formulating alternative strategies for the future.

Another important consideration in financial analysis is how to manage the shareholder's value in the company. Outsourcing has been used as a means of eliminating the need for funds for capital investment, which affects stakeholder value.

What has been termed the "miracle mill," Utah's Geneva Steel, has confounded all the experts by turning out profits from what was considered a hopeless plant (Ansberry, 1991). How did Geneva managers accomplish the miracle? They took an "ancient" open-hearth furnace facility and, by holding down costs, were able to outperform the nation's six largest steelmakers, who all were losing money. The payoff came from encouraging workers to find new but simple ways of reducing cost. One example was storing finished coils of steel indoors rather than leaving them outside to rust. Geneva also caters to mid-sized or small users rather than coping with what it calls "Detroit gorillas." The result was earnings of $16 million, or $1.10 per share on a share price of $19, giving Geneva a 17.3 PE ratio.

The costs that competitors incur are inferred via analogy, research, and estimates based on known advantages or disadvantages that each competitor has, such as access to cheap labor or length of shipping distances. Strategic managers can use models to predict a competitor's strategic moves and, in turn, develop strategies to take advantage of the competitor's cost disadvantages. Using knowledge gained through a competitive-cost analysis, a company could, for example, develop strategies to

- Engage in price competition if the company enjoys a cost advantage
- Avoid price competition if the company has a cost disadvantage
- Implement marketing maneuvers that exploit and expand sources of market premiums

Another method that strategic managers can use to identify sources of cost advantage is cost de-averaging. *Cost de-averaging* is an accounting procedure that allocates costs to particular products or business units, rather than averaging and allocating costs equally. This procedure shows which products or businesses actually contribute to the company's competitive advantage. Using cost de-averaging, a company can focus its resources where they will result in the greatest competitive cost advantage and profitability.

Financial analysis and planning are important aspects of strategic management because they help managers to answer the following questions about a proposed strategy:

- Is the strategy appropriate, given the company's current financial position in the industry?
- Does the company have the financial resources to initiate the strategy and carry it out?
- Are financial resources being allocated correctly to achieve the firm's strategy?

Additional issues that need to be addressed include

- When to expand capacity

- Which new products should be developed
- Whether acquisitions should be considered
- How much is needed for advertising
- How must research and development is needed
- How much maintenance and replacement is required
- Whether outsourcing should be considered

Many of these questions are related to assumptions that are made about funds availability, price elasticity, projections of income and expenses, estimate of cash-flow requirements, economic conditions, competitor actions, consumer demand, taxes, and regulatory requirements.

Answers to these questions can be obtained through the application of methods such as financial ratio analysis, strategic funds programming, and financial planning models. *Financial ratio analysis* is particularly useful for (1) determining a company's financial position relative to that of competitors in an industry and (2) projecting the company's probable future financial position. This analysis involves computing various financial ratios that indicate profitability, liquidity, leverage, and activity, and comparing them to averages for the industry, to ratios from periods during the past, or to absolute standards.

Strategic funds programming helps to identify sources of funds that could be used to initiate a strategy and to implement it over the long term. This method involves assessment of (1) cash flow generated by operations, (2) funds generated by total debt, and (3) the company's ability to generate additional funds by increasing long-term debt. Strategic funds programming enables managers to determine not only whether sufficient funds are available for a given strategy but also whether the company is likely to have sufficient funds to sustain its rate of growth throughout the implementation period.

For over a decade, Intel has used its net income and depreciation to bolster its research and development, which has run as high as 80% of its net income (Flannigan, 1984). In 1982 Intel sold 17% of its stock to IBM in order to obtain the capital needed to be a leader in the chip and semiconductor marketplace. Profits are viewed as another source of funds needed to compete in the extremely volatile semiconductor business.

A number of *financial planning models* have been used to determine the company's ability to implement its strategy or to adapt that strategy to changing environmental conditions. Three of these are baseline projections, what-if analysis, and assessing capital risk analysis.

In addition to these methods, a number of other approaches are used in financial planning. They include break-even, payback period, inflation accounting, cash-flow management, return on value added, risk assessment, shareholder value analysis, activity costing, and cost de-averaging. Qualitative forecasting has also been included in this chapter to supplement the financial risk analysis that is covered.

Computerized financial planning systems have contributed to the financial aspects of strategic planning and implementation. The use of financial planning programs can help managers avoid major mistakes and enables them to

- Create and edit their own financial models using a simple language

- Generate reports, such as pro-forma balance sheets, income statements, and cash-flow analyses
- Test the assumptions on which a plan is based by asking "what-if" questions and performing sensitivity analyses
- Examine alternative goals to ensure that the stated corporate goals and objectives are properly incorporated in the plan
- Perform, for each of the alternatives, a risk analysis that takes into account the uncertainty and risk inherent in every major strategic decision

Many of the problems confronting strategic managers include a large number of factors. Each factor can have different levels of importance and priority. To assist the strategic manager in making these decisions, multiattribute decision making analysis is employed. Considerations to take into account in preparing a budget close the chapter.

A number of related types of analyses are shown in the appendices to this chapter. Appendix A covers the learning curve and its implications for cost analysis. Appendix B shows how to prepare a discounted cash flow. Appendix C illustrates a cost/benefit analysis. Appendix D shows how to apply computer analysis to evaluate financial factors. Appendix D includes a number of printouts from the fisCAL computer program, which provides computerized support for strategic financial analysis.

MANAGING SHAREHOLDER VALUE AND OUTSOURCING

An important concern emerging in financial analysis is how to resolve the apparent conflict between competitive advantage and shareholder value. *Shareholder value analysis* attempts to define which strategies improve shareholder value while sustaining a competitive advantage. By focusing on productivity, financial planners can increase the value of products produced and at the same time lay the foundation for a competitive edge in the marketplace (Rappaport, 1992). Obviously, factors such as competitor costs, market share, product life cycle, and product niche all influence a company's competitive position and may not depend on productivity improvement alone. One of the reasons why companies focus on short-term profitability rather than long-term improvements is the former's potential for lowering stock prices. Apple introduced the Macintosh in 1984 and was able to achieve a highly differentiated market position because of its user-friendly language. The result was that from 1986 to 1990, Apple achieved a 30% return on equity and its annual earnings exceeded 30%. This performance increased shareholder value on the basis of product differentiation rather than productivity. It also illustrates that shareholder value can be increased by long-term investment. Difficulty often arises because shareholder value is not the same as sustainable competitive advantage. Unfortunately, shareholder value is often overlooked when a firm is making investments needed to sustain market position (Day and Fahey, 1990). However, a sustainable competitive advantage can lead to a sustainable shareholder value.

Too often shareholder value is viewed from the perspective of stock prices rather than growth potential, which ultimately is the real shareholder value. Wenner and LeBer (1990) describe shareholder value analysis as the process of analyzing the economic value determined by the net present value of expected cash flows, discounted at the cost of capital. They cite four key factors that create shareholder value:

- Performance of the company's product portfolio
- Assumptions underlying its strategy
- Level of potential improvement
- The company's priorities and goals

An illustration of how goals can affect strategy is the restructuring of companies and retention of businesses. Disney owns or has shares in only those businesses that meet its expected return on capital and growth potential. Marriott Corporation sold off its hotels and increased its ROS from 9% to over 20%. The company felt that its core competency was in managing hotels, not owning them (Willigan, 1990). Using other people's financing, Marriott built hotels that it could manage and achieved an annual growth of over 20%.

Shareholder value is measured by the return received from an investment to compensate for the risk involved. A comprehensive framework for determining shareholder value proposed by McLean (1990) includes

- The net present value of future cash flows
- The value of stock options
- The value of restructuring
- Costs of the corporate office
- Outstanding claims based on liabilities or pending litigation

An approach that can be used to determine shareholder value would cover

1. Which strategies increase cash returns
2. A forecast of cash flow by asset and tax base
3. Determination of equitable return for a specified risk

Ultimately, where equity is a critical source of funds, strategies must incorporate shareholder value as a critical aspect of any analysis. One of the approaches being used to reduce a firm's asset base and thereby increase its cash flow is *outsourcing*. Outsourcing has become critical for computer service, where the cost of computers is high and it is difficult to attract and retain competent employees. One of the more successful companies in outsourcing services is Electronic Data Systems. The industry has grown from sales of $25 billion in 1989 to $38 billion in 1992 and is projected to grow to $49 billion in 1994 (Weber, 1992). Merrill Lynch analyst Stephen McClellan describes outsourcing as a rapidly developing tidal wave. The rapid growth in outsourcing goes along with the financial benefits derived. However, Bettis, Bradley, and Hamel (1992) claim that improperly used outsourcing may account for our declining competitive position in world trade. Outsourcing amounts to giving up the firm's ability to control its manufacturing or other processes needed to deliver a product to market. Akio Morita, CEO of Sony Corporation, describes the effect of outsourcing as the "hollowing of American industry where the U.S. is abandoning its status as an industrial power." The consumer electronics industry has seen the decline in competitiveness of once-prestigious companies such as RCA. For example, in 1960 the United States had a 100% share of the color television market; that share had shrunk to 55% in 1990. This decline resulted from improved economics of scale in the supplier countries, who eventually took over the manufacture of the entire products, not just the portion that was outsourced. U.S. computer manufacturers such as AST and Everex started as suppliers of boards and components to other PC manufacturers, but as they perfected their components, they turned around and manufactured the entire computer. The critical assumptions made by companies who choose outsourcing are

1. Strategy is primarily having a strong market position.
2. A brand name is sufficient even without manufacturing capability.
3. Manufacturing can be separated from engineering design.
4. Manufacturing knowledge is not critical for understanding the marketplace.

The result of these assumptions is that firms that scale back manufacturing in favor of outsourcing find it difficult to introduce new designs that take advantage of the latest technology, often because suppliers are unwilling to make the necessary investment without assurance of its paying off. In short, there are a number of hazards associated with outsourcing.

Another perspective on outsourcing is described by Welch (1992), who claims that the make-or-buy decision is too often based on unit cost without regard for the strategic or technological implications. The advantages claimed for outsourcing have been that it

- Changes fixed costs to variable costs
- Creates a better balance of the workforce
- Reduces capital investment
- Reduces cost where a supplier offers economies of scale
- Encourages a focus on product development rather than manufacturing
- Enables the firm to benefit from suppliers' innovations
- Focuses resources on those activities that have a high added value

Outsourcing is most effective where

- Process technology is unavailable, as in chip manufacturing
- Competitors have superior technology
- The supplier has lower scrap, rework, returns, recalls, or warranty costs
- Capital for investment is limited and there is a need to focus on high-value-adding activities
- There is flexibility in changing suppliers or where outsourcing could readily be discontinued by either acquisition or new investment in strategic capability

COMPETITIVE-COST ANALYSIS

To compete successfully, a company must analyze its cost position relative to that of competitors. The aim of *competitive-cost analysis* is to get an accurate picture of the competitive situation in an industry. If all competitors' costs are known, the company can project future price levels, anticipate competitors' moves, prepare countermoves, and assess the potential of its strategies for success.

Data that reflect what has transpired in the manufacturing and distribution of a company's products are required for cost analysis. What managers need is accurate and timely information that can help them introduce more effective operating procedures. Kaplan (1988) maintains that not one but three cost systems are required for meeting managerial needs. The first is inventory valuation to allocate production costs between goods that are sold and goods in stock. The second system should supply the feedback needed for operational control; it should focus especially on the resources consumed. Third is a basis for measuring product cost. This same theme is echoed by Ohmae (1989), who contends that company-centered accounting does not adequately deal with overcapacity and can lead to the ruin of companies and industries. Ohmae suggests that to deliver value requires adopting a flexible operating outlook, not simply spending more money to gain market share. Companies must change to fit the changing customer, which implies that accounting systems must accommodate these changing requirements rather than relying on "last year's data."

Cooper (1989) has proposed a number of measures for determining when a new cost system is needed. A new system should be designed when

1. Managers want to drop unprofitable lines
2. Profit margins can't be explained
3. Difficult products show the largest profits
4. The company is introducing increased automation
5. Functional areas develop their own cost system
6. Every decision requires a special accounting team

Cooper maintains that a good cost system should last 10 years, although it may need to be redesigned sooner in a highly volatile environment.

STRATEGIC COST-DRIVING FACTORS

Competitive-cost analysis begins with an analysis of *strategic cost-driving factors:* those factors that determine a company's relative long-run position. These include product design, factor costs, productivity, scale, experience, focus, and capacity utilization. Before the company's relative cost position can be determined, its own cost behavior must be known and differentiated by business segments.

The initial question is "Which costs are relevant in a strategic sense?" That is, which can be influenced by a new strategy? Compared to operational cost control, the goal of which is to cut costs in the short run by "doing things right," strategic cost analysis has the goal of positioning the firm for long-term cost advantages by "doing the right things." Managers sometimes confuse their ability to reduce cost in the short run, such as by laying off personnel, with the fundamental need to achieve strategic cost-competitiveness. Massive layoffs and plant closures can be only a short-term measure to adjust capacity. The roots of the long-term cost disadvantage must be addressed differently.

When considering which products should be produced, where, and for what customers, the strategic manager should ask questions about the following cost-driving factors.

1. *Product design.* Does product design influence product cost? How much of an advantage can be gained by designing a lighter-weight product, a product with fewer parts, a product with more functions integrated into individual components, or a more rugged product that results in lower cost to produce a given quality?
2. *Factor costs.* How much do the basic factor costs (labor, capital, and energy) influence the final cost of the product? How much of an advantage could be gained, for example, by moving production to a country with lower labor costs?
3. *Productivity.* How does productivity differ among competitors in this industry (for example, in terms of sales per employee or value added per employee)? What factors determine these differences (for example, level of employee skills or education, level of automation, differences in applied technology)? With productivity factored in, what advantage would production in a country having lower-cost labor really yield?
4. *Scale/sales.* What is the impact of overall sales volume on costs? Which costs can be shared among businesses or functions (such as overhead, sales costs)? Would building a larger production facility have an impact on costs?
5. *Experience.* How much learning—and thus time and cost—does it take for a relative newcomer in this business to reach a competitive level of efficiency? What future cost and price level can be projected?
6. *Focus.* What are the potential advantages of increased focus with respect to production or distribution? Is it better to invest in single-purpose, specialized machines or in multipurpose, flexible machines? Should all potential customers be addressed in order to maximize volume, or should the sales effort be concentrated on one specific customer group?
7. *Capacity utilization.* What are the cost penalties of overinvesting or underinvesting in new capacity? What cost penalties are associated with underuse of a plant? How would the industry react if actual demand were to exceed expectations?

Figure 8.1 shows the impact of these different cost-driving factors on the cost structure of a company's product. The X's indicate which parts of the cost structure a particular factor affects. The cost structure itself gives an indication of the size of each factor's potential impact. This simple evaluation can be a useful check to remind management of the sources of strategic advantage. The analysis illustrated in Figure 8.1 enables managers to see the relative importance of the different cost-driving factors underlying the company's competitive advantage. Management at AMP may conclude that the focus should be on overall volume and product design because these factors have an impact on many parts of the cost structure. (It might be desirable at this point to review the AMP case in Chapter 6.)

Given a set of product and infrastructure decisions, the analysis of cost-driving factors can be used to determine the firm's relative cost position in the future. It can also be used to determine the competitors' positions, once their products and infrastructures are analyzed in detail. Analysis of competitors enables the firm to gauge its competitive-cost position. AMP, for example, has a size and factor cost disadvantage relative to its main competitors. AMP may be able to overcome this disadvantage with better product design, a stronger focus on production and marketing, and better utilization of its resources. Before making any detailed comparisons, however, AMP must thoroughly investigate its own cost situation.

FIGURE 8.1   Strategic Cost-driving Factors for AMP, Inc.

Cost Element	Percentage of Total Costs	Cost-Driving Factors							
		Product Design	Factor Costs	Productivity	Scale/ Volume	Volume per Product Group	Volume per Customer	Capacity Utilization	Experience
Material	31	X	X		X				
Parts treatment and manufacturing	9	X	X	X	X	X		X	X
Assembly	18	X	X	X	X	X		X	X
Quality control	4	X			X	X			
Packaging	5	X			X	X	X		
Warehousing and distribution	8				X		X		
R&D	2	X			X	X			
Applications engineering	3	X				X			X
Sales and marketing	12				X		X	X	
General administration	8				X		X	X	
Total	100								
AMP's relative position		+	–	0	+	–	+	0	+

Note: Volume per product group and volume per customer involve the issue of focus. In bottom line of table, + = better than competitors; 0 = equal to competitors; and – = worse than competitors.

COST DE-AVERAGING

Normal accounting procedures assign some costs directly to particular products sold to specific customers. All other costs are averaged—that is, divided among all products and customers—on the basis of a specified allocation. The broader the product line and the larger the number and variety of customers, the greater the use of cost averaging. This often leads to a misstatement of real costs. Overhead and other costs can differ greatly from one product to another, but this fact is obscured through existing accounting practices.

Cost averaging can lead to a loss of market share. The leading company in any industry often has the lowest costs, unless some competitor has exclusive use of better technology. Yet, in business after business, new entrants gain on the leader and eventually displace it because they are able to take advantage of the leader's practice of cost averaging. This happens because a specialized factory, for example, can produce a high volume of products much more cheaply than a factory designed for flexibility. Similarly, a focus on the uniform needs of certain customers can reduce costs. It costs less to serve large, sophisticated buyers who care about price and delivery than to serve smaller buyers who require education, service, and support. In a company serving both markets, cost averaging leads to price averaging, which means that some customers are overcharged while others are subsidized. By focusing on a market segment where the leader is either overcharging or undercharging the customer, a new competitor can gain a foothold. The companies that produce clones of the IBM PC are a good example. Using low-cost components made overseas, they are able to underprice IBM.

An even more subtle and often more damaging effect of cost averaging is that, as the leader increases its product offerings in order to gain sales volume, the overhead charges for all products go up as a result of increased complexity. This effect of product proliferation is demonstrated in Figure 8.2, which shows how in one company, overhead charges for all products went up in three years from 235% to more than 310% as the number of product varieties increased from 8 to 20.

The market leader can prevent some of these problems by averaging costs for the basic product configuration and *then* adding market-segment-specific costs related to product complexity, higher quality, and price. To do this, the company's strategic managers practice cost de-averaging. *Cost de-averaging* requires that they

1. Analyze costs by products as well as by customer groups.
2. Intentionally bias cost allocations, where they are necessary, away from rapidly growing, vulnerable market segments.
3. Differentiate the service to each market segment as required, and organize and price accordingly.

Figure 8.3 shows how costs can be separated by market segments. In this case, a manufacturer produced different-quality products that were targeted at different price points in the market. Basic costs, such as for manufacturing, distribution, and selling, were shared among all products, while segment-specific costs, such as for better quality and advertising, were allocated to specific brands (A, B, and C). This way,

---

FIGURE 8.2 | **Effect of Product Proliferation**

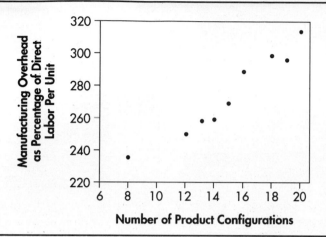

Source: Courtesy of The Boston Consulting Group, Inc. Reprinted with permission.

---

the manufacturer was able to reduce its basic or necessary costs by increasing volume overall without overcharging customers in the price-sensitive segment (brand A).

The isolation of market-segment-specific costs is seldom this simple, or more firms would do it on a regular basis. Figure 8.4 is an analysis of costs for a producer of stock forms (continuous computer printout paper) by job size. The company's current accounting data showed that small accounts were most profitable, and management considered investing more in machinery for this segment and increasing its marketing to smaller customers. But a more detailed cost analysis revealed the astonishing fact that small accounts were *not* as profitable as large ones.

First, the cost of waste during startup had not been accounted for regularly. On the average, all jobs had a 7% waste (see Figure 8.4). Yet when managers accounted for the minimum startup waste inherent in all jobs regardless of run length, they saw that the smaller jobs had startup waste factors as high as 57%. Because materials represented a significant percentage of total costs, failure to account for this difference in waste costs led to grave errors in statements of total manufacturing costs.

Second, the cost of selling to small accounts turned out to be higher. When segment-specific sales activities were analyzed, it turned out that sales to small accounts, even over the telephone, involved greater costs per ton than sales to large accounts because of the complex and varying demands of customers in the small-account segment. As Figure 8.4 shows, cost averaging did not reflect actual selling costs to accounts of any size. The average of 18% is way above actual selling costs for large accounts, most of which merely required negotiation of a basic contract for the year and a few visits after that.

When the company de-averaged its job costs per ton of paper sold, it learned that small jobs were twice as expensive as originally reported, medium-sized ones

| FIGURE 8.3 | Basic and Segment-specific Costs |

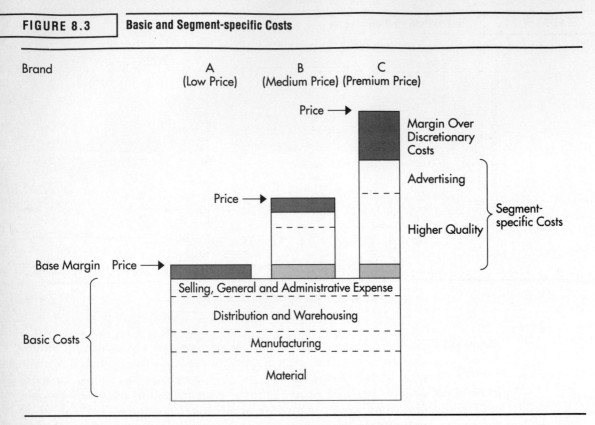

Source: Courtesy of The Boston Consulting Group, Inc. Reprinted with permission.

were 8% more expensive, and large jobs were 14% less expensive. Given the company's pricing policy, it was losing a substantial amount on small jobs while gaining substantial profits on the large ones. As a result of cost de-averaging, management decided to invest in larger machines and automated warehousing. Small jobs were eliminated from the production program, but a separate organization was installed to customize forms produced by other companies.

COMPETITIVE-COST MODELING

Once the firm's costs have been properly allocated, they can be compared to those of competitors in particular market segments. Competitive-cost analysis generally begins by examining the firm's own costs. Competitors' costs are estimated by using an appropriate analogy. To model competitive costs, managers need data covering

- Internal cost behavior
- Competitive microeconomics
- Financial performance of the firm
- Knowledge about competitors

FIGURE 8.4 | Cost De-averaging

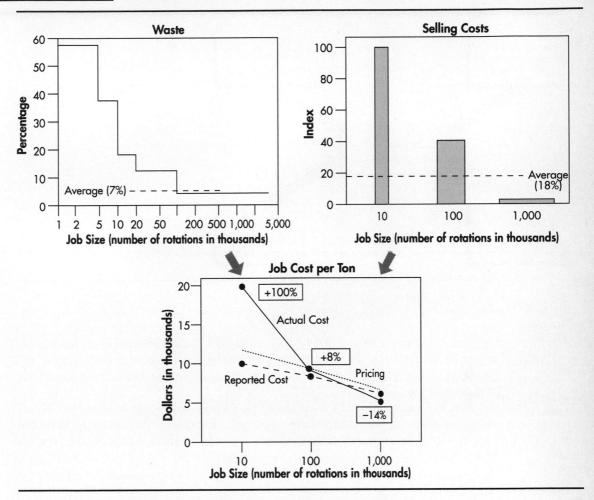

Source: Courtesy of The Boston Consulting Group, Inc. Reprinted with permission.

Figure 8.5 is a competitive-cost model based on these sets of data. Using data about the firm's own costs, managers establish microeconomic relationships to explain how costs behave relative to changes in the cost-driving factors (see Figure 8.1). Next they acquire data on the competitors' infrastructure, such as plant size, location, sales by market segment, number of employees, and technology used. These data can be obtained from public sources such as annual reports, Form 10-Ks, analysts' reports, and other publications. Other important sources include industry specialists, academics, suppliers and customers of the competitors, and sometimes even the competitor itself. The competitor's financial performance is

FIGURE 8.5	Competitive-Cost Modeling

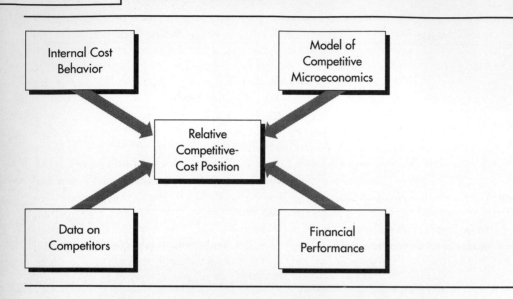

another important element; it can be used to spot inconsistencies between performance as predicted by the competitive-cost model and the competitor's actual performance. Discrepancies may, for example, reveal important facts about operations or technology use.

The key question to ask in performing a competitive-cost analysis is "Where are the firm's sources of competitive advantage, and can the advantage be defended over time?" The answer to this question depends on those posed in the sections that follow.

Product Design

What would our costs be if we produced our competitor's product (in our existing plant)? In other words, what are the production costs, given the weight, complexity of design, number and quality of parts, and performance of a competitor's product characteristics? This analysis enables managers to draw some immediate conclusions about the material costs of competitive products and to make inferences concerning the competitor's technology and production process. It is important to recognize that the competitive product would often cost more to produce using the firm's machines even if it were, for example, lighter and had fewer parts, because production technology and process are optimized as a product is developed. Either specialized machines are bought to produce a particular design, or the product is designed such that it optimally utilizes existing processes and technology.

Differences in product design and the resulting cost differences can be significant and can also reveal differences in production philosophy among competitors. For example, Japanese electronics manufacturers tend to integrate product components more than Western countries do. Such a practice means higher initial costs for development and production, but its long-term effects on quality overcome the short-term cost disadvantages by far. Similarly, the designs of European cars tend to fulfill expectations about performance and longevity, enabling European car manufacturers to dominate the luxury segment of the market.

Factor Costs

What would our costs be if our plant were in the same location as the competitor's? The purpose of this hypothetical question is to assess the competitor's factor costs. What if, for example, the competitor's plant is in South Korea or Taiwan instead of the United States? The potential savings in labor costs can be substantial, as is shown in Table 8.1. It is important to recognize that these data are average and that regional differences exist within each country. Furthermore, when one isolates those parts of the cost structure that really are comparable, it is often surprising how little total costs are affected by labor costs. Wages paid to sales personnel, for example, typically depend on where the product is marketed, not on where it is manufactured, and

TABLE 8.1	International Comparison of Labor Costs

Country	Hourly Wages ($)*	Index
High Labor Rates		
United States	14.45	100
Germany	17.45	121
Medium Labor Rates		
Japan	11.90	82
France	12.10	84
Great Britain	10.25	71
Italy	11.15	77
Sweden	12.95	90
Finland	11.80	82
Low Labor Rates		
Taiwan	2.30	16
South Korea	2.00	14

* Average hourly wages in machinery manufacturing, including additional compensation, at currency exchange rates of July 1987.

Source: U.S. Bureau of Labor Statistics, 1987.

tend to be the same whether the plant is in the United States or Taiwan. Low labor costs are beneficial if manufacturing and assembly still dominate the product's value chain and if the upstream activities of sales and marketing are difficult to differentiate.

Productivity

How do differences in productivity affect the costs of competitors? Productivity comparisons can be based on a number of indicators, such as value added per employee, sales per employee, or fixed-asset turnover. These comparisons should be done at the plant level and, if possible, on the machine level. Discussions with machine suppliers can help managers understand a competitor's approach to achieving productivity gains.

Production technology is a major determinant of productivity. In recent years, for example, considerable progress has been made in factory automation and machine flexibility, at little or no additional cost. Many leading Western competitors have recognized the potential of the "factory of the future" and are using production technology to retain their competitive edge, while at the same time maintaining employment in countries with high labor costs. In textile manufacturing, for example, so-called quick-response systems are helping to restore jobs to high-cost countries.

Figure 8.6 shows how the production costs of standard bolts declined as new technologies emerged. Currently, a machine shop with many workers has cost

---

FIGURE 8.6 | **Technological Evolution in the Production of Standard Bolts**

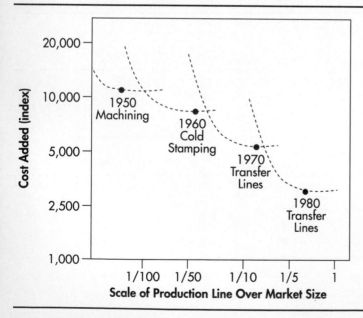

Source: Portfolio and Competitive Systems, Paris, © November 1985. Courtesy of The Boston Consulting Group, Inc. Reprinted with permission.

added that is at least four times the cost added for a competitor employing the most recently developed transfer lines. As can be seen in the figure, the volume supplier needs to retain a significant portion of the total market in order to maintain its productivity advantage in the face of the competition from alternative technologies.

As many Japanese competitors proved in the early 1980s, significant gains in productivity can also be made without massive investments in new technology. Table 8.2 shows the increases in labor and capital productivity of a number of Japanese manufacturing firms. These companies achieved gains by pioneering new concepts, such as Kanban or just-in-time (JIT), on the shop floor. What makes these productivity gains particularly impressive is the fact that they were accomplished while product variety was increasing.

Scale Effects: Total Volume

What would our production costs be if our production facility were the same size as our competitor's? Total volume of production is a cost-driving factor for virtually every element in the cost structure (see Figures 8.7 and 8.8). Other advantages of scale depend on the size of plant or machines (Figure 8.9). Production costs in the paper industry, for example, are strongly influenced by the width of the paper machine used. Paper machines today have sophisticated automation systems, and the employee-hours per ton required to operate a paper machine decrease as the machine size increases. As a result, the labor cost per ton of paper declines as machine size increases. In the machine-tool industry, on the other hand, more volume means more machines and more personnel to operate them. Therefore, increased investment in machines does not reduce production costs. Yet costs at the plant level (such as quality control, warehousing, repair and maintenance, and general administration) do not tend to increase with higher volume.

TABLE 8.2	Productivity Improvements: Japanese Manufacturing Firms, 1976–1982

Company	Product	Increases		
		Labor Productivity	Capital Productivity	Product Variants
Yanmar	Diesel engines	1.9×	2.0×	3.7×
Hitachi	Refrigeration equipment	1.8×	1.7×	1.3×
Komatsu	Industrial equipment	1.8×	1.7×	1.8×
Toyo Kogyo	Automotive components	2.4×	1.9×	1.6×
Isuzu	Automobiles	2.5×	1.5×	NA
Jidosha Kiki	Brakes	1.9×	NA	NA
Average		2.0×	1.8×	2.1×

Source: Introduction to Time-Based Competition and Operational Effectiveness, Vol. 1, p. 10, © August 1987. Courtesy of The Boston Consulting Group, Inc. Reprinted with permission.

FIGURE 8.7 | The Leader's Advantage: Advertising Costs of Tire Companies

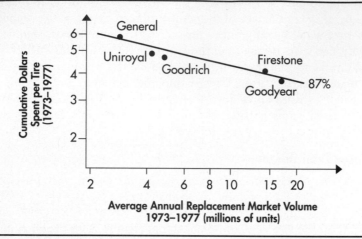

Source: Courtesy of The Boston Consulting Group, Inc. Reprinted with permission.

FIGURE 8.8 | Purchasing Scale Economics for Hydraulic Components
(Price per unit includes full amortization of tooling costs)

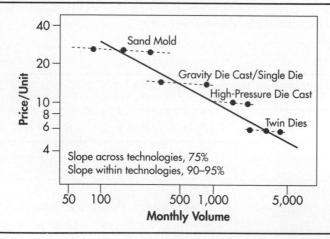

Source: Courtesy of The Boston Consulting Group, Inc. Reprinted with permission.

Figure 8.9 also illustrates how different scale effects are determined. Through discussions with management as well as suppliers, different machine configurations and their labor requirements can be modeled and then plotted. The scale effects can then be calculated or read directly from the chart. When all the scale effects for

FIGURE 8.9	Effects of Machine Size and Plant Capacity on Labor Costs

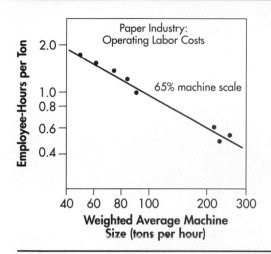 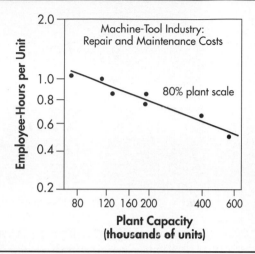

Source: Courtesy of The Boston Consulting Group, Inc. Reprinted with permission.

every part of the cost structure have been derived, the company's total potential cost advantage or disadvantage relative to that of a competitor can be established.

Focus: Volume per Product Group or Customer

How would a change of focus alter our competitive-cost position? In today's competitive environment, few companies can base their success on an overall volume advantage, particularly in a shrinking market. In this kind of environment, the focused competitor beats the broad-line supplier every time. General Motors' massive lead in market share, for instance, today is being eroded by competitors who "build a car like a car" (Ford), make an automobile "engineered like no other car in the world" (Mercedes-Benz), or "sell cars you can afford" (Hyundai). Focus involves better understanding of the business and greater attention to detail. The more focused a company is, the better it can identify and increase the value of its products to customers.

A focused company concentrates on activities that it does best. Focus is usually associated with closing or selling off weak businesses and pruning unprofitable products. Therefore, focus is driven by a thorough understanding of markets and customers, an understanding that can be converted directly to cost advantages and higher profitability.

Figure 8.10 shows the relationship between production lost and the annual volumes of different models of a ceramic product. Clearly, the higher the volume per model, the lower the percentage of production rejects. Small-volume models had rejection rates of up to 30% at the end of the production line, whereas some high-volume models had rejection rates of less than 5%. Yet customers were

| FIGURE 8.10 | Production Lost versus Volume per Model of a Ceramic Product |

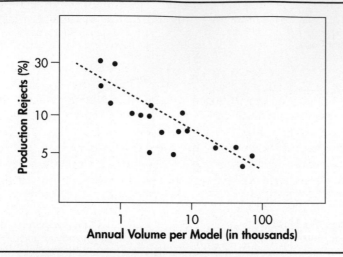

Source: Courtesy of The Boston Consulting Group, Inc. Reprinted with permission.

willing to pay a higher price for the unique (low-volume) designs, and this market segment was growing fastest. Therefore, the company decided to focus on the low-volume, unique items, manufacture all of its products in a single factory, and arrange the production process so that the low-volume products would benefit from production economies made possible by their high-volume counterparts. With this system, the company was able to reduce the rejection rate of all products, but particularly that of the low-volume items. Focusing on these items enabled the company to establish itself firmly as the leader in the high-priced, designer market.

Focus can also involve concentrating marketing in particular geographic regions. Figure 8.11 shows how regional focus affected the profitability of seven U.S. supermarket chains. Independent of their size, supermarkets tend to be more profitable if they dominate particular regions. The regional leader has logistical advantages, such as distribution efficiency and collective advertising in local newspapers. Because of its lack of geographic focus, A&P, though about equal in size to the market leader (Safeway), had a significantly lower profitability, even compared to smaller regional competitors such as Winn-Dixie and Stop & Shop. Once A&P recognized this, it closed its unprofitable stores and expanded in areas where it had a strong position. As a result, A&P has recovered from near bankruptcy to become very profitable.

Capacity Utilization

How do we compare with respect to optimal use of product capacity? Capacity utilization is most important for industries with high capital investments and declining markets. Competitors in this situation often enter into intense fights over volume leadership to avoid having to reduce capacity and lay off personnel in response to lower market demands. The ensuing price-cutting wars often lead to vicious circles in which competitors convert any cost reductions into immediate price cuts, thereby pushing all competitors' break-even points further out of reach. Eventually, the industry undergoes a shake-out and consolidation, after which capacities are brought back in line with market demands through competitive restructuring.

Price Realization

What is our relative position with respect to price realization? Pricing is often ignored in comparisons among competitors. Yet, in one industry after another, patterns of differing price realization for almost identical products emerge. Figure 8.12 shows how the prices charged for radial tires vary, even though it would be difficult for the average buyer to distinguish one brand of radials from another if the brand names were removed. Some reasons for greater price realization are based on customers' perceptions of the product. Customers may, for example, associate certain features with the product because of their perception of a supplier's image. A more typical reason is that the leading supplier is in a position to influence price realization through better or more numerous locations, a loyal base of existing customers, better employees and better service, or better availability and shorter delivery times. These advantages combined to allow the market leaders, Goodyear and Firestone, to charge about 5% to 10% more per tire than their smaller competitors. In stalemated industries with little potential for cost differentiation, a difference in price realization can often make the difference between failure and long-term survival.

FIGURE 8.11	Regional Focus of U.S. Supermarkets

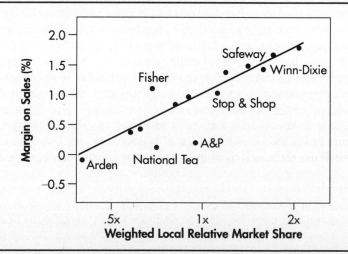

Source: Courtesy of The Boston Consulting Group, Inc. Reprinted with permission.

FIGURE 8.12	Retail Weighted Average Price Realization of Steel and Economy Radial Tires, 1978

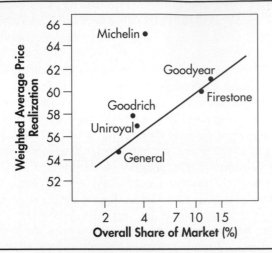

Source: Courtesy of The Boston Consulting Group, Inc. Reprinted with permission.

A COMPLETE COMPETITIVE-COST COMPARISON

The purpose of competitive-cost analysis is to obtain an accurate picture of the supply situation in an industry. A company that knows all its competitors' costs can readily make projections concerning the industry price development, anticipate competitive moves, prepare countermoves, and assess the potential success of strategic moves.

Figure 8.13, for example, shows the result of a competitive-cost analysis for a commodity product in the paper industry. In the graph, the cost of each competitor, as calculated, is plotted along with its supply. The largest competitor (competitor A) has the lowest cost. When the supplies from all competitors are added, the total supply from the industry can be shown relative to market demand. As seen in this example, the total industry supply exceeds the market demand of about 1.25 million tons. In such a situation, the price level typically is reduced to the cash operating cost of the marginal competitor. Competitors with higher cash costs are often forced to leave the market. As new capacity comes on stream, the price level is brought down to the cash operating cost of the new marginal competitor, and those with higher cash costs become noncompetitive. Because it takes at least two years to complete a new paper mill after announcing the investment decision, there is sufficient time for marginal competitors to adjust their strategies and switch to more specialized paper grades.

A recently suggested approach to costing is to link activities with resource usage. Cooper and Kaplan (1991) recommend substituting activity-based costing for traditional cost accounting systems. The key, they contend, is to separate expenses based on the level of activity that consumes resources. Thus expenses would be allocated not by individual products, but by the activity level needed to "produce different products or to serve different customers, independent of how many units are produced or sold." Activities are grouped as follows:

FIGURE 8.13 | **Paper Product Supply Curve and Its Effects on Price Realization**
(Full cost equals cash operating cost plus depreciation and capital costs)

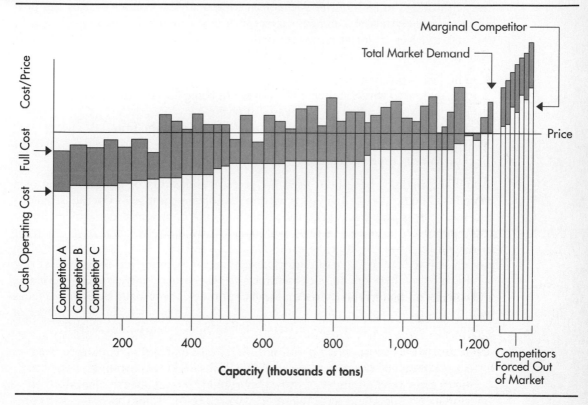

Source: Courtesy of The Boston Consulting Group, Inc. Reprinted with permission.

1. Facilities—expenses of maintenance and operations
2. Products—expenses to design and improve products
3. Batch level—support for producing products
4. Unit level—direct cost of producing products

They conclude by stating, "Bad information on product costs leads to bad competitive strategy."

Understanding the strategic cost drivers in an industry and doing a competitive-cost analysis can be very helpful in defining areas that offer the best potential for future profitability. A carefully done competitive-cost comparison can also yield direct conclusions on how to maintain or improve the company's competitive position, such as by

- Investing in improved product design to match a rival
- Moving a new factory to a lower-cost country
- Raising productivity to projected levels on the experience curve
- Increasing volume in specific segments to gain scale advantage and focus
- Closing plant sites to achieve better capacity utilization

FINANCIAL RATIO ANALYSIS

One widely used technique for evaluating performance and for comparing a business with others in an industry is financial ratio analysis. Financial ratios can provide a quick overview of a company's recent or past profitability, liquidity, leverage, and activity. Key financial ratios are defined in Table 8.3. Financial ratios, which often are employed for merger or acquisition decisions, can be used to show

1. The firm's position in its industry
2. The degree to which strategic objectives are being accomplished
3. The firm's vulnerability to decreases in revenue
4. The future borrowing power and growth potential of the firm
5. The firm's ability to react to unforeseen changes in the environment
6. The risk of corporate failure

Financial ratios have been used for years as indicators of the well-being of a company. Financial ratio analysis is used in assessing a company's internal strengths and weaknesses and, because considerable amounts of financial data are available about competitors, and for making comparisons within an industry. It is important to recognize, however, that these ratios reflect the past; therefore, they are often more useful for evaluating past performance than for planning future strategies.

Each of the four key areas chosen for analysis—profitability, liquidity, leverage, and activity of the firm—comprises a number of ratios. It is usually sufficient to focus on only a few, such as the ones defined in Table 8.3. To evaluate the performance of a company with respect to these ratios, the following three methods are used.

1. *Industry comparisons.* To perform this analysis, managers compare the company's financial ratios to those of similar firms in the same industry. The other firms must be comparable; that is, they should be of about the same size, sell similar products, and serve the same markets. If this is not the case, results of the comparison can be misleading.
2. *Time-series analysis.* This method involves computing the company's financial ratios for several past years and plotting them on a graph to detect changes and trends over time and project future performance.
3. *Comparison to absolute standards.* In many organizations, minimum financial ratios serve as absolute standards for performance. Such absolute standards include
   a. Profitability: net profit, the ratio of profits after taxes to sales: no less than 3%
   b. Liquidity: ratio of current assets to current liabilities: greater than 1
   c. Leverage: ratio of long-term debt to total equity: less than 1
   d. Activity: average collection period: less than 60 days

A complete financial analysis generally includes all three of these methods.

These methods are often supplemented by doing an industry comparison. An example is shown in Appendix D, where the fisCAL program is used. Managers also rely on comparative data from companies such as Dun & Bradstreet to assess their relative profitability, liquidity, leverage, and activity ratios.

1. *Profitability.* Profitability ratios indicate how well a company is allocating its resources in relation to income generated.

TABLE 8.3 | **Key Financial Ratios**

Ratio	Definition	Ratio	Definition
1. Profitability		**3. Leverage**	
a. Gross profit margin $$\frac{\text{Sales} - \text{cost of goods sold}}{\text{sales}}$$	Total margin available to cover operating expenses and yield a profit	a. Debt-to-assets ratio $$\frac{\text{total debt}}{\text{total assets}}$$	The extent to which funds are used to finance the firm's operations
b. Net profit margin $$\frac{\text{profits after taxes}}{\text{sales}}$$	Return on sales	b. Debt-to equity ratio $$\frac{\text{total debt}}{\text{total equity}}$$	Ratio of funds from creditors to funds from stockholders
c. Return on assets $$\frac{\text{earnings before interest and taxes (EBIT)}}{\text{total assets}}$$	Return on the total investment from both stockholders and creditors	c. Long-term debt-to-equity ratio $$\frac{\text{long-term debt}}{\text{total equity}}$$	The balance between debt and equity
d. Return on equity $$\frac{\text{profits after taxes}}{\text{total equity}}$$	Rate of return on stockholders' investment in the firm		
2. Liquidity		**4. Activity**	
a. Current ratio $$\frac{\text{current assets}}{\text{current liabilities}}$$	The extent to which the claims of short-term creditors are covered by short-term assets	a. Inventory turnover $$\frac{\text{sales}}{\text{inventory}}$$	The amount of inventory used by the company to generate its sales
b. Quick ratio $$\frac{\text{current assets} - \text{inventory}}{\text{current liabilities}}$$	Acid-test ratio; the firm's ability to pay off short-term obligations without having to sell its inventory	b. Fixed-asset turnover $$\frac{\text{sales}}{\text{fixed assets}}$$	Sales productivity and plant utilization
c. Inventory to net working capital $$\frac{\text{inventory}}{\text{current assets} - \text{current liabilities}}$$	The extent to which the firm's working capital is tied up in inventory	c. Average collection period $$\frac{\text{accounts receivable}}{\text{average daily sales}}$$	The average length of time required to receive payment

2. *Liquidity.* Liquidity measures are based on the simple notion that a business cannot operate if it is unable to pay its bills. A sufficient amount of cash and other short-term assets must be available when needed. On the other hand, because most short-term assets do not produce any return, a great amount of

liquidity damages profits. The goal is to keep liquidity as low as possible while ensuring that short-term obligations will be met. This means that industries competing in a stable and predictable environment generally require smaller current ratios than more volatile industries.

3. *Leverage.* Leverage ratios show how a company's operations are financed. Too much equity often means that management is not taking advantage of the leverage associated with long-term debt. Outside financing does, however, become more expensive as the debt-to-equity ratio increases. Therefore, managers have to consider leverage in light of the company's profitability and the volatility of the industry.

4. *Activity.* Activity ratios are used to measure the productivity and efficiency of a firm. Comparing the fixed-asset turnover ratio to the industry average, for example, shows how well the company is using its productive capacity. The inventory-turnover ratio indicates whether the company used too much inventory in generating sales and whether the company is carrying obsolete inventory.

Worksheet 8.1 is a complete financial ratio analysis for AMP. The evaluation of the different ratios can be summarized in a financial ratio profile, such as the one shown in Worksheet 8.2. AMP's position is indicated by the shaded areas.

FINANCIAL IMPLICATIONS OF THE PRODUCT LIFE CYCLE

As one traces the changes that take place in the life cycle of a typical product, it becomes obvious that there are significant impacts on the financial performance of a firm as well as on its competitive advantage. As can be seen in Figure 8.14, the expected revenue for any given product reaches a maximum at what is termed maturity and then declines until the product is totally obsolete. One of the major reasons why products become obsolete is the investments made in R&D that lead to new technology, which helps new products surpass mature products in performance, service, reliability, cost, and so on. A consequence of this technology's forcing out the old product is a decline in profit, despite the lower unit cost that results from the learning curve. Figure 8.14 shows that it is necessary to make continuous investment in new products in order to have a sustainable competitive advantage.

Another significant effect of the product life cycle is the change in strategy needed to sustain a competitive advantage. Depending on the firm's market position, the strategy needs to be continuously modified to meet competitive forces and market demands. Table 8.4 shows the changes required as the product moves through its life cycle. This table also shows when investment is required to improve the product's features and when funds are required because of reduced prices or a need to advertise or improve the product. Cash flow thus changes in each phase of the product life cycle.

WORKSHEET 8.1	Financial Ratio Analysis

Case   <u>AMP</u>
Date   <u>1990 Company Data</u>
Name   <u>John Doe</u>

1. Profitability

   a. Gross profit margin

   $$\frac{\text{sales} - \text{cost of goods sold}}{\text{sales}} = \frac{3,043 - 2,092}{3,043} = \underline{33.9\%}$$

   b. Net profit margin

   $$\frac{\text{profit after taxes}}{\text{sales}} = \frac{287}{3,043} = \underline{9.4\%}$$

   c. Return on assets

   $$\frac{\text{EBIT}}{\text{total assets}} = \frac{488}{2,929} = \underline{16.7\%}$$

   d. Return on equity

   $$\frac{\text{profits after taxes}}{\text{total equity}} = \frac{287}{1,793} = \underline{16.0\%}$$

2. Liquidity

   a. Current ratio

   $$\frac{\text{current assets}}{\text{current liabilities}} = \frac{1,618}{953} = \underline{1.70}$$

   b. Quick ratio

   $$\frac{\text{current assets} - \text{inventory}}{\text{current liabilities}} = \frac{1,618 - 482}{953} = \underline{1.19}$$

   c. Inventory to net working capital

   $$\frac{\text{inventory}}{\text{current assets} - \text{current liabilities}} = \frac{482}{1,618 - 953} = \underline{0.72}$$

(continued)

| WORKSHEET 8.1 | Financial Ratio Analysis (continued) |

3. Leverage

   a. Debt-to-assets ratio

   $$\frac{\text{total debt}}{\text{total assets}} = \frac{1,136}{2,929} = \underline{39\%}$$

   b. Debt-to-equity ratio

   $$\frac{\text{total debt}}{\text{total equity}} = \frac{1,136}{1,793} = \underline{63\%}$$

   c. Long-term debt-to-equity ratio

   $$\frac{\text{long-term debt}}{\text{total equity}} = \frac{69}{1,793} = \underline{3\%}$$

4. Activity

   a. Inventory turnover

   $$\frac{\text{sales}}{\text{inventory}} = \frac{3,043}{482} = \underline{5.5}$$

   b. Fixed-asset turnover

   $$\frac{\text{sales}}{\text{fixed assets}} = \frac{3,043}{1,122} = \underline{2.7}$$

   c. Average collection period

   $$\frac{\text{accounts receivable}}{\text{average daily sales}} = \frac{557}{3,043/365} = \underline{67 \text{ days}}$$

| WORKSHEET 8.2 | Financial Ratio Profile |

Case　　AMP
Date　　1990 Company Data
Name　　John Doe

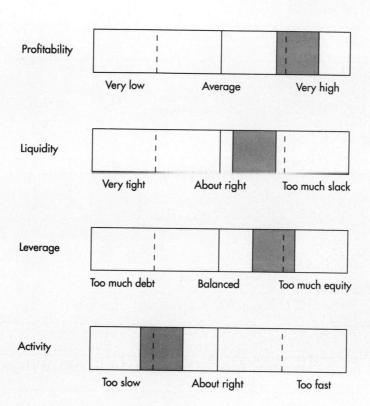

Profitability

Very low　　Average　　Very high

Liquidity

Very tight　　About right　　Too much slack

Leverage

Too much debt　　Balanced　　Too much equity

Activity

Too slow　　About right　　Too fast

Comments:

Excellent profitability, high liquidity. AMP applies a very conservative financial policy in financing the company. Very little debt is used. The activity ratios indicate potential for improvement, especially in the inventory turnover.

The product life also has a direct impact on financial ratios. As described in the previous section, financial ratios reflect a static perspective on the performance of a firm. But when we look at them from the point of view of the product life cycle, we obtain a dynamic perspective on the significance of the financial ratios. Table 8.5 shows how the financial ratios change with each of the four principal

---

FIGURE 8.14 | **Financial Implications of the Product Life Cycle**

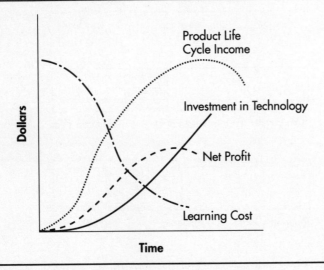

TABLE 8.4 | **Typical Product/Market Strategies Based on the Experience Curve and Product Life Cycle**

Market Share	Product Life Stage			
	Introduction	Growth	Maturity	Decline
High: market leader	Sacrifice current profits in order to gain market share as fast as possible	Reduce prices as costs come down to discourage new competitors	Hold market share by improving quality and increasing sales effort and advertising; utilize capacity fully	Maximize cash flow by reducing investment and advertising; allow market share to decline in order to maximize short-term profits
Low: market follower	Invest to increase market share	Concentrate on a market segment that can be dominated	Withdraw from the market or maintain share by keeping prices and costs below those of market leaders	Withdraw from the market

phases of the product life cycle. Table 8.6 is a summary of the general effects on financial ratios and how they should be interpreted.

As is apparent, industry norms are at best an average over the life cycle for a product or in some cases an SBU, where the business unit concentrates on a specific product line.

Another factor that affects financial ratios is the change that takes place in given industries. For example, Boise-Cascade experienced wide fluctuations in its ratios over a ten-year period, as shown in Table 8.7. The ratio of current assets to current liabilities had almost a threefold variation, from 3.4 to 1.3, during this period. Net profit over net worth was more stable, with a maximum variation of 6.2 to 12.6. Inventory over net working capital ranged from 71.3% to 137.0%, again almost a 2-to-1 variation. Like changes attributable to the product life cycle, financial ratios should be averaged over a number of years.

TABLE 8.5	Summary of Table 8.4 Strategies

Market Position	Introduction	Growth	Maturity	Decline
High	Sacrifice current profits	Reduce prices	Improve, quality, advertise	Maximize cash flow
Low	Invest	Concentrate on segment	Withdraw from market	Withdraw

TABLE 8.6	Relationship of Financial Ratios and Product Life Cycle

Phase	Introduction	Rapid Growth	Maturity	Decline
Impact on financial ratios	Ratios are lower than industry	Ratios are near or higher than industry	Ratios are higher than industry	Ratios are lower than industry

OTHER ANALYSES USING FINANCIAL RATIOS

As we have seen, much can be learned by examining how ratios change over time. Financial ratios can also be used to assess several other factors.

1. *The degree to which objectives are being accomplished.* For this purpose, any of the ratios discussed so far can be plotted against a projected or targeted rate of change in order to reveal the firm's ability to close performance gaps. Many companies aim for above-average performance, in which case, the company's ratios are compared to those of the industry leaders rather than to averages for the industry.

2. *The firm's vulnerability to decreases in revenue.* This assessment is particularly valuable as the company's products reach the maturity phase of the product life cycle. The *DuPont formula* (see Appendix D) is a method of using financial ratios to determine return on assets (ROA). Here, ratios for earnings as percent of sales (operating margin) and for asset turnover are particularly useful. Because ROA is equal to the product of these two ratios, profitability depends to a large measure on the firm's ability to maintain or improve these ratios over time.

TABLE 8.7	Changes Over 10 Years in 3 Financial Ratios at Boise-Cascade

Ratio	Year									
	1	2	3	4	5	6	7	8	9	10
Current assets / Current liabilities	3.4%	3.1	2.3	2.0	2.6	2.9	2.3	1.6	1.6	1.3
Net profit / Net worth	7.2%	6.2	9.7	11.4	9.0	10.3	8.8	10.7	12.6	9.8
Inventory to net working capital	71.3%	77.3	91.3	100.0	84.3	73.8	90.0	123.4	137.0	100.5

3. *The future borrowing power and growth potential of the firm.* The growth potential of a firm is based on its ROI, the average interest rate on total debt, and on its degree of financial leverage (debt-to-equity ratio). A significant change in one of these indicators suggests a change in the firm's growth pattern. By plotting these ratios over time, strategic managers can often see behind the "window dressing" that a firm may employ to make financial data for a specific period look good.

4. *The firm's ability to react to unforeseen changes in the environment.* Market-oriented ratios, such as the price/earnings (P/E) ratio or the market-to-book-value ratio, can reflect a firm's ability to deal with unforeseen changes. These ratios reflect investors' estimations of how well the company will be able to cope with such environmental changes as a turnaround of the economy, entry of a major new competitor into the market, or development of a new technology.

5. *The chances for company survival in the long run.* In 1968, Edward Altman developed a useful predictor of corporate bankruptcy for manufacturing companies. His predictor of corporate survival is the value of *factor Z*, which is based on a discriminant function with five significant ratios, X_1 through X_5.

$$Z = .012X_1 + .014X_2 + .033X_3 + .006X_4 + .999X_5$$

where

X_1 = Working capital/total assets (%). This ratio measures net liquid assets relative to total capitalization. Ordinarily, a firm experiencing consistent operating losses has shrinking current assets relative to total assets.

X_2 = Total retained earnings/total assets (%). This is a measure of cumulative profitability over time, so the age of a firm is implicitly considered in this ratio. In general, the incidence of failure is much higher among young firms.

X_3 = Earnings before interest and taxes (EBIT)/total assets (%). This ratio, which measures the productivity (or earning power) of the firm's assets, seems to be particularly useful for predicting corporate failure.

X_4 = Market value of equity/book value of total debt (%). This measure shows how much the firm's assets can decline in value before the liabilities exceed the assets and the firm becomes insolvent.

X_5 = Sales/total assets. The asset-turnover ratio measures management's ability to deal with competitive conditions.

In some cases, the Z-factor can be approximated with the simplified equation

$$Z \approx \frac{sales}{total\ assets}$$

Altman found that companies with a Z-factor higher than 2.99 have a minimum risk of corporate failure, whereas companies with a Z-factor less than 1.81 have a significant risk of bankruptcy. Companies with a Z-factor between 1.81 and 2.99 fall into a "zone of ignorance," where it is not possible to predict which way the company will go. A single Z-factor in this zone may not be cause for immediate concern, but Z-factors in this zone over several periods indicate financial and competitive difficulties that could become quite serious. As with other ratios, the Z-factor must be related to companies in a given industry and at a given phase of their organizational life cycle. In the case of AMP, the Z-factor is above 6 which indicates that AMP is in a good financial situation.

STRATEGIC FUNDS PROGRAMMING

Attempting to introduce a new strategy is like trying to rebuild a ship at sea. The current business must be kept operating properly so that it generates enough funds to carry out the new strategic programs. A common error in strategic planning is for managers to become so enamored of the possibilities and opportunities of a new strategy that they fail to provide enough support for the current business.

Strategic funds programming helps managers to avoid this pitfall by identifying the funds required to meet the new conditions. Strategic funds programming is a budget and control system that provides managers with the decision-making information they need to implement strategy. It is designed to balance the financial requirements of maintaining current business with the financial needs of launching a new strategy.

FLOW-OF-FUNDS ANALYSIS

A first step in strategic funds programming is to identify how a company uses its financial resources. Table 8.8 shows how AMP managed its flow of funds during the fiscal year 1989–1990. By examining these numbers, managers can identify additional sources of funds that can be obtained by renegotiating long-term debt and can see where adjustments might be made to free funds for strategic use. As Table 8.8 shows, AMP increased its allocation of funds to inventory and accounts receivable.

Funds can be obtained either by selling off a company's assets or by increasing its liabilities or owners' equity. The funds so obtained are used to increase other assets of the company or to reduce liabilities or equity. If a company pays off some of its long-term debt, for example, its cash position diminishes, thereby keeping the flow of funds in balance.

GENERATING STRATEGIC FUNDS

Organizations can generate new funds from three sources, which constitute the company's resources for strategic growth.

1. Regular operations and other internal sources (examples include profits after taxes, depreciation, and distress sales or auctions to dispose of excess inventory or unused buildings)
2. Expansion of debt consistent with the financial structure of the organization (having banks or suppliers provide extended lines of credit, factoring accounts receivable, leasing rather than buying equipment)
3. The addition of new long-term debt or equity funds through changes in the financial structure of the firm (issuing new stock, negotiating additional long-term loans)

TABLE 8.8	**Flow-funds Analysis for AMP** (Dollar amounts in millions)

Category	1989–1990	Amount
Sources of Funds (Inflow)		
Cash	460 – 334 =	126
Accounts receivable	557 – 520 =	37
Inventories	482 – 495 =	–13
Fixed assets	1,122 – 954 =	168
Other investments and receivables		81
Total		399
Uses of Funds (Outflow)		
Accounts payable	245 – 225 =	20
Short-term loans	708 – 501 =	207
Long-term debt	183 – 179 =	4
Common stock and retained earnings	1,793 – 1,625 =	168
Total		399

SUSTAINABLE RATE OF GROWTH

A company's sustainable growth rate is limited by (1) the rate at which it can generate the funds necessary to achieve its growth target and (2) the return it can expect to earn on these funds. The critical variable in generating strategic funds is the growth in shareholders' equity. Shareholders' equity generates internal sources of funds in the form of retained earnings, and it also serves as collateral for raising new debt. In other words, a firm's growth potential is directly linked to its return on equity (ROE).

Sustainable growth rate is computed as follows:

Sustainable growth rate =

$[D/E \times (ROA - i) + ROA] \times k$

or = f (return on equity $\times k$)

where

D/E = total debt-to-equity ratio

ROA = return on assets

i = average interest rate on total debt

k = retention rate = 1 – dividend payout rate

In a strategic context, therefore, leverage, dividend policy, and equity funds exhibit an important interrelationship. By using ROE as a standard performance target, a firm can often improve performance and growth through a careful reevaluation of its different businesses. As long as ROA exceeds the average interest rate on total debt, a firm can achieve a higher growth rate by increasing its financial leverage. This is accomplished without changing the firm's characteristic rate of return on assets. In fact, a firm could accept lower returns on investment than its competitors and still grow at a more rapid rate by assuming a significant amount of debt. This tactic does, however, change the risk characteristics of the business, because creditors normally demand a higher interest rate as the debt-to-equity ratio increases. There is a limit to how much a company can increase its growth rate by taking on more debt.

Dividend policy is another variable that has a critical influence on the growth of a firm. There is a direct tradeoff between current and future dividends, because higher retention rates (or lower payout rates) support higher growth rates. Also, in the majority of cases, it is substantially cheaper to finance growth by reducing the dividend payout than by issuing new stock.

AMP in 1990 has a sustainable growth rate of 9.5%.

$$[0.63 \times (16.7\% - 13\%) + 16.7\%] \times 0.50 = 9.5\%$$

In order to grow faster than that—for example, at the rate of 15% that it hopes to achieve—AMP will have to assume more debt, raise its profitability further, gain lower-cost financing, or retain a larger portion of earnings.

ALLOCATION OF STRATEGIC FUNDS

The funds a firm generates are used to

- Support the organization's current business and its ongoing operation. These are called *baseline funds*.
- Invest in the new programs required to meet the organization's strategic objectives and goals. These are called *strategic funds*.

Baseline funds are used to pay current operating expenses, maintain adequate working capital, or maintain current plant and equipment. Depending on product/market dynamics, baseline funds are used to maintain a specified level of production, market share, or growth rate.

Strategic funds are allocated to purchase such new tangible assets as facilities, equipment, and inventory; to increase working capital; and to fund direct expenses for research and development, marketing, advertising, and promotions. They are also used for mergers and acquisitions if these growth alternatives are the most attractive ones for the firm.

Strategic funds programming is conducted in eight basic steps, through which managers seek to

1. Identify the strategic business units (SBUs).
2. Formulate goals and objectives for each SBU.
3. Determine the amount of strategic funds available:
   Strategic funds = total funds available – baseline funds

4. Formulate a strategic program to meet the goals and objectives of each SBU.
5. Estimate the funds needed for each strategic program.
6. Rank the programs according to their contribution to the strategy, taking into account the amounts of strategic funds used and the level of risk involved.
7. Allocate the available strategic funds to each program in order of program priority. Key decision points concerning risk and return are reached when the funds available from internal operating sources are exhausted and when readily available credit sources are used up. Managers evaluate the proposed strategy in terms of the change in financial structure it requires.
8. Establish a management planning and control system to monitor the generation and application of funds and to ensure that the desired results are achieved.

Worksheet 8.3 is an illustration of strategic funds programming for AMP. AMP will require significant investments in fixed assets (about $300 million a year) and in market development (about $100 million a year) if it wants to grow at the projected 15%. Baseline funds are therefore estimated at $400 million.

The calculation of total funds available from internal sources is reasonably straightforward. When calculating the augmented debt, managers should keep in mind that they need to estimate how much additional debt capacity can be obtained in the next period. Using the current total debt-to-equity ratio as a multiplier, they obtain a first estimate (but not necessarily the best estimate) of additional leverage to be gained from retained earnings. AMP's debt-to-equity ratio, for example, is very high, and it is likely that a more conservative estimate for augmented debt will be below $439,000. The newly negotiated long-term debt-to-equity ratio is an estimate of the firm's additional future leverage from long-term debt. This estimate of $536,000 may be viewed as a "ceiling" on additional long-term debt from which management can "borrow" when necessary.

The worksheet shows a sample calculation of the total funds available to AMP under different financing options, and it also shows a strategic funds analysis of the three identical options.

It is important to point out that strategic funds programming only identifies *feasible options* under different financial assumptions. The strategic manager should also make a capital assessment (discussed later in this chapter) before choosing the final strategic option.

FINANCIAL PLANNING MODELS

Executives increasingly are looking for planning tools that enable them to project financial statements, test key assumptions on which a plan is based, explore the impact of possible changes or disruptions in the plan, and factor in the risk or uncertainty associated with different projections. To meet these needs, managers usually turn to commercially available software packages. The first step in using a computer spreadsheet or similar software package is to create a financial planning model that reflects the financial structure of the company. This section will

WORKSHEET 8.3	Strategic Funds Programming

Case __AMP (in $ millions)__
Date __1992__
Name __Mary Doe__

Internal Sources

Profit after taxes   287

   Less dividends   145

Retained earnings   142

   Plus depreciation   207

     Other non-cash expenses   000

Cash flow from operations | 349 |

Augmented debt

Retained earnings   142

   Times current <u>total</u> debt-to-equity ratio
   = augmented debt   0.63 | 90 |

Funds from within current structure   439

Expanded debt capacity

Newly negotiated <u>long-term</u> debt/equity ratio   0.10

   Minus current long-term debt/equity ratio   0.03

Equals unused debt factor   0.07

Times shareholders equity = expanded   1,763 | 126 |
  debt capacity

Total funds available (maximum)   565

(continued)

WORKSHEET 8.3	Strategic Funds Programming (continued)

Analysis of funds use	Source of funds (in $ thousands)		
	Internal sources	Internal plus augmented	Internal, augmented, and expanded
Total funds available	349	439	565
Baseline requirements	400	400	400
Strategic funds	−51	39	165
Option A			
Option B			
Option C			

Comments:

AMP cannot finance its future growth from operational cash flow alone. That debt will have to be increased. Should AMP consider any additional strategic moves, such as an acquisition, the financing with debt would have to be increased substantially.

describe such a model, based on projections of AMP's income statements, cash-flow statements, and balance sheets.

BASELINE PROJECTIONS

What will happen to AMP's profitability and growth if sales trends are as forecast and everything else remains the same? To answer this question, AMP's managers start with a set of plausible assumptions about significant relationships in a spreadsheet, such as the one in Table 8.9. As a starting point, they use a sales forecast as the driving force and project the remaining numbers by linking them to this sales forecast by means of a set of constant financial ratios. After this baseline projection has been completed, it can serve as the vehicle for developing alternative financial scenarios.

AMP used the following step-by-step approach to develop a baseline projection. In Table 8.9, the entries A1, B1, and so on identify individual cells in the spreadsheet. AMP's managers begin by calculating the expected sales revenues for 1991 and 1992. Sales growth is forecast to be 3,043 times A1 for 1991 and times B1 for 1992.

TABLE 8.9 | **Baseline Projections: Pro-forma Financial Statements for AMP**
(Dollar amounts in millions)

| | Pro-Forma Income Statements | | |
| | Actual | Projected | |
	1990	1991	1992
Sales revenue	3,043	A1	B1
Cost of goods sold	2,012	A2	B2
Gross profit	1,013	A3	B3
Selling, general and administrative	543	A4	B4
EBIT	488	A5	B5
Interest expenses	26	A6	B6
Taxable income	462	A7	B7
Taxes	175	A8	B8
Net income	287	A9	B9
Dividends	145	A10	B10
Retained earnings	142	A11	B11

(continued)

| | | Pro-Forma Balance Sheets | |
| | Actual | Projected | |
	1990	1991	1992
Assets			
Cash	460	A12	B12
Accounts receivable	557	A13	B13
Inventories	482	A14	B14
Other current assets	119	A15	B15
Total current assets	1,618	A16	B16
Property, plant and equipment	2,303	A17	B17
Less accumulated depreciation	1,181	A18	B18
Equals net property, plant, and equipment	1,122	A19	B19
Investment	189	A20	B20
Short-term debt	379		
Accounts payable	254		
Other short-term liabilities	329		
Total assets	2,929	A21	B21
Total current liabilities	953	A22	B22
Long-term debt and deferred liabilities	183	A23	B23
Liabilities			
Beginning equity	1,651	A24	B24
+ Retained earnings	142	A25	B25
= Ending equity	1,793	A26	B26
Total liabilities	2,929	A27	B27

TABLE 8.9 — Baseline Projections: Pro-forma Financial Statements for AMP (continued) (Dollar amounts in thousands)

WHAT-IF ANALYSIS

Though baseline projections merely extrapolate current trends, they are quite valuable when it comes to building a financial planning model. The next step is to use this model to ask "what-if" questions in order to test the plausibility of the different assumptions underlying the model and to determine their impact on the firm's financial performance. The what-if analysis is carried out as follows.

1. *Review the assumptions that were used to arrive at the baseline projections.* If some of the figures appear to be unreasonable or implausible, make adjustments

to the projections or define a different relationship. This is very important, because all of the numbers in the spreadsheet are interdependent. Consequently, an error in projecting one particular item can easily cause errors in many other numbers.

2. *Incorporate any additional information or forecasts to ensure the relative accuracy of projections.* For example, because of economies of scale, some of the fixed costs and sales revenues may not be related in a strictly linear fashion. On the other hand, some of the expense items may grow faster than the company's sales revenues because of general inflation or growing complexity.

3. *Enter all of the strategic decisions that have already been approved for the planning period.* Although this particular step may appear to be out of sequence, it reflects the fact that many strategic decisions are made without an assessment of their financial impact.

4. *Propose any changes that can improve profitability or lead to a sounder financial structure.* The baseline projection for AMP suggests several improvements. EBIT is expected to decline in 1990, despite an increase in gross profit. Therefore, AMP should make every effort to check increases in operating expenses, particularly administrative expenses. Also, by reducing its inventories and accounts receivable, the company would reduce interest expenses, generate much-needed cash flow, and reduce the debt burden.

5. *Simulate different financial scenarios to test the sensitivity of results to changes in different variables.* One could ask, for example, "What would happen to AMP's financial position if sales unexpectedly grew by only 5%, or even less?" or "What if AMP cuts its R&D budget to improve short-run profitability?" or "How would a 1% rise in interest rates affect AMP's profitability?" or "How would a change in the depreciation method affect cash flows and profits?" These what-if scenarios can help managers to detect and reduce areas of potential vulnerability.

6. *Evaluate strategic alternatives.* Finally, and perhaps most important, different strategic proposals are evaluated. For example, AMP may want to consider different financing options for each of its three strategic alternatives in order to maximize the company's net worth at an acceptable level of risk. For this purpose, the basic model would have to be expanded to incorporate additional variables and relationships, such as might be seen in a discounted cash-flow analysis.

ASSESSING CAPITAL RISK

Assuming too much debt can place a company in jeopardy. The Cloud Tool Company used a worst-case scenario to address the potential risk of a $15 million investment for expansion of capacity. One year after the investment was made, the bottom fell out of the oil business and Cloud Tool was facing bankruptcy. Only then did management realize that what it thought was a worst-case scenario was, in fact, too optimistic (Arnold, 1986). How can managers who are constantly faced with such situations avoid the dire consequences of a miscalculation? To avoid the potential for disaster, they must

1. Define the company's staying power in a hostile environment.
2. Estimate the possible market erosion and the dollar consequences.

3. Project the future cash flow needed for working capital.
4. Determine what options are available if they are needed, such as cost cutting.
5. Determine future source of funds if they are needed. Unfortunately, many estimates tend to be based on assumptions rather than verifiable data. Or they may simply be expressions of opinion, which may or may not reflect the reality of a situation.

An example of how to forecast the potential impact of alternative scenarios is shown in Table 8.10. Factor forecasts provide a base-line projection for key economic indicators. This can be used for the pro-forma projections shown in Table 8.11.

The financial models generally are *deterministic;* that is, the manager can specify a single estimate for each of the input variables. Yet many estimates are based on assumptions made with a great deal of uncertainty. As Hertz (1964) pointed out, behind any precise calculation are data that are not precise. Together, these uncertainties can result in considerable uncertainty.

An assessment of risk can be carried out using the approach shown in Tables 8.10 and 8.11. Each factor that is relevant to an investment can be examined on a risk basis of pessimistic (risky), most likely (average risk) and optimistic (least risky). The strategic manager can examine the results to determine whether or not to proceed.

RISK ANALYSIS

To deal with the risk inherent in strategy, a manager can perform a *risk analysis,* which consists of the following steps:

1. *Identify the key variables that have an impact on the decision.* For instance, in the AMP case, the important variables for determining what strategy the company should follow include
   a. Market growth rate
   b. Company's market share
   c. Investment required
   d. Cost of production
   e. Selling price of product
   f. Useful life of technology
2. *Assign a subjective probability distribution to each variable.* A subjective probability distribution can be estimated, first by determining the range of values that can occur. In Figure 8.15, for example, the range for market growth is −10 to +20%, and the range for the useful life of strategic option A is 2–16 years. Next, the frequency for a reasonable number of intermediate values is estimated. These values are now plotted and a smooth curve drawn through the points to obtain a frequency distribution.
3. *Identify what criterion will be used to determine whether the strategy in question is successful.* The criterion might focus on the financial aspects of the strategy, such as whether the strategy increased the return on investment. Another criterion might be whether the strategy contributed to sustainable growth. Each of these criteria becomes the goal or objective that is related to achieving success for a given strategy.

TABLE 8.10　Factor Forecasts

Factor	Current	1991 PE	1991 ML	1991 OPT	1992 PE	1992 ML	1992 OPT	1993 PE	1993 ML	1993 OPT	1994 PE	1994 ML	1994 OPT	1995 PE	1995 ML	1995 OPT
Consumer confidence (growth factor)	0.05	-0.02	0.05	0.08	-0.05	0.07	0.1	-0.07	0.08	0.12	-0.1	0.09	0.14	-0.12	0.1	0.16
Gross National Product (GNP factor)	4.1 TR. -0.03															
Tax level Internal Revenue Service (IRS)	0.34	0.36	0.34	0.34	0.37	0.34	0.33	0.38	0.34	0.32	0.39	0.34	0.37	0.40	0.34	0.30
Interest rate (debt factor)	0.09															
Banking (debt available)																
Oil prices (transportation factor)																
Inflation																
Unemployment (unemployment factor)	0.07															
Economic forecast (combination-growth factor)	0.02															
Market forecast (market growth potential)	0.03															
Productivity (cost of goods sold factor)																
Capital spending (equipment profit factor)																
Durable goods orders (capacity growth)																
Materials prices (raw-materials factor)																

PE = Pessimistic　ML = Most likely　OPT = Optimistic

TABLE 8.11   **Pro-forma Projections**

Factor	Current*	1991 PE	1991 ML	1991 OPT	1992 PE	1992 ML	1992 OPT	1993 PE	1993 ML	1993 OPT	1994 PE	1994 ML	1994 OPT	1995 PE	1995 ML	1995 OPT
Sales/revenue	$100	98	105	108	93	112	119	86	121	133	77	132	152	68	145	176
Cost of goods sold																
Materials	10															
Subcontractors	5															
Freight	2															
Direct labor	12															
Manufacturing overhead	3															
Total	32															
Gross profit	68															
Expenses																
Marketing/selling																
Advertising	5															
Commissions	2															
Promotion/co-op	1															
Other	0															
Total marketing	8															
Administrative expense																
Rent/lease/mortgage	5															
Salaries	7															
Heat/light	1															
Telephone	1															
Office Supplies	1															
Depreciation	2															
Total administrative	17															
Total expense	25															
Operating income	43															
Other charges																
Interest	2															
Sale of assets	0															
Misc.	0															
Total other	2															
Before tax income	41															
Income tax	14															
Loss carry-over	–1															
Investment credit	–1															
Net income	29															
Dividends	2															
Retained/reinvestment	27															

*Dollars × 10,000.

PE = Pessimistic   ML = Most likely   OPT = Optimistic

FIGURE 8.15	**Risk Analysis: Examples of Subjective Probability Distribution for Two Key Decision Variables, Rate of Market Growth and Useful Life of AMP's Strategic Option A**

(Relative frequency stands for the probability with which an event occurs)

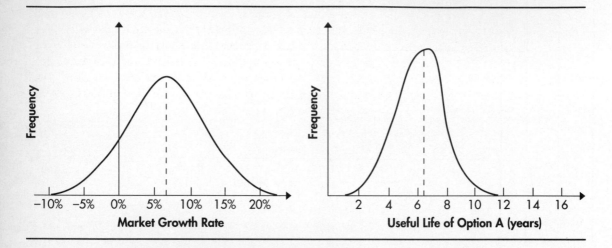

4. *Use a random sampling procedure as the basis for computing whether the criterion for success has been achieved.* To prepare for a random sample, one can use a table of random numbers or a computer program that generates random numbers. The random number is used to select a value from each frequency distribution.

Random sampling is a fairly straightforward statistical procedure that allows the manager to sample from any distribution of values without introducing bias. The steps involved in generating a random number and then using it to select a value from a frequency distribution are described in most books on statistical methods.

Applying the random sampling procedure to AMP, the manager can examine how ROI can be used as a criterion for evaluating which strategic option is most likely to be successful. Using this approach, AMP's management can evaluate the effect of alternative strategic options and see how the financial variables are related. Sounder judgments are possible when random sampling procedures are used to determine which goals are most likely to be achieved.

MULTIATTRIBUTE DECISION MAKING

All strategic decisions are subject to uncertainty and risk. In addition, there inevitably are conflicting values. Thus it is important that strategic managers consider all the factors, or attributes, inherent in each strategic alternative under consideration.

An *attribute* is a characteristic, quality, or desirable aspect of a given situation. It must be measurable in order for managers to determine the relative value or worth of the attribute for each alternative strategy. A criterion is the basis used to choose that combination of attributes, goals, or objectives that is judged relevant to reaching a decision. For example, growth is a criterion that could be used to determine which attributes would best achieve the desired objective. A multiattribute approach to decision making simultaneously considers each of the factors that is likely to sway a decision.

Multiattribute decision making uses a weighting scheme to establish the relative importance or impact of each attribute of a strategy. The weighting scheme enables managers to compute a single, combined score for each strategy. The computation helps to increase the decision makers' confidence in whichever solution or alternative is chosen.

To understand multiattribute decision making, it is helpful to consider single-attribute decision making first. Suppose a building contractor in Southern California wishes to expand his operations. The contractor is considering four possible alternative strategies for growth:

A1. Expand the level and type of advertising.
A2. Hire additional personnel to increase sales.
A3. Subcontract to expand the sales base.
A4. Enter a new market to expand the sales base.

Having stated some strategic alternatives, the contractor needs criteria by which to evaluate them. Suppose he chooses to judge each alternative on the basis of a single criterion, profitability, and that he decides to judge profitability on the basis of a single measurable attribute, growth of net profits. The next task is to rate the profitability of each alternative. Table 8.12 shows how he rated profitability on a scale of 1 to 10. Table 8.13 shows how the contractor rated each alternative. A rating of 7 indicates the contractor's opinion that entering a new market might be

TABLE 8.12 | **Profitability Rating: Single-attribute Decision Making**

Level of Profitability	Rating
Marginal	1–2
Below average	3–4
Average	5–6
Above average	7–8
Outstanding	9–10

TABLE 8.13 | **Profitability Ratings of Four Strategic Alternatives**

Alternative	Rating
A1 Expand advertising	5
A2 Hire sales personnel	6
A3 Subcontract	6
A4 Enter new markets	7

the most profitable alternative. Should he choose this alternative? Not necessarily: profitability is not the only important consideration. A more extensive list of criteria is shown in Table 8.14.

At this point, the contractor begins to apply the multiattribute approach. To do this, he must decide which criteria are most important to his strategic goal of expanding his business.

Table 8.15 shows how he rated each criterion on a scale of 1 (least important) to 10 (most important). In employing this scheme, the contractor defined *importance* as his best judgment of the chance of success and relative value in contributing to meeting his personal objectives.

Having assigned values to the criteria, the contractor realized that they would be different for each alternative. Profitability's relative value of 6, for example, would not be appropriate for each alternative. Table 8.16 shows how he felt profitability (C1) would change from alternative to alternative.

Why should the contractor change the relative value of each criterion for each alternative? Why would he give profitability (C1) a value of 5 for the advertising alternative (A1) and a value of 7 for the new-markets alternative (A4)? These ratings reflect the contractor's belief that the profit potential changes with each alternative (see Table 8.16).

Using similar reasoning, the contractor assigned cost (C2) a value of 10 for the advertising alternative (A1). Even though the overall relative value for cost is 8 (Table 8.15) he felt that the advertising strategy would have a better cost/benefit payoff than the personnel strategy (A2), so he assigned (A2) a value of only 4.

Table 8.17 is a decision matrix that shows values for each criterion depending on which alternative is being considered. Once all the values are entered in the matrix, the contractor averages the values for each alternative (see the far-right column of Table 8.17).

TABLE 8.14	Multiple Criteria and Attributes

Criterion (C)	Attribute (Basis for Measurement)
C1 Profitability	Net profit (dollars)
C2 Cost	Cost/benefit ratio
C3 Control	Ability to meet requirements
C4 Adaptability	Speed of response to change
C5 Work load	Amount of time spent in executive activities
C6 Organization	Information flow and control
C7 Market potential	Revenue from sales

TABLE 8.15 | Judged Importance (Value) of Each Criterion

Values Assigned by the Contractor

Criterion	Values
C1 Profitability	6
C2 Cost	8
C3 Control	5
C4 Adaptability	6
C5 Work load	6
C6 Organization	5
C7 Market potential	7

Weighting Scheme Used to Assign Values

Ranking	Value Range
Very important	9–10
Important	7–8
Moderately important	4–6
Unimportant	1–3

TABLE 8.16 | Values for the Profitability Criterion by Strategic Alternative

Alternative	Profitability Value
A1 Expand advertising	5
A2 Hire sales personnel	6
A3 Subcontract	6
A4 Enter new markets	7

The averages shown in Table 8.17 do not differ significantly. It is dangerous to choose the alternative with the highest average (in this case A3), because averages do not consider intangible factors, such as risk propensity, prior experience, and personal values. What the contractor needs, therefore, is to apply the 10-point weighting scheme that accounts for the judged importance of each criterion (Table 8.15). Next, the contractor takes the values shown in Table 8.15 and multiplies them by the values for each alternative strategy (Table 8.17) to obtain a weighted

TABLE 8.17	Decision Matrix 1: Values for Each Criterion by Strategic Alternative

	Criteria							
Alternative	C1	C2	C3	C4	C5	C6	C7	Average
A1	5	10	8	4	4	9	3	6.1
A2	6	4	4	6	8	4	8	5.7
A3	6	6	5	6	9	5	7	6.3
A4	7	6	4	7	3	5	9	5.8

value for each alternative. This is shown in Worksheet 8.4 where he obtained a total for each alternative by adding its seven weighted scores. Alternative 3(A3)—subcontract to expand the sales base—has the highest weighted total. But the contractor chooses alternative 1 (A1), to expand advertising. Why? A1's weighted total is almost as high as that of A3; therefore, it is legitimate to choose either one if other considerations are important. The subjective aspects of choice and uncertainties associated with criteria or goals can influence decisions, as can interdependence among the criteria. Profitability and market potential may, for example, be interdependent. Rather than incorporating all such considerations in the formal method, it is preferable to start with a few simplifying assumptions that can be removed, one by one, after the weighted scores are obtained (see Worksheet 8.4). Ultimately, the choice of an alternative depends on the objective results of multiattribute decision making and subjective factors, which often have to do with acceptance of the choice.

The multiattribute approach can be summarized as follows.

1. Specify the strategic goal (such as to expand the business).
2. State the available strategic alternatives.
3. Identify criteria to be used in evaluating the degree to which the strategic goal is achieved.
4. Determine how each criterion will be measured on the basis of attributes.
5. Rank the criteria to establish their overall value or importance.
6. Establish the value of each criterion with respect to each alternative.
7. Examine the sensitivity of each alternative to changes in each criterion's value.
8. Determine the weighted score of each alternative with respect to each criterion. This yields relative importance.
9. Compute the weighted total score for each alternative.
10. Rank the alternatives according to their weighted totals.
11. Choose an alternative, taking into account the objective and subjective benefits of each.

WORKSHEET 8.4 | **Multiattribute Decision Making**

Case   <u>Contractor Example</u>
Date   <u>1989</u>
Name   <u>Southern California Building Contractor</u>

Decision Matrix

Alternative	C1 (6)	C2 (8)	C3 (5)	C4 (6)	C5 (6)	C6 (5)	C7 (7)	Other ( )	Weighted Total
A1	×5 = 30	×10 = 80	×8 = 40	×4 = 24	×4 = 24	×9 = 45	×3 = 21		264
A2	×6 = 36	×4 = 32	×4 = 20	×6 = 36	×8 = 48	×4 = 20	×8 = 56		248
A3	×6 = 36	×6 = 48	×5 = 25	×6 = 36	×9 = 54	×5 = 25	×7 = 49		273
A4	×7 = 42	×6 = 48	×4 = 20	×7 = 42	×3 = 18	×5 = 25	×9 = 63		258
Other									

(Criterion / Weight headers span columns C1–C7; "Other" is its own column.)

Justification of the alternative chosen:

The contractor feels that he has limited time available to manage the business. He is also reluctant to risk the money required either to expand his staff or to advertise to increase sales. He feels that earnings, ease of operation, and low risk justify adopting alternative A1, which will change the way the business is being run because he would have less direct marketing effort. If he selected A3, subcontract, this would require additional involvement on the contractor's part, which he did not want.

An example of how the ABC Entertainment Company used multiattribute decision making appears in Table 8.18, which shows how it rated the benefit that could accrue from an attribute. Criteria C1 through C11 are listed in the first column. The next column identifies the criteria and gives the attributes used for measurement. For example, criterion C1, profitability, is measured in terms of the attribute internal rate of return (IRR), or the net profit for the project. The weights for benefits and importance are shown in the next two columns. The alternatives are shown along the top of the figure, and the computed values are shown for each criterion and each alternative. When the computed values are added for each alternative, Primetime TV (with a value of 85) emerges as best, and Video Rentals (with a value of 78) is second best. Through weighting, the results clearly reflect the preference and judgment of the strategic manager who must choose one of the alternatives to pursue.

THE STRATEGIC BUDGET

Budget preparation is usually the final step in strategic planning. Money and other resources must be allocated to translate a strategic plan into programs of action. A budget is the principal place where current decisions are made in accordance with longer-range plans. Therefore, operating plans and capital investment plans are the financial base of the strategic plan.

Although preparing a strategic budget is generally the last stage of resource allocation, it can be made an integral part of long-range financial planning. For example, financial information (such as an income forecast) depends on strategic decisions and

---

TABLE 8.18 | **Multiattribute Decision Making for the ABC Entertainment Co.**

Benefit-of-Attribute Rating		Weighting for Criteria		Alternatives
	0		0	A1 Primetime TV
Marginal	1	Unimportant	1	A2 Commuter Talk Radio
	2		2	A3 Movie Channel
Below Average	3	Low Importance	3	A4 Video Rentals
	4		4	
Average	5	Moderately Important	5	
	6		6	
Above Average	7	Important	7	
	8		8	
Outstanding	9	Very Important	9	
	10		10	

(continued)

TABLE 8.18   Multiattribute Decision Making for the ABC Entertainment Co. (continued)

Criterion	Attribute Basis for Measurement	Benefit ×	Importance	A1	Importance	A2	Importance	A3	Importance	A4
C1	Profitability (IRR, or net profit on the project)	7	7	49	4	28	1	7	6	42
C2	Low cost/investment (resource requirement)	1	5	5	8	8	3	3	5	5
C3	Capability/control (ability to carry out)	1	8	8	3	3	2	2	5	5
C4	Contingency demands (speed of response)	1	3	3	5	5	7	7	3	3
C5	Management demands (executive time needs)	1	3	3	7	7	3	3	2	2
C6	Organizational demands (information flow and control)	1	5	5	2	2	3	3	8	8
C7	Growth potential (market potential)	1	7	7	3	3	5	5	3	3
C8	Product life cycle (long-lived)	1	2	2	5	5	8	8	3	3
C9	Risk level (favorable risk)	1	3	3	3	3	5	5	7	7
C10	Ease of exit (if worst case)	0	0	0	0	0	0	0	0	0
C11	Other	0	0	0	0	0	0	0	0	0
				85		**64**		**43**		**78**
				Primetime TV		Commuter Talk Radio		Movie Channel		Video Rentals

assumptions, including pricing policy, product life cycle, and so on. The following outline summarizes some of the strategic factors that affect the budget process.

1. Income estimate using sales forecast
   a. Basis for the forecast
   b. Market dynamics (impact on sales)
2. Depreciation
   a. Adequacy of reserves for capital replacement
   b. Length of time for depreciation
   c. Technological forecast and obsolescence of investments
3. Research and development expenditures
   a. Requirements to meet competition or technological changes
   b. New products or product mix required
   c. Relation to profitability (PIMS approach)
4. Acquisitions and mergers
   a. Impact on cash flow or growth
   b. Ability to obtain funds
   c. Consolidated financial statements
5. Employee benefits
   a. Incentives, bonuses, training
   b. Management development programs and career planning
6. Production requirements
   a. Inventory: amount, variety, safety stock, vendors
   b. Delivery and production cycles
   c. Required capacity
7. Pricing policy
   a. Tradeoff between quality and cost
   b. Experience curve effect
8. Marketing requirements
   a. Product-life-cycle effects
   b. Advertising cost and effectiveness
   c. Funds for market research
9. Cost
   a. Basis for estimating (history or formulas)
   b. Standards and variances to be used in budget
10. Profit desired
    a. Basis for allocating general, administrative, and overhead expenses
    b. Use of profit centers
    c. Joint profits

Each of the factors listed requires analysis of financial data relevant to the firm. The budget for strategy implementation is based on decisions about the source, use, and allocation of funds.

SUMMARY

Traditionally, financial analysis has focused on an historic explanation of facts. Financial ratio analysis compares a company to its competition with respect to profitability, liquidity, leverage, and activity for the *preceding* period(s); the DuPont formula uses past data to show how the firm has managed its assets; and the flow-of-funds analysis shows the past use of discretionary funds. Though all these techniques are widely used in industry, they were not designed for strategic planning. Nonetheless, they provide valuable data that can be used in formulating alternative strategies for the future.

Financial ratio analysis provides the strategic manger with a direct analysis of the company's financial well-being. It is a widely used approach in industry and provides an easy way of comparing one company with another.

Strategic funds programming is a future-oriented financial planning approach. It helps strategic managers to identify potential sources of discretionary funds and to plan their allocation on the basis of the concept of sustainable rate of growth.

Competitive-cost analysis can be a very useful tool in defining the right strategy and focus for a company. Competitive-cost analysis identifies the strategic cost-driving factors and de-averages costs prepared for the company's accounting system. Once strategic managers understand the firm's own costs in detail, they can model competitors' costs through microeconomic analysis of the cost structure. Managers who model competitors' costs gain an understanding of each competitor's situation in great detail, which helps them to anticipate their competitors' strategic moves.

Computerized financial planning systems have revolutionized the financial aspects of strategic planning and implementation. The use of financial planning programs can help managers to avoid major mistakes and enables them to create and edit their own financial models, generate reports, test the assumptions on which a plan is based, examine alternative goals, and perform a risk analysis for each of the alternatives.

The strategic budget is the final output of a financial analysis. It reflects the decisions made regarding allocation of funds and which strategies can be pursued.

REFERENCES AND SUGGESTIONS FOR FURTHER READING

A matter of opinion. 1992. *The Economist,* April 4, p. 106.

Altman, Edward J. 1968. Financial ratios, discriminant analysis and the prediction of corporate bankruptcy. *Journal of Finance* 23, no. 4.

Ansberry, Clare. 1991. Utah's Geneva Steel, once called hopeless, is racking up profits. *The Wall Street Journal,* November 10, pp. A-1 and A-5.

Arnold, Jasper. 1986. Assessing capital risk: You can't be too conservative. *Harvard Business Review,* September–October, pp. 113–120.

Bettis, Richard, Stephen Bradley, and Gary Hamel. 1992. Outsourcing and industrial decline. *Academy of Management Executive* 6, no. 1, pp. 7–22.

Boston Consulting Group. 1974. *Segmentation and strategy.* BCG Perspective No. 156. Boston, Mass.

Boulden, James B. 1976. *Computer-assisted planning systems.* New York: McGraw-Hill.

Chen, Kung H. and Thomas A. Shimerda. 1980. An empirical analysis of useful financial ratios. *Financial Management* 10 (Spring), pp. 51–60.

Cooper, Robin. 1989. You need a new cost system when.... *Harvard Business Review,* January–February, pp. 77–82.

Cooper, Robin and Robert Kaplan. 1991. Profit priorities from activity-based costing. *Harvard Business Review,* May–June, pp. 130–135.

Cooper, Robin and Robert Kaplan. 1988. Measure costs right: Make the right decisions. *Harvard Business Review,* September–October, pp. 96–103.

Day, George and Liam Fahey. 1990. Putting strategy into shareholder value analysis. *Harvard Business Review,* March–April, pp. 156–162.

Donaldson, Gordon. 1985. Financial goals and strategic consequences. *Harvard Business Review,* May–June, pp. 57–66.

Dun & Bradstreet. 1981. *Key Business Ratios.* New York.

Flanigan, James. 1984. The formula that makes a business succeed: Invest, invest, and reinvest. *Los Angeles Times,* February 1.

Hamilton, William F. and Michael A. Moses. 1974. A computer-based corporate planning system. *Management Science,* October.

Hedge, Gary W. 1987. Designing modern accounting software. *Byte,* Summer, pp. 47–52.

Hertz, David B. 1964. Risk analysis in capital investment. *Harvard Business Review* 42, no. 1 (January–February), and 1979, 57, no. 6 (November–December).

Kaplan, Robert. 1988. One cost system isn't enough. *Harvard Business Review,* January–February, pp. 61–66.

Mason, Richard O. and E. Burton Swanson. 1981. *Measurement for management decision.* Reading, Mass.: Addison-Wesley.

McLean, Robert. 1990. Planning for value. *Managing Value,* Spring, pp. 75–82.

Ohmae, Kenichi. 1989. Companyism and do more better. *Harvard Business Review,* January–February, pp. 125–132.

Porter, Michael E. 1985. *Competitive advantage: Creating and sustaining superior performance.* New York: The Free Press.

Rappaport, Alfred. 1992. CFOs and strategists: Forging. *Harvard Business Review,* May–June, pp. 84–91.

Rappaport, Alfred. 1981. Selecting strategies that create shareholder value. *Harvard Business Review,* May–June, pp. 139–149.

Rock, Milton L. 1987. *The mergers and acquisitions handbook.* New York: McGraw-Hill.

Rudden, Ellen M. 1982. Why DCF doesn't work. *The Wall Street Journal.* November 1.

Troy, Leo. 1980. *Almanac of business and industrial financial ratios.* Englewood Cliffs, N.J.: Prentice-Hall.

Wang, Penelope. 1987. What-if accounting. *Forbes,* May 30, pp. 112.

Warren, F. M. and F. P. Shelton. 1971. A simultaneous equation approach to financial planning. *Journal of Finance* 26, no. 5.

Weber, Jonathon. 1992. Computer services for hire: Outsourcing thrives as firms shed data processing chores. *Los Angeles Times,* August 2, pp. D-1 and D-2.

Welch, James and P. Ranganath Nayak. 1992. Strategic sourcing: A progressive approach to the make-or-buy decision. *Academy of Management Executive* 6, no. 1, pp. 23–41.

Wenner, David and Richard LeBer. 1990. Managing for shareholder value—from top to bottom. *Managing Value,* Spring, pp. 95–109.

Willigan, Geraldine. 1990. The value-adding CFO: An interview with Disney's Gary Wilson. *Harvard Business Review,* January–February, pp. 85–93.

Worthy, Ford S. 1987. Accounting bores you? Wake up. *Fortune,* October 12, pp. 43–52.

APPENDIX A

Learning Curve

How much of an impact on cost does learning have? Competitors accumulate know-how over time. This accumulated experience can be measured, and it has been shown for many industries that the total cost per unit can decline between 20% and 30% every time total accumulated production is doubled. This assumption is portrayed graphically by what is known as a *learning curve* or *experience curve* (Figure 8A.1).

The experience curve results from four basic effects:

1. *Learning effects.* Efficiency increases as operators, supervisors, and staff personnel become familiar with the required tasks. As these individuals gain experience, planning, tooling, and coordination become more cost-effective.
2. *Economies of scale.* These occur as the total fixed cost of productive capacity is allocated among a larger number of products. In addition, materials can be more economically purchased, handled, and processed as production volume increases.
3. *Substitution.* The substitution of less expensive materials helps to reduce costs.
4. *Innovation and value engineering.* Cost benefits are realized as improved methods, procedures, and technologies emerge.

A simple way of demonstrating this relationship between the cost per unit and the cumulative volume is to plot it on a log–log scale (Figure 8A.2) Obviously, as costs come down, profit opportunities go up. Prices, however, generally do not parallel the cost curve; rather, they follow a pattern similar to the one shown in Figure 8A.2. During phase A, the new product struggles to establish a position in the market, and price is frequently lower than cost. At the end of this phase, the experience effect takes over and the price remains relatively constant. During phase B, supply is relatively low compared to demand. Price cuts, therefore, are very moderate. Toward the end of the growth phase, the competitive situation becomes very unstable as new competitors are attracted by high profit margins. As a result, prices drop dramatically, and marginal producers are forced out of the market. At the end of this shakeout, the competitive situation usually stabilizes as the product matures and market growth slows (phase C). Profits also tend to stabilize, while the costs of production and marketing (the cash

FIGURE 8A.1	Experience Curves

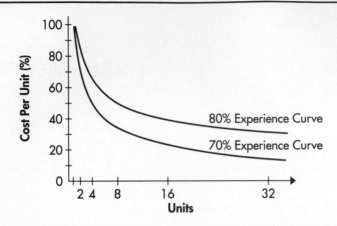

FIGURE 8A.2	Typical Price/Cost Relationship

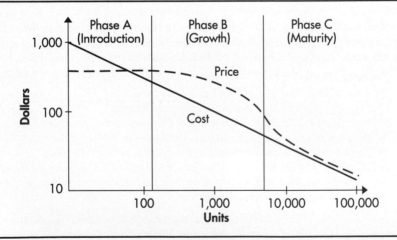

requirements of a product) decrease. Products with high market shares tend to generate increasing amounts of cash during this phase. Finally, profit margins become smaller and smaller as the demand for the product starts to decline, and the majority of competitors phase out the product. The product/market effects of the experience curve are very similar to those of the product life cycle.

From its analysis of experience curves and cost–price relationships, The Boston Consulting Group concluded that the best strategy is one in which the price of a product is closely related to cost (BCG, 1974). The BCG argued that this pricing strategy would discourage competition while allowing market share to build and would result in larger profit margins in the long run.

APPENDIX B

Discounted Cash Flow

The discounted cash flow (DCF) method is an important factor in all cash generation by a business. To arrive at the DCF, managers use

1. A financial pro-forma statement projecting AMP's future free cash flow as shown (see Table 8B.1). Free cash flow is defined as *net income* plus *depreciation* minus *capital expenditures* minus *change in net working capital*. Because only a limited number of years can be projected with fair accuracy, managers establish a terminal value in the form of an annuity for the last year.

2. The discount factor. The discount factor is based on the weighted average cost of capital (WACC), which is derived as follows:

$$WACC = k_e \times e + i \times (1 - t) \times d$$

where

k_c = cost of equity capital
e = share of equity in total capitalization
i = average interest rate on debt
t = tax ratio
d = debt share of total capitalization

If, for AMP, $k = 15\%$, $i = 8\%$, and $t = 40\%$, then

$$WACC = .15 \times 1,793/2,929 + .08 \times (1 - .4) \times 1,136/2,929 = 11.04\%$$

AMP sales revenues projected for 1991 are $1.15 \times 3,043 = 3,499$, for 1992 they are $1.15 \times 3,499 = 3,989$, and so on. The assumptions for the entries in the pro-forma statements are contained in Table 8B.1.

TABLE 8B.1	Assumptions Used for AMP Projections

Item	Assumption
Sales revenue	Grows at 15% per year
Cost of goods sold	66% of sales
Selling, general and administrative	18% of sales
Interest	13% interest paid on short- and long-term debt in previous year; 9% interest earned on investments
Taxes	40% of taxable income
Dividends	50% payout rate
Accounts receivable	19% of sales
Inventories	Inventory turnover of 6
Other current assets	Grow at 15% per year
Property, plant, and equipment	Grows at 10% per year
Depreciation	11% of property, plant, and equipment from previous year
Investments	Grow at 30% per year
Current liabilities	30% of sales
Long-term debt and deferred liabilities	Constant
Beginning equity	Equals ending equity from previous year
Ending equity	Equals beginning equity plus retained earnings
Cash	A plug-in to balance total liabilities and total assets

The results of these assumptions and calculations are given in Table 8B.2.

The DCF value can now be calculated as shown in Table 8B.3. If managers at AMP can realize their ambitious growth plans of 15% per year, the value of equity will be $7.275 billion. Compared to a current market capitalization of about $6 billion, this would add a substantial value to shareholders.

Unfortunately, discounted cash flow is often misunderstood. Critics claim that it has led to a decline in the competitive advantage of U.S. companies by discouraging them from making investments that could have improved productivity. *Discounted cash flow (DCF)* is, in fact, a sound financial model that evaluates financial health on the basis of cash flow rather than accounting profits, which may prove elusive because they are not always based on operations. Evaluations based on earnings may not take into account (1) the importance of the flow of funds needed to conduct the business or (2) the cost of funds so employed. DCF explicitly takes into account the interest that a comparable investment could have earned by discounting future cash flows and showing what cash the business would have now if it had made the alternative investment.

TABLE 8B.2	**Completed Baseline Pro-forma Projections for AMP***

(Dollar amounts in millions)

Income Statements	1990	1991	1992	1993	1994	1995	1996	1997	1998	1999	2000
Sales revenue	3,043	3,499	3,989	4,508	5,049	5,604	6,165	6,720	7,257	7,765	8,231
Cost of goods sold	2,012	2,310	2,633	2,975	3,332	3,699	4,069	4,435	4,790	5,125	5,433
Gross profit	1,031	1,190	1,356	1,533	1,717	1,905	2,096	2,285	2,467	2,640	2,799
Selling, general and administrative	543	630	718	811	909	1,009	1,110	1,210	1,306	1,398	1,482
EBIT	488	560	638	721	808	897	986	1,075	1,161	1,242	1,317
Interest	−26	−40	14	21	29	41	55	74	99	131	172
Taxable income	462	520	652	742	837	937	1,042	1,149	1,260	1,373	1,489
Taxes	175	208	261	297	335	375	417	460	504	549	596
Net income	287	312	391	445	502	562	625	690	756	824	894
Dividends	145	156	195	222	251	281	313	345	378	412	447
Retained earnings	142	156	196	223	251	281	312	345	378	412	447

Balance Sheets	1990	1991	1992	1993	1994	1995	1996	1997	1998	1999	2000
Cash	460	452	551	653	725	848	914	953	942	858	668
Receivables	557	665	758	857	959	1,065	1,171	1,277	1,379	1,475	1,564
Inventories	482	583	665	751	841	934	1,027	1,120	1,210	1,294	1,372
Other current assets	119	137	157	181	208	239	275	317	364	419	481
Total current assets	1,618	1,837	2,131	2,442	2,761	3,081	3,388	3,666	3,895	4,046	4,086
Property, plant, and equipment	2,303	2,533	2,787	3,065	3,372	3,709	4,080	4,488	4,937	5,430	5,973
Less accumulated depreciation	1,181	1,434	1,713	2,020	2,357	2,728	3,136	3,584	4,078	4,621	5,218
Net property, plant, and equipment	1,122	1,099	1,074	1,046	1,015	981	944	904	859	809	755
Investments	189	246	319	415	540	702	912	1,186	1,542	2,004	2,606
Total assets	2,929	3,182	3,524	3,903	4,316	4,764	5,245	5,756	6,295	6,859	7,446
Total current liabilities	953	1,050	1,197	1,352	1,515	1,681	1,849	2,016	2,177	2,330	2,469
Long-term debt	183	183	183	183	183	183	183	183	183	183	183
Beginning equity	1,651	1,793	1,949	2,145	2,367	2,618	2,900	3,212	3,557	3,935	4,347
Retained earnings	142	156	196	223	251	281	312	345	378	412	447
Ending equity	1,793	1,949	2,145	2,367	2,618	2,900	3,212	3,557	3,935	4,347	4,794
Total liabilities	2,929	3,182	3,524	3,903	4,316	4,764	5,245	5,756	6,295	6,859	7,446
Return on equity	17.3%	16.0%	16.0%	18.8%	19.2%	19.4%	19.5%	19.4%	19.2%	19.0%	18.6%

*(See Chapter 6, p. 230.)

Perhaps more important than earnings is a company's value to shareholders. In an article about strategies that create shareholder value, Alfred Rappaport (1981) pointed out that conventional five-year pro-forma accounting statements do not accurately reflect a company's value to management or shareholders. He claimed that the ultimate test of a strategic plan is whether it creates shareholder value. Rappaport posed three questions:

TABLE 8B.3	Discounted Cash Flow (DCF) for AMP
	(Dollar amounts in millions)

	1990	1991	1992	1993	1994	1995	1996	1997	1998	1999	2000
Net income	287	312	391	445	502	562	625	690	756	824	894
Plus depreciation	207	253	279	307	337	371	408	449	494	543	597
Minus capital expenditures	−375	−230	−253	−279	−307	−337	−371	−408	−449	−494	−543
Minus net working capital change[1]	46	−122	−147	−155	−157	−153	−139	−112	−67	1	100
Free cash flow[2]	165	213	269	318	376	443	523	618	734	874	1,048
Discount factor	1.110	1.233	1.369	1.520	1.688	1.874	2.081	2.311	2.566	2.850	
Present value	191	219	233	247	263	279	297	317	341	368	
Sum of present values	2,754										
+ Terminal value[3]	4,704										
− Long-term debt	183										
Total company DCF	7,275										

[1] Capital expenditures equal to increase in fixed assets
[2] Net working capital = current assets minus current liabilities; change from previous year
[3] Terminal value = discounted market value from final period
= net income times P/E-ratio divided by discount factor
= $894 \times 15/2.850 = 4,704$

1. Does the strategic plan create shareholder value, and how much?
2. Are some of the company's SBUs more profitable than others?
3. Would an alternative strategic plan increase shareholder value more than the one in use or under consideration?

Rappaport believes that earnings per share (EPS) can, in fact, be misleading. Of 400 industrial companies rated by Standard and Poor's, only 172 had EPS of 15% or better. More than 50% of the 172 companies had EPS that were negative or inadequate to cover inflation. In part, this is due to the fact that EPS does not reflect the unique status of each SBU. The SBUs usually differ with respect to the risk taking inherent in their strategies, their use of working capital, their need for fixed investments, and their dividend payouts.

Rappaport recommended the use of DCF to determine shareholder value. This approach involves anticipating cash flow discounted by the cost of capital. DCF is analyzed as follows:

1. Estimate the pretax operating return on incremental sales that is needed to create shareholder value.
2. Compare the rate of return on incremental sales realized during the previous five-year period to that for the projected five-year period.
3. Estimate the contribution that alternative strategies would make to shareholder value.
4. Determine whether the proposed growth strategy is financially feasible, taking into account return on sales, investments required, capital structure, and dividend policy.

5. Determine whether the financial evaluation shows that the company is a potential takeover target. If the aggregate value of the individual components of the company is greater than the present equity of the shareholders, then the company may become a takeover target.

A major advantage of the shareholder-value approach is that the data are already available in most companies.

DCF has some disadvantages. It is often difficult to apply for evaluating single investments. It also relies on assumptions about the future sales of products, price levels, competitor actions, government tax policies, and interest rates. For strategic managers, the real value of DCF is its use in determining what would happen to market share, cost of production, or similar considerations, given the returns expected on an investment.

DCF is most readily applied to assessment of labor-saving or cost-reducing investments. But even these kinds of investments require assumptions regarding the learning curve, quality, supplier prices, and overhead costs. Assumptions become increasingly problematic in times of widely fluctuating interest rates or inflation. Again, the question is what alternative investments, such as government bonds, would yield.

Another important consideration that is often overlooked is the fact that running a successful business requires expenditures for such items as advertising and warehouse facilities, without which the business could not function effectively. Toys-R-Us, a major sales outlet for children's toys, maintains a large inventory of toys year-round. This chain of stores would not be competitive without a large inventory and a huge display area. If Toys-R-Us completed a discounted cash flow on the investment in warehouse and display space, Toys-R-Us might find that the return was not justified; its liquidated values might exceed the discounted cash flow from operations. For another example, the cash flow in many high-tech companies in the Los Angeles area is quite low, yet the replacement value of their facilities and land has risen dramatically, leading to handsome potential returns on the sale or exchange of those assets. Discounted cash flow might have suggested divesting assets, whereas the real value, because of appreciation, exceeded the discounted value. Because of these considerations, many financial planners now take into account a number of factors, in addition to discounted cash flow, when recommending an investment. They look at what contributes to maintaining a sustainable competitive advantage, because decisions that rely solely on discounted cash flow can create an unfavorable competitive position. Relying on a single approach can adversely affect pricing, market share, customer service, or other factors needed for a competitive advantage.

APPENDIX C

Cost/Benefit Analysis

A company that plans to invest large sums of money in a new strategy cannot ignore the costs and benefits associated with each strategic alternative. An alternative can be considered efficient when it meets objectives at the lowest possible cost, and yet it can still be a poor choice. Efficiency alone is not a sufficient measure. The desirability of any given strategic alternative depends on both cost and value. Factors that need to be considered include efficiency, ability to implement, urgency of the strategy, and politics that often play a major role in strategic decision making.

A cost/benefit analysis helps managers to determine whether the benefits of a strategic alternative exceed its cost and to choose the alternative that provides the maximum net benefit. The analysis includes both tangible and intangible costs and benefits. Potential tangible benefits might include

Lower administrative costs	Effective work-load balancing
Reduced inventory	Reduced communication costs
Faster delivery to customers	Reduced scrap and rework
Reduced workforce	Reduced transportation
Reduced overtime	Improved utilization of workforce
Reduced cost of new-plant start-up	

The tangible benefits can usually be related directly to their costs, so that each strategic alternative can be ranked according to its net monetary benefit. The net value of a strategy's intangible benefits is much more difficult to assess. This does not mean, however, that intangible benefits cannot be quantified. In fact, under some circumstances, the analysis of intangible benefits is fairly straightforward, and the choice of an alternative can often be justified on the basis of intangible benefits alone. Benefits that fall into the intangible category include

Improved customer service	Improved product decisions
Better control	Competitive product advantage
Earlier information	Improved cost control and performance measurement
Industry leadership	Organizational flexibility
Decentralized management	Improved forecasting and business planning
Improved employee morale	Improved resource utilization
Improved planning for long-range capacity	

Once managers have determined the net benefit of each strategic alternative, they compare the alternatives that have positive net benefits to determine which one can best meet the goals and objectives of the main strategic thrust. To do this, they first assign each alternative a score of 0 to 1 for the three main success factors shown in Table 8C.1.

Table 8C.2 shows how the scores might be weighted.

TABLE 8C.1 | **Factors That Determine Strategic Success**

Main Success Factors	Contributing Factors
1. Impact	Long-run profitability (ROI)
	Number of strategic business units and people affected
	Number of needs served
	Ability to accomplish overall objectives
2. Implementation	Ability to estimate implementation cost
	Degree of acceptance
	Ability to plan implementation
	Degree of certainty of implementation
	Resources available
3. Urgency	Desirability of proposed strategy
	Political support expected
	Urgency of need for solution

TABLE 8C.2 | **Scores Indicating Level of Support for a Strategy**

Potential for Success	Score
Strong	0.8–1.0
Moderate	0.5–0.79
Weak	0–0.49

The maximum potential of each alternative is obtained by multiplying the alternative's scores for the three main factors. If, for example, an alternative's scores were 0.7 for impact, 0.8 for implementation, and 0.3 for urgency, its maximum potential would be

$$0.7 \times 0.8 \times 0.3 = 0.168$$

which represents the likelihood that the alternative under consideration will succeed. In this example, the low score for urgency (0.3) lowers the strategy's chance of success.

Cost/benefit analysis, then, involves

1. Determining the net benefits of each alternative and eliminating alternatives with low net benefits.
2. Rating the maximum potential of each remaining alternative with respect to impact, implementation, and urgency.
3. Applying judgment to ensure that some obvious critical factor (such as meeting the needs of a key customer) is not overlooked.

An application of the cost/benefit analysis is shown in Worksheet 8.5.

WORKSHEET 8.5 | **Cost/Benefit Analysis**

Case   AMP – example
Date   1993
Name   Mary Doe

	A	Related	B	Advanced	C High Technology	D
Incremental benefit						
Tangible		$430,000[1]		$570,000[2]	$710,000[3]	
Intangible		50,000[4]		100,000[5]	500,000[6]	
Incremental cost		50,000[7]		190,000[8]	940,000[9]	
Net incremental value						
Tangible alone		380,000		380,000	–230,000	
Total		430,000		480,000	270,000	

Alternatives

Footnotes:

[1]Assuming 3% increase in growth; [2]4% increase; [3]5% increase; [4]additional benefits from new technology; [5]additional benefits from new markets and new technology; [6]benefits from improved market position; [7]initial outlays distributed over four periods; [8]same as note 7, [9]same as note 7, plus yearly operating expenses of $840,000.

Analysis:

Options A and B have roughly the same tangible value. The investment in related technology is lower, but benefits from advanced technology appear to be higher. The total value of option B seems to be highest, but the final decision has to consider available funds for investment. Costs for high technology (option C) exceed tangible benefits, and the total net incremental value is the lowest of all three options.

(continued)

WORKSHEET 8.5 Cost/Benefit Analysis (continued)

Alternative	Criterion: Impact ×	Implementation ×	Urgency =	Belief in success ×	Investment level =	Potential
A. Related	0.85	0.95	0.9	0.73	430	312.5
B. Advanced	0.9	0.8	0.95	0.68	480	328.3
C. High tech.	0.99	0.5	0.85	0.42	270	113.6
D.						

Interpretation and Recommendations:

Option B is the most attractive alternative for AMP. It has a high impact on long-run profitability as well as on overall objectives. It is, however, riskier than option A and uses more resources. Therefore, an overbearing reason (such as timing, availability of funds, high interest rates, or similar factors) could make option A the best choice because there is little difference in the potential between options B and A.

APPENDIX D

The fisCAL Computer Program

A number of computer programs are available for preparing detailed financial analyses. One that is especially helpful for analyzing cases or for strategic evaluations is fisCAL. This computer program is available from the Halcyon Group at 447 Fleming Road, Charleston, SC 29412. This appendix shows a sample set of printouts, which simplify many of the calculations needed for a financial analysis. Included are programs for

- Comparison of financial statement and ratio analysis with industry norms
- Balance sheet—operating capital requirements
- DuPont formula for return on assets
- Trend analysis
- Net worth diagram

Comparison with industry standards provides an important base for evaluation. The program also does pro-forma statements and strategic evaluation.

INTRODUCTION TO fisCAL

Before using fisCAL, one needs to read the basic diagnostic reports described in Chapters 1–5 of the *fisCAL Key Disk & Manual*.

The videotape that comes with the fisCAL package can be particularly useful as an introduction.

To better understand fisCAL, use it for reports for which the same data were analyzed by hand. To prepare the fisCAL reports, follow these steps:

1. Read Chapters 1–5 and 8 of the *fisCAL Key Disk & Manual*.
   Chapter 8 of this manual provides a step-by-step description of how to enter data into fisCAL and how to print reports. The earlier chapters explain the specific reports to be run and provide information on how to interpret the output.
2. Read the tips handout provided with the teaching guide.

3. Go over the company's financial statements and insert three years of data into *copies* of the data entry sheets provided in the manual.

At the end of the teaching note in the *fisCAL Key Disk & Manual,* you will find copies of fisCAL's data entry screens. We have found that transcribing the correct figures onto these copies prior to starting a fisCAL computer session saves a great deal of time, because it takes new fisCAL users extra time to translate company data to correspond with pre-set categories. Examples of computer printouts follow.

TABLE 8D.1	Industry Standard Data for Company Comparisons

INDUSTRY STANDARDS DATA

NAME - OFFICE SUPPLIES AND EQUIPMENT

SIC # - 59431

ASSETS

Cash and Equivalents	7.2
Accounts Receivable - Trade (net)	31.0
A/R Progress Billing	0.0
A/R Current Retention	0.0
Inventory	37.5
Cost & Est Earnings in Excess of Billings	0.0
All Other Current	1.3
TOTAL CURRENT	77.1
Fixed Assets (Net)	16.8
Joint Ventures & Invest	0.0
Intangibles (net)	1.7
All Other Non-Current	4.5
TOTAL ASSETS	100.0

LIABILITIES

Notes Payable - Short Term	9.7
Current Matured Long Term Debt	4.5
Accounts Payable - Trade	23.9
Accounts Payable - Retention	0.0
Billings in Excess of Costs & Est Earnings	0.0
Income Taxes Payable	0.0
All Other Current	7.7

(continued)

TABLE 8D.1	Industry Standard Data for Company Comparisons (continued)

TOTAL CURRENT   46.5
   Long Term Debt   18.2
   Deferred Taxes   0.1
   All Other Non-Current   2.7
   Net Worth   32.5
TOTAL LIABILITIES & NET WORTH   100.0

INCOME DATA
   Net Sales   100.0
   Gross Profit   37.1
   Operating Expenses   34.3
   Operating Profit   2.8
   All Other Expenses (net)   0.7
   Profit Before Taxes   2.1

RATIOS	L	M	U
Current	1.3	1.7	2.4
Quick	0.6	0.8	1.1
Receivables/Payables	0.0	0.0	0.0
Sales/Receivables	8.3	10.8	15.2
Cost of Sales/Inventory	3.3	5.1	9.0
Cost of Sales/Payables	6.0	9.0	13.5
Sales/Working Capital	22.1	10.1	6.0
EBIT/Interest	1.1	2.4	5.2
Cash Flow/Cur Mat LTD	0.5	1.3	3.7
Fixed/Worth	1.4	0.5	0.2
Debt/Worth	5.7	2.1	1.1
% Profit Bef Taxes/Networth	3.5	16.4	44.3
% Profit Bef Taxes/Total Assets	0.7	6.1	13.6
Sales/Net Fixed Assets	13.7	26.1	48.1
Sales/Total Assets	2.1	3.2	4.1

Source: Reprinted from fisCAL Analysis Software with permission of The HALCYON Group, Inc.

TABLE 8D.2	Balance Sheet

FINANCIAL STATEMENT COMPARISONS
BY DOLLARS
STUDY FOR GENERIC RETAIL, INC. STUDY CASE

ANALYSIS PROCESSED ON 4/25/1989 FOR INCOME/BALANCE ON 12/31/00

	STUDY CASE ($)	SIC# 9999 ($)	VARIANCE ($)
ASSETS			
Cash and Equivalents	1,000	1,825	−825
A/R - Trade (net)	9,500	7,325	2,175
A/R Progress Billings	0	0	0
A/R Current Retention	0	0	0
Inventory	10,500	10,025	475
Cost & Est Earnings in Excess of Billings	0	0	0
All Other Current	900	275	625
TOTAL CURRENT	21,900	19,450	2,450
Fixed Assets (Net)	3,100	4,275	−1,175
Joint Ventures & Invest	0	0	0
Intangibles (net)	0	150	−150
All Other Non-Current	0	1,150	−1,150
TOTAL ASSETS	25,000	25,000	
LIABILITIES			
Notes Payable - Short Term	1,950	3,050	−1,100
Current Matured Long Term Debt	1,050	1,325	−275
Accounts Payable - Trade	950	5,400	−4,450
Accounts Payable - Retention	0	0	0
Billings in Excess of Costs & Est Earnings	0	0	0
Income Taxes Payable	0	300	−300
All Other Current	1,150	2,350	−1,200
TOTAL CURRENT	5,100	12,425	−7,325
Long Term Debt	2,000	3,750	−1,750
Deferred Taxes	0	125	−125
All Other Non-Current	0	575	−575
Net Worth	17,900	8,100	9,800
TOTAL LIABILITIES & NET WORTH	25,000	25,000	
INCOME DATA			
Net Sales	100,000	100,000	
Gross Profit	49,000	37,100	11,900
Operating Expenses	36,200	33,800	2,400
Operating Profit	12,800	3,300	9,500
All Other Expenses (net)	3,700	800	2,900
Profit Before Taxes	9,100	2,500	6,600

Source: Reprinted from fisCAL Analysis Software with the permission of The HALCYON Group, Inc.

TABLE 8D.3	DuPont Formula for Return on Assets

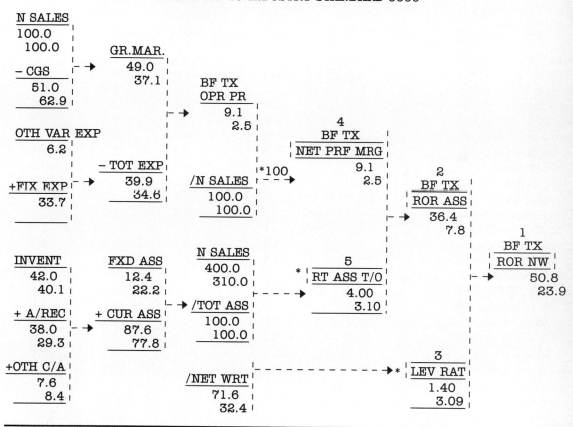

STRATEGIC PROFIT MODEL
FOR GENERIC RETAIL, INC. STUDY CASE DATED 12/31/00
COMPARED TO INDUSTRY STANDARD 9999

```
N SALES
100.0
100.0              GR.MAR.
                    49.0
- CGS               37.1        BF TX
 51.0                           OPR PR
 62.9                            9.1              4
                                 2.5            BF TX
OTH VAR EXP                                    NET PRF MRG
  6.2                                            9.1            2
              - TOT EXP                          2.5          BF TX
+FIX EXP        39.9         /N SALES   *100                 ROR ASS
 33.7           34.6         100.0                           36.4           1
                             100.0                            7.8         BF TX
                                                                         ROR NW
INVENT        FXD ASS       N SALES                                        50.8
 42.0          12.4         400.0            5                            23.9
 40.1          22.2         310.0        RT ASS T/O
                                     *    4.00
+ A/REC       + CUR ASS     /TOT ASS      3.10
 38.0           87.6        100.0
 29.3           77.8        100.0
                                                            3
+OTH C/A                    /NET WRT                      LEV RAT
 7.6                         71.6        *                 1.40
 8.4                         32.4                          3.09
```

Source: Reprinted from fisCAL Analysis Software with the permission of The HALCYON Group, Inc.

Learning Resources
Centre

TABLE 8D.4	Trend Analysis

fisCAL TREND ANALYSIS FOR GENERAL RETAIL, INC.

RUN DATE: 4/25/1989

	STUDY CASE 12/31/00 $000	STY CS +01 12/31/01 $000	STY CS +02 12/31/02 $000	SIC # 9999 $000	VARIANCE $000
BALANCE SHEET DATA					
Cash and Equivalents	1.0	7.0	10.9	2.2	8.7
Accounts Receivable	9.5	7.5	6.5	8.8	−2.3
Inventory	10.5	10.0	11.0	12.0	−1.0
All Other Current	0.9	0.9	0.9	0.3	0.6
TOTAL CURRENT ASSETS	21.9	25.4	29.3	23.3	6.0
Fixed Assets (Net)	3.1	1.9	0.7	5.1	−4.4
Intangibles (Net)	0.0	0.0	0.0	0.2	−0.2
All Oth. Non-Current	0.0	0.0	0.0	1.4	−1.4
TOTAL ASSETS	25.0	27.3	30.0	30.0	
Notes Pay-Short Term	2.0	0.9	0.5	3.7	−3.2
Cur Mat Lng Term Dbt	1.1	1.1	0.0	1.6	−1.6
Accounts Payable	1.0	3.0	3.1	6.5	−3.4
Income Taxes Payable	0.0	0.0	0.0	0.4	−0.4
All Other Current	1.2	1.1	1.3	2.8	−1.5
TOTAL CURRENT LIAB	5.1	6.1	4.9	14.9	−10.0
Long Term Debt	2.0	0.9	0.0	4.5	−4.5
Deferred Taxes	0.0	0.0	0.0	0.2	−0.2
All Oth. Non-Current	0.0	0.0	0.0	0.7	−0.7
NET WORTH	17.9	20.3	25.1	9.7	15.4
TTL LIAB & NET WORTH	25.0	27.3	30.0	30.0	
INCOME STATEMENT DATA					
Net Sales	100.0	99.0	120.0	120.0	
Gross Profit	49.0	45.0	60.0	44.5	15.5
Operating Expenses	36.2	36.7	47.1	40.6	6.5
Operating Profit	12.8	8.3	12.9	4.0	8.9
All Other Exp (Net)	3.7	4.6	5.2	1.0	4.2
Profit Before Taxes	9.1	3.7	7.7	3.0	4.7
Profit After Taxes	7.6	3.7	7.7		
CASH FLOW-OPERATIONS		8.3	9.0		
CASH MARKET VALUE	56.0	30.2	55.0	21.4	33.6
BREAKEVEN POINT	78.7	89.6	101.6		
OPERTNG CAPITAL RQRD	20.1	21.5	25.3	16.5	8.8
RATIOS					VAR %
CURRENT RATIO	4.3	4.2	6.0	1.6	273.7
QUICK RATIO	2.1	2.4	3.6	0.7	407.3

(continued)

TABLE 8D.4	Trend Analysis (continued)

SALES/RECEIVABLES	10.5	13.2	18.5	10.7	72.5
COST OF SALES/INVTRY	4.9	5.4	5.5	5.0	9.1
COST OF SALES/PAYBLS	53.7	18.0	19.4	10.7	80.9*
SALES/WORKING CAPTIAL	6.0	5.1	4.9	10.5	−53.2*
EBIT/INTEREST	14.0	6.3	39.5	3.1	1174.2
CASH FLOW/CUR MAT LTD	9.8	4.5	inf	1.9	inf
FIXED/WORTH	0.2	0.1	0.0	0.5	−94.4
DEBT/WORTH	0.4	0.3	0.2	2.1	−90.7
%PFT BF TX/NET WORTH	50.8	18.2	30.7	21.9	40.1
%PTF BF TX/TTL ASSETS	36.4	13.6	25.7	6.9	272.0
SALES/NET FIXED ASSETS	32.3	52.1	171.4	25.0	585.7
SALES/TOTAL ASSETS	4.0	3.6	4.0	3.1	29.0
DEG OF OPER LEVERAGE	5.26	5.66	4.82		
BANKRUPTCY PREDICTOR	8.50	7.79	10.09		

NET WORTH DIAGRAM

```
A/P                L/T LIA        TOT ASS
  3.8                8.0          100.0
 21.6               17.8          100.0            NET WORTH
                                     |-- - - →        71.6
+NT/PAY           + TOT C/L     └─→ −TOT LIA             32.4
 12.0   |- →         20.4            28.4
 17.5               49.7            67.5

+OTH C/L
  4.6
 10.6
```

1 = BEFORE TAX RATE OF RETURN ON NET WORTH, %
2 = BEFORE TAX RATE OF RETURN ON ASSETS, %
3 = FINANCIAL LEVERAGE RATIO, TOTAL ASSETS/NET WRT
4 = NET PROFIT MARGIN, %
5 = RATE OF ASSET TURNOVER, SALES/TOTAL ASSETS

Source: Reprinted from fisCAL Analysis Software with the permission of The HALCYON Group, Inc.

CHAPTER NINE

Entrepreneurship, Mergers and Acquisitions, Restructuring, and the Service Sector

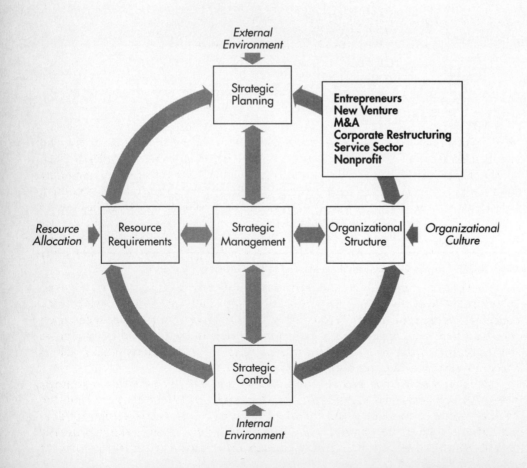

Chapter 1 A Framework for Strategic Management	**Chapter 2** Strategic Analysis	**Chapter 3** Strategic Visioning, Goals, Ethics, and Social Responsibility	**Chapter 4** The Competitive Environment	**Chapter 5** Capability-based Strategy	**Chapter 6** Market Dynamics and Sustainable Competitive Advantage
How to approach strategic management	*Application of strategic analysis*	*Understanding vision, values, ethics*	*Coping with competitive forces, stakeholders*	*Assessing company capability, timeliness, quality*	*Determining trends, gap analysis, and market dynamics*

Chapter 7 Strategy in a Global Environment	**Chapter 8** Financial Planning and Competitive-Cost Analysis	**Chapter 9** Entrepreneurship, Mergers and Acquisitions, Restructuring, and the Service Sector	**Chapter 10** Leadership Factor in Strategy and Implementing Strategic Change	**Chapter 11** Information Technology and Future Directions in Strategy
Assessing global trade, foreign markets, monetary exchange	*Preparing a financial plan and competitive-cost analysis*	*Importance of small business, entrepreneurs, restructuring*	*Strategy implementation, leadership, culture*	*Information technology, trends, new management*

INTRODUCTION

Smaller, entrepreneurial businesses are a driving force in the nation's economy, and small business management is taught to business majors in over 400 colleges. Even so, the entrepreneurial or small business sector is often not considered a candidate for strategic management. The service and public sectors also are often neglected. Nevertheless, now more than ever, strategic management methods can be utilized by the small business, service, and public sectors to achieve more effective performance. Although these sectors may look different on the surface, there are many similarities and strategic management approaches could be used more widely by both the small business and the service sectors.

M&A (merger and acquisition) activity is another area where strategic analysis is important. Recently, those involved with mergers and acquisitions have become concerned with strategic fit. The majority of deal makers in the past focused on short-run financial considerations. Strategic fit needs to be analyzed in relation to the long-term impact of merger. Because mergers and acquisitions often result in corporate restructuring, this also is included in this chapter.

Although many small business owners may not choose to develop a strategic plan, every business that seeks capital funding must provide a business plan. No bank or venture capitalist would consider providing funds to a business that does not have up-to-date information. The strategic plan for a small business is usually an abbreviated one containing only enough information to satisfy a bank or venture-capital group. Though it may be more operationally oriented than a strategic plan for a large corporation, it is a document that can determine the long-term survivability of the business. The action plan, or tactical plan for carrying out a strategy, ultimately determines how well strategic management functions.

Problems confronting service businesses and businesses that manufacture, distribute, market, and/or sell a product are often similar. A product is a tangible item that can be seen, felt, weighed, or measured, whereas a service is generally intangible. A service business, such as a law practice, has no visible results or impact other than a decision handed down by a judge. A service can be highly subjective, as is the case with food service; here the value is determined by the person who receives the service. The personality or attitude of the person providing the service can also directly affect the value perceived. Thus the exact same service may be perceived by one person as valuable and by another as worthless. In many cases, a service can be considered equivalent to a product. Tangible products also can have psychological value, such as that inherent in the prestige they confer. Although the majority of service providers are small businesses, large entities such as government agencies, hospitals, and schools also provide services. Many of these may be not-for-profit, but strategic analysis is still critical to their performance.

With a high of almost 4,000 acquisitions in 1986, merger mania has subsided to approximately 2,000. The highest dollar amount, almost $240 billion in 1989, dropped to approximately $80 billion in 1991 (Woolley, 1992). Serious questions have been raised concerning the efficacy of acquisitions. Some claim that acquisitions threaten the basis of the capitalist system because of the exploding corporate debt. By 1988 there was almost $1.8 trillion of debt outstanding, propelled largely by the cost of acquisitions. As an example of the outcome of an acquisition, the RJR Nabisco deal had the following results (Greenwald, 1988):

1. Shareholders: $8–14 billion in profit
2. New owners: $2 billion or more
3. LBO investors: a 40% annual yield
4. Investment bankers received: $170 million
5. Commercial bankers received: $170 million
6. Lawyers were paid: $100–200 million
7. Junk bond holders: 14.5% annual return
8. Corporate bond holders: loss of $1 billion
9. Taxpayers: loss of $2–5 billion

The fear is that greed, debt, and buyout are spiraling out of control. Furthermore, of the 25 best-performing U.S. companies, twelve made acquisitions in 1988 but only three of these acquisitions showed significant value for the companies' shareholders (Coley and Reinton, 1988).

The divestiture of a strategic business unit (SBU) or division of a company is different from the selling of an entire company. In many respects, a strategic business unit can be considered a "small business" within a larger company. Many small businesses are acquired and become SBUs in larger companies. When these small companies are acquired, the small business ceases to exist. This does not mean that these small companies fail, even though statistics show them as "no longer in business."

Finally, a merger and acquisition deal may actually determine whether a company survives or grows. The deal itself is a strategic decision but it may or may not involve a strategic analysis or a strategic plan. And although in many cases there is no impact, research has shown that the majority of mergers fail. For example, W. T. Grimm and Company reported that in 1985 there were 1,237 divestitures and 1,764 acquisitions, reflecting a 70% failure rate for acquisitions. By comparison, in 1985 approximately 700,000 new businesses were started. In that year the failure rate for new businesses was lower than that for M&As.

Most businesses do not suddenly appear as large corporate entities, fully functioning and mature. Most businesses start relatively small. They usually start as entrepreneurial activity in a garage, basement, or some small rented area. There is a "natural" organizational life cycle from birth through growth and maturity to decline and death. This is much like the product life-cycle metaphor. As businesses grow, they may decide to speed growth through merger, or they may be acquired and merged with larger organizations as a business unit or even as a separate division or company. Some businesses, however, tend to stay small. Most service businesses remain small because of their labor-intensive nature. All the topics addressed in this chapter—entrepreneurship, mergers and acquisitions, restructuring, and the service sector—reflect aspects of the development and evolution of growing businesses. That is why they are grouped together in this chapter. And, because they all start with entrepreneurial activity, the first main area we shall discuss is entrepreneurship and small business.

ENTREPRENEURSHIP AND THE SMALL BUSINESS SECTOR

In the business press, small business is said to account for 80% to 90% of all new jobs created. If businesses employing fewer than 100 people are considered small businesses, then over 87% of all businesses are small. If 500 employees is taken as the cut-off point, 99% fall in the small business category! These figures are from the U.S. Small Business Administration and the National Federation of Independent Business. The U.S. Chamber of Commerce (1988) stated that small businesses represent 98% of the 14 million non-farm businesses and that they employ 48% of the total workforce. They also provide two-thirds of all first jobs and initial training.

The economic welfare of the United States is closely linked to a favorable environment for small business. When national and local laws have favored small business, the economy has been strong. When these laws have hurt small businesses, the economy has suffered. Recent laws in many states, such as those that require small businesses to provide a comprehensive medical plan and those that mandate the taxing of service businesses at 5 to 6%, have seriously threatened the existence of many small businesses.

Small business is widely considered "the American way." From the beginning, many Americans have wanted to be in control of their own lives, to be independent. Such "rugged individualists" believe the entrepreneurial spirit is what made this country strong. Today, many national, state, and municipal officials encourage the development of small business and recognize its contribution to the economy. A survey of law makers by the National Conference of State Legislatures, reported in the *Wall Street Journal* in 1992, showed that 29 states favor measures to spur economic development in hard-hit communities. Even in the face of severe budget crises, these states are expected to pass laws aiding new and small businesses and promoting development in rural areas.

Unfortunately, the weakened banking industry, the numerous leveraged buy-outs that created highly unbalanced corporate debt, and the federal deficit that demands unreasonably high debt service have all eaten away at the pool of capital available for small business. Without this capital, the potential for small business is very poor. It is highly desirable for new state programs to come to the rescue.

Definitions of the term *small business* are numerous and varied. Some definitions are based on how a business is taxed or pays for services. In some organizations the fee structure is based on size and/or number of employees. Most definitions are based on a combination of the number of employees, the volume of sales, and the size of the capital structure. In manufacturing, capitalization is more important than the number of employees. In a retail business, sales volume is more important, and for service firms, the number of employees is given more weight.

Often, 100 employees is considered the magic number. These definitions tend to change from time to time, making it necessary to keep up with specific legislation affecting the business and the industry. Many books on small business give different measures. Megginson et al. (1988) give the following guidelines for classifying a company as a small business.

Manufacturing—maximum employee range between 500 and 1,500, depending on the industry

Construction—average annual receipts less than $17 million for the past three years

Wholesale—maximum of 500 employees

Retail—annual sales not over $3.5 to $13.5 million

Service—annual sales not over $3.5 to $14.5 million

Between being a small business and a large business, a company may go through several stages, which include being a "mid-sized" firm. In time, a special discipline for mid-sized companies may emerge. A classic measure of growth stages is Greiner's (1972) "Evolution/Revolution" stages or "crises." From startup to the *crisis of control* is the first stage. When a business grows to a size where the entrepreneur can no longer stay on top of all business activities, the business has reached a crisis of control. The delegation of authority and the division of activities into functional areas with independent managers are required. This is often a wrenching experience for the entrepreneur, who may find it hard to let go. At this point, the entrepreneur must become a small business manager who can delegate and plan strategically if he or she is to survive. Many entrepreneurs are unable to make the transition to being a strategic manager. One of the most important reasons for the failure of so many small businesses and mergers is a lack of strategic analysis, strategic fit, and strategic management.

The small business sector is often a special focus of the national media. Magazines such as *Inc.* and *Entrepreneur* have become successful by concentrating on small business concerns. For several years the *Wall Street Journal* has published a special section that takes an in-depth look at small business, and it has a column called "Enterprise" that focuses on small business and entrepreneurial issues.

ENTREPRENEURS

Entrepreneurship is more than starting a new business—it is a style of managing. Consider Digital Equipment Corporation (DEC), for example, which by being entrepreneurial outfoxed IBM in the mini-computer market. Another strategy used by DEC was to introduce XCON, an expert-systems approach to manufacturing and distribution that is said to have saved the company $80 million. DEC was expected to post a loss for 1992, but its entrepreneurial spirit has resurfaced with the introduction of the Alpha chip that is reputed to operate at 150 million calculations per second. This is twice the speed of any current computer. Even industries can have an entrepreneurial spirit. Consider biotechnology (Hamilton et al., 1992), which looks like it will be the dominant growth industry of the 1990s. Its range of products is mind boggling: recombinant DNA, gene therapy, chemical synthesis, and many others.

Most often, however, entrepreneurship is associated with individuals who have the vision, drive, and courage of their convictions, such as Land at Polaroid and, more recently, Steven Jobs, who helped start Apple Computer, and William Gates, who started Microsoft. In a study of why some new businesses succeed while others fail, Brokaw (1991) found that although cash is indispensable, flexibility in responding to the unpredictable was a key requirement for a startup business. Furthermore, she found that "nobody likes your product as much as you do," that ignoring competitors can be deadly, and that upper management's ability to delegate is vital to the company's survival.

Three major reasons why small businesses fail are a lack of planning, severe competition, and a lack of working capital. Successful entrepreneurs, however, are creative individuals who have vision (conceptual style); have little patience, and want to control everything (directive style); are able to motivate others (behavioral style), and finally are willing to take risks (analytic style).

A study by Rowe (1987), based on the initial validation of a test instrument called the Decision Style Inventory (DSI) with members of the Young Presidents Organization (YPO), revealed these four styles. That study showed that YPO members are extremely flexible and can use all four decision styles. In a second study, of 57 company presidents identified as "up-and-comers" by *Forbes* magazine, Rowe found that 17 exhibited the entrepreneurial style (a combination of the conceptual and the directive styles). Twenty of the young presidents had a planning or executive style (analytical and conceptual decision styles). These findings help explain why startup companies need the entrepreneurial style but growth companies need to emphasize strategic management.

Barbara Bird's 1989 research on entrepreneurs explodes some of the old myths. In general, however, research supports the view that most entrepreneurs had difficult childhoods and tended to be misfits in "normal" society. They were impatient with rules and formal education. Once they had an idea, they became fanatical about it and would not give up. Failure was not a crushing defeat; rather, it spurred them on to try harder. If they failed, they did not give up or get depressed. Instead, they persisted until they succeeded or found a new idea to pursue.

Although entrepreneurs tend to see the big picture, they often jump to conclusions. The Rowe (1989) profile of the entrepreneur reveals that he or she has a conceptual and directive style, which is consistent with the studies by Bird. Hodgetts and Kuratko (1989) list five characteristics that are crucial to entrepreneurial success:

1. *Technical competency*—Entrepreneurs must have technical know-how and know what they are doing.
2. *Mental ability*—Primary is the ability to view operations in broad terms and see how everything fits together.
3. *Human relations skills*—The entrepreneur must get along with others and must communicate, motivate, and influence.
4. *High achievement drive*—The entrepreneur must be action-oriented and should gauge success according to results through feedback. (David McClelland's seminal work on the achieving society equated the achievement orientation of most Americans with the success of America as a land of opportunity.)
5. *Creativity*—It is important to process information in a way that results in new, original, and meaningful ideas, concepts, processes, and products.

The research by Jeff Hansen (1985) shows the importance of relating decision style to the conditions confronting the entrepreneur. For example, we can describe the development of a new venture as shown in Figure 9.1. Table 9.1 shows what style(s) of decision making Hansen found to be most effective in each stage of development.

| FIGURE 9.1 | New-Venture Development |

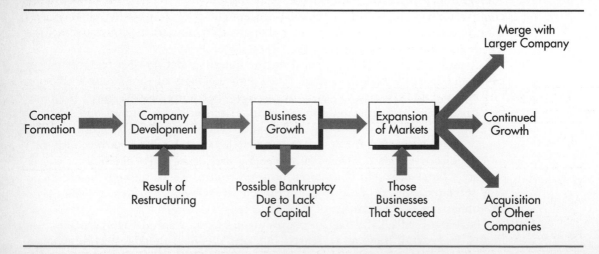

TABLE 9.1	The Decision Style That Tends to Be Most Effective at Each Stage of the Company Life Cycle

Life Cycle Stage	Number of Employees	Most Effective Decision Style
1. Concept development	1 to 9	High conceptual Low analytic
2. Company development	10 to 25	High analytic High behavioral Low conceptual Low directive
3. Company positioning	26 to 75	High conceptual Low behavioral
4. Process operation	75 or more	High directive

Hansen studied entrepreneurs who were funded by venture capitalists. He found that decision style could assist venture capitalists in the funding decision. Of the 59 individuals studied, 41% had a decision style pattern that was consistent with the data shown for entrepreneurs in Table 9.2.

As can be seen in Table 9.2, entrepreneurs were higher in the directive and conceptual styles than either typical managers or the population at large. The high conceptual is typically creative and has the vision needed to create new endeavors. When such an individual is also a high directive (energetic and results-oriented), she or he is clearly an appropriate person to start a new venture. Interestingly, the shortcoming of typical entrepreneurs is the low analytical score, which may account for their lack of planning, low use of data, and tendency to have financial difficulties. Rowe's (1983) study of CEOs and chairmen of the board also showed a pattern similar to that of entrepreneurs. They have high conceptual scores and average directive scores. Thus they have the vision for creating change but tend to rely on subordinates to carry it out. The entrepreneurs, however, not only had the vision but also were able to carry the vision out.

TABLE 9.2	Decision Style Scores for Entrepreneurs, Managers, and the General Population

	Entrepreneurs (score)	Managers (score)	Population (average score)
Directive style	83	71	75
Analytical style	76	88	90
Conceptual style	97	84	80
Behavioral style	44	57	55

Brokaw (1991) pointed out that there are a number of lessons that have been learned which can help new ventures.

1. If cash is considered king, then flexibility must be god.
2. What has broken many startups is their inability to respond to the unpredictable.
3. New ventures often overlook the fact that nobody likes their products as much as they do.
4. New ventures may ignore the fact that competitors who are ensconced have a viable business, which the startup does not have.
5. Experience is generally needed to run a successful business, and startups are often reluctant to buy it.
6. Underestimating competitors can lead to disastrous results.
7. Founders who are able to delegate responsibility are best able to survive.
8. Few founders correctly estimate the time or money needed to penetrate a market.
9. Founders do not realize how much time it will take to start and run their own business.
10. Entrepreneurs may not be aware of the risk and the emotional drain that running their own business entails.

The Barnett tape of Mo Siegel, who started Celestial Seasonings teas, also supports the entrepreneurial profile. According to Siegel, "niche picking" is the key to success in a small business. Siegel was a formal-education dropout who was a fanatic about his herb teas, especially Red Zinger. He says he has an "M.B.A." based on experience gained from the streets and a "Ph.D." in "marginality." "Being on the streets" consisted of 15 years of listening to Peter Drucker tapes while bicycling to work. The "marginality" was his fanatical scrutiny of expenses and cost of goods sold. However, he believes in a good business education, because a person needs to have the knowledge to succeed. He said he became autodidactic, reading and studying everything he could. Every morning he would tell himself and his employees to take care of the "customer's needs" not one's own "greed." He added that if this is done in an intelligent, businesslike way and if basic rules of good business are followed, a lot of money will be made. (Many business leaders and professors of business agree that management is a "people business." If one can develop and maintain good relationships with customers and employees, one will be successful. Making lots of money is only a "side benefit" of being able to deal effectively with people.)

In describing growth, Siegel says the problem is first not having enough product, then distribution, and finally too much inventory. Different problems arise at each level of growth. Because people tend to disappear, new people have to be hired for the next level. Picking the right people for each job, position, and project is extremely important. Siegel says he always hires people smarter than himself for the job that needs to be done. Managers who are afraid to hire people who are smarter than they are make a big mistake.

Siegel identifies three stages of corporate development by sales level. Sales of up to about $9 million characterize the *entrepreneurial stage*. Strategic planning starts at about $5 million. At this stage, Siegel brought in an expert in planning who stayed for three years and whose efforts led to the growth that became the core of a crisis. Many of the people who were initially with the business did not like to plan, so they left. Between $5 and $10 million in sales, there was a complete house cleaning. People who did not grow were out.

Siegel's experience reflects the fact that the levels of financial activity and analysis are quite different at the various stages of growth. When comparing small business with large corporations, one must interpret ratio analysis differently. For large corporations, industry averages are useful benchmarks, although that has changed for firms saddled with huge debt as the result of LBO or junk-bond activity. These firms are more like small businesses in that a deteriorating economy may threaten their existence. Small businesses focus on avoiding large debt in the event that the economy turns down. Entrepreneurs typically have a low equity position at the start and make maximum use of an accounts payable "float." They also contribute many hours of "sweat equity" that does not show up on a financial statement.

The next stage of growth for Mo Siegel was between $10 and $25 million in sales. He describes this as the *corpreneurial stage.* Most of the people hired at this stage were mavericks who left large companies so that they could get experience and later start their own businesses. One of these was Keith Brenner, who later started Wishbisquetts. Most of the people at this stage did not like planning.

The last stage of growth was from $25 million up. At this level, personnel changed to those who were comfortable with planning and wanted the certainty of knowing what the policies were. In this traditional *corporate stage,* planning dominates and is the focus of strategic management. People who are comfortable at the corporate level are easier to manage. They prefer structure and want policy guidelines. They like to fit in. They dislike uncertainty and ambiguity. Therefore, it is easier to devise planning systems, to formulate strategy, and to implement policies, procedures, and rules.

The entrepreneur dislikes all this. The transitional stage from entrepreneurial to small business management has talent that is quite "mavericky" and resists structure. If the business passes this transition and becomes a large successful company, the mavericks tend to be replaced by "corporate types" who like structure.

According to Kuratko and Hodgetts (1989), the reasons why most small businesses do not plan are

1. Time scarcity: many owners work 14–16-hour days, seven days per week with continual day-to-day operating problems.
2. Lack of knowledge of the processes, components, or sequence of factors involved.
3. Lack of expertise: owners tend to be generalists with no specialized expertise in planning.
4. Lack of trust and openness: owners may be guarded about their business and decisions and may refuse to share information with employees or outside consultants.

APPLICATION OF ANALYTICAL METHODS TO SUPPORT ENTREPRENEURS

The National Federation of Independent Business (NFIB), the largest small business trade group, collects data on small business members, but, as NFIB concedes, there are no averages that apply to all small businesses. Smaller "industry" trade groups may have data more useful to that specific industry. Nevertheless, ratios for a startup are very different from those of a well-established and well-run business. Furthermore, the success of a small business is much more dependent on the drive and dedication of the entrepreneur than on financial ratios.

According to Baruch Lev (1974) only two ratios are good predictors of corporate failure. These are cash flow to total debt and net income to total assets. These tend to give a five-year lead time. Two others give a lead time of about three years: total debt to total assets and working capital to total assets. All others give a warning of only a year or less. For small business, these important ratios are less favorable in general (lower cash flow and net income in the early years). Of course, total debt and total assets are also lower. And the so-called unfavorable ratios can be more than compensated for with drive, hard work, and long hours. These rules of thumb vary somewhat according to the author or source, but one example is the suggestion of a 30% debt-to-equity ratio for a corporation and a 50% ratio for a small business.

Looking at the bright side, however, the methods and analytical models described in this book are useful at any stage of growth. Furthermore, the use of these tools will change the odds for success in favor of the entrepreneur. Entrepreneurial managers with conceptual/directive profiles resist analytical rigor, and it is a real challenge for them to apply these approaches. One way to gain acceptance of a methodological approach is to keep it simple and amenable to "guestimates" rather than insisting on rigorous data. The models and tools set forth here can be used in a variety of ways and are helpful even if data are weak. The methodologies in this book can be used with subjective data as well as with well-analyzed, objective input. The degree of risk a manager is willing to live with determines the level of uncertainty in data that he or she is willing to tolerate. Because entrepreneurs are moderate-to-high risk takers, they tend to use intuition and hunches rather than careful analysis.

"Corporate types," on the other hand, tend to be risk-averse and prefer hard, objective data. However, this data can also lead to fatal errors.

The advantage of a systematic approach is that it reduces the likelihood of overlooking important factors or of not understanding basic principles such as product life cycle, balanced portfolios, or strategic funds programming. But because many entrepreneurs are intuitive thinkers, they make spur-of-the-moment decisions on the basis of minimal information. They also avoid analysis paralysis (defined as immobility caused by substituting data analysis for courage). Steven Greenberg, Anametrics chairman, says, "Don't dillydally. Make decisions in a hurry" (Rowan, 1986).

It is difficult to convince entrepreneurs to use a structured analysis, but they do realize that there is a need for planning when they must raise money from a bank or venture capitalist. This effort requires the use of careful analysis, which can help the entrepreneur make the transition to the small business stage and then to the large corporation stage. However, the desire for growth is dependent on the psychological makeup and decision style of the entrepreneur. He or she may not want to grow and many bail out before reaching the small business stage. Those who leave tend to be the rugged individualists who cannot stand structure. Rather than succumb to structure, they strike out in a new direction with a new idea and start another new business. They seem to be driven to do this. Some entrepreneurs "fail" many times before they finally succeed; and often they fail and start right over again in the same business.

Henry Ford failed twice before he produced a car that captured the imagination of a mass market and became the most successful automobile manufacturer in the twenties. Ford started small but did not stay small. In the beginning, entrepreneurs focus all their energies on market forces and economic impacts. They do not have the time, personnel, or energy to deal with government regulations, taxes, and other considerations. To a large company, such impediments to doing business may be no more than minor annoyances, but to the small company, these "interferences" can be fatal. (As William F. Buckley said in a television debate on April 3, 1992, the best thing the government could do for small businesses is just get out of the way.)

Do founders learn from these sobering experiences? Brokaw's 1991 studies suggest that most do not and in turn, most do not survive.

NEW-VENTURE DEVELOPMENT

To better understand the new-venture development process, let's consider the wide range of conditions found in the new-venture arena.

1. *New products*. The list of new ventures built on products is legion. Successes include billion-dollar Sun Microsystems, Apple Computer, and Lotus Development Corporation. The first product of The Games Gang, called Pictionary (a way to play Charades on paper), went from zero in 1986 to more than $125 million annual sales in just two years (Deutsch, 1989).
2. *A new technology*. In December 1982, three young Harvard MBAs started Orbital Science Corporation (OSC). The product introduced by this space transportation company was a winged rocket booster, called Pegasus, that is launched from an airplane rather than from the ground. This innovation makes it possible to carry heavier payloads into space, and at much lower cost. The unusual aspect of this venture, one of the largest private ventures ever undertaken in space technology, is that the three founders functioned as "project managers." They neither invested their own money nor manufactured the rocket (Martin Marietta did that). They put the deal together with NASA and raised money from private investors (Perry, 1989). The first successful Pegasus was launched in April 1990 ("Petite Payloads," 1990).
3. *A new approach to retailing by mail*. A number of mail-order firms thrived in the 1980s by selling sportswear to baby boomers who had little time to shop: J. Crew started in the early 1980s and had sales close to $150 million in 1989; Tweeds started in 1987 and had an estimated revenue of $37 million in 1989; Lands' End started in 1963 and had sales close to $500 million in 1989 (Rudolph, 1989).
4. *New retailing services*. These ranged from fingernail decorating and polishing to high-priced barber shops, 24-hour mailbox and mailing services, and video-game parlors. Various segments of this wide range of services have flourished

at one time or another in the past decade. When carefully planned, they have all been fairly effective in generating good cash flow.

5. *A new entrant into an existing area.* It is generally agreed that in order to succeed, a new venture has to have something different. The difference, however, does not have to be an innovative product or service. For example, in real estate during the mid-1970s and early 1980s, it was possible to conservatively buy property in metropolitan areas such as New York and be able to make a substantial amount of money simply by doing well what was already being done. Converting apartment buildings into cooperatives required little more than following well-established legal patterns and dealing effectively with a variety of complex operational and regulatory problems. Many of these ventures resulted in returns of over 500% in less than three years.

6. *A new approach to pet care.* Pet sitting in an owner's home is an example of smaller new ventures. Patti Moran's service called "Crazy 'bout Critters," in Winston-Salem, N.C., for example, employs 39 part-time pet sitters, She wrote a book, *Pet Sitting for Profit,* and in 1989 started the National Association for Pet Sitters. Membership was expected to be over 300 by the end of 1990.

7. *A new airline service.* More than 50 applications are filed each year for new airline services. North American found out that before starting its one-plane operation, it had to file more than 10,000 pages of manuals. In addition, it had to pass a battery of inspections by federal regulatory agencies, buy $500 million of insurance, spend $300,000 on training and $250,000 on FAA testing, arrange financing to lease a new Boeing 757, and enter into a cooperative arrangement with El Al Israel Airlines, which own 2.9% of the company. All this had to be done in the ten-month period preceding North American's first commercial flight (Dahl, 1990).

The accelerating pace of entrepreneurial activity experienced during the 1980s, which is expected to continue throughout the 1990s, seems to be an international phenomenon. For example, during the 1980s Italy experienced an entrepreneurial boom that rivaled and in some cases exceeded that in the United States and in other European countries (Haberman, 1980). Entrepreneurial activity is also beginning to show up in Eastern Europe, especially in Hungary (Greenhouse, 1990).

Contrary to popular belief, many new ventures are well planned and well managed. Often, what is needed by new ventures is help in managing the business more effectively. As in any business, the strategic-planning processes described in this book include tools and approaches that can help the new venture be more successful.

TASKS INVOLVED IN STARTING NEW VENTURES

Starting a new venture takes a special kind of mentality and strategic approach. The major tasks involved in planning and management include

1. Identifying an opportunity
2. Deciding to explore and proceed with the venture
3. Formulating the business concept and plans
4. Acquiring resources and determining future source of funds

5. Managing the venture within an appropriate organizational structure
6. Controlling cost, quality, and value (important after the venture has been started)
7. "Growing" the venture (important after a successful start)

IDENTIFYING AN OPPORTUNITY

An in-depth survey of the general economic social system and marketplace will turn up any number of needs and wants not being met or will suggest where needs and wants could be satisfied more efficiently and effectively. For example, Rupert Murdoch's publishing organization identified a market niche, a magazine for women aged 38 to 50. Those who make up this market niche are much older than readers of *Glamour* and *Mademoiselle,* a little older than those of *Harper's Bazaar* and *Vogue,* and younger than those of *Lear.* This niche is growing with the aging of baby boomers and looks promising because of the high incomes in the target market. The new magazine Murdoch produced is called *Mirabella* (Kleinfield, 1989).

DECIDING TO EXPLORE AND PROCEED

After opportunities are identified, the decision to explore further depends on a number of other factors. In most cases, the first considerations are whether the opportunity is something you want to do, whether it fits your style or personality, and whether it fits your budget or provides the lifestyle you want. At this point there are no "right" answers, but asking the right questions is absolutely essential. The kind of person who could work well with a group of high-tech professionals, as at Orbital Science Corporation, may not be the kind who would succeed at running a retail health food store or chain of stores. A high-powered developer of innovative financial packages, such as mortgage-backed bonds, may be a very different entrepreneurial type from the person who can succeed at developing a fashion magazine, a toy company, a mail-order clothing company, a real estate venture, or a retail store. Decision style and/or personality may or may not be a major consideration. In many entrepreneurial ventures, drive, commitment, hard work, and persistence often overcome many so-called "personality handicaps."

FORMULATING THE BUSINESS CONCEPT

The formulation of a viable strategic approach often is the key to the success of the business. Von Clausewitz, one of the early writers on military strategy, is now widely quoted as saying that a war is won or lost before the first shot is fired, depending on what strategic decisions were made beforehand. The same can be said for a new venture. The success of a business depends on the strategic decisions made before the doors are opened for business. The strategic plan must establish an effective working relationship between the opportunities and threats in the external environment and the internal strengths and weaknesses organized for implementation of the plan.

The Games Gang, which developed Pictionary, followed "fad-product strategy" and did not sink a lot of money into building a manufacturing plant. Companies that *did* incur that cost include Atari (home video games) and Caleco (Cabbage Patch dolls). Both of these companies suffered when the fad died. The Games Gang farmed out productions, owned no distribution units, and avoided building a plush corporate headquarters. Its strategy was focused on keeping costs low and was based on finding a game that was already selling well in a local market, testing it for "playability," setting up a royalty arrangement, subcontracting manufacturing, and letting publicity and word of mouth build sales (Deutsch, 1989).

Strategy formulation is an iterative process that cycles continually from beginning to end. The best one can do is relax between cycles and then jump back into the race.

ACQUIRING RESOURCES

Once a plan has been developed, it is a relatively straightforward matter to determine the cost. Typically, cost is more than was planned, which gives rise to the need to raise capital. Orbital Science Corporation did not have to invest its own money because it had an arrangement with Martin Marietta and NASA. It also raised several million from private sources, including $50 million from selling R&D limited partnership units. Orbital's situation illustrates that capital can be raised from many sources. The primary sources of capital for new ventures include

1. The entrepreneur's personal savings
2. Friends and relatives
3. Banks, insurance companies, and so on
4. Private investors
5. Venture-capital firms
6. Mortgage financiers
7. Potential suppliers and customers
8. SBA loans

Each source of capital has its own special requirements. Some require a substantial equity position and/or control or insist on final authority in decision making. There are always tradeoffs, but without sufficient capital, there is no business. As Harvey Mackay says in *Swim with the Sharks,* 1% of something is worth more than 100% of nothing.

MANAGING THE VENTURE

After an initial success raises the prospects for continued survival, attention shifts to managing an on-going business. This sometimes requires a change in both approach and personnel. As Mo Siegel (of Celestial Seasonings) indicated, managers eventually replace the entrepreneurs, who go on to start other new ventures.

Within seven years, Sun Microsystems grew to over $2 billion in sales, but earnings dropped and resulted in a loss in 1989. The crisis was due to their lack of capable management for that stage of growth. Sun needed to abandon the seat-of-the-pants style for a more structured and disciplined approach. Failure to train managers or change management style has derailed many new ventures. Sun managed to recover and make the necessary transition successfully and more quickly than anyone expected (Fisher, 1990).

Some entrepreneurs have successfully undergone the necessary metamorphoses and have stayed with the business for years. Digital Equipment and Hewlett-Packard offer good examples. Here the owners developed and grew with the business. Scott McNealy has likewise expressed his determination to stay with Sun Microsystems and grow with the company. Thus far, prospects look good (Pollack, 1989). At DEC, Ken Olsen finally departed in July 1992. For a long time he had refused to go, but things had gotten so bad that he had to face reality and leave.

Probably a more interesting example of how new ventures can lose their way is found in the experience of *Venture* magazine. In mid-1989 *Venture* suspended publication for two months and laid off much of its staff. This was done after a deal to sell the magazine fell through. As a result, Arthur Lipper, the founder, lost a substantial amount of money because the magazine had failed to keep pace with the market (Scardino, 1989). Unfortunately, when strategy is poorly planned and not continuously updated, it is easy to lose sight of what's happening in the marketplace and of the needs and wants of customers.

ACHIEVING A COMPETITIVE EDGE

Clearly, small and entrepreneurial businesses have much to contribute to the overall economy. In a number of cases, these companies have produced significant exports and actually have reduced the trade deficit. As Table 9.3 shows, the potential for global exports is enticing (Holstein and Kelly, 1992).

TABLE 9.3 Global Exports in Billions of Dollars

	1986	1991
Canada	55	85
Japan	27	48
Mexico	12	33
Germany	10	21
Britain	11	22
Korea	6	15
France	7	15
Taiwan	5	13
Other (including capital goods)		153
Total		415

For example, Vita-Mix now exports 20% of its $15 million a year in sales. The key is serving a niche market that is too small or too difficult for competitors to penetrate. Relying on the toll-free 800 number, faxes, and translators offered by phone companies, small businesses are increasingly able to compete in the global marketplace. With a stagnant U.S. market, the global marketplace is increasingly inviting.

Franchises are beginning to "teach the corporate elephants to dance" (Matusky, 1990). For example, Union Carbide is recruiting personnel for a new "intrapreneurial" program within specialty chemicals. To change Union Carbide from a production-driven company to a service-oriented business, franchising may be the answer. Within nine weeks, Union Carbide started a national network for Mobile Care. A radical change in culture may be impossible in an established entity, but a new organizational division can create its own culture.

Who are the "hottest growth companies" in the United States, and what makes them run? While the big three auto makers lost $7.5 billion in 1991, Spartan Motors, an auto parts manufacturing firm, doubled its sales to $51 million. What accounted for this difference was the highly innovative chassis that Spartan made. *Business Week*'s 100 best small companies represent those where sales grew 48.3%, compared with 6.2% for Standard and Poor's industrial-stock index. The same companies' earnings grew 100.9%, compared with a decline of 14.3% for the industrials (Touby, 1992). What contributed most to the growth of these companies was focusing on a niche market, reacting rapidly to change, being highly innovative, and—most important—serving a customer need.

One of America's fastest growing companies is Connor Peripherals. Using non-stop innovation, Connor has been able to fend off the competition, including the Japanese. In addition, Connor listens to its customers, has smart manufacturing, and utilizes rapid product development. Connor improves its products incrementally, thus ensuring quality and reliability (Kupfer, 1990).

In spite of the many success stories, simply being a nimble entrepreneurial company is not enough to survive in an environment that has stable, concentrated, and well-protected industrial alliances (Ferguson, 1988). To illustrate this, in 1981 the United States exported $27 billion in high-technology products. For high-technology industries to succeed, they require increased investment in wide marketing and customer support. Since 1980 the U.S. semiconductor world market share has slipped from 60% to 40%. Japan has twice as many integrated-circuit patents as the United States. Table 9.4 illustrates some of the differences between U.S. and Japanese semiconductor companies.

Considering the relative size of the workforce in the two countries and their relative gross domestic product (GDP), the Japanese have significantly outperformed the United States. Interestingly, U.S. GDP grew by 2% in the first quarter of 1992 and is projected to grow by as much as 4% by the second quarter of 1993 (Liscio, 1992).

Fragmentation, instability, and entrepreneurism have contributed to the structural problems in the U.S. semiconductor industry. It is projected that without a coordinated development process in semiconductor technology, the U.S. industry will doom itself. Evidence of this prophecy can be seen in the once-successful Wang

TABLE 9.4	Comparison of Capital and R&D Spending Between U.S. and Japanese Semiconductor Companies (Dollar amounts in millions)

Year	U.S. Companies		Japanese Companies	
	Capital	R&D	Capital	R&D
1976	306	228	237	165
1977	179	300	413	200
1978	453	384	650	376
1979	656	470	887	428
1980	956	624	1,300	484
1981	1,047	776	1,424	621
1982	1,301	875	1,188	725
1983	2,234	944	1,323	941
1984	3,508	1,114	3,010	1,078
1985	2,961	1,596	1,789	1,314
1986	2,585	1,582	990	NA

Laboratories, Inc., which filed for protection under Chapter 11 of the Bankruptcy Code after it fell $550 million in debt. The reason given was Wang's inability to keep pace with change. In the absence of a more cohesive policy of support for the small business segment, Wang may be only one of many future failures.

One bright spot is the number of recent joint venture deals for developing and manufacturing microchips. On July 13, 1992, Toshiba, IBM, and Siemens announced that they would collaborate in developing advanced memory chips. Shortly thereafter, the Pentagon proposed a cut in the funds to support Sematech, a consortium designed to boost U.S. semiconductor competitiveness. Congress, however, restored the amount to the $100 million level previously authorized. Shortly afterward, a National Science Foundation study revealed that the United States is losing its technology edge (Bloomberg, 1992). In their article on industrial policy, Christopher and Mandel (1992) clearly point up the problem caused by not having a national policy that supports technology growth. They cite the R&D gap, productivity lag, investment drops, erosion of high-tech trade, and the decline in factory jobs as evidence of the need for a national strategy to spur growth. Their recommendations include the following:

1. Increase federal spending above $20 billion per year for R&D, and reduce defense spending below its current $43 billion per year.
2. Increase federal spending for technical assistance to industry.
3. Improve data collection on R&D.
4. Rebuild the U.S. infrastructure to encourage high-tech industries.
5. Expand the Export-Import Bank to make export financing easier.

6. Increase funds for scientific education.
7. Provide tax incentives for R&D investment.

The new-growth agenda will not come cheaply, but to fail to implement it could adversely affect the quality of life in the U.S. for years to come.

MERGERS AND ACQUISITIONS

Because many new ventures are acquired, the merger–acquisition process is a natural part of the business life cycle. One of the differences between U.S. and Japanese industry is that the businesses in the United States focus on short-term acquisitions, whereas in Japan the emphasis is on growth. Furthermore, the sales of smaller U.S. companies have increased from approximately 30% of all mergers and acquisitions to over 50% in 1990. Mergers and acquisitions will undoubtedly continue for many years.

A January 1992 business news program on CNN stated that in 1991 mergers were down 32% from 1990. Other reports had mergers down 34%. In 1992, Colgate-Palmolive raised $446 million in a public offering in order to restructure debt and committed $900 million to acquisitions, including the Mennen takeover. *Fortune,* discussing the "Deals of the Year," stated that companies are turning to equity financing and that leverage-laden companies are paying down debt. In the eighties over $640 billion of equity disappeared from corporate books. A little is creeping back. Of the 50 biggest deals in 1991, 16 were stock transactions, compared to only 2 in 1990. Former junk-bond gurus are now claiming to be "restructuring experts." In the *Fortune* article, Fisher (1992) says this is like a fire department made up of reformed pyromaniacs.

Mergers effected for strategic reasons can be beneficial to both the acquiring company and the company acquired. Strategic fit implies that the merger is synergistic and that the new, combined firm produces more benefits to the stakeholders than the two did separately before the merger. Most mergers based on strategic fit perform well and are enduring. Those that were formed to reap financial gain or to raid corporate assets have caused more harm than good. The use of the LBO (leveraged buyout) saddled so many firms with so much debt that they could not survive when the economy turned down. These over-leveraged companies just could not service their enormous debt.

As in all strategic analysis, it is important to examine each SBU and evaluate the fit among all those affected by a proposed merger. The methods described here can be used to evaluate the strategic fit between an SBU and the acquiring company. As we noted earlier, each SBU is similar to a small business entity. This suggests that a similar culture may prevail. Whether cultural differences can be accommodated and clashes minimized can make or break a merger.

CULTURAL ISSUES IN A MERGER

To effectively implement a strategy designed to achieve specific goals and objectives, it is imperative to put appropriate rewards in place. Rewards either reinforce or inhibit certain activities, depending on how the reward system operates.

A merger or acquisition attempt tends to drive up the stock price of the target company, and if a company is acquired by issuing junk bonds, the capital structure is changed. In these cases, although stock prices may rise in the short run, shareholder value can suffer in the long run.

Another serious consideration is that after an acquisition, many so-called "non-essential" positions are cut; some of these may be in research and development. Because R&D typically is a critical "life force" to many companies, cutting research and development can lead to the eventual demise of the company.

Conflicting corporate cultures account for much of the criticism of acquisitions and explain why so many fail. One large national consulting group (Selkirk) insists that culture must be considered because people often cling to ingrained values and beliefs about what they are willing to do, even when logical analysis should convince them otherwise. The mores, values, norms, roles, and relationships that define a particular culture determine the organization's ability to introduce or adapt to change. The ability to adapt is a key determinant of the success of a merger. Organizational culture questionnaires can be very helpful in analyzing the fit between two companies contemplating a merger.

The large-company mentality and structure can destroy the enthusiasm that makes high-tech and entrepreneurial companies so successful. The large-company culture demands management discipline, but the imposition of tight controls and red tape is anathema to the undisciplined flow of the creative genius. When the Ford team that designed the successful Taurus was interviewed on CNN (December 1991), various members of the team complained that the "corporate types," who have authority over their R&D activities, are constantly looking over their shoulder and interfering with their creativity. Members of the team said their enthusiasm, creativity, and morale are down and that they had recently been unable to come up with any new ideas. Under these conditions, morale declines and the dedication to be the best often disappears. In some cases, the affected managers just depart from such intolerable situations.

The introduction of *any* change creates anxiety and fear. When a major change is in the offing due to a proposed merger, fear and anxiety may cause high levels of fight, flight, or "freeze" (those who are paralyzed because they just don't know what to do). The result is that the change flounders in a morass of opposition, sabotage, neglect, and inaction. The company taking over promises that no one will be fired. Whether or not this is the acquiring company's intention, those in the acquired company who don't fit the new corporate culture soon take "flight," even when the company taking over wants them to stay.

The USAir takeover of PSA and Piedmont teetered on the verge of disaster for several years but is now beginning to stabilize. This takeover was plagued by a really bitter cultural war between USAir and Piedmont, which ended in USAir's firing 3,800 employees and closing the Dayton hub. USAir also closed out service to many smaller cities previously served by PSA. Piedmont had a relaxed culture, and the employees balked at the rigid and bureaucratic rules imposed by PSA. The result was chaos, canceled flights, missed connections, misplaced baggage, and hostile or nonexistent service. The outlook is considered favorable, but USAir has high fuel costs because of short hops with many takeoffs and landings. This makes

USAir one of the highest-cost airlines in business. If the economy does not improve, cash flow could cause serious problems and USAir's life might be short.

Smart managers generally jump ship before the merger or acquisition talks reach a serious stage. That is what happened at Celestial Seasonings when it reached $25 million in sales, and the departure of key executives put the company in a precarious position after it was acquired by Kraft. Celestial's managers were knowledgeable about the other company as well as their own, and they knew whether the deal would actually take place and whether the "fit" would work. They also knew whether they would be able to work in the new cultural environment. These managers had an early-warning "radar" that gave them the edge in finding the best relocation alternatives. Unfortunately, such managers are often the better managers, and when those at Celestial left, the company was without the managers who understood how the company ran and how to protect its vital resources.

Because of a cultural mismatch, six months after a merger, the exodus of managers heats up with 20–25% leaving; it peaks in the second year at about 35–40%, and then declines to barely a trickle after three years. On average, some 52% of top management personnel are gone in less than three years after a merger. Eventually, two-thirds to three-quarters of the managers find greener pastures elsewhere.

MAKING A MERGER WORK

To make a merger work, the decision makers must deal with more than the desirability of the merger (in strategic or financial terms) to the acquired organization. It may be more critical to the success of a merger to consider the acceptability of the change, in terms of cultural expectations, to those individuals who must carry out the activities involved.

Whether a merger is successful involves the following four considerations:

1. The executive who becomes the change agent
2. The culture, which reflects the change environment
3. The values of individuals whose activities affect the change process
4. The match between pre-merger values and culture and those of the new entity

The change agent is the key executive (often the founder of the company) whose values dominate the culture of the company. Such key executives determine the company's strategy in accordance with their own preferences. They expect others to support them. When the change agent is ready to make a change, the "team" needs to be to be ready to follow and support him or her. (See Chapter 10 for a further discussion of organizational change.)

The change environment is a second factor to be considered. The internal change environment reflects the corporate culture. It is largely created by the key change agent but must be responsive to the external environment. The "corporate culture" is immediately affected by actions taken at top levels of management. If the internal environment does not fit the needs and demands of the external market environment, the corporate culture can inhibit performance. And if it ignores the realities of the marketplace, there will be conflicts.

Rothchild (1991) has detailed one of the biggest financial disasters of the 1980s and described how Robert Campeau's decision style (he charmed, cajoled, and bullied with audacity and ego) was both an asset and a fatal flaw. Campeau was the change agent. He also determined the culture and the values of the company. The conflict between Campeau's values and culture and those of the acquired companies eventually spelled financial disaster.

The values and beliefs of those whose activities are needed to implement the strategic change constitute the third ingredient of the change process. Some values are so ingrained and may be so irrational that they seriously inhibit or prevent the implementation of strategic change. Another factor is the mind set of the managers charged with the implementation process. Managers who are not supportive of change often continue to carry out an inappropriate strategy even in the face of obvious problems and changed market conditions.

The concept of fit is also a vital concern. Gaining acceptance of a merger plan is critical, and it is often where a deal breaks down. It is not until the proposed changes are accepted, internalized, and made a part of the values of those involved that the merger has any chance of success.

For companies to operate effectively in a particular market environment, the internal corporate culture must blend with the external cultural imperatives. Over years of successful operations, a company tends to evolve into an appropriate fit. However, when the external environment changes enough to affect the way business is done, the internal corporate environment must adapt or suffer failure.

The sale of Microflat Corporation to Esterline Inc. turned into a problem for the founder of the small company because there was conflict with management of the acquiring company. The initial offer was fair, and the final offer included a five-year contract to the seller. However, after the sale the corporate office started interfering in management, countermanding orders and making life difficult for the former owner. There was a conflict that made managing almost impossible. After three years of valiant effort, the former owner of Microflat resigned his position because he was not allowed to perform in the entrepreneurial mode that made him successful in his own company.

Making an acquisition is often only the tip of the iceberg. Making the merged company a cohesive, compatible company can become a nightmare. Anthony D'Amato, CEO of Borden, is finding that acquiring good companies is not enough. Borden has recently acquired Creamette and Prince Pastas, Classico and Aunt Millie's pasta sauce, Eagle condensed milk, ReaLemon lemon juice, Wise potato chips, Cheez Doodles, Cracker Jack, Cremora, and Elmer's glue, which add up to $7.2 billion in revenue. The outcome in 1991 was a $72 million loss due to layoffs. Between 1986 and 1991, Borden spent $1.9 billion making 90 acquisitions, and it has the leading market position in six major product lines. But having made these acquisitions so rapidly, management was unable to integrate them and to take advantage of economies of scale. The result was a "patchwork of loosely related fiefdoms." D'Amato, as a consequence, has instituted a crash integration process that is beginning to pay off. D'Amato, who is considered outspoken and pugnacious, is spending 80% of his time visiting and grilling managers to avoid complacency. He says he won't hesitate to "make changes that will get the job done" (Lubove, 1992).

In many mergers, changes are too rapid, and in any merger it is impossible to make changes "by decree." Some people have a need for stability and tend to resist any change. They must be able to see and understand the value of the change. Trying to convince someone with very strong contrary beliefs is difficult. Recognizing that many entrepreneurial ventures will eventually be acquired, it is doubly important to develop strategies for growth and for making the new venture attractive to a potential buyer. Most of the approaches described in this text can provide the kind of support needed to ensure growth and to make possible an eventual merger or acquisition that is successful.

CORPORATE RESTRUCTURING

Mergers and acquisitions during the 1980s often were a result of "restructuring" organizations to focus on core competency. In many companies, divestitures become available for another company's acquisition. Figure 9.2 shows the changing emphasis in mergers from conglomerate to leveraged reorganization, which typically leads to corporate restructuring.

| FIGURE 9.2 | **Waves of Mergers and Acquisitions** |

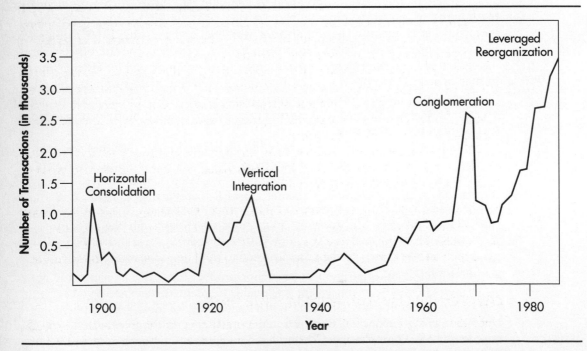

Source: Data from Devra Golbe and Lawrence White, *Mergers and Acquisitions*, University of Chicago Press. Courtesy of The Boston Consulting Group, Inc. Reprinted with permission.

Leveraged reorganization is beginning to pay off for companies that have used the process to become "leaner and meaner." Among other things, leveraged reorganization inspires strategies that cut costs, increase productivity, and boost profit margins. In numerous instances, poorly performing operations are sold or eliminated, and assets are redeployed to those with better promise of returns. This process has led to a boom in divestitures, mergers, and acquisitions. If management is not ready to make adjustments, an outside raider will come in to break up a company's assets and reduce the bloated corporate staff, usually to the benefit of the company's shareholders. The results of such moves are significantly lower break-even points for a number of companies and significant gains in earnings.

This kind of restructuring occurs in five partly overlapping phases:

1. Formulation of a corporate vision
2. Divestment or closure of underperformers
3. Acquisition search
4. Strategic valuation
5. Postmerger integration

These phases are addressed in the sections that follow.

CORPORATE VISION FORMULATION

The first step in corporate restructuring is to develop a clear understanding of the new direction the company wants to take. The key strategic question is, "Where can the firm gain a long-term competitive advantage?" In other words, in which strategic and market segments can the firm (1) maintain or create a competitive cost advantage, and (2) generate new customer values?

Figure 9.3 is a competitive-advantage matrix for the strategic business units (SBUs) of a large, diversified company. As the shaded circles show, several businesses had entered into decline and were losing money. Competitive-cost analysis quickly showed that the company had only four leading businesses. Some had irreversibly lost their ability to compete.

Through its competitive analysis, top management came up with a new vision of the company's position for the 1990s. This vision was based on the two types of successful businesses the company had:

1. A core of specialized businesses in the company's main fields of operation. These had good potential for becoming international and dominating the industry.
2. A range of fragmented and stalemated domestic businesses that could be sold as opportunities arose and the proceeds used to fund new businesses in the future.

DIVESTMENT OR CLOSURE OF UNDERPERFORMERS

Once the strategic direction was clear, the company's top management was ready for some fairly major changes. Within a single year, more strategic decisions were made and implemented than within the previous 10. Among other things, three major businesses were sold, despite strong resistance from certain stakeholders.

| FIGURE 9.3 | Competitive-Advantage Matrix Showing Strategic Business Units of a Large, Diversified Company (Circle size indicates size of business) |

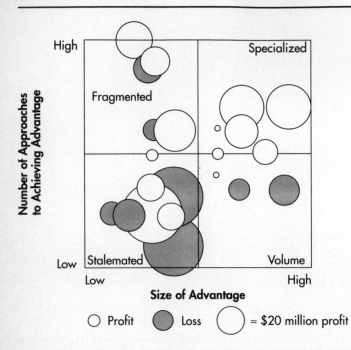

Source: Courtesy of The Boston Consulting Group, Inc. Reprinted with permission.

The result of divestment is shown in Figure 9.4. Now the business portfolio consisted mainly of profitable businesses with good potential for development. Two of the money losers were retained for their technology and growth potential.

The projection of sales and return on investments for the remaining business signaled a significant turnaround in earnings (Table 9.5). Sales growth, however, was severely cut by divestment. Therefore, the next step was to explore possible areas for growth in the new business structure.

ACQUISITION SEARCH

Having reduced the company to a few businesses with long-term profitability, management sought to acquire similarly focused businesses that had the same potential for sustained advantage. The most attractive targets were quickly identified and screened on the basis of

1. Their inherent, stand-alone capabilities
2. The synergistic effects they were likely to have if merged with the company
3. The risks of the merger

FIGURE 9.4	Competitive-Advantage Matrix After Divestment: Same Company as in Figure 9.3

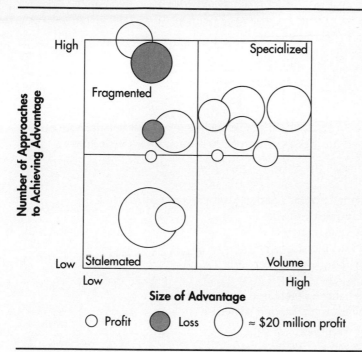

Source: Courtesy of The Boston Consulting Group, Inc. Reprinted with permission.

TABLE 9.5	Results of Focused Portfolio Structure

(Dollar amounts in millions)

Indicators	Before Restructuring	Projections 3 Years After Restructuring	Difference
Sales	9,300	7,600	−1,700
Capital invested in operations	6,500	3,800	−2,700
Operating profit	−250	+430	+680
Return on investment	−3.8%	+11.3%	

This preliminary phase of acquisition is often termed the *strategic logic phase.* Its purpose is to help managers determine whether an acquisition makes sense strategically.

During the strategic logic phase, the company analyzed each candidate based on available data. Then each firm was ranked with respect to a number of criteria, including

Size	Efficiency of operations
Growth	International network
Brand awareness	Quality of management
Market share	Information and reporting systems
Profitability	Proprietary technologies and patents
Asset utilization	Availability of the firm
Leverage	

The next part of the strategic logic phase included identifying the synergistic interfaces for the combined businesses. These were broken down as follows:

1. Cost synergies
   a. Joint R&D
   b. Joint manufacturing locations and greater capacity utilization
   c. Joint marketing and distribution
   d. Joint administrative management
   e. Combined (greater) buying power
   f. Financing options/bond ratings
2. Price synergies
   a. Combined market shares; increased selling power
   b. Influence on the industry's pricing structure
   c. Segment dominance
   d. International roll-out potential
3. Other synergies
   a. Access to larger customer base
   b. Attractiveness to its own personnel

Finally, the risks of merging the two business operations were evaluated. These risks included

- Potential for loss of key personnel
- Potential for loss of market share
- Threat of competitive retaliation
- Legal issues
- Potential loss of image in the marketplace

The company decided to concentrate further research on the three best candidates in each business.

STRATEGIC VALUATION

During the next phase of acquisition, the *financial logic phase,* managers established what the company stood to gain financially. Each of the remaining candidates was evaluated with respect to its

1. Book value
2. Replacement value
3. Market-to-book value

4. Price–earnings value
5. Discounted cash flow (DCF) value

Because these methods are covered in detail in finance textbooks, only a simple application will be described here. Suppose that MPS was one of the candidates being evaluated and that the acquiring company was AMP.

AMP's 1988 book value, or shareholders' equity, is $2.8 million. To determine AMP's replacement value, its balance sheet would have to be audited and estimates made for particular assets. This usually is not possible until after an agreement has been reached—that is, during the due diligence period of acquisition. A first estimate should be attempted, however, because it helps managers to determine possible proceeds from sales of assets that will not be needed after the merger—particularly hidden assets, such as prime office locations or proprietary technologies.

Table 9.6 shows how a first estimate of MPS's replacement value was made by obtaining basic information about the company and its assets, especially its real estate holdings. This approach yields a value of the assets closer to $9 million than to the $7.8 million shown in the books.

The market-to-book value can be derived from similar transactions in the industry. If the average market-to-book value ratio in the industry is 3.5, then the market value of MPS based on this analysis is 9.8 (2.8 × 3.5).

Another method of valuation is to use price–earnings ratios typical for the industry. If the price–earnings ratio for companies comparable to MPS is 18, and

---

| TABLE 9.6 | **Book Value and Replacement Estimates for AMP** (Dollar amounts in millions) |

	Book Value	Replacement-to-Book Multiple (%)	Replacement Value
Assets			
Cash	0.5	100	0.50
Accounts receivable	3.4	95	3.23
Inventories	2.8	90	2.52
Property, plant, and equipment	1.1	250	2.75
Total	7.8		9.00
Liabilities			
Accounts payable	2.3	100	2.30
Short-term loans	1.2	100	1.20
Long-term debt	1.5	100	1.50
Total	5.0		5.00
Valuation	2.8		4.00

MPS's net profit for 1988 was $550,000, then the company is worth $9.9 million ($18 \times 550,000 = 9.9$ million).

Perhaps the best method of valuation is the discounted cash flow (DCF) method, because DCF "factors in" all future cash generation by the business. (DCF is explained in Chapter 8.) To arrive at the DCF, managers at AMP used

1. A financial pro-forma statement projecting MPS's future free cash flow. Free cash flow is defined as *net income* plus *depreciation* minus *capital expenditures* minus *net working capital change*. Because only a limited number of years can be projected with fair accuracy, managers establish a terminal value in the form of an annuity for the last year.
2. The discount factor. The discount factor is based on the weighted average cost of capital (WACC), which is derived as follows:

$$WACC = k_e \times e + i \times (1 - t) \times d,$$

where

k_e = cost of equity capital

e = share of equity in total capitalization

i = average interest rate on debt

t = tax ratio

d = debt share of total capitalization

Based on financial projections, MPS's cash flow stream can be projected as shown in Table 9.7.

If, for MPS, k_e = 14%, i = 12%, and t = 40%, then

$$WACC = .14 \times 2,800/7,800 + .12 \times (1 - .4) \times 5,000/7,800 = 9.64\%$$

Now the DCF value can be calculated as shown in Table 9.8. MPS's most probable worth is $9.975 million based on DCF valuation. Estimates of MPS's worth were fairly consistent—between $9.8 and $10 million—whether market-to-book value, price earnings ratio, or DCF value was computed.

TABLE 9.7 | **Free Cash Flow Projection for MPS**
(Dollar amounts in millions)

Computation	1988	1989	1990	1991	1992	1993	1994	1995
Net income	0.6	0.5	0.6	0.8	1.2	1.4	1.5	1.6
Plus depreciation	0.2	0.3	0.2	0.2	0.3	0.3	0.3	0.4
Minus capital expenditures	−0.3	−0.3	−0.3	−0.4	−0.4	−0.4	−0.4	−0.4
Minus net working capital change	−0.3	−0.4	−0.4	0.0	−0.2	−0.3	−0.2	−0.3
Free cash flow	0.2	0.1	0.1	0.6	0.9	1.0	1.2	1.3

TABLE 9.8	Calculation of MPS's Discounted-Cash-Flow Value	
	(Dollar amounts in millions)	

Year	Free Cash Flow	Discount Factor	Present Value
1988	.2	1.0000	.200
1989	.1	0.9036	.090
1990	.1	0.8165	.082
1991	.6	0.7378	.443
1992	.9	0.6666	.600
1993	1.0	0.6024	.602
1994	1.2	0.5443	.653
1995	1.3	0.4919	.639
Terminal value	16.6	0.4919	8.166
Total NPV			11.475
Long-term debt			−1.500
Total company DCF			9.975

Note: Terminal value = net profit 1995/WACC = 1.6/.0964 = 16.6   NPV = net present value

Once the stand-alone value of a potential acquisition is known, managers also estimate the candidate's potential for restructuring and synergy. First, they need to estimate the cash-flow impact of the synergistic interfaces listed earlier. If, for example, AMP can absorb all MPS's administrative functions within its existing management structure, it will save about $1 million per year. The after-tax impact of eliminating the administrative functions on the free cash flow will result in an increase of over $7 million in MPS's present net value. If the cost of eliminating MPS's administrative functions were $3 million, the net effect of this synergy alone would be $4 million. Once all the synergies have been estimated and added, the acquirer can set an upper limit on any premium paid to the seller and establish a negotiating strategy accordingly.

According to Drexel Burnham Lambert (1988) to restructure or not to restructure is not the question. Nine out of ten executives are looking at restructuring as a way to concentrate energies and resources, increase efficiency of operation, and become more cost-competitive, thereby increasing the value of their companies. A number of qualifications are necessary to carry out restructuring successfully, including knowledge about mergers and acquisitions, leveraged buyouts, securities, and public and private fundraising. Restructuring is not for the amateur. It has to be carefully thought out, skillfully executed, and effectively managed.

Some companies have difficulties with restructuring. When in 1987, the word came out that Western Union would be out of cash in 10 days, Robert Laventhal, the president, threatened to file for Chapter 11 bankruptcy if Wall Street security holders called for a restructuring vote. For the previous three years, Western Union had survived a strike, losses of $1 billion, junk bonds, and then the October 1987 stock crash. Unfortunately, Western Union had few growth businesses and had sustained massive losses. A restructuring plan presented in 1986 was badly flawed, and the outlook for Western Union was dim. In 1986 Western Union reported a loss of $531 million. For the first nine months of 1987, the company reported a $17.2 million loss. Finally, the company had to attempt a major refinancing of $500 million to purchase and merge with ITT's Worldcom. The merger took place in 1987. The 136-year-old company's salvation came on the very last day of 1987, when debt holders voted to exchange their debentures for stock in the restructured company. This step rescued Western Union from the brink of bankruptcy.

Other companies have fared better. A successful restructuring was accomplished by TRW, which sold off $800 million worth of low-growth and low-return subsidiaries so that it could concentrate on its core business: automotive accessories and parts, electronics, and defense. TRW sold a money-losing foundry that made aircraft castings to Precision Castparts, which proceeded to turn it into a winner, with half the scrap rate and increased sales.

Although the cutbacks, spin-offs, and buyouts may bring pain to some employees, restructuring really does work (Magnet, 1987). Restructured companies are more competitive in the world market. In fact, restructuring is imperative precisely because of global competition. The theory that greater size leads to economies of scale and therefore to competitive advantage does not hold true if low performance and inefficiency creep in, as has happened in American industry since World War II.

POSTMERGER INTEGRATION

Actions taken immediately after contracts have been signed are critical to the success of a merger. In too many cases, the managers who prepared the acquisition move on to new positions or tasks, and promises that were made are not kept. Consequently, the synergistic potential of the merger is only partially realized. The following proven guidelines can often prevent these negative effects and ensure the success of a merger.

1. *Keep your promises.* The new relationship will sour if employment and other guarantees are not honored. The resulting decline in morale will damage the new business.
2. *Convey a clear vision.* The new management team needs immediate information about the firm's philosophy and about changes that are to be implemented during the first months after the merger.
3. *Demonstrate competence in the new business.* Displaying knowledge about and interest in the acquired business shows the new employees the advantages of the merger and builds their confidence in the success of the new venture.
4. *Provide sufficient resources for success.* Adequate resources include both funds and technical resources.
5. *Implement a new organization rapidly.* Integration of another business invariably leads to management changes. It is important to clarify the new structure and relationships between managers of the two firms quickly.
6. *Change the rules of the game gradually.* Integration should not result in loss of identity for individuals or the acquired corporation. The corporate culture of the acquired firm should not abruptly be renounced.

7. *Improve compensation.* Reductions in personnel usually mean more responsibility for those who remain. Better pay and more incentives can go a long way toward ensuring the success of the new company.

These dos and don'ts of postmerger integration demonstrate how critical it is to prepare well for this phase even before entering into acquisition negotiations.

Restructuring and downsizing are often viewed as a means of bringing new life to troubled companies. By abandoning declining products and focusing on innovation and new lines of business, many companies have gained a second life. Williams Company of Tulsa, for example, exchanged a pipeline business for fiber optics and landed MCI Communications as its major west coast customer. Goodyear had been the number-3 tire maker in the United States but gave it up to produce polyvinyl chloride, specialty chemicals, and aircraft parts. Although Goodyear lost $53 million in 1991, its managers agreed this was better than staying in the tire business. Chesapeake Corporation, known for production of wood pulp, gave it up to become the leading producer of customized cartons, store displays, and paper products. Conversion is not easy, but it's better than remaining in a declining business or in one where the competition prevents growth or profitability (Hage and Geier, 1992).

The problem with downsizing is the potential loss of qualified personnel and the resulting frustration, resentment, and possible disloyalty. Recognizing these problems, management needs to take appropriate action to minimize the damage. An approach called transformational leadership that was developed by Noel Tichy (1986) emphasizes people's response to change and loss. Losing middle managers along with widespread layoffs creates in the "survivors" a feeling comparable to the loss due to death or divorce. A period of mourning is normal and should be considered legitimate. Employees should be encouraged to bring their grief out into the open where it can be dealt with (Fisher, 1988). When contemplating a change, management should consider the following guidelines:

1. Make sure employees understand the new strategy, how it affects them, and why it is needed.
2. Those who must be let go should be given an opportunity to transfer, should be treated with kindness and respect, and should be assisted in any way possible.
3. Those whom management wants to stay need to be given reinforcement, a clear description of their new role, and an idea of what they might expect in the future.
4. Build a new culture that is responsive to the needs of employees and promotes the organization's ability to cope with the changing external environment.

THE SERVICE SECTOR

When one examines the relationship between gross national product (GNP) and the number of new businesses started, it is apparent that enterprise formation is alive and well (see Table 9.9). Even so, according to the SBA (Small Business Administration), one in every five new ventures fails within two years, and only 5% really take off (Pouschine and Kripalani, 1992).

TABLE 9.9	Growth of New Enterprises	

Year	GNP (in $ trillions)	New Enterprises
1970	2.8	22,000
1975	3.0	28,000
1980	4.0	49,000
1985	4.3	59,500
1990	4.7	50,000
1991	4.75	55,000

Why does U.S. enterprise formation continue to grow? In part it's the entrepreneurial spirit, and in part it's the individual's desire for independence. As one individual put it, "I got tired of forcing myself to go to the office." What is not obvious is that approximately 75% of the U.S. workforce will soon be in the service industry. This sector of the economy is often overlooked but in health care, for example, gross income is approaching 20% of the GNP (approximately $900 billion for 1992). Because manufacturing has been the focus of study over the years, the special needs of the service industry have tended to be ignored.

Linda Grant's recipe for the survival of the service sector is to slim down and work "smarter" (Grant, 1992). Although the service sector is approaching 75% of private employment in the United States, and manufacturing accounts for less than 20%, productivity in the service sector is a little over 105% (1982 = 100), whereas that in manufacturing is almost 130%. This condition exists despite the high investment in computers that was supposed to "slim down" information workers and provide support so they could work smarter. Unfortunately, the service industry allowed white-collar employees to grow without a comparable payback in productivity. Although it is clear that banks, phone companies, the credit card industry, and other aspects of the service industry could not exist without computers, more needs to be done to utilize fully the mammoth capability that computers offer.

A number of companies have risen to the challenge of helping to shape up the service sector. The need is overwhelming, as Connecticut Mutual Life found out. It was taking this company 2 weeks and as many as 30 people just to process a claim. Using specialized equipment, the same job now takes two people 4 days and is expected to repay the $6 million invested in just 2 years (Pomice, 1991). Among the companies providing support to the service sector are

- Octel: high-tech communications
- FileNet: systems to reduce paperwork
- Kelly Services: temporary work support to reduce overhead
- Telxon: portable computers for inventory control
- Medco Containment: mail-order pharmaceuticals that help reduce health care costs

These are a small sample of the "service" companies that can help the service industry become more efficient.

Without a strategy, service companies are likely to falter because they don't know their customers, competitors, and funding sources or how to use technology to reduce cost. What may be even more bothersome are the low wages and dead-end jobs. The percentage of the workforce that is stuck in dead-end jobs has been approximately 70% since 1983 (Schlesinger and Haskett, 1991). Most of the failures in the service industry are a result of the way the system has been designed. For example, Sears experimented with reducing cost by shifting to 70% part-time salespeople; the result was a significant drop in customer satisfaction. Attracting skilled employees is difficult because of limited opportunities for growth and low pay, which leads to a "cycle of failure." For example, Merck & Co. found that the total cost of turnover equaled 150% of employees' annual salary. In spite of massive investment in technology, the service industry has as many employees as before. Compounding the problem are foreign competition, deregulation (in the phone and airline industry, for instance), and the fact that the United States spends more than twice what Japan does for services and 20 times what Canada does (Roach, 1991).

For service companies to be successful, they need to focus on "serving" customers' needs while making the services more affordable. Shouldice Hospital near Toronto, Canada, has reduced the stay for surgery (5 to 8 days for the typical hospital) to 3½ days. Doctors perform more surgeries than at other hospitals at a salary less than what they could charge in private practice. Allowing patients to care for themselves whenever possible reduces the nurses' work load. To cap it all, Shouldice is 10 times more effective in eliminating the need for repeat treatment for the same problem, and patients rate them very high. Shouldice accomplished all this by segmenting the market so that it could focus its efforts (Davidow and Uttal, 1989).

There is considerably more psychology involved in selling a service than in selling a product. But computer programs and consulting service often can be considered as much a tangible output as a service. Developing a computer program or designing a system is merely a different way of providing a product. Some states include software development under "manufacturing" in their planning for improving the state's economy.

A service that is highly intangible is the "900" telephone number services that sell information only. There is no product; nevertheless, even this service is amenable to the strategic management approach. Market research is needed to determine how many people in various geographic areas would use a given service. There are laws and government regulation controlling this business, and there are opportunities and threats even in this environment.

NOT-FOR-PROFITS

Not-for-profit organizations often have the same problems as profit-making organizations. The differences are shown in Table 9.10 (adapted from Cornwall and Perlman, 1990, Table 13-1).

Although not-for-profit organizations may appear to be more ambiguous and less focused than profit-oriented businesses, Peter Drucker (1989) maintains that "the best management practices and the most innovative methods come from the

TABLE 9.10	Profit-Making Versus Not-for-Profit	

Function	Profit-Making	Not-for-Profit
Mission	CEO or board of directors	Legislation or committees
Goals	Provide products and services for a profit	Serve community or constituents
Measures of performance	Return on investment, return on assets, equity or sales growth, market share, competitive position	Improvement in quality of life, improvements in community services provided
Need for change	Needed for adaptation in a competitive marketplace and customer needs	Population requirements, demographics, taxation
Control systems	Managerial and budget-based	Constituencies
Life cycle	Changes in organization	Reacts to societal needs
Government regulation	Responds to regulatory agencies and laws	Reports directly to political bodies

Girl Scouts and the Salvation Army." For businesses to become more effective, they will have to learn more about the way not-for-profit organizations motivate knowledge workers, achieve productivity, and work out policies and practices. The average American volunteer spends 5 hours a week at a not-for-profit. Thus these 80 million volunteers are equivalent to 10 million full-time people. Another way of describing this is to say that it amounts to $150 billion a year. For example, using a strict work program, the Salvation Army is able to rehabilitate 20,000 young criminals each year for less than it would have cost to keep them in jail.

The not-for-profits have to be more concerned about funding because of the difficulty in raising money. They also are less able to exercise tight control. Rather, the CEO of a nonprofit has to rely on convincing others by a clear mission statement with which they can identify. Making a board operate as an effective unit requires carefully organizing the work to be done and defining the board members' role in helping to carry out the organization's functions. The lesson for businesses that manage knowledge workers is that such workers need clear communications, role definition, challenging assignments, empowerment to perform their jobs, and accountability for results.

An interesting approach to introducing efficiency into the public sector has been proposed by de Conink-Smith (1991). With increasing pressure on budgets and slowing growth, ways are being sought to provide more value for the available dollars. The implication is that public-sector activities need to find ways to deliver products that better satisfy the needs of constituents (customers), especially in a competitive environment. A classic example is the post office, which is using technology to improve efficiency and is also being innovative to fend off competitors such as UPS and Federal Express. Smith estimates that a 15% to 20% saving is possible without reducing the level of service provided. Restructuring and better management will be the critical challenge of the 1990s. This can be achieved by a program that introduces "competition" into activities that have been "protected." Unfortunately, the indiscriminate introduction of efficiency or privatization can create serious dislocations and unemployment, which means it must be planned carefully.

Privatization has become increasingly popular around the world because it provides a source of income to the public coffers at the same time as it introduces deregulation and competition. This typically is not possible for natural monopolies such as the TVA authority. However, such public enterprises often outsource subcontract work to private companies that specialize in a given area, such as computers. Another approach is to make public entities more businesslike by

1. Separating the purchasing decisions from the political arena
2. Introducing business approaches such as strategic management, organizational change, and so on
3. Separating administration from operating roles
4. Introducing incentives and recognition for achievement
5. Introducing empowerment and creative problem solving

Introducing change of this magnitude is formidable, but the payoff can be astounding.

AN EXAMPLE OF STRATEGIC MANAGEMENT IN A SMALL BUSINESS

Strategic fit is a key priority in a merger, for growth, and in other kinds of change. Strategic analysis that evaluates opportunities, threats, strengths, and weaknesses and the way they "fit" is the first step. There are a number of methodologies that are useful in accomplishing this task. What follows is an example of their application for a small business.

The company, TTS (a real company, disguised), was in a very competitive niche in the textile industry and was losing customers, market share, and money. TTS had fewer than 100 employees, under $5 million in plant and equipment, and under $1 million in sales. In addition to standard financial analysis, the methodologies applied included a company capability profile, industry analysis, strategic positioning and action evaluation (SPACE), organizational culture evaluation, and decision style analysis. A modified Delphi approach and an in-depth questioning of each executive on the basis of the ten managerial roles defined by Mintzberg (1971) was undertaken. These roles were then compared to the roles expected of executives in their positions. (As is true for any case analysis, the methodologies used for TTS were the ones deemed most appropriate. Rarely are all the methodologies covered in this book applied for a given situation.)

INDUSTRY AND SPACE ANALYSIS

The annual industry rate of growth was estimated to be 3% to 4% and slipping. This parallels the general economic growth of the U.S. economy. There are few barriers to entry for new firms, and there is a high intensity of competition among firms in the industry. An increasing number of substitutes are being developed for various products, and there is a high dependency on complementary, or supporting, products and services. In most cases, the buyers seem to be able to dictate terms as well as prices. The degree of bargaining power of suppliers and vendors varies with the product but is not generally a problem. The degree of technological sophistication in the industry is moderately low. There has been very little (if any) innovation in the industry for a number of years. In addition, there are few capable managers available with experience in this industry. New management talent is not being trained, and young potential managers are not being attracted to the industry. Many managers in the industry who currently hold top positions are approaching retirement age.

The SPACE analysis indicated either a defensive or a competitive posture, depending on the general economic outlook.

- The *defensive* position would be suggested by a lack of strong competitive products and/or a lack of financial strength in an unattractive industry. The critical factor is the level of competitiveness. Indicated alternatives are
  - Prepare to retreat from the market.
  - Discontinue marginally profitable products.
  - Reduce costs aggressively.
  - Reduce capital investments.
  - Defer or minimize investments.

- The *competitive* position for TTS would be suggested by a moderate competitive advantage in a somewhat unstable environment. The critical factor is low financial strength. The indicated alternatives are
  - Acquire resources to increase market penetration.
  - Increase the sales force.
  - Extend or improve product lines.
  - Invest in productivity.
  - Reduce cost.
  - Protect advantages in declining markets.
  - Increase prices for products that are relatively "inelastic."
  - Attempt to merge with a cash-rich firm.

Which actions are recommended depends on what the company is able to implement satisfactorily. As an example, the ability to merge with a cash-rich firm depends on whether there is an actual firm available that satisfies the company's needs. Adding to the sales force would require hiring salespeople and training them at reasonable cost within a reasonable time. The expected increase in sales volume would have to justify the cost of implementing this alternative.

DECISION STYLES AND FIT WITH CORPORATE CULTURE

The strategic alternatives to be chosen also depend on the fit among the strategic needs of the company, the decision styles of the executives who will implement the strategy, and the constraints of the culture. At the first meeting with TTS, decision styles and corporate culture were discussed. Then the general profiles for the positions involved were drawn up and used to develop requirements for the positions. The ten managerial roles described by Mintzberg (1973) were discussed to determine whether the actual jobs of the executives conformed to the profiles commonly accepted. All the positions studied were very close to generally accepted profiles. In addition, the decision styles of the executives were very close to what was considered appropriate. Let's look at the specifics for several positions.

General Manager

The typical profile for this position emphasizes the analytical and conceptual characteristics. Top managers generally need more conceptual strength, whereas line managers generally need more directive strength with strong analytical ability. According to the decision style inventory, the profile of the general manager at TTS was a combination of directive and conceptual, with an analytical backup. The corporate culture profile showed that the incumbent had an appropriate fit. The following decision style analyses for individuals currently employed at TTS were performed to determine whether they were suited to their jobs based on how their style matched the job characteristics.

Operations Manager

The decision style profile of the operations/manufacturing manager was directive and analytical. The position requirements at TTS are almost identical to the general norm. The incumbent has a higher than average analytical decision style and a strong emphasis on the directive style. The culture in the manufacturing department emphasizes productivity. However, the overall fit indicates that it is flexible and able to adapt to what the conditions require. The incumbent needs to make difficult decisions related to conflicts among people and the financial requirements.

Sales Manager

The sales manager's position requires someone who is able both to understand customers and to close the sale. This typically requires a combination of drive and empathy and is reflected in a combination of the directive and behavioral styles. The job as described at TTS was a combination of directive and conceptual, with a low behavioral score. These results suggest that this job may need to be re-engineered. The decision style of the incumbent was consistent with what is required of the sales management position, where both directive and behavioral styles are present. On the other hand, a marketing manager's job would require a combination of conceptual and directive styles. This distinction is reasonable because the sales manager had been involved with marketing. There is currently some confusion about the distinctions between marketing management and sales management.

Marketing Manager

As we have noted, the ideal marketing manager profile is conceptual/directive. The marketing manager's job as described at TTS was highly analytical with a directive backup. This is due to the fact that the marketing manager was heavily involved in marketing research rather than marketing management. Marketing research requires a strong analytical component. The incumbent had an analytical/behavioral/conceptual profile and was low in directive. This may be the result of wearing two hats and of the emphasis on marketing research. The incumbent might have trouble exercising control and making the hard decisions necessary of the marketing manager. It is suggested that the functions be realigned.

Financial Manager

The typical profile for a financial manager is one that is both analytical and directive, with analytical being the dominant factor. The job description at TTS is identical to this requirement. The incumbent, however, has a very strong behavioral profile but is low in both directive and analytical styles. There is a backup in the directive style, but the analytical portion is very low. This presents a problem for matching the incumbent to this position. Immediate attention to this position is required. One solution would be to have the incumbent attend a quantitatively oriented program. This person desires to succeed in the position and has a very strong wish to please his superiors as well as his fellow workers. It is questionable whether this person is capable, at present, of doing the sophisticated analysis and making the hard decisions required in future allocation.

RESULTS

The company struggled to find a buyer, a company to merge with, or a source of cash. This effort was not successful. Two salespersons were hired on a commission basis, and reorganization of the financial and marketing functions was undertaken. Informal training is starting to show minor but encouraging results. The financial manager enrolled in an MBA program on his own time. Things are still tenuous, but the company has stopped losing money, and a small profit was achieved in the face of very poor and deteriorating economic conditions. Had it not undertaken this analysis and implemented the actions suggested by the analysis, TTS would have had to file under Chapter 11 over two years ago.

 UMMARY

This chapter addressed an important and growing concern in United States: entrepreneurship, which is one of our major competitive weapons in a global environment. The relationship of entrepreneurship to small business was discussed, as were the characteristics of the entrepreneur. Entrepreneurism is not only the style of an executive but can also be a company's spirit or that of a whole industry.

Growth often involves mergers and acquisitions, which in turn have a profound influence on the culture of an organization. Because mergers appear to be a normal part of the business environment, how to introduce organizational change was covered. Along with change, we discussed the corporate restructuring whereby many companies are divesting parts of their business portfolios, which often wind up as the small businesses of employees who want to be entrepreneurs.

Other sectors of the economy were covered, including the service sector and not-for-profits. Often a service business is a small or entrepreneurial business. And not-for-profit organizations have a similar need for strategic planning as other industries, a fact that is becoming increasingly important for HMOs and other health care providers.

REFERENCES AND SUGGESTIONS FOR FURTHER READING

Barnett, John H. and William D. Wilsted. 1988. *Strategic management concepts and cases.* Boston: PWS-Kent.

Bianco, Anthony and John J. Keller. 1987. The sad saga of Western Union's decline. *Business Week,* December 14, pp. 108–114.

Bird, Barbara J. 1989. *Entrepreneurial behavior.* Glenview, Ill.: Scott, Foresman.

Bloomberg Business News. 1992. U.S. losing technology edge, panel says. *Los Angeles Times,* August 13, p. D-1.

Boroughs, Don. 1992. Amputating assets. *U.S. News & World Report,* May 4, pp. 50–52.

Boston Consulting Group. 1987. Growth: The vital imperative. Paper presented at the Conference for Chief Executives, Phoenix, AZ. Summary of Discussion. Boston: The Boston Consulting Group.

Brokaw, Leslie. 1991. The truth about start-ups. *Inc.,* April, pp. 52–67.

Changing a corporate culture. 1984. *Business Week,* May 14, pp. 130–138.

Chip diplomacy. 1992. *The Economist,* July 18, pp. 65–66.

Coley, Stephen and Sigurd Reinton. 1988. The hunt for value. *The McKinsey Quarterly,* Spring, pp. 29–34.

Cornwall, Jeffrey R. and Baron Perlman. 1990. *Organizational entrepreneurship.* Homewood, Ill.: Irwin.

Cornwall, Jeffrey R. and Baron Perlman. 1980. Corporate culture: The hard-to-change values that spell success or failure. *Business Week,* October 27, p. 148.

Curtis, David A. 1983. *Strategic planning for smaller businesses.* Lexington, Mass.: D.C. Heath.

Dahl, Jonathan. 1990. Starting up an airline is not an easy process, even a one-jet outfit. *Wall Street Journal,* January 22, pp. A1 and A8.

Davidow, William and Bro Uttal. 1989. Service companies: Focus or falter. *Harvard Business Review,* July–August, pp. 77–85.

Davis, Bob. 1990. Space gamble: Start-up firm faces big risks in launching rocket from plane. *Wall Street Journal,* March 23, pp. A1 and A4.

Debono, E. 1969. Virtues of zig-zag thinking. *Think,* June.

De Coninck-Smith, Niels. 1991. Restructuring for efficiency in the public sector. *The McKinsey Quarterly,* no. 4, pp. 133–150.

Deutsch, Claudia. 1989. A toy company finds life after Pictionary. *New York Times,* Business Section, July 9, pp. 6 and 7.

Diebold, John. 1990. *The Innovators.* New York: Dutton.

Drexel Burnham Lambert. 1988. To restructure or not to restructure. That isn't the question. *Business Week* advertisement.

Drucker, Peter. 1989. What business can learn from nonprofits. *Harvard Business Review,* July–August, pp. 88–93.

Farrell, Christopher, Michael Mandel, Karen Pennar, John Carey, Robert Hof, Zachary Schiller, and bureau reports. 1992. Industry policy. *Business Week,* April 6, pp. 70–75.

Ferguson, Charles. 1988. From the people who brought you voodoo economics. *Harvard Business Review,* May–June, pp. 55–62.

Fisher, Anne B. 1992. Deals of the year. *Fortune,* January 27, pp. 104–111.

Fisher, Anne. 1988. The downside of downsizing. *Fortune,* May 23, pp. 42–52.

Fisher, Lawrence M. 1990. Sun's rebound in work stations. *New York Times,* March 5, p. D6.

Flanigan, James. 1986. As U.S. firms merge, Japan's keep growing. *Los Angeles Times,* Tuesday, August 19.

Grant, Linda. 1992. Recipe for survival: Service sector forced to slim down, work smarter. *Los Angeles Times,* May 31, pp. D-1 and D-3.

Greenhouse, Steven. 1990. "A new formula in Hungary: Speed service and grow rich." *New York Times,* June 5, pp. A1 and D20.

Greenwald, John. 1988. Where's the limit? *Time,* December 5, pp. 66–70.

Greiner, Larry E. 1972. Evolution and revolution as organizations grow. *Harvard Business Review,* July–August.

Haberman, Clyde. 1989. For Italy's entrepreneurs, the figures are bella. *New York Times Magazine,* July 16, pp. 32–34 and 62–63.

Hage, David and Thom Geier. 1992. Corporate reincarnation. *U.S. News and World Report,* June 15, pp. 43–50.

Hamilton, Joan, Emily Smith, Larry Armstrong, Geoffrey Smith, and Joseph Weber. 1992. Biotech: America's dream machine. *Business Week,* March 2, pp. 66–74.

Hanson, Jeff. 1985. Meeting the challenge of entrepreneurial growth—CEO management style. Atkinson Graduate School of Management, Willamette University.

Harris, Roy J. 1990. After entrepreneurial studies, the real learning begins. *Wall Street Journal,* June 27, p. B2.

Holstein, William, Kevin Kelly, and bureau reports. 1992. Little companies, big exports. *Business Week,* April 13, pp. 70–72.

Jespersen, Fred. 1992. The top 100 deals. *The 1992 Business Week 1000,* pp. 65–72.

Kleinfield, N. R. 1989. Grace Mirabella, at 59, starts over again. *New York Times,* Business Section, April 30, p. 13.

Koff, Richard M. 1984. *Using small computers to make your business strategy work.* New York: Wiley.

Kupfer, Andrew. 1990. America's fastest-growing company. *Fortune,* August 13, pp. 48–51.

Kuratko, Donald and Richard Hodgetts. 1989. *Entrepreneurship.* New York: Dryden Press.

Lawrence, John F. 1985. A company's culture shapes performance. *Los Angeles Times,* January 27.

Liscio, John. 1992. The ABCs of GDP. *U.S. News & World Report,* May 4, p. 55.

Loss at Sun Microsystems. 1989. *New York Times,* July 29, p. 34.

Lubove, Seth. 1992. Pulling it all together. *Forbes,* March 2, pp. 94–95.

Magnet, Myron. 1987. Restructuring really works. *Fortune,* March 2, pp. 38–46.

Main, Jeremy. 1987. Wanted: Managers who can make a difference. *Fortune,* September 28.

Mann, Richard. 1982. *Relationship between the decision-making styles of corporate planners and other planning executives.* Dissertation, University of Southern California, p. 55.

Matusky, Gregory. 1990. The competitive edge: How franchises are teaching the corporate elephants to dance. *Success,* September, pp. 58–70.

McClelland, David C. 1961. *The achieving society.* New York: Wiley.

Megginson, Leon C. 1988. *Successful small business management.* Homewood, Ill.: Irwin.

Mergers and Acquisitions. 1987. *The elements of restructuring.* Philadelphia: MLP Publishing Company.

Merwin, John. 1987. Not the next 30 days. *Forbes,* July 13, pp. 72–80.

Mintzberg, Henry. 1971. Managerial work: Analysis from observation. *Management Science,* October, pp. B97–B110.

Mockler, Robert J. 1991. *Strategic management: An integrated situational decision making orientation.* New York: D&R Publishing Company.

Mockler, Robert J. 1989. *Knowledge-based systems for strategic planning.* Englewood Cliffs, N.J.: Prentice-Hall.

Nasar, Sylvia. 1987. Competitiveness: Getting it back. *Fortune,* April 27.

Outrageous! Master the art of everyday showmanship. 1992. *Success,* March, pp. 40–42.

Pentagon to cut funds to chip consortium. 1992. *Los Angeles Times,* August 18, p. D-3.

Perry, Nancy D. 1989. Shooting for the stars. *Harvard Business School Bulletin,* June, pp. 47–55.

Petite payloads: Pegasus puts into orbit the first of a new class of small satellites. 1990. *Time,* April 16, p. 62.

Petruno, Tom. 1992. Simple plan makes Sunrise Medical a Wall Street star. *Los Angeles Times,* February 27, pp. D-1 and D-5.

Pollack, Andrew. 1989. For Sun, a difficult world. *New York Times,* July 20, pp. D1 and D7.

Pomice, Eva. 1991. Shaping up services. *U.S. News & World Report,* July 22, pp. 42–44.

Porter, Michael E. 1985. *Competitive advantage: Creating and sustaining superior performance.* New York: The Free Press.

Pound, John. 1992. Beyond takeovers: Politics comes to corporate control. *Harvard Business Review.* March–April, pp. 83–93.

Pouschine, Tatiana and Manjeet Kripalani. 1992. I got tired of forcing myself to go to the office. *Forbes,* May 25, pp. 104–114.

Prokesch, Steve E. and William J. Howell, Jr. 1985. Do mergers really work? *Business Week,* June 3, p. 89.

Quinlan, Michael. 1991. How does service drive the service company? *Harvard Business Review,* November–December, pp. 146–158.

Rappaport, Alfred P. 1981. Selecting strategies that create shareholder value. *Harvard Business Review,* May–June.

Reston, James Jr. 1982. Genius hunting. *Omni,* November, pp. 78–86.

Roach, Stephen. 1991. Services under siege—the restructuring imperative. *Harvard Business Review,* September–October, pp. 82–91.

Rock, Milton L. 1987. *The mergers and acquisitions handbook.* New York: McGraw-Hill.

Rothchild, John. 1991. Betting the store. *Esquire,* November, pp. 104–113.

Rowe, Alan J. and Richard O. Mason. 1987. *Managing with style.* San Francisco: Jossey-Bass, pp. 189–205.

Rudden, Ellen M. 1982. Why DCF doesn't work. *Wall Street Journal,* November 1.

Rudolph, Barbara. 1989. The chic is in the mail. *Time,* July 17, pp. 74–75.

Sathe, Vijay. 1983. Implications of corporate culture: A manager's guide to action. *Organizational Dynamics,* Autumn.

Sauriders, Laura. 1988. How the government subsidizes leveraged takeovers. *Forbes,* November 28, pp. 192–196.

Scardino, Albert. 1989. The magazine that lost its way. *New York Times,* Business Section, June 18, pp. 1 and 10.

Schlesinger, Leonard and James Heskett. 1991. The service-driven service company. *Harvard Business Review,* September–October, pp. 71–81.

Schumpeter, Josef. 1962. *Capitalism, socialism, and democracy.* New York: Harper & Row.

Stevenson, Howard H., Michael J. Roberts, and H. Irving Grossbeck. *New business ventures and the entrepreneur,* 2nd ed. Homewood, Ill.: Irwin.

Tannenbaum, Jeffrey A. Entrepreneurs and second acts. *Wall Street Journal,* May 17, p. B1.

Tichy, Noel M. and Marv A. Devanna. 1986. *The transformational leader.* New York: Wiley.

Timmons, Jeffrey A. 1985. *New venture creation,* 2nd ed. Homewood, Ill.: Irwin.

Touby, Laurel. 1992. Hot growth companies. *Business Week,* May 25, pp. 89–90.

Toy, Stewart. 1985. Splitting up. *Business Week,* July 1, pp. 50–55.

Troubled Wang decides to file for Chapter 11. 1992. *Los Angeles Times,* August 18, pp. D-1 and D-4.

Tunstall, W. Brooke. 1983. Cultural transition at AT&T. *Sloan Management Review,* Fall (Vol. 25, no. 1), pp. 1–12.

Utall, Bro. 1983. Corporate culture vultures. *Fortune,* October 17, p. 66.

Western Union clears last hurdle for reorganization. 1987. *Los Angeles Times.* December 31, Part IV, p. 3.

Woolley, Suzanne. 1992. The top 100 deals. *Business Week,* April 13, pp. 65–73.

Worthy, Ford S. 1987. Accounting bores you? Wake up. *Fortune,* October 12, pp. 35–38.

CHAPTER TEN

The Leadership Factor in Strategy and Implementing Strategic Change

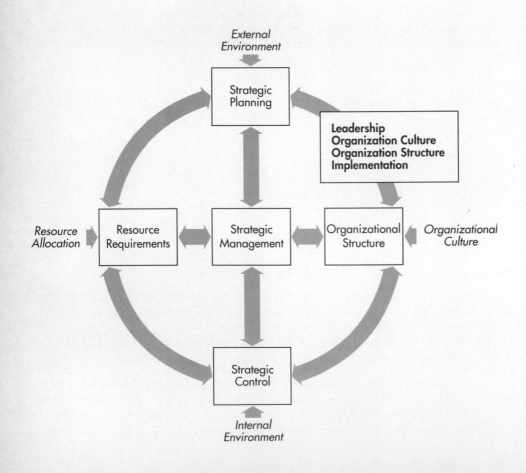

Chapter 1 A Framework for Strategic Management	**Chapter 2** Strategic Analysis	**Chapter 3** Strategic Visioning, Goals, Ethics, and Social Responsibility	**Chapter 4** The Competitive Environment	**Chapter 5** Capability-based Strategy	**Chapter 6** Market Dynamics and Sustainable Competitive Advantage
How to approach strategic management	*Application of strategic analysis*	*Understanding vision, values, ethics*	*Coping with competitive forces, stakeholders*	*Assessing company capability, timeliness, quality*	*Determining trends, gap analysis, and market dynamics*

Chapter 7 Strategy in a Global Environment	**Chapter 8** Financial Planning and Competitive-Cost Analysis	**Chapter 9** Entrepreneurship, Mergers and Acquisitions, Restructuring, and the Service Sector	**Chapter 10** Leadership Factor in Strategy and Implementing Strategic Change	**Chapter 11** Information Technology and Future Directions in Strategy
Assessing global trade, foreign markets, monetary exchange	*Preparing a financial plan and competitive-cost analysis*	*Importance of small business, entrepreneurs, restructuring*	*Strategy implementation, leadership, culture*	*Information technology, trends, new management*

INTRODUCTION

To remain successful, organizations must change with changing conditions. In many cases, the alternative is simply to fade away. Why is it imperative that organizations be capable of change? And how should the change be carried out? The answers to these questions are found in the material covered in this chapter.

Creating the kind of "learning organization" that can change successfully is a challenge and opportunity that confronts management. Global demands increase the importance of strategic learning in an organization, even though it involves doing things differently than in the past. Meen and Keough (1992) make the following points about achieving a "learning organization."

1. Large organizations have difficulty with learning that crosses functional lines.
2. The impetus for change should come from the people in the organization rather than change being imposed from outside.
3. The central task of management is the continuous building of a knowledge base that contributes to the learning process.

Supporting the concept of a "knowledge-creating company," Nonaka (1991) points out that Japanese companies have in place the organizational roles, structures, and practices needed to guide continuous innovation. Knowledge is typically generated by individuals who have gained insight into a problem area. The ability to develop new knowledge depends on the culture and values of an organization. Managing a knowledge-creating organization requires

1. Understanding the creation of knowledge and how it affects managerial roles and responsibilities
2. Continuously challenging employees to re-examine things they have always taken for granted
3. Responding quickly to customer needs by modifying existing products or developing new products
4. Dominating emerging technology by being able to create new knowledge

Creating technology is described as

1. Sharing specific knowledge with others
2. Combining specific knowledge about a problem into a pattern that leads to new knowledge
3. Converting this new knowledge into a usable form
4. Applying the new knowledge to previously unknown problems

Although creating knowledge can be understood, unless it is shared in an organization, it has limited value. Using teams or other organizational forms to work together on creating new knowledge that is shared freely helps lead to the knowledge-creating organization.

Creative organizations require a culture that helps to link a company's values and norms with its performance. Dumaine (1992) describes research suggesting that "the single most visible factor that distinguishes major cultural changes that succeed from those that fail is competent leadership at the top." This chapter describes the strategic change models that show the relationship of leadership style, organizational culture, and individual values (willingness to change) to the organization's ability to implement change.

In discussing basic truisms about leadership, Warren Bennis (1991) describes leaders as people who know the right thing to do. Individuals follow a leader who is consistent, even if they have different viewpoints. Bennis describes the role of leadership as empowering the collective effort of the organization toward meaningful goals. This becomes evident when

1. People feel important
2. Learning and competence are reinforced
3. People feel they are part of the organization
4. Work is viewed as exciting, stimulating, and enjoyable

Phillips (1991) describes Abraham Lincoln's approach to leadership as

1. Communicating your vision clearly
2. Being accessible at all times
3. Being discreet and never losing your temper
4. Building a team that can achieve results
5. Not compromising, but rather searching until you find the right person for the job
6. Creating a culture in which high achievers flock together

These ideas and others are covered in the section on leadership.

It is usually easier to think about things than to do them. As Vince Lombardi, the great football coach of the Green Bay Packers, once said, "The best game plan in the world never blocked or tackled anybody." It is for this reason that the implementation of strategies, policies, and plans is a crucial and very challenging part of strategic management. Consider, for example, the implementation problems that President Kennedy encountered in 1962. During the Cuban missile crisis he assured Khrushchev that the U.S. missiles located in Turkey would be removed, and several times he issued very clear orders to the military to do so. Nevertheless, as Kennedy learned later, the missiles were never removed (Allison, 1971).

The Ford Motor Company faced a slightly different implementation problem. In the early 1970s, Ford embarked on its "European car" strategy. Ford sought to unify its diverse product lines, to manufacture spare parts in the country with the lowest cost, and to focus its sales efforts on the most promising growth markets. Among the countries involved were England, Germany, Belgium, France, Ireland, the Netherlands, and Portugal. Ford undertook this strategy in hopes of obtaining the economy-of-scale advantages of the "experience curve," focusing its advertising and marketing efforts in a more efficient and effective manner, and eliminating the cost of duplicate facilities.

After the first several years of the strategy, almost *none* of these advantages had materialized. Instead, Ford ran into problems in integrating the differing levels of precision that existed in manufacturing, in standardizing on the metric system, and in dealing with currency fluctuations and exchange rates. Additional difficulties resulted from its effort to centralize paperwork and management systems in order to encourage cooperation rather than "back-biting" and price wars, as well as from its attempt to integrate the different cultural outlooks and views of the many diverse workers and managers in the countries involved. In short, a strategy that was grand in conception was thwarted in implementation. Even so, the European design now provides Ford with all its new models in the United States. Nonetheless, Ford has recently sustained a $2.3 billion loss, the worst it has had in its 89-year history (Woutat, 1992).

Why is introducing strategic change such a difficult problem? According to *Fortune* (Utall, 1983), only one in ten big-league companies successfully implements a complex new strategy. Is one of the problems that planners concentrate on the technical or financial requirements of change without due regard for organizational considerations?

What are the social dimensions of strategic change? For a strategic change to succeed, it must be accepted and supported by the people who are involved in the change. The style of the change agent, the values of individuals, the corporate culture as a whole, the structure of the organization, and the organization's position in its life cycle all affect the implementation of a change—and, in turn, all are affected by the change.

Strategic decision making involves a continued assessment of the current situation confronting an organization in light of the leader's vision for the future. One of the best illustrations of effective decision making is that of Jack Welch, CEO of General Electric Company. His leadership style encouraged teamwork and transformed General Electric from a ponderous organization into one that is profitable and growth-oriented. How executives like Welch make strategic decisions and demonstrate leadership styles is another important subject of this chapter.

Strategic decision making can be best understood by examining the factors that influence the decision and the individual who makes it. Here we will use a decision style inventory that examines how individuals think and process information as the basis for determining how choices among strategic alternatives are made. Both the mode of processing information in the brain (whether the decision maker relies more on left- or right-hemisphere processing) and the cognitive complexity of that individual influence the style of decision making. For example, managers who are planning-oriented in their decisions tend to rely on their "left brain," whereas those who are leader-oriented in their thinking tend to rely on their "right brain."

LEADERSHIP—THE FORCE THAT MAKES THINGS HAPPEN

In her provocative article "Will George Bush Really Change?", Dowd (1992) raises a critical issue in leadership. The American public is concerned about a lingering recession, the "Iran-gate" scandal, race riots, abortion rights, health care, unemployment, and the incomplete Iraq affair. George Bush claimed that the Democratic Congress was to blame for the lack of progress. President Clinton likewise has been confronted with a Republican Senate that has refused to go along with his stimulus package in what is called "porklock" instead of "gridlock." Clinton is faced with resolving the Bosnian crisis, job stimulus program, gays in the military, and lack of a definitive plan to reinvigorate the U.S. His ability to lead America out of its current miasma will determine whether he really is an effective leader.

SEVERAL EFFECTIVE LEADERS

By contrast, others who have a grand vision have been able to create an environment where change can and does take place. For example, there are "masters of the impossible" who break down barriers, recognize opportunity, exploit change, build teams, and turn problems into opportunities (Maren and Wallace, 1992). Examples of such leaders include Rene Anselano, who managed to break a global monopoly that was controlled by Intelsat for all international communications. He formed Alpha Lyracom/Pan American Satellite against all odds, including country regulations on communications. His break came when the Intelsat monopoly charged exorbitant rates during the Persian Gulf War.

Another example of a trend setter is Jack Welch. The CEO of General Electric is a villain or a hero, a rejuvenator or a destroyer. There is little question that Welch has a dynamic style and has made a flexible, lean machine of the once-ponderous GE. There is also little doubt that he has raised considerable controversy since taking office in 1981. He is noted for having made GE less bureaucratic. He has pushed authority down to the lowest level possible, while still fostering teamwork and expecting candor and trust. The results of Welch's leadership are unmistakable: in five short years, GE's revenues increased from $28 billion to $40 billion and its operating profits increased from $3 billion to $5 billion.

On his tenth anniversary, Jack Welch is again reinventing General Electric (*The Economist*, 1991). Now he intends to create an organization that is "boundaryless" by transforming its culture in such a way as to blur the distinctions among internal divisions and encourage everybody to work as a team. GE is a partner with its customers, and there is no distinction between domestic and foreign operations. The results in 1990 showed an annual growth of 8%, profits of 11% per year for a total of $4.3 billion in 1990, a workforce reduced from 410,000 to 300,000, and return on equity of approximately 19% per year. He fixed, closed, or sold businesses that were not number one or two in their industry. Over the 10-year period, he sold $10 billion worth of GE companies and bought others worth $25 billion. "Neutron Jack" has the reputation of being arrogant and ruthless, but he claims he is "hard-headed but warm-hearted." His leadership style would be described as inspirational and directive.

In an interview with Tichy and Charan (1989), Welch commented that insecure managers use complexity and clutter to distract others. Self-confident leaders, however, use speed and simplicity to achieve a transformation of attitudes that releases "emotional energy, encourages creativity and creates a feeling of ownership and self worth." This is consistent with what a directive/inspirational leader would say and do. Having a leadership style paradigm makes us better able to understand different leaders and to predict how they would behave in transforming their organization in terms of the vision they propose.

A very different style of leadership is that of James Dutt, the controversial boss of Beatrice Companies. At one time Dutt was considered easygoing and amiable, but he has become short-tempered and autocratic. At management meetings he shouts and demoralizes his executives. He is a driven man, who expects his management to work incredibly hard and to be absolutely loyal. Dutt's goal for Beatrice is to make it attractive to investors. In pursuit of this vision, he sold off profit centers that did not meet his standards. Yet he then acquired Esmark for $2.7 billion—23 times the price–earnings ratio. In an effort to make Beatrice the world's premier marketeer, he has so far made it bigger but not better or more profitable. Profits are down, top executives have quit or have been fired, and some describe Dutt's vision as a mirage.

Dutt's tight-fisted style of leadership eventually led to a leveraged buyout through Drexel Burnham Lambert for $8.4 billion. In 1986 the deal was called Drexel's greediest. Frederick B. Reutschler, the new president and chief executive officer, is attempting to reduce Beatrice's debt by using various recapitalization alternatives, including redeeming outstanding debenture bonds. Beatrice was initially hailed as the deal of the century but now is proving very disappointing because of its inability to obtain sufficient funds from the sale of a number of divisions.

Lee Iacocca is a person many people think of when asked to name a strong leader. He was able to turn the nearly defunct Chrysler Corporation into a viable entity. He claims that he was not looking for a challenge when he took over Chrysler Corporation and that the people who made the turnaround happen were not looking for challenges either. They did have the desire to accept new leadership that had the potential to help the company survive and grow. His lessons for success include the following (Iacocca, 1984).

1. Don't look for easy answers neatly tucked away in some ideology, because you won't find them.
2. Don't let the people with pat answers take over—they will always mess things up if they are put in charge.
3. Don't be afraid to compromise when you can't win, but also don't be afraid to dig in your heels when you think that you are right.
4. Don't be overly idealistic and miss the world around you; don't be so overly pragmatic that you take no strong stands.
5. Don't be afraid to make mistakes, but don't make the same big mistake twice.
6. Finally, don't let anyone tell you that you can't go up the mountain—you can if you really want to.

WHAT IS LEADERSHIP?

Leadership has often been characterized as the ability of management to create an environment that fosters commitment on the part of workers and that evokes performance beyond normal expectations. This has been called "transformational leadership." True leadership involves a complex transaction between leaders and followers. Zaleznick (1977) describes managers and leaders as having fundamentally different world views. *Leaders* think about goals in a way that creates images and expectations about the direction a business should take. Leaders influence changes in the way people think about what is desirable, possible, or necessary. *Managers*, on the other hand, tend to view work as a means of achieving goals based on the actions taken by workers. Thus leaders make decisions that are systematic and pragmatic in marshalling resources, designing organizations, motivating workers, solving problems, and controlling activities.

In his book *Mind of a Manager, Soul of a Leader* (1990), Hickman describes how managers and leaders differ. The manager is a person who typically is analytical, who prefers structure and control, and who is deliberate and orderly. At the other end of the spectrum, the leader (who is conceptual) typically is a visionary who is willing to experiment and be flexible, uncontrolled, and creative. Managers and leaders deal with organizational problems in a different manner because of their differences in style and perspective. Hickman claimed it is important that both be respected and work for the benefit of the organization. A leader tends to make a poor manager, however, and vice versa.

Zaleznick (1990) characterized the leader as the one who induces change and often is a disruptive force in an organization. Leadership inevitably requires using power to influence the thoughts and actions of other people and to develop fresh approaches and open new options. To be effective, the leader must be able to project her or his ideas into images that excite people in their work. Leaders who are concerned with ideas relate in intuitive and empathetic ways and arouse strong feelings of identity, difference, love, or hate. Warren Bennis (1976) warned that leaders may be a beleaguered species. He felt that to lead others, the leader must first know himself or herself. Further, he stated that "the leader must be a social architect who studies and shapes what is called the culture of work—those intangibles that are so hard to discern but are so terribly important in governing the way people act, the values and norms that are subtly transmitted to individuals and the group and that tend to create binding and bonding." Warren Bennis further describes leaders as people who have a passion for the promise of life. Leaders transform vision into action by harnessing diffused power to empower others who can then translate the vision into reality. "Leaders have to lead under uncertain, risky conditions where it is virtually impossible to get ready for something when you have to be ready for anything." Bennis identified the following dictums as characterizing the strategies of the 90 exceptional CEOs he studied (Bennis, 1985).

1. *Vision.* Create a compelling vision.
2. *Communication and alignment.* Communicate that vision to gain the support of constituencies.
3. *Persistence, consistency, and focus.* Maintain the organization's direction under all conditions.
4. *Empowerment.* Create environments—the social architecture—that can harness the energies of those in the organization to bring about the desired results.
5. *Organizational learning.* Find ways and means for the organization to monitor its performance and to compare its results with objectives. Access an evolving database on which to review past actions and base future ones. Determine how to restructure the organization and key personnel when faced with new conditions.

Bennis elaborated on these five dictums by identifying the ways in which they can be made operational:

- Make your intentions simple, complete, and easily communicable.
- Transform the organization into an integral unit by using symbols, such as ceremonies, that demonstrate leadership.
- Provide creative space for leaders to make their intentions aesthetically attractive and compelling.

James Zumberge, president of the University of Southern California, singled out three fundamental abilities of leaders, which are highly consistent with Bennis's observations. Zumberge says that leaders (1) see opportunities for change that are consistent with their concept of what the organization should be, (2) possess qualities that enable them to share their vision with others, and (3) know how to mobilize the power base needed to bring about changes in the behavior of others (Zumberge, 1988).

The headline in a *Fortune* magazine article (1987) read, "Wanted: Leaders Who Can Make a Difference." The thesis was that good management is no longer sufficient to tackle the tough problems confronting American industry in the face of new economic realities and foreign competition. In particular, the writers disclaimed the value of the rational decision maker who coolly prepares plans for growth and competitive advantage. Rather, the executive of the future will have to have a vision and the ability to inspire others to join him or her in making that vision a reality. The most important difference between the old-style decision maker and the new-style leader is that the new leader recognizes the need for change and then makes it happen.

Although the natural tendency of an organization is to preserve the status quo, the new leader is not content with things as they are. Whereas an old-style decision maker might say, "We've been doing it this way for the last twenty years and it works," thus adhering to the old adage "If it ain't broke, don't fix it," the new leader would look at the organization and see not what it is, but what it could be. In today's dynamic environment, anything that is more than a year or two old is probably in some sense obsolete. The skills needed to create and carry out a vision are different from those needed to keep an organization going. A leader is not afraid to change the structure of the company in order to carry out the new vision.

In examining what leaders really do, Kotter (1990) found that whereas managers are good at "controlling" complex situations, leaders are effective change agents who produce useful results. He describes leaders as people who

1. Set direction vs. planning or budgeting
2. Align individuals with organizational goals vs. developing organizational structures
3. Motivate employees by satisfying basic human needs vs. using controls to enforce performance
4. Create exciting opportunities for young employees
5. Develop a culture that encourages participation
6. Create a sense of belonging that values strong leadership

Others have commented on the question of vision. Langeler (1992), for example, describes the vision trap. He maintains that abstract visions can be too grand and inspirational and can wind up weakening a company because it lacks focus. Ultimately, a vision must satisfy customers as well as employees. Kiechel (1989) warns that executive vision can sometimes ignore the realities of experience and the demands of customers and stockholders. He questions the value of such lofty aspirations as being the best in the industry or making the highest-quality products. Unless it is possible to deliver on these visions, they may turn out to be no more than sources of frustration.

If the new-style leader is in fact unique, what are the ways in which he or she is different? Is it possible to determine ahead of time which people are most likely to be successful leaders? Decision-style analysis shows that leaders combine elements of the conceptual style, which gives them vision and creativity; the behavioral style, which helps them understand people; and the directive style, which focuses on getting results. Note that the only style missing (see Chapter 9) is the analytical style—the one most characteristic of the rational decision maker. What we can conclude is that leadership ability is related to the executive's personality and cognitive skills. In a study of senior executives, the decision style that stood out was the conceptual style (Rowe and Mason, 1987). Although conceptual-style executives have been successful so far, the question is whether they will continue to be successful in dealing with an increasingly complex environment characterized by the ongoing electronic revolution; very sophisticated and vocal pressure groups of employees, customers, and stakeholders; changing economic and monetary systems; and foreign competition. Their future success will depend on their ability to bring to bear other styles of leadership as warranted by the situation.

Fortunately, the decision style inventory is ideally suited to measuring the attributes identified above as leadership qualities. The fact that this instrument has been validated with a large number of senior executives creates confidence that it can be used to determine who has these qualities. To support this approach, a leadership style model has been developed that is shown in Figure 10.1. This model identifies the leadership styles associated with different change emphasis and goal orientation. As with decision styles, we have found that leaders exhibit various combinations of leadership styles.

Jeff Hansen's study of successful entrepreneurs clearly showed that leadership style, in conjunction with the phase of the organization life cycle, can be used to predict the likelihood that a particular individual will succeed (Hansen, 1984). The truly effective leader is the one whose style best matches the requirements of the situation. For example, Lee Iacocca needed both a strong authoritarian style (directive) and a creative style (inspirational) to undertake the radical transformation that was needed at Chrysler. President Zumberge, on the other hand, needed a more creative

| FIGURE 10.1 | Leadership Styles |

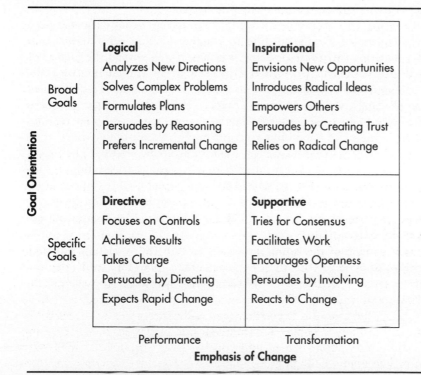

	Logical	Inspirational
Broad Goals	Analyzes New Directions Solves Complex Problems Formulates Plans Persuades by Reasoning Prefers Incremental Change	Envisions New Opportunities Introduces Radical Ideas Empowers Others Persuades by Creating Trust Relies on Radical Change
Specific Goals	**Directive** Focuses on Controls Achieves Results Takes Charge Persuades by Directing Expects Rapid Change	**Supportive** Tries for Consensus Facilitates Work Encourages Openness Persuades by Involving Reacts to Change

Goal Orientation (vertical axis)

Performance   Transformation
Emphasis of Change

Source: ©Alan J. Rowe and Kathleen K. Reardon, Rev. August 1, 1992.

(inspirational) and considerate (supportive) style of leadership, because a highly authoritarian style would conflict with the cultural values of a university.

Using an approach such as that shown in Figure 10.1, strategic managers can match individuals' leadership styles to the situation confronting the organization to determine who is most likely to succeed.

STRATEGIC CHANGE

INTRODUCING STRATEGIC CHANGE

Before strategic change can take place, there must be trust in management on the part of employees. Farnham (1989) maintains that there is a "trust gap" wherein corporate America is split between top management and employees and that it is crucial to regain employee confidence. In part, the gap exists because management does not know what employees really want. A Harris poll done for Steelcase Corporation revealed that employees value respect, management ethics, recognition for contributions and closer, honest communications above even high pay, better working conditions, and benefits. Unfortunately, many differences separate employees and top management. When top managers do not hear about products, markets, competitors, operating problems, or creative opportunities, they are in danger of losing touch with reality. Managers need to earn people's confidence if they expect acceptance of and commitment to strategic change.

Could American workers themselves be at fault for the gulf that exists between them and top management? Not according to Magnet (1992), who claims that those who accuse American workers of being lazy haven't examined the facts. For example, the real gross domestic product (GDP) grew at an annual rate of 1.3% for the past decade and remains the highest in the industrial world. Thus the men and women who are employed in the United States hold their own against global competition. The culprits are managers who fail to channel the pent-up energy and creativity that many employees are willing to contribute to their organization.

There are two approaches that have been used for strategic change. The first is working with the people in the organization to achieve mutual understanding. This is largely an informal approach. The second is making formal changes in the organizational structure, culture, or relationships. Effective implementation generally requires that both approaches be used in order for the change to be appropriate and to be accepted by participants.

Globe Metallurgical, the first small company to win the Malcolm Baldrige Award, believes that to achieve strategic change, managers must be tenacious and must be willing to get some dirt under their fingernails (Rayner, 1992). The company has achieved strategic change through

1. A management-led leveraged buyout
2. Flexible work teams
3. A strong focus on R&D, leading to high quality and low cost
4. Following a high-value niche strategy
5. Tight control of quality

6. Continuous improvement of operations
7. Insisting on obtaining agreement from all employees

The transformation from an old-line metallurgical company to the new vision was a traumatic experience described as "trial-by-fire transformation." The change was led by Arden Sims, the slow-speaking CEO who used total quality management and flexible work teams to bring about the strategic change he wanted.

In order for a strategic plan to be successful, the organization and many of its stakeholders need to accept the plan. There are, however, individuals whose behavior is especially crucial to the success of strategic change. Most successful implementation requires active participation from the CEO and other senior executives in an organization. Top executives provide the power, authority, and resources necessary to carry out the strategic plan. Next, someone has to champion the change. This could be the CEO (as was the case with Jack Welch at General Electric), or it could be a junior executive who has the vision and inspiration and is given an opportunity to move the organization in a new direction. Finally, there are all the other members of the organization—production workers, sales personnel, office workers and the like—who must change how they work in accordance with the new strategic plan. Of particular importance are the middle managers whose expertise is often rooted in the old ways of doing things and who are in a position to control the flow of information and activities. Middle managers are often the principal source of resistance to change. The new strategy's champion must play the role of change agent and influence the behavior of senior management, middle management, and all other members of the organization. Participation and the effective use of authority are the change agent's key tools. These and other tools are used to obtain commitment on the part of all involved parties. As Drucker (1974) observed, "The best plan is only a plan; that is, it shows good intentions. Unless there is a commitment made, there are only promises and hopes, but no plan." Thus effective strategic change absolutely requires acceptance and commitment on the part of the organization's members.

CREATING CHANGE

In an era when people are often suspicious that they are being manipulated (in contrast to being motivated), workers face a battle of beliefs. Most people concentrate on a small percentage of what they are exposed to and exclude all the competing stimuli. Marshall McLuhan dubbed those elements in the environment with which one chooses to interact the "environmental surround." Unfortunately, most workers do not experience the "revolution in ideas, concepts, values, traditions, ideologies or human relations" (Ledford, 1991). Recognizing this lost opportunity, management needs to find ways to release the potential that exists in most employees. Rod Canion, Compaq's CEO and president, understood the need to achieve consensus in his organization (Webber, 1990). He created a culture where teamwork and consensus management contributed to Compaq's phenomenal growth. Compaq believes in a careful and methodical approach to making new-product decisions, even though it also believes in bringing new products to market rapidly. With a low labor cost and well-designed products, Compaq has enjoyed remarkable financial results. It has been flexible enough to respond to a market where new products often show up in six to twelve months. Considering the high-tech nature of Compaq's business, Rod Canion has a culture that fits the needs of his industry.

Four key elements are needed to bring about strategic change. They are

1. The *style* of the executive who is the change agent.
2. The *corporate culture*, which reflects the change environment.
3. The *values* and *beliefs* of the individual performers who affect the change process.
4. The *match*, or *fit*, between the values of the individual performers and the corporate culture. This match determines whether the change is acceptable and whether change will take place or will become distorted or blocked.

These four factors are shown in Figure 10.2.

THE STYLE OF THE CHANGE AGENT

The *change agent* is generally a key executive whose values are strong and dominate the culture. This person may be a founder of the company, the strategic planner, or any other key executive.

FIGURE 10.2 | **Elements of Strategic Change**

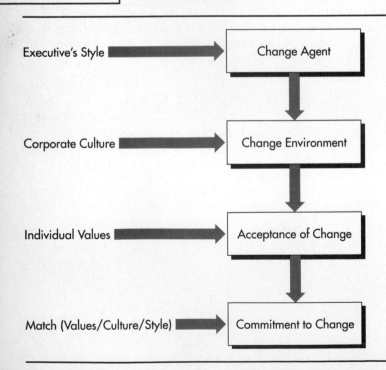

The founders' vision is generally so strong and powerful that others "buy into" it. This vision is built on a recognition of opportunities, needs, and requirements. The founders determine the company's strategy based on their preferences about the means of implementing what they believe to be in the best interests of the company. The classic example of such a founder is Thomas J. Watson of IBM. Watson created an enduring culture that had made IBM a world leader in computers. Watson's vision and support of people still permeate the organization. In his son's book *A Business and Its Beliefs* (1963), Watson is quoted as saying, "I believe the real difference between success and failure in a corporation can very often be traced to the question of how well the organization brings out the great energies and talents of its people." He also expressed the opinion that the single most important factor in success is adherence to "a sound set of beliefs."

Howard Schwartz, a vice president of Management Analysis Corporation, is actively involved with organizations that are dealing with changing culture (Sethia, 1984). He believes that if the chief executive is to be an effective change agent, he or she must place any new strategy in the context of the organization's core values and guiding beliefs.

When implementing a new strategy, the change agent should

1. Communicate the need for changes that will enable the organization to meet competitive forces in the environment
2. Develop a vision that can be shared by members of the organization
3. Determine what beliefs, values, norms, structures, and protocol must be changed for the new strategy to succeed
4. Make the CEO's office the focal point of support for the proposed changes
5. Ensure that the changed culture is reinforced and supports the new strategy

The success of the social change process often depends on the decision style of the change agent. An overly analytical manager will often focus on current problems without regard to the need to employ an appropriate change process. On the other hand, a broadly conceptual manager may be overly concerned with examining many options and involving other employees in the organization in the decision-making process and thus may miss opportunities or diffuse the means of bringing about a change. Once again, a combination of styles provides the best balance.

THE CORPORATE CULTURE

Why is it that intelligent, well-thought-out strategies are so often thwarted in the implementation phase? Often it is the organizational culture that prevents the strategic change from taking place. Indeed, one large international consulting group insists that a strategy cannot be executed without first considering corporate culture, because people often cling to well-established beliefs about what they are willing to do, even when logical analysis should convince them otherwise.

Heirs and Pehrson (1982) described stakeholders' collective and collaborative thinking on behalf of the organization as the "organization's mind." However, because the thinking process is different for each individual, figuring out how all these diverse perspectives can be brought together to produce a harmonious whole that will bring about the desired activities is difficult.

Corporate culture is the sum total of shared values, attitudes, beliefs, norms, rituals, expectations, and assumptions of the people in the organization (see Chapter 3). The culture is affected by the organization's structure, power centers, and climate (the degree of openness and level of trust and consensus in the organization). In his bestselling book on corporate cultures, Terrence Deal (1984) observed that culture meets social needs by defining relationships, specifying roles and duties, and establishing standards to be followed. Corporate rituals provide a means of demonstrating the values and beliefs of the organization and thus define the culture, the social interaction, the priorities, and the way individuals deal with one another.

Culture depends on key decision makers as well as on the history of the organization. Just as civilizations grow and develop their own cultures, organizations mature and incorporate the culture of the founders and their key executives.

Defining corporate culture is one thing—making it work is another. Companies whose cultural values have worked in the past include

- Hughes Aircraft, which had pursued Howard Hughes's vision of dedication to science and innovation
- IBM, where Thomas Watson's dedication to customer service was paramount
- ITT, where financial discipline demanded total dedication
- Digital Equipment, which focused on freedom with responsibility by emphasizing innovation
- Delta, which still promotes teamwork and customer service
- ARCO, which encourages action by fostering intrapreneurship
- J. C. Penney, which considers long-term employee and customer loyalty more important than being an aggressive competitor
- Wal-Mart, which follows a modern version of Penney's ideals

These companies have produced significant results in different fields, all by adhering faithfully to a corporate culture that fit the organization and helped it to meet competitive challenges.

When a change agent introduces a new strategy, it is critical that the culture be ready to lend support. The fact that the corporate culture at the top level is supportive does not necessarily mean that the entire organization is ready to pursue the same goals. Members of the organization who must implement the change are often insulated from the dynamics of the corporate culture at the top. Thus the corporate culture may be very different at different levels. The prevailing viewpoint at some levels may even be antithetical to that of top management. For example, union workers on the production lines may believe management is out to exploit them.

When two organizations are merged, cultures often conflict because their underlying values, norms, and beliefs differ. Drucker (1982) reported that from one-half to two-thirds of mergers turn out to be counterproductive or fall far short of expectations. In the face of such findings, why does merger mania still have a strong hold on so many corporate executives? The answer appears to be that the potential financial gains overshadow consideration of the factors that are needed to make a merger work.

As the following examples show, the sad reality is that many mergers should never have taken place.

- Reports indicate that Exxon spent over $600 million for an office systems company it acquired. What started as a great concept wound up as an implementation fiasco. Exxon's purchase of Reliance Electric, which cost some $1.2 billion, produced elusive benefits.
- When Honeywell bought Synertek, some managers of Synertek grumbled that rather than concentrate on the job, they had to spend their time haggling over resources. Finding the haggling culturally unacceptable, many of the managers left.
- North American's merger with Rockwell is an example of an attempt to marry the science and technology of one company with the commercial prowess of the other. The effort to combine North American's high technology with the cost-conscious market orientation of Rockwell has met with only limited success.
- After Wells Fargo paid $1.07 billion to buy Crocker National Bank from the British Midland Bank, the *Los Angeles Times* business headline read, "Wells Fargo Is Ready to Crack Whip at Crocker" (Broder, 1986). Given Wells Fargo chairman Carl Reichardt's relentless drive to cut costs, an estimated 19% of the Crocker workforce was eliminated over a two-year period. Ten out of the top 50 Crocker officers remained after the takeover, and as many as 100 of the combined 626 offices were closed.

A strategic change that is incompatible with corporate culture often flounders in a morass of opposition, sabotage, neglect, and inaction. Even if a takeover company promises that no one will be fired, those in the acquired company who do not fit in with the new corporate culture will soon take flight or else try to sabotage the change.

In evaluating or planning for a strategic change such as a merger, it is important to consider both how the corporate culture will affect the proposed change and how the change will affect the culture. Corporate culture provides clues to appropriate change strategies. There are many examples of cases in which the culture's norms, values, beliefs, and assumptions determined what actions were taken and how they were carried out. By studying the elements of the corporate culture and their potential effect on proposed strategies, a change agent can greatly increase the likelihood of successfully implementing a strategic change.

The various combinations of organizational values and orientations produce four types of cultural environments within which organizations function (Figure 10.3). *Organizational values* range from performance in a controlled system to achievement in an open system. The *organization's orientation* can be technical, and hence differentiated, or social, with high levels of integration and coordination.

An organization's values and orientation combine to bring about a particular cultural environment. For example, valuing the achievement of individuals leads to the development of a quality culture if there is a strong technical orientation or to a creative culture if there is a more social focus. When organizational values and norms stress performance, a technical orientation leads to a productive culture, whereas a focus on interpersonal competency brings about a supportive or cooperative culture.

FIGURE 10.3	Organizational Cultural Model

Quality Culture
Effective Planning
Problem Solving

Accepts Change

Creative Culture
Innovation
Entrepreneurship
Risk Taking

Initiates Change

Achievement (open system)

Productive Culture
Efficiency
Consistency
Procedure
Rituals

Resists Change

Supportive Culture
Teamwork
Cooperation
Growth

Responds to Change

Performance (controlled system)

Organizational Values/Norms

Technical (differentiation)   Social (integration)
Organization's Orientation

These four cultures have different characteristics. The productive culture concentrates on efficiency and consistency, whereas the quality culture focuses on the growth of employees within the organization through effective planning and problem solving. In practice, the productivity-oriented organization tends to employ many rigid procedures and rules, whereas the quality-oriented organization is more flexible in its approaches. The creative culture tends to be innovative and entrepreneurial, inclined toward risk taking. Change is most easily made in this type of culture. Most organizations would like—or think they would like—to have a creative culture. They may even go about trying to make change as though they did have one. But more often than not, they have some other type of culture, and the change fails. The supportive culture produces an environment characterized by teamwork, cooperation, and reinforcement.

Worksheet 10.1 is an example of cultural elements that are likely to affect the success of a strategic change at General Electric. The scores reflect the culture of GE in 1992. The first column of blanks is used to rate the culture in each of these categories. The importance of the various cultural elements depends on their pervasiveness, strength, and relation of a specific element to acceptance of change.

The second column is used to evaluate the compatibility of the proposed strategy with each of the elements as they exist in the present culture. A high score means that the strategy is likely to go in a direction that is consistent with that of the existing culture. This approach was proposed by Snyder (1984).

The four ways in which culture and strategic change can be related are shown in Figure 10.4. If the scores in the two columns in Worksheet 10.1 are high, the fit is supportive: elements that are important in the culture are strongly compatible with the strategic change. A low score in the first column and a high score in the second indicate that the culture is related to the strategy, so little attention to cultural elements is required. Low scores in both columns suggest that the change is inconsistent with the culture and that factors other than culture should be considered. A high score in the first column and a low score in the second signify a seriously constrained relationship between the culture and the strategy. The stronger the elements in the culture and the more incompatible the proposed strategy, the more difficult it is for the strategy to succeed. Thus Worksheet 10.1 provides a way of focusing on the elements of culture that must be changed if the proposed strategy is to succeed.

INDIVIDUAL VALUES AND BELIEFS

The values and beliefs held by those who are expected to implement the change are the third factor in the effectiveness of strategic change.

Values are the fundamental premises that we all use to determine what is important and what we believe in. They are intrinsic, deep-seated beliefs so pervasive that they influence every major decision one makes, moral judgments, reactions to others, willingness to make commitments, and support for organizational goals. Values determine what "really counts." Values can be so ingrained and strongly held that they can seriously inhibit or prevent change, even when the connection between the change and the values is irrational. Thus values must be

---

FIGURE 10.4 | **Importance of Cultural Fit to Strategic Change**

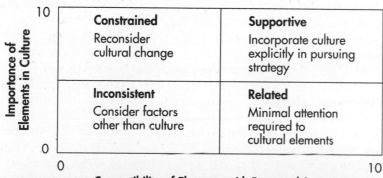

| WORKSHEET 10.1 | Assessment of Cultural Elements |

Case   General Electric
Date   1992
Name   John Doe

Score (0–9) for each

	Importance of culture	Compatibility with strategic change
1. Founder's beliefs and values	5	3
2. Key executive's style	9	9
3. Maturity of organization	8	3
4. Cohesiveness and collaboration	7	5
5. Openness and trust	7	5
6. Climate of organization	8	6
7. Recognition of individual	8	7
8. Rewards for performance	9	8
9. Support of individual	6	5
10. Participation in decisions	6	6
11. Consistent communication	8	7
12. Enforcement of policies	9	6
13. Degree of social interaction	7	5
14. Opportunity for growth	8	6
15. Level of job security	7	5
16. Level of technology	9	9
17. Degree of innovation	8	9
18. Sense of belonging	8	8
19. Latitude in job execution	8	8
20. Sense of urgency	7	8

understood and dealt with to ensure commitment to a proposed change. Examples abound of cases in which strategies ran into serious conflicts with values. Ross Perot's shock troops ran into flak at GM when proposing change (Mason and Brandt, 1985), and in the end the company chose to buy Perot out for about $1 billion rather than change GM's culture. Culture shock also shook up the Bell system when it was deregulated. In short, recognition of potential differences can help smooth transitions and forestall confrontation.

When strategies and individual values mesh, the results can be impressive. Recognizing the importance of the social values of employee security, welfare, and happiness, the president of National Duplicating chose to emphasize slow but steady growth of a high-quality product rather than compete on price (Guth and Taguiri, 1965). Although he was aware of the economic risks, the president chose a strategy that fit the personal values of his employees. Unlike the chairman of People Express (see page 478), the president of National chose not to let changing market conditions affect basic values.

Acoustic Research has maintained a policy of providing high quality at the lowest possible cost to the consumer (Guth and Taguiri, 1965), in spite of pressure and unfounded claims by competitors. For many years Hewlett-Packard has emphasized concern, trust, and respect for employees. During a downturn in business, the company opted to reduce the work week by 10% rather than lay off employees. The result has been employees' unflinching loyalty and dedication, which has helped Hewlett-Packard maintain a technological lead. Tandem Computers is another company that has upheld values such as loyalty, hard work, self-esteem, and respect for co-workers. These values are reinforced by rites, rituals, and extras such as parties and jogging trails. Tandem still has a unique niche in the "non-stop" computing system arena. Sales have continued to increase rapidly; however, profit growth has not kept pace.

The importance of values cannot be underestimated. They go way beyond normal incentives or rewards in creating a hidden source of strength, commitment, and dedication. In a study involving nearly 1,500 managers across the United States, Posner and Schmidt (1984) found that those who felt that their values were consistent with the goals of the organization were more committed to realizing those goals. The strength of commitment leads to a sense of success and fulfillment, a healthy attitude toward work, and an understanding of the values and ethics of colleagues, subordinates, and management, along with a more positive attitude toward organizational objectives and organizational stakeholders. Obviously, values alone do not make the difference. But if the values of individuals match the strategy of the organization, a synergy is created that transcends almost any other relationship in an organization.

THE FIT OF VALUES TO CULTURE

Behavior within organizations and between organizations ultimately depends on the match, or fit, between individual values and the corporate culture. Management often must alter the corporate culture in order to introduce a strategic change. If the new culture conflicts with individual values, however, it might not be accepted. It is at the acceptance stage, called "the third level" by Sathe (1983), that the change process often breaks down. Not until the proposed change has been accepted, internalized, and made a part of the values of those involved can the change be successfully implemented.

If an organization focuses on conformity and emphasizes production and control, and if the individual worker is very self-oriented and internally focused, the result is likely to be avoidance on the part of the worker. This individual shows up for work but, at best, does as little as possible or, at worst, sabotages the strategy at every opportunity. If an organization demands conformity and the individual is externally focused, the result is generally a compromise. The person meets demands, but that is all. Internalization of goals and performance demands does not occur. Acceptance takes place only when the corporate culture is characterized by values consistent with individual values. When workers who are externally oriented are exposed to such a culture, the result is accommodation: they become committed, and there is goal congruence and support for the organization. The more internally focused employee working in a corporate culture of openness relates closely with the organization, and the result is identification with the goals of the organization and collaboration. This is the "secret" of Japanese management style. It works particularly well in Japan because of Japan's relatively monolithic culture.

Acceptance and internalization of cultural change is by no means easy to come by (see Figure 10.4). Even when individuals have shown unswerving loyalty in the past, growth, competition, or dramatic changes in the environment can bring about changes in the corporate culture that are hard to accept. Take, for example, the case of People Express. Donald Burr, founder and chairman, started the airline with his humanistic vision of a company where every employee would be an owner–manager. His most important goal was developing people. As revenues grew from zero in 1980 to an estimated $1 billion in 1985, Burr's goal changed. Mounting competition made it imperative that he acquire Frontier Airlines to meet the demand for a broader geographic system. His decision to install a layer of managers in what had been a lean organization disturbed the match between the corporate culture and the values and beliefs of the individual performers. Unable to accept the new culture, in which employees were prevented from asking questions and a humane style was replaced by a more autocratic one, employees substituted fear for commitment. People Express was acquired by Texas Air, Inc. in September of 1986 because the airline was facing bankruptcy (*Business Week,* 1989).

The final effects of the change in culture at AT&T have yet to be determined. Before the process of divestiture began at AT&T, Chairman Charles L. Brown started the process of culture change with a speech in which he emphasized that the telephone company had to satisfy customer requirements by utilizing high technology and applying advanced marketing strategies. The new strategy included starting a joint venture with a Dutch firm, Phillips, and reorganizing Western Electric and Bell Labs. The reorganization involved reassigning 13,000 corporate staff employees (Tunstall, 1983). The result was described in *Fortune*: "Waking Up at AT&T: There's Life After Culture Shock" (Mendes, 1984). After 103 years, suddenly AT&T's culture, with its focus on lifetime employment, promoting from within, consensus decision making, and high-quality service, was obsolete. The new culture emphasized the marketplace, lower costs, and a streamlined organization. AT&T employees are learning, and time will tell whether the culture will be internalized or will be replaced. The evidence appears to favor bringing in new personnel, such as Archie McGill, a former IBM vice president, to establish a new AT&T marketing department.

How did AT&T go about shifting to a new culture? It started by changing the managerial mind-set and then followed up by creating a new environment. First a new system of management was developed that was carefully related to the change in corporate values. Training was then used to create a new cultural environment consistent with the new strategy. Ultimately, however, the success of implementation will depend on acceptance of the new culture by the employees who will be needed to carry out the plans.

Today, AT&T is still forging ahead with the culture it changed in 1983. Having acquired NCR, their CEO, Bob Allen, is now pursuing the seemingly impossible dream of uniting computers and telecommunications (Verity and Coy, 1992). He had to battle a culture that was known for its turf battles, yes-men, and internal bickering. Building on a culture of teamwork, Allen considers this the driving force that will help AT&T achieve its goals. He empowers people by giving all employees a role in the organization and the opportunity to do their best.

Other companies have used a similar approach to introduce a new culture. In one organization, the decision to change from a low- to a high-technology company was made by the CEO and his executive committee, at the urging of outside consultants. The executive's decision style was clearly entrepreneurial—a combination of the conceptual and directive styles. The culture of the company was primarily production-oriented, with cost, delivery, and availability being dominant objectives. To change the cultural environment, a combination of approaches was used. Training was provided to help personnel understand the strategic change and the management systems that would be needed to support it. In addition, a major reorganization was undertaken, which involved shifting individuals to new responsibilities, hiring technically qualified personnel, and establishing an R&D lab. The development of new, higher-technology products required putting the company's resources on the line. The payoff was a new strategic direction and a changed cultural environment in which the focus had shifted from daily shipments to new-product development.

Changing culture is tantamount to asking a person who is mean to become friendly. More often than not, changing a culture requires bringing in a new team that does not have entrenched habits that are hard to break. What a leader does is develop a sense of loyalty based on three factors (Sashkin, 1990): compliance (where reward and punishment are used), identification (where employees psychologically find that they identify with the leader's characteristics), and internalization (where employees endorse the leader's values and accept them as their own). The outcome is a sense of loyalty that is a natural consequence of transformational leadership, an "unwritten contract" in which employees and management share common goals.

The survival of U.S. companies depends on their ability to change strategy to meet the new challenges as markets and competition become more global in nature. In making changes, however, management must take into account the fit between the values and beliefs of the individuals affected and the new cultural environment. Learning about and adapting to all types of individuals on a global scale will help managers deal more effectively with the diversity that exists in America. Only if a match can be made between individual values and the culture of the organization will proposed changes work smoothly.

In addition to working directly with people to change their behavior, implementing strategic change also requires designing and managing *systems* to achieve effective integration of people, structures, processes, and resources. As Miesing (1984) has found, successful implementation of strategies requires the right organizational structure, resource allocation, and compensation programs. These formal methods include policies, programs, budgets, procedures, and information systems.

Policies are broad guidelines for the behavior of the organization's members and are intended to ensure that the organization achieves its stated objectives. They include guides to decision making and rules to follow in various situations. A discount store, for example, may have the policy "We are never undersold." Policies about hours, advertising, and reporting may also be established for the purpose of securing the desired change within the organization.

Programs are specifications of activities or steps needed to accomplish some aspect of the overall plan. Frito-Lay, for example, embarked on a multi-product-line strategy during the early 1980s. It changed its investment policy so that a new product needed to have an annual market potential of only about $10 million instead of $100–$500 million. Consistent with these strategies and policies, Frito's management developed advertising and promotion programs for each of its product lines, such as the new sour-cream-flavored Lay's potato chips. Among the most important policies are those that specify how people will be rewarded and paid for their contributions. These compensation and incentive policies must be consistent with the demands of the strategy.

Budgets detail the allocation of the organization's resources to particular activities and programs. They are statements of the organization's operational plans and programs, expressed in dollars or sometimes in terms of the assignment of people and assets to tasks. Every Frito-Lay product has an advertising budget.

Procedures consist of a detailed, usually step-by-step, set of actions required to carry out a day-to-day task. They are sometimes called standard operating procedures, or SOPs. Frito has very precise steps that each of its 10,000 route sales representatives are to follow in displaying individual bags of chips in a retail customer's store so that sales potential is maximized. These procedures are coordinated with the advertising programs.

Information is the glue that holds a strategy together. *Information systems* are required to inform members of the strategies, policies, programs, and plans to be followed; to provide the data that members need to make decisions and take appropriate actions; and to track and measure performance. If a strategy is to be implemented successfully, the organization's information system must be designed and operated in such a way as to get the right information to the right people at the right time. Policies, programs, budgets, procedures, and information systems are all executed within the context and constraints of the organization's structure.

LOGICAL INCREMENTALISM AND INTRAPRENEURSHIP

Logical incrementalism and intrapreneurship are two alternative approaches that have been proposed for introducing strategic change. *Logical incrementalism* is an alternative to the rational-analytical process that is often suggested by formal planning systems. In real life, the strategic planning process is typically fragmented and evolutionary and is often based on intuition or dearly held beliefs. Quinn (1978) claimed that the support for an evolving strategy that generates widely shared consensus among key top executives is so strong that logical incrementalism provides a more realistic description of the planning process than does the step-by-step approach generally proposed.

Logical incrementalism incorporates crucial organizational and behavioral factors into the process of strategy formulation. Multiple goal structures, politics, bargaining, negotiation, and coalitions all enter into the choice of particular substrategies for dealing with specific issues. Decisions on each issue, such as acquisitions, reorganization, or new-product development, blend incrementally and opportunistically to create a cohesive pattern that ultimately becomes the organization's strategy. The overall strategy thus is developed after, not before, the substrategies. Because the organization has only a limited ability to link all of the major considerations and factors that need to be taken into account when a strategy is developed, logical incrementalism facilitates the integration of both formal analytical and behavioral aspects of strategy.

Clearly, assessment of internal capabilities or strengths, forecasts of future conditions, analysis of competitors' actions, and identification of performance gaps are at best tenuous. Communicating assumptions, integrating divisional and corporate plans, taking politics into account, and providing the means for implementing strategy and measuring performance are equally difficult. It is small wonder, therefore, that effective strategies tend to *emerge* rather than springing full-blown from the mind of the executive. Logical incrementalism allows the organization to respond continuously to changing environmental conditions and to do so in a way that builds cohesion and commitment. At the same time, it in no way precludes the use of the relevant information or appropriate analyses necessary to determine which strategy to pursue.

Change also can be brought about by fostering what is presently called *intrapreneurship*—that is, entrepreneurial behavior "inside" the organization. A focus on intrapreneurship shifts the emphasis from planning to fostering innovation and productivity. The actual changes are introduced by the people responsible for carrying out specific strategic decisions.

IBM's move into the personal computer market is a case in point. The company broke with all previous traditions by establishing a separate development group that was allowed to function like a startup company. The IBM parent organization acted as a venture capitalist, providing guidance, money, and a building in Boca Raton, Florida. The building was not swank—it was a converted warehouse with few windows, a leaky roof, and malfunctioning air conditioning. Don Estridge, a go-getting entrepreneurial type, was put in charge. Under his direction, design team members were allowed to work on their own, with only quarterly corporate reviews. With this freedom and under these spartan conditions, working 80 to 100 hours a week, they were able to bring out their product, the IBM PC, on time. They opted not to use proprietary electronic circuitry—a move hitherto unheard of at IBM—and settled on the Intel microprocessor as the heart of the system. They also went to outside vendors for the software programs and used over 800 retailers, such as Computerland and Sears, to market the PC. A highly automated factory kept costs low, enabling them to pursue an aggressive pricing policy. Because IBM allowed Don Estridge and his PC team to operate in an entrepreneurial mode, without having to worry about corporate policy or the fit with other IBM product lines, IBM became a dominant factor in the PC market in less than a year.

The tried and true ways of pursuing new developments are not always the best. By giving employees the freedom to pursue their own ideas, management can achieve the desired innovation and at the same time provide opportunity and challenge to valued employees.

IMPLEMENTATION OF STRATEGY

Implementation is one of the most critical components of strategic management. A strategy that is not implemented is no strategy at all. In fact, as Thomas Bonoma has observed, good execution may save a poor strategy, whereas poor implementation ensures trouble or failure regardless of how appropriately the strategy has been formulated (Bonoma, 1984). Although implementation is covered here among the last steps in the strategic management process, the astute manager starts thinking about implementation at the very outset of strategy development. Each step in strategy formulation, evaluation, and choice should be undertaken with the implementation requirements clearly in mind.

Judson (1966), in *Manager's Guide to Making Changes,* delineated five phases of managerial action necessary to implement change:

1. Analyzing and planning the change
2. Communicating about the change
3. Gaining acceptance of the required changes in behavior
4. Making the initial transition from the status quo to the new situation
5. Consolidating the new conditions and continuing to follow up

Gibson, Ivancevich, and Donnelly (1988) elaborate on these phases as follows:

1. Examine the internal and external forces that require a change.
2. Diagnose the reasons for change.
3. Determine an appropriate intervention to introduce the change.
4. Examine the constraints and limitations that may inhibit change.
5. Identify the performance objectives and outcomes.
6. Apply methods (such as those suggested by Judson) to implement the change.
7. Provide means for evaluating the effectiveness of implementation and feedback mechanisms to correct the implementation if required.

The ideal in strategic implementation is to reach a state in which everyone in the organization understands what she or he is to do and why. This is the state of mutual understanding. Although it is the only state in which implementation can be secured for an extended period of time, few organizations fully achieve it. Generally speaking, there are four possible relationships that can exist between strategic managers and those they plan for (see Figure 10.5). These relationships depend on how well the managers understand the needs, wants, and capabilities of the organization's members and on how well the members understand the goals, objectives, tasks, and assumptions of the plan.

Managers can either make an effort to understand the members or not. Members can either be encouraged to understand the plan or not. This results in four possible outcomes. If the managers do not understand the members and the members do not understand the plan, then they are acting at cross purposes. Managers can attempt to implement the plan by fiat, drawing on their authority, but this approach is unlikely to succeed. (It is, in large measure, what happened to Ford's European car plan.) If, on the other hand, the managers understand the members but the members do not understand the plan, the managers must sell the plan to the members and motivate them by means of rewards and incentives. Because the members do not understand the reasons for the plan, however, it is

---

FIGURE 10.5	Understanding Strategic Change

	Members do not understand the plan.	Members do understand the plan.
Managers do not understand the members' needs, wants, and abilities.	**Failed Implementation** Power and authority are the only available approaches.	**Partial Implementation** Participation and education are possible approaches.
Managers do understand the members' needs, wants, and abilities.	**Partial Implementation** Motivation and selling are possible approaches.	**Full Implementation** Requires full use of the social change process.

unlikely that the plan will be fully implemented or that the organization will achieve its maximum potential. If the managers do not understand the members but the members are educated to understand the plan and its underlying assumptions—a condition reached because of the participation and education activities that the organization has engaged in—some of the plan will be implemented and some of the organization's potential may be realized. The U.S. military officers who let Kennedy's orders get "stalled" in red tape understood the directive perfectly. They just didn't believe in its assumptions and objectives. At the time, Kennedy did not understand how to get orders carried out effectively within the military establishment. The only way to ensure full realization of an organization's potential is for its managers to understand its members well and for the organization's members to understand and believe in the plan fully. This involves the coordinated use of research, education, participation, motivation, and authority. One of the reasons why Wal-Mart has been so successful is that all its members understand the reasons behind the company's creed, its policies, and its plans. Reaching this level of mutual understanding requires the use of a social change process.

Social change is a key element of implementation. There are very few instances where introducing a strategy does not involve changing the social system. Yet managers become so concerned with the economic aspects of strategy that they fail to see that it requires changes in the social system as well. Organizations are composed of people, and unless the manager can introduce a strategy in a way that leads people to accept and support it, the strategy may be doomed to failure.

Thus social change must be considered part of any strategic change. The phases in implementing a strategy should include

- Determining what social change is required for a proposed strategy and then introducing that change.
- Obtaining commitment to the change.
- Carrying out the implementation, utilizing managerial controls that balance behavioral and technical requirements to achieve specified objectives. This phase often requires re-evaluation of the original strategy or its adaptation to new environmental demands. Management may have to engage in many "unfreezing, changing, and refreezing" cycles over several years. How is the strategic manager to make these choices? The social change model has been designed to help in this difficult but exceedingly important undertaking.

A method for carrying out the social change process is presented in Appendix A.

Organizational Structure and Strategy

Present-day approaches to relating strategy and organizational structure evolved from two important efforts. The first was Chandler's (1962) study on strategy and structure, based on an analysis of four of the largest U.S. corporations: Sears Roebuck, General Motors, Standard Oil, and DuPont. He found that strategy determines structure and that environmental changes result in strategic options, which may, in turn, necessitate changes in organizational structure.

Later, Lawrence and Lorsch (1967), in their empirical work on organization and environment, examined differentiation and integration in three different types of industries. *Differentiation* implies breaking organizational units and functions apart and distributing them throughout the organization. *Integration* brings them back together again so that they are coordinated and unified. The amount of differentiation in an organization influences the way people are oriented toward goals and time, the role of interpersonal relationships, and the degree of formality of the organizational structure. The extent of integration affects the degree of collaboration and the mode of communication among departments with respect to common projects.

Lawrence and Lorsch found that the appropriate degrees of differentiation and integration were contingent on the organization's environment. In turbulent environments, successful companies tended to be both highly differentiated and highly integrated (a finding also reflected in Peters and Waterman's simultaneous "loose–tight" properties).

In stable environments, however, far less differentiation was needed and lower levels of integration were utilized.

In general, four factors determine the amount of differentiation needed. These are

1. The degree of certainty of the information used. Manufacturing would typically have well-defined information, whereas a market research department would be likely to utilize rather uncertain information.
2. The importance of rapid response.
3. The functions of the unit and the stakeholders with whom it interacts. Units with broad goals or objectives typically require less specialization than do those that focus on specific areas of the organization's environment.
4. The decision style of key executives. Decision styles determine the type of response to the manner in which the organization is structured.

Integration coordinates diverse groups within an organization. The factors that determine the amount of integration needed are similar to those that determine the appropriate degree of differentiation: the level of certainty, the response required, the goals that need to be met, and the orientation of the managers.

In many organizations it is necessary to differentiate activities and at the same time to provide for integration. Both processes have to be considered in dealing with the inevitable conflicts that arise in the process of formulating a strategy and designing a structure to carry it out.

Mintzberg (1979) developed a taxonomy of organizational structures, which include

1. Entrepreneurial structures
2. Bureaucratic structures
3. Divisional structures
4. Matrix structures

In addition to the four categories developed by Mintzberg, an intermediate structure, the strategic business unit (SBU), is often used as the basis for developing strategic plans. We will review all five organizational forms here to determine their strategic requirements.

ENTREPRENEURIAL STRUCTURE

A formal organizational chart or structure is typically nonexistent or of little consequence in an entrepreneurial firm.

The principal advantages of such an organization are that

- It permits maximum opportunity for flexibility and innovation.
- It allows rapid response to a startup situation.
- It permits initiative and informality.

The principal disadvantages are that

- The organization is critically dependent on the president.
- Employees must be very flexible and willing to assume multiple responsibilities.
- Nonspecialization may lead to inefficiencies in operation and lack of responsibility.

BUREAUCRATIC STRUCTURE

As a company evolves from the introductory stages of its life cycle to the growth stage, the organization is often formalized into a centralized structure. This type of structure is referred to as a bureaucratic, or *functional,* form of organization.

The principal advantages of the bureaucratic form of organization are that

- It provides centralized control of policies and procedures.
- It requires specialized knowledge on the part of each functional manager.
- If each functional area is staffed and managed effectively, product opportunities receive more thorough analysis.

The principal disadvantages are that

- Problems of functional coordination often occur.
- Overspecialization may result.
- Tight control may stifle creativity.
- An overload is often forced on the chief executive.

The functional form of organization requires effective leadership and integration by the chief executive. Coordination at the strategic level is needed to offset a tendency for one or more functional areas to dominate the company. The chief executive must provide the long-term focus, because the individual managers of functional areas are not likely to possess an integrated view of the firm.

DIVISIONAL STRUCTURE

In *decentralized,* or divisional, organizational structure, each division manager is typically in charge of a specific product. An alternative form of divisional structure is based on geographic areas, with a division manager for each region.

The advantages of a divisional structure are that

- It permits shared authority and responsibility.
- It allows more rapid response to changing environmental and market conditions.
- It allows direct measurement of product or geographic performance.

- Shared authority and responsibility help develop future management.

The principal disadvantages are that

- A duplication of effort often results.
- A large staff is needed.
- Divisions may become too independent.

This structure requires a long-range planning process based on shared authority and responsibility. The planning process must enable division managers to retain responsibility for product market decisions and must enable top management to coordinate allocation of resources.

STRATEGIC BUSINESS UNITS

As a company moves through the mature stages of its life cycle, the focus often shifts to consolidation of effort and efficiency of operations. In a large multi-product company, there may be many divisions or product managers. To manage the diverse products effectively, management may seek ways to group products logically. The basis for logical groupings may be production processes, marketing methods, demand for the product, or channels of distribution. The logical grouping of products into strategic business units (SBUs) permits management to take advantage of synergy. For example, because of leverage, the divisions' combined market potential may be greater than that of individual divisions.

When a company is organized into strategic business units, resource allocation can more easily be evaluated in terms of each product group.

Each strategic business unit can be systematically examined as though it had its own product portfolio. Of course, effective and forward-looking strategic management of a firm made up of SBUs requires considerable skill. A comprehensive plan for an SBU entails the same analytical steps that are required for the overall strategic plan of an enterprise, and consolidation of all SBU plans can be a formidable task. In the case of General Electric, for example, resource allocation among approximately 40 identifiable SBUs represents a significant undertaking. It is an easier task, however, than integrating the more than 170 product departments that existed at GE prior to reorganization or attempting to group the departments on some functional basis.

The advantages of the SBU approach are that

- Synergistic effects are obtained from product groupings.
- Coordination of functional activities within each SBU is improved.
- It fosters a broad and long-range management viewpoint at the SBU level.

The disadvantages of this structure are that

- Rivalries and competition over resource allocation may develop among product groups.
- A proliferation of staff functions may result.
- Empire building may occur at the SBU level.

In 1989, GE restructured into 14 business segments, which are an aggregation of SBUs based on major industries.

MATRIX STRUCTURE

In recent years, another form of organizational structure called the *matrix* organization has evolved. The matrix form of organization combines the product form with the functional form.

The matrix structure operates by vesting authority in a particular project manager (such as the interest-bearing checking accounts manager) so that he or she can use functional experts (marketing, systems design, administration) to carry out the project. The performing individual at any given point in the matrix has dual authority and responsibility relationships with his or her functional superior and project manager.

The matrix organization is not a panacea for a poorly designed or ineffective functional or divisional organizational structure. The shared responsibility, the different reporting channels, and the different superiors for each subordinate present potential difficulties for a firm that operates as a matrix organization. A complex set of relationships is required to utilize a matrix structure. Among the many corporations that have adopted this approach are Citibank, Dow Chemical, Shell Oil, and Texas Instruments.

The principal advantages of the matrix structure are that

- It permits major projects to be worked on within the functional structure.
- It focuses on specific requirements of a given market, product, or project.
- Decisions can be made by project managers with the input and perspective of top management.
- Management of new projects that do not fit into a current product or functional structure is facilitated.

Disadvantages of this structure are that

- Problems may develop from dual command and multiple responsibilities.
- Authority relationships are constantly changing.
- Problems of organizational continuity and conflict of authority may arise.
- It is difficult to reward adequately individuals who perform well.

In the past, a hierarchic or structured form of organization dominated industry. But in today's complex environment, structured relationships are often an impediment to effective strategy formulation and implementation. The matrix form was one of the first to deviate from the simple linear relationship among units of an organization. The matrix form of organization required the crossing of classic organizational boundaries and necessitated multiple reporting relationships. To have an effective matrix, one focuses on building an organization whose concern is strategic innovation rather than structural complexity. The characteristics of a successful transition to the matrix form include

1. A clear and consistent vision, carefully communicated
2. Emphasis on the individual's identification with company goals

3. Integration of the thinking and activities of the individual with the broad agenda of the company, which builds a shared vision

GE failed to achieve these three conditions in their Brazilian subsidiary, where they shifted from TV manufacturing to large appliances and finally to housewares. After the RCA acquisition, GE sold off its Brazilian subsidiary because it really was engaged in international outsourcing rather than building a responsive and self-sufficient subsidiary (Bartlett and Ghoshal, 1990).

The matrix form of organization was the first major break with conventional hierarchic forms of organization. The matrix is a transitional step toward the evolving concept of a "boundaryless," or open, organization wherein relationships are what is important, not the rigid lines of authority. In this organizational form, the emphasis is on coordination, involvement, shared vision, and individual empowerment. In the boundaryless organization, employees question activities and it is incumbent on managers to listen. Hirschhorn and Gilmore (1992) consider four key elements that need to be addressed in the new organizational form.

1. *Authority boundary*: defining who is in charge of what
2. *Task boundary*: defining who is responsible for doing which tasks
3. *Political boundary*: defining who gets what in return for organizational support
4. *Identity boundary*: finding the feelings of individuals and how they relate to the organization

Teams often replace departments or divisions in the boundaryless organization and erase group labels. To be effective, however, teams require a leader who can balance the four elements of authority, task, politics, and identity. In one example of team failure, the leader did not specify a clear authority boundary, and the team reacted by emphasizing an identity boundary. The overly strong identity boundary kept the team members from developing the task and political boundaries needed to do the job. Authority boundaries, then, are needed, but they are designed to define limits rather than control the effort.

STRATEGY/STRUCTURE LINKAGES

Organizations ideally function as coordinating mechanisms that facilitate coping with strategic problems. As a result, organizational structures vary from simple hierarchies to complex divisional arrangements.

The structured relationships shown on organizational charts, however, are static. They identify titles of incumbent managers and the roles and formal authority associated with the structure. Although these relationships have a pervasive influence on how strategies are determined and executed, they do not reflect the continuous adjustment that is made to accommodate environmental demands. The link between strategy and structure will now be examined from three perspectives: the organizational life cycle, integrative mechanisms, and the contingency approach to determinants of structure.

ORGANIZATIONAL LIFE CYCLE

The dynamics of organizational change are often referred to as the *organizational life cycle*. On the basis of his research on organization life cycles, Kimberly (1976) argued that a dynamic perspective on organizations is badly needed. An understanding of organizational cycles, which include creation, transformation, and decline, can help change agents to determine what intervention strategies are appropriate for organizational change and at what stage in the organization's development they should be introduced.

In another work about organizational change, Child (1972) described growth as a means of fulfilling the aspirations of organizational members, enhancing the chance of survival, and improving the organization's performance. Growth can contribute to economies of scale, reduce vulnerability, and improve the firm's ability to bargain with other constituents. However, growth also leads to organizational complexity, which in turn requires more staff and support to sustain growth. The unpredictability of environmental demands further complicates the task of the organization. Thus the benefits of increased size often give way to problems, in the classic biological pattern of birth, maturation, and decline. Small companies particularly tend to follow this pattern because of an inability to cope with externally imposed requirements and lack of adequate resources.

Pfeffer and Salancik (1978) distinguished between growth based on internal decisions to achieve organizational or individual goals and growth based on a biological model, which is limited by resources and constraints. In their view, growth represents an "intentional" response to problems of interdependence such as uncertainty or external control. For example, mergers are seen as a means to control interdependence by domination or avoidance of exchanges. Although increased size does not necessarily lead to the economies of scale often attributed to large companies, growth often does stabilize profits, reduce uncertainty, and enhance the organization's ability to apply leverage in the environment—benefits that increase the organization's survival potential. Thus firms merge and grow in an attempt to manage environmental dependence.

Filley, House, and Kerr (1976) suggested that regular growth patterns are predicted fairly well by a biological model that reflects the strategic adaptive behavior (provided no overt departures, such as mergers, affect the organization's product and structural base). Because of the interdependence between the firm and its environment, strategic adaptation leads to cyclical patterns of change.

Mintzberg (1979) maintained that there is strong evidence that organizations undergo structural change as they grow. The four basic stages of growth parallel the types of organizational structure described previously.

The nature of the transition from stage to stage depends on whether the firm starts in a simple or a complex environment. In any case, structural change is difficult to accomplish because of resistance by individuals in the firm.

Another perspective on organizational growth and the crisis of transition was described by Greiner (1972). He identified five phases in the growth cycle and characterized each as leading to a crisis that is resolved by a change in the form of management or organizational structure.

A typical organizational growth curve is shown in Figure 10.6. The first phase is characterized by an entrepreneurial management style. The organizational structure is informal, and the main emphasis is on creating a product and a market. As the company grows, however, the founders find themselves burdened with unwanted management responsibilities. This situation leads to a crisis, because the firm needs a manager who has the skills to introduce more effective control. In many cases, the founders lack such skills but still do not want to step aside.

The next phase of growth is characterized by increased efficiency in operations and centralized and directive management. At some time, however, these methods in turn become inappropriate. As the organization becomes larger and more complex, lower-level executives find themselves restricted by a centralized hierarchy. When these managers possess more knowledge about their operations and markets than does top management, they begin to demand greater freedom in their decision making. Thus the critical choice for top management is whether to give up some of its responsibility or lose creative middle management.

| FIGURE 10.6 | **Organizational Life Cycle: The Curve Identifies Crises That Lead to Changes at Different Stages of Growth** |

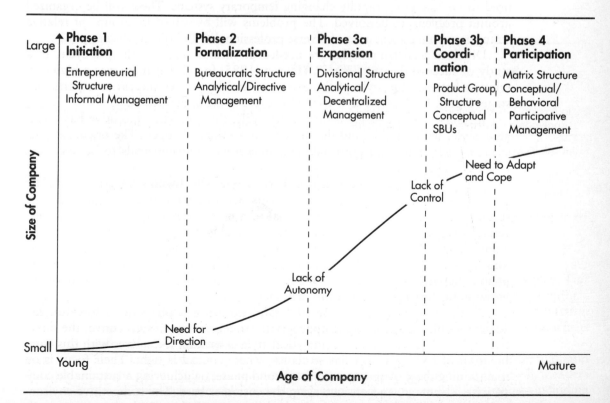

Group cohesiveness is reduced

1. When false expectations are raised about the group
2. When a few members dominate group activities and decision making
3. When disagreement or failure is experienced too often

The administrator reading this list may feel overwhelmed by the many things to keep in mind when forming a problem-solving group. Yet each factor, considered by itself, can readily be controlled by relatively simple effort on the part of the group leader or the administrator responsible for the group.

It is not a simple matter, however, to assess individual personality traits and thus to assemble groups whose members are compatible. Such groups should be more productive than groups with incompatible members. Generally, the assessment of personality is a complex process and raises questions about the feasibility of selecting compatible group members in any precise fashion in an organizational setting.

Successful groups appear to follow similar patterns. In a series of studies of airplane crews that had to solve the problem of surviving after bailing out over enemy territory, three principal procedures were followed by successful crews. These crews were able

1. To make sense of an initially unstructured, unclear situation (a necessary first step in many problem situations)
2. To resume communication among members
3. To establish a goal to work toward

The problems of business groups are rarely so critical, and are rarely presented in such a challenging setting, yet the procedures for solving problems are presumably the same.

Margerison and McCann (1985) have developed a team approach that is used for training, development, and more effective problem solving. They have an index called the TMI (team management index) that has been used by a number of companies, including Hewlett-Packard, DuPont, Mobil, and Shell. The index covers four basic behaviors that have been observed when people work together in teams: exploring, advising, controlling, and organizing. The key aspects of work behavior that the TMI measures are

1. *Advising:* These individuals obtain and disseminate information to others who can use it.
2. *Innovating:* These individuals are very creative and willing to experiment with new ideas and to pass these ideas along.
3. *Promoting:* These individuals search for new opportunities and are constantly looking for ways to persuade others to pursue what they have found.
4. *Developing:* These individuals are very good at assessing and testing how well new approaches apply to the particular problems the team is addressing.
5. *Organizing:* These individuals are very good at establishing and implementing the means for making things work, including relationships, assignments, and organizational structure.

6. *Producing:* These individuals focus on establishing procedures and practice so that the performance can be done on a more systematic basis and the desired results achieved.
7. *Inspecting:* These individuals are the ones who check and audit the performance of the system to ensure that it is meeting its targets and goals.
8. *Maintaining:* These are the people who ensure that processes continue and that standards are met.

There is considerable similarity between the team approach and the use of the TMI in management control systems. The team approach involves planning effectively and facilitates performance appraisal as well as career planning. The TMI is very helpful in training for team building as well as individual development. It is a tool that makes managers more effective in carrying out their functions.

Teamwork is a means for developing creative collaboration. In an open organization, team members communicate across divisions and can even report to a manager who may not be the team leader. In some respects, a team operates in a manner similar to projects in a matrix organization. The key is flexibility in the assignment of team members and an increase in information flow among individuals and among groups, which contributes to consensus decision making (Nunamaker, 1992). Because teams often consist of peer experts, it is critical to have a sensitive team leader who understands the need for communication and coordination.

Many new computer tools that can enhance the effectiveness of teams are becoming available for use in the strategy arena. They include

1. Brainstorming software
2. Idea organizers using IBM's TeamFocus tool kit
3. Electronic voting using Option Finder
4. Group support systems, including electronic mail
5. Expert choice for issue exploration
6. Mathematical decision support programs
7. Stakeholder analysis using the Strategic Models program

(The above section, The Team Approach, is reprinted with the permission of Macmillian Publishing Company from *Managerial Decision Making* by Alan J. Rowe and James D. Boulgarides. Copyright © 1992 by Macmillian Publishing Company.)

IMPLEMENTING STRATEGY: CONTROL

Strategies are, after all, only a means toward an end. Thus determining how best to implement a strategy requires an analysis of what controls are needed to achieve the desired results.

If one takes a broad view of achieving productivity and performance, control must be viewed from an organizational rather than a purely technical perspective. The following considerations need to be taken into account prior to establishing strategic control.

1. Identification of critical factors using decision criteria as the basis for analysis or comparison between actual and desired performance. In many respects, this is comparable to problem formulation, because before controls can be put to work, one must identify what needs correction.

2. Operating on symptoms is an inappropriate control approach. Rather, what is needed is a way of identifying the underlying causes of any problems and of using the symptoms as flags or indicators that there may be a serious situation that needs correction.

3. Before corrective action is taken, the costs and benefits should be examined. Then the appropriate corrective action can be determined. In many respects, this is comparable to problem solving, because the decision maker must understand the constraints limiting what can be done to correct a system.

4. The decision environment is an important concern, and the manager must take this into account when attempting to change or correct any aspect of performance.

5. Corrective action is needed when performance is poor or decisions are wrong. Corrective action should lead to improved performance.

6. A management control system must relate the needs of the organization to the needs of the individual. The functions of an organization must be consistent with the task demands, technology, external environmental forces, and members' personal needs.

Management controls in organizations are different from controls used in technical systems, such as quality control and inventory control. Drucker (1954) has stated this succinctly:

> Controls in a social institution are goal setting and value setting, they are not objective, they are of necessity moral. The only way to avoid this is to flood the executive with so many controls that the entire system becomes meaningless, becomes mere noise, and this means that the basic question is not how do we control but what do we measure in our control system. That we can quantify something is no reason at all for measuring it. The questions that should be asked: Is this what the manager should consider important? Is this what a manager's attention should be focused on? Is this a true statement of the basic realities of the enterprise? And is this the proper focus for control, i.e. effective direction with maximum economy of effort?

Some work environments require strict and demanding management control systems that ensure quality output, as in mass-production manufacturing. In the United States, quality control is often separated from manufacturing and is carried out by sampling methods. Thus problems are identified after the fact. Parts are scrapped and new parts made, which results in additional costs and time delays. In Japan, the manufacturing and quality control functions are combined in the worker responsible for producing quality parts. This simultaneity yields savings in both cost and time. When a worker is held responsible for the quality of work produced, responsibility is taken more seriously. The worker—not a checker—examines the product. Making the worker responsible for the quality of the work produced is "control at the point of action."

As the organizational structure evolves, so must the control process. We shall examine the following six types of control:

- *Management control*, which is based on past performance, historical data, or performance measurement.

- *Management by objectives*, which emphasizes the setting of objectives and frequent evaluation to be sure that those objectives are being met. MBO has been widely used to achieve personal commitment and motivation and to improve both performance and job satisfaction. Typically, if individuals participate in setting their own goals and objectives, they tend to be committed to achieving them.
- *Performance management*, which is concerned with goal congruence and organizational effectiveness. The performance management system (PMS) is an extension of MBO; it also attempts to ensure that subordinates receive constructive feedback on their performance. This feedback is provided by using a profile to evaluate the individual's strengths and developmental needs with respect to performance goals.
- *Adaptive control*, which focuses on responding to required changes rapidly and in an effective manner.
- *Strategic control*, which involves anticipating and minimizing potential deviations from the desired outcome.
- *Real-time control*, which uses computers to provide information as current as possible.

This list reveals that control is multidimensional and that it affects many aspects of strategic management. All six types of control are involved in ensuring implementation of strategic decisions.

In the following discussion of control, the measurement aspects of management control and performance management are combined. Likewise, adaptive, strategic, and real-time control are covered together. For other purposes, each of these approaches could be considered separately.

MANAGEMENT CONTROL

An important question in control is "How frequently and in what form should performance be measured?" Frequent interaction and multidimensional measures are needed to assess performance. Evaluation of such factors as cohesiveness, responsiveness, adaptability, and effectiveness provides additional insight into the organization's performance.

The identification and measurement of deviations in performance—a crucial aspect of implementation—cannot be accomplished simply by adopting a set of standards. Dependencies and interactions, along with change, give rise to a variety of problems in implementing any strategy; thus it is almost impossible to predict precisely the course that should be followed or the standard of performance that is appropriate.

The estimates that form the basis for standards are typically determined from historical data, which, by definition, are "after the fact." Furthermore, estimates rarely include any provision for variability. Absolute standards such as the following are often used: "keep equipment busy 100% of the time" or "meet 100% of quotas." However, 100% utilization of capacity can rarely be achieved. The use of averages is equally problematic; they tend to hide variability in performance.

Arbitrary allocations, such as for overhead, also create difficulties, because there is little relationship between performance and the standard.

It is almost axiomatic that because of the problems inherent in establishing standards, goals, and objectives and in defining the basis on which measurement is made, measuring performance is difficult.

Unfortunately, the manner in which control is imposed often has unintended consequences, such as widespread antagonism, successful resistance, noncompliance, unreliable performance, need for close surveillance, and high administrative costs. Ridgway (1956) showed that there are many dysfunctional consequences of performance measurement and that using a single criterion of performance or a single standard generally leads to undesirable or suboptimal results.

MANAGEMENT BY OBJECTIVES

Management by objectives (MBO) is an approach in which individuals are involved in determining milestones for improving performance. Table 10.1 shows how MBO was applied in a large aerospace company. Five vice presidents, each in charge of a major function, first identified key milestones they hoped to achieve in their specific areas of responsibility. The milestones were specific targets to be reached in pursuit of the company's overall strategy. For example, in the financial area, the milestones included a 5% reduction in overhead costs, a profit objective of 15%, and the hiring of two additional controllers for the decentralized operations. The marketing vice president's objectives included analyzing 13 new products and increasing sales per employee to $90,500 per year. In the personnel area, the targets included hiring 16 new key personnel and reducing the ratio of indirect to direct costs to 10%. In the area of engineering, not only did managers plan to recruit 25 additional senior engineers, but they also agreed to start a minimum of 5 research and development projects related to advanced technology. The operations vice president wanted to increase capacity by 150% and also had other targets, such as increasing interdivisional sales by $200,000 per year and installing 15 new computer systems.

Each month the president held a performance review meeting to compare the current status with the plan. At the time MBO was instituted, a reduction of 2% in overhead had already been achieved, and the forecast was that 3% would be possible by the end of the year. Thus a deficit of 2% is shown in the column labeled Projected Deviation. Because all aspects of the milestones are defined, including the target, current status, future forecast, and what has to be achieved, management is in a position to examine alternative actions that might be taken in order to meet the objectives.

In some instances, the target underestimated the vice president's ability to meet objectives. For example, in marketing, the plan for increasing sales effort called for a 20% increase, but 30% was actually achieved. Because this value overshot the target, a reduction to a 25% increase was planned, for a residual net 5% increase. In the case of product mix, the plan was for a 50% shift in product mix, but an 80% shift was achieved; the revised forecast of a 75% change for the year exceeded the initial target by 25%. Some of the targets did not exhibit the degree of precision that one might think was desirable, such as those for personnel development.

TABLE 10.1	Management by Objectives: Key Milestone Plan

Key Milestones for Each Major Functional Area	Plan/Objective	Current Performance	Forecast Performance	Projected Deviation
Financial				
Reduction in overhead cost	5%	2%	3%	−2%
Profit on sales	15%	12%	13%	−2%
Hiring of new controllers	2	1	2	0
Marketing				
Analysis of new products	13	2	10	−3
Increase in sales effort	20%	30%	25%	+5%
Shift of product mix (civilian/military)	50%	80%	75%	+25%
Sales per employee	$90,500	$90,000	$90,000	−$500
Personnel				
Number of key personnel needed	16	10	13	−3
Standard of labor efficiency	88%	80%	82%	−6
Personnel development	400	418	418	+18
Ratio of indirect to direct cost	10%	17%	15%	+5
Engineering				
Recruitment of senior engineers	25	16	18	−7
Application of project control systems	3	0	1	−2
Increase percentage of R&D per sales	5%	6%	6%	+1
New technological programs	15	10	12	−3
Operations				
Increase in production capacity	150%	110%	150%	0
Reduction in labor variance	10%	0	2%	−8
Increase in interdivisional sales	$200,000	$20,000	$50,000	−$150,000
Application of new computer systems	15	3	4	−11

It was estimated that 400 managers would be sent to various training courses. As it turned out, 418 actually went to courses, a difference of 18. This difference, however, should not be construed as indicating a lack of control or bad estimating. Obviously, 400 was only an estimate. An allowable variation should have been specified so that the variance of +18 would not be considered as reflecting poor performance. One of the most difficult targets for the company to achieve was increased interdivisional sales. The results showed only a $20,000 increase in sales, whereas the target was $200,000. The difference of $150,000 between the latest forecast and the target indicated that new strategies must be selected if performance is to match the desired objectives.

The MBO approach shown here illustrates how information, properly utilized and properly displayed, can provide management with a tool for achieving more effective performance. However, it is important to recognize that both the measurement aspects and the behavioral aspects of control must be considered jointly. These vice presidents set their own targets or objectives and were held accountable for their own estimates. Typically, if individuals determine their targets, they will be committed to achieving them. And the data they report will give management the information needed to assess performance and evaluate the basis for the targets. What has made MBO so popular is that it both provides meaningful measures and takes behavior into account.

PERFORMANCE MANAGEMENT

Performance management is concerned with a multidimensional way of measuring output, including

1. Behavioral measures, which relate to the actions required and rely on observable, behaviorally anchored rating scales
2. Objective measures, which directly focus on the outcomes rather than on the process of achieving them
3. Evaluation techniques, which rely on the judgment and experience of the individual conducting the performance appraisal

Performance management is often equated with performance appraisal that has had mixed success in implementation. Successful programs, however, tend to have the following three elements in common.

1. Objectives are specific and are set jointly with management.
2. Feedback is concrete and periodic.
3. Top management is involved in the program and supports it.

Because it is a system-oriented approach, performance management takes into account the degree of specificity with which work can be defined and the reaction or expectation of the individual who will perform the task. Objective measures, such as those used in MBO, can create problems merely because of the way in which the objectives are established or the way measurement is conducted.

On the other hand, where the task can be defined in specific terms, such as by objectives, direct measurement of output may be the most appropriate approach.

Behavioral measures are most useful where the work is well defined and the individual's expectations can be taken into account. Finally, subjective evaluation is generally required where the task cannot easily be defined or where no direct measurement is possible.

An approach to performance appraisal that builds on MBO is called the *performance management system (PMS)*. Developed by Beer and Ruh (1976), it was applied at Corning Glass Works with 3,800 managerial and professional employees. The PMS approach provides subordinates with constructive feedback about their performance. It emphasizes the manager's role in meeting organizational goals and in developing and evaluating subordinates. A profile is used to determine the individual's strengths and development needs. The results are then used to identify goals and means for achieving them.

Some of the factors considered in a performance profile include initiative, priorities, accomplishment, accuracy, communication, cooperation, decisiveness, and flexibility. With the profile as a starting point, a development program is designed to improve the employee's attitude, abilities, or interpersonal skills. Given this base, evaluation interviews are held covering the subordinate's current performance, promotion potential, and salary increase. At Corning, merely identifying performance dimensions helped improve organizational effectiveness.

The principal difference between PMS and MBO is in the process of arriving at performance standards. MBO starts with agreed-upon objectives and then allows individuals to establish their own criteria and plans for achieving these objectives. PMS starts with a description of the subordinate's behavior, showing his or her strengths and weaknesses. Using a sequence of interviews, the manager and subordinate jointly identify areas where improvement is required. Plans are then established for developing the abilities the individual needs to perform effectively.

In the past, the emphasis in performance management has been on a closed-loop feedback approach. In such a system, however, objectives are often unclear, missing, or changing; accomplishment is difficult to measure with unambiguous, quantitative output standards; and feedback information is often not relevant or usable. Because of the complexity of control, the emphasis is increasingly being placed on behaviorally oriented systems, such as a combination of MBO and PMS.

More recent approaches emphasize a relaxation of the rigid control systems that have been applied in the past. For example, Chaparral Steel, which operates in an extremely competitive environment, has been able to produce steel at a record low of 1.6 hours per ton, compared with 2.4 hours for mini-mills and 4.9 hours for integrated steel mills. This was accomplished by relaxing controls and emphasizing the contributions that workers can make. Gordon Forward, CEO of Chaparral, has developed a "classless" organization. Workers receive a salary and a bonus based on individual performance, the company's profits, and the skills they have learned. There are no time clocks; lunch hours and breaks are set by the workers themselves. There is an open parking lot and executive offices are also open. Forward was seeking the commitment of employees by providing extraordinary freedom, and they, in turn, were expected to show initiative in their work. The result has been significant improvements in equipment design, inventions, and overall performance. Chaparral has emerged as a quality, low-cost producer that is highly profitable in an industry most would shun (Dumaine, 1992).

The opposite was the case at TopChem, where CEO Sam Verde based employee compensation on incremental improvements (Ehrenfeld, 1992). The following were specified targets:

1. Base pay would be 75% of former pay
2. Flexible pay would be 25% of former pay based on
   a. The team's ability to show a 5% annual improvement defined as follows: achieving a 30% improvement in quality, keeping unit cost to market at 25%, improving speed to market by 20%, and increasing safety and environmental compliance by 10%
   b. Improving divisional financial performance by 15%

The feeling at TopChem was that teamwork was a motivational kick that did not reflect the way people worked. The pay plan proposed at TopChem provided a negative rather than positive incentive. It set arbitrary targets in difficult-to-define areas that simply "justified" the salary with no bonus or incentive attached. It failed.

ADAPTIVE, STRATEGIC, AND REAL-TIME CONTROL

Because the basic strategy of a firm undergoes continuous modification, so must its implementation. Although adaptive controls have been used principally at the operating level, modifying *all* aspects of the internal environment to match the changing external requirements is critical for achieving desired strategies. An obvious approach is to anticipate possible deviations, just as is done in statistical quality control. For example, if an expenditure is proposed, the possibility that it might exceed the budget should be considered ahead of time rather than after the fact.

Dell Computers offers an example of control that is done on a timely basis. Increasingly, customers are demanding on-time delivery from their suppliers. When the product cannot be delivered promptly, customers go elsewhere. Dell managers meet at 7:30 A.M. every Friday to review the week's performance from the point of view of customer satisfaction. Dell has set as a target to be number one in customer satisfaction. To achieve this objective, Dell simplifies products and components and transmits customer order information to the factory, where a "made-to-order" operation ensures delivery within three or four days. Just as was the case with AHSC (see Chapter 1), when this system was launched, sales increased by 70% in less than two years (Kumar and Sharman, 1992).

A strategic control system permits management to change both the desired objectives and the methods of control. Organizations with many products, or with large and complex projects, may need a computer-based system to achieve strategic control. Evaluating a complex system generally requires large amounts of data, and the system must be continuously monitored if appropriate corrective action is to be taken "in time" to achieve desired objectives. Thus an adaptive computer-based approach often depends on a system that utilizes large-scale databases and simulation models to forecast the future states of the system. Such systems are closely tied to decision support systems as shown in Figure 10.10.

The operation of a realtime, adaptive computer-based system is shown in Figure 10.10. The data gathered by the computer are used to update the database and to produce management reports or other displays for real-time inquiries. Appropriate simulation models supply the strategic information that is an essential part of a decision support system. Expert support systems are beginning to emerge as another tool for adaptive controls, because they can answer "what if" questions and provide useful advice (Mockler, 1989).

An important question is "When has the system changed sufficiently to warrant a modification?" Because performance involves randomness and uncertainty, deviations from a narrow target, objective, or budget do not necessarily indicate a need for correction; most deviations will be due to chance. To deal with this problem, management can use appropriate control limits. Furthermore, because objectives are often based on estimates derived from experience, comparable work, or some arbitrarily determined standard, considerable uncertainty exists about the validity of the objective itself. Therefore, it is inappropriate to use the estimate as a "rigid" base for measuring performance or to adapt the system. It is precisely because of rapid and often unpredictable change that a strategic control system is needed to pinpoint the need for corrective action.

Managerial and strategic control are so intimately intertwined with behavioral and analytical considerations it is small wonder that no simple, straightforward solution has emerged to the problem of strategy implementation. Rather, there are

FIGURE 10.10	Adaptive Computer-based Control System

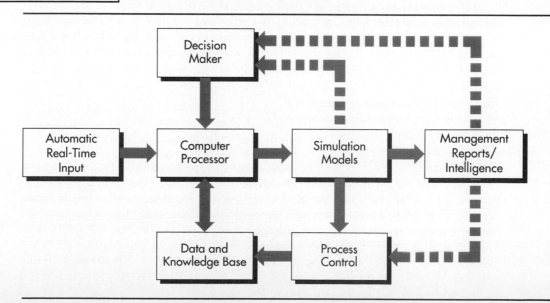

multiple perspectives. Managers with behavioral styles contend that quantitative controls are dysfunctional. The analytic school claims that without numbers, sub-optimization is inevitable. Computer specialists tout the need for decision support systems that can provide adaptive, real-time control. Where does the answer lie? Obviously, the answer is with none of the above taken singularly. The approach must be an integrative one that recognizes the strengths, pitfalls, and problems of each individual approach and attempts to reconcile them into a single effective method. For a strategy to be implemented, it is necessary to create a supportive organizational culture and to bring consensus and commitment to the control process so that organizational goals and objectives are achieved. This task is an essential one for strategic management.

SUMMARY

As soon as a strategic repositioning of the company is proposed, a plan of action is needed. A well-conceived strategy is one that has been planned with the company's capability to carry out the proposed change in mind.

A strategy that is not implemented is no strategy at all. Therefore, the astute manager incorporates implementation into the plan from the very beginning. After the strategic change has been instituted, continuous and systematic follow-up is necessary to ensure that resistance is minimized, that the strategy is executed, and that its full potential is realized. Thus both formal and informal methods are needed to ensure stakeholder acceptance of proposed changes, to maximize motivation and commitment on the part of those who have to carry out the plan, and to evaluate completely and objectively the results achieved.

Four factors affect the implementation of any strategy:

1. The style of the executive who is the change agent
2. The corporate culture—the norms, values, and beliefs that guide the organization
3. The values held by individuals in the organization
4. The fit, or match, of corporate and individual values

Using the implementation model presented, the decision maker can determine how compatible a particular culture is with a proposed change.

The executive's decision style and leadership style affect the strategic alternatives and direction an organization will pursue. Few decisions have as significant an impact on the organization as the choice of an overall strategy. Therefore, it is not surprising that the decision styles of those in charge play a major role in determining the overall success of an organization.

The decision style model provides insights into both how and why decisions are made. Decision style analysis shows how much information and what approach a manager generally uses in solving strategic problems. It also helps to identify the focus of the manager in terms of technical versus organizational problems. Given this perspective, one can determine the approach most likely to be taken by the decision maker, provided no extraneous factors influence the decision.

Not only is a knowledge of decision styles helpful in determining how someone will respond to a situation, it also lends insight into who has leadership qualities. Most leaders today have the conceptual style as their dominant style. They have a vision and are more idea-oriented than those who are predominantly concerned with operational management activities. Visions are turned into reality when the leader has a supportive, directive style that focuses on results. The increasing number of factors affecting business decisions may make the rational or analytical decision maker unable to cope with the social and political requirements of an organization. Furthermore, those with leadership qualities may not succeed if they do not have the power or authority to carry out their ideas. The way in which power is exercised within an organization depends on the kinds of uses of power that a particular manager prefers, as well as on his or her level of authority.

The structure of an organization is a function both of its size and of its complexity. Mintzberg's (1979) four basic categories of organizational form provide a means for examining the relationship of organizational structure to strategy. The traditional view of the structure of an organization as a response to a given strategy is no longer adequate, given the rapid change in environmental forces and in the contextual variables internal to the organization. A structure is not simply a rigid artifact that reflects the manner in which strategies are carried out. Rather, organizations are constantly changing and adapting to external exigencies and to internal political coalitions and technology requirements.

Organizations exhibit a cyclical pattern that often follows the familiar biological growth curve. This pattern, called the organizational life cycle, provides useful insights into how the size of the organization and the rate of change influence both strategies and controls. The most appropriate leadership style also changes with the organization life cycle. The start-up phase requires an entrepreneurial style, whereas a mature organization needs the vision and direction that an analytical or conceptual style can provide. Although the exact pattern an organization follows depends on competition, product life cycle, technology, general economic conditions, and managerial career life cycle, the general pattern can be used to guide strategic decisions.

The organizational structure matrix relates the level of environmental uncertainty to the degree of integration needed; that is, it shows the strategy/structure linkages. The amount of integration and coordination required is in turn related to the stage in the organizational life cycle.

The contingency approach relates the organizational structure to the external environment, individual and group factors, and the internal work system. The model proposed by Tosi and Hamner shows the factors that contribute to the constant realignment of the organization.

When all three approaches are combined—the life cycle, the uncertainty/integration matrix, and the contingency model—it is readily apparent that no one structure is most appropriate nor will any structure remain best for a long period of time. The structure must be tailored to the external constraints as well as the internal culture of the firm, and it must be fine-tuned and adjusted regularly.

Logical incrementalism and intrapreneurship are two alternative means of gaining acceptance of strategic change. These approaches rely on motivational and political bases for influencing behavior. However, they do not eliminate the need for an analytical basis for determining which alternatives are viable and consistent with the overall mission of the organization.

REFERENCES AND SUGGESTIONS FOR FURTHER READING

Allison, Graham T. 1971. *Essence of decision: Explaining the Cuban missile crisis.* Boston: Little, Brown.

Anderson, Carl R. and Frank T. Paine. 1975. Managerial perceptions and strategic behavior. *Academy of Management Journal,* December.

Barnes, Louis B. and Mark P. Kriger. 1987. The hidden side of organizational leadership. *The McKinsey Quarterly,* Winter, pp. 15–35.

Bartlett, Christopher and Sumantra Ghoshal. 1990. Matrix management: Not a structure, a frame of mind. *Harvard Business Review,* July–August, pp. 138–145.

Beer, Michael and Robert A. Ruh. 1976. Employee growth through performance management. *Harvard Business Review,* August.

Bennis, Warren G. 1991. Learning some basic truisms about leadership. *Phi Kappa Phi Journal,* Winter, pp. 12–15.

Bennis, Warren G. 1976. Leadership a beleagured species. *Organizational Dynamics,* Vol. 5, no. 1, pp. 3–16.

Bennis, Warren and Burt Nanus. 1985. *Leaders.* New York: Harper & Row.

Bonoma, Thomas V. 1984. Making your marketing strategy work. *Harvard Business Review,* March–April.

Broder, John M. 1986. Wells Fargo is ready to crack whip at Crocker. *Los Angeles Times,* February 16, pp. IV 1–2.

Bryon, Christopher. 1981. How Japan does it. *Time,* March 30, p. 54.

Byrne, John A. 1989. Donald Burr may be ready to take to the skies again. *Business Week,* January 16, pp. 74–75.

Byrne, John A. 1985. Up, up and away? *Business Week,* November 25, pp. 80–94.

Chandler, Alfred D. 1962. *Strategy and structure.* Cambridge, Mass.: M.I.T. Press.

Changing a corporate culture. 1984. *Business Week*, May 14, pp. 130–138.

Child, J. 1972. Organizational structure, environment and performance. *Sociology*.

Clark, Rolf. 1992. TQM from the trenches: The role of the individual. *Program Manager*, March–April, pp. 28–32.

Corporate culture: The hard-to-change values that spell success or failure. 1980. *Business Week*, October 27, pp. 148–160.

Deal, Terrence. 1984. *Corporate cultures: The rite and rituals of corporate life*. Reading, Mass.: Addison-Wesley.

Deshpande, Rohit and A. Parasuraman. 1986. Linking corporate culture to strategic planning. *Business Horizon*, May–June, pp. 28–37.

Diesing, Paul. 1962. *Reason in society*. Westport, Conn.: Greenwood Press.

Dowd, Ann Reilly. 1992. Will George Bush really change? *Fortune*, June 29, pp. 61–64.

Driver, Michael and Alan J. Rowe. 1979. Decision-making styles: A new approach to management decision making. In *Behavior problems in organizations*, ed. Cary Cooper. Englewood Cliffs, N.J.: Prentice-Hall.

Drucker, Peter. 1982. Why some mergers work and many more don't. *Forbes*, January 18, p. 34.

Drucker, Peter. 1974. *Management: Tasks, responsibilities, and practices*. New York: Harper & Row.

Dumaine, Brian. 1992a. The corporate culture connection. *Fortune*, May 4, p. 119.

Dumaine, Brian. 1992b. Unleash workers and cut costs. *Fortune*, May 18, p. 88.

Ehrenfeld, Tom. 1992. The case of the unpopular pay plan. *Harvard Business Review*, January–February, pp. 14–18.

Epstin, Edwin M. 1974. Dimensions of corporate power, part 2. *California Management Review*, Summer.

Epstin, Edwin M. 1973. Dimensions of corporate power, part 1. *California Management Review*, Winter.

Farnham, Alan. 1989. The trust gap. *Fortune*, December 4, pp. 56–78.

Fiedler, Fred E. 1958. *Leadership attitudes and group effectiveness*. Urbana: University of Illinois Press.

Filley, Alan C., Robert J. House, and Steven Kerr. 1976. *Managerial processes and organizational behavior*. Glenview, Ill.: Scott, Foresman.

Galbraith, Jay R. 1973. *Designing complex organizations*. Reading, Mass.: Addison-Wesley.

Galbraith, Jay R. and Robert K. Kazanjian. 1986. *Strategy implementation*. Los Angeles: West Publishing Company.

Galbraith, Jay R. and Daniel A. Nathanson. 1978. *Strategic implementation: The role of structure and process*. St. Paul: West.

Gibson, John L., John M. Ivancevich, and James H. Donnelly, Jr. 1988. *Organizations*. Plano, Texas: Business Publications Inc.

Greiner, Larry E. 1972. Evolution and revolution as organizations grow. *Harvard Business Review*, August.

Guth, William D. and Renato Taguiri. 1965. Personal values and corporate strategy. *Harvard Business Review*, September–October, pp. 123–132.

Hampton, William. 1984. Why Honeywell and Synertek couldn't make a go of it. *Business Week*, December 17, p. 39.

Hampton, William J. 1980. Corporate culture: The hard-to-change values that spell success or failure. *Business Week*, October 27, p. 148.

Hansen, Jeffrey A. 1985. CEO management style and the stages of development in new ventures. Unpublished paper. Salem, Oregon: Atkinson Graduate School of Management.

Hansen, Jeffrey A. 1984. Decision and management styles in emerging companies. Unpublished paper, Atkinson Graduate School of Management, Willamette University, Oregon.

Heiko, Lance. 1989. Some relationships between Japanese culture and just-in-time. *The Academy of Management Executive* III, no. 4, pp. 319–321.

Heirs, Ben and Gordon Pehrson. 1982. *The mind of the organization*. New York: Harper & Row.

Heller, Frank A. and Bernard Wilper. 1981. *Competence and power*. New York: Wiley.

Here comes the intrapreneur. 1983. *Business Week*, July.

Hickman, Craig R. 1990. *Mind of a manager, soul of a leader*. New York: Wiley.

Hillkirk, John. 1991. AT&T chief makes teamwork a driving force. *USA Today*, March 12, pp. 12–13.

Hinings, Christopher R. et al. 1974. Structural conditions of intraorganizational power. *Administrative Science Quarterly* 19.

Hirschhorn, Larry and Thomas Gilmore. 1992. The new boundaries of the "boundaryless company." *Harvard Business Review*, May–June, pp. 104–115.

Iacocca, Lee and William Novak. 1984. *Iacocca*. New York: Bantam Books.

Jack Welch reinvents General Electric—again. 1991. *The Economist*, March 30, pp. 59–62.

A Japanese boss whose "consensus" is an iron fist. 1984. *Business Week*, November, pp. 176–178.

Judson, Arnold S. 1966. *A manager's guide to making changes*. London: Wiley.

Kiechel, Walter, III. 1989. A hard look at executive vision. *Fortune*, October 23, pp. 207–210.

Kilman, Ralph H. and Mary J. Saxton. 1983. *Kilman-Saxton culture gap survey*. Pittsburgh: Organizational Design Consultants.

Kimberly, J. R. 1976. Organizational size and the structuralist perspective. *Administrative Science Quarterly.*

Kimberly, John R. and Robert H. Miles. 1980. *The organizational life cycle.* San Francisco: Jossey-Bass.

Kotter, John. 1990. What leaders really do. *Harvard Business Review*, May–June, pp. 103–111.

Kotter, John P. 1988. The leadership factor. *The McKinsey Quarterly*, Spring, pp. 71–78.

Kouzes, James M. and Barry Z. Posner. 1988. From manager to leader. *Newsweek—Management Digest Quarterly*, Fall.

Kumar, Anil and Graham Sharman. 1992. We love your product, but where is it? *The McKinsey Quarterly*, no. 1, pp. 24–44.

Langeler, Gerard. 1992. The vision trap. *Harvard Business Review*, March–April, pp. 46–55.

Lawrence, John F. 1985. A company's culture shapes performance. *Los Angeles Times*, January 27.

Lawrence, Paul R. and J. W. Lorsch. 1967. *Organization and environment.* Homewood, Ill.: Irwin.

Ledford, Bruce. 1991. The battle of beliefs: In the age of manipulation. *Phi Kappa Phi Journal*, Winter, pp. 33–35.

Levinson, Harry. 1973. Asinine attitudes toward motivation. *Harvard Business Review*, February.

Lewin, Kurt. 1951. *Field theory and social science.* New York: Harper & Brothers.

Lindblom, Charles E. 1965. *The intelligence of democracy.* New York: The Free Press.

Lord, Mary. 1991. How Nabisco solved its labor problem. *U.S. News & World Report*, May 20, p. 60.

Lundberg, Olof and Max D. Richards. 1972. A relationship between cognitive style and complex decision making: Implications for business policy. *Proceedings of the Academy of Management*, August.

Magnet, Myron. 1992. The truth about the American worker. *Fortune*, May 4, pp. 48–65.

Main, Jeremy. 1987. Wanted: Managers who can make a difference. *Fortune*, September 28, pp. 92–98.

Mann, Richard B. 1982. Relationship between the decision-making styles of corporate planners and other planners. Unpublished dissertation. Los Angeles: University of Southern California.

Maren, Michael and Don Wallace. 1992. Masters of the impossible. *Success*, January–February, pp. 22–32.

Margerison, C. J. and D. J. McCann. 1985. *The team management index.* New Berlin, Wis.: National Consulting and Training Institute.

Maruyama, Magoroh. 1991. Policy for international talent utilization. *Technology Analysis & Strategic Management* III, no. 4, pp. 323–331.

Maruyama, Magoroh. 1991. Contracts in cultures. *Human Systems Management*, 10, pp. 33–46.

Maslow, Abraham H. 1954. *Motivation and personality.* New York: Harper & Row.

Mason, Todd and Richard Brandt. 1985. How Ross Perot's shock troops ran into flak at GM. *Business Week*, February 11, p. 118.

McClelland, D. C. 1971. *Assessing human motivation.* New York: General Learning Press.

McConkey, Dale D. 1973. MBO—Twenty years later, where do we stand? *Business Horizons*, August.

Meen, David and Mark Keough. 1992. Creating the learning organization. *The McKinsey Quarterly*, 1, pp. 58–86.

Mendes, Joshua. 1984. Waking up AT&T: There's life after culture shock. *Fortune*, December 24, pp. 66–74.

Miesing, P. 1984. Integrating planning with management. *Long-Range Planning*, October, pp. 118–124.

Miles, Robert H. 1982. *Coffin nails and corporate strategies.* Englewood Cliffs, N.J.: Prentice-Hall.

Miller, Danny. 1983. The correlates of entrepreneurship in three types of firms. *Management Sciences* 29, no. 7 (July).

Mintzberg, Henry. 1979. *The structuring of organizations.* Englewood Cliffs, N.J.: Prentice-Hall.

Mockler, Robert J. 1989. *Knowledge-based systems for strategic planning.* Englewood Cliffs, N.J.: Prentice-Hall.

Morse, John J. and Jay W. Lorsch. 1970. Beyond theory Y. *Harvard Business Review*, June.

Nonaka, Ikujiro. 1991. The knowledge-creating company. *Harvard Business Review*, November–December, pp. 96–104.

Nunamaker, Jay. 1992. Teamwork tools lead the way to creative collaboration. *Corporate Computing*, August, pp. 196–198.

Patz, Alan L. and Alan J. Rowe. 1977. *Management control and decision systems.* New York: Wiley.

Perot, Ross. 1988. How I would turn around GM. *Fortune*, February 15, pp. 44–50.

Pfeffer, Jeffrey and Gerald R. Salancik. 1978. *The external control of organizations.* New York: Harper & Row.

Phillips, Donald. 1992. *Lincoln on leadership: Executive strategies for tough times.* New York: Warner Books.

Platt, John R. 1966. *The step to man.* New York: Wiley.

Posner, Barry Z. and Warren H. Schmidt. 1984. *The significance of values compatibility between managers and their organization.* Unpublished paper, Academy of Management, Western Regional Meeting, Vancouver, Canada, April, pp. 1–16.

Prokesch, Steve E. and William J. Howell, Jr. 1985. Do mergers really work? *Business Week*, June 3, p. 89.

Quinn, James B. 1978. Strategic change: Logical incrementalism. *Sloan Management Review*, Fall.

Raia, Anthony P. 1974. *Managing by objectives.* Glenview, Ill.: Scott, Foresman.

Rayner, Bruce. 1992. Trial-by-fire transformation: An interview with Globe Metallurgical's Arden C. Sims. *Harvard Business Review*, May–June, pp. 117–129.

Reddin, William J. 1970. *Managerial effectiveness*. New York: McGraw-Hill.

Ridgway, V. P. 1956. Dysfunctional consequences of performance measurements. *Administrative Science Quarterly*.

Rowe, Alan J. 1981. Decision making in the 80's. *Los Angeles Journal of Business and Economics*, Winter.

Rowe, Alan J. and James D. Boulgarides. 1992. *Managerial decision making*. New York: Macmillan.

Rowe, Alan J. and James D. Boulgarides. 1983. Decision styles—A perspective. *Learning and Organizational Development Journal* 4,4.

Rowe, Alan J. and John Carlson. 1974. Adaptive control systems for operating management. *Logistics Spectrum Journal*, September.

Rowe, Alan J. and Richard O. Mason. 1988b. Are you in the right job? *Newsweek—Management Digest Quarterly*, Winter.

Rowe, Alan J. and Richard O. Mason. 1988a. The impact of style, values, and culture on strategic change. Paper presented at the International Planning Conference, Boston.

Rowe, Alan J. and Richard O. Mason. 1987. *Managing with style*. San Francisco: Jossey-Bass.

Sanchez, Jesus. 1991. Cooperation forges a success story. *Los Angeles Times*, April 26, P. D1.

Sashkin, Marshall. 1990. What causes loyalty? Unpublished paper, pp. 1–16.

Sathe, Vijay. 1983. Implications of corporate culture: A manager's guide to action. *Organizational Dynamics*, Autumn.

Schein, Edgar H. 1985. *Organizational culture and leadership*. San Francisco: Jossey-Bass.

Schumacher, Ernst F. 1973. *Small is beautiful*. New York: Harper & Row.

Sethia, Nirmal. 1984. Observations on *Shaping the Culture of the Firm: The Role of Management*. Unpublished review of the conference at Pepperdine University, Los Angeles, April 10.

Shaw, Russell. 1990. Robert E. Allen: Chairman & CEO, AT&T. *Sky Magazine*. October, p. 50.

Sherman, Straford P. 1989. The mind of Jack Welch. *Fortune*, March 27, pp. 39–50.

Sirota, David and Alan D. Wolfson. 1972. Job enrichment: Surmounting the obstacles. *Personnel*, July.

Smith, Lee. 1985. Japan's autocratic managers. *Fortune*, January 7, pp. 56–64.

Snyder, Richard C. 1984. To enhance innovation, manage corporate culture. Unpublished paper, University of Southern California.

Springer, Sally P. and Georg Deutsch. 1981. *Left brain, right brain*. San Francisco: W. H. Freeman.

Starbuck, William H. and Paul C. Nystrom. 1981. Designing and understanding organizations, in *Handbook of organizational design*, Vol. 1. Ed. Paul C. Nystrom and William Starbuck. New York: Oxford University Press.

Steers, Richard M. 1977. *Organizational effectiveness*. Santa Monica, Calif.: Goodyear.

Tandem computers. 1988. *Value Line*, Vol. 1110, November 4.

Tichy, Noel and Ram Charan. 1989. Speed, simplicity, self-confidence: An interview with Jack Welch. *Harvard Business Review*, September–October, pp. 112–120.

Tosi, Henry L. and W. Clay Hamner. 1974. *Organizational behavior and management*. Chicago: St. Clair Press.

Toy, Stewart. 1985. Splitting up: The other side of merger mania. *Business Week*, July 1, pp. 50–55.

Tunstall, W. Brooke. 1986. The breakup of the Bell System: A case study in cultural transformation. *California Management Review*, Winter, pp. 110–125.

Tunstall, W. Brooke. 1983. Cultural transition at AT&T. *Sloan Management Review*, Fall, pp. 1–12.

Utall, Bro. 1983. Corporate culture vultures. *Fortune*, October 17, p. 66.

Verity, John and Peter Coy. 1992. Twin engines: Can Bob Allen blend computers and telecommunications at AT&T? *Business Week*, January 20, pp. 56–61.

Vroom, Victor H. and Philip W. Yetton. 1973. *Leadership and decision-making*. Pittsburgh: University of Pittsburgh Press.

Watson, Thomas J., Jr. 1963. *A business and its beliefs: The ideas that helped build IBM*. New York: McGraw-Hill.

Webber, Alan. 1990. Consensus, continuity, and common sense: An interview with Compaq's Rod Canion. *Harvard Business Review*, July–August, pp. 115–123.

Weber, Max. 1969. *Bureaucracy*. New York: Wiley.

Weber, Max. 1947. *Theory of social and economic organization*. New York: Oxford University Press.

White, F. B. and L. B. Barnes. 1971. Power networks in the appraisal process. *Harvard Business Review*, May–June.

Woutat, Donald. 1992. Ford loses $2.3 billion; Diahatsu quits U.S. market. *Los Angeles Times*, February 14, pp. D-1 and D-2.

Zaleznick, Abraham. 1977. Managers and leaders: Are they different? *Harvard Business Review*. May–June.

Zumberge, James. 1988. Presidential address, University of Southern California.

APPENDIX A

The Social Change Model

The *social change model* can help a manager determine how a new strategic plan will be perceived by the stakeholders and how management can cope with possible resistance. The purpose of the model is to identify the target area for introducing strategic change and the best means of communicating the plan. Management must make clear to those involved why the proposed change is necessary and how it can be accomplished.

PRELIMINARY ANALYSIS

The first step in the preliminary analysis is to prepare a description of the social system required to carry out the new strategy. In other words, identify the stakeholders and their primary motivating interests. This involves identifying the role of each stakeholder in the system, discovering how that role is related to other roles, and investigating the sentiments, norms, values, and ideals that operate in the interactions between each pair of roles. This description enables strategic managers to analyze the attitudes and probable reactions of individual stakeholders and the organization as a whole.

The following method can be used to gauge stakeholders' support for a strategic plan. First, each stakeholder is identified and assigned a weight from 1 to 10, indicating the importance of that stakeholder in implementing the strategy. If a strategy plan cannot be carried out without the involvement of a given stakeholder, this stakeholder should be assigned an importance weight of 10. A weight of 1 indicates that the plan can be implemented without this stakeholder's support.

Next, the attitude of each stakeholder toward the expected results of a strategy should be evaluated. There obviously is a wide spectrum of sentiments concerning change, ranging from active resistance at one extreme to enthusiastic support at the other. Possible behaviors in between these two extremes include cooperation, acceptance, protests, and simply doing what is ordered. The introduction of change often creates anxiety and fear. When a major change is in the offing as the result of some newly proposed strategy, anxiety may cause undesirable reaction that needs to be countered. Table 10A.1 can be used to score the attitude of each stakeholder.

By multiplying the importance weights by the attitude scores, one can determine the approximate effect that each stakeholder will have on implementation of a new strategy. Often the best one can do with important stakeholders who actively resist the implementation of a strategy is to attempt to neutralize their effect. If they are less resistant, managers may try to convert them. Stakeholders with little importance can usually be ignored, whereas strong supporters should be reinforced. The weighted total of all the scores will indicate the overall disposition of a system toward translating a strategic plan into action. Table 10A.2 lists some potential causes of resistance and suggests ways of dealing with them.

The second step in the preliminary analysis is to assess the level of social resources the manager has available for implementing the strategy. Social resources, as distinct from economic resources, are particular and unique to each stakeholder. Friendships, loyalties, habits, perceptions, psychological style, anxieties, prejudices, shared beliefs, identification

---

TABLE 10A.1 | **Attitude Scales for Stakeholders**

Behavior	Score
Active resistance	1
Passive resistance	3
Indifference	5
Cooperation	7
Enthusiastic support	10

TABLE 10A.2 | **Resistance to Change**

Typical Problems Causing Resistance	Technique for Overcoming Resistance	Expected Outcome
1. Those affected lack knowledge about the proposed change	Communicate in meetings, encourage involvement	Achieve understanding and acceptance
2. Groups are exerting power to maintain the status quo	Encourage participation and power sharing or cooperation	Integrate group members into change strategy
3. Change is having dysfunctional consequences	Negotiate or provide inducements to obtain consensus	Avoid major confrontation
4. Timing of the change is critical	Facilitate change and provide support	Help to accelerate change
5. The change is so radical as to be mistrusted	Provide open climate, accept ideas, create respect	Gain acceptance by including others in the decision

with purpose, will power, and dedication are examples of social resources. They are very specialized, and generally they cannot be allocated or used for other purposes.

The third step is to form a general opinion of the social change problem. The problem statement describing the current situation is critical. The social dimension of a strategy generally involves righting some current misalignment, disorganization, or conflict that is serving as a barrier to executing the strategy. A method is needed for achieving a new pattern of integration and organizational equilibrium.

PRINCIPLES OF NONECONOMIC DECISION MAKING

Once these three preliminary steps have been accomplished, the three *principles of noneconomic decision making* can be employed (Diesing, 1962). As the application of the principles unfolds, the information obtained during the three preliminary steps can be augmented and reorganized. All three of Diesing's principles should be applied. If required, the process should be repeated until a final social change solution emerges. Here is the first principle of noneconomic decision making:

Principle of changeability: *Select the easiest possible relevant changes within the organization.*

The easiest changes are most likely to be successful. They will generate less conflict and resistance. The ease of change is based on two variables: introducibility and acceptability.

Introducibility, in turn, depends on two factors. First, roles must exist in the social system that permit one to put new changes in place. Second, people must have sufficient skill to execute these roles effectively. The first requirement for introducibility is evaluated by examining the activities and interactions inherent in each role, the second by assessing the social resources available in the system and available to those who might occupy the role of change agent. Ideally, the role of those who introduce a new strategy is to win over people who play roles that must be changed if the strategy is to be effective. Thus the change agent should be a credible source for the change. For example, a county agricultural agent is a credible and presumably skillful source for initiating changes in agricultural practice but might not be a credible or skillful source for introducing changes in, say, a computer system.

The success of a new strategy may lie with a single individual and the social resources he or she can bring to bear. For example, John Platt (1966) credits the scientist Leo Szilard with playing a crucial role in formulating and implementing U.S. atomic energy policy during the early years of World War II. Szilard used his status in the scientific community to persuade British and American atomic scientists to keep their activities secret during the prewar years. Later he drew on his friendship with Einstein to encourage Einstein to write the letter to President Roosevelt that started the U.S. Atomic energy project in 1940. From the standpoint of introducibility, Szilard was the right man, in the right place, at the right time.

Acceptability depends on something more than just acquiring the conscious approval of the stakeholders. The new strategy must be capable of being integrated into the existing organizational system with a minimum of disruption, incompatibility, and conflict. A new strategy is more likely to be accepted if it is functionally similar to the one it replaces. For example, a school district policy that requires teachers to employ a new text that embodies the same educational philosophy as previous texts is more likely to be accepted than is a policy that calls for a major redesign in texts, teaching style, facilities, grading systems, and administrative support. Educational innovations such as team teaching, open classrooms, and curricular revision often have not been accepted because they require changing many social relationships.

A similar point is made by E.F. Schumacher (1973) with respect to the field of economic development. He argues that smaller innovations are more likely to be accepted than major changes. For example, new agricultural implements that fit into the existing Indian peasant culture—tightly organized communities, small land holdings, traditional furrowing methods—are more likely to be accepted by the community than large-scale agricultural equipment. Intermediate technology—such as a scientifically designed steel plow or a small, one wheel, hand-held motorized plow—is more appropriate than, say, a large tractor or combine. Many businesses that have tried to export U.S. manufacturing and sales methods into foreign countries have learned the very same lesson, often at a great expense.

Acceptability, then, is greater if *functional similarity*—the pattern of activities and interactions among the stakeholders—remains substantially the same and only the content changes. A new strategy is less acceptable if it destroys old activities and interactions and institutes completely new ones. The stronger the sentiments for an old activity or interaction and the more deeply ingrained the norms and habits related to participating in it, the less likely it is that a new strategy will be acceptable. Exceptions occur if subordinates feel a strong need for change in the system or if an intense conflict has been held in check. At that point the system is ready (occasionally too ready) to accept changes.

In applying the principle of changeability, the strategic manager should ask the following questions:

- What change is possible? Can it be introduced? Is it acceptable?
- Which is the easiest change to effect with the social resources available?

The second principle of noneconomic decision making is as follows:

Principle of separability: *Select a target area that is sufficiently independent from its context to be susceptible to separate implementation while protected from outside pressures.*

Implementation of strategies takes time—often several years and sometimes decades. Consequently an entire strategy can seldom be implemented all at once. Instead, a workable target area or substrategy must be identified and a change proposed that can be implemented in that limited area. For any given strategy many target areas can typically be identified. Separation is needed because large, highly interconnected target areas are too massive for full implementation at once. The likelihood of success is improved if the strategy can be focused on manageable, smaller target areas or substrategies.

This task is often a difficult one for the strategic manager because problems are generally highly interconnected, complex, uncertain, ambiguous, and political in nature. Yet this complexity is also to some extent organized. *Organized complexity* implies that some parts of the strategy are relatively separable from the others and that the relevant relationships can be changed to a limited extent without simultaneous change in the entire system. Identifying a relatively independent target area in the organization may involve observing social relationships within a single group or class of stakeholders, such as a work group, a kinship group, an age group, a particular organization, a geographic region, or an occupational class. Alternatively, it may involve changing a cluster of roles, beliefs, drives, values, rituals, or symbols.

The principle that is being applied here differs from Lindblom's (1965) concept of incrementalism, or "muddling through." Although both concepts recommend a small, manageable increment of change, the principle of separability requires that the choice of a target area be guided by a concept of the strategy as a whole. This point will take on more force in light of the next principle.

Principle of growth: *Begin a change in such a way that extension of the change is possible.*

This principle is equivalent to initiating a *social chain reaction*. Organizations are typically conservative and foster mechanisms that reject innovation. When properly triggered, however, the same mechanisms can be used to encourage the change, expand it, and facilitate its diffusion.

When a positive feedback loop is activated, a change escalates. The positive feedback loop acts as a multiplier, amplifying the output for every cycle that occurs. It is this phenomenon that causes a child's quarrel to escalate into a brawl, each step louder and noisier than the previous one. The snowball effect comes into play, each cycle adding exponentially to the mass of the underlying problem.

John Platt (1966) has argued that it is possible to select points of entry into a social system where the multiplier is greater than 1, and thus a chain reaction is released. He calls the initial, narrowly defined implementation the *seed operation*. Usually changes in a few activities and interactions lead to changes in sentiments and norms, thus reinforcing the changes and permitting new activities and interactions to be started. Then the process is repeated. During each iteration, the target area gradually increases in size and in complexity. More social resources become available to deal with the problem because each iteration leads to a decrease in conflict and tension in the original target area, freeing the psychic and physical energy that was tied up in these conflicts. The new energy is now available to deal with the new, larger, and more difficult strategic target area.

Examples of this effect can be found in virtually every field. The invention of metal coins eliminated barter and permitted modern commerce to take off. The advent of the horse collar, according to one theory, increased the productivity of the farmer, leading to enlarged medieval farms, which, in turn, created a surplus of production, releasing people so that they could move into the cities and thereby making the Renaissance possible.

Ideally, the chain reaction ends when the entire strategy has been fully implemented and relationships in the organization have all been modified according to the prescriptions of the strategy. The chain reaction can stop prematurely, however, if it encounters a barrier somewhere in the process—that is, if an iteration of the cycle exposes too large and difficult a strategic target for the energy accumulated thus far. Anticipation of these barriers permits seed operations to be begun in places with relatively low positive feedback at first, but with a growth pattern that will permit the accumulation of enough energy to overcome the barriers when they are encountered. For this reason, successful social change often takes a long time.

In applying the principle of growth, the strategic manager should ask where the seed operation should be begun. That is, what social relationships can be changed so that a chain reaction is triggered in the direction specified by the policy?

Targets for change that satisfy one of the three basic principles may not fulfill the requirements of the other two. If this is the case, the strategic manager must re-examine the options until a strategy is found that begins with a relatively separable strategic target area, introduces an acceptable change rather easily, and then triggers a social chain reaction.

APPLYING THE SOCIAL CHANGE MODEL

Once the overall strategy has been identified, the social change model can be applied by means of the following steps.

1. Identify a series of possible change tactics, such as starting a new advertising program, installing new equipment, implementing a new compensation package, or instituting a new information system. *Summarize each change tactic as an action to be taken in a target area.*

2. Evaluate each change tactic in relation to its changeability, separability, and growth characteristics. Use a scale ranging from 1 to 10, with 10 the highest score possible.
3. Multiply the changeability, separability, and growth scores ($C \times S \times G$) to obtain a total score. The change tactic with the highest total score is the most effective change tactic.

An application of the social change model applied to the AMP company is shown in Worksheet 10A.1. This example illustrates how the process can be applied to determine an appropriate strategic action. Three strategic options have been identified. (Refer to Chapter 6 for details on the AMP company.)

- Option A: New design involving improved, but not advanced, technology, promising savings of between 2% and 3% in direct cost. This option would require a minimum investment of $200,000 for new equipment and engineering design.
- Option B: Advanced technology requiring an investment of up to $750,000 for special-purpose equipment and assembly devices. This technology could save up to 5% in direct cost.
- Option C: High technology involving new approaches that have not been fully tested. If successful, this technology would give AMP a clear edge in the connector field for many years to come. Some experimentation is required, however, and its cost could run as high as $70,000 per month for an extended period, although the investment in equipment would not exceed $400,000.

The principles of social change have been applied to these three options in Worksheet 10A.1. With respect to an evaluation of the social change possibilities, option B rates the highest. The evaluation points out the following features of option B:

- Option B is rather easy to introduce, and because of the technical and professional nature of AMP's personnel, it should be acceptable. Moreover, its potential cost savings makes it attractive to management.
- Because it is based on advanced technology, option B is undoubtedly easier to protect from outside interference than is option A.
- Option B also provides growth opportunities through advanced research. This should give AMP a sound foundation for moving toward the high-technology capability required by option C.

In making a final choice, the strategic manager must balance the social change evaluation against the economic and other evaluations covered earlier in this book. The correct approach is the one that best incorporates the advantages offered by all the evaluation methods utilized.

WORSHEET 10A.1	Social Change Model

WORKSHEET 10A.1 | Social Change Model

Case ___AMP___
Date ___1992___
Name ___Mary Doe___

Change Option	Comment	Evaluation	Score C × S × G
A	*Changeability:* Easy to change from a technological and cost point of view.	8	
	Separability: Not very separable.	2	
	Growth: Provides minimum growth because it is focused on current technology.	4	64
B	*Changeability:* Relatively easy to introduce and get accepted. Economical if investment can be made advantageous.	6	
	Separability: Reasonably separable.	5	
	Growth: Provides relatively high growth potential because it builds on an advanced technological base.	5	150
C	*Changeability:* Because of uncertainty and heavy investment required, very difficult to introduce and get accepted.	2	
	Separability: Very separable.	9	
	Growth: Would provide maximum growth if successful, but is very uncertain now.	6	108

APPENDIX B

Decision Styles

McDonnell Douglas, at one point, was described as the Pentagon's most proficient and lowest-cost producer. What contributed most to this reputation was "Mr. Mac's" style. He was an engineer and aircraft designer who developed a company with thrift and paternalism. Because of Mac's style, an infatuation with engineering permeates every aspect of the company's activities and decision making. It was the basis of Mac's power in the organization, and it was reflected in the organization's structure.

An important conclusion is that the manager's style has a direct effect on strategy. The entrepreneurial risk taker who is highly innovative, for example, may not do well supervising the cost cutting that must be emphasized during the second and third phases of an organization's life cycle.

It takes a hard-driving spirit to lift a company out of the doldrums. Joe Alibrandi, the wiry, fast-talking, energetic president of Whittaker Corporation, dumped almost 100 operating units in order to launch the company into a new phase of the life cycle. As a result, Whittaker has enjoyed a startling turnaround. Lee Iacocca transformed Chrysler from a company plagued by a loss of $1.7 billion into a profitable enterprise with a whole new outlook. In both of these cases, the style of management matched the requirements of the organization's life cycle. As organizations mature and change, so must management if it is to ensure continued and profitable growth. Thus a key element of meeting strategic objectives is to find the right manager to fit the situation. Knowing the decision styles of potential managers can help one determine who would be most likely to succeed in a particular situation.

Table 10B.1 lists characteristics that distinguish flexible decision styles from focused, or rigid, ones. Style flexibility affects the manager's ability to deal with highly ambiguous or changing conditions. Although the flexible manager is better at handling complex problems, the focused manager is better able to deal with problems that require quick decisions or rapid action.

TABLE 10B.1	Style Flexibility

Factor	Rigid Style	Flexible Style
Tolerance for ambiguity	Low	High
Need for structure	High	Low
Use of power	Authoritarian	Sensitive
Need for control	High	Low
Values that are important	Rules	Honesty
Dealings with others	Expects results	Supportive
Personal orientation	Self	Others

COGNITIVE ASPECTS OF DECISION STYLE

Cognitive processes help to explain the differences that individuals exhibit in thinking and perceiving. These processes determine the way information is used and conceptual ability applied in formulating and evaluating strategies.

Information Processing. Springer and Deutsch's (1981) research on the left and right hemispheres of the brain has shown that each hemisphere has specific functions. The left hemisphere deals with logical thought, is analytical, processes information serially, and is used for processing language. It handles speaking, pointing, and smiling, as well as the abstract logical reasoning needed for mathematics. Individuals whose left hemisphere is dominant tend to be able to readily differentiate diverse elements in a set of data. The right hemisphere specializes in intuition and creativity. Individuals whose right hemisphere is dominant tend to perceive things as a whole, have a comprehensive sense of timing, and consider many ideas at the same time (parallel processing of information). They appreciate space, imagery, fantasy, and music. These individuals tend to integrate data into a broad or cohesive perspective leading to more general constructs. Dreams seem to be predominantly right-brain functions. Many right-brain thinkers are artistic.

Cognitive Complexity. *Cognitive complexity* refers to a person's ability to consider a number of interdependent variables at once. One element of cognitive complexity is the ability to differentiate a number of dimensions in perceived data or to discriminate among bits of data (a left-hemisphere function). Another element of cognitive complexity is the ability to combine data in such a way as to find new constructs or complex rules (a right-hemisphere function). This ability is called *integration.* Because strategy involves many complex, interdependent variables, the manager's ability to comprehend and deal with a given situation depends on his or her cognitive complexity. Individuals with a high level of cognitive complexity have little difficulty in perceiving patterns of interrelatedness among data. Individuals with low cognitive complexity tend to rely on a few specific rules as the basis for interpreting the data in a given strategic situation.

MODELS OF DECISION STYLE

The decision style model shown in Figure 10B.1 applies the concept of cognitive complexity to strategy. This model relates decision style to cognitive complexity and to values orientation, which in turn reflects a propensity toward left- or right-hemisphere dominance. The degree of cognitive complexity is high at the top of the model and low at the bottom. The values orientation is toward technical or task-oriented matters on the left, reflecting left-hemisphere processing, and toward organizational or people-oriented matters on the right, suggesting right-hemisphere processing.

The four basic decision styles are as follows:

1. *Directive style*. Directive managers have a low tolerance for ambiguity and tend to be oriented toward technical matters. Often, people with this style are autocratic and have a high need for power. Because they use little information and consider few alternatives, they are typically known for speed and results. Directive managers tend to prefer structure in their environment and to want detailed information given orally. They also tend to follow procedures and to be aggressive. Although they are often effective at getting results, their focus is internal to the organization and short-range, with tight controls. They generally have the drive required to control and dominate others, but they need security and status.

2. *Analytical style*. Analytical managers have a much higher tolerance for ambiguity than directive managers; they also have more cognitively complex personalities. They desire considerable amounts of information, preferably in written form, and consider many more alternatives than does someone with a directive style. Like directive managers, however, they have a technical orientation and an autocratic bent. Individuals with this style are oriented to problem solving; they strive for the best that can be achieved in a given situation. They enjoy variety and challenge but emphasize control. Analytical individuals tend to be innovative and good at abstract or logical, deductive reasoning.

| FIGURE 10B.1 | Cognitive Decision Style Model |

3. *Conceptual style.* Having both high cognitive complexity and a focus on people, conceptual managers tend to be achievement-oriented and yet to believe in trust and openness in relations with subordinates. In making decisions, they look at considerable data and explore many alternatives. Conceptual managers are often creative in their solutions and can visualize complex relationships. Their main concern is with long-range problems, and they have high organizational commitment. Conceptual managers are often perfectionists, emphasizing quality. Preferring loose control over the more directive use of power, they frequently invite subordinates to participate in decision making and goal setting. They value praise, recognition, and independence.

4. *Behavioral style.* Although low on the cognitive complexity scale, behavioral managers have a deep concern for the organization and for the development of people. Behavioral-style managers have a high need for acceptance and tend to be supportive of others, showing them warmth and empathy. They enjoy counseling others. Preferring persuasion to direction, they provide loose control. Behavioral managers are receptive to suggestions and communicate easily. They require relatively little data and prefer verbal communication to written reports. They tend to focus on short- or medium-range problems.

Although the preceding discussion makes the styles appear to be distinct, in reality a manager's style rarely falls neatly into one category. Most managers have multiple styles; the style adopted in a particular situation depends on the context in which the decision is made. Typically, however, even the most flexible managers have a dominant style and use the others as backup styles. Thus, style categories describe general ways of thinking.

Even though it is never possible to gauge another's decision styles exactly, having an idea of an individual's dominant style can be useful information. The manager who can identify another's dominant cognitive style and orientation to values can better predict that person's decision-making behavior. An application of decision styles was illustrated in the section on entrepreneurship in Chapter 9.

The decision style inventory (DSI) in Worksheet 10B.1 can be used to determine how frequently an individual uses each decision style. Answers to the questions in the inventory, when scored, provide a valid indicator of a person's style. The worksheet has been left blank so that readers can fill it in to determine their own style.

The total score for the appropriate column of the inventory is used to determine the level of dominance of each style. A standard deviation of 15 has been found for each of the four style categories. Given that scores follow a normal probability distribution, 49% of the scores will fall within the following ranges: directive, 68–82; analytical, 83–97; conceptual, 73–87; and behavioral, 48–62. If a person's score for a style is 7 or more points (approximately ½ standard deviation) above the mean (average) for that style, the style is considered to be dominant. If it is more than 1 standard deviation (15 points) over the mean, that style is considered to be very dominant. A score within 7 points (plus or minus) of the mean indicates that the style is a backup style. A score more than 7 points below the mean indicates that the style is a least-preferred style; the style either is latent and used only when needed or is seldom used.

A decision style graph can be generated from the results of the decision style inventory. Each bar indicates how much the individual's score deviates from the mean for that score. Bars for scores that are greater than the mean extend to the right of the average score line; bars for scores that are lower than the mean extend to the left. Worksheet 10B.2 displays scores for Pfeffer and Palma, two managers at Lift Inc.

The first graph shows that Pfeffer uses the directive style as his dominant style and the analytical style as a backup. The second graph shows that Palma uses the conceptual style as

WORKSHEET 10B.1	Decision Style Inventory

Case _____

Date _____

Name _____

The following decision style inventory is used to determine the manager's self-perception in terms of the cognitive-contingency model. Each question is answered by assigning an 8 to the answer that is most like them, a 4 to the next answer most like them, then a 2, and finally a 1 for the answer least like them. For example, in the first question an individual may want to assign an 8 to "be recognized for my work," a 4 to "have a position with status," a 2 to "feel secure," and a 1 to "be outstanding in my field." Remember that each score can be assigned only once to each question. In other words, all four numbers, 8, 4, 2, and 1, must be used for each question. Do not repeat any of these four numbers for any one question. Thus using two 8s would not be a correct response to any given question. An interpretation of the scores follows the inventory.

One should relax when filling in the inventory and recognize that it reflects one's self-image. There are *no* right or wrong answers. Each person is different and will, therefore, score the questions differently. Generally the first answer that comes to mind is the best to put down.

Decision Style Inventory III*

Please score the following questions based on the instructions given. Your score reflects how you see yourself, not what you believe is correct or desirable, as related to your work situation. It covers typical decisions that you make in your work environment.

1. My prime objective is to:	Have a position with status		Be the best in my field		Achieve recognition for my work		Feel secure in my job	
2. I enjoy jobs that:	Are technical and well defined		Have considerable variety		Allow independent action		Involve people	
3. I expect people working for me to be:	Productive and fast		Highly capable		Committed and responsive		Receptive to suggestions	
4. In my job, I look for:	Practical results		The best solutions		New approaches or ideas		Good working environment	
5. I communicate best with others:	In a direct one to one basis		In writing		By having a group discussion		In a formal meeting	
6. In my planning I emphasize:	Current problems		Meeting objectives		Future goals		Developing people's careers	
7. When faced with solving a problem, I:	Rely on proven approaches		Apply careful analysis		Look for creative approaches		Rely on my feelings	
8. When using information I prefer:	Specific facts		Accurate and complete data		Broad coverage of many options		Limited data that is easily understood	
9. When I am not sure about what to do, I:	Rely on intuition		Search for facts		Look for a possible compromise		Wait before making a decision	
10. Whenever possible, I avoid:	Long debates		Incomplete work		Using numbers or formulas		Conflict with others	
11. I am especially good at:	Remembering dates and facts		Solving difficult problems		Seeing many possibilities		Interacting with others	
12. When time is important, I:	Decide and act quickly		Follow plans and priorities		Refuse to be pressured		Seek guidance or support	
13. In social settings I generally:	Speak with others		Think about what is being said		Observe what is going on		Listen to the conversation	
14. I am good at remembering:	People's names		Places we met		People's faces		People's personality	
15. The work I do provides me:	The power to influence others		Challenging assignments		Achieving my personal goals		Acceptance by the group	
16. I work well with those who are:	Energetic and ambitious		Self confident		Open minded		Polite and trusting	
17. When under stress, I:	Become anxious		Concentrate on the problem		Become frustrated		Am forgetful	
18. Others consider me:	Aggressive		Disciplined		Imaginative		Supportive	
19. My decisions typically are:	Realistic and direct		Systematic or abstract		Broad and flexible		Sensitive to the needs of others	
20. I dislike:	Losing control		Boring work		Following rules		Being rejected	

© A.J. Rowe, revised 3/3/83. Reprinted with permission of the author.

Interpretation of Scores

To score the decision style inventory, simply total each of the four columns. The first column total score is associated with the *directive* style, the second column total is the *analytical* style, the third column total is the *conceptual* style, and the fourth column total is the *behavioral* style. Enter each of these totals into the four respective boxes of the decision style diagram. The combined score should total 300 points.

WORKSHEET 10B.2 | **Decision Style Graph**

Case LIFT Inc.
Date 1992
Name Pfeffer (top); Palma (bottom)

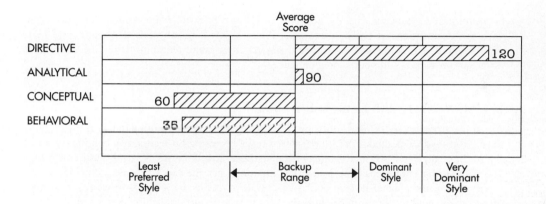

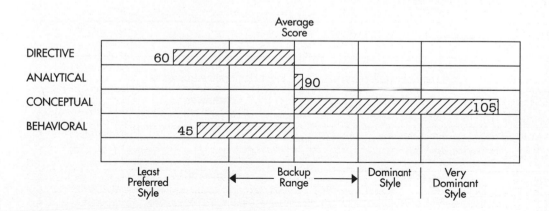

© A.J. Rowe, revised 3/3/83. Reprinted with permission of the author.

TABLE 10B.2	Style Scores of General Population

Style	Average Score
Directive	75
Analytical	90
Conceptual	80
Behavioral	55

his dominant style, again with the analytical style as a backup. These findings are consistent with the descriptions of these individuals. Pfeffer's left hemisphere is dominant, and he is task-oriented. Palma delegates authority, prefers long-range planning to day-to-day operations, is innovative, and wants independence.

DECISION STYLES AND LEADERSHIP ABILITIES

Are some decision styles used more by those who concentrate on managing, and others by those who lead? Zaleznick (1977) considered tasks requiring little cognitive complexity to be the maintenance functions of *management*; in those areas, the focus is on obtaining results and motivating employees. The *leadership* functions are the tasks that deal with ideas and therefore require a higher level of cognitive complexity. A leader is a person who is more concerned with the direction or outlook of the firm than with accomplishing detail assignments.

Figure 10B.2 focuses on the differences among the decision styles in terms of thinking versus action and leader qualities versus manager qualities. This table suggests that leaders, who are proactive and change-oriented, would be more likely than managers to have as a dominant style one of the styles in the upper half of the model—either the analytical style or the conceptual style.

FIGURE 10B.2	Cognitive Decision Style Model

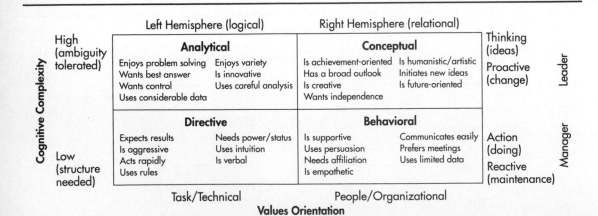

This hypothesis has been supported by studies of scores shown for managers and leaders on the decision style inventory. Over 20,000 managers and professionals have taken the decision style inventory since 1977. The average scores for the population at large are shown in Table 10B.2. Managers, on the whole, have been found to have scores similar to the population norms. For example, in a study of 194 managers in the southern California area (Mann, 1982), the average scores were as follows: directive, 74; analytical, 89; conceptual, 83; and behavioral, 54.

The scores of 26 young presidents who took the decision style inventory were also nearly the same as those of the overall population in all four categories.

Specific groups, however, have been found to have characteristic patterns of style that reflect the demands of their positions and the selection processes that brought them there. In a research study based on interviews with 80 senior executives (including chief executive officers, chairpersons, presidents, executive vice presidents, and directors of major industrial corporations, financial institutions, foundations, and consulting firms), Rowe found distinct style patterns (Rowe and Mason, 1987). The results clearly showed the central role that conceptual thinking plays in high-level management. For 90% of these executives, the conceptual style was either dominant or backup. For 76%, the analytical style was dominant or backup, and for 70%, the directive style was dominant or backup. The executives' mean scores for each style are graphed in Figure 10B.3.

An especially revealing insight into differences in style is contained in Mann's study of financial and strategic planners (1982). The scores of the two groups are shown in Table 10B.3. Note that among financial planners the dominant style is the analytical style needed to collect and analyze large amounts of financial data. Among strategic planners, on the other hand, the very dominant style is the conceptual style needed to think of the business as a whole and to create new options for it to pursue. Strategic planners have profiles similar to those of executives, reflecting the importance of intuition and creative thinking.

Table 10B.4 summarizes the differences in style patterns of various demographic and occupational groups. The exhibit reveals that female managers have higher directive and behavioral scores than do female architects, who are more analytical and conceptual. One

FIGURE 10B.3	**Decision Styles of 80 Senior Executives**

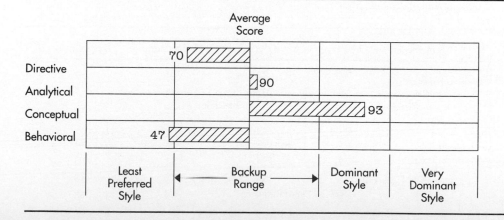

would expect these results, considering that the manager's job involves directing others and the architect's job involves analysis and visualization of structures to be built.

In one study, police chiefs were compared with engineering executives. This study showed that, typically, police chiefs are more analytical and behavioral than engineering executives, who are more directive. The conceptual scores of both groups were comparable. On the surface, this finding seems surprising inasmuch as it is often assumed that police are highly directive.

Table 10B.4 shows that U.S. managers, in general, have high analytical scores. One group of male engineering executives, however, had an analytical score of only 83.0, which is below the typical male score. The same group had a directive score of 82.9, which means that these engineering executives were focusing more on results than does the typical manager.

The comparison of U.S. and Japanese managers is very revealing. Japanese managers had an average score of 84 for the conceptual style and 68 for the behavioral style, which would make them predominantly right-brain-oriented, in contrast to male managers in the United States.

TABLE 10B.3 | **Style Scores of Financial and Strategic Planners**

Planning Function	Number	Decision Style			
		Directive	Analytical	Conceptual	Behavioral
Financial	19	75	100*	74	51
Strategic	11	62	81	100*	57

* Dominant style

Source: Richard B. Mann, 1982.

TABLE 10B.4 | **Comparison of Decision Styles**

	Number	Directive	Analytical	Conceptual	Behavioral
Female managers	93	74	88	74	64
Female architects	224	65	95	85	55
Police chiefs	151	71	90	81	58
Ph.D. psychologists	5	62	75	103	60
Male architects	141	65	95	86	54
Male U.S. managers	54	72	94	81	53
Male engineers	39	78	96	73	53
Japanese managers	21	69	79	84	68

CHAPTER ELEVEN

Information Technology and Future Directions in Strategy

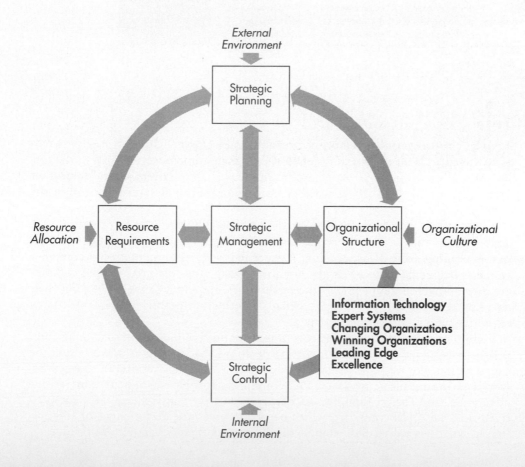

Chapter 1 A Framework for Strategic Management	**Chapter 2** Strategic Analysis	**Chapter 3** Strategic Visioning, Goals, Ethics, and Social Responsibility	**Chapter 4** The Competitive Environment	**Chapter 5** Capability-based Strategy	**Chapter 6** Market Dynamics and Sustainable Competitive Advantage
How to approach strategic management	*Application of strategic analysis*	*Understanding vision, values, ethics*	*Coping with competitive forces, stakeholders*	*Assessing company capability, timeliness, quality*	*Determining trends, gap analysis, and market dynamics*

Chapter 7 Strategy in a Global Environment	**Chapter 8** Financial Planning and Competitive- Cost Analysis	**Chapter 9** Entrepreneurship, Mergers and Acquisitions, Restructuring, and the Service Sector	**Chapter 10** Leadership Factor in Strategy and Implementing Strategic Change	**Chapter 11** Information Technology and Future Directions in Strategy
Assessing global trade, foreign markets, monetary exchange	*Preparing a financial plan and competitive-cost analysis*	*Importance of small business, entrepreneurs, restructuring*	*Strategy implementation, leadership, culture*	*Information technology, trends, new management*

INTRODUCTION

Today's strategic managers must be prepared to invoke new and flexible approaches to strategic management in order to ensure their companies' survival in the turbulent and uncertain business environment. This chapter covers several important areas that are likely to affect whether an organization will succeed or fail in the years ahead.

One of the principal changes on the horizon is the role of information as a strategic imperative. The rate of increase in the application of information technology is nothing short of astounding. A mere ten years ago, the personal computer was just beginning to come on the horizon. Today, not only are personal computers more powerful than some of the mainframe computers of the 1970s, but their cost has been reduced to the point where "information power" is available to any executive who is willing to utilize it.

This chapter will explore the role of information technology in sustaining competitive advantage as well as supporting decisions that managers make within the organization. For example, telemarketing today is used by over 80,000 companies, IBM is banking on super-fast RISC computers to help sustain its competitive advantage, and Digital Equipment Corporation has just introduced, at a competitive price, the Alpha computer, which boasts the awesome performance of 150 million instructions per second—double that of any computer available at this time.

How is all this powerful technology utilized to enhance strategic management? The applications explored in this chapter include decision support systems, expert systems for strategic management that include knowledge-based systems.

Technology by itself no more changes an organization than a written score creates a symphony. The organization must implement strategies for coping with massive technological innovations, extreme uncertainties, and a rapidly changing world environment. Thus the counterpoint to more sophisticated applications of information technology is the role of the organization in the future. Previous chapters have covered organizational structure, organizational change, strategy implementation, and leadership. This chapter takes a broader perspective: how managers will have to deal with problems in the 1990s. A reading on "Sustaining Competitive Advantage from IT," by John Cecil and Michael Goldstein, concludes the chapter.

THE CHANGING OUTLOOK

Tomorrow's companies will have to think strategically about new products, new markets, and new competition (Peters, 1989). By adapting their core expertise to a new view, large companies that can move toward a flatter structure, that continuously innovate, and that cope with chaotic conditions can survive. As markets become increasingly fractured, products become more customized. Timely response, quality design, high value, and customer focus will be the key to meeting these challenges.

But how does a company reinvent itself? It is not sufficient to create new products in the absence of an organizational structure that emphasizes continuous innovation. In 1970, Xerox created the Palo Alto Research Center (PARC) to pursue advanced research in the areas of computers, electronics, and materials. This center contributed

1. Fundamental innovations in computer technology
2. Bit map computer screens
3. Local area networks
4. Mouse editing
5. Object-oriented language
6. The first prototype laser printer

In 1991 the Center was focusing on the relationship of technology to work and on how information technology can support group collaboration.

The continuously innovating company improves operating practices as well as products, innovates at all levels in the organization, and innovates with the customer. GE is an example of a company that is trying to tap employee brainpower. Welch's vision for GE's success is "speed, simplicity, and self-confidence." He feels that removing the domination of the boss is tantamount to eliminating whips and chains. This helps to release the innovative power of workers, which, in turn, leads to greater satisfaction and improved performance. Over the past ten years, GE has improved its productivity by a total of 4% going from an improvement of 2% to 6%. U.S. manufacturers, on the other hand, have witnessed a decline of 2% over the same time period, going from a 1% productivity improvement to a 1% loss (Stewart, 1991).

Because of the importance of environmental factors in the determination of strategy, future manufacturers will need a better understanding of market structures and market dynamics. Porter (1980) clearly pointed out the need to take marketing forces into account in determination of strategy. The profit impact of market strategy (PIMS), which was discussed in Chapter 6, is used to maintain a current database of information for determining what strategies are most effective in a given industrial sector.

As the influence of stakeholders in the conduct of the organization becomes greater, the importance of such methods as stakeholder analysis will become apparent. Both consumers and the government are increasingly demanding that organizations be more socially responsible. Companies are responsible for not polluting the environment, making safe and durable products, being concerned with the well-being of their employees, not discriminating in hiring practices, and contributing to the good of society while meeting investor expectations. No longer does an organization choose to be socially responsible purely for altruistic reasons; rather, management recognizes that the external environment now plays a key role in determining the ultimate success or failure of the enterprise.

Certainly resources, investments, and technology still play key roles in determining both the effectiveness of operations and the ability to penetrate or defend a market. These three factors, however, are no longer considered synonymous with strategy. Although it would be foolhardy to ignore the importance of resources, investments, or technology in formulating strategic alternatives, coping with the market and with the formulation and implementation of strategy are equally important. In the microcomputer field, for instance, the first company to market a portable model, Osborn Inc., went bankrupt despite its technology, whereas IBM, which had no technological advantage in the personal computer area, came to dominate the field because of its reputation, resources, and marketing expertise.

Poor profitability or inadequate funding typically necessitates a defensive strategy. The innovative leader, however, can turn a defensive position into a positive approach, as occurred at Chrysler under Lee Iacocca. Strategic funds programming (see Chapter 8) permits planners to determine what resources are required for strategic alternatives. The resources available can have a significant impact on the level of expenditures for products in the firm.

The strategic managers need better methods to assist in allocating the available resources. Improved means to allocate limited resources and alternative strategies for accomplishing goals can substitute for technology or other capabilities that are not available in the firm. The strategic manager ensures that requirements of the strategic plan are met, while at the same time meeting external requirements and satisfying stakeholder demands.

After technological, marketing, and other problems are overcome, there still remain the human problems of implementing change and ensuring desired performance. We have discussed the importance of commitment on the part of the individual as a basis for ensuring performance. The performance management system (PMS) approach, combined with management by objectives (MBO), is widely used to match jobs to behavioral as well as skill requirements. (PMS and MBO are described in Chapter 10.)

In an article entitled "Meeting the Challenge of Global Competition," Gluck (1982) pointed out that a company's skill at responding rapidly to change is no guarantee of eventual competitive success. Rather, he maintained, managers will have to radically alter their thinking and behavior to cope effectively with the new environment. Planners will have to become change agents, and top management will have to shift from reactive to proactive leadership and achieve a quantum leap in corporate performance. (The next section examines in more detail the characteristics needed for excellent management in the future.) Gluck stated that strategic approaches based purely on analyses and forecasting will be inadequate to deal with the turbulence and instability that most companies will be encountering in the 1990s. It appears that he accurately predicted future requirements.

Strategic managers will have to "create the future" and at the same time integrate it with operational performance. Management will shift from a prescriptive approach to a more creative approach based on insights and tolerance for ambiguity. External conditions will be viewed as opportunities rather than problems, and planning will be concerned as much with understanding requirements as with involving those who must carry out the strategy. Thus the planner will become a change agent, matching the internal and external requirements with the motivational and structural needs of the organization.

Whereas the structure of an organization was at one time considered a key factor in carrying out strategy, the current trend is to consider more flexible structures, or "adhocracies," as preferable to bureaucracies. The typical life cycle of an organization illustrates the need to change the organizational structure to meet the demands of the environment. As the level of uncertainty and the size of an organization increases, there is a need for greater levels of differentiation to meet the new requirements. (The organizational life cycle is discussed in Chapter 10.)

The change models discussed in Chapter 10 show that there are effective means for bringing about change in an organization. With the many rapid changes now taking place, conventional approaches to strategy and structure do not suffice. Thus managers are increasingly turning to temporary structures or to the team approach. In addition, the consensus approach advocated by Japanese management is receiving increased attention as a means of improving communication and dedication to performance.

EXCELLENCE IN MANAGEMENT

A company's success is measured not solely by financial indicators but also by factors such as growth, competitiveness, ability to attract and retain excellent individuals, innovation, quality, responsiveness, adaptability, and social responsibility. Thus the "bottom line," although important, does not by itself ensure excellence in management. Rather, it is the combination of a leader's vision, plans, and action that contribute to effective organizational performance.

Japanese managers have demonstrated what many consider to be excellence in management. What makes their management excellent? Studies indicate that it is the great natural talent of the founder or chief executive who grasps intuitively the basic

survive on the planet in a harmonious manner, simple profit-driven goals can no longer be the prime objective of strategy. Rather, being a good corporate citizen may go a long way toward curing the ills of the twentieth century. Leading-edge strategists can contribute to this effort, but a new government-industry paradigm is needed to ensure progress in the twenty-first century.

What is being recommended to propel the United States back into a dominant position for the year 2000 and beyond? First, if one examines U.S. productivity closely, the findings are very interesting (Stewart, 1992). At present, for example,

1. The average U.S. worker produces $40,000 worth of goods and services.
2. The average German worker produces $37,850 worth.
3. The average Japanese worker (who has the longest work week) produces $34,500.

Even so, the United States cannot be complacent. Although it is ahead in productivity, the rate of improvement has declined. Only substantial investments in new technology and worker innovation will stop the downward trend. Recommendations include the following:

1. Redesign work and the reward system.
2. Emphasize total quality management.
3. Re-engineer manufacturing processes to allow for teamwork and concurrent design.
4. Eliminate low-value-adding components.
5. Upgrade the skill of the workforce by more training.

The "new gurus" of management (Byrne, 1992) extend this list to include

1. Create a learning organization that can change as requirements change.
2. Re-engineer the organization to focus on outcomes rather than on functional departments.
3. Focus on core competencies rather than on products or markets.
4. Re-examine organizational architecture to incorporate new thinking on leadership, autonomous work groups, empowerment, job ownership, entrepreneurial spirit, and a flexible structure that includes strategic alliances.
5. Employ time-based management and emphasize quality, value, service, and energizing innovation.

Other suggestions for repositioning the United States in a more competitive environment include

1. Develop a more effective global communication approach that enhances customer perceptions of the product (Makovsky, 1992).
2. Build the infrastructure by dealing effectively with the environment, telecommunications, technology, transportation, energy, education, and services (Jacobson, 1992).

Business Week's special 1992 edition on "Reinventing America" also emphasized a broad range of issues from managing change to creating a government for the people.

CHANGING ORGANIZATIONAL REQUIREMENTS

Why is concern so often expressed about the future of U.S. management? In part, this concern is a result of the impressive advances that have been made by Japan and other advanced countries. The literature on what constitutes excellent management illustrates the need for a redefinition of what we must look for in developing strategies that will carry U.S. industry successfully into the next century. The major changes in store for future businesses have been identified by Naisbitt and Aburdene (1985). They include a greater emphasis on information, high technology, a world economy, and use of participation as an organizational style. Organizations are clearly entering an era of increased ambiguity, complexity, and turbulence and will need to draw on all their resources to compete effectively in a world market.

The search for an ideal organization continues unabated because structure alone does not determine effectiveness. Recognition of the "adaptive" organization merely points to the need for a new or different perspective on how organizations are viewed and on how to achieve effective performance in a diverse workforce that expects to satisfy ever more complex needs.

Consider Table 11.2 where the corporate environments of Japanese and American firms are compared (Tsurumi, 1991). The obvious difference between the U.S. and Japanese corporate environments is the U.S. focus on the "bottom line" compared with the Japanese recognition of the importance of employee contributions. The employee-centered environment fosters strong group norms, a paternalistic culture, job rotation for flexibility, and job security for commitment and trust.

Can American managers manage as well as the Japanese? When dealing with American workers, who are a very heterogeneous group (compared to Japanese workers) with a low sense of company loyalty, can American managers achieve the same level of output in terms of quality and cost as their Japanese counterparts?

Consider two General Motors plants: one in Fremont, California, and the other in Van Nuys, California. The Fremont plant is a joint venture between Toyota and GM. The Fremont plant had been closed by GM in 1982. There had

TABLE 11.2	Comparison of Corporate Environments

Environmental Factors	Japanese Firms	American Firms
Strategic orientation	Long-term growth	Short-term profitability
Strategic goals	Global market share	Primarily domestic
Job security	Ensure long-term commitment and innovation	Considered costly and not attainable
Executive staffing	Promote from within	Fill positions both from within and from outside
Organizational control	Use of implicit rules and shared goals	Explicit rules, MBO, and cost control

been a high level of unrest in that plant, and there were 800 unresolved grievances at the time of the plant closing. In 1983 Toyota, GM, and the United Auto Workers embarked on a historic effort to fuse the dramatically different American and Japanese labor-management traditions. A form of Japanese management that applied quality circles was introduced as a way of improving performance.

During the same period, the GM plant in Van Nuys was having difficulties and faced the threat of being closed. While the Fremont plant was managed by the Japanese, the Van Nuys plant was managed by Americans. In 1990 the Fremont plant was highly successful, whereas the Van Nuys plant was still experiencing major problems (Stavro, 1990).

Some new employees of the New United Motor Manufacturing, Inc., The GM-Toyota joint venture, were flown to Japan for training. One American commented that "while there is more work per man, they make it easier for the worker. They listen to suggestions from the worker on how to improve his job" (Jameson, 1984). In 1992 workers at the GM Van Nuys plant suffered the traumatic experience of being laid off when the plant was finally closed.

WINNING ORGANIZATIONS

The top 100 of America's fastest-growing companies are exploiters of change and exemplify the entrepreneurial spirit that still pervades the United States. Deutschman (1991) admonishes that "old-line giants had better learn from them." Table 11.3 profiles ten of the top 100 growth firms and suggests that the effect covers most industries, especially those that are not so capital-intensive as the industries in which GE and GM operate. Note further that a number of the top 100 growth

| TABLE 11.3 | Ten of the Top 100 Growth Companies |

Rank in Growth	Company	Sales Growth (%)	Growth in Earnings/Share (%)	Price-Earnings Ratio
1.	Zeos International	256	—	17
4.	Synoptics Communications	209	129	16
8.	American Waste Services	180	116	21
12.	Columbia Hospital	153	81	14
14.	California Energy	151	—	31
17.	Ivax Pharmaceuticals	139	—	367
29.	Symantec	97	—	55
31.	First Financial Management	89	41	15
46.	Amgen	76	—	125
59.	Centex Telemanagement	69	72	27

companies were startup organizations. This reflects the power and advantage enjoyed by a cohesive and nimble organization that has a good product or service.

Reinforcing the requirement for speed and for satisfying a more demanding workforce, the winning organization is able to outperform the larger, more sluggish organization by being responsive to customer needs, providing individual service, making decisions quickly, and adapting products and organizations to fit changing requirements. The 1990s will have even more stringent requirements in fast and extraordinary global competition (Main, 1988). Speed is not limited to small, nimble companies. IBM, for example, uses computer simulations to skip two to three generations of prototypes in developing new integrated circuits. And Limited Inc. tracks daily sales of clothing by using point-of-sale computers that provide the base for orders sent by satellite around the globe.

It is predicted that corporate staffs will virtually disappear, as will dozens of layers of management. The horizontal organization described by Ostroff and Smith (1992) will replace the traditional vertical/hierarchic structure that impedes information flow, restricts empowerment, and limits worker satisfaction. A horizontal organization leverages capability by allowing greater cross-functional work flow that adopts and responds to customers and suppliers. The primary defect of vertical organizations is their inability to be responsive. The horizontal form of organization is built around a small number of business processes or the flow of work that links employer with customers and suppliers. The result is reduced cycle time, reduced cost, and greater throughput. Performance evaluation and resource allocation focus on continuous improvements. In effect, this structure is organized around processes, not specific tasks. To create a horizontal structure, the company needs to identify a limited number of core processes (three to five), which include activity flows, information flow, and material flow.

Motorola has shifted from a fragmented vertical organization to an integrated horizontal organization in its Government Electronics Group. The results have been a reduction in the workforce, linked flows, and the elimination of non-value-adding activities. Team leaders and technical experts provide overall guidance, and there are only two levels between the group head and the teams. "Ownership" of processes and performance is at the team level, as is evaluation of the extent to which the team has met objectives and satisfied customers. Teams become the building block for performance and design and combine managerial with non-managerial activities whenever possible. Self-management builds on intrinsic motivation rather than on control that imposes constraints and frustration. Flexibility is achieved because team members assume multiple competencies. Finally, team performance and skill development are emphasized over individual performance. Of course, this requires that team members hold themselves mutually accountable and that they be rewarded on the basis of joint performance. It is true that changing to a horizontal form of organization can be frustrating, but Motorola achieved a significant reduction in cycle time, a 30% reduction in workforce, and an astounding tenfold improvement in supplied quality. Others, including IDS, GE, and Knight-Ridder, have had similar results (Ostroff and Smith, 1992).

This same theme is echoed by Stewart (1992), who describes the organization of tomorrow as one with a bold new look that is flat and lean. High-performance teams use redesigned work and unbridled information to achieve their goals. Lawrence Bossidy, CEO of Allied Signal, predicts a corporate revolution in the way organizations will be structured to cope with the dramatically new environment. The consensus is that the hierarchic structure of the past will wither away and will be replaced by an organization that fosters high involvement, self-managing teams, and the use of business processes to replace functional departments and to bring information technology to the point where accountability depends on knowledge. The key is an integrated activity flow that can enhance performance.

Byrne (1989) poses an intriguing question when he asks, "Is your company too big?" Perhaps he is alluding to the dinosaurs of the past that could not survive in the rapidly changing environment of the Ice Age. Are our monster organizations of today facing extinction because of their inability to adapt? Table 11.4 compares large companies with small ones. Large companies and small, agile, entrepreneurial companies also differ in other ways. These include the ability to obtain funding, to develop capital-intensive products, and to compete effectively in the global market place. Largeness does not guarantee competitiveness, and we must not forget that large corporations have to satisfy stockholders. Finally, responsiveness depends primarily on information flow, which is horribly sluggish in large organizations.

Can large organizations act the same as small ones? Some evidence suggests that they can. AT&T has split into 6 major businesses and 19 smaller groups to encourage individual risk taking. At GE, Jack Welch wants to avoid encumbering the divisions. He has reduced the number of levels of management from 9 to 4 and uses staff only for advice. GM's Roger Smith vowed to eliminate entrenched layers of management. Hewlett-Packard emphasizes self-direction by individuals, which leads to ownership. It also subdivided the business into 50 units, each with responsibility for its own performance. McDonald's relies on incentives, awards, and autonomous operation.

TABLE 11.4   **Comparison of Large and Small Companies**

Factor	Large Companies	Small Companies
Size	Sprawling plants	Unitized factories
Integration	Vertical	Subcontracting
Cost-effectiveness	Economies of scale	Flexibility
Organization	Hierarchic	Flat
Orientation	Organization	Innovation
Market share	Large	Create new markets
Distribution	Mass marketing	Niche markets
Manufacturing focus	Quantity	Quality

M.I.T.'s Ferguson claims that a small company can succeed in a niche market but that to compete effectively with Japanese giants, a small company must either grow or join in the coordinated efforts of a number of small companies. Only a large, strong company such as IBM or GE is in a position to compete effectively in the global marketplace. Although size confers some important advantages, it does not effectively confer job ownership or worker commitment, the lack of which can lead to difficulty when dealing with complex organizational problems. The answer may well be that to compete effectively, the United States needs a combination of small entrepreneurial companies and large ones that organize for agility, creativity, and commitment from employees.

A final consideration in redesigning the corporation is how to accelerate change at the middle-management level, which appears to be the major obstacle to the flattening of organizations. Organizational change can be a wrenching, challenging, and time-consuming process. Redesigning structures in such a way that critical skills are retained means changing the mass of middle and front-line managers who currently are responsible for performance. One reason why Japan has found change and adaptability easier is its relatively homogeneous population that believes in harmony in the workplace. As pressures mount and the need for redesigning U.S. businesses becomes acute, a new approach to the management of change will be required. It will be necessary to utilize information technology and careful planning to fit the varied organizational pieces back together again in a new pattern. Heygate (1992) cites the case of a major bank that had a maximum of only three years to cut costs by 30%, increase profit by 100%, restructure the branch network, and teach new skills to 20,000 members of the staff. The redesigned positions meant a reduction of 50% in the workforce, and 80% of the remaining jobs were changed. Also required was information technology support that could easily have been sabotaged.

To achieve its objective, the bank had to overcome several obstacles, including middle-management resistance, the need for training in new skills, inflexible information systems, and an inflexible program for implementing changes in strategy.

To overcome these barriers to accelerated front-line change, the bank took the following steps:

1. Used precise redefinition of tasks and roles.
2. Used computer workstations to support training.
3. Sidestepped inflexible approaches to redesign of the computer system by using incremental improvements.
4. Used logical modules to proceed in parallel with the design process.
5. Applied program management techniques to avoid the traditional sequential approach to design.
6. Kept improvements flowing via communications and empowerment.
7. Remained current by using a disciplined release of new updates.
8. Kept key team leaders and senior management involved at every stage.
9. Maintained a central logistics unit to ensure appropriate delegation of the line and functional units.
10. Relied on active participation of team leaders to ensure effective communications.

Clearly, implementing an accelerated massively parallel change requires new approaches and new support tools, because conventional approaches are much too slow and do not ensure meeting the overall design objective.

To be competitive in the 1990s, organizational structure will need to embrace a new model that is more entrepreneurial and that focuses on increasing value and customer satisfaction (Dichter, 1991). The GE Salisbury plant had five levels of management and separate design and manufacturing departments. After restructuring, the plant has only three levels of management, and the workforce consists of self-managing teams. Cross-functional committees meet weekly and performance reports are available from computers, which facilitate being flexible. This resulted in a 10% cost reduction, an average delivery time of 3 days instead of 3 weeks, and only one-tenth as many complaints as there were before. Since the early 1980s, over 400 companies or divisions have created similar organizational structures.

To be successful, organizations of the 1990s will need to

1. Provide superior value to customers
2. Continuously improve performance
3. Operate as self-leading teams
4. Have an organizational structure that is flat and flexible
5. Empower workers and share values
6. Exhibit leadership that has value-driven vision
7. Create fundamental changes in culture
8. Involve workers in the redesign process
9. Provide guidelines for redesign that are based on
    a. A new corporate vision
    b. A challenge to improve performance
    c. Simpler structures and systems
    d. A new change process
    e. The provision of intensive training and support
10. Accelerate change by
    a. Loosening control
    b. Providing clearly defined performance standards, training, rewards, shared values, and motivation
    c. Making teams accountable for performance
    d. Making individual performance the responsibility of the team
    e. Reducing the influence of the remaining hierarchy
    f. Making all decisions participatively and by consensus

Does this model apply to all organizations equally well? Certainly, some organizations are more amenable than others to introducing the changes described here. But those that do not change will be in jeopardy of losing their competitive position and may even risk failing to survive.

One of the key elements of organizational change is the CEO, who becomes an "organizational architect" (Howard, 1992). Some companies achieve the creativity that small units nourish while preserving the strength and vision of a large organization. The structure that makes this possible has been referred to as the C^2D^2 of organization design, where C^2 stands for centralized coordination and D^2 for decentralized decision making. Restructuring is not merely redesigning an organization. Rather, it calls for a major paradigm shift that leads to new thinking, culture, and flexibility. A redesign will not by itself lead to improved performance. Implementing a change requires a new set of relationships, such as the teamwork or cluster groups that were used for GM's Saturn car. It requires empowerment, ownership, rewards that match effort and commitment, and a changed set of values that contribute to a new work ethic.

INFORMATION TECHNOLOGY

Redefining the role of information is perhaps the most critical aspect of using computers as a competitive tool. Information can play three key roles in a firm's strategy.

1. *Information can be used to report the transactions of the business.* In this role it performs the stewardship function. It keeps track of "what things are where" and "who owes what to whom." The ability to scan local and global markets rapidly has fundamentally altered the processes of planning and distribution. Retail stores such as Wal-Mart can now determine when a particular item is selling well in one store and not moving well at all in another. Rather than let the merchandise remain dormant, they can move it around as needed. American Hospital Supply Corporation (see Chapter 1) used its computer system to deal directly with the needs of hospitals and thereby gained a competitive advantage.
2. *Information can be used to guide business decision making.* In this role it informs the decision maker how well the business is functioning, what problems need attention, and what alternatives should be considered. Management science, management information, and decision support systems all address this role of information in business. (The next section will describe some decision support systems in use today.)
3. *Information can be an integral part of the product or service the business offers to its customers.* In this special role, information becomes—in the customer's eyes, at least—indistinguishable from facilities, people, and commodities. Hence it becomes part of the business's product/market planning. This role is perhaps the most crucial one that information plays—the one that has the tightest link to strategic planning, as well as the most potential.

It is the third function of information that opens opportunities to businesses to make information systems the vanguard of their strategy. Being close to the customer is one of the keys to excellence in business. A strategy that emphasizes closeness focuses on revenue generation as opposed to cost reduction and requires that a business be obsessed with providing service and quality as distinctive competencies.

Among the many companies that have used information services to achieve a competitive advantage are American Airlines, with its Sabre reservation system; Avis, with the "Wizard"; Merrill Lynch, with its cash management system; and Citibank, with its international telecommunications system. Sears is using videodiscs and personal computers to automate its customer catalogs and provide information to customers in their homes. Mobil Oil is using point-of-sale terminals to link the gasoline pumps to automated tellers of local banks. The list of applications is growing exponentially; the possibilities seem to be limited only by the creativity of planners and strategists. What all this portends is radical change, not only in the way information is viewed and used but also in the impact of information processing as a competitive weapon.

The formula for successfully using information systems as a part of the product is straightforward:

1. Identify an unfulfilled customer need or want.
2. Create a means by which information services can fill that need in a manner that enhances the level of service, improves the quality and reliability of the product, and distinguishes both from the offerings of all competitors.
3. Bring the information systems and services to the marketplace as an integral part of the corporate product and marketing strategy.

DECISION SUPPORT INFORMATION SYSTEMS

Information systems can play an important supporting role in developing and carrying out business strategies. There are several approaches to using information systems in strategy formation.

Warren McFarlan and Gregory Parsons developed a technique for applying Porter's concepts (Porter's concepts are described in Chapter 4, beginning on page 123) to information technology. They initially assess the threat (low to high) of each of the five competitive forces affecting the firm and then determine how information technology can influence each threat. They use a two-dimensional matrix to show the firm's competitive position and the role of information systems. This matrix becomes a planning tool for determining new strategies and forecasting changes.

The MAIN Information System

Kodak focuses its information system, the MAIN system, on answering managers' strategic questions. J. Phillip Samper, group vice president and general manager of Kodak's Photographic Marketing Group, summarized the intent of Kodak's information system as follows:

> Our job is to insure, on a worldwide basis, that the information about the marketplace, about technology, about competition, about our performance—that all these are joined together to develop a scenario that allows us to properly position ourselves in the marketplace.

> I am convinced that the Kodak *MArket INtelligence* System (the MAIN system) can enhance these functions greatly with the availability of a worldwide data bank—retrievable on demand—that ties business objectives to critical issues.

A basic premise of the MAIN system is that there is no limit to the amount of information that can be obtained about markets and customers. A basic pitfall, unfortunately, is that there is no limit to the amount of money that can be spent on acquiring marketing information. Spending too much money to acquire information is the common error that Russell Ackoff (1967) considered in his classic paper,

"Management Misinformation Systems." The solution is to focus the firm's information systems and services on a few high-payoff areas. The MAIN system does so by translating important yet uncertain strategic-planning assumptions into critical market research questions (CMRQs). The CMRQs cover technical issues (hardware and software), environmental forces, and interpersonal considerations within the organization, as well as design criteria for decision support information systems. After the CMRQs have been prioritized and budgets allocated accordingly, a search is made for data that will answer the questions they pose.

A second basic premise of the MAIN system is that information is not just a "thing in itself," but rather part of a complex relationship among four key entities:

1. The marketplace, which provides signals as to what customers need or say they need
2. The firm's market research department, which collects information, assesses its reliability and validity, analyzes it, and reports it to decision makers
3. The organizational decision makers, who determine what products and services the business is able and willing to present to the marketplace and what the economic results will be
4. The strategic managers, who are responsible and accountable for the performance of the other three

The MAIN system is an information utility that coordinates the activities of these four entities. It contains market data, a library of past studies, a system bibliography, analytical software, graphic and portrayal software, communications software, user help (both automated and interpersonal), a support organization, and, of course, the requisite hardware. All of these information resources are focused on the prioritized CMRQs and the planning process.

Thus the MAIN system has four functions:

1. It helps strategic management to determine what information about the marketplace is needed.
2. It is used, in conjunction with the market research function, to collect data from the marketplace.
3. It provides an interface between the market research department and the organizational decision makers—largely product planners, market managers, brand managers, and so forth—so that information can be summarized, stored, retrieved, and disseminated as needed.
4. It analyzes and interprets the organizational decision-making process so that strategic management can evaluate it.

Critical Success Factors

Jack Rockart and Christine Bullen developed an approach for helping businesses identify what information is required for strategic planning (Rockart, 1979). Their approach uses critical success factors (CSFs) to define strategic objectives and meaningful action steps. (Critical success factors are described in Chapter 5.) Arthur Young and other consulting firms have used CSFs for three related purposes:

1. To clarify managerial focus by highlighting similarities and differences among executives' CSFs

2. To develop top management's information needs by relating CSFs to specific items of decision support information

3. To set information systems priorities by defining the gap between available and required information as it is related to the importance of the CSF

Used in these ways, CSFs help managers to establish a businesswide perspective and define initial requirements.

The CSF approach focuses on critical high-payoff factors, it is relatively fast and inexpensive to administer, and it frequently reveals new insights to the executives involved. Its major disadvantages are that it is not comprehensive and that it results in a snapshot of the business, which can quickly become obsolete if any major change occurs.

Information Needs and the Product Life Cycle

Analysts at Nolan Norton and Company have developed a methodology for linking corporate strategic planning with information systems planning. The primary support needs of a product are determined by considering its stage in the product life cycle (see Chapter 6) and its relative market share. The Nolan and Gibson (1974) model distinguishes four stages:

- *Initiation*, in which technological specification, systems creation, and original investment are crucial
- *Expansion*, in which learning and adaptation are crucial
- *Control*, in which rationalization and elaboration are crucial
- *Maturity*, in which a careful review of projects for continued viability and the need for integration is crucial

In general, early-life-cycle/low-market-share products tend to need strategic information support, early-life-cycle/high-market-share products tend to need operational support, later-life-cycle/high-market-share products tend to need management control support, and later-life-cycle/low-market-share products tend to need strategic support. The market needs for each product can then be identified and placed into one of three categories—cost reduction, improved productivity, and product differentiation. Finally, existing and proposed applications of information systems are reviewed via a functional portfolio model. The functional portfolio model represents all the key activities in the business, shown in a portfolio similar to the product portfolio.

The results of these analyses can then be used to answer broad questions:

- How are the product needs related to market needs?
- How are the stages of the information system related to the product needs?
- How are the product needs related to the functional portfolio?
- How are the stages of the information system related to market needs?
- How are the market needs related to the functional portfolio?
- How are the stages related to the functional portfolio?

Each of these questions can be answered in terms of costs, coverage, and systems support. The result is an overall evaluation of the application and information systems. Guidelines emerge for budgets, improvements in existing systems, and opportunities for new systems.

ASSESSMENT OF INFORMATION-SYSTEMS NEEDS

Mark Porat, Alvin Toffler, and others have asserted that society has entered an information age (Porat, 1977; Toffler, 1990). A large number of people are involved in the production and dissemination of information. Many firms spend 1% to 3% of total revenues on information systems. They draw heavily on the more than 500 databases and other commercial information services available. How can managers determine whether a company is using information systems appropriately? One method is to compare the company's usage of information (and the return received therefrom) to that of its competitors. Another approach is to consider the value added by the systems.

Industry Comparisons

Information services can contribute to the total value added by every business. Moreover, the percentage of value added by information has been increasing over the past two decades. This percentage is, however, greater in information-processing and financial services industries than in manufacturing industries. Robert Hayes, dean of the UCLA Graduate School of Library and Information Science, has produced econometric evidence suggesting that manufacturing industries in the United States are *underinvesting* in information (Hayes, 1982). His results, based on data from 51 industries, indicate that the manufacturing segment is utilizing less information than is needed to maintain a competitive position in a global economy. As the potential for information systems to contribute to total value added increases (2–3% per year has not been unusual), alert managers must maintain their company's ability to obtain information services at the optimal level.

One way to determine whether a business is making optimal use of information is to

1. Make a list of the business's major information and communication functions.
2. Rate the company and its competitors on each of these functions in terms of (a) their dependence on information technology and (b) the effectiveness of the technology in use.
3. Combine the two ratings to yield an information-systems "absorption" rate.
4. Compare the results. A firm whose absorption rate is below the industry average may have some catching up to do. A firm whose rate is above the average may be a technological innovator or may have assumed too much risk.

Value-Added Approaches

Another approach is to consider the total value-adding chain within the business and ask how improved information services might result in improved performance. The value chain, which was discussed in Chapter 5, helps to determine those activities in which a company performs better in terms of technology and cost (Porter and Millar, 1985). Although a product's value is whatever the buyer is willing to pay, its ultimate cost depends on the interdependent activities linked together by the value chain.

Along with capital and labor, information adds value during production. Information is used in raw-materials acquisition, materials processing, manufacturing, distribution, and customer service. Value chain analysis reveals not only promising business opportunities but also opportunities to improve profits.

In determining whether information systems will add value, strategic managers should ask

- What major decisions are made?
- What are the constraints and problems?
- What role does information play?
- How can improved use of information lead to improved performance of the business?
- Could better information lead to better profits?

Value is added through the transformation of inputs into outputs. Thus the key to understanding a business is to identify the dominant features of the transformation. Information can play two key roles in the transformation process. First, it can be used to coordinate and smooth the flow of activity from one stage to another. Second, it can be used in production. For example, by using information systems technology in the design process, a firm can improve performance and thereby secure a competitive edge. Long-linked technology is likely to uncover some strategic opportunities for the application of information technology to a business. A long-linked technology accomplishes its task by sequential interdependence between tasks and relies on effectiveness through planning and control. An example of a long-linked technology is an assembly line that mass-produces a standard product at a constant rate and is dependent on feeder lines supplying material to the right place at the right time.

James Thompson first identified the basic technological cores that underlie the transformation of inputs into outputs (Thompson, 1967). He labeled these cores long-linked technology, extensive technologies, intensive technologies, and mediating technologies. Long-linked technology is described above.

1. *Extensive technologies* convert one input into two or more distinct outputs. Examples of this type of input/output process are the conversion of timber into lumber and paper; of grapes into raisins, table grapes, and wine; and of sheep into mutton and wool. In the cases of timber and grapes, a firm can decide how much input to allocate to each output. In the case of sheep raising, the conversion ratios are relatively fixed; one cannot change the proportions of input used to produce mutton and wool. Many industries (notably oil) fall somewhere between these two extremes. In the petroleum industry, the chemistry of hydrocarbon bonding constrains the range of alternative outputs that can be produced. Within these constraints, however, the chemistry is flexible enough to offer a considerable number of options.

Information systems can have several important functions in these highly technological industries. First, the demand and price characteristics of each of the potential output areas can be closely monitored so that the business can shift its emphasis to the most profitable products. Anticipating changes in demand and price is part of strategic product-portfolio management. Second, the technological environment can be scanned in order to find ways of increasing the range of outputs and the flexibility to shift among them. Third, information can be used to allocate the cost of inputs used to produce each output. Only with a logical system for allocating joint costs can a company establish profitability and determine whether to shift its emphasis from one product output to another.

2. *Intensive technologies* are the mirror image of extensive technologies. Intensive technologies combine a variety of inputs into a single output. Construction projects and one-time events, such as rock concerts, are generally intensive in nature. Information must be used to guide the application of inputs to output so that time/cost objectives can be met.

Case-management systems are archetypical intensive technologies. A *case* in this context is a business transaction with an individual that is opened, processed, and closed. Examples of case-management systems include transactions with patients in a hospital, claimants in an insurance firm, and clients for a professional's services. Stephen Rosenthal (1982) pointed out that case-management systems have four principal phases:

- *Identification,* in which new cases are sought, received, screened, and either rejected or accepted for further processing
- *Analysis,* in which data about each case are collected and interpreted and the case is diagnosed, prioritized, and scheduled
- *Response,* in which the resources are actually applied to the case and an output (such as a finding, verdict, or cure for a patient) is reached
- *Resolution,* in which the case is closed, although it may be monitored for performance and possible chronic relapse.

Each of these phases requires information and thus is a good target for the application of information-services technology.

3. *Mediating technologies* add value by matching diverse inputs with diverse outputs. They constitute a combination of intensive and extensive technologies. An example is a real estate brokerage system, in which an input case is opened for each property listing and an output case is opened for each prospective buyer. Then the firm seeks to match properties with buyers.

Reservation systems, such as American Airlines' Sabre system and Avis's Wizard, fall into this category. Wizard permits an Avis customer anywhere in the United States to order a particular style of car to be available in another city at a specified time. A complex telecommunications and computer system does the matching, informs Avis decision makers, and keeps track of accounting transactions once the entry is made. Both American Airlines and Avis gained strategic advantages over their competitors by designing systems that facilitated their mediating activities. By improving their mediating function, they were able to provide better services to their customers and reduce their cost of performance.

As financial intermediaries, banks and other financial institutions are classic users of mediating technologies. They can separate the two technologies, however. Operations dealing with deposits and sources of funds are intensive technologies, whereas those dealing with loans and investments are extensive technologies. This separation is possible because money can be used to transfer a debt, and because bank management uses indicators such as the loan-to-deposit ratio to balance the flows of inputs and outputs. Today, more financial institutions are trying to manage a diverse customer base by matching customers to the combination of deposit, loan, and investment services they want. This practice also gives bankers an opportunity to estimate the profit (loss) contribution of a customer—information that has eluded them in the past.

Information is central to mediating technologies. It is used to identify and service suppliers (input) and customers (output) and to match them in an effective and profitable manner.

INFORMATION TECHNOLOGY AND STRATEGY

There is a new meaning of power in today's economic and political world. As Alvin Toffler (1990) observes, a new system of wealth creation has emerged. Information and knowledge—including facts, art, science, moral values, intelligence, and even misinformation—provide the raw material for creating wealth. But information was not always a principal source of power. To the ancient Athenians, Thucydides tells us in his account of the Peloponnesian war, "might made right." For the ensuing nearly 2,500 years, the capability to do violence and to inflict harm on others has been a major source of power. Starting in the sixteenth century, however, as market economies began to form, money began to be used more pervasively in all political and economic relationships. In the process, money emerged as a second, and in a sense a more flexible, source of power (Braudel, 1981). Then, as the Industrial Revolution unfolded in England and the United States, and especially as the modern corporation came into being, money became a dominant source of power. With money one could buy goods, services, influence, and if necessary, war-making capacity.

Yet the sheer complexity of bigger businesses and governments themselves (as expressed in the form of railroads, steamship companies, automobile makers, nationwide mail order houses, steel makers, chemical companies, and agencies) created a massive problem of managerial control. In response, new information-based technologies such as the telegraph, the telephone, the adding machine, the typewriter, and the punched-card accounting machine were invented. These new technologies were used to provide the information needed to cope with the increased distance, speed, volume, and complexity involved in doing business. Sociologist James Beniger (1986) calls this phenomenon the "control revolution." These events, he argues, form the technological and economic origins of the information society. After World War II, major advances in computers and telecommunications technology and an expanding global economy worked together to change the fundamental nature of the economy and of society. Western capitalist societies became information-based. And this occurrence, Toffler states, brought about another shift in the basis of power. Knowledge and information replaced money as the fundamental source of power.

Information, it turns out, is a higher-quality source of power. Toffler continues:

> High-quality power is not simply clout. Not merely the ability to get one's way, to make others do what you want, though they might prefer otherwise. High quality implies much more. It implies efficiency—using up the fewest power resources to achieve a goal. Knowledge can often be used to make the other party *like* your agenda for action. It can even persuade the person that she or he originated it.

Knowledge also serves as a wealth and force multiplier. It can be used to augment the available force of wealth or, alternatively, to reduce the amount needed to achieve any given purpose. In either case, it increases efficiency, permitting one to spend fewer power "chips" in any showdown. (p. 16)

The shift to information and knowledge as a basis of power has profound effects for corporate strategy. For many years, information played an auxiliary role in business affairs. It was used primarily for stewardship purposes—for record keeping and to keep track of labor, capital, and other resources. As time passed, the potential role of information as an input to decision making and as a fundamental element in the delivery of goods and services was discovered, and strategies for the effective linking of information with operations and decision making were developed. Businesses embarking on these strategies changed the concept of information itself. Information ceased being merely a way of accounting for other resources and *became a resource in its own right*. Information, it was soon learned, could be acquired, manipulated, and allocated just as any other economic resource could. Thus information became a major source of corporate power, and information technology became the instrument for harnessing this power.

Information technology (IT) is the means used to gather, process, store, and transmit data, text, sound, graphics, and other symbolic images. It has strategic significance. In an information-rich economy, a company can use information technology to "reduce costs, upgrade product quality, improve customer service, or even integrate a customer's operations with its own, thus assuring repeat business." Insofar as it achieves these goals, information technology is a tool for increasing the economic power of a firm.

The potential sources of this power are expanding almost daily as new technologies are developed and made available. Parallel computers, optical networks, massive data storage, and a whole host of new information processing and handling technologies are being released, and several decades more of new technologies are currently moving through the research and development pipeline. As a consequence, the information networks of the 1990s and well beyond will dwarf those of today in size, level of sophistication, and efficiency. They will link hundreds of suppliers (that offer thousands of products) with who knows how many millions of customers.

A prototype firm of the future is Rosenbluth Travel. Rosenbluth, which operates out of Philadelphia, is one of the five largest travel agencies in the United States. Since 1980 it has grown from a regional agency with annual sales of $40 million into a "global virtual corporation" with annual sales well over $1.3 billion. The company formed Rosenbluth International Alliance (RIA) by entering into partnerships with some 34 local travel agents spanning over 37 countries. Information technology was the tool for linking them. According to Rosenbluth executive David Miller,

Information technology enables the company to coordinate travel services throughout the world. Through IT, specific information concerning clients and travelers is available anywhere in the world to provide superior travel support. A U.S. executive traveling in the U.K. will find that the local RIA representative is aware of her itinerary and travel preferences as well as her company's travel policies and special rate programs. And through IT, information can be consolidated across the world to coordinate decision making and leverage global purchasing power. (Personal interview, January 1992)

We need not travel around the globe, however, to see IT being used as an effective strategic tool. Just visit the local Wal-Mart or Sam's. During the first quarter of 1991, Wal-Mart Stores, the brainchild of pioneering discounter Sam Walton, surpassed Sears and became America's largest retailer. Sears' annual sales reached $32 billion; Wal-Mart's were in excess of $32.6 billion and still growing. Wal-Mart was also considerably more efficient. Its expenses were only 16% of sales, and its employees generated an average of $95,000 in sales per employee. Sears' costs, on the other hand, were a lofty 29% of sales, and its employees averaged only about $85,000 each in sales. IT played a crucial role in this remarkably successful strategy. As *Time* magazine reported,

> Walton—Mr. Sam to his 350,000 employees—invested in a state-of-the-art corporate satellite system that has enabled the company to perfect round-the-clock inventory control so that the products customers want are nearly always in stock. In Bentonville (Arkansas), a computer center the size of a football field controls the widespread operations, tracking inventory, credit, and sales via a Hughes satellite. (Castro, 1991)

Wal-Mart's network provides real-time data and voice and video links to about 1,600 stores. In addition to making possible just-in-time inventory replenishment to the stores from distribution centers, the network is linked to suppliers. In early 1992 over 2,200 suppliers were on line to Wal-Mart; about 2,000 more were slated to join. The satellite network is also used for direct television broadcasting of messages to the stores and for training employees. Buyers use the network to tell stores what new items are available in a particular department and how those items should be displayed. Executives use the network to share ideas about what is selling well and what merchandising ideas work for particular products (Booker, 1990).

Telemarketing has become another IT-based tool of strategy. It is already being used by over 80,000 companies large and small, and the list is growing every day. Although applications such as telemarketing have succeeded in increasing direct sales, the greatest potential of IT still lies in adding a new capability to the company's competitive arsenal. IT allows companies to enter new markets rapidly, differentiate their products through better service and response, dramatically improve sales performance, and gather the intelligence needed to compete in a dynamic marketplace.

Warren McFarlan (1984) has shown that companies can use IT to build barriers to entry, to increase customer switching costs, or to change the basis for competing, thereby throwing the competition off balance. A notable example of such a strategy is that of Digital Equipment Corporation (DEC). Severely hurt by its failure to compete in the personal computer field, DEC needed a new strategic thrust. A computer-based expert system proved to be a key part of the answer.

DEC found that it could outperform IBM, Apple, and other competitors when it used an artificial-intelligence-based system called XCON (Expert Configurator) to communicate directly with customers. When customers place orders, XCON provides them with complete specifications and delivery dates and at the same time sends the information to the factory so that work on orders can commence. This competitive advantage saved the ailing giant, making DEC a formidable competitor once again.

Another example is a new expert system, Business Insight, that is being employed to help determine the best strategies for introducing new products

(Lewis, 1991). Business Insight is the most comprehensive of a number of available computerized strategic-planning programs. The business development manager for the Dynatel Systems Division of 3M claims that this program provides the broadest perspective of any. The program operates in an interactive mode and starts by asking questions such as "How likely is it that a competitor will retaliate?" The value of the program is that it forces a systematic evaluation of the factors that a company must consider when introducing a new product.

At Rockwell International, engineers use an object-oriented expert system to design payloads on the computer screen. This allows them to see how well the payload fits into a space shuttle's cargo bay. Engineers have been enthusiastic about using the program and say that it saves them considerable time and effort (Callahan, 1992). Numerous accounts of the successful application of expert systems have been published in recent years. The expanding use of expert system technology to support more effective design and strategic analysis paints a bright picture for its future use.

Professor Eric Clemons has summarized some of the ways in which information technology can empower a firm:

1. *Increased efficiency.* "Use information technology to address fundamental requirements of the business or its customers and suppliers, thereby gaining competitive advantage." (p. 23)
2. *First-mover advantage.* "Hustle and continuously improve your uses of information technology; or rely on switching costs to keep customers tied to you and thus defend your gains in the face of competitors' response." (p. 24)
3. *Leverage resource advantages.* "Use information technology to add value to resources you already enjoy and that your competitors lack and cannot readily acquire." (p. 24)
4. *Achieve parity.* Once a competitor has innovated in an industry, the use of information technology can become a strategic necessity. This has happened, for example, in the airline and banking industries. In these industries, applications involving computers and communications have become an unavoidable part of the cost of doing business.
5. *Interorganizational cooperation.* Companies are increasingly crafting strategies that are based on strategic alliances with other companies, often located in other countries.

Rosenbluth Travel is a case in point, and there are many others that use electronic data interchange (EDI). For example, Levi Strauss has formed cooperative electronic arrangements with its suppliers of denim and other textiles so that orders are placed and goods arrive just in time for manufacture (in retailing this is called "quick response"). Similarly, Levi's has links to its retail customers, such as J.C. Penney, for automatic replenishment of apparel inventory at retail stores.

There are several strategic objectives that can be achieved by employing information technology as an integral part of a corporate strategic plan. They include

1. Improved economies of scale
2. Improved economies of scope

3. Creation of proprietary information
4. Enhanced organizational learning and skills development
5. Compression of time to market

Are open systems the wave of the future in information technology? An open system relates more to information than hardware. It can be understood by users who readily can apply information in their work. Knowledge workers—persons who are primarily responsible for managing information systems—will soon represent the single largest occupational group. The real advantage that open systems confer from a strategic perspective is that they enable companies to compete with the benefit of a sounder technological base. Open systems allow companies to run computer programs on more than one computer system and thus make programs portable (White, 1991). The competitive advantage of using information technology derives from its being almost universally available, which facilitates the electronic transmission of all kinds of records, forms, and raw data. This allows a company to readily expand services, products, distribution, and timeliness. For example, American Express can respond to a credit card inquiry from any of its millions of subscribers in a matter of seconds. The question is not whether to use information technology but how to use it to achieve a significant competitive edge.

EXPERT SYSTEMS IN STRATEGIC MANAGEMENT

The magnitude of the problems confronting strategic managers is such that they often appear overwhelming. The ability to evaluate all available information and to maintain a knowledge base is beyond most managers. More effective means than are now used are required to cope with the avalanche of data that confronts strategic decision makers and to advise them regarding strategic options. Much more is involved than industry and competitor analysis. Factors to be considered include

1. Interdependencies among organizational functions
2. Interactions in the network of manufacturing activities
3. Timing and concurrency of product manufacturing
4. Periodicity and life cycles of products
5. Trends and discontinuities in customer demand, growth, and so on
6. Uncertainty and vulnerability in the external environment
7. Technology advances and their impact on products, growth, and position
8. Leadership and culture requirements to provide an environment conducive to change
9. Balance in product and business portfolios
10. Requirements for a sustainable competitive advantage

DEVELOPING A KNOWLEDGE BASE FOR STRATEGY

Mockler (1989) views the development of an expert system for strategy as built on a knowledge base. He examines strategy by using a frame hierarchy, as shown in Figure 11.1. The frame provides a basis for determining what factors make up the

FIGURE 11.1 | Frame Hierarchy

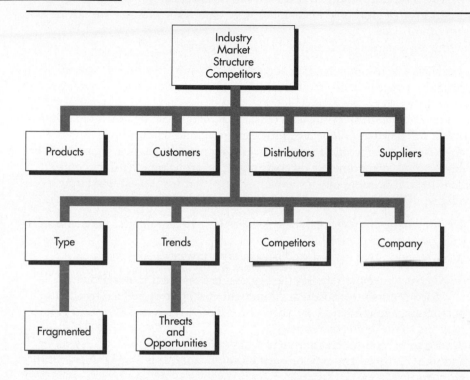

knowledge base when one is assessing the desirability of strategic alternatives. For example, he considers whether the industry is fragmented, declining, mature, or emerging when determining a strategy recommendation.

In developing a marketing strategy, he examines the recommendations that the expert system could make:

1. Introduce an existing product without alterations but change the brand name.
2. Introduce the product as an extension to an existing product line.
3. Introduce the product as a replacement of an existing product.
4. Change the product and introduce it with a new brand name.
5. Change some elements of the product and then introduce it as a new brand.
6. Change some elements of the product and then introduce it as a replacement for an existing product.
7. Reject the proposed product and do not introduce it.

The expert system chooses from among these recommendations using appropriate heuristic decision rules. Industry data such as rate of growth, financial ratios, fragmentation, concentration, and elasticity can also be included in a knowledge base. For example, a high debt-to-equity ratio might be perfectly acceptable for certain industries but not for others. The knowledge base is thus used to support which strategic options will be recommended. In addition, an explanation of why a specified option was chosen can be included. Table 11.5 lists possible strategic options that are stored in the knowledge base. They illustrate the advice such a program can provide.

The four basic strategies that Mockler identifies are

1. *Aggressive:* this recommendation suggests that the firm exploit its strong position by concentric diversification, vertical integration, overall cost leadership, and the like.
2. *Competitive:* this strategy includes concentric mergers, conglomerate mergers, turnaround, product uniqueness, differentiation, and value added.
3. *Conservative:* this recommendation focuses on niche or market segment, global diversification, conglomerate diversification, or protecting the status quo.
4. *Defensive:* this is essentially a survival strategy that focuses on harvesting products, divestitures, retrenchment, cost reduction, liquidation, or merger.

These four basic strategies can be considered generic strategies. A generic strategy matrix is shown in Figure 11.2.

These strategic alternatives are consistent with Porter's generic strategies.

1. *Overall cost leadership* requires the aggressive construction of efficient facilities, vigorous pursuit of cost reduction, tight cost control, reduction of marginal customers, and reduction of expenses for R&D, sales, and advertising. It is analogous to the *aggressive* strategy.
2. *Differentiation* requires creating something that is unique, such as design, brand image, special features, or outstanding quality. It is comparable to the *competitive* strategy.

TABLE 11.5	Strategic Options

Pricing level	New market penetration
De-averaging cost	Joint venture
Quality required	When to buy competitors
Guarantee level	Level of R&D expenditure
Service level	Product innovations required
Timing of delivery	Advertising level
Uniqueness of products	Comparative productivity
Value-added level	Customer information
Market niche to pursue	Competitor information
Opportunities and product gaps to pursue	Portfolio balance
Barriers needed	Strategic restructuring required
Market potential	Competitive posture
Location	Vertical integration
Technology required	Resource allocation

| FIGURE 11.2 | Generic Strategies |

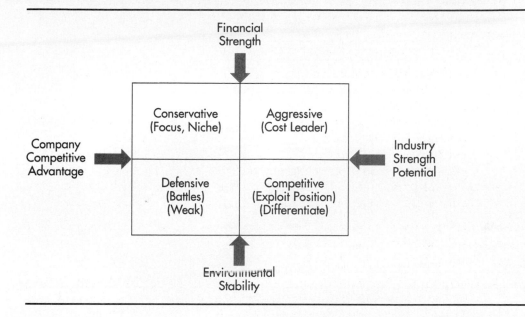

3. *Focus* deals with a specific buyer group, market segment, product line, or geographic market. This strategy is based on the premise that the firm can do something specific better than other firms and thus is able to capture a limited market share. It is comparable to the *conservative* strategy.
4. *"Stuck in the middle"* is what Porter calls a company that has an extremely weak strategic position and finds it difficult to extricate itself. This is analogous to the *defensive* strategy.

Mockler (1989) also describes the use of a strategic decision rule matrix for making strategic decisions. An example is shown in Figure 11.3. The rule matrix displays the "if" conditions (sometimes called premises) and the "and" conditions (sometimes referred to as rules) and relates them to the "then" decisions (or recommendations or classifications, depending on the problem being considered). The matrix format has the advantage of ease of construction and ease of reading. Note that different combinations of conditions may lead to the same decision or action. For example, *consider* occurs twice, as does *pursue*.

A SPACE output is shown in Figure 11.4. The company is low on all four factors, and as a result, the defensive strategy is indicated. This survival strategy is consistent with the fact that the company is weak competitively and financially. It is operating in an industry that is not attractive and in an environment that is not very stable.

Expert systems have provided important support in many areas of managerial decision making. And the use of such systems for strategy formulation is sure to become one of the critical aspects of operating in a complex, sometimes hostile, and always highly competitive global environment.

FIGURE 11.3	Strategic Decision Rule Matrix

If-Conditions	And-Conditions				
	1	2	3	4	5
1. Competitors	Many	Few			
2. Elasticity	Yes	No			
3. Differentiation	Yes	No			
4. Market Share			Small	Medium	Large
5. Growth Potential			Low	Moderate	High
6. Technology			Not Critical	May Be Critical	Critical
7. Barriers			Low	Increasing	High
8. Substitutes			Many	Increasing	Few
9. Change in Customer Base			No	Some	Yes
10. Change in Distribution			No	Some	Yes
Then-Decision	Avoid	Consider	Consider	Pursue	Pursue

FIGURE 11.4	SPACE Analysis

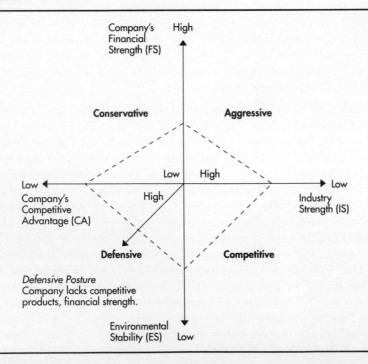

Company's Financial Strength (FS) — High

Conservative   Aggressive

Low ← Company's Competitive Advantage (CA)   Low   High   Low — Industry Strength (IS)
High

Defensive   Competitive

Defensive Posture
Company lacks competitive products, financial strength.

Environmental Stability (ES)   Low

INTELLIGENT DECISION SUPPORT SYSTEMS

The CEO of Information Technology, Richard Heygate (1990) believes that the key role of decision support systems is to leverage information in order to provide analytical support, control current activities, enhance performance, and make trans-organizational information available. His emphasis is on the use of information, not on the methodologies used to obtain or store data. Given this perspective, how should one go about the design and use of knowledge bases so that they can serve as an intelligent decision support system?

A number of approaches can be employed to add intelligence when using a knowledge or database. For example, the Pareto law can be used to partition knowledge into "currently significant" information versus "archival information" that is needed only for reference or audit (Rowe and Watkins, 1992). Research by Kandelin (1990) suggests that in order to have intelligence added to data, one has to form an "events database." As economic events occur, they are recorded as such in the database. The intelligence component is based on the automatic updating of reports as new data, information, or knowledge, in the form of events, is recorded. This automated updating serves to "signal" the users of changes in activities that may be of interest and concern. Thus relevant data are quickly and efficiently put to use, whereas data that are not relevant are ignored or not stored at all.

Current technology permits images to be stored in large-scale databases. Thus, image data that were not needed for current operations could be kept in permanent archival storage devices such as optical discs. If such data were ever needed to support an audit or provide backup, they would be available. American Express, for example, processes all credit card transactions by image processing and also stores all the scanned images. What should be stored, and for how long, are the critical issues for a large-volume transaction processor; clearly, an economic solution is required.

From their inception, the objective of computer-based systems has been to provide decision makers with information in a more meaningful and useful form. Unfortunately, most current systems do not really "support" decision making (Dickinson, 1991). There are efforts underway to ameliorate this situation. Lotus Development introduced the personal information manager ("AI + database," 1988) that allows users to enter information into an "Agenda" database in natural, free-form units called "items" without the normal structure required in the typical database system. Lotus Agenda assists the user by applying intelligence to an expert's knowledge using contextual cues and historic information to perform logical inferences. Storey and Goldstein (1990) suggest that what is needed to improve the design of a database is an expert system to elicit user views in order to determine storage requirements. This approach avoids inconsistencies, ambiguities, and redundancies because they can be detected and resolved ahead of time.

To overcome the sheer magnitude of the task of handling data more efficiently, one needs to utilize data more intelligently. For example, what is the value of increased information? When would aggregate data be more appropriate for decision making than all the elemental or detail data? When inundated with mountains of details, most decision makers go into "information overload." What is needed is a process whereby decision making leads to appropriate actions that accomplish specified strategies. However, strategic decisions involve actions that take place in the future, and the outcome is uncertain. In order to reach an acceptable level of risk, data and knowledge are needed. Adding intelligence to data in accordance with the following formula can reduce the risk to a level that is acceptable.

Acceptable risk = Uncertainty + Intelligent use of data and knowledge

The following guidelines are suggested for adding intelligence to data and knowledge.

1. Define the data requirements for critical issues.
2. Structure problems so that the intelligent use of data and knowledge is possible.
3. Devise intelligent methods of storing and retrieving data and knowledge.
4. Use expert systems and heuristics to explore ways of storing data efficiently.
5. Determine what is an acceptable level of risk for given strategic decisions.

THE GROWING IMPORTANCE OF KNOWLEDGE-BASED SYSTEMS (KBS) IN BUSINESS

The importance of knowledge-based systems in business is increasingly being recognized, judging by the number of companies involved in developing them, the amount of money spent on them, and the number of systems already developed and in operation.

The importance of these systems is likely to increase in the future, especially systems designed to support and replicate lower- and middle-level management tasks. This is the level at which shortages of managerial personnel arising from the "baby bust" will be occurring over the next twenty years. These shortages are already showing up in the retail and service areas today. A wide range of knowledge-based systems can be useful in helping fill this management gap.

Their importance is also likely to increase as KBS become more and more integrated with conventional computer systems. KBS are ultimately just another technology information tool among the many available, which can be used to help managers make more effective decisions.

PROBLEMS INHIBITING THE GROWTH OF KBS

Enormous problems have been encountered in introducing KBS technology into business. One study (Cullen, 1988) found that half the systems failed. Rose (1988) describes another somewhat typical project, in which two years and $300,000 were spent in developing an 80-rule system that is not being used. Such stories can be discouraging to those thinking about entering this area.

In addition to technological limitations, a key problem inhibiting rapid growth of these systems is that considerable work still needs to be done in defining in precise detail how the thousands of management and operational decisions occurring daily in business are made. Solving this problem is difficult, largely because not enough business managers and experts have the time or financial incentive to do this work. Yet, as with other types of decision support systems, input from these managers about the thinking processes (heuristics) involved in their decision making is an extremely important ingredient in creating effective KBS (Mockler, 1991,

1992). These kinds of difficulties and failures are not unexpected at this stage of a newly emerging technology such as knowledge-based systems.

Introducing any computer technology into an organization requires integrating technological and user requirements. The job is especially difficult when introducing knowledge-based system technology, because

- The technology (hardware and software) is relatively new and still developing rapidly, so that neither the technology nor its benefits and applications are yet widely understood.
- Many advocates of the technology have promised more than the technology can deliver, given the present state of the art (Bulkeley, 1990), causing many to become disenchanted with the technology.
- Developing these systems requires skills that are substantially different from those required for conventional computer system development, creating major problems for computer systems personnel.

Although the development and use of knowledge-based systems continue to grow, they have not been implemented to any significant degree in strategic management. This is due in part to lack of experience in their use, but to a larger extent, the problem involves the issues discussed in Chapter 10: leadership and bringing about organizational change. A bright light on the horizon is the growing use of large-scale networks that can interact more readily than before. New programs are being developed to handle what are called large-scale distributed heterogeneous databases. Simply stated, this refers to the large number of computer systems scattered around the country that have to interact in an "open system" format so that divisions of companies, no matter how widely dispersed, can interact in real time and utilize the latest technological approaches available. The future is bright, but only for those with the foresight and courage to make the vision a reality which requires

- Expert/user involvement in the development process much greater than that found in conventional computer system development, creating substantial management and organization problems in efforts to develop knowledge-based systems.
- There are few readily available, detailed accounts of (1) how these expert systems affect an existing company organization situation and the people in it or (2) what type of organization and management style is best for developing and deriving maximum benefit from these systems.
- There is resistance to KBS because the need for such systems is not as apparent to managers as is the need for conventional computer systems, such as those found in the financial and accounting areas.

Planning and carrying out KBS development efforts involves integrating technical, human, and organization factors. This process can be complicated by the fact that development situations vary so widely.

At one extreme, a company situation may involve smaller systems and a single or small group of users/operating managers who are computer-literate or have access to expert systems development shells and who perceive expert systems as being potentially useful in their jobs. At the other extreme, application development situations may involve a large, diversified group of users who are in sales or other primarily nontechnical jobs, who have varying degrees of computer literacy, who are not aware of the potential benefits of expert systems, who vary widely in ages and work experience, and who work in widely dispersed geographic locations for a large, diversified company.

The range of system technology and complexity can also vary, from small user-developed systems employing personal computers (PCs) and PC expert system shells, to very large systems developed by computer scientists using mainframe or dedicated computer hardware technology.

Summary

In describing information and decision technology in the 1990s, Forgionne (1990) indicated that new information systems will be required to support all phases of decision making. Included are problem recognition, formulation, analysis, solution, interpretation, and implementation. These new systems will be required to provide all the technology needed by management and to provide an integrated system so that individuals or group decision makers will have the best possible information to support their decisions. This complete technology for management will include all the various approaches and decision tools (such as simulation models, expert systems, forecasting, and various kinds of economic and accounting models), as well as the system hardware needed to network computers. Everybody will have access to the same data and will receive the kinds of displays that will make information more meaningful.

The application of expert knowledge in expert systems will introduce an important consideration into such future systems. Using the decision maker's knowledge makes him or her a part of the system. Such "ownership" is an important aspect of introducing motivation, and managers who are unfamiliar with systems tend to disregard them. On the other hand, if such information systems provide data, trends, analysis, forecasts, tables, graphs, or whatever the decision maker wants, then he or she is more likely to use that system. The computer will become interactive and will enable managers to incorporate many more insights and judgments into evaluating problems, so the technology that involves a computer

will change from decision support to augmenting the manager's ability to make better decisions. This will also tap into the creativity and intelligence that managers have and will allow them to enhance that creativity through their ability to use available information in databases or knowledge bases.

A look far into the future suggests some startling possibilities in the application of information to support decision making. Neural networks provide a frontier that may change the way managers look at decision making and at support systems. Neural networks are crude but powerful simulations of the nervous system that try to mimic the way the brain works. Neural networks are hybrid analog/digital computers with speeds about 1,000 times faster than current systems. They are able to process information 1 billion times faster than current conventional digital computers. Applications include a variety of tasks from machine vision and robotics to speech recognition, tests, and handwriting recognition. They have been able to solve very complex problems that involve patterns, such as interpretation or evaluation of military vehicles and analysis of integrated computer circuitry. In banking, neural networks have helped Chase Manhattan detect credit card fraud. Security Pacific Bank uses such a system to analyze commercial and automobile loan risks. In addition to such applications, neural networks have been applied in medicine to detect abnormal heart sounds and interpret electrocardiograms. At Roarck University in England, an electronic nose that recognizes smells has been developed. A similar system is used in Japan to test the freshness of sushi. Ford Motor Company is developing a computer, which is actually on the automobile, that simultaneously monitors all aspects of the automotive operation—the engine, power train, suspension, electronic steering, brakes, climate control, and so forth (Moore, 1990).

In addition to the capabilities mentioned, neural networks have been used in Japan for a variety of applications that try to simulate human behavior. They incorporate a concept of "fuzzy logic." This logic does not deal with precise values but with concepts, such as a very bright finish. *Bright* can have a range of values, which is why this logic is called fuzzy. On the other hand, the Japanese have applied it to washing machines, where the water can be determined as being dirty or not dirty. Again, a fuzzy concept. We will also see a drastic change in the way computers are built and in the kinds of software they use. In particular, parallel architecture that allows the program to process over a large number of electronic routes provides the ability to do things that we cannot do very efficiently with digital computers. This will enhance the processing speed but will also introduce some interesting new, and yet untested, capabilities.

The future presents untold opportunities for those who have the appropriate tools and approaches to deal with the requirements of the long-term growth and survival of the organization. Changing markets, changing expectations, and changing stakeholders all portend a change in the approach managers will need for successful organizations in the future. The emphasis on the entrepreneurial and leadership styles of management will contribute to greater use of newer methodologies, complex scenarios, and interactive computer-based systems.

With more and more data becoming readily available as the information age progresses, managers are asking, "How can any given information become a strategic resource?" Information has evolved from being merely a tool for tracking the use of labor, capital, and other resources to being a resource and a product itself. By using information systems, companies can gain a strategic edge over competitors. Here again, balance is crucial. Simply having the relevant data does not ensure that decisions will be made correctly or carried out properly. Although decision makers may avoid serious errors because they have the data needed to evaluate alternative futures, data are only a means to an end. Effective performance in a highly turbulent environment requires leaders with the ability to integrate the individual performer into the formulation and implementation of strategy.

In the coming years, leaders, managers, researchers, and educators will continue to grapple with the question of how best to utilize information systems for strategy. Those who find answers will benefit most.

Changes in organizational structure and managerial approaches to improving performance are the key to success. The evidence suggests that flatter organizations with fewer layers of management exhibit improved communication and enhanced worker responsibility. De facto reliance on teams has been adopted by many companies. Team leaders assume responsibility for performance, design, motivation, innovation, and commitment on the part of team members. Teams become self-monitoring and can reduce the need for traditional management control approaches such as MBO. Most important, teams in flatter organizations seem to achieve significant performance and to improve the company's competitive position.

Innovation and technology are key determinants of competitive advantage. Companies such as Lincoln Electric, GE, Xerox, and Hewlett-Packard are shining examples of how effective innovation leads to breakthrough new products and helps fend off competition while creating customer needs that did not previously exist.

This book has been directed toward helping managers determine strategies for success. The methods and approaches presented here can help ensure that an appropriate analysis has been done so that the creative manager knows where to start and what is needed. To bring these ideas to fruition requires an appropriate way of thinking and a managerial process that recognizes the role and the needs of the individual as a key element in implementing strategic change.

REFERENCES AND SUGGESTIONS FOR FURTHER READING

Ackoff, Russel E. 1967. Management misinformation systems. *Management Science,* December, pp. 147–156.

AI + database = personal information manager. 1988. *AI Week,* September 1, p. 9.

Allman, William. 1992. Shrinking the future. *U.S. News & World Report,* March 9, pp. 52–53.

Anderson, Howard. 1991. The open corporation. *Forbes,* October 28, advertisement.

Bender, Paul S., William D. Northrup, and Jeremy F. Shapiro. 1981. Practical modeling for resource management. *Harvard Business Review,* January–February, pp. 163–173.

Beniger, James R. 1986. *The control revolution.* Cambridge, Mass.: Harvard University Press.

Bennis, Warren and Burt Nanus. 1985. *Leaders.* New York: Harper & Row.

Bleeke, Joel. 1989. Peak strategies. *The McKinsey Quarterly,* Spring, pp. 19–27.

Booker, Ellis. 1990. IS trailblazing puts retailer on top. *Computerworld,* February 12, pp. 69–73.

Braudel, Fernand. 1981. *Civilization and capitalism, 15th–18th century,* vol. 1. New York: Harper & Row.

Broderick, Renae and John Boudreau. 1992. Human resource management, information technology, and the competitive edge. *Academy of Management Executive* 6, no. 2, pp. 7–17.

Brooks, Nancy and Jesus Sanchez. 1992. U.S. firms map ways to profit from the accord. *Los Angeles Times,* August 13, pp. D-1 and D-2.

Brown, John Seely. 1991. Research that reinvents the corporation. *Harvard Business Review,* January–February, pp. 102–111.

Bulkeley, William M. 1990. Bright outlook for artificial intelligence yields to slow growth and big cutbacks. *Wall Street Journal,* July 5, pp. B1 and B3.

Byrne, John. 1992. Management's new gurus. *Business Week,* August 31, pp. 44–52.

Byrne, John. 1989. Is your company too big? *Business Week,* March 27, pp. 84–94.

Callahan, Tom. 1992. The changing strategist. *Beyond Computing,* Premier Issue, pp. 12–14.

Castro, Janice. 1991. Mr. Sam stuns Goliath. *Time,* February 25, pp. 62–63.

Clemons, Eric. 1991. Corporate strategies for information technology. *IEEE Computers,* November, p. 23.

Clemons, E. K., M. C. Row, and D. B. Miller. 1992. Rosenbluth International alliance: Information technology and the global virtual corporation. *Proceedings of the Hawaii International Conference on Systems Science.* IV, pp. 678–686.

Cook, William. 1992. Dialing the future. *U.S. News & World Report,* February 3, pp. 49–51.

Cullen, J. and A. Bryman. 1988. The knowledge acquisition bottleneck. *Expert Systems,* August, pp. 216–250.

Day, George S. 1986. *Analysis for strategic market decisions.* St. Paul, Minn.: West.

Deutschman, Alan. America's fastest. *Fortune,* October 7, pp. 46–68.

Dichter, Steven. 1991. The organization of the 90's. *The McKinsey Quarterly,* no. 1, pp. 145–155.

Dickinson, John. 1991. An intelligent user interface should possess business smarts. *PC Computing,* May, p. 52.

Drucker, Peter. 1988. The coming of the new organization. *Harvard Business Review,* January–February, p. 45.

Dumaine, Brian. 1991. Closing the innovation gap. *Fortune,* December 2, pp. 56–62.

The fastest-growing occupations (1990–2005) for careers requiring a bachelor's degree. *Florida Leader* 9, no. 4.

Ferguson, Charles H. 1990. Computers and the coming of the U.S. keiretsu. *Harvard Business Review,* July–August, pp. 55–71.

Flint, Jerry. 1992. Platform madness. *Fortune,* January 20, pp. 40–42.

Forgionne, Guisseppi A. 1990. OR/MS and decision technology in the 1990s. *OR/MS Today* June, pp. 20–21.

Fromson, Brett. 1988. Where the next fortunes will be made. *Fortune,* December 5, pp. 185–196.

Gittelson, Steven. 1992. Future edge: Find tomorrow's opportunity now—or else! *Success,* April.

Grunwald, Henry. 1992. The year 2000: Is it the end or just the beginning? *Time,* March 30, pp. 73–76.

Gwynne, S. C. 1990. The right stuff. *Time,* October 29, pp. 74–84.

Hanna, Alistair and Jerold Lundquist. 1990. Creative strategies. *The McKinsey Quarterly,* no. 3, pp. 56–79.

Heygate, Richard. 1992. Accelerating front-line change: Cross-border alliances. *The McKinsey Quarterly,* Winter, pp. 134–147.

Howard, Robert. 1992. The CEO as organizational architect. *Harvard Business Review,* September–October, pp. 107–121.

Huey, John. 1991. Nothing is impossible. *Fortune,* September 23, pp. 135–140.

Jacob, Rahul. 1992. The search for the organization of tomorrow. *Fortune,* May 18, pp. 93–98.

Jacobson, George. 1992. Are we producing a future work force of Bart Simpsons? *Business Forum,* Winter, pp. 18–21.

Jamison, Sam. 1984. U.S. trainees praise Toyota system. *Los Angeles Times,* June 19, p. 1.

Kahalas, Harvey and Kathleen Suchon. 1992. Interview with Harold A. Poling, chairman, CEO, Ford Motor Company. *Academy of Management Executive* 6, no. 2, pp. 71–82.

Kanter, Rosabeth Moss. 1989. *When giants learn to dance: Mastering the challenge of strategy, management, and careers in the 1990s.* New York: Simon and Schuster.

Kanter, Rosabeth Moss. 1987. Increasing competitiveness without restructuring. *Management Review,* 76 (June), p. 21.

Kiechel, Walter III. 1988. Corporate strategy for the 1990's. *Fortune,* February 29, pp. 34–42.

Koselka, Rita. 1992. Distribution revolution. *Forbes,* May 25, pp. 54–61.

Lewis, Peter. 1991. Software to help introduce products. *New York Times,* October 6, pp. F-8N and F-8L.

Main, Jeremy. 1988. The winning organization. *Fortune,* September 26, pp. 50–60.

Makovsky, Kenneth. 1992. How to make your company a powerhouse in the 21st century. *Business Forum,* Winter, pp. 9–12.

Mason, Richard O. and Ian I. Mitroff. 1981. *Challenging strategic planning assumptions.* New York: Wiley.

McFarlan, F. Warren. 1984. Information technology changes the way you compete. *Harvard Business Review,* May–June, pp. 98–104.

McFarlan, F. Warren. 1981. Portfolio approach to information systems. *Harvard Business Review,* September–October, pp. 142–150.

McFarlan, F. Warren, Richard L. Nolan, and David P. Norton. 1973. *Information systems administration.* New York: Holt, Rinehart and Winston.

McNamee, Patrick B. 1985. *Tools and techniques for strategic management.* New York: Pergamon.

Meeting the challenge of sustainable development. 1992. *Forbes* advertising supplement, May 25.

Mockler, Robert J. 1992. *Developing knowledge-based systems: A managerial decision-making approach.* Columbus, Ohio: Merrill.

Mockler, Robert J. 1991. *Computing software to support strategy formulation decision making.* Columbus, Ohio: Merrill.

Mockler, Robert J. 1989. *Knowledge-based systems for strategic planning.* Englewood Cliffs, N.J.: Prentice-Hall.

Moore, John L. 1990. Transportation: Planning the future. *Governing,* December, pp. 43–55.

Morrison, Ann. 1992. *The new leaders: Guidelines on leadership diversity in America.* San Francisco: Jossey-Bass.

Naisbitt, John and Patricia Aburdene. 1985. *Re-inventory the corporation: Transforming your job and your company for the new information society.* New York: Warner.

New products, new markets, new competition, new thinking. 1989. *The Economist,* March 4, pp. 19–22.

Nolan, Richard L. and C. F. Gibson. 1974. Managing the four stages of EDP growth. *Harvard Business Review,* January–February, pp. 76–88.

Nulty, Peter. 1987. How managers will manage. *Fortune,* February 2, pp. 47–50.

O'Toole, James. 1985. *Vanguard management.* New York: Doubleday.

Ohmae, Kenichi. 1991. The boundaries of business: Commentaries from the experts. *Harvard Business Review,* July–August, pp. 127–140.

Ohmae, Kenichi. 1982. *The mind of the strategist.* New York: McGraw-Hill.

Ostroff, Frank and Douglas Smith. 1992. The horizontal organization. *The McKinsey Quarterly,* no. 1, pp. 148–167.

Parsons, Gregory L. 1983. Information technology: A new competitive weapon. *Sloan Management Review,* Fall, pp. 3–14.

Peters, Tom. 1989. Tomorrow's companies: Thriving on chaos. *The Economist,* March 4, pp. 19–22.

Peters, Tom. 1988. *Thriving on chaos: Handbook for a management revolution.* New York: Knopf.

Peters, Thomas J. and Robert H. Waterman, Jr. 1982. *In search of excellence: Lessons from America's best-run companies.* New York: Harper & Row.

Porat, Marc. 1977. *The information economy.* Washington, D.C.: U.S. Department of Commerce.

Porter, Michael E. 1980. *Competitive strategy.* New York: The Free Press.

Porter, Michael E. and Victor E. Millar. 1985. How information gives you competitive advantages. *Harvard Business Review,* July–August, pp. 149–160.

Rockart, John F. 1979. Chief executives define their own data needs. *Harvard Business Review,* March–April, pp. 81–92.

Rose, Frederick. 1988. An electronic clone of a skilled engineer is very hard to create. *Wall Street Journal,* August 12, pp. 1 and 14.

Rosenthal, Stephen R. 1982. *Managing government operations.* Glenview, Ill.: Scott, Foresman.

Rowe, Alan J. and Paul R. Watkins. 1992. Intelligent use of knowledge and data. *Proceedings,* Symposium on Expert Systems in Finance and Business, Pasadena, California.

Saporito, Bill. 1989. Companies that compete best. *Fortune,* May 22, pp. 36–44.

Sharing the environment. 1992. *The Economist,* May 30, pp. 1–14.

Skrzycki, Cindy. 1989. Corporate America learns to listen to workers. *Los Angeles Times,* August 10.

Stavro, Barry. State's two car plants—Study in sharp contrasts. *Los Angeles Times,* January 28, p. D1.

Stewart, Thomas. 1992. U.S. productivity: First but fading. *Fortune,* October 19, pp. 53–64.

Stewart, Thomas. 1991. GE keeps those ideas coming. *Fortune,* August 12, pp. 41–49.

Storey, Veda C. and Robert C. Goldstein. 1990. An expert view creation system for database design. *USC Expert System Review,* pp. 19–45.

Sustainable development. 1992. *Forbes—Special Supplement,* May 25.

Taylor, Alex, III. 1992. The road ahead at General Motors. *Fortune,* May 4, pp. 94–95.

Thompson, James D. 1967. *Organizations in action.* New York: McGraw-Hill.

Toffler, Alvin. 1990. *Powershift.* New York: Bantam.

Toffler, Alvin. 1985. *The adaptive corporation.* New York: Bantam Books.

Tsurumi, Yoshi. 1991. Adaptive corporations for the global age. *Pacific Basin Quarterly,* Summer–Fall, pp. 5–18.

Turban, Efraim. 1988. *Decision support and expert systems.* New York: Macmillan.

Turban, Efraim and Paul Watkins. 1988. *Applied expert systems.* New York: Elsevier.

Vincent, Barbara and Gerald Zaltman. 1991. *Hearing the voice of the market: Competitive advantage through creative use of market information.* Boston: Harvard Business School Press.

Vogel, Todd. 1989. Where 1990s style management is already hard at work. *Business Week,* October 23, pp. 92–100.

White, John. 1991. Open systems: The puzzle and the payoffs. *Optiv,* I, no. 1, Fall, pp. 6–15.

Willenz, Nicole V. 1988. Electronic data interchange. *Price Waterhouse Review* 32, no. 3, pp. 33–45.

Woutat, Donald. 1992. Two top GM executives demoted. *Los Angeles Times,* April 7, pp. D-1 and D-15.

APPENDIX A

Sustaining Competitive Advantage from IT

John Cecil and Michael Goldstein

It's common to hear about yet another successful installation of IT. Then why is it that most CEOs can't point to one in their companies? The authors argue that it is because managers have focused their attention primarily on the technology of IT and not enough on gaining sustainable advantage from IT. Gaining advantage from IT depends on how you use it to change what you do; technical advances aren't enough.

The most commonly cited examples of companies using information technology (IT) to achieve competitive advantage go back 10 years or more. Both American Airlines' SABRE system and McKesson's Economost system for pharmacies were introduced in the 1970s. But CEOs of most companies are hard put to cite even a single example of having achieved more than a short-lived advantage from their investments in information technology.

CEOs frequently complain that the famous examples don't offer much practical guidance about managing their businesses. Most of the famous examples exploit "first-mover" advantage. This sounds great but often bears no relation to the IT investments being funded. Moreover, whenever one company today does get to the market first, competitors seem to catch up before the investment starts to pay back.

Thus, today, after a decade of "strategic" systems investments, few CEOs invest in IT to achieve sustainable advantage. Most view IT only as a necessity to remain competitive. Is this the best that can be achieved? We don't think it is.

IT Benefits "Old Games"

The notion that IT works only for companies that radically redefine their business is wrong. IT can be extremely valuable to companies pursuing established business or "old-game" strategies.

Source: John Cecil and Michael Goldstein, "Sustaining competitive advantage from IT," *The McKinsey Quarterly*, 1990, no. 4. Copyright © 1990 by McKinsey & Company, Inc. All rights reserved.

We'll describe how you can use IT to leverage (or drive) one or more existing sources of sustainable advantage (the "Extend" strategy). We'll also look at how companies that trail on some basis of competition can use IT to reduce their disadvantage (the "Reduce" strategy). Both the Extend and Reduce strategies are available to virtually any company, not just overall industry leaders and followers.

Helps "New Games" Too

Companies that are prepared to pursue a "new-game" strategy have more than one way to achieve sustainable competitive advantage. One way is the "First-Mover" strategy, which was followed by such classic IT implementers as McKesson. However, being first is only the initial stage of the strategy and additional actions are necessary if that advantage is to be sustained. In addition, we'll describe a second valid way to achieve advantage, called "Focused Hustle," which is not so well known as the First-Mover model.

The balance of this article will explore the importance of and impediments to achieving competitive advantage using IT. It will discuss the Extend strategy as a model of IT investment and the First-Mover and the Focused-Hustle models as alternatives.

WHY ACHIEVING SUSTAINABLE ADVANTAGE FROM IT IS SO HARD

Despite the attention to and investments in IT over the past decade, it seems more difficult, not less, to achieve sustainable competitive advantage from IT. A sustainable advantage is a capability of one competitor that cannot be duplicated by another. It is a standard that is difficult to achieve or maintain. As more companies invest in IT capabilities, it becomes even harder for someone to carve out a unique, defensible position.

Indeed, we believe that it is virtually impossible for major IT users (excluding vendors) to gain advantage based on IT technology alone. Two issues demand attention:

1. Information technologies (except for application systems) are almost universally supplied by vendors to user companies, and are freely available to all competitors in an industry.
2. Application systems, while custom developed by large user-companies, rarely confer advantage in themselves.

IT Alone Doesn't Deliver

There are several reasons why IT by itself fails to deliver a sustainable competitive edge:

- *Peer competitors generally start with equivalent application knowledge.* There may be differences after an application has been developed, but it's usually difficult to protect. Competitors can hire away key employees or use the same vendors and system integrators to take advantage of the leader's experience.
- *Differences in IT development capabilities among competitors can usually be evened out by vendors.* For many applications, followers can purchase packages or hire systems integrators and end up with equivalent functionality at lower cost than the leaders.
- *Larger scale rarely translates into a cost advantage.* Larger companies generally have more complex requirements, increasing development costs. They are more likely to need (or think they need) customized systems instead of vendor-supplied packages.

A couple of examples illustrate these points. In the early 1970s Procter & Gamble and General Electric led other major consumer companies in developing integrated marketing decision–support systems. These were mainframe systems that allowed users to track and analyze market share and promotion effectiveness, and perform demand analysis, combining both internal and vendor-supplied market research data. At the time this was a leading-edge technical application, and presented the pioneers with technical challenges they couldn't meet without vendor support. While the vendors helped make the original implementations successful, they soon turned around and sold packaged systems to competitors. For example, by 1975 both Kraft and General Foods had installed equivalent functionality.

Involving vendors in new application development continues today. Indeed, it is often the only way—given the endemic shortage of IT skills and the increasing complexity of integrated IT technologies—that companies can hope to develop new, leading-edge applications. Monsanto, for example, is today developing a state-of-the-art flexible manufacturing system for a major fiber plant. Its development strategy is keyed to working with a limited number of "technology partners," including IBM, DEC, and H-P. Monsanto managers acknowledge that competitors will learn from their experience, but feel that it is better to co-develop the system with vendors than to go it alone.

WHY SUSTAINABLE ADVANTAGE IS IMPORTANT

Does it matter if many businesses take advantage of IT at roughly the same rate?

We think it does. *Without competitive advantage, heavy IT investors tend to lose.* Industries that adopt IT uniformly are likely to suffer eroding profitability because IT destroys conventional forms of differentiation and forces businesses to compete head-on. As a result, competitors can't hold on to the benefits of their own investment. They pass them on as lower prices to customers.

How IT Restructured Merchant Credit-Card Banking

The merchant-servicing side of the bank credit-card business, conducted by more than 10,000 institutions in the United States, consists of processing the sales drafts from Visa and Mastercard transactions, and depositing the collected funds, less a discount, to the merchant's account.

Traditionally, this was a paper-intensive business in which the merchant's local bank held a significant advantage. The issue was convenience: the sales drafts needed to be physically deposited with the processor. Since the merchant already needed to travel to a bank branch to deposit cash, it made sense to deposit the Visa and Mastercard sales drafts at the same time.

In the mid-1980s, the industry made a concerted effort to eliminate the paper sales draft, and to replace it with electronic draft capture (EDC) at the point of sale. As the cost of all computer technology fell rapidly, it became economically feasible for even the smallest merchants to submit electronically.

It also seemed to make a lot of sense for the industry. EDC totally eliminated keying in of the sales draft information, as well as the errors which keyboarding introduced. The terminals ensured that end-of-day balances were correct and matched the sales draft totals. And the electronic transmission eliminated several days of unproductive float. In order to encourage widespread adoption, and to pay back the necessary investment in point-of-sale terminals, Visa and Mastercard both lowered their key "interchange" rate for EDC transactions.

By one measure, the incentives were an enormous success. Between 1987 and mid-1990, the share of electronic draft capture transactions grew from roughly 25 percent to 75 percent. However, for most participants in the industry, the transition has been a profitability disaster.

The problem for the many small banks in the business is that their local branch networks no longer conferred advantage. Merchants could dial up the host computer of an out-of-state bank or a non-bank processor as easily as a local bank's host. In any case, funds could be cleared electronically to the merchant's local bank account, if necessary on the next day. Out-of-state banks and low-cost, nonbank processors cut price in order to capture market share from existing players.

For example, in the mid-1980s, a small retailer might have expected to pay a 3 percent discount rate to his local bank. By 1990, the same retailer might pay only 1.5 percent (although he would probably have to lease his EDC terminal). The promised savings to the industry ended up being passed on to consumers. Overall, the industry now operates at a significant deficit, and many players, large and small, have sold their portfolios and exited the business.

Low Cost and High Quality

Paradoxically, as the EDC example shows, the competitive problem with IT that is often both the lowest-cost and highest-quality way to do something. In many service businesses, for example, consumers would rather interact with a well-designed system than face-to-face. In manufacturing business, flexible automation often provides both low cost and high quality. Once an application is automated, therefore, the ability to differentiate can diminish. If an average customer never experiences an error or defect, the ability of one competitor to lower defect rates even further will no longer increase differentiation.

The bottom line is that businesses employing IT should do so in a way that gives them a sustainable advantage. If they don't, they risk competing away the benefits created.

But is it possible to achieve sustainable advantage from IT, given the use of vendor-supplied technology and the difficulty in keeping experience proprietary? We would argue that it can only happen if the underlying strategy is robust enough to survive duplication by competitors. Specifically, gaining advantage with IT depends on how you use IT to change what you do in your business; attaining technical proficiency in IT isn't good enough.

How the "Extend" Strategy Ensures Sustainable Advantage

We mentioned earlier that companies can use IT to achieve sustainable advantage while pursuing an established business or "Extend" strategy, the key to which is that it leverages or extends existing forms of sustainable advantage in a business.

Take a consumer packaged goods manufacturer, for example, that holds the largest share in a product segment and, as a result, enjoys scale advantage in purchasing, manufacturing, and logistics over its smaller competitors. In this segment, because of the high cost of transportation relative to price, all major competitors manufacture and compete regionally.

Improves Scale Advantage

An Extend strategy here would be to focus IT investments on applications that improve scale advantages: for example, a centralized purchasing system that minimizes raw materials costs across multiple manufacturing plants, trading off volume discounts and shipping costs.

This application could be duplicated by any competitor, but it doesn't help them much. Regional competitors do not benefit at all (since they purchase for only a single plant), and smaller national competitors benefit little because their smaller scale limits their savings.

What makes the advantage sustainable is not the system itself, but the scale advantage the leader originally held, and the way the business reorganized purchasing to leverage that scale. IT is essential to achieving the advantage, however, because without IT the cost of coordination and the impact of lowered flexibility would have offset the savings it might have achieved.

An Extend strategy, on the other hand, would make us less inclined to invest in, say, an IT-based process improvement that simply lowered cost independent of scale—a capability that is bound to be matched by all competitors. Such investments though are a strategic necessity since we can't afford to fall behind our competitors in process improvements, However, leadership in such IT investments shouldn't be the priority.

Other Advantages Too

Extend strategies don't have to leverage scale; they can leverage any structural advantage enjoyed by a business. Moreover, companies don't need to be industry leaders to take advantage of Extend. Most companies enjoy some advantage over competitors on some factor of competition. Any such advantage is a candidate for Extend. Common structural advantages, in addition to scale, which can be leveraged include:

- *Economies of scope*—enjoyed by sharing costs across two or more distinct product/market segments such as in banking, where leading banks have been developing integrated systems to shift from a product to a customer focus. In the credit-card business, for example, a bank which cross-sells credit cards to its mortgage customers enjoys roughly 50 percent higher profitability than banks selling credit cards to the general market. Here, although the IT-based systems enable cross-selling, the *advantage* is created not by the systems, but by the fact that some competitors do not participate in both markets.
- *Proprietary information*—which can be of any form, but the most common and powerful is usually customer information. American Airlines, for example, identifies its best customers through its frequent flyer program, and offers special benefits to the top 2–3 percent of flyers (who make up over half of American's total seat miles). These benefits—allowing customers to book flights that are "full" to others or offering free upgrades to first class—differentiate American's service to its top customers. Again, other airlines can develop and, to some extent, have developed similar systems. But these work only with their own customer bases, while American's works with the strongest franchise among its frequent business travellers. (Delta won't know who the frequent American flyer is when he takes an occasional Delta flight. Thus, the passenger will experience standard Delta service, which will be inferior to the enhanced American service, preserving American's franchise.)
- *Institutional skills or experience*—which are impossible for competitors to duplicate, can be effectively leveraged by IT. One international consulting firm, for example, has achieved in several industries a broader range of consulting experience, spread across a large number of offices, than its competitors. By capturing non-confidential aspects of this experience in written form, and creating a bibliographic database of this information, the firm is able to leverage this experience even in offices that have not worked first-hand in these industries. Again, the IT application is straightforward, and could be duplicated by any major competitor, but, without the extensive experience base, duplication will be less effective.

REDUCING DISADVANTAGE

A flip-side to the Extend strategy, which we call "Reduce," exploits the leveling tendencies of IT, hitherto presented as a problem.

Here, the objective is to use IT to play competitive catch-up: a competitor that suffers a disadvantage on some basis of competition uses IT to improve its abilities in this area. We would expect the current leader to match the application. Nevertheless, a company that today is at a disadvantage would be better off at parity. Analogous to Extend, Reduce is available to most companies, even industry leaders, which may suffer a disadvantage on some factors of competition.

Compressed Time to Market

A shoe company, for example, that possesses no design skills may compete by producing low-cost knock-offs. However, it realizes low prices because it can't deliver the hottest designs at the peak of a fashion trend. By installing a CAD/CAM system, the company compresses the product development cycle and is able to provide timely deliveries. The design leaders can also install the same system, but it helps them less, because the design-to-manufacture interval is less critical if a company originates a design.

In principle, Reduce can apply to virtually any form of competitive disadvantage suffered by a company.

- *Scale disadvantage.* For example, a small-scale industrial products company may suffer a disadvantage because it cannot keep extensive inventories of spare parts in regional warehouses. However, moving to a centralized spare-parts inventory, and using an overnight delivery service and systems that permit same-day shipment of orders, the small-scale company provides equivalent service as large-scale competitors, at equivalent or lower cost.
- *Skill disadvantage,* which includes competitors that may suffer an institutional skill deficiency as compared with industry leaders. A systems company, for example, that lags in providing on-line technical support can install an expert system to catch-up. The technical support leader can also install a similar system, but its distinctive advantage has already been eroded.

Old game versus new game

Both Extend and Reduce are really "old-game" strategies: they reinforce the existing business strategies of a company. Management doesn't need to redefine the product or business. Basically, Extend and Reduce focus attention on what should be the highest leverageable, sustainable opportunities in their current strategy.

These strengths of Extend and Reduce, which make them widely useful and relatively straightforward to execute, are also, in some sense, the strategies' weakness. They ignore the possibility of a "new game" that might obsolete the "old game" entirely.

The "new game" most often described is what we call a "First-Mover" strategy. We'll also argue that there's a second "generic" new-game strategy as well, which we call "Focused Hustle."

How "First-Mover" strategies create sustainable advantage

Classic outcomes of "First-Mover" strategies, such as McKesson's Economost or Merrill Lynch's CMA account, work not because these companies achieve sustainably better IT capabilities, but because they are able to convert a temporary IT advantage into sustainable forms of conventional advantage such as scale, customer loyalty, and brand image.

A fully executed First-Mover strategy has three stages, requiring companies to:

1. Develop a vision of how to change the business using IT to deliver improved value to customers or to achieve better operating capability.
2. Be the first to use the enhanced operational capability to achieve one or more "first-mover advantages," including the opportunity to grow rapidly, to penetrate distribution networks, or to build a unique reputation.
3. Exploit these first-mover advantages to achieve other sustainable advantages, such as scale, customer loyalty, and brand franchises, which will survive even after competitors duplicate the systems capabilities.

How IT Revolutionized Drug Distribution

The classic example of how McKesson Drugs revolutionized the drug distribution business illustrates the point. In the mid-1970s drug distribution was under attack from two sides. From the bottom, chains were rapidly displacing independent drugstores and were beginning to supplant the traditional independent distributor with captive distribution. From the top, drug manufacturers were finding it cheaper to sell direct to the central purchasing departments of chains than through distributors. McKesson, the only national drug distributor at the time, faced the dilemma of either fixing the business or selling it.

Three-Step Process

Management's vision (step 1 of our three-step process) focused on electronic order-entry as a way to differentiate the company. McKesson sold portable electronic devices to the drugstores that could connect via modem to its computers. Instead of ordering through a telephone clerk, the druggist could walk through the aisles of his store, key in the stock numbers of items that needed to be reordered, and then automatically send the complete order in to McKesson. The company in turn would process the order overnight and deliver it the next day. The value to the druggist was significant. The new process reduced clerical effort and shipping errors. Overnight delivery made it feasible to cost shelf stock. In addition, McKesson was able to provide useful management reports for controlling inventory and profitability.

McKesson, by launching it nationally in 1975, did, in fact, offer this kind of system before any other drug distributor and achieved several first-mover advantages (step 2 of our three-step process). The primary first-mover advantage was rapid acceleration of sales volumes. Druggists who had previously spread orders among two or three different distributors now concentrated all orders with McKesson. The system also differentiated McKesson with new customers. From 15 percent of orders entered electronically in 1975, it grew to handle 50 percent by 1982, and total volume more than doubled from $0.9 billion to $1.9 billion.

However, by 1982, several competitors had matched the order-entry functionality that McKesson offered. What distinguished McKesson is that it pursued step 3 of our three-part process to leverage its first-mover opportunities into a sustainable advantage as the scale-based cost leader. During the early 1980s McKesson changed from an organization where each warehouse acted as an autonomous business, responsible for order entry, billing, and purchasing as well as fulfillment, to one where all functions, except fulfillment, were centralized to maximize scale economies. The savings were significant: order-entry staff was cut from 700 in 1975 to 15 in 1985 (when electronic orders reached 97 percent); purchasing staff from 140 to 12. Subscale warehouses were replaced by fewer, highly automated distribution centers that captured scale benefits in logistics.

WHY FIRST-MOVER SUCCESS STORIES AREN'T MORE COMMON

As we noted earlier, the First-Mover strategy is potentially powerful, but there are only a handful of documented examples. The key problem is that a First-Mover strategy requires not only a powerful vision of how to use IT in a business, but also the ability to implement it quickly.

These conditions are difficult to meet. Worse, in many ways, they are significantly more difficult today than they were 10 years ago because:

- *There are a lot more companies in the game today and basic IT skills are more widely available.* Today, when a company is experimenting with a promising technology, it's likely that its competitors are, too. That wasn't as true in the 1970s. McKesson piloted its order-entry system for close to five years in one region before rolling it out nationally in 1975. It would be much harder today for an industry leader to experiment with a new technology and expect competitors to take 5 to 7 years to match it.
- *Today's more complex installed base slows the roll-out of new systems.* Gradual implementation may also alert competitors before the first mover can capture any real advantage. McKesson, on the other hand, was able to roll out its new system relatively quickly. It was running only simple batch accounting applications on standalone IBM 360/20s in each warehouse. It could install its new order-entry applications without worrying about how it would interact with other applications, or how to preserve data integrity of a mix of on-line and batch applications, or any of the other concerns that systems developers have today in integrating a new application with the existing portfolio.

Another problem with the First-Mover strategy is that it's a very high-risk strategy. By the time you make sure your applications deliver value you may already have alerted competitors and reduced lead-time as a first mover.

Nevertheless, the rapid evolution of information technology is probably increasing the number of opportunities for attempting a First-Mover strategy, particularly in industries that may not have been able to exploit IT in the past—though, given the risks involved, we think many more opportunities are squandered than realized.

Whenever new IT capabilities allow businesses to deliver fundamentally better value to customers, top management needs to consider whether the opportunities for first-mover advantage might not outweigh the risk. If the changes needed to the business can be feasibly implemented in a relatively short period of time, First Mover may be the strategy of choice.

However, there are many businesses in which IT can have a powerful transforming effect, but where the complexity of the business system and the information architectures that support it don't permit rapid roll-out. For such companies, an alternative model is needed.

HOW A "FOCUSED-HUSTLE" STRATEGY CREATES ADVANTAGE

How can you create fundamentally new advantages based on IT, if you can't keep your information technology investment proprietary, if your business is too complex to permit radical changes all-at-once, and if you can't achieve a significant lead-time advantage over your competitors? We think the answer is, in some sense, a synthesis of the Extend model and the First-Mover model of how to achieve advantage:

- *Figure out the most powerful changes you can make in your business.* Consider not simply business changes, and not simply IT changes, but both together.
- *Focus resources*—initially on achieving a breakthrough level of performance in the most important of the IT and business changes identified.

- *Apply development resources* to extend advantage across the entire business system once the basic breakthrough is achieved.
- *Repeat the whole cycle as quickly as possible.* The key is to have a vision guiding the process that is setting a consistent direction and guiding the choice of what is the most important thing to do next.

Restructuring Machine Tool Building

One company that has successfully executed a Focused-Hustle strategy is Yamazaki Mazak, the world's largest manufacturer of machine tools and flexible manufacturing systems. In the mid-1960s, Yamazaki was a small manufacturer of conventionally controlled lathes. It pursued a low-cost manufacturing strategy, and was more aggressive than most Japanese manufacturers at the time in pursuing export markets. A major opportunity occurred a few years later when Yamazaki was one of the Japanese companies selected by MITI to manufacture computer numerically controlled (CNC) machine tools based on the standard Fanuc controller.

Helped by rapid growth in the low-cost CNC segment of the market, Yamazaki continued to grow and expand its product line throughout the 1970s. However, by the end of the 1970s, despite extensive use of CNCs in its own facilities, Yamazaki faced a real bottleneck to further growth: adding new products was forcing Yamazaki to extend shipping intervals. Machine tools took, on average, 90 days to build.

Cutting Throughput Time

Yamazaki's management developed a vision based on cutting throughput time. The idea was not to cut just physical manufacturing time, but total throughput time from product design to shipment of finished product. The first major breakthrough involved developing a basic flexible manufacturing concept* and implementing it in the most bottlenecked parts of the manufacturing process.

Initial implementation of the concept was modest and focused. Between 1979 and 1981, Yamazaki developed two new production lines at its main factory at Oguchi. The effort required significant skill-building and organization change: production management, the key function in Yamazaki's conventional operations, had to be placed under the control of the central engineering department developing the new technology.

Results were spectacular. The most bottlenecked operations fell from 90 days using conventional production to three days with flexible manufacturing. Other operations that were not automated now became the bottlenecks, so that overall throughput averaged 30 days.

Between 1981 and 1983, Yamazaki extended the design concepts proven at Oguchi to a "greenfield" plant at Minokamo. The new plant had five lines (not two as at Oguchi),

---

*Throughput lengthens as product line complexity increases in conventional manufacturing systems, because of a tradeoff between run-length and set-up time. To keep average costs down, manufacturers need to amortize set-up costs over a long production run. As the product line increases, different set-ups are required. Given the thousands of parts needed to make a machine tool, it becomes impossible to schedule production of all parts without experiencing bottlenecks. Flexible manufacturing attacks this tradeoff by driving the set-up times close to zero. The machinery is also built to perform multiple manufacturing operations at a single station. This simplifies scheduling, eliminates time lost in physical movement of work-in-process, and allows operations to be performed in parallel instead of sequentially.

extending the system to include automatic rotational operations. Tool changes and materials movements were performed by robots and the precision of the machinery was improved to handle operations that were previously performed off-line.

Integrating Design and Manufacturing

The second major breakthrough in developing Yamazaki's flexible manufacturing vision was to integrate its CAD with its CAM system. Yamazaki engineers developed software that could evaluate a design specification and decide whether it could be manufactured with the flexible manufacturing system at Minokamo. Designs that could were accepted; those that couldn't were sent back for redesign; in effect, they were standardizing designs to speed throughput. They weren't standardizing parts—which is how you do it in a conventional manufacturing environment; they were standardizing around flexible manufacturing capabilities.

The skills needed to create the Minokamo breakthrough didn't come without organizational change, however. Whereas the emphasis at Oguchi had been on developing individual machines, at Minokamo it was on the system and on the interactions across machines. Software was as important as hardware, and developers organized into multidisciplinary teams combining engineering, production management, and software designers.

Yamazaki extended the Minokamo breakthroughs both by building a greenfield plant in Worcester, England (exploiting even more advanced concepts) and by installing additional flexible manufacturing lines in its conventional plants around the world. This required still another reorganization: Yamazaki's engineering and technical function, historically centralized at the company's headquarters in Japan, was now distributed to the individual plants.

Today, Yamazaki is the largest machine tool builder in the world, enjoying dominant market share in low-cost lathes and several segments of flexible manufacturing systems. Its advantage lies not in the individual pieces of technology it has developed, but in the scope of its manufacturing concepts and in the skills it has developed over the years. Another machine tool builder could attempt to leapfrog from a conventional manufacturing system to the current Yamazaki system, but the odds of it succeeding are remote, and Yamazaki itself would render it obsolete by the time the competitor was finished.

Importance of Vision

This example offers a number of lessons about how Focused Hustle creates sustainable advantage. Initially, competitors that don't share the strategy implementer's vision won't match it step-for-step. The circumstances that motivated Yamazaki to start the small-scale plant at Oguchi were unique to its competitive positioning. Competitors had different agendas. As Yamazaki changed, its manufacturing system and those of its competitors diverged even further. Ultimately, competitors couldn't copy Yamazaki without adopting an entirely new philosophy and system of production.

At the root of the advantage is a difference in skills; not simply IT skills, but in *all* of the skills necessary to manage a transformed business system. It's no longer simply a problem of copying a set of applications. It's a problem of fundamentally changing the business and developing a new set of skills—from the shop floor to the executive suite—that are needed to be successful in the new business. Few competitors are capable of such extensive transformation.

Long-Term Strategy

The Focused-Hustle strategy is not without risks and problems. It's a long-term strategy requiring leadership and patience. Top management's vision has to be farsighted and meaningfully better than that of the competitors. And finally, it is difficult to execute. People in the business need to accept rapid and significant change, which, by definition, will stretch their capabilities.

FOUR MODELS, NOT ONE, FOR SUSTAINABLE ADVANTAGE FROM IT

The four models offer top management a much broader range of options for using IT than they may have considered.

For the CEO pursuing an established, successful strategy, Extend provides a new tool for focusing his, and his organization's, thinking on how IT can help. Extend can either be used proactively by top management to trigger new IT projects or simply as a tool for project evaluation. Similarly, Reduce provides a way to make up for a weakness in an existing strategy.

Most companies can take advantage of both strategies at any given time, since they both apply to specific sources of competition, not to overall positioning. Industry leaders and followers can both leverage Extend and Reduce against different mixes of advantages and disadvantages.

For other businesses the biggest opportunity comes from trying to establish a "new game." Here the choice between a First-Mover strategy and Focused Hustle increases the range of companies that might attempt them.

For companies where the increased value can be realized quickly, a First-Mover strategy may offer the highest potential reward. However, for companies where full realization of the potential is measured in years and decades, Focused Hustle offers a new model for gaining maximum advantage from IT investments.

CASE 1 Akron Zoological Park, 1991

F. Bruce Simmons, III

As custodians of our wildlife heritage and animal preservation efforts, zoos remain an important educational and recreational resource. This case serves to illustrate the efforts made by the local zoo community in response to changes in consumer preferences, general price levels, governmental priorities, and international ownership of the rubber industry. The zoo's history, mission, relationship to its area competitors, administration, organization, and financial status are presented. The zoo has lowered its per-visitor operating costs and increased its annual attendance. It has embarked on a building program and engages in strategic planning. In recognition of its achievements as an outstanding micro zoo, it has recently been awarded accreditation by the American Association of Zoological Parks and Aquariums.

BACKGROUND

Zoos are perceived as custodians of our cultural wildlife heritage and as educators in the skills of conservation. Acting alone, zoos can collectively maintain about 1,500 species of rare and endangered birds and animals. This represents less than one-half of 1% of the species that are expected to become extinct during the next ten years. Zoos are strategically placed to inform and educate the public. More people annually visit zoos than enter all U.S. national parks. Collectively, more people attend North American zoological facilities and programs than the combined number of persons who attend professional football, basketball, baseball, and hockey games. Zoos have remained a strong attraction for the people of the United States.

During 1990, member institutions of the American Association of Zoological Parks and Aquariums had 102,187,739 visitors; over $711 million in operating budgets; $408,072,905 in combined capital improvements; 3,681,570 support organization members; over 24,267 acres in parklands; and more than 842,000 specimens from among 36,746 species of mammals, birds, reptiles, amphibians, fish, and invertebrates. Zoological parks, aquariums, and botanical gardens come in all sizes. For example, the largest institution had 4,300,000 visitors and an annual operating budget of $50 million. The smallest institution had 3,000 visitors. Another had a $96,325 budget.

Approximately 38% of A.A.Z.P.A. member institutions had annual operating budgets of less than $1 million. However, 17% had budgets in excess of $6 million. The association, at its annual 1989 meeting, awarded membership to the Akron Zoological Park. This recognition established that the zoo is one of the best 160 institutions in the Western hemisphere.

Prepared by F. Bruce Simmons, III, the University of Akron. The cooperation and assistance of the Akron Zoological Park are acknowledged and appreciated. All rights are reserved to the author. © 1992.

During the late 1970s, changes in consumer preferences for radial automobile tires, the internationalization of the rubber industry, the economic ravages of rapidly increasing general price levels, and changes in governmental priorities almost resulted in the permanent closing of the Akron Children's Zoo. Sagging attendance and a low level of family memberships did not help matters. Faced with the uncertain prospect of continuing its zoo operations, the city of Akron sought to reduce, or eliminate, its financial commitment. As a response, the Akron Zoological Park was organized as an eleemosynary corporation under Section 501(c)3 of the Internal Revenue Code. The board of trustees contracted with the city to operate the zoo.

During the 1980s, the major employers in the Akron area were buffeted by the winds of change. For example, Firestone was purchased by Bridgestone, General Tire changed its name and sold off its broadcasting affiliates and its tire operations, Michelin acquired the combined Uniroyal–Goodrich company, and Goodyear had to sell several of its divisions to fend off an attempted takeover. In the 1980s and 1990s, many area corporations are pursuing strategies of delayering, destaffing, and operating under the just-in-time manufacturing philosophy.

Although the zoo made it through these turbulent and difficult times, its president and CEO are aware that yesterday's achievements do not guarantee tomorrow's survival. Under the guidance of this CEO, the zoo expanded its operations and facilities, increased its annual attendance, and received A.A.Z.P.A. accreditation. In order to keep the zoo open and financially solvent, the CEO believes she needs to develop more animal exhibits, restroom facilities, parking spaces, and community outreach programs. Yet she must balance the costs of this approach with the flows of operating revenues. The zoo CEO is currently searching for a course of action to follow. What would you recommend? If you advise adding employees, exhibits, or events, how would you obtain the funds to build, operate, and employ them?

HISTORY

Residents of Akron, like people in many other cities, created their zoo by donating animals to their city. Earlier this century, two brown bears were given to the city of Akron. The city fathers constructed an appropriate facility in a neighborhood park. Subsequently, other individuals established a Museum of Natural History near the Perkins Park bears. In 1953 both facilities were combined to create the Akron Children's Zoo. By the late 1970s, the city's ability and willingness to satisfactorily husband its animals were questioned. The future of the zoo as a community resource and its continuing operation were in grave danger. In response to this turmoil, the trustees of the Akron Zoological Park contracted with the city to manage and operate the zoo.

While contemplating the future direction of the zoo, and mindful of the severe financial constraints, the zoo's trustees decided to restrict their animal husbandry to North, South, and Central American birds, animals, and reptiles. The old Mother Goose exhibits were eliminated. They were replaced by more natural and native animal environments. These animal exhibits contain the zoo's collection of 183 specimens that represent 66 different species of birds, reptiles, and animals.

During the past seven years, the zoo has expanded its operations. Although it continues to focus on the Western hemisphere, the zoo opened an animal clinic, renovated its "petting zoo" barnyard, and constructed a gift shop, an alpaca exhibit, a concessions area, a reptile building, and a North American river otter exhibit. New maintenance facilities and educational display areas were built. Also, the zoo has completed the first phase in its installation of educational signs.

PURPOSE

The mission of the Akron Zoological Park is to manage its resources for the recreation and education of the people of Akron and surrounding communities and to promote the conservation of wildlife. To be successful, the Akron Zoological Park must maintain its image as a quality place where its visitors desire to spend their time. The park seeks to keep its animal exhibits clean and neat so that they are easy for all to see and enjoy. Flowers and plants abound. As resources become available for construction and continuing operations, new exhibits and new activities are added. Attendance increased from 63,034 people in 1986 to a record of 133,762 people in 1988. As a unique institution, the Akron Zoological Park presents a balanced program of education, recreation, conservation, and scientific activities.

OPERATING SEASON

In deference to its northern climate, the zoo conducts its open season from mid-April until mid-October. Except for Halloween and the winter holidays, the zoo is closed for the winter months. It reopens for one week during Halloween. For the month of December, it is decked out in over 150,000 yuletide lights. Its operating season is shorter than many of its local competitors. Also, it is totally dependent on the largess of nature. For the 1990 year, the Akron area experienced the wettest weather in its recorded history. More than 57 inches of rain and snow were received. New Orleans; San Juan, Puerto Rico; Miami, Florida; and Mobile, Alabama, are among the lush locales that generally have this type of wet weather. Additionally, in December 1989, local records were broken for the coldest temperature on this date, the lowest wind-chill factors, and the most snow. Because of this extreme cold and snow, several evenings of the "Holidays Lights" were canceled. Attendance at this event in 1988 was over 48,000 patrons. In December 1989, the Holiday Lights attendance did not exceed 21,000 people. Weather influences zoo admissions.

The variations in weather also affect crop yields and the prices of fresh animal foods. A drought in 1988 and too much rain in 1989 and 1990 inflated the costs of feeding the animals.

In less extreme climatic circumstances, the zoo may be able to achieve its target attendance goal. Although its surrounding community suffered a declining population level (from 524,472 people in 1980 to 514,990 people in 1990), the zoo seeks to attract an annual attendance equal to 40% of its community. This goal may be too ambitious. The target audience for any zoological park tends to be young children and their parents. The Akron Zoo's community contains a high percentage (approximately 40%) of senior citizens. As indicated in Exhibit 1.1, since the zoo has become better known as an innovative community resource, the annual attendance has doubled.

MEMBERSHIP

Membership in the Akron Zoological Park is available to all. Becoming a zoo member means one has unlimited, no-charge admission to the zoo grounds during the operating season plus reciprocal admission at over 130 other zoological parks, aquariums, and botanical gardens. Members receive a quarterly newsletter and invitations to members-only events. The different types of memberships include family, grandparents, donor, patron, zookeeper, safari leader, and director's club. Each type of membership reflects different levels of financial support for zoo activities. As shown in Exhibit 1.2, the number of memberships has increased during the past several years. As the variety and number of activities increased, membership and attendance more than doubled.

Providing good customer service to the zoo's clientele pays dividends. Part of customer service is providing exciting events at the zoo. As indicated in Exhibit 1.3, during 1991 the zoo promoted several newsworthy and special events. These events serve to attract community media attention, which in turn boosts annual memberships.

EXHIBIT 1.1	Annual Attendance: Akron Zoological Park

		Admission Fee		
Year	Total	Adult	Child	Group
1991	125,363	$3.00	$2.00	$1.00
1990	126,853	3.00	2.00	1.50
1989	108,363	2.50	1.50	1.00
1988	133,762	2.50	1.50	1.00
1987	95,504	2.00	1.00	.50
1986	63,034	1.50	.75	.50
1985	63,853	1.50	.75	.50
1984	61,417	1.50	.75	.50
1983	53,353	1.50	.75	.50

Source: Akron Zoological Park.

EXHIBIT 1.2	Annual Memberships: Akron Zoological Park

Year	Total
1991	1,825
1990	1,365
1989	1,100
1988	1,158
1987	1,200
1986	1,036
1985	1,295
1984	986
1983	492
1982	437
1981	312

Source: Akron Zoological Park.

EXHIBIT 1.3	Special Events in 1991: Akron Zoological Park

Activity	Month
Snow Bowl	January
Spring Fling	April
Earth Day Observance	April
Super Saturday & Keep Akron Beautiful	April
Mother's Day	May
Little Spot Day	May
Sunday Sundae: Zoobilation	June
Reptile Day	July
Costa Rica Trip	July
Nocturnal Golf Classic	July
The Rhino Walk with Michael Werikhe	August
Recycle with Ohio Zoos	August
Members' Night	September
Boo at the Zoo	October
Annual Bird Seed Sale	October
Downtown Yule Display	November
Holiday Lights Celebration	December

Source: Akron Zoological Park.

EDZOOCATORS

This unpaid volunteer group began in the 1970s. These volunteers have no responsibility for the direct operations of the zoo. In 1983 the zoo created the position of education curator, one of whose responsibilities is to coordinate this group's educational activities. As volunteers, members of this group are trained to provide on-site and off-grounds educational programs using the zoo's birds, reptiles, and animals. They conduct guided tours of the zoo grounds, give presentations at local schools, provide a speakers' bureau, and appear on radio and television programs. They also receive free admission to the zoo grounds.

OUTREACH PROGRAMS

Two zoomobile programs exist to take the zoo's services to those who are not able to visit the zoo. The fur, feathers, and scales and the rain forest offerings give people an opportunity to learn about the zoo's conservation mission and its animals in a personal way. These individuals are taught to respect the animal and to preserve its dignity. For a nominal fee, plus gas mileage if travel outside the city is involved, the zoo's educational services are available for citizens' groups, day care centers, schools, and other community organizations. If you are not able to travel to the zoo, it can come to you. If you can visit the grounds, the zoo offers a summer day zoocamp program and the opportunity for your child to celebrate a zoorific birthday party. Also, the zoo established a highly popular and well-known teen volunteer program. Young adults between the ages of 14 and 18 are trained and permitted to handle the animals while working one or two days per week at the zoo.

ADVERTISING

Akron and Summit County are situated just south of Cleveland, Ohio. Cleveland is a major metropolitan area. It has television stations that are affiliated with all four major networks. It has one public and three independent broadcasting stations. By contrast, Akron has one affiliate, one independent, and one public broadcasting station. Because many people view Cleveland television broadcasts, the local residents are generally more conversant with Cleveland events than with Akron's.

To gain media exposure in this market, the zoo must create media events. It must develop exciting activities that "make the cut" as newsworthy. Unlike the Cleveland MetroParks Zoo, the Akron zoo cannot afford to advertise on commercial television. The zoo remains totally dependent on public service announcements, the zoo's public television series, and press coverage of activities at the zoo.

PROMOTIONAL PROGRAMS

The zoo creates newsworthy activities and conducts several promotions. For example, in the spring when the animals give birth to their young, the zoo conducts a contest to name the new arrivals. In order to create the opportunity for members of the community to learn firsthand about the animals in the zoo's collection, the zoo sponsors an annual expedition. In the past, these expeditions have taken participants to the Amazon of Peru, the forests of Belize, the sea turtles and rain forests of Costa Rica, and the Galapagos Islands of Ecuador. In July 1992, the zoo offered its members the opportunity to travel to Kenya. The local press has been quite supportive in reporting these globe-trotting activities. In Exhibit 1.3, the events scheduled for 1991 are listed. These events generated considerable media attention and are a major reason why zoo attendance increased.

SAFETY

In the event of an animal escape, zoo employees have a written procedure to follow for the recapture of the animal. Through its risk management and safety audit program, the zoo management aims to ensure a safe environment for visitors, employees, and the animals that inhabit the zoo. The zoo management remains committed to improving the quality of its exhibits and the habitats of the animals. For example, in conformance with A.A.Z.P.A.'s Code of Professional Ethics mandatory standards, exhibit animals are marked with identifying numbers. This animal marking system facilitates the proper care and security of the animal, bird, or reptile. Animal acquisition and disposal, breeding cooperation, and research for the health and preservation of endangered species are coordinated with other zoos. Cooperative research with colleges and universities is performed within written policy guidelines. As part of its strong commitment to customer service, the personnel of the zoo constantly strive to adhere to high standards of safety and professional conduct.

ADMINISTRATION

The president and CEO of the zoo is Patricia Simmons. She believes that her main function is to ensure the fiscal and conservational integrity of the zoo. She strives to maintain and improve the zoo's excellent customer service. A zoo employee for seven years, her contributions have resulted in increases in her operational authority and various promotions. She has a diverse background. Her training and education are in fishery administration, fund raising, fine arts, and management. She possesses a graduate degree in arts management. A community organization, Leadership Akron, honored her by enrolling her in its 1989 class. On April 17, 1989, the trustees adopted the business corporation structure of governance and elected Mrs. Simmons president and CEO. Mrs. Simmons holds a seat and a vote on the board of trustees and is a member of the executive committee.

The board of trustees oversees the policies of the zoo and sets the guidelines for memberships and promotional activities. The board sees that all financial statements are audited by independent public accountants. Each trustee is elected to serve a three-year term. There are currently 24 trustees. The executive committee consists of the president and CEO, the five elected trustee officers, and the chairs of three standing board committees. The officers, who are elected annually and may serve a limited number of years in office, are the chairman of the board, two vice chairmen, a secretary, and a treasurer. The three standing committees are planning and finance, promotion and sales, and animal care and education. The board has quarterly and annual meetings.

ORGANIZATION

The director of zoo operations, Pat Barnhardt, is provided via a grant from the city of Akron. He supervises the animal curator and keeping staff as well as the maintenance and security crews. When his father was the Akron Park's superintendent, he learned firsthand, as a volunteer, about the daily aspects of zoo operations.

The employees of the zoo are nonunion and non–civil service. As depicted in Exhibit 1.4, there exist twenty full-time zoo employees. The education curator is responsible for the informational activities and coordinates the efforts of the volunteer groups. The public relations person seeks to obtain recognition for zoo events in the local media. The business manager supervises the accounting procedures and the daily commercial operations.

EXHIBIT 1.4   Administrative Structure: Akron Zoological Park

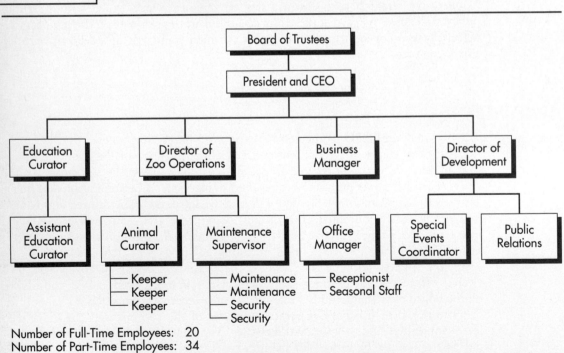

Source: Akron Zoological Park.

It is the zoo's policy that hiring, promotion, and employee transfer are based strictly on individual merit without favoritism or discrimination. A strong anti-nepotism policy is in place. For example, the zoo will not hire an applicant for employment to work under the direct supervision of, or within the same department as, a relative.

OTHER AREA NOT-FOR-PROFIT INSTITUTIONS

With greater competition for private gifts and grants, the decline in donations resulting from changes in the federal tax law, and weather-related effects on gate receipts, the zoo must consider the actions of its competitors. The Akron Zoological Park must successfully compete for resources within its community. Four other museums currently exist: the Historical Society, Hale Farm and Village, the Art Museum, and Stan Hywet Hall and Gardens. A brief description of each institution is provided in Exhibit 1.5. The most recent addition to the local museums is the National Inventors' Hall of Fame. Its organizers have announced an intention to raise $40 million from the community to construct a physical facility. Funds raised for this endeavor will necessarily not be available for other community institutions. When coupled with local universities' fund-raising activities, the competition for the community's resources and their allocation will be very intense.

A survey of current admission prices and operating statistics appears in Exhibit 1.6. The other institutions charge higher fees and have different sources of funding. For example, the Historical Society receives its funding from the county government.

FINANCIAL STATUS

The zoo's ability to survive remains a function of its gate receipts, its memberships, its creative special events, the donations it receives, and its many volunteers.

Nearly 75% of all operating funds are generated from zoo events and activities. During four of the past five years, excluding the grant contracted for with the city, the zoo received an average of $124,000 in donative grants. During the same period, membership sales increased by a net 144% and ticket and merchandise sales increased by more than 78%.

Financing the zoo's activities remains an important consideration. Zoo managers have looked into alternative sources of financing. They have explored the feasibility of placing before the voters a property tax levy to sustain zoo operations. They have also discussed with the other area not-for-profit organizations the possibility of a joint tax levy. These other institutions receive funding from other sources and believe that entering into a joint effort with the zoo would place their access to these other funds in serious jeopardy. The zoo has been left alone in its struggle for fiscal integrity. Recently, a committee of the regional chamber of commerce (A.R.D.B.) studied the financial feasibility of merging the zoo with the county MetroPark system. At this time, the committee report has not been made public.

EXHIBIT 1.5	Brief Description of Competitors

Institution	Description
Historical Society	Consists of the General Simon Perkins Mansion and the abolitionist John Brown's home. Mansion, built in 1837, is 15 rooms of nineteenth-century items. Located near the zoo.
National Inventors' Hall of Fame	Museum intended to recognize holders of U.S. patents. Soliciting funds from community to construct a permanent site. Although not yet open, it conducts an annual event. It raised $35 million from state and local governments and community foundations and citizens.
Hale Farm and Village	A living history museum, with authentic renovated buildings with costumed guides, that depicts rural life in mid-nineteenth-century Northeast Ohio.
Art Museum	The major exhibition of modern art between New York state and Chicago. It houses the E.C. Shaw collection and contains the finest art from 1850 to the present.
Stan Hywet Hall and Gardens	An English country manor with 65 rooms that once was a self-sufficient estate of 3,000 acres. It is decorated with treasures

Source: Summit Visitors and Convention Bureau.

Audited financial statements are provided in Exhibits 1.7 through 1.12. Because not-for-profit accounting is somewhat different from conventional business accounting, a brief description of the accounts is necessary. The unrestricted fund accounts for all revenues and expenditures that are not accounted for in other funds. The unrestricted expenditures for each calendar year are financed principally by admissions, donations, memberships, concessions, and a grant from the city of Akron. The restricted fund accounts for all grants and other revenues that are designated for specific uses by their benefactors. The plant fund accounts for all the acquisition and deletion of building and equipment plus related depreciation. Land is leased from the city of Akron for nominal consideration. Depreciation is straight-line over an applicable five-to-twenty-year period. Buildings typically represent approximately 80% of the amount. Deferred membership income is recognized at the time of receipt but is amortized to operations over the one-year membership period. Deferred restricted contributions are recognized at the time of receipt and are recorded in operations when the expenditure for the specific purpose is made. Inventories are stated at the lower of FIFO cost or market. Contributed utilities and benefits are provided by the city of Akron. The city supplies the utilities to the zoo and provides the salary and benefits for one city worker.

Along with the skyrocketing increases in veterinary and trash disposal costs, the rapid escalation in health and liability insurance is also a major concern. The

EXHIBIT 1.6	Summit County Museums, 1990 Operating Statistics

| | | Visitors | | | |
Institution	Operating Budget	1990	1989	Open Hours	Membership
Historical Society	$ 228,000	12,000	10,000	1,432	1,200
Zoological Park	594,759	126,853	108,363	1,467	1,365
National Inventors' Hall of Fame	700,000	5,000	15,000	160	5,000
Hale Farm and Village	850,500	80,000	77,000	1,357	1,200
Art Museum	1,000,000	52,000	52,000	2,345	1,300
Stan Hywet Hall and Gardens	1,383,000	61,000	109,126	2,100	2,500

Survey of Competitors' Pricing, 1991 Admission Fees

| | Admission Fee | | |
Institution	Adult	Child	Group
Historical Society	$ 3.00	$ 2.00	$ 1.00
Zoological Park	3.00	2.00	1.50
National Inventors' Hall of Fame		Not yet open.	
Hale Farm and Village	6.50	4.00	none
Art Museum		There is no charge.	
Stan Hywet Hall and Gardens	6.00	3.00	none
Cleveland Zoo	3.50	1.50	1.75
Sea World of Ohio	18.50	14.50	15.50

Source: Telephone survey.

availability of health care insurance is not guaranteed. Few insurance companies are interested in writing a policy for an employer with only 17 employees. The few who are interested want to select only a few employees and leave the others without insurance. Should the zoo have one employee whom the issuing company deems a high risk, there may be no insurance available for any employee. The dilemma remains how to obtain health insurance for all employees at an affordable rate.

As the costs of fringe benefits increase, the salary level available for the employee cannot rise. This places the dedicated zoo employee at a distinct financial disadvantage relative to an employee at the city of Akron. The city of Akron wages are among the highest for municipal employees in the state of Ohio. By contrast, the basic wage rate at the zoo is the legally prescribed minimum wage. Recent increases in the federal minimum wage have significantly raised annual wage costs.

EXHIBIT 1.7	Combined Balance Sheet: Akron Zoological Park (As of December 31, 1990)

	Unrestricted Fund	Restricted Fund	Plant Fund	Total
Assets				
Cash	$197,055	$109,363	$105,145	$ 411,563
Inventories	26,498	0	0	26,498
Accounts receivable	2,776	0	0	2,776
Other assets	1,000	0	0	1,000
Total current assets	227,329	109,363	105,145	441,837
Buildings and equipment	0	0	936,251	936,251
Less accumulated depreciation	0	0	308,371	308,371
Total fixed assets	0	0	627,880	627,880
Total assets	$227,329	$109,363	$733,025	$1,069,717
Liabilities				
Accounts payable	$ 35,674	$ 0	$ 1,695	$ 37,369
Accrued payroll	4,242	0	0	4,242
Accrued payroll taxes	7,686	0	0	7,686
Accrued bonus	20,000	0	0	20,000
Deferred membership	15,155	0	0	15,155
Deferred income	9,403	0	0	9,403
Deferred restricted contributions	0	109,363	103,450	212,813
Total liabilities	92,160	109,363	105,145	306,668
Fund Equities				
Fund balance	89,875	0	627,880	717,755
Board restricted	45,294	0	0	45,294
Total fund equities	135,169	0	627,880	763,049
Total liabilities and fund equities	$227,329	$109,363	$733,025	$1,069,717

Source: Akron Zoological Park.

EXHIBIT 1.8	Combined Balance Sheet: Akron Zoological Park (As of December 31, 1989)

	Unrestricted Fund	Restricted Fund	Plant Fund	Total
Assets				
Cash	$138,303	$1,938	$160,739	$300,980
Inventories	26,203	0	0	26,203
Accounts receivable	4,213	0	17,892	22,105
Other assets	824	0	0	824
Total current assets	169,543	1,938	178,631	350,112
Buildings and equipment	0	0	843,142	843,142
Less accumulated depreciation	0	0	250,167	250,167
Total fixed assets	0	0	592,975	592,975
Total assets	$169,543	$1,938	$771,606	$943,087
Liabilities				
Accounts payable	$ 25,828	$ 0	$ 36,745	$ 62,573
Accrued payroll	2,808	0	0	2,808
Accrued payroll taxes	6,745	0	0	6,745
Deferred membership	14,055	0	0	14,055
Deferred income	8,779	0	0	8,779
Deferred restricted contributions	0	1,938	141,886	143,824
Total liabilities	58,215	1,938	178,631	238,784
Fund Equities				
Fund balance	54,686	0	592,975	647,661
Board restricted	56,642	0	0	56,642
Total fund equities	111,328	0	592,975	704,303
Total liabilities and fund equities	$169,543	$1,938	$771,606	$943,087

Source: Akron Zoological Park.

EXHIBIT 1.9	Combined Balance Sheet: Akron Zoological Park

(As of December 31, 1988)

	Unrestricted Fund	Restricted Fund	Plant Fund	Total
Assets				
Cash	$197,519	$4,514	$113,480	$315,513
Inventories	9,088	0	0	9,088
Accounts receivable	4,166	0	12,920	17,086
Other assets	824	0	0	824
Total current assets	211,597	4,514	126,400	342,511
Buildings and equipment	0	0	734,724	734,724
Less accumulated depreciation	0	0	198,941	198,941
Total fixed assets	0	0	535,783	535,783
Total assets	$211,597	$4,514	$662,183	$878,294
Liabilities				
Accounts payable	$ 22,571	$ 0	$ 12,920	$ 35,491
Accrued payroll	2,202	0	0	2,202
Accrued payroll taxes	5,981	0	0	5,981
Deferred membership	17,082	0	0	17,082
Deferred income	10,668	0	0	10,668
Deferred restricted contributions	0	4,514	113,480	117,994
Total liabilities	58,504	4,514	126,400	189,418
Fund Equities				
Fund balance	55,573	0	535,783	591,356
Board restricted	97,520	0	0	97,520
Total fund equities	153,093	0	535,783	688,876
Total liabilities and fund equities	$211,597	$4,514	$662,183	$878,294

Source: Akron Zoological Park.

Half of the employees received a pay raise from the enactment of this recent legislation. Without corresponding increases in revenue, the zoo could become a victim of this legislation.

Although it possesses federal not-for-profit status, the zoo must seek to ensure that its sources of income equal or exceed its operating and physical plant costs. Its continued existence and its promotion of wildlife conservation remain totally dependent on its ability to generate revenues and to reduce its expenses.

EXHIBIT 1.10	**Combined Balance Sheet: Akron Zoological Park**
	(As of December 31, 1987)

	Unrestricted Fund	Restricted Fund	Plant Fund	Total
Assets				
Cash	$70,657	$6,021	$119,728	$196,406
Inventories	4,611	0	0	4,611
Accounts receivable	2,330	0	0	2,330
Other assets	824	0	0	824
Total current assets	78,422	6,021	119,728	204,171
Buildings and equipment	0	0	661,947	661,947
Less accumulated depreciation	0	0	154,098	154,098
Total fixed assets	0	0	507,849	507,849
Total assets	$78,422	$6,021	$627,577	$712,020
Liabilities				
Accounts payable	$19,766	$ 0	$ 3,677	$ 23,443
Accrued payroll	1,325	0	0	1,325
Accrued payroll taxes	5,286	0	0	5,286
Deferred membership	5,229	0	0	5,229
Deferred income	4,840	0	0	4,840
Deferred restricted contributions	0	6,021	116,051	122,072
Total liabilities	36,446	6,021	119,728	162,195
Fund Equities				
Fund balance	19,455	0	507,849	527,304
Board restricted	22,521	0	0	22,521
Total fund equities	41,976	0	507,849	549,825
Total liabilities and fund equities	$78,422	$6,021	$627,577	$712,020

Source: Akron Zoological Park.

ADMISSIONS POLICY

The park is open to all persons who follow the general admission rules. These rules are printed on the visitor's brochure. All visitors must wear a shirt and shoes. No alcoholic beverages are permitted. The zoo reserves the right to remove visitors who prove to be unruly, harass the animals, feed the animals, enter into the exhibit areas, or litter the park.

EXHIBIT 1.11	Combined Balance Sheet: Akron Zoological Park
	(As of December 31, 1986)

	Unrestricted Fund	Restricted Fund	Plant Fund	Total
Assets				
Cash	$64,654	$12,171	$242,892	$319,717
Inventories	6,242	0	0	6,242
Accounts receivable	4,247	1,000	0	5,247
Due from unrestricted fund	0	7,718	0	7,718
Other assets	824	0	0	824
Total current assets	75,967	20,889	242,892	339,748
Buildings and equipment	0	0	416,996	416,996
Less accumulated depreciation	0	0	119,602	119,602
Total fixed assets	0	0	297,394	297,394
Total assets	$75,967	$20,889	$540,286	$637,142
Liabilities				
Accounts payable	$ 2,351	$11,579	$ 0	$ 13,930
Accrued payroll	1,910	0	0	1,910
Accrued payroll taxes	4,549	0	0	4,549
Deferred membership	3,915	0	0	3,915
Deferred income	0	0	0	0
Deferred restricted contributions	7,718	9,310	242,892	259,920
Total liabilities	20,443	20,889	242,892	284,224
Fund Equities				
Fund balance	20,524	0	297,394	317,918
Board restricted	35,000	0	0	35,000
Total fund equities	55,524	0	297,394	352,918
Total liabilities and fund equities	$75,967	$20,889	$540,286	$637,142

Source: Akron Zoological Park.

MASTER PLAN

The zoo is located in Perkins Park. The shade trees serve to keep the grounds relatively free from the harsh effects of the sun. The zoo consists of 25 acres and stretches across two plateaus. Between the upper and lower levels there is a comparatively

EXHIBIT 1.12	Statement of Support, Revenue, Expenses, and Changes in Fund Balances: Akron Zoological Park

	Operating Funds				
Years Ended December 31	1990	1989	1988	1987	1986
Support and Revenue					
City of Akron grant	$180,000	$180,000	$175,000	$165,000	$160,000
City services in kind	58,597	55,367	51,160	49,722	50,398
Donations	152,289	155,143	227,102	311,263	201,842
Admissions	167,307	109,523	113,840	71,725	47,297
Concessions	76,788	55,177	54,419	41,054	42,297
Memberships	38,800	27,247	24,666	15,891	26,502
Interest	32,112	22,291	15,634	13,768	13,901
Total revenue	705,893	604,748	661,821	668,423	542,857
Expenses					
Program					
Animal collections	133,819	127,410	113,037	113,897	118,789
Buildings and grounds	233,121	189,763	169,870	161,605	141,914
Cost of concessions	13,489	14,267	14,434	13,888	26,336
Education	26,510	28,509	22,699	25,169	23,277
Strategic planning	0	3,838	0	0	0
Total expenses	406,939	363,787	320,040	314,559	310,316
Supporting					
Administration	228,391	206,217	175,426	131,327	95,629
Promotion	8,277	15,795	23,903	23,130	17,534
Legal and accounting	3,540	3,522	3,401	2,500	26,073
Total supporting	240,208	225,534	202,730	156,957	139,236
Total expenditures	$647,147	$589,427	$522,770	$471,516	$449,552
Excess of support and revenue over expenses	58,746	15,427	139,051	196,907	93,305
Operating fund balance: Beginning of year	$704,303	$688,876	$549,825	$352,918	$259,613
Operating fund balance: End of year	$763,049	$704,303	$688,876	$549,825	$352,918

Source: Akron Zoological Park (Auditors: Deloitte & Touche).

steep natural incline. This incline runs throughout the middle of the zoo. Nationally, zoos are responding to rapid changes in accreditation requirements, and because the Akron Zoo is now an accredited institution, it too must change. The terrain hinders access to the grounds for the handicapped and disabled. Also, to improve zoo access, higher-quality washroom facilities are necessary.

To continue to provide great customer service, the zoo will also need to expand its parking area. On days of special events when the crowds number near 3,000 people or more, the parking space is inadequate. The zoo does have some space within its fenced perimeter where it can expand parking. And by expanding into Perkins Park, the zoo could double its size. Yet this presents a dilemma. To expand and to construct new exhibits will increase admissions, but it will require increases in both capital and operating funds. Without additional parking and concession areas, the zoo will not be able to increase its gate receipts. Further, extra exhibits can mean that customers will remain longer in the zoo and are likely to purchase more concessions and souvenirs. Continued pursuit of its educational and recreational objectives can become a financial burden. Failure to follow its expansion strategy would mean the risk of organizational decline and acceptance of the uncertainty of present financing. Zoo executive management will not accept a secondary community status.

SURVEY REPORT ON THE ZOO

The zoo contracted with the local university to conduct a study of zoo clientele. Telephone surveys were made the last week of September 1989. Interviewers received 757 usable responses. In general, those people who patronize zoos have a positive overall evaluation of the facility. They rate favorably its cleanliness, safety, convenience, and animal displays. Approximately half of the respondents avail themselves of the opportunity to use the Akron zoo. However, nearly two-fifths of the people interviewed report never going to a zoo. The results of this survey are reviewed in Exhibit 1.13. The basic reasons given for not attending a zoo are a "dislike of zoos," "no time for a visit," "lack of transportation," "the children are grown," and simply "I do not have an answer."

When asked about the zoo, many people responded that it is too small. Three-quarters of its patrons and two-thirds of the general public expressed concern at the relative smallness of the facility. The respondents offered suggestions for five additional facilities they would like the zoo to construct. These requests include "more exhibits for the children with visitor involvement," "a railroad," "bring back the black bears," and "add more small cats and monkeys."

To better understand the needs of zoo customers, the survey asked whether the respondents visited any other attractions in the area during 1989. The responses indicated that the zoo's clientele attended five other area institutions: the Cleveland Zoo, Sea World, Stan Hywet Hall and Gardens, Hale Farm and Village, and Geauga Lake Park Amusements. Three-fifths of those who attend the Akron Zoological Park also visit these competing facilities.

EXHIBIT 1.13	Visitor Surveys: Akron Zoological Park
	(December 1989)

Other Attractions Visited in 1989	Percent
Cleveland Zoo	51.8
Sea World	45.2
Stan Hywet Hall and Gardens	41.2
Hale Farm and Village	32.2
Geauga Lake Park Amusements	31.2

Reasons Not to Attend	Percent
Lack of time	27.2
Not personally able	16.7
Do not like zoos	16.3
No interest	13.6
Kids are grown	12.2
Unable to supply an answer	12.0
Transportation problems	6.1
Unsafe urban neighborhood	2.4
New to area	1.7

Preferred New Projects	Response Ranking
Build exhibits for children	First (tie)
Addition of a railroad	First (tie)
Bring back the bears	Second
Addition of small cats to collection	Third
More monkeys	Fourth

Source: The University of Akron Survey Research Center *Project Report*, 1989.

Zoos, aquariums, and botanical gardens are evolving away from their origins in the museum community. They are caretakers of life in an age of extinction. They focus on life and its diversity. The employees and board members are concerned with the zoo's future viability, prosperity, and perspective. What recommendations would you make to enable the zoo to continue its operations?

CASE 2 Alterenergy, Inc.: The Packaged Cogeneration Industry

Robert J. Mockler ▪ Assaf Harel ▪ Gabriel Leung ▪
Paul Poppler

Alterenergy, Inc. is a publicly held company that operates in the packaged cogeneration system (PCS) segment of the electricity industry. Exhibit 2.1 shows the segmentation of the electricity industry. The PCS industry consists of manufacturers who offer PCSs that produce electricity and heat simultaneously. The PCSs are usually sold to small and medium-sized companies through the manufacturers' salespersons and independent dealers. A PCS has two advantages: it produces electricity at a lower cost and with less interference caused during transmission.

Rapid changes and cost overruns are characteristic of the PCS industry. The industry had grown from its beginnings in 1981 to $46 million in 1988 and was expected to grow to over $80 million by 1992 (Toulson, 1989). The powerful public utility companies that had been trying to discourage the industry were changing their attitude. Some utility companies were considering entering the industry as manufacturers. Other utilities are providing incentives to companies that use the PCS.

Due to the infancy of the industry, many manufacturers lack the necessary experience to control installation and maintenance costs. As a result, cost overruns had caused some companies to withdraw from the industry. However, other companies were entering the industry because they expected the growth stage of the industry would arrive in the next few years.

Incorporated in 1981, Alterenergy pioneered the packaged cogeneration system. It manufactures, installs, and maintains the PCSs. In 1992, Alterenergy was considered the leader of the industry and enjoyed the best reputation in product quality and performance. However, Alterenergy had not been able to show a profit since its inception due to the infancy of the industry and cost overruns in installation and maintenance operations. Over the years, Alterenergy had employed various strategies without success. Exhibit 2.2 shows the strategies used and net losses from 1981 to 1988.

In light of the rapid changes in the industry and the company's problem of cost overruns, Alterenergy is exploring key strategic decision areas, including its core operation, product line, distribution channel, and level of maintenance support.

INDUSTRY AND COMPETITIVE MARKET

THE ELECTRICITY INDUSTRY

The electricity industry can be divided into two sectors: the regulated public utility companies and independent power producers. The "birth" of the independent

EXHIBIT 2.1	Segmentation of the Electricity Industry

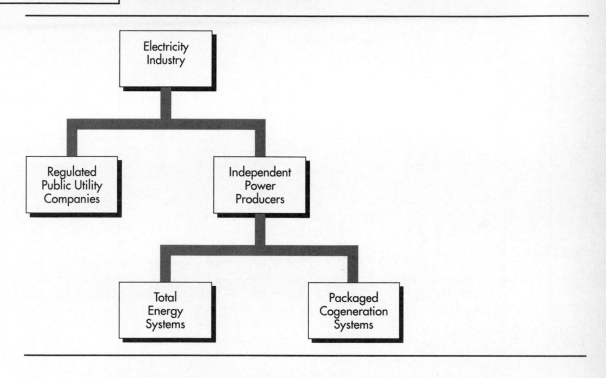

power producers was a result of the electricity supply shortage and the rising cost of electricity.

The electricity industry is dominated by the regulated public utility companies. However, some major corporations such as UNISYS and New York Telephone have turned to producing their own electricity when the supply and demand of electricity became imbalanced. As shown in Exhibit 2.3, the electricity demand increased at a rate of 5% per year from 1984 to 1988. In 1988 the demand reached approximately 96% of supply capacity during peak time, such as summer between the hours of 8 A.M. and 6 P.M.

The demand for electricity was increasing due to (1) the growing population and (2) technological advancement such as the invention of microwave ovens and micro-computers and (3) the growing insistence of the Environmental Protection Agency (EPA) on the use of clean and efficient energy. While the demand for electricity was increasing, the supply of electricity remained relatively unchanged. The production capacity of the power plants owned by the public utilities is fixed. In other words, there is a maximum level of electricity that can be produced.

At a 5% rate of increase per year, demand will exceed supply in the next few years. To meet anticipated demand, new power plants must be built. However, utility companies were reluctant to build conventional power plants because of increasing environmental concerns (Paul, 1989). Another method of producing

EXHIBIT 2.2 | **Strategies Used by Alterenergy, Inc., 1981–1988**

Strategic Decision Area	1981	1982	1983	1984	1985	1986	1987	1988
Core operation	• Manufacturing • Installation • Full Maintenance							
Product line	100–450 kw				100–1000 kw (Prototype of 65 kw was built. Project was abandoned in the same year.)	Concentrated on 400 kw and above		
Distribution channel	Direct sales		Direct sales and dealer network		Concentrated on dealer network		Dealer network and engineering firms	
Product financing	Company owned (no cost to customer, shared cost saving)			Direct financing and direct purchase		Direct purchase and third-party		
Profit/loss[a]	0.00	(0.50)	0.10	(4.00)	(3.30)	(4.20)	(5.20)	(4.80)
Cumulated losses[a]	0.00	(0.50)	(0.40)	(4.40)	(7.70)	(11.90)	(17.10)	(21.90)

[a] In millions.

EXHIBIT 2.3	Peak Demand for and Supply of Electricity, 1984–1988

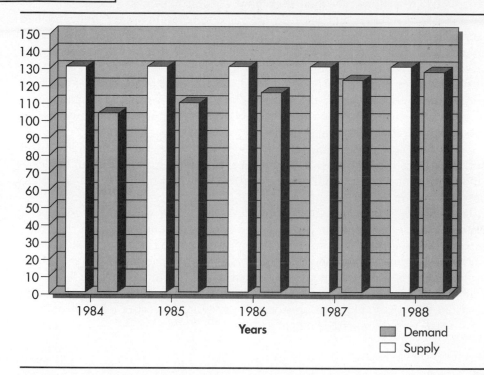

Source: Compilation of peak demand data of New York, New York; Boston, Massachusetts; San Diego, California; and Chicago, Illinois. Data supplied by the company.

electricity is by nuclear reaction. However, the general public had been opposing this alternative electricity production method due to massive cost overruns and safety concerns. The public concerns about safety in nuclear power production make it an unlikely future alternative. In 1989 a group of nuclear industry executives, government officials, energy experts, and environmentalists gathered in Sundance, Utah, in an attempt to determine whether the "second-age" nuclear reactor is feasible. Opinions were sharply divided. "You haven't got a lot of open minds left. It's obvious that the environmental community is never going to [accept nuclear power production] until they are convinced there is no alternative," said Kenneth M. Carr, chairman of the Nuclear Regulatory Commission (Wald, 1989).

The electricity supply shortage problem was especially noticeable during summertime when the demand reaches the highest in a year. When the demand exceeded the capacity of the power plants, the utility companies shut off or reduced the electricity supply, resulting in blackouts or brownouts. During the blackouts, factories and offices were shut down, causing loss of productivity and revenue. For example, for the twelve-month period ended August 1988, companies in Massachusetts lost approximately $87 million in productivity due to blackouts and brownouts (Paul, 1989).

The demand and supply imbalance was not the only reason that led a number of corporations to construct their own power plants. The cost of electricity had been increasing steadily, and the PCS (power cogeneration system) industry had become a mature industry. As a result, many cogeneration facilities operated much more efficiently and produced cleaner energy. Exhibit 2.4 shows the average electricity rates in five major cities in New York, Massachusetts, Illinois, Texas, and California for the period from 1981 to 1988. The increase in the price of crude oil was the primary reason for the upward trend in electricity cost. As a result, companies such as General Motors and Coca-Cola had constructed their own power plants to reduce electricity costs.

As the problem of electricity shortage and increasing cost grew, independent power producers began to emerge. The independent power producers can be divided into two segments: the total energy system (TES) and the packaged cogeneration system (PCS) segments.

Total energy systems provide 100% of the electricity users' needs for operations or productions. The user of a TES is normally disconnected from the utility company and, therefore, has no alternative power supply if the TES is shut down for any reason. Since it is independent of the utility company, the TES must have adequate backup equipment to guarantee continuous power supply. The TES, with its elaborate backup equipment, is a very expensive investment. A typical TES costs from $4 to $20 million to construct. As a result, the cost of a TES is prohibitive for small to medium-sized companies.

EXHIBIT 2.4 | **Average Electric Rate of Five Major Cities, 1981–1988**
(Cents per kw)

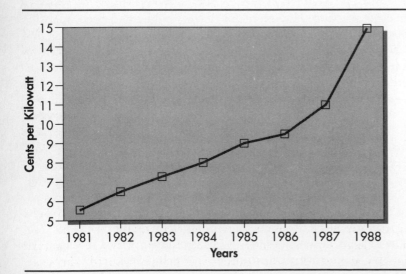

Source: Compiled from Electric and Gas Rates for the Industrial and Commercial Sectors, 1981–1988.

Packaged cogeneration systems, on the other hand, provide approximately 80–85% of the electricity needs of a customer. The balance of the electricity needed is supplied by the utility company. An installed PCS costs between $150,000 and $1,000,000. Cost saving is a major incentive for the end users of a PCS.

THE PRODUCT

The Packaged Cogeneration System basically generates electricity and reuses the waste heat produced during electricity generation. The PCSs are installed on the premises of a user.

Basic Components

The basic components of a PCS are a prime mover (generally an engine), a generator, a waste heat recovery system, a control system, and an interface with the electric utility company. The engine is powered by oil or gas and moves the generator that generates electricity. During this process, heat is also generated. The waste heat recovery system recaptures the waste heat and converts it into steam, hot water, or cool air. The efficiency of a PCS is determined by the design of the waste heat recovery system and how well it is integrated with the user's existing plumbing system. The more waste heat that can be recaptured, the greater the savings.

Selling Price

In 1989 the cost of a PCS ranged from $75,000 to $600,000, excluding installation. The engine usually makes up approximately 30% of the total cost. For example, in a PCS costing $75,000 prior to the installation, the engine costs approximately $23,000. Further advancement in engine technology will allow a 40% reduction in cost. This will further increase the economic merit of the PCS and allow a larger market. However, such technical advancement is not expected in the near future.

Manufacturers usually offer a range of product capacities from 60 kw to 1,000 kw. Product selection is based on current and anticipated electric and thermal needs. All products can be engineered to generate the required electric load.

Even though most manufacturers offer products with different capacities, from 1981 to 1988, more units of 100 kw or less were sold than units above 100 kw. Exhibit 2.5 shows the size distribution of units sold from 1981 to 1988. However, it is believed that the number of larger units sold will be higher than the units of 100 kw or less. Exhibit 2.6 shows the projected size distribution in the next 10 years (Williams, 1989).

Advantages

The advantages of installing a PCS, compared with purchasing electricity from a public utility company, are cost savings and better electricity quality.

The PCS reduces electricity cost because it produces electricity and recaptures the otherwise-wasted heat generated while electricity is being produced. The recaptured heat is used for hot water, steam, or heating and cooling. The recaptured

---

| EXHIBIT 2.5 | Size Distribution of Units Sold, 1981–1988 |

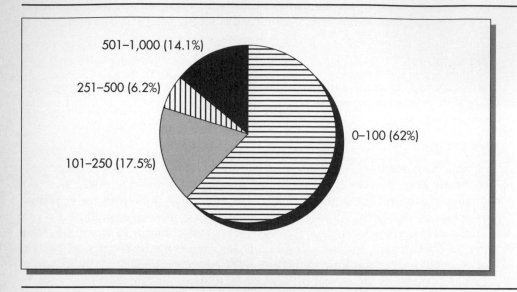

Source: Information obtained from James H. Williams, "Market Trend," *Packaged Cogeneration Systems Proceedings Conference,* February 14, 1989, p. 2.

| EXHIBIT 2.6 | Size Distribution of Units Sold, 10-Year Projection |

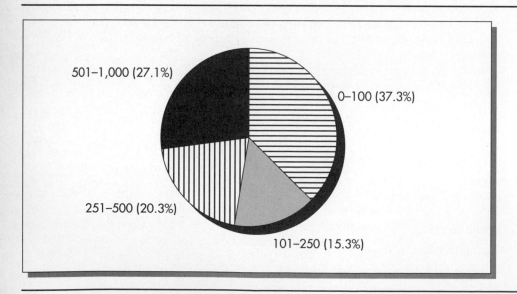

Source: Compiled from a study conducted by Alterenergy, Inc.

heat is in essence free. Therefore, a PCS system can reduce the user's electricity cost by about 20%. The cost savings can be higher in areas that have higher electricity rates. A user can generally recover its investment in four to five years.

In addition to cost savings, the PCS produces electricity of better quality. The PCS produces electricity on the customer's premises, whereas electricity purchased from the utility company is transmitted from miles away. The transmitted electricity normally carries interference, which can cause damage to sensitive equipment such as computers. The electricity produced on the premises has substantially less interference than that which is transmitted from the utility. Companies that depend on computer operations, such as AT&T, have established divisions focusing on incorporation of the PCS into general operations.

DISTRIBUTION

Packaged cogeneration systems are usually sold through three different distribution channels: in-house salespersons, independent dealer networks, and developers. In 1989 a fourth channel began to emerge: engineering consulting firms.

In-House Salespersons

Most manufacturers sell their PCSs through in-house salespersons. The manufacturers usually concentrate on the areas that have high electricity rates and select potential customers. A system is proposed to the customer. If the customer is interested in the proposal, an economic study is conducted to determine the economic feasibility. The primary criterion used in the feasibility studies is the number of years required to recover the money paid for the system through cost savings. It is considered feasible if the number of years required is five or less. If it is considered feasible, the manufacturer solicits the customer to purchase the system. In addition, many sales are also referred by existing customers.

Typically, a manufacturer builds and installs the PCS at a fixed price; this is called a turnkey service. In a turnkey project, the price of the contract covers all costs from the design stage to the stage where the PCS is operational, including equipment that is necessary to connect with the utility company. Usually, the cost of the installation is approximately equal to the cost of the PCS equipment. However, if major modification to the customer's premises is necessary, then the cost of installation exceeds the cost of the PCS.

The manufacturers of PCSs also provide maintenance service. A typical maintenance agreement covers all costs, including parts and labor for preventive maintenance, minor repairs, and major repairs such as overhauls. The price of the maintenance service is generally $0.01 to $0.015 per hour when the engine is in operation. An industrial graded engine requires a major overhaul every 20,000 to 40,000 hours of operation. In 1989 the price of such an overhaul varied from $15,000 to $25,000 in parts and labor. General preventive maintenance costs from $2,000 to $5,000 per month and requires four to six hours of system shutdown each month.

Independent Dealer Networks

In addition to selling through in-house salespersons, manufacturers also use outside independent dealers to generate sales on a commission basis. These dealers are usually sales representatives of engine manufacturers or other energy-related equipment manufacturers. The economic feasibility studies are carried out by the PCS manufacturers.

Developers

In addition to the manufacturer, a promoter referred to as a developer also sells the PCSs. The developer does not manufacture or install the system. He or she proposes a system to a potential user in the same way a manufacturer does. After the user signs a contract to purchase a system, the developer sells the contract to a third party, such as a nonregulated subsidiary of a public utility company, at a higher price. After the user and buyer are found, the developer purchases the PCS system from a manufacturer on a turnkey basis. Some developers also provide financing to customers.

Engineering Consulting Firms

Prior to 1989, engineering consulting firms took a passive role in all packaged cogeneration system projects. Their participation was limited to installation consultation services. For the most part, the engineering consulting firms were not experienced in the design and operation of the PCS. In 1989, however, several consulting firms had begun to act as manufacturers' representatives.

THE LEGAL DEVELOPMENTS

When the packaged cogeneration system was first introduced, utilities took a defensive position by disallowing access to their power lines. Since the PCS supplies only 80–85% of the electricity needs of a customer, it is important to be able to access the utility's power line for additional power supply. However, in 1978 Congress passed the Public Utility Regulatory Policies Act (PURPA), which mandated that all utilities allow interconnecting and required utilities to purchase any excess electricity produced by a PCS at a non-discriminatory rate (a rate equivalent to the cost of creating new capacity at today's cost). Several large public utilities filed a complaint alleging that the act is unconstitutional, but the U.S. Supreme Court ruled against the utilities in 1983.

In June 1990, the Solar, Wind, and Geothermal Power Production Incentive Act was introduced. This act removed the size limitation contained originally in PURPA. Prior to this, cogeneration plants were not allowed to operate or produce an electric facility that generated more than 80 megawatts. The new act removed any size limitation on renewable energy projects.

After being defeated in court, the utilities required elaborate and expensive electronic connecting devices to reduce the PCSs' economic advantage. In addition, the approval process usually takes months to years. According to Mr. Richard Newton, president and CEO of Alterenergy, Inc., it took two and a half years for Alterenergy's project in Riverhead, New York, to receive interconnecting approval from Long Island Lighting Company. The interconnection equipment costs from $30,000 to $200,000. This additional cost often makes a project economically not feasible.

Beginning in 1987, three significant events occurred. First, a number of public utilities began to relax some compliance requirements and lowered interconnection charges. Second, several public utilities began to form wholly owned nonregulated subsidiaries to engage in owning and operating PCS facilities. For example, in 1989 Public Service Electric and Gas in New Jersey, and San Diego Gas and Electric in California invited bids for PCSs from several manufacturers. In addition, in 1987 Eastern Utilities Associates, a utility holding company headquartered in Andover, Massachusetts, formed a subsidiary to purchase PCS facilities, and Boston Gas Company was contemplating entering the market as manufacturer and operator of PCSs. The third and the most significant event was the rebate program offered by Consolidated Edison and Long Island Lighting Company in early 1989. Consolidated Edison and Long Island Lighting Company will pay electricity users a certain amount for every kilowatt of electricity they produce using the user's PCS during summer peak-demand hours. In mid-1989, several other major utility companies were considering a similar rebate program.

However, some utilities were still trying to reduce the attractiveness of the packaged cogeneration systems. The most commonly used method was changing the electricity rate structures from fixed to different rates for different amounts of electricity used. The higher the amount of electricity used, the lower the rate. Thus the PCS, which is replacing the lowest electricity rate, is economically unattractive. In addition, a new stand-by charge is imposed on a user for the utility to stand by and provide electricity in the event of a system shutdown. The stand-by charge is imposed whether or not an actual shutdown occurs. On top of the stand-by charge, if actual system shutdown occurs and the utility "steps in" to provide electricity, there is an additional demand charge.

The changes of the utility companies' attitude toward PCSs and their participation in the market were the turning point for the industry. The relaxation of the interconnection requirements and the lowering of charges improved the PCSs' economic advantage. Although only a limited number of utility companies relaxed the requirements and reduced charges, others were considering making similar changes.

CUSTOMERS

The customers of a packaged cogeneration system include any establishment that uses a lot of electricity and heat or cooling. However, the PCSs are particularly attractive to hospitals, hotels and motels, supermarkets, restaurants, nursing and retirement homes, and computer facilities.

According to a study conducted by Forst & Sullivan, Inc., a leading consulting firm in the energy industry, in 1988 200 units of PCSs were sold to various businesses. Exhibit 2.7 shows the breakdown of these purchases by business type.

EXHIBIT 2.7	PCS Sales by Business Type, 1988

Business Type	Amount of Investment	Units
Supermarkets	$2,500,000	10
Schools	4,500,000	20
Restaurants	4,800,000	20
Remote locations	3,600,000	15
Offices	3,400,000	15
Municipal	4,500,000	20
Hotels	3,600,000	15
Health care	3,500,000	15
Farms	4,800,000	20
Apartments	4,500,000	20
Varied industrial	6,900,000	30

Total amount: $46.6 million
Total number of units: 200

Source: Information obtained from "New Study Sees Big Market for Packaged Cogeneration," *World Cogeneration,* Summer 1989, p. 15.

Hospitals

Hospitals are large units and use electricity and heat 24 hours a day. PCSs are considered most economical for hospitals with 150 beds or more, because of their large demand for electricity and large heat consumption. In addition, all hospitals have an emergency generator that can be incorporated into the PCS as a component, reducing the cost of the PCS.

Hotels and Motels

Hotels and motels use more electricity and heat during vacation seasons. During these periods, rooms are usually occupied and most equipment in the hotels is operating close to maximum capacity. Like hospitals, most hotels and motels have emergency generators that can be used as a component of the PCS and, therefore, reduce the capital investment. PCSs are not economical in hotels with 50 or fewer rooms, however, because of their low demand for electricity or heat.

Supermarkets

Supermarkets have moderate continuous electrical demand. However, they are potential customers because of their constant need for large amounts of heat to produce cool air for refrigeration systems. In addition, supermarkets generally have large, open spaces. The space heating during the winters demands a large amount of electricity. The refrigeration and winter space heating make the PCS economically attractive to supermarkets.

Restaurants

Restaurants are a potential application for smaller PCSs because of their need for large space air-conditioning in the summers and heating during the winters. The cost savings is particularly appealing to full-service chains.

Nursing and Retirement Homes

Nursing and retirement homes generally operate on a very tight budget. The cost savings is a very attractive advantage. In addition, nursing and retirement homes incorporate features of both hospitals and hotels. Laundry facilities, if present, further enhance the economic advantage of using a PCS.

Computer Facilities

Computer facilities use large amounts of electricity and usually operate around the clock. Computer equipment also generates a large amount of heat and operates under only a narrow range of temperature. Therefore, computer facilities must be air-conditioned all year round. In addition, computer equipment is sensitive to electrical interference. The need for electricity, climate control, and low electrical interference makes the PCS attractive.

PRODUCT FINANCING

There are three ways to finance the purchase of a packaged cogeneration system: manufacturer's financing, third-party financing, and direct purchase.

Manufacturer's Financing

In the early days of the PCS industry, the product was relatively new and the customers were uncertain about the PCS equipment. "It has taken us 30 years to learn how to make good cottage cheese. Now you want us to learn how to make electricity?" said a plant manager of a large dairy ("Small," 1987). In order to consummate a sale and overcome the fear of the customer, manufacturers often provide financing. In addition, some manufacturers were installing PCS systems at the customer's premises for free. This was done primarily for the purpose of increasing the number of PCS systems in the industry and thereby increasing awareness.

Third-Party Financing

Another method of financing the purchase of a PCS system is through a third party. In third-party financing, the manufacturer sells the PCS to a third party that enters into a contract with a user, sharing the energy savings with the user at a predetermined percentage split. At the end of the contract term, the user has an option to purchase the system from the third party.

Direct Purchase

In 1981 there was no user direct purchase; all PCSs were sold through manufacturer or third-party financing. Then in 1983, the United States Coast Guard purchased ten systems directly from the manufacturer. In 1988 many users, such as

Ralston Purina, New York Telephone, and Holiday Inn, made direct purchases of the PCS from manufacturers. In 1988 AT&T formed a cogeneration division. The purpose of the division was to make direct purchase of the PCSs and incorporate them into the company's general operations.

COMPETITION

The packaged cogeneration system industry consists mainly of small firms, many operating on a regional basis. These firms manufacture PCSs capable of producing from 60 kw to 1,000 kw of electricity. A small business application such as a 20-room hotel requires approximately 100 kw of electricity per hour. Alterenergy, Inc. (Alterenergy) is the pioneer and leader in the industry. Tecogen is the second-largest competitor. Tecogen is a wholly owned subsidiary of Thermo Electron whose revenue in 1989 was $578 million. From September 29, 1990, to September 28, 1991, the total sales of Tecogen Inc. was within the range of $17–$18 million.

Most manufacturers offer a limited product line that is capable of producing 50 kw to 150 kw of electricity. Alterenergy is the only manufacturer that offers a product line ranging from 100 kw to 1,000 kw. All manufacturers provide application design, engineering, and turnkey services. However, Alterenergy has the best reputation and track record in interconnecting with the utility companies successfully. Incorporating the PCS operations with utilities is of the utmost importance, because PCSs replace only 80–85% of the customer's electricity needs. The remaining 15–20% must be supplied by the utility company.

Alterenergy leads the industry in terms of total kilowatts (production capacity) installed, although its product has the highest selling price among all manufacturers. Alterenergy installed a total of over 35,000 kilowatts of capacity and had interconnection experiences with more than five major utilities, such as Consolidated Edison, Southern California Edison, and San Diego Gas and Electric. In 1989 Alterenergy was the only manufacturer that had been able to interconnect with Long Island Lighting Company. No other single manufacturer in the industry was seriously challenging Alterenergy's leadership in capacity installed and expertise in interconnection engineering design. Exhibit 2.8 shows the total capacity installed, by manufacturer, from 1981 to 1988. Tecogen, on the other hand, led the industry in total number of systems sold. Exhibit 2.9 shows the total units sold, by manufacturer, from 1981 to 1988.

The difference in leadership between Alterenergy and Tecogen is largely due to their different marketing efforts. Alterenergy concentrates on the market for 100 kw and above whereas Tecogen concentrates on the market for 100 kw and below.

On the supply side of the industry, the PCS industry has its problems. Because the industry is still in its infant stage, many of the engineering designs are untested. Therefore, cost overruns caused by last-minute changes are common. In addition, a construction cost budget was as good as an educated guess. Contractors were unwilling to enter into fixed-price contracts because on-site changes due to technical problems and site conditions were driving the cost higher.

Since the inception of the PCS industry, only a few companies have been able to achieve profitable operations. Turner Construction Company sold its 51% stake

EXHIBIT 2.8	Total Capacity Installed, by Manufacturer, 1981–1988
	(Kw in thousands)

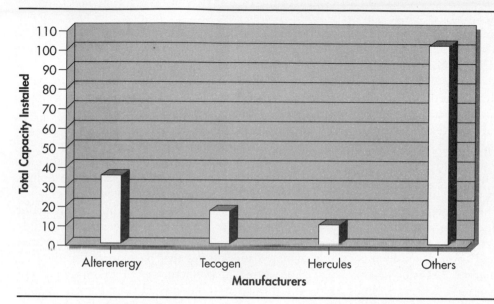

Source: Information obtained from company data.

EXHIBIT 2.9	Total Units Sold by Manufacturer, 1981–1988

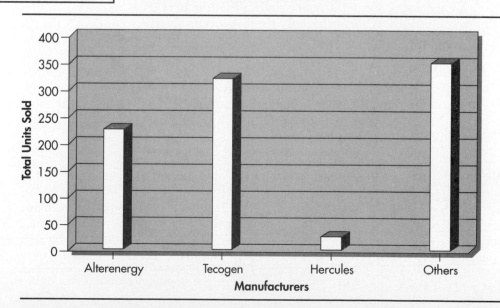

Source: Information obtained from company data.

in its cogeneration division in 1987, after losing $6 million since 1985. Hawthorne Electric Co., a major Caterpillar dealer in California, closed its cogeneration subsidiary in September 1989. Cogeneration of America, in New Jersey, laid off 85% of its 112 employees in early 1989. Alterenergy, Inc., the pioneer and leader of the industry, filed Chapter XI bankruptcy in August 1989, after losing $25 million. The problem stems from the infancy of the industry. There were not enough experienced professionals in the areas of engineering, operation, and finance.

Maintenance was another factor that caused some major "players" to withdraw. All of the systems installed were "experimental" facilities in nature, because the technology used was largely untested. Therefore, design flaws manifested themselves after the system was in operation. In addition, due to the infancy of the industry, the number of facilities was not sufficient to create a critical mass for maintenance operations, which are labor-intensive and require skilled mechanics. The engine broke down more often than anticipated, costing thousands of dollars in repairs and loss of revenue. Customer satisfaction was also dampened.

However, there were also new contenders. In 1988 a small number of major equipment manufacturers, such as Ajax Cooper Group, had formed special study groups or divisions exploring the PCS market. In addition, some public utilities had formed wholly owned nonregulated subsidiaries that participated in the PCS market in various forms, such as investing, manufacturing, or maintaining. For example, Eastern Utilities Associates formed a wholly owned subsidiary to acquire and operate PCS facilities.

On the buying side of the industry, customers' level of awareness and acceptance of the PCS had been increasing. As indicated in Exhibit 2.10, over 32,000 kw of system applications were expected to be built in various states in 1988.

Market experts' opinion on the short-term potential of the industry is mixed. ". . . the market is due for a major shake up in the next three years. [It] will be intense competition as major vendors try to maintain [market] position while the market retracts." So said an international marketing consulting firm, citing concern about stiffer air-quality standards and regulations aimed at reducing acid rain. Some professionals do not believe the PCSs can produce a long-term economic advantage because they believe the long-term operating costs will outweigh the advantages. However, other marketing consultants see a steady growth in the market. Sales will increase to $81 million in 1992 (1988 dollars) from $46 million in 1988 ("Packaged," 1989).

Almost all industry experts agreed that PCSs require many improvements to enhance their reliability and performance. In addition, the market seriously lacks professionals who have enough knowledge and experience in the engineering, legal, and finance areas (Calvin, 1989).

FOREIGN OPPORTUNITIES

Power-shortage problems are not confined to the United States. Europe and Asia have also had their share of problems, and PCSs are popular in these parts of the world.

EXHIBIT 2.10	Small Power Projects for the Top Ten States (In millions of kilowatts)

	Capacity on Line	Planned Capacity Filed with FERC[a]
California	5,218	6,498
Texas	5,178	4,023
New Jersey	250	4,404
Pennsylvania	548	3,581
Virginia	236	2,874
New York	53	3,949
Florida	213	1,643
Michigan	753	1,871
Louisiana	643	2,064
Massachusetts	170	1,690

[a] Federal Energy Regulatory Commission.

Sources: Information obtained from Hagler, Bailly Cogeneration and Small Power Generation Database, April 1, 1988; Purpalines PURPA Annual State-by-State Survey for 1988.

Europe

In Europe, the Netherlands and West Germany are the top markets for foreign PCSs. More than 100,000 kw costing $150 million are installed in West Germany each year. About 70,000 kw worth $105 million will be installed in the Netherlands over the next 10 years. According to A.A.M. Jenge, president of Nedalo BV, Uithoorn, there were more than 1,000 packaged units operating in the Netherlands in 1989.

Asia

In Asia, Japan is the forerunner in alternative energy supply. Although problems in the social system for energy supply restrict independent productions, Japan formed the Cogeneration Research Society of Japan in April 1985. The society was formed following a decision by the Ministry of International Trade and Industry supporting cogeneration ("Cogeneration," 1989). The objective was to utilize cogeneration as a means to better use the heat that was being produced and was currently being wasted. In 1989 a number of Japanese trading companies were seeking U.S. manufacturers to provide PCSs.

In addition, countries such as Taiwan and Korea have been seeking manufacturers in the United States to provide similar PCSs.

The Company

HISTORY

Alterenergy, Inc. (Alterenergy) was incorporated under the laws of the state of Delaware in 1981 for the purpose of engaging in the design, manufacture, and installation of packaged cogeneration systems. It had its first public offering shortly thereafter. In the same year, Alterenergy opened offices in Virginia, Massachusetts, California, and Hawaii. Since its inception, Alterenergy has not been able to achieve profitable operations with the exception of 1983. In 1989 the company had a net operating loss of $23 million and negative net worth of $4 million. Exhibit 2.11 shows the condensed statements of operations of Alterenergy from 1984 to 1988.

Since the introduction of its packaged cogeneration system, Alterenergy had been considered the industry leader in terms of kilowatt capacity installed. By 1989 Alterenergy had installed 228 PCSs with total capacity of over 35,000 kw.

Alterenergy's marketing effort had been concentrating on the market for 100 kw or above. "You have to understand that almost all the units Tecogen sold are 60-kw units. Of course they have a higher number of units sold. But you have to look at the kw capacity installed. That's what determines the superiority in leadership," said Mr. Richard Newton, the founder and chief executive officer of Alterenergy, Inc.

Alterenergy has a better reputation in customer satisfaction. Customers of Alterenergy include such major corporations as Ralston Purina, Coca-Cola, Holiday Inn, Ramada Inn, Johnson & Johnson, and New York Telephone and government agencies such as the U.S. Coast Guard, the Custom House, the U.S. Post Office, and the Internal Revenue Service.

EXHIBIT 2.11	Consolidated Statements of Operations: Alterenergy, Inc. (In millions of dollars, except per share data)

	1989[a]	1988	1987	1986	1985	1984
Revenue	6.1	4.3	7.6	5.5	5.0	2.4
Operating loss	(5.0)	(4.0)	(4.6)	(3.8)	(3.2)	(3.8)
Other, net	(0.9)	(0.8)	(0.6)	(0.4)	(0.1)	(0.2)
Net loss	(5.9)	(4.8)	(5.2)	(4.2)	(3.3)	(4.0)
Shares outstanding	18.2	15.2	10.3	9.6	8.6	7.3
Net loss per share	(0.32)	(0.31)	(0.51)	(0.43)	(0.39)	(0.55)
Total assets	2.8	4.6	7.1	9.0	7.4	8.2
Long-term debts	4.7	4.6	6.4	5.2	1.8	1.8

[a] Projected.

Source: Company's Form 10-Ks filed with the Securities and Exchange Commission.

In early 1989, Alterenergy entered into negotiations with AT&T, MCI, and United Airlines for potential direct purchases. These negotiations were suspended pending further development of Alterenergy's financial situation. Although AT&T proceeded to contract with Alterenergy in April 1989, it canceled the contract on August 16, the day after Alterenergy filed for Chapter XI bankruptcy protection with the United States Bankruptcy Court.

Alterenergy enjoys a better product quality reputation because it uses Caterpillar engines, considered the "Cadillac" of industrial engines. Tecogen, on the other hand, uses the Chevrolet automotive engine, which is not an industrial engine and therefore is less efficient and reliable. However, the cost of a Chevrolet engine is approximately 50% of that of a Caterpillar engine. Other manufacturers use various less desirable and less expensive nonindustrial-grade engines, such as Cumins and Hercules. Alterenergy's products, in addition, provide the highest efficiency of wasted-heat recovery.

In 1987 Alterenergy began to offer a special monitoring device that is attached to the PCSs. This specially designed high-tech device continuously monitors the system for maximum efficiency and keeps track of all performance data for further analysis. The device can also correct certain part failures through remote manual control via personal computers. The introduction of such a device was considered an important breakthrough because remote corrective measures significantly reduce cost and response time.

THE MARKETING DEPARTMENT

Alterenergy's marketing department consists of a senior vice president and two regional sales managers. The sales managers solicit contracts and coordinate and supervise the sales activities. Alterenergy also uses independent dealers on a commission basis; they are supported by the sales managers. In addition, the department is supported by two technical analysts responsible for performing feasibility studies. Most of the contracts were obtained by a small number of the dealers.

James Tucker joined Alterenergy in 1984 as senior vice president of sales after many years as director of marketing for a major computer hardware distributor. Jefferson, a regional sales manager, joined Alterenergy in 1982 and had not yet obtained a contract. "Jefferson is a very hardworking fellow. I don't think we should blame him. This company has never been serious about its dealer network," said Mr. Tucker when asked about Mr. Jefferson's inability to obtain contracts.

One of the first things James Tucker did after joining Alterenergy was to establish a dealer network. In 1985 Alterenergy had 35 independent dealers. Despite its large number of dealers, Alterenergy's sales remained sluggish. A further analysis of the backgrounds of the dealers revealed that most had been used car salesmen, used engine salesmen, shoe salesmen, and attorneys.

Alterenergy uses a category and product specification sheet as its primary sales tool. It also had a cooperative advertisement with the American Gas Association. The advertisement, which had never been updated, could be seen in a variety of professional journals. The category and product specification sheet were four years out of date.

Alterenergy offers a wide product line from 100 kw to 1,000 kw. In 1985 a prototype of 65 kw was built. The project was abandoned in the same year after the company concluded that the performance was unsatisfactory. Some engineers believed that the profit margin could be improved by using a lower-quality engine. Most of the units sold over the years are 100–450 kw. However, in the last few years, the focus of Alterenergy's sales effort has shifted toward the higher-kilowatt systems. "Closing a 100 kw and a 1,000 kw take the same amount of time and effort, but the 1,000 kw's margin is much higher," said Mr. Richard Newton.

THE MANUFACTURING AND ENGINEERING DEPARTMENT

The manufacturing and engineering department is headed by Mr. James MacDonald. MacDonald is a graduate of the Merchant Marine Academy and was a second officer of a cargo ship before joining Alterenergy as project manager in 1985. He was promoted to vice president of engineering in 1986.

The engineering department consists of one director of engineering, four project managers, one project engineer, two maintenance managers (one in New York and one in California), and ten field service mechanics (five in California and five in New York). After a contract is signed with the customer, the project engineer makes a preliminary site visit to determine the site condition. The project manager then prepares the equipment specifications and forwards them to the plant manager for production scheduling and purchasing. The director of engineering supervises the work of the project managers.

The PCS is manufactured in a factory located in Akron, Ohio. The finished system is then shipped to the project site for installation. All installation work is subcontracted to outside contractors. There is one plant manager who is responsible for production scheduling, quality control, purchasing, and shipping. In addition, there are eight full-time shop foremen and two skilled workers. No layoff has ever been made, even during slow periods.

In late 1988, Alterenergy began a new-product prototype called engine driven chiller (EDC). The EDC unit is an enhancement of the packaged cogeneration system. The development of the EDC product was a direct result of the new rebate program announced by Consolidated Edison Company and Long Island Lighting Company in 1988. The rebate program will pay any commercial electricity user for the amount of electricity it replaces by generating its own electricity during the summer peak-demand hours. The EDC unit, working as a component of the PCS, replaces the aging air conditioner. The EDC unit is powered by a gas-fired engine instead of an electrical engine and substantially reduces the electricity needed from the utility company during the summer peak hours. Therefore, it can potentially generate significant rebates.

THE FINANCIAL POSITION

Since its inception in 1981, Alterenergy has had several public offerings, raising over $10 million in financing the company's operations. By the end of 1988, the company had over 18 million shares of common stock outstanding and over 5,000 shareholders. With the exception of 1983, Alterenergy has been incurring losses.

As of the end of 1988, Alterenergy had a net operating loss of $4 million, its current liabilities exceeded its current assets by over $1 million, and it had a negative net worth of approximately $4.5 million. Alterenergy's cash flow had reached a point where over 85% of its $1.5 million accounts payable were 90 days or more past due. By May 1989, Alterenergy defaulted, for the first time, on its public debenture interest payment.

By mid-1989 Alterenergy was actively seeking a buyer for its assets. On August 15, 1989, Alterenergy filed a petition for reorganization under Chapter XI of the United States Bankruptcy Codes.

Analysis of the records shows that Alterenergy's loss is attributable largely to construction cost overruns and loss on maintenance operations. Charles Hertz believed that Alterenergy should withdraw from the maintenance business. "We have not yet reached the critical mass. Until then, we should leave this headache to someone else." Exhibit 2.12 shows the distribution of facilities that Alterenergy is maintaining.

Richard Newton, on the other hand, believed that providing full maintenance support is important in obtaining new contracts. "Customers will definitely want to know who is going to take care of their machine. These [machines] are delicate equipment; you just can't have some unknown party maintain them. Besides, if the job is not done right, it will cost us more money to correct the mistakes."

Both Newton and Hertz agreed that Alterenergy should not be in the construction business. They believed that Alterenergy should be strictly a manufacturer of PCSs. The chief financial officer, Michael Lourda, strongly disagreed. A certified public accountant and attorney, Lourda has been a top executive of major construction companies for many years. "Unless there are two separate contracts, one for equipment purchasing and one for construction with another party, we are ultimately liable for manufacturing to the point where the system is operational. Unfortunately, this will complicate the transaction and reduce the chance to obtain a contract."

Suggestions to subcontract out all work with guaranteed contract prices had also been rejected by Lourda. "Guaranteed contract means nothing. If there is a problem in cost overrun, you will find your contractor nowhere to be found. The key is to have a good cost estimate, a good set of shop drawings, and bid specifications. In addition, we have to hold the respective department accountable for cost overruns or inadequate profit margin. There is no accountability around here," he added.

Alterenergy was precluded from trading on the NASDAQ National Market System, through which the company's stock was traded in the public market, when its net worth fell below the positive $1 million requirement. The company's stock is being traded in the over-the-counter market. The price of Alterenergy's stock was approximately $0.25 per share in April of 1989. Alterenergy's stock was selling as high as $8.00 per share in 1983.

TOWARD THE FUTURE

In light of the dynamics of the industry and the company's inability to achieve profit since 1981, Alterenergy's top management is reviewing its strategic decision areas in an attempt to formulate a strategic plan for the company.

EXHIBIT 2.12	Distribution of Facilities under Maintenance Agreement, by State: Alterenergy, Inc. 1992

Location	Number of Facilities
Arizona	
Phoenix	1
California	
Anaheim	1
Hollywood	2
Los Angeles	3
San Diego	6
Santa Barbara	1
Massachusetts	
Taunton	1
New Jersey	
Freehold	1
New York	
Brooklyn	2
Jamaica	1
La Guardia	2
Riverhead	2
Staten Island	2
Yaphank	1
Yonkers	3

Source: Information obtained from company data.

The electricity industry has been changed by the enactment of the Public Utilities Regulatory Policy Act of 1978. In 1992, more than 17 billion kw of electricity were produced by cogeneration facilities installed from coast to coast. An additional 34 billion kw were planned or under construction (Toulson, 1989). The packaged cogeneration system segment of the industry was expected to step into the growth stage in the next few years.

The president of the company believed some of the best market opportunities are in new, immature markets such as the market of packaged cogeneration systems. In such markets, the competition is often not as heavy as in more mature markets, although the risk of failure is usually higher. He suggested that the company should remain the way it is: a manufacturer that provides turnkey and full maintenance support services. The advantage of this strategy is its simplicity in selling. A customer does not have to get involved in contracting with another contractor for the installation of the PCS. In addition, the customer does not have to look for another party to maintain the system. A further advantage of this strategy is that the customer is "locked in." The president believed that because the industry was immature, customer knowledge about the PCS was insufficient. Therefore, simplicity in the sales transaction is important.

Some managers did not agree with the president's view. They argued that the cost of installation was very difficult to control due to the immaturity of the industry. The majority of the installation designs were untested, so last-minute changes were frequent and costly. These managers believed that the company should not provide installation service and should concentrate on manufacturing only.

In terms of product line, Alterenergy had been concentrating on the 400 kw and above for the last few years. Some managers believed that the company should continue to focus its products in the larger units, because the profit margins were higher for the same amount of effort necessary to sell a smaller unit. In addition, the managers believed that the company should avoid direct competition with the financially stronger Tecogen. Alterenergy's products have a higher selling price than the competition's. Other managers, however, believed that the company's products are superior to its competitors' and cost less in the long run because of lower maintenance cost and better performance. Therefore, there was no reason for the company to ignore a major market.

Opinions on maintenance support were also sharply divided. The senior vice president of sales and marketing believed that full maintenance support was important because most customers were still not familiar with the operation of packaged cogeneration systems. The vice president of operation argued that there were not enough facilities to create the critical mass needed to break even. He believed the company should stay away from installation and maintenance. The company can resume offering maintenance services when the number of facilities reaches the critical mass. Other managers, however, argued that such a strategy would damage the company's good reputation in maintenance. In addition, one of the justifications of the company's higher product price is better performance and therefore lower operating cost. If the equipment is not maintained properly, the performance will be impaired, thereby negating the justification of higher price.

Alterenergy depended heavily on its dealer network to effect sales. However, some managers questioned the effectiveness of the dealer network. They argued that in some cases the sale of a packaged cogeneration system was in competition with other products that the dealer carried. For example, a dealer for an engine manufacturer may sell an engine to a customer instead of taking the opportunity to sell the PCS. This is because it is much easier and involves less work to sell an engine than a PCS. In addition, the dealers may carry competitors' products, and the company will be under great pressure to reduce the selling price or increase the commission to the dealer or both. The senior vice president of sales and marketing believed the dealer network is the only way to ensure adequate market coverage at a reasonable cost. He also argued that the dealer network is a good source of information about market movements.

REFERENCES

"Cogeneration Makes Sense for Japan's Energy Mix." *World Cogeneration,* Spring 1989, pp. 21–22.

Kostzewa, Lawrence J. "The Maturing of Packaged Cogeneration Technology." Gas Research Institute, 1988.

"New Study Sees Big Market for Packaged Cogeneration." *World Cogeneration,* Summer 1989, p. 15.

"Packaged Cogeneration Market to Double, Says Study." *CEE News,* September 1989, p. 8.

"Packaged Plants Popular in Europe." *World Cogeneration,* Spring 1989, p. 32.

Paul, Bill. "Get Set to Lose Your Cool This Summer." *Wall Street Journal,* May 18, 1989, p. B1.

Sims, Calvin. "Expertise Needed for Cogeneration." *The New York Times,* October 18, 1988, p. D1.

"Small-scale Cogeneration: Why Is Industry Holding Back?" *Engineer's Digest,* March 1987, pp. 23–24.

Toulson, Dana. "Can Independent Producers Meet Future Generation Needs?" *Strategic Planning and Energy Management,* Winter 1989, p. 46.

Wald, Matthew L. "Renewed Debate on Nuclear Power." *The New York Times,* October 23, 1989, pp. D1–D2.

Williams, James H. "Market Trend." *Packaged Cogeneration Systems Proceedings Conference,* February 14, 1989, p. 2.

CASE 3 American Airlines: Deregulation Strategies and Establishment of North/South Hubs

Hooshang Kuklan ▪ Mei-Lung Chen ▪ Youngil Cho ▪ Raphael Thompson

The Airline Deregulation Act of 1978 amended the Federal Aviation Act of 1958 and ended an era of far-reaching federal control over the operations of airlines. The law intended to encourage price competition; to eliminate restrictions on fares, routes, and frequency of flight changes; to remove several barriers to mergers and acquisitions; and to make the airline industry more competitive generally.

In late 1985, about seven years after enactment of the deregulation law, an executive of American Airlines characterized the impact of this legislation on American Airlines as follows:

> Deregulation, as anticipated, opened the industry to intense competition and made it highly cost-conscious. Only the low-cost airlines had a chance to succeed. American Airlines just could not compete with such low-cost carriers as People Express, New York Air, and Northeast. American had to get its cost down to the new marketplace levels.

> In brief, American was confronted with a number of most challenging tasks. To survive in a highly competitive deregulated environment, American had to find ways of changing its fleet and route structure, expanding its ground facilities, lowering its cost to competitive levels, and changing the nature and scope of its operations.

HISTORY AND BACKGROUND

COMPANY HISTORY

The first regularly scheduled flight of what was to become American Airlines was made on April 15, 1926, when Charles Lindbergh, chief pilot of Robertson Airline Company, flew the mail in a DH-4 airplane from St. Louis to Chicago. Robertson Company and several other small airline companies were consolidated in 1929 into Aviation Corporation. Aviation Corporation comprised Colonial Airways, the Embry-Riddle Company, Interstate Airlines Inc., Southern Air Transport, and Universal Air Lines.

Colonial Airways consisted of Colonial Transport, Colonial Western Airways, and Canadian Colonial Airways. Colonial Air Transport, organized in 1923, won the contract to carry mail over Boston–Hartford–New York and began service in

The authors wish to express their sincere appreciation to the management of American Airlines for sharing with us American's deliberations on the establishment of North/South hub(s) in the East. Our special thanks go to President Robert L. Crandall and Brad Jensen, managing director of schedules planning. This case heavily relies on the generous supply of data provided to us by American Airlines. We would also like to thank Professor Tyronza Richmond of North Carolina Central University for his support and leadership in paving the way for this case study. Reprinted with permission.

July of 1926. Passenger service was inaugurated on April 4, 1927, with what is believed to have been the first night passenger flight in the United States. Colonial Western Airways started service in December 1927, linking Albany, Syracuse, Rochester, Buffalo, and Cleveland. Canadian Colonial Airways began service in 1928 between New York and Montreal via Albany.

Embry-Riddle, based in Cincinnati, operated the first scheduled service on the Cincinnati–Indianapolis–Chicago route starting in December 1927.

Interstate Airlines flew between Atlanta and Chicago starting in November 1928.

Southern Air Transport, a strong and successful airline, resulted from the merger of Texas Air Transport and St. Tammany Gulf Coast Airways. Texas Air Transport began scheduled service at Dallas, Fort Worth, and other Texas cities in February 1928. St. Tammany began flying between Atlanta and New Orleans in January 1929.

Universal Air Lines, having originated as Continental Air Lines, started scheduled service between Cleveland and Louisville in August 1928. After acquiring a number of other airlines, in June 1929 Universal joined with the New York Central and the Atchison, Topeka and Santa Fe railroads to inaugurate the first transcontinental air–rail service.

To put together an airline system from this conglomeration, all airline subsidiaries of the Aviation Corporation were incorporated in 1930 into American Airways, Inc.

In February of 1934, the government abruptly canceled the air mail contracts, and thus ended the first chapter of commercial airline history. American Airways became American Airlines that year, and the new company emerged with a more integrated route system. American Airlines quickly made itself known through its initiative in the development of an airways traffic control system that was later adopted by all airliners and administered by the U.S. government (Exhibit 3.1).

Ranking high among the important airline industry events of the mid-1930s was the development of an airplane, the DC-2. The DC-2, though a good airplane, was not an economical passenger-carrying aircraft. American Airlines collaborated with McDonnell Douglas, and the result was a new airplane, the DC-3, destined to become one of the most famous commercial airplanes in history. American inaugurated commercial flights with the DC-3 between Chicago and New York on June 25, 1936. By the end of the decade, American was the nation's number-one domestic air carrier.

During the 1930s, American introduced a "sell and record" reservations system that gradually became antiquated. Later, in the early 1950s, American developed a new electronic reservations system, and in 1962 it took another step with installation of SABRE. This highly sophisticated airline reservations system was expanded in 1972 and again in 1975. In 1987 SABRE was the largest and most widely used computer reservations system in the industry.

Development of new commercial airplanes stopped during World War II, but with the end of the war came a series of famous airplanes to fill a greatly expanded need for air transportation. The first of 50 American DC-6s entered service in 1947. American retired its last DC-4 in 1948 and its last DC-3 in 1949. Thus, by 1949 American had become the only airline in the United States with a completely post-war fleet of pressurized passenger airplanes.

EXHIBIT 3.1 | **Early Genealogy of American Airlines**

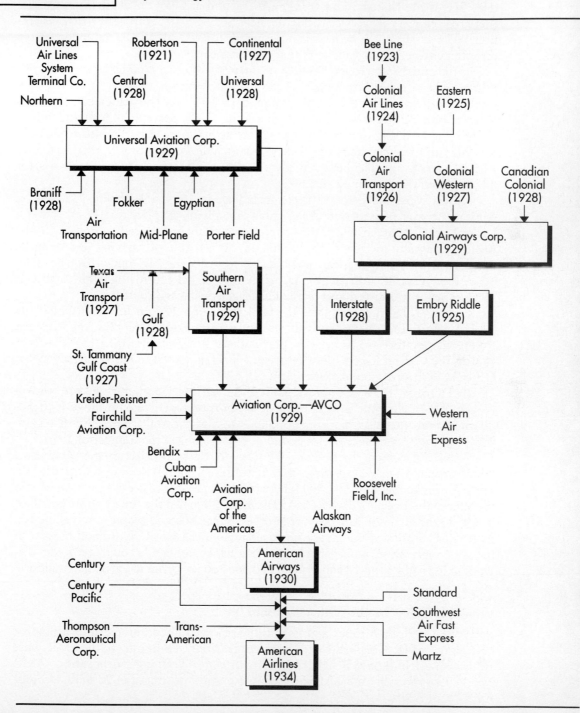

In 1953 American pioneered nonstop transcontinental service in both directions across the United States with the DC-7; and in 1959 the company began the first cross-country jet service, using the new Boeing 707s. American's first-generation 707 jets shortly became second-generation jets with the introduction of the turbofan engine, another industry first for American.

In the mid-1950s, American became the first airline to establish a special facility for flight attendant training. The installation, built on a 40-acre tract between Dallas and Fort Worth, Texas, opened in 1957 as the American Airlines Stewardess College. It was later renamed the Flight Service College and subsequently the Learning Center. The size of the facility more than doubled from 1957 to 1987, and training activities widened to include instruction of other American Airlines personnel. The center is also made available to outside companies for meetings and other business functions.

As jets were added to the fleet—including, in 1964, the Boeing 727—piston equipment was phased out. American's last piston airplane, a DC-6, flew on December 17, 1966, at which time American already had placed an order with the Boeing Company for the 747, a wide-body jet capable of carrying 360 or more passengers. In 1968 American was the first to order the McDonnell Douglas DC-10, a big, versatile, quiet trijet that made its first scheduled flight on August 5, 1971, when it was introduced on the Los Angeles–Chicago route.

In 1977 American completed the final phase of a 1975 plan to consolidate its 11 U.S. mainland reservations offices into four regional centers: the Western Reservations Office at Los Angeles, the Southern Reservations Office at Dallas/Fort Worth, the Central Reservations Office at Cincinnati, and the Eastern Reservations Office in Hartford, Connecticut.

In October 1978, Congress passed the Airline Deregulation Act, and in November of the same year, American announced that it would move its headquarters from the New York metropolitan area to the Dallas/Fort Worth region. The relocation took place over a period of two months in the summer of 1979.

American retired the Boeing 707 from its fleet in 1981. In the same year, "AAdvantage," a marketing program to reward frequent travelers, was introduced. In 1982 American welcomed its 500 millionth passenger, began service to London, and introduced the Boeing 767 to its fleet. The Super 80 joined the American Airlines fleet in 1983, and in 1984 American ordered 67 Super 80s and placed options on 100 more; this constituted the largest single aircraft purchase in U.S. aviation history. In the same year, American began the American Eagle program, a commuter feeder network at its major airports, and inaugurated nonstop jet service to Paris and Frankfurt.

ORGANIZATIONAL STRUCTURE AND WORKFORCE

In 1982 American Airlines and its subsidiaries were incorporated into a holding company, AMR Corporation. The organizational components of AMR were American Airlines, Sky Chefs, American Airlines Training Corporation, AMR Energy Corporation, and AMR Services Corporations. American Airlines accounts for 95% of AMR.

By early 1986 American was organized on a functional basis consisting of nine functional departments: Airline Planning, Marketing, Operations, Government Affairs, Finance, Legal, Information Systems, Employee Relations, and Personnel Resources. The first seven departments were headed by senior vice presidents and the last two by vice presidents (Exhibit 3.2). In January 1986, the upper organizational echelon of American included 50 senior executives: the chairman and president, 9 senior vice presidents, 17 vice presidents, 6 assistant vice presidents, and 14 directors.

By the end of 1985, the 44,000 workforce of American Airlines consisted of 6,421 (15%) management/specialists, 5,072 (12%) pilot/flight engineers, 8,392 (19%) flight attendants, 12,159 (28%) ground-service personnel, 10,608 (24%) agent/clerical staff, and 808 (2%) persons working in various other jobs. Labor unions represented about 62% of American's employees. Exhibit 3.3 lists unions representing different categories of American employees and their membership as of the end of 1985.

OPERATIONS

In terms of scheduled services, in 1985 American had over 463,000 departures with a daily average of 1,271. This represented an increase of 17.5% over the performance in 1984. During 1985 over 41 million passengers boarded American flights. The daily average was about 113,000 passengers. Those numbers for 1984 were 34 million and 93,000 passengers, respectively. The available seat miles (total seats available multiplied by miles flown) rose by 60% from 1979 to 1985. The increase was 11.9% in 1984 and 16.5% in 1985. The passenger load factor (percentage of seats filled) went up in 1981, 1982, 1983, and 1985, but it dropped in 1980 and 1984. The load factor jumped from 62.6% in 1984 to 64.6% in 1985 (Exhibit 3.4).

The ton-mile load factor experienced a somewhat similar change during the period. In 1984, the break-even ton-mile load factor, an indication of the firm's profitability, was 6.5 points lower than in 1979. The difference between ton-mile load factor and break-even ton-mile load factor—a measure of operating cost efficiency—was positive in 1983 and 1984. It was 3.9 points and 4.3 points for 1983 and 1984, respectively (Exhibit 3.4). Further, total commissions paid to travel agents, as a measure of the carrier's passenger revenues, increased consistently during the period, from 6% in 1981 to about 9% in 1985 (Exhibit 3.5).

From its inception through December of 1985, a total of 623 million scheduled and charter passengers were boarded by American Airlines and its predecessor companies. From the start of scheduled jet service on January 25, 1959, through December 1985, American cumulatively had a total of over 18 million scheduled passenger departures and arrivals.

In January 1986, American served 99 points on the U.S. mainland and 31 points outside the U.S. mainland (in Alaska, the Caribbean, Canada, Europe, Mexico, and the Pacific). In total, American flew to 117 cities and 130 airports. Furthermore, through American Eagle—American's franchise partners to provide

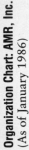

EXHIBIT 3.2   **Organization Chart: AMR, Inc.**
(As of January 1986)

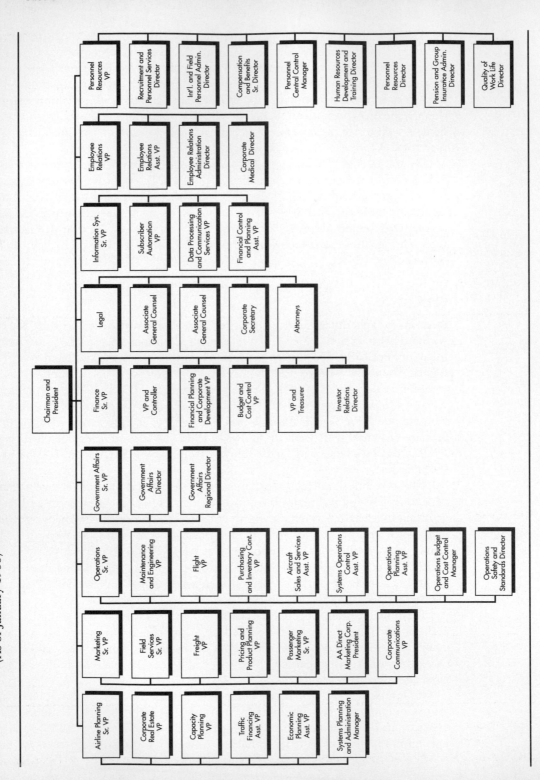

Chairman and President

Personnel Resources VP
- Recruitment and Personnel Services Director
- Int'l. and Field Personnel Admin. Director
- Compensation and Benefits Sr. Director
- Personnel Central Control Manager
- Human Resources Development and Training Director
- Personnel Resources Director
- Pension and Group Insurance Admin. Director
- Quality of Work Life Director

Employee Relations VP
- Employee Relations Asst. VP
- Employee Relations Administration Director
- Corporate Medical Director

Information Sys. Sr. VP
- Subscriber Automation VP
- Data Processing and Communication Services VP
- Financial Control and Planning Asst. VP

Legal
- Associate General Counsel
- Associate General Counsel
- Corporate Secretary
- Attorneys

Finance Sr. VP
- VP and Controller
- Financial Planning and Corporate Development VP
- Budget and Cost Control VP
- VP and Treasurer
- Investor Relations Director

Government Affairs Sr. VP
- Government Affairs Director
- Government Affairs Regional Director

Operations Sr. VP
- Maintenance and Engineering VP
- Flight VP
- Purchasing and Inventory Cont. VP
- Aircraft Sales and Services Asst. VP
- Systems Operations Control Asst. VP
- Operations Planning Asst. VP
- Operations Budget and Cost Control Manager
- Operations Safety and Standards Director

Marketing Sr. VP
- Field Services Sr. VP
- Freight VP
- Pricing and Product Planning VP
- Passenger Marketing Sr. VP
- AA Direct Marketing Corp. President
- Corporate Communications VP

Airline Planning Sr. VP
- Corporate Real Estate VP
- Capacity Planning VP
- Traffic Financing Asst. VP
- Economic Planning Asst. VP
- Systems Planning and Administration Manager

| EXHIBIT 3.3 | American Employees Represented by Labor Unions |

Union	Categories	Number of Employees
Transport Workers Unions (AFL/CIO)	Maintenance	12,655
	Stores	487
	Flight/Ground instructors	157
	Dispatchers and assistants	86
	Simulator technicians	57
	Meteorologists	12
	Guards	12
Allied Pilots Association	Pilots	4,808
Flight Engineers International Association (AFL/CIO)	Flight engineers	299
Association of Professional Flight Attendants	Flight attendants	8,418

| EXHIBIT 3.4 | Operating Statistics, 1979–1985 |

	1979	1980	1981	1982	1983	1984	1985
Seat miles flown* (in millions)	43,109	40,672	41,756	44,605	48,203	58,667	68,336
Passenger load factor	67.4	60.4	61.4	63.5	65.0	62.6	66.8
Ton-mile load factor	56.6	51.4	53.3	54.3	56.0	53.7	NA
Break-even ton-mile load factor	55.9	53.7	52.0	54.7	52.1	49.4	NA
Domestic load factor:							
American Airlines			61.4	63.9	64.5	62.0	64.2
Industry	NA	NA	57.8	58.3	59.9	56.9	60.9
Commissions paid to travel agents (as a percentage of passenger revenue)	NA	NA	6.5	7.2	7.8	8.2	8.6

*Scheduled service.
NA: Not available

Source: Aerospace and Air Transport, Industry Surveys, January 9, 1986; American Airlines, Inc., *1985 Annual Report.*

| EXHIBIT 3.5 | Commissions Paid to Travel Agents |

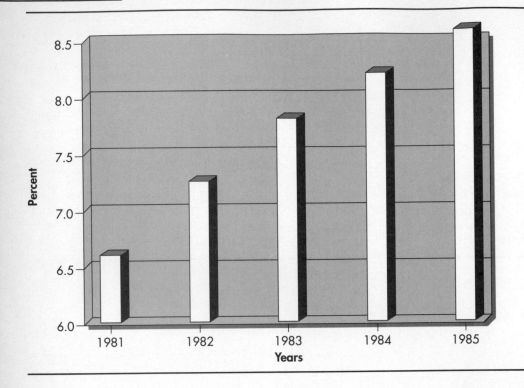

feeder traffic at major airports—American served 20 additional cities in Texas, Virginia, North Carolina, Arkansas, Louisiana, Oklahoma, and Missouri.

During the 12 months ending September 1985, American's top 10 markets ranked by revenue passenger miles were Los Angeles–New York, Dallas/Fort Worth–Hawaii, Dallas/Fort Worth–New York City, Chicago–Greater San Francisco, Dallas/Fort Worth–Greater San Francisco, Los Angeles–Hawaii, New York–San Juan, and Chicago–New York City.

International Services

American was primarily a domestic airline during the 1930s. Then it began service to Toronto in 1941 and to Mexico in 1942. For a period of about five years— 1945 to 1950—American operated a transatlantic division, American Overseas Airlines, which served a number of European countries. That division was sold to Pan American World Airways in September 1950.

American became an international airline again in August 1970, when flights were started from the U.S. mainland to Hawaii, American Samoa, the Fiji Islands, New Zealand, and Australia. Service to all those points except Hawaii was suspended in March 1974 because of government-imposed route restrictions and limited profitability. In June 1975, American conducted a route exchange agreement with

Pan American World Airways, under which American traded its Pacific routes (except Boston/St. Louis–Honolulu) for Pan Am's U.S.–Bermuda, New York–Santo Domingo, and New York–Barbados authority. In March 1978, American suspended its nonstop flight between Boston/St. Louis and Honolulu. However, nonstop flights between Los Angeles and Honolulu and between Dallas/Fort Worth and Honolulu were inaugurated in December 1980 and June 1981, respectively. Dallas/Fort Worth–Maui and Chicago–Honolulu nonstop service began in December 1984 and May 1985, respectively.

American started service to Montreal, Jamaica, Guadeloupe, and Martinique in 1976 and 1977. And in early 1979, service on 19 new domestic and international routes was launched, including St. Maarten in the Caribbean and Nassau in the Bahamas. Joining the system later in the year were Guadalajara and Puerto Vallarta, Mexico.

In May 1982, American returned to the European market. It introduced service to London's Gatwick Airport with five 747 flights a week, increasing this service to daily frequency in June of the same year. European service was expanded in the spring of 1985 to include nonstop service between Dallas/Fort Worth–Frankfurt and Chicago–Frankfurt.

Freight Services

In 1944 American introduced the first domestic scheduled U.S. freight service with two DC-3s. As the business grew, DC-4, DC-6A, and DC-7 freighters were put into service in the 1940s and 1950s.

By 1964 American was operating Boeing 707 jet freighters, each capable of carrying 90,000 pounds of freight over a range of 3,000 miles. On November 5, 1974, American put into service the first 747 freighter on domestic routes. The airplane, capable of carrying 221,000 pounds of cargo, was introduced in New York, Chicago, Los Angeles, San Francisco, and Dallas/Fort Worth. By the summer of 1981, American was operating six 747 freighters, and the 707 freighters had been retired. American retired its freighter fleet in the fall of 1984.

The Fleet

As of the end of December 1985, American's fleet consisted of 39 Boeing 727-100, 125 Boeing 727-200, 56 McDonnell Douglas Super 80, 46 McDonnell Douglas DC-10, 10 McDonnell Douglas DC-10-30, and 13 Boeing 767. By January 1986, American had 79 aircraft on order (5 Boeing 767-ER, 10 Boeing 767, and 64 Super 80) to become available for service between 1986 and 1988. Exhibit 3.6 shows American's fleet mix by the end of 1986 and the seat configuration in each aircraft.

THE FINANCIAL OUTLOOK

The airline industry experienced back-to-back recessions during 1981–1982. American Airlines' financial performance slid in 1980–1982 but improved consistently from 1983 to 1985. The years 1983–1985 were American's best years since deregulation.

EXHIBIT 3.6	Aircraft Fleet Mix at Year End

	Fleet Count		Seat Configuration			
	1985	1986	First Class	Business Class	Coach/ Economy	Total
Boeing 727-100	36	36	10		105	115
	3	3	10		108	118
Boeing 727-200	125	125	12		138	150
McDonnell Douglas Super 80	56	56	12		130	142
McDonnell Douglas DC-10	2	2	16		297	313
	5	5	16		293	309
	8	8	34		256	290
	31	31	34		234	268
McDonnell Douglas DC-10-30	2	2	16		297	313
	2	2	16		288	304
	6	6	25	36	180	241
Boeing 767	13	13	24		180	204
	2	7	24		180	204
Total	291	296				

Aircraft on Order (as of 12/1/86)		
Aircraft	Number	Available for Service
Boeing 767	10	No later than 1989
Super 80	64	No later than 1988
Boeing 767-ER	5	No later than 1988

From 1979 to 1985, total operating revenues rose by over 80% but total operating expenses increased by under 68%. The operating income increased about 17 times, net earnings rising by 29%. During the same post-regulation years, American's current assets and its total assets more than doubled. Despite an $8 billion capital spending commitment for the period 1985–1991, the airline's operating earnings and net earnings rose by 74% and 52%, respectively, from 1983 to 1985 (Exhibits 3.7, 3.8, and 3.9).

EXHIBIT 3.7

Consolidated Statement of Operations, 1979–1985: American Airlines
(Dollar amounts in thousands, except per-share amounts)

Years Ended	1985	1984	1983	1982	1981	1980	1979	Increase/(Decrease) from 1979 to 1985 (%)
Revenues								
Passenger	$4,985,565	$4,335,779	$3,885,347	$3,414,222	$3,377,016	$3,154,426	$2,752,981	80
Other	1,145,463	1,017,492	877,960	762,752	731,752	666,552	602,310	90
Total operating revenues	6,131,028	5,353,721	4,763,307	4,176,974	4,108,699	3,820,978	3,355,291	83
Expenses								
Wages, salaries, and benefits	2,115,027	1,892,088	1,726,989	1,583,645	1,512,518	1,453,536	1,325,940	60
Aircraft fuel	1,141,848	1,091,799	1,038,556	1,070,236	1,115,733	1,114,812	801,506	42
Other operating expenses	2,337,520	2,001,306	1,716,280	1,513,956	1,408,231	1,388,885	1,197,434	95
Total operating expenses	5,594,395	4,985,193	4,481,825	4,167,837	4,036,482	3,907,233	3,324,880	68
Operating income	536,633	368,528	281,482	9,137	72,217	(86,255)	30,411	16.65
Other income (expense)								
Interest income	131,898	134,678	77,012	65,857	63,361	52,507	62,043	126
Interest expense	(152,888)	(153,006)	(152,010)	(148,491)	(136,115)	(91,434)	(82,040)	86
Interest capitalized	19,726	19,964	11,254	16,160	13,877	9,145	7,670	157
Miscellaneous—net	(16,323)	29,426	81,345	27,380	23,731	(50,041)	28,445	(157)
	(17,587)	31,062	17,601	(39,094)	(35,146)	(79,823)	16,118	(210)
Earnings before income taxes	519,046	399,590	299,083	(29,957)	37,071	(166,078)	46,529	1015
Provision for income taxes	173,206	165,710	71,216	(10,344)	20,231	(14,418)	(29,450)	688
Earnings (loss) from extraordinary items)						75,868	11,466	
Net earnings	345,840	233,880	227,867	(19,613)	16,840	(75,792)	87,455	295
Preferred dividend requirements	9,052	21,789	21,356	12,033	12,033	12,033	12,033	(25)
Earnings applicable to common share shares	$ 336,788	$ 212,091	$ 206,511	$ (31,646)	$ 35,407	$ (87,825)	$ 75,412	347
Earnings per common share primary	$ 5.94	$ 4.37	$ 4.79	$ (1.00)	$ .16	$ (3.06)	$ 2.63	126
Fully diluted	$ 5.88	$ 4.16	$ 4.48	$ (1.00)	$ .26	$ 0	$ 2.54	131

EXHIBIT 3.8　Selected Consolidated Financial Data: American Airlines
(Dollar amounts in thousands, except per-share amounts)

	1985	1984	1983	1982	1981	1980	1979	Increase/(Decrease) from 1979 to 1985 (%)
Total operating revenues	$6,131,028	$5,353,721	$4,763,307	$4,176,974	$4,108,699	$3,820,978	$3,355,291	83
Total operating expenses	5,594,395	4,985,193	4,481,825	4,167,837	4,036,482	3,907,233	3,324,880	68
Operating income	536,633	368,528	281,482	9,137	72,217	(86,255)	30,411	1,665
Earnings (loss) before extraordinary item	345,840	233,880	227,867	(19,613)	16,840	(151,660)	75,979	355
Net earnings (loss)	345,840	233,880	227,867	(19,613)	47,440	(75,792)	87,445	295
Earnings (loss) before extraordinary item per common share								
Primary	5.94	4.37	4.79	(1.00)	.16	(5.70)	2.23	166
Fully diluted	5.88	4.16	4.48	(1.00)	.26	(5.70)	2.18	169
Net earnings (loss) per common share								
Primary	5.94	4.37	4.79	(1.00)	1.21	(3.06)	2.63	126
Fully diluted	5.88	4.16	4.48	(1.00)	1.16	(3.06)	2.54	131
Total assets	6,421,101	5,260,896	4,728,165	3,896,813	3,738,221	3,277,883	3,186,897	101
Long-term debt	920,542	774,821	726,580	751,798	717,873	669,386	680,019	35
Obligations under capital leases	910,183	766,585	784,961	764,811	798,553	601,727	509,590	77
Redeemable preferred stock	88,621	126,753	105,399	110,600	109,505	108,410	107,314	(17.4)
Convertible preferred stock	—	125,000	125,000	—	—	—	—	
Common stock and other stockholders' equity	2,180,914	1,513,407	1,299,627	836,155	731,199	695,064	785,746	177
Common shares outstanding at year-end	58,681	48,453	48,374	37,241	28,766	28,698	28,696	104
Book value per common share	$ 37.00	$ 30.98	$ 26.59	$ 22.07	$ 24.88	$ 23.64	$ 26.77	38
Preferred shares outstanding at year-end								
Redeemable preferred stock	2,971	4,602	4,749	5,000	5,000	5,000	5,000	
Convertible preferred stock	—	5,000	5,000	—	—	—	—	

EXHIBIT 3.9 — Consolidated Balance Sheet: American Airlines
(Dollar amounts in thousands)

	1985	1984	1983	1982	1981	1980	1979	Increase/(Decrease) from 1979 to 1985 (%)
Assets								
Current assets								
Cash and short-term investments	$1,357,016	$1,353,683	$1,070,042	$465,862	$459,884	$292,418	$455,374	198
Receivables, less allowances for uncollectible accounts	631,600	587,341	556,637	514,134	532,028	530,549	493,571	28
Inventories, less allowances for obsolescence	224,600	197,521	192,605	193,634	186,065	185,081	146,404	53
Other current assets	57,557	42,010	46,180	40,802	33,540	41,623	10,880	429
Total current assets	2,270,773	2,180,555	1,865,464	1,214,432	1,211,517	1,049,671	1,106,229	105
Equipment and property								
Flight equipment, at cost	3,190,404	2,411,932	2,411,737	2,157,106	1,879,668	1,686,847	1,967,776	62
Less accumulated depreciation	1,143,134	970,228	945,522	885,607	785,328	687,622	953,072	20
	2,047,270	1,441,704	1,466,215	1,271,499	1,094,340	999,225	1,014,704	102
Purchase deposits for flight equipment	141,279	133,148	73,382	89,993	103,946	102,829	111,179	27
	2,188,549	1,574,852	1,539,597	1,361,492	1,198,286	1,102,054	1,125,883	94
Other equipment and property at cost	1,407,752	1,196,052	1,049,753	953,777	861,638	775,326	671,819	110
Less accumulated depreciation and depletion	666,989	611,912	558,037	501,665	426,265	365,533	305,968	118
	740,763	584,140	491,716	452,112	435,373	409,793	365,851	105
	2,929,312	2,158,992	2,031,313	1,813,604	1,633,659	1,511,847	1,491,734	96
Equipment and property under capital leases								
Flight equipment	934,760	813,171	885,543	852,439	858,320	642,284	656,803	42
Other equipment and property	193,932	204,910	208,505	203,828	181,606	171,269	163,194	19
	1,128,692	1,018,081	1,094,048	1,056,267	1,039,926	813,553	819,997	38
Less accumulated amortization	409,271	363,443	439,554	382,470	335,053	290,622	370,490	10
	719,421	654,638	654,494	673,797	704,873	522,931	449,507	60
Other assets								
Route acquisition cost—net	36,054	37,146	38,238	39,330	40,423	41,515	42,608	(15)
Other	465,541	229,565	138,656	155,650	147,749	151,919	96,819	381
	501,595	266,711	176,894	194,980	188,172	193,434	139,427	260
Total assets	$6,421,101	$5,260,896	$4,728,165	$3,896,813	$3,738,221	$3,277,883	$3,186,897	101

EXHIBIT 3.9 **Consolidated Balance Sheet: American Airlines (continued)**
(Dollar amounts in thousands)

Liabilities, Redeemable Preferred Stock, Convertible Preferred Stock, Common Stock and Other Stockholders' Equity

	1985	1984	1983	1982	1981	1980	1979	Increase/(Decrease) from 1979 to 1985 (%)
Current liabilities								
Accounts payable	$ 516,307	$ 476,769	$ 494,697	$ 420,000	$ 404,354	$ 357,857	$ 313,558	65
Accrued salaries and wages	269,516	226,943	186,845	172,304	167,150	149,624	150,879	79
Other accrued liabilities	421,680	358,077	275,253	245,256	260,880	157,256	142,166	197
Air traffic liability and customers' deposits	452,207	382,420	368,665	305,332	280,296	300,522	260,531	74
Current maturities of long-term debt	99,666	66,823	64,215	48,921	55,105	50,824	57,696	73
Current obligations under capital leases	43,565	41,814	48,262	51,377	53,469	42,439	41,592	5
Total current liabilities	1,802,941	1,552,846	1,437,937	1,243,190	1,221,254	1,058,522	966,422	87
Long-term debt, less current maturities	920,542	774,821	726,580	751,798	717,873	669,386	680,019	35
Obligations under capital leases, less current obligations	910,183	766,585	784,961	764,811	798,553	601,727	509,590	77
Other liabilities								
Deferred federal income tax	299,718	241,384	131,330	81,374	99,469	112,322	118,239	153
Other liabilities and deferred credit	218,182	160,100	117,331	108,885	60,368	32,452	19,567	1,015
	517,900	401,484	248,661	190,259	159,837	144,774	137,806	276
Redeemable preferred stock	88,621	126,753	105,399	110,600	109,505	108,410	107,314	(17)
Convertible preferred stock, common stock and other stockholders' equity								
Convertible preferred stock		125,000	125,000					
Common stock	58,681	48,453	48,374	37,241	28,766	28,698	28,696	104
Additional paid-in capital	1,030,123	709,632	708,022	461,309	333,182	332,522	332,511	210
Retained earnings	1,092,110	755,322	543,231	337,605	369,251	333,844	424,539	157
	2,180,914	1,638,407	1,424,627	836,155	731,199	695,064	785,746	178
Total liabilities and stockholders' equity	$6,421,101	$5,260,896	$4,728,165	$3,896,813	$3,738,221	$3,277,883	$3,186,897	101

Within the same time frame, American's current ratio and acid-test ratio improved slightly, while its fixed asset turnover and debt to total assets experienced a modest drop. Return on total assets doubled. Return on net worth rose from 9.8% to 15%. The profit margin on sales more than doubled from 1979 to 1985 (Exhibit 3.10).

Over the three-year period from 1983 to 1985, AMR Corporation experienced a significant profit growth. The operating revenue rose by 12.4% in 1984, primarily due to higher passenger revenues. The operating revenue for 1985 increased 14.5% to $6,131 million. During 1984 and 1985, operating income rose by $87 million (30.9%) and $168 million (45.6%), and net earnings advanced by $6 million (2.6%) and $111 million (47.9%), respectively. The 1985 operating margin was 8.8%—up from 1984's level of 6.9%. The revenue passenger miles (one passenger flown one mile) saw an increase of 20.3% in 1985. Revenue ton miles (one ton of cargo or mail transported one mile) also went up by over 10% in 1985. Despite strong traffic growth, the revenue yield per passenger mile (the average amount received per passenger mile) decreased by 4.3% in 1985. The decrease in yield was caused primarily by substantial fare discounting in the industry during this period.

Labor costs rose by only 1.5% in 1984, the lowest increase in more than 15 years and slightly below the U.S. industry average. Fuel costs, which typically account for about 25% of each revenue dollar, experienced a steady decline due to American's fuel management programs and the worldwide drop in oil prices.

Exhibit 3.11 provides a comparison of 12 major carriers' operating statistics for 1984 and 1985.

DISTINCTIONS

In November 1975, the Flight Safety Foundation presented a special Distinguished Performance Award to American in recognition of the 6 million hours of safe flying the airline had compiled over a 10-year period. It was the greatest total of safe flying hours ever amassed by an airline in the history of aviation.

EXHIBIT 3.10	Financial Analysis Ratios: American Airlines						
Ratio	1985	1984	1983	1982	1981	1980	1979
Current ratio	1.26%	1.40%	1.30%	.98%	.99%	.99%	1.14%
Acid-test ratio	1.13	1.28	1.16	.82	.84	.82	.99
Fixed asset turnover	1.48	1.74	1.66	1.56	1.63	1.71	1.61
Profit margin on sales	5.6	4.4	4.8	(.5)	.4	(2.0)	2.6
Returns on total assets	5.4	4.4	4.8	(.5)	.5	(2.3)	2.7
Returns on net worth	15.0	12.0	14.0	(2.1)	2.0	9.4	9.8
Debt to total assets	28.1	29.5	30.4	31.9	32.7	32.2	30.3

EXHIBIT 3.11	**Comparative Operating Results of Twelve Major Carriers**
	(Dollar amounts in thousands)

	Revenues			Operating Expenses		
Carrier	1984	1985	%Chg	1984	1985	%Chg
American[2]	5,067,382	5,859,334	+15.2	4,748,317	5,352,850	+12.7
Continental	1,185,378	1,704,773	+43.8	1,077,278	1,548,110	+43.7
Delta	4,458,837	4,690,194	+5.2	4,167,325	4,454,979	+6.9
Eastern	4,383,898	4,815,070	+10.3	4,174,267	4,593,454	+10.0
NWA	2,444,974	2,655,491	+8.6	2,348,698	2,578,404	+9.0
Pan Am[2]	3,304,218	3,090,324	−6.5	3,411,594	3,287,950	−3.6
Piedmont[1]	1,282,879	1,527,231	+19.0	1,143,599	1,407,003	+23.0
Republic	1,547,232	1,734,397	+12.1	1,447,230	1,568,067	+8.3
TWA	3,525,070	3,725,418	+5.8	3,447,939	3,787,827	+9.9
UAL[2]	6,218,720	5,291,609	−14.9	5,654,590	5,534,265	−2.1
USAir	1,629,696	1,749,126	+7.3	1,436,972	1,582,204	+10.1
Western	1,181,900	1,306,500	+10.5	1,170,500	1,230,000	+5.1
Total	36,230,184	38,149,467	+5.3	34,228,309	36,925,113	+7.9

[1]Systems operations: includes nonairline subsidiaries.
[2]Airline operations only.
[3]Corporate totals.
[4]Before extraord. items. NM-Not meaningful. d-deficit

Source: Company reports.

In 1982 American earned the distinction of being selected number one for domestic service in an International Airline Passengers Association survey for the fourth time. More than 14,000 of IAPA's members took part in the survey. American has finished first in every poll ever taken by the association.

In January 1982, American was named "Airline of the Year" for 1981 by *Air Transport World* magazine. In February the *Wall Street Transcript* announced that its annual gold award for outstanding airline industry management had been awarded to the American Airlines team of Chairman Casey and President Crandall. *Financial World* magazine in March named Casey the top airline management executive of the year.

DEREGULATION STRATEGIES

American Airlines responded to the deregulation of 1978 with four major strategies in order to improve its competitive posture:

1. Improve the aircraft mix and increase the seating density of the fleet.
2. Minimize labor costs.

Operating Income			Net Income[4]		Rev. Passenger Miles		Passenger Load Factor (%)	
1984	1985	%Chg	1984	1985	1984	1985	1984	1985
339,065	506,484	+49.4	233,880[3]	345,840[3]	36,702	44,138	62.6	64.8
108,100	156,663	+44.9	50,270	60,884	10,923	18,405	62.7	64.8
291,512	235,215	−19.3	258,641	156,775	27,040	30,071	52.9	58.5
189,631	221,616	+16.9	d37,927	5,875	29,409	33,140	58.9	60.3
96,276	77,087	−19.9	86,857	73,119	20,127	22,912	60.9	60.7
d107,376	d197,626	NM	d206,836[3]	48,750[3]	28,406	27,332	64.4	63.0
139,280	120,228	−13.7	58,175	66,712	6,352	8,307	52.4	65.7
100,002	186,330	+68.3	13,709	69,231	8,594	10,737	60.2	68.8
77,131	d62,409	NM	29,885	d208,433	28,304	32,052	62.2	65.2
564,130	d242,656	NM	235,857[3]	d88,223[3]	46,687	41,640	60.4	63.0
192,724	166,922	−13.4	118,331	109,850	8,191	9,732	58.1	59.2
11,400	78,500	+571.1	d29,200	35,400	9,412	10,441	57.7	59.8
2,001,875	1,224,354	−38.8	811,652	675,780	260,147	288,907	59.3	61.7

3. Maximize revenues by expanding the use of American's computer reservations system, developing new frequent-flyer programs, establishing a system of feeder service to American's major cities, and initiating structural readjustments.
4. Restructure and strengthen the route system.

IMPROVING FLEET MIX AND INCREASING SEATING DENSITY

Improvement in the Fleet Mix

In 1978 fuel accounted for about 30% of American's total operating expenses. One of the biggest tasks confronting American at the time was to ground the inefficient portion of its fleet. Twenty-six of the 707s, a fuel-inefficient aircraft, were removed from service in January 1981, and the remaining 36 aircraft (including nine 707 freighters) were retired by summer of the same year.

In anticipation of the retirement of 707s, American placed an order in November of 1978 to buy 30 transcontinental twin-engine 767s. The 767 accommodates 200 passengers in a mixed first-class and coach arrangement. It performs the same mission as the 707 but does so while providing greater comfort and achieving greater fuel efficiency. The airplane carries up to 1,000 pounds of baggage and cargo. In November 1982, American introduced into service the first of 30 Boeing 767 jetliners.

In 1983 American further expanded its fleet with the acquisition of 20 Super 80 aircraft from McDonnell Douglas. Later, 13 more Super 80s were acquired. On February 29, 1984, American announced the largest airplane buy in commercial aviation history up to that point, when it placed an order for 67 Super 80s and acquired options to purchase an additional 100 planes.

From 1978 to 1985, the percent of American's fleet that was fuel-efficient increased from 15% to 44%, and the percent of seats in the fuel-efficient fleet jumped from 29% to 53% during the same 7-year period following deregulation. The fuel-efficient portion of American's fleet and that of its seat capacity are expected to increase to 64% and 69%, respectively, by 1991.

The restructuring of the fleet mix resulted in a drop in fuel cost from about 30% of the airline's total operating expenses in 1978 to 21.3% by the end of 1985, a reduction of about 9%. This reduction occurred despite an increase of over 20% in the fleet size from 1978 to 1985. American's aircraft fuel statistics for the period from 1981 to 1985 are given in Exhibit 3.12.

Increase in Seating Density

From 1978 to 1985, American undertook measures to increase seating density in DC10 and B727 aircraft through the use of slimline seats, compact galleys, and centerline bins. During this period the number of seats in DC10-10 aircraft was increased from 264 to 290 (an improvement of 9.8%). The increase in B727-100 aircraft was from 100 to 118 seats, and in B727-200 aircraft the number of seats was raised from 127 to 150, an increase of 18% in both cases.

EXHIBIT 3.12	Aircraft Fuel Statistics: American Airlines				
	1981	1982	1983	1984	1985
Gallons consumed	1,087,364,643	1,106,763,564	1,169,938,000	1,277,845,000	1,411,146,045
January–December price/gallon spread	95.77¢–$1.031	$1.03–95.08¢	96.24¢–86.79¢	86.80¢–84.39¢	83.70¢–82.39¢
Average price/gallon	$1.026	96.70¢	88.77¢	85.44¢	80.96¢
Total fuel cost	$1,115,733,000	$1,070,236,000	$1,038,556,000	$1,092,614,000	$1,141,289,000
Percent of total operating expenses	28.8%	26.8%	24.2%	23.0%	21.3%

PROGRAMS TO MINIMIZE LABOR COSTS

Deregulation required implementation of various cost-reduction programs. The deregulation-generated competition made the industry significantly more cost-conscious than before. An American Airlines executive characterized the situation as follows:

> After the deregulation, American Airlines just couldn't compete with the low-cost carriers. We had to get our cost down to the new marketplace levels. The cost differential was quite significant. The cost structure at some airlines was up to 35 percent lower than ours. Regarding the labor cost, there were two ways to go about getting the cost down. One way was to cut down the pay of existing employees which, we all agree, is a very painful and hard thing to do. Continental did it successfully. They filed for bankruptcy and took the position that they could not survive with their existing contractual obligations including their labor contracts. They arbitrarily proposed their own new conditions and pay scale. The Continental situation could never happen again the same way it happened for Continental. The strategy that the senior officers of American adopted was to seek a negotiated solution to the problem. American could not unilaterally lower wages and risk a strike. A strike could not achieve our goal. American negotiated with the unions to protect current employees at their existing salaries, but hire new employees at market rates. We succeeded in convincing our labor unions that this was the only way we could survive in the deregulated environment.

The collective bargaining agreement signed by American and by the Transport Workers Union and the pilot and flight attendant unions in 1983 was the first airline agreement to include the so-called "two tier," "new hire," or "market-rate" wage scale. Under this system historical rates of pay for existing employees were preserved, but new employees could be hired at market rates. In return for the unions agreeing to the two-tier scheme, American promised to grow internally rather than through mergers and acquisitions. Labor costs rose by only 1.5% in 1984 (the lowest increase in more than 15 years), the first full year that American had the benefit of the new system. In September of 1985, the Transport Workers Union agreed to a continuation of the market-rate scales approved in 1983.

An important statistical measure of airline employee productivity is the number of available seat miles produced per employee. According to this measure, the productivity of American's personnel has consistently increased since 1981; a 7% increase was recorded in 1985. The available annual seat miles per employee increased from about 1.25 million in 1981 to 1.65 million in 1985.

The two-tier pay scale has given American a strong incentive to grow and reduce cost through growth. By the end of 1985, the proportion of American's market-rate employees had increased to 36% of its work force of nearly 44,000. American expects 50% of its employees to belong to the "B" (market-rate) pay scale by 1989.

In 1985, due to a tight market, American revised and increased its 1983 pay for the newly hired pilots by about 15–36%. To hold down labor costs, in August of 1986, American was negotiating with its pilots' union, Allied Pilots Association, to almost double the time it would take new pilots to reach the top of their pay scale.

In November 1986, AMR (which in 1982 became the parent company of American Airlines) revealed plans to buy ACI, the parent company of AirCal, in an attempt to strengthen its market position on the west coast. AMR's chairman and president, Robert L. Crandall, stated that this was not a departure from the company's commitment to internal growth. The decision was defended as a tactical move in response to the strong consolidation forces present in the industry.

In addition to the new cost-saving labor agreements that American reached with its unions, the airline also managed, as we have noted, to reduce its fuel consumption as a percentage of total operating expenses from 28.8% in 1981 to 21.3% in 1985 through fleet mix improvement and fuel management programs.

PROGRAMS TO MAXIMIZE REVENUES

American's efforts to maximize profit in the deregulated environment focused primarily on its SABRE computer reservation system, frequent-flyer program, American Eagle commuter airline, and programs of internal diversification and consolidation.

SABRE

The airline industry has five computer reservation systems (owned by American, United, TWA, Eastern, and Delta), which collectively generate a total annual revenue of over $800 million. American's SABRE is the largest in the industry; United's APOLLO ranks second. These two systems together account for 70% of the market. Computer reservation systems (CRSs) are sources of significant revenues for airlines. American's 1985 revenue from its SABRE was $338 million, representing an increase of 89% over the preceding year. United expected the revenue from its APOLLO system to increase by 66% to $246 million in 1985.

By the end of 1985, SABRE had more than 11,000 subscriber locations, over 50,000 CRTS, about 1,200 airlines for which the system had information, and 2,911 participating carriers (Exhibit 3.13). In an effort to maximize their CRS-related revenues, by late 1986 American Airlines and United were aggressively pushing their sophisticated reservation systems into Europe.

Frequent-Flyer Program

Following deregulation, the low-cost airlines began promoting several forms of systemwide deep-discount fares. Instead of offering such across-the-board discount fares, American responded to this challenge by introducing, in 1981, a focused discount program intended to reward loyal and frequent customers. The program was called "AAdvantage." AAdvantage grew rapidly; by early 1986 its membership exceeded 3 million.

EXHIBIT 3.13	SABRE at a Glance

Number of locations (Travel agency, corporate, and government accounts)	over 11,000
Number of CRTs	over 50,000
Number of printers	over 25,000
Number of airlines for which SABRE schedules information	1,200
Number of fares in SABRE	over 13 million
Number of participating carriers	291
Number of hotel properties and condominium firms	over 10,000
Number of car rental companies	20

Advance boarding passes available for:

American Airlines	Ozark Airlines
Delta Air Lines	Trans World Airlines
Eastern Airlines	United Airlines
Frontier Airlines	Western Airlines

Another innovation of American in 1981 was "AAirpass," a concept that guaranteed fixed personal and business air travel cost for periods ranging from 5 years to a lifetime.

American Eagle

American Eagle, a commuter airline, was formed in 1984 as a network of regional airlines integrated into the American Airlines domestic route system. American Eagle provides franchise feeder service into American's major cities and also serves markets that are not economically feasible to serve with American's aircraft.

The first partners in this marketing venture were Metro Airlines and Chaparral Airlines, which fed passengers through the Dallas/Fort Worth hub. American Eagle schedules are integrated into American's timetable. Eagle in-flight personnel are trained by American. Eagle reservations are handled through American's SABRE terminals, which can automatically print both tickets and boarding passes. American Eagle planes are painted in a color scheme complementing the American look. By January 1986, American Eagle served 35 cities.

Internal Diversification and Consolidation

American has experienced several structural changes since deregulation. During this period AA Training Corporation, AMR Corporation (a parent holding company) and AA Services Corporation were formed. Further, American sold its catering business, AA Sky Chefs.

American Airlines Training Corporation

AA Training Corporation (AATC) was created in 1979 to service various commercial and military contracts awarded to American for pilot and mechanic training. The subsidiary has its headquarters near the airline's pilot training center, the Flight Academy, at Dallas/Fort Worth. A new training facility at London's Gatwick Airport—operated by a subsidiary, American Airlines Training, Ltd.—was opened in 1981.

Although 1985 was the third consecutive profitable year for AATC, revenues and earnings from continuing operations declined from the record highs of 1984 as activity on several major programs began to wind down. Contributing to the decline in earnings was a $1.6 million loss realized on the sale of AATC's London-based training subsidiary. In 1985 a training contract with the U.S. Air Force continued to be AATC's principal source of revenue.

AATC also manufactures training equipment pursuant to contracts with NASA, the U.S. Navy, and Beech Aircraft. Lack of new markets for such equipment prompted a decision in 1985 to discontinue manufacturing operations following completion of the existing contractual commitments in 1986.

AMR Corporation

On May 19, 1982, American Airlines stockholders voted to approve a plan of reorganization under which a new holding company, AMR Corporation, was formed and became the parent company of American Airlines, Inc. The holding company was established to provide increased flexibility for financing and investment.

American Airlines Services Corporation

AA Services Corporation, the ground-services subsidiary, began operations in 1984. The company performed a variety of aircraft service functions, including loading and unloading, baggage handling, cabin cleaning, and de-icing. Other services included freight warehousing, passenger processing, building cleaning, sky cap services, security, and ground transportation.

The company experienced substantial growth in 1985. Revenues were $15.8 million, up from $3.2 million in 1984. After-tax net income was $1.4 million. Apart from the work it performed under its own contracts, the company also administered American Airlines' ground handling contracts, revenues from which increased from $55 million in 1984 to $60 million in 1985.

American Airlines Sky Chefs

In 1942, American entered the airline catering business with the formation of Flagship International (known as Sky Chefs) to provide food service for American as well as other airlines. Starting with 218 employees at 8 catering locations, Sky Chefs served about 1 million meals during the first year.

In 1985 American sold its food service subsidiary to Onex Capital Corporation, a diversified company based in Toronto, Canada. It was believed that because of its affiliation with American, Sky Chefs had limited chances of growth in the future.

Sky Chefs' revenues amounted to $352.3 million in 1985. The net income was $15.9 million, compared with $13.6 million in 1984. Sky Chefs operated 29 airline catering kitchens and 238 airport restaurants and concessions at 30 airport terminals. At the time of sale, Sky Chefs catered over 43 million airline meals annually, served about 7 million airport restaurant meals, and catered approximately 449 thousand flights.

Sky Chefs will continue to meet the majority of American's catering needs under a multi-year contract.

STRENGTHENING AND RESTRUCTURING OF THE ROUTE SYSTEM

Route Expansion

During the period from deregulation to mid-1985, American Airlines opened 72 new cities, including 6 cities reinstated and 2 Alaskan cities served through the American/Alaska Airlines interchange. During the same time, the airline started nonstop service in 114 new city pairs and increased the number of airports served from 65 to 129.

In addition to domestic routes, American increased its daily service to Europe. In 1985 American carried more than 383,000 passengers between the United States and Europe. The company expects to operate a total of 8 trips a day between the United States and Europe during the peak season.

Hub Expansion

Air travel can be either point-to-point or through a connecting hub supported by smaller feeder lines. In the point-to-point market, the airplane flies from point A to point B and so do all the passengers on that airplane. In a more complex system, passengers are taken from point A to an intermediate point, a hub, where they can connect to any of the many points on the other side of the hub. The hub system creates connections and so is less desirable than the nonstop service, but it serves many more markets. American Airlines adopted the strategy of evolving from a largely point-to-point system to a primarily hub structure.

In 1982 American Airlines started major expansions at its two existing hubs in Chicago and Dallas/Fort Worth. In July 1982, a $76 million expansion program at Dallas/Fort Worth Airport was announced, and in September 1983, an additional $15 million was committed to expansion at this hub. A 75,000-square-foot terminal expansion was completed in 1984, permitting the addition of 1,600 seats to the departure lounges. American also acquired 9 additional terminal gates in 1984 to handle future expansion. In 1985 American expanded the operations at its Dallas/Fort Worth hub to 321 daily nonstop flights to 94 destinations. In

September 1983, American also launched a 5-year, $100 million expansion and improvement program at its Chicago hub. Forty-nine new flights were added to the Chicago hub in 1984, a 32% increase. Service to 15 new cities was introduced in 1984. The service grew in 1985 to 237 daily nonstop flights to 66 cities.

Hub Development

In addition to expanding its two east–west hubs at Chicago and Dallas, American concluded that as part of its deregulation strategies, it also had to establish a major new hub to serve the strong north–south market in the eastern part of the country.

ESTABLISHING A NORTH/SOUTH HUB

GROWTH STRATEGY

Under the deregulated system, carriers were free to decide which markets to enter and which to exit. The intense competition and cost-consciousness forced airlines to change their operating efficiencies and systems. In general, the industry's response to deregulation centered around cost-reduction measures, expansion of existing operations, and consolidation through mergers and acquisitions.

The senior officers of American Airlines concluded that without major adjustments the airline could not effectively compete in the new environment. Efficiency improvement through growth and expansion constituted the thrust of American's coping response. Here's how an American Airlines executive put it:

> The two-tier plan gave American a strong incentive to grow. The faster we grew, the more market-rate employees we took in and the faster our average cost got down to market rate. Subsequently, we adopted an aggressive growth plan as a means of lowering average labor cost.

> To grow, we needed to expand the markets we served. We defined some areas of the world that could bring us new business. We divided the country into sections— north/south services in the east, point-to-point services on both coasts, and east/west services. We concluded that the eastern half of the country, where we did not have a strong presence, held the most promise.

> We thoroughly examined the north/south market in the east and gradually became convinced that the focal point of our growth strategy had to be this market. As part of our analysis, we did a study of Piedmont Airlines. Piedmont operates out of three major hubs, Charlotte, Baltimore, and Dayton. Piedmont has been a very successful carrier in that part of the country. We tried to determine why Piedmont was so successful. Piedmont had realized that there were some underserved markets out there. During deregulation, major carriers pulled back from a lot of these point-to-point services. Piedmont identified the fact that these areas provided a strong potential because they were not served by any carrier. Piedmont opened a hub and collected all the traffic from a lot of small markets which because of their size no other carrier was interested in. We concluded that we needed a hub in the east to serve the north/south traffic.

Hubbing in the east was judged to provide American with access to wholly new sources of passenger and freight revenue, as well as to several ancillary benefits, including increased "frequent-traveler plan" coverage; better personnel, facility, and equipment productivity at many existing stations; and improved productivity of national advertising.

Hubbing

Throughout the country, there are 33 major hubs located in 25 cities (Exhibits 3.14 and 3.15). Predominantly north/south hubs are limited in number. The majority of the hubs are east/west, and multi-directional hubs rank second in number.

Typically, east/west hubs have a larger local traffic base. However, they are individually more competitive as well as substantially more competitive with other hubs for flow traffic. By contrast, north/south hubs are less competitive both individually and in relation to other hubs. On average, each east/west hub city faces strong competition from 8 other hub cities. The comparable number for north/south cities is 2.3 (Exhibit 3.16). Exhibit 3.17 shows predominantly east/west, north/south, and multi-directional hubs broken down by the relative local origin and destination—using Chicago as a base—and the complexing carriers for each hub.

EXHIBIT 3.14	Major Hubs in the United States

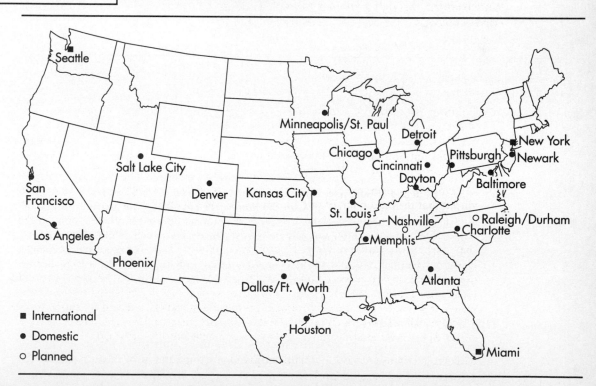

- ■ International
- ● Domestic
- ○ Planned

EXHIBIT 3.15	Major Airline Hubs
	(Working or planned)

American	Charlotte
Chicago	Dayton
Dallas/Fort Worth	Texas Air
Nashville	Atlanta
Raleigh/Durham	Denver
Delta/Western	Houston
Atlanta	Kansas City
Cincinnati	Newark
Dallas/Fort Worth	New York
Los Angeles	Trans World
Salt Lake City	New York
Northwest	St. Louis
Detroit	United
Memphis	Chicago
Minneapolis/St. Paul	Denver
Pan American	San Francisco
Miami	Washington, D.C.
New York	USAir
Piedmont	Philadelphia
Baltimore	Pittsburgh

Assumes completion of all pending major airline mergers.

Source: AP Newsfeatures.

As an aviation executive expresses it,

Hubbing is, in fact, an economical way of market expansion. The math is simple, 10 airplanes in and 10 airplanes out take 10 gates. If it takes 10 gates, it takes 10 crew to feed them. Cost tends to go up with the number of aircraft on the ground at the time, but the revenue goes up with the product of the number of aircraft on the ground at the time. Ten airplanes at a time mean we have 100 markets served. Thirty airplanes at a time serve 900 markets. Roughly, three times more cost and nine times more revenue, so revenue builds exponentially with the size of the hub. A hub is like a heart-beat in the circulatory system pumping traffic from one side to the other.

THE SELECTION PROCESS

American Airlines used geography, market size, and competitive forces as the primary criteria for the selection of its intended north/south hub. More specifically, the selection criteria included:

EXHIBIT 3.16   Level of Competition at East/West and North/South Hub Cities

East/West Hub City	Highly Competitive	Competitive Hubs											
		CHI	DFW	IAH	DEN	ATL	DTW	MSP	STL	PIT	MCI	SLC	MEM
Chicago	(10)	—	x	x	x	x	x	x	x	x	x	x	0
Dallas/Fort Worth	(8)	x	—	x	x	x	0	0	x	x	x	0	x
Houston	(8)	x	x	—	x	x	0	0	x	x	x	0	x
Denver	(10)	x	x	x	—	x	x	x	x	x	x	x	0
Atlanta	(8)	x	x	x	x	—	0	0	x	x	x	0	x
Detroit	(6)	x	0	0	x	0	—	x	x	0	x	0	0
Minneapolis/St. Paul	(6)	x	0	0	x	0	x	—	x	x	x	x	0
St. Louis	(11)	x	x	x	x	x	x	x	—	x	x	x	x
Pittsburgh	(8)	x	x	x	x	x	x	0	x	—	x	0	0
Kansas City	(11)	x	x	x	x	x	x	x	x	x	—	x	x
Salt Lake City	(5)	x	0	0	x	0	0	x	x	0	x	—	0
Memphis	(5)	0	x	x	0	x	0	0	x	0	x	0	—
Average	(8)												

North/South Hub City	Highly Competitive	Competitive Hubs					
		ATL	PIT	BWI	CVG	MEM	CLT
Atlanta	(2)	—	0	0	0	x	x
Pittsburgh	(3)	0	—	x	x	0	x
Baltimore	(2)	0	x	—	x	0	0
Cincinnati	(2)	0	x	x	—	0	0
Memphis	(2)	x	0	0	0	—	x
Charlotte	(3)	x	x	0	0	x	—
Average	(2.3)						

x Highly Competitive
0 Competitive

EXHIBIT 3.17	East/West, Multidirectional, and North/South Hubs by Hub Location, Local Origin and Destination and Complexing Carriers

	Hub Locations	Local Origin and Delivery Index (Chicago = 100)	Carriers Complexing
Predominantly East/West Hubs	Chicago	100	AA, UA
	Dallas/Ft. Worth	82	AA, DL
	Houston	63	CO
	Denver	50	CO, UA, FL
	Detroit	37	RC
	Minneapolis/St. Paul	33	NW, RC
	St. Louis	28	TW, OZ
	Kansas City	21	EA
	Salt Lake City	14	WA
Multi-directional Hubs	Atlanta	49	DL, EA
	Pittsburgh	25	AL
	Memphis	10	RC
	Dayton	7	PI
Predominantly North/South Hubs	Baltimore	19	PI
	Cincinnati	12	DL
	Charlotte	10	PI
	Nashville[a]	10	AA
	Raleigh/Durham[a]	10	AA

[a]Potential hub cities.

- Geographic location relative to the area to be served
- Potential flow traffic as well as potential local market size
- Competitive environment
- Facility options
- Relative operating conditions such as weather and airport capability

The new hub was to be centrally located to balance cities north and south of the hub, to minimize overlap, to optimize American's competitive positions, and to minimize long thin "spokes." American followed a process of elimination in selecting a hub city. In the beginning, there were 16 cities under consideration: LaGuardia, Kennedy, Philadelphia, Newark, Pittsburgh, Baltimore, National, and Dulles in the northeast and Atlanta, Memphis, Nashville, Charlotte, Norfolk, Greensboro/High Point, Raleigh/Durham, and Richmond in the southeast. Data collected on the 16 potential north/south hub cities included such factors as local population base that would use the airport, industry O&D (origin and destination) passengers to and from the city, industry passengers enplaned at the city, passengers per operation, load factor, and carriers with high enplanement shares at each airport (Exhibits 3.18 and 3.19).

Some cities were eliminated early in the process because they failed to meet all or most of the selection criteria. Several locations were difficult to eliminate because they met all or most of the selection criteria. At the end of the first phase of screening, 7 cities were eliminated and 9 remained in competition (Exhibit 3.20).

In the second phase, special attention was given to the local market and the connecting O&D flow (passengers per day each way, PDEW), using the city pairs likely to be served by each hub. The top five sites for connecting traffic flow were Nashville, Greensboro/High Point, Atlanta, Raleigh/Durham, and Charlotte. On the basis of local plus connecting flow, the top six choices were Atlanta, Nashville, Charlotte, Raleigh/Durham, National, and Greensboro/High Point (Exhibit 3.20).

Out of these six top contenders, Atlanta was already the hub city for Eastern and Delta. Piedmont had one of its hubs at Charlotte. Geographically, National was viewed as not quite centrally located to serve the intended markets. Greensboro/High Point presented some potential expansion problems. According to an executive of American Airlines who visited Raleigh/Durham and Greensboro/High Point airports as part of the selection process,

> In Greensboro the airport configuration of the terminal is different from Raleigh/Durham. The Greensboro airport has a main concourse with two concourses off of it at 90 degree angles. The master plan designed for the airport included an extension at either end of the terminal. The airport authorities stated that it was a relatively easy matter to extend the terminal and create another concourse off of it. Our concern, however, was that because of leasing arrangements between the airport and the tenants such an extension required the approval of other airlines to the airport. That was a hindrance. We wanted to be able to go in and start the project. We did not want to be subject to perhaps competing airlines saying yes or no. Further, Greensboro did not have a second runway. At Raleigh/Durham a second runway was already in the process of being built and a new terminal did not require any consideration from the other airlines at the airport.

Thus the process of elimination left American Airlines with two choices: Nashville, Tennessee, and Raleigh/Durham, North Carolina.

MARKET ANALYSIS

Nashville, Tennessee

The economy of Tennessee is expected to continue to grow at a healthy rate through the end of the century. Total employment in the state is expected to grow 1.33% a year, on the average, through 2005. Over that period, the state will create 709,520 new jobs, the eighteenth largest increase of any state in the nation. The population of Tennessee is expected to grow steadily over the next two decades, increasing at an average rate of 0.9% a year. The total population of the state will grow from 4.68 million in 1983 to about 5.7 million by the turn of the century.

EXHIBIT 3.18	Five-Year Plan Status, North/South Hub

(Population and historical local traffic, year ending second quarter 1983)

	(1) Population Base (1/1/84 Estimate)	(2) Industry O&D Passengers PDEW[a]	(3) Industry Enplaned Passengers per Day	(4) Annual Travel Rate (O&D Trips/ Population)	Carriers with High Enplanement Shares			
Northeast								
LaGuardia	⎧ 11,658,821	19,188	22,797	1.00	EA-31%	AA-14%	DL-10%	
Kennedy	⎩	12,605	17,484	.49	TW-20%	AA-18%	EA-18%	PA-16%
Philadelphia	6,403,109	8,641	10,510	.49	AL-26%	EA-18%	UA-14%	
Newark	5,610,795	17,423	16,594	1.13	PE-18%	EA-17%	AL-15%	UA-12%
Pittsburgh	3,728,852	6,805	3,747	.67	AL-75%			
Baltimore	2,993,090	4,714	5,176	.57	AL-19%	EA-16%	DL-13%	
National	1,854,842	13,849	17,082	2.73	EA-25%	AL-12%	UA-12%	
Dulles	1,544,695	2,115	3,121	.50	UA-30%	AA-22%	NW-12%	
Southeast								
Atlanta	3,348,178	12,889	48,430	1.41	DL-51%	EA-41%		
Memphis	2,063,733	2,858	6,292	.51	RC-44%	DL-33%		
Nashville	1,770,424	2,490	2,936	.51	AA-25%	RC-20%	DL-14%	
Charlotte	1,642,418	2,636	8,863	.59	PI-68%	EA-27%		
Norfolk	1,446,731	3,068	3,435	.77	PI-45%	AL-21%	EA-16%	
Greensboro/High Point	1,353,019	1,489	1,931	.40	PI-44%	EA-31%	DL-18%	
Raleigh/Durham	1,311,595	2,276	2,737	.63	EA-35%	PI-22%	DL-20%	
Richmond	1,079,327	1,112	1,275	.38	PI-55%	EA-37%		

[a]Per day each way
(4) = (2) * 365/(1)

EXHIBIT 3.19	**Five-Year Plan Status, North/South Hub** (Historical local traffic, year ending second quarter 1983)

	Industry O&D RPMs[a] PDEW[b]	Industry Onboard RPMs[a] PDEW[b]	Passengers per Operation	Load Factor
Northeast				
LaGuardia	14,420	14,578	84	59.6
Kennedy	19,760	26,653	118	65.1
Philadelphia	9,076	7,993	74	56.7
Newark	14,949	13,010	94	65.3
Pittsburgh	4,851	7,732	66	60.7
Baltimore	4,823	4,177	68	60.6
National	9,853	7,855	72	58.1
Dulles	3,396	5,601	90	62.1
Southeast				
Atlanta	9,075	30,942	80	56.6
Memphis	2,120	3,645	54	54.4
Nashville	1,850	1,568	64	55.9
Charlotte	1,696	3,991	64	57.1
Norfolk	2,050	1,430	62	54.6
Greensboro/High Point	1,044	866	53	48.7
Raleigh/Durham	1,617	1,211	54	58.3
Richmond	773	615	51	50.3

[a]Revenue passenger miles, in thousands
[b]Per day each way

The Nashville metropolitan area led the state in durable manufacturing job growth during the 1970s. Between 1983 and the year 2000, Nashville is expected to create approximately 100,000 manufacturing and service jobs. Nashville is a dynamic city with continued high-growth potential. The Association of American Geographers selected Nashville as one of the four "best places to live." *Advertising Age* ranked Nashville as one of the "top ten growth markets in the nation." During the height of the 1981–1982 recession, the unemployment rate in Nashville was 7%; the national average 9–10%. Nashville has a balanced work force: 23% manufacturing, 22% trade, 21% service, and 17% government. The area has 16 universities, colleges, and technical schools. There is low union membership. Nashville is famous for the music industry. It is the sixth largest publishing center and the state capital.

EXHIBIT 3.20	Five-Year Plan Status, North/South Hub

(Local and connecting O&D over hub passengers PDEW, year ending third quarter 1983; based on the city pairs likely to be served by each hub)

Hub City	Local Markets	Flow Markets	Nonstop in Flow Markets	Connecting Flow	Local Plus Connecting Flow
Atlanta	9,524	32,980	20,701	12,279	21,803
Nashville	1,695	43,351	28,701	14,650	16,345
Charlotte	1,995	36,946	24,851	12,095	14,090
Raleigh/Durham	1,817	38,283	26,033	12,250	14,067
National	5,661*	29,661	21,576	8,085	13,746
Greensboro/High Point	1,130	38,970	26,586	12,384	13,514
Baltimore	2,322*	29,661	21,576	8,085	10,407
Dulles	2,322*	29,661	21,576	8,085	10,407
Philadelphia	4,329	14,144	8,584	5,560	9,889

*Local Washington traffic divided among three area airports on basis of airport preference shown in Washington Council of Governments 1981/1982 Air Passenger Survey: DCA 55% BWI 22.5% IAD 22.5%

The closest hub city to Nashville is Memphis. Using the eight reference cities of Charlotte, New York, Washington, Philadelphia, Tampa, Kansas City, Houston, and New Orleans, the local O&D for Nashville—compared to that for Memphis—is larger in the first four cities and smaller in the remaining four. For each of the reference cities, Exhibit 3.21 shows the comparative nonstop, one-stop, and local O&D service as well as the Nashville O&D as a percentage of Memphis.

Serving the eastern half of the country diagonally through Nashville would provide American with a relative advantage in terms of travel time, mileage, and yield (Exhibit 3.22). Four examples of this comparative advantage are given in Exhibit 3.23. This exhibit shows that for the sample pair cities of Detroit–Huntsville, Philadelphia–Little Rock, Minneapolis/St. Paul–Birmingham, and Chicago–Huntsville, American would enjoy a significant time, mileage, and yield advantage if it used Nashville as its connect station. The time advantage could be as high as 65 minutes; indexed mileage and yield superiority could be 32 and 48 points, respectively.

Raleigh/Durham, N.C.

The population of North Carolina is expected to grow at an average rate of 0.84% a year between 1983 and the beginning of the twenty-first century. In 2005 North Carolina will be the twelfth most populous state in the nation with a population of 7.3 million. Total employment in North Carolina will grow at an average annual rate of 1.18% during the period from 1983 to the end of the century. It is estimated that by the year 2000, the state will have about 850,000 more jobs than it had in 1983.

EXHIBIT 3.21	Examples of Comparative Service and Traffic, Nashville vs. Memphis and Raleigh/Durham vs. Charlotte

Reference City	Nashville			Memphis			Nashville O&D
	Non-Stop	One-Stop	Local O&D	Non-Stop	One-Stop	Local O&D	As a % of Memphis O&D
Charlotte	4	—	52.2	2	2	34.0	153%
New York	3	5	262.3	6	6	211.2	124
Washington	4	1	119.1	6	1	98.4	121
Philadelphia	2	1	66.8	2	3	55.7	120
Tampa	0	0	47.0	3	1	50.0	94
Kansas City	0	1	29.8	5	0	37.6	79
Houston	0	0	72.7	6	1	94.4	77
New Orleans	1	0	39.9	9	0	73.8	54

Reference City	Raleigh/Durham			Charlotte			Raleigh/Durham O&D
	Non-Stop	One-Stop	Local O&D	Non-Stop	One-Stop	Local O&D	As a % of Charlotte O&D
Washington	10	—	191.0	10	5	108.6	176%
New York	15	3	567.7	15	9	366.9	155
Boston	2	6	113.8	5	3	81.4	140
Orlando	1	1	49.1	5	—	45.6	108
Chicago	2	2	108.9	9	3	126.5	86
Philadelphia	2	—	75.5	7	—	99.3	76
Miami	1	—	52.9	5	3	84.7	63
Pittsburgh	3	—	36.7	8	—	59.8	62

Raleigh/Durham/Chapel Hill (Wake, Durham, and Orange counties) is also a highly dynamic and growth-oriented area. It experienced an annual population growth rate of 1.8% between 1983 and 1987, more than double the statewide rate for the same period. The average household income for the area rose from $25,000 in 1983 to $42,000 in 1987, an increase of 68%. In 1983 gross retail sales in the three-county area exceeded $4.4 billion. The Rand McNally "Places Rated" Almanac ranks Raleigh/Durham number three as "The most desirable area in which to live." The area has four major universities: North Carolina State University in Raleigh, Duke University and North Carolina Central University in Durham, and University of North Carolina at Chapel Hill. Though the area has a diversified economic base, tobacco and textiles remain strong industries in the region. Durham contains the

EXHIBIT 3.22 | Geographic Area Served North/South by Nashville Hub

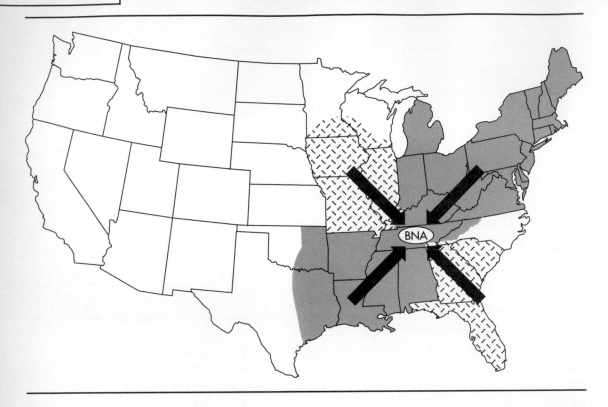

Research Triangle Park, a nationally unique planned research center for private and public scientific/medical research and high-tech development. The park employs more than 22,000 people with an annual payroll of over $700 million. During the height of the 1981–1982 recession, the unemployment rate was 4.2% in the area; the national average was 9–10%. The area has the highest concentration of Ph.D.s per square mile in the nation. Raleigh is the state capital.

The closest hub city to Raleigh/Durham is Charlotte. The relative position of Raleigh/Durham and Charlotte in terms of nonstop, one-stop, and local O&D traffic is given in Exhibit 3.22 for the eight reference cities of Washington, New York, Boston, Orlando, Chicago, Philadelphia, Miami, and Pittsburgh. This exhibit shows that the true local O&D demand at Raleigh/Durham may well be larger than at Charlotte. Serving the most eastern north/south corridor through a potential Raleigh/Durham hub would give American a consistent time, mileage, and yield advantage over the competing carriers (Exhibit 3.24). Exhibit 3.25 provides examples of this comparative advantage for four sample pair cities of LaGuardia–Jacksonville, Philadelphia–Savannah, Pittsburgh–Ft. Meyers, and Baltimore–Orlando.

EXHIBIT 3.23	Examples of Implied Cost and Yield Advantage: Nashville

Carrier	Connect Station	Elapsed Minutes	Indexed	
			Mileage	Yield[a]
Detroit–Huntsville				
Eastern	ATL	204	100	100
Delta	ATL	210	100	100
Republic	MEM	195	106	94
American	BNA	153	75	133
Philadelphia–Little Rock				
TWA	STL	242	100	100
Delta	ATL	245	100	100
Republic	MEM	210	91	110
American	BNA	210	90	110
Minneapolis/St. Paul–Birmingham				
Delta	ATL	215	100	100
Eastern	ATL	224	100	100
Republic	MEM	200	88	114
American	BNA	182	84	119
Chicago–Huntsville				
Delta	ATL	205	100	100
Eastern	ATL	209	100	100
Republic	MEM	175	89	112
American	BNA	144	68	148

[a]Percentage of $100 over mileage

Nashville and Raleigh/Durham versus Atlanta, Charlotte, and Memphis

American's new north/south hub had to compete with a number of established hubs in the east. Atlanta and Memphis (two multi-directional hubs) as well as Charlotte (a predominantly north/south hub) posed the highest level of competition. A close review of the relative merits of Nashville and Raleigh/Durham suggested that collectively they would provide access to virtually all north/south markets of significance.

| EXHIBIT 3.24 | Geographic Area Served North/South by Raleigh/Durham Hub |

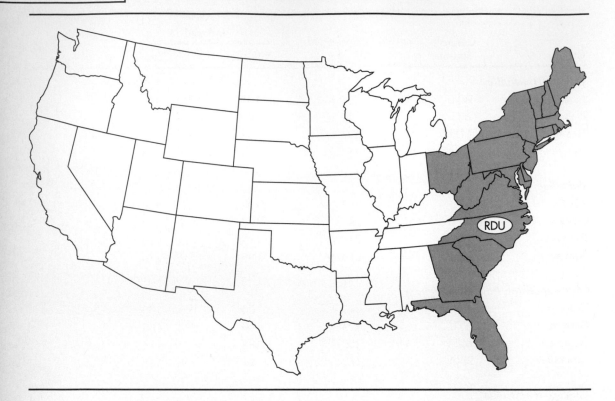

Among the five competing hub cities of Atlanta, Memphis, Nashville, Raleigh/Durham, and Charlotte, Nashville and Raleigh/Durham had two of the highest population growth rates for 1970 to 1985. In terms of average daily local O&D, Charlotte, Nashville, and Raleigh/Durham experienced the sharpest growth during the five-year period of 1979–1984 (Exhibit 3.26). The Nashville and Raleigh/Durham flow markets were estimated to be competitive with 73 of Delta's top 100 revenue markets served via Atlanta, 70 of Eastern's top 100 revenue markets served via Atlanta, 78 of Piedmont's top 100 revenue markets served via Charlotte, and 75 of Republic's top 100 revenue markets served via Memphis.

Elapsed time from origin to destination has always been an important consideration influencing buyer selection of a particular airline or flight. In the existing computer reservation systems (CRS), both "screen presence" and "line position" are influenced by elapsed time. American's service through Nashville and Raleigh/Durham was estimated to involve less mileage in over 65% of the flow occurrences by an average of about 5–6%. American's scheduled elapsed time (flying time plus ground time) would be shorter in over 78% of the cases because of (a) reduced circuitry with the potential of resulting in lower costs, higher yield, and improved CRS positioning; (b) less congestion at the hub airports; and (c) reduced ground/connection time at smaller, less complex directional hubs.

EXHIBIT 3.25	Examples of Implied Cost and Yield Advantage: Raleigh/Durham

Carrier	Connect Station	Elapsed Minutes	Indexed	
			Mileage	Yield[a]
LaGuardia–Jacksonville				
Eastern	ATL	234	100	100
Delta	ATL	240	100	100
Piedmont	CLT	209	82	121
American	RDU	192	81	123
Philadelphia–Savannah				
Piedmont	CLT	160	100	100
Eastern	CLT	163	100	100
Delta	ATL	217	133	75
American	RDU	155	95	105
Pittsburgh–Ft. Meyers				
Delta	ATL	215	100	100
Eastern	ATL	225	100	100
People Express	EWR	305	133	74
American	RDU	200	96	105
Baltimore–Orlando				
Delta	ATL	215	100	100
Eastern	ATL	220	100	100
Piedmont	CLT	194	85	118
American	RDU	173	81	124

[a]Percentage of $100 over mileage

Thus American Airlines, already committed to establishing a hub in the east as an integral part of its deregulation and growth strategies, had to choose between Raleigh/Durham and Nashville, two equally attractive sites for a new north/south hub. The survival and prosperity of American Airlines during the highly competitive post regulation years were believed to depend on this strategic decision.

RANKING IN THE INDUSTRY SEVEN YEARS AFTER THE DEREGULATION

Among the major carriers, in 1979 American ranked number eight in terms of its operating earnings and number two with respect to its net earnings. By 1985 the company had improved its position in both of these areas to number one in the

EXHIBIT 3.26	Population Growth and Average Daily Local Origin and Delivery Among Potential North/South Hub Cities

North/South Hub Cities	Population Growth Trends		
	Population, 1985 Estimate	1970–1980 Growth	1980–1985 Growth
Atlanta	3,361,000	23.2%	6.4%
Memphis	2,137,000	10.9	3.8
Nashville	1,853,000	20.8	5.3
Charlotte	1,715,000	15.5	7.2
Raleigh/Durham	1,335,000	17.6	8.5

	O&D Growth Comparisons		
	Avg Daily Local O&D, Year Ending 9/30/84	5–Year Growth 9/79–9/84	3–Year Growth 9/81–9/84
Atlanta	13,959	6.6%	10.2%
Charlotte	2,931	20.3	27.4
Memphis	2,925	(21.5)	(2.6)
Nashville	2,809	7.5	13.0
Raleigh/Durham	2,793	33.8	41.8

industry. In terms of operating margin, American was number eight in 1979 but advanced to number two in 1985 (Exhibit 3.27). From an operational point of view, American's load-factor ranking dropped from number one in 1979 to number three in 1985. When 1985 ended, however, not only was American the second largest carrier in the nation in terms of fleet size and passengers carried, but it ranked number one in available seat miles, revenue passenger miles, and profitability.

EXHIBIT 3.27	American's Ranking Among the Major Carriers, 1979–1985

	1979	1980	1981	1982	1983	1984	1985
Operating earnings	8	10	3	4	1	2	1
Net earnings	2	11	3	4	1	3	1
Operating margin	8	8	4	4	2	5	2
Load factor	1	5	2	1	1	3	3

CASE 4 The Black & Decker Corporation
Timothy W. Edlund ▪ Sandra J. Lewis

Black & Decker's worldwide competitive position had been profoundly altered. The firm made major acquisitions, including General Electric's small appliance group (1984), Rank Electric's housewares operations in Australia and New Zealand, and all of Emhart Corporation in 1989. These and other acquisitions were intended to complement and enhance Black & Decker's traditional power tool product lines.

Nolan D. Archibald, formerly with Beatrice Company, was elected CEO in 1986. He reorganized the firm, abolishing country-based product/market division, intending to build worldwide product-design and marketing teams, to restore the company's competitive abilities. As fiscal 1989 ended, income did not cover debt service, outside observers predicted that debt repayment requirements would be missed, and the company's stock price declined sharply. Archibald must develop strategies that will keep the company solvent. Could he continue to build and grow the company, or was retrenchment necessary for survival?

COMPANY HISTORY

The Black & Decker Manufacturing Company was incorporated in 1910 by S. Duncan Black and Alonzo Decker in Baltimore, Maryland. They initially made milk bottle capping machines. In 1916 the first product, a portable electric drill, was produced and sold under the Black & Decker trademark. Subsidiaries were established in Canada in 1922, in England in 1925, and in Australia in 1929.

Black & Decker manufactured a wide range of electric and cordless portable power tools, small home appliances and tools, and lawn care equipment and tools. In 1979 portable electric tools accounted for nearly 75% of the company's overall sales. Corporate annual growth goals were 15% in sales and earnings per share.

The company was the world's largest and oldest power tool manufacturer. It segmented its power tool products into two markets: individual consumers and the professional or commercial market. Black & Decker's distribution channels included national merchandisers (K mart, J.C. Penney, Sears, Payless, etc.); department stores (Hechts, Bon Marche, etc.); hardware stores and home centers (Hechingers, 84 Lumber, etc.); and government contracts (Army and Air Force Exchange Stores). On the industrial side, distribution was primarily through mill supply outlets using sole sourcing with dominant regional distributors; it also included contractor supply houses and plumbing and electrical supply firms.

Timothy W. Edlund, Morgan State University, and Sandra J. Lewis, United States Army. This refereed case was written using published materials and was presented to the Decision Science Institute in 1991. It is intended as a basis for class discussion rather than to illustrate effective or ineffective handling of an administrative situation. © 1991 by Timothy W. Edlund.

Black & Decker was an international company with over 100,000 distribution outlets worldwide, 104 company-owned service centers in the United States, 221 centers in 45 countries, and 31 manufacturing plants in 10 countries. The corporation was substantially decentralized. Each division in each plant in each country was responsible for the design, production, supply and sourcing, and engineering of its products. In addition, marketing and advertising in its own market were the responsibility of each foreign subsidiary. Research and development were partially decentralized and conducted in the United States and four other countries with a 1979 budget of over $15 million.

The diverse product line consisted of over 280 models for both the consumer and professional markets. The product lines were built around nearly 200 motor sizes. Standardization of parts and components had not yet been fully implemented. Some of the manufacturing plants were just beginning to move into automated assembly processes and to take advantage of computerization.

Although Black & Decker enjoyed a world portable electric power tool market share of 31.1% and a U.S. market share of 43.1%, it still faced competition at home and abroad. Its major U.S. competitors and their market shares (shown as U.S. market share/world market share) were Skil Corporation, 12.1%/7.1%; Sears, Roebuck & Company/Singer, 13.3%/4.3%; Milwaukee Tools, 10.9%/3.5%; and Rockwell International Corporation, 6.2%/1.9%. Its major international competitors were Makita Electric Works Ltd., 2.8%/11.1%; Robert Bosch Gmbh, 2.9%/10.7%; Hitachi, 0%/8.3%; and AEG Telefunken, 1.1%/5.0%.[1]

RECENT DEVELOPMENTS

Black & Decker experienced a downturn in the early 1980s. The management operated under a sense of complacency, manufacturing costs were too high, marketing efforts were loose, and product quality was poor. The dollar was overvalued, and competitors, such as Makita Electric of Japan and Robert Bosch of Germany (the second- and third-ranked companies in the world tool market), were quickly taking over much of Black & Decker's market share in the United States. In 1981 the recession decreased sales of Black & Decker's most important line, power tools. By 1985 the business had deteriorated to the point where the company posted a loss of $158 million on sales of $1.7 billion.[2] This loss was due in large part to a $215 million write-off for plant shutdowns and other cost-saving measures.

Black and Decker fought back, complementing its power tool business by purchasing General Electric's small-appliance division in April 1984. In addition, B&D purchased Rank Electric's Housewares Operations of Australia and New Zealand. These purchases increased Black & Decker's access to the European market and provided both access to their distribution channels and a wide range of small-appliance products (irons, mixers, etc., to which was added Black & Decker's popular line of Dustbuster® vacuums and other battery-driven appliances).[3] The company dropped "Manufacturing" from the corporate name in February 1985.[4]

In 1985 Nolan Archibald, formerly a marketing and operations specialist with Beatrice Foods, began reorganizing Black & Decker's operations. According to Archibald, Black & Decker previously had "little geographical fiefdoms" around the world, each with its own product-design center and marketing team.[5] Under the old organization, the company still had over 100 different motor sizes. Furthermore, it split consumer and professional tools into two separate groups that seldom communicated with each other.

Archibald organized plants around motor sizes and, in the process, reduced product variations and streamlined manufacturing. In 1985 the company closed plants in Allentown, Pennsylvania; Barrie, Ontario, Canada; Sao Paulo, Brazil; and Hampstead, Maryland. By 1987 Black & Decker had 19 plants, 5 of which were inherited from General Electric—a substantial reduction from 25 plants in 1984.

In this reorganization over 2,000 workers, including many highly paid managers, were let go. The resultant savings were used for new-product development, quality control, and advertising. These recovery actions paid off: in 1988 the company earned nearly $100 million on sales of $2.3 billion.[6] Sales by product group are shown in Exhibit 4.1; Exhibit 4.2 breaks down sales growth from 1987 through 1989.

In March 1986 Archibald was elected CEO.

COMPANY FINANCIAL PROFILE

Sales during fiscal 1989 (October 1988 through September 1989) reached $3.2 billion, an increase of 40% over 1988 sales.

This substantial increase was due primarily to the April 1989 acquisition of Emhart Corporation and to continued strong growth in worldwide power tool operations. Sales amounts and growth by geographic area were as follows: United States, $1.7 billion, up 46%; Europe, $936 million, up 24%; and all other areas, $520 million, up 53%.

For the first quarter of 1990, the corporation had net earnings of $10 million, or $0.17 per share. Operating income rose 148% for this period to $108.2 million, from $43.6 million last year. Sales for the quarter were $1 billion, 76% higher than in the same 3-month period of 1989.

Earnings before income taxes were $62.9 million in 1989, compared to $125.7 million in 1988 and $69.8 million in 1987. The significant decline in earnings from 1988 to 1989 was attributed primarily to acquisition-related interest and other costs. The acquisition of Emhart was financed principally through long-term debt. Interest expense rose from $36.5 thousand in 1988 to $201.1 thousand in 1989; and net earnings dropped from $97.1 thousand in 1988 to $30.0 thousand in 1989. The effects of the Emhart purchase were still felt as 1990 began, with $10,014 net earnings for the first three months of fiscal 1990, compared to $25,858 for the same period the prior year.[7] Financial data are given in Exhibits 4.3, 4.4, and 4.5.

EXHIBIT 4.1	1989 Sales by Product Group: Black & Decker Corporation

	$ Millions	% Sales	% Change from Last Year
Power tools	$1,077	34%	+13%
Household products	833	26%	+11%
Accessories and fastenings			
Existing	250	8%	+2%
Acquired[1]	20	—	—
Outdoor products			
Existing	208	7%	+8%
Acquired[1]	93	3%	—
Locks and hardware—acquired[1]	169	5%	—
Mechanical fasteners—acquired[1]	157	6%	—
Other commercial products			
Acquired[1]	162	5%	—
Service—existing	154	4%	+6%
Plumbing fixtures—acquired[1]	67	2%	—
Totals Existing	$2,522	79%	+11%
Acquired[1]	668	21%	—
Grand total	$3,190	100%	

[1] Sales of acquired Emhart businesses, excluding those identified for sale, for the five-month period from the date of acquisition.

Source: Black & Decker Corporation, Form 10-K, fiscal year ending September 24, 1989, p. 3.

EXHIBIT 4.2	Results of Operations—Sales: Black & Decker Corporation (Dollar amounts in millions)

Analysis of Sales Growth	1989	1988	1987
Consolidated sales	$3,190	$2,281	$1,935
Volume Existing	11%	14%	3%
Acquired	29%	—	—
Price	2%	—	1%
Currency exchange	–2%	4%	4%
Total growth	40%	18%	8%

Note: Percentages are year-to-year changes.

Source: Black & Decker Corporation, 1989 Annual Report.

EXHIBIT 4.3	**Results of Operations—Geographic Areas: Black & Decker Corporation**
	(Dollar amounts in millions)

Analysis of Sales Growth	1989	1988	1987
United States sales	$1,734	$1,185	$1,018
Volume Existing	9%	17%	2%
Acquired	35%	—	—
Price	2%	–1%	—
Total growth	46%	16%	2%
Europe sales	$ 936	$ 755	$ 612
Volume Existing	10%	10%	1%
Acquired	18%	—	—
Price	2%	2%	3%
Total growth	24%	23%	19%
Other sales	$ 520	$ 341	$ 305
Volume Existing	21%	12%	11%
Acquired	32%	—	—
Total growth	53%	12%	11%

Source: Black & Decker Corporation, *1989 Annual Report.*

EXHIBIT 4.4	**Quarterly Results (unaudited): Black & Decker Corporation**
	(Dollar amounts in thousands)

Fiscal Year Ending September 24, 1989	1st Quarter	2nd Quarter	3rd Quarter	4th Quarter
Net sales	$705,519	$570,722	$854,732	$1,059,337
Gross margin	$257,430	$209,294	$296,919	$ 360,124
Net earnings	$ 38,360	$ 25,858	$ (5,174)	$ (29,018)
Earnings per share	$ .65	$ .44	$ (.09)	$ (.49)

Fiscal Year Ending September 25, 1988	1st Quarter	2nd Quarter	3rd Quarter	4th Quarter
Net sales	$612,279	$537,787	$539,331	$591,526
Gross margins	$229,697	$202,166	$200,857	$217,439
Net earnings	$ 31,118	$ 21,145	$ 21,393	$ 23,439
Earnings per share	$ .53	$ .36	$ .36	$ .40

Source: Black & Decker Corporation, *1989 Annual Report.*

EXHIBIT 4.5	**Consolidated Statement of Earnings, 1987–1989: Black & Decker Corporation**
	(Dollar amounts in thousands, except per share data)

Years Ending	September 24, 1989	September 25, 1988	September 27, 1987
Net sales	$3,190,310	$2,280,923	$1,934,799
Operating costs and expenses			
Costs of products sold	2,066,543	1,430,764	1,229,989
Marketing and administrative expenses	853,409	691,044	592,337
Total operating costs and expenses	2,919,952	2,121,808	1,822,326
Operating income	270,358	159,115	112,473
Interest expense	201,066	36,502	43,385
Other income (expense)	(6,366)	3,082	678
Earnings (before income taxes)	62,926	125,695	69,766
Income taxes	32,900	28,600	14,200
Net earnings	$ 30,026	$ 97,095	$ 55,566
Net earnings per share	$ .51	$ 1.65	$ .95

Source: Black & Decker Corporation, *1989 Annual Report.*

INTERNATIONAL OPERATIONS

Black & Decker is an international corporation with manufacturing plants and sourcing covering 6 continents and 26 countries of the world. Black & Decker has manufacturing plants in Brazil, Mexico, the United States, Canada, England, France, Germany, Italy, Switzerland, Singapore, and Australia. Purchases come from those countries and also from Ireland, Spain, Italy, Holland, Belgium, Sweden, Austria, Finland, Yugoslavia, India, Hong Kong, Taiwan, Korea, and Japan. Black & Decker markets its products in over 100 countries worldwide.

GLOBAL MANUFACTURING AND PURCHASING STRATEGY

The (1984) General Electric acquisition marked a turning point in the corporate strategy at B&D. The purchase boosted sales by one-third, gave the company access to the household market, and provided a strategic base in the Far East. Subsequently, Nolan Archibald stated that operations had to be streamlined and made more efficient. His "cut-and-build" strategy was planned to trim worldwide manufacturing capacity by one-third. It would also eliminate duplication in manufacturing and design by reorganizing plants by motor size.

B&D had used over 100 different motor sizes in its products. By 1988 this figure was trimmed to 20, and the goal was to be down to about 5 motor sizes by the early 1990s. Plants would be designed as either small, medium, or large motor facilities, and the decision to produce at a specific plant—be it household appliances or power tools—would depend on motor size, similarities in the manufacturing process, and level of plant utilization.

According to Frank Rosenthal, vice president of global manufacturing and technical development, "one cannot separate the manufacturing, engineering, and purchasing functions. Purchasing was not only included in the restructuring plans; in many respects it has led the way."[8] Gene Richter, vice president for corporate purchasing, reported directly to Rosenthal. Purchasing's mission is to out-buy the competition, both in the United States and overseas.

A Hybrid Purchasing Approach

The purchasing division has taken ideas from both a decentralized and a centralized philosophy in developing its global procurement strategy. This has resulted in a hybrid system that combines the free-wheeling style of a decentralized purchasing operation and the critical intelligence and buying muscle of centralization. In the program worked out by Gene Richter, corporate purchasing has two heads under his guidance. One group of commodity managers operates out of world headquarters in Towson, Maryland, and oversees purchases for North America. The second group, operating out of Slough, England, handles purchases for all of Europe.

The cornerstones of B&D's buying policy are centralization of key commodities, dominant supplier strategy, long-term agreements, and international buying. In addition to being responsible for big-ticket purchases such as plastic resins, corporate purchasing was given jurisdiction over key commodities. Any item that meets one of the following criteria is centrally purchased by the Towson group: items deemed strategically important (such as small, direct-current motors); items whose availability is limited to a relatively few global suppliers (such as nickel–cadmium batteries); items that are critical to product quality (such as electrical switches, the leading cause of product failure); and items that have a high degree of technical content (such as printed circuit boards).

This strategy is designed to capitalize on Black & Decker's worldwide presence and to make purchasing more efficient. Policy still leaves plant purchasing managers a lot of latitude. Richter deliberately left under plant control those items that local buyers could do a better and faster job of sourcing: components that are readily available from local sources, involve extensive tooling expense, or are just impractical to handle in a centralized mode. Purchases of accessories and finished products from outside manufacturers were also left decentralized. It should be noted that B&D plants in Mexico, Brazil, and Singapore operate on their own because they are "too far outside the mainstream geographically."[9] Other factors that affect sourcing of these plants include high tariffs and freight costs.

Richter calls his plan a dominant-source strategy. The dominant supplier of a major commodity gets 70% of the business, 25% goes to a capable backup source, and 5% is reserved for a promising new supplier that can offer advanced technology and may later develop into a dominant source. The purpose is to create and maintain competition while providing all the benefits of single sourcing (cooperative partnership with world-class suppliers, improved quality, and, ultimately, lower total costs) without the attendant risks (supply disruption and supplier complacency). The dominant supplier must be "world-class" in quality and technology. The "world-class" supplier status was to be tested annually by purchasing.

The culmination of Black & Decker's sourcing strategy was the long-term agreement (LTA) negotiated with all dominant suppliers. These agreements could run from two to five years in length and averaged three years long. An LTA required the supplier "to remain competitive in quality, delivery, and technology."[10] Supplier pricing was also required to be competitive. One of purchasing's long-range goals was to negotiate with its major suppliers global pricing that would allow products to be transferred between countries without incurring a materials-cost penalty. By 1989 B&D had achieved hemispheric pricing for all European plants on certain commodities. Roughly 20% of Black & Decker's purchases were covered by LTAs. This strategy was a means of gaining control and leverage over suppliers.

Far East Operations

With the purchase of GE and its Singapore manufacturing plant, Black & Decker acquired one of the best "on-site" intelligence gathering networks. Vice president Gene Richter believed that there was no place in the world to buy everything. It was necessary that the company take advantage of technology or currency ebb and flow through these on-site intelligence networks. The showcase of these networks was the creation of a Far East purchasing operation (FEPO).

Until the creation of the FEPO, Black & Decker's purchases in the Far East were done through trading companies. B&D paid a price for this service, not only in monetary terms, but also in not being able to develop the person-to-person relationships that are very important to doing business in the Far East. The FEPO eliminated the middleman. All purchase orders from the United States, Europe, or other B&D plants were to be funneled through the FEPO. The FEPO contracted with dedicated agents who resolved supplier quality problems, recommended sources to the plant buyer, conducted audits before shipments, and, in effect, served as a purchasing office in Singapore. A similar purchasing operation was established in Brazil.

To coordinate the whole purchasing operation and ensure that it remained consistent with the long-range goals of the corporation, Richter developed three purchasing councils to review tactics and strategy. One council covers operations in the Western hemisphere, one covers Europe, and the third is a "world council" that focuses on policy matters and long-term strategies. These purchasing councils, attended by plant buyers and corporate staff, meet quarterly.

Worldwide Manufacturing Rationalization

Nolan Archibald's "cut-and-build" strategy included reducing overhead and consolidating plants so the company could be profitable at a modest level of sales. Part of this strategy included aligning the production staffing with expected sales and, as mentioned earlier, concentrating production around motor sizes. Standardizing motor sizes allowed B&D to develop a global product strategy. It designed a limited number of common motors, which permitted longer runs at manufacturing plants. Its common product is then adapted to the individual overseas markets by changing specific features to suit local tastes.

By designing for manufacturing, Black & Decker modularized the functional parts and automated assembly, thus ensuring cost and quality gains. Manufacturing lead times were reduced substantially, which made it easy to switch rapidly between products in response to volatile market demand. "Just in time" sourcing was instituted, along with quality circles (called Total Customer Service groups), to meet the challenge of the global marketplace. Using these and other Japanese-style manufacturing methods, Black & Decker worked to become the world's low-cost producer of power tools.

Localized Product Marketing Approaches

Although Black & Decker had an overall global product strategy, and although sourcing was accomplished through a hybrid system, advertising and promotions were tailored to the needs of the individual markets and end users. The company marketed products differently in various locations, taking into account cultural factors and local customs of each country.[11]

OTHER DEVELOPMENTS AND INITIATIVES

Black & Decker's restructuring drew attention. It developed an approach to simultaneous engineering, in which manufacturing engineering meets regularly with product engineering—an approach aimed at reducing lead times and costs.[12] A 1988 *Fortune* article chose B&D's cordless tools as one of the five best-designed mass-market U.S. products.[13] In October 1988, it was reported as growing twice as fast as any other power tool firm, after earlier share losses to Makita Electric's invasion of the U.S. and world markets.[14] B&D's factory in Spennymoor, County Durham, England, was cited as one of six "superplants" in the United Kingdom.[15] It should be noted that earlier, by 1979, B&D's U.K. company had reduced its power tool models from 130 to 50 and that it had a 90% share of the U.K. market. Archibald's cut-and-build concept drew compliments as an effective approach to cost cutting.[17]

Additional key personnel had been brought on board: George Sherman, former head of Emerson Electric's Skil division, to head power tools; and Dennis Heiner, formerly with Beatrice Foods, to head household products. Not only were power tools growing rapidly, but B&D retained market leadership in the small-appliance line acquired from General Electric.[18] Organization structure also drew attention. In today's competition, whether global or local, a single source of competitive advantage no longer suffices; it is necessary to combine many perspectives. White and Poynter stated that in a worldwide context, exploiting such opportunities is primarily an organizational issue.[19] Structures require continual adjusting and flexibility. We have already noted Black & Decker's flexibility in manufacturing and sourcing. In the U.S. Power Tool Group in Hunt Valley, Maryland, product and brand managers worked together in a parallel channel manager organization, with product managers having ultimate authority for the marketing program in place in every channel.[20]

Meanwhile, Black & Decker attempted to broaden its product line through acquisition. Its pursuit of American Standard Inc. was coolly regarded and fought off in early 1988.[21] Archibald continued to look for acquisitions that would provide a strategic fit.[22]

THE EMHART PURCHASE

In 1989, playing the role of "white knight," Black & Decker bought the Emhart Corporation for $2.8 billion, to save it from an unwanted suitor. Some judged that this move was intended both for growth and to increase market share in the world power tool market. The purchase was financed with low-interest bank financing, and B&D intended to pay off the long-term debt with expected increases in overall international sales. The bank loan agreement required that Black & Decker sell approximately $150 million in assets by the end of 1990.[23] Archibald stated the goal of selling $1 billion of Emhart assets by mid-1990. Additional debt payments were due: $250 million in March 1991, and $50 million in June 1991.

Several business writers were enthusiastic about this deal. Emhart provided many well-known consumer-product brand names, marketed through many of the same channels. They looked to see B&D's product-design expertise applied to the Emhart lines. The match was found in both power tools (53% of B&D's 1988 volume) and in household appliance products (33% of 1988 volume). The ratio of debt to total capital would rise above 82%. Earnings would be hurt for a time, with analysts predicting $36 million in 1989 with a rebound to $100 million in 1990. Retailers carrying B&D lines were being pushed to consider carrying Emhart's lines as well—even before the merger was final. And Archibald immediately embarked on a 5-week trip, visiting 40 plants in 11 countries. He predicted that the merger would double B&D's earning capacity.[24]

Having committed himself, Archibald needed to review his strategic plans, revise them as necessary, and implement those plans effectively. There was little margin for error.

NOTES

1. Cheng G. Ong and Michael E. Porter. "Skil Corporation." Harvard Business School Case 9-389-005, 1988.
2. Stuart Flack. "All Leverage Is Not Created Equal." *Forbes*, March 19, 1990, pp. 39–40.
3. *Ibid.*
4. Moody's *Industrial Manual, 1990*, p. 992.
5. Christopher S. Eklund. "How Black & Decker Got Back in the Black." *Business Week*, July 13, 1987, p. 86.
6. Stuart Flack, *op. cit.*
7. Black & Decker Corporation, *1989 Annual Report* and *1990 First Quarter Report*.
8. Ernest Raia. "Purchasing 1988 Medal of Professional Excellence: Black & Decker." *Purchasing*, September 29, 1988, p. 56.
9. *Ibid.*, p. 57.
10. *Ibid.*, p. 75.
11. *Ibid.*; also see John H. Sheridan. "Purchasing's New Clout." *Industry Week*, 1988, 237(9), pp. 49–65.

12. John M. Martin. "The Final Piece to the Puzzle." *Manufacturing Engineering*, 1988, 101(3), pp. 46–51.

13. Brian Dumaine. "America's best designs," *Fortune*, 1988, 118 (12), pp. 129–130.

14. Bruce Nussbaum. "Comeback Style." *Business Week*, October 21, 1988, pp. 13–14.

15. Simon Caulkin. "Britain's Best Factories." *Management Today* (UK), September 1988, pp. 58–80.

16. Ong & Porter, *op. cit.*, p. 8.

17. Daniel J. McConville. "How To Be a Cost-Cutting King." *Financial Manager*, 1989, 2(2), pp. 16–22.

18. John Huey. "The New Power in Black & Decker." *Fortune*, January 2, 1989, 119(1), pp. 89–94.

19. Roderick E. White and Thomas A. Poynter. "Organizing for Worldwide Advantage." *Business Quarterly* (Canada), Summer 1989, 54(1), pp. 84–89.

20. Keven T. Higgins. "Firms Tune Up Their Management." *Marketing News*, September 25, 1989, 23(20), pp. 2 and 26.

21. "A Quick Rebound for M&A." *Mergers & Acquisitions*, 1988, 22(6), pp. 7–8.

22. Huey, *op. cit.*

23. Stephen Goldstein. "Black & Decker Sells 3 More Units." *The Washington Times*, October 5, 1990, p. D3.

24. Janet Meyers. "Black & Decker Ups Share in Hardware." *Advertising Age*, July 24, 1989, 60(32), p. 28; and Joseph Weber. "Black & Decker Cuts a Neat Dovetail Joint." *Business Week* (Industry/Technology Edition), July 31, 1989, pp. 52–53.

CASE 5 Cadbury Schweppes, PLC

Franz T. Lohrke • James G. Combs •
Gary J. Castrogiovanni

> All large (food) companies have broken out of their product boundaries. They are no longer the bread, beer, meat, milk or confectionery companies they were a relatively short time ago—they are food and drink companies. Sir Adrian Cadbury, Chairman, (retired) Cadbury Schweppes, PLC. (Smith, Child, and Rowlinson, 1990, p. 9)

In the early 1990s, Cadbury Schweppes embodied the archetypal modern food conglomerate. With extensive international operations in confectionery products and soft drinks, the company maintained a diversified global presence. Although Cadbury had enjoyed a relatively stable competitive environment through much of the company's history, contemporary developments in the international arena presented Cadbury management with many diverse and critical challenges.

THE HISTORY OF CADBURY

The company started up in 1831 in the United Kingdom (UK), when John Cadbury began processing cocoa and chocolate to be used in beverages. In 1847 the company became Cadbury Brothers, and in 1866 it enjoyed its first major achievement when the second generation of Cadburys found a better way to process cocoa. By using an imported cocoa press to remove unpalatable cocoa butter from the company's hot cocoa drink mix instead of adding large quantities of sweeteners, Cadbury capitalized on a growing public distaste for adulterated food.

The company further prospered when it found that cocoa butter could be used in recipes for edible chocolates. In 1905 Cadbury introduced Cadbury Dairy Milk (CDM) as a challenge to Swiss firms' virtual monopoly in British milk chocolate sales. A year later, the firm scored another success with the introduction of a new hot chocolate drink mix, Bournville Cocoa. These two brands provided much of the impetus for Cadbury's early prosperity (Jones, 1986).

Cadbury faced rather benign competition throughout many of the firm's early years. At one point, in fact, Cadbury provided inputs for the UK operations of the American firm Mars, Inc. (Smith, Child, and Rowlinson, 1990). Cadbury also formed trade associations with its UK counterparts, J. S. Fry and Rowntree & Co., for the purpose of (among other things) reducing uncertainty in cocoa prices. The company later merged financial interests with J. S. Fry, but it spurned offers to consolidate with Rowntree in 1921 and 1930 (Jones, 1986).

Prepared by Franz T. Lohrke, James G. Combs, and Gary J. Castrogiovanni, Louisiana State University. Copyright 1992, Franz T. Lohrke. Reprinted with permission.

Facing growing protectionist threats in overseas markets following World War I, Cadbury began manufacturing outside the UK, primarily in Commonwealth countries (see Exhibit 5.1). This international growth was also prompted by increasing competition. For example, by 1932 Cadbury management considered the Swiss company Nestlé its primary competitor in the international arena (Jones, 1986).

In 1969 Cadbury merged with Schweppes, the worldwide maker of soft drinks and mixers. The merger offered both companies an array of advantages, both defensive and offensive. First of all, both companies faced potential takeover threats from larger firms, so the merger placed the new company in a better defensive posture to ward off unwanted suitors. On the offensive side, the marriage allowed the new company to compete better on a worldwide scale. Cadbury had invested primarily in Commonwealth countries, and Schweppes had branched out into Europe and North America, so the new company enjoyed greater geographic dispersion. The increased international presence also enabled the company to defray product development costs over a wider geographic base. Furthermore, the new company enjoyed greater bargaining power with suppliers. For example, following the merger, Cadbury Schweppes became the largest UK purchaser of sugar (Smith, Child, and Rowlinson, 1990).

The British confectionery companies historically pursued a different strategy than their American counterparts. Whereas U.S. companies, such as Mars, manufactured narrow product lines and employed centralized production, Cadbury maintained 237 confectionery products until World War II forced the company to scale back to 29. While it was faced with little competition, Cadbury's brand proliferation strategy could be effective. As rivalry heated up in the mid-1970s, though, Cadbury's share of the UK chocolate market fell from 31.1% to 26.2% between 1975 and 1977. Management then began to realize that the lower-cost, American-style strategy of rationalized product lines and centralized production represented the only viable means to compete (Child and Smith, 1987).

Cadbury had long been famous for its unique management style. "Cadburyism" drew upon the founders' Quaker heritage, providing for worker welfare and harmonious community relations. Following Cadbury's reorientation toward core products and rationalized production, though, the company's old management style underwent a transformation. Confectionery manufacturing personnel were reduced from 8,565 to 4,508 between 1978 and 1985 (Child and Smith, 1987). In the process, management's traditional close relationship with

EXHIBIT 5.1	Cadbury's Foreign Direct Investment				
World War I					World War II
1914–1918	1921 Australia	1930 New Zealand	1933 Ireland	1937 South Africa	1939–1945

workers, which had been built through years of maintaining employment stability, began to erode as reduction in numbers of workers became a professed goal of Cadbury executives.

THE ENVIRONMENT

As is the case with several products in the food industry, many of Cadbury's product lines enjoyed very long product life cycles. (Exhibit 5.2 lists assorted confectionery products of Cadbury and its rivals.) Food and beverage companies derived substantial benefit from their long-established products, such as Cadbury's CDM bar, and the occasional new-product introductions required little technological investment. The food companies, therefore, competed primarily by seeking cost reduction by incorporating process improvements such as automation, by finding alternative inputs to replace expensive cocoa, and by introducing creative packaging and marketing (Child and Smith, 1987).

Successful new-product introductions remained sporadic, and many of the most successful confectionery products, such as the Mars bar and Rowntree's Kit Kat (taken over by Nestlé), had been around since the 1930s (Tisdall, 1982). Some unsatisfied demand seemed to persist, however, as evidenced by Rowntree's successful 1976 launch of its Yorkie bar, Mars' profitable introduction of Twix a few years later, Cadbury's notable 1984 launch in the UK of its Whispa bar, and Hershey's 1988 introduction of Bar None (Weber, 1989).

Nevertheless, new-brand introductions required immense investments in development and marketing costs and offered only limited possibilities for success. For instance, various research suggests that approximately 60% of new food product introductions are withdrawn within five years, and this figure may be an underestimate (Smith, Child, and Rowlinson, 1990). Consequently, established brands with customer loyalty represented crucial assets for food and beverage companies.

MODERN CADBURY SCHWEPPES

Expansion was key to Cadbury's plans to improve its international position. Chief Executive Officer Dominic Cadbury commented, "If you're not operating in terms of world market share, you're unlikely to have the investment needed to support your brands" (Borrus, Sassen, and Harris, 1986, p. 132). In 1986 Cadbury shared third place in the world with Rowntree and Hershey, each having approximately 5% of the market. Nestlé held second place with about 7.5%, and Mars dominated internationally with approximately 13% (van de Vliet, 1986).

To generate the worldwide expansion it deemed necessary, Cadbury had two primary markets in which to gain positions. Enjoying a dominant position in its home market, the company realized that the United States and the remaining countries of the European Economic Community (those besides the UK) provided critical markets for a worldwide standing. According to Terry Organ, director of international confectionery, "Rightly or wrongly. . .we decided to tackle the US

| EXHIBIT 5.2 | Assorted Major Brand Names of Cadbury Schweppes and Its Confectionery Competition |

Cadbury Schweppes		Nestlé	
Cadbury Dairy Milk (CDM)	Whole Nut	Nestlé Crunch	Polo
		Kit Kat	Quality Street
Milk Tray	Roses	Smarties	Yorkie
Crunchie	Fruit and Nut	After Eight	Aero
Whispa	Trebor	Rolo	Black Magic
		Dairy Box	Fruit Pastilles
		Butterfinger	Baby Ruth

M&M/Mars		Hershey	
Mars	Galaxy	Hershey Bar	Reese's Peanut Butter Cup
Twix	Maltesers	Hershey Kisses	Reese's Pieces
Bounty	Milky Way	Mounds	Almond Joy
M&Ms	Snickers		

Philip Morris
Milka
Toblerone
E. J. Brachs candy

first" (van de Vliet, 1986, p. 45). Earlier, Cadbury had taken steps toward competing more vigorously in the United States by acquiring Peter Paul in 1978. By 1980, however, the company still controlled only about 3.5% of the U.S. confectionery market, far eclipsed by its bigger rivals, Hershey and Mars.

Cadbury was not large enough to employ a sales force comparable to that of its competitors. The company therefore had to rely on food brokers to push products to wholesalers, which left the firm far removed from the consumer. Furthermore, its two larger rivals could easily outspend Cadbury in advertising (Borrus, Sassen, and Harris, 1986).

To compound problems, the company also committed two marketing blunders in the U.S. market. When Cadbury introduced Whispa, the company's marketing success of the decade in the UK, management did not realize that distribution channels in the United States were longer than those in the UK. Consequently, the candy bars aged seven to nine months by the time they reached test markets in New England, and consumers reacted accordingly.

The company's second mistake occurred following an effort to standardize its candy bar size across countries. When Cadbury first introduced its CDM bar in the

EXHIBIT 5.7	Cadbury Schweppes' 1990 Worldwide Sales
	(In millions of pounds[1])

Region	Total Sales	Confectionery	Beverages
United Kingdom	1,476.0	715.4	760.6
Continental Europe	638.0	195.6	442.4
Americas	403.7	18.3	373.5
Pacific Rim	495.5[2]	NA	NA
Africa and other	132.9	91.2	38.8

[1] 1 pound = $1.93
[2] Sales primarily in Australia and New Zealand
NA = Not available
Note: Total Sales will not always equal Confectionery plus Beverages. In the United States (Americas region), for example, Cadbury Schweppes also generated sales from its Mott's subsidiary.

Source: Compact Disclosure; Wall Street Journal.

emphasis on Europe and instead attempt to exploit new opportunities in the under-developed Asian market? Whatever Cadbury Schweppes management decided to do, it had to move quickly. The list of available name-brand food and beverage products was shrinking fast. (See financial statements, Exhibits 5.8 and 5.9.)

EXHIBIT 5.8	Balance Sheet: Cadbury Schweppes
	(In thousands of pounds)

Fiscal Years Ending	December 29, 1990	December 30, 1989	December 31, 1988
Assets			
Cash	£ 62,600	£ 57,400	£ 41,300
Marketable securities	118,000	33,300	200,700
Receivables	554,100	548,200	434,500
Inventories	328,200	334,800	253,400
Total current assets	1,062,900	973,700	929,900
Net property, plant, equipment	978,800	822,500	602,200
Other long-term assets	320,700	332,600	20,700
Total assets	£2,362,400	£2,128,800	£1,552,800

(continued)

EXHIBIT 5.8	Balance Sheet: Cadbury Schweppes (continued) (In thousands of pounds)

Fiscal Years Ending	December 29, 1990	December 30, 1989	December 31, 1988
Liabilities			
Notes payable	£ 60,100	£ 57,400	£ 92,200
Accounts payable	272,100	263,900	409,500
Current capital leases	76,200	76,300	21,900
Accrued expenses	320,900	305,900	52,100
Income taxes	78,200	95,800	81,800
Other current liabilities	154,700	143,600	118,800
Total current liabilities	962,200	942,900	776,300
Long-term debt	407,900	381,400	124,700
Other long-term liabilities	108,401	124,000	74,600
Total liabilities	1,478,500	1,448,300	975,600
Preferred stock	300	NA	3,300
Net common stock	174,400	173,600	150,400
Capital surplus	95,800	36,700	33,000
Retained earnings	115,800	167,600	88,800
Miscellaneous	381,600	217,400	210,500
Total shareholders' equity	767,900	595,300	486,000
Minority interest	116,000	85,200	91,200
Total liabilities and net worth	£2,362,400	£2,128,800	£1,552,800

Note: 1 pound = | $1.93 | $1.61 | $1.81
NA = Not available

EXHIBIT 5.9	Income Statement: Cadbury Schweppes (In thousands of pounds)

Fiscal Year Ending	December 29, 1990	December 30, 1989	December 31, 1988
Net sales	£3,146,100	£2,766,700	£2,381,600
Cost of goods sold	1,738,400	1,596,900	1,365,000
Gross profit	1,407,700	1,179,800	1,016,600
General, selling and administrative expenses	1,074,700	907,500	787,800
Income before interest and taxes	333,000	272,300	228,800

(continued)

EXHIBIT 5.9	Income Statement: Cadbury Schweppes (continued) (In thousands of pounds)

Fiscal Year Ending	December 29, 1990	December 30, 1989	December 31, 1988
Non-operating income	3,800	3,100	4,400
Interest expense	57,200	31,100	17,500
Income before taxes	279,600	244,300	215,700
Taxes and miscellaneous expenses	100,200	85,500	75,200
Income before extraordinary items	179,400	157,800	140,500
Extraordinary items	NA	15,200	28,400
Net income	£ 179,400	£ 173,000	£ 168,900

Note: 1 pound = $1.93 $1.61 $1.81
NA = Not available

Source: Compact Disclosure; *Wall Street Journal.*

REFERENCES

Borrus, A., J. Sassen, and M. A. Harris. "Why Cadbury Schweppes Looks Sweet to the Raiders." *Business Week,* January 13, 1986, pp. 132–133.

Browning, E. S., and M. Studer. "Nestlé and Indosuez Launch Hostile Bid for Perrier in Contest with Agnellis." *Wall Street Journal,* January 21, 1992, p. A3.

Child, J., and C. Smith. "The Context and Process of Organizational Transformation—Cadbury Limited in Its Sector." *Journal of Management Studies,* 24 (1987), pp. 565–593.

Gofton, K. "Has Cadbury Got His Finger on the Button?" *Marketing,* July 31, 1986, pp. 20–25.

House, K. E. "The 90's and Beyond: The U.S. Stands to Retain Its Global Leadership." *Wall Street Journal,* January 23, 1989, p. A8.

Jones, G. "The Chocolate Multinationals: Cadbury, Fry and Rowntree, 1918–1939." In G. Jones, ed., *British Multinationals: Origins, Management and Performance.* Brookfield, Vt.: Gower, 1986, pp. 96–118.

Mergers and Acquisitions. "The Nestlé–Rowntree Deal: Bitter Battle, Sweet Result." September/October, 1989, pp. 66–67.

Smith, C., J. Child, and M. Rowlinson. *Reshaping Work: The Cadbury Experience.* Cambridge, England: Cambridge University Press, 1990.

Standard and Poor's Industry Surveys. England: "Food, Beverages, and Tobacco." June 27, 1991, pp. F23–F27.

Swarns, R. L., and B. Toran. "Hershey to Buy U.S. Business from Cadbury." *Wall Street Journal,* July 25, 1988, p. 30.

Templeman, J., and R. A. Melcher. Supermarket Darwinism: The Survival of the Fattest. *Business Week,* July 9, 1990, p. 42.

Tisdall, P. "Chocolate Soldiers Clash." *Marketing,* July 29, 1982, pp. 30–34.

van de Vliet, A. "Bittersweet at Cadbury." *Management Today,* March, 1986, pp. 42–49.

Weber, J. "Why Hershey Is Smacking Its Lips." *Business Week,* October 30, 1989, p. 140.

Winters, P. "Cadbury Schweppes' Plan: Skirt Cola Giants." *Advertising Age,* August 13, 1990, pp. 22–23.

CASE 6 Compaq Computer Corporation

Thomas Goeller • Robert J. Mockler •
Chiang-nan Chao • Jennifer A. Finn

Compaq Computer Corporation is a publicly owned personal computer maker that was founded in 1982. Compaq designs, develops, manufactures, and markets personal computers for business and personal use. The Compaq product lines offer customers the broad range of industry standard desktops and portable computers.

In 1991 Compaq sold its products exclusively through about 3,800 full-service computer specialty dealers for resale to end users. Of these 3,800 dealers, 2,000 were located outside the United States. Foreign business accounted for about 54% of sales in 1991. Research and development accounted for 5.2% of sales (*Value Line*, November 1, 1991, p. 1086).

As shown in Exhibits 6.1 and 6.2, Compaq's sales grew rapidly from 1983 to 1990. The company's sales in 1990 soared to a record $3.6 billion, an increase of 25% over 1989 sales of $2.87 billion. Net income in 1990 rose 35% to a record $432 million, compared with the company's net income of $319.2 million in 1989. In 1991 Compaq's sales dropped to $3.27 billion, net income sank to $130.87 million, far below 1990 record level; and the net profit margin dropped from 12% in 1990 to 4% (Blumenthal, 1991; *Value Line*, November 1, 1991; and Scheier, February 3, 1992).

At the end of 1991, over 100 million personal computers were in use around the world, and the U.S. market was fast approaching saturation. Since then the personal computer industry has begun losing some buoyancy. Competition has been increasing, demand flattening, and margins decreasing. Early in 1990, Compaq was becoming concerned about sustaining this rate of growth. The company saw its profits fall by 14% in the fourth quarter of 1989. The computer industry as a whole grew at slow rates of 10% in 1989 and 9% in 1990 (*Value Line*, November 1, 1991).

Things did not improve at Compaq Computer in 1991. In the second quarter, Compaq reported a net profit of $104 million, or an 81% drop from the quarter a year earlier. It blamed slower-than-expected European sales and a U.S. market battered by price competition and a glutted distribution channel. In an interview, Compaq's then president and chief executive officer, Joseph R. Canion, said third-quarter profit could be lower than $20 million if the dollar remained strong and Compaq's European business turned in its usual seasonally soft performance. Compaq said that it was stung especially hard in the United States, where mergers involving 8 of its 10 largest dealers, including Computerland, Businessland, and Computer Factory, left dealers with excess inventory (Bartimo, 1991).

The situation became more troublesome in the third quarter of 1991, as the company reported its first loss. Compaq took a $135 million charge to cover the cost of laying off 12% of its work force (*Wall Street Journal*, 1991). Compaq improved its fourth quarter's sales to only $873 million, 13% down compared to the same quarter a year earlier, and net income to only $67 million due to a price

EXHIBIT 6.1	**Compaq's Sales**
	(Dollar amounts in millions)

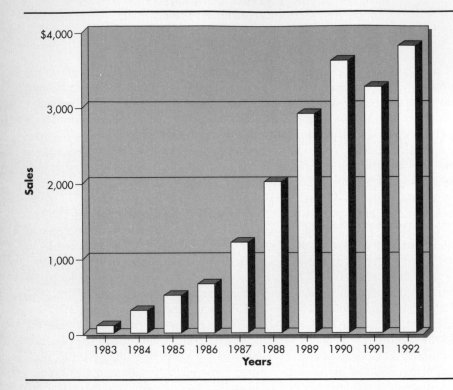

Source: Value Line, November 1, 1991, p. 1086.

cut on its popular notebook computers. A weaker dollar helped international operations (Fisher, 1992; Blumenthal, 1992; Scheier, 1992).

Compaq built its success and its profits on product reputation, not on price; on personal computers, not on other products; on retail distribution, not on direct sales. These strategies enabled Compaq to maintain its forceful presence in the marketplace—but how long would this last? In light of the current unpredictable market, should the company expand into direct sales, or should it expand by widening its product line? If so, to sell what? If it had ample cash flow, should it do both? These were the questions the industry analysts were asking in early 1992.

INDUSTRY AND COMPETITIVE MARKET

THE COMPUTER INDUSTRY

The computer industry is defined as a subgroup in the technology industry, including seven specific industries: electronic computers, computer storage devices, computer terminals, computer peripheral equipment, computer programming services,

EXHIBIT 6.2	Compaq's Net Income
	(Dollar amounts in millions)

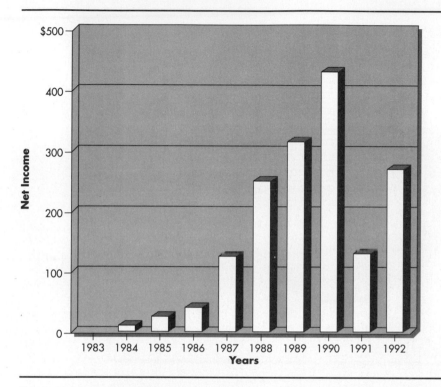

Source: Value Line, November 1, 1991, p. 1086.

prepackaged software, and computer integrated systems design (*U.S. Industrial Outlook*, 1991).

The personal computer is a segment of the computer hardware industry—specifically, the microcomputer segment. The other segments are the mainframes (supercomputers are also in this category) and minicomputers. Workstations, although a distinct segment, are classified as part of the microcomputer segment. Exhibits 6.3, 6.4, and 6.5 show the segment percentages of each of these categories for 1984, 1989, and 1992 (estimate). Clearly, the computer industry is downsizing.

It was not a good year for the computer industry in 1991, as the companies contended with tough economic times. The big computer makers, such as IBM, Digital Equipment Corporation (DEC), and Compaq were hit hardest. IBM posted a $2.8 billion loss for 1991, its first loss ever, and its first drop in annual sales since 1946. IBM officials confirmed that personal computers (PC) sales in 1991 dropped for the first time ever, down 10% from 1990 to less than $9 billion. DEC posted a $138.3 million loss on sales of $3.5 billion (Fisher, 1992). Compaq Computer posted a 51% drop in the fourth-quarter profit on a 13% decline in sales. Its profits of the same period a year ago were $131 million, and sales were

EXHIBIT 6.3	The Computer Hardware World Market by Segment, 1984 ($84.8 billion)

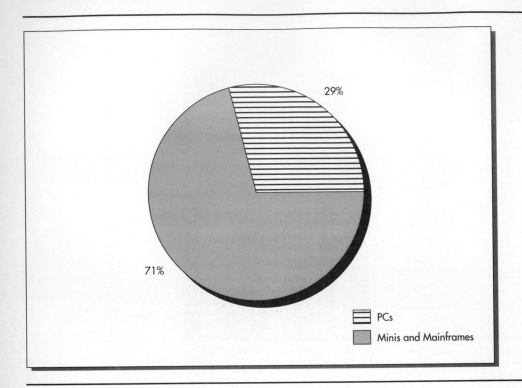

29%

71%

PCs

Minis and Mainframes

Source: S & P Industry Surveys, October 17, 1991.

$873 million (Wilke, January 10, 1992, and January 21, 1992; Allen, 1992; Scheier, 1992). Meanwhile, price cutting further eroded profit margins of the personal computer makers and their suppliers, while mainframe makers saw sales shrink as potential customers waited for a new generation of machines.

Despite slowing growth in the computer industry from PCs to mainframes, PCs continued to account for an increasing share of total computer sales. According to *Value Line*'s estimate, the total worldwide unit shipments of PCs increased by 10% in 1991 (*Value Line*, November 1, 1991).

Overall, the world computer industry was undergoing rapid restructuring, as technological and commercial changes greatly affected its basic structure. Almost all computer companies in the U.S. and the world experienced a decline in profitability in 1991. Computer companies responded by restructuring, slashing prices, consolidating, and forming alliances with other manufacturers. In October 1991, IBM cut the prices of its high-performance workstations by up to 60% (reducing the price of some models to $52,000 from $130,000) in response to fierce competition from Sun Microsystems, Hewlett-Packard, and others. For the first time in its history, IBM discounted the price of the new mainframe to stimulate sales. Price

EXHIBIT 6.4	The Computer Hardware World Market by Segment, 1989
	($145 billion)

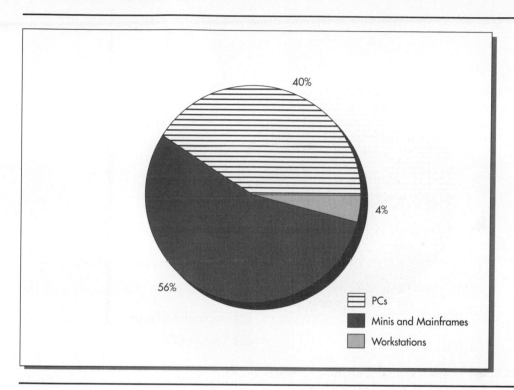

40%

4%

56%

PCs

Minis and Mainframes

Workstations

Source: S & P Industry Surveys, November 17, 1991.

competition in the personal computer sector became extremely intense. Meantime, intensive consolidation and alliances had taken place in the computer industry. Examples include AT&T's purchase of NCR (the fifth-largest U.S. computer manufacturer), Computer Associates' acquisition of On-line Software, and Borland International's purchase of Ashton-Tate. In April 1991, Compaq, DEC, Microsoft, Silicon Graphics, MIPS Computer, and other major companies formed the Advanced Computing Environment (ACE) Consortium to develop a new desktop computing standard. Apple Computer entered into agreements with IBM to swap technologies. As the profit margins in the industry declined and the costs of developing new products increased, the trend toward mergers and partnerships seemed likely to continue (*Standard & Poor Industry Surveys*, 1991).

As technology advanced, the older-generation machines were facing less expensive, newer products such as minicomputers, which were winning business that otherwise would have gone to mainframes. The more recent challenge of personal computers and workstations was at the expense of both minicomputers and mainframes. Networking of a number of workstations could perform many tasks

EXHIBIT 6.5	The Computer Hardware World Market by Segment, 1992 ($214 billion)

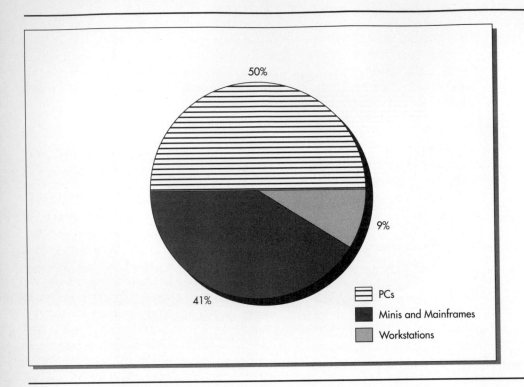

Source: S & P Industry Surveys, November 17, 1991.

formerly done by the mainframe (Markoff, 1992). For many organizations, these tied together an enterprise's computer resources, with the goal of allowing users to access data easily no matter where it was on the network.

Mainframes

Mainframe computers have a broad range, which includes supercomputers and mainframes defined as computers with the highest processing speed, and are sold for the highest prices in any given period of time. *Supercomputers* are often described as the most powerful computers with the fastest performance and a very large main memory. They are used for highly complex computational problems that could not otherwise be solved in a practical amount of time or at a lower cost than either physical modeling or slower computers.

The supercomputer industry experienced mild growth in 1991, reaching a total value of $1.7 billion, up 13% globally from 1990. The mainframe shipments by U.S.-based manufacturers increased by 3% in 1991, to $13.4 billion (*U.S. Industrial Outlook, 1991*). The recession in the United States and other parts of the world forced many potential buyers of supercomputers to put their spending plans on hold or to spend more time studying whether new equipment was needed. As these potential buyers' business slowed, the need for additional data processing power was lessened. For example, IBM saw demand sag as it brought out its next generation of machines. The shipments of these new powerful machines did not start until September 1991.

Nevertheless, the supercomputer and mainframe segment would continue to exhibit slow growth in both product technology and user demand. Several U.S. suppliers were combining their hardware and software capabilities to supply more powerful systems. U.S. firms continued to lead the world in the production of multiple processor computer systems.

Minicomputers

A minicomputer is a mid-range computer with processing and storage capabilities smaller than those of a mainframe but larger than those of a microcomputer. This segment of the computer industry consists of multiuser systems ranging in price from $25,000 to $500,000. Some of these machines are designated general-purpose computers; others are designed for specific applications. Mid-range computers serve a broad spectrum of applications but are used predominantly in services and durable-goods manufacturing and to a lesser degree in education and government markets.

The minicomputer segment remained at about $20 billion in 1990. Many suppliers in this category broadened their offerings to include networking equipment, software, technical workstations, portables, and system integration services. Others focused on specific market niches, offering their minicomputers as network servers. Users of minisystems were carefully watching the development of open systems—those employing nonproprietary or standardized hardware components and operating systems. Most suppliers, while seeking to preserve their installed base of proprietary systems, also introduced some form of open system. Open systems garnered a share of the mid-range market, and as such limitations as the lack of specific applications software were overcome, these systems would account for an even larger share. Minisystems were predicted to continue slower growth into the mid-1990s (*U.S. Industrial Outlook,* 1991).

Microcomputers

The microcomputer segment is the largest segment of the computer hardware market, including personal computers and workstations. In 1991 this segment was estimated to be $100 billion worldwide (*Standard & Poor's Industry Surveys,* 1991).

Personal computers (PCs) are primarily single-user, general-purpose systems that are based on a microprocessor. Personal computers span a range of products from commodity-like models at the low end to workstation-like models at the high end. A typical low-end system sells for $500 to $2,000; machines that serve as network hubs cost about $25,000.

In 1977 companies such as Apple, Commodore, and Tandy took the concept of a personal computer, pioneered by technically innovative entrepreneurs who sold microcomputer kits to hobbyists, and ignited the PC boom. By 1980 Steve Jobs's Apple Computer Corp. had grown into a $117 million company and its multicolored apple logo was beginning to be seen in the large corporations where IBM's mainframes had dominated.

In 1981 IBM launched a program to bring itself into the personal computer business. However, in the mid-1980s, IBM was losing control over its outside suppliers. Intel and Microsoft, more than IBM or any of the companies producing clones of IBM's PC, began to determine how PC technology progressed and, to a large degree, how much PCs would cost. Instead of taking pricing cues from IBM, as minicomputer and mainframe makers had always done, a growing mob of PC clone companies slashed prices to as much as 30–50% below IBM's, while maintaining relatively good quality or better.

Toward the end of the 1970s and into the early 1980s, the PC industry had been able to ignore the general economic health of the nation and had easily expanded at a pace that outstripped overall growth levels. However, this was no longer true. The personal computer market was approaching its maturity, characterized by greater competition and less industry concentration.

In the middle of the 1980s and the early 1990s, the PC industry ran into turmoil. Computer companies were beginning to become more dependent on the state of the economy (Niemond, 1990). In an effort to bolster sales, IBM introduced the PS/2, incorporating the company's proprietary Micro Channel Architecture (MCA) into a design that would be more difficult to copy. However, by 1987, the original PC standard (in its slightly updated PC-AT format) had become a force that even IBM couldn't stop. The clone makers continued to build sales and market share by improving on the old standard. As IBM's market share dropped from 27% in 1985 to 16.5% in 1990 (*Standard & Poor's Industry Surveys,* 1991), the company began slashing prices in order to compete, but IBM's cost of producing PCs was much more than that of the clone makers, particularly if they came from off shore.

In 1987 the majority of personal computer manufacturers formed an industry alliance to support a major advance in the Industry Standard Architecture (ISA). It provided for an industry-standard expansion bus. The bus is the device that controls the flow of data among the processor, disk drives, keyboard, display, and other peripherals attached to the personal computer. This alliance was formed after IBM (1987) had deviated by developing the Micro Channel Architecture (MCA), which differed from the industry standard and had developed a different bus, making the IBM line incompatible with thousands of existing hardware products that could be attached to the majority of today's business PCs. Later, more PC models and plug-in boards were introduced that were based on the Extended Industry Standard Architecture (EISA).

EISA allows personal computers to deliver the performance demanded for sophisticated jobs in network communications and work group applications, yet it enables customers to use their existing software and peripherals. EISA also enables customers to employ new, high-performance peripherals designed specifically to take advantage of EISA capabilities. Among the group of companies that formed this alliance in establishing specifications for EISA were Compaq, AST Research, Epson America, Hewlett-Packard, NEC Information Systems, Olivetti & Co., Tandy Corporation, and Zenith Data Systems. Additional industry support came from over 100 other companies, including Intel Corporation, Microsoft Corporation, and Digital Communications Associates. The support of these companies ensured availability of hardware, software, chip sets, and peripheral devices capable of using EISA features ("President's Letter," 1989).

Powerful new software encouraged the replacement of 16-bit 80286 and 8088 machines with 32-bit 80386 and 80486 PCs. Slow economic growth could force information center managers to consider more cost-effective ways of automating an increasing number of complex tasks. Powerful PC multiprocessor file servers capable of minicomputer and mainframe performance could become the next stage in the desktop revolution.

The technological developments were spurring demand for notebook computers, with global sales expected to top $8 billion in 1991. This new sub-segment of the PC industry would represent the fastest-growing sub-segment in the overall computer industry. The technological development had enabled notebooks to perform nearly all functions the desktop performed, and users could take them wherever they went. According to *PC World*, notebook shipments in 1991 were 1.5 million units with about 10,000 colored units. The shipment of more powerful notebooks in 1992 would top 2.1 million units with 30,000 colored units (Hoga, 1991). Downsizing trend in the computer industry was accelerating. Exhibit 6.6 breaks down the units of notebooks shipped by vendor.

EXHIBIT 6.6 | **The U.S. Notebook Market by Vendor, 1990**
(840,000 units)

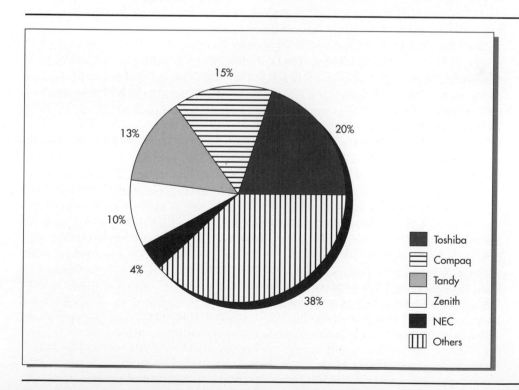

Source: S & P Industry Surveys, November 17, 1991.

Workstations are within the same microcomputer segment as personal computers. They are single-user, high-performance computer systems with advanced graphics capabilities. The principal use of workstations is in computationally intensive scientific and engineering applications. Workstations are usually based on microprocessors that offer users greater processing power and capabilities of handling multitasking and networking.

Workstation systems, created in 1981 by Apollo and legitimized in 1985 by Sun Microsystems, were retailed between $10,000 and $100,000, but substantial price improvements were expected because of the availability of faster microprocessors. Sales of U.S.-based vendors soared by a compound annual rate of more than 110% between 1986 and 1988. A high-performance workstation could cost less than $1,000 every million instructions per second (MIPS) of computer power, compared to more than about the $100,000 for every MIPS commanded by a typical mainframe. For many tasks—though not all—low-cost workstations were an affordable alternative to mainframe computer power. In this area Sun Microsystems was in the lead, followed by Hewlett-Packard, Digital Equipment Corp., IBM, and many other, smaller companies. Compaq had already introduced a multiprocessor machine called SystemPro, but due to the lack of operating system software to take advantage of this new architecture, the product was slow to catch on.

The marriage of workstation performance with the PC's best software base might lure dozens of computer manufacturers and software developers into this emerging market, thus pushing the demand for workstations. Workstations were projected to offer the greatest opportunity in the computer industry in the early 1990s. The market for workstations grew 40.3% and 21.5% in 1989 and 1990, respectively (*Wall Street Journal,* 1991). Although the growth slowed in 1991, the worldwide market for workstations hit $11 billion. This market segment was one of the fastest-growing areas in the overall computer industry, but it represented only 5% of the sales of all computers (*Standard & Poor's Industry Surveys,* 1991; *U.S. Industrial Outlook,* 1991).

Workstations, together with PCs, squeezed the mid-range market with the arrival of Intel 486-based and Motorola 68040-based systems, as well as workstations based on reduced instruction set chips (RISC). The single-CPU microcomputer already appeared to match the power of the classic minicomputer. The traditional PC vendors had introduced products that carved out a new multiprocessing market. Examples included Compaq Computer's Systempro, which supported two Intel CPUs, and Olivetti's CP486, which coupled an Intel 486 microprocessor with an i860 RISC chip. In a UNIX-based, 60-user configuration, Compaq's Systempro was more than six times faster than the HP 9000 Series 835, even though the $25,000 Systempro sold for about $135,000 less than Digital's VAX and for about $68,000 less than HP's 9000. In addition, Systempro offered an impressive 15 million instructions per second (MIPS). This sub-segment would continue to outpace other segments in the computer industry.

PERSONAL COMPUTERS

The products in the personal computer industry could have been grouped into two categories: desktops and portables. Although desktops accounted for about 90% of the market, demand for portables exhibited a much higher growth rate. The introduction of lighter and smaller computers had blurred the distinctions between these two categories (*U.S. Industrial Outlook*, 1990).

Desktops

A *desktop computer* is a microcomputer system that can fit on a desktop (Parker, 1992). Desktop computers make up 90% of all personal computer industry sales. They were available in an increasing number of sizes and configurations. Although workstations and desktops had largely targeted different markets, their fundamentals were very similar. Workstations were for the scientific and engineering marketplace, desktops for the commercial marketplace. Keeping the two separate and distinct were software applications.

Portables

Portable computers are microcomputers compact enough to be carried about easily (Parker, 1992). In 1989 the U.S. market for portable computers totaled $3.7 billion, a 24% increase from 1988, according to Dataquest, Inc. Portable computers were designed in a broad range of shapes and sizes and were divided into three major categories: transportables, laptops, and notebooks. *Transportables* had been around the longest, required AC power, and weighed approximately 20 pounds. *Laptops,* defined as portable computers light enough to be operated while they rest on the operator's lap, became serious contenders in the business sector because of improvements in technology, such as increased battery life, screen visibility, and memory capacity. The laptops have a slimmer line, weigh between 10 and 20 pounds, and have a rechargeable battery. *Notebooks* are defined as portable computers that weigh between 4 and 8 pounds, are 8.5 by 11 by 2 inches in size, and extend operating time up to 8 hours on battery power. Liquid crystal display (LCD) technology is used in manufacturing screens for notebook computers. Color screens have been available at a premium since late 1991. All these categories are designed to be compatible with desktop models (Parker, 1992).

All of the portable market leaders introduced a notebook system, with a wide range of prices from $800 for a 286-12 based system to $10,000 for a 486-33 based color system (*PC Week,* March 23, 1992, p. 1). Notebook computers provide a convenient means of information processing, allowing immediate order placement and the elimination of redundant data entry. The emerging notebooks based on the Intel 386 and 486 chips, as well as the color screen, were accelerating sales.

The market for notebook computers became the fastest-growing sector in the computer industry. The increase in notebook computer sales came as sales of desktop personal computers were slowing, particularly in the United States. The unit shipment of notebooks in 1990 was 840,000 units; this figure was expected to reach 1.5 million units, of which 10,000 were color (Hoga, 1991). By 1995 notebook sales were expected to be about 50% of all personal computers, and the demand for notebooks in Europe was expected to increase 30%. In Japan, laptop computers accounted for more than 40% of all PC sales, as the notebook computers were especially well suited for use in Tokyo's crowded offices. Of recent significance was the Bush administration's lifting of trade sanctions against imports of laptops manufactured in Japan.

Two other different kinds of portable computers are palmbook computers and slate computers. Poqet Computer pioneered the palmbook technology with a 1.1-pound IBM-compatible PC that fits easily into a coat pocket, and Hewlett-Packard offered a similar product for about $400, $300 less than the price at which it was first offered. The slate computer is about notebook-size with an electronic pen. Software enables the computer to interpret handwritten characters. These two sub-categories would grow at a much faster pace once they were compatible with desktops.

CUSTOMERS

The customers in the industry can be broken down into four categories: business, home, scientific, and education (*U.S. Industrial Outlook,* 1989). Exhibits 6.7 and 6.8 show a breakdown of sales units and dollar value by application from 1986 to 1992 (the sales from 1989 to 1992 are estimated).

Business

Business customers range from small businesses to major corporations in all industries. As shown in Exhibits 6.7 and 6.8, the business/professional market sector purchased more than 60% of the units sold in the United States, which represented more than two-thirds of the total market value. The 21% increase in total units sold in 1988, reaching a level of 6.3 million units, was well below the exceptional growth rate of 54% in 1987. This could have been explained by the fact that managers tended to wait for new-product developments before approving the purchase of new systems, trying to assess the cost-effectiveness of a new purchase.

Home

Sales to the home market sector were expected to decline for a number of reasons. Included was the growing utility of portable computers, which are used in both the home and the office. Also, the home market was purchasing items such as video game systems and TV-interactive home services, which are more popular in the home than personal computers. Unit shipments to the home market rose only 4% to 2.5 million units, while the value of shipments to this market sector increased 16% to $3.3 billion in 1988.

EXHIBIT 6.7 | **The U.S. PC Market**

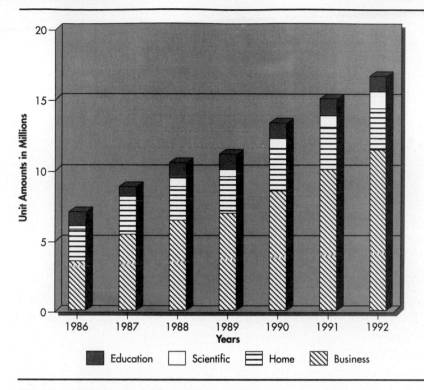

Source: U. S. Industrial Outlook, 1989, pp. 26–27.

Scientific

The scientific market sector was the fastest-growing customer in the industry. Technological developments enabled this sector to design, for use in its field, parts and machinery, schematics, complex diagrams, and complex calculations that previously had taken too long to be efficient. Unit shipments in this market segment had double-digit increases in the late 1980s.

Education

Sales to the education market segment have two dimensions. The education market itself is targeted for computer use in institutions and for the prospect of obtaining future purchases from the students and faculty for personal or professional use. Unit shipments to this market increased by 12% in 1988 and should continue to increase in the early 1990s.

EXHIBIT 6.8

The U.S. PC Market
(Dollar amounts in billions)

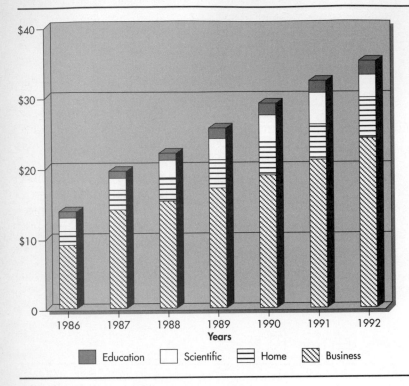

■ Education   ☐ Scientific   ☰ Home   ▨ Business

Source: U. S. Industrial Outlook, 1989, pp. 26–27.

DISTRIBUTION

Dealership

Computers and computer products have been distributed largely through authorized dealers, or resellers, such as Businessland, Computerland, and Computer Attic.
The authorized dealers have been trained in the functions and capabilities of the
various computers and should be able to advise prospective purchasers on what
product or manufacturer will suit their needs. The manufacturer usually provides
the training and sometimes offers support and/or incentives to the sales force,
which were the keys to success in ensuring good relations between them and the
authorized dealers. Some companies, such as Tandy, have distributed PCs through
their own retail stores. An advantage of this type of distribution is the direct customer contact involved.

Direct Marketing

An alternative to the dealership in the PC industry is direct marketing, by which the
PC manufacturers sell directly to the customers. An example of direct marketing is

mail-order sales. This way the manufacturers bypass the "middlemen" and reduce the costs of distributing PCs to the customers. Meantime, the customers can avoid sales tax if they order from an out-of-state source. Direct marketing has been emerging strongly. 1991 was the banner year for direct marketers such as Gateway 2000, Dell Computer Corp., Zeos International, and AST Research. "Now, PC purchases are on the same level as purchasing paper supplies," said Brian Clarke of International Data Corp. "The end user is an educated consumer. He's more prone to shop around for the best deal" (*PC Week,* 1991). PC components, like circuit boards (mother boards), cases, floppy drives, and hard disks, can be swappable among different brands. These direct marketers have been operating on slim margins, and with minimal R&D budgets and low overhead, so they were able to undercut the prices of first-tier vendors. "For $1,399, IBM has a 286-10. For $1,450, I can buy a Gateway 2000 386SX with two floppy-disk drives and a color monitor," said Glen Bell, director of academic computing at Spring Hill College in Mobile, Alabama. In addition, the top direct marketers have developed a reputation for offering solid, reliable machines and have proved that they are in the PC business for the long term. At the same time, each of these firms has gained market share. As these firms expanded, the long-held belief that PC managers must buy from top-tier vendors to purchase quality machines began to fade. As their reputations matured, the direct marketers also become known for offering service that was usually on a par with—and sometimes better than—support offered by local dealers or resellers.

MARKETS

Domestic Market

The U.S. PC market is very competitive because barriers to entry and exit are insignificant. This market consists of the major and well-known computer manufacturers as well as of many clone makers. The growing presence of many small- and middle-sized PC clone makers is the major force eroding the major market share. The costs of establishing a PC clone manufacturing are relatively small, as most of the components are standardized. Exhibit 6.9 illustrates the division of PC sales in the United States among vendors in 1991.

Global Market

The U.S. PC makers follow global manufacturing strategies, and many depend on overseas suppliers and markets for a major share (typically 20–40%) of their revenues. The U.S. PC industry's major overseas market is Europe, which accounted for over $10 billion in sales. The U.S. manufacturers purchase equipment, parts, and labor from the lowest-cost suppliers, which are primarily located in the Far East. Imports have been growing at a strong pace, though this pace will be slowed in the future by foreign manufacturers moving inshore to be closer to the U.S. market, to avoid trade sanctions, and to minimize the effects of devaluation of the dollar (*U.S. Industrial Outlook,* 1989). In 1992 several trade barriers were lifted, which opened up a prosperous new market for many companies and offered opportunities to those that have had an existing strong presence in Europe. Exhibit 6.10 illustrates the division of PC sales in Western Europe among vendors in 1991.

EXHIBIT 6.9

U.S. PC Market by Vendor, 1991
(9.5 million units)

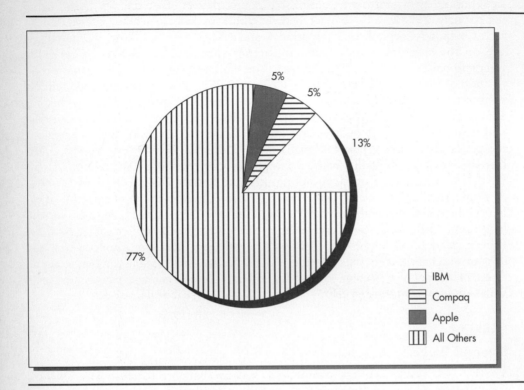

5%
5%
13%
77%

IBM
Compaq
Apple
All Others

Source: *S & P Industry Surveys*, November 17, 1991.

COMPETITION

Competitive Environment

While experiencing both supplier consolidation and the formation of new firms, the worldwide PC industry has been exhibiting maturation at the low end and rapid technical changes at the high end. The commodity-like nature of lower-priced PCs, based on high production volumes, standardized designs, off-the-shelf components, and low support and service requirements, made new firms' entry costs relatively small. This resulted in a significant increase in systems vendors worldwide and a lowering of market concentration. Even though the top two suppliers, IBM and Apple, still have almost one-fifth of the U.S. market, the market share of the top 10 suppliers dropped from 75% in 1983 to less than 50% in 1990 (*Standard & Poor's Industry Surveys*, 1991).

The move to low-end machines, which carried lower profit margins, put the squeeze on the bottom line of most manufacturers. Also, more and more computers were utilizing off-the-shelf central processors, which make products from different manufacturers more interchangeable and thus less profitable, giving the

EXHIBIT 6.10	Western Europe PC Market by Vendor, 1991
	(7.8 million units)

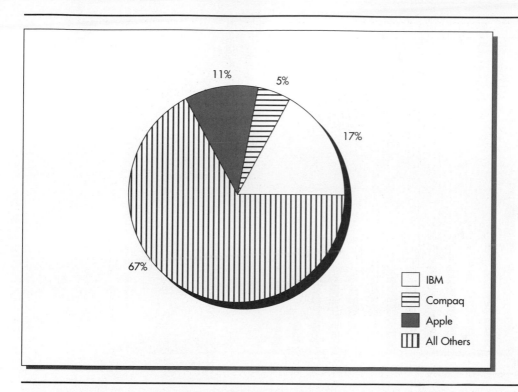

Source: S & P Industry Surveys, November 17, 1991.

advantage to IBM-compatible users. As a direct result, many companies moved to make their products tie into other computer gear (Niemond, 1990).

Exhibit 6.11 ranks the 20 leading U.S. computer makers in terms of profit margins for 1991. Exhibits 6.12 and 6.13 rank them in terms of sales growth for the latest 5 years and 12 months, respectively. Exhibits 6.14 and 6.15 rank them in terms of ROE for the latest 5 years and 12 months, respectively.

The majority of the companies ranked in these exhibits were widely diversified within the computer industry, which included such areas as mainframe computers, minicomputers, microcomputers, peripherals, software, and maintenance. Compaq was top ranked in terms of the 5-year ROE but only ninth in terms of ROE for the latest 12 months. Exhibit 6.13 shows that Compaq had a negative increase in sales in 1991.

Competitors

IBM in 1981 introduced its first PC, setting the standard for the personal computer industry, and immediately claimed about half of the PC market share.

EXHIBIT 6.11 | **20 Major Computer Makers' Profit Margin, 1991**

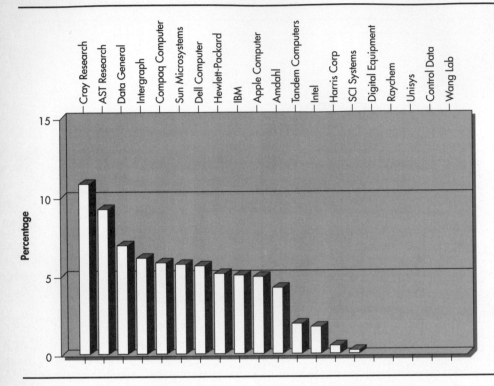

Source: *Forbes*, January 6, 1992, p. 113.

In 1985, when the U.S. computer industry slump started, IBM's profits began to slide, and so did those of many other computer makers. In 1988 IBM reorganized after three years of disappointing profits (Bernstein, 1988). This did not stop the downward trend of IBM's dominance in the PC market, as its market share dropped to about 29% in early 1989. IBM entered the workstation segment early in 1990. The company had a strong balance sheet, which should have enabled it to get through the predicted slow industry growth. Nineteen-ninety-one witnessed IBM's first loss in over 45 years, although IBM held about 17.3% of the U.S. PC market and 12.7% of the Western European market (*Standard and Poor's Industry Surveys*, 1991).

Apple Computer is a California-based computer manufacturer founded in 1977. The company makes personal computers and related software and peripherals. It also offers several different personal computer products, which are marketed toward different customers. The original Apple II line was sold to education and home markets. The new Macintosh line, sold largely to businesses, consists of user-friendly computers that make use of graphic icons (pictorial representations of functions) and of a mouse input device.

EXHIBIT 6.12	20 Major Computer Makers' Sales Growth, Latest 5 Years

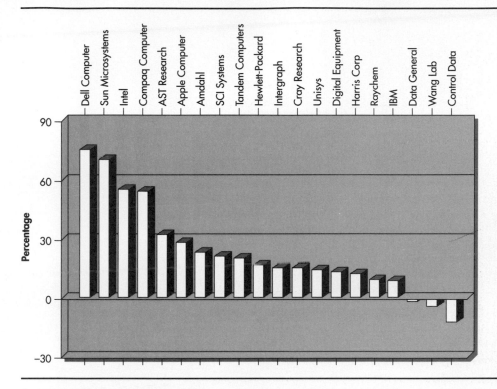

Source: Forbes, January 6, 1992, p. 113.

Apple products used to be sold at a premium price, but as buyers became more price-sensitive, the company had to make significant price reductions. The education market was a large customer of Apple products. This field tended to buy low-end machines, which carried less profit. Apple consistently had to keep costs to a minimum in this area, and the company took a $224 million pretax charge in June 1991 to cover the cost of reducing its work force by 10%, to consolidate facilities, and to move manufacturing to lower-cost regions (*Value Line,* November 1, 1991).

A possible weakness of the Apple product line was that the computers were not IBM-compatible. The company stressed their easy-to-learn interface, which gave users a consistent look no matter what application they were running. The joint venture between Apple and IBM in 1991 should make Apple machines compatible with IBM PCs. The company's strong balance sheet should enable it to ride out the tough times predicted.

Tandy Corporation was first incorporated in New Jersey in 1899 and was reincorporated in Delaware in 1967. The company is a manufacturer and marketer of consumer electronic products for the home, office, and education markets. It is a

EXHIBIT 6.13 | **20 Major Computer Makers' Sales Growth, 1991**

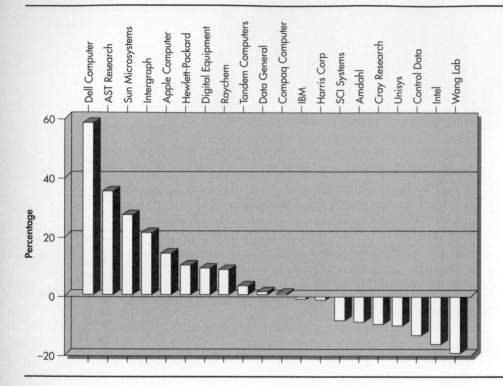

Source: Forbes, January 6, 1992, p. 113.

leading retailer of a broad range of consumer electronic products, with some 4,812 owned and 2,233 franchised Radio Shacks and other outlets. Tandy owned and operated 27 plants in the United States and abroad, manufacturing about half of the private label sold exclusively through its Radio Shack division in 1991.

Tandy is also an important manufacturer of microcomputers that are offered through the Radio Shack stores. Tandy acquired GRID Systems, a portable computer manufacturer, in the hope of increasing sales to corporations and the government.

Radio Shack sales were flat between 1989 and 1991. This was because there were few new products and because the existing products were priced too high in comparison with the competition. Another reason might have been Radio Shack's image. The chain sold a lot of low-ticket, obscure electronic parts and hence was not often thought of as the place to buy things mass-marketed by others. This image needed to be upgraded.

Commodore International, through its subsidiaries, is a fully integrated, independent manufacturer and marketer of personal computers and related microcomputer products. It was first incorporated in Canada in 1958 and was reincorporated in the Bahamas in 1976. It markets its products to homes, educational institutions, and businesses.

EXHIBIT 6.14	20 Major Computer Makers' ROE, Latest 5 Years

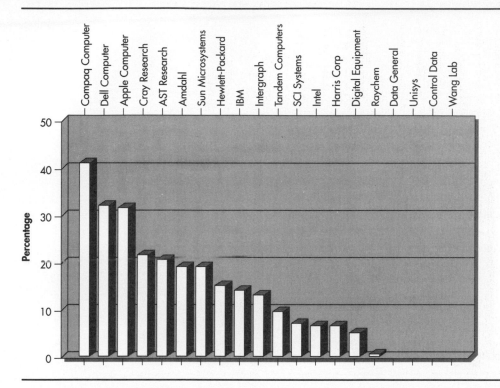

Source: Forbes, January 6, 1992, p. 113.

Commodore's PC line was IBM-compatible, and the company had strengthened the high end of its IBM-compatible personal computer series by basing the models on the powerful Intel processors.

Commodore's products had long been accepted as strong contenders in Europe (85% of the company's revenue was booked in Europe, where Commodore ranked second only to IBM in units sold), but its efforts lagged in the United States. The U.S. market viewed Commodore products as low-powered computers suitable only for entertainment. To dispel this image, the company installed a new management team and mounted a $15 million advertising campaign. Given that continued sluggish demand was expected for low-end personal computers, performance was not expected to be very high for this company (*Value Line,* November 1, 1991).

The first generation of PCs revolved around the IBM Corporation. These machines were built with IBM personal computer compatibility in mind. However, many PC makers did not follow IBM's microchannel technology. The major selling point for most of these *clone manufacturers* was lower prices and better quality (Bright, 1986). The improvements IBM made in hardware and software did not make cloning any more difficult. Though many who bought IBM considered it

| EXHIBIT 6.15 | 20 Major Computer Makers' ROE, 1991 |

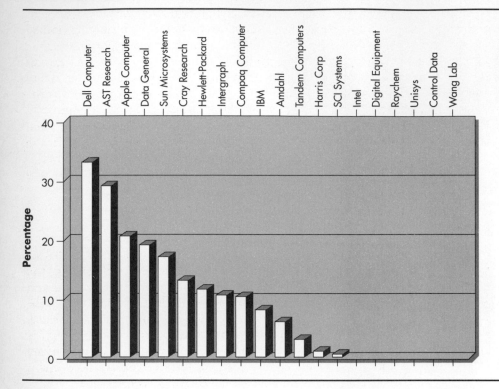

Source: Forbes, January 6, 1992, p. 113.

safest to buy the best, not everyone saw IBM as setting the standard anymore (Schnorbus, 1988). The IBM-compatible PC market was a potentially lucrative source of royalty revenue for IBM; in 1990 royalty revenue was estimated at $78.7 million (Keefe, 1989). But these clone makers have become a real threat to the major computer manufacturers, because they have been grabbing more and more market share. Nineteen-ninety-one was a banner year for many clone makers, including AST Research, Dell Computer, Gateway 2000, Northgate, and many others.

THE COMPANY

HISTORY

Compaq Computer Corporation was founded in 1982. Joseph Canion, known as one of the most famous baby-boom bosses, was co-founder and chief executive of the company. "Rod" Canion started out at Texas Instruments, designing computer printers. He was frustrated by the bureaucracy and all the paperwork, and he had a better idea. He quit his middle-manager position after 13 years there. Along with some Texas Instrument colleagues, he set out to build personal computers that were compatible with the industry-standard architecture established by IBM in 1981, but technologically superior ("Managing," 1988).

Compaq built a reputation in the personal computer market for providing powerful, reliable systems that set performance standards that other companies, including IBM, inevitably followed (Furger, 1989). At Compaq, growth was phenomenal. In 1988 it became the first company to reach $2 billion in sales in only five years of existence ("Company Profiles," 1989). Compaq consistently demonstrated its ability to redefine the existing standard of personal computers with engineering excellence and innovation (Honan, 1988). Michael S. Swavely, president of the North American division of Compaq Computer Corporation, said in an interview that a combination of factors contributed to the spectacular growth of the company. For example, the underlying market growth was very high during the time that Compaq was growing, and the firm was able to position itself correctly from a strategic perspective to take maximum advantage of that market growth ("Rapid Rise to the Top," 1989).

PRODUCTS

Compaq's computers were IBM-compatible and held a leading share of the IBM-compatible desktop market. The desktop personal computer market was the mainstay of Compaq's business. Desktops made up the majority of its sales and accounted for 90% of all industry sales. Compaq's product line featured high-performance desktops, portables, and laptops for business and professional use. Compaq emphasized quality, reliability, additional features, and full functionality of its products and, with each new generation of microprocessors, had emphasized the higher-performance end of the market. Compaq believed performance was a more important factor than price in the purchase decision for its products.

Compaq was able to bring new products to market more quickly than its competitors because the firm focused its time and resources on understanding the needs of business personal computer users. Compaq spent about 5.2% of revenues on research and development (*Value Line,* November 1, 1991). By focusing on marketing, Compaq was able to provide the right mix of product features at the precise moment when the market could support them. Changes in the computer industry should have made Compaq revise its strategy.

Desktops

The fastest-growing segment of the desktop computer market was composed of personal computers based on the latest Intel Corporation technology—more specifically, the Intel 386 and 486 microprocessors. Introduced in September 1986, before IBM's product, the Compaq 386-based PC remained the premium supplier to this market. The speed and power of these machines enabled them to be used as engineering and scientific workstations, file servers in networks, and productivity tools for managing businesses and organizations.

Laptops

Numerous lightweight, battery-powered PCs came on the market in 1988. Compaq waited to enter this market until the right combination of technology and packaging became available to meet the needs of its users. The company introduced its SLT/286 personal computer late in October 1988, believing it was the first real business-class laptop. Technologically, however, laptop computers had their limits because they had to be light. Laptops were quickly losing their significance in 1991.

Notebooks

Once the sales and technology leader with its notebooks, Compaq was losing customers as many PC makers shifted to notebooks (1.5 million units were sold, of which 10,000 were color). AST Research, Dell Computer Corp., and other competitors seized the notebook technology initiative. While Compaq was slow to update its notebooks, those competitors were adopting the latest processors, screens, and communications capabilities. Compaq's main problem, according to users, is price (Boudette, 1992).

Recently Compaq planned to announce its first notebooks based on 386SL (power-saving) chips. However, Compaq representatives declined to comment on the unannounced products, simply acknowledging both the company's notebook development efforts and its expected price points. Compaq announced its 486-chip-based notebooks for delivery in the middle of 1992 (Zimmerman, 1992).

DISTRIBUTION

Compaq Computer Corporation distributes its products only through authorized dealers. The company does not sell products directly, nor does it offer any type of leasing arrangements. In 1991 about 3,800 authorized dealers distributed Compaq's products worldwide (*Value Line,* November 1, 1991). A weakness existed in that the company's success depended on the dealer's success. For example, Businessland Inc., one of Compaq's largest dealers, and Compaq had a falling out for over a year that hurt both companies' sales. In 1988 Businessland accounted for 7%, or $147 million, of Compaq's $2.1 billion in sales, and Compaq products accounted for 15% of Businessland's 1988 revenues (Calkins, 1989).

Compaq provides support to its dealers in selling, servicing, and training programs. Compaq expanded its sales force and doubled the size of its field systems engineering staff, believing that these groups played important sales and technical support roles between major businesses and authorized dealers. The company developed incentives to dealers for employing systems engineers, creating special demonstration centers, and attending advanced Compaq training classes.

After suffering the first quarterly loss in its history for the three months which ended September 30, 1991, Compaq was scrambling to reshape its distribution. It started looking toward its own sales force instead of to resellers to shore up sagging sales. Compaq began granting more authority to its sales staff by allowing them to accept orders instead of forcing them to turn all sales over to dealers. Although Compaq officials maintained that resellers were a key component of its business, there were many signs that Compaq no longer viewed the resellers' role to be as crucial as it once had been. One sign was that Compaq no longer had a vice president of corporate marketing to act as ambassador to the reselling community. Responsibility for that job was split among many different executives after the restructuring of

October 1991. In addition, Compaq indicated that it might reallocate the 2–3% of sales that the company gave to resellers for marketing and support. Compaq was also considering other methods of developing closer ties to customers, from extending telephone support lines to 24-hour-a-day service, to establishing on-line support service for customers and starting a mail-order business (Fisher, 1991).

CUSTOMERS

In 1987 and again in 1988, Compaq's share of the U.S. business PC market, as measured by dealer revenue, was 24%. IBM's share decreased in 1988 to 34% from 41% in 1987. Apple's share was 11% in 1988 and 12% in 1987.

Compaq's weakness in this area was that it ignored 33.4% of the remaining PC market. This market was left to Compaq competitors to target, especially the clone makers. Compaq's advertising techniques exemplified this. In 1989 Compaq spent in the range of $25–30 million on advertising—all geared toward the business customers. In March 1989, a $10 million network and cable TV campaign focused on what experts said about Compaq, while showing business PC users benefiting from the brand's high performance and illustrating the theme "it simply works better" (Lawrence, 1989).

INTERNATIONAL MARKETS

At the end of 1988, international sales accounted for nearly 40% of the company's revenues. The largest portion of this revenue came from Europe, where Compaq held a strong presence. A new manufacturing facility in Scotland was purchased to enhance European operations. The company felt that through the mid-1990s the growth rate in Europe, combined with its size, would be the major factor in Compaq's growth.

At the end of 1989, international sales grew 62% to $1.3 billion, contributing 45% of Compaq's revenue. International sales accounted for 54% of its revenue in 1991. North American revenues increased 24%, which reinforced Compaq's number-two position in the business PC market in the United States and Canada. Again the largest portion of these sales came from Western Europe, where Compaq had a substantial business-customer base in the large financial, insurance, and manufacturing companies. The company saw further opportunities in this market with the 1992 European Community lifting of trade barriers.

COST/EARNINGS

Exhibit 6.16 compares Compaq's performance ratios to the industry average from 1987 to 1991.

Things did not improve in 1991 at Compaq. In the second quarter of 1991, Compaq's net income fell 81% and sales fell 17%. In the third quarter of 1991, Compaq, for the first time in the company's history, took a $135 million charge to cover the cost of laying off 12% of its work force. In the fourth quarter of 1991, the company earned about $40.3 million net income on sales of $800 million, far below the fourth quarter of 1990 (Wilke, 1992). For the year, Compaq was the biggest casualty in the PC industry as a result of competition. Meanwhile Apple, Stratus Computer, AST Research, Dell Computer, Gateway 2000, and Sun Microsystems had a better year, as did hundreds of small IBM clone makers.

According to International Data Corp., 3.8 million computers were sold for home use in 1991, down from 4 million in 1990. During that time, the market shifted from lower-speed Intel 286-based machines to faster Intel 386 machines and notebooks. As a result, when IBM and Tandy were still trying to get rid of these old machines as PS/1 and 1000RL, they suffered losses (Lancaster, 1992).

At the same time, Compaq Computer's recent restructuring cut deeper into its work force than previously acknowledged. Stung by stagnant demand and a vicious price war, Compaq struggled unsuccessfully for most of 1991 against nimbler, more cost-effective makers of PC clones. Then Compaq's board surprised the computer world by jettisoning Compaq founder Joseph R. Canion, a soft-spoken engineer, in favor of Eckhard Pfeiffer, who is believed to be an aggressive marketing whiz (Fisher, 1991). Pfeiffer quickly signaled his intention to shake up Compaq, mainly by bringing its cost structure somewhat closer to that of competitors such as Dell Computer Corp. and AST Research Inc. "Everybody knows that when you have to cut, you go as deep as you can without hitting the bone," Mr. Pfeiffer said. "We went very deep: our intent clearly has been not to have any more cuts" (Hooper, 1991).

Some analysts noticed the differences in style between Compaq's former boss and the current CEO. Canion warned in December 1991 that the "autocratic" management style of his replacement, Pfeiffer, could cause the company problems: "When there is turmoil in the industry, if you get caught making changes too rapidly and not waiting to see if they are working, you can get into serious trouble. That is just one of the pitfalls of the type of manager Eckhard is. Pfeiffer is likely to create a more autocratic environment rather than the participative environment. I believe what I did well was to look carefully, decide on a course and stay the

| EXHIBIT 6.16 | Compaq Performance versus That of the Industry |

	1987	1988	1989	1990	1991	1992
Industry operating margin	20.00	20.00	17.90	18.10	17.00	17.50
Compaq operating margin	20.90	19.80	20.00	21.80	12.00	14.00
Industry net margin	8.50	8.80	6.30	6.40	5.30	5.70
Compaq net margin	10.90	12.00	11.10	12.00	4.09	7.00
Industry % earned capital	12.50	13.30	10.20	10.50	8.50	9.50
Compaq % earned capital	25.00	24.10	22.80	23.50	8.50	11.50
Industry % earned net worth	13.70	15.30	11.90	11.90	9.50	10.50
Compaq % earned net worth	33.40	30.50	27.20	23.20	9.00	12.00

Source: Value Line, November 1, 1991, p. 1077.

course." According to *PC Week,* Canion was shocked by the abruptness with which Compaq's chairman Rosen pushed his resignation (Burke, 1991).

According to Compaq's new president, Compaq's new strategies will be the PC market first, systems second. Pfeiffer said, "We are refocusing very clearly on the PC market opportunity. We cannot let ourselves drift into a niche, high-performance environment only, or we'll miss the volume opportunity." He splits the PC market into high-performance, low-cost, and mass-market segments for the number-four PC maker (Dodge, 1991).

TOWARD THE FUTURE

In early 1992, Compaq was restructuring. It was undertaking a 12% reduction in headcount and was expected to separate into two business entities—personal computers and systems. The board named COO Eckhard Pfeiffer to replace chairman and CEO Rod Canion, who left to pursue other interests. Market conditions remained lackluster. The company indicated that there were as yet no signs of a recovery in its markets. However, the restructuring was expected to make Compaq leaner and meaner in an industry that had become increasingly differentiated. On the PC side, customers were much more cost-conscious as personal computers continued to be considered a commodity. Smart shoppers would buy clones in which the components were made by those well-known original-equipment manufacturers whose components were sold in whole pieces, as the circuit boards, drives, and hard disks. Compaq had to maintain its perceived premium-performance image but lower its prices, resulting in tighter margins. It had to alter its distribution strategy, such as by expanding its marketing channel to include office supply and computer superstores, in order to compete effectively. On the systems side, the chore was to make inroads against the workstation and minicomputer manufacturers in an already competitive market segment (*Value Line,* November 1, 1991).

Compaq was expected to face another tough year in 1992, as it had more than a 100% decrease in its 1991 net profit. The company still believed that Compaq would regain its market position. It expected to continue growth in Western Europe, and it was optimistic also with its lineup of new products for the 1990s.

With industry experts predicting a general softening of the desktop personal computer market (mainly because the U.S. PC market and the European PC market were approaching maturity), Compaq was facing difficult strategic decisions. For example, one decision under consideration involved what to do in the workstation market. Industry experts expected the workstation market to quadruple through the mid-1990s. The majority of workstation sales came from the business and educational communities. Workstation systems carried a price tag of about $100,000, with relatively higher margins than the low-end desktop computers. On one hand, three companies (Hewlett-Packard, Digital, and Sun Microsystems) accounted for roughly 80% of the workstation segment revenue. With Compaq's ability to move on ideas, changing user requirements, market trends, and the availability of new technology, it should be able to enter this segment with the same ease with which it entered the personal computer segment. On the other hand, the industry giant,

IBM, was notable for its presence in this market segment, which would make the workstation segment very competitive. Compaq was already established in the business community, but it would have to expand into the educational community in order to compete in this segment.

Some Compaq managers felt that it would be too risky to expand to the workstation segment of the computer industry. New-product introductions offering greater performance at lower costs had already been seen. Also, in the near future, advances in components and software, along with the adoption of a common graphical user interface standard, might eliminate performance differences that currently distinguish low-end workstations from high-end personal computers. Research and development costs were high in this area, and Compaq was not expected to increase its R&D spending. Competition was expected to intensify: some leading U.S. personal computer firms were using their experience in retailing and a broad base of applications software to win commercial customers, and Japanese electronics companies and many hundreds of clone manufacturers in the Pacific Rim countries, as well as in the United States, were able to offer low-cost, high-volume, and high-quality products.

Another alternative, supported by many of Compaq's executives, was to expand Compaq's distribution channels to include leasing arrangements. With cash flow slowing, credit costs rising, and computer hardware technology advancing at a rapid pace, more and more corporate managers were seeking special leasing arrangements to help them reduce the risk of an outright purchase.

Some managers felt that Compaq should offer its own leasing arrangements, which would provide simultaneous expansion into the retail market. They felt that with Compaq's quality recognition, worldwide presence, and IBM-compatibility, this strategy would provide greater opportunities for increased sales.

Other Compaq executives felt that this strategy would not be in their best interest, because computer users who needed to live on the leading edge of technology would be forever demanding upgrades in the middle of the lease. This would cause tremendous problems for the company's manufacturing and proposed financing activities.

In early 1992, Compaq was wondering what to do about these and other possible strategic alternatives. Some actions definitely had to be taken, but at that point no consensus had been reached.

REFERENCES

Allen, Michael. *Wall Street Journal,* January 29, 1992, p. A3.

Bartimo, Jim. *Wall Street Journal,* July 25, 1991, p. B5.

Bernstein, Aaron. "Big Changes at Big Blue." *Business Week,* February 15, 1988, pp. 92–98.

Blumenthal, Karen. *Wall Street Journal,* January 8, 1991, p. B2.

Boudette, Neal. "Compaq Struggles to Maintain Its Share of Notebook Market." *PC Week,* December 2, 1992, p. 140.

Bright, David. "Microcomputers." *Computer World,* October 20, 1986, pp. 41–42, 47–54.

Burke, Steve. "A Tale of Two Presidents." *PC Week,* December 16, 1991, p. 1.

Calkins, Laurel B. "Their Compact Is Broken." *Business Month,* April 1989, p. 17.

"Company Profiles." *Datamation,* June 15, 1989, pp. 68–162.

Compaq Computer Corporation, *1989 Annual Report.*

"Computer and Peripherals Industry." *Value Line,* May 4, 1990, pp. 1078–1079.

"Computer Equipment and Software." *U.S. Industrial Outlook 1990,* pp. 30.1–30.14.

"Computer Equipment and Software." *U.S. Industrial Outlook 1989,* pp. 26.1–26.11.

"Computers and Office Equipment." *Standard & Poor's Industrial Survey,* June 15, 1989, pp. C75–C91.

"Computers—Current Analysis." *Standard & Poor's Industrial Survey,* November 16, 1989, pp. C61–C65.

Corporate Performance Review, Third Quarter 1991. *Wall Street Journal,* November 4, 1991, p. A10.

Dubaski, Jagannath. "Computers: A Global Report." *Financial World,* November 28, 1989, pp. 42–55.

Fisher, Susan E. "Computer Giants Take a Beating in Fourth Quarter." *PC Week,* January 20, 1992, p. 93.

Fisher, Susan E. "Fourth Quarter Gives Large PC Makers Glimmer of Hope." *PC Week,* January 13, 1992, p. 120.

Fisher, Susan E. "Compaq Boots Sales Force to Shore up Bottom Line." *PC Week,* December 2, 1991, p. 137.

Fletcher, James A. "In Defense of Compaq." *Computerworld,* August 25, 1986, pp. 33 and 35.

Francis, Bob. "The Desktop Dimension." *Datamation,* November 1, 1989, pp. 28–113.

Furger, Roberta. "Compaq Tries to Top Itself." *Infoworld,* December 4, 1989, pp. 46–50.

"The Greatest Capitalist in History." *Fortune,* August 31, 1987, pp. 24–35.

Hoga, Mike. *PC World,* November 1991, p. 15.

Honan, Patrick. "Compaq Computer Corporation: Upholding the Standard." *Personal Computing,* August 1988, pp. 92–98.

Hooper, Laurence. "Compaq Pares 300 More Jobs in Revamping." *Wall Street Journal,* December 16, 1991, p. B6.

Keefe, Patricia and Michael Alexander. "Compaq to Pay IBM Patent Bill." *Computerworld,* July 17, 1989, p. 1.

Kelly, Joseph. "Three Markets Shape One Industry." *Datamation,* June 15, 1989, pp. 6–14.

Lancaster, Hal. "Growth of Home PC Market Is Impeded by Confusing Array of Products, Prices." *Wall Street Journal,* January 3, 1992, p. B1.

Lawrence, Jennifer. "Compaq Gets Down to Business." *Advertising Age,* March 20, 1989, p. 61.

"Managing." *Fortune,* August 15, 1988, p. 60.

Markoff, John. "David Gelernter's Romance with Linda." *New York Times,* January 19, 1992, Section 3, p. 6.

Moody's Handbook of Common Stock, 1989.

Niemond, George A. "Computer and Peripherals Industry." *Value Line,* May 4, 1990, pp. 1078-1079.

Parker, Charles S. *Understanding Computer and Information Processing,* 4th ed. Fort Worth, Texas: Dryden, 1992, pp. g-5 and g-12.

PC Week, December 30, 1991, p. 25.

PC Week, December 23, 1991, p. 25.

"Rapid Rise to the Top: An Interview with Compaq's Michael S. Swavely." *Journal of Business Strategy,* November/December 1989, pp. 4–7.

Savitz, Eric J. "Pulling the Plug: The Great Boom in PCs May Be Coming to an End." *Barron's,* July 24, 1989, pp. 8–9, 28–29.

Scheier, Robert L. *PC Week,* February 3, 1992, p. 109.

Schnorbus, Paula. "Business Adds Byte." *Marketing and Media Decisions,* January 1988, pp. 57–68.

"Spotlight Profiles." *Datamation,* June 15, 1989, p. 36.

Standard & Poor's Industry Surveys, October 17, 1991, pp. C61–95.

"Standard NYSE Stock Reports." *Standard & Poor's,* February 28, 1990.

U.S. Industrial Outlook, 1991, pp. 28.1–28.18.

Value Line, November 1, 1991, p. 1086.

Value Line, May 4, 1990, p. 1086.

Value Line, February 2, 1990, p. 1086.

Wall Street Journal, January 20, 1992, p. A1.

Wall Street Journal, November 4, 1991, p. A11.

"What the Leaders Think." *Electronic Business,* March 19, 1990, p. 73.

Wilke, John R. *Wall Street Journal,* January 10, 1992, p. B3 and January 21, 1992, p. A1.

Wise, Ray. "Falling Profits, Tight Credit Boost Demand for Lease Deals." *Electronic Business,* March 19, 1990, pp. 115–116.

Zachary, G. Pascal and Andy Zipser. "Businessland Is Compaq's Land Again." *Wall Street Journal,* March 8, 1990. pp. B1 and B8.

Zimmerman, Michael. "Compaq Readying Its First 386SL-Based Notebooks." *PC Week,* January 6, 1992, p. 4.

Zipser, Andy. "Compaq Profit Decreased 14% in 4th Quarter." *Wall Street Journal,* February 2, 1990, p. A4.

CASE 7 Crowley Inn: "Une Bonne Place pour Rester"

Arthur Sharplin

Crowley, Louisiana, hometown of colorful Louisiana governor Edwin "Fast Eddie" Edwards, is in the heart of Cajun country 60 miles west of Baton Rouge. Crowley Inn, with 59 rooms, a restaurant, and a bar, is at the intersection of Louisiana Highway 13, the main north-south route through Crowley, and Interstate Highway 10. Also at that intersection are a Texaco and an Exxon station, a Kentucky Fried Chicken store, and a Burger King restaurant. But many townspeople took special interest in the inn. Mayor Bob Istre said, "Crowley Inn is the first business you see, the only one out there that calls itself 'Crowley' anything." Inn manager Shirley Miller explained, "C'est pour du monde de la village au Crowley [It is for the people of the village of Crowley]."

The inn was completed in 1973. The owner defaulted on his $800,000 loan in 1986, resulting in seizure by the lender, a savings and loan company. The S&L was taken over by the Resolution Trust Corporation (RTC) in 1990. Then, on May 21, 1991, the RTC sold the inn to Art and Kathy Sharplin, of Lake Charles, 45 miles west of Crowley. Art taught business at McNeese State University in Lake Charles.

They formed Crowley Motel, Inc. (CMI) to hold the property and assigned Art's associate Debbie King to manage the investment with the help of an on-site manager. Debbie, 35, had been one of Art's MBA students, and he had employed her part-time after she dropped out of the program. At various times Debbie had worked for the regional "Baby Bell" telephone company and had managed a parcel delivery service and two credit and collection agencies.

The RTC's manager, Pam Potts, quit without notice in June. Debbie had been preparing to terminate Pam anyway, with a month's pay, and immediately promoted Shirley Miller, the daytime front-desk clerk, to manager. Shirley was high school educated, was active in local society, and was in her forties.

The bar, called "Martin's Tavern," had been rented to Burnell Martin, a local barber, and CMI assumed that lease, which was to expire at the end of 1992. The tavern had become a popular night spot for Crowleyites and frequented by the mayor, the sheriff, and other leading citizens, as well as by rice farmers, crawfishers, and oilfield hands. A true Cajun, Martin had talked of setting up an off-track betting parlor and then arranged to get two of Louisiana's first video poker machines, which were to be legal beginning in June 1992.

Arthur Sharplin, McNeese State University. Originally presented at a meeting of the Southwestern Case Research Association, a regional affiliate of the North American Case Research Association, March 1992. This case was written with the cooperation of management, solely for the purpose of stimulating student discussion. All data are based on field research in the organization. All incidents and events are real. Faculty members in non-profit institutions are encouraged to reproduce this case for distribution to their own students, without charge or written permission. All other rights reserved jointly to the authors and the North American Case Research Association (NACRA). Copyright 1992 by NACRA and Arthur Sharplin. Reprinted by permission.

In February 1992, famous Cajun chef Roy Lyons agreed to lease the restaurant for two years, naming it "Chef Roy's Café Acadie." Debbie breathed a sigh of relief. She remarked, "The restaurant has been one big headache. It required more employees than the motel, took most of our management time, ate us alive with repairs, and lost money every month." Art had helped his brother build and operate several other motels years earlier and knew that motel restaurants typically lose money.

The Sharplins had intended to sell the inn after fixing it up, and that remained a possibility. But Art had asked Debbie and Shirley to assume a ten-year holding period in management decisions. Given that time horizon, the managers were looking for ways to improve motel operations and to implement a marketing plan. And the idea of getting a national franchise, such as Best Western or Red Carpet, was only temporarily on hold.

FACILITIES

The physical plant had presented quite a challenge to Debbie, who said she knew "less than nothing about running a motel, let alone fixing one." Most rooms were distinctly substandard—sagging and stained bedding; broken furniture; 20-year-old TVs and room air conditioners; ceilings de-spackled and discolored by leaks; faded curtains hanging loose at one end; plumbing fixtures pitted and coated with white scum; washroom counters spotted with cigarette burns; mouse holes in walls; and tacky traps behind credenzas, each holding a grizzly menagerie of dehydrated bugs and roaches. It all seemed even worse in the dim hue cast by the cheap, old incandescent lamps with their yellowed and tattered shades.

Outside, water seeped through cracked pavement from a broken underground pipe, nurturing a patch of green slime. The clack, clack, clack of the sewer plant blower gave notice of imminent failure in that vital system. From the sewer plant, it was possible to see into the small equipment room, where an aging water heater had piled clumps of damp rust on the floor, and to see past the dumpster, overflowing with customer and trespasser refuse, to where a pothole in the truck parking area had grown into a muddy pond.

The lobby building was little better. Art discovered that in addition to the usable space, the air conditioning system heated and cooled the void above the hung ceilings. And one of the two main condenser units had been inoperative for months. Someone had poured tar on leaks in the roof overhang, and the black goo hung in stringy drops from the pegboard soffit and the shrubs beneath. In the restaurant kitchen, only one of the overhead exhaust systems worked; an oven door was tied shut with a stocking; cold air leaked from the walk-in freezer through a cocked door; and a long-disabled deep fryer still held its last charge of grease, stale and mantled with scorched meal.

But the inn had originally been well built—and it was still attractive. The guest room building was made of concrete blocks and steel-reinforced slabs, with front and back walls of grooved wood paneling over pine studs. Piping was copper and cast iron, not plastic. One wall in each room was latex enameled, and the others had vinyl wall covering, torn and unglued in a few places, but of good quality. The lobby building, of brick veneer, was shrouded with ninety-year-old live oaks and much younger pines, giving a sense of homeyness and comfort. And the neat grey and blue decor, though not striking, added a subdued welcomeness.

From May 1991 to February 1992, Crowley Inn's cash flow was applied to upgrading the property. Art and Kathy bought sixty rooms of used furniture, drapes, lamps, and bedspreads from the refurbishment contractor for a Holiday Inn in Beaumont, Texas. Debbie purchased sixty each of new RCA TVs with remote controls, GE clock radios, and chrome clothes racks with hangers. She also got new shower rods and curtains, bed linens, pillows, and a full complement of new beds and foundations. Kathy modified and helped install the drapes, advised on aesthetics, and livened the lobby with greenery and art work. Shirley arranged for several local men—unemployed artisans she could hire for minimum wage—to help as needed. As each shipment arrived, they came in to take out the old and install the new. They did much more—sanding the cigarette burns off the washroom counters, painting, stopping mice holes, patching concrete, and so on. An air conditioning contractor replaced or repaired twenty room air conditioners; renovated the lobby building heating, ventilating, and air conditioning system; and worked long hours on the restaurant coolers and freezers. A roofer replaced the leaky third of the motel roof and put proper patches on that of the lobby building. Total cost of the renovations: about $130,000.

Two prospective franchisors were asked to inspect the property. Best Western identified about $100,000 in needed improvements—more modern room lights and furniture, new carpeting, covering the concrete block walls with vinyl, and so on—but seemed anxious to do the deal. Red Carpet Inns was ready to franchise immediately, suggesting only minor changes. Debbie concluded the inn was then essentially up to standard for low-end franchises, such as Days Inns, Comfort Inns, Scottish Inns, and Red Carpet, but not for lower mid-range ones, like Best Western and Quality Inns. Bubbly front-desk clerk Josie Forrestier put it differently: "Crowley Inn used to be just a dump. Now, it is *une bonne place pour rester* [a good place to stay]."

PERSONNEL AND ORGANIZATION

When the RTC's manager resigned, the motel employed six housekeepers plus a supervisor, a maintenance man, and five front-desk clerks, all at minimum wage. There was no written job description for Pam's job or for any other. The RTC had balked at paying overtime, and it had become standard practice to show eight-hour shifts on time cards, although employees often worked more, or less. A housekeeper explained, "Pam gave us more than we could do. So we had to punch out and then go back and finish the work." In fact, most time cards for that period show handwritten checkout times, with no indication of who made the entries. This was allegedly done because Pam could not keep the time clock working properly. The industry standard for room cleaning time was about half an hour per room, including laundering. Of course, expensive hotels allowed more, inexpensive ones less.

However much time the housekeepers actually spent, the rooms stayed dirty. Two large dogs, or maybe camels, had been left alone for a time in room 112. Pale spots in the soiled mauve carpet marked where they had "done their business" and the stench gushed out to greet new guests. One guest, a nurse from Florida, chose another room. In July 1991, she wrote Mayor Istre,

> I am writing to express my concern re the deplorable condition of the Crowley Inn. The mattresses and springs in our room would probably have been rejected by the worst flophouse in the country. The mattresses had a permanent swag, not to mention, sir, a URINE STAIN about 36 inches in length. The tub has mildew all around the caulking. The drapes and spreads haven't seen a laundry in years, it appears. The carpet has stains. The pillows also are stained, not to mention lumpy. Neither mattresses nor pillows have protective covers that can be wiped down between customers. The swimming pool looked cloudy and green our entire stay, and though the desk clerk assured us it was okay, we declined.

No housekeeper, not even the head one, had worked at any other motel. Each was left to decide the best way to clean rooms. And there was no regular inspection by any manager. During June and July 1991, two or three people a night refused to stay after seeing their rooms.

Inspecting the motel after receiving a copy of the nurse's letter, Art and Debbie agreed with her assessment. Many of the problems, Art felt, reflected the discouragement of his people. In one room, toilet paper came off the bottom of the roll; in another, off the top. Here was a bed with a small, flowered pillow and a large, white one; next door, an identical set. In room 124 a double bedspread was stretched to half-cover a king bed, while a king spread in 122 fell in clumps around a double bed. In this room, five tiny bars of soap; in that one, none at all. Waste baskets of various sizes—one, two, or none per guest room; pint freezer boxes for ice buckets; shower curtains loose from hanger rings; a stiff bath cloth behind a commode, another hung on a shower curtain rod; a KFC box, with dehydrated chicken parts, peeping from under a bed. And the furniture, old, cheap, and stained though it was, need not have been so misdistributed. Chair counts ranged from four to none. An orange sled chair was paired with a puce overstuffed one. Chairs with no tables, tables with no chairs.

Wallace Mayer, the maintenance man, was responsible for cleaning the parking areas, mowing the lawn, taking waste to the dumpster, making bank deposits, moving heavy items, adding chlorine to the sewer plant, maintaining the swimming pool, and fixing anything that broke. Sixty-seven years old, but physically strong and unfailingly good-natured, Wallace went about his tasks with consistency, if not speed. A motel begets refuse, and housekeepers often stacked bulging bags of it in the vending machine areas until Wallace could take them to the dumpster, fifty feet away. It was just as well; the bags hid the grey-matted residue next to the machines and the cans and candy wrappers cast behind them by long-forgotten guests. Wallace kept the lawn and shrubs trimmed, but dairy cups and flattened cans were often left for another day. And six-packs of defeated soldiers could sometimes be seen standing at the parking lot curb in mute, noontime tribute to Bacchus.

The province of neither housekeeping nor maintenance, room windows and screens suffered neglect. Rain splatter had formed rivulets on the dusty panes, and layers of ancient cobwebs gave the half-screens a fuzzy translucence.

As the renovation progressed, Debbie and Shirley began frequent, though sporadic, inspections. Art decreed, "No employee walks past a piece of trash. Nobody!" Cards saying "It was my pleasure to clean your room" were given to housekeepers to sign and leave on credenzas. Debbie obtained videos on proper bed making and room cleaning. She asked the head housekeeper to train her charges and to inspect all guest rooms daily. Of the six housekeepers, only Sandra Guillotte adapted—and survived. The head housekeeper, a holdover from the RTC, soon decided she, too, could not meet Shirley's and Debbie's escalating demands. The new one, Carol Hoffpauir, promised she could. In February 1992, Shirley told of the improvement:

> We're getting compliments. We used to be afraid to ask if a guest enjoyed their stay. But today, at least five people commented on how nice the rooms were. Carol checks every room every day, and I do twice a week. We set a new record last week, a whole week without a complaint. The housekeepers still miss things—a bath cloth, or something left in a drawer—but they are doing so much better.

Art asked Shirley, "Why are the housekeepers doing better?" "Because we keep demanding more," she replied. "If we didn't demand it, they wouldn't do it." Carol Hoffpauir agreed, adding,

> I write them up every day, which rooms they clean and what they do wrong. We talk, and they can all read my notes on the clipboard, which I leave on the desk. If they do good, I tell them and I tell Shirley. I wish I could find five workers who take pride in cleaning the way I do. Two of the girls do, but the others seem to just tolerate it. I can hire and fire; I just have to tell Shirley my reasons. But I would rather get them out of their old routine.

Art asked, "Doesn't the improved situation here inspire them?" "I reckon so," Carol replied, "But you have to tell them when they mess up." Debbie added, "We know that new surroundings don't motivate."

Exhibit 7.1 shows the organization and employees at the end of February 1992. The desk clerks and Wallace were paid $5 an hour; the housekeepers, minimum wage; Shirley, $300 a week; and Carol, $200. Art had instituted paid one-week vacations, but there was no company medical insurance or retirement plan. Shirley talked about her job:

> I have a little problem supervising these people. You see, going from housekeeper, to the front desk, to being a manager—I was one of them; I can't come out and fuss at them. It was really hard at first. I called them together and told them it was business for eight hours. After that, we can go have a beer together. I told them, "I don't demand respect—don't call me 'Ma'am' or screen my calls. But when I say I want this done, I want it done. I don't want to stay on your butt." They are not kids. And I'm not running an old folks home, or a community center.
>
> Everybody is from Crowley or Church Point, all Cajun. They take things very lightly. They are all struggling. But they leave their problems at home, unless they get too big. Sometimes, you just need to talk. I listen. I cried when I had to fire Joanne [the former head housekeeper]. She's happier though, drinking and trying to get unemployment. Marie works in the restaurant after she finishes here, because she needs the money. Her mother is sick—over ninety percent stoppage in her heart. I could go on and on. This is a second home, for all of us.
>
> Mr. Wallace is part of the furniture. He has been here six, seven, maybe eight years. He does not want forty hours—says it will cut his Social Security. Takes off Friday noon.

He is good; you just have to point it out. He loves his job, and we all depend on him. We took a poll the other day on what Mr. Wallace enjoys most; we think he likes blowing off the parking lot best.

You get to know the customers. We talk; give them a little Cajun flavor: "Oh, you're from Texas. Well, we went to San Antonio last year . . . blah, blah, blah." It makes them come back. The truck drivers and oilfield hands holler at us when they come in the door. Whether we use the right English they don't care. It's like being a bartender. Our regular guests will just about tell you their life story. You even get to know the ones who come here for a couple of hours. They trust us; park their girlfriend right here in front. Some men leave women behind here. The other day, one stood on the interstate an hour with her thumb up, until somebody stopped.

Cajuns may seem a little stand-offish at first. Not at the front desk; this is *our* territory, and we feel secure. The girls always have a smile and gab for a guest. But at other places you're afraid to say the wrong thing. I was in Wisconsin with Byron [her son, a priest] last year and I told someone, "Catch me a Coke." They kidded me about it. Byron took me aside and said, "Mom, you don't *catch* a Coke; you just get one." He used to bring his priest friends home. I would beg him, "Byron, don't bring these educated people here." But, once I got to know them I get the biggest kick when they come. And I can't get them out of the house. We shouldn't be ashamed of our language, anyway. Listen to Governor Edwards: "Dis, dat, and dem." And he's a lawyer, definitely an educated man.

Jo Ann and Josie were at the front desk, just outside Shirley's office, and stepped to the door to listen. Jo Ann said, "All the improvements make us proud and we want to do better—makes me smile more. We bring a problem to Shirley and it gets

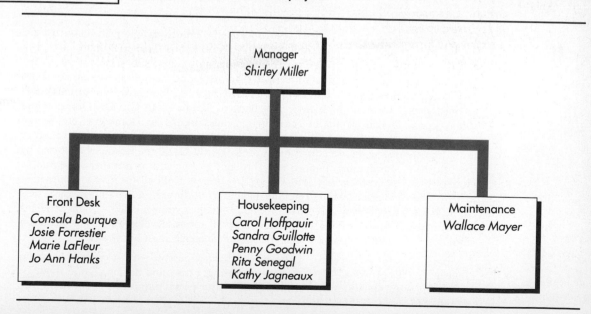

EXHIBIT 7.1	Crowley Inn Organization and Employees

Manager
Shirley Miller

Front Desk
Consala Bourque
Josie Forrestier
Marie LaFleur
Jo Ann Hanks

Housekeeping
Carol Hoffpauir
Sandra Guillotte
Penny Goodwin
Rita Senegal
Kathy Jagneaux

Maintenance
Wallace Mayer

taken care of, immediately. If it is a big one, Shirley gets on the phone with Debbie and it gets solved." Josie added, "It's exciting. Every day, I look forward to coming to work." Jo Ann's shift was over, and she excused herself. Josie continued:

> Customers like to hear us talk. They can't get over how friendly we are. Some say they expected to see a mean type of people. They think Cajuns are ignorant, uneducated, barefooted people with web toes. We are different. But we're Americans—Texas is over here and Mississippi is over there. I tell customers everybody around here is friendly. I make people feel welcome. I want them to feel they are getting their money's worth. I want them to know I am their friend and to think of this as a home away from home. I say, "It's a quiet little place," except on Saturday night, when the band gets too loud and some of the people are—what's a nice way of putting it?—highly intoxicated.

> The other night, a guy had invited two girls to his room and the second one showed up early. They were fighting and screaming, disturbing the other guests. So I called the sheriff. The one in the room reached right over the deputy and "Pow!" laid the other one out. The deputy brought her up here in handcuffs and threw her in the car.

> The inn is like my home, too. When Kenny and the Jokers [a Lafayette, Louisiana, band] play in the bar, I come about an hour early to hear them. And my kids [17, 15, 14, and 13 years old] love to come here, sometimes to go swimming. There is nowhere else to do that. We eat in the restaurant sometimes. When I worked in housekeeping, I would come by sometimes just to visit. I always try to be here thirty minutes early, and I usually hang around that long after my shift.

Ninety-two-year-old retired Catholic priest Msgr. Jules O. Daigle, of nearby Welsh, Louisiana, would agree with Shirley that Cajuns should not be ashamed of the way they talk. He insisted that Cajun was a true language, saying, "To call Cajun bad French is to call French and Italian bad Latin." Daigle fought for years to preserve the Cajun language and culture. In the preface to his Cajun language dictionary [Jules O. Daigle, *A Dictionary of the Cajun Language* (Ann Arbor, Mich.: Edwards Brothers, 1984), pp. viii–x], he wrote,

> Historically, the Cajuns are the descendants of the French people who colonized the general area of ancient Acadia, now known as Nova Scotia, beginning in 1604. . . . In 1755, the British began a cruel, systematic program of deportation of our ancestors. Penniless, ill-clad and, worst of all, being both French and Catholics, nothing but scorn and hatred awaited them in the colonies. . . . After serving their indenture to the British colonists, some of them made their way back to Acadia or to Canada. Others found refuge in the French islands of Martinique, Guadaloupe, St. Domingue, etc. In the meanwhile, many of the Acadians who had evaded capture by the British sought refuge in the forests among the friendly Indians of the north. Of all the Acadians deported by the British, a considerable number were brought to England as prisoners: eventually, most of these found their way into France. . . . It was from all the above groups that many of the Acadians came to Louisiana, beginning in the early 1760s. Free at last, they had to begin a totally new and different kind of life, in a strange land. . . . The Acadians had to invent a new vocabulary, find new types of foods, develop a new cuisine and a whole new way of life. Thus was born the Cajun language and Cajun culture.

> To some, a Cajun is a crude, ignorant, backward person who speaks little or no English. . . . His principal interest in life is boozing, eating and having a good time. To be sure, there are such Cajuns, but they are an infinitesimal minority and are in no way characteristic of the Cajun people.

Daigle added that the Cajuns are bishops, judges, lawyers, contractors, professors, beauticians, bricklayers, farmers, teachers, and so forth. He concluded, "Yes, and sure enough some of them are lazy, ignorant bums and drunks: all in about the same proportion as the rest of the American population."

During the annual rodeo and the monthly horse show, the inn's regular guests merged with equestrians—from sprite barrel racers to wrinkled Marlboro men. Drowsy tourists' senses were jostled by the too-metallic jangle of spurs on concrete stairs and the too-earthy aroma of a dozen horse trailers. Wide-brimmed hats were worn everywhere—at restaurant tables, on the crowded dance floor in the tavern, even in the bathroom. One inebriated October cowboy thought his bed a dance floor, until it collapsed. Another, dispirited by lost love, conjectured to aim at his head but blew just his palm away, spraying scraps of flesh and bone into a new mattress. And a famous Cajun musician, held hostage during drug withdrawal by two burly friends, broke a table and ripped a towel rack from the wall.

Mostly, though, Crowley Inn was, as Josie said, a quiet little place, a place where Texaco could house visiting executives and straying locals could enjoy secret liaisons. And it seemed so much a part of the employees' and townspeoples' lives that Art wondered if he and Kathy were really the sole owners of the inn.

MARKETING

Art and Kathy had initially been inclined to seek a franchise—Best Western was the leading candidate, Quality Inns a close second. In February 1992, they were continuing to discuss the matter. Debbie and Shirley expressed ambivalence about franchising, but both were excited about promotion and other aspects of marketing.

CROWLEY BEST WESTERN?

Most motels are franchised. Franchisors typically provide a reservation system, advice on pricing, national advertising, a franchisee directory showing locations and amenities, quality control standards, yearly inspections, training, informational services, design help, and an approved-supplier catalog. Best Western's charge for Crowley Inn would be about $21,000 up front and that much each year. Other franchisors get a certain percentage of room revenue. For example, Red Carpet quoted 4.5% for Crowley Inn, with no initial fee. Holiday Inns was collecting as much as 7% then.

Art believed Crowley Inn could qualify for a Best Western franchise within six months by making the following expenditures (in addition to paying the annual fee).

Initial franchise fee	$21,000
Best Western signs	12,000
Reservation and accounting system	15,000
Required renovations	96,000
Total	$144,000

Debbie, Shirley, and Art reached consensus that this would allow hiking average daily rate (ADR) by $4.00 or increasing average occupancy by 15%, or some combination of the two. Art concluded, "Assuming 64% occupancy, which I think is about the industry average, the added revenue would be $56,000 a year, a good return on $144,000." Debbie objected.

> Well, 68% has been about our average. Even that should jump this year with or without a franchise. We have really improved this property since last summer, when we ran 76%. Besides, some of the renovations Best Western requires won't improve customer service—things like covering the concrete-block wall with vinyl and replacing the two-by-four ceiling tiles in the baths and lobby with two-by-two squares. I'll bet we could do the worthwhile renovations, which would cost maybe $60,000, and raise ADR by $3.00, without a franchise.

"What about Red Carpet?" asked Art. "We can have their sign up in a month." "I don't think they add a thing," replied Debbie. Shirley nodded concurrence.

Art said, "Okay, but you know there has been talk of a Days Inn just seven miles away, in Rayne. If we were Best Western, no one would dare do that."

After a few more minutes of discussion, they all agreed to defer the decision on franchising for at least six months. "We haven't taken a cent out of this thing," said Art, "and I would like for you to produce some cash before we reinvest any more big chunks."

THE MARKETING PLAN

Art asked Debbie to help prepare a marketing plan. "What should be our main objective?" she asked. "What's wrong with 'maximize shareholder wealth'?" he replied. A few days later Debbie brought Art her rough draft. The final version is presented in Exhibit 7.2.

EXHIBIT 7.2 | **The Marketing Plan**

MISSION

The mission of Crowley Inn is to maximize return on invested capital by providing quality lodging and related services delivered by competent and enthusiastic employees operating a clean, well-maintained facility—at prices fully reflecting the quality of service.

MARKETING OBJECTIVE

The objective of the marketing plan is to maximize motel revenue while keeping expenses low. Revenue targets for 1992 are

Room revenue ($33.00 ADR; 72% occupancy)	$512,000
Telephone revenue (1991 rate + 10%)	24,453

(continued)

| EXHIBIT 7.2 | The Marketing Plan (continued) |

TARGET MARKET

Our current guests are mostly blue-collar persons on business travel, about 20% from Louisiana and the rest from all regions of the country. About 45% pay with cash or check, 36% use credit cards, and 19% have us bill a third party. Here are data taken from 247 folios [forms that guests fill out upon check-in] completed in February 1992:

Purpose of Travel		Home address		Payment	
Work crew	48	Louisiana	52	Employer	47
Truck driver	38	Northeast	27	Credit card	89
Local	15	Southeast	17	Cash	111
Tourist	10	Northwest	13		
Business	38	Southwest	21		
Military	2	Foreign	11		
Cannot tell	96	Cannot tell	106		

[Marie LaFleur, who knew most regular inn guests, sorted the folios by purpose of travel. The "local" category, she said, mainly involved romantic liaisons.]

With average occupancy of 41 rooms, we serve a tiny percentage of those who pass our door. Daily traffic counts near the inn during 1990 were as follows (provided by the Louisiana Department of Transportation):

I-10 east of Crowley (both directions)	29,530
I-10 west of Crowley (both directions)	26,600
Hwy 13 north of I-10 (both directions)	7,570
Hwy 13 south of I-10 (both directions)	18,430

Visitors to families and businesses in Crowley (1990 population, 14,038) and surrounding Acadia Parish (1990 population, 55,882) may also be potential new customers. The Cajun tradition of fais-dodo (a country dance, usually involving staying overnight) and family togetherness in general frequently pull back many who leave the area.

In addition to our present customer base, we will seek to attract more up-scale guests, including (1) white-collar business travelers, (2) tourists, and (3) sojourners in the local area.

PRODUCT

Our main product is a room-night, which includes the elements listed below.

1. An attractive, comfortable, secure room—well-supplied, clean, and with all amenities in good order.
2. Attractive, functional vending machines.
3. Attractive, clean, neat grounds and paved areas.
4. Easy access to good food, drink, and entertainment.
5. Daily servicing of room by attractive, well-dressed personnel to exceed standards set by Best Western or comparable franchisors.
6. Guest services provided by enthusiastic, competent, attractive, articulate, well-dressed personnel who reflect the local culture.

(continued)

| EXHIBIT 7.2 | The Marketing Plan (continued) |

A room-night is more perishable than a bruised tomato. We accept delivery of 59 room-nights every day, and unsold ones spoil sometime around midnight.

Shirley and Debbie plan to enhance the value and salability of room-nights in 1992 by

1. Aggressive training and supervision of housekeepers.
2. Aggressive training of front-desk clerks, including role-playing of common types of guest contacts.
3. Inspections of all rooms daily by the head housekeeper.
4. Aggressive training and supervision of the maintenance person.
5. Inspection of all rooms and facilities at least weekly by Shirley, and at least monthly by Debbie.
6. Setting up control systems to ensure creative compliance with vital policies.
7. Upgrading of the work team, through training, supervision, and/or replacement of employees.

PRICE

Current prices at Crowley Inn are shown below. Pricing of room-nights is done by front-desk clerks, who have a list of "approved" commercial customers.

1. Basic room-night $31.00 ($29 commercial)
2. Each guest above one/room $4.00/night
3. Local telephone calls $0.50
4. Long-distance calls   AT&T rates plus 40%
5. Facsimile transmissions $2.00/page
6. Rollaway bed or crib $5.00/night

Members of the American Association of Retired Persons and others over 65 are eligible for commercial rates. ADR has been about $32.50 since a $2 per room-night price increase in July 1991. Two factors tend to pull ADR down. First, few customers are charged the $4 per extra guest. In fact, only about one in twenty (based on a check of February 1991 folios) completes the "No. of persons in room" blocks on the folio. Second, front-desk clerks give commercial rates to most who ask for a discount. Shirley says pricing policies are clear and are understood by all front-desk clerks, but they do not follow policies well.

Shirley and Debbie plan to

1. Review pricing policies and change them or enforce them.
2. Set up control systems to identify and correct improper pricing practices.
3. Insure that telephone billing equipment and practices are correct.
4. Price room-nights at no less than the double-occupancy rate during special events, when the inn normally fills up.
5. Price room-nights at no less than the double-occupancy rate whenever as many as 40 rooms are reserved.
6. Review pricing frequently, and quickly implement justified changes, such as when occupancy moves reliably above 75%.

PROMOTION

Crowley Inn relies primarily on billboards for advertising. For eastbound traffic there are two signs, on the left 16 miles out and on the right 4 miles out. For westbound traffic, signs are on

EXHIBIT 7.2	The Marketing Plan (continued)

the left at 13 miles and on the right at 7. The signs carry the slogan, "Comfort you can afford," and have a large inset saying, "24 hr Grill." They are yellow and white on a black background.

Debbie is developing an image, involving a slogan, a logo, and sign designs. A consultant is helping. The new slogan is "Comfortable, caring, and Cajun." This is intended to suggest comfortable lodging supplied by caring personnel with a Cajun flair. The logo is a large C containing a rice design, used alone or in spelling "Crowley Inn."

Debbie plans to rent two additional billboards on I-10, one each direction, and have all billboards repainted. Chef Roy agreed to pay a fifth of the cost, and a fifth of the sign space will be devoted to advertising Café Acadie. A "board" across the bottom of each sign will announce special features such as HBO–Showtime, Martin's Tavern, and live entertainment. Each billboard costs about $400 to repaint and about $400 per month.

She also plans to place two signs along Highway 13 a few miles on either side of the inn. Each of these is expected to cost about $300 to paint and $200 per month.

Debbie just purchased space on electronic bulletin boards at the Tourist Information Centers at the east and west I-10 entry points to Louisiana. Users will dial a two-digit code that will connect them to the front desk at the inn.

Crowley Inn will join the Louisiana Travel Promotion Association (LTPA). LTPA publishes the *Louisiana Tour Guide* annually and helps members with advertising, printing, and the like.

Though the inn is right beside I-10, an informal survey suggests that many people pass without noticing it. So Kathy and Shirley plan to have the guest-room doors painted a noticeable color, such as burgundy, and to use bright colors elsewhere to make the inn more conspicuous.

Shirley and Debbie plan to start making sales calls on present and prospective direct-bill customers and to send them direct-mail advertisements from time to time. They also are seeking ways to entice tour groups to the inn.

PLACE

Crowley Inn is 16 miles east of its nearest competitor, a TraveLodge in Jennings. The Jennings Holiday Inn is three miles further west. East of Crowley, the larger town of Lafayette has a Holiday Inn, a La Quinta Inn, a Motel 6, and several other motels and hotels.

Crowley is home to the Louisiana Rice Festival, held annually in May, and nearby towns sponsor festivals celebrating crawfish, frogs, ducks, and other animals and plants. During the days surrounding each festival, the inn normally is booked solid. The inn also fills up during the monthly horse show in Crowley and during the annual rodeo.

Crowley is the seat of Acadia Parish (county), and Art suggested that this makes it the "Capital of Acadiana" (Cajun country is often called Acadiana). A famous Cajun restaurant, Belizaires', is a half-mile south of the Crowley Inn, and its signs attract many visitors. Debbie and Shirley plan to feature the "Capital of Acadiana" theme in ads and signs and to encourage the Crowley Chamber of Commerce to do so. Mayor Istre thought this was a good idea.

Debbie and Shirley were in essential agreement about each element of the marketing plan. During the last week of February 1992, they met to discuss both the process and the time frame for implementing it.

| EXHIBIT 7.3 | Income Statement: Crowley Inn |

	May–December 1991	January 1992
Revenue		
Room revenue[1]	$ 272,011	$48,770
Telephone revenue	7,351	1,334
Restaurant revenue[2]	136,977	18,085
Rental income[3]	5,400	1,120
Miscellaneous revenue	9,218	637
Total revenue	$ 430,957	$69,946
Expenses		
Food purchases	$ 45,994	$ 5,857
Telephone	11,789	1,224
Salaries and wages	128,029	16,101
Payroll tax expense	14,478	3,085
Operating supplies	11,147	2,376
Office supplies	4,209	127
Taxes, licenses, and fees	6,755	1,709
Credit card fees	1,348	715
Professional fees	14,529	1,520
Travel and entertainment	1,199	0
Advertising	12,223	4,984
Repairs and maintenance	14,707	7,447
Miscellaneous	1,358	440
Utilities	36,285	6,655
Cable television	1,307	148
Insurance	15,293	2,002
Interest	31,487	6,344
Depreciation	23,100	3,300
Total expenses	$ 375,237	$64,034
Income before taxes	$ 55,720	$ 5,912
Income taxes (22%)	12,258	1,301
Net income	$ 43,462	$ 4,611

[1] Monthly room revenue for May 21, 1991 through December 1991 was as follows: May, $16,648; June, $36,941; July, $46,720; August, $48,303; September, $38,240; October, $40,221; November, $38,738; and December, $23,364.

[2] The restaurant was leased beginning February 1, 1992 for $2,300 a month, including utilities (estimated at $600 a month). Up to that point, it had accounted for about 60% of salaries and wages, food purchases, and shares of several other expense items.

[3] This includes $900 a month for the bar. The remainder is for rental of the banquet room.

EXHIBIT 7.4	Balance Sheet: Crowley Inn

	May 21, 1991	December 31, 1991	January 31, 1992
Assets			
Cash	$ 7,745	$ 12,007	$ 9,389
Accounts receivable		17,274	12,277
Land	40,000	40,000	40,000
Improvements	358,728	438,963	441,963
Furniture and fixtures	75,647	132,269	133,069
Accumulated depreciation		(23,100)	(26,400)
Security deposits	11,930	11,930	11,930
Total assets	$494,050	$629,344	$622,228
Liabilities			
N/P, A&K Sharplin	$493,050	$570,969	$555,700
Accrued and withheld tax		13,913	17,455
Total liabilities	$493,050	$584,882	$573,155
Equity			
Common stock	$ 1,000	$ 1,000	$ 1,000
Retained earnings		43,462	48,073
Total equity	$ 1,000	$ 44,462	$ 49,073
Total claims	$494,050	$629,344	$622,228

FINANCE

Art and Kathy paid the RTC $475,000 cash for the inn. They advanced another $21,000 to Crowley Motel, Inc. then and more later for working capital. CMI gave the Sharplins demand notes earning 10% interest for all but $1,000 of their investment and issued common stock for that. Exhibits 7.3 and 7.4 provide financial reports for CMI.

THE BANK LOAN

After buying Crowley Inn, Art and Kathy applied for a $380,000 loan from Evangeline Bank, in Crowley, to partly reimburse themselves and to fund improvements. The bank offered a half-percent under bank prime (then 10.5%) for a 7-year loan with 15-year amortization. But the bank's attorney delayed approving the title, noting that the inn sign and the sewer plant encroached over the adjacent property and that 10 guest rooms had been built over an existing right-of-way (for a road to property behind the inn). Art knew this when he bought the inn and had thought it a small matter, because the problem had existed without complaint for 20 years. However, he suggested the loan amount be cut to $200,000 in view of the title problems.

The bank continued to delay closing, and after a few weeks Art and Kathy resolved not to bother with the loan. Art explained,

> We might be happier taking eight or ten thousand a month in interest, principal, and fees than we would getting, say $380,000 at once. I never have believed this "optimum debt ratio" stuff anyway. Of course, having the inn financed might make it easier to sell. But we will cross that bridge if we come to it.

Besides, Art acknowledged, there was no certainty they could get the loan anyway.

COST STRUCTURE

The motel business typically involves high fixed costs, partly because of the capital required. For example, Holiday Inns claimed its cost for a new motel averaged $65,000 per room. And Art's brother Jerry said a new 60-room Best Western would cost about $22,000 a room, including land cost.

The problem was not severe for CMI. Its debt was held by its owners, and interest charges had been accrued rather than paid. But Art directed Shirley to pay interest out, along with half the cash flow (which would be treated as payment of principal), beginning in April 1992.

Debbie calculated the variable cost per room-night at Crowley Inn as follows:

Housekeeping labor	$3.21
Supplies	2.61
Laundry	.80
Avoidable utilities and telephone	1.70
Total	$8.32

Debbie had been keeping close tabs on room cleaning costs, supplies, and other variable items. After studying CMI's cost structure, she decided to concentrate more on marketing. Debbie explained,

> At a $32.50 ADR, each extra room-night produces $24.18 for fixed costs and profit. That's $725 per month, about $8,700 a year, almost enough to pay for two billboards on I-10. If we raise prices, rather than let occupancy rise, the result may be even better. At 72% occupancy, we sell about 1,275 room-nights a month. So anything that lets us raise rates by $1 produces $15,000 a year.

To Art's chagrin, Shirley also became less tight-fisted. On February 21, 1992, Debbie called from Crowley to say she was excited about all the nice improvements Shirley was making. "The oak trees have been pruned and fertilized, she got someone to edge the lawn, and there is new paint all around," said Debbie. Later that day, Kathy told Art she had learned that Shirley wanted to paint the entire motel and lobby building.

POSSIBLE SALE OF THE INN

In February 1992, Art was approached by two prospective buyers, Mahesh Patel, who owned an Econo-Lodge motel in Huntsville, Texas, and Fred Gossen, Jr., a businessman from Rayne, Louisiana, seven miles east of Crowley. The Patel name was familiar to Art. It was the surname used by thousands of émigrés from western India, many of whom invested in low-end motels and convenience stores in the United States. In fact, Art believed that Patels owned half the economy motels in Louisiana and adjoining states.

Art convinced Kathy they should offer to sell the inn real estate, chattels, and leases to Gossen for $800,000, with $200,000 down and seller financing of the remainder at 12% for 7 years, with 180-month amortization. They made a similar offer to Patel, but at $900,000 with $250,000 down and a 5-year balloon.

Kathy had changed her mind by the next day. "Why don't we take out, say, $10,000 a month for a couple of years," she said. "We can probably still sell the motel for $800,000."

Art called Debbie to meet them at his campus office. "If we refuse an $800,000 offer," he began, "it is as if we just bought the inn for that amount." Debbie and Kathy agreed.

"Assuming Kathy is right," Art continued, "what discount rate should we use to settle the question?"

After a moment's thought, Debbie said, "This is effectively an equity investment in an entrepreneurial business. So I would suggest something like 40%."

"But can't we treat the project as a normally financed one; that is, say, $600,000 in 12% debt and $200,000 in equity?" Art asked. "If you stick with your 40% for equity, that gives a discount rate of 19%."

Kathy interjected, "I don't understand this discount rate stuff, Art. But if we get $200,000 in cash, we will have to put it in the Merrill Lynch account at about 5%. That's a far cry from 19%."

"Instead of doing that, we could pay off the 11% debt on the Pepsi building [a building Art and Kathy owned in Pineville, Louisiana]," said Art.

After a few minutes more discussion, Art promised to fax a note to Gossen withdrawing the offer. "What about Patel?" asked Kathy. "That offer is not in writing," replied Art. "Besides, there is zero chance a Patel is going to accept without negotiating. And when he makes the first counter, the law deems my offer withdrawn. Besides, real estate deals have to be in writing to be enforceable."

"By the way," Debbie asked, "why did you quote $100,000 higher to Patel?"

"Three reasons: I think Fred will treat our people better, I would not be as confident of getting paid with Patel, and a broker is involved on that deal," answered Art.

The next day, Art asked Shirley, "What do you think about the sale idea?"

She replied, "It's your decision, but $800,000 is a lot of money." Art knew Shirley hoped he would not sell. She had often said she loved her job; a sale would put it at risk.

He asked, "Do you know that if I put $800,000 in the bank at 6% it would only draw $4,000 a month?" "Is that all?" exclaimed Shirley. "Debbie and I can get you a lot more than that without selling."

Art stopped by to see Chef Roy and get his input about a possible sale. Roy said, "I personally hope you keep the motel. But I can't advise you to turn down a profitable deal."

When Art saw Burnell Martin, the lounge operator, Burnell volunteered, "I hear you are thinking about selling. Art, keep this place. It's a gold mine."

CASE 8 CSX Transportation, Inc.

Timothy W. Edlund ▪ Michael T. Avara

On February 15, 1990, CSX Corporation announced the appointment of Robert L. Kirk to head its railroad division. Kirk was to assume his new post on March 30. Kirk had just completed the installation of a new management team at Reflectone, Inc. Sixty-one years old, he had previously served as chairman and CEO of Allied-Signal Aerospace; he had also served LTV for several years, first heading its aerospace division and then serving briefly as its president. One analyst said that appointing someone without rail experience may be helpful in an industry that is trying to reorient itself.[1]

Kirk would report to John W. Snow, then president and CEO of CSX Corporation and also of CSX Transportation, its giant transport component. Kirk and Snow have at least one common experience: Snow was recruited into railroad management from teaching economics twelve years earlier, by the current chairman, Hays T. Watkins. Watkins had seen the expansion by mergers and into extensive diversification.[2] Its rail operations are the result of the merger of the Seaboard Coast Line and the Chessie System, in 1980. (The Chessie had resulted from the earlier merger of the Chesapeake and Ohio and the Baltimore and Ohio railroads.) Based on operating revenues, CSX is the largest railroad in the United States.[3]

Although it was the largest road (or nearly so, depending on the measurement used), CSX transportation had faced difficult challenges. In 1988 the company had taken large write-offs, resulting in losses for the railroad and very little profit for the overall corporation. 1989 was much better, but it was not certain that the firm was firmly on the path to recovery. Kirk would have his hands full learning the business and guiding strategic choices.

THE CORPORATION

CSX is based in its railroad origins. For over a decade, U. S. railroads have been rationalizing their systems, and merging with each other to create a small set of lines, each of which serves a substantial portion of the country. Deregulation has been an integral part of this process. The elaborate regulatory structure built in the nineteenth century when railroads held substantial monopoly power was, at last, largely dismantled, with the aim of freeing railroads to compete more effectively. (See the industry note, reprinted at the end of the case.)

CSX acquired other transportation capabilities: American Commercial Lines, providing barge transport on the Mississippi River and its tributaries; Sea-Land Service, Inc., the largest transporter of containers by ship; and the Texas Gas

Timothy W. Edlund, Morgan State University, and Michael T. Avara, MBA graduate, Loyola College in Maryland. This refereed case was written using published sources and was presented to the North American Case Research Association in 1990. It is intended as a basis for class discussion rather than to illustrate effective or ineffective handling of an administrative situation. © 1990 by Timothy W. Edlund.

Transmission pipeline system. It also acquired resorts, gas and oil properties, and manufacturing plants. It developed realty projects and a fiber-optic communications network (together with Southern New England Telephone Company). And it established a technology group charged with supporting CSX's transportation units, as well as serving external customers.[4] CSX was an early supporter of intermodal shipping, in which freight in containers is carried on whichever of a variety of carriers is most effective for each portion of its trip. Exhibits 8.1 through 8.3 give corporate financial data, and in Exhibits 8.4 through 8.6 the impact of transportation generally and of rail operations on the corporation may be ascertained.

RECENT DEVELOPMENTS

In its 1988 annual report,[5] management discussed the restructuring then underway. There were three prime objectives: (1) to become the premier international transportation services company; (2) to improve service quality and company profitability; and (3) to focus on the basics of CSX's business. Among the steps taken to increase shareholder value were the repurchase of up to 60 million outstanding common shares and the sale of gas pipelines, gas processing holdings, and most resort properties.

Management took these steps because it believed that CSX's common was not selling at full value. Investment bankers advised that non-transportation assets were being undervalued as a result of a "conglomerate" discount. There existed a perception that such assets were outside the main stream of CSX's business. With the sales made in 1988 and early 1989, management states that CSX is more focused and leveraged and that it will generate good earnings and cash flow.

Management emphasized the need to modernize and upgrade facilities and equipment, while cutting expenses at all levels. Goals were a 15,000-mile system and 30,000 employees. Agreements permitting immediate reduction of crews from 4 to 3 on 38% of the system were reached with the principal union.

On June 27, 1989, CSX announced the appointment of Jerry R. Davis, then with Union Pacific Railroad, to head CSX Rail Transport, one of the three functional divisions of CSX Transportation. His predecessor, A. R. "Pete" Carpenter, was freed to concentrate on his duties as president of CSX Distribution Services, the independent marketing unit for the railroad.

On Wall Street, there were many doubters about the CSX turnaround. In August, John Gormley reported Lazard Frere's evaluation: "The management of CSX has been accused of many things . . ., but running a railroad effectively is not one of them."[6] Yet Lazard went on to recommend purchase, as did others. Past implementing of plans and goals was rarely satisfactory, but several factors led research analysts to change their minds. It was pointed out that CSX's crew reduction agreements were the first reached without intervention of the federal government. Branch-line sales are also important. Though they had been stalled by a court decision in 1987, the Supreme Court had issued a ruling on June 21 that appeared to permit at least some branch-line sales.

Standard & Poor's survey of the rail and trucking industry,[7] newly revised in October, brought out several interesting points. A series of major rail mergers,

---

EXHIBIT 8.1	Consolidated Statement of Earnings: CSX Corporation
	(In millions of dollars except per share amounts)

Years Ended December 31	1989	1988	1987
Operating Revenue			
Transportation	$7,428	$7,259	$6,699
Non-transportation	317	333	251
Total	7,745	7,592	6,950
Operating Expense			
Transportation	6,725	6,517	6,016
Non-transportation	151	166	139
Special charge (Note 3)	—	738	—
Total	6,876	7,421	6,155
Earnings (Loss)			
Operating income	869	171	795
Other income	166	116	117
Interest expense	343	347	324
Earnings (loss) from continuing operations before income taxes	692	(60)	588
Income tax expense (benefit)	265	(22)	215
Earnings (loss) from continuing operations	427	(38)	373
Discontinued operations, net of income taxes			
Earnings from energy segment	2	5	59
Gain, disposal, energy segment	23	180	—
Earnings before cumulative effect of change in accounting	452	147	432
Cumulative effect on years prior to 1987 of change in accounting for income taxes	—	—	(294)
Net earnings	$ 452	$ 147	$ 138
Per Share			
Earnings (loss) per share			
From continuing operations	$4.09	$(.33)	$2.40
From discontinued operations			
Earnings from energy segment	.02	.03	.38
Gain, disposal, energy segment	.23	1.23	—
Earnings per share before cumulative effect of change in accounting	4.34	.93	2.78
Cumulative effect on years prior to 1987 of change in accounting for income taxes	—	—	(1.90)

(continued)

EXHIBIT 8.1	**Consolidated Statement of Earnings: CSX Corporation (continued)**
	(In millions of dollars except per share amounts)

Years Ended December 31	1989	1988	1987
Earnings per share	$4.34	$.93	$.88
Common shares outstanding at year-end (thousands)	97,696	106,683	155,446
Average common shares outstanding (in thousands)	101,230	146,451	154,814

Selected notes to Financial Statements (abbreviated):

2. Restructuring and Common Share Repurchase. In September 1988, the company announced a restructuring program, which included the sale of the company's natural gas transmission businesses and certain of its resort properties, and the repurchase of up to 60 million shares of common stock. The company's energy segment has been reduced substantially with the 1988 sale of Oil & Gas and with the 1989 sale of Texas Gas Transmission Corp.

Rockresorts Inc. and certain related properties were sold in July 1989. Pretax income from the sale is included in Other Income.

3. In June 1988, the company recorded a pretax special charge of $738 million to continuing operations. Included was a provision of $592 million for separation pay liabilities and $146 million for various costs and claims, which were expected to result from litigation and negotiated settlements. The separation pay provision related to the cost of the planned separation of 8,200 (6,500 active and 1,700 furloughed) rail employees by 1991. Such a reduction is necessary to meet competitive pressures within the industry and to bring the rail labor force into balance with the planned core track system of 15,000 route-miles. As of December 31, 1989, approximately 6,100 employees have been separated from rail service, accounting for 60% of the separation pay liability, and the core track system has been reduced to 19,700 route-miles.

necessitated by changing market factors and stimulated by changes in regulation, have boosted profitability and opened new markets. New single-line, long-haul corridors have been created, facilitating piggyback operations and avoiding inter-line transfers, while achieving lower rates through cost economies. More restructuring in the western railroads is expected. And branch-line sales are expected to resume, now that the Supreme Court has given qualified approval to such sales.

Pertinent to CSX is the status of coal hauling. CSX is the industry leader in hauling coal. In 1987 it generated $.15 billion from hauling 182.9 million tons, which was almost 35% of all coal handled. Coal's profitability was felt to be greater than seemed to be the case. Per ton, it generated just $11.65 in revenues in 1987—less than half the revenue generated for all other traffic. But costs are lower too. There are lower handling costs, lower claims, and lower insurance costs. And finally, the unit-train concept (all cars filled with the same product—preferably all going to the same destination) sharply slashes the handling required.

Unit-trains have increased as increased amounts of coal are mined in the western states, where there are larger and fewer mines. By 1988 over 75% of all coal

EXHIBIT 8.2	Consolidated Statement of Cash Flows: CSX Corporation
	(Dollar amounts in thousands)

Years Ended December 31	1989	1988	1987
Cash Provided by Continuing Operations			
Earnings (loss) from continuing operations	$ 427	$ (38)	$ 373
Adjustments to reconcile earnings to cash provided			
Depreciation	447	467	452
Deferred income taxes	213	18	233
Special charge—provision	—	738	—
Payments	(257)	(147)	—
Proceeds from real estate sales	133	256	145
Gain on disposition of properties	(141)	(235)	(77)
Gain on sales of affiliates	(164)	—	—
Changes in operating assets and liabilities			
Sale of accounts receivable	200	—	300
(Increase) decrease in other accounts receivable	51	(166)	(19)
(Increase) decrease in other current assets	40	(95)	(36)
Decrease (increase) in current liabilities other than debt	121	22	(78)
Other	44	(37)	(73)
Cash provided by continuing operations	1,114	783	1,143
Cash Provided by (Used for) Discontinued Operations			
Earnings from discontinued energy segment	25	185	59
Adjustments to reconcile earnings to cash provided			
Gain of disposition of assets	(54)	(314)	—
Changes in operating assets and other	(78)	157	75
Cash provided by (used for) discontinued operations	(107)	28	134
Total cash provided by operations	1,007	811	1,277
Investment Activities			
Property additions	(815)	(1,151)	(744)
Proceeds from sale-leaseback transactions	830	493	877
Acquisition and refurbishment costs for sale-leaseback transactions	(479)	(178)	—
Proceeds from disposition of properties	126	149	26
Proceeds from sales of affiliates	360	—	—
Investment in other affiliates	(37)	(135)	(76)
Other investment activities	(21)	(73)	(79)

(continued)

EXHIBIT 8.2	Consolidated Statement of Cash Flows: CSX Corporation (continued)

(Dollar amounts in thousands)

Years Ended December 31	1989	1988	1987
Discontinued operations			
Property additions	(10)	(65)	(69)
Proceeds from disposition of assets	577	630	167
Cash provided by (used for) investment activities	531	(330)	(98)
Financing Activities			
Short-term debt—net	(766)	900	37
Long-term debt issued	14	314	334
Long-term debt repaid	(285)	(325)	(998)
Preferred stock issued	—	—	150
Common stock reacquired	(324)	(1,598)	—
Cash dividends paid	(145)	(198)	(186)
Other financing activities	3	20	47
Discontinued operations—net	(9)	99	(59)
Cash used for financing activities	(1,512)	(788)	(675)
Cash and Cash Equivalents			
Increase (decrease) in cash and cash equivalents	26	(307)	504
Cash and cash equivalents at beginning of year	508	815	311
Cash and cash equivalents at end of year	$ 534	$ 508	$ 815

moved in unit-trains. Barges are also vying for coal traffic, and they commonly serve those coal-burning plants located on inland waterways. Barge transport is inherently cheaper but has several disadvantages, including limited accessibility, longer transit times, and vulnerability to the weather (ice in winter and sometimes, as in 1988, low water due to severe drought).

Coal production is gradually shifting to the western states, where good, low-sulfur coal can be economically surface-mined from the extensive seams that lie near the surface of relatively flat land. Such coal does less environmental damage when burned, and mining damage to the land can be readily repaired. Its marketability has been limited by transport costs, but the factors we have noted above will reduce this disadvantage. Moreover, eastern coal is hurt by the acid rain problem.

Intermodal shipping (including piggyback trailers and containers and also the RoadRailer, an innovative vehicle with both road and rail wheels that is placed directly on rails) is not showing the growth rates that had been anticipated. Overall, rail intermodal generated revenues of $3.8 billion, about 13% of the (rail) industry total in 1988. Double-stack holds great promise for growth. This involves placing one container on top of another on a modified rail flatcar. It was

| EXHIBIT 8.3 | Consolidated Statement of Financial Position: CSX Corporation |

(Dollar amounts in millions)

Years Ended December 31	1989	1988	1987
Assets			
Current assets			
Cash and cash equivalents	$ 534	$ 508	$ 815
Short-term investments	57	117	113
Accounts receivable	645	896	730
Materials and supplies	237	241	216
Discontinued energy segment	41	440	538
Other current assets	197	233	163
Total current assets	1,711	2,435	2,575
Properties and other assets			
Properties	9,652	9,631	9,295
Affiliates and other companies	284	380	261
Discontinued energy segment	—	—	229
Other assets	651	580	358
Total properties and other assets	10,587	10,591	10,163
Total assets	$12,298	$13,026	$12,738
Liabilities			
Current liabilities			
Accounts payable and other current liabilities	$ 1,867	$ 1,865	$ 1,492
Current maturities of long-term debt	261	227	254
Short-term debt	203	969	69
Total current liabilities	2,331	3,061	1,815
Long-term debt	2,727	3,032	3,009
Deferred income taxes	2,378	2,176	2,158
Long-term debt and deferred gains	1,341	1,249	578
Minority interest	124	116	170
Shareholders' Equity			
Preferred stock, $100,000 stated value	150	150	150
Common stock, $1 par value	96	107	155
Other capital	1,136	1,228	1,771
Retained earnings	2,013	1,907	2,932
Total shareholders' equity	3,397	3,392	5,008
Total liabilities and shareholders' equity	$12,298	$13,026	$12,738

| EXHIBIT 8.4 | **Business Segment Data: CSX Corporation**
(Dollar amounts in millions) |

Years Ended December 31	1989	1988	1987
Operating Revenue			
Transportation	$ 7,428	$ 7,259	$ 6,699
Properties	284	307	219
Technology	207	142	128
Eliminations and other	(174)	(116)	(96)
Consolidated	$ 7,745	$ 7,592	$ 6,950
Operating Income			
Transportation	$ 703	$ 12	$ 683
Properties	171	173	101
Technology	207	142	12
Eliminations and other	(8)	(1)	(1)
Consolidated	869	171	795
Other income	166	116	117
Interest expense	343	347	324
Earnings (loss) from continuing operations before income taxes	$ 692	$ (60)	$ 588
Identifiable Assets			
Transportation	$12,151	$11,858	$11,477
Properties	485	547	472
Technology	46	145	154
Eliminations and other	(384)	476	635
Consolidated	$12,298	$13,026	$12,738

developed by shipping lines (primarily American President Lines) to offer faster, more economical service inland from ports and to avoid delays by using the Panama Canal. Both handling and fuel costs are lower en route, more than making up for higher costs to load and unload. Some domestic traffic is now being double-stacked; some roads intend to phase out conventional piggy-back service.[8] In December 1989, Daniel Machalaba reported concrete signs of attention by CSX to its railroad operations.[9] One sign seems quaint but is symbolic. Shortly after being appointed president of CSX in April 1989, John W. Snow moved to a new house—30 yards from the railroad tracks. He reports problems he sees there. Interest in operating details is new at CSX. Earnings had fallen both because of slighting day-to-day operations and because of outside factors such as Hurricane Hugo, the Pittston Co. coal strike, cold weather, and lower auto shipments. Snow won't change Watkins's policies radically until Watkins retires. Among policies questioned by the writer are

EXHIBIT 8.5	Operational Analysis: CSX Transportation
	(Dollar amounts in millions)

	1989		1988		1987	
	Total	Rail	Total	Rail	Total	Rail
Operating revenue	$7,428	$4,988	$7,259	$5,089	$6,699	$4,486
Operating expense						
Labor and fringe	2,758	2,028	2,736	2,090	2,593	2,014
Materials, etc.	2,291	1,325	2,172	1,308	1,941	1,056
Rents	875	460	806	473	667	439
Depreciation	433	339	452	352	438	341
Fuel	368	247	351	238	377	255
Special charge	—	—	730	724	—	—
Total	6,725	4,399	7,247	5,185	6,016	4,105
Operating income (loss)	$ 703	$ 589	$ 12	$ (96)	$ 683	$ 579
Operating ratios		88.2%		101.9%		87.6%
Property additions	$ 739	$ 589	$1,053	$ 479	$ 666	$ 421

Note: Figures for non-railroad transport operations are not shown in this chart.

EXHIBIT 8.6	Commodities Carried by Rail: CSX Transportation

	Carloads (thousands)			Revenue (dollar amounts in millions)		
Commodity/Year	1989	1988	1987	1989	1988	1987
Automotive	279	310	307	$ 355	$ 386	$ 359
Chemicals	378	378	354	565	561	508
Minerals	410	444	454	315	326	311
Food and consumer products	205	214	230	198	210	218
Agricultural products	278	252	264	284	265	262
Metals	252	305	298	237	264	242
Forest products	557	622	664	476	501	493
Phosphates and fertilizer	518	510	469	267	285	258
Coal	1,909	1,931	2,006	1,568	1,562	1,536
Total	4,786	4,966	5,046	4,265	4,360	4,187
Intermodal (loads)	865	1,032	1,023	590	608	362
Total freight revenue				4,855	4,968	4,549
Other revenue				133	121	135
Total operating revenue				$4,988	$5,089	$4,684

the unusual tripartite management described earlier, and rapid changes of command, there having been four chiefs of the rail operating unit in as many years.

The road had lost the confidence of some important shippers. United Parcel changed to Norfolk Southern, and Quaker Oats tries to avoid CSX, as does Maersk Lines. Snow conceded that diversification in the past may have distracted management. He has vigorously pursued divestment of such assets and expects the line to become much more focused. New equipment has been obtained, and old equipment has been repaired or junked. A central computer dispatching station has been installed in Jacksonville. CSX pointed to service improvements, and to success in obtaining the General Motors business formerly handled by Norfolk Southern.[10]

A survey of several customers by *The Journal of Commerce*[11] indicates that CSX's commitment to service is being noticed. Attitudes have improved; so has the service delivered. Snow indicated that early hopes for synergy among the various units of CSX have been disappointing. He prefers to concentrate on running each unit well; then, when synergy does happen, each unit will deliver effective service to customers.

KIRK'S DILEMMA

Because he is new both to the railroad industry and to CSX, Kirk can use all the advice he can get. He has asked that a strategic analysis of CSX's strategic position be prepared for his review. That should enable him to understand the analyst's view of strengths, weaknesses, opportunities, and threats; how CSX's rail unit might best interact with other CSX units; how the economic factors bear on strategic choice; and any suggested strategies.

Exhibit 8.7 shows the line structure of the railroad (and of the inland barge system as well).

NOTES

1. John H. Gormley, Jr. "CSX Names New Chief for Its Railroad Division." *The Sun,* February 2, 1990, p. 1D; and Daniel Machalaba. "CSX Names Kirk, a Non-Railroader, to Head Rail Unit." *Wall Street Journal,* February 16, 1990, p. B8.

2. Stanford Erickson. "Putting It Together: CSX Chief Tries to Integrate Global Transport Units." *The Journal of Commerce,* January 2, 1990. pp. 1A and 2B.

3. 1988 figures. CSX and Burlington Northern had almost exactly the same amount of revenues.

4. CSX Corporation, *1988 Annual Report.*

5. *Ibid.*

6. John H. Gormley, Jr. "CSX Is Working on the Railroad, and Wall Street Says It Shows." *The Sun,* August 9, 1989, pp. 1C and 4C.

7. Stephen R. Klein. *Standard & Poor's Industry Analysis: Railroads & Trucking, Including Coal,* October 19, 1989.

8. *Ibid.*

9. Daniel Machalaba. "CSX Is Returning to Its Basic Business: Engines and Boxcars." *Wall Street Journal,* December 28, 1989, pp. A1 and A10.

10. *Ibid.*

11. Erickson. "Putting It Together."

EXHIBIT 8.7   Domestic Routes, Rail and Barge (inset): CSX Transportation

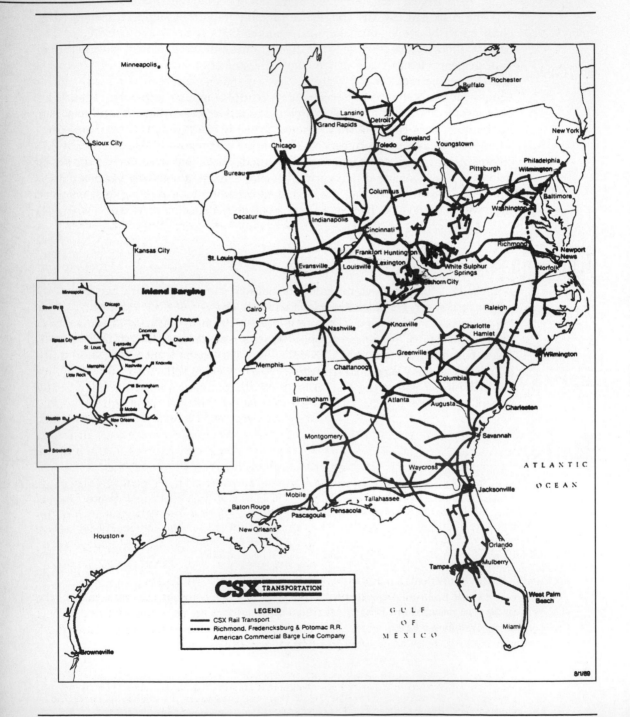

The Railroad Industry in 1990: An Industry Note

INTRODUCTION

Evolutionary changes in the U.S. railroad industry have occurred over most of the twentieth century. However, in recent years changes in the railroad industry have been especially dramatic. In the past decade, the combined forces of fundamental changes in the national economy; increased market competition among transportation modes, products, and geographic regions; and partial economic deregulation of the railroad industry have had a substantial impact on railroads. The rail industry has increased its productivity, improved its safety record, rationalized its physical and human resources, and bettered its financial posture. At the same time, freight rates have increased only modestly, and the industry remains revenue inadequate by regulatory standards.[1]

INDUSTRY ASSESSMENT

The glory days of the railroads have long since passed. Once the first truly modern enterprise, involved in creating new managerial and accounting methods as well as spearheading the taming of the American continent in the nineteenth century, the industry has been declining for decades.[2] Operating and financial statistics suggest that the railroads are in the fourth stage of the industrial life cycle, since the industry is experiencing a slow, but steady, decline.

Railroads move more freight than ever before, but their percentage share has declined drastically. Exhibit A depicts the volume of U.S. intercity freight traffic by the various transport modes. Although rail still carries more tonnage of freight than any other type of transport, it no longer dominates. Moreover, much of rail freight is high bulk/weight commodities, yielding relatively low returns.[3]

An examination of the volume of U.S. intercity passenger traffic paints an even bleaker picture for the railroads, as shown in Exhibit B. Railroads' share in both absolute and percentage terms has fallen severely from 1929 to 1988. Note that air carriers had not yet begun to transport passengers in 1929, but by 1988 had captured 90.3% of the market, generating 334,200 million revenue passenger miles. U.S. intercity bus passenger miles quadrupled from 1929 to 1988, but still lost substantial market share. Inland waterways lost their entire share, as they no longer transport intercity passengers.[4]

Exhibit C presents operating revenues and net income of U.S. railroads for the period 1928 through 1988. Although both operating revenues and net income increased in absolute terms, when adjusted for the consumer price index both financial measures were lower in 1988 than in 1929.[5]

Timothy W. Edlund, Morgan State University, and Michael T. Avara, MBA graduate, Loyola College in Maryland. This refereed note was written using published sources and was presented to the North American Case Research Association in 1990. It is intended as a basis for class discussion rather than to illustrate effective or ineffective handling of an administrative situation. © 1990 by Timothy W. Edlund.

EXHIBIT A

Volume of U.S. Intercity Freight Traffic
(Millions of revenue freight tons—Miles)

Year	Railroads	%	Trucks	%	Inland Waterways	%	Oil Pipelines	%	Air	%	Total Volume
1929	454,800	74.9	19,689	3.3	105,983	17.4	26,900	4.4	3	.0	607,375
1939	338,850	62.4	52,821	9.7	96,249	17.7	55,602	10.2	12	.0	543,534
1944	746,912	68.6	58,264	5.4	150,155	13.8	132,864	12.2	71	.0	1,088,266
1950	596,940	56.2	172,860	16.3	163,344	15.4	129,175	12.1	318	.0	1,062,637
1960	579,130	44.1	285,483	21.7	220,253	16.8	228,626	17.4	778	.0	1,314,270
1970	771,168	39.8	412,000	21.3	318,560	16.4	431,000	22.3	3,295	.2	1,936,023
1980	932,000	37.5	555,000	22.3	407,000	16.4	588,000	23.6	4,840	.2	2,486,840
1987	972,000	36.8	661,000	25.1	411,000	15.6	587,000	22.2	8,670	.3	2,639,670
1988	1,034,000	37.0	704,000	25.2	434,000	15.6	612,000	21.9	9,300	.3	2,793,300

EXHIBIT B

Volume of U.S. Intercity Passenger Traffic
(Millions of revenue passenger—Miles)

Year	Railroads	%	Buses	%	Air Carriers	%	Inland Waterways	%	Total Volume
1929	33,965	77.1	6,800	15.4	—	—	3,300	7.5	44,065
1939	23,669	67.7	9,100	26.0	683	2.0	1,486	4.3	34,938
1944	97,705	75.7	26,920	20.9	2,177	1.7	2,187	1.7	128,989
1950	32,481	47.2	26,436	38.4	8,773	12.7	1,190	1.7	68,000
1960	21,574	28.6	19,327	25.7	31,730	42.1	2,688	3.6	75,319
1970	10,903	5.7	25,300	14.3	109,499	77.7	4,000	2.3	149,702
1980	11,000	4.5	27,400	11.3	204,400	84.2	Nil	—	242,800
1987	12,200	3.3	23,000	6.3	329,200	90.4	Nil	—	364,400
1988	12,800	3.5	23,100	6.2	334,200	90.3	Nil	—	370,100

The rate of return on net investment was lower in 1988 than in 1929. The rate of return was 5.30% in 1929 compared to 4.21% in 1988.[6] The rate of return on net investment represents the relationship of net railway operating income to net investment in transportation property. Net railway operating income is defined as operating revenues after deducting operating expenses, current and deferred taxes, and rents for equipment and joint facilities, but before recording non-operating income and deducting fixed charges.

Exhibit D presents information on working capital and on equipment debt, the principal type of long-term debt utilized by railroads. Working capital for the railroad industry declined from $530.6 million in 1951 to a negative $190.2 million in 1988, while equipment debt increased from $2.3 billion in 1951 to $3.2 billion in 1988.[7]

An examination of operating statistics lends further credence to the proposition that railroads are in the fourth stage of the industrial life cycle. Exhibit E presents various operating statistics for the period from 1929 to 1988. Revenue carloadings declined from 52.9 million in 1929 to 21.6 million in 1988. This decline is deceiving because car capacity has increased significantly in this time period. A better indicator is originated tonnage, since this measure remains constant. Originated tonnage is slightly greater than in 1929, but is substantially greater than in the depression year of 1939. Freight train miles have decreased, partly due to greater hauling capacities of cars and trains, while miles of road owned have been slashed sharply. Railroad employment in 1988 was less than one-seventh the 1929 level.[8] This statistic can be deceiving; much of the decline in employment has been brought about by productivity improvements and attempts to decrease costs.

INDUSTRY PARTICIPANTS

Class I railroads are the industry's largest participants and are defined annually by the Interstate Commerce Commission (ICC), based upon an operating revenue threshold. The 1988 threshold for Class I railroads is $92 million in annual operating revenue. In 1988 there were 14 Class I railroad systems that reported operating and financial data to the ICC. There are 476 other railroads defined by the Association of American Railroads as being one of two types: regional railroads, which earned between $40 million and $92 million in 1988 operating revenue, or operate at least 350 miles of track; and local railroads, which were below both the regional railroad thresholds. In 1988, there were 30 regional railroads and 446 local railroads, the latter including switching and terminal railroads.[9] The following table shows the components of the freight railroad industry in the United States. Class I railroads operate about 81% of the mileage and employ over 90% of the railroad labor force.

Railroad Type	Number	Miles	Employees
Class I	14	140,767	231,299
Regional	30	15,310	12,092
Local	280	14,556	6,431
Switching and Terminal	166	4,181	7,255
Total	490	174,814	257,077

EXHIBIT C	**Railroad Income Statement Statistics**

(Dollar amounts in thousands)

Year	Operating Revenue		Net Income		Consumer Price Index
	Unadjusted	Adjusted	Unadjusted	Adjusted	
1929	$ 6,279,521	$12,254,066	$ 896,807	$1,748,774	1.95
1939	3,995,004	9,588,010	93,182	93,182	2.40
1944	9,436,790	17,929,901	667,188	1,267,657	1.90
1947	8,684,918	12,940,528	478,875	713,524	1.49
1951	10,390,611	13,403,888	693,176	894,197	1.29
1955	10,106,330	12,632,913	927,122	1,158,903	1.25
1960	9,514,294	10,404,994	444,640	202,318	.82
1965	10,207,850	10,727,852	814,629	254,910	.80
1970	11,991,658	11,077,562	226,583	269,507	.75
1975	16,401,860	10,169,153	144,362	89,504	.62
1979	25,219,115	11,600,793	938,254	431,597	.46
1980	28,102,946	11,522,208	1,129,392	463,051	.41
1981	30,898,610	11,432,486	2,041,265	755,268	.37
1982	27,503,503	9,626,226	1,151,548	403,042	.35
1983	26,729,392	9,087,993	1,777,916	604,491	.34
1984	29,453,446	9,425,103	2,653,814	849,220	.32
1985	27,586,441	8,275,932	1,788,151	536,445	.30

Source: Railroad Facts, 1989.

We focus on the seven largest rail systems in the United States: (1) Burlington Northern, (2) CSX Transportation, (3) Union Pacific, (4) Norfolk Southern, (5) Conrail, (6) Atchison, Topeka & Santa Fe, and (7) Southern Pacific. Most of these companies are engaged in other industries. For comparability purposes, only those statistics relating to railroad operations will be included.

Exhibit F provides information on operating revenue and net income for these carriers and Class I railroads in the aggregate. Total 1988 operating revenue for all Class I railroads was in excess of $27.9 billion. The seven largest Class I railroads accounted for $24.4 billion or 87.3% of the total. The largest Class I railroad in terms of 1988 operating revenue was Burlington Northern with nearly $4.5 billion and 16.1% of the total for all Class I railroads. Burlington Northern was followed by CSX Transportation, Union Pacific, Norfolk Southern, Conrail, Atchison, Topeka & Santa Fe, and Southern Pacific.[10]

Total net income for Class I railroads in 1988 was nearly $2.4 billion. In terms of net income, Norfolk Southern was the most profitable member of the group with $632 million or 26.5% of the total, followed by Union Pacific, Conrail, Southern Pacific, Burlington Northern, Atchison, Topeka & Santa Fe, and CSX Transportation.[11]

EXHIBIT D	**Balance Sheet Statistics**

(Dollar amounts in millions)

Year	Working Capital	Equipment Debt
1951	$ 530.6	$2,284.7
1955	933.8	2,532.2
1960	677.9	2,352.5
1965	636.3	2,771.4
1970	109.1	3,913.3
1975	67.9	4,669.1
1979	566.9	5,624.4
1980	921.3	6,164.1
1981	1,691.6	6,204.4
1982	1,371.7	5,740.8
1983	1,325.4	5,130.8
1984	1,844.2	4,690.7
1985	1,083.5	4,352.9
1986	742.7	3,927.3
1987	34.1	3,454.0
1988	(190.2)	3,176.9

Source: Analysis of Class I Railroads.

Exhibit G presents various financial ratios for these seven companies and the industry averages. Operating ratio measures the percentage of operating expense relative to operating revenue. Other ratios have their ordinary meaning.[12]

Strategic Constraints

Adversities facing the railroad industry are clear: a hostile environment of limited growth, severe competition and structural cost increases in the near term. Railroads face threats on both the revenue and expense side. Revenue rate levels assume approximately two-thirds of inflation can be recovered through pass-through increases. Although higher demand should sustain such increases, actions of competition may have an adverse effect on revenues. Expense levels are highly contingent on the planned pace of line dispositions. To the extent that this pace is not achieved, expenses will be impacted adversely.

Opportunities open to the industry are in the areas of customer satisfaction, the industry labor productivity, and effective downsizing. Specific strategic action plans must emphasize several important themes in order to survive and prosper in this hostile environment:

EXHIBIT E	Operating Statistics

Year	Revenue Carloadings	Originated Tonnage (Thousands)	Freight Train-Miles (Thousands)	Miles of Road Owned	Railroad Employment
1929	52,827,925	1,339,091	613,444	229,530	1,660,850
1939	33,911,498	901,669	451,991	220,915	987,943
1944	43,408,295	1,491,491	698,761	215,923	1,413,679
1947	44,502,188	1,537,546	616,071	214,486	1,351,961
1951	40,499,182	1,477,402	528,573	213,401	1,276,000
1955	37,636,031	1,396,332	476,444	211,459	1,058,216
1960	27,886,950	1,240,654	404,464	217,552	780,494
1965	28,344,381	1,387,423	420,962	211,925	639,961
1970	27,015,020	1,484,919	427,065	206,265	566,282
1975	23,217,158	1,395,055	402,557	191,520	487,789
1979	23,891,735	1,502,251	437,835	169,927	482,789
1980	22,597,816	1,492,414	428,488	164,822	458,994
1981	21,612,363	1,453,021	407,520	162,160	436,397
1982	18,498,165	1,268,645	344,936	159,123	378,906
1983	18,814,584	1,292,607	345,916	155,879	322,030
1984	20,257,427	1,429,388	369,403	151,998	323,030
1985	19,418,382	1,319,794	347,292	145,764	301,879
1986	19,588,666	1,305,839	347,234	140,061	275,817
1987	20,602,204	1,372,262	360,692	132,220	248,526
1988	21,599,993	1,429,510	379,271	127,555	235,880

Source: Railroad Facts, 1989.

1. Continuous quality improvement in all aspects of the business.
2. Unit cost improvements through productivity gains and continued downsizing of the workforce.
3. Serving the customer well but with targeted marketing aimed at matching market efforts with strengths and unused capacity.
4. Faster implementation of a core rail system by eliminating unproductive lines.
5. Continuing to raise the productivity of capital by more intensively utilizing assets and improving capability without capacity additions.

QUALITY IMPROVEMENT

A history of poor service is a primary reason for the decline in the railroad industry's share of intercity freight traffic. All too frequently, trains have not run on time, customers have found the cars provided to be of unacceptable quality, and goods have been damaged in transit. Postponement of capital expenditures in

| EXHIBIT F | 1988 Financial Statistics (Railroad only) |

Railroad	Operating Revenues (Millions $'s)	% of Total	Net Income (Millions $'s)	% of Total
Burlington Northern	$ 4,499	16.1%	$ 256	10.7%
CSX Transportation	4,443	15.9	(48)[1]	(2.0)
Union Pacific	4,295	15.4	497	20.9
Norfolk Southern	3,617	12.9	632	26.5
Conrail	3,408	12.2	306	12.8
Atchison, Topeka & Santa Fe	2,140	7.7	153	6.4
Southern Pacific	1,948	7.0	299	12.6
Other Class I Railroads	3,584	12.8	287	12.1
Total	$27,934	100.0%	$2,382	100.0%

[1] In 1988, CSX Transportation recorded a pretax charge of $724 million comprised of a $592 million charge for separation liabilities and a $132 million charge for various costs and claims resulting from litigation and negotiated settlements. Without the special charge, CSX Transportation's 1988 net income would have been $409 million.

Source: Analysis of Class I Railroads.

earlier years has resulted in aged equipment and deteriorating track. The challenge facing the industry is to achieve overall quality improvement, especially in the key areas of train service quality and car quality.

Rail shippers say that consistency is the missing ingredient in rail service. Why is consistent service so tough to deliver? One reason is the network itself. Carriers feel forced by economic necessity to shrink the physical plant, equipment, and workforce. However, the process cuts margin for error by cutting assets. Consequences cascade through the system when even a minor delay occurs at one location. Even when things are running right, railroading is a difficult, intricate business. It's tough to manage a one-lane railroad when vehicles move in different directions on the same track, at different speeds in different sized units. Network problems and delays aren't the only barriers to consistent service. Unlike those truckers who concentrate on a single type of service, railroads have to address wide variations of service demands that are driven by product characteristics.[13]

Four specific steps can be undertaken to improve the performance of rail service:

1. Encourage more realistic expectations.
2. Simplify internal systems.
3. Expand service design.
4. Focus on smaller units.

Railroads should educate shippers for more realistic expectations regarding consistent service. A promise of perfect service should not be made since it can never be

| EXHIBIT G | 1988 Financial Ratios |

Item	Burlington Northern	CSX Transportation
Operating ratio	85.29%	102.28%
Return on total capitalization	9.46%	(.91)%
Return on shareholders' equity	8.97%	(1.24)%
Current ratio	.9	.6
Debt/equity ratio	60.07%	35.36%
Ratio of cash flow to debt due within one year	5.6	1.4

Source: Analysis of Class I Railroads.

provided. Railroads should commit to an achievable level of high-quality, consistent service. Railroads and shippers should work together toward solutions when service consistency is not satisfactory. When service is important, perhaps shippers should pay more for it, assuming railroads would pay penalties when they don't meet standards.[14]

Simplification of internal systems should also lead to better service. State-of-the-art customer service centers are really improving, but they're still at the mercy of complicated internal systems. No matter how good, the customer service center can be tripped up by the service delivery process. For example, one carrier has a 106-step process from the time a car is ordered until it is available for reload. On a big carrier, that means a potential exists to make one million mistakes a day on cars alone.[15]

Another means of improving rail services is the expansion of service design. Service design tries to harmonize the customer's needs with an efficient operating plan. In practice, that means both shippers and internal power centers, operating, marketing and financial, seek to bring about changes in the way freight is moved. As the critical interface where marketing ideas turn into transportation service, this concept blends marketing skill and operating savvy to balance diverse needs within each company. Service design is a pragmatic, real-world approach to balance forces of efficiency, profitability, and consistency.[16]

A focus on small units that concentrate on responsibility, control and service delivery, will improve rail service. With a single contact point and broad responsibility, the carrier-customer relationship becomes more personal and healthy by providing better service control.

Railroad management should make the achievement of quality improvement the number one priority throughout the entire organization. Formal quality training programs should be developed and all employees should be enrolled in them. Emphasizing quality service enhances work productivity and points the way to the elimination of unnecessary work. The quality emphasis means doing things right the first time in order to meet the customer's requirements and to avoid costly

Union Pacific	Norfolk Southern	Conrail	Atchison, Topeka & Santa Fe	Southern Pacific	Industry Averages
81.39%	74.10%	86.43%	89.79%	105.09%	88.82%
13.03%	12.90%	7.99%	7.35%	14.09%	12.89%
14.66%	13.49%	7.77%	6.75%	14.66%	9.09%
.7	1.7	1.4	1.1	.6	1.0
41.50%	13.63%	20.69%	24.37%	37.15%	31.30%
8.1	10.3	6.8	5.4	8.0	5.1

duplication of effort. Employees must find better ways to do their jobs, by focusing on customer needs whether that customer is a shipper or a co-worker.

Customers should also be consulted in order to determine how railroad service can be improved. Railroads should start by surveying their largest customers concerning service problems and service enhancement suggestions. Members of management should then be assigned to one of the large shippers. The management personnel should see that all service problems relating to the shipper assigned them are resolved. This process should be an ongoing one where surveys are conducted on a routine basis and service performance is closely monitored. Managers' compensation should directly reflect the results they achieve in improving service to their assigned shippers.

One relatively inexpensive way to make gains in service is to improve existing monitoring systems for train service quality and customer acceptance of cars. An augmented measurement system should be utilized to place direct responsibility on division managers and engineers to provide timely reliable service and acceptable cars to customers. Daily reports on actual performance relative to these measures should be provided to top management. Compensation rates for all levels of non-union operating personnel from vice-presidents to division managers should be directly tied to the achievement of quality improvements in general, as well as these two specific areas. Financial commitments must be made to acquire new locomotives and cars, to improve the quality of the existing equipment fleet and to properly maintain track and structures.

COST REDUCTION

The railroad industry's losing struggle to retain its share of intercity freight traffic during the past few decades reflects more than just technological obsolescence. Railroads have an inherent cost disadvantage relative to their main competitors, trucks. The industry is both capital *and* labor intensive service business, which has contributed to the erosion of its competitive position. Railroads built their infrastructures and spend millions of dollars per year to maintain them. The infrastructure utilized by trucks, the interstate highway system, was paid for and is maintained by the federal and state governments. User taxes that trucks pay are insignificant compared to railroads' capital costs. While years of heavy investment in new technologies has boosted productivity of physical plant and rolling stock, there has been less progress correcting inefficiencies on the labor side.

The railroad industry's total labor costs currently stand at approximately 50% of operating revenues. According to a report published by the Association of American Railroads during 1985, the average cost per rail employee was $40,972, or some 53% greater than the $26,779 earned by the typical trucking employee. The report further noted that wage and fringe benefit costs were higher than those for 97.4% of all industrial workers. Since 1985, labor costs for both railroad and trucking employees have increased, but there has been no significant change in the cost differential.

Railroads must lower prices in those areas where they compete directly with trucks. In order to be able to do this and still earn a profit, costs must be cut. The following steps are essential:

1. Archaic union work rules must be eliminated.
2. Future salary increases must be made contingent on productivity increases.
3. Downsizing of the work force must continue.

The railroad industry is burdened by unnecessary and costly work rules, some of which have changed very little since the beginning of the century. These work rules severely restrict the operational flexibility available to railroads and limit the quantity and type of work that rail employees perform in a normal work day. As a result of these rules, railroads must keep certain employees whose jobs have been rendered obsolete by technological advances. For example, train crews receive an extra day's pay whenever their train exceeds a stated mileage, based on older, slower trains of many decades ago. Elimination of these rules would make the industry more efficient and allow it to recapture some ground lost to motor carriers during the past few decades. A more competitive railroad industry would be a more reliable employer and traffic increases would allow it to eventually employ more people in required positions. In national bargaining negotiations, railroads should attempt to obtain agreements on the following points:

- The relaxation of work rule restrictions in all crafts
- Elimination of unnecessary train crew members
- Increased basic day miles in through-freight service
- Modification of job protection arrangements
- Working full 8-hour days for 8 hours of pay

Annually, the railroad industry faces increasing labor costs without obtaining matching productivity gains. With a revenue base that is stable or declining, this is a sure prescription for continued financial difficulties. Rather than being faced with blanket future salary increases, railroads must make them contingent on productivity increases. Productivity increases can be obtained by the following actions:

- The aforementioned work rule reductions
- Phase in an equitable pay structure that is compatible with market rates
- Containment of and increased employee participation in health and welfare costs
- Reduced pay and benefit levels for new employees, as has been negotiated by many members of the air transport industry

MARKET SEGMENTATION

Before computers, the transportation industry could only grope for ways to identify costs. The result sometimes was disastrous, because railroads never could be sure how much each different freight movement was costing them. Some railroads even deluded themselves into thinking the costs were lower than they were so they could set lower rates and capture more tonnage from their competitors. To get volume and increase market share, they often made rates that literally gave their services away, charging far less than they were spending. This parallels the rate wars between railroads in the nineteenth century, with equally adverse results.[18]

With computers and more sophisticated market-analysis tools, railroads are able to better determine costs of carrying each different commodity over each different route. Direct operating expenses required for each move must be computed and replacement costs of locomotives and cars must be determined and apportioned to the move.

It is important that replacement cost of equipment rather than original cost be utilized in calculations. There is a substantial gap between what railroads originally paid for their fleets and current replacement costs. Much of the equipment utilized by railroads is 10 to 15 years old or older. Inflation has multiplied purchase prices of locomotives and cars only a few years old. The more immediate reason for setting values at replacement cost is that the industry is launching an ambitious equipment replacement program. Moreover, Betterment Accounting, specified for use by the entire industry until recently, provides even greater distortion of actual values than do accounting methods used in other industries. When marketing managers make new multi-year contracts it is imperative that fully allocated cost of new equipment be utilized when calculating associated costs.

SYSTEM RATIONALIZATION

As a result of the decline in demand for rail services, the industry is burdened with many miles of track that are unprofitable or only marginally profitable. The obvious required action is to dispose of these lines. Track lines can be disposed of by two methods: abandonment or sale. In the case of abandonment, railroads must apply with state authorities for the permission to terminate rail service over a designated section of track. After an assessment of the alternative transportation options for the remaining shippers on the line, the states will rule on whether railroads can abandon the lines. Alternatively, railroads can attempt to sell these lines to regional or short line carriers who may be able to restore them to profitability because they do not face the burden of unionized labor. Obviously, the sale of excess track is preferable to outright abandonment since the railroads are able to recover a portion of their investment in these lines.

Another important rail issue, involving the sale of regional or short lines, has been the subject of conflicting court rulings. Late in 1988, the U.S. Supreme Court agreed to hear two cases with some application to the issue, but held up appeals on several other cases with direct bearing on the sales of short lines by major rail carriers. The debate turns on whether and under what circumstances labor protection payments would be required for rail workers whose jobs are affected by the sale of a short line.

As a result, the creation of regional railroads was virtually halted, and the pace of downsizing through short line sales—the most efficient method and the only one which provides continued service—has been slowed for major railroads nationwide. Without such sales, more small communities would be left without rail service, as the only alternative would be abandonment of these lines. Railroads, shippers, and these small communities should jointly attempt to convince the U.S. Supreme Court of the merits of and need for short line sales without overly burdensome labor protection contingencies, or to have new legislation passed liberalizing procedures.

CAPITAL PRODUCTIVITY GAINS

Railroads are entering a period of transition. Having cut labor forces and shed unwanted track significantly, they must now move from downsizing to increasing productivity through better management of capital assets. Capital productivity opportunities are of three kinds:

1. Better utilization of existing fleets.
2. Judicious acquisitions of new equipment.
3. Technological improvements.

Fleet utilization is enhanced by improving the availability and reliability of locomotives and freight cars. Locomotive availability is measured by an index entitled "mean time between failures" (MTBF). As the name implies, MTBF measures the average length of time between locomotive problems that require temporary removal from service. The out-of-service ratio for locomotives runs as high as 10%. Freight car availability is measured by a term referred to as "bad order ratio." This ratio indicates the percentage of the rail car fleet that is out of service due to various conditions requiring repair. Measurement of availability can help to improve fleet availability.

Utilization of existing fleets can also be enhanced by improving management information systems. Locomotive and freight car scheduling are performed via the utilization of information systems. These systems help management decide where and in what quantities locomotives and cars are required.

Although the aim is to improve the productivity of capital by more intensively utilizing existing assets, some equipment additions will be required. The challenge facing management is to make capital additions in the most effective manner possible.

The third area that offers the potential for capital productivity to railroads is technology. Railroads should constantly explore ways to improve the productivity of locomotives, cars, and other equipment through new technology. Joint exploration with other railroads and manufacturers could be more effective in developing such improvements.

Conclusion

The railroad industry reached its peak in the 1920s and has been experiencing a slow but steady decline ever since. The current and longer term prospects for those industries that are the railroads' primary customers vary, but are collectively mediocre. As more and more heavy industry leaves the United States, the potential revenue base for the railroad industry diminishes. On a percentage basis, railroads are experiencing market share losses to trucks annually. Railroads are also burdened with a very expensive unionized workforce. Yet changes in customer requirements and cost structures, together with changes in cost structure of trucking and intermodal transport all offer significant opportunities to improve performance in the industry.

Notes

1. Association of American Railroads. *Railroad Facts 1989* (Washington, D.C.: Association of American Railroads, 1989), p. 4.
2. Alfred D. Chandler, Jr. *The Visible Hand: The Managerial Revolution in American Business.* Cambridge, MA: Harvard University Press, 1977; pp. 79–205.
3. Association of American Railroads, op. cit., p. 32.
4. *Ibid.*
5. *Ibid.,* pp. 12, 21.
6. *Ibid.,* p. 18.
7. *Ibid.,* pp. 22, 23.
8. *Ibid.,* pp. 24, 27, 33, 42, 56.
9. *Ibid.,* p. 2.
10. Association of American Railroads. *Analysis of Class I Railroads, 1988* (Washington D.C.: Association of American Railroads, 1989), pp. 1–6.
11. *Ibid.*
12. *Ibid.,* pp. 61–66.
13. Ripley Watson, III. "Consistent Rail Service: Making the Gruel Tastier." *Modern Railroads,* February 1990, p. 80.
14. *Ibid.*
15. *Ibid.*
16. *Ibid.*
17. Standard & Poor's Corporation. *Standard & Poor's Industry Surveys* (New York: Standard & Poor's Corporation, 1989), p. R15.
18. Chandler, op. cit.

Reference

Watson, Ripley, III. "How to Tackle the Service Equation." *Modern Railroads,* February 1990.

CASE 9   W. L. Gore & Associates, Inc.

Frank Shipper ▪ Charles C. Manz

"To make money and have fun."—W. L. Gore

THE FIRST DAY ON THE JOB

On July 26, 1976, Jack Dougherty, a newly minted M.B.A. from the College of William and Mary, bursting with resolve and dressed in a dark blue suit, reported for his first day at W. L. Gore & Associates. He presented himself to Bill Gore, shook hands firmly, looked him in the eye, and said he was ready for anything.

What happened next was one thing for which Jack was not ready. Gore replied, "That's fine, Jack, fine. Why don't you look around and find something you'd like to do." Three frustrating weeks later he found that something: dressed in jeans, he was loading fabric into the mouth of a machine that laminates the company's patented GORE-TEX membrane to fabric. By 1982 Jack had become responsible for all advertising and marketing in the fabrics group. This story is part of the folklore that is heard over and over about W. L. Gore. Today the process is slightly more structured, but new "Associates" take a leisurely journey through the business before settling into their own positions, regardless of the specific position for which they were hired. A new sales Associate in the Fabric Division may spend six weeks rotating through different areas before beginning to concentrate on sales and marketing. Among other things, she or he may learn how GORE-TEX fabric is made, what it can and cannot do, how Gore handles customer complaints, and how it makes its investment decisions.

Anita McBride related her early experience at W. L. Gore & Associates this way:

> Before I came to Gore, I had worked for a structured organization. I came here, and for the first month it was fairly structured because I was going through training and this is what we do and this is how Gore is and all of that, and I went to Flagstaff for that training. After a month I came down to Phoenix and my sponsor said, "Well, here's your office," (it's a wonderful office) and "Here's your desk" and walked away. And I thought, "Now what do I do," you know? I was waiting for a memo or something, or a job description. Finally after another month I was so frustrated, I felt, "What have I gotten myself into?" And so I went to my sponsor and I said, "What the heck do you want from me? I need something from you." And he said, "If you don't know what you're supposed to do, examine your commitment and opportunities."

Prepared by Frank Shipper, Department of Management, Franklin P. Perdue School of Business, Salisbury State University, Salisbury, MD 21801, and Charles C. Manz, Department of Management, College of Business, Arizona State University, Tempe, AZ 85287. Reprinted by permission.

BACKGROUND

W. L. Gore & Associates is a company that evolved from the late Wilbert L. Gore's personal, organizational, and technical experiences. He was born in Meridian, Idaho, near Boise, in 1912. He claimed that by age six, he had become an avid hiker in the Wasatch Mountain Range in Utah. In those mountains, at a church camp, he met Genevieve, his future wife. She is called Vieve by everyone. In 1935 they got married. In the partnership they envisioned, he would make breakfast and she would make lunch. The partnership lasted a lifetime.

Gore received both a Bachelor of Sciences degree in chemical engineering in 1933 and a Master of Sciences degree in physical chemistry in 1935 from the University of Utah. He began his professional career at American Smelting and Refining in 1936. He moved to Remington Arms Company in 1941. He moved once again, to E. I. DuPont de Nemours, in 1945. He held positions as research supervisor and head of operations research. While at DuPont, he worked on a team to develop applications for polytetrafluoroethylene—frequently referred to as PTFE in the scientific community and known as Teflon by DuPont's consumers. (It is known by other names by customers of other companies.) On this team, Wilbert Gore felt a sense of excited commitment, personal fulfillment, and self-direction. He followed the development of computers and transistors and believed that PTFE had the ideal insulating characteristics for use with such equipment.

He tried, without success, a number of ways to make a PTFE-coated ribbon cable. Then a breakthrough came in his home basement laboratory. He was explaining the problem to his son Bob. Bob saw some PTFE sealant tape made by 3M and asked his father, "Why don't you try this tape?" His father then explained to his son that everyone knows you cannot bond PTFE to itself. Bob went on to bed.

Bill Gore remained in his basement lab and proceeded to try what everyone knew would not work. At about 4 A.M., he woke up his son, waved a small piece of cable around, and shouted excitedly, "It works, it works!" The following night father and son returned to the basement lab to make ribbon cable coated with PTFE.

For the next four months, Bill Gore tried to persuade DuPont to make a new product, PTFE-coated ribbon cable. By this time in his career, Bill Gore knew some of the decision makers at DuPont. After he talked to a number of them, it became clear that DuPont wanted to remain a supplier of raw materials, not a fabricator.

Bill began to discuss with his wife Vieve the possibility of starting their own insulated wire and cable business. On January 1, 1958, their wedding anniversary, they founded W. L. Gore & Associates. The basement of their home served as their first facility. After finishing dinner on their anniversary, Vieve turned to her husband of 23 years and said, "Well, let's clear up the dishes, go downstairs, and get to work." They viewed this as another partnership.

Bill Gore was 45 years old with five children to support when he left DuPont. He left behind a career of 17 years, a secure job, and a good salary. To finance the first two years of operation of their new business, they mortgaged their house and took $4,000 from savings. All of their friends told them not to do it.

The first few years were rough. In lieu of salary, some of their employees accepted room and board in the Gore home. At one point 11 Associates[1] were living and working under one roof. The order (which was almost lost) that put the company on a profitable footing came from the City of Denver's water department. One afternoon, Vieve answered a phone call while sifting PTFE powder. The caller indicated that he was interested in the ribbon cable but wanted to ask some technical questions. Bill was out running some errands. The caller asked for the product manager. Vieve explained that he was out at the moment. Next he asked for the sales manager and finally for the president. Vieve explained that they were also out. The caller became outraged and hollered, "What kind of company is this anyway?" With a little diplomacy, however, the Gores were able to secure an order for $100,000. This order put the company over the hump and it began to take off.

W. L. Gore & Associates has continued to grow and develop new products primarily derived from PTFE, including its best-known product, GORE-TEX fabric.[2] In 1986, Bill Gore died while backpacking in the Wind River Mountains of Wyoming. Before he died he had become chairman, and his son Bob president, a position he continues to occupy. Vieve remains as the only other officer, secretary-treasurer.

THE OPERATING COMPANY

W. L. Gore & Associates is a company without titles, hierarchy, or any of the conventional structures associated with enterprises of its size. The titles president and secretary–treasurer are used only because they are required by the laws of incorporation. In addition, Gore is a company that does not have a corporate-wide mission or code of ethics statement, nor does Gore either require such statements or prohibit business units from developing them for themselves. Thus the associates of some business units who have felt a need for such statements have developed them for themselves. The majority of business units within Gore do not have such statements. When questioned about this issue, one Associate stated, "The company belief is that (1) its four basic operating principles cover ethical practices required of people in business; (2) it will not tolerate illegal practices." Gore's management style has been referred to as un-management. The organization has been guided by Bill's experiences on teams at DuPont and has evolved as needed.

For example, in 1965 W. L. Gore & Associates was a thriving and growing company with a facility on Paper Mill Road in Newark, Delaware, with about 200 Associates. One warm Monday morning in the summer, Bill Gore was taking his usual walk through the plant. All of a sudden he realized that he did not know everyone in the plant. The team had become too big. As a result, he decreed that no facility would have over 150–200 Associates. Thus was born the expansion policy of "Get big by staying small." The purpose of maintaining small plants is to cultivate a close-knit and personal atmosphere.

Today W. L. Gore & Associates consists of 44 plants worldwide with over 5,300 Associates. In some cases the plants are clustered together on the same site, as in Flagstaff, Arizona, where four plants occupy the same site. Twenty-seven of those plants are in the United States. The 17 that are overseas manufacture electronics, medical, industrial, and fabric products in Scotland, Germany, France, and Japan.

Gore electronic products are found in unconventional places where conventional products will not do—in space shuttles, for example, where Gore wire and cable assemblies withstood the heat of ignition and the cold of space. In addition, they are found in fast computers, transmitting signals at up to 93% of the speed of light. Gore cables are even underground, in oil drilling operations, and undersea, on submarines that require superior microwave signal equipment and no-fail cables that can survive high pressure. The Gore electronic products division has a history of anticipating future customer needs with innovative products. Gore electronic products are well known in industry for their ability to last under adverse conditions.

In the medical arena, GORE-TEX-expanded PTFE is considered an ideal replacement for human tissue in many situations. In patients suffering from cardiovascular disease, the diseased portion of arteries is often replaced by tubes of expanded PTFE that are strong, biocompatible, and able to carry blood at arterial pressures. Gore has a dominant share in this market. Other Gore medical products include patches that can literally mend broken hearts by patching holes and repairing aneurysms, a synthetic knee ligament that provides stability by replacing the natural anterior cruciate ligament, and sutures that allow for tissue attachment and offer the surgeon silk-like handling coupled with extreme strength. In 1985 W. L. Gore & Associates won Britain's Prince Philip Award for Polymers in the Service of Mankind. The award was bestowed in recognition of the life-saving achievements of the Gore medical products team.

The industrial products division makes a number of products, including sealants, filter bags, cartridges, clothes, and coatings. These products tend to have specialized and critical applications. Gore's reputation for quality appears to influence the industrial purchasers of these products.

The Gore fabrics division, which is the largest division, supplies laminates to manufacturers of foul-weather gear, ski wear, running suits, footwear, gloves, and hunting and fishing garments. Firefighters and U.S. Navy pilots wear GORE-TEX fabric gear, as do some Olympic athletes. The U.S. Army has adopted a total garment system built around a GORE-TEX fabric component.

GORE-TEX membrane has nine billion pores randomly dotting each square inch and is feather light. Each pore is 700 times larger than a water vapor molecule yet thousands of times smaller than a water droplet. Wind and water cannot penetrate the pores, but perspiration can escape. As a result, fabrics bonded with GORE-TEX membrane are waterproof, are windproof, and breathe. The laminated fabrics bring protection from the elements to a variety of products—from survival gear to high-fashion rain wear. Recently other manufacturers, including 3M, have brought out products to compete with GORE-TEX fabrics. Gore, however, continues to have a commanding share of this market.

Bill Gore knew that products alone do not a company make. He wanted to avoid smothering the company in thick layers of formal "management," which he felt stifled individual creativity. As the company grew, he knew that a way had to be devised to help new people get started and to follow their progress. This was seen as particularly important when it came to compensation. W. L. Gore & Associates has developed what it calls its "sponsor" program to meet these needs. When people apply to Gore, they are initially screened by personnel specialists, just as in most companies. For those who meet the basic criteria, there are interviews with other Associates. Before anyone is hired, an Associate must agree to be that candidate's sponsor. The sponsor is to take a personal interest in the new Associate's contributions, problems, and goals. The sponsor is both coach and advocate, tracking the new Associate's progress, helping and encouraging, dealing with weaknesses, and concentrating on strengths. Sponsoring is not a short-term commitment. All Associates have sponsors, and many have more than one. When individuals are first hired, they have a sponsor in their immediate work area. If they move to another area, they have a sponsor in that work area. As Associates' responsibilities grow, they may acquire additional sponsors.

Because the sponsoring program looks beyond conventional views of what makes a good Associate, some anomalies in hiring practices occur. Bill Gore has proudly told the story of "a very young man" of 84 who walked in, applied, and spent five very good years with the company. This individual had 30 years of experience in the industry before joining Gore. The other Associates had no problems accepting him, but the personnel computer did. It insisted that his age was 48. The individual success stories at Gore come from diverse backgrounds.

An internal memo by Bill Gore described as follows three kinds of sponsorship and how they might work.

1. The sponsor who helps a new Associate *get started* on his job. Also, the sponsor who helps a present Associate get started on a new job (starting sponsor).
2. The sponsor who sees to it that the Associate being sponsored *gets credit* and recognition for contributions and accomplishments (advocate sponsor).
3. The sponsor who sees to it that the Associate being sponsored is *fairly paid* for contributions to the success of the enterprise (compensation sponsor).

A single sponsor can perform any one or all three kinds of sponsorship. A sponsor is a friend and an Associate. All the supportive aspects of friendship are also present. Often (perhaps usually) two Associates sponsor each other as advocates.

In addition to the sponsor program, Gore Associates are asked to follow four guiding principles:

1. Try to be fair.
2. Use your freedom to grow.
3. Make your own commitments, and keep them.
4. Consult with other Associates prior to any action that may adversely affect the reputation or financial stability of the company.

The four principles are often referred to as Fairness, Freedom, Commitment, and Waterline. The waterline terminology is drawn from an analogy to ships. If someone pokes a hole in a boat above the waterline, the boat will be in relatively little real danger. If someone pokes a hole below the waterline, however, the boat is in immediate danger of sinking.

These operating principles were put to a test in 1978. By this time, word about the qualities of GORE-TEX fabric was spreading throughout the recreational and outdoor markets. Production and shipment had begun in volume. At first a few complaints were heard. Next some of the clothing started coming back. Finally, much of the clothing was being returned. The trouble was that the GORE-TEX fabric was leaking. Being waterproof was one of the two major properties responsible for GORE-TEX fabric's success. The company's reputation and credibility were on the line.

Peter W. Gilson, who led Gore's fabric division, says, "It was an incredible crisis for us at that point. We were really starting to attract attention; we were taking off—and then this." In the next few months, Peter and several Associates made a number of those below-the-waterline decisions.

First, the researchers determined that oils in human sweat clogged the pores in the GORE-TEX fabric and altered the surface tension of the membrane, allowing water to pass through. They also discovered that a good washing could restore the waterproof property. At first this solution (known as the "Ivory Snow Solution") was accepted.

A single letter from "Butch," a mountain guide in the Sierra, changed the company's position. Butch wrote how he had been leading a group and, "My parka leaked and my life was in danger." As Gilson says, "That scared the hell out of us. Clearly our solution was no solution at all to someone on a mountain top." All of the products were recalled. As Gilson says, "We bought back, at our own expense, a fortune in pipeline material. Anything that was in the stores, at the manufacturers, or anywhere else in the pipeline."

In the meantime, Bob Gore and other Associates set out to develop a permanent fix. One month later, a second-generation GORE-TEX fabric had been developed. Furthermore, Gilson told dealers that if at any time a customer returned a leaky parka, they should replace it and bill the company. The replacement program alone cost Gore roughly $4 million.

ORGANIZATIONAL STRUCTURE

W. L. Gore & Associates has been described not only as un-managed but also as unstructured. Bill Gore referred to the structure as a lattice organization. A lattice structure is portrayed in Exhibit 9.1. The characteristics of this structure are

1. Direct lines of communication—person to person—with no intermediary
2. No fixed or assigned authority
3. Sponsors, not bosses
4. Natural leadership defined by followership
5. Objectives set by those who must "make them happen"
6. Tasks and functions organized through commitments

The structure within the lattice is described by the people at Gore as complex. It evolves from interpersonal interactions, self-commitment to group-known responsibilities, natural leadership, and group-imposed discipline.

Bill Gore once explained this structure by saying, "Every successful organization has an underground lattice. It's where the news spreads like lightning, where people can go around the organization to get things done." Another description of what is occurring within the lattice structure is constant cross-area teams—the

EXHIBIT 9.1 | **The Lattice Structure**

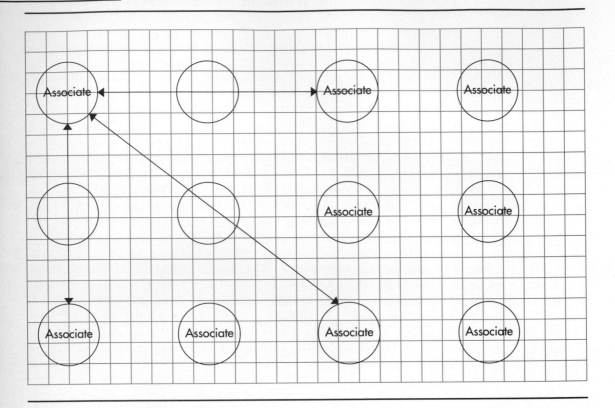

equivalent of quality circles going on all the time. When a puzzled interviewer told Bill that he was having trouble understanding how planning and accountability worked, Bill replied with a grin, "So am I. You ask me how it works, every which way."

The lattice structure does have some similarities to traditional management structures. For instance, 30 to 40 Associates who make up an advisory group meet every six months to review marketing, sales, and production plans. As Bill Gore has conceded, "The abdication of titles and rankings can never be 100%."

One thing that might strike an outsider in the meetings and other interactions in the Gore organization is the informality and amount of humor. Meetings tend to be only as long as necessary. As Trish Hearn, an Associate in Newark, Delaware, said, "No one feels a need to pontificate." Words such as "responsibilities" and "commitments" are, however, commonly heard. This is an organization that seems to take what it does very seriously, but its members do not take themselves too seriously.

Gore may have the shortest organizational pyramid in existence for a company of its size. The pyramid consists of Bob Gore, the late Bill Gore's son, as president, and Vieve, Bill Gore's widow, as secretary–treasurer. All the other members of the Gore organization are referred to as Associates. Words such as "employees," "subordinates," and "managers" are taboo in the Gore culture.

Gore does not have any managers, but it does have many leaders. Bill Gore described the kinds of leadership and the role of leadership in the following internal memo.

1. The Associate who is recognized by a team as having a special knowledge, or experience (for example, this could be a chemist, computer expert, machine operator, salesman, engineer, lawyer). This kind of leader gives the team *guidance in a special area.*

2. The Associate the team looks to for coordination of individual activities in order to achieve the agreed upon objectives of the team. The role of this leader is to persuade team members to *make the commitments* necessary for success (commitment seeker).

3. The Associate who proposes necessary objectives and activities and seeks agreement and team *consensus on objectives.* This leader is perceived by the team members as having a good grasp of how the objectives of the team fit in with the broad objective of the enterprise. This kind of leader is often also the "commitment seeking" leader.

4. The leader who evaluates relative contribution of team members (in consultation with other sponsors), and reports these contribution evaluations to a compensation committee. This leader may also participate in the compensation committee on relative contribution and pay and *reports changes in compensation* to individual Associates. This leader is then also a compensation sponsor.

5. The leader who coordinates the research, manufacturing and marketing of one product type within a business, interacting with team leaders and individual Associates who have commitments regarding the product type. These leaders are usually called *product specialists.* They are respected for their knowledge and dedication to their products.

6. *Plant leaders* who help coordinate activities of people within a plant.

7. *Business leaders* who help coordinate activities of people in a business.

8. *Functional leaders* who help coordinate activities of people in a "functional" area.

9. *Corporate leaders* who help coordinate activities of people in different businesses and functions and who try to promote communication and cooperation among all Associates.

10. *Intrapreneuring Associates* who *organize new teams* for new businesses, new products, new processes, new devices, new marketing efforts, new or better methods of all kinds. These leaders invite other Associates to "sign up" for their project.

It is clear that leadership is widespread in our lattice organization and that it is continually changing and evolving. The situation that leaders are frequently *also* sponsors should not confuse that these are different activities and responsibilities.

Leaders are not authoritarians, managers of people, or supervisors who tell us what to do or forbid us doing things; nor are they "parents" to whom we transfer our own self-responsibility. However, they do often advise us of the consequences of actions we have done or propose to do. Our actions result in contributions, or lack of contribution, to the success of our enterprise. Our pay depends on the magnitude of our contributions. This is the basic discipline of our lattice organization.

Many other aspects are arranged along egalitarian lines. The parking lot does not have any reserved parking spaces except for customers and the handicapped. There is only one area in each plant in which to eat. The lunchroom in each new plant is designed to be a focal point for Associate interaction. As Dave McCarter of Phoenix explains, "The design is no accident. The lunchroom in Flagstaff has a fireplace in the middle. We want people to like to be here." The location of the plant is also no accident. Sites are selected on the basis of access to transportation, the presence of a university nearby, beautiful surroundings, and climate appeal. Land cost is never a primary consideration. McCarter justifies the selection by stating, "Expanding is not costly in the long run. The loss of money is what you make happen by stymieing people into a box."

Not all people function well under such a system, especially at first. For those accustomed to a more structured work environment, there are adjustment problems. As Bill Gore said, "All our lives most of us have been told what to do, and some people don't know how to respond when asked to do something—and have the very real option of saying no—on their job. It's the new Associate's responsibility to find out what he or she can do for the good of the operation." The vast majority of the new Associates, after some initial floundering, adapt quickly.

Gore's flexible work place is not for those who require more structured working conditions and cannot adapt. According to Bill, "It's an unhappy situation, both for the Associate and the sponsor. If there is no contribution, there is no paycheck."

As Anita McBride, an associate in Phoenix, says, "It's not for everybody. People ask me whether we have turnover, and yes we do have turnover. What you're seeing looks like utopia, but it also looks extreme. If you finally figure the system, it can be real exciting. If you can't handle it, you gotta go. Probably by your own choice, because you're going to be so frustrated."

In rare cases an Associate "is trying to be unfair," in Bill's words. In one case the problem was chronic absenteeism, and in the other the individual was caught stealing. "When that happens, all hell breaks loose," said Bill Gore. "We can get damned authoritarian when we have to."

Over the years, Gore & Associates has faced a number of unionization drives. The company neither tries to dissuade Associates from attending an organizational meeting nor retaliates when flyers are passed out. Each attempt at unionization has been unsuccessful. None of the plants has been organized to date. Bill believed that no need exists for third-party representation under the lattice structure. "Why would Associates join a union when they own the company? It seems rather absurd."

Overall, the Associates appear to have responded positively to the Gore system of un-management and un-structure. The year before he died, Bill estimated that "The profit per Associate is double" that at DuPont.

The lattice structure is not without its critics. As Bill Gore stated, "I'm told from time to time that a lattice organization can't meet a crisis well because it takes too long to reach a consensus when there are no bosses. But this isn't true. Actually a lattice, by its very nature, works particularly well in a crisis. A lot of useless effort is avoided because there is no rigid management hierarchy to conquer before you can attack a problem."

The lattice has been put to the test on a number of occasions. For example, in 1975 Dr. Charles Campbell, the University of Pittsburgh's senior resident, reported that a GORE-TEX arterial graft had developed an aneurysm. An aneurysm is a bubble-like protrusion that is life-threatening. If it continues to expand, it will explode. Obviously, this kind of problem has to be solved quickly and permanently.

Within only a few days of Dr. Campbell's first report, he flew to Newark to present his findings to Bill and Bob Gore and a few other Associates. The meeting lasted two hours. Dan Hubis, a former policeman who had joined Gore to develop new production methods, had an idea before the meeting was over. He returned to his work area to try some different production techniques. After only three hours and twelve tries, he had developed a permanent solution. In other words, in three hours a potentially damaging problem to both patients and the company was resolved. Furthermore, Hubis's redesigned graft has gone on to win widespread acceptance in the medical community.

Other critics have been outsiders who had problems with the idea of no titles. Sarah Clifton, an Associate at the Flagstaff facility, was being pressed by some outsiders about what her title was. She made one up and had it printed on some business cards: SUPREME COMMANDER. When Bill Gore learned what she had done, he loved it and recounted the story gleefully to others.

Another critic is Eric Reynolds, founder of Marmot Mountain Works Ltd. of Grand Junction, Colorado, and a major Gore customer.

> I think the lattice has its problems with the day-to-day nitty-gritty of getting things done on time and out the door. I don't think Bill realizes how the lattice system affects customers. I mean after you've established a relationship with someone about product quality, you can call up one day and suddenly find that someone new to you is handling your problem. It's frustrating to find a lack of continuity. But I have to admit that I've personally seen at Gore remarkable examples of people coming out of nowhere and excelling.

Bill Gore was asked a number of times whether the lattice structure could be used by other companies. His answer was "No. For example, established companies would find it very difficult to use the lattice. Too many hierarchies would be destroyed. When you remove titles and positions and allow people to follow whomever they want, it may very well be someone other than the person who has been in charge. The lattice works for us, but it's always evolving. You have to expect problems." He maintained that the lattice system works best when put in place in startup companies by dynamic entrepreneurs.

RESEARCH AND DEVELOPMENT

Like everything else at Gore, research and development are unstructured. There is no formal Research and Development Department. Yet the company holds many patents, although most inventions are held as proprietary or trade secrets. Any Associate can ask for a piece of raw PTFE, known as a silly worm, with which to experiment. Bill Gore believed that all people have it within themselves to be creative.

The best way to understand how research and development work is to see how inventiveness has previously occurred at Gore. By 1969 the wire and cable division was facing increased competition. Bill Gore began to look for a way to straighten out the PTFE molecules. As he said, "I figured out that if we ever unfold those molecules, get them to stretch out straight, we'll have a tremendous new kind of material." He thought that if PTFE could be stretched, air could be introduced into its molecular structure. The result would be greater volume per pound of raw material with no adverse effect on performance. Thus fabricating costs would be reduced, and profit margins would be increased. Going about this search in a scientific manner with their son Bob, the Gores heated rods of PTFE to various temperatures and then slowly stretched them. Regardless of the temperature, and regardless of how carefully they were stretched, the rods broke.

Then, working alone late one night in 1969 after countless failures, Bob in frustration yanked at one of the rods violently. To his surprise, it did not break. He tried it again and again with the same results. The next morning Bob demonstrated his breakthrough to his father, but not without some drama. As Bill Gore recalled, "Bob wanted to surprise me so he took a rod and stretched it slowly. Naturally, it broke. Then he pretended to get mad. He grabbed another rod and said, 'Oh the hell with this,' and gave it a pull. It didn't break—he'd done it." The new arrangement of molecules not only changed the wire and cable division but also led to the development of GORE-TEX fabric and what is now the largest division at Gore, plus a host of other products.

Initial field-testing of GORE-TEX fabric was conducted by Bill and Vieve in the summer of 1970. Vieve made a hand-sewn tent out of patches of GORE-TEX fabric. They took it on their annual camping trip to the Wind River Mountains in Wyoming. The very first night in the wilderness, they encountered a hail storm. The hail tore holes in the top of the tent, but the bottom filled up like a bathtub from the rain. As Bill Gore stated, "At least we knew from all the water that the tent was waterproof. We just needed to make it stronger, so it could withstand hail."

The second-largest division began on the ski slopes of Colorado. Bill was skiing with his friend Dr. Ben Eiseman of the Denver General Hospital. As Bill Gore told the story,

> We were just about to start a run when I absentmindedly pulled a small tubular section of GORE-TEX out of my pocket and looked at it. "What is that stuff?" Ben asked. So I told him about its properties. "Feels great," he said, "What do you use it for?" "Got no idea," I said. "Well give it to me," he said, "and I'll try it in a vascular graft on a pig." Two weeks later, he called me up. Ben was pretty excited. "Bill," he said "I put it in a pig and it works. What do I do now?" I told him to get together with Pete Cooper in our Flagstaff plant, and let them figure it out.

Now hundreds of thousands of people throughout the world walk around with GORE-TEX vascular grafts.

Every Associate is encouraged to think, experiment, and follow a potentially profitable idea to its conclusion. For example, at a plant in Newark, Delaware, a machine that wraps thousands of feet of wire a day was designed by Fred L. Eldreth, an Associate with a third-grade education. The design was done over a weekend. Many other Associates have contributed their ideas through both product and process breakthroughs.

Without a Research and Development Department, innovations and creativity work very well at Gore & Associates. The year before he died, Bill Gore claimed that "The creativity, the number of patent applications and innovative products is triple [that of DuPont]."

ASSOCIATE DEVELOPMENT

As Ron Hill, an Associate in Newark, said, Gore "will work with Associates who want to advance themselves." Associates are offered many in-house training opportunities. They do tend to be focused on technology and engineering because of the type of organization Gore is, but the company also offers in-house programs in leadership development. In addition, it has cooperative programs that enable Associates to obtain training through universities and other outside providers. Gore will pick up most of these costs. But in Associate development, as in many other areas at Gore, the Associate must take the initiative.

PRODUCTS

The products that Gore makes are arranged into four divisions: electronics, medical, industrial, and fabrics. The Electronic Products Division produces wire and cable for various demanding applications in aerospace, defense, computers, and telecommunications. The wire and cable products have earned a reputation for unequaled reliability. Most of the wire and cable is used where conventional cables cannot operate. For example, Gore wire and cable assemblies were used in the space shuttle Columbia, because they would stand the heat of ignition and the cold of space. Gore wire was used in the Moon vehicle shuttle that scooped up samples of Moon rocks, and Gore's microwave coaxial assemblies have opened new horizons in microwave technology. Back on Earth, the electrical wire products help make the world's fastest computers possible; electrical signals can travel through them at up to 93% of the speed of light. Because of the physical properties of the GORE-TEX material used in their construction, the electronic products are used extensively in defense systems, electronic switching for telephone systems, scientific and industrial instrumentation, microwave communications, and industrial robotics. Reliability is a watchword for all Gore products.

In medical products, of course, reliability is literally a matter of life and death. GORE-TEX-expanded PTFE is used to combat cardiovascular disease. When human arteries are seriously damaged or plugged with deposits that interrupt the flow of blood, the diseased portions can often be replaced with GORE-TEX artificial arteries. GORE-TEX arteries and patches are not rejected by the body, because the patient's own tissues grow into the graft's open porous spaces. GORE-TEX vascular grafts of many sizes are employed to restore circulation to all areas of the body. They have saved limbs from amputation and have saved lives. Some of the tiniest grafts relieve pulmonary problems in newborns. GORE-TEX-expanded PTFE is also used to help people with kidney disease. Associates are developing a variety of surgical reinforcing membranes, known as GORE-TEX cardiovascular patches, that can literally mend broken hearts by patching holes and repairing aneurysms.

Through the Fabrics Division, Gore technology has traveled to the roof of the world on the backs of renowned mountaineers. GORE-TEX fabric is waterproof and windproof, yet it breathes. Those features have qualified GORE-TEX fabric as essential gear for mountaineers and adventurers facing extremely harsh environments. The PTFE membrane blocks wind and water but allows sweat to escape. That makes GORE-TEX fabric ideal for anyone who works or plays hard in foul weather. Backpackers have discovered that a single lightweight GORE-TEX fabric shell will replace a poplin jacket and a rain suit and will dramatically outperform both. Skiers, sailors, runners, bicyclists, hunters, anglers, and other outdoor enthusiasts have also become enthusiastic consumers of garments made of GORE-TEX fabric. General sportswear and women's fashion footwear and handwear of GORE-TEX fabric are as functional as they are beautiful. Boots and gloves, both for work and recreation, are waterproof thanks to GORE-TEX liners. GORE-TEX garments are even becoming standard items issued to many military personnel. Wetsuits, parkas, pants, headgear, gloves, and boots keep the troops warm and dry in foul-weather missions. Other demanding jobs also require the protection of GORE-TEX fabric because of its unique combination of chemical and physical properties.

The Industrial Products Division's GORE-TEX fiber products, like the fabrics, end up in some pretty tough places. The outer protective layer of NASA's spacesuit is woven from GORE-TEX fibers. GORE-TEX fibers are in many ways the ultimate in synthetic fibers. They are impervious to sunlight, chemicals, heat, and cold. They are strong and uniquely resistant to abrasion.

Industrial filtration products, such as GORE-TEX filter bags, reduce air pollution and recover valuable solids from gases and liquids more thoroughly than alternatives; they also do it more economically. They could make coal-burning plants completely smoke free, contributing to a cleaner environment. Other Gore divisions also serve the needs of industry.

The Industrial Products Division also produces joint sealant, a flexible cord of porous PTFE that can be applied as a gasket to the most complex shapes, sealing them to prevent leakage of corrosive chemicals even at extreme temperature and pressure. Steam valves packed with GORE-TEX valve stem packing are guaranteed for the life of the valve when used properly.

The Coatings Division applies layers of PTFE to steel castings and other metal articles by a patented process. Called Fluroshield[3] protective coatings, this fluorocarbon polymer protects processing vessels used in the production of corrosive chemicals.

GORE-TEX microfiltration products are used in medical devices, pharmaceutical manufacturing, and chemical processing. These membranes remove bacteria and other microorganisms from air or liquids, making them sterile and bacteria-free.

COMPENSATION

Compensation at W. L. Gore & Associates takes three forms: salary, profit sharing, and an Associates' Stock Ownership Program (ASOP).[4] Entry-level salary is in the middle for comparable jobs. According to Sally Gore, daughter-in-law of the founder, "We do not feel we need to be the highest paid. We never try to steal people away from other companies with salary. We want them to come here because of the opportunities for growth and the unique work environment." Associates' salaries are reviewed at least once a year and more commonly twice a year. For most workers, the reviews are conducted by a compensation team in the facility in which the employee works. The sponsors for all Associates act as their advocates during this review process. Before meeting with the compensation committee, the sponsor checks with customers or whoever uses the results of the person's work to find out what contribution has been made. In addition, the evaluation team considers the Associate's leadership ability and willingness to help others develop to their fullest.

Besides salaries, W. L. Gore & Associates has profit sharing and ASOP plans for all Associates. Profit sharing typically occurs twice a year but is dependent on profitability. The amount is also dependent on time in service and annual rate of pay. In addition, the firm buys company stock equivalent to 15 percent of the Associates' annual income and places it in an (ASOP) retirement fund. Thus an Associate becomes a stockholder after being at Gore for one year. Bill wanted all Associates to feel that they are themselves the owners.

The principle of commitment is seen as a two-way street. W. L. Gore & Associates tries to avoid layoffs. Instead of cutting pay, which is seen at Gore as disastrous to morale, the company has used a system of voluntary layoffs and temporary transfers within a plant or cluster of plants.

MARKETING STRATEGY

Gore's marketing strategy is based on determining that it can offer the best-valued products to a marketplace, that people in that marketplace appreciate what it manufactures, and that Gore can become a leader in that area of expertise. The operating procedures used to implement the strategy follow the same principles as other functions at Gore.

First, the marketing of a product revolves around a leader who is referred to as a product champion. According to Dave McCarter, "You marry your technology with the interests of your champions, because you've got to have champions for all these things no matter what. And that's the key element within our company. Without a product champion you can't do much anyway, so it is individually driven. If you get a person interested in a particular market or a particular product for the marketplace, then there is no stopping them."

Second, a product champion is responsible for marketing the product through commitments with sales representatives. Again according to Dave McCarter,

We have no quota system. Our marketing and our sales people make their own commitments as to what their forecasts are. There is no person sitting around telling them that that is not high enough, you have to increase it by 10%, or whatever somebody feels is necessary. You are expected to meet your commitment, which is your forecast, but nobody is going to tell you to change it. . . . There is no order of command, no chain involved. These are groups of independent people who come together to make unified commitments to do something and sometimes, when they can't make those agreements, you may pass up a market place, . . . but that's O.K. because there's much more advantage when the team decides to do something."

Third, the sales representatives are on salary. They are not on commission. They participate in the profit sharing and ASOP plans in which all other Associates participate.

As in other areas of Gore, the individual success stories are exciting. Dave McCarter related one of these success stories as follows:

I interviewed Sam one day. I didn't even know why I was interviewing him actually. Sam was retired from AT&T. After 25 years, he took the golden parachute, and went down to Sun Lakes to play golf. He played golf a few months and got tired of that. He was selling life insurance.

I sat reading the application; his technical background interested me. . . . He had managed an engineering department with 600 people. He'd managed manufacturing plants for AT&T and had a great wealth of experience at AT&T. He said, "I'm retired. I like to play golf but I just can't do it everyday so I want to do something else. Do you have something around here I can do?" I was thinking to myself, this is one of these guys I would sure like to hire but I don't know what I would do with him. The thing that triggered me was the fact that he said he sold insurance and here is a guy with a high degree of technical background selling insurance. He had marketing experience, international marketing experience. So, the bell went off in my head that we were trying to introduce a new product into the marketplace that was a hydrocarbon leak protection cable. You can bury it in the ground and in a matter of seconds it could detect a hydrocarbon (gasoline, etc.). I had a couple of other guys working on it who hadn't been very successful with marketing it. We were having a hard time finding a customer. Well, I thought that kind of a product would be like selling insurance. If you think about it, why should you protect your tanks? It's an insurance policy that things are not leaking into the environment. That has implications, big-time monetary. So, actually, I said, "Why don't you come back Monday? I have just the thing for you." So he did. We hired him; he went to work, a very energetic guy. Certainly a champion of the product, he picked right up on it, ran with it single-handed. . . . Now it's a growing business. It certainly is a valuable one too for the environment.

In the implementation of its marketing strategy, Gore relies on cooperative and word-of-mouth advertising. Cooperative advertising is especially used to promote GORE-TEX fabric products. Those products are sold through a number of clothing manufacturers and distributors, including Apparel Technologies, Lands' End, Austin Reed, Timberland, Woolrich, North Face, Grandoe, and

Michelle Jaffe. Gore engages in cooperative advertising because the Associates believe positive experiences with any one product will carry over to purchases of other and more GORE-TEX fabric products. Apparently this strategy is paying off. Richard Zuckerwar, president of the Grandoe Corporation, said about his company's introduction of GORE-TEX gloves, "Sports activists have had the benefit of GORE-TEX gloves to protect their hands from the elements. With this handsome collection of gloves. . . you can have warm, dry hands without sacrificing style."

The power of informal marketing techniques extends beyond consumer products. According to Dave McCarter, "In the technical end of the business, company reputation probably is most important. You have to have a good reputation with your company." He went on to say that without a good reputation, a company's products would not be considered seriously by many industrial customers. In other words, the sale is often made before the representative calls. Using its marketing strategies, Gore has been very successful in securing a market leadership position in a number of areas ranging from waterproof outdoor clothing to vascular grafts.

FINANCIAL INFORMATION

W. L. Gore is a closely held private corporation. Financial information is as closely guarded as proprietary information on products and processes. About 90% of the stock is owned by Associates who work at Gore.

According to Shanti Mehta, an Associate, Gore's return on assets and sales rank it among the top 10% of the *Fortune* 500 companies. According to another source, W. L. Gore & Associates is working just fine by any financial measure. It has had 31 straight years of profitability and positive return on equity. The compounded growth rate for revenues at W. L. Gore & Associates from 1969 to 1989 was over 18%, discounted for inflation.[5] In 1969 total sales were about $6 million, and in 1991 $700 million. This growth has been financed without debt.

ACKNOWLEDGMENTS

A number of sources were especially helpful in providing background material for this case. The most important sources were the W. L. Gore Associates who generously shared their time and viewpoints about the company. We especially appreciate the input received from Anita McBride, who spent hours recounting her personal experiences and providing many resources, including internal documents and video tapes. In addition, Trish Hearn and Dave McCarter added much to this case by sharing their personal experiences as well as ensuring that the case accurately reflects the Gore company and culture.

Notes

1. In W. L. Gore & Associates' literature, the word "Associate" is always used instead of "employee" and it is always capitalized.
2. GORE-TEX is a registered trademark of W. L. Gore & Associates.
3. Fluroshield is a registered trademark of W. L. Gore & Associates.
4. Gore's ASOP is similar legally to an ESOP (Employee Stock Ownership Plan). Gore simply does not use the word "employee" in any of its documentation.
5. In comparison, only 11 of the 200 largest companies in the Fortune 500 have had positive ROE each year from 1970 to 1988, and only two other companies missed only one year. The revenue growth rate for these 13 companies was 5.4%, compared to 2.5% for the entire *Fortune 500*.

References

Aburdene, Patricia and John Nasbitt. *Re-inventing the Corporation.* New York: Warner Books, 1985.

Angrist, S. W. "Classless Capitalists." *Forbes,* May 9, 1983, pp. 123–4.

Franlesca, L. "Dry and Cool." *Forbes,* August 27, 1984, p. 126.

Hoerr, J. "A Company Where Everybody Is the Boss." *Business Week,* April 15, 1985, p. 98.

Levering, Robert. *The 100 Best Companies to Work for in America* (chapter on W. L. Gore). New York: New American Library, 1985.

McKendrick, Joseph. "The Employees as Entrepreneur." *Management World,* January 1985, pp. 12–13.

Milne, M. J. "The Gorey Details." *Management Review,* March 1985, pp. 16–17.

Posner, B. G. "The First Day on the Job." *Inc.,* June 1986, pp. 73–75.

Price, Kathy. "Firm Thrives Without Boss." *AZ Republic,* February 2, 1986.

Rhodes, Lucien. "The Un-manager." *Inc.,* August 1982, p. 34.

Simmons, J. "People Managing Themselves: Un-management at W. L. Gore, Inc." *The Journal for Quality and Participation,* December 1987, pp. 14–19.

"The Future Workplace." *Management Review,* July 1986, pp. 22–23.

Trachtenberg, J. A. "Give Them Stormy Weather." *Forbes,* March 24, 1986, pp. 172–174.

Ward, Alex. "An All-Weather Idea." *The New York Times Magazine,* November 10, 1985, Sec. 6.

Weber, Joseph. "No Bosses. And Even 'Leaders' Can't Give Orders." *Business Week,* December 10, 1990, pp. 196–197.

"Wilbert L. Gore." *Industry Week,* October 17, 1983, pp. 48–49.

CASE 10 Great Lakes Chemical Corporation

Charles C. Nielson ▪ Gary J. Castrogiovanni

INTRODUCTION

Great Lakes Chemical Corporation has come a long way in the sixteen years since president and CEO Emerson Kampen attended a seminar for emerging companies. The main advice he got there: hire a high-powered management consulting firm. Kampen ignored that advice and developed his own path to an enviable record of earnings and sales growth. The company has carved a strong position in specialty chemicals and created a family of products based on the chemical bromine. In addition, it has aggressively pursued diversification through an acquisition program building on the company's technical and market strengths.

By 1988 the success of Kampen's growth strategy had become apparent. The company had grown by a factor of 14 since 1975. It had expanded into European operations and was actively exporting to the Far East. A decade of acquisitions had moved the company into many new product areas. Yet such changes do not occur without risks and threats. Kampen recognized that Great Lakes faced numerous challenges as the firm entered a new era as a major diversified, worldwide company.

As the company increases in size, what management programs and organizational plans are required to help ensure the continued success of the Great Lakes aggressive business approach? Will the company maintain the competitive advantages it owes to rapid decision making and close customer relationships? Will the increased size of the company and additional major business lines necessitate the increased divisionalization of Great Lakes? How can the company improve on its existing multidivisional organizational structure?

Continuing environmentalist activism and government regulations pose a possible threat to the bromine-based businesses. Is Great Lakes' diversification program diverse *enough*, in terms of products and markets, to provide a hedge or buffer against this threat? The increasing scope of the company's international operations suggests that Emerson Kampen can no longer play an active personal role in many of the detailed business decisions. Can he devise a global organization in which he has sufficient trust to allow it to operate autonomously? Finally, how will its two major competitors, Dow Chemical and Ethyl Corporation, strategically respond to Great Lakes' success and aggressive growth?

Prepared by Charles C. Nielson and Gary J. Castrogiovanni, Louisiana State University. Reprinted with permission.

EARLY HISTORY

Charles S. Hale was the founder of what has come to be known as Great Lakes Chemical Corporation. Hale, a geologist by academic training, also had an entrepreneurial streak. He wished to buy and run a small company, preferably one involved in some form of natural resources, as a hedge against inflation and to match his interest in geology. It also had to be cheap. McClanahan Oil Company, in Mount Pleasant, Michigan, met those criteria perfectly. In 1946 Hale purchased the company and was elected president.

By late 1947, revenues had increased and profits were projected in the near future, so Hale set his acquisition sights on another company with a natural resource base, Great Lakes Chemical Corporation. Great Lakes in 1947 was a $200,000 company with its headquarters in Filer City, Michigan. The rechristened Great Lakes Oil and Chemical Company struggled through the 1950s. The era of the small oil company was quickly disappearing, and the oil segment of Great Lakes was a serious financial drain. In 1960 Hale decided to reestablish Great Lakes as a chemical company and sold off the oil and gas properties. 1960 marked another important event in the new beginning for Great Lakes. A joint venture with another chemical company was formed to exploit the bromine-rich brine fields in south Arkansas. Using this low-cost source of bromine as a base, Great Lakes began a period of rapid growth. The company's revenues grew from $1.4 million in 1960 to $6.6 million by 1967. Hale partially retired in 1967. Over the next 6 years Great Lakes' revenues increased to $23 million. By 1974 Great Lakes had grown to $34 million in revenues, based largely on bromine-derivative products. The company was poised for an era of growth through implementation of aggressive strategies in the bromine-based businesses, coupled with a program of ambitious acquisitions.

MANAGEMENT AND ORGANIZATION

Emerson Kampen was elected chairman of Great Lakes Chemical Corporation in 1988. After receiving his degree in chemical engineering from the University of Michigan in 1951, Kampen began his career with Great Lakes as a chemical engineer. Advancing through a series of marketing and manufacturing positions, he was named vice president–marketing in 1962. A series of promotions followed, beginning with his advancement to vice president–manufacturing in 1968, to executive vice president in 1971, to president in 1972, and to CEO in 1977.

The career of Emerson Kampen and the success of Great Lakes are closely interwoven. Kampen established his mark shortly after assuming the presidency in 1972. At this juncture his strategies centered on growth in the core business:

> [We are following] a strategic plan which calls for the company to prepare for and to aggressively seize upon the unprecedented growth opportunities in bromine chemicals. . . . The opportunities are there. As the only company in the U.S. dedicated to exploiting the chemistry of bromine as its primary mission, we intend to capitalize upon the opportunities to the maximum extent possible (Great Lakes, 1974).

Rapid growth in the bromine business did occur. In the 5-year period ending in 1979, Great Lakes' revenues grew at an annual rate of 29.6% to $125 million. This growth was largely due to the core, bromine-based products, which by 1979 still contributed more than 90% to revenues. Over that same period, the value of Great Lakes' stock (traded on the NYSE) increased by almost 600%! In comparison, the value of the Standard & Poor's 400 index increased by only 50%. Great Lakes was becoming a "darling" of the stock market.

Performance of this magnitude draws attention, and in 1983 the *Wall Street Transcript* awarded Kampen its Gold Medal Award for being the most outstanding chief executive officer in the specialty chemical industry. Kampen captured this honor again in 1984, 1985, and 1988—an unprecedented four times in the history of this publication.

Emerson Kampen has an established reputation as a difficult man to work for. He is reportedly a tough task master who expects his employees to be very loyal and to work intensely. He involves himself in many lower-level decisions that are generally regarded the preserve of subordinates to the president/CEO. In a report profiling Kampen's successful acquisition program, one financial analyst noted: "You certainly have to give the top guy credit for that. There's no question that he runs the company" (Great Lakes, 1987). Great Lakes could be characterized as a "one-man show."

As recently as 1983, Great Lakes had no major operating divisions. Vice-presidential positions (including engineering, marketing, manufacturing, finance, and R&D) were largely functional in nature. By 1988, only four operating divisions of significance were in place: three product groups and the European operations.

PRODUCTS AND MARKETS

Bromine remains the core of the Great Lakes product portfolio. However, two recent, major acquisitions have diversified the company somewhat. In 1988 the company's major businesses were organized as follows:

BROMINE-BASED PRODUCTS

Fire-control Chemicals

Bromine-containing compounds used as flame retardants and fire-extinguishing agents. Flame retardants are incorporated in plastics, fibers, and other combustible products to inhibit burning. End uses include applications in electronics, furniture, and appliances. Halons (brominated fire-extinguishing agents) are used in buildings for fire protection.

Agricultural Specialities

Bromine-containing chemicals used in soil fumigation to kill insects and other pests in agriculture.

Bromine Derivatives

Compounds used as chemical intermediates in the manufacture of other chemical products. End uses include pharmaceuticals, papers, and photographic chemicals.

Derivatives of bromine are also used as recreational and industrial water-treatment chemicals. Clear brine fluids, another major derivative, are used in oilfield extraction operations to enhance oil recovery.

OTHER CHEMICAL PRODUCTS/SERVICES

Furfural Specialty Chemicals

Through its largest subsidiary, QO Chemicals, Great Lakes is the world's leading producer of furfural-based specialty chemicals. Furfural is produced from readily available agricultural waste material and is then reacted to manufacture furfuryl alcohol and other specialty products used in foundry resins, urethanes, and chemical intermediates and as refining solvents.

Customer Synthesis

Provides facilities for the manufacture of chemical products by other single customers.

Fluorine-based Chemicals

Fluorine-based products are beginning to emerge. End uses include electronic chemicals and intermediates.

Motor Gasoline and Oil Additives

A recent acquisition, Associated Octel, will serve to add depth to the bromine-based businesses and will extend Great Lakes into supplying fuel additives to the petroleum refining industry. Octel's principal product is tetraethyllead, used as an octane booster in motor fuels.

NON-CHEMICAL BUSINESSES

Other small, diversified businesses include engineered surfaces, printed circuit boards, and toxicological testing.

FINANCIAL CONDITION

By 1988 Great Lakes' revenues had grown to $616 million—an average rate of increase of 19.4% per year since 1979. Net income grew to $103 million in 1988, an annual growth rate of 20.9%. In 1988 the company's after-tax return on sales and return on total assets were 19% and 16%, respectively. This performance compares very favorably to the chemical industry averages of 13% and 9%. Over the last 5 years, the company's earnings per share (EPS) grew at an annual rate of 27% per year, compared to the chemical industry average of 9%, reflecting extraordinary corporate performance. A 10-year summary of Great Lakes' financial operating results is included in Exhibit 10.1. Exhibit 10.2 profiles a summary of key financial measures for Great Lakes and for the chemical industry. Exhibit 10.3 shows company balance sheets for 1987 and 1988.

EXHIBIT 10.1 **Financial Summary: Great Lakes Chemical Corporation**
(Dollar amounts in thousands)

	1988	1987	1986	1985	1984	1983	1982	1981	1980	1979
Summary of Earnings										
Revenues	$616,046	$501,010	$305,703	$281,952	$283,261	$225,220	$174,712	$153,515	$128,906	$124,961
Income before taxes	143,488	85,036	42,717	45,368	56,543	39,180	25,621	26,378	29,379	30,651
Percent of revenues	23.3	17.0	14.0	16.1	20.0	17.2	14.7	17.2	22.8	24.5
Net income	$103,288	$ 55,536	$ 26,817	$ 28,818	$ 35,568	$ 23,842	$ 16,408	$ 18,031	$ 18,948	$ 18,606
Per share	5.93	3.34	1.79	1.93	2.38	1.63	1.13	1.25	1.33	1.32
Percent of revenues	16.8	11.1	8.8	10.2	12.6	10.4	9.4	11.7	14.7	14.9
Financial Position at Year End										
Working capital	$100,238	$101,083	$113,370	$ 78,009	$ 66,728	$ 50,856	$ 42,353	$ 34,692	$ 38,156	$ 31,680
Capital expenditures	47,017	35,186	18,327	25,601	28,770	20,370	28,483	47,335	20,496	18,315
Total assets	$663,838	$577,087	$491,567	$323,121	$284,414	$227,040	$202,058	$170,198	$118,407	$ 99,323

Source: Great Lakes Chemical Corporation, 1988 *Annual Report.*

EXHIBIT 10.2	Key Financial Ratios, 1987: Great Lakes Chemical Corporation

Ratio Percentages	Great Lakes Chemical Corporation	Chemical Industry Comparison			
		Upper Quartile	Median	Lower Quartile	RMA
Profitability					
Return on sales	12.0	7.2	3.8	1.4	4.8
Return on assets	10.0	10.7	6.6	3.7	NA
Return on net worth	22.0	28.9	15.0	8.1	NA
Efficiency					
Sales to inventory	19.6	18.0	9.7	6.2	6.1
Sales to net working capital	4.7	10.9	6.1	3.8	NA
Solvency					
Quick ratio	0.9	2.3	1.1	0.7	0.8
Current ratio	1.9	4.0	2.0	1.3	1.6

RMA: Robert Morris Associates' industry mean. NA: Not available.

Sources: Great Lakes Chemical Corporation, *1987 Annual Report;* Dun & Bradstreet Credit Services, *Industry Norms and Key Business Ratios,* 1987–1988 (SIC 2869, Industrial Organic Chemicals); Robert Morris Associates, *RMA Annual Statement Studies,* 1989 (SIC 2861, 2865, 2869, Industrial Chemicals).

EXHIBIT 10.3	Consolidated Balance Sheet: Great Lakes Chemical Corporation (Dollar amounts in thousands)

	1988	1987
Assets		
Current assets	$222,885	$209,735
Plant and equipment	234,405	218,403
Excess of investment over net assets of affiliates	51,596	53,722
Investment in unconsolidated affiliates	126,905	74,656
Other assets	28,047	20,571
Total assets	$663,838	$577,087

(continued)

EXHIBIT 10.3	Consolidated Balance Sheet: Great Lakes Chemical Corporation (continued)

(Dollar amounts in thousands)

	1988	1987
Liabilities and Stockholders' Equity		
Current liabilities	$122,647	$108,652
Long-term debt, less current portion	19,266	42,149
Deferred income taxes	39,700	33,684
Stockholders' equity	482,225	392,602
Total liabilities and stockholders' equity	$663,838	$577,087

Source: Great Lakes Chemical Corporation, *1988 Annual Report.*

THE CHEMICAL INDUSTRY

The chemical industry originated around the turn of the century. Its impact as a major industrial factor began in the 1920s, so the industry can be regarded as 60 to 70 years old. Viewed as a whole, the industry is in its maturity stage. Total industry sales growth rate from 1974 to 1988 was about 7%. The growth rate from 1981 to 1988 slowed to between 2% and 3%, well below GNP growth. Of course, within the whole industry there are sectors growing at relatively slower or faster rates. Many of these industry sectors are subject to cyclical variation, as is the industry as a whole. Industry sales and profitability are highly dependent on general economic conditions. Individual sector performance is also dependent on the economic conditions of the particular end-use markets served.

TECHNOLOGY

Technology remains a major force in the chemical industry. Industry firms' R&D expenditures as a percent of sales average about 5%, reflecting the need to maintain technological competence. R&D efforts are directed at both product and process development. The objective of process development is largely efficiency improvement and cost reduction. Innovation in the industry is largely incremental. Major, quantum jumps in innovation, such as the discovery of nylon or synthetic dyes, have been infrequent. Thus, although technology plays a key role in the corporate strategy of individual firms, it cannot be regarded as highly dynamic from an industry point of view.

GLOBALIZATION

One very dynamic feature of the chemical industry, however, is increasing globalization. U.S. firms are seeking expansion through positions in the Far East, in Europe, and to a lesser extent in Third-World countries. This emphasis on globalization places demands on the management and organization of chemical firms. The need to understand the demands of local markets and customs is critical. Furthermore, product quality and specifications are becoming increasingly stringent. At the same time, foreign chemical companies such as Bayer, ICI, and Mitsubishi are establishing positions in the U.S. domestic market. These companies are creating new sources, and higher levels, of competition in the industry.

GOVERNMENTAL AFFAIRS

Finally, environmental forces and related government regulations are sources of change and uncertainty. Special-interest groups (such as the Sierra Club and the Environmental Defense Fund) are major forces counterbalancing the interests of the industry. But the impact of their influence waxes and wanes, and the targets of their efforts often change. U.S. and state regulatory bodies are also sources of inconsistent direction and focus. Their objectives are often determined by the changing political winds blowing at any given time. The chemical industry is subject to the vagaries of all these dynamic situational factors.

THE COMPETITIVE SITUATION

Great Lakes, with revenues of $34 million in 1974, was a virtual pygmy in an industry dominated by giant companies. Great Lakes' major domestic competitor, Dow Chemical, was a $3.1 billion company in 1974. Ethyl Corporation, with $700 million in revenues, was poised to enter the bromine business on the strength of its Arkansas brine reserves located adjacent to those of Great Lakes. Dow also controlled brine reserves in Arkansas, so all three companies had captive sources of low-cost raw materials.

By virtue of their size, these two major competitors would seem to have possessed several advantages over Great Lakes. First, their financial "muscle" could be brought to bear during periods when price-cutting tactics were required. The larger companies could use the cash from their sister divisions to make up for the depressed profits in bromine that resulted from price reductions. Second, during cyclical periods when the bromine-based businesses were depressed, these multidivisional chemical giants, with their diversified business portfolios, were better poised to withstand the economic downturn in a given sector. Third, Dow and Ethyl possessed certain economies of scope not enjoyed by Great Lakes—in R&D, for example. The chemical industry is influenced by technological change affecting products and processes. Larger companies, with large, centralized R&D facilities, enjoy synergies in R&D. They can use engineers and scientists, equipment, and innovation in one product area to enhance work in another.

These advantages accruing from size might be regarded as partially offset by the fact that Great Lakes had positioned itself as a "specialty" chemical company.

In contrast to commodity chemicals, specialty chemicals rely more on specific customer knowledge, applications technology, and the ability to move quickly in response to changing customer demands. Smaller companies are typically more flexible and faster at making decisions than large companies.

THE REGULATORY/ENVIRONMENTAL SITUATION

Another major issue facing Great Lakes in the early to mid-1970s was the potential for government regulation resulting from toxicological/environmental problems associated with bromine-based chemicals. Certain bromine-containing organic compounds are considered toxic—much like compounds containing chlorine, such as PCBs and dioxins. The EPA and certain state agencies in this country were investigating the toxic properties of several products produced by Great Lakes. In 1975, for example, the EPA ordered the recall of one million cans of the Great Lakes pesticide ethylene dibromide because of a leaking problem. The agency said that this odorless and colorless gas "is extremely toxic, and exposure to skin or inhalation of high concentrations can cause death" (Great Lakes, 1975). Environmental problems with ethylene dibromide have persisted into the 1980s. In 1983, after discovering that the state's ground water had been contaminated, the state of Florida ordered a permanent ban on the sale, distribution, and use of the product.

The use of ethylene dibromide was also curbed in the 1970s as a result of federal EPA-mandated regulations on leaded motor gasoline. Ethylene dibromide is used in conjunction with tetraethyllead in compounds to increase the octane ratings of gasoline. Environmental concern about toxic lead particulates in air dictated the removal of lead (and consequently of ethylene dibromide) from gasoline. Prior to these regulations, ethylene dibromide had been the largest-selling bromine-based product in the industry.

Thus Great Lakes faced two main issues at this juncture. The first was the competitive disadvantages resulting from its relatively small size. The second was its high dependence on a class of products potentially facing severe environmental regulation as a result of alleged toxic properties. Growth and business diversification appeared to provide a solution.

STRATEGY

Great Lakes' stated business strategy in the early 1970s centered on growth in bromine-based products. The "unique chemistry of bromine" was still the linchpin of Kampen's growth outlook in 1976: "Great Lakes is uncommonly well positioned to seek out and develop this chemistry. . . [based on our technology, our market and production expertise,] and our concentrated focus on bromine" (Great Lakes, 1976). The underlying concept was to extend the use of bromine into high-return, high-value-added, new businesses.

By focusing on a specific product area and customer base, the company had carved out a dominant worldwide market share in the majority of its bromine-based businesses. It had achieved a reputation as an aggressive, flexible, and responsive supplier in the industry. As one securities analyst explained,

> Great Lakes Chemical has been doing very well. . . . They had a product that was losing a great part of its market, bromine additives that went into gasoline, and they shifted around and developed a new kind of end market for bromine chemicals. They did a lot of very innovative things in that area, really carving out a niche for themselves in a very specialty chemistry (Great Lakes, 1987).

Great Lakes' centralized organization and reliance on Kampen's decision-making skills may be important ingredients in that success. Kampen notes that "Great Lakes has been one of the few companies that has consistently made money with bromine chemistry. We have done it by being the best at developing new products, and the lowest-cost producer and marketer of those products" (Great Lakes, 1988).

Great Lakes also embarked on acquisition and major internal development programs that, adhering to Kampen's stated strategy, largely maintained some connection to the bromine-based businesses. However, some important non-bromine exceptions also occurred. By 1988 Kampen had broadened his perspective to encompass growth in non-bromine-related businesses. He identified five growth areas for Great Lakes. Two of these, flame retardants and water treatment chemicals, are bromine-centered. However, three of the growth areas are directed toward securing Great Lakes a position in certain non-bromine fields: furfural chemicals, fluorine-based chemicals, and custom manufacture. A summary of the acquisitions and the major new-product, internal development programs entered into by Great Lakes since 1974 appears in Exhibit 10.4.

Kampen's strategy involved "possible acquisitions in certain areas that fit our additives business very well. I anticipate making some acquisitions over the next couple of years in businesses that are more closely associated to our basic bromine and furfural businesses" (Great Lakes, 1988). The fluorine business, according to Kampen, "represents another important addition to our diverse technology. We have just brought on stream a new fluorine derivative plant, which produces a very high-value-added product. We're looking at building a plant in which we will make six to eight new fluorine monomers that we would sell to customers who would in most cases convert these to polymers" (Great Lakes, 1988).

The water treatment field presents an opportunity for Great Lakes to become "more of the consumer products company. . . than we have been in the past. So I think, in that whole water treatment field, we would certainly be doing a lot more advertising than we have, and I think some of our new products are products that could be marketed through some of the mass merchandising type of operations, which are used to serve water treatment retail customers" (Great Lakes, 1988).

Regarding the expanding global opportunities for his company, Kampen notes that

> We view the world as the geographic area we serve. [For example,] China could probably add $1 billion per year to its bottom line just utilizing bromine chemistry in agriculture—and I do believe that. We do have a number of projects underway where we're having the Chinese do some research and development for us. . . . I would hope that those things will expand the vistas of working with the Chinese. But, I don't know that

EXHIBIT 10.4	Acquisitions and Major New-Product Developments, 1974–1988

Year	Product Development or Acquisition	Type of Product(s)
1974	Everlube Corp.	Industrial lubricants.
1975	Halon	Introduced Halon fire-extinguishing fluids from a joint venture formed in France.
1976	Drug Research, Inc.	Swimming pool chemicals.
1977	Tesco	Swimming pool chemicals.
	WIL Labs	Toxicology testing of chemicals.
1980	Merichem	Joint venture to manufacture and market an insecticide.
	ABM Chemicals	Bromine-based specialty compounds producer in the U.K.
1981	Velsicol Chemical Corp.	Bromine-based flame retardants.
	DuPont Joint Venture	Joint agreement to manufacture and market Halon. The French joint venture was dissolved.
1982	OSCA	A leading marketer of clear completion fluids. Moves Great Lakes downstream in this market.
	Enzyme Technology	Partial interest in an embryonic biotechnology firm.
1983	Inland Specialty Chemicals	Manufacturer of electronic chemicals.
1984	Syntex Chemicals	Purchased a specialty chemicals manufacturing facility.
1985	Purex Pool	Supplier of chemicals and equipment for swimming pools and other residential uses. Moves Great Lakes further downstream in the home pool market.
	High-Purity Silicon	Application of halogen chemistry to the manufacture of super-high-purity silicon for use in electronics.
1986	Q.O. Chemicals	World's leading producer and marketer of furfural and furfural-based chemicals.
1987	Sucralose	Agreement to provide Johnson & Johnson an intermediate required to manufacture this sweetener.
	Fluorine	Announced plans to build a plant to produce fluorine-based specialty chemicals.
1988	Octel Company, Ltd.	Acquired majority interest in U.K.-based manufacturer and marketer of fuel additives to the petroleum refining industry. Octel has interests in bromine reserves, manufacturing capability in Europe, and some technology in bromine chemistry.

I would expect China and Russia to be a major part of our business in the next three or four years. It's going to be slower growing than that (Great Lakes, 1988).

These strategies, according to Kampen, are intended to translate into a continuation of Great Lakes' historic growth rates: "I think over the past 15 years we have grown at a compound rate of 25%. Our earnings have not been far off of that figure either. Certainly, as you get bigger, it's difficult to achieve that kind of growth, but I would be very disappointed if we could not achieve a 15% growth over each of the next 3 to 5 years" (Great Lakes, 1988). However, with Great

Lakes growing at the current rate, Kampen believes that "the biggest single problem I have becomes a 'people problem,' recruiting those kinds of people who have the drive, the desire to move ahead themselves, and with them the company. We have not been big enough to grow these people in-house, as some of the major companies have been able to do" (Great Lakes, 1988). Kampen adds that "the second area of major concern involves the environmental issues."

REFERENCES

Great Lakes Chemical Corporation. *Wall Street Transcript,* August 8, 1988.

Great Lakes Chemical Corporation. *Wall Street Transcript,* July 16, 1987.

Great Lakes Chemical Corporation. *1985 Annual Report.*

Great Lakes Chemical Corporation. *1976 Annual Report.*

Great Lakes Chemical Corporation. *1974 Annual Report.*

"Great Lakes Chemical Pesticide Is Recalled Due to Container Leak." *Wall Street Journal,* March 3, 1975, p. 16.

CASE 11 Hewlett-Packard Company: The Workstation Segment of the Computer Industry

Robert J. Mockler ▪ Thomas Goeller ▪
Stephen Persek ▪ Christopher Pryce

Hewlett-Packard Company (HP) is a publicly held company that designs, manufactures, and services electronic products and systems for measurement and computation. HP helps customers worldwide improve their personal and business effectiveness. In 1990 HP was in second place (behind Sun Microsystems) in the workstation segment of the computer industry, with a 21.2% market share. In 1991 the company had more than 11,000 products and employed 89,000 people worldwide. Its net revenues were $14.4 billion; international sales accounted for just over 55% of that amount. HP had 600 sales and support offices, as well as distributorships in 110 countries. Slightly more than half of the company's 1991 product revenues were derived through the efforts of its own sales organization.

Exhibit 11.1 shows the overall structure of the computer industry. Experts projected worldwide sales of over $19 billion in the workstation segment by 1992, up from $6.4 billion in 1989 (Standard & Poor's, 1991). To achieve success in this rapidly growing market in an ever-changing competitive environment, HP was examining several strategic issues.

Hewlett-Packard needed to integrate its various commercial and technical lines of workstations to reduce market confusion. In order to attract new customers, HP's management was also considering new uses and applications for its workstations. In addition, in response to the shift in the selling function to resellers, the company was considering ways to restructure its distribution channels. An increasing number of customers were buying their products from value-added resellers (VARs), to whom HP granted discounts. This lowered selling prices and increased HP's sales costs. In addition, HP had continued its long-standing strategy of promptly positioning itself in emerging markets by entering into joint ventures in Asia and Central Europe. HP was wondering how to extend this strategy to new areas overseas.

THE INDUSTRY AND COMPETITIVE MARKET

THE WORKSTATION SEGMENT OF THE COMPUTER INDUSTRY

Workstations were similar in appearance to the single-user general-purpose personal computer (PC) in that they both had a terminal and a console or keyboard. However, their internal designs were different. The single-user, general-purpose PCs had a disk drive, a single microprocessor chip with a resident operating system, and

| EXHIBIT 11.1 | Computer Industry Structure |

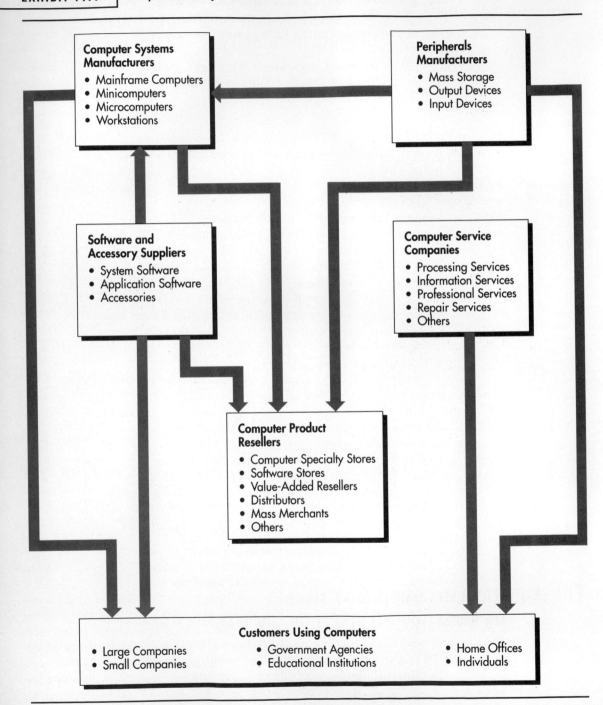

Source: Adapted from Juliussen and Juliussen, *The Computer Industry Almanac*, 1991.

local programming capability; hence they were called "stand-alone" systems. The original workstations were diskless "dumb terminals" without resident operating systems and local programming capabilities. Instead, they were connected to a mainframe computer that provided central processing and file storage capabilities. Today, workstations are single-user, stand-alone computer systems that can perform scientific calculations at extremely high speeds. Workstations use one or more high-performance microprocessors and special-purpose hardware to achieve very advanced graphics capabilities. Compared to the PC, modern workstations offer users greater processing power and at least 4 million bytes of random access memory (RAM). They also feature high-resolution monitors and sophisticated software capable of handling multi-tasking (more than one task at a time) and of communicating via networks with other computers, such as PCs, workstations, and mainframes.

In 1991 the workstation segment was one of the fastest-growing areas in the overall computer industry. Created in 1981 by Apollo (now a division of Hewlett-Packard) and legitimized in 1985 by Sun Microsystems, workstation sales of U.S.-based vendors soared by a compound annual rate of more than 110% between 1986 and 1988. Growth slowed in 1990 as overall revenues advanced 21.5%, down from 40.3% in 1989 (Standard & Poor's, 1991). Contributing to the sluggishness of the overall computer industry were the U.S. recession, deep price cutting, the transition from proprietary to open-based systems, maturation of traditional technical markets, and the lengthening of sales cycles. However, U.S. workstation vendors nonetheless enjoyed another year of strong demand for their systems from both domestic and foreign customers in 1991. U.S. suppliers stimulated demand by offering new products with substantially improved price/performance ratios and by slashing prices as much as 25% to 40% on selected existing entry-level and high-end systems. The battle for market share among leading manufacturers and their efforts to displace personal computers in certain commercial accounts drove the price per millions of instructions per second (MIPS) for a low-end workstation to less than $300 retail. This translated to less than $240 after volume discounts (U.S Department of Commerce, 1992).

The workstation segment, like the entire computer industry, was characterized by extremely high levels of competition, the rapid development of new products and technologies, and a strong dependence on foreign suppliers for computer memory chips. This segment was still in the early stages of its growth cycle, so it presented opportunities for future growth in the 1990s. Workstations were projected to account for only 3% of the entire computer industry's sales in 1992, as seen in Exhibit 11.2, but this segment had great potential. Exhibit 11.3 compares price and performance of different computer product segments.

Since their introduction in the early 1980s, workstations had been used primarily for computationally intensive engineering and scientific applications. In the late 1980s and early 1990s, however, U.S. manufacturers aggressively moved into such commercial markets as electronic publishing, business graphics, financial services, and office automation. This move was facilitated by having application software developers transfer a number of PC-based business software to workstation systems and by the commitment of software firms to develop more applications for workstation systems. The joining of workstation performance with the personal

EXHIBIT 11.2	Computer Industry World Market in 1992,* by Segment

Segment	Market Share (percent)	Market Share (in billions of dollars)
Services and other software	38.5	249.9
Peripherals	19.0	123.3
PCs	16.5	107.1
Minis and Mainframes	13.5	87.6
PC Software	5.5	35.7
Datacommunications	4.0	26.0
Workstations	3.0	19.4
	100%	$649.0

* Projected by Price Waterhouse

Source: Information obtained from Standard & Poor's, *Industry Surveys*, 1991.

EXHIBIT 11.3	Computer Product Segments

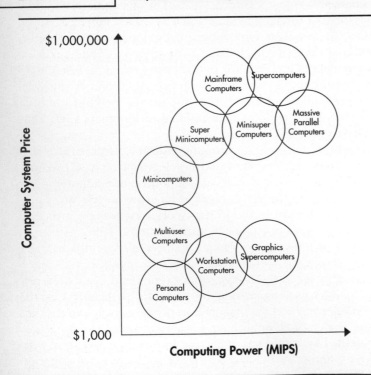

Source: Adapted from Juliussen and Juliussen, *The Computer Industry Almanac*, 1991.

computer's vast software base and networking capabilities lured dozens of computer manufacturers and software developers into this emerging market. The raw data processing power of the PC vied with that of low-end workstations, and the technological features that once distinguished PCs from workstations began to converge. As a result, the PC and workstation segments began to consolidate.

Workstation manufacturers such as Sun Microsystems, HP, Digital Equipment Corporation (DEC), and IBM were targeting business and commercial users in addition to their traditional engineering and scientific markets. More business applications were being modified to run on UNIX operating systems, which were widely used on workstations. PC companies such as Apple and Compaq were planning to build more powerful desktop machines using Reduced Instruction Set Computing (RISC) microprocessors borrowed from the world of engineering workstations.

Distribution patterns were also changing in the workstation market. Traditionally, workstations had been sold primarily by direct sales forces or through value-added resellers (VARs). Increasingly, workstations were being offered by the same computer dealers and retail outlets that served the PC market. Some workstation suppliers had begun to use mass distribution channels for their products.

As workstations entered the business market, a conflict between PC and workstation software standards arose. Although Microsoft's DOS and IBM's OS/2 operating systems dominated the PC world, UNIX (in its various forms) was the operating system of choice for workstations. Members of the Advanced Computing Environment (ACE) initiative, an industry consortium of 84 companies, supported both a future unified version of UNIX and a future version of the OS/2 operating system. This strategy suggested that members were hedging their bets until it became clearer which direction the business workstation market would take.

THE PRODUCTS

There were three major types of workstations on the market in 1991. The first was the personal workstation, which bore the greatest resemblance to the PC. These low-end workstations were similar to high-end PCs. These models offered the workstations' increased capabilities, as well as ease of use and the capacity for future expansion. The second type of workstation was the graphic workstation. These models were usually middle-of-the-line workstations that could create and manipulate images and/or text. The third type was the high-end design workstation used by engineers, scientists, and architects for computer-aided design, manufacturing, and engineering (CAD/CAM/CAE) applications.

The price and performance distinctions between workstations and other types of computer systems blurred at both the low and high ends of the market in the early 1990s. At the low end, personal workstations had experienced a price reduction of more than 60% since 1981 and had added features that made them more accessible and user-friendly. Units had an internal memory of 400–840 megabytes (MB) that could be expanded to 4.4–9.45 gigabytes (GB). Performance speeds ranged from 13.7–50 MIPS. These improvements placed the entry-level, low-end workstation in the cost range of the PC, which also featured improved operating speeds and increased storage capabilities. At the high end, design workstations offered the greatest amount of memory, typically around 800 MB–2.6 GB, expandable to 26.5–236 GB. These units achieved operating speeds ranging from 28.5 to 76.7 MIPS. Systems with up to 8 central processing units (CPUs) operating at 230 MIPS were introduced for approximately $200,000 in 1991 (U.S. Department of Commerce, 1991).

Workstation performance was enhanced by improvements in the internal design of workstation systems and by the acceptance and adoption of new software architectures. Manufacturers had been able to reduce the total number of components used in workstation systems without adversely affecting the units' dependability and performance.

Software is required by every computer system, including workstations. Because software applications add value and can be cost-effective compared to new hardware, software development had become an essential component of workstation systems. The new Reduced Instruction Set Chips (RISC) software architecture was an approach to computer design that yielded breakthroughs in computers' performance and price. Computer system performance is a function of the number of instructions in a program and of the average time it takes a processor to execute an instruction. In order to improve performance, Complex Instruction Set Chips (CISC) focused on reducing the number of instructions per program by adding complex instructions to the processors' instruction set. In contrast, RISC architectures focused on reducing the average time needed to execute an instruction by streamlining the processor to include only simpler, more frequently used instructions. RISC's streamlined architecture made possible the more effective use of optimizing compilers, powerful hardware, and software techniques, which generally decreased total execution time.

CISC had been the architecture of choice in desktop computers, but RISC architectures were used by the workstation industry. According to Dataquest Inc., RISC workstations accounted for 35% of the value and 25% of the number of units shipped in 1989. Dataquest predicted that by 1993 more than 60% of all workstations sold worldwide would be based on RISC. Furthermore, RISC was being adopted by minicomputer makers and by every major Japanese computer supplier (Standard & Poor's, 1991).

American manufacturers were increasingly abandoning hardware production to pursue value-added activities such as systems design and integration, software development, and after-sale service and support. This shift in emphasis resulted from the comparative advantage held by the United States in this area, as opposed to Japan's advantage in hardware production.

Technological innovations in workstation products were expected to continue in the future. The rapid pace of product introductions had reduced the product life cycle of traditional 32-bit workstations to only 1 year. Industry analysts projected that by 1994, workstation products would be 10 to 15 times more powerful than the units of 1989. This meant that in order to remain competitive, the major workstation producers would have to continue to devote significant portions of their sales revenue to the improvement of their products.

The majority of the new systems used RISC microprocessors as their central processing units and UNIX as their operating system environment. Low-end models introduced in 1991 had average performance speeds of 32.8 MIPS and a minimum total disk capacity of 4 GB. Models introduced at the high end had average performance speeds in excess of 50 MIPS and a minimum total disk capacity of 26.5 GB. Some workstations featured superscalar architectures in which several instructions could be executed simultaneously per clock cycle, significantly boosting system performance over that of competitive products. A number of suppliers marketed models with three-dimensional graphics capabilities for under $10,000. At the high end, some graphics supercomputer systems with up to 8 central processing units had performance speeds of over 200 MIPS and up to 2.6 GB of main memory. Workstation manufacturers would not be able to continue to compete on the basis of technological advantage alone. Their ability to develop products that could easily be modified to take advantage of future technological developments, as well as to comply with changing industry standards, would be one of their keys to success. Giving the customer the freedom to mix and match hardware and software was commonly referred to as providing "open systems."

CUSTOMERS

The workstation industry targeted a broad range of customers worldwide, including organizations and individual users. Organizations included high-technology and business corporations of all sizes, government agencies, and not-for-profit organizations. In addition, workstations were designed to meet the needs of the ultimate or actual users of the machines: technical users (scientists and engineers), business and commercial users (analysts, controllers, and programmers), and individual users.

Technical users, or traditional customers, provided manufacturers with more than half of their workstation revenues. Revenue growth from technical users of workstations was expected to remain steady throughout the mid- to late 1990s. Technical users worked for engineering and high-technology firms, government research laboratories, and not-for-profit institutions such as hospitals and educational institutions. The characteristic common to all members of this group was their need to solve complex computing and research problems. This demanded the increased capabilities and applications of the workstation, rather than the traditional PC. Technical users generally used high-end design workstations for their CAD/CAM/CAE applications. Compared to other users of workstations, technical users were not very price-sensitive. They desired substantial memory and graphics capabilities, and they often utilized add-on components, such as graphics accelerators, to increase their hardware's flexibility.

Business and commercial users traditionally used mid-range computer systems that supported individual terminals for office automation, financial services, electronic publishing, graphics design, and animation. The increased price/performance ratios offered by workstations had caught the attention of business and commercial customers. These users needed additional software applications and placed greater emphasis on high levels of after-sale service and support. This group of users had become an important source of revenue to the workstation industry by 1992, and the trend was expected to continue.

The declining price levels of the low-end models made the individual user very important to the workstation segment. As the PC's life cycle matured, the individual user continued to look for ways to boost efficiency and effectiveness at work. These needs were increasingly being fulfilled by the personal workstation and the development of software packages for individual applications. Individual users purchasing workstations would demand a high level of service and competitively priced systems from workstation manufacturers.

SALES AND DISTRIBUTION

In the domestic market, workstation manufacturers sold their products directly to computer users or through a variety of resellers. Generally speaking, open-based system hardware was essentially a commodity, and application software ran on such systems without modifications. Gross margins on a mainframe sale could be 70% or more, whereas gross margins on open-based workstations could be as low as 30%. These margins were too small for manufacturers to rely solely on an extensive direct sales force (Standard & Poor's, 1991). Therefore, workstations were commercially distributed through a variety of channels, mainly direct sales forces, value-added resellers (VARs), and other resellers such as computer specialty stores.

In the early stages of the industry, the primary channel used to sell workstations was direct sales. This method was appropriate because it offered the customer—usually a large corporation, government agency, or not-for-profit institution—who was investing large sums of money in the product, a higher degree of individual attention and technical support. This consideration was particularly important when sales representatives were trying to sell government contracts and large corporate accounts. However, as the personal workstation gained the attention of the individual customer, workstation manufacturers diversified their distribution channels in the United States to compete with high-end PC manufacturers.

The workstation sales function had shifted from direct sales to value-added resellers (VARs). Value-added resellers were vendors who specialized in narrow segments called vertical markets. They assembled hardware components into a computer system and "added value" to it by installing customized software before selling the complete package to the final consumer. This method of sales met the needs of price-sensitive small-to-medium-sized firms and institutions.

Although VARs were the principal sellers of workstations between 1989 and 1991, U.S. manufacturers had broadened their distribution channels to include other resellers—such as computer specialty shops—in order to lure commercial customers away from PC suppliers into traditional workstation markets. Computer specialty stores, which focused on selling personal computers and related products, were the most important sales channel for such computers, especially to individual users. Workstation manufacturers were attracted by the success of this channel and were establishing footholds in computer specialty stores. These stores were fast becoming important sales channels for workstations and related products. In 1990 almost 250 specialty shops and dealers distributed workstation products in the United States, according to a report from Summit Strategies, a Boston-based consulting firm (U.S. Department of Commerce, 1991).

In the international market, a mixed distribution strategy that included direct sales and value-added reselling was used. Selling in foreign markets had certain inherent problems: foreign currency risks, import/export controls and duties, and economic and political uncertainties. The European market, with a population of 320 million, was expected to continue to be a major source of revenue for U.S. producers. An appropriate mix of direct sales and value-added reselling was expected to be a successful strategy for this market.

THE WORKSTATION MARKET

The major companies operating in the workstation segment of the computer industry produced a wide range of workstation models that were distributed both domestically and internationally.

The Domestic Market

The domestic market for workstations was approximately $5 billion in 1990, and it was expected to grow to over $11.4 billion by 1992 as a result of continued expansion of product lines and the customer base (Juliussen and Juliussen, 1991; and Standard & Poor's, 1991). By 1993 sales in this segment were expected to account for almost 30% of all computer revenues and for 76% of computer industry growth (Juliussen and Juliussen, 1991). Given the lingering recession, the U.S. computer equipment industry expected moderate domestic growth over the short term. A majority of this growth was expected to come from traditional workstation users (scientists and engineers) who worked for engineering and high-technology firms. However, the number of business and commercial users and individual users was also expected to increase rapidly, as the number of software applications and support programs for these two groups continued to expand.

Workstation manufacturers were attempting to reach an agreement on the standard operating format for workstations. In 1990 the dominant system in the United States was the UNIX system (and its derivatives, POSIX and XENIX). However, some workstation manufacturers had adopted alternatives such as Apple's A/UX and IBM's AIX formats. Furthermore, some manufacturers were using the OS/2 format found in the high-end PCs as a base for their workstation systems. Reaching an agreement on which standards to use was a risk that could produce unsatisfactory results for U.S. manufacturers. On the one hand, an agreement could lead to lowered prices, expanded potential markets, and increased consumer choice. On the other hand, it could benefit foreign producers by allowing them to use their high-volume, low-cost production methods to capture market share.

The Foreign Markets

The foreign markets, most notably Europe and Japan, were expected to grow at a much faster rate than the U.S. market and so were expected to become significant revenue sources, as shown in Exhibit 11.4. In recent years, several U.S. firms had either established new production facilities or expanded existing ones in Europe and Asia to serve these rapidly growing markets more effectively.

EXHIBIT 11.4	**Worldwide Workstation Market** (Dollar amounts in billions)

Market Segment	1989	1990	1992*
United States	$4.1	$5.0	$11.4
Foreign	$2.3	$2.8	$ 8.0
Total	$6.4	$7.8	$19.4

* Projected by Price Waterhouse.

Sources: Information obtained from Standard & Poor's, *Industry Surveys,* 1991; and Juliussen and Juliussen, *The Computer Industry Almanac, 1991.*

U.S. companies accounted for roughly 93% of the 76,850 units produced in Europe during 1990, according to estimates by Dataquest Inc. The size of the European market, and the 1992 unification of Europe in particular, could have long-term impacts on the workstation industry's future. With the formation of a "United States of Europe," there would be few, if any, restrictions on travel between member countries. There would also be a unification of the major tax rates, shared technical and operating standards, and possibly a common currency. The adoption of uniform standards and the elimination of individual duties and tariffs would make the production and marketing of new products less costly for U.S. manufacturers. A real danger, however, was that a united Europe could increase protectionist policies aimed at U.S. manufacturers and their products. In anticipation of this possibility, many U.S. firms had acquired or entered into joint ventures with European firms in order to establish a European base. This was not a perfect solution, however, because it required that 80% of a company's production take place within Europe, with no more than 20% of parts and labor coming from outside its borders. In spite of these restrictions, U.S. firms expected to manufacture locally more than half of what they sold to European users by 1994, up from only 22% today (U.S. Department of Commerce, 1992).

The United States led Japan in the workstation industry and had been active in the Japanese market since the mid-1980s. The U.S. presence in the Japanese market was largely through original equipment manufacturer (OEM) marketing arrangements with major Japanese consumer electronics and computer suppliers, or through contracts assigning production to Japanese partners. OEMs are vendors who assemble computer systems from components originally manufactured by other suppliers. In 1990 Sun Microsystems, Silicon Graphics, and Hewlett-Packard/Apollo opened plants in Japan (U.S. Department of Commerce, 1992).

The Japanese market had grown annually at an average rate of 61% from 1988 to 1990, to almost $1.5 billion in 1990. In Japan, workstations were used primarily for software development, but computer-assisted design (CAD) and artificial intelligence (AI) were also important applications. In 1990 U.S. suppliers garnered a 75% share of this market and generally enjoyed price and performance advantages over Japanese manufacturers.

MATERIALS SUPPLIERS

The two main resources used in the U.S. workstation industry were (1) raw materials or commodities and (2) semiconductors and other electromechanical subassemblies. The first group of materials included aluminum, copper, brass, steel, plastic resins, silicon, and gold. The materials and supplies necessary for manufacturing operations were available in the required quantities from several suppliers, in addition to the commodities market. Thus, shortages in materials and delays in shipment did not adversely affect production schedules.

Exhibit 11.5 lists the top ten semiconductor suppliers by sales in 1980 and 1990. As shown in Exhibit 11.6, Japanese and Far Eastern manufacturers had been the major suppliers of these chips since overtaking the United States in 1986. Of the second type of materials (semiconductors) necessary for the production of workstations, dynamic random access memory chips (DRAMs) were in sufficient supply, though problems were expected in the future. As shown in Exhibit 11.7, Japan's top four memory chip manufacturers captured 49% of worldwide DRAM production in 1989. In fact, Texas Instruments and Micron Technology were the only two U.S. producers of DRAMs in 1990. At full capacity, these two firms combined could satisfy only 25% of the U.S. demand in 1989.

The continued low output of U.S.-made DRAMs drove up prices and forced U.S. manufacturers to delay the introduction of several new product lines until 1991. This strategic weakness contributed to the erosion of profit margins for U.S. companies. It was feared that in the near future, the Japanese could demand the licensing of proprietary design information from U.S. producers, in exchange for

EXHIBIT 11.5	The Top Ten Semiconductor Suppliers' Worldwide Sales (Dollar amounts in millions)		

1980		1990	
Texas Instruments (U.S.)	1,580	NEC (Japan)	4,952
Motorola (U.S.)	1,110	Toshiba (Japan)	4,905
Phillips	935	Hitachi (Japan)	3,927
NEC (Japan)	787	Motorola (U.S.)	3,692
National	747	Intel (U.S.)	3,135
Toshiba (Japan)	629	Fujitsu (Japan)	3,019
Hitachi (Japan)	622	Texas Instruments (U.S.)	2,574
Intel (U.S.)	575	Mitsubishi (Japan)	2,476
Fairchild	566	Matsushita (Japan)	1,945
Siemens	413	Phillips	1,932
Total	$7,964	Total	$32,557

Source: Information obtained from *Sematech, Annual Report 1991.*

EXHIBIT 11.6	Estimated Worldwide Semiconductor Market

(As percentage of total market)

Region	1982	1983	1984	1985	1986	1987	1988	1989	1990	1991
Japan	33%	38%	39%	42%	47%	49%	51%	50%	47%	47%
United States	56%	54%	52%	48%	42%	40%	38%	38%	40%	39%
Other	11%	8%	9%	10%	11%	11%	11%	12%	13%	14%
Total	100%	100%	100%	100%	100%	100%	100%	100%	100%	100%

Purchasers of Semiconductors in 1991
(Dollar amounts in billions)

Region	1991
Japan	$20.9
United States	$15.4
Europe	$10.1
Other	$ 8.2
Total	$54.6

Source: Adapted from Pollack, 1992.

increased supplies of these chips. This would permit the Japanese to make great strides in the development of their workstations, which were considered to be about two generations behind the U.S. products.

Because of these anticipated problems, some U.S. manufacturers decided to take action. Seven companies, including IBM, DEC, and HP, decided to help U.S. Memories raise $1 billion to form a startup DRAM manufacturing company. This

EXHIBIT 11.7	DRAM Market Leaders

(Estimated 1989 market: $9,200 million)

Firm	Country	Sales (in millions of dollars)	Percentage of Market
Toshiba	Japan	$1,525	16.6%
NEC	Japan	$1,100	11.9%
Hitachi	Japan	$1,000	10.9%
Samsung	S. Korea	$ 950	10.3%
Mitsubishi	Japan	$ 900	9.7%

Source: Information obtained from *Electronic Business,* April 16, 1990.

effort later collapsed because an unforeseen overcapacity in the open DRAM market led to saturation in the computer industry. This resulted in the unwillingness of major industry players (notably Apple, Compaq, and Sun) to contribute funds to the venture. In addition, the lack of involvement of the federal government ensured the demise of U.S. Memories in January 1990.

THE COMPETITIVE MARKET

The workstation industry was highly concentrated and was dominated by U.S. manufacturers. Increasing levels of competition were expected in the workstation segment of the computer industry, which was projected to grow from $6.4 billion in 1989 to more than $30 billion by 1995. This meant that each producer would be vying for market share (U.S. Department of Commerce, 1991). More U.S. personal computer firms were expected to branch into business workstation manufacturing. Large, vertically integrated Japanese electronics companies (as well as manufacturers in South Korea and Taiwan) were expected to use their strengths as low-cost, high-volume hardware and semiconductor producers to offset their current lack of software offerings and distribution channels in the United States.

The major computer manufacturers (both foreign and domestic) were expected to increase their market presence by introducing new software packages as well as dramatic pricing strategies. Some industry observers were expecting that by 1993, an onslaught of low-priced clone manufacturers in Japan and the Far East would force U.S. vendors to rethink their research and development and marketing strategies. Industry observers predicted that by the mid-1990s, several U.S. firms would leave hardware design and manufacturing to concentrate on software development or systems integration, or to market foreign-made workstations on an OEM basis, whereas others might produce only the more profitable, higher-performance systems (U.S. Department of Commerce, 1992).

Competition in this industry could be divided into two categories: domestic producers (competitors) who led in the development of new technologies and foreign producers who specialized in the production of clone products and the development of computer memory (DRAM) chips. In general, U.S. manufacturers were developing increasingly complex workstations, networked systems, and support software, whereas foreign producers were involved mainly in the development and production of computer memory chips and clone products. However, Japanese manufacturers were expected to begin concentrating on the development of low-end workstations, improved software packages for workstations, and the creation of software applications in the Japanese language—an area traditionally ignored by U.S. manufacturers. There was no major effort to create software applications in the various European languages because the character set used by the Romance and Slavic languages of Europe were easily adaptable to the Roman characters used in English.

Domestic Competition

Apollo Computers, which was acquired by Hewlett-Packard in 1989, was the pioneer of the early stand-alone workstations. Founded in 1980, Apollo's first offering was a fully configured (set-up) system with a price tag close to $60,000. In 1985

Sun Microsystems entered the market with a competitive UNIX workstation that sold for roughly $30,000 in full configuration. From the very beginning, the workstation market had been characterized by fierce competition among a number of small, young, innovative companies that were leading the industry.

Domestic competition consisted of an assortment of well-known firms and some lesser-known firms. These included Apollo, Compaq, Control Data, Data General, DEC, HP, IBM, Intergraph, NCR, NeXT, Stardent, Sun Microsystems, and Unisys. Each of these firms intended to move aggressively in order to become the market leader while the segment was young, so they could capitalize on its future growth. HP's acquisition of Apollo is an example of this aggressive strategy. Other major competitors were also acquiring smaller firms, especially software development firms. Such an acquisition gave the acquiring firm access to complicated new supporting software without the heavy development costs. This in turn freed companies' research and development budgets for the creation of new hardware. Despite the many players in the domestic workstation market, only Sun, Hewlett-Packard, Digital Equipment Corporation, and IBM had captured significant market shares as of 1990 (Exhibit 11.8).

In 1990 Sun Microsystems dominated the workstation market with a 32.4% market share and sales of $4.8 billion. Sun's Sparc RISC-based microprocessor and its SunOS version of UNIX attracted several licensed clone manufacturers who offered Sun-compatible computers. The company's strategy was to establish Sparc as the industry standard, and, thanks largely to the success of its other products, it was succeeding.

Hewlett-Packard, with a 21.2% market share and $3.1 billion in 1990 workstation revenues, was the number-two workstation vendor. HP's position was expected to be strengthened by the introduction of its HP Apollo Series 700 workstations in

EXHIBIT 11.8	RISC-Based Workstation Market Share (Percent)	

Firm	1990[1]	1992[2]
Sun	32.4	35.0
HP	21.2	16.0
DEC	16.2	12.0
IBM	6.7	9.0
Other	23.5	28.0
Total	100%	100%

Note: The figures for 1992 were from projections made in 1991 before release of the HP's Series 700 workstations.

Sources: [1] Adapted from Standard & Poor's, *Industry Surveys,* 1991.

[2] Adapted from Radding, 1992.

1991. Using an enhanced version of the RISC architecture on which its minicomputers were based (called Precision Architecture), HP made a technological leap by producing systems that greatly outperformed its competitors' comparably priced systems. HP claimed that its new Series 700 Model 730 workstation was twice as fast as IBM's fastest workstation and that it offered three and a half times the performance of Sun's Sparcstation 3.

Digital Equipment's share of the workstation market declined from 23% in 1989 to 16.2% in 1990. Sales for 1990 were $2.4 billion. DEC was aggressively supporting the ACE consortium and planned to upgrade its DECstation product line with new workstations based on the powerful R4000 RISC microprocessor from MIPS Computer Systems.

IBM has had a resurgence in the workstation market since its 1990 introduction of a range of products based on its own RISC design. Sales of its RS/6000 workstations totaled $1 billion in 1990, resulting in a market share of 6.7%. Sales of its workstation products were expected to total $2 billion in 1991, up from $1.7 billion in 1990. IBM has made moves to aggressively challenge Sun Microsystems. According to International Data Corp., Sun and IBM may be tied for first place among workstation vendors by 1993.

Japanese Competition

The major Japanese competitors in the workstation market were Fujitsu, Matsushita, NEC, Sony, and Toshiba. During 1988 and 1989, the Japanese companies attempted to penetrate the U.S. workstation market by targeting CAD/CAM/CAE users and increasing software development. They concentrated on the price-sensitive low-end market in order to take advantage of high-volume, low-cost production methods. However, they had few established distribution channels and lacked applications software.

Early on, the Japanese had adopted a somewhat different strategy, which was to design better chips for initial use in their own machines, and by this means they became innovators in the industry. The Japanese had some major technological advantages: workstations required large amounts of DRAMs (which they produced). Thus they could build workstations without buying microprocessors from Intel or Motorola (U.S. companies). By mid-1989, the Japanese had begun to offer RISC-based clone workstations in the United States.

Japanese firms were expected to intensify their challenge to U.S. firms both in the U.S. and foreign markets. They planned to expand their operations in the United States. Furthermore, workstation shipments from Japanese facilities for U.S. consumption and exports were expected to more than double, surpassing 80,000 units by the end of 1992 (U.S. Department of Commerce, 1992).

THE COMPANY

Hewlett-Packard was incorporated in 1947 as the successor to a partnership founded in 1939 by William Hewlett and David Packard, developers of the audio oscillator. The company became the leading manufacturer of electronic testing and measuring instruments for the science, telecommunications, and aerospace industries. In the early 1960s, this expertise and technology were applied to the analytical chemistry and medical fields.

HP went public in 1961 and introduced its first computer in 1966. This computer was designed to gather and analyze the data produced by the company's electronic instruments. In 1972 HP developed the first scientific hand-held calculator. In the mid-1970s, the company branched into the business computing segment with the HP 3000 Series. The HP 9000 Series and the Vectra Series were added in the 1980s. The 1989 acquisition of Apollo Computers helped HP become the number-one producer of computer workstations. HP acquired Avantek, Inc., a company whose product line expanded and complemented the radio- and microwave-frequency segment of HP's business, in November 1991. In 1991 Hewlett-Packard had 89,000 employees worldwide. As shown in Exhibit 11.9, gross sales for 1991 were $14.4 billion and net earnings were $755 million. Gross sales of $16 billion and net earnings of $955 million were projected for 1992 (Niemond, 1992).

EXHIBIT 11.9	**Consolidated Statement of Earnings: Hewlett-Packard Company and Subsidiaries** (In millions of dollars, except per-share amounts)

For the years ended October 31	1991	1990	1989
Net revenue			
Equipment	$11,019	$10,214	$ 9,404
Services	3,475	3,019	2,495
Total	14,494	13,233	11,899
Cost and expenses			
Cost of equipment sold	5,634	5,072	4,513
Cost of services	2,224	1,921	1,578
Research and development	1,463	1,367	1,269
Selling, general and administrative	3,963	3,711	3,327
Total	13,284	12,071	10,687
Earnings from operations	1,210	1,162	1,212
Interest income and other income (expense)	47	66	65
Interest expense	130	172	126
Earnings before taxes	1,127	1,056	1,151
Provision for taxes	372	317	322
Net earnings	$ 755	$ 739	$ 829
Net earnings per share	$ 3.02	$ 3.06	$ 3.52

Source: Information obtained from Hewlett-Packard, *1991 Annual Report.*

CORPORATE STRUCTURE AND PHILOSOPHY

In 1991 David Packard served as chairman of the board, John Young served as president and chief executive officer, and Dean O. Morton served as executive vice president and chief operating officer. In October 1990, HP implemented a major change in its management structure. This reorganization was undertaken to simplify structure, to streamline decision making, and to give managers more direct control over the technologies and sales activities required for the company's success.

The company's new structure consisted of three main organizations, as shown in Exhibit 11.10; each of these contained several groups and divisions. The Computer Systems Organization brought together the workstation and multiuser systems businesses. Executive vice president Lew Platt was in charge of this group. The Computer Products Organization combined the PC and peripherals business and was headed by executive vice president Dick Hackborn. The Test and Measurement Organization, under vice president Ned Barnholt, combined the activities of the Electronic Instruments and Microwave and Communication Groups. All three groups reported to John Young through the respective vice presidents.

EXHIBIT 11.10 | **Organizational Structure: Hewlett-Packard Company**

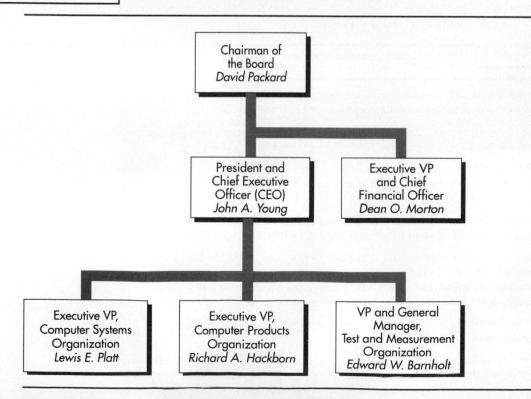

Source: Information obtained from Hewlett-Packard, *1991 Form 10K.*

The company's reputation as a good employer was legendary in the industry. HP fostered an innovative, nonauthoritarian atmosphere that encouraged employees to develop their own ideas, while at the same time stressed the importance of teamwork and cooperation. To this end, the company practiced management by objectives (MBO). This policy was based on seven written corporate objectives that provided a framework for individual and group goal setting. These objectives are shown in Exhibit 11.11.

Under the direction of Young, HP had become more computer systems-oriented. This was evidenced by a 31.2% annually compounded increase in computer sales from 1982 to 1991. In 1991 computer sales accounted for 65.5% of HP's revenues. 34.4% of that amount came from computer information systems and 31.1% coming from the sales of peripheral devices such as printers, disk drives, and networked products.

The company's computer systems, personal peripheral products, and other peripherals were used in various applications, including engineering and scientific computation and analysis, instrumentation and control, and business information management. HP's core computing products and technologies included its PA-RISC architecture for systems and workstations and its software infrastructure for open systems. Key products included the HP 1000, designed for factory automation and real-time data acquisition; the HP 3000 Series of computer systems,

---

EXHIBIT 11.11 | **Hewlett-Packard's Corporate Objectives**

Profit: To achieve sufficient profit to finance our company's growth and to provide the resources we need to achieve our other corporate objectives.

Customers: To provide products and services of the highest quality and the greatest possible value to our customers, thereby gaining and holding their respect and loyalty.

Fields of Interest: To participate in those fields of interest that build upon our technology and customer base, that offer opportunities for continuing growth, and that enable us to make a needed and profitable contribution.

Growth: To let our growth be limited only by our profits and our ability to develop and produce innovative products that satisfy real customer needs.

Our People: To help HP people share in the company's success which they make possible; to provide employment security based on their performance; to ensure them a safe and pleasant work environment; to recognize their individual achievements; and to help them gain a sense of satisfaction and accomplishment from their work.

Management: To foster initiative and creativity by allowing the individual great freedom of action in attaining well-defined objectives.

Citizenship: To honor our obligations to society by being an economic, intellectual, and social asset to each nation and each community in which we operate.

Source: Adapted from Hewlett-Packard, *Corporate Objectives,* 1990.

designed for commercial applications; the HP 9000 Series, which runs HP-UX (HP's implementation of the UNIX operating system), consisting of workstations with powerful computational and graphics capabilities, as well as multiuser computers for both technical and commercial applications; the HP Vectra Series of IBM-compatible personal computers for use in business, engineering, manufacturing and chemical analysis; and the new HP 95LX palmtop personal computer. The company's peripheral products included a variety of system and desktop printers, such as the industry-leading HP LaserJet and the HP DeskJet families. The company also produced measurement systems for use in electronics, medicine, and analytical chemistry.

Hewlett-Packard continued to demonstrate its ability to combine measurement and computation and to provide service for its equipment, systems, and peripherals. The company promoted industry standards that recognized customers' preferences for open systems in which different vendors' products could work together. The company often based its product innovations on such standards.

WORKSTATION PRODUCTS

The HP Apollo Series 700 workstations were HP's high-end products. Based on price/performance standards and on networking, and graphics capabilities, HP had the best RISC-based workstations in the industry. Designed for power, the Series 700 products were the fastest PA-RISC desktop and deskside workstations on the market (Radding, 1992). Before the Series 700, performance like this could be obtained only with mainframe systems. HP's commitment to open systems and standards was inherent in the Series 700 family. The UNIX-based HP-UX operating system provided a path to OSF/1, the industry-standard operating system of the 1990s. In addition, HP's client/server and transparent networking technologies allowed the user to build a distributed cooperative computing environment.

Models 720, 730, and 750 were on the market in 1991. According to HP's technical literature, the 720 was the industry's best price/performance expandable workstation in a desktop. Integrated graphics included the leading-edge X11, 2D/3D vector performance, and outstanding 3D-color modeling and rendering. The 730, which used a 66-MHz PA-RISC processor, was the industry's highest-performance desktop workstation. It boasted the industry's fastest X11, 2D/3D vector performance, and 24-plane solids performance on a desktop. The Model 750 offered the industry's leading performance and expandability in a deskside system. Large random access memory (RAM) and disk capacities made the 750 ideal for server applications. This model supported all the graphics options available on the 720 and 730.

In January 1992, Hewlett-Packard introduced additions to the Series 700 line of workstations, as well as more than 16 multiuser systems and servers. HP demolished existing standards in low-price RISC workstations when it announced two new machines: the Series 700 Model 705 for $4,990 and the Model 710 for $9,390. Based on 11 benchmark tests run by the Systems Performance Evaluation Cooperative (SPEC), a consortium involving about 24 RISC vendors, HP's new machines came in at a price/performance rating of $147 per "SPECmark." This performance catapulted HP past the previous low-price RISC market leaders: Sun

($246 per SPECmark), DEC ($245 per SPECmark), Solbourne Computer, Inc. ($300 per SPECmark), and Data General ($434 per SPECmark). This HP announcement dampened enthusiasm for IBM's January announcement of its RISC System/6000 Model 220, a 25-SPECmark machine with a $6,345 base price and a rating of $254 per SPECmark (Radding, 1992). Other HP hardware introductions included a line of X-terminals, which are low-cost alternatives to workstations.

HP had already started to warm up for the next round of workstation wars by announcing its next-generation Precision Architecture-RISC microprocessor. The superscalar PA-RISC 7100 chip, which was to show up in new HP computer systems in late 1992, would reportedly deliver 50% more performance than current HP 9000 and 3000 mid-range systems. Company officials said that full compatibility with previous PA-RISC chips would be guaranteed. The next generation of chips was expected to have clock speeds doubling the current 50–100 MHz and a performance rating of 120 SPECmarks. According to Jack Jeffers, quality assurance manager at Quaker Oats Co. in Jackson, Tennessee, where HP's workstation systems were used to run a statistical process control system, "Anything that gives us faster response time for people on the factory floor is welcome." This attitude testifies to the effectiveness of HP's research and development program in helping to keep the firm competitive. The company's product developments were expected to continue to fulfill the market's demand for decreased price and increased performance standards, helping to make the company the dominant player in the workstation market.

CUSTOMERS

Hewlett-Packard offered its products to technical, business and commercial, and individual customers in a variety of settings—for example, high-tech and industrial corporations, business firms, government agencies, and educational institutions. In 1991, with the exception of the U.S. government, no single account represented more than 5% of the company's orders. Compared to its major competitors, HP had fewer extremely large customers.

Most of HP's workstation revenues were earned by supplying technical users with graphics and design workstations. Technical users, including scientists and engineers, were the traditional mainstay of the workstation market. Orders from this group were expected to grow at a steady pace.

Business and commercial users, as a group, accounted for the next-highest portion of HP's workstation revenues. These users constituted a relatively new target customer base, because they traditionally utilized mid-range computer systems that supported individual terminals for office automation, financial services, and electronic publishing. The improvement in the price and performance competitiveness of workstations, compared to mid-range systems, persuaded many customers to switch to workstation systems. The performance, network, and connectivity features that workstation systems offered were expected to lead to a steady increase in the number of business and commercial users abandoning mid-range computer systems in favor of personal and design workstation systems.

Individual users, such as the business and commercial users, constituted a new target customer. In the past, the high cost of workstations had proved unattractive to the individual user who traditionally purchased PCs. But the improved performance, coupled with intense price competition, had made personal workstations very attractive to the individual user. As the differences between high-end PCs and personal workstations became less well defined, individual users were expected to purchase more workstations and to be significant customers for the industry to target.

SALES AND DISTRIBUTION

Slightly more than half of Hewlett-Packard's product revenue was derived through the efforts of its own sales organization selling to end users. The remaining revenue was derived through value-added resellers (VARs) and other resellers such as computer specialty stores. In 1991 a higher proportion of net revenue was generated from products such as personal peripherals, which were sold mainly through outlets such as mass merchandisers. Mass merchandisers included consumer electronics stores, department stores, and discount stores such as Sears and Montgomery Ward. Sales operations were supported by a team 34,000 strong comprising field service engineers, sales representatives, and service and administrative personnel.

As shown in Exhibit 11.12, the company's total orders originating from outside the U.S. increased steadily since 1986 to $8.1 billion in 1991. International orders accounted for 53% of total orders in 1989, for 54% in 1990, and for 56% in 1991 (*Hewlett-Packard Annual Report,* 1991). The majority of these international orders were from customers other than foreign governments. Approximately 66% of HP's international orders from 1989 to 1991 originated in Europe; others came largely from Japan, the Far East, and Canada. Most of the sales in international markets were made by foreign sales subsidiaries. Other sales were made directly from the parent company in the United States. For international markets with low-volume sales, sales were made through various representative and distributorship arrangements.

Hewlett-Packard's international business was subject to the risks customarily encountered in foreign operations, including fluctuations in monetary exchange rates, import/export controls, and political risks. However, the company believed its international diversification gave worldwide operations stability and reduced the impact of adverse economic shocks in any single country. In 1991 HP expanded its presence in Eastern Europe and the Commonwealth of Independent States by a variety of means, including formation of various joint ventures and sales and support subsidiaries.

During 1991 the company sold its products through a mix of direct sales and value-added resellers. Direct sales were the largest channel in previous years; however, HP began selling its low-end workstations through independent resellers in 1988. In 1991 HP began offering its entire workstation family through a new direct-mail unit.

EXHIBIT 11.12	Selected Financial Data: Hewlett-Packard and Subsidiaries (In millions of dollars, except per-share amounts and employees)

For the years ended October 31	1991	1990	1989	1988	1987	1986
U.S. orders	$ 6,484	$ 6,143	$ 5,677	$ 4,780	$4,262	$ 3,826
International orders	8,192	7,342	6,483	5,290	4,117	3,375
Total orders	$14,676	$13,485	$12,160	$10,070	$8,379	$ 7,201
Net revenue	$14,494	$13,233	$11,899	$ 9,831	$8,090	$ 7,102
Earnings from operations	$ 1,210	$ 1,162	$ 1,212	$ 1,084	$ 905	$ 752
Net earnings	$ 755	$ 739	$ 829	$ 816	$ 644	$ 516
Per share						
Net earnings	$ 3.02	$ 3.06	$ 3.52	$ 3.36	$ 2.50	$ 2.02
Cash dividends	$ .48	$ .42	$ .36	$ .28	$ .23	$ .22
At year-end						
Total assets	$11,973	$11,395	$10,075	$ 7,858	$8,547	$ 6,770
Employees	89,000	92,200	94,900	86,600	82,300	82,300

Source: Information obtained from Hewlett-Packard, *1991 Annual Report.*

HEWLETT-PACKARD'S COMPETITIVE POSITION

The company encountered aggressive competition in all areas of its business activities. Its competitors were numerous, ranging from some of the world's largest corporations to many relatively small and highly specialized firms. Hewlett-Packard competed primarily on the basis of technology, performance, price, quality, reliability, distribution, and customer service and support.

Several important strategic strengths had helped HP become a serious contender in the workstation segment. The company was financially strong and compared favorably to other firms in its industry. The company had extensive, well-developed distribution networks and a large and highly trained sales force that served both domestic and international markets. HP also maintained complete and competitive product lines with good price/performance ratios. Workstation models utilized the UNIX operating system, the de facto industry standard. In 1991 HP had an experienced management team and a solid research and development program in place. Research and development expenditures were 10.1% of net revenues (*Hewlett-Packard 10K Report, 1991*). HP's excellent research and development program enabled the product developers to maintain a current and competitive product line. New products were essential in this industry in which technology and success went hand-in-hand. More than half of HP's 1991 orders were for products that had been introduced since 1989.

HP had some weaknesses to correct before its overall competitive position could be improved, especially in the workstation market. Market research suggested that HP had fallen behind some of its competitors in providing satisfactory after-sale service and support. The company lagged in the development of software that could take advantage of its improved hardware systems designs. The two families of computer systems—the HP 9000 UNIX-based computers and the HP Apollo 700 Series—were at times competing with each other and creating confusion in the market and among customers. Furthermore, the improved price/performance ratio of its own PC line meant that Hewlett-Packard's PCs were beginning to compete with its low-end workstations.

TOWARD THE FUTURE

The challenge for all workstation companies was to maintain profit margins as average workstation prices fell and to adjust to new distribution channels as the market for workstations expanded. In 1992 Hewlett-Packard was considering strategies that recognized the importance of balancing efforts to improve the effectiveness of the firm in the workstation segment. There was universal agreement that HP should aggressively continue to offer its wide product line to both domestic and foreign markets. In addition, HP should continue to compete on the basis of technology, price, performance, quality, distribution, and customer service and support. However, there was disagreement on the specific strategies the company should pursue.

One manager suggested that the best strategy would be to concentrate on the high end of the proprietary workstation market. HP's proprietary RISC-based Precision Architecture had allowed the company to surpass its competitors. The company's workstations had superior price/performance ratios coupled with the high quality for which HP was legendary. By focusing on this niche, it was argued, the company could realize high margins while expanding its domestic and foreign customer base.

John Young, the president and CEO of Hewlett-Packard, did not agree with this strategy. He felt the company had to compete in both the low and high ends of the workstation market. He suggested that HP manufacture both proprietary and open-systems hardware for its entire line of workstations. HP's workstation segment had not gotten high marks for customer service and support, compared to the rest of the computer industry. Young wanted to continue matching product quality with marketing quality for HP's workstations, while maintaining a lead position in workstation price/performance against Sun, DEC, and IBM. Although proprietary system platforms carried greater profit margins than did open, or nonproprietary, systems, the trend toward open systems was unstoppable.

Given the dynamic nature of the industry and its intensely competitive environment, management was considering what it should do about these and other major strategic problems facing the company.

REFERENCES

Alster, Norm. "Drowning in DRAMs." *Forbes,* November 11, 1991, p. 41.

Anthens, Gary. "Bush Trip Yields High-Tech Silver Lining." *Computerworld,* January 20, 1992, p. 85.

Bayer, Tony. "Open Systems Slowly Gaining Steam in Factory." *Computerworld,* October 28, 1991, p. 78.

Burrows, Peter. "A 'Single Industry Voice' Gets Results in Chip Wars." *Electronic Business,* May 6, 1991, p. 11.

David, Bernard J. "ACE Promises Unity and Fragmentation." *Systems 3X/400,* October 1991, pp. 90–94.

Electronic Business, April 16, 1990, p. 48.

Francis, Bob. "Workstations Enter the Third Dimension." *Datamation,* September 1, 1991, pp. 34–38.

Hewlett-Packard. *1991 Annual Report,* Hewlett-Packard, 3000 Hanover Street, Palo Alto, California 94304.

Hewlett-Packard, Corporate Objectives–1990, Hewlett-Packard, 3000 Hanover Street, Palo Alto, California 94304.

Hewlett-Packard, 1991 Form 10K, Securities and Exchange Commission, Washington, D.C. 20549.

Hughes, David. "Hewlett-Packard, Digital and IBM Race to Create Faster Workstations." *Aviation Week & Space Technology,* August 19, 1991, pp. 103–107.

Johnson, Maryfran. "HP Announces Next-Generation PA-RISC Chip." *Computerworld,* February 24, 1992, p. 8.

Johnson, Maryfran. "Sun Storage Prices Plummet." *Computerworld,* March 30, 1992, p.16.

Juliussen, Karen and Egil Juliussen. *The Computer Industry Almanac, 1991.* (Dallas, Texas: Computer Industry Almanac Inc., 1991.)

Mockler, Robert J. *Strategic Management: An Integrated Situational Management Orientation.* Yorkville Station, N.Y.: D & R Publishing Company, 1990.

Pollack, Andrew. "U.S. Chip Makers Stem the Tide in Trade Battles with Japanese." *New York Times,* April 9, 1992, p. A1.

Radding, Alan, "RISC Desktop Machines: PCs in Disguise?" *Computerworld,* March 23, 1992, pp. 85–87.

Sematech, Annual Report 1991. Sematech, 2706 Montopolis Drive, Austin, Texas 78741.

Standard & Poor's, *Industry Surveys,* October 17, 1991, pp. 75–83.

U.S. Department of Commerce. *U.S. Industrial Outlook, 1991.* Washington, D.C. 20549.

Verity, John. "From Mainframes to Clones, a Trickery Time." *Business Week,* January 13, 1992, pp. 97–98.

C ASE 12   Johns-Manville and Riverwood-Schuller

Arthur Sharplin

In 1898 Henry Ward Johns, inventor of many asbestos products and founder of Johns-Manville Corporation (J-M), died of scarring of the lungs, presumably asbestosis.[1] But his company survived, and for most of the next century it would be the world leader in mining and distributing the fiber and in developing, manufacturing, and marketing asbestos goods. The insert that follows on page 817 discusses asbestos applications and health issues. Exhibits 12.1 through 12.9 provide financial data.

EXHIBIT 12.1	**Comparative Income Statements, 1976–June 1982: Johns-Manville** (Dollar amounts in millions*)

	1982 6 mos.	1981	1980	1979	1978	1977	1976
Net sales	$949	$2,186	$2,267	$2,276	$1,649	$1,461	$1,309
Cost of sales	784	1,731	1,771	1,747	1,190	1,066	983
Selling, general and administrative	143	271	263	239	193	174	166
R&D and engineering	16	34	35	31	33	28	25
Operating income	6	151	197	259	232	193	135
Other income	1	35	26	21	28	2	1
Interest expense	35	73	65	62	22	20	15
Income before tax	(28)	112	157	218	238	175	121
Income tax	(2)	53	77	103	116	89	48
Net income	(25)	60	81	115	122	86	73
Preferred stock dividends	12	25	25	24	—	—	—
Net income for common stock	$(37)	$ 35	$ 55	$ 91	$ 122	$ 86	$ 73

* Totals may not check, due to rounding.

Arthur Sharplin, McNeese State University, July 1992. Reprinted with permission.

EXHIBIT 12.2 | **Comparative Business Segment Information, 1976–1981: Johns-Manville**
(Dollar amounts in millions*)

	1981	1980	1979	1978	1977	1976
Revenues						
Fiberglass products	$ 625	$ 610	$ 573	$ 514	$ 407	$ 358
Forest products	555	508	497	—	—	—
Nonfiberglass insulation	258	279	268	231	195	159
Roofing products	209	250	273	254	204	171
Pipe products and systems	199	220	305	303	274	218
Asbestos fiber	138	159	168	157	161	155
Industrial and specialty products	320	341	309	291	301	309
Corporate revenue, net	12	9	11	20	12	(22)
Intersegment sales	(95)	(84)	(106)	(94)	(74)	(56)
Total	$2,221	$2,292	$2,297	$1,677	$1,480	$1,291
Income from operations						
Fiberglass products	$ 90	$ 91	$ 96	$ 107	$ 82	$ 60
Forest products	39	37	50	—	—	—
Nonfiberglass insulation	20	27	27	35	28	18
Roofing products	(17)	9	14	23	14	8
Pipe products and systems	0	(5)	18	26	24	(3)
Asbestos fiber	37	35	56	55	60	60
Industrial and specialty products	50	55	43	36	25	19
Corporate expense, net	(23)	(38)	(23)	(23)	(24)	(49)
Eliminations and adjustments	3	11	(2)	1	3	2
Total	$ 198	$ 223	$ 280	$ 260	$ 212	$ 116

* Totals may not check, due to rounding.

EXHIBIT 12.3 | **Comparative Balance Sheets, December 1976–June 1982: Johns-Manville**
(Dollar amounts in millions*)

	June 30	December 31					
	1982	1981	1980	1979	1978	1977	1976
Assets							
Cash	$ 10	$ 14	$ 20	$ 19	$ 28	$ 39	$ 25
Marketable securities	17	12	12	10	38	121	66
Accounts and notes receivable	348	327	350	362	328	263	239

(continued)

EXHIBIT 12.3	**Comparative Balance Sheets, December 1976–June 1982: Johns-Manville (continued)** (Dollar amounts in millions*)

	June 30	December 31					
	1982	1981	1980	1979	1978	1977	1976
Inventories	182	211	217	229	219	149	144
Prepayments	19	19	20	31	32	30	26
Total current assets	$ 576	$ 583	$ 619	$ 650	$ 645	$ 601	$ 501
Land and improvements	—	119	118	114	99	64	64
Buildings	—	363	357	352	321	264	259
Machinery and equipment	—	1,202	1,204	1,161	1,043	642	598
		$1,685	$1,679	$1,627	$1,462	$ 970	$ 921
Accrued depreciation and depletion	—	(525)	(484)	(430)	(374)	(337)	(327)
Total	—	$1,160	$1,195	$1,197	$1,088	$ 633	$ 594
Timber and timberland	—	406	407	368	372	0	0
Total plant, property, and equipment	$1,523	$1,566	$1,602	$1,565	$1,460	$ 633	$ 594
Other assets	148	149	117	110	113	99	93
Total assets	$2,247	$2,298	$2,338	$2,324	$2,217	$1,334	$1,188
Liabilities and Stockholders' Equity							
Short-term debt	$ 0	$ 29	$ 22	$ 32	$ 23	$ 18	$ 20
Accounts payable	191	120	126	143	114	69	58
Accrued compensation and benefits	0	77	80	54	45	37	32
Income tax	0	30	22	51	84	57	32
Other liabilities	149	58	61	50	63	54	48
Total current liabilities	$ 340	$ 316	$ 310	$ 329	$ 329	$ 235	$ 189
Long-term debt	499	508	519	532	543	203	208
Other noncurrent liabilities	93	86	75	73	60	23	11
Deferred income tax	186	185	211	195	150	130	108
Total liabilities	$1,116	$1,095	$1,116	$1,129	$1,083	$ 591	$ 516
Preferred stock	$ 301	$ 301	$ 300	$ 299	$ 299	—	—
Common stock	60	59	58	56	55	54	54
Capital above par	178	174	164	152	142	134	134
Retained earnings	642	695	705	692	643	561	492
Current transactions, adjustments	(47)	(22)	0	0	0	0	0
Treasury stock	(3)	(3)	(4)	(4)	(6)	(7)	(9)
Total stockholders' equity	$1,131	$1,203	$1,222	$1,196	$1,134	742	672
Total liabilities and stockholders' equity	$2,247	$2,298	$2,338	$2,324	$2,217	$1,334	$1,188

* Totals may not check, due to rounding.

EXHIBIT 12.4	Comparative Income Statements, 1982–1988: Johns-Manville
	(Dollar amounts in millions*)

	1988	1987	1986	1985	1984	1983	1982
Net sales	$ 2,062	$1,935	$1,803	$1,880	$1,814	$1,729	$1,685
Cost of sales	1,545	1,440	1,368	1,473	1,400	1,370	1,329
Selling, general and administrative	203	206	213	246	238	224	256
R&D and engineering	36	32	35	35	36	35	28
Restructuring costs	139	(3)	47	153	2	—	—
Other income (loss)	69	50	39	63	61	61	32
Income from operations	207	310	180	36	200	161	104
Interest expense	40	25	20	23	21	26	52
Chapter 11 and A-H cost	12	15	28	61	43	39	18
Deposition of assets	—	—	—	—	—	(3)	46
Income tax	66	113	54	(2)	58	40	8
Income, continuing operations	89	157	78	(45)	77	60	(21)
Income, discontinued operations	7	7	4	—	—	7	(77)
	96	164	81	(45)	77	67	(98)
Extraordinary charge	(1,288)	(91)	0	0	0	0	0
Accounting change	(107)	0	0	0	0	0	0
Net income	$(1,299)	$ 73	$ 81	$ (45)	$ 77	$ 67	$ (98)

* Totals may not check, due to rounding.

EXHIBIT 12.5	Comparative Business Segment Information, 1982–1988: Johns-Manville
	(Dollar amounts in millions*)

	1988	1987	1986	1985	1984	1983	1982
*Revenues***							
Fiberglass products	$ 937	$ 877	$ 809	$ 803	$ 780	$ 720	$ 609
Forest products	678	596	541	459	451	427	436
Specialty products	501	506	494	674	254	248	285
Nonfiberglass insulation	—	—	—	—	203	209	232
Roofing products	—	—	—	—	190	228	211
Corporate and eliminations (net)	15	6	(-2)	8	—	—	—

(continued)

EXHIBIT 12.5	**Comparative Business Segment Information, 1982–1988: Johns-Manville (continued)** (Dollar amounts in millions*)

	1988	1987	1986	1985	1984	1983	1982
Corporate revenue, net	—	—	—	—	39	35	14
Intersegment sales	—	—	—	—	(43)	(76)	(69)
Total	$2,131	$1,985	$1,842	$1,943	$1,873	$1,791	$1,717
Income from Operations							
Fiberglass products	$ 123	$ 151	$ 120	$ 69	115	$ 97	$ 75
Forest products	127	100	62	34	63	53	48
Specialty products	38	36	27	(38)	22	18	28
Nonfiberglass insulation	—	—	—	—	16	9	11
Roofing products	—	—	—	—	(11)	(10)	(6)
Corporate and eliminations (net)	(81)	23	(29)	(28)	—	—	—
Corporate expense, net	—	—	—	—	(4)	(6)	(22)
Eliminations and adjustments	—	—	—	—	—	1	7
Total	$ 207	$ 310	$ 180	$ 36	$ 200	$ 161	$ 141

* Totals may not check, due to rounding.
** Includes net sales and other income, net.

EXHIBIT 12.6	**Comparative Balance Sheets, 1982–1988: Johns-Manville** (Dollar amounts in millions*)

	December 31						
	1988	1987	1986	1985	1984	1983	1982
Assets							
Cash and equivalents	$ 219	$ 210	$ 137	$ 7	$ 9	$ 19	$ 11
Marketable securities	54	385	307	314	276	240	206
Accounts receivable and notes receivable	298	309	292	314	285	277	310
Inventories	146	160	153	153	164	141	152
Prepayments	14	27	24	29	17	22	17
Total current assets	731	1,091	914	817	752	700	696

(continued)

EXHIBIT 12.6	Comparative Balance Sheets, 1982–1988: Johns-Manville (continued)

(Dollar amounts in millions*)

	December 31						
	1988	1987	1986	1985	1984	1983	1982
Land and improvements	95	97	99	95	96	97	108
Buildings	253	261	312	304	308	303	332
Machinery and equipment	1,366	1,330	1,234	1,156	1,121	1,056	1,090
Accrued depreciation and depletion	(645)	(597)	(586)	(538)	(513)	(472)	(547)
Timber and timberland	357	367	376	385	392	395	402
Plant, property, and equipment, net	1,427	1,458	1,434	1,402	1,405	1,379	1,385
Other assets	235	204	165	174	182	174	154
Total assets	$2,393	$2,753	$2,513	$2,393	$2,339	$2,253	$2,236
Liabilities and Stockholders' Equity							
Short-term debt	$ 77	$ 21	$ 30	$ 26	$ 20	$ 14	$ 12
Accounts payable	103	104	93	84	102	94	86
Accrued compensation and benefits	97	101	103	94	81	65	63
Income tax	31	14	16	12	18	10	32
Other accrued liabilities	113	73	62	69	35	26	29
Total current liabilities	421	312	304	286	256	208	221
Long-term debt	869	223	80	92	84	4	12
Liabilities subject to Chapter 11	0	547	575	578	574	713	736
Other noncurrent liabilities	208	101	118	115	67	61	60
Deferred income tax	97	198	161	144	162	136	140
Total liabilities	1,595	1,381	1,239	1,214	1,142	1,122	1,170
Preferred stock	418	301	301	301	301	301	301
Preference stock	89	—	—	—	—	—	—
Common stock	0	60	60	60	60	60	60
Capital above par	761	178	178	178	178	178	178
Retained earnings	(479)	821	749	667	713	635	568
Current transaction adjustments	8	12	(11)	(26)	(53)	(41)	(39)
Treasury stock	0	(2)	(2)	(2)	(2)	(2)	(2)
Net worth	798	1,370	1,275	1,178	1,197	1,131	1,066
Total liabilities and stockholders' equity	$2,393	$2,753	$2,513	$2,393	$2,339	$2,253	$2,236

* Totals may not check, due to rounding.

EXHIBIT 12.7	Comparative Income Statements, 1989–1991: Johns-Manville (Dollar amounts in millions*)

	1991	1990	1989
Net sales	$2,025	$2,127	$2,081
Cost of sales	1,640	1,649	1,553
Selling, general and administrative	220	212	206
R&D and engineering	36	41	39
Restructuring costs	(64)	(27)	4
Other income (loss)	10	34	21
Income from operations	76	232	308
Interest expense	74	83	76
Profit sharing	10	0	0
Disposition of assets	—	—	—
Income tax	22	61	75
Income, continuing operations	(30)	88	157
Income, discontinued operations	(18)	22	39
Income before charge	(13)	111	197
Extraordinary charge	0	0	0
Accounting change	47	0	0
Net income	$ 35	$ 111	$ 197

* Totals may not check, due to rounding.

EXHIBIT 12.8	Comparative Business Segment Information, 1989–1991: Johns-Manville (Dollar amounts in millions*)

	1991	1990	1989
*Revenues***			
Paperboard and packing	$1,019	$ 906	$ 789
Engineered products	486	581	631
Building products	568	720	725
Corporate and eliminations	(37)	(46)	(42)
Total	$2,036	$2,161	$2,103
Income from Operations			
Paperboard and packing	$ 145	$ 159	$ 186
Engineered products	34	90	109
Building products	(39)	54	68
Corporate and eliminations	(63)	(71)	(55)
Total	$ 76	$ 232	$ 308

* Totals may not check, due to rounding.
** Includes net sales and other income, net.

EXHIBIT 12.9	Comparative Balance Sheets, 1982–1988: Johns-Manville (Dollar amounts in millions*)

	December 31		
	1991	1990	1989
Assets			
Cash and equivalents	$ 127	$ 88	$ 280
Marketable securities	36	37	47
Accounts receivable and notes receivable	251	295	277
Inventories	190	192	162
Prepayments	10	25	18
Deferred tax assets	61	6	0
Total current assets	675	642	785
Property, plant and equipment, net	1,437	1,483	1,295
Timber and timberland	347	353	354
Deferred tax assets	246	14	0
Other assets	297	304	210
Total assets	$3,003	$2,796	$2,645
Liabilities and Stockholders' Equity			
Short-term debt	$ 41	$ 60	$ 137
Accounts payable and accruals	401	382	386
Accrued dividends, common stock	128	0	0
Total current liabilities	570	442	523
Long-term debt	823	870	802
Accrued dividends	267	0	0
Other long-term liabilities	564	343	326
Total liabilities	2,223	1,655	1,651
Preferred stock	418	418	418
Preference stock	100	119	103
Common equity	262	604	472
Net worth	780	1,141	994
Total liabilities and stockholders' equity	$3,003	$2,796	$2,645

* Totals may not check, due to rounding.

OVERVIEW

By 1930 the second generation of J-M managers had taken over and would remain with the company into the 1960s. A trickle of asbestos-health (A-H) lawsuits in the 1920s and 1930s would swell to a flood in the 1970s.

A third generation of J-M managers and directors took office about 1970 and started to diversify the company and change its image. Four events made the strategy more urgent: J-M lost its first major A-H case (to Clarence Borel) in 1973; a steep recession in 1974–1975 cut profits in half; in 1976 the former medical director admitted that in the 1940s and 1950s, the firm had knowledge of dangers associated with asbestos; and in 1977, A-H lawyers found a batch of incriminating correspondence among industry officials of the 1930s and 1940s.

ASBESTOS APPLICATIONS AND HEALTH ISSUES

Asbestos is a mineral fiber obtained by crushing asbestos-containing rock, mainly from open-pit mines, and sifting and blowing away the unwanted material. The fine strands are fireproof and almost impervious to most acids, to body fluids, and to oxygen. Before about 1978 (and afterwards in many countries), asbestos cloth was used to make such household items as drapes, rugs, pot holders, and ironing board covers. Asbestos was mixed into slurry and sprayed onto building walls and ceilings. It was used in most industrial insulations, in roofing and floor tiles and wallboards, in a wide range of putties and sealants, and in automobile brakes, clutches, and mufflers. The substance was present in practically every ship, automobile, airplane, home, factory, and school completed before the mid-1970s and in many completed afterwards.

As asbestos products are worked or disturbed, they exude dust containing microscopic pieces of fiber. Ingested, the fibers cut and penetrate moving tissue, especially in the lungs. Intense or prolonged exposure leads to asbestosis, a progressive and irreversible scarring, thickening, and calcification of the lungs and their linings (the pleura). Mesothelioma, a rare and fatal cancer of the pleura (it may also affect the peritoneum, the lining of the abdomen), is strongly connected with prolonged occupational exposure to asbestos, as are increased incidence and severity of lung cancer and many other respiratory ailments. The first symptoms of asbestos disease typically appear ten to thirty years after exposure begins. But early damage is easily detectable by x-rays, and some cancers and respiratory deficiencies show up after only a year or two. Cigarette smokers are several times more susceptible to respiratory diseases, especially those related to asbestos, than are non-smokers. It is widely agreed that as long as asbestos is "encapsulated"—as in floor tiles or painted insulating blocks—the danger of disturbing it in the process of removal exceeds that of leaving it in place.

Lawyer John A. McKinney became chief executive in 1976. He arranged to acquire Olinkraft Corporation, a large wood products firm, paying half in cash and half in preferred stock. In 1981 J-M was renamed Manville Corporation and reorganized. By August 1982, A-H claims totaled 20,000, and some juries were awarding punitive damages. Also, Manville's businesses were losing money.

On August 26 that year, the company filed for bankruptcy reorganization. No A-H claims would be paid for over six years, although commercial creditors were soon assured of full payment. A plan to emerge from Chapter 11 protection would be approved by the court in 1986 and would become final in 1988.

The managers and directors got improved pay and benefits, continued indemnity against the A-H claims, and added tenure to retirement. Some set up groups to buy assets out of the bankruptcy, including the main asbestos mine and factories. By 1988 the remaining third-generation executives chose successors and retired, several with large severance checks as well as pensions.

The fourth-generation managers set about sorting Manville's $3 billion in assets and cash into divisions to be renamed "Riverwood International" and "Schuller International." They began a public relations campaign. Soon Stephens would express confidence that the company would escape the asbestos mess altogether.

Meanwhile, bankruptcy judge Burton R. Lifland issued an injunction directing the A-H claims to a trust. The trust was to be funded with $150 million from the company and $695 million from its insurers. It also received common and preferred stock but could not trade or vote the shares for several years.

The trust paid its first claim in 1989 and ran short of funds three months later. By late 1991, the chief executive of the trust and all but one trustee had resigned. Sixteen thousand A-H claimants had received an average of about $20,000 each (after attorneys' charges). Payment of another 12,000 claims was promised by the year 2020. But 160,000 still awaited processing,[2] and new claimants were told to expect their first payment in 23 years.[3] The average life expectancy of claimants was estimated at 17 years.[4]

Lifland reaffirmed the injunction. Company legal chief Richard B. Von Wald said, "That's the kind of certainty we were after. Manville is a company which has put the asbestos risk questions behind us." But many victims faced a less favorable certainty, the one Johns himself had confronted nearly a century before. Exhibit 12.10 outlines the Manville story, which is told in more detail in the pages that follow.

EXHIBIT 12.10	Outline of the Manville Story

1898	Founder, Henry Ward Johns, dies of asbestosis.
1920s	Early lawsuits; second generation of managers in charge.
1930s	Incriminating correspondence among industry officials.
1970s	Third-generation managers take charge; Borel case; diversification efforts; Olinkraft acquisition.
1981	J-M renamed Manville and reorganized.
1982	A-H claims total 20,000; punitive damages awarded; businesses losing money; Chapter 11 filing in August; asbestos claims and other debts stayed.
1984–1986	Manager pay and benefits increase; asbestos mine and other assets sold free of asbestos claims; Chapter 11 plan approved by court.
1987–1988	Manville begins public relations campaign; Chapter 11 plan becomes final; unsecured creditors receive full value; injunction directs asbestos claims to trust.
1989	A-H trust runs short of funds within three months of paying first claim.
1991–1992	A-H trust in disarray and expected to sell Manville shares to survive; 16,000 A-H claims have gotten an average $20,000 each; 12,000 more promised payment by the year 2020; 160,000 claims await processing; Manville, with $3 billion in assets, prepares to divide itself and break free of past.

THE EVIL IS VERY INSIDIOUS

The year Johns died, a British factory inspector had described a common fate of asbestos textile workers: "In the majority of cases the evil is very insidious. . . . The worker falls into ill health and sinks away out of sight in no sudden or sensational manner."[5] And in 1918, Prudential Insurance Company's chief actuary wrote, "[I]n the practice of American and Canadian life insurance companies asbestos workers are generally declined on account of the assumed health-injurious conditions of the industry."[6]

Studies reported in the medical literature in 1924, 1928, and 1930 began to show the nature of the asbestos-health (A-H) problem. The 1930 research revealed that 26.3% of the workers studied had fairly serious asbestosis, a name given the disease in 1927.[7]

A PRINCIPAL DEFENSE

By 1929 J-M was defending lawsuits for asbestos deaths. In court, the company claimed employees assumed the risks of employment, knew or should have known the dangers, and were contributorily negligent. Legal documents in these cases bore the signatures of senior J-M officials who would remain with the company until the late 1960s. Through the 1950s, most A-H claimants were present and former J-M employees who had been exposed in the company's mines and factories; later claimants were mainly asbestos insulation workers employed by others.

Prominent among J-M's insurers was Metropolitan Life Insurance Company. In 1930 Dr. A. J. Lanza, of Metropolitan, began a four-year study on the "Effects of Inhalation of Asbestos Dust Upon the Lungs of Asbestos Workers."[8] His preliminary report, written the next year, showed 87% of the workers with over 15 years of exposure and 43% with under 5 years had x-ray-visible fibrosis.[9] J-M vice president Vandiver Brown reviewed a draft of Dr. Lanza's report and wrote him,

> All we ask is that all of the favorable aspects of the survey be included and that none of the unfavorable be unintentionally pictured in darker terms than the circumstances justify. I feel confident that we can depend upon you and Dr. McConnel to give us this "break."[10]

Although the insurers had some liability, J-M remained primary defendant in the lawsuits. In 1934 J-M's chief outside attorney, George Hobart, wrote Brown:

> [I]t is only within a comparatively recent time that asbestosis has been recognized by the medical and scientific professions as a disease—in fact one of our principal defenses in actions against the company on the common law theory of negligence has been that the scientific and medical knowledge has been insufficient until a very recent period to place on the owners of plants or factories the burden or duty of taking special precautions against the possible onset of the disease in their employees.[11]

A half-century later, Brown's successor, John A. McKinney, would be claiming to have just recently learned that asbestos "can sometimes cause certain lung diseases."[12] And McKinney would hire Hobart's firm, then called Davis Polk Wardwell, to defend the company.

THE MINIMUM OF PUBLICITY

In October 1935, Brown wrote Raybestos-Manhattan Corporation president Sumner Simpson, "I quite agree that our interests are best served by having asbestosis receive the minimum of publicity."[13] He was commenting on Simpson's response to the editor of the industry journal *Asbestos*, who had written,

> You may recall that we have written you on several occasions concerning the publishing of information, or discussion of, asbestosis. . . . Always you have requested that for certain obvious reasons, we publish nothing, and naturally your wishes have been respected.[14]

Brown and Simpson convinced nine other asbestos companies to provide an average of $450 each per year for the industry's own three-year study of the effects of asbestos dust on guinea pigs and rabbits. Brown wrote the researcher, Dr. LeRoy U. Gardner, "In the event it is deemed desirable that the results be made public, the manuscript of your study will be submitted to us for approval prior to publication."[15] Gardner later advised the companies of "significant changes in guinea pigs' lungs within a period of one year" and "fibrosis" produced by long fibers and "chronic inflammation" caused by short fibers.[16] He made several requests for funding but died in 1946 without reporting final results.

LET THEM "LIVE AND WORK IN PEACE"

World War II brought J-M spiraling sales, as thousands of tons of asbestos were used in building war machines, mainly ships, thus exposing hundreds of thousands of shipyard workers and seamen, many of whom would die of asbestos diseases decades later.

In 1947 a study by the Industrial Hygiene Foundation of America found that from 3% to 20% of asbestos plant workers had asbestosis. A J-M plant employing 300 was reportedly producing "5 or 6 cases annually that the physician believes show early changes due to asbestos."[17]

In 1950 J-M chief physician Dr. Kenneth W. Smith gave superiors a report showing that of 708 workers he studied, only 4 had "essentially normal and healthy lungs" and 534 had "fibrosis extending beyond the lung roots," "advanced fibrosis," or "early asbestosis."[18] Concerning the more serious cases, he wrote,

> The fibrosis of this disease is irreversible and permanent so that eventually compensation will be paid to each of these men but as long as the man is not disabled it is felt that he should not be told of his condition so that he can live and work in peace and the company can benefit from his many years of experience.[19]

Dr. Smith later said he tried to convince senior J-M managers to put caution labels on the bags of asbestos in 1953. In a 1976 deposition, he characterized their response: "We recognize the potential hazard that you mentioned [and] the suggested use of a caution label. We will discuss it among ourselves and make a decision." Asked why he was overruled, Smith said, "Application of a caution label identifying a product as hazardous would cut out sales."[20]

By 1952 John A. McKinney, Fred L. Pundsack, Chester E. Shepperly, Monroe Harris, and Chester J. Sulewski had all joined the company in various capacities. They would be the firm's top five officers as it prepared for bankruptcy 30 years later.

DISASSOCIATE THIS RELATIONSHIP

In 1956 the Board of Governors of the Asbestos Textile Institute (made up of J-M and other asbestos companies) met to discuss the increasing publicity about asbestos and cancer and agreed that "Every effort should be made to disassociate this relationship until such a time that there is sufficient and authoritative information to substantiate such to be a fact."

The next year, the Asbestos Textile Institute rejected a proposal by the Industrial Health Foundation that asbestos companies fund a study on asbestos and cancer. Institute minutes reported, "There is a feeling among certain members that such an investigation would stir up a hornet's nest and put the whole industry under suspicion."[21]

NOT UNTIL 1964 WAS IT KNOWN

An increasing number of articles connecting asbestos with various diseases appeared in medical journals over the next few years. And in 1963 Dr. I. J. Selikoff, of Mt. Sinai Medical Center in New York, presented his study of asbestos insulation workers to the American Medical Association. Like the earlier research, the Selikoff study implicated asbestos in many thousands of deaths and injuries. Selikoff would soon estimate that at least 100,000 more Americans would die of asbestos diseases before the year 2000.

In later congressional testimony, Selikoff told of a group of 632 insulation workers he had followed from 1942 through 1962.

> During these years, 27 men have died of asbestosis, of a total of 367 deaths. . . . [In addition,] while we would have expected approximately six or seven deaths due to lung cancer among these men, there were 45. While we would have expected nine or ten cancers of the stomach or colon, there were 29. . . . Incidentally, since 1963 the figures have been, if anything, even worse. While we would have expected approximately 50 of the remainder of these men to have died in the past five years, there have been 113 deaths. And while we would have expected 3 to have died of cancer of the lungs or pleura, 28 have died of this disease.[22]

J-M officials claimed Selikoff's 1964 report was their first knowledge of the danger, a position they would consistently maintain over the next two decades. For example, on August 27, 1982, McKinney would write,

> Here's the bottom line. Not until 1964 was it known that excessive exposure to asbestos fiber released from asbestos-containing insulation products can sometimes cause certain lung diseases.[23]

And the *1982 Annual Report and Form 10-K* would state, "The company has maintained that there was no basis for product warnings or hazard controls until the results of scientific studies linking pulmonary disease in asbestos insulation workers with asbestos exposure were made public in 1964."[24]

In 1964 J-M placed its first caution labels on certain asbestos products. The labels read, "Inhalation of asbestos in excessive quantities over long periods of time may be harmful" and suggested that users avoid breathing the dust and that they wear masks if "adequate ventilation control is not possible." The company's most profitable product, bags of asbestos fiber for distribution to other manufacturers and insulators throughout the world, would not be caution-labeled for another five years.

Use of asbestos in the United States had risen from around 200,000 metric tons a year in the 1930s to about 700,000 tons during the 1950s, 1960s, and early 1970s. Then it dropped sharply, to just over 100,000, in the 1980s.[25] Worldwide, production plateaued at about 4.6 million metric tons a year in the mid 1970s. This would drop only a little in the 1980s, as increased shipments to developing countries offset declining usage elsewhere.[26] Canada, the world's dominant marketer of asbestos in the 1980s and early 1990s, sold an estimated 42% of its output to Asia in 1988, up from just 16% in 1979. Other leading producers were Russia, Zimbabwe, and Brazil.[27]

THE SMOKING GUN

Always lucrative, the asbestos trade became even more so as the industry came under suspicion during the 1960s and 1970s. For example, sales of the raw fiber alone produced 41% of J-M's operating profit in 1976, though it accounted for just 12% of revenues. By that time, J-M had accumulated about $2.8 billion (1991 dollars) in assets and $1.6 billion in book value net worth, practically all from asbestos and asbestos products.[28]

Like R.J. Reynolds and American Tobacco, J-M had already begun to invest its wealth in "clean" businesses—first fiberglass, then a variety of unrelated enterprises. A prestigious new slate of directors had taken over in the late 1960s. Among them were college deans at Princeton and New York Universities, the chief executive of Ideal Basic Industries and former three-time governor of Colorado, the head of Phelps-Dodge Corporation, and the top managers of three other firms.

The directors installed psychologist-consultant Richard Goodwin as president in 1970. Goodwin promised to diversify the company and change its image. He moved J-M headquarters from its old Madison Avenue brick building to a new, modern structure in the Denver countryside and arranged 20 or more small, diverse acquisitions. But he would not have time to finish his program.

In 1972 J-M and its codefendants lost their first big A-H case, to Clarence Borel, a Texas asbestos victim. According to a later news report, this loss "triggered the greatest avalanche of toxic tort litigation in the history of American jurisprudence."[29] A short, steep recession in 1974–1975 cut J-M profits in half. It made matters worse when, in 1976, former J-M medical director Smith told of his earlier knowledge and research on asbestos and health. Later that year, the directors fired Goodwin and replaced him with long-time J-M lawyer John A. McKinney. A later chief executive would claim Goodwin had been a womanizer and an alcoholic,[30] but Goodwin would deny that and say he was not given a reason for his firing.[31]

Then, in April 1977, A-H attorneys found what they called J-M's "smoking gun," the "Raybestos-Manhattan Correspondence." Included were many letters and memoranda among Manville officials and other asbestos industry executives. Most were written during the 1930s. A South Carolina judge reviewed the material and wrote,

> The Raybestos-Manhattan Correspondence very arguably shows a pattern of denial of disease and attempts at suppression of information which is highly probative [and] reflects a conscious effort by the industry in the 1930s to downplay, or arguably suppress, the dissemination of information to employees and the public.[32]

By April 1978, J-M would be defendant in 623 A-H lawsuits asking as much as $4 million for each plaintiff[33]—but the annual report did not mention the lawsuits.

A liberal new bankruptcy code, which would provide J-M a way out, would be passed by Congress that October. Chapter 11 of the law so favored big debtors that public-company assets in bankruptcy would soon increase more than tenfold.[34] Exhibit 12.11 describes bankruptcy reorganization under the new law.

| **EXHIBIT 12.11** | **Chapter 11 Bankruptcy Reorganization** |

A voluntary Chapter 11 petition acts as an order to stay all legal and administrative proceedings against the debtor, which becomes Debtor in Possession (DIP). Neither good faith nor insolvency is required. Unless removed for cause, the DIP may pursue the ordinary course of business and has the powers and duties of a trustee. Except as modified by the court, the stay remains in effect throughout the proceeding. Often, a secured creditor requests the stay be lifted with respect to its claim. The DIP can usually prevent this by showing the liened asset is needed and providing "adequate protection" of the secured claim.

Reorganization is accomplished through implementation of a written plan. At first, only the DIP may file a plan. But if a plan is not submitted within 120 days and accepted in 180 days, any party in interest may file one. Both time limits may be extended or shortened for cause. A committee is appointed to represent unsecured creditors. A stockholders committee and other representatives may also be appointed.

A confirmed plan binds all parties. Here are the main requirements for confirmation:
(1) The plan must be proposed in good faith and disclose "adequate information" (done by means of a written "disclosure statement"). (2) Each holder of a claim or interest who has not accepted the plan must receive at least as much value, as of the plan's effective date, as Chapter 7 liquidation on that date would provide. (3) Each class of claims or interests that is "impaired" under the plan must have "accepted" the plan unless the judge rules the plan "does not discriminate unfairly and is fair and equitable with respect to the class." The DIP, or the trustee if one is assigned, sorts claims and interests into classes, usually when a plan and disclosure statement are filed. A class of claims or interests is unimpaired if reinstated

and the holders compensated for damages or if paid in cash. Acceptance of a plan by a creditor class requires approval by over half the claims representing at least two-thirds in amount of allowed claims in the class that are voted. For classes of interests, such as shareholders, the requirement is two-thirds in amount of interests that are voted. Imposition of a plan on a class of impaired claimants that has not accepted it is called "cramdown" and is allowed only if at least one class of claimants (equity is an "interest," not a "claim") has accepted the plan. (4) Confirmation must not be deemed likely to be followed by the need for further financial reorganization or liquidation.

Executory contracts, except financial accommodations (such as agreements by banks to extend additional borrowing), may be assigned, assumed, or rejected by the debtor at any time before plan confirmation—or in an approved plan. "Executory" means neither party has completed its legal obligations under the contract. The rejection of executory contracts may create allowable claims, which are usually treated as prefiling, unsecured claims. While collective bargaining agreements are executory contracts, Code Section 1113 sets special requirements for their assumption or rejection.

In 1984 the U.S. Supreme Court ruled, "The *fundamental* purpose of reorganization is to prevent the debtor from going into liquidation, with an attendant loss of jobs and possible misuse of economic resources" (*NLRB* v. *Bildisco & Bildisco,* 108 S Ct 1188, 1984). Ideally, the company will remain viable and will propose to pay its creditors more than they could get through liquidation. The first claim to payment goes to administrative costs of the proceeding and any post-filing obligations, especially any that are assigned "superpriority" status by the judge. It is generally believed that any remaining value should be distributed to the claimant and interest groups in order of their prebankruptcy entitlements: (1) secured debt (up to the value of respective collateral as of the effective date of the plan), (2) unsecured debt (including nominally secured debt above the value of respective collateral), and (3) equity interests in order of preference (for example, preferred, then common). Claimants within each group, again ideally, share pro rata according to the value of their respective claims. The value may be distributed as cash, securities, or other real or personal property. Negotiation among stakeholders and court intervention often result in departures from such an "ideal" distribution. In general, claims not provided for in the plan or the order confirming it are discharged. Unlike debt forgiveness, the discharge of debts in bankruptcy does not create income.

AGGRESSIVE DEFENSE AND A SUBSTANTIAL ACQUISITION

Upon taking office, McKinney had vowed "aggressive defense" of the A-H lawsuits and a "substantial acquisition." J-M purchased Olinkraft Corporation in late 1978. The price was $595 million ($1.2 billion in 1991 dollars), over twice recent market value. But only half was to be cash; the remainder was debt-like preferred stock, required to be repurchased at par starting in 1987. The repurchase requirement was canceled by the bankruptcy filing in 1982. W. Thomas Stephens, who would later become Manville chief executive, was Olinkraft's chief financial officer at the time and was an early advocate of the sale. Olinkraft's main assets were several paper mills and 600,000 acres of prime timberland, with many trees over 50 years old. J-M soon doubled the division's plywood capacity and adopted a 32-year life for the tree farms, enhancing the subsidiary's cash-producing capability.

J-M changed its name to Manville Corporation in 1981 and reorganized itself, segregating its various businesses in separate divisions. Also that year, juries began awarding Manville A-H claimants punitive damages, over $1 million each in some cases. Actually, J-M paid few A-H claims—such expenses never amounted to even half a percent of sales—but the operating businesses were in trouble. In real terms, the company's sales fell 20% from 1978 to 1982 and profits disappeared. Manville's auditor, Coopers and Lybrand, qualified its opinion on the company's 1980 and 1981 annual reports.[35] Of course, Standard & Poor's and Moody's downgraded Manville debt.[36]

Manville's insurers stopped paying for most of the asbestos claims by 1981[37] and generally could not pay punitive damages anyway. The firm's insurers of the 1970s and 1980s, when many asbestos-health problems appeared, argued that the claims should be paid by insurers from decades earlier, when most of the claimants were exposed. The insurers from the earlier period took the reverse position. This "manifestations versus exposure" debate was used by the insurers as a rationale for refusing to pay claims.[38]

Recording the A-H liabilities would justify a bankruptcy filing, but accounting rules required that they be reasonably estimable to be recorded. A committee of directors assessed the liabilities with the help of consultants. In mid-1982, the committee reported that the A-H liabilities would total "at least $1.9 billion." Selikoff's associates said that was "a serious underestimate." The directors suggested as much, by saying the estimate involved "conservative assumptions favorable to Manville."[39] By mid-August 1982, Manville's stock dropped below $8, less than one-fourth its 1977 high.

IN FULL READINESS FOR CHAPTER 11

There were five main reasons to consider the company well prepared for bankruptcy.[40] First, assets were dispersed in separately incorporated divisions. The divisions could file joint or separate petitions and reorganization plans.

Second, a large part of Manville (the former Olinkraft) had never been in the asbestos business. And the company had other nonasbestos divisions, such as fiberglass. This would be a public relations advantage, at least.

Third, management was cohesive: tough, long-tenured, rich with lawyers, and cohesive in the face of attacks from without. The company had opposed asbestos claims since the 1920s and had a reputation for effectiveness in court. Eight of the eleven prefiling directors had been with the firm since the fifties and sixties. They were distinguished in business, government, and academe. McKinney and four others were attorneys. Each of the top five officers in 1982 had at least thirty years' tenure. Only one, President Fred Pundsack, objected to the forthcoming Chapter 11 filing, and he resigned. The A-H claims totaled 20,000 by then, and three new ones were being filed per business hour.[41]

Fourth, the firm had competent counsel, resolute leadership, and access to the nation's preeminent pro-debtor bankruptcy court. McKinney retained top bankruptcy lawyer Michael Crames as well as New York law firm Davis Polk Wardwell and investment banker Morgan Stanley and Company. The latter two firms had been Manville allies since the thirties. McKinney insisted on one fundamental principle: the reorganized Manville must not have asbestos liabilities. McKinney later wrote that his resistance to compromise was considered stubbornness, adding, "In this context, I am proud to be called stubborn."[42] The company met requirements for filing in the Southern District of New York, where Burton R. Lifland was chief bankruptcy judge. Lifland administered more big cases than any other bankruptcy judge and was known for favoring debtors.[43]

Finally, the firm's debt was practically all unsecured, and the debt-like preferred stock would not have to be repurchased, ensuring that the firm would have plenty of cash and borrowing capacity. McKinney would soon boast of "nearly $2 billion in unencumbered assets." The company's "cash portfolio" would increase to $760 million during bankruptcy. And cash would exceed $300 million even after implementation of the reorganization plan.[44]

THE BANKRUPTCY REORGANIZATION

On the evening of August 25, 1982, the directors met in New York and were briefed on bankruptcy. A Chapter 11 petition had been prepared and was filed the next day. The required committee of unsecured creditors was formed. The usual, but optional, committee was set up for shareholders. A committee of 19 contingent-fee attorneys and one victim represented present A-H claimants. New York lawyer Leon Silverman was appointed to represent future claimants.

Certain shareholders would demand a special meeting, at which they might elect new directors. In response, Lifland would disband the shareholders committee and eject shareholders from the proceedings.

Leading A-H attorney Ronald Motley spoke of criminal prosecution of the company or its executives. Other A-H attorneys called for liquidation, which Manville later said would yield $2–$2.4 billion ($2.8–$3.4 billion in 1991 dollars).[45] The directors and officers consistently opposed liquidation.

Shortly after the filing, many "property damage" (PD) claims—soon totaling $90 billion—poured in. These were mostly for asbestos removal and abatement in buildings. McKinney successor W. Thomas Stephens later said the PD claims had been his main reason for opposing liquidation.[46] But a trust set up to pay them would run out of money and soon cease operating. Lifland would rationalize the limited funding for PD claims as compared to A-H claims: "Blood and bones are more important than bricks and mortar."

The largest division, Manville Forest Products Corporation (MFP, formerly Olinkraft), emerged from Chapter 11 March 26, 1984. MFP paid its commercial debt but was ordered immune from asbestos claims.[47] Various other units, notably the main asbestos fiber subsidiaries and certain asbestos-cement pipe operations, were sold that year, also shielded from asbestos liabilities.[48]

A reorganization plan for the remaining divisions was filed in 1986. It promised commercial creditors full payment with 12% interest. A trust was to be set up to pay A-H claims, and Lifland issued an injunction that shielded from asbestos claims Manville; its past, present, and future managers and directors; its insurers; and even its codefendants. Morgan Stanley affirmed that Manville's plan was feasible but added elsewhere in its report, "No representations can be made with respect to the accuracy of the projections. . . . Morgan Stanley did not independently verify the information considered in its reviews." To explain its plan to the A-H claimants, Manville distributed 100,000 copies of its 550-page "Information Packet." Accompanying the packet were brief, glossy "Vote yes" fliers provided by the A-H committee and emphasizing its members' trustworthiness. Later the A-H attorneys voted claimant proxies overwhelmingly for the plan. Lifland confirmed the plan just before Christmas 1986. It survived two appeals and became effective two years later.

RESULTS OF REORGANIZATION FOR STAKEHOLDERS

The plan promised the A-H trust a "$1.65 billion bond." That number was the sum of 44 semiannual payments that would start six years later. Discounted at 16%, the 44 bond payments were worth just over $200 million. In 1987 Stephens would estimate the value of the bond at $350 million.[49]

The trust was to own 50% of Manville's common stock. Manville would vote these shares until November 1992, and the stock could not be traded until a year later.[50] The trust would also get 7.2 million preferred shares convertible to bring common stock ownership to 80%. A description of the stock would say it "does not pay a dividend; has no maturity or mandatory sinking fund; has restrictions on convertibility, transferability, and voting rights; is nonredeemable by Manville; and has a liquidation preference of $89 per share."[51]

Bankruptcy's practical results for Manville's main stakeholders were becoming clear by 1992.

BENEFITS FOR THE MANAGERS AND DIRECTORS

The third generation of Manville executives and directors retired in the mid-1980s, some with bonuses in addition to their pensions.[52] For example, McKinney left in 1986 with $1.3 million in severance pay. His annual cash compensation had gone from $408,750 in 1982 to $638,005 in 1985, his last full year of employment. And legal chief G. Earl Parker got $1.2 million after he stepped down. McKinney was replaced by his protégé W. Thomas Stephens, and Parker by his, Richard B. Von Wald.

Other managers arranged to buy company assets. A group headed by the chief of J-M Canada, which owned the world's largest asbestos mine, bought that division in 1983.[53] All but a small, borrowed downpayment was to be paid "out of 85.5% of available future cash flows."[54] Payment took less than four years, prompting division president Peter Kyle to remark, "As far as leveraged buyouts go, I don't think there are any as good as this one."[55] John Hulce, Manville president for a short while in 1986, retired and paid $7 million for Manville plants with annual sales of $17.5 million.[56]

Staying behind with the fourth-generation managers was long-time board chairman and Stephens mentor George C. Dillon. Dillon signed a consulting agreement with Manville and stepped down to act as director and chairman of the executive committee. He later compared Manville to such companies as Johnson & Johnson, whose handling of the Tylenol scare made it the nation's most respected firm; to Union Carbide, whose chief executive was arrested when he rushed to India after a disastrous gas leak at a subsidiary's plant there; and to Perrier, which discovered a trace of benzene in its mineral water and soon corrected the problem. Dillon ended by quoting his "granddaddy," who said, "If you ain't got a choice, be brave."[57]

Stephens surrounded himself with loaves and fishes and posed as Jesus Christ for the cover of *Corporate Finance*. The article inside expressed wonder at Stephens' "miracle."[58] *Fortune* featured him as one of 1988's "25 most fascinating business people" and proclaimed the company "Free at Last." And chief financial officer John Roach appeared under the caption "Redeeming Manville" on the cover of *CFO*. Inside, a recurrent theme: "Manville is out to redress past wrongs— by growing big enough to repay its victims."

The 15 executive officers' cash pay went to an average $359,826 in 1990— Stephens' went from $330,000 in 1985 to $866,583 in 1990. Manville sorted its assets into divisions named "Riverwood International" (paperboard and packaging products, formerly Forest Products—see Exhibit 12.8) and "Schuller International" (engineered products and building products—see Exhibit 12.8). The consolidated company would have $307 million in "deferred tax assets" (see Exhibit 12.9), created by nuances of the Bankruptcy Code and a large special charge in 1988.

The managers were confident that they would be free of the A-H trust before November 1992, when it could vote its shares. Stephens remarked, "We know the change in ownership is going to happen. What we've tried to do is have the maximum flexibility, in case the market puts more value on the pieces than the whole."[59] "Change of ownership" was interpreted to mean a sale of Manville stock or of one or both divisions by the A-H trust.

But a management-led buyout was an obvious possibility. Stephens himself had strong connections with Riverwood. The division's main plant was in his home town of West Monroe, Louisiana, where he had been Olinkraft's chief financial officer before the 1978 acquisition. Plans were made in April 1992 to restructure Riverwood and for it to buy Macon Kraft, Inc. for $210 to $220 million, which was to include the assumption of $175 million in debt. Macon Kraft had an annual capacity of 525,000 tons of corrugated paperboard. Stephens said, "If the transaction is successfully completed later this year [1992], we would expect to make substantial investments to equip the Macon mill to produce our proprietary coated boxboard grades of paperboard." Stephens expected to fund the project through a "primary public offering of up to 20% of Riverwood International's common stock and a concurrent offering of long-term debt."[60] This would further shield Riverwood from possible A-H trust control. At the time, Manville owned all the stock of Riverwood, and the trust was to gain control of Manville, and therefore

Riverwood, in November 1992—if it resisted pressures to sell its interest. After the restructuring, outsiders were expected to own 18% of Riverwood.

BENEFITS FOR UNSECURED CREDITORS AND INSURERS

The unsecured commercial (as opposed to asbestos-related) creditors received full value, with 12% interest. The secured debt was variously paid or reinstated. And Manville's insurers settled billions in contingent liabilities by contributing about $695 million for the A-H trust.

RESULTS FOR THE ASBESTOS VICTIMS

The asbestos claimants were often painted as opportunists—even charlatans—represented by "ambulance-chasing lawyers." Several thousands of the 1982 claimants died before 1989, when the A-H trust made its first payments. Many surviving plaintiffs were old and sick. Smoking had multiplied the risk of asbestos disease for many. And few knew whom to blame, because most had been exposed to asbestos from several companies.

They had generally discovered their diseases after years of declining health. Most had fared poorly in state courts. Manville had usually been able to delay A-H lawsuits if not to win them. The company had employed top law firms and had certain valid defenses. Therefore, few large judgments against the company had come down, and fewer yet had been paid.

Finding the Raybestos-Manhattan papers had promised to change that. But it had taken A-H attorneys several years to get them before juries. The first big awards remained unpaid when Manville filed its bankruptcy petition—which McKinney said "preserved the position of the victims as equal creditors (virtually all unsecured) in the event of a financial calamity."[61] And prefiling A-H claimants were soon joined in line by thousands of new ones. Many of these had been recruited by Manville, which in 1986 advertised nationally for potential claimants. The A-H committee assisted with the advertising program. Whatever the committee's purposes, its members thus obtained thousands of potential new clients—and as many proxies, which would be voted for Manville's plan.

Representatives of both present and future victims appear to have been preempted in the bankruptcy court. In the five months ending January 1984, the A-H committee tried to dismiss the bankruptcy,[62] rejected Manville's plan,[63] requested that management be replaced with a trustee,[64] and asked the court to cut executive pay.[65] But in November 1983, Manville pronounced the contingency-fee contracts "completely unconscionable."[66] And in January 1984, a hearing was set on its motion to void them.[67] In March 1984, the A-H Committee withdrew its motion to cut management salaries.[68] And Manville stopped questioning the fees. For the ensuing two years, the committee filed no action in opposition to management.[69] In fact, the committee became a management ally, providing glossy brochures to promote the company's plan.[70] In defense of his committee, chairman Ronald Motley wrote, "[The] intimation that there is some relationship between Manville's withdrawal of its objection to contingency fees [and] the A-H Committee's not opposing certain management decisions is both false and insulting."[71] As to future claimants, their representative, Leon Silverman, got $2.3 million and a commendation from Lifland for helping design the plan, which would essentially disenfranchise future victims.

The A-H trust spent millions on salaries, offices, and expert help. Lifland had appointed the executive director of the U.S. Trial Lawyers Association, Marianna S. Smith, to head the trust at $250,000 a year. She hired three assistants, at salaries above $150,000 each. The six lifetime-tenured trustees received $30,000 each per year, plus expenses, and plus $1,000 a day for meetings. The trustees together got $440,555 plus expenses before any A-H claim was paid,[72] and Smith got at least $500,000. In addition to directors' and officers' insurance, $30 million of trust funds was set aside to indemnify the trustees and others. The trust leased 32,038 square feet of Washington, D.C., office space for $26.50 annually per square foot. During 1990 and 1991, trust expenses would average $3.5 million a month—about 50% more than would be paid to A-H claimants in those years.[73]

The trust ran short of money three months after paying its first claim. Silverman remarked, "This recent flurry of publicity should not lead to disquiet. All of these problems were anticipated in the original plan and should not result in diminution of payments to claimants."[74] And Smith told a reporter, "Based on current projections over the life of the trust, there will be enough money to pay all the claimants, although there will be temporary cash shortfalls."[75]

By the end of 1991, the trust had received over $900 million. It had dispensed $696 million for 15,864 A-H claims, an average $43,902 each. A-H attorneys presumably got a third ($232 million) plus estimated expenses of $140 million. This left perhaps $325 million for claimants, an average of $20,487 each for the one in ten who got paid. "Settled" but unpaid claims totaled $523 million—to be paid by the year 2020. Over 160,000 claims were waiting to be processed.[76] And prospective new claimants had been told they might expect their first payment 23 years after filing a claim.[77]

By March 1992, the A-H trust was in chaos. The directors' and officers' insurance had not been renewed. Smith and all but one trustee had resigned.[78] New trustees were hired in early 1992, but Smith's position remained vacant. Lifland's superior, district judge Jack B. Weinstein, had ordered claims processing suspended until the existing "first-come, first-served" waiting line could be rearranged and payments cut further. Under the new system, the "most urgent" claims would be paid first. Initial payments would be 12% of *settlement* value, and payments could never total more than 45 percent of that amount. The new chief trustee said, "That could create a lot of heat and fire. But I'd rather it come to the surface now."[79]

PREPARING FOR THE 1992 ANNUAL MEETING

At the 1991 annual meeting, Stephens had said,

> The situation with the Trust has been stabilized and while our businesses are operating in a recessionary environment, the situation is under prudent control. . . . Manville is a

company where 18,000 skilled and hard-working people have committed themselves to making your company a special place to invest their careers as well as your money.

At the 1992 meeting, scheduled for June 5, he was expected to map the company's corporate strategies for the next year and to set forth, with finality, the firm's attitude toward the asbestos claims.

NOTES

1. David Ozonoff, "Failed Warnings: Asbestos-Related Disease and Industrial Medicine." In Ronald Bayer, ed., *The Health and Safety of Workers: Case Studies in the Politics of Professional Responsibility* (Oxford: Oxford University Press, 1988), p. 151.

2. Manville Personal Injury Settlement Trust, "Financial Statements and Report of Manville Personal Injury Settlement Trust for the Period Ended December 31, 1991," *Stockholders & Creditors News Re. Johns-Manville Corp., et al.*, March 11, 1992, pp. 12,614–12,625.

3. "Your Check Is Not in the Mail." *Time,* September 17, 1990, p. 65.

4. Author's calculation based on conversations with Dr. Irving J. Selikoff, of Mt. Sinai Medical Center in New York, and standard mortality tables.

5. Quoted in Ozonoff, pp. 155–156.

6. Quoted in Ozonoff, p. 157.

7. Ozonoff, pp. 155 and 167.

8. Vandiver Brown to A.J. Lanza, December 10, 1934.

9. Ozonoff, p. 167.

10. Vandiver Brown to A.J. Lanza, December 21, 1934.

11. George S. Hobart to Vandiver Brown, December 15, 1934.

12. Manville Corporation. "Beleaguered by Asbestos Lawsuits Manville Files for Reorganization." News release, August 27, 1982.

13. Vandiver Brown to S. Simpson, October 3, 1935.

14. Anne Rossiter to Sumner Simpson, September 25, 1935.

15. Vandiver Brown to LeRoy U. Gardner, November 20, 1936.

16. LeRoy U. Gardner, M.D. "Interim Report on Experimental Asbestosis at the Saranac Laboratory." Enclosure to letter from Vandiver Brown to Sumner Simpson, December 26, 1939.

17. W.C.L. Henderson. "Industrial Hygiene Foundation of America, Inc.: Report of Preliminary Dust Investigation for Asbestos Textile Institute." June 18, 1947, pp. 2 and 15.

18. Kenneth W. Smith. "Industrial Hygiene—Survey of Men in Dusty Areas." Enclosure to memorandum marked "*Confidential*" from A. R. Fisher (J-M president) to Vandiver Brown, February 3, 1949, p. 2.

19. *Ibid.,* p. 3.

20. Dr. Kenneth W. Smith, discovery deposition, Louisville Trust Company, Administrator of the estate of William Virgil Sampson, v. Johns-Manville Corporation, File no. 164-122, (Court of Common Pleas, Jefferson County, Kentucky, April 21, 1976).

21. David A. Shaw. "Memorandum in Opposition to Motions for Summary Judgment Filed by the Wellington Defendants and Defendant Raymark Industries." Reprinted in *Asbestos Litigation Reporter,* November 18, 1988, p. 18,051.

22. Irving J. Selikoff, testimony before House of Representatives, Select Committee on Labor, Committee on Education and Labor, U.S. Congress, March 7, 1968.

23. Manville Corporation. "Beleaguered by Asbestos Lawsuits, Manville Files for Reorganization." News release, August 27, 1982.

24. Manville Corporation, *1982 Annual Report and Form 10-K,* December 31, 1982, p. 49.

25. Barry I. Castleman. *Asbestos: Medical and Legal Aspects.* 3rd Ed. Englewood Cliffs, N.J.: Prentice-Hall, 1990, p. 658.

26. *Ibid.*

27. Alan Freeman. "Canadian Asbestos Mining Enjoys a Modest Recovery." *Wall Street Journal,* March 10, 1989, p. B2.

28. Conversion to 1991 dollars, here and elsewhere, employs the Consumer Price Index for All Urban Consumers (CPI-U), not seasonally adjusted, as reported in Ibbotson Associates, *Stocks, Bonds, Bills, and Inflation: 1992 Yearbook* (Chicago: Ibbotson Associates, 1992), especially p. 84.

29. "Arkansas Plane Crash Kills Marlin Thompson, Robin Steele, Four Others." *Asbestos Litigation Reporter,* December 2, 1988, pp. 18,086–18,087.

30. W. Thomas Stephens, conversation with author, October 16, 1987.

31. Richard Goodwin, conversation with author, January 21, 1988.

32. Amended Order (Survival and Wrongful Death Actions), Bennie M. Barnett, Administrator, for Gordon Luther Barnett, deceased, v. Owens-Corning Fiberglass Corp., et al., (Court of Common Pleas, Greenville County, South Carolina, August 23, 1978), pp. 10 and 5.

33. Manville Corporation, *Form 10K,* December 31, 1977, pp. 26–27.

34. Christopher McHugh, ed. *The 1992 Bankruptcy Yearbook and Almanac.* Boston: New Generation Research, 1992, p. 40.

35. Manville Corporation, *1980 Annual Report,* p. 21, and *1981 Annual Report,* p. 15.

36. See, for example, "Manville Ratings Cut by Standard and Poor's." *Wall Street Journal,* June 11, 1982, p. 36.

37. Manville Corporation, *U. S. Securities and Exchange Commission Form 10-Q,* June 30, 1982, II-11 through II-14.

38. An argument for the conspiracy theory is found in David A. Shaw, "Memorandum in Opposition to Motions for Summary Judgment Filed by the Wellington Defendants and Defendant Raymark Industries." Reprinted in *Asbestos Litigation Reporter,* November 18, 1988, pp. 18,048–18,053.

39. Manville Corporation, *1982 Annual Report and Form 10-K,* p. 9.

40. See Arthur Sharplin, "Chapter 11: A Machiavellian Analysis." In Samuel M. Natale and John B. Wilson, eds., *The Ethical Contexts for Business Conflicts.* Lanham, Md.: University Press of America, 1989, pp. 23–28.

41. G. Earl Parker. "The Manville Decision," paper presented at the symposium "Bankruptcy Proceedings— The Effect on Product Liability," conducted by Andrews Publications, Inc., Miami, March 1983, p. 3.

42. John A. McKinney to editor, *Business Month,* February 1989, p. 5.

43. See, for example, Beth Lubove, "A Bankrupt's Best Friend," *Forbes,* April 1, 1991, pp. 99–102.

44. John D.C. Roach. "Reshaping Corporate America: Chapter 11 Forced Manville to Reexamine the Way It Did Business." *Management Accounting,* March 1990, p. 22.

45. Manville Corporation, *First Amended Disclosure Statement, Second Amended and Restated Plan of Reorganization, and Related Documents,* August 22, 1986, p. M-399.

46. Conversation with author, October 1987.

47. Manville Corporation, *1983 Annual Report and Form 10K,* p. 13.

48. *Ibid.,* p. 15.

49. Speech at National Conference on Business Ethics, October 1987.

50. A-H trust, *1991 Annual Report.*

51. *Ibid.*

52. A sympathetic story of several of the departing executives is told in Greg Barman, "Life after Manville," *Colorado Business Magazine,* November 1989, pp. 15–23.

53. "Hearing on Sale of J-M Canada Scheduled for August 30," *Stockholders and Creditors News Service,* August 15, 1983, p. 1,315.

54. *Ibid.*

55. Alan Freeman. "Canadian Asbestos Mining Enjoys a Modest Recovery." *The Wall Street Journal,* March 10, 1989, p. B2.

56. "3 Manville Manufacturing Plants Sold to Former President Hulce." *The Denver Post,* January 5, 1988, p. 2C; and "Manville Sells Three Plants for $7 Million," *Stockholders and Creditors News Service,* January 11, 1988, 7, pp. 261–262.

57. George C. Dillon. "Does It Pay To Do the Right Thing? Not Necessarily. But for Manville Corporation, That's the Wrong Question to Ask." *Across the Board,* July 1991, pp. 15–17.

58. Stephen W. Quickel. "Miracle at Manville: How Tom Stephens Raised the Bread to Overcome Bankruptcy," *Corporate Finance,* November 1987. (No page numbers; reprint of article provided by Manville Corporation). Jesus's miracle of the loaves and fishes is described in Matthew 14:15–21.

59. Marj Charlier. "For Manville, a Sale or Breakup Appears Imminent." *Wall Street Journal,* March 3, 1992, p. B4.

60. See Marj Charlier, "Manville's Rating on Debt and Stock Is Cut By Moody's," *Wall Street Journal,* April 13, 1992, p. C15; and W. Thomas Stephens, letter to shareholders, Manville Corporation, *MvL* (1992 Summary Annual Report Issue), pp. 1–4.

61. John A. McKinney to Arthur Sharplin, May 11, 1987.

62. "Committee of Asbestos-Related Litigants Again Asks Bankruptcy Court to Dismiss Johns-Manville Bankruptcy," *Asbestos Litigation Reporter.* September 23, 1983, p. 7,148.

63. "Asbestos Claimants Committee Rejects Plan," *Asbestos Litigation Reporter,* November 25, 1983, p. 7,416.

64. "Asbestos-Related Litigants Move to Have Bankruptcy Court Appoint Trustee." *Asbestos Litigation Reporter,* January 6, 1984, p. 7,625.

65. "Committee of Asbestos-Related Litigants and/or Creditors Withdraws Its Motion to Reduce Salaries of Manville Officers." *Asbestos Litigation Reporter,* March 16, 1984, p. 7,999.

66. "Johns-Manville Asks Court to Void Asbestos-Claimants Attorney Fees." *Asbestos Litigation Reporter,* November 25, 1983, p. 7,411. In general, such contracts give attorneys a third of gross receipts. The attorneys' expenses are reimbursed out of the other two-thirds, with the remainder going to clients.

67. "Hearing Set on Replacement for Plaintiff Contingency Fee Arrangements." *Asbestos Litigation Reporter,* February 3, 1984, p. 7,785. Lifland later made it clear that he would have cut the fees. For example, see "Judge Lifland Refuses to Stop Trust Payments to Claimants," *Stockholders and Creditors News Re. Johns-Manville Corp., et al.,* May 8, 1989, p. 8,799, which reports that Lifland complained that the victims were not told how to contest the fees.

68. "Committee of Asbestos-Related Litigants and/or Creditors Withdraws Its Motion to Reduce Salaries of Manville Officers." *Asbestos Litigation Reporter,* March 16, 1984, p. 7,999.

69. "In re Johns-Manville Corp." *Asbestos Litigation Reporter: Eight-Year Cumulative Index, February 1979–July 1987,* August 1987, pp. 37–38.

70. The Committee of Asbestos-Related Litigants and/or Creditors Representing Asbestos-Health Claimants of Manville Corporation. "Questions and Answers on Asbestos-Health Claims and the Manville Reorganization Plan" and "A Very Important Message for People With Asbestos-Related Diseases." Undated, distributed in August–October 1986.

71. Ronald L. Motley to Arthur Sharplin, April 1, 1988.

72. "Manville Personal Injury Settlement Trust Financial Statements." *Stockholders and Creditors News Re. Johns-Manville, et al.,* March 6, 1989, pp. 8,639–8,655.

73. A-H trust annual report for 1991. Claims payments would average $4.7 million a month, of which perhaps $2.2 million a month would go to claimants. Again, the calculations assume standard contingency fees and expenses totaling 20% of gross payments.

74. Stacy Adler. "Payouts Do Not Imperil Manville Trust: Director." *Business Insurance,* February 13, 1989, p. 2.

75. *Ibid.*

76. *Ibid.*

77. "Your Check Is Not in the Mail." *Time,* September 17, 1990, p. 65.

78. "Marianna S. Smith Resigns as Executive Director of Trust." *Stockholders and Creditors News Re. Johns-Manville Corp., et al,"* December 9, 1991, p. 12,279. Smith said she was resigning because the directors' and officers' insurance was not being renewed.

79. "Manville Trust to Hold Regional Meetings on Claims Process." *Stockholders & Creditors News Re. Johns-Manville Corp., et al.,* March 25, 1992, p. 12,638.

CASE 13 The Kellogg Company

Robert J. Mockler ▪ Larry Boone ▪ Richard Gordon ▪ Valerie Donnelly

In the late 1800s, Dr. W. K. Kellogg, while operating a sanitarium in Battle Creek, Michigan, invented wheat and corn flakes to add variety, taste, and nutrition to his patients' diets. He believed that most health problems were caused by too much drinking and excessive consumption of meat and harmful condiments. At first, his corn flakes were made from the whole kernel and found limited acceptance. Kellogg discovered that a much tastier flake could be produced by adding malt flavoring and by using only the heart of the corn. In 1902, Kellogg decided to form a company dedicated to the production of his food products, and in 1906, Kellogg officially came into being, quickly establishing a reputation for excellence that still prevails.

In the first quarter of 1991, although it still commanded approximately 38.8% of the domestic cereal market, Kellogg was losing market share to its chief rival, General Mills, because the company underestimated the strength of the nation's oat bran binge (Biesada, 1991). Its share in 1987 had been 42%, and top management had talked of attaining more than 50% of the market by 1992.

Moreover, Kellogg now had to deal with attacks on its latest product, Heartwise, an oat bran cereal containing psyllium, a grain reported to lower cholesterol level, and particularly with FDA requirements that it demonstrate the safety of psyllium as a source of dietary fiber in cereals. If psyllium were proved unsafe, Kellogg would have to eliminate or reduce its content in Heartwise, jeopardizing potentially significant sales growth.

Also, Kellogg's world leadership position in the cereal market was being threatened in Europe by a joint venture agreement between two major competitors and in Japan where several competitors were introducing new products.

Kellogg's management was faced with decisions concerning all these issues. Should it become more competitive in the oat bran wars, withdraw Heartwise from the market, and/or defend its world leadership position in the increasingly competitive international market?

INDUSTRY AND COMPETITIVE MARKET

THE CEREAL INDUSTRY

Grains boiled in water have been consumed all over the world for thousands of years. The practice of grinding grains before cooking appears to be as old as grain farming; grinding stones were found at the excavated sites of some of the earliest agricultural settlements. Another primitive means of processing grains involved roasting, which also made it easier to remove tight-fitting hulls. These items bear a slight resemblance to some of our modern-day toasted cold breakfast cereals. Modern types of cold breakfast cereals owe their development to Seventh-Day Adventists who, in 1866, established the Sanitarium of Battle Creek, Michigan, where diets were based mainly on minimally refined grain products. There, Dr. Kellogg invented his wheat and corn flakes.

In 1988 cereal processing technology around the world concentrated on wheat (28.3%), rice (23.4%), corn (22.6%), and barley (12.8%) because these four grains accounted for over 85% of the world's grain production. However, cereal products were also made from oats, rye, millets, and sorghums, which accounted for 3.4%, 1.9%, 3.5%, and 3.5% of world grain production, respectively.

The cereal industry can be divided into breakfast cereals, cereal bars, and other cereals. Other cereals consist of rice, barley, oats, buckwheat, corn, wheat, and rye consumed at meals other than breakfast. Breakfast cereals can be broken down into two categories: cold cereals (or ready-to-eat cereals), which are the topic of interest in this case, and hot cereals:

- *Ready-to-eat cereals* are made from wheat, corn, rice, and oats and, as the name indicates, do not require any cooking but are eaten cold with or without milk.
- *Hot cereals* are made from wheat and oats and need to be cooked in water or milk prior to consumption.

The ready-to-eat cereal industry segment is dominated by six large American producers: Kellogg, General Mills, Post (General Foods), Quaker Oats, Ralston Purina, and Nabisco Brands (see Exhibit 13.1). Only three competitors also produce hot cereals and all of them operate on a worldwide basis, either by selling cereals or by selling other types of food products.

EXHIBIT 13.1	General Mills: Gaining in the Breakfast Race

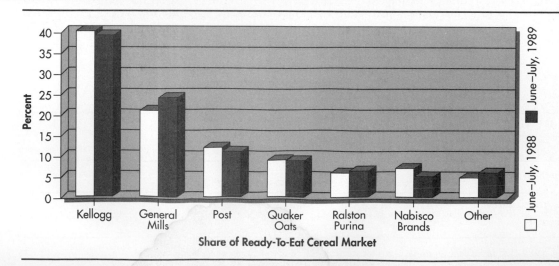

Source: Russell Mitchell. "Big G Is Growing Fat on Oat Cuisine." *Business Week,* September 18, 1989, p. 29.

In 1989 the breakfast cereal industry shipped $6.13 billion worth of product. The ready-to-eat cereal segment of the market had reached a mature stage. Household penetration of ready-to-eat cereals in the United States was at 92.4% (Messenger, 1987). However the ready-to-eat cereal market had improved from a −1% annual growth rate in 1979 to a rate of 4% in 1989. This sector of the industry had seen a record year in 1987, with volume up 3.9% to 2.37 billion pounds of product shipped. In dollars, this amounted to an increase of 8.9% to what was a $5.6 billion market in 1989. The hot cereal sector, which accounted for approximately 10% of overall cereal sales, was up by 10% in dollars to $630 million. Exhibit 13.2 indicates annual shipments of cereal breakfast foods from 1986 to 1989.

Strong growth in breakfast cereal sales has been attributed to consumers' voracious appetites for oat bran, in both hot and ready-to-eat varieties. This is due to the fact that oats, oat brans, and fibers have been reported to reduce cholesterol levels and the chance of developing certain types of cancer. Since consumers are strongly interested in health and fitness, they had increased their consumption of cereals, especially oat bran–based cereals. This consumer interest led to the introduction of many new cereals containing oat bran. Manufacturers tried to develop better oat bran products that provided more fiber, better taste, or both. While the ready-to-eat market segment increased moderately in dollar sales in 1989, products containing either oats or bran posted a large 31.4% gain, and oat bran product sales rose a sensational 364.9% in 1989 (Weinstein, 1989).

Americans are the world's fourth-largest consumers of cereals (after the Irish, British, and Australians), with a per capita consumption of approximately 10 pounds a year (Kellogg, *1988 Annual Report*); see Exhibit 13.3. Not surprisingly, cold cereals comprise the largest part of the breakfast foods market, accounting for 81% of the $5.81 billion spent in 1986 on breakfast foods such as sausage, bacon and eggs, doughnuts, and hot cereals.

Per capita consumption abroad has been expanding rapidly. In Japan, both hot and ready-to-eat cereals have become the fastest-growing food product. Rice, eggs, and fermented soybean soup breakfasts are being set aside in favor of grain. Total cereal sales shot up more than 60% in 1988, reaching $142 million (Ono, 1989). The Japanese market is still small compared to the U.S. market. It has an average

---

EXHIBIT 13.2	Shipments of Cereal Breakfast Foods from 1986 to 1989 (Dollar amounts in millions)			
	1986	1987	1988	1989
Ready-to-eat cereal	4,161.8	4,523.9	4,963.2	5,591
Hot cereal	495	536.1	579	630.8

Source: 1989 U.S. Industrial Outlook, U.S. Department of Commerce, Bureau of Census and International Trade Administration, January 1989, pp. 39–41.

EXHIBIT 13.3	1988 Per Capita Cereal Consumption by Country (In pounds)

Ireland	15.4	France	1.1
Great Britain	12.8	Venezuela	0.6
Australia	12.3	Spain	0.4
United States	9.8	Central America	0.3
Canada	8.7	Japan	0.2
Denmark	4.6	South Korea	0.1
Germany	2	Colombia	0.09
Mexico	1.9	Brazil	0.07
South Africa	1.4	Argentina	0.04

Source: Kellogg, *1988 Annual Report,* p. 7.

consumption of only half a box in a year, but the market is expected to explode. Some predict a 100-billion-yen market within five years.

The rest of the world is also beginning to change its diet to include more ready-to-eat cereals. The German and French markets, for example, experienced 20% growth in 1987. In 1989 Europe represented a $1.6 billion cereal market. However, it has been predicted that by the year 2000, the European market could be as large as the U.S. market in 1989: $6.5 billion.

TYPES OF BREAKFAST CEREALS

Ready-to-eat cereals can be classified into two main categories (Nielsen, 1986).

Natural, Unsweetened, Nutritious Cereals

This type of cereal is made of unsweetened, unadulterated grains. Some are also high in fiber, added vitamin, protein, and fruit. They are consumed by people interested in cereals that are "good for you," either via inclusion of positive ingredients or the absence of negative ones, or by people interested in basic, familiar cereals. Examples of such cereals are Quaker Oat Squares from Quaker Oats and Heartwise from Kellogg.

Even though this entire category enjoys growing demand, fiber cereals are a favorite, showing up in the bran and shredded products. It is estimated that a fifth of total dollars spent in the ready-to-eat category are going to this segment. Fiber and bran ready-to-eat cereal sales rose almost 200% in 1987. The fiber/bran segment rose 25% between 1984 and 1988 and increased its share of the overall cereal category from 14.7% to 20% of total volume. This translates into an increase from 309 million pounds in 1984 to 387 million pounds at the end of fiscal 1987. Perhaps more important, this growth has been accelerating. In the first two quarters of 1988, the fiber/bran segment rose 50% in volume compared to a drop in demand for pre-sweetened cereals.

Oat bran cereals have been given a substantial boost as part of the general health craze. The three top-selling oat bran products, for example, accounted for about $109 million in sales in 1987. One year earlier, the same three cereals—Kellogg's Nutrific Oatmeal, Kellogg's Cracklin' Oat Bran, and General Mills' Oatmeal Raisin Crisp—accounted for only $36 million in sales.

In the twelve months between February 1987 and February 1988, sales of oat bran cereals jumped 215% to more than $100 million. At the same time, the entire oat cereal category soared 30.7% in sales to $1.1 billion. This was approximately one-fifth of the sales in the entire cereal industry.

Highly Sweetened, Fun-to-Eat Cereals

These cereals have a high sweetness level. Consumers perceive them as sweet-tasting and fun for kids to eat. They also appeal to adults looking for sweet taste. Examples of such cereals are Frosted Flakes from Kellogg and Ghost Busters from Ralston Purina. Pre-sweetened cereals accounted for more than one-quarter of total breakfast cereal sales in 1987.

Hot cereals cannot be further classified into categories because they all are generally natural and nutritious, appealing to health-conscious people. Sales of hot cereals with oats or bran rose 22.3% in 1989, and sales of oat bran products soared 469.3% (Weinstein, 1989).

CONSUMERS

Consumers of ready-to-eat cereals are readily divided into three categories.

Children Under Age 17

This segment accounts for about 20% of all cereal sales. Children tend to consume sweetened cereals.

Adults Age 25 to 49

The adult consumer group favors nutritious cereals and accounts for approximately 35% of the cereal market. The aging of the baby boomers means that the largest segment of the domestic population is now between the ages of 30 and 49. By the year 2000, those 45 and older will make up 36% of the population, and in 2010, this group will constitute 42% of the population.

Kellogg led the move toward nutritious cereals by linking consumption of oat bran cereal with reduction of cancer risk. Concern about cancer and the need for fiber helped stimulate consumption in the baby boom group. The age group below 17 was also turning to a more nutritious product line. While it is true that the largest consumers of ready-to-eat cereals on a per capita basis are between the ages of 6 and 17, the 35-and-over crowd is catching up. As Exhibit 13.4 indicates, in 1987, consumption per capita in the 35–49 age group was up 6% from 1986.

Hot cereals enjoy most of their popularity with the health-conscious older population.

EXHIBIT 13.4	Ready-to-Eat Cereals: U.S. Per Capita Consumption by Age Group

Age	1983	1986	1987	Percent Change 1986/1987
Under 6	11.6	11.5	12	+.04%
6–11	14.8	15.5	16.5	+.06%
12–17	11.6	13.7	15.4	+12%
18–24	7.1	7.3	6.7	−8%
25–34	5.4	6.3	6.6	+4%
35–49	5.3	6.5	6.9	+6%
50–64	7.8	9.1	9	−1%
Over 64	—	10.6	11	+3%
Total per capita consumption	8.6	9.3	9.6	+3%

Source: Kellogg, *1988 Annual Report,* p. 8.

Adults Over Age 50

Traditionally, cereal consumption has been a practice of the young and the old. Children 17 and under and adults 50 and older, who represent 40% of the population, accounted for over half of cereal consumption in the United States. The difference between the two groups is that children are much more inclined to eat pre-sweetened cereals, whereas older adults are disposed toward eating the more healthful fiber or bran cereals. In fact, 82% of those in the 50-to-64 age group who are cereal eaters eat fiber or bran cereals rather than pre-sweetened cereals. People in the 50–64 age group eat breakfast 79% of the time, about 10% more than the general population. The final important fact concerning this age segment is, of course, that it will include the aging baby boomers over the next decade. Realizing the importance of this demographic inevitability, marketers started to focus their penetration among the baby boomers in the mid-1980s.

Due to the increasing number of working mothers, who often lack time to prepare breakfast, more and more families are turning to ready-to-eat cereals because of the convenience they offer. If one adds the promise of good nutrition to the convenience factor, it is easy to see why analysts forecast 7–8% annual growth in ready-to-eat cereals.

REGULATIONS

A recent development in regulations is threatening the high-growth adult segment and the extension of its product lines. In 1987 the Reagan administration abandoned an 81-year-old ban on making specific health claims on packaged foods (Hilts, 1989). Since then, various claims have been made linking certain cereals and other foods with reduction in the risk of heart disease, cancer, and other illnesses. Food producers had not been required to support these claims with rigorous scientific proof, as had been drug companies when they made similar claims. This new regulatory situation has several important aspects.

Interim Regulation

The Food and Drug Administration (FDA) is drafting an interim regulation that is intended to ensure that manufacturers make only claims that are supported by the evidence cited in two major federal studies of diet and health, the 1988 "Surgeon General's Report on Nutrition and Health" and the 1989 National Academy of Sciences report titled "Diet and Health" (Hilts, 1989).

Psyllium Safety

The FDA is also requiring two cereal makers, Kellogg and General Mills, to prove that a new high-fiber cereal containing psyllium, a grain reported to lower blood cholesterol levels, is safe to eat and presents no long-term health risk. There is no indication that the FDA believes psyllium represents a potential health hazard. In fact, psyllium is the primary ingredient in such popular laxatives as Metamucil and Fiberall. However, the agency has yet to determine what it considers a safe level of psyllium in cereals.

Psyllium and Advertisement

The use of psyllium poses another issue for the FDA: should it permit the grain's reputed cholesterol-lowering property to be touted in advertisements for products? Procter & Gamble, the largest U.S. user of psyllium husks, has raised that question. Psyllium is a major ingredient in P&G's Metamucil laxative, but so far the FDA has refused to approve a P&G request to advertise the grain's cholesterol-lowering property.

If companies such as Kellogg are forced to trim their advertising claims or to eliminate psyllium from their cereals, it could make the continued manufacturing and marketing of cereals containing ingredients reported to bring health benefits unprofitable. This could also affect the highly profitable health-conscious segment of the ready-to-eat cereal market. If consumers start to believe that they have been fooled, they could reduce their purchases.

DISTRIBUTION

Breakfast cereal manufacturers purchase commodity ingredients to produce their ready-to-eat cereals and then distribute their products through independent wholesalers and chain store–owned warehouses to supermarkets that sell the cereals to consumers.

In 1988 grocery store sales, which include sales of chains and independent supermarkets, grocery stores, and convenience stores, accounted for 94% of total industry sales. This represents a 5.2% increase over 1987 figures. Grocery chain stores increased sales marginally in 1988 to about $181 billion, 55% of all food store sales.

Traditionally, retail supermarkets had been the only distributors of breakfast cereals. Now distribution opportunities are available through health-food stores. Such distribution could effectively promote nutritious breakfast cereal as more than just cereal but also as a health-food product.

Distribution channels are clogged with a constant flow of new products. Because each manufacturer obtains shelf space in approximate proportion to its sales, the three primary manufacturers dominate supermarket shelves while small brands compete for the remaining space. Food stores are taking advantage of this situation by requiring high slotting allowances. During 1988 cereal manufacturers continued to protest against food store operators' levying these allowances in return for accepting new products. Traditionally, manufacturers had supported new-product introduction through national advertising and local trade promotions but had not paid any other fees to retailers. Many retailers, while still insisting on these traditional incentives, also required the payment of the slotting allowances and became more selective in adding new products. A typical retailer reviewed about 2,700 new products annually but accepted less than one-half of those evaluated.

Because of their growing computer sophistication, retailers now exercise a great deal of purchasing power over their suppliers. Some analysts estimate that as much as 70% of the slotting fees represented pure profit to the retailer.

In an attempt to regain the initiative, many food-retailing processors and suppliers are using regional and local marketing strategies such as chain-specific advertising and promotion programs. Some also are trying to renew partnership relationships with retailers by developing computer shelf space simulation, profit-related sales presentations, and other tools to influence retailers' buying decisions.

It is forecast that in the 1990s, customer trends will include desires to shop less often and demands for fresh food without preservatives. It is also forecast that the superstore concept will grow in suburban and inner-city areas; that the role of the specialist, independent food retailer will increase; and that in the long term, the distribution role of medium-sized supermarkets will continue to diminish.

COMPETITION AND POTENTIAL NEW COMPETITORS

Though there are over 220 cereal brands (in 1990), only six companies control roughly 89.3% (first quarter 1991) of the ready-to-eat cereal market, and the three leading firms dominate by accounting for approximately 73.8% of sales (Biesada, 1991). Only three of these producers are involved in the hot cereal segment. Quaker Oats leads with a 68% market share, Nabisco follows with a 17% share, and General Mills accounts for 9% of the market. Other smaller manufacturers make up the final 6% of the hot cereal segment.

Analysis of Competitors

Kellogg is the market leader with 38.8% of sales in the ready-to-eat segment. The runner-up, General Mills, sold approximately half as much; General Foods trailed with 11.2%. However, General Mills' share increased in 1989 and threatened Kellogg's goal of achieving a 50% market share. Smaller producers, such as

Quaker Oats, Ralston Purina, and Nabisco, control 7.4%, 4.7%, and 3.4%, respectively. A description of the main competitors follows.

General Mills   General Mills entered the ready-to-eat cereal market in 1921 and by 1943 was producing Wheaties, Corn Kix, and Cheerios, which established the firm as the second major processor of breakfast cereals after Kellogg. However, while Kellogg's share of the market (based on revenues) totaled about 40%, nearly the same as the previous decade, Big G's share had risen from 21% in 1979 to almost 23.8% in 1991. Recent figures indicate that General Mills is taking market share from Kellogg, and not only from the weaker rivals.

Much of General Mills' success is related to its use of oat bran in its products. In 1989 40% of General Mills' cereals by volume were made from oats, and the firm has benefited from the health craze more than Kellogg. Oat-rich Cheerios are now the most popular cereal in America, displacing Kellogg's Frosted Flakes.

On a number of fronts, General Mills has been putting Kellogg on the defensive. Big G's Raisin Nut Bran, Oatmeal Raisin Crisp, and Total Raisin Bran have dealt a heavy blow to Kellogg's Raisin Bran, whose sales are shrinking. General Mills also entered the hot cereal market with its Total brand, supported by a $24 million marketing blitz in 1987. Moreover, General Mills introduced Benefit in the spring of 1989. It is a cereal made from psyllium, the grain reported to reduce blood cholesterol levels. Kellogg introduced its own version, Heartwise, later in the year (August).

However, General Mills' success is closely tied to the health craze and could be threatened by the recent FDA move to limit health claims on food packages and to lower the psyllium content in cereals or even eliminate it.

General Mills has undergone a massive restructuring since 1985 and is now focusing on cereal, Betty Crocker Foods, and the Red Lobster and Olive Garden restaurant chains, which are all forecast to perform well in 1989. For most of these businesses, the market position is expected to be number one, as Exhibit 13.5 illustrates. General Mills earned $414.3 million on $5.6 billion in sales in fiscal 1989, up 46% from the previous year.

Furthermore, over the past few years, General Mills has significantly expanded its snack foods activity, adding new products to its leading fruit snack line. In 1987 it continued to hold the dominant share in the $280 million fruit snacks market.

One of the weaknesses of General Mills has been its late entry into international markets. Only in the late 1980s did the company begin to consider expanding overseas where Kellogg already derived 36% of its revenue. However, General Mills and Nestlé SA, the world's number-one food company, have announced a joint venture whereby Nestlé would use its enormous sales and distribution muscle, as well as its factories, to stock European grocery shelves with ready-to-eat cereals from General Mills. A similar distribution arrangement was anticipated in Asia, Africa, Australia, and elsewhere. Nestlé commands about 35% of Portugal's ready-to-eat cereal market and 10% of France's and Spain's markets.

General Foods   GF holds the third position in the market and has seen its market share slide to 11.2% in 1991 from 16.6% in 1983. Post's market share (the company's main cereal line) started to decline because of a lack of new-product

EXHIBIT 13.5 | General Mills' Businesses and Respective Market Shares Forecast for 1989

Business	Forecast 1989 Sales (in millions)	Forecast 1989 Market Share	Forecast Market Position
Consumer Foods			
Big G RTE cereals	$1,340	29%	2
Betty Crocker desserts	420	42%	1
Family Flour & Bisquick	270	55%	1
Yoplait yogurt	200	21%	2
Gorton's frozen seafood	190	25%	1
Helper dinners	170	65%	1
Fruit snacks	100	39%	2
Pop Secret microwave popcorn	80	21%	2
Restaurants			
Red Lobster USA	1,220	24%	1
The Olive Garden	300	8%	1

Source: General Mills, *Third Quarterly Report,* p. 4.

introductions. From 12% in 1987, Post's market share decreased to 11.8% in 1988 and to 10% in September of 1989 (Deutsch, 1989). The company brought to market only two new cereals in six years, and it had not had a successful new product since 1982 (Sellers, 1988).

In the bran/fiber cereal segment, General Foods was the second-largest marketer after Kellogg, with a 32.7% share of the segment (Maxwell, 1986).

General Foods' new creative campaign for its Raisin Bran could help the company gain share against Kellogg. Another move by GF has been its introduction of a resealable Zip-Pak technology for its cereals, beginning with Raisin Bran in 1987. These bags increase product freshness: the package stays fresh for one year when unopened (General Foods, *1988 Annual Report*).

Though GF's Post cereals hit a low 11.2% share in 1991, GF can still be a fierce competitor. Its parent, Philip Morris, with total sales of $25 billion, possesses the capital resources to revitalize GF's cereals.

Two recent moves by GF seem to confirm this assumption: Post introduced Post Oat Flakes targeted at one of the strongest segments, the health-conscious, adult market. Furthermore, GF is building a 150,000-square-foot Post ccreals plant in Jonesboro, Arkansas. This plant will feature the latest in cereal-making and -packaging technology (Messenger, 1987).

Quaker Oats   Quaker Oats markets a variety of breakfast products, and all enjoy significant sales (see Exhibit 13.6).

Quaker Oats holds fourth place in the ready-to-eat cereal industry and has seen its market share consistently erode since 1983. The company's share rose to 8% in 1989 from 7.4% in 1986 and 7.9% in 1987 (Deutsch, 1989) but dropped back down to 7.4% in the first quarter of 1991 (Biesada, 1991).

Quaker Oats has recently shifted its strategy. The company has introduced unique, new products that meet the needs of health-and value-conscious consumers (Quaker Oats, *1988 Annual Report*). Quaker's introduction of Quaker Oat Squares in 1988 already represents a strong entry in the adult cereal category. The company also introduced Quaker Oat Bran, a biscuit-shaped cereal, in April 1989.

Marketing expenditures as a percentage of sales declined in 1989. However, "Our key brands now have positive, sustainable sales momentum," said executive V.P. James Tindall (Erickson, 1989).

The latest developments within Quaker Oats are related to the current concern of regulators about health claims and cereal contents. Texas filed a suit against the company on September 7, 1989, to challenge a two-year ad campaign by Quaker Oats claiming that oatmeal and oat bran could help reduce cholesterol levels by 10% and the risk of heart attack by nearly 20%. Those claims helped spur a 25% jump in sales of the company's oat cereals in the first year (Carey, 1989).

Quaker Oats' hot cereals are its most profitable products. This category holds 68% of the market. Hot cereal sales grew substantially in 1988 due to Quaker's aggressive advertising and merchandising programs, in addition to a greater awareness of oatmeal's health benefits.

Quaker Oats is the leader in wholesome snacks, with a 50% market share, and with a 20% share in the granola segment (Quaker Oats, *1988 Annual Report*).

EXHIBIT 13.6	Quaker Oats' Business Sales from 1983 to 1988 (Sales in millions of dollars)

Fiscal Year	1988	1987	1986	1985	1984	1983
Ready-to-eat cereals	$ 397.4	$ 346.3	$ 289.9	$ 264.9	$ 280.7	$ 258.5
Hot cereals	326.8	260.3	254.8	236.8	219.6	194.2
Wholesome snacks	139.9	138.2	168.2	184.3	125.8	61.1
Aunt Jemima products	226.9	205.5	181.8	171.2	155.4	150.4
Celeste Pizza, corn products, and other	199.1	191.1	193.3	190.5	194.0	194.6
Total U.S. food division	$1,290.1	$1,141.4	$1,088.0	$1,089.7	$ 975.5	$ 858.8

Source: Quaker Oats, *1989 Annual Report*, p. 20.

Ralston Purina   With a 4.7% market share, Ralston Purina does not pose a major threat in the ready-to-eat cereal segment because it is not positioned in the fastest-growth segment of the industry, the adult segment. While other companies have begun to pay closer attention to the adult cereal market, this company continues to focus on the children's segment, which is declining in proportion to the other segments. In 1987 Ralston Purina introduced two pre-sweetened cereals aimed at children, Fruit Islands and Freakies (Ralston Purina, *1988 Annual Report*). However, Ralston Purina does offer its own version of oat bran cereal, Oat Bran Options, which has received wide acceptance so far. The product has been billed as an "appealing way to add oat bran to the diet without sacrificing taste." The company is counting heavily on new-product introductions.

Ralston Purina started to increase production capacity at three cereal plants in 1988 in order to relieve capacity constraints that existed in certain key items and to better capitalize on market-proven items, as well as other new opportunities in the growing ready-to-eat cereal market.

Ralston Purina also manufactures hot cereals, such as Ralston High Fiber Hot Cereal.

Nabisco   Nabisco's ready-to-eat cereals are part of Nabisco Brands, which is the largest component of RJR Nabisco's food business. The company's food sales were $9.4 billion in 1987, an increase of $184 million over 1986.

Though Nabisco ranks last with its 3.4% share of the market, the company still has a strong 23% position in the adult cereal market (Deutsch, 1989). The company increased its marketing expenditures by 19% from 1986 to 1987 and rolled out successful new products such as Shredded Wheat'n Bran and Fruit Wheats. Fruit Wheats and Wholesome'N Hearty Oat Bran hot cereal have also met with consumer acceptance. Nabisco promotes the taste attribute of its product, noting that research showed that consumers were not satisfied with the taste of existing oat bran cereals. In 1988 Nabisco introduced Frosted Wheat Squares, offering consumers the nutrition of shredded wheat with the taste of light sweetening (Nabisco, *1988 Annual Report*).

General Competitive Environment

The breakfast cereal industry is highly competitive. Several underlying factors support its competitiveness.

Rivalry Among Existing Firms   Rivalry among existing firms is intense because

- The cereal industry has reached the mature stage.
- Since the United States population growth is flat, the high percentage household penetration of 92.4% makes it difficult for firms to achieve significant new gains in sales volume.
- Six companies control 89.3% of the market, and the three leading firms hold 73.8% of the market (Biesada, 1991).
- Consumers show little brand loyalty, even among established brands.

Threat of Potential Entrants   The high level of industry concentration is a direct result of the high entry barriers that exist in the industry. They include

- *Technology:* Firms are working to transform cereal manufacturing from traditional batch processing to computerized, less energy-intensive continuous production. The twin-screw extruder, a recent innovation, can combine various grains into cereal in as little as 20 minutes. Previously the process required as long as 24 hours because ingredients passed through a tube for mixing, kneading, and cooking. A length of manufactured breakfast cereal emerged through dies under high pressure. Rotating knives then cut the cereal to form the final product. The new extrusion technique enables a greater variety of cereals to be made available to consumers, generates less waste in production, and provides for lower labor costs, inventory overhead, and energy usage.
- *High Advertising:* Brand building is crucial because consumers exhibit little brand loyalty. This stems from the fact that almost three-quarters of cereal consumers eat from 3 to 6 servings a week and therefore desire variety. The total industry devoted $651 million to advertising in 1987. Kellogg accounted for 44% of these advertising dollars, as can be seen in Exhibit 13.7, which indicates the advertising expenditures of the top six cereal manufacturers in 1987.

Suppliers' Relative Power   Most cereal ingredients are supplied by farmers or farm marketing cooperatives who do not possess significant bargaining power because they are fragmented (they do not act in groups) and because there is little difference in quality among the commodities offered by different suppliers. However, the great majority of oats used in the cereal processing industry are imported. This means that a greater demand for imported oats caused by increased consumer demand for oat bran may force upward the price of bran and perhaps increase the power of the suppliers of an increasingly scarce commodity. In fact, high oat

---

EXHIBIT 13.7	Advertising Expenditures of the Top Six Cereal Advertisers in 1986 and 1987 (Dollar amounts in millions)		

	1986	1987	% Change
Kellogg	$188.6	$286.6	52
General Mills	$154.8	$162.1	5
General Foods	$80.4	$93.1	16
Quaker Oats	$40.1	$47.7	19
Ralston Purina	$19.7	$28.5	45
RJR Nabisco	$28.4	$33.7	19

Source: BAR/LNA Multi-Media Service Class/Brand Summary, 1986, 1987.

imports for the past several years have already doubled the import price per bushel. Although the United States increased oat imports from 33 million bushels in the 1986–1987 crop year to 60 million in the 1988–1989 period, the price soared from $1.21 per bushel to $2.80 per bushel.

Substitutes   Substitutes are products that can be consumed in place of breakfast cereals. The pressure from such products has been increasing as manufacturers of breakfast foods (such as grocery stores and fast food restaurants with their take-out orders and their drive-through facilities) have sought to position their products in a way that directly competes with breakfast cereals—by stressing the convenience and/or the nutritional aspects of their products. Substitute products include

- Bacon and eggs, sausages, doughnuts: Grocery stores and fast-food restaurants emphasize the convenience of such products. In fact, the marketers of these substitutes are continually attempting to make it easier for consumers to pick up such breakfast items.
- Yogurt, cereal bars, and natural fruit bars: The advantage of these products is that they can be positioned as either convenient or nutritious, or both. After a galloping growth during the early 1980s, the value of yogurt shipments rose 2.8% in 1988 to $729.7 million.

Though consumers are increasingly adopting low-fat, low-cholesterol diets, breakfast sausage is still a very competitive item. One study reported that cereal sales increased 128% when a 10% price cut was combined with an in-store display and an advertising feature. Breakfast sausage was far more promotable, with sales increasing 447% when the same ad display and price cut were combined (Johnson, 1987).

THE COMPANY

In 1991 Kellogg remains the industry leader, with a substantial 38.8% share of the ready-to-eat cereal market. Until then, the company's strategy had been very aggressive, reflecting management's determination to reach its goal of achieving a 50% market share in 1992. However, this goal attainment was threatened by General Mills which has recently gained market share at the expense of Kellogg. General Mills' market share is about 23.8%, having gained an estimated 2% in 1989 and 1% in 1990.

HISTORY

Since its foundation, Kellogg has remained committed to providing customers with high-quality, nutritious products. Along this line, Kellogg pioneered nutrition labeling in the late 1930s, sugar content labeling in 1977, and sodium content labeling in 1979 (Kellogg, *1987 Annual Report*).

From 1980 to 1989, Kellogg issued a steady stream of new products, some of which depended on new high-tech manufacturing processes.

- Crispix, introduced in 1982, was the first cereal with identity separation of two grains (corn and rice) in a single manufactured cereal form. Crispix allowed Kellogg to compete directly with Ralston Purina's Chex family of cereals, which had about $125 million in annual sales and no significant competition.
- Raisin Squares, introduced in 1984, was the first cereal to enrobe fruit. It allowed Kellogg to crack Nabisco's Shredded Wheat niche (Sellers, 1988).
- Just Right, introduced in 1985, was also unique: the cereal offered four-grain separation that retained individual qualities of each grain and provided 100% of the U.S. Recommended Allowance of 11 nutrients (Kellogg, *1987 Annual Report*). This technology is still exclusive to Kellogg, and no competitor has been able to produce a copycat product.

OPERATING RESULTS

The bulk of Kellogg's sales and operating profits are derived from the manufacture and marketing of ready-to-eat cereals, which accounted for approximately 75% of U.S. revenues in 1988 (MacMillin, 1988). Other businesses include yogurt production, food service distribution, and frozen foods, primarily pies and waffles. The company's Mrs. Smith line held a dominant 60% market share in the $285 million frozen pies category. Pop Tarts held a 75% share of the $200 million dry toaster market, and Eggo held a 50% share of the $155 million frozen waffles market. Whitney's yogurt was not winning the yogurt war and tonnage volume had dropped 15% in 1987 (MacMillin, 1988). Exhibit 13.8 shows the dollar sales for ready-to-eat cereals, Mrs. Smith, and Whitney's Foods, from 1983 to 1988.

During 1988 approximately 36% of total corporate sales and 27% of pretax earnings were generated abroad, the vast majority coming from Europe and Canada (Larson, 1989).

After Kellogg made major gains against competitors during most of 1988, the year ended with a weak fourth quarter and a final 41.4% share of the ready-to-eat cereal market. While this was up from 1987's 41.1%, it was down from the 42% midyear level (Erickson, 1989). This downward trend continued in 1989 and 1990 but was reversed in 1991, with a first-quarter market share figure of 38.8% (Biesada, 1991). Exhibit 13.9 shows Kellogg's operating performance in 1988 and 1989.

MARKET NICHES

Kellogg initiated the resurgence of the ready-to-eat cereal market in the early 1980s by capitalizing on adults' growing concern over eating a more healthful breakfast. Instead of concentrating on children, cereals' customary consumers, Kellogg decided instead to focus on the expanding adult population. "We looked at demographics and saw this big group—80 million baby boomers. We knew they were health oriented, they were joggers. People said, 'Forget about them. They don't eat breakfast.' We knew they were too big to forget about," said Mr. Lamothe, Kellogg's CEO.

EXHIBIT 13.8	Operating Income and Estimates: Kellogg

(Dollar amounts in millions, except per-share data)

	1983	1984	1985	1986	1987	1988	% Change	1989E	% Change
Sales									
Ready-to-eat cereals	$1,846.0	$2,034.0	$2,280.0	$2,585.0	$2,947.0	$3,423.9	16.2%	$3,770.0	10.1%
Salada (ex cereal)	25.0	30.0	35.0	35.0	38.0	9.0	−76.3%	10.0	11.1%
Fearn, International	171.0	186.0	210.0	250.0	279.0	319.0	14.3%	350.0	9.7%
Mrs. Smith	211.0	219.0	246.0	280.0	320.0	370.0	15.6%	430.0	16.2%
Whitney's Foods, Inc.	16.1	25.4	40.0	49.0	59.0	75.0	27.1%	90.0	20.0%
Other	112.0	108.0	119.1	141.7	150.0	152.0	1.3%	155.0	2.0%
Total	$2,381.1	$2,602.4	$2,930.1	$3,340.7	$3,793.0	$4,348.9	14.7%	$4,805.0	10.5%
Operating Income									
Ready-to-eat cereals	$395.0	$422.0	$508.0	$591.5	$644.5	$739.5	14.7%	$766.5	3.7%
Salada (ex cereal)	1.0	1.2	1.5	2.0	2.0	0.1	−95.0%	0.3	200.0%
Fearn, International	14.4	16.3	19.9	21.0	21.5	26.2	21.9%	29.7	13.4%
Mrs. Smith	15.9	17.0	19.3	21.0	19.0	23.0	21.1%	30.0	30.4%
Whitney's Foods, Inc.	2.0 NM	1.4	1.7	−2.0	−2.0	0.0	NM		0.0
Other	4.0	5.3	8.0	8.5	6.2	5.4	−12.9%	6.0	11.1%
Total	$432.3	$463.2	$558.4	$642.0	$691.2	$794.2	14.9%	$832.5	4.8%
Net interest 168.0%	11.7	12.9	−31.0	−39.5	−25.5	−19.4		NM	−52.0
Pretax income	$444.0	$476.1	$527.4	$602.5	$665.7	$774.8	16.4%	$780.5	0.7%
Income taxes	201.3	225.6	246.3	267.7	269.8	294.3	9.1%	286.4	−2.7%
Net income	242.7	250.5	281.1	334.8	395.9	480.5	21.4%	494.1	2.8%
Earnings per share	$1.59	$1.68	$2.28	$2.71	$3.20	$3.90	21.9%	$4.05	3.8%
Average shares outstanding	152.8	149.1	123.3	123.5	123.7	123.2	−0.4%	122.0	−1.0%
Operating Margin									
Ready-to-eat cereals	21.4%	20.7%	22.3%	22.9%	21.9%	21.6%			20.3%
Salada (ex cereal)	4.0	4.0	4.3	5.7	5.3	1.1			3.0
Fearn, International	8.4	8.8	9.5	8.4	7.7	8.2			8.5
Mrs. Smith	7.5	7.8	7.8	7.5	5.9	6.2			7.0
Whitney's Foods, Inc.	12.4	5.5	4.3	−4.1	−3.4	0.0			0.0
Other 3.9	3.6	4.9	6.7	6.0	4.1	3.6			
Total	18.2	17.8	19.1	19.2	18.2	18.3			17.3

NM: Not meaningful

[1] 1986 earnings per share of $2.71 excludes $0.13 per share nonrecurring charges.

Source: Eric J. Larson. Equity Research, First Boston Corporation, November 7, 1989, p. 8.

EXHIBIT 13.9	Third Quarter and First Nine Months Fiscal Operating Performance: Kellogg

(Dollar amounts in millions, except per-share data)

	Third Quarter			First Nine Months		
	1989	1988	% Change	1989	1988	% Change
Sales	$1,195.4	$1,140.3	4.8%	$3,563.5	$3,256.8	9.4%
Cost of goods sold	611.8	563.5	8.6%	1,798.8	1,636.7	9.9%
Gross profit	583.6	576.8	1.2%	1,764.7	1,620.1	8.9%
Selling, general and administrative expense	374.8	341	9.9%	1,144.6	996.8	14.8%
Operating profit	$ 208.8	$ 235.8	–11.5%	$ 620.1	$ 623.3	–0.5%
Interest expense	7	9.2	–23.9%	34.9	24.2	44.2%
Interest (income) and other	11.8	–8.1	NM	13.5	–16.6	NM
Interest, net	18.8	1.1	NM	48.4	7.6	NM
Pretax profit	$ 190.0	$ 234.7	–19.0%	$ 571.7	$ 615.7	–7.1%
Income taxes	66.9	89	–24.8%	207.5	236.2	–12.2%
Net income before accounting change	$ 123.1	$ 145.7	–15.5%	$ 364.2	$ 379.5	–4.0%
Cumulative effect of accounting change	0	0		48.1	0	
Net income	$ 123.1	$ 145.7	–15.5%	$ 412.3	$ 379.5	8.6%
Tax rate	0.352	0.379	–7.1%	0.363	0.384	–5.5%
EPS-continuing operations	1.02	1.18	–13.6%	2.99	3.08	–2.9%
EPS from accounting change	0	0	—	0.39	0	—
EPS reported	1.02	1.18	–13.6%	3.38	3.08	9.7%
Dividends per share	0.43	0.38	13.2%	1.29	1.14	13.2%
Average shares outstanding	122.1	123.5	–1.1%	122.1	123.2	–0.9%
As a Percentage of Sales						
Gross profit	48.8%	50.6%		49.5%	49.7%	
Operating profit	17.5%	20.7%		17.4%	19.1%	
Pretax profit	15.9%	20.6%		16.0%	18.9%	
Net income	10.3%	12.8%		10.2%	11.7%	
Selling, general and administrative expenses	31.4%	29.9%		32.1%	30.6%	

NM: Not meaningful

Source: Eric J. Larson. Equity Research, First Boston Corporation, November 7, 1989, p. 8.

Kellogg's move started in 1984 when the company promoted its bran cereals by claiming that these products may reduce some kinds of cancer because of their high-fiber, low-fat qualities. Kellogg offered as evidence the dietary research of such groups as the American Cancer Society, the American Heart Association, and the American Institute of Cancer Research (Messenger, 1987).

In February 1988, Kellogg launched "Project Nutrition," a three-part, multimillion-dollar health and nutrition education campaign, which sought to encourage Americans to improve their diets. One part employed Kellogg-hosted symposia to reach medical, health, and science leaders. A second part targeted adult consumers, health professionals, and school-age children with the "Get a Taste for the Healthy Life" print advertising and educational campaign. "Resolution 88" was the third part of the campaign and, along with other corporations, supported the American Health Foundation cholesterol-screening effort (Sellers, 1988).

This led to a 26% increase in cereal consumption by people aged 25 to 49, and cereals for adults accounted for about 40% of total ready-to-eat cereals in 1988 (Sellers, 1988).

Even though Kellogg initiated and was first to benefit from the health craze, it failed to keep up with the increasing demand for new oat bran cereals; instead of emphasizing more good-for-you cereals, it decided to go after nostalgia. Kellogg thought that S.W. Graham, a sweet cereal named after the founder of the popular cracker, would be its next winner; its sales peaked in October of 1989 with a tiny 0.66% share of the market. Kellogg seemed to treat the demand for oat bran as a passing fancy (Gibson, 1989). Nearly 80% of Kellogg's cereals are corn- or wheat-based, and only 20% are made with oat bran versus 40% for General Mills (Mitchell, 1989). Moreover, when Kellogg introduced Heartwise, containing psyllium, in August of 1989, it looked more like a follower than a leader. Indeed, General Mills introduced its own psyllium-based cereal, Benefit, in the spring of the same year.

MARKETING POLICY

Most of the money Kellogg spent on marketing went into brand-building advertising. Kellogg boosted total U.S. advertising a substantial 52% in 1987 (Multi Media Service, 1986/1987).

Annual spending tripled from 1983 to 1987 to an estimated $865 million, or 20% of sales (Sellers, 1988).

Advertising and promotion expenses rose at approximately twice the rate of sales growth in the third quarter of 1989 (Larson, 1989). Selling and administration expenses reached as high as 32–33% of total sales, compared with 29.4% in 1988. This was due to the fact that Kellogg was aggressively promoting new products in order to face General Mills and Quaker Oats, whose market shares had recently increased from large exposure to oat-based products.

Though Kellogg was busy opening up and defending new market niches, the company continued to strongly support its established brands, such as Rice Krispies, Frosted Flakes, Special K, Froot Loops, and Corn Flakes. Quite recently, however, General Mills' Cheerios displaced Kellogg's Frosted Flakes as the most popular cereal in America.

In addition to increased advertising support, Kellogg came up with more contemporary advertisements. Kellogg dropped its lifestyle type commercials and opted instead for more focused commercials that communicated product benefits. Some examples of Kellogg's more modern commercials showed tennis players being beaten by fiber-eating opponents and romantic couples strengthening their bond by eating right (Kellogg cereals).

Kellogg also reevaluated its media expenditures, increasing its magazine advertisement by 222% in 1987 (Maxwell, 1988). Instead of relying on a typically heavy TV schedule, Kellogg now favored highly selective lifestyle magazines to explain the uniqueness of its adult cereals.

Finally, annual price increases of 11–12% were offset by aggressive trade allowances and promotions. Trade discounting is usually accounted for as an off-invoice transaction in the food industry (Larson, 1989).

PRODUCTION AND PRODUCTION FACILITIES

From 1983 to 1987, Kellogg quadrupled capital spending, and the 1988 budget was close to $600 million (Maxwell, 1987). In February 1987, Kellogg completed the construction of a factory called "Building 100." Billed as the most efficient cereal factory in the world, it houses computer-monitored machines that perform every step of the cereal-making process, from mixing the grains to packing the boxes in cartons, 24 hours a day, 7 days a week. The technologically advanced equipment helped Kellogg improve product quality. Building 100's products were 20% to 25% more consistent in quality than cereal that came out of Kellogg's older plants (Sellers, 1988).

As Kellogg's two toughest competitors, General Mills and General Foods, added their own new plants, Kellogg began to construct a new plant in Memphis to increase domestic capacity by as much as 35% and cost by nearly $1.2 billion. General Mills was limited in boosting its sales because its plants were already operating at full capacity. The plant it was building in Covington, Georgia, was to be ready in 1989. However, Kellogg had just announced that it was delaying construction because of current market conditions. Since the facility was not to start operating before 1993, this delay revealed a pessimistic long-term outlook. But Kellogg had indicated that it could grow without adding the facility. The company still had five other U.S. plants, including Building 100, which added bran- and rice-processing capacity in 1990. A company spokesperson warned that the plant might never be built.

PRODUCT POLICY

In this mature, highly competitive marketplace, new products provide a key growth opportunity. In 1987 Kellogg's R&D budget was $42 million, about 1.1% of sales, compared with General Mills' $41.2 million or 0.7% of sales in May of 1987 (Sellers, 1988).

Despite its heavy introduction of new products, Kellogg failed to introduce as many oat bran–based cereals as General Mills had in 1988. In fact, analysts say much of Kellogg's erosion was in such core brands as Corn Flakes, Rice Krispies, and Frosted Flakes, which represented nearly one-third of its sales volume (Gibson, 1989).

During 1987, Kellogg introduced five new products:

- Nutrific, a multi-fiber, low-fat, cholesterol-free cereal. This new brand boldly capitalized on the health craze. A box of Nutrific came with a small booklet that had height and weight tables, cholesterol counts, a nutrition guide, and a checklist for exercise habits.
- Strawberry Squares, the company's third product in the fruit-filled biscuit category.
- Pro Grain, a specially fortified, multi-grain product developed to respond to the nutritional needs and taste preferences of active teenagers and young adults.
- Nutri Grain Nuggets, the first whole-grain nugget cereal, providing more dietary fiber than any other nugget cereal.
- Mueslix, a premium-quality cereal based on the European "Museli" cereals. Though the cereal costs 10% more than other premium-priced cereals, Mueslix achieved a 1% share of the market within one year, about twice that projected by Kellogg (Maxwell, 1987).

Kellogg also became the first to bring out a snack pack of high-fiber cereals. Kellogg's Fiber Pack contains single-serving portions of six high-fiber cereals.

In 1988 the company continued the new-product momentum it established in 1987, introducing six new cereals:

- Nutri Grain Biscuits, the only whole grain, shredded wheat cereal without preservatives.
- Bite-sized Frosted Mini-Wheats.
- Nut&Honey Crunch Biscuits.
- Two varieties of S.W. Graham Shredded Biscuits.
- Common Sense Oat Bran.
- Blueberry Squares, Kellogg's fourth fruit-filled biscuit cereal.

Kellogg's strategy of rapid product introduction paid off through 1988. But in 1989, with a lack of new cereals made of oat bran, Kellogg lost market share to General Mills. Still Kellogg did have three oat cereals: OatBake, Common Sense, and Heartwise.

In August 1989, Kellogg introduced Heartwise, an oat bran cereal containing the controversial grain psyllium. If the FDA were to limit health claims on food and were to ban psyllium in cereals, Kellogg would have to reevaluate its strategy. Because the adult segment was considered the most profitable market, this could be a blow to Kellogg. However, Kellogg could still capitalize on the past education provided to consumers and continue manufacturing healthful cereals for health-conscious people.

Heartwise followed two other new Kellogg cereals: OatBake and a new Golden Crunch variety of Mueslix. OatBake was made of whole oats, corn, wheat bran, and other ingredients, including nuts, fruit, coconut, and honey—all shaped into rings and baked in an oven. Because its texture and ingredients were different from those of typical toasted cereals, Kellogg promoted OatBake as both a hot and a ready-to-eat cereal. Common Sense grabbed a 2% share—a worthy debut, but nowhere near the 10% that the Cheerios varieties had cornered (Deutsch, 1989).

As far as substitutes were concerned, Kellogg failed in its attempt to introduce granola bars. The reason for this failure was thought to be a lack of good taste. Recently, Kellogg decided to bet five of its best-known trademarks on its new Smart Start cereal bars. The new bars offered consumers a portable version of such cereal brands as Kellogg's Corn Flakes, Raisin Bran, Rice Krispies, Nutrigrain, and Common Sense. Each bar had an outer layer, made with a Kellogg cereal, surrounding fruit or nut fillings. However, Smart Start has been plagued with production problems, threatening its success.

Kellogg has been sharply focused for a long time, with ready-to-eat cereals accounting for 80% of its total sales. As the cereal market was declining in the late 1970s, many of the cereal producers began to diversify. General Mills got further into upscale retailing and fast foods, and Quaker Oats got into retailing and direct marketing (Fannin, 1988). Even when Kellogg diversified, it stuck to the breakfast table, with acquisitions such as Mrs. Smith microwave pies, Eggo Nutri Grain waffles, and Salada caffeine-reduced tea (Mitchell, 1988).

INTERNATIONAL MARKET

Kellogg is the world leader in the ready-to-eat cereal market with a 51.1% market share and is present in almost 130 countries (Biesada, 1991).

Kellogg's market shares outside the United States are 46% in the United Kingdom, and 50%, 80%, 60%, and 50% in France, Spain, Belgium, and Italy, respectively. Latin American countries saw RTE cereals virtually dominated by Kellogg products (MacMillin, 1988). Kellogg holds a 70% market share in Japan. Recently, however, Switzerland-based Nestlé S.A. launched a series of new cereals, challenging the long-standing market dominance of Kellogg. Nestlé is now trying to expand its 12% market share by sprinkling vegetable powder on corn flakes. Nestlé's slightly salted Vegetable Time cereal, launched in March 1989, quickly became the best seller of the company's seven cereal brands in Japan (Ono, 1989).

General Mills started to bring in Cheerios through ties with Japan's biggest potato chip maker, Calbee Foods Co. Cisco Co., the only long-time Japanese cereal maker, recently expanded its selection in the Japanese market to 17 brands, surpassing Kellogg's 13.

TOWARD THE FUTURE

Kellogg is facing many different problems and challenges. Kellogg has been losing much of its market share to General Mills, down from 42% in 1987 to 38.8% in 1991. This decline is due to Kellogg's failure to capitalize adequately on the adult segment and its preoccupation with health. It has not introduced enough oat bran–based products aimed at the health-conscious. Only 20% of its products are oat bran–based, compared with 40% for General Mills (Mitchell, 1989). Moreover, its long-time domination of basic products has come to an end. General Mills' Cheerios has displaced Kellogg's Frosted Flakes as the most popular cereal in America. Kellogg's domination of foreign markets may also be threatened, as is presently the case in Japan, with Nestlé and General Mills gaining ground, and in Europe, with the recent agreement between Nestlé and General Mills to form a joint venture. Furthermore, future FDA regulations could mean that the health-conscious segment of the ready-to-eat cereal market will not remain profitable to Kellogg if consumers believe they have been misinformed, or if certain grains, such as psyllium, are banned from cereals. Finally, Kellogg has failed to impose a strong presence in substitutes for ready-to-eat cereals.

Kellogg's CEO, Mr. Lamothe, is contemplating future actions for his company. He believes that emphasis should be placed on regaining domestic market share by developing more oat bran–based cereals targeted at the health-conscious segment of the market. However, this may be restrictive, considering the strong potential growth that exists in other consumer segments such as older cereal eaters and teenagers. As far as product is concerned, hot cereals also have strong potential growth because older people are the main consumers of these cereals and, with the advent of the microwave, hot cereals have become very convenient to prepare. Moreover, Kellogg has all the resources needed to introduce new oat bran–based cereals, both hot and cold, and cereals based on other grains.

On the other hand, some managers feel that although emphasizing oat bran–based cereals is necessary, it needs to be combined with a regard for cereals based on wheat, corn, rice, and the like. Hot cereals need to be marketed to appeal to the older segment of the population. Ready-to-eat cereals can be slightly sweetened with honey to appeal to more health-conscious young people. Kellogg has a strong presence on supermarket shelves; it has a high marketing budget and high capital investment. Most of its competitors have production problems because they have reached full capacity. Kellogg has an edge in that area, because most of its large plants have not been operating at full capacity.

Few managers expect the FDA to draft regulations that threaten to slow the rapid growth of the adult segment of the ready-to-eat cereal market. Most believe, however, that consumers are well educated and that elimination of health claims from cereal boxes is not the most important problem. The psyllium issue is considered to be a greater concern. However, no consensus on possible strategies and solutions has yet been reached.

How will Kellogg, the number-one ready-to-eat cereal maker in the world, respond to these challenges in the 1990s? How will it proceed both domestically and internationally in response to a changing environment? These are the pressing questions Kellogg's management has to address.

REFERENCES

Bennett, Stephen and Erin Sullivan. "Breakfast Foods." *Progressive Grocer,* September 1987, p. 122.

Biesada, Alexandria. "Life After Oat Bran." *The Financial World,* June 11, 1991, pp. 46–49.

Carey, John, Lois Therien, Wendy Zellner, and Todd Mason. "Snap, Crackle, Stop." *Business Week,* September 25, 1989, pp. 42–43.

Deutsch, Claudia H., "Has Kellogg Lost Its Snap?" *New York Times,* September 24, 1989, pp. 1 and 14.

Erickson, Julie Liesse. "Kellogg Tests Bar Cereals." *Advertising Age,* May 8, 1989, p. 24.

Erickson, Julie Liesse. "Cereal Makers Roll More Oats." *Advertising Age,* March 6, 1989, p. 34.

Erickson, Julie Liesse. "New Cereals Stir Up Food Market." *Advertising Age,* November 7, 1988, p. 57.

Erickson, Julie Liesse. "General Mills Refills Cereal Bowl." *Advertising Age,* October 10, 1988, p. 30.

Erickson, Julie Liesse. "Kellogg Company." *Advertising Age,* September 28, 1988, p. 102.

Erickson, Julie Liesse. "Cereal Giants X-Cited." *Advertising Age,* May 9, 1988, p. 8.

Fannin, Rebecca. "Crunching the Competition." *Marketing and Media Decisions,* March 1988, pp. 70–74.

General Foods, *1988 Annual Report.*

General Mills, *1987 Annual Report.*

Gibson, Richard. "Nestlé to Help General Mills Sell Cereals in Europe." *Wall Street Journal,* December 1, 1989, p. B6.

Gibson, Richard. "Personal Chemistry Abruptly Ended Rise of Kellogg President." *Wall Street Journal,* November 28, 1989, pp. A1 and A9.

Gibson, Richard. "Kellogg Pours Water on Plans to Build Big Cereal Plant." *Wall Street Journal,* October 30, 1989, p. B1.

Gibson, Richard. "Kellogg Co. to Post Lower Period Net, Competition Cited." *Wall Street Journal,* October 3, 1989, p. A16.

Gibson, Richard. "FDA Raises Safety Questions About Use of Psyllium by General Mills, Kellogg." *Wall Street Journal,* October 2, 1989, p. B2.

Hilts, Philip J. "FDA Considering New Rules to Curb Food Label Claims." *New York Times,* October 31, 1989, p. A1.

Johnson, Bill. "Breakfast Foods." *Progressive Grocer,* September 1987, p. 122.

Kellogg, *1988 Annual Report.*

Kellogg, *1987 Annual Report.*

Larson, Eric J. Equity Research, First Boston Corporation, November 6, 1989.

Larson, Eric J. Equity Research, First Boston Corporation, September 22, 1989.

MacMillin, John M. Equity Research, Prudential Bache Securities, March 8, 1988.

Maxwell, John C., Jr. "Marketers Milk Cold Cereal Sales." *Advertising Age,* September 26, 1988, p. 64.

Maxwell, John C., Jr. "Products for Adults Increase." *Advertising Age,* September 28, 1987, p. 88.

Maxwell, John C., Jr. "Kellogg." *Advertising Age.* July 7, 1986, p. 49.

Messenger, Robert. "No More Blues in Battle Creek." *Prepared Foods,* February 1987, pp. 44–45.

Mitchell, Russell. "Big G Is Growing Fat on Oat Cuisine." *Business Week,* September 18, 1989, p. 29.

Mitchell, Russell. "The Health Craze Has Kellogg Feeling Great." *Business Week,* March 30, 1988, p. 59.

Multi Media Service BAR/LNA. Class Brand Summary 1986/1987.

Nabisco, *1988 Annual Report.*

Ono, Yumiko. "Japanese Are Snapping Up Cereals as Market Crackles with Entries." *Wall Street Journal,* July 13, 1989, p. B6.

Quaker Oats, *1988 Annual Report.*

Ralston Purina, *1988 Annual Report.*

Samuelson, Robert J. "The Great Cereal War." *Newsweek,* September 7, 1987, p. 49.

Sellers, Patricia. "How King Kellogg Beat the Blahs." *Fortune,* August 29, 1988, pp. 54–64.

U.S. Department of Commerce, *U.S. Industrial Outlook 1989.*

Weinstein, Steve. "Main Courses and Entrées." *Progressive Grocer,* July 1989.

CASE 14 LIN Broadcasting Corporation: The Cellular Telephone Industry

Robert J. Mockler ▪ Alan Lockman ▪ Brenda Massetti

With the flick of an ankle, TV's bumbling secret agent Maxwell Smart could pick up his shoe and dial himself out of a jam. In 1989, the cellular telephone industry is a $3 billion business, and it is the 25 major service providers that are falling over themselves, signing up subscribers, and swallowing up rivals (Pomice, 1989, p. 40).

LIN Broadcasting is a communications corporation that has interests in cellular telephone systems in five of the top ten United States markets. In 1989 LIN is ranked fifth in the number of subscribers it carries in the United States. Donald A. Pels, Chairman of the Board and President, claimed that LIN would look to expand through mergers and acquisitions in regions where the company lacks properties in the 1990s: "We're looking for opportunities to get bigger, . . . significantly bigger over the next few years," he says. "We'll be buyers" (Keller, 1989, p. 45).

Donald A. Pels faced many challenges to his dream for LIN to become a truly nationwide cellular service. Leading companies within the cellular phone industry were acquiring cellular interests across the United States, causing a consolidation trend in the industry. At the same time, the industry was attempting to increase the level of cellular penetration through mass distribution and competitive pricing strategies. It remained questionable whether LIN would stay independent in this consolidating environment and keep up with continuing technological changes. As it prepared for the 1990s, LIN management was exploring different strategic decisions in several areas, such as the kind of service to provide, the type of customers to target, the amount of distributors, and whether to invest in a select group of cellular geographic areas.

INDUSTRY AND COMPETITIVE MARKET

THE CELLULAR TELEPHONE INDUSTRY

The cellular telephone industry, as shown in Exhibit 14.1, has four basic sectors:

- Subscriber equipment (cellular telephones)
- Cell site or radio base station equipment
- Switching equipment
- Cellular services (system operators)

The subscriber equipment (also known as the cellular telephone) is purchased by customers for use in the car or anywhere else they can transport the phone within the cellular network. The cell base site (or tower) is used in cellular systems to communicate with mobile units. The mobile telephone switching office coordinates all elements of each cellular system and connects the system to the public telephone

---

| EXHIBIT 14.1 | The Four Basic Sectors of the Cellular Telephone Industry |

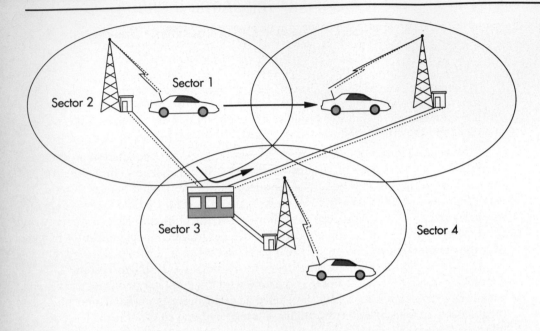

Sector 1 Cellular Telephone
Sector 2 Cell Base Site
Sector 3 Mobile Telephone Switching Office
Sector 4 Systems Operators Control the Cellular Network (Sectors 2 and 3)

Source: Adapted from the U.S. Department of Commerce, Washington, D.C., "A Competitive Assessment of the Cellular Radiotelephone Industry," June 1988, p. 4.

network. The second and third sectors are treated together as the cellular system or network, which is the focus of this study, and are controlled by the system operator. Companies such as LIN Broadcasting and McCaw Cellular Communications manufacture the cellular network and control these systems.

A cellular geographic service area is an independent cellular "market" that is granted to system operators through a licensing process by the Federal Communications Commission. Once companies such as LIN Broadcasting and McCaw Cellular had manufactured the cellular system within a designated cellular geographic service area, they were able to provide a service that allowed for the operation of a cellular phone. Cellular phones were available to customers through various distributors, such as automobile accessory stores, automobile manufacturers and national retailers, who receive their supplies from cellular phone manufacturers, such as Motorola Incorporated, NEC, and AT&T. The latter have the responsibility of advertising and promotion through select media such as magazines, newspapers, television, and radio.

EXHIBIT 14.2	The Estimated Growth in the Number of Cellular Subscribers, 1984–2000

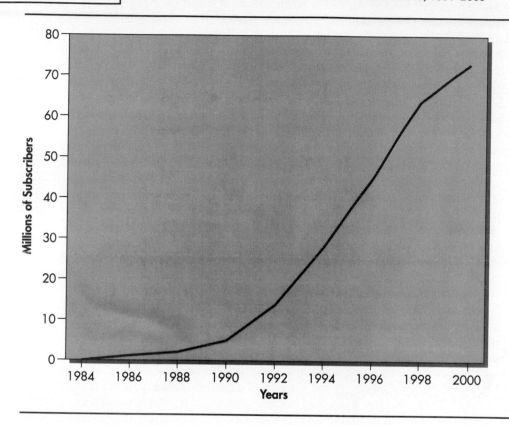

Note: Data for 1989 to 2000 are estimates.

Source: Information obtained from Southwestern Bell, *1988 Annual Reports,* p. 9.

Sources of revenue for system operators in the cellular telephone industry are twofold. The value of a cellular geographic service area, which is based on the number of potential subscribers, is only one measure of revenue. The second measure of revenue is based on the amount of phone usage by customers within that area.

INDUSTRY BACKGROUND

The industry under study is the cellular mobile telephone industry. This is a relatively new and emerging industry developed to provide more efficient, superior-quality, and higher-capacity mobile communications. Both small and large manufacturers in this industry bid on construction permits in specific areas of the United States, known as Cellular Geographic Service Areas. Each such area is the geographic area for which the cellular system operator is obliged to provide cellular service. These areas can further be divided into Metropolitan Statistical Areas (MSA) and Rural

Service Areas (RSA), which are both designated areas developed by the Bureau of the Census. An MSA is defined in terms of counties and their populations and is the outermost limit of the cellular geographic service area ("Telecommunications...," 1988). There are 305 MSAs in the United States. An RSA is similar to the MSA; however, it is much smaller and is usually located between the larger MSAs.

The structure of the cellular industry, as it exists today, is a result of the federal regulatory process. Under the framework created, each cellular "market" in the United States is eligible for two separate operating licenses. One license is granted to a wireline company, which is a conventional telephone company that uses land-line facilities to provide local exchange services. The second license is granted to a non-wireline company, a provider of cellular services that does not own land-based telephone transmission equipment. For example, in the New York area the wireline company is NYNEX, and the non-wireline company is Metro One Cellular Telephone Company. Bids are presented to the Federal Communications Commission (FCC), which has the right to regulate the acquisition, construction, and operation of the cellular systems and, most important, allocates the frequency spectrum, which is the amount of radio channels available for cellular use. Presently, the FCC has allocated 59 megahertz of spectrum within the 800-megahertz radio band for cellular use for a total use of 808 channels for voice use. A megahertz refers to the unit of broadcast frequency.

In the beginning of 1989 there were about 3 million cellular telephone subscribers in the United States, as shown in Exhibit 14.2. It is estimated that this number will rise to over 10 million by the end of 1991 and to 16 million by 1993 (Southwestern Bell, 1988).

The two key factors driving this rapid growth in cellular subscribers are availability and price. Cellular systems need to be built if there are to be subscribers. As of June 1989, the last MSA had commenced cellular telephone service. Cellular telephone service is available to approximately three-quarters of the United States population. The second factor, price, is important because the subscriber of the future who might want a cellular telephone for safety or convenience will be less willing to pay the big up-front costs and the large monthly fees that were paid when the industry was in its early stages.

Future growth of the cellular phone industry will depend greatly on the rate at which technological developments continue, the speed at which the FCC licenses the Rural Service Areas, and the pace at which system operating costs decline and prices to the customer decrease.

SERVICE

As mentioned earlier, companies such as LIN Broadcasting provide a service that allows cellular telephones to function in a designated area. How this service works is very important, as are the new technologies being developed to enhance this service. The cellular telephones also play a key role in the cellular network.

How the Cellular Network Works

The cellular telephone derives its name from small regions, called cells, into which a service area is divided. Each cell is equipped with a low-power transmitter/receiver (base station or tower). The radius of a cell can range from two to ten miles, depending on local terrain, projected user dispersion, and placement of the transmitter. The base station (or tower) of each cell is connected to a mobile telephone switching office (MTSO) by telephone lines. The MTSO is a central switching point where a computer coordinates calls for the entire service area ("Telecommunications. . .," 1989). Construction of the cellular system involves setting up this equipment, connecting the MTSO to a landline carrier, and testing the system.

When calling from a cellular phone, the subscriber enters the number and presses the "send" button. This is then sent to the local tower in its vicinity and is locked onto the strongest signal. The tower decodes the information, forwarding it to the mobile telephone switching office. This switch processes the call into the landline system and connects the selected trunk to the tower link associated with the designated voice channel (U.S. Department of Commerce, 1988). Similarly, calls originating outside the cellular system are routed through a long-distance .company or local phone company to the MTSO and on to the tower.

During conversation, as the cellular telephone user crosses a cell boundary, control of the call is transferred from cell to cell to ensure the highest possible signal quality. This process is known as "hands-off."

Technological Changes

In 1989 digital technology was in the process of being developed so that the cellular networks could handle the high demand of cellular phone calls in large metropolitan areas. Because of this high demand, the current cellular networks are facing capacity constraints that cause interference during cellular phone use. Three ideas are currently being employed to combat this strategic problem: adding channels to the frequency spectrum, cell splitting, and digital technology.

Adding New Channels to the Frequency Spectrum   The first solution is for the Federal Communications Commission (FCC) to add channels to the system. The FCC has allocated 59 megahertz of spectrum that adds up to 808 channels for voice use. Increasing this number of channels does not seem likely because the FCC added channels in 1986 to reach this total. Adding more channels was expected to take a few years of processing.

Cell Splitting   Cell splitting refers to dividing a cell by adding more, less powerful base stations. For example, a system initially set up with cells having a radius of eight miles may be split into smaller cells of perhaps four miles and, later, two miles. With an increase in the number of cells, a system operator is able to increase the level of frequency reuse (the system's ability to use the same channel simultaneously for several calls) ("Telecommunications. . .," 1989). Problems can arise from this procedure, however, because the number of times a cell can be split is limited. Extreme cell density (the amount of cells in one area) can eventually result in channel interference.

Digital Technology   Cellular companies are looking ahead to digital technology, which the Cellular Telecommunications Industry Association asked manufacturers

EXHIBIT 14.6	The Top Ten Companies in Terms of Subscribers and Potential Customers

	Subscribers (thousands)	Potential (millions)
Pactel	262	15
McCaw	258	50
BellSouth	255	13
Southwestern Bell	244	18
LIN	228	18
Ameritech	146	17
GTE Mobilinet	127	22
NYNEX	127	18
Bell Atlantic	100	19
US West Newvector	83	12

Source: Adapted from Calvin Sims, "Cellular Phone Growth Starts Investor Rush," *New York Times,* June 23, 1989, p. D1.

Cellular, it had holdings in the San Francisco–San Jose, Miami, Seattle, Portland (Oregon), Denver, and Minneapolis markets (Shriver, 1989). McCaw had a variety of subscriber plans with monthly charges ranging from $10 to $150, accompanied by air time usage charges generally ranging from $0.15 to $0.65 per minute.

BellSouth Corporation This corporation had made big headlines with moves in the United States and the international cellular communications business and had stayed ahead of the ever-changing telecommunications industry by building on the expertise of 100 years in the telephone business. BellSouth, in a $710 million stock transaction, acquired Mobile Communications Corporation of America, a national cellular telephone company. That acquisition, along with existing operations in the United States, the United Kingdom, and Australia, gave BellSouth 320,000 cellular customers worldwide. Domestically, BellSouth had 235,000 subscribers in an area of 13 million people. BellSouth provided cellular service in 11 markets.

Regional Competitors

A few selected examples of direct competitors with LIN in specific markets such as Los Angeles and Dallas/Fort Worth were Pactel Corporation and Southwestern Bell, respectively. Each such competitor had substantial assets and resources and extensive experience in the telecommunications industry.

Pactel Corporation The largest competitor in terms of number of subscribers was Pactel, a division of Pacific Telesis Group, with 1988 revenues of $9.5 billion. In

1988 Pactel had 262,000 subscribers, an increase of 94,000 over 1987, in a potential market of 15 million and had begun to turn substantial profits. The company continued to hold its lead as the nation's largest provider of cellular telephone service, and at the end of 1988, Pactel expanded its operations in Detroit, Atlanta, and other markets. It offered various usage rates to appeal to different customers and was represented by a wide range of distributors and retailers.

Southwestern Bell This company had 244,000 subscribers in a potential market of 18 million. During each business day of 1988, an average of 355 new customers were added to Southwestern Bell's cellular networks nationwide (89,000 new customers for the year). Southwestern Bell operated in 6 of the top 15 markets and was expected to see its first profits from the cellular business during 1989. This company had filed for licenses to serve 76 Rural Service Areas within its 5-state area, which allowed people in smaller towns and along interstate highways to obtain cellular service. Its major areas of operation were in Texas, Illinois, and Washington, D.C. In addition, Southwestern Bell developed a major accounts program, which provided discount service packages in markets it served and helped its customers secure the best rates in other cities. It also reached an agreement with 57 area K mart stores to offer a sales and service program through those stores.

Changing Competitive Environment

During 1988 and 1989, a significant level of consolidation in the cellular industry occurred. FCC rules designated that, once a system was licensed, a wireline carrier could acquire a non-wireline carrier, or vice versa, though no single company could hold both licenses in a single market. The largest players in the acquisition game were some of the regional Bell companies, a few independent telephone companies, and McCaw Cellular Communications.

Following a landmark ruling by U.S. District Court Judge Harold Greene in early 1986 permitting the regional Bell operating companies to provide service beyond their own regions, the wireline carriers began purchasing non-wireline interests (U.S. Department of Commerce, 1988). This began with Pacific Telesis Group's purchase of Communications Industries for $429 million. Subsequent acquisitions included Southwestern Bell's purchase of several cellular franchises from Metromedia and BellSouth's April 1989 acquisition of Mobile Communications Corporation of America for $710 million.

The largest battle during 1989 involved McCaw, BellSouth, and LIN Broadcasting. After McCaw's pockets were deepened by British Telecom's purchase of a 22% stake in the company in January 1989, McCaw attempted a takeover of LIN. LIN was an extremely attractive takeover target because it had cellular operations in five of the country's top ten markets. McCaw, already owning 9.8% of LIN, offered to acquire the remainder for $120 a share. LIN's managers rejected the bid and sought other bidders. On September 11, 1989, LIN announced a merger agreement of its cellular operations with BellSouth Corporation, which could stop an unfriendly takeover by McCaw. However, McCaw was unlikely to give up this easily, and before this deal could go through, McCaw was likely to make a counteroffer ("Telecommunications. . . ," 1989).

Combining properties would encourage more subscribers to make calls as they drove between cities. In the long run, there would be more lucrative long-distance revenues and a greater chance of luring large corporate accounts for those companies that were spending large sums of money for others. For example, a large company like Eli Lilly, which has a sales force of over 500 people who travel across the United States, would take full advantage of a cellular system wherein its sales force could communicate with customers from anywhere in the United States.

In addition, as shown in Exhibit 14.7, the level of cellular penetration (the proportion of Americans with a cellular phone) was a little above 1% and the number of new subscribers was growing at a rate of 50% a year.

A model of the cellular phone industry drawn by Moram Asset Management Incorporated, showed that 15% of Americans would use cellular phones by the year 2000, assuming no new regulation of the industry and few competing technologies (Hof, 1989b).

THE COMPANY

COMPANY HISTORY

LIN Broadcasting Corporation, based in New York, is a communications corporation operating in cellular radiotelephones, as well as commercial broadcasting and specialty publishing. The businesses of LIN were:

- Interests in cellular telephone operations in five major United States markets
- Ownership and operation of seven network-affiliated television stations
- Publication of hardcover and softcover magazines for placement in the rooms of distinguished hotels in major metropolitan areas

The interests in cellular radiotelephone operations is the segment of LIN that is discussed in this study. LIN held significant ownership interests in non-wireline cellular ventures in the New York (50%), Los Angeles (50%), Philadelphia (51%), Dallas–Fort Worth (60%), and Houston (50%) markets, each of which constituted one of the ten largest markets in the United States.

LIN had initially acquired small minority interests in cellular partnerships formed to serve certain smaller markets for which the company had filed a license. Eventually, the company sold all these small interests in order to concentrate its efforts on the five major markets cited. Each of LIN's current cellular ventures had completed construction of its cellular system and had obtained operating authority for its system to provide service to customers within each area by 1989.

All of LIN's ventures relied on a network of distributors that, according to agreements with LIN's ventures, solicited customers for a commission, usually on an exclusive basis. LIN had been exploring the use of retailers as a source of distribution. In addition, LIN offered a variety of service plans in its operating markets and provided services such as call-forwarding, call-waiting, three-way calling (conference calling), and no-answer transfer (LIN Broadcasting Corporation, 1988).

EXHIBIT 14.7	The Level of Cellular Penetration of the Top Ten Companies

Company	Subscribers (thousands)	Potential (millions)	Penetration Rate
Pactel	262	15	1.746%
McCaw	256	50	0.516%
BellSouth	255	13	1.961%
Southwestern Bell	244	18	1.350%
LIN	228	18	1.267%
Ameritech	148	17	0.856%
GTE Mobilinet	127	22	0.577%
NYNEX	127	18	0.705%
Bell Atlantic	100	19	0.526%
US West Newvector	83	12	0.690%
Average penetration for top ten companies			**1.0198%**

Source: Adapted from Calvin Sims, "Cellular Phone Growth Starts Investor Rush," *New York Times,* June 23, 1989, p. D1.

LIN Seeks Interests in Metromedia

In September 1986, LIN had commenced actions against Metromedia, Inc. to enforce its right to acquire Metromedia's interests in both the New York and Philadelphia markets. LIN sought to enforce its "right of first refusal" agreement, which stated that if Metromedia decided to sell to a third party, LIN had the right of first refusal to buy out Metromedia at the same price.

In October 1986, Metromedia filed motions to dismiss these actions alleging that the modification of its agreement with Southwestern Bell to remove the New York and Philadelphia cellular interests from its sale agreement with Southwestern Bell nullified LIN's rights to acquire those interests (LIN Broadcasting Corporation, 1988). The following October, the trial court judge upheld LIN's right to acquire the interests of Metromedia. Then, in July, the Appellate Division of the New York State Supreme Court reversed the lower courts decision and granted Metromedia's motion to dismiss LIN's lawsuit.

LIN Obtains Rights to Metromedia

In February 1989, the New York Court of Appeals granted LIN an appeal of its dispute with Metromedia. Finally, as of October 28, 1989, LIN was granted the right of first refusal and acquired Metromedia's interests in the New York market for $1.9 billion (Sims, 1989a).

EXECUTIVE ORGANIZATION

LIN Broadcasting was headed by Donald A. Pels, Chairman of the Board and President. The president of LIN's Cellular Group was Robert S. Cecil, who reported directly to Pels. In addition, there were five presidents of each cellular subsidiary that reported to Cecil. Exhibit 14.8 illustrates LIN Broadcasting's Executive Organization.

EXHIBIT 14.8 | **1988 Directors: LIN Broadcasting Corporation**

Directors	Officers	
Leland S. Brown Retired, formerly Senior Vice President, Citibank, N.A.	Donald A. Pels	Chairman of the Board and President
	Robert S. Cecil	President–LIN Cellular Group
William G. Herbster Financial Consultant	Gary R. Chapman	President–LIN Television Group
	Frank O'Neil	Vice President
Wilma H. Jordan President, The Jordan Group, Inc. (publishing consultants)	Peter K. Orne	Vice President
	Ronald E. Smith	Vice President
	Harold N. Spitz	Vice President
Richard W. Kislik Publishing Consultant	Arnold S. Blauweiss	Vice President–Finance
	Ronald E. Graiff	Vice President–Engineering
Thos. H. Law President, Law, Snakard & Gambill (a law firm)	David M. Naseman	Vice President–General Counsel and Secretary
	Michael Plouf	Vice President–Corporate Development and Treasurer
Donald A. Pels Chairman of the Board	Daniel B. Stokes	Vice President–Corporate Controller
	Eli V. Bakofsky	Director of Accounting
	Peter E. Maloney	Director of Taxation

Cellular

Robert S. Cecil, President–LIN Cellular Group

Joseph H. Grenuk, Vice President–Operations

Jordan M. Roderick, Vice President–Marketing

Jan S. Zwaik, Controller

	President and General Manager	Location	Equity	Management
Metro One Cellular Telephone Company	E. Lee Kaywork	New York	45%	50%
Los Angeles Cellular Telephone Company	Howard B. Frantom (Acting)	Los Angeles	35%	50%
Metrophone	Michael E. Kalogris	Philadelphia	51%	51%
Metrocel Cellular Telephone Company	Daniel Yost	Dallas	60%	60%
Houston Cellular Telephone Company	Steve R. Skinner	Houston	56%	50%

Source: Information obtained from LIN Broadcasting Corporation, *1988 Annual Report,* p. 21.

The people who represented LIN were among the hardest working in the industry because of the many challenges presented by each of LIN's businesses.

FINANCES

In 1989 third-quarter earnings rose 19.4%, to $24.6 million, or 46 cents a share, from $20.6 million, or 39 cents a share, in 1988. Revenues rose 12.6%, to $61.7 million, from $54.8 million a year earlier (Associated Press, 1989). Income from operations increased to $82,121,000 in 1988, a 48% increase over the previous year. From 1984 to 1989, as shown in Exhibit 14.9, LIN's sales increased at a rate of 22.0% per year, and net income increased at a rate of 45.8% per year.

In 1989 LIN had no debt, and its cellular holdings had helped boost its share price by 55% annually from 1984 to 1988. 1988's cellular revenues were $67 million and had outpaced 1987's by 29%. In the quarter ended June 30, 1989, LIN's cellular operating income climbed 62%, to $21 million on revenues of $44 million—a 47% rise (Keller, 1989). Exhibits 14.10 through 14.14 provide supplemental cellular financial data for LIN: consolidated statements of income, consolidated balance sheets, consolidated statements of cash flows, and selected quarterly data.

KEY EVENTS IN 1989

During the year 1989, many exciting events took place for LIN Broadcasting. Earlier in the year, LIN planned to spin off its television stations to concentrate fully on its growing cellular interests. As the year progressed, LIN became the talk of the cellular industry, and companies such as McCaw Cellular Communications and BellSouth offered large amounts of cash to acquire LIN's cellular interests.

EXHIBIT 14.9 | Five-Year Summary of Sales and Net Income: LIN Broadcasting Corporation

Year	Sales (in $ thousands)	Net Income	EPS
1988	$225,535	$ 82,121	1.54
1987	208,651	87,431	1.56
1986	183,759	66,240	1.19
1985	141,718	85,788	0.70
1984	119,892	29,088	0.65
Annual growth rate	22.0%	45.8%	34.2%

Source: Information obtained from LIN Broadcasting Corporation, *1988 Annual Report*, p. 6.

EXHIBIT 14.10	Consolidated Statements of Income: LIN Broadcasting Corporation and Subsidiaries

(Dollar amounts in thousands, except per share data)

Years Ended December 31	1989	1988	1987
Net revenues	$250,748	$225,535	$208,651
Operating costs and expenses			
Direct operating	59,583	56,606	54,570
Selling, general and administrative	70,798	60,256	57,206
Corporate expense	6,648	6,028	5,453
Depreciation	12,623	10,427	10,085
Amortization of intangible assets	3,953	3,842	3,847
	153,605	137,159	131,161
Operating income	97,143	88,376	77,490
Other income (expenses)			
Equity in income of unconsolidated affiliates	68,144	42,392	11,267
Investment income	22,709	9,064	7,671
Nonrecurring charges	(76,629)	—	—
Interest expense	(3)	(1,673)	(1,885)
	14,221	49,783	17,053
Income before provision for income taxes and minority interest	111,364	138,159	94,543
Provision for income taxes	43,435	47,286	35,150
Income before minority interest	67,929	90,873	59,393
Minority interest in net income of consolidated subsidiaries	10,563	8,752	3,949
Income from continuing operations	57,366	82,121	55,444
Discontinued operations			
Income from operations of discontinued radio business (less applicable income taxes)	—	—	862
Gain on sale of radio business (less applicable income taxes)	—	—	31,125
Income from discontinued operations	—	—	31,987
Net income	$ 57,366	$ 82,121	$ 87,431
Income per share			
Income from continuing operations	$ 1.07	$ 1.54	$ .99
Income from discontinued operations	—	—	.57
Net income	$ 1.07	$ 1.54	$ 1.56

Source: Information obtained from LIN Broadcasting Corporation, 1989 Annual Report, p. 7.

LIN's Television Stations Spun Off

In May of 1989, LIN announced a spinoff of its seven television stations, which left LIN focused on a strong and growing cellular telephone business and specialty publishing. This in turn enhanced the possibility that this side of the business could be

EXHIBIT 14.11	**Consolidated Balance Sheets: LIN Broadcasting Corporation and Subsidiaries**

(Dollar amounts in thousands)

December 31	1989	1988
Assets		
Current assets		
Cash and cash equivalents	$154,652	$ 78,565
Marketable securities	83,521	146,233
Accounts receivable, less allowance for doubtful accounts (1989–$5,225,000; 1988–$4,688,000)	62,049	51,909
Film contract rights and other current assets	17,253	9,379
Total current assets	317,475	286,086
Property and equipment, at cost, less accumulated depreciation	114,721	95,082
Other noncurrent assets	21,084	17,041
Investments in and advances to unconsolidated affiliates	88,443	46,502
Intangible assets, less accumulated amortization (1989–$28,149,000; 1988–$24,196,000)	133,157	137,383
Total assets	$674,880	$582,094
Liabilities and Stockholders' Equity		
Current liabilities		
Accrued income taxes	$ 28,311	$ 29,867
Film contract rights	6,644	9,010
Accounts payable	10,990	7,668
Unearned revenues	9,820	7,767
Other accruals	28,668	27,278
Total current liabilities	84,433	81,590
Long-term debt—cellular	—	4,250
Deferred federal income taxes	34,814	29,033
Film contract rights and other noncurrent liabilities	20,952	15,500
Minority interests in equity of consolidated subsidiaries	37,873	27,222
Commitments and contingencies		
Stockholders' equity		
Common stock 1989 and 1988 — $.01 par value, 150,000,000 shares authorized, 55,329,000 shares issued	553	553
Paid-in capital	191,054	185,164
Retained earnings	465,449	408,083
	657,056	593,800
Less common stock in treasury, at cost (1989–3,746,000 shares; 1988–4,263,000 shares)	160,248	169,301
Total stockholders' equity	496,808	424,499
Total liabilities and stockholders' equity	$674,880	$582,094

Source: Information obtained from LIN Broadcasting Corporation, *1989 Annual Report,* p. 8.

EXHIBIT 14.12	Consolidated Statements of Cash Flows: LIN Broadcasting Corporation and Subsidiaries

(Dollar amounts in thousands)

Years Ended December 31	1989	1988	1987
Cash Flows from Operating Activities			
Net income	$ 57,366	$ 82,121	$ 87,431
Adjustments to reconcile net income to net cash provided by operating activities			
Depreciation and amortization	16,576	14,269	13,995
Provision for losses on accounts receivable	4,364	3,675	4,41
Provision for losses on marketable securities	—	6,525	9,900
Gain on sale of radio business	—	—	(31,125)
Increase in deferred federal income taxes	5,781	4,082	2,614
Increase in minority interests	10,651	14,448	3,949
Equity in income of unconsolidated affiliates	(68,144)	(42,392)	(11,267)
Cash received from unconsolidated affiliates	30,909	12,962	—
Increase in accounts receivable	(14,504)	(4,703)	(1,309)
Increase (decrease) in accrued income taxes	(1,556)	2,727	(3,404)
Increase in other current liabilities	4,399	9,544	149
(Increase) decrease in film contract rights and other current assets	(7,874)	(567)	303
Other, net	1,621	(271)	1,470
Total adjustments	(17,777)	20,299	(10,315)
Net cash from operating activities	39,589	102,420	77,116
Cash Flows from Investing Activities			
Proceeds from disposal of discontinued radio business	—	—	63,682
Proceeds from marketable securities sold	383,272	333,206	422,997
Payments to acquire marketable securities	(320,560)	(303,569)	(460,934)
Capital expenditures	(31,893)	(17,132)	(7,584)
Increase in notes receivable	—	(10,618)	—
Loans to unconsolidated affiliate	(7,001)	—	—
Net cash from investing activities	23,818	1,887	18,161
Cash Flows from Financing Activities			
Repayment of long-term debt	(2,213)	(22,987)	(6,102)
Proceeds from common stock issued for stock purchase plan, stock options and related tax benefits	14,893	20,530	13,522
Purchase of common stock for treasury	—	(49,723)	(110,612)
Purchase of common stock upon option exercises	—	(1,034)	(3,775)
Net cash from (used in) financing activities	12,580	(53,214)	(106,967)
Net increase (decrease) in cash and cash equivalents	76,087	51,093	(11,690)
Cash and cash equivalents at beginning of year	78,565	27,472	39,162
Cash and cash equivalents at end of year	$154,652	$ 78,565	$ 27,472

Source: Information obtained from LIN Broadcasting Corporation, *1989 Annual Report*, p. 9.

EXHIBIT 14.13	**Supplemental Financial Data (Unaudited): LIN Broadcasting Corporation**

(Dollar amounts in thousands)

	Three Months Ended September 30		Nine Months Ended September 30	
	1990	1989	1990	1989
Cellular				
Net revenue	$ 82,693	$ 47,577	$209,344	$128,094
Direct costs and expenses	19,526	12,356	50,151	32,307
Marketing	16,902	9,645	45,720	26,713
	36,428	22,001	95,871	59,020
Cash flow [1]	$ 46,265	$ 25,576	$113,473	$ 69,074
Cash flow as a percentage of net revenue	55.9%	53.8%	54.2%	53.9%
Cash flow before marketing	$ 63,167	$ 35,221	$159,193	$ 95,787
Cash flow before marketing as a percentage of net revenue	76.4%	74.0%	76.0%	74.8%
Proportionate subscribers	304,000	147,000	304,000	147,000
Media				
Net revenues	$ 36,070	$ 38,631	$112,864	$117,003
Operating expenses	20,625	20,101	60,770	58,493
Cash flow [1]	$ 15,445	$ 18,530	$ 52,094	$ 58,510

[1] Income from operations before depreciation and amortization.

The cellular operating data reflects proportionate consolidation of the accounts of the cellular operations in which LIN has an interest. For the periods ending September 30, 1990, the proportionate consolidation also includes an additional 48% direct and indirect interests of the New York City Cellular Telephone Company and a decrease of 1.01% in the Philadelphia Cellular Telephone Company from August 10, 1990, the date the transactions were completed.

Note that LIN's consolidated statements of operations for the quarter and nine months ended September 30, 1990 and 1989 does not reflect proportionate consolidation for the cellular ventures but consolidation and equity accounting as required for each of those periods.

Source: LIN Broadcasting Corporation, *Report to Stockholders*, Third Quarter 1990.

acquired (Kneale, 1989). The spinoff meant that LIN would partition its TV station group as a separate entity. Analysts expected that this move was designed to make the company a more attractive takeover candidate, because former Bell companies are prohibited from owning broadcast outlets (Guyon, 1989).

McCaw's Tender Offer

On Tuesday, June 6, 1989, McCaw Cellular Communications offered to buy LIN for $6 billion in a deal that would establish a communications giant (Shriver, 1989). The deal proposed $120-a-share buyout that would create a company with possible annual revenues of more than $500 million. LIN said it would study the

EXHIBIT 14.14	Consolidated Statements of Operations (Unaudited): LIN Broadcasting Corporation

(Dollar amounts in thousands, except net income (loss) per share)

	Three Months Ended September 30		Nine Months Ended September 30	
	1990	1989	1990	1989
Net revenues	$94,853	$61,702	$ 272,069	$180,835
Operating costs and expenses				
Direct costs and expenses	46,400	34,030	134,767	96,206
Corporate expense	2,175	1,595	5,653	4,983
Depreciation	5,701	3,140	15,847	9,247
Amortization of intangible assets	9,205	980	11,385	2,965
	63,481	39,745	167,652	113,401
Operating income	31,372	21,957	104,417	67,434
Other income (expenses)				
Equity in income of unconsolidated cellular affiliates	19,398	18,996	52,857	50,310
Investment income	1,055	5,774	5,666	16,350
Nonrecurring charges	—	(3,381)	(292,884)	(6,742)
Gain on sale of cellular interests	15,397	—	15,397	—
Interest expense	(36,822)	—	(60,093)	(3)
	(972)	21,389	(279,057)	59,915
Income (loss) before provision (benefit) for income taxes and minority interest	30,400	43,346	(174,640)	127,349
Provision (benefit) for income taxes	8,403	16,059	(58,017)	46,874
Income (loss) before minority interest	21,997	27,287	(116,623)	80,475
Minority interest in net income of consolidated cellular subsidiaries	9,024	2,696	33,032	8,104
Provision for preferred stock dividends of a subsidiary	18,772	—	18,772	—
	27,796	2,696	51,804	8,104
Net income (loss)	$ (5,799)	$24,591	$(168,427)	$ 72,371
Net income (loss) per share	$ (.11)	$ .46	$ (3.27)	$ 1.36
Average common and equivalent shares outstanding	51,379	53,428	51,482	53,392

Source: Adapted from LIN Broadcasting Corporation, *Report to Stockholders,* Third Quarter 1990.

offer and do what was best for its shareholders. LIN's stock jumped up $1.25 to $103.50 following this announcement.

The following day, June 7, the stock market anticipated a bidding war for LIN and pushed the stock up $26 to $129.50, $9.50 higher than McCaw's offer.

Therefore, one could assume that McCaw's offer would not elicit much of a response. There were also many questions within the industry about McCaw's finances and how the company would come up with the cash required for the proposed purchase of LIN. McCaw's large debt, coupled with first-quarter losses of $98 million, seemed to make it a poor applicant for $6 billion more in takeover loans (Brown, 1989). In addition, McCaw filed suit against LIN's anti-takeover measures, which required that if any party bought more than 15% of the company, all other shareholders would be entitled to buy LIN's stock at half price and that, in the event of a merger, its shareholders would be entitled to buy back stock in the acquiring company at half price (Guyon, 1989).

McCaw's New Tender Offer

As of October 19, 1989, McCaw introduced a new strategy to sweeten its bid without having to pay a lot of money up front. This strategy stipulated paying $125 a share now, but for only half of LIN's outstanding stock, with the balance being purchased five years from now. This would allow the shareholders to get immediate cash and an opportunity to cash in again in the mid-1990s, as long as LIN remained a leader in the industry. This prompted BellSouth Corporation, the other bidder for LIN, to announce that it would sweeten its bid, which was about $125 a share (Fabrikant, 1989b).

BellSouth Sweetens Offer and LIN Acquires Metromedia's Interests in New York

On October 27, 1989, BellSouth Corporation sweetened its offer to LIN shareholders for the merger of the cellular companies (Sims, 1989b). Also, LIN exercised its right of first refusal to purchase the interests of Metromedia in the New York market, which happened to have blocked McCaw in this deal. LIN believed that the purchase prices could be met from its working capital on hand or its ability to borrow funds from financial and other institutions. In this merger, BellSouth would own 50% of the new cellular company, and the rest will be owned by the current LIN shareholders. The combined company would be the largest cellular company, with 480,000 subscribers, as shown in Exhibit 14.15.

"This plan is worth more to LIN shareholders because it offered them more cash initially through tax incentives, provided for guaranteed long-term investment and allowed shareholders to keep full ownership of the company" (Sims, 1989b).

As of November 7, 1989, the time period for the BellSouth Corporation and LIN Broadcasting merger expired. LIN's proxy statement was expected to be mailed to the shareholders for a meeting in January 1990. It was questionable whether LIN's shareholders would approve the deal (Reuters, 1989).

McCaw Sweetens Its Bid

As of November 21, 1989, McCaw offered $150 a share in cash for 22.5 million shares, or 46% of LIN's stock. This offer came in response to BellSouth's bid on October 27, 1989. LIN had been resisting McCaw's bids and had agreed to merge with BellSouth Corporation. An additional feature of McCaw's bid was that once the acquisition was completed, LIN would buy $425 million of McCaw class A common stock and distribute it as a dividend. LIN investors would receive $16.17 of that

EXHIBIT 14.15	The Next Cellular Giant?

	Subscribers* 1989	Service Revenues (in $ millions)
BellSouth–LIN	480,000	$576
Pacific Telesis	460,000	415
Southwestern Bell	303,000	365
McCaw	296,000	355
GTE	168,000	202

*Estimates

Source: John J. Keller, "This Cellular Hookup Could Jam the Competition," *Business Week,* September 25, 1989, p. 45.

stock for each LIN share retained. If successful, McCaw would have controlling interest in LIN because presently it owned 10% of the stock (Fabrikant, 1989a).

In addition, McCaw had committed itself to buying the remaining shares or selling them to another company within five years at "private market value." Analysts had put the value of this offer at $130–$135 a share. Many analysts were saying that BellSouth had to come back with a higher offer. Also, McCaw had received firm commitments totaling $3 billion from a 22-bank syndicate. Craig McCaw, the company's CEO, had asked for the McCaw proposal to be put to a vote at LIN's annual shareholders meeting on January 12, 1990, when the BellSouth bid was to be considered.

TOWARD THE FUTURE

Large companies in the cellular phone industry were creating a consolidating environment by acquiring cellular interests in other companies across the United States. In addition, the industry was exploring various strategies to increase the level of cellular penetration through mass distribution and competitive pricing strategies.

Having reviewed the facts presented, LIN managers were studying future actions for the company. They believed that through a merger with either McCaw Cellular Communications or BellSouth Corporation, the new company would be strategically positioned to expand through acquisitions in regions where the company lacked properties. They believed that a larger, merged company would not only ensure survival but also place the new company in a better position to provide a truly nationwide cellular service, which would allow a customer to travel from city to city and use the same system without any interference. The company was in a good position to do this, because it had interests in five of the top ten markets that were vital in producing a nationwide service. At the same time, the company had not yet realized the true potential of its existing markets, cellular use penetration being just over 1%. If this type of merger went through, it would create a cellular giant with large amounts of resources and assets, which would enable the company to invest more in acquiring new subscribers.

Some managers felt that in the future, much of the growth in cellular phone usage would come from nonbusiness users. They believed that tapping this market would require making a major capital investment in the new digital system (as the competitors were doing), as well as investing selectively in other Metropolitan Statistical Areas and Rural Service Areas. This strategy, they felt, would be more feasible and profitable in the long run for LIN. Instead of pursuing a major merger with BellSouth or McCaw, LIN would offer various usage rates to appeal to different customers and would be represented by a large number of distributors. The company was in a good position, because it had the resources to implement digital technology. Also, it would realize more revenues when the level of cellular penetration increased past the 1% rate.

These were just a few of the many major strategic questions being explored by LIN's management as the company prepared to meet the competitive challenges of the 1990s.

REFERENCES

Associated Press. "LIN's Profit Up 19.4% in Period." *New York Times,* October 25, 1989, pp. D13 and D22.

Bean, Clifford A. "Trends in Mobile Communications." *Telecommunications,* January 1989, pp. 72–75.

Benoit, Ellen. "Now You Hear It. . . ." *Financial World,* October 14, 1986, pp. 18–19.

Brown, Warren. "Cellular Phone Industry's Big Numbers." *Washington Post,* June 8, 1989, pp. E1 and E6.

Dworkin, Peter. "How Four Brothers Cashed in on the Car-Phone Boom." *U.S. News & World Report,* August 1, 1988, pp. 42–43.

Dworkin, Peter and Roberta Ostroff. "The 'Celling' of America." *U.S. News & World Report,* August 31, 1987, pp. 45–46.

Fabrikant, Geraldine. "McCaw Sweetens Its Offer for LIN." *New York Times,* November 21, 1989a, p. D22.

Fabrikant, Geraldine. "McCaw Strategy in Seeking LIN." *New York Times,* October 19, 1989b, p. D2.

Gannes, Stuart. "Behold, The Bell Tel Cell War." *Fortune,* December 22, 1986, pp. 97–102.

Gossack, Linda L. "Communications Equipment–Cellular Radiotelephone Systems." *U.S. Industrial Outlook 1989,* 1989, pp. 27-5 and 27-6.

Guyon, Janet. "LIN Shares Soar Past McCaw Offer, Spurring Other Cellular-Phone Stocks." *Wall Street Journal,* June 8, 1989, pp. A3 and A13.

Hamel, Ruth. "Living in Traffic." *American Demographics,* March 1989, pp. 49–51.

Hinds, Michael deCourcy. "Mobile Phones, as Prices Drop, Aren't Just for Work Anymore." *New York Times,* June 10, 1989, p. A33.

Hof, Robert D. "Hello, Reality Calling: Slower Growth in Cellular Has Investors Cashing Out." *Business Week,* August 7, 1989a, pp. 22–23.

Hof, Robert D. "The Cellular Bidding War Will Get Even Hotter." *Business Week,* June 19, 1989b, pp. 39–40.

Keller, John J. "This Cellular Hookup Could Jam the Competition." *Business Week,* September 25, 1989, p. 45.

Keller, John J. "Will Cheaper Cellular Put a Phone in Every Pocket?" *Business Week,* December 5, 1988, p. 142.

Kneale, Dennis. "LIN to Spin Off 7 TV Stations, Raising Chance for Takeover Bid." *Wall Street Journal,* May 26, 1989, p. B4.

Lee, William C. Y. "How to Evaluate Digital Cellular Systems." *Telecommunications,* December 1987, pp. 45–47.

Levine, Jonathan, J. "Craig McCaw's High Risk Empire." *Business Week,* December 5, 1988, pp. 140–151.

LIN Broadcasting Corporation, *1988 Annual Reports.*

Mandell, Mel. "Calling All Cars: The Cellular Connection." *Nation's Business,* November 1988, pp. 46–48.

McCarthy, Robert F. "Churning the Cellular Phone Channels." *Business Marketing*, June 1988, pp. 49–58.

Meeks, Fleming. "Calling More Than Cars." *Forbes*, October 31, 1988, p. 141.

Olsen, William. "Customer Profiles." *Cellular Business*, January 1988, pp. 44–49.

Pomice, Eva. "Have Phone, Will Travel." *U.S. News & World Report*, July 24, 1989, pp. 40–41.

Rudnitsky, Howard. "Great Expectations." *Forbes*, April 18, 1988, pp. 56–59.

Sextro, Darren. "Analysis: Growing the Typical Cellular User." *Cellular Business*, January 1989, pp. 104–107.

Shriver, Jube, Jr. and Linda Williams. "McCaw Cellular Offers to Buy LIN Broadcasting for $6 Billion." *Los Angeles Times*, June 7, 1989, p. 27.

Sims, Calvin. "LIN and BellSouth Sweeten Proposal to Thwart McCaw." *New York Times*, October 28, 1989a, pp. 31 and 33.

Sims, Calvin. "If Your LIN Is Cellular, Give A Ring." *New York Times*, October 1, 1989b, pp. 29 and 31.

Sims, Calvin. "Cellular Phone Growth Starts Investor Rush." *New York Times*, June 23, 1989c, pp. D1 and D3.

Slutsker, Gary. "Gotta Go, I'm Heading into the Canyon." *Forbes*, March 6, 1989, pp. 138 and 140.

Southwestern Bell Corporation, *1988 Annual Reports*.

Taylor, Thayer C. "New Capabilities for Cellular Phones." *Sales and Marketing Management*, July 1989, pp. 66–67.

"Telecommunications–Cellular Telephones." *Industry Surveys*, Standard & Poor's Corporation, October 5, 1989, pp. T24–T28.

"Telecommunications–Cellular Mobile Telephones." *Industry Surveys*, Standard & Poor's Corporation, December 22, 1988, pp. T24–T27.

U.S. Department of Commerce, Washington D.C., "A Competitive Assessment of the Cellular Radiotelephone Industry." June 1988.

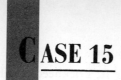

CASE 15 Lockheed Corporation

Robert N. McGrath • Franz T. Lohrke • Gary J. Castrogiovanni

By 1990 the Lockheed Corporation was a national institution and had been one for many decades. Its pioneering efforts in the fields of aviation and space were legendary. In fact, Lockheed's contributions during times of both war and peace suggest that it was an instrument of national security as well as a profit-seeking enterprise.

A business it was, however, and like other aerospace companies, it had experienced dramatic boom-to-bust cycles due primarily to shifts in government expenditures. The U.S. government, and principally the Department of Defense (DoD), were the corporation's major customers by far. Their political and military strategies had been principal determinants of Lockheed's corporate strategy.

At the end of the 1980s, Lockheed found itself in a crisis of uncertainty. It had survived the post-Vietnam cutbacks, several contracting scandals, a disastrous attempt to get back into the civilian sector, and the changing tides of defense policy. It had then healed and profited through the initiatives of the Reagan administration. Headquartered in Calabasis, California, having its airplane-related component in Burbank, and having its space-related component a few hundred miles north in Sunnyvale, Lockheed prospered in the graces of a Californian president devoted to matching global military threats. Sales doubled from 1983 to 1988. At the close of the decade, however, world events seemed to conspire against its business once again: the Soviet hegemony was crumbling in metaphor as the Berlin wall crumbled in fact. The Defense Department, based on Secretary of Defense Cheney's voluntary proposal in 1989, was poised to cut spending by about $180 billion and to reduce the overall size of the armed forces by 25% in just a few years. Naturally, these events caused a severe political and military reassessment of programs under development, and companies such as Lockheed suddenly found themselves likely to become big losers.

The Lockheed posture was not a slave to the situation, though. Dan Tellep, a corporate veteran of over three decades of service, became CEO at the end of 1988. A Renaissance-man type of executive, Tellep doted on innovation and encouraged non-traditional thinking. His proudest achievement had been to garner sales of $1 billion in space station and Star Wars contracts. For four years he ran the Lockheed Missiles and Space Company and was the driving force behind the D-5 missile program, which the chairman of the House Armed Services Committee dubbed the "best-managed program I've seen." Though Tellep admitted to knowing nothing about airplanes (perhaps the proudest part of the Lockheed legacy), corporate-wide changes in strategy certainly seemed imminent.

Prepared by Robert N. McGrath, Franz T. Lohrke, and Gary J. Castrogiovanni, Louisiana State University. Reprinted with permission.

became a worldwide mainstay for decades. Also of critical importance was the sale of 856 Constellation airliners, modified into everything from the PanAm and TWA flagships to Air Force One.

During this era, Lockheed also established a firm foothold in the narrow area of maritime patrol aircraft and anti-submarine warfare (ASW) technology. Between 1946 and 1962, 1,052 Neptune aircraft were built for many countries, giving Lockheed unrivaled expertise in the maritime patrol niche. Then, building on the Electra design, Lockheed produced the new Orion, which eventually became the standard maritime patrol aircraft through at least the end of the century. Lockheed's prowess in ASW also produced the ungainly Viking (S-3), a carrier-based aircraft that took the ASW mission to new levels of aviation technology. Though a narrow business, ASW technology provided a steady cash flow that was to be instrumental in saving the corporation during hard times ahead.

In 1954 Lockheed again demonstrated its technological prowess by introducing the F-104 Starfighter, the first Mach-2 aircraft, known as the "missile with a man in it." Over 2,500 were sold to many air forces. Another of Kelly Johnson's masterpieces, in 1958 it set an altitude record the same day it won the prestigious Collier Trophy for the Year's Greatest Achievement in Aviation. It was so "hot" that even NASA bought versions to train astronauts and do exotic performance tests.

It is difficult to underestimate the importance of the Skunk Works during this period, and especially that of Kelly Johnson up to his retirement in 1975. His leadership, born of technical genius, may have been the most significant single contribution to aviation ever. In addition to the projects mentioned, the Skunk Works produced the U-2 Spy Plane, famed not only because of its use in Cold War crises but also because of its technical capabilities. It was eventually replaced by the TR-1, so remarkably similar that it stood as testimony to the original design. Perhaps the most mysterious project, though, was the Mach-3 (and up) SR-71 Blackbird. This spyplane, with a theoretically unlimited (and never divulged) top speed, holds all speed records. Every detail of the airplane had to be invented to withstand high-speed/high-altitude rigors, such as oil that must withstand getting so hot that it is solid until the plane warms up and titanium skin that expands so much from the heat at those speeds that it is porous at ground conditions. Its advanced state was still unmatched at its retirement after almost thirty years. (Only arrays of satellites could do more.) The SR-71 became "the" symbol of Lockheed excellence. Additionally, the Skunk Works produced the F-117 Stealth Fighter, secretly operational for the better part of a decade before the Northrop Stealth Bomber even flew as a prototype. It is hard to imagine what would have happened to Lockheed without the Skunk Works and Kelly Johnson.

Lockheed was strong in other areas of aviation as well. In 1951 a simple contract to take the B-29 Bomber production line "out of mothballs" for the Korean War effort evolved into one of the strongest businesses Lockheed ever had. At a plant in Georgia, the Air Force subsequently contracted Lockheed to build a new, rugged cargo aircraft. This was to be the C-130 Hercules, which was designed so well that over 30 distinct derivatives were sold for at least as many purposes in over 45 countries. Production was almost continuously sold out for at least 40 years. This established a tradition of heavy aircraft, for next came the C-141 Starlifter, the Air Force's workhorse airlifter. The next step was to build the C-5 Galaxy, which was for years to be the largest airplane in the world, holding outsize and gross-weight cargo records for many years.

Ironically, the C-5 program almost crippled the company. Although the Air Force agreed to buy the plane, the rival Boeing 747 was successfully marketed commercially, killing hopes for volume efficiencies. Also, the technical problems of building a plane so big and yet so versatile were costly. Overruns inspired the Pentagon to cancel 31 of the 115 originally ordered. Corporate losses in 1970 were $187.8 million, the worst in Lockheed's history. The value of common stock dropped by almost half. In the end, $250 million was written off. Eventually, though, the C-5A established a good technical reputation such that 50 follow-on C-5B versions, worth $6.6 billion, were ordered.

Confident in its success with big airplanes, Lockheed decided to reenter the civilian sector in the late sixties. It had not produced an airliner since the mid-1940s, the Constellation. Nevertheless, Lockheed saw an unmistakable market for at least 300 250-passenger airliners and invested over $1 billion in the development of the L-1011 TriStar. Unfortunately, McDonnell Douglas saw the same opportunity, and eventually the L-1011 split the market with the DC-10. Nevertheless, Lockheed continued. Part of its strategy was to contract Rolls-Royce as its engine manufacturer, hoping for inroads to subsequent European markets. Rolls-Royce went bankrupt in the meantime, though, and efforts to save the engine manufacturer for the sake of the TriStar almost destroyed Lockheed financially. Because of Lockheed's importance for national defense, Congress saw fit to guarantee a $250 million line of credit. Though the government eventually profited to the tune of $30 million from that guarantee agreement, negative publicity gave Lockheed a scandalous reputation. After the L-1011 write-off in 1981, net income began to increase again. From $207.3 million in 1982, it increased in three years to $401 million, while sales increased from $5.6 billion to $9.5 billion. Predictably, TriStar demonstrated technical superiority, establishing records in the civilian aviation industry and admiration for Lockheed.

Of equal technical excellence, Lockheed established itself as a leader in the missiles and space segment of the aerospace industry. In the 1950s, Kelly Johnson again proved his genius by participating in the development of a series of "X" (for eXperimental) aircraft that were the pioneers into ranges of air and near-space necessary for further exploration. From this experience, Lockheed was to produce the Polaris, Poseidon, and Trident missiles, which together constituted the entire U.S. Navy submarine-launched ballistic missile capability. These programs in themselves were models of managerial acumen, achieving results ahead of schedule and pioneering organizational techniques. Involvement with the national space programs developed into steady, understated, but vital business as well.

Present Business Environment

As noted, the Reagan administration ushered in a new era for defense contractors, raising real spending 55% during the first five years. Reagan's advocacy of the Stealth Bomber, the "Star Wars" concept of nuclear deterrence, and a 600-ship Navy are examples. Defense spending peaked in 1985, though, and from that point until the end of the decade, the defense industry outlook eroded at an increasing rate. It was predicted that by 1995 defense spending would fall by 13.6% to $261 billion, and to $225 billion by 2000. Military aerospace and missiles were expected to drop at least 10% a year, mostly by cancellation of new programs. By 1990, up to 1,000,000 defense-related jobs might be lost. Lockheed was extremely vulnerable to these forces.

By the mid-1980s, public opinion and burgeoning defense budgets had led to a fairly strict policy of "fixed price." This term is almost self-explanatory. A contract stipulated (in voluminous detail) a product to be delivered and one price to be paid for it. Again, almost all front-end risk had been shifted to the contractor, for major contracts always needed some level of engineering development and R&D. A strategy of winning business by bidding low became popular, though it was often financially ruinous to do so. In concept, "fixed price" might be good free-market economics, but in practice it threatened to undermine national security by driving out important players, reducing incentives for innovation, and discouraging participation in defense contracting itself.

The hostility of this environment became exacerbated by other issues. A policy of separating development and production awards, with no guarantee that a production contract would be awarded, aggravated the risks of development. Further, the loser of a contract competition often won second-source contracts. In other words, in the interest of national security, the government frequently contracted a second company for a major product as a back-up source. This player, usually the runner-up in the original competition, was frequently *given* the results of developmental work expensively performed by the "winner." Runners-up were winners in their own way, avoiding technological risk.

Additionally, the DoD adopted policies of (a) requiring contractors to pay for tooling and test equipment, (b) demanding long-term warranties, (c) establishing strict guidelines for calculating allowable profits, and (d) making progress payments more modest. Finally, a policy of criminal liability took effect. Periodic accusations of fraud and abuse induced a trend of pursuing criminal action against not only contractors but also their employees. Many veteran players simply opted out of this environment. The risks were just too severe.

The geopolitical scene and the Cheney reduction plan also made the industry consider major restructuring. A 25% reduction in force, massive base closings, the crumbling Soviet bloc, and a serious domestic economic agenda made prospects for enormously expensive new systems increasingly speculative. Obviously, the major companies would be pursuing fewer programs. Even within existing (already fielded) systems, costly technological upgrades would be competing for scarce resources. On the other hand, an equally likely possibility would be for the DoD to pursue upgrades as cheaper alternatives to buying new systems. It was impossible to predict what would be sacrificed to finance what. The Advanced Tactical Fighter program, for example, undergoing fierce competition between a Lockheed-led team and a Northrop-led team and still in R&D, might be scrapped in favor of upgrading existing fleets of F-15 and/or F-16 Fighters or producing enhanced derivatives. Or a limited number of Advanced Fighters might be bought as a short-term budget compromise, destroying economies of scale. Any acquisition combination was possible, and no one could make an accurate prediction.

In the industry, long-range marketing and operating strategies began to emerge. Principally, industry wisdom emphasized reorganizing production/operations, securing subcontracting work, upgrading existing programs, and diversifying into stronger growth areas in order to maintain a business base on which to compete for future programs. However, most past efforts to diversify out of this industry had been catastrophic. After Vietnam, Grumman had tried its hand at subway cars. McDonnell Douglas had forayed into computer services. Hundreds of millions were lost. There were some success stories, but horror stories were the rule. One explanation is that defense contractors build up huge bureaucracies in order to serve the Pentagon, while commercial companies must stay flexible. It is not uncommon for a defense contract to take five times as long as a civilian program. Also, defense contractors build to specifications with minimal risk. Technical prowess is valued over cost control. Fixed-price concepts, common in the civilian sector, wreaked havoc in the defense sector.

However, the lure of the civilian sector was powerful. Operating profits in that industry in 1988 alone were $2.5–$3.0 billion. The demands there were huge and long-term. World traffic was expected to grow at a rate of 5.4% a year through 2005. Generally favorable economic conditions and airline deregulation, favorable tourism policies, and a favorable investment climate sustained a buying spree augmented by concerns of airlines over aging fleets and a trend toward larger aircraft. The key elements for market share were affordable equipment and low operating and maintenance costs. Consequently, major steps toward advanced technology or all-new aircraft programs were avoided. Long-range market prospects were for $516 billion by 2005, including a $96 billion backlog and a $420 billion open market (comprising $125 billion for replacements and $295 billion for aircraft to accommodate growth). There was little doubt that civilian aviation had a bright future in almost every segment.

In strategic defense, the environment was somewhat different again. Arms limitations talks notwithstanding, there was little or no evidence that Soviet economic troubles were affecting Soviet growth in strategic capability: missiles, submarines, military adventurism in space, and the like. To balance the threat, American strategic funding had grown faster in real terms than that for conventional forces, absorbing about 15% of the defense budget. Despite the need for balance, the administration was forced by economic constraints to take a gradualist approach to new systems and modernizations. Three major modernization programs were expected to consume the lion's share of the strategic budget: the Navy's Trident 2 D-5 missile (a Lockheed product), Rockwell's B-2 Bomber, and a replacement for the aging Intercontinental Ballistic Missile force—all many years into development. Despite its cost of $35 billion, the Trident missile seemed to be the most politically secure. The Northrop B-2 Stealth Bomber, in the prototype stage, was in the greatest danger. The future of the Strategic Defense Initiative (Star Wars) was almost totally unpredictable.

LOCKHEED'S POSITION

ORGANIZATION

By the end of the 1980s, Lockheed was organized into five major business groups. The largest was the Aeronautical Systems Company (LASC), employing about half of the corporation's over 90,000 people and headquartered in Burbank, California. Most of the rest of the company was employed at Marietta, Georgia, just outside Atlanta.

Activities in California included production of the P-3 Orion anti-submarine aircraft and the TR-1 reconnaissance aircraft. Production of these aircraft would be completed soon. There was a good deal of service/support business related to the S-3 Viking carrier-based ASW aircraft and the L-1011 TriStar. The Advanced Development Projects (Skunk Works) office was also part of this organization, having recently delivered the last of about 50 F-117 Stealth Fighters. The Skunk Works was also currently developing the F-22 Advanced Tactical Fighter (ATF).

| **EXHIBIT 15.2** | **Organizational Chart (Case-simplified): Lockheed Corporation** |

Lockheed Aeronautical Systems Company	Lockheed Missiles and Space Company
Lockheed–California (Burbank, Calif.)	LMSC (Sunnyvale, Calif.)
Lockheed–Georgia (Marietta, Ga.)	Engineering and Management (Houston, Texas)
Lockheed Aeromod Ctr. (Greenville, S.C.)	Space Operations (Titusville, Fla.)
Murdock Eng. Co. (Irving, Texas)	Advanced Marine (Santa Clara, Calif.)
Lockheed Support Sys. (Arlington, Texas)	Marine Systems Group (Seattle, Wash.)
Lockheed Aircraft Svcs. (Ontario, Calif.)	Electronics Systems (Sanders)
Information Systems Group CADAM (Burbank, Calif.) DataCom (New York) DIALOG (Palo Alto, Calif.) CalComp (Anaheim, Calif.) Metier Mgt. (Overseas) Air Terminal (Burbank, Calif.)	Lockheed Finance Corp. Lockheed Corporation International Lockheed Arabia

In Georgia, ongoing activities included production of the last C-5B's under contract, steady but modest production of the venerable C-130 transport, and almost continuous modernization/support projects for existing fleets of C-141, C-130, and C-5 transports.

Niche and service-oriented components of LASC included the Lockheed Aeromod Center in Greenville, South Carolina; the Murdock Engineering Company in Irving, Texas; Lockheed Support Systems in Arlington, Texas; and Lockheed Aircraft Services in Ontario, California.

While LASC was essentially half the corporation, the other half was essentially the Lockheed Missiles and Space Company (LMSC). Headquartered in Sunnyvale, California, its principal activities included the development and production of all U.S. Navy fleet ballistic missiles and that of spacecraft and space systems for NASA and the U.S. Air Force. The long list of projects included the D-5 Trident Missile, advanced observation satellites, information retrieval systems, advanced materials (such as Space Shuttle exterior silica tiles and lithium batteries), physical sciences research (such as atomic and molecular physics, astronomy, nuclear physics, nuclear weapons effects, plasma physics, and re-entry physics), ground vehicles, ocean systems (deep-diving vehicles), ocean mining (and vehicles), advanced tactical systems (radiometric area correlation guidance, airfield destruction, and offensive suppression systems), extensive Star Wars R&D (accredited with "major" breakthroughs), remotely piloted vehicles, and the pride-and-joy Hubble Telescope. (With resolution up to 10 times better than any earth-based telescope, it would allow a view into 350 times more of the universe than ever seen before and revolutionize our understandings through an array of sensors unprecedented in technological capacity.) Futuristic possibilities included a rejuvenated idea for a supersonic transport, a role in the hypersonic national aerospace plane, and liquid hydrogen aircraft fuel.

Components of LMSC included the Engineering and Management Service Company in Houston, Texas; the Space Operations Company in Titusville, Florida; and Advanced Marine Systems in Santa Clara, California.

Lockheed's Information Systems Group (the corporation's smallest) included CADAM (Computer-Aided Design and Manufacturing) in Burbank, California; DataCom Systems of New York City; DIALOG Information Services of Palo Alto, California; CalComp of Anaheim, California; Metier Management Systems (five computer companies with offices in the Far East and Europe); and Lockheed Air Terminal, established in 1941 to manage the company-owned Burbank Airport. (The airport was eventually sold, but Lockheed stayed in the airport management business.)

The Marine Systems Group, headquartered in Seattle, Washington, concerned itself with ship designs, engineering, construction, overhaul, repair, and logistical support. It employed about 1% of Lockheed's work force.

The Electronics Systems Group was formed in 1986 with the acquisition of Sanders Associates, Inc. It developed and manufactured advanced electronic systems for both military and civilian applications.

Unassigned to company groups were the Lockheed Finance Corporation, formed to help customers finance business with Lockheed; Lockheed Corporation International, which provided marketing and support services for all of Lockheed worldwide; and Lockheed-Arabia, a joint venture concerned with a broad spectrum of basic aviation needs.

"Oh, What a Difference a Year Makes." *Business Week,* February 25, 1991, p. 37.

"The $75 Billion Question: Whose Fighter Will Win?" *Business Week,* April 8, 1991, pp. 64–65.

Standard & Poor's Industrial Manual, Lockheed, 1991.

"Tactical Aircraft Producers Face Diminishing Returns." *Aviation Week and Space Technology,* February 22, 1989, p. 34.

"U.S. Armed Forces Vary Means of Coping with Tight Budgets." *Aviation Week and Space Technology,* March 20, 1989, pp. 52–53.

"Who Pays for Peace?" *Business Week,* July 2, 1990, pp. 64–70.

Yenne, W. *Lockheed.* New York: Crown, 1987.

CASE 16 Marriott Corporation and the U. S. Hotel Industry

Robert J. Mockler ▪ John Angelides ▪
Geetu Jedhani

Marriott Corporation, a publicly held company, was founded in 1927 by the late J. Willard Marriott. It owned, managed, and franchised hotels. In 1992 it had over 4,000 units, with operations and franchises in 50 states and 26 countries. In lodging, it offered 161,379 rooms and developed over $1 billion of real estate each year (Marriott Corp., *1992 Annual Report*).

Exhibit 16.1 provides financial data on Marriott Corporation for the years 1988–1991. During 1991 the revenues of the company reached $8.331 billion, an 8.9% increase from the revenues of the previous year. This rate of growth was higher than the growth rate the corporation realized between 1989 and 1990 (1.5%) but less than the growth rate of 1988 and 1989 (13.8%). At the same time, corporate earnings improved from $47 million in 1990 to $82 million in 1991.

During the 1980s, the average annual growth rate of Marriott was 15–20%, reflecting a great improvement over the average growth of 11% that the company achieved in the 1970s. In the beginning of the 1990s, however, Marriott was concerned about its ability to sustain a healthy rate of growth, especially since its debt reached $2.779 billion by the end of 1991 and its growth had slowed considerably in recent years.

The basic problem the hotel industry faced was the overbuilding of rooms that took place in the 1980s. As a result, half of America's hotel companies faced various economic problems. Some hotels were unable to service their debts, and others were unable to finance necessary capital improvements. Many were in the hands of lending institutions and other "reluctant owners" who had been forced to foreclose on the properties. Still more hotels were in immediate danger of being downgraded to a lower level of quality and losing market share.

The measures Marriott had already taken included a substantial layoff of employees, significant cutting of operating costs, $1 billion in asset sales, and (starting in 1990) a complete halt of new hotel construction. The company also planned to reduce overhead cost by more than 10% in the coming years and to delay merit pay increases for top management.

In light of these problems, the company faced many strategic choices in 1992. Marriott could reduce its debt by slowing or halting its expansion, but that might adversely affect its long-term earnings growth. Because of this, should it continue aggressively building more hotels or focus just on renovating the already existing ones? Should it rely on owning, managing, franchising, or some combination of the three? What type of customers should be sought? Which specific market niches of products should be targeted? What pricing strategy should the company pursue?

EXHIBIT 16.1	Four-Year Financial Summary: Marriott Corporation

(Dollar amounts in millions, except per-share data)

	1991	1990	1989	1988
Summary of Operations				
Sales	$8,331	$7,646	$7,536	$6,624
Earnings before interest expense and income taxes	410	263	483	448
Interest expense	265	183	185	136
Income before income taxes	145	80	298	312
Income taxes	63	33	117	123
Income from continuing operations	82	47	181	189
Net income	82	47	177	232
Cash Flow Information				
Cash from continuing operations	$ 549	$ 385	$ 423	$ 411
Proceeds from asset sales	84	975	1,359	1,016
Capital expenditures	427	1,094	1,368	1,359
Cash dividends and share repurchases	27	321	306	381
Capitalization and Returns				
Total assets	$6,400	$6,926	$6,496	$5,981
Total capital	5,065	5,289	5,080	4,689
Long-term debt	2,979	3,598	3,050	2,857
Percent to total capital	58.8%	68.0%	60.0%	60.9%
Shareholders' equity	679	407	628	710
Return on average common shareholders' equity	18.3%	9.7%	23.8%	30.4%
Per Common Share and Other Data				
Earnings per common share				
Continuing operations	.80	.46	1.62	1.59
Net income	.80	.46	1.58	1.95
Cash dividends declared	.28	.28	.25	.21
Common shareholders' equity	5.02	4.35	6.11	6.53
Market price at year end	16.50	10.50	33.38	31.63
Common shares outstanding	95.5	93.6	102.8	108.7
Hotel rooms				
Total	161,379	150,416	134,349	117,789
Company operated	132,125	124,622	109,561	94,253
Employees	202,000	209,000	229,900	229,600

Source: Marriott Corporation, *1991 Annual Report.*

INDUSTRY AND COMPETITIVE MARKET

THE HOTEL INDUSTRY

The hotel industry is a hospitality industry, which consists of hotel companie offering the same or similar products and services for its customers.

Hotels based their plans and strategies on the needs of the travelers and so offered a range of lodging products with different brand names at different hotel chains. Given a diverse population, there were many different occasions that stimulated the need for hotel accommodations. Occasions like conventions, trade shows, business meetings, sightseeing, touring, and other events all generated a need for hotel services. In addition to price, convenient location and amenities played a major role in the customer decision.

The hotel industry was highly competitive. To survive in the 1990s and beyond, experts felt that hotels would have to meet the following requirements:

Marketing   Marketing to the general population via media needed to be improved. Trends such as changing demographics and global political reforms were likely to result in an increased number of international travelers (Jesitus, 1991c). Growing interest in environmental issues and healthful lifestyles were expected to affect hotel consumers' buying behavior. Marketing to specific markets (such as Hispanic, Asian, etc.) would be needed to increase brand awareness in diverse population groups. In addition, marketing of hotels' amenities would be needed to appeal to the different customer groups.

Service   Service remained a critical success factor. Upgraded facilities, well-trained employees, and good management would be necessary elements in providing superior service (Marinko, 1991). In 1990 service was the hardest problem to solve. Employee turnover rate was high, and good management was hard to find. Often, this led to the retaining of inexperienced workers and to poor service. As a result, training and development had become greater challenges for the hotel manager. This was especially true because it was assumed that the importance of guest satisfaction would increase in the future (Hogan, 1992).

Technology   Hotels would need a wide range of networking systems to improve the interaction of their own hotel systems with airline reservation networks. This would replace the outdated systems and improve the quality of service.

In 1990, after a decade of fast growth and large profits, the $57.1 billion American hotel industry lost approximately $350 million. It was generally estimated that about 60% of all hotels had experienced a net operating loss (Mcdowell, 1991). One of the major financial problems many companies were facing was their debt servicing burden. A study revealed that in 1990, interest expense amounted to almost 12% of every dollar generated by a full-service hotel. In 1980 interest expense amounted to only 4.5%. In addition, in 1990 borrowing capacity was weak in the lodging industry. Other indicators of the industry's weakness: the 0.8% increase in room rates through August 1991, compared to the inflation rate of 4%; and room demand up only 0.3%, in contrast to the room supply, which had increased by 2.7% (Smith, 1991).

Major restructuring of the industry had begun taking place in response to the adverse conditions. The major forces influencing the shape of the hotel industry included overbuilding; owning, managing, and/or franchising; and consolidating.

The supply of U.S. hotel rooms had grown in the 1980s by 37.5%, with 774,000 rooms being added. New construction averaged $6.1 billion (in 1982 dollars) from 1983 to 1989, compared with $2.6 billion from 1974 to 1982, a period that included two recessions ("Industry Facing. . . ," 1990). The result of this building boom of the 1980s was that supply far outstripped demand. In addition, the 1990-1992 recession of the U.S. economy and the Persian Gulf war led to a decline in traveling, which in turn negatively affected hotel occupancy rates (Jusko, 1991).

Overbuilding was the result of many factors, including an initial shortage of rooms and the prospect of continued appreciation of real estate values and easily obtainable financing. Tax legislation also had an impact: 65% of the hotel rooms built between 1981 and 1986 were built in the full expectation that they would lose money and so generate tax losses. The 1986 Tax Reform Act eliminated many of the existing tax write-offs, but by then the oversupply of hotel rooms was in place.

In 1990–1991, the oversupply of hotel rooms caused a reduction in the average occupancy rate, which kept the increase in the average per-room rate far below the inflation rate. Because costs in the lodging industry were basically fixed, the occupancy rate was a crucial factor in a hotel's performance.

In the 1980s, hotel occupancy rates tended to average close to 70%. In contrast, in 1990 the hotel occupancy rate was about 63%—below the break-even point of 65 to 70% (U.S. Industrial Outlook, 1990)). In 1991, the hotel occupancy rate was 61.8 percent ("Hotels and Motels," 1990). Due to the lag of four to five years between the time a project was planned and the time it opened, even more rooms had opened in 1990 and 1991.

In 1991 the construction of new hotels declined. The U.S. Department of Commerce indicated that the value of new hotel and motel construction declined by 29% during the first 8 months of 1991 from the corresponding period of 1990. Similarly, the construction of new hotel rooms had significantly decreased. According to F.W. Dodge in 1990, only 67,000 new rooms were built compared to 100,000 rooms in 1989. In 1991 the number of new rooms declined even further, to 25,000. This trend suggested that if the construction slowdown continued, the industry could recover from the building boom of the 1980s and the recession by the mid-1990s ("Overbuilt. . . ," 1991).

Another indicator supporting relative optimism for the hotel industry was the 1991 occupancy rates. In 1991 there had been more properties reporting occupancies above 90% and revenues of more than $100 per available room than in 1990. In general, it was believed that room rates and occupancies would reach profitable levels by 1994 and that by that time, occupancy would be between 64% and 65% (see Exhibit 16.2).

Consolidation of hotel companies was another force shaping the hotel industry. Small chains were selling out to larger chains or were combining with each other. This merger and acquisition activity was intensified by foreign buyers. For example, in August 1990, the French company Accor S.A. purchased for $1.3 billion Motel Six L.P., a chain that owned and operated more than 500 economy

EXHIBIT 16.2	Forecast of Industrial Performance

	1993	1992	1991	1990
Occupancy	63.5%	62.9%	62.3%	63.4%
Daily rate (dollars)	56.24	56.05	55.78	55.12
Room demand (thousands/day)	1,977	1,922	1,863	1,840
Room supply (thousands/day)	3,116	3,057	2,989	2,905

Source: Coopers & Lybrand, *Hospitality Direction*, Vol. 3(1), Winter 1993.

lodging properties. Many national chains were becoming international, and many regional chains were becoming national. It was estimated that the 25 largest hotel companies controlled about 50% of all U.S. hotel rooms in 1991.

Participation in the hotel industry took a variety of forms. Companies could choose to own, manage, and/or franchise properties; some did all three.

Owning a property required considerable capital but offered both control and the possibility of future gains from appreciating asset values. Providing management services was a low-capital way to participate in the hotel business. Franchising a brand name to properties that a company neither owned nor managed was attractive, because it enabled the franchisor to generate revenues (typically a percentage of room sales) on a limited capital investment. Moreover, the addition of franchise properties gave visibility to the overall company name and provided more marketing dollars for brand promotion. Exhibit 16.3 gives a list of the top ten franchisors

EXHIBIT 16.3	The Top Ten Franchisors in August 1991

Top 10 Total Properties		Top 10 Franchised Rooms or Suites	
1. Best Western	3,400	1. Best Western Intern.	274,000
2. Choice Hotels Intern.	2,190	2. Holiday Inn Worldwide	269,110
3. Holiday Inn Worldwide	1,432	3. Choice Hotels Intern.	207,687
4. Days Inn of America	1,200	4. Hospitality Franchise Systems	154,500
5. Hospitality Franchise Systems	1,020	5. Days Inn of America	134,000
6. Super 8 Motels Inc.	843	6. ITT Sheraton	64,702
7. Treadway Inns Partners	395	7. Radisson Hotels Int.	61,600
8. The Promus Cos.	377	8. The Promus Cos.	56,813
9. Hospitality Intern.	302	9. Super 8 Motels Inc.	52,137
10. Forte Hotels Intern.	275	10. Hilton Hotels Corp.	49,833

Source: Jesitus, 1991a.

in terms of total number of properties and total number of franchised rooms or suites. Best Western is ranked highest in both categories, followed by Holiday Inn Worldwide, Choice Hotel International, and Days Inn of America.

Due to room oversupply, franchisors and operators were under pressure to maintain profits, to grow, and to improve quality. To maintain quality, franchisors could drop some aging hotels from the system. But this was not often done for fear of network shrinkage. Such shrinkage undermined other goals, such as growth and maintaining earnings. It also meant having to use up-front fees from new operators to cover revenue lost as old properties were closed.

Not surprisingly, foreclosures were more common in the early 1990s. Lenders were more aggressive than ever. Many had asset-management staffs, which allowed them to take over and manage foreclosed hotels more easily. Also, many former actively lenders were no longer in the market; some were not even in business.

CUSTOMERS

The customer base of the hotel industry consists of business travelers, leisure travelers, and international travelers to the United States.

Business Travelers

A business traveler is a person making at least four business trips in a year during which he or she stays overnight in a hotel. In 1989 one out of four trips Americans took was for business. Total spending of business travelers was estimated to be $28 billion. Business travelers accounted for 30% of the hotel industry revenues. And 39% of all business travelers were women (Cutler, 1990).

Hotel location, price, service, and comfort were among the most significant criteria that business travelers applied when making a hotel reservation (Weaver and McCleary, 1991). Hotels provided services specific for the business traveler. Such services included sophisticated communication technology in the guest room itself, as well as the development of business centers. A typical business center included copying machines, facsimile service, and personal computers and their respective printers (Wolff, 1991). Hotels also developed meeting facilities to facilitate business transactions (Jaquette, 1991).

The number of business travelers was expected to increase in the 1990s (Rowe, 1992). And the percentage of women business travelers was increasing compared to their male counterparts.

Leisure Travelers

A leisure traveler is a person who makes two or more leisure trips in a year during which he or she stays overnight in a hotel. Leisure travelers have a wide range of preferences. Outdoor recreation, entertainment, and family visits are some of the main reasons for leisure travel.

In 1989, 70% of all U.S. travel was leisure-related. Between 1984 and 1989 the number of weekend vacations taken by Americans grew by 28%. Over 41 million households took one or more vacation trips of all kinds each year (Zelinsky, 1990).

The number of leisure travelers was expected to grow at an annual rate of 10% (Rowe, 1992). As baby boomers got older, leisure travelers on average were also expected to be older with greater discretionary income (Yesawich, 1991). Middle-aged Americans were the biggest leisure time spenders, and this trend was expected to continue in the 1990s. Family-oriented travel would supply the most growth from these customers. Weekend getaways were on the rise since most couples were working. Another important age group included customers 50 and older. This segment would outpace the growth of those under 50 by 15% (Whelihan, William, and Kye-Sung, 1991).

International Travelers to the United States

Although international travelers in general come to the United States for a combination of business and leisure purposes, most international travelers come on vacation.

In 1989 overseas travelers spent an average of 20 nights in the United States. Male travelers were twice as numerous as female travelers, and children accounted for 4%. The average age of the international traveler was 40 for males and 36 for females. Of the $74 a day that such visitors spent, 26% was for hotels. International travel had shown substantial increases in the period 1985–1991, and this trend was expected to continue in 1992, reaching 44 million international travelers for the year 1992.

American travel agents were predicting 44.6 million international visits in 1992, a 7% increase from 1991. This number of foreign visitors would generate $7.2 billion of trade surplus (Seal, 1991). Among the international travelers, the ones who spent the most were the Japanese, followed by Canadians, British, Mexicans, and Germans (Peterson, 1992).

PRODUCTS/SERVICES

The hotel industry was highly competitive. To grow, competitors identified different market segments and developed specific products and services to satisfy individual segment needs. Hotel companies used different brands for lodging facilities targeting different market segments. This practice led to brand proliferation.

Brands fell into two categories: those offering a range of services (ranged-service hotels) and those centered around airports or hospital areas (strategically oriented hotels).

Ranged-Service Hotels

The hotel industry had attempted to gain leverage by segmenting its hotel products. These hotel products were divided into three levels of services: limited service, mid-range service, and full service.

Limited-Service Hotels   These types of hotels were low-priced, provided high quality rooms, and offered limited food service. They did not have costly restaurants, huge lobbies, or meeting rooms.

Families traveling on a budget price were their primary target market. By going the limited-budget route, larger chains targeted a large group of customers that the higher-priced chains had not been able to reach yet. *Economy hotels* were the lodging products that fitted into this segment.

A typical economy property had 100–125 rooms (Braus, 1989). Room rates ranged between $40 and $50, 20–50% below the average market rate (Hasek, 1992). As the economy slowed down at the beginning of the 1990s, economy hotels expanded their facilities to provide meeting places for price-conscious business travelers and low-budget-meeting planners. This strategy attracted not only the traditional leisure customers at the economy hotels but also business travelers. The result was that the economy segment benefited from the recessionary times at the beginning of the '90s (Bard, 1991).

In 1991 the top 50 economy hotel chains had a total of 7,626 properties and 701,800 rooms. The actual growth from 1990 to 1991 was 598 properties and 41,300 rooms (Daniele, 1992). Exhibit 16.4 is a list of the fastest-growing economy chains.

Mid-Range Service Hotels   These hotels were moderately priced. Their target market was the individual business and leisure travelers as well as their families. Mid-range service hotels had about 150 rooms with rates ranging from $49 to $89 per night, depending on location (Marriott, 1992). All-suite hotels were the fastest and latest of the mid-range service hotels.

All-suite hotels targeted the extended-stay travelers. A typical all-suite hotel had one- or two-bedroom suites equipped with a kitchen area and separate living and sleeping quarters (Murino, 1989). Some all-suite hotels provided supporting

| EXHIBIT 16.4 | Ten Fastest-Growing Economy Chains in 1991 |

Chains	Opened as of 1/1/91		Opened as of 1/1/92		Increase in Rooms
	Properties	Rooms	Properties	Rooms	
Motel 6	551	63,300	639	72,800	9,500
Hojo Inns	10	900	113	9,600	8,700
Comfort Inns	690	61,800	778	68,700	6,900
Hampton Inns	248	31,100	295	36,800	5,700
Super 8 Motels	785	48,800	863	53,300	4,500
Days Inns	1,112	129,900	1,218	134,000	4,100
Holiday Inn Express	3	500	31	3,700	3,200
Econo Lodge	637	48,600	692	51,400	2,800
Travelodge	463	37,500	488	39,500	2,000
Fairfield Inns*	76	9,900	92	11,300	1,400
Friendship Inns*	96	5,000	130	6,400	1,400

*Tied for tenth place.

Source: Daniele, 1992.

office services that included 24-hour fax sending and receiving and access to professional typists (Brown, 1991).

As shown in Exhibit 16.5, the top 16 all-suite chains had a combined total of 498 properties and 82,400 suites as of January 1991. This represented a 19% increase in properties since January 1990 and a 21% increase in suites.

Full-Service Hotels Luxury, high price, image, convenience, and service were the main characteristics of these hotels. They were the flagships of the hotel companies. Their location varied from downtown, where they were often the hallmark of a city, to the resorts. Their clientele consisted of (1) relatively rate-insensitive, discriminating, transient guests and (2) more price-sensitive business and leisure guests (Boyer and King, 1991). Their upkeep and eventual renovation was expensive. It took three years and $100 million to renovate St. Regis of New York, for example, when the hotel's total rooms were reduced from 557 to 359. The strategy was to downsize in order to create a better product (Conner, 1991). The slow economy at the beginning of the nineties had an adverse effect even on the full-

---

EXHIBIT 16.5	Suite Growth in 1991

	As of January 1, 1991		Expected to Add by December 31, 1991
	Number of Properties	Number of Suites	Number of Properties
Embassy Suites	94	22,900	100
Residence Inns	162	19,300	176
Guest Quarters Suite Hotels	30	6,200	31
Radisson Hotels Internat.	27	5,500	30
Comfort Suites	32	3,400	46
Marriott Suites	15	3,800	17
Quality Suites	22	3,100	27
Hawthorn Suites Hotels	13	2,200	19
Summerfield Suites Hotels	8	1,000	23
Lexington Hotel Suites	17	2,500	20
Homewood Suites	16	1,900	24
Manhattan East Suite Hotels	9	1,900	9
Woodtin Suites	8	1,100	12
Studio Plus	14	1,000	19
Amerisuites	8	900	11
Park Suites Hotels	5	1,200	5

Source: Daniele, 1991.

| EXHIBIT 16.11 | Marriott's Involvement in the Economy Segment |

	Inns	Rooms
Company-operated:		
Owned	30	3,633
Under management or lease agreement	50	6,681
Franchised	13	1,185
Total Fairfield Inns system	93	11,499

Source: Marriott Corp., *Form 10-K*, January 1992.

---

as Motel 6, Days Inns, and Hojo Inns. Aimed at budget-conscious individual business and leisure travelers, Fairfield Inns typically had 63 to 135 rooms with rates ranging from $30 to $45 per night, depending on location. Since there was limited public space, this chain did not have any restaurants.

In 1991 this sector of the lodging industry had been outperforming the national industry's occupancy rates. Fairfield Inns appealed to its customers by providing excellent value relative to its price.

Fairfield Inns was able to offer packages that had been very appealing to the business and leisure traveler. In 1991 this segment of the industry was growing at an 8.5% rate, well above the industry average of 2 to 3%. In 1991 Fairfield Inns was ranked number 10 among the fastest growing chains.

Courtyards

Courtyard hotels served the mid-range service segment of the hotel industry (see Exhibit 16.12). As of January 1992, there were 196 Courtyard hotels in the Marriott Corporation located in 35 states (Marriott Corp., *Form 10-K*, January 1992).

Marriott's Courtyard hotels were moderately priced. Their market position in the industry enabled them to compete directly with major franchised hotel chains. They targeted individual business and pleasure travelers as well as families. In 1991 a typical Courtyard hotel had 150 rooms with rates ranging from $49 to $89 per night, depending on location.

Courtyard hotels looked like residential condominiums. The operating systems developed for these hotels enabled them to be very competitive in pricing while providing the customer with superior product and service. In 1986 Marriott sold 50 Courtyards in a limited partnership and an additional 70 in 1987. In 1992 Marriott intended to sell 14 new Courtyards, while retaining long-term operating leases for the properties.

Marriott Hotels and Resorts

As of January 1992, the full-service Marriott system included 233 Marriott hotels, resorts, and suites located in 41 states, the District of Columbia, and 18 foreign

EXHIBIT 16.12	Marriott's Involvement in the Mid-Range Segment

	Hotels	Rooms
Company-operated:		
Owned	65	9,373
Under management or lease agreement	126	18,390
Franchised	5	1,061
Total Courtyard Hotels system	196	28,824

Source: Marriott Corp., *Form 10-K,* January 1992.

countries with a total of 99,079 guest rooms (Marriott Corp., *Form 10-K,* January 1992). Most of the Marriott hotels in this segment provided 300 to 500 rooms. Marriott also had 18 convention hotels (totaling 18,931 rooms), each one containing up to 1,900 rooms. The room rates in this sector ranged from $80 to $225, depending on location.

Room rentals contributed 62% of Marriott hotel and resort sales in 1991, with the remainder coming from food and beverage operations, recreational facilities, and other services.

This segment of the Marriott Corporation catered primarily to business and pleasure travelers and to group meetings at locations in downtown and suburban areas and near airports. Individual business and pleasure travelers accounted for approximately 58% of occupied-room nights at Marriott hotels and resorts in 1991; group meetings represented another 37%.

To stimulate pleasure-travel business, Marriott began offering nonrefundable advance-purchase discounts to its customers, and additional advance-purchase promotions were scheduled for 1992. The nonreturnable advance-ticket discounts were first introduced in the airline industry in 1987. Marriott was the first to introduce this concept into the hotel sector of the industry. In December of 1991, it introduced $49-a-night rates to travelers who would pay for their entire stay in advance and who made reservations 14 days prior to their stay.

Brighton Gardens

Brighton Gardens were Marriott's hospital-area hotels (see Exhibit 16.13). Marriott entered this market in the early 1980s. This Senior Living Services operation developed and managed "full-service living communities" for the elderly.

Marriott recognized that it had in place two of the three essential components needed to succeed in this segment of the market. Through its real estate organization, it developed and planned new retirement facilities. And because of its hospitality experience, it met property-maintenance and food-service needs. The only area it had no direct experience in was health care. Therefore, Marriott contracted with health-care providers who offered on-site services.

EXHIBIT 16.13	Marriott's Involvement in Hospital-Area Hotels

	Communities	Apartments/Beds
Owned: Brighton Gardens	4	516
Independent full-service	7	2,765
Operated under management agreements	2	439
Total Retirement Community System	13	3,720

Source: Marriott Corp., *Form 10-K,* January 1992.

MARKETING AT MARRIOTT

Traditionally, the Marriott Corp. had focused on upscale hotel users and provided services and amenities that catered to this market segment. Its slogan—"Service, The Ultimate Luxury"—was quite appropriate for such a target audience. As the industry grew and changed, however, Marriott saw the need to segment its markets. Segmentation in the lodging industry meant establishing different levels of price, service, and space for different kinds of guests. As a result, Marriott carefully designed its product portfolio to offer many different products, creating a diversity that has kept it alive and successful in a highly competitive market.

Two major factors were contributing to Marriott's success. The first was its ability to manage its financial assets effectively, and the second was its effort to become the provider of choice, or the preferred provider, in the hotel industry. In guest satisfaction surveys, Marriott consistently ranked at the top (Ulrich and Lake, 1991).

In the 1980s, the motto of the hotel industry was location, location, location. In the 1990s, the motto became service, service, service. Marriott Corporation had a strong focus on world-class customer service to gain a competitive edge and reinforce customer loyalty. It also developed an effective market feedback, which served as a basis for differentiation. For example, Marriott received more than 80,000 comment cards each year from member hotels. Each hotel was rated using a "guest satisfaction index."

Sophisticated marketing research methods, including focus groups and surveys, were used to define Marriott customers' needs. The development of an extended data base of frequent fliers was another product of market research. This database had vital implications for marketing programs at Marriott. It offered great segmentation possibilities by distinguishing heavy, medium, and light users. This allowed for the customization of mailing lists and the future development of products geared specifically to different user segments.

As a large hotel chain, Marriott had a clear advantage over smaller competitors. For example, in the frequent-guest programs, the biggest hotel chains had the largest memberships because they could offer travelers a wider choice of hotels in more areas. In 1991 Marriott had the largest membership, approximately 3.5 million.

Marketing Strategies

Marriott's top-of-the-line, full-service, luxury hotels enjoyed a strong position in the business, convention, and upscale pleasure customer segment. The recession of 1991 had an adverse effect on the upscale hotel revenues. The upscale pleasure customer segment was the only segment that had an increased occupancy rate for 1991 (to 65.5%, up 0.3% from 1990). Even though this trend was expected to continue, Marriott was taking precautionary methods to cut back on expenses and tried to attract more customers by using expanded advertising campaigns.

During the 1991 hotel slump, Marriott and its competitors succumbed to heavy discounting. Marriott employed one of the most drastic discounting strategies: nonrefundable advance-purchase rates, which were quite common in the airline and rental car industries. This strategy was first put to work in May of 1991, when Marriott began a summer promotion offering nonrefundable discounted room rates at Marriott hotels, resorts, and suites for travelers paying in advance.

Customer reaction to this strategy was very favorable. Aside from the savings, Marriott allowed its customers a structured, rational set of rules that defined the discount rates, which made it easier for guests to understand the lodging-purchase process. The "rack rate," or posted rate, no longer had any meaning because every knowledgeable business or leisure traveler negotiated and got cheaper rates.

In April of 1992, however, ITT Sheraton Corporation introduced a similar simplified lower-rate structure called the "SureSaver." The main difference between these two promotions was that no prepayment and penalties were required by Sheraton's "SureSaver." Industry analysts believed that this type of discounting would catch on in the industry.

Because most upscale hotels were located in city business centers and catered to business travelers, Marriott and its competitors alike constantly offered discounts for weekend stays to fill the rooms with leisure travelers when the business travelers were not around.

Travelers attending conferences provided a great opportunity for upscale hotels. Marriott Hotels and Resorts developed the "No-Risk Meeting," in which services not delivered were deducted from the account. Marriott saw this program as an excellent selling tool.

Another marketing strategy included the attraction of hotel guests to Marriott's lounges and its Champions Sports bar by a variety of promotions. Because an increasing number of people were avoiding drinking alcoholic beverages, marketing tactics such as "Happy Hours" and "2 for 1" drinks became less effective. Marriott applied new marketing concepts by providing sports on big-screen television, interactive video trivia games, Sing A' Lounges, performers, college alumni parties, and more. Another marketing strategy included the promotion of food and drinks with Marriott Hungry Hours. In the upscale Marriott lobby bars, the attractions included wine and food matching (such as offering combinations of shrimp mousse and a glass of chardonnay for one price). Marriott's aim was to position itself as a one-stop shop for eating, drinking, and entertainment. The result was that food sales from the bar increased from 3% in 1989 to 20% of total food sales in 1992.

In the resort segment, Marriott developed strategies that focused on families and children. Due to the success of these strategies, the firm expanded them to other market segments. An example of this strategy was the "Friday Night Family Night" package offered at nine Chicago-area hotels, which provided accommodations for up to five family members, a "kid's fun-pak" with snacks and crayons, a kids-eat-free deal for those aged six and under, a $30 dinner certificate for parents, free breakfast, and a free in-room movie.

OPERATIONS

Facilities

In the beginning of the 1990s, Marriott Corporation cut its new construction drastically. Known for its aggressive building of hotels for sale to investors in the 1990s, Marriott diverted from that strategy and by 1992 was expanding its hotel business by acquiring already-built facilities. Fairfield Inns units were the only hotels Marriott was constructing from the ground up (because financing was still available).

In 1992 the stagnant U.S. economy did not hinder Marriott's expansion of its product line of lodging facilities. Eight full-service hotels were opened in U.S. locations, and a major construction program to achieve national distribution of the company's Courtyard, Residence Inns, and Fairfield Inns brands neared completion during 1991 (Marriott Corp., *1991 Annual Report*). Marriott also benefited from the addition of a large number of franchised properties in 1991 and from the acceleration of converted brands. Twelve of the properties added to Marriott in 1991 were conversions. At the end of the first quarter of 1992, Marriott had 162,000 rooms in 709 hotels, 11 of which were opened in the first quarter.

Technology

In the 1980s the hotel industry lagged behind the airline and car industries in technological support systems, but that began changing in the 1990s. The most outstanding product through June of 1992 was the Confirm Reservation System. It was a joint venture of American Airlines, Hilton Hotels Corporation, Marriott Corporation, and Budget Rent A Car Corporation. "The consortium was called Intrico (International Reservations and Information Consortium) and was designed to enhance marketing opportunities for hotel chains and car rental companies, while providing greater global distribution capabilities. The system would provide agents with more detailed information about availability and rates worldwide" (Lawrence, 1991).

On a smaller scale, Marriott improved its technology by capitalizing on the existing equipment by increasing its functionality. For example, it introduced voice mail via the television and attached a jack on all its phones so that guests with portable computers could get hooked up. It examined the prospects of voice recognition, extensive selections on "pay per view" television, and robotics to do cleaning. It added fax machines and conference telephone capabilities to make the business traveler more comfortable.

CORPORATE FINANCIAL OVERVIEW

Despite the difficult operating environment (economic conditions, oversupply of domestic hotel rooms, and soft airline enplanements at many airports), Marriott Corporation achieved a record level of operating cash flow in 1991 and significantly strengthened its financial position. The major financial highlights of 1991 were as follows:

- Operating cash flow increased by nearly 50%.
- The company reduced its long-term debt by over $600 million and extended maturities on another $700 million of debt.
- Cash flow coverage of interest increased to 2.1 times, compared to 1.8 times in 1990.
- Shareholders' equity increased 67% to $679 million.
- Earnings per share of common stock increased substantially compared to 1990.
- Despite weakness in the U.S. economy and hotel industry, occupancy rates and profits were higher in three of the company's four major lodging product lines and were down only slightly for Marriott Hotels, Resorts, and Suites.
- Substantial progress was made in international lodging and contract services development and in the expansion of lodging franchise programs (Marriott Corp., *1991 Annual Report.*)

The company funded its capital requirements with a combination of cash flow from operations (including money generated by properties held for sale, proceeds from sales of hotels and other properties, and debt and equity financing). Marriott Corp. disposed of businesses that no longer met its financial return or growth objectives. In 1989 the company divested itself of its airline catering business for over $500 million. In 1990 the company sold its fast-food restaurant division for more than $365 million. In 1991, 138 family restaurants were sold for cash proceeds of approximately $43 million. The company sold an additional 107 for total proceeds of $67 million in early 1992 and expected to sell many of its remaining 177 family restaurants by year end 1992 (Marriott Corp., *Form 10-K,* January 1992).

On March 27, 1992, there were 100,211,270 shares of common stock outstanding, held by 59,135 stockholders (insiders own 30% of stock). The company's common stock was traded on the New York Stock Exchange, Midwest Stock Exchange, Pacific Stock Exchange, Philadelphia Stock Exchange, and Tokyo Stock Exchange.

Corporate expenses increased 18% in the first quarter of 1992, reflecting higher profit sharing and foreign exchange costs and startup losses in a foreign hotel joint venture. Interest expense, net of interest income, decreased 6% as lower average borrowing and interest rates were partially offset by reduced interest capitalization (see Exhibits 16.14 and 16.15).

HUMAN RESOURCES

One of the major sources of competitive advantage in the hospitality industry was quality of human resources. Marriott Corporation was one of the industry leaders in the development of its human resources. It worked hard to ensure that its people were well trained to take care of its customers and provided an environment that fostered personal achievement.

| EXHIBIT 16.15 | Key Annual Financial Ratios: Marriott Corporation (continued) |

Fiscal Year Ended	January 3, 1992	December 28, 1990	December 29, 1989
Leverage			
Current debt/equity	0.08	0.18	0.05
Total liab/total assets	0.89	0.94	0.90
Total liab/invested capital	1.56	1.63	1.60
Total liab/common equity	11.94	16.02	9.34
Long-term debt/equity	4.39	8.84	4.86
Total debt/equity	4.46	9.03	4.90
Total assets/equity	9.43	17.02	10.34

Source: Value Line, January 3, 1992.

With a work force of more than 200,000, Marriott was one of the largest employers in America, and it was widely recognized for its successful human resource programs. Marriott received many honors, including "one of the best places to work" by *Working Mother, Black Enterprise,* and *Hispanic* magazines. Approximately 40% of Marriott's employees were members of minority groups, and over half were female, with management made up of approximately 15% minority and 40% female. Though this was one of the best records among major companies, Marriott was constantly striving to improve it and had specific programs to do so. Marriott also had a long-standing record of employment for people with disabilities and had received many awards for its programs in this area.

Marriott's approach to management included its Business Council system, wherein managers of various company operations in more than 50 geographic locations met periodically to address common issues, share information, and work cooperatively in areas such as recruiting, purchasing, and sales generation.

In 1989 Marriott established the Department of Work and Family Life at company headquarters in Washington, D.C., because studies of company employees revealed that family issues affected productivity (Solomon, 1991). In response to these findings, Marriott also developed a pretax salary set-aside program for dependent care, a child-care resource and referral service, an on-site child-care center at corporate headquarters, and a child-care discount program in which Marriott employees got a 10% discount at 3,000 child-care centers nationwide.

For its efforts, Marriott won *Personnel Journal*'s 1991 Optima Award, given annually to companies that displayed excellence in human resources management in one of 10 categories ranging from managing change to global outlook. Marriott was the winner in the "Quality of Life" category.

With the exception of autistic and psychotic individuals, and those suffering from progressive physical infirmities, handicapped persons could find work at Marriott. Marriott's comprehensive employment program for mentally and physically challenged workers was based on the belief that with proper job matching, training, and support, such workers could benefit themselves and the company (Burgess and Zhu, 1990).

By approving the Americans with Disabilities Act (ADA) in May 1989, the House of Representatives theoretically opened the doors (and expanded doorways) for the nation's estimated 43 million handicapped people. Under the bill, the Civil Rights Act of 1964—which outlaws discrimination on the basis of race, religion, sex, and national origin—was extended to cover the physically and mentally disabled, including AIDS and cancer patients, as well as treated or recovering substance abusers.

To comply with the law, businesses had to make "reasonable accommodations" to workers and job applicants with disabilities unless the required changes presented an "undue hardship." The Torrance (California) Marriott teamed up with Employ America, a not-for-profit agency that seeks to employ persons who might not otherwise have job opportunities—persons with such disabilities as cerebral palsy, learning disabilities, or traumatic brain injury. Chainwide, Marriott employed some 6,000 disabled persons.

POWER AND POLITICS

In 1989 Bill Marriott, 57, suffered a minor heart attack in October and underwent a bypass operation in December. In November, his heir apparent, John H. Dasburg, left to help run NWA Inc. This latest in a series of key departures raised questions about whether Marriott had the management talent to navigate one of its toughest periods. Without Bill Marriott, a renowned workaholic, it was speculated that the company could face serious problems (Foust and Maremont, 1990).

J.W. (Bill) Marriott, Jr., emphasized excellence in decorum and cleanliness. Marriott's hotel employees had to follow a rigid 54-step procedure in making up a room, with various tasks addressed in sequence (mirrors had to be cleaned, for example, before the wastebaskets were emptied). Some experts felt that was one of the reasons this family business was one of the most consistently successful service companies in America.

Bill Marriott's family and the Mormon Church were the priorities in his life—he was religious head of eight Mormon wards—but he still routinely put in 14-hour days. He traveled 200,000 miles a year visiting Marriott operations and various competitors. He liked to hear what his employees had to say.

Bill Marriott sometimes dropped by a hotel kitchen unannounced to check on the cleanliness and the flow of food, a habit he picked up from his father. A few workers were chilled by the boss's unexpected appearance. "There's a mixed reaction," Marriott admits. "I'm not a yeller or a screamer, but I expect my people to make profits" (*Fortune,* January 2, 1989, p. 62).

In 1992 the Marriott family owned slightly less than 30% of the company stock. The family's religion, the Church of Jesus Christ of the Latter Day Saints—or Mormonism—rarely influenced major business decisions affecting the hospitality company, and when such influences were felt, it was always to the benefit of the company.

There were, however, times when Bill Marriott's philosophy entered into a business decision, such as Marriott's decision a couple of years ago not to acquire a gaming business.

"The very definite, strong work ethic in this company is probably associated with some of the family's philosophy of life, which was, in turn, affected by its religion," said senior vice president Ehrlich, "and it has served Marriott well." There were very high levels of integrity, and that influenced Marriott's human resource philosophy.

REFERENCES

Barker, Julie. "Airport Hotels: Pamper Your Meeting." *Successful Meetings,* July 1989, pp. 61–70.

Bard, Susan M. "Industry Profitability Still Down on the Road." *Hotel & Motel Management,* November 4, 1991, pp. A-3, A-84, and A-112.

Boyer, Cheryl and Ellen King. "Upscale Markets: New York City and Washington, D.C." *Cornell Hotel & Restaurant Administration Quarterly,* December 1991, pp. 35–38.

Braus, Paul. "Hold the Frills: Meeting at Economy Hotels." *Successful Meetings,* June 1989, pp. 77–81.

Brown, Ann. "Your Home Away from Home." *Black Enterprise,* October 1991, pp. 131–134.

Buglass, Karen. "The Business of Eldercare." *American Demographics,* September 1989, pp. 32–39.

Burns, John. "Move to Outpatient Settings May Boost Medical Hotels." *Modern Health Care,* June 8, 1992, pp. 57–58.

Burgess, Charles and Guangli Zhu. "Should All Mentally Challenged People Work?" *Personnel,* January 1990, pp. 20–22.

"C. H. R. A. Q. News & Reviews." *The Cornell H. R. A. Quarterly,* April 1992, p. 17.

Conner, Fred L. "NYC Hotels Show the Reasons Why." *Cornell Hotel & Restaurant Administration Quarterly,* December 1991, pp. 24–34.

Coopers & Lybrand, *Hospitality Direction,* Vol. 3(1), Winter 1993.

Daniele, Daniel W. "Down Before the Rebound." *Hotel & Motel Management,* April 27, 1992, pp. 17–22.

Daniele, Daniel W. "All-Suite Companies' Rise Cut Short in 1991." *Hotel & Motel Management,* April 8, 1991, pp. 55–58.

Foust, Dean and Mark Maremont. "The Baggage Weighing Marriott Down." *Business Week,* January 29, 1990, pp. 64–66.

Gonzalez, Arturo and Maureen Gonzalez. "Meetings: So Why Not an Airport Hotel?" *Sales & Marketing Management,* November 1989, pp. 60–66 and 93.

Grover, Ronald and Eric Schine. "Can Hilton Draw a Full House?" *Business Week,* June 8, 1992, pp. 88–89.

Hanks, Richard D., Robert G. Cross and Paul R. Noland. "Discounting in the Hotel Industry: A New Approach." *Cornell Hotel & Restaurant Administrative Quarterly,* February 1992, pp. 15–23.

Hasek, Glenn. "Room Demand Boosts Upper Segment." *Hotel & Motel Management,* April 27, 1992, pp. 17 and 24.

Helliker, Kevin. "Weak Links: How a Motel Chain Lost the Moorings After 1980's Buy-Out." *Wall Street Journal,* May 26, 1992, pp. A1–A8.

Hogan, John J. "Turnover and What To Do About It." *The Cornell H.R.A. Quarterly,* February 1992, pp. 40–45.

"Hotels and Motels." *U.S. Industrial Outlook 1990,* pp. 45-1, 45-5, 44-1, and 44-4.

"Industry Facing 80's Building Boom." *Standard & Poor's,* March 15, 1990, pp. 37–39 and 52.

Jesitus, John. "Duking It Out." *Hotel & Motel Management,* August 19, 1991a.

Jesitus, John. "The New Labor Pool." *Hotel & Motel Management,* December 16, 1991b, pp. 23–24.

Jesitus, John. "U.S. Tourism Needs Coordinated Sales Pitch." *Hotel & Motel Management,* June 24, 1991c, pp. 3–37.

Jesitus, John. "Risk in Troubled Hotels Fuels Management Team Turnover." *Hotel & Motel Management,* May 27, 1991d, pp. 39 and 41.

Jusko, Jill. "Forum Indicates Industry Recovery Will Take a While." *Hotel & Motel Management,* December 16, 1991, pp. 2 and 44.

Lawrence, Jennifer. "Travel Marketing: Data Base Opening Doors." *Advertising Age,* November 4, 1991, p. 56.

Marinko, Barbara. "In-Room Amenities." *Hotel & Motel Management,* October 7, 1991, pp. 35–36.

Marriott Corp., *10-K Report,* January 3, 1992.

Marriott Corporation, *1991 Annual Report.*

Mcdowell, Edwin. "Hotels Await the Wake-Up Call." *New York Times,* September 24, 1991, p. D1.

Murino, Catherine. "Travelers Come Home to Temporary Housing." *Personnel Journal,* June 1989, pp. 140–143.

Olsen, Michael D. and Katherine Merna. "Trends." *Hotel & Motel Management,* December 16, 1991, pp. 23–24.

"Overbuilt Hotel Industry in Slump." *Industry Surveys,* March 12, 1991, pp. L34–L36.

Pesmen, Sandra. "Super Resorts Entice Super Meetings." *Business Marketing,* January 1992, pp. 46–49.

Peterson, Robin T. "Importing People Will Ease U.S. Trade Deficit." *Marketing News,* February 3, 1992, p. 4.

Rock, Stuart. "London's Luxury Blues." *Director,* February 1992, pp. 65–71.

Rowe, Megan. "Travel Looks Up." *Lodging Hospitality,* May 1992, pp. 51–52.

Seal, Cathy. "Sheraton Differentiates Its Inns from Hotels," *Hotel & Motel Management,* July 29, 1991, pp. 2 and 38.

Smith, Randell A. "Vision of Industry's Future Remains Cloudy." *Hotel & Motel Management,* November 4, 1991, pp. 1 and 4.

Solomon, Carlene Marmer. "Marriott's Family Matters." *Personnel Journal,* October 1991, pp. 40–42.

"Travel Services." *U.S. Industrial Outlook 1992,* pp. 42-1 to 42-4.

Ulrich, Dave and Dale Lake. "Organizational Capability: Creating Competitive Advantage." *Academy of Management Executive,* February 1991, pp. 77–92.

Weaver, Pamela and Ken McCleary. "Basics Bring 'Em Back: Extras Are Appreciated, but Business Travelers Still Value Good Service and Good Management." *Hotel & Motel Management,* June 24, 1991, pp. 29–38.

"Which Hotel? Try One of the New Breed of Airport Hotels." *Agency Sales Magazine,* February 1992, pp. 37–38.

Witham, Glenn. "Bustin' Loose." *Cornell Hotel & Restaurant Administration Quarterly,* August 1991, p. 13.

Wolff, Carlo. "Getting Back to Basics: The Recession Seems to Spur Creativity and Scope as Guestroom Amenities Contract." *Lodging Hospitality,* August 1991a, pp. 83–84.

Wolff, Carlo. "An Essential Amenity." *Lodging Hospitality,* February 1991b, pp. 57–58.

Woolsey, Christine. "Hospital Hotels: Hospital Alternatives Offer Cost Savings, Rapid Recovery." *Business Insurance,* April 22, 1991, pp. 3 and 22.

Word was losing out to WordPerfect and others for a very different reason than Multiplan lost to Lotus 1-2-3. Multiplan failed in the United States because IBM coerced Microsoft into gauging the program to IBM's low-end machines. Word was losing because Microsoft, in its zeal to create the most powerful word processing program available, failed to consider the full array of user needs.

Just as the success of Multiplan was resurrected by turning to the European market, Word also fared better there. When Word arrived in France in 1984 to mixed reviews, WordStar and Textor (produced by a French company) were already well positioned. Gates and his European staff decided on a three-pronged penetration strategy. First, to encourage distributors to sell Word, Microsoft France provided distributors with free training and a free copy of Word. Second, Microsoft arranged to have all retailer demonstrations of Hewlett-Packard's new LaserJet printer performed using Word. Third, Microsoft France convinced many printer manufacturers to promote Word because of its ability to port to sophisticated, high-end multifont printers. Michael Lacombe, CEO of Microsoft France, explained:

> When a client went to a retailer and asked to see how Word worked with a printer, in 95% of the cases, the distributor would not be able to answer the question. We visited all the printer manufacturers and sold them on the idea of a Microsoft Word binder with several pages of printing samples.

As a result of this aggressive marketing effort, Word began making inroads into the French market in 1985. After a much-refined Word 3.0 was released in April 1986, sales of Word rose fast. In 1987 it was the best-selling word processing software in France, with sales of 28,700 copies compared to 10,300 for IBM VisiOn, 7,000 for Textor, 3,800 for WordPerfect, and 3,300 for WordStar.

While Microsoft was again enjoying phenomenal success in Europe with a program that had been unsuccessful in the United States, the great improvements made in the 3.0 version of Word also substantially increased its U.S. market share. In this version, the problems previously experienced by users in learning Word were solved. Included with all 3.0 versions of Word was a step-by-step on-line tutorial that replaced the traditional user's manual. U.S. sales of Word climbed substantially. By 1989 Word's sales had reached 650,000 compared to 937,000 for WordPerfect. Although Word was by many standards a superior product, WordPerfect had firmly established itself as the word processing software of choice for PC users. Once customers learned and grew comfortable with a program, it was often difficult and costly for them to switch.

While Microsoft was having difficulty capturing market share with its earlier versions of Word in 1984 and 1985, it was working feverishly on a Word program for the Apple Macintosh computer that was the only substantial challenger to the IBM standard. When Word for the Mac was released in 1985, the only other word processing program available for the Macintosh was Apple's own software, MacWrite, which was included with the sale of each machine. Although Word for the Mac had some bugs, it began to attract a following among Macintosh users. When the 3.0 version was released in 1986, it was a tremendous success. By 1988, with annual sales of 250,000 copies, it was second only to the PC versions of WordPerfect and Word. WordPerfect released its own version for the Macintosh in 1988, but it was too late. Just as WordPerfect had beaten Microsoft to the U.S. PC market, Microsoft had preempted WordPerfect in the Macintosh market. When Word 4.0 was released in 1989, 100,000 copies were sold immediately, confirming Word's preeminence with the Macintosh.

GRAPHICAL USER INTERFACES

Although the IBM PC was the best-selling microcomputer in the industry and was copied by a great number of other manufacturers, the Apple Macintosh surpassed all others in "user-friendliness" because of Apple's unique work with graphical user interfaces. Whereas users of IBM PCs and compatibles had to interact with their machines using learned text commands such as *delete,* the Macintosh user employed a mouse to connect icons or simple images on the screen. For instance, instead of typing the command *delete,* the Mac user could use a mouse to point to a file icon and pull it to an icon of a trash can. Both Gates and Apple co-founder Steve Jobs believed that the future of microcomputing was in graphical interface technology because it made computers extremely user-friendly, opening up the world of computers to the most unsophisticated user.

In 1981 Apple asked Microsoft to write applications programs for the Macintosh, realizing that the availability of high-demand software could determine the success of the Macintosh just as the popularity of VisiCalc had launched the Apple II. Microsoft and Apple began a close collaboration aimed at designing an optimum match between the Macintosh configuration and Microsoft's applications programs. The agreement specified that Microsoft versions of Multiplan, Chart, and File would be shipped with each Macintosh machine and that Microsoft could not publish software with a graphical user interface until one year after the Macintosh was released, or December 1983 at the latest.

In the following years, Microsoft enjoyed tremendous success with its Macintosh applications programs. In addition to Word for the MAC, Microsoft's new spreadsheet program, Excel, sold at a rapid rate, beating out Lotus's new integrated software called Jazz. In 1986 Microsoft sold 160,000 copies of Excel to Mac users compared to 10,000 copies of Lotus's Jazz. By 1989 Lotus had decided to stay away from the Macintosh market altogether. Microsoft's success with Macintosh users made it the number-one developer of applications software for the first time. The key lesson learned from Microsoft's experience in the Macintosh market was that Microsoft's primary competitive advantage was in graphical user interfaces. It was clear that the PC market would inevitably move toward graphical interface technology, so Microsoft appeared to be in a commanding position to expand its influence in the development of software for that market.

WINDOWS

Windows was Microsoft's attempt to change MS-DOS into a graphical user interface. Although IBM had been successful in establishing its hardware and operating system (MS-DOS) as industry standards, no such standardization applied to PC applications software. Each applications program written for the PC was unique in the method demanded to modify or print a file. In addition, the popular PC applications programs communicated with printers differently. Different printers demanded different intermediary programs—called drivers—to enable printers to receive data from applications. Consequently, when a customer bought a copy of a particular applications software, she or he often received as many as a dozen diskettes, only one of which carried the applications program. The extra diskettes contained drivers to adapt the program to various printers.

To address this problem, Microsoft decided in 1981 to develop a program that would act as a layer between the operating system and applications software, interpreting the particular communications requirements of the printer and monitor being used. The second purpose of this program would be to place over MS-DOS a graphical interface that would standardize the appearance of applications so that they would share common commands for such actions as modifying texts or printing files.

While Microsoft was working on its graphical interface, dubbed Windows, other companies began develop their own versions. VisiCorp, for example, released VisiOn in 1983. More perturbing, however, was that some industry analysts were speculating that IBM was working on its own version of a graphical interface. In the past, powerful IBM had largely looked to Microsoft to develop the software for its PC; however, Gates suspected that IBM wanted to grab a piece of the highly lucrative software market for itself. Past dealings with Big Blue had proved that the computer giant was intent on expanding its control to include standardization of the entire computer configuration—not only hardware but also software. When IBM announced in 1983 that it was releasing TopView, a graphical interface to rest on top of DOS, it was a clear signal that IBM was no longer content to remain in the domain of hardware. This action by IBM, although disturbing to Microsoft, was not at all surprising. The computer industry in general was characterized by Machiavellian moves and countermoves. Although companies were often dependent on others to develop and position their products in a dominant or advantageous hardware–software configuration, collaborative efforts and contracts were usually characterized by ulterior motives and covert countervailing thrusts.

Recognizing that IBM was attempting to squeeze Microsoft out of future software sales, Gates acted quickly. He contacted the manufacturers of IBM-compatible computers and tried to persuade them to follow Microsoft's lead with Windows and thus isolate IBM. A large group of IBM-compatible manufacturers did not want IBM to monopolize standards further and were amenable to waiting for Microsoft's version of Windows rather than following IBM's lead by including TopView with its machines. Although competitors, many software companies also pledged their support to Microsoft Windows. The support of Lotus, the primary supplier of applications software for the PC and compatibles, was particularly appreciated. It was apparent that Lotus did not relish the thought of a stronger, more influential IBM and was willing to accept Microsoft's lead to prevent it. The software publishers were also confident that Microsoft would create an interface environment into which they could easily port their applications programs. IBM, on the other hand, had released a version of TopView configured in such a way that, if it was successful, would give Big Blue a significant advantage in the development of future applications.

Gates's success in this effort would prove critical to the success of Windows. He had never hesitated to play hardball in the past with larger, more powerful companies. While some criticized Gates as an opportunist, others saw him as an astute and resolute visionary.

The Windows project was characterized by lengthy and embarrassing delays. Although Gates announced the imminent release of Windows in 1983, it did not hit the market until November of 1985. Over 20 software publishers had to delay their Windows-ported applications software. By 1985 most of these companies had put all Windows-associated software projects on hold. Nevertheless, shortly after its introduction, Windows was a great success. After sales exceeded 1 million copies of Windows, the 2.0 version was released in 1987. This version offered a user interface that was very similar to that of the Macintosh. When Microsoft released its PC version of Excel that same year, the credibility of Windows increased even more, and PC manufacturers began positioning their machines against Apple's Macintosh.

THE APPLE LAWSUIT

On March 17, 1988, Apple announced that it was suing Microsoft over Windows 2.03 and Hewlett-Packard over New Wave, its graphical interface environment. What made the announcement particularly unsavory to Gates was that he had just seen the CEO of Apple, John Sculley, and no mention was made of it. Apple announced the news of the suit to the press before notifying Microsoft.

Apple argued that it had spent millions creating a distinctive visual interface that had become the Macintosh's distinguishing feature and that Microsoft had illegally copied the "look and feel" of the Macintosh. Microsoft countered that its 1985 contract with Apple granted it license to use the visual interface already included in six Microsoft programs and that this license implicitly covered the 1987 version, Windows 2.03. In July of 1989, Judge Schwarzer dropped 179 of the 189 items that Apple had argued were copyright violations. The ten remaining items were related to the use of certain icons and overlapping windows in Windows 2.03. In February of 1990, Judge Walker of the Federal District Court of San Francisco took over the case. He had previously ruled against Xerox in its suit against Apple over the same copyrights. In March 1990, Walker ruled that the portions of 2.03 under debate were not covered by the 1985 agreement between Apple and Microsoft. As of late 1991, the case is still in litigation. If Apple should lose the case, it would also lose the competitive advantage of a distinctive visual interface. If Microsoft should lose, it might have to take all current versions of Windows off the market and pay royalties on past sales to Apple.

A DISTINCTIVE ORGANIZATION

Computer programming is an activity dominated by the young. It is also an extremely intense activity that demands sharply focused concentration on the part of the programmer for extended periods of time. The software industry can be characterized as competition between groups of minds. It is an utterly innovative industry in which relatively few resources are spent on anything but the support of the imaginative process.

Finding its genesis in the early days of Microsoft when Gates and Allen and a small coterie of programmers literally slept at work for weeks at a time under incredible pressure, the Microsoft culture has gelled into its present and unique form. The working atmosphere at Microsoft counterbalances the intensity of activity with an offbeat emphasis on an unstructured and informal environment. Working hours are extraordinarily flexible, dress and appearance extremely casual. Many programmers work in bare feet. It is not unheard of for a team of programmers working on an intense project to take a break at 3 A.M. and spend 30 minutes making considerable racket with their electric guitars and synthesizers.

The present Microsoft complex in Redmond, Washington, looks more like a college campus than the headquarters of a Fortune 500 company. It can be almost surrealistic. Most of the 5,200 employees have offices with windows. The courtyards adjoining the principal structures are often rife with the activity of employees juggling, riding unicycles, or playing various musical instruments.

Microsoft employs many people from foreign countries, which gives the company grounds an international flavor. Some of these employees work on the many foreign translations of Microsoft's software. Others are simply many of the best programmers in the world whom Microsoft attracts to its fold.

Microsoft hires the very best and hardest-working programmers and then allows them wide discretion in their work. When hiring, Microsoft cares little about a candidate's formal education or experience. After all, neither Bill Gates nor Paul Allen ever graduated from college. No matter how lofty applicants' credentials appear to be, they are not hired until they have been thoroughly questioned on programming knowledge and skills. Charles Simonyi, chief architect of the developers groups for Multiplan, Word, and Excel, insisted for some time on personally interviewing each applicant. He explained,

> There are a lot of formulas for making a good candidate into a good programmer. We hire talented people. I don't know how they got their talent and I don't care. But they are talented. From then on, there is a hell of a lot the environment can do.

Microsoft employees earn relatively modest salaries, compared to the rest of the industry. Bill Gates himself has never earned more than $175,000 in salary per year. (He is, however, a billionaire as a consequence of owning 35% of Microsoft stock.) Employee turnover is about 8%, well below the industry average.

Microsoft is loosely structured. Programmers are usually assigned to small project teams. Gates explains that "it takes a small team to do it right. When we started Excel, we had five people working on it, including myself. We have seven people working on it today."

Communications at Microsoft are open. Everyone is tied together in a vast electronic network, and anyone can send a message to anyone else via electronic mail, regardless of relative status.

One of the keys to Microsoft's success is that it attracts the finest programmers in the industry and creates an environment that not only pleases and retains employees but is also conducive to high computer programming productivity. No amount of financial might can make a software company successful. There are no apparent economies of scale to be realized. The primary asset that determines success or failure of a software company is the creativity and performance of its people.

POSITIONING FOR THE '90s

In 1987 Microsoft began collaborating with IBM on the development of a new operating system called OS/2 and a new, more powerful graphical interface named Presentation Manager. In late 1989, IBM released OS/2 version 1.2 for IBM PCs. Microsoft released OS/2 version 1.21 for IBM-compatible machines in mid-1990. Sales of OS/2 have been far lower than hoped.

Many industry observers consider OS/2 the inevitable replacement of DOS. However, DOS version 5.0 was released in 1991, fueling speculation and confusion about in what direction Microsoft was leading the industry. In fact, IBM appears to believe it was double-crossed. When the introduction of OS/2 went poorly, Microsoft continued to upgrade and push MS-DOS and Windows, at the expense of OS/2 and Presentation Manager. IBM has since taken over the majority of the development on OS/2 and has distanced itself from Microsoft.

In June of 1991, IBM and Apple began a joint venture to develop an entirely new PC standard in which they will control the rights to the operating system and the microprocessor. This cooperation between the two largest microcomputer manufacturers could have a tremendous impact on the software industry. If IBM and Apple are successful in developing and controlling a new industry standard operating system, Microsoft's will lose its preeminent position in the industry. Right now, nearly all applications programs written are ported through Microsoft's MS-DOS/Windows environment, enabling Microsoft to determine the direction and makeup of future computer applications. If the IBM–Apple initiative proves successful, Microsoft could find itself following another company's lead for the first time in its history.

The IBM–Apple venture is not a sure bet, though. The advanced technology they are working on is extraordinarily complex, and the risks are high for both companies. John Sculley, CEO of Apple, has said, "This is something only Apple and IBM could pull off. Still, it's a big gamble, and we're betting our whole company on it." Another concern is that the radically different cultures of the two manufacturers and their historical disdain for one another may make progress difficult.

In addition, Microsoft still holds significant sway over the applications development efforts of other software companies. Over time, customers have made significant investments in hardware and software that operate in the MS-DOS/Windows environment. It is questionable whether software publishers or customers would make wholesale changes so readily. Bill Gates comments:

> Sure, we're being attacked on all sides, but that's nothing new. Customers will vote on all of this. I think ours will thank us for preserving their current investment in PCs, while improving that technology. That has always been our strategy.

CASE 18 Newmarket Regional Health Center (NRHC)
Michael J. Merenda • Timothy W. Edlund

In 1985, the Newmarket Regional Health Center (NRHC) and its satellite facility, the Lamprey River Clinic (LRC) recorded their 13th consecutive year of growth in both revenues and patients served. This growth was expected to continue through the 1980s, especially in those towns served by the Center that were designated medically underserved areas (MUAs). For 1985 NRHC expected to pass the million-dollar mark in total revenues for the first time in its history. Since 1981 the Center's revenues had risen an average of 25% per year. Visits by outpatients had grown as follows:

Year	Visits	Year	Projected Visits
1980	8,490	1985	17,700*
1981	9,872	1986	20,000*
1982	12,309		
1983	14,700		
1984	16,000		

* Totals forecast by Long-Range Planning Committee

The Center had several problems, however. These concerns were articulated through the Center's long-range strategic planning process. The Center utilized a three-year planning process, which was updated annually.

STRATEGIC CONCERNS

Ann Peters, executive director of NRHC, had just completed the first session of the annual strategic planning process with the Strategic Planning Committee of the Center's board of directors. She was extremely pleased with the Center's performance over the last several years (see Financial Statements, Exhibits 18.1 through 18.4) but was concerned about several issues. The issues labeled critical by the planning committee for the 1985 through 1988 strategic plan were:

Complete a capital fund drive to build a new 6,200-square-foot medical facility for the Lamprey River Clinic (LRC) in Raymond, New Hampshire, and to

This case was prepared by Michael J. Merenda of the University of New Hampshire and Timothy W. Edlund of Morgan State University and was published in *Annual Advances in Business Cases, 1991* (Case 30). It is intended to be used as a basis for class discussion rather than to illustrate either effective or ineffective handling of the situation. The names of selected individuals have been disguised to preserve their desire for anonymity. All rights reserved to the authors. Copyright © 1986, 1991 by Michael J. Merenda and Timothy W. Edlund.

renovate the existing headquarters facility in Newmarket, New Hampshire. The existing inadequate facility used for the LRC in Raymond was leased. That lease would expire December 31, 1985.

Develop and implement an inpatient hospital policy, choosing among two area hospitals for patients requiring inpatient service, and provide prearranged obstetrician coverage at one or both of these hospitals whenever the NRHC obstetrician might not be available.

Retain, recruit, and develop key medical providers and staff in light of changes in the medical care needs of patients, the changing nature of the medical care industry, and potential cutbacks in government funding for health and welfare programs.

Stem the drain on financial resources and operating funds resulting from the recently created prenatal program.

Assess the impact of current and projected growth on the stated mission of the Center, its programs, employees, systems, and patients.

Develop a healthier payer mix to provide funds to meet the needs of those patients with limited ability to pay.

Strive for financial independence—that is, less dependence on government grants and funds.

EXHIBIT 18.1	Financial Highlights: Newmarket Regional Health Center, Inc.		
	1984	1983	1982
Total assets at June 30	$328,608	$282,577	$184,304
Total revenues from services	320,668	226,657	149,002
Total grants received	296,904	275,974	257,515
Other revenues and services received	137,569	158,702	48,278
Total expenses	732,468	631,748	417,995
The percentage breakdown of revenues is as follows:			
Patient services	42.5%	34.3%	32.8%
Operating grants	39.3	41.7	56.7
In-kind services	9.2	18.1	—[1]
Other operating revenues	9.0	5.9	—[1]
	100.0%	100.0%	100.0%
Operating expenses (as a percent of operating revenues)	97.0%	95.5%	91.9%

[1] Breakdown not available for 1982. Total for these two categories, 10.6%. Percentages may not add up to 100% due to rounding.

Source: NRHC documents.

GROWTH IN FOR-PROFIT HOSPITALS

In the recent past, health care units ". . . tend[ed] to compete on the basis of their availability and sophistication of their services and facilities."[4] However, the entry of new "competitors" into the medical arena is altering the way in which medical services were provided. *U.S. News & World Report,* in a December 10, 1984 article, reported that there appeared to be shrinkage in the total number of hospitals since the 1970s but that the number of institutions belonging to for-profit corporations had more than doubled.[5] Competition from for-profit providers increased the pressure on not-for-profit organizations to rethink past practices and strategies. Coddington et al. reported that hospital administrators were beginning to talk like *Fortune* 500 company executives. Some new strategies being considered were downsizing, specialization (coronary by-pass surgery, high-risk maternity), low-cost providers, diversification into for-profit businesses, merging, and joint ventures.[6]

RISING HEALTH CARE COSTS

Spiraling health care costs have forced many outside the health care industry to lobby for cost reduction and control. Between 1965 and 1978, health care costs rose at annual rates of 10% to 14%. And the future is not much brighter. *Business Week* (July 25, 1983) noted,

> . . . the rising average age of Americans virtually guarantees that the U.S. will continue to demand more medical care. And the advent of modern, high-cost medical techniques means that care is going to cost more. (p. 52)

A *Business Week* survey of reasons for rising health care costs found 82% agreement that the major reason for spiraling health care costs was the purchase of expensive new equipment by hospitals and doctors.[7] This was followed by increased third-party medical coverage (government, insurance companies), increased patient testing, and long hospital stays. The survey asked, "Several reasons have been advanced for the big increase in health costs. Do you think each of these reasons is important or unimportant?" The questions and responses were as follows:

	Important	Not Sure	Not Important
The purchase of expensive new equipment by hospitals and doctors	82%	5%	13%
The existence of such federal programs as Medicare and Medicaid	76%	8%	16%
Insurance companies paying claims without questioning whether treatment really was necessary	74%	8%	18%
Doctors ordering more laboratory tests than are necessary	69%	7%	24%
Doctors permitting longer stays than are necessary for minor ailments	65%	7%	29%

In another study,[8] rising health care costs were attributed to five dimensions:

1. *Demand pull.* Rising personal incomes and increased growth in medical insurance have created new and increased demand on a relatively inelastic supply of medical providers.
2. *Labor cost push.* Rising hospital staffing costs, along with decreased provider productivity, have driven expenses and overall medical costs up.
3. *Scientific progress.* New technology and methods of care have been achieved at a higher cost.
4. *Capacity.* Prices have risen in response to increased capital investments and increased expenses in maintaining facilities that are underutilized.
5. *Cost reimbursement.* Increases in medical supplies, equipment, staffs, and salaries have occurred with the increased growth in insurance coverage and other third-party reimbursement plans.

Some users of medical services have begun to flex their muscles in light of rising medical costs. Susan Lee reported that business had every reason to be concerned with rising medical costs. On average, medical insurance was running about 10% of payroll, and health bills were rising 15–35% a year, outstripping inflation and payroll increases. According to Lee,

> Business's newest weapon is the health care coalition. These are groups of employers dedicated to heavy-duty dealings with the medical establishment. The prevailing sentiment is that the private sector must do something.[9]

One option being touted by business executives was the promotion and development of preferred provider organizations (PPOs). These were groups of physicians who agreed to provide medical services at negotiated rates in exchange for set contracted services.

ETHICAL CONCERNS

The appearance of for-profits in the medical arena, along with increased medical costs and an aging American population, raised several moral and ethical questions. Questions were raised about the health care industry's new concern for profitability. Is health care a service, a business, or both? One argument that was advanced was that for-profit medical providers should not be expected to take on the responsibility of caring for the poor or medically disadvantaged. If profit is the objective, these critics argued, then to cater to the underprivileged would be a poor business decision and would drive the provider out of business. Furthermore, these critics claimed that the predominant and traditional not-for-profit structure in the medical care industry is the antithesis of private for-profit competition and market constraints. *Business Week* reported that rising costs and the aging population " . . . raise extremely difficult moral and ethical questions, including whether Americans want to pay $50,000 to $100,000 to care for an 85-year-old patient whose quality of life is gone." Observed Dr. Harvey B. Karsh, a Denver internal medicine physician, "People are unwilling to talk about such issues, but someone soon is going to have to make some decisions."[10]

NRHC's SERVICE AREA

NRHC was founded, and had its first clinic and headquarters, in Newmarket, New Hampshire, a small manufacturing town about 10 miles west of Portsmouth and the Atlantic Ocean. Rockingham County includes the city of Portsmouth (population 26,254) and stretches 35 miles west to the outskirts of Manchester, New Hampshire's largest city (population 90,936).[11] Along the county's southern border are a string of boom towns, which became a tax haven for many seeking relief from high taxes in Massachusetts. But the upper central portion of the county contains a number of towns that are still rural and have high proportions of poor and indigent people. Six Rockingham towns (Deerfield, Candia, Epping, Fremont, Nottingham, and Raymond) are classified as medically underserved areas (MUAs). NRHC's medical service area includes these towns and also Brentwood, Newfields, and Newmarket in Rockingham County and Lee, Durham, and Barrington in Strafford County immediately to the north. The University of New Hampshire, a medium-sized land grant institution, is in Durham, immediately north of Newmarket.

Travel in the service area was primarily by local roads and highways except that State Highway 101 ran East–West through the service area, connecting Manchester to the coast, with a spur to Portsmouth, 40 miles away. In the center of the county, this was a two-lane highway utilizing older roads; but both near Manchester and near the coast a new four-lane limited-access highway had replaced the old road. Reconstruction of the middle portion was underway; completion was expected to take three or four years. Exhibit 18.5 is a map of Rockingham County and surrounding areas.

New Hampshire in 1985 had no general state sales taxes or income taxes, and it retained the tradition of local control over most spending. Silber reported that New Hampshire schools derived 90% of their funding from local sources, the highest in the nation;[12] this pattern is typical of all categories of spending.

New Hampshire towns retain the town meeting, in which spending for each year is determined by vote of all citizens in attendance. The state legislature has been reluctant to undertake new enterprises, generally leaving such initiatives to the towns and, in some cases, to the counties.

NRHC's BACKGROUND

In 1969 a Volunteers in Service to America (VISTA) group began a referral and coordinating agency in Newmarket, New Hampshire. From this beginning as an information and referral (I&R) agency, the Center expanded first into blood pressure screening and eventually into providing lifelong preventive health care for individuals of all ages and incomes. NRHC in 1985 was the only not-for-profit, community-based health center in New Hampshire to provide primary health care and social services. "Since Day 1 we have had a tremendous amount of community support," noted Ms. Peters, "and we have found a great sense of community that you just don't see everywhere."

EXHIBIT 18.5	Rockingham County and Vicinity

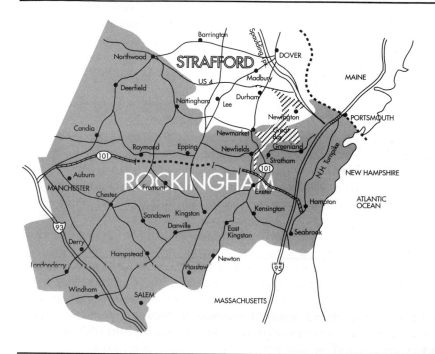

Source: NRHC documents.

"We really make an effort to take care of the whole person," observed Dr. Sally Oxnard, NRHC's medical director. Care of the "whole person" was provided at the Center through six interconnected and closely related programs (Exhibit 18.6). At the hub was the primary-care medical services program. The medical program was strongly supported, like the spokes in a wheel, by several social service and administrative programs, including Senior Citizen Transportation, Health Promotion and Disease Prevention, Self-Care for the Elderly, Social Services (Community Health Workers), and the original Information and Referral Program. Dr. Oxnard continued, "While not actually a program, the Administrative Service and System function is considered an integral part of the Center's medical and social services programs."

MEDICAL PROGRAM

The preceding three years were unprecedented years of growth and development for the Newmarket Regional Health Center, and specifically for the medical program. The opening of a second facility and the addition of two new physicians and other support staff enlarged the size and scope of the medical program.

open in January 1986. Ann noted, "The prenatal program is still in the process of being fully integrated into the overall agency operations. The new building in Raymond and the prenatal program problems have precipitated a need for change. We need to revise the Center's management and supervisory functions, as well as its fiscal operating procedures." "Just how the management and supervisory functions will be revised is not clear at this time, but it is considered a major concern that needs to be addressed in the 1985–1988 strategic plan," John Russell added.

Capital Fund Drive

The Center was in the midst of a major $550,000 capital fund raising effort. The funds would be used for renovation of the Newmarket facility and construction of the Raymond facility. This expansion will mark the fifth time in 13 years that the Center has enlarged its facilities in order to meet demand for its services. Exhibit 18.8 contains excerpts from the market study that helped support the expansion decision. It was estimated that there would be unmet demand for 2.32 (conservative estimate) to 5.22 FTE (full-time equivalent) medical providers in the Center's service area by 1990, even with the proposed Raymond facility.

Operating Statistics

Ann Peters, along with the Center's Planning Committee, viewed the capital fund drive as necessary and important to the future viability of the Health Center. Nevertheless, they were concerned with its timing. They were aware of the drastic changes occurring in the health care industry. Recent speeches by the secretary of health, education, and welfare and President Reagan, announcing an all-out effort to combat the massive federal budget deficit, presented a major threat to the health care industry. Although the Center had set fiscal autonomy and independence as an objective, only 42% of its revenues were provided by patient fees. Bad debt for the prenatal program was projected to be almost $100,000 for 1985–1986. Exhibits 18.9, 18.10, and 18.11 contain excerpts from the executive director's report on operating statistics. This report was presented monthly to the Center's board of directors.

At the first board meeting of the new year, a new director inquired why the last three months' receivables and collection rates were not posted. Ann Peters explained, "Those entries show how much of each month's adjusted charges are paid within 90 days. October's can't be posted until the end of January, and so forth." She went on, "You may spot what looks like another discrepancy, but it isn't. The medical visit data for each clinic in the management reports include hospital stays. Such stays were eliminated from the data given to the Long-Range Planning Committee."

EXHIBIT 18.8	Market Projections: Newmarket Regional Health Center, Inc., 1984–1990

ABSTRACT

1. The service area population is 23,905.
2. There is a need for one to two more primary-care physicians on the staff of the Newmarket Regional Health Center based on conservative Method A.
3. The 1990 need for primary care physicians would increase by approximately 0.5–1.0 FTE.*
   The above conclusions are very conservative based on the following assumptions that may prove to underestimate actual demand:
   A. We estimated that total service-area population will increase 20% from 1982 to 1990. From 1980 to 1982 there has been a 7.5% increase. If that rate continues to 1990, the increase will be 37%.
      The impact of the reconstruction of state route 101 has not been estimated. Completion of this superhighway connecting Manchester and Portsmouth should lead to additional population increase.
   B. We assumed that NRHC would capture only 50% of the unmet need for services. This may be too conservative, considering that the Center is located in the service area and that current unmet need is being serviced in the contiguous market areas of Manchester and Exeter.
   C. Our estimates do not consider the addition of other services and specialties to the staff of NRHC that may provide a multiplying effect on demand.

* FTE = full-time equivalent medical providers.

Source: NRHC document.

DEMAND FOR FULL-TIME PRIMARY-CARE PROVIDERS

Method A (Conservative)

1984 PROVIDERS (FTE)
NRHC 4.03–4.03
Others 2.25–2.25
Total (FTE) 6.28–6.28
Need (FTE) 8.60–10.32[A]
Unsatisfied Need 2.32–4.04

[A] 1984 Need: Based on standards of 1:2,500–3,000
25,800 divided by 3,000 = 8.60 FTE
25,800 divided by 2,500 = 10.32 FTE
Assume NRHC could capture 50% of need.
NRHC = 50% FTE level.
FTE needed by NRHC to satisfy needs of 1984 population = 1.16–2.02 FTE

1990 PROVIDERS (FTE)
NRHC 4.03–4.03
Others 2.25–2.25
Total (FTE) 6.28–6.28
Need (FTE) 9.60–11.50[B]
Unsatisfied Need 3.32–5.22

[B] 1990 Need: Based on standards of 1:2,500–3,000
28,686 divided by 3,000 = 9.6 FTE
28,686 divided by 2,500 = 11.5 FTE
Assume NRHC could capture 50% of increased service population.
Therefore, NRHC needs 50% FTE level.
FTE needed by NRHC to satisfy needs of 1990 population = 1.66–2.61 FTE

Total
Actua
Actua
Actua

Tota
Actu
Actu
Actu

EXH

Cha
Gen.
Ad
Pren
Ad
In-h
Ad
Tota
Tota

Rev
Cas
% a
Mec
Mec
Oth
Dir
Tot
Rec
Rec
Col

*Ex
Sou

The 1987 stock market crash caused a slowing of sales, earnings, and return on sales for major retail companies. As a result, 1987 sales only marginally surpassed 1986 sales (Marsh, 1989). Exhibit 19.1 shows sales of all retail stores for 1990 and 1989. Wearing apparel sales are included in two categories: general merchandise stores and apparel and accessory stores.

As illustrated in Exhibit 19.1, sales in the apparel and accessory category increased only 3.3% from 1989 to 1990, compared to a 3.8% increase in the general merchandise category. Consumer spending on clothing continued to rise in 1990, although the approximately 1% increase recorded was considerably less than the 4.8% increase recorded from 1988 to 1989 (U.S Department of Commerce, 1991). Many factors contributed to this slow growth: the lack of fashion direction in women's apparel, consumer resistance to higher prices, and rapid overexpansion by retailers.

Nonetheless, retailers planned to open as many stores in 1992 as they had in 1991, and stores were expected to be even larger. With this strategy, stores were attempting to maximize sales, raise market share, and capitalize on the concept of one-stop shopping. However, many analysts believed that this was not the answer to the problems plaguing the overall retail industry. The main problem, according to a study conducted by Smith Barney Harris Upham, a New York investment firm, was that the growth rate of sales per store had slowed in the last decade, so size did not matter. The report showed that in 1987, dollar sales per store grew at an average annual rate of 3% between 1948 and 1977. Since 1977, the average annual rate of sales growth has slowed to six-tenths of 1%. In one analyst's opinion, the answer to the retail industry's problems was increased efficiency. One suggested solution was using technology more effectively to automate backroom operations and to allow customers to serve themselves (Barmash, 1992).

During 1991 and 1992 an increasing number of retailers, including Macy's, filed for bankruptcy protection. Another popular retailer, the Oklahoma-based Street's, closed its doors after the 1991 Christmas selling season. Street's, which operated 10 stores, had been in operation since the 1930s, but heavy competition from outlets such as Dillard's Department Stores, The Limited Inc., and Wal-Mart Stores forced the half-century-old chain to shut down (Helliker, 1991).

Other retailers that filed for bankruptcy between 1988 and 1992 included Federated Department Stores (1990), Allied Stores (1990), Carter Hawley Hale (1991), Revco Department Stores (1988), Ames Department Stores (1990), and Hills Department Stores (1991) (Norris, 1992).

Mergers, acquisitions, and corporate restructuring were also on the rise during the early 1990s. As earning potential lessened, companies acquired or merged with other companies. This trend in the retail wearing apparel industry was expected to continue (Norris, 1992).

Retail square footage increased dramatically during this period. In 1990, 15 square feet of retail space existed for every woman, man, and child in the country. This growth surpassed consumer population growth and created a buyer's market. Retail apparel stores were attempting to gain market share by expanding geographically. Malls especially were becoming overcrowded with specialty and department stores, resulting in market saturation in many areas.

EXHIBIT 19.1	**Sales of Retail Stores by Kind of Business, 1990 and 1989** (Dollar amounts in millions)

Kind of Business	1990	1989	Percent Change
Retail trade, total	1,826,293	1,747,804	+4.5
Total (excluding automotive group)	1,441,204	1,363,653	+5.7
Durable goods stores, total	661,594	652,739	+1.4
Building materials, hardware, garden supply, and mobile home dealers	95,132	92,700	+2.6
Building materials, supply, hardware stores	82,117	79,612	+3.1
Building materials and supply stores	69,703	67,045	+4.0
Hardware stores	12,414	12,576	−1.2
Automotive dealers	385,089	384,151	+0.2
Motor vehicle and miscellaneous automotive dealers	352,892	353,765	−0.2
Motor vehicle dealers	334,859	335,278	−0.1
Motor vehicle dealers (franchised)	312,983	309,714	+1.1
Auto and home supply stores	32,197	30,386	+6.0
Furniture, home furnishing, and equipment stores	91,937	91,493	+0.5
Furniture and home furnishing stores	50,420	51,082	−1.3
Furniture stores	27,436	29,720	−7.7
Floor covering stores	12,979	12,136	+6.9
Household appliances, radio, and TV	32,561	32,387	+0.5
Household appliance stores	9,071	9,462	−4.1
Radio and television stores	23,490	22,925	+2.5
Sporting goods stores and bicycle shops	13,936	13,531	+3.0
Book stores	7,356	6,492	+13.3
Jewelry stores	14,667	14,049	+4.4
Nondurable goods stores, total	164,699	1,095,065	+6.4
General merchandise group stores	212,140	204,387	+3.8
Dept. stores (excl. leased depts.)	169,681	164,358	+3.2
Dept. stores (incl. leased depts.)	175,684	169,506	+3.6
Conventional dept. stores (incl. leased depts.)	53,149	52,844	+0.6
Discount dept. stores (incl. leased depts.)	84,494	78,744	+7.3
National chain dept. stores (incl. leased depts.)	38,041	37,918	+0.3
Variety stores	7,410	7,356	+0.7
Miscellaneous general mdse. stores	35,049	32,673	+7.3

(continued)

The fastest-growing population segment is the over-55 age category. This group made about 30% of apparel purchases in 1990. As a whole, this group was at its peak spending capabilities and was expected to be a strong market for many types of career, casual, and active-wear apparel. This group had been known to spend $13 billion on apparel in a single year (U.S. Department of Commerce, 1992).

Special Markets

The special market known as the large-size market was an increasingly important segment of the women's market. In 1990 more than $10 billion was spent on apparel by the 40 million American women who wear size 14 or larger. This was expected to continue to be a lucrative market, because demand was high and supply was low.

"This is a great market to be in because customers' appreciation is so high," said Susie Phillips, vice president of marketing at Lane Bryant. Large-sized women had faced extremely limited choices in selection, quality, and fashion in the past, so opportunities existed in select or diverse lines of large-size apparel (Adams, 1988).

Petite women, those under 5 feet 5 inches tall, also found it difficult to purchase apparel that fit. Petite customers frequently encountered ill-fitting sleeves and hem lengths. This segment was sometimes ignored because of the belief that these customers could alter the clothes to fit. However, this was costly. The popular catalog merchandiser Clifford & Wills was one of several marketers to offer a select group of merchandise that could be purchased in petite sizes at the same cost as the similar regular-size items.

Historically, women have spent more than any other demographic group on wearable apparel and they were considered to be the number-one target of apparel merchants. Women favored department stores, discounters, and factory outlets for apparel, although specialty stores seemed to be gaining in popularity in the late 1980s. Women tended to purchase apparel that was moderately priced and had a designer look. Stores that offered designer-look, quality apparel at low prices were the most suitable for their shopping needs (Lee, 1992).

Men

Men accounted for only a small portion—about 10%—of retail apparel industry sales. Men's dollar sales totaled only $8.9 billion in 1990. In general, men spent a larger portion of their time working, so they had less time to shop. However, when they did find time, chain stores such as The Gap were the most popular for sportswear items such as shirts, sweaters, and trousers, according to 47% of the men interviewed in a nationwide fashion study. Department stores were the preferred sales outlet for suits and business attire by 37% of those interviewed ("Upfront," 1991). Men also shopped more often at stores that were conveniently located.

Children

The children's market accounted for the smallest portion of retail sales within the apparel industry in 1990: 5% of the market. This segment's customers were under the age of 18 and for the most part relied on other family members to purchase for them or fund their apparel purchases. The industry generally divides this category on the basis of sex and combines market data with that for men and women.

PRODUCTS

The range of products offered in the retail wearing apparel industry was vast. Items included outerwear products (blouses, jackets, and trousers), accessories (belts, hats, and scarves), and shoes. Retailers offered all of these products at various prices and in many types, styles, colors, and sizes for men, women, and children. Exhibit 19.3 lists several merchandise categories and their values in 1988, 1989, and 1990.

Price

Price was determined by many factors: the cost of labor and shipping, the fabrics used to make a garment, the length of time it took to produce a garment, and the fashion or style of the garment. In 1991 sales of higher-priced fashions slowed and sales of moderately priced products rose, as demand increased for reasonably priced apparel. Shoppers spent the largest amounts on inexpensive apparel in 1991 ("Retail Apparel Industry," 1992). Major retailers, such as Wal-Mart, were planning on cutting out middlemen. These retailers wanted to deal directly with the manufacturer instead of a wholesale broker or merchandise representative. The 2–3% saved on wholesalers' commissions would result in savings for the consumer, because this amount would otherwise be added to the price of a retailer's merchandise (Barmash, 1992).

EXHIBIT 19.3	Value of Apparel Shipments from Wholesalers to Retailers, 1990
	(Selected merchandise categories)
	(Dollars amounts in millions, except as noted)

				Percent Change	
Item	1988	1989	1990	1988–1989	1989–1990
Industry Data					
Value of shipments	$15,101	$15,468	$15,288	2.4%	−1.2%
Men's/boys' suits/coats	3,169	3,102	3,137	−2.1	1.1
Men's and boys' shirts	4,031	4,170	4,101	3.4	−1.7
Men's and boys' neckwear	500	502	501	0.4	−0.2
Men's/boys' trousers	5,767	6,061	5,915	5.1	−2.4
Men's/boys' work clothing	1,633	1,633	1,634	0.0	0.1
Value of shipments	14,315	14,288	14,307	−0.2	0.1
Women's/misses' blouses	3,573	3,810	3,691	6.6	−3.1
Women's/misses' dresses	6,037	5,771	5,908	−4.4	2.4
Women's suits/coats	4,705	4,707	4,708	0.0	0.0
Value of shipments	3,884	3,921	3,904	1.0	−0.4
Women's/children's underwear	2,621	2,716	2,669	3.6	−1.7
Bras and allied garments	1,263	1,205	1,235	−4.6	2.5

Source: Information obtained from U.S. Department of Commerce, "Apparel," U.S. *Industrial Outlook 1991*, pp. 34-1 to 34-7.

COMPETITORS

The retail wearing apparel industry was in the maturity stage of its life cycle in 1992. Growth in both the number of customers and the amount of money they were spending on apparel was slowing. In addition, a large number of firms were competing in the same market. The increase in the number of stores selling apparel had caused the supply of goods to exceed demand in an already saturated market.

Competition in this industry came from a variety of sources, including department stores, specialty stores, mass merchandisers, catalog retailers, discount stores, and off-price stores, as well as numerous boutiques and small shops. Exhibit 19.4 lists the top retailers within each of these segments.

Department Stores

Department stores sell a wide variety of merchandise, including apparel, accessories, and cosmetics, in a convenient shopping atmosphere. Department stores carry a wide range of merchandise and cater to customers' many needs. However, department stores did not achieve the same levels as specialty stores in terms of ambiance and customer service, nor did they compete with off-price chains that carried designer clothes at lower prices (Sack, 1989). Department store sales totaled more than $70 billion in 1990. The top five department stores and their sales volumes in 1990 are shown in Exhibit 19.4.

To improve sales, many department stores targeted their merchandise at higher-income customers. Also, many stores developed the "store within a store" format, dividing apparel departments into separate sections based on design and fashion.

Specialty Stores

Specialty stores offered ambiance, strong fashion statements, and good customer service. They took advantage of the growing segmentation of the mass market by targeting merchandise at distinct market segments. Specialty stores carried apparel that was targeted mainly at upscale customers.

Specialty stores usually were distinguished from competitors by merchandise selection and presentation. They frequently offered a unique type of quality merchandise. Total 1990 sales were more than $35 billion—an increase of 7.3% from the previous year. The top four apparel specialty outlets and their sales volumes in 1990 are shown in Exhibit 19.4.

Mass Merchandisers

Mass merchandisers offered customers a wider variety of goods, increased convenience, and lower prices than most department stores. The wearing apparel sold in mass-merchandise stores was generally less fashionable and usually of lower quality than that sold in other types of apparel stores. Unlike specialty and department stores, mass merchandisers were not known throughout the industry as leaders in service. Total sales for this segment were $85.5 billion in 1990. The top three mass merchandisers and their sales volumes in 1990 are listed in Exhibit 19.4.

EXHIBIT 19.4	The Top Companies in the Retail Apparel Industry by Type of Company, 1990
	(Dollar amounts in billions)

	Sales		Sales
Department Stores		*Catalog Retailers*	
J.C. Penney	$14.6	Best Products	$2.30
Marvin's	4.1	Lands' End Inc.	1.40
Dillard's	3.6	CML	0.74
Macy's Northeast	3.1	Luria & Sons	0.33
Nordstrom	2.89		
		Discount Stores	
Specialty Stores		Rose's Stores	$2.0
The Limited	$5.5	Dollar General	1.2
Marshalls	2.2	Jamesway Corp.	1.1
T.J. Maxx	2.0		
Gap, Inc.	2.0	*Off-Price Stores*	
		Ross Stores	$1.65
Mass Merchandisers		Burlington Coat Factory	1.62
Wal-Mart	$3.26	Dress Barn	0.60
K mart	3.21	Syms Corp.	0.45
Sears	3.20		

Catalog Retailers

Catalog retailers were a growing force in the retail wearing apparel industry. The number of mail-order catalog retailers has exploded since 1980, a boom fueled primarily by low startup costs. In an effort to compete directly with catalog retailers, many department stores increased catalog mailings in the 1980s. However, the saturated market and increased postal rates have caused many department stores to discontinue their catalogs.

Catalog retailers took advantage of demographic changes affecting the retail industry. These changes include the two-income family, rising disposable incomes, customers' limited shopping time, the increased use of credit cards, and Americans' fondness for dialing toll-free numbers. In 1990 total mail-order sales volume was $200.7 billion, a 9.49% increase from 1989 ("Mail Orders Top 250+," 1991). The top four catalog retailers and their sales volumes for 1990 are listed in Exhibit 19.4.

Discount Stores

Discount stores offered lower prices and more convenience than mass merchandisers and off-price stores. However, one problem was that consumers sometimes perceived lower prices to mean lower quality and less service. Discount stores were shifting their attention away from selling a broad assortment of goods to selling large selections of targeted products, such as lower-priced apparel. Total discount store sales for 1990 were $85.5 billion, a 7.3% increase from 1989. The top discount stores and their sales volumes in 1990 are listed in Exhibit 19.4.

Off-Price Stores

These apparel stores attracted the price-conscious, fashion-conscious customer. They carried designer fashions at lower prices than department or specialty stores. The major disadvantage of off-price stores was a lack of available capital to invest in their stores. Total sales for 1990 were over $5 billion. The top four off-price stores and their sales volumes for 1990 are listed in Exhibit 19.4.

THE COMPANY

HISTORY OF THE COMPANY

In early 1992, Nordstrom, Inc. operated 69 retail stores. The stores were located mainly in the northwestern and western regions of the country, with the exception of its newest stores, which were located in Virginia; Washington, D.C.; and New Jersey.

During World War I, business was slow and it was difficult to sell shoes, the company's original product. Wallin and Nordstrom worked very hard to keep the business flourishing. In 1923 post-war prosperity caused business to boom. During this time Wallin and Nordstrom opened their second store. They were dedicated to keeping the company a family-run business, with each partner employing family members. In 1928 John W. Nordstrom sold his share of the partnership to his three sons, who had started with the company as stock boys.

Nordstrom continued to prosper throughout the decades, first increasing the size and locations of stores and then expanding the product line to include wearing apparel and accessories (Nordstrom, Inc., *1988 Annual Report*).

PRODUCTS

Nordstrom began as a retailer of high-quality, good-value shoes in a wide variety of styles and sizes for men, women, and children. In 1992 Nordstrom was still dedicated to selling quality merchandise at a good value. However, in addition to shoes, products now included women's, men's, and children's wearing apparel and accessories. The company sold a limited number of styles, considered classic rather than trendy, because Nordstrom targeted customers who preferred traditional apparel. Nordstrom aimed at broad customer appeal and based its stores' inventories on geographic location.

Exhibit 19.5 shows Nordstrom's sales by major merchandise category.

CUSTOMERS

Nordstrom offered high-priced items for customers with above-average incomes. It targeted customers who were unwilling to purchase fashion-forward apparel, so it carried only classic merchandise. Nordstrom's stores were equipped with large traditional designer areas, as well as departments that offered basic items such as bluejeans.

EXHIBIT 19.5   Percentage of 1990 Sales by Merchandise Category: Nordstrom, Inc.

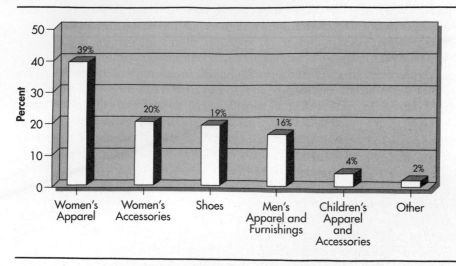

Source: Nordstrom, Inc., *1990 Annual Report.*

Nordstrom entered existing population centers rather than "blazing new trails." It served mainly "upwardly mobile" markets. For example, Nordstrom's new store in Paramus, New Jersey, was located in an upscale neighborhood. This store included the standard valet parking and piano music that Nordstrom insisted its customers wanted.

Decisions regarding Nordstrom's merchandise purchases were made by regional buyers. The theory was that individual buyers knew the actual needs of their customers and were experienced enough to select appropriate inventory. New stores opening in East Coast areas were expected to be geared toward career-oriented individuals. Nordstrom was convinced that customers wanted wearable fashions at good values, and it targeted merchandise buys accordingly (Nordstrom, Inc., *1990 Annual Report*).

CUSTOMER SERVICE

The basic philosophy of the Nordstrom organization was to provide superior customer service, selection, quality, and value. Customer service has been a distinguishing characteristic for Nordstrom, Inc. throughout its history. For Nordstrom, customer service did not stop with a cheerful smile and an available salesperson. Its stores were known for their elaborate attempts to please their customers. Many Nordstrom stores did not play recorded music but provided live piano music! Coat checking services were available so customers were not burdened with carrying extra loads while shopping (Schwadel, 1989).

In an age of incompetent and elusive sales service, shopping had become a chore for most customers. Nordstrom, with its legendary reputation for customer service, had an edge over its competition. Its commitment and dedication to customer service had built a strong base of loyal customers in an age when store loyalty was a thing of the past.

Nordstrom provided sales training sessions and motivational seminars for its staff. Salespeople were expected to make merchandise suggestions to customers, ring up sales, and assist customers with returns and exchanges. Nordstrom employed more floor staff people than any other store chain. Sales staff were also expected to call loyal customers and thank them for their patronage, as well as sending personal notes to alert them to new lines and special incentive sales. Nordstrom's experienced sales staff even went to new stores to train new customer service personnel.

The strong dedication to customer service did not always have good results. Many salespeople felt too much pressure to sell and "put on a happy face" at all times. They were expected to follow a dress code, which some employees felt signaled a loss of individuality. This caused some problems, and in 1991 Nordstrom was accused of unfair labor practices. Employees reported that they were not being compensated for overtime and extra duties performed. The State of Washington Department of Labor and Industries issued an order against Nordstrom, directing it to change its practices. Also, a lawsuit was filed on behalf of the employees seeking damages. These lawsuits were pending in early 1992 (Solomon, 1992).

Nordstrom's excessive expansion may also cause customer service problems in the future. Only a limited number of the employees were willing to relocate and train future employees at new locations (Schwadel, 1989). As a result, Nordstrom may find it difficult to maintain standards.

EXPANSION

Nordstrom, Inc. has undergone many expansions since the company's earliest days. John W. Nordstrom, the founder of Nordstrom, Inc., started the expansion in the early part of the century when he and his partner opened their second shoe store in 1923. In 1961 Nordstrom owned and operated 8 shoe stores and had 600 employees. Gross sales were $12 million that year. This success led Nordstrom to expand its business to include wearing apparel, so the company bought an existing chain store and offered a full range of apparel.

Nordstrom opened its first store outside the Northwest region in Southern California in 1978, and by 1990 its stores were located in six states. Exhibit 19.6 shows the geographic distribution of Nordstrom stores in 1990.

When Nordstrom opened a new store in Sacramento in 1980, the crowds were so overwhelming that the company was forced to request merchandise shipments from its other California stores in order to meet customer demand. Rather than predicting customer needs in this geographic area, Nordstrom executives decided to put everything in the store and let the customers decide what should be stocked (Ginsberg, 1989b).

The drive to expand nationally was largely attributable to the fact that Nordstrom had been successful in all of its store openings. This success convinced

| EXHIBIT 19.6 | Square Footage by Market Area at End of 1990: Nordstrom, Inc. |

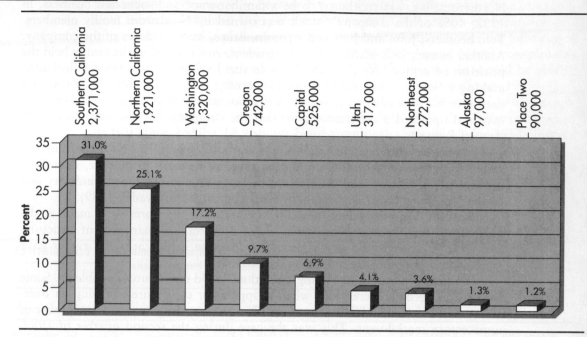

Source: Nordstrom, Inc., *1990 Annual Report.*

company executives to try their expertise in picking locations on a national level (Stevenson, 1989). At first, Nordstrom stores were located only in the northwestern and western regions of the United States. Then, in 1988, it opened its first East Coast store in McLean, Virginia. This suburban Washington, D.C., store was an instant success. Thanks to Nordstrom's decentralized management structure, the apparel buyers for this store were able to test the market prior to the store's opening and to choose merchandise they felt would be successful in that area of the country. This method of buying was successful, and sales for the store's first year were in excess of $100 million (Born, 1989).

In the third quarter of 1989, another East Coast store opened in the Pentagon area of Washington, D.C. Again the store was stocked with the traditional apparel deemed appropriate for Nordstrom's upwardly mobile, affluent customers. Trained staff members were transferred to the Washington area to train new employees in the Nordstrom philosophy of selling and customer service. Long-term success was predicted for this store, which was located directly above the Metroliner train service. This location was expected to serve customers who stopped and shopped on a whim, as well as tourists visiting Washington, D.C. (Schwadel, 1989).

By 1992 Nordstrom had built 4 stores in the eastern United States and had opened 12 clearance stores called Nordstrom Rack in Washington state, Oregon, California, and Maryland. Nordstrom also leased shoe departments in stores in Hawaii (Nordstrom, Inc., *1990 Annual Report*).

EXHIBIT 19.8	Balance Sheets 1987–1990: Nordstrom, Inc.

(Dollar amounts in thousands)

Years Ended January 31	1988	1989	1990	1991
Assets				
Current assets				
Cash and equivalents	$ 4,949	$ 16,058	$ 33,051	$ 24,662
Accounts receivable net	404,615	481,580	536,274	575,508
Inventories	312,696	403,795	419,976	448,344
Prepaid expenses	7,922	22,553	21,847	41,865
Total current assets	730,182	923,986	1,011,148	1,090,379
Property, plant and equipment, net	502,661	594,038	691,937	806,191
Other noncurrent assets	1,424	3,679	4,335	6,019
Total noncurrent assets	504,085	597,717	696,272	812,210
Total assets	$1,234,267	$1,521,703	$1,707,420	$1,902,589
Liabilities and Stockholders' Equity				
Accrued income taxes	$ 17,085	$ 20,990	$ 12,491	$ 24,268
Notes payable	88,795	95,903	102,573	149,506
Accounts payable	166,524	190,755	195,338	204,266
Accrued expenses, salaries, and taxes	101,204	120,821	151,687	163,365
Current portion of long-term debt	21,091	19,696	27,799	10,430
Total current liabilities	394,699	448,165	489,888	551,835
Long-term debt	215,300	356,471	418,533	457,718
Obligations under capitalized leases	23,952	23,049	22,080	21,024
Deferred taxes	67,107	54,077	43,669	45,602
Other noncurrent liabilities				
Total noncurrent liabilities	306,359	433,597	484,282	524,344
Total liabilities	701,058	881,762	974,170	1,076,179
Stockholders' Equity				
Preferred stock				
Common stock	146,317	147,629	148,857	NA
Paid in capital				
Retained earnings	386,892	492,312	584,393	NA
Total stockholders' equity less: Treasury stock (520,000 shares) at cost	533,209	639,941	733,250	826,410
Total stockholder's equity	533,209	639,941	733,250	826,410
Total liabilities and stockholders' equity	$1,234,267	$1,521,703	$1,707,420	$1,902,589

Source: Adapted from Nordstrom, Inc., *1989 Annual Report*.

Net Sales, 1981–1990: Nordstrom, Inc.
(Dollar amounts in millions)

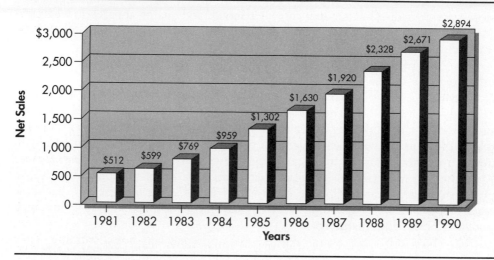

Source: Nordstrom, Inc., *1990 Annual Report.*

Net Earnings, 1981–1990: Nordstrom, Inc.
(Dollar amounts in millions)

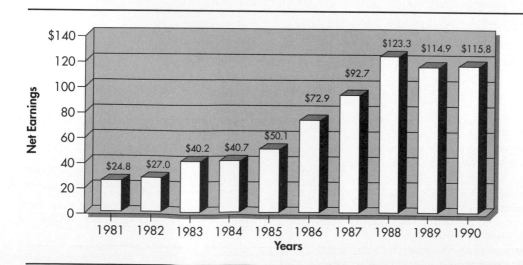

Source: Nordstrom, Inc., *1990 Annual Report.*

TOWARD THE FUTURE

In early 1992, Nordstrom management was considering strategic alternatives for the company's future. Nordstrom had a reputation among industry members and customers for providing outstanding customer service and quality apparel. In a saturated industry where consumers were spending less on wearing apparel, Nordstrom was looking for ways to expand the company.

Some Nordstrom executives argued that the company should enter markets in other regions of the United States. These executives argued that the affluent Nordstrom customer bought traditional-style apparel and was looking for a conveniently located outlet. These executives wanted to search out upscale markets because they knew this was where to find the Nordstrom customer. They believed that if they approached their expansion efforts in this fashion, they would obtain more customers. For example, a study showed that 23% of the residents of Riverside and Monroe Valley—cities that attracted affluent and upwardly mobile population segments—shopped in other areas. This study also indicated that these residents would prefer shopping at more convenient locations and so represented potential Nordstrom customers.

However, other managers believed this approach was not justifiable. They wanted to put plans for expansion on hold until there were definite signs of an economic recovery and a long-term increase in consumer spending. They felt that because company earnings had declined over the past 2 years and because the value of a share of stock had dropped 13.5 points, it would be unwise for the company to expand. These executives felt customers were balking at Nordstrom's moderate to high prices. They believed customers were not just waiting for an economic recovery before spending, but rather that the trend that lower prices was a long-term trend that would cause these customers to turn to Nordstrom's competitors.

Nordstrom was considering the foregoing alternatives as well as many other strategies and their long-term effects on the company.

REFERENCES AND BACKGROUND READINGS

Adams, Muriel. "Large (Size) and Growing." *Stores,* May 1988, pp. 33–52.

Baldo, Anthony. "Nordstrom: Success Has Its Price." *World,* July 25, 1989, p. 15.

Barmash, Isadore. "Down the Scale with the Major Chains." *New York Times,* Business Section, February 2, 1992, p. 5.

Benkelman, Susan. "Taking Stock at Macy's." *Newsday,* March 9, 1992, pp. 25–27.

Born, Pete. "Macy's, Nordstrom: Pentagon Faceoff." *Women's Wear Daily,* September 28, 1989, p. 11.

Ciampi, Thomas. "December Big-Store Sales Mostly Weak." *Women's Wear Daily,* January 6, 1992, p. 19.

Donston, Scott. "Media Reassess as Boomers Age." *Ad Age,* July 1991, p. 12.

Gill, Penny. "Moderate Sportswear: Moderately Optimistic." *Stores,* January 1989, pp. 19–32.

Gill, Penny. "Who's Counting?" *Stores,* May 1988, pp. 33–52.

Ginsberg, Steve. "Commission Sales Growing in Big Stores." *Women's Wear Daily,* January 4, 1989a, p. 16.

Ginsberg, Steve. "Nordstrom's Sacramento Store Has Robust Start." *Women's Wear Daily,* October 24, 1989b, p. 16.

Helliker, Kevin. "Final Markdown." *Wall Street Journal,* December 4, 1991, pp. A1 and A6.

Koselka, Rita. "Fading into History." *Forbes,* August 19, 1991, pp. 70–71.

Lee, Georgia. "Lower Prices Key at Atlanta Show." *Women's Wear Daily,* February 12, 1992, p. 8.

Levin, Gary. "Boomers Leave a Challenge." *Ad Age,* July 1991, pp. 1 and 14.

"Mail Orders Top 250+." *Direct Marketing,* July 1991, pp. 30–49.

Marsh, Lisa. "Analysis of Retail Performances for Fiscal 1988." *Women's Wear Daily,* August 24, 1989, pp. 4–5.

McCusker, Tom. "The Message Is Integration." *Datamation,* August 15, 1991, pp. 31–32.

Mitchell, Russell. "Inside the Gap." *Business Week,* March 9, 1992, pp. 58–64.

Nordstrom, Inc., *1990 Annual Report.*

Nordstrom, Inc., *1988 Annual Report.*

"Nordstrom Plugs Tyler Leak." *Chain Store Age Executive,* September 1989, pp. 40–42.

Norris, Floyd. "Win or Lose, Buyouts Do It Big." *New York Times,* January 28, 1992, pp. D1 and D8.

"Retail Apparel Industry." *Value Line,* February 28, 1992, pp. 1601–1711.

Robins, Gary. "Automating Reorders." *Stores,* November 1988b, pp. 20–27.

Robins, Gary. "Auto ID." *Stores,* September 1988a, pp. 1–16.

Robins, Gary. "EDI: Closing the Loop." *Stores,* April 1988c, pp. 53–62.

Sack, Karen J. "Nordstrom, Inc." *Standard & Poor's Corp.,* October 2, 1991, pp. 4,793–4,794.

Sack, Karen J. "Retailing: A Basic Analysis." *Standard & Poor's Industry Surveys,* April 20, 1989, pp. 75–112.

Sack, Karen J. "Retailing: An Industry at the Crossroads." *Standard & Poor's Industry Surveys,* December 22, 1988, pp. 61–63.

Schechter, Dara. "Howell Says J.C. Penney Is Ready for Big Growth; Cites Technology as Aid." *Women's Wear Daily,* October 27, 1989, p. 10.

Schiffman, Michael. "Nordstrom, Inc." *Value Line,* September 1, 1989, p. 1651.

Schneider, Bart. "Retail Store Industry." *Value Line,* September 1, 1989, pp. 44–45.

Schwadel, Francine. "Nordstrom's Push East Will Test Its Renown for the Best Service." *Wall Street Journal,* August 1, 1989, pp. A1 and A4.

Schwartz and Kraft. "Managing Consumer Diversity: The 1991 American Demographic Conference." *American Demographics,* August 1991, p. 22.

Silverman, Edward R. "Supplier Trouble for Alexander's." *Newsday,* March 7, 1992a.

Silverman, Edward R. "Macy's Cutbacks Coming." *Newsday,* March 8, 1992b, p. 7.

Solomon, Charlen-Marmer. "Nightmare at Nordstrom." *Personnel Journal,* September 1990, pp. 76–83.

Stevenson, Richard W. "Watch Out Macy's Here Comes Nordstrom." *New York Times Magazine,* August 27, 1989, pp. 34–40.

"Top 100 Department Stores." *Stores,* July 1991, pp. 31–43.

"Top 100 Specialty Stores." *Stores,* August 1991, pp. 25–41.

"Upfront: Salon International, Mode Masculine." *Stores,* March 1991, p. 14.

U.S. Department of Commerce. "Retailing." *1989 U.S. Industrial Outlook,* January 1989a, pp. 54-1 to 64-3.

U.S. Department of Commerce. "Apparel." *1989 U.S. Industrial Outlook,* January 1989b, pp. 41-1 to 41-6.

U.S. Department of Commerce. "Apparel." *U.S. Industrial Outlook 1991,* pp. 34-1 to 34-7.

U.S. Department of Commerce. "Retail Trade: 1990." *Current Business Report 1992,* pp. 1–29.

Yang, Dori Jones and Laura Zinn. "Will the Nordstrom Way Travel Well?" *Business Week,* September 3, 1990, pp. 82–83.

PURPOSE

A flyer distributed by the Society to solicit members provides a statement about the purposes of the organization:

1. Fostering an interest in all the peoples who contributed in any way to the establishment and perpetuation of the state of Ohio.
2. Searching for the reasons and forces behind the migrations of early settlers into the state.
3. Preserving and safeguarding manuscripts, books, and memorabilia relating to the early settlers of Ohio.
4. Securing and holding copyrights, master copies, and plates of books, periodicals, tracts, and pamphlets of genealogical and historical interest to the people of Ohio.
5. Publishing, printing, buying, selling, and circulating literature regarding the purposes, records, acquisitions, and discoveries of the Society.
6. Aiding others in the publication and dissemination of materials pertaining to Ohio, including biography and family and local history.
7. Receiving and holding gifts and bequests from any source for the benefit of the Society, disposing of such gifts and bequests not needed, and using funds derived therefrom solely for the purposes of the Society.
8. Doing all things incidental to the perpetuation of the purposes of the Society and exercising the powers legally and properly requisite thereto.

PUBLICATIONS

The regular publications of the Society are *The Report, The OGS Newsletter,* and *Ohio Records and Pioneer Families.* The first (published quarterly) contains book reviews, genealogical articles, court records, Bible records, First Family of Ohio rosters, and articles submitted by members. The *Newsletter* is published monthly and contains genealogical news, state information, chapter announcements, projects, meeting notices, classified ads, publications for sale, questions and answers, lists of Society library holdings, and queries. The *ORPF* is published quarterly and contains abstracts of original records.

Other publications include history reprints, census indexes, source materials, pamphlets, and books. Some materials are produced outside the Society but are sold by the Society as a service to its members.

PROJECTS

The Society has a number of ongoing projects for the collection of genealogical data. One of the largest is its collection of ancestor cards and charts, better known as family trees. Members submit 3-by-5 note cards and 5-generation ancestor charts. If a match with another member's ancestor card is found, the member is notified. The library has a collection of over 200,000 ancestor cards.

In the distant past, the family Bible was used to record the family tree, including dates of births and deaths. Accordingly, the Society collects copies of the family pages of Bibles. The church is one of the best sources of such vital statistics as baptisms, deaths, and marriages for the years preceding the time that local and state governments assumed this function. The Society is surveying all church records in Ohio to locate materials for genealogical research. The Society has also identified all Ohio cemeteries and encouraged chapters to publish transcriptions. It also offers advice on cemetery law and preservation methods.

A major project just completed was the creation of an index to the 1880 Federal Census. The resulting publication is used to look up the name of the ancestor of interest. The index gives the user the information needed to select the proper roll of microfilm and find the frame containing the ancestor. Finding the name in the index is the first step for anyone using census data.

A new project is to publish a statewide index to marriage records through 1820. Projects such as this require considerable time (creating the 1880 Census Index mentioned above required 5 years).

Society members are also urged to prepare manuscripts based on their research. They are encouraged to copy, abstract, and publish source records.

MEMBERSHIP

The basic fee for single membership is $25 per year. Life membership is $350. A joint membership is $30 annually, or $525 for life. Membership includes subscriptions to *The Report* and *The Ohio Genealogical Society Newsletter,* use of the Society's library in Mansfield, help from the library's staff and volunteers, and access to membership in the honorary organization First Families of Ohio if the member is directly related to someone who settled in Ohio before 1820. Members live in all 50 states and in a number of foreign countries. As we have noted, membership grew rapidly from the Society's founding in 1960 until about 1983. It then leveled off and has remained constant since 1988. Exhibit 20.1 shows membership levels for the years 1983 to 1991.

To attract new members, the Society sends out brochures and advertises in genealogical magazines. The advertising budget is limited.

Membership activities can include tours to popular genealogical sites such as Salt Lake City, where the Mormons (LDS) have the largest genealogical collection in the world, and to Washington, D.C., for the National Archives. The tours have been very popular.

The highlight of the year is the annual convention. It is a time to meet people from across the state and nation, purchase publications, learn from leading speakers, and attend to the business of the society. The annual meeting is held in different locations each year.

FACILITIES

As the Society has expanded, it has outgrown its facilities twice. Each was formerly a home. The current headquarters building is a large, imposing sandstone mansion of Romanesque design built in 1893. Located on the edge of the downtown area,

| EXHIBIT 20.1 | Growth in Membership, 1983–1991: Ohio Genealogical Society |

Year	Members	Percent Change from Prior Year
1983	5,546	
1984	5,778	4.2
1985	5,934	2.7
1986	6,056	2.1
1987	6,240	3.0
1988	6,348	1.7
1989	6,332	–0.3
1990	6,343	0.2
1991	6,350	0.1

the home originally was owned by Martin Bushnell, a banker. When the family sold the house, it went through the typical uses of old mansions. From 1947 to 1953 it was a funeral home. At that time an addition was made to the rear of the building for funeral home vehicles. The building was next occupied by the AAA automobile club, and much of the second floor was divided into offices. In 1987 the Society was able to purchase the building, and in less than 5 years, it was able to pay off the note. It has also been able to raise over $150,000 that will be used for additions to the library in the future.

The library is located in the addition made for the funeral home vehicles, because the structure of the house proper is not considered strong enough to carry the weight of the books, shelving, and filing cabinets. The addition floors are made of concrete. Because the addition was not insulated, the heating system can barely hold the temperature at 60 degrees on cold winter days. The library is accessible to the handicapped, but the restrooms—up a short flight of stairs into the main house—are not.

The basement of the house is used for storage of First Family of Ohio records (in heavy, fireproof file cabinets), back issues of monthly and quarterly publications, and the Society's inventory of books for sale. The foundation is made of large sandstone blocks, common to buildings of that time, that allow water vapor to pass through. The humidity level is high and not easily managed; most dehumidifiers do not work at temperatures below 60 degrees. Most basements are about that temperature in the summer.

The first floor houses the office of the manager in what was the dining room of the mansion. The room is complete with elaborate woodwork. The living room and parlor are large, making them suitable as meeting rooms and work rooms for volunteers preparing documents for microfilming.

The second floor was previously divided into offices. The Society is fixing and painting some rooms for reading and study areas and one room for a place where staff members can eat. It has considered renting out office space on this floor, but the inconvenient, single staircase limits easy access and may also violate fire code for business rental use.

The entire third floor under the vaulted roof was a ballroom at one time. Properly restored, it would be grand. It would make a fine meeting room for at least 75 people, but today's fire codes would not allow that without the addition of fire escapes. Furthermore, it is not accessible to the handicapped. Currently, it is put to no use other than storage.

The location at the edge of downtown in the central city in a declining area brings problems of security. The building has been broken into a number of times in the past year. A security system has been installed that detects the motion of individuals after hours.

OPERATIONS

The Society has one full-time employee, its manager Tom Neel. One part-time employee handles some secretarial duties. The remainder of the work force is composed of volunteers. The library is staffed by volunteers who can help members and visitors find information. They also answer genealogical correspondence and assist the office manager as needed. Tom directs the volunteers and handles research problems that are beyond their skills. Volunteers also help in filing and preparing paperwork, sorting documents, and performing other activities. Many of the volunteers appear to be retired or nearing retirement. The Society could not function without them. The interactions with visitors to the library seem to be friendly and positive.

For a short period the Society had an executive director, but she left for other employment. The Society has thought of hiring another executive director. The salary and fringe benefit package for this position would run about $35,000.

ORGANIZATION

The Ohio Genealogical Society is a private not-for-profit organization. It has its headquarters in Mansfield and chapters throughout the state and the country. The Society is governed by the Board of Trustees, which is made up of 15 elected district trustees, 9 trustees elected at large, the immediate past chairman of the board, the immediate past president, and all past presidents and past chairmen who were elected before 1986 and who remain in good standing.

The officers and trustees were elected with the purpose of giving each chapter and district a voice at the state level. The chairman of the board, currently Diane Gagel, is elected by the board from among its members and presides at all board meetings. The Board of Trustees formulates policy and handles the finances of the Society. Committees governing the policy and finances are appointed by the Board. These committees are listed in Exhibit 20.2. All other committees are appointed by the president and the chairman of the board. These committees are listed in Exhibit 20.3.

The president, currently Mary Bowman, and the various committees carry out all the directives of the board. The president and the district trustees are liaison

The Society has only one full-time employee, but continued increases in health insurance and other premiums could increase the reluctance to hire additional employees.

The use of home computers with modems attached is increasing. Data services from the competition, such as the LDS, could eliminate the need for some to belong to the Society.

POTENTIAL FUTURE BENEFITS

It is usually the older population who have the time and interest to engage in genealogical research. The number of older people in the population is increasing. The Society should be able to increase membership if it can reach these people.

There are a number of foundations that give money to not-for-profit, nongovernmental organizations. The Society will need to investigate the possibilities of grant writing to tap this source of funds.

CASE 21 Peat Marwick and KMG: To Merge or Not to Merge

Philip D. Cooper · Timothy W. Edlund

As competition within the public accounting industry intensified, many firms were considering mergers. Two of the world's largest accounting firms, Price Waterhouse and Deloitte Haskins & Sells, announced plans to merge and form the biggest firm in the world in 1984. Many competitors were greatly relieved when the deal was canceled. Following suit were Peat Marwick International (PMI) and KMG in 1985. These negotiations also collapsed. Yet both KMG and PMI continued evaluating their relative market positions and considering strategies to propel their respective firms to the forefront of the industry for the 1990s. As calendar 1986 drew to a close, a future merger remained under consideration, possibly with each other. The forces that caused PMI and KMG to consider merging were also felt by competing firms, but no major accounting firm mergers were known to be under active discussion in late 1986.

EARLY HISTORY: PEAT MARWICK (PMI)

James Marwick, a Scotsman, founded his firm in 1895 by opening a practice in New York City. He joined forces with Simpson Roger Mitchell in 1897, and their business continued to expand. Using the firm name of Marwick, Mitchell & Co., the firm opened offices across the United States as the railroads took its clients to new locations. Marwick maintained his business contacts in Europe and traveled there frequently. On one such trip in 1911, he met William B. Peat, another Scotsman, with a public accounting firm headquartered in London. The two men decided to merge their respective firms and finalized the agreements later that year. With its solid Anglo-Saxon tradition, Peat Marwick, Mitchell & Co. expanded through mergers and acquisitions into Peat Marwick International (PMI), a multi-million dollar worldwide accounting and consulting firm.

EARLY HISTORY: KMG

In 1917 Piet Klynveld opened an accounting practice in Amsterdam. As its clients grew, so did the Dutch firm: throughout Europe and into South America. In Frankfurt several bankers got together in 1890 and created DTG (Deutsche

THE FUTURE

Each firm still faced the same strategic dilemmas. If they chose to, the partners could reflect on the past negotiations and decide whether the proposed merger could still be successful. Alternative strategies could be identified and pursued. The data in Exhibits 21.1 and 21.2 were available to help in this examination. In PMI's Annual Review, issued following the fiscal year ended June 30, 1986 for its Fall Partners Meeting, chairman Jim Brown presented PMI's view of the coming years:

> What is PMI's program for the next few years? Rather than overhaul our organization, which after all set new records for accountancy income and profitability in 1986, we will build on the solid base of what we have achieved in the past. We have added a task force, headed by the chairman of our Personnel Development Committee, charged with substantially increasing the number of practice-related international transfers. We have asked another task force to reexamine the process of serving the multinational client: What should the auditor of a parent company be entitled to expect of the auditor of subsidiary companies, and vice versa? We will continue to develop new ideas for delivering total client service, with the goal of determining how we can best bring to each client the appropriate skills from among our 32,000 personnel. And we will continue our research and development efforts in several areas of management consulting.

> In the near future, we will also be updating our strategic plan. An effective, truly multinational strategic plan must not only incorporate the goals of all the member firms, but must also build on the collective strengths of our individual industry practices, functional groups, and local offices. PMI will be a key player in the communication, coordination, and constant feedback that is necessary for our strategic plan to have the multinational perspective that will be essential in the years ahead if we are to effectively compete in an increasingly global economy. (Peat Marwick, 1986, p. 13)

| EXHIBIT 21.1 | PMI Chargeable Hours Geographically | | | | | |

Region	1984 Hours	%	1985 Hours	%	1986 Hours	%
North America	16.7	53.9	17.6	53.7	18.2	52.3
South America	1.7	5.5	1.8	5.5	1.8	5.2
Europe	6.7	21.6	7.0	21.3	7.8	22.4
Africa and Middle East	1.6	5.2	1.9	5.8	1.9	5.5
Asia Pacific	4.3	13.9	4.5	13.7	5.1	14.7
Totals	31.0		32.8		34.8	

Note: Percentages do not necessarily total to 100% due to rounding.

Source: PMI, *1986 Annual Report.*

EXHIBIT 21.2	Comparative Statistics for KMG and PMI as of 1986

	KMG	PMI
Worldwide		
Revenues (million U.S. $)	1,044	1,665
Client service hours (million chargeable hours)	26.3	34.6
Partners	2,827	2,733
Staff	23,372	28,300
United States		
Revenues (million U.S. $)	234	1,000
Partners	529	1,356
Staff	3,000	10,356

Note: Figures may vary from other sources.

Source: Cypert, 1991.

Comparative Revenues by Service (Million U.S. $)

	KMG[a]	PMI[b]
Audit	664	1,031
Tax	149	371
Management consulting	232	263

[a] Year ended March 31, 1986; excludes Canada and the Philippines.
[b] Year ended June 30, 1986.

REFERENCES

Berton, Lee. "KMG Main Hurdman's Merger Interest May Portend a Marriage of Necessity." *Wall Street Journal,* September 24, 1985, p.1.

Cypert, Samuel A. *Following the Money: The Inside Story of Accounting's First Mega-Merger,* New York: American Management Association, 1991.

Horner, Larry D. "Ethics." *Management Accounting,* June 1990, pp. 16–17.

Klott, Gary. "Marwick Ends Hurdman Talks." *New York Times,* September 25, 1985, p. D5.

Peat Marwick Mitchell & Co. "The Year in Review." 1986.

Sasseen, James. "Shotgun Wedding." *International Management,* September 1988, pp. 27–34.

Sommer, A. A., Jr. "Commentary on the Challenge of the Mergers." *Accounting Horizons,* December 1989, pp. 103–106.

Stevens, Mark. *The Accounting Wars.* New York: Macmillan, 1985.

Stevens, Mark. *The Big Eight.* New York: Macmillan, 1981.

Wise, T. A. *Peat Marwick Mitchell & Co.: 85 Years.* New York: Peat Marwick Mitchell, 1982.

Wootton, Charles W., Stanley D. Tonge, and Carel M. Wolk. "From the Big Eight to the Big Six Accounting Firms." *The Ohio CPA Journal,* Spring 1990, pp. 19–23.

CASE 22 Procter & Gamble and the Introduction of BC-18

Paul Olk

Procter & Gamble is one of the largest consumer product companies in the world. With 70 U.S. brands and over 100 international brands, the company currently operates in over 40 countries and competes globally with such companies as Colgate-Palmolive, Unilever, Kao, and L'Oreal. With a growing international business, P&G continually researches products that have the potential for significant overseas sale. This case focuses on one such product innovation: BC-18. BC-18 is a combination shampoo and conditioner product that is sold in the United States as Pert Plus and was developed in the mid-1980s. After reviewing the company's operations and the shampoo market, the case discusses the development of BC-18 and the decision(s) facing P&G managers.

PROCTER & GAMBLE MANAGEMENT PHILOSOPHY

The Cincinnati-based company began in 1837 when William Procter and James Gamble joined together to make candles and soap. They distinguished themselves from other regional companies with their commitment to providing a quality product at a fair price. Their first major achievement, Ivory Soap (noted for its purity), was the result of painstaking research to find the best mixture of ingredients to create a pure soap. Based on the success of Ivory, Procter & Gamble (P&G) expanded its business beyond the midwest and began operating nationally. This devotion to product development continued, as P&G created other products in the soap business (such as Camay) and in the related product lines of detergent (Cheer), toothpaste (Crest), and shampoo (Head and Shoulders). Today the company prides itself on meeting the needs of consumers by developing innovative products that are technologically superior to the competition's.

Accompanying the focus on product innovation is P&G's attention to marketing. The company has developed a reputation for being one of the top marketing companies. It maintains this status by following well-documented procedures for conducting thorough market analyses. Managers admit that P&G may not be the first company to the market with a product, but when it enters, it is prepared. P&G's marketing philosophy also dictates that the company will enter into a market only if it can stay in the market for the long term. Managers believe they can make up any ground lost to earlier entrants by offering a superior product implementing product introduction effectively.

The key to P&G's marketing analysis, product launch implementation, ar ongoing business activities is the brand manager. Each brand in a region has on manager who oversees all aspects of the product within the assigned market. Usually working with a team of 5 or 6 individuals, the brand manager is responsible for testing, manufacturing, and marketing the product.

These three attributes—innovative technology, attention to marketing, and brand management—are the cornerstones in the development of the P&G outlook and have helped the company become a market leader.

INTERNATIONAL EXPANSION

To remain in this dominant position, P&G's managers continually search for new opportunities in existing markets and for new markets to enter. Recently the focus of this search has shifted to international markets. Observers have separated P&G's international expansion into three time periods: pre-World War II, 1950s to 1970s, and 1980s to the present.[1]

Prior to World War II, P&G operated outside of the United States only in Canada and England. It established independent subsidiaries in these markets but had very little international focus. In the second phase, during the 1940s and 1950s, P&G began to expand into additional countries. Avoiding acquisitions, it established new subsidiaries in most of Western Europe in the 1950s; in Venezuela, Mexico, and Costa Rica in the 1950s; and in Japan in the 1970s. The organizing strategy in each country was to develop mini-P&Gs. The management and marketing approaches developed in the United States were simply exported. Often this was done through the use of expatriate American managers, trained in Cincinnati. Headquarters, however, typically did not interfere with the operations inside the country. Each country was managed separately, local managers controlling what products were sold in the country and how they were marketed.

The third phase is distinguished not only by a movement into other countries (such as Taiwan, Thailand, Saudi Arabia, Brazil, Chile) but also by an attempt to integrate the activities among the various subsidiaries. A clear example of this integration took place in Europe in the 1970s with the development of Euro-brand teams. These teams, consisting of managers from each country where a product was sold, were created in an effort to reduce some of the costs of duplication. The teams coordinated production and marketing strategies and shared information about effective operations. The result was an interdependence, created from cross-subsidiary teamwork, among countries. Additionally, P&G began to use fewer U.S. managers to staff these positions and used more domestically born managers.

A critical part of P&G's expansion into new markets was the acquisition of Richardson-Vicks (R-V) in 1985. R-V, a beauty care company, has operated in Europe and Southeast Asia since the 1950s. The company was able to introduce P&G's products to the Asian markets through the R-V subsidiary, making use of the existing personnel and distribution channels. This helped P&G establish a market presence in most regions of the world (Appendix 1 provides more detailed information on P&G's international operations).

P&G's recent efforts to be competitive in each geographic market have been very successful. The company's sales are increasing in countries in every region of the world and across a wide range of product categories. The international division currently accounts for more than a third of total sales and is growing faster than the domestic rate, achieving double-digit unit volume growth in many of the countries. International sales are projected to be 60% of total sales by the mid-1990s. The shampoo market in these countries represents an opportune area for further growth.

SHAMPOO MARKET

Shampoo products at P&G are part of the Personal Care Products groups. This largest division of the four product groups had sales of $7.5 billion in 1987. This represents slightly over 44% of the company's total sales in 1987. The remaining three groups are Laundry and Cleaning (selling such products as Tide, Spic and Span, and Bounce)—sales of $5.8 billion; Food and Beverage (selling such products as Folgers coffee, Jif peanut butter, and Pringles)—$3 billion; and Pulp and Chemicals (manufacturing wood pulp)—$1.1 billion.

Although Personal Care Products is the largest division in Procter & Gamble, shampoo products make up only a small part of the overall division. The leading product in the group is disposable diapers, sold as Pampers and Luvs. Other paper products include Always feminine protection products and Puffs facial tissues. Other personal care products include Panteen and Vidal Sassoon shampoos, NyQuil, Vicks cough drops, and Crest toothpaste.

Internationally, the shampoo market has not been a strategically important category for P&G. In 1987 only about 20% of its shampoo business was outside the United States. Though Head & Shoulders had a strong position in the U.S. market, most shampoos sold outside the United States were products picked up from the Richardson-Vicks acquisition. This was due in part to the nature of the shampoo market. Historically, the shampoo market had very low entry barriers; there were over 100 major brands of shampoo worldwide. Analysts comment that each year, 20 new shampoos enter the market and 20 shampoos exit the market. Developing and maintaining a competitive edge was difficult.

BC-18 TECHNOLOGY

The development of the BC-18 shampoo represented a sustainable competitive advantage for Procter & Gamble. The concept of combining shampoo and conditioner into one product was not a new one. Turning the idea into a product was the real problem, because it was not technologically feasible. Competitors were also researching the idea and had introduced products that combined shampoo and conditioner. These products never caught on with the consumer, however, because they required shaking before using—the shampoo and conditioner would otherwise separate—and product performance was not outstanding.

In 1985 researchers in Cincinnati developed a silicon-based product that successfully emulsified the shampoo and conditioner. The shampoo and conditioner did not separate and did not require shaking. This technological advance could be turned into a sustained advantage. The product envisioned would lather, clean, and rinse as well as any leading shampoo, condition as well as any leading conditioner, and remain "shelf-stable."

With the knowledge that product development was feasible, attention shifted toward how to position the product to attract consumers. An early attempt introduced it as a new product line, called Ambria, in the United States. This met with limited success. It was then decided to revive an existing product line, Pert. Pert shampoo was introduced in the 1970s with the image of leaving a consumer's hair bouncy yet manageable. The image was good, but the product did not support the image. After initial success, Pert's performance began to lag and it had just 2% of the market in 1985. P&G decided to reformulate Pert with the BC-18 product and label it Pert Plus.

In positioning Pert Plus, managers decided to emphasize the convenience of the product, rather than health or beauty considerations. It continued the "Wash 'N Go" position. One ad showed a woman who had just finished playing racquetball extolling the advantages of being able to get back to work very quickly. The product was test-marketed in Seattle with promising results, indicating that the product would sell very well.

The decision facing P&G managers now was whether the product should be introduced to international markets and, if so, where and how. Several issues needed to be considered in making this decision. A major factor was the positioning of the product. Managers in other countries argued that the positioning was geared too much toward U.S. lifestyles. For example, one concern was that women in some of the countries do not work out in gyms and do not have professional careers. More important, the managers argued that consumers in their countries do not use conditioners. Therefore, having a conditioner combined with a shampoo would not make any difference.

A second issue was how to enter particular markets. Whereas in the United States it was convenient to reformulate Pert, that option was not available in other countries because Pert was not sold overseas. Even though P&G sold shampoo—primarily Richardson-Vicks products—in many countries, it did not have the market coverage it had in the U.S market. One option would be to introduce BC-18 as a product extension of a brand already in the market. However, that also presented problems. For example, Vidal Sassoon had developed a strong market position in England based on a three-step hair treatment process. Introducing an all-in-one shampoo to the same consumers, under the Vidal Sassoon name, would risk destroying that product line's image. A similar problem would occur for the Panteen product line, which had cultivated a health-care image in parts of Europe. Another option would be to create a new product name for the shampoo to use around the world. This alternative, however, would be more expensive and time-consuming.

An important element of the decision of where to introduce the product is the reaction expected of competitors. The major competitors in the shampoo market are profiled in Appendix 2.

CHALLENGE

Design a detailed plan of action for P&G. In developing your plan, be sure to consider the marketing and manufacturing challenges and competitors' reactions to P&G's actions. Specify what factors are important for P&G to consider in this decision. The following questions are offered as a guide.

1. Should P&G introduce BC-18 to international markets?
2. If it should not:
   a. How can it get a return on its R&D investment?
   b. What type of product should it introduce to international markets?
3. If it should:
   a. What countries should it enter and in what order?
   b. Should it introduce the product to different countries sequentially, in what is sometimes referred to as a waterfall approach; sequentially to a host of countries; or via a combination of these two strategies?
   c. Should P&G maintain the marketing approach it has successfully used in the United States? If the approach should be changed, what should be emphasized?
   d. Should P&G sell the same product it manufactures in the United States or reformulate it for local demands? If it should change the product or marketing approach, how much time should P&G spend product testing and repositioning the product before introducing it to the new markets?
   e. Overall, how long should it take P&G to introduce the product globally?

| **APPENDIX 1** | **Profile of P&G Operations in Various Regions** |

CANADA

P&G started operating in Canada in 1915. Its Canadian headquarters are located in Toronto, Ontario, and P&G manufactures and sells a full line of products: disposable diapers, feminine hygiene products, laundry and food products, cake mixes, and pulp and lumber products. P&G markets its products similarly to the approach used in its U.S. operations and is structured in much the same way as in the United States.

(continued)

SUBJECT INDEX